ANNUAL REVIEW OF PSYCHOLOGY

ANNUAL REVIEW OF PSYCHOLOGY

VOLUME 33, 1982

MARK R. ROSENZWEIG, *Editor*
University of California, Berkeley

LYMAN W. PORTER, *Editor*
University of California, Irvine

ANNUAL REVIEWS INC. 4139 EL CAMINO WAY PALO ALTO, CALIFORNIA 94306 USA

AR ANNUAL REVIEWS INC.
Palo Alto, California, USA

International Standard Serial Number: 0066-4308
International Standard Book Number: 0-8243-0233-8
Library of Congress Catalog Card Number: 50-13143

PRINTED AND BOUND IN THE UNITED STATES OF AMERICA

This volume is dedicated to
WILLIAM KAUFMANN
Editor-in-Chief of Annual Reviews Inc. 1973 to 1981
In appreciation for his helpful and friendly support
of the *Annual Review of Psychology*

PREFACE

A regular feature of ARP volumes has been the inclusion of one or two "special topic" chapters that are commissioned on subjects not regularly included in the basic coverage of areas under our Master Plan and which are prepared under a shorter deadline. This year's chapter in the special topic category is a review of "Endorphins and Behavior," by Robert S. Bolles and Michael S. Fanselow. With respect to this type of chapter, the Editors welcome suggestions from readers for future timely topics that merit consideration for special coverage.

Another feature that appears at periodic intervals is an invited chapter on developments in psychology in some country other than the United States. This year we are pleased to include an article on "Psychology in Latin America," by Ruben Ardila. Through these chapters devoted to what is happening in psychology in a particular country or area, and through the inclusion of non-U.S. literature whenever possible in the coverage of topic areas in the standard chapters, the Editorial Committee hopes that the *Annual Review of Psychology* can serve as an important source of information about worldwide developments in this field of science. Again, suggestions from readers outside the U.S. as to future topics for this section of ARP will be welcome.

We would like to remind readers that the basic topic areas regularly covered under the Master Plan can be ascertained by referring to the list of recent chapter titles that is placed at the end of this volume. This list provides a view of both the broad categories of topics and the type of specific coverage they have received in the last five years. Also, the interested reader may wish to refer to the Preface in Volume 32 (1981) concerning the instructions given to authors with regard to the scope and intent of ARP chapters.

We have had to bid adieu to Lewis R. Goldberg, who completed his five-year term on the Editorial Committee. We and his Committee colleagues will miss his wide-ranging knowledge of the field of psychology and his many insightful contributions to the planning of these volumes. Norman Garmezy is the new member replacing Lew. The Editorial committee was expanded this past year, and we welcome two other new members: Bert F. Green and Jeanne S. Phillips.

L.W.P.
M.R.R.

Annual Review of Psychology
Volume 33, 1982

CONTENTS

SOME ARTICLES IN OTHER *ANNUAL REVIEWS* OF INTEREST TO PSYCHOLOGISTS

From the *Annual Review of Sociology,* Volume 7 (1981)

Observational Field Work, Robert M. Emerson

The Role of Cognitive-Linguistic Concepts in Understanding Everyday Social Interactions, Aaron V. Cicourel

Sociological Aspects of Criminal Victimization, Michael R. Gottfredson and Michael J. Hindelang

Self-Help and Mutual Aid: An Emerging Social Movement? Alfred H. Katz

Organizational Performance: Recent Developments in Measurement, Rosabeth Moss Kanter and Derick Brinkerhoff

The Social Control of Sexuality, John DeLamater

From the *Annual Review of Anthropology,* Volume 10 (1981)

Endocrine-Environment Interaction in Human Variability, Frances E. Purifoy

A Critical Review of Models in Sociobiology, B. J. Williams

Sign Language in its Social Context, William Washabaugh

Anthropology and Industry: Reappraisal and New Directions, Carol S. Holzberg and Maureen J. Giovannini

From the *Annual Review of Public Health,* Volume 3 (1982)

Labor-Management Aspects of Occupational Risk, Robert B. DesJardins, William J. Bigoness, and Robert Harris

Social Influences on Smoking Behavior, S. Leonard Syme and Rina Alcalay

The Psychological Control of Cigarette-Smoking, Robert C. Benfari, Judith K. Ockene, and Kevin M. McIntyre

The Chronically Mentally Disabled and "Deinstitutionalization," Janet Archer and Ernest M. Gruenberg

Defining the Health Problems of the Elderly, Joseph G. Ouslander and John C. Beck

From the *Annual Review of Neuroscience,* Volume 5 (1982)

Electroreception, Theodore Holmes Bullock

Signaling of Kinesthetic Information by Peripheral Sensory Receptors, P. R. Burgess and Jen Yu Wei

Where Does Sherrington's "Muscular Sense" Originate? Muscles, Joints, Corollary Discharges? P. B. C. Matthews

Human Memory: Neuropsychological and Anatomical Aspects, Larry R. Squire

From the *Annual Review of Medicine,* Volume 33 (1982)

Rehabilitation of Leprous Deformities, Carl D. Enna

Behavioral Pharmacology of the Endorphins, Philip A. Berger, Huda Akil, Stanley J. Watson, and Jack D. Barchas

Undiagnosed Physical Illness in Psychiatric Patients, Erwin K. Koranyi

The Development of Reliable Diagnostic Criteria in Psychiatry, Andrew E. Skodol and Robert L. Spitzer

From the *Annual Review of Pharmacology and Toxicology,* Volume 22 (1982)

The Neurochemical Basis of Acupuncture Analgesia, J. S. Han and L. Terenius

Cholinergic Systems in Behavior: The Search for Mechanisms of Action, Roger W. Russell

ANNUAL REVIEWS INC. is a nonprofit corporation established to promote the advancement of the sciences. Beginning in 1932 with the *Annual Review of Biochemistry,* the Company has pursued as its principal function the publication of high quality, reasonably priced *Annual Review* volumes. The volumes are organized by Editors and Editorial Committees who invite qualified authors to contribute critical articles reviewing significant developments within each major discipline. Annual Reviews Inc. is administered by a Board of Directors, whose members serve without compensation.

Publications

PLANNED FOR 1983: Annual Review of Immunology

ANNUAL REVIEWS OF
Anthropology
Astronomy and Astrophysics
Biochemistry
Biophysics and Bioengineering
Earth and Planetary Sciences
Ecology and Systematics
Energy
Entomology
Fluid Mechanics
Genetics
Materials Science
Medicine
Microbiology
Neuroscience
Nuclear and Particle Science
Nutrition
Pharmacology and Toxicology
Physical Chemistry
Physiology
Phytopathology
Plant Physiology
Psychology
Public Health
Sociology

SPECIAL PUBLICATIONS
Annual Reviews Reprints:
Cell Membranes, 1975–1977
Cell Membranes, 1978–1980
Immunology, 1977–1979
Excitement and Fascination of Science, Vols. 1 and 2
History of Entomology
Intelligence and Affectivity, by Jean Piaget
Telescopes for the 1980s

For the convenience of readers, a detachable order form/envelope is bound into the back of this volume.

Ann. Rev. Psychol. 1982. 33:1–39

SOCIAL PSYCHOLOGY OF INTERGROUP RELATIONS

Henri Tajfel[1]

Department of Psychology, University of Bristol, Bristol BS8 1HH, England

---

CONTENTS

Intergroup relations represent in their enormous scope one of the most difficult and complex knots of problems which we confront in our times. This is why their study in social psychology (and in other disciplines) has been more a matter of "approaches" or perspectives than of tight theoretical articulations.

Intergroup behavior will be understood in this chapter in terms proposed by Sherif (1966): "Whenever individuals belonging to one group interact, collectively or individually, with another group or its members *in terms of*

[1]I wish to express my gratitude to Margaret Wetherell for her work on the initial stages of the preparation of this review, to Penny Oakes for making available to me an unpublished review of the literature on the salience of intergroup categorization, and to Alma Foster for her invaluable help in the presentation of the material.

0066-4308/82/0201-0001$02.00

their group identification, we have an instance of intergroup behavior" (p. 12). This definition needs to be anchored to its two underlying concepts: "group" and "group identification."

A "group" can be defined as such on the basis of criteria which are either external or internal. External criteria are the "outside" designations such as bank clerks, hospital patients, members of a trades union, etc. Internal criteria are those of "group identification." In order to achieve the stage of "identification," two components are necessary, and one is frequently associated with them. The two necessary components are: a cognitive one, in the sense of awareness of membership; and an evaluative one, in the sense that this awareness is related to some value connotations. The third component consists of an emotional investment in the awareness and evaluations.

The empirical reality of the internal criteria is a *necessary* condition for the existence of a group in the psychological sense of the term; but it is not a *sufficient* condition for the emergence of intergroup behavior. There can be no *inter*group behavior unless there is also some "outside" consensus that the group exists. But this in turn cannot be a sufficient condition since a classification by others of some people as a group does not necessarily mean that the individuals so classified have acquired an awareness of a common group membership and the value connotations associated with it. We shall adopt a definition of "group identification" as consisting of the two (and sometimes three) internal components referred to above; and a conjunctive definition of a "group" as requiring a combination of *some* external criteria with the internal criteria.

The 1970s have seen a revival of interest in intergroup behavior. Several recent reviews varying in their scope are now available (e.g. LeVine & D. Campbell 1972, Ehrlich 1973, Kidder & Stewart 1975, Billig 1976, Austin & Worchel 1979, Turner & Giles 1981) of which Billig's is the most extensive in its historical and critical coverage.

The general emphasis of most of the work done since Allport (1954) wrote his classic integration of research on prejudice is reflected in the very first paragraph of the review by Ehrlich (1973):

> Two types of theory are required to explain the state of ethnic group relations in a society. One must be a theory of intergroup behavior, sociological in orientation and using for its evidence materials that are primarily historical. The other theory is social psychological. Its concern is primarily cognitive factors and the relations of these factors with the interpersonal behavior of individuals (p. vii).

These views represent a considerable narrowing of scope as compared with the range of issues that Allport (1954) attempted to cover 20 years earlier. Is it justifiable to establish a dichotomy between a "theory of intergroup behavior" which must remain "sociological" and "historical" as constrasted with a "social psychological theory" which is focused upon cognition and interpersonal behavior? As Sherif (1966) wrote: "Our claim is the study of relations between groups and intergroup attitudes of their respective members. We therefore must consider both the properties of the groups themselves and the consequences of membership for individuals. Otherwise, whatever we are studying, we are not studying intergroup problems" (p. 62).

The plan of this review will reflect in its sequence the transition from "individual" to "group" approaches. We shall start with research concerned with individual processes in their direct applications to intergroup behavior. The remainder of the review will concentrate on the effects that group membership has on intergroup behavior; i.e. it will be concerned with research in which individuals are considered as members of groups rather than as self-contained entities. It will be seen that in many cases the effects of group membership on intergroup behavior can hardly be considered without simultaneously taking into account the nature of the relations between the individuals' membership group and other groups which are interdependent with it. The final section of the review will summarize some of the studies concerned with reducing intergroup conflicts and tensions.

INDIVIDUAL PROCESSES IN INTERGROUP BEHAVIOR

One of the important trends of theory and research in the recent revival of interest in intergroup behavior has focused upon the role played by general cognitive processes in determining the individuals' "ideas" about ingroups and outgroups. This work is closely related to certain strands of cognitive theory which it applies to the functioning of stereotypes. We shall adopt Stallybrass's (1977) definition of a stereotype as "an over-simplifed mental image of (usually) some category of person, institution or event which is shared, in essential features, by large numbers of people . . . Stereotypes are commonly, but not necessarily, accompanied by prejudice, i.e. by a favorable or unfavorable predisposition toward any member of the category in question" (p. 601).

From Individual to Group Impressions

The above title reproduces the title of an article by Rothbart et al (1978); both reflect the recent upsurge of interest in attentional processes as they affect the formation and functioning of social stereotypes. In this work the emphasis has been on individuals or events *singled out* for attention; in other words, the interest has focused upon the derivation or strengthening of stereotypes which are due to the salience, in certain situations, of information which stands out, which is unusual or unexpected in its context. This "availability heuristics" of certain items of information (e.g. Tversky & Kahneman 1973, Rothbart et al 1978) is assumed to have marked generalizing effects, the direction of inference being from the characteristics of certain individual members of groups to groups as a whole. In a similar way, the idea of "category prototypes" formulated by Rosch and others (e.g. Rosch et al 1976, Rosch 1977, 1978) is reflected in the search for the particular levels of these category prototypes which may affect the conception of the category as a whole. The "levels" may vary in the centrality of their impact upon the conception of a category, and once again the direction of inferences tends to be from individual items to a category which these items represent.

Rothbart et al (1978) summarized the general conception underlying much of this research. The focus of it is "on how people amalgamate their impressions of discrete individuals to form a perception of the group as a whole, and our theoretical emphasis will be on the cognitive mechanisms that enable us to distill relatively simple impressions from a complex stimulus array" (p. 238). It is possible to argue that this emphasis creates a break in the study of intergroup relations between psychological functioning and the social fabric within which this functioning takes place. On the other hand, this interest in the accumulation of individual impressions is itself part and parcel of the social context from which it derives. As S. E. Taylor (1981) wrote, "recent trends toward desegregation [in the United States] have resulted in the creation of a situation uniquely suited to testing the implications of distinctiveness. This situation is solo status. Solo status is the case in which there is one member of a different race, sex, or ethnicity in a group which is otherwise homogeneous on that attribute." It remains true, however, that this is only one of many social situations in which intergroup behavior and attitudes are displayed.

Rothbart et al (1978) were able to show that under high memory loads the assumed typicality of certain distinctive instances tends to be retrospectively overestimated. This is the case in the association of "extreme" individuals, such as would be one or a few members of a social minority in groups of mixed composition, with some forms of "unusual" behavior which would tend to be "unfavorable." As Rothbart et al pointed out, findings of this kind may be relevant to our understanding of the effects of mass media on the formation of negative stereotypes about selected minority groups. The studies point to selective memory retrieval of information as the locus of the process. There is, however, some evidence (Upmeyer & Layer 1974, Upmeyer et al 1976) that when a division into ingroups and outgroups is used as one of the independent variables, the stage of the assimilation of information about groups ("input accentuation") has a stronger effect on selectivity than its subsequent retrieval ("output accentuation"). This evidence is congruent with some of the findings of later studies by Rothbart et al (1979) and by Howard & Rothbart (1980).

The effects on stereotyping of attention being directed to individual members of certain social groups who become salient because of their minority or "solo" status in a group of mixed composition have recently been the subject of a series of studies by S. Taylor and her associates (S. Taylor et al 1978, 1979, S. Taylor 1981).

This research is closely related to field studies (Wolman & Frank 1975, Kanter 1977) which showed that women who are on their own among men in relatively new professional settings, such as middle-level business managers or medical students in work groups, tend to be stereotyped in terms of a variety of traditional feminine roles. The opposite of this phenomenon, which indirectly confirms the "solo" findings, was described by Novarra (1980) in her report about recent pilot schemes in West Germany in which young women trained in "men's work," such as precision tool making, avoid much of the discomfort and/or stereotyping by being in female working groups which consist of no less than 20 members in any one firm.

The main findings on "solo" status are as follows: one woman in a group of men or one black in a group of whites leave a relatively "stronger impression"; the evaluations of that person are polarized as compared with the evaluations of the same person identified as belonging to the majority in the group, in the sense that both positive and negative evaluations become more extreme in the solo condition. The findings do not, however, apply equally to various social categories. For example, there is some evidence in the studies that blacks tended to be stereotyped whether they were solo or members of evenly balanced mixed groups. As to gender differences, little evidence was found that solo status led to stereotyping in terms of *traits;* there was, however, evidence of stereotyping in terms of *roles.*

S. Taylor (e.g. 1981) relates these findings to Rosch's views (e.g. Rosch et al 1976) about the "basic level" of category prototypes in the perception of objects (i.e. the objects which carry the most information about the category as a whole and are thus the most clearly differentiated from prototypes of other categories). She finds support in the work by Cantor & Mischel (1979), who applied the prototype ideas to the study of person perception, for her argument that the stereotypic aspects of person perception find their "basic" or "prototype" equivalent to object perception at the level of social roles rather than in other taxonomies. In other words, personality traits would be, on Taylor's argument, less important in these contexts than what people are assumed to be *doing.* There is, however, some evidence from Canadian studies (Aboud & D. Taylor 1971, Aboud et al 1973) that traits associated with ethnic stereotypes tend to be assigned more often to the outgroup than to the ingroup, while the converse is true of role stereotypes. The conception about the "prototype" nature of role stereotypes may need to take into account the ingroup vs the outgroup target of stereotyping. The evidence reported by S. Taylor and her colleagues applies mainly to the stereotyping of women. Women as a disadvantaged social category present a number of similarities with other such categories; but the differences from other social categories (e.g. ethnic groups, immigrant populations, religious or political minorities, etc) are also important (e.g. Williams & Giles 1978). It is therefore fairly hazardous to generalize from data about women, "solo" or not, to other instances of social stereotyping.

The general conception that stereotypes accumulate as a result of focusing attention on unusual people or events is also at the background of the studies on "illusory correlations" reported by D. Hamilton (e.g. 1976, 1979, D. Hamilton & Gifford 1976). The studies showed that when certain actions were attributed to members of two groups in a design in which more information was provided about one of the groups, and the ratio of desirable to undesirable behaviors was varied, the subjects "grossly over-estimated the extent to which the infrequent group . . . performed the 'uncommon' type of behavior" (D. Hamilton 1979, p. 63) whether the behavior was desirable or undesirable. As Hamilton argues, these findings have a general significance for social stereotyping, since members of minority groups often represent "infrequent" stimuli and therefore a conjunction of their relatively rare appearance with some of their actions lends itself to the construction of "illusory correlations" and thus to stereotyping.

Most of the work on stereotypes described so far follows Ehrlich's (1973) prescription (see above) that the aim of a social psychological theory of intergroup behavior should be to relate cognitive processes to interpersonal behavior. The result has been an impressive body of research which focused upon the accretion of information about individuals leading to the building up of stereotypic views about their groups. The underlying and clearly stated conception has been that the study of cognitive processes is both necessary and sufficient for the understanding of the attitudinal (or stereotypic) aspects of intergroup behavior (e.g. D. Taylor & Aboud 1973, D. Hamilton & Gifford 1976, Rothbart et al 1978, S. Taylor et al 1978, S. Taylor 1981).

We have been led to new insights about one specific intergroup social situation: small groups of mixed composition which include one or a few members of certain social minorities. As has been pointed out earlier, this particular situation does relate to some of the social realities of partial desegregation; but one must ask whether the research succeeded in justifying the two claims made for it: the *sufficiency* of the study of cognitive processes in intergroup stereotypes, and the demonstration of this sufficiency in the work about the cognitive salience of selected individuals.

Some doubts must be raised. Social stereotypes are by no means confined to situations in which members of a target group are unfamiliar. This is not to say that individuals do not sometimes create their stereotypes on the basis of a few contacts with members of outgroups. It is, however, improbable that the genesis of widely diffused intergroup stereotypes can be found in the social summing up of the cognitive effects of "rarity" or "unfamiliarity" or "singling out" of isolated individuals. In some ways the argument begs the question, since it fails to provide a rationale as to why some individuals are singled out as a basis for the formation of stereotypes and others are not. For example, it is unlikely that "solo" red-haired or fat persons in groups of "mixed" composition would generate widely diffused social stereotypes of "groups" of red-haired or fat people. The behavior of certain individuals often becomes relevant to the stereotype of their group because they are representatives of a category which has a preexisting social significance enmeshed with preexisting value connotations. Attention-focusing becomes important for stereotyping mainly when it happens in the context of these preexisting evaluative social differentiations and when it is determined by them. There is still no evidence that, outside of this context, attention-focusing on individuals who are in some ways "different" is a primary condition of the process of stereotyping.

GROUP MEMBERSHIP AND INTERGROUP BEHAVIOR

The focus of the research just reviewed was on the question of how cognitive structures determine certain aspects of intergroup attitudes. In the present section, several trends of research will be considered which have adopted a different order of priorities. Group membership is here the starting point of the analysis which then considers various psychological processes which follow from that membership.

One of the classic examples is the concept of "ethnocentrism." Sumner (1906) was the first to use the term together with those of "ingroup" and "outgroup." In their wide-ranging review of theories concerned with ethnocentrism, LeVine & D. Campbell (1972) made the term "to cover both the ingroup-outgroup polarization of hostility and the self-centered scaling of all values in terms of the ingroup folkways" (p. 8). As they pointed out, for Sumner ethnocentrism was a "syndrome" in the sense that it encompassed "a number of (mutually related) attributes of social life"; it played a function in group formation and intergroup competition, and it was universal. LeVine & Campbell described and compared in their book a formidable array of sociological, anthropological, and psychological theories trying to account for ethnocentrism at various levels of explanation.

The Scope and Range of Ethnocentrism

The "universality" of ethnocentrism was one of Sumner's basic assumptions. "Universality" is a notoriously slippery notion. As we can assume from common experience that ethnocentrism in its various manifestations is a widespread phenomenon, a useful empirical question is possible: what are the conditions which lead to an increase or decrease in ethnocentrism or even perhaps sometimes to its disappearance?

It is this clarification of the *realities* of ethnocentrism which was the aim of the most ambitious cross-cultural study to date on the subject. A large-scale survey of ethnocentric attitudes (LeVine & D. Campbell 1972, Brewer 1968, 1979a, 1981, Brewer & D. Campbell 1976) combined ethnographic, social psychological, and field-anthropological methods of inquiry. The C.C.S.E. (Cross-Cultural Study of Ethnocentrism) encompassed data from 30 ethnic groups in East Africa at a time when the region was undergoing rapid social and political changes, as well as from West Africa, Northern Canada, and some of the Pacific islands. Attachment to the ingroup was found in all the groups studied. But this was not related in any simple way, such as was posited by Sumner, to outgroup attitudes and intergroup differentiations. For example, value connotations of stereotypes about outgroups did not systematically vary with open intergroup conflict; such conflict was not, in turn, directly related to various measures of social distance; ingroup favoritism was "relatively independent" of outgroup attitudes, etc. In sum, "which differences are emphasized under what circumstances appears to be flexible and context dependent; this flexibility permits individuals to mobilize different group identities for different purposes" (Brewer 1981, p. 350).

A similar flexibility and diversity of ingroup attachments and outgroup attitudes was found in two other field studies which, in common with the C.C.S.E., were concerned with comparing a number of ethnic groups seen in their historical and sociocultural context. Klineberg & Zavalloni (1969) worked with samples of students from several African countries which were, at the time of the study (and still are), engaged in the difficult process of nation building within boundaries determined more directly by the recent colonial past than by the older tribal loyalties. Using samples and methods very different from those employed by the C.C.S.E., Klineberg & Zavalloni also found close relationships between the variety of group identities assumed by their respondents and the "different purposes"—tribal or national —which these identities served.

A similar point of historical transition to nation building has been reached in Indonesia whose population, consisting of 300 separate ethnic groups, was estimated in 1972 at 124 million. Jaspars & Warnaen (1982) worked, using various types of questionnaires, with young people from several of these groups. The main purpose of the questionnaires was to elicit descriptions and evaluations of ingroups and outgroups in Jakarta, where many of the ethnic groups live side by side, and in the original locations of the groups where this is not the case. As a result of salience of group membership, more significant in the mixed environment of Jakarta than elsewhere, ingroup favoritism and outgroup discrimination were more marked in the capital than in the provinces. More generally, "groups do not necessarily evaluate outgroups more negatively than their own group. They do, however, in general have a more positive view of themselves than other groups have of them" (Jaspars & Warnaen 1982). As in the C.C.S.E., the absence of a simple relationship between ingroup favoritism and outgroup attitudes is thus reported again in the Indonesian study. Jaspars & Warnaen related their findings to processes of social identity and social comparison which will be discussed later.

The Development of Ethnocentrism

The difficulties of organizing and conducting large-scale cross-cultural field studies on ethnocentrism, such as those described above, resulted in the fact that much of the data we have on ingroup and outgroup attitudes and behavior relating to ethnic, national, or racial groups originate from experimental or semiexperimental research on more easily available groups or subgroups in Western societies. These studies were generally concerned with eliciting children's identifications and preferences through inducing them to make choices between concrete stimuli (such as dolls, pictures, etc) representing their own group and relevant outgroups. The conclusions of the earlier research have been that at a very early age children from underprivileged groups tended to reflect the social consensus about the status and the image of their group by adopting outgroup identifications and preferences, while the majority children clearly showed ethnocentric attitudes (for recent reviews see e.g. Pushkin & Veness 1973, Milner 1975, 1981, P. Katz 1976).

These findings led to methodological controversies followed by many replications. In addition to invalidating simple notions about the "universality" of ethnocentrism, the data pose more specific questions about the stages of cognitive development underlying children's attitudes and concepts about ingroups and outgroups (e.g. P. Katz 1976, Williams & Morland 1976). They also raise issues connected with what appears to be the immense sensitivity, shown both by the "majority" and the "minority" children, to the surrounding "social climate" of intergroup differentials and evaluations.

There is little doubt about sensitivity. A good deal of evidence exists about children's early assimilation of the socially available systems of values and preferences even in conditions where obvious interracial cues are not present. This is the case for the expression of preferences between foreign nations which seem to crystallize in children earlier than the assimilation of even the simplest items of factual information about these nations (e.g. Middleton et al 1970, Stillwell & Spencer 1973, Tajfel 1981, Chap. 10[2]). There is also evidence from several European countries of the early acquisition of "liking" or "preference" for one's own nation (e.g. Simon et al 1967, Jaspars et al 1973, Barbiero 1974, Tajfel 1981, Chap. 9). Evidence that in the case of lower status ethnic groups, neither acute intergroup tensions nor obvious visual cues are necessary for outgroup favoritism to make its appearance is also available from Israel and Scotland (Rim 1968, Tajfel 1981, Chap. 9).

The methodological debate about the validity of some aspects of the earlier findings concerned mainly the misidentification of "black" children with white figures presented to them (see Greenwald & Oppenheim 1968, Hraba & Grant 1970, P. Katz 1976, Williams & Morland 1976, Milner 1981). There was, however, little doubt from the earlier studies about the data concerning outgroup *preferences*.

In some of the more recent studies on children and adults (see Brigham 1971, Bourhis et al 1973, Fox & Jordan 1973, P. Katz & Zalk 1974, Giles & Powesland 1975, Berry et al 1977) the pattern of outgroup preferences so often documented in the earlier work on children was not replicated. Commenting on some of these studies, P. Katz (1976) wrote that "it is tempting to attribute such changes . . . to societal changes that have occurred over the past few years. The importance of black people's developing pride in their blackness is certainly a factor" (p. 128). She added, however, that "there are several problems with the societal change interpretation" (p. 128), most of them arising from further replications in the late sixties and in the seventies of the earlier results showing outgroup favoritism. These reservations lost some of their strength after the elegant demonstration by Vaughan (1978a,b) of a direct relationship in New Zealand between indices of social change and the decrease of outgroup favoritism in Maori children. Vaughan's data originated from four studies using very similar methods and conducted in several locations over a period of about 10 years. As Pettigrew (1978) wrote: "proud strong minorities are possible despite the 'marks of oppression' " (p. 60). There is also supporting evidence for the effects of social change from two field studies on young adults conducted in Italy in 1963 and 1978–79 with similar methods and populations (Capozza et al

[2]This is a reference to a collection of theoretical articles and empirical studies revised and edited as one volume. It will be used here instead of the original sources for the sake of brevity and convenience.

1979). It was found that the self-stereotypes and reciprocal stereotypes of northern and southern Italians living in the north changed in the intervening period in accordance with what would be expected from changes in the social and political climate and conditions in the country.

Despite some evidence from the United States and New Zealand that racial minority children of various ages begin to shed the older patterns of "ingroup devaluation," there are also recent findings from elsewhere of its persistence. In addition to the work by Jahoda et al (1972) and Milner (1973, 1975), there have been more recent studies in Britain (e.g. Davey & Mullin 1980, Davey & Norburn 1980) showing that Asian and West Indian children continue to express outgroup preferences. Some aspects of these studies may enable us to gain a further understanding of the phenomenon. Direct comparisons with the higher status groups are explicitly and directly built into the studies on ingroup devaluation. The recent work in Britain shows that the Asian children, although expressing outgroup preference toward the white majority, do it to a lesser extent than is the case for the West Indian children. Milner (e.g. 1973) suggested that this finding can be accounted for by more protection of their self-image offered to the children by the Asian than by the West Indian group, as the Asian immigrant communities in Britain preserve a stronger cultural, familial, linguistic, and religious separate identity than do the West Indians.

Social comparisons made by an individual may focus toward the ingroup or the outgroup. In the former case, the ingroup may provide a basis for the building up of a positive self-image, if it managed to preserve a system of positive evaluations about its "folkways," mode of life, social and cultural characteristics. When the group suffers at the same time from low status in the society at large, the strength drawn by its members from its internal and positive social identity may come into conflict with the negative evaluations from the "outside" whenever comparisons with the higher status groups become salient—as has been the case in the studies showing the outgroup bias of minority children. Results reported by I. Katz (e.g. 1973), based on data from the sixties about academic performance of black pupils in recently desegregated schools, can be subsumed within the same process of social comparisons with the higher status outgroup. In Katz's research, the performance and the expectations of the black pupils were often lower than might have been expected from independent assessments of their potential ability. It is reasonable to assume that the growth of *group* self-respect in underprivileged minorities, closely related to socioeconomic, political, and psychological changes both inside the group and outside of it, would result in a corresponding decrease of ingroup devaluations and of low comparative expectancies.

But this is a long process in which sociopsychological transformations must be seen as the *effects* of socioeconomic and political change rather than being in some way autonomous and determined by the vagaries of haphazard assimilation by individual members of minority groups. For the present, there is a good deal of evidence (see Tajfel 1981, Chap. 15) that members of groups which have found themselves for centuries at the bottom of the social pyramid sometimes display the phenomenon of "self-hate" or self-depreciation. It was one of the merits of the studies on ingroup devaluation in children to have provided an accumulation of clear and explicit data on the subject. The self-depreciation, relating to social comparisons with the outside world, leads to a variety of internal conflicts (e.g. Weinreich 1979), some of which achieve their resolution in seeking and finding responsibility for the social discrepancies in an external "locus of control," i.e. in the social system at large (Lao 1970, Louden 1978). Several of these conflicts are described in some detail in the extensive field study by Geber & Newman (1980) based on data about African high school pupils gathered some years ago in Soweto, the African township bordering on Johannesburg. As the authors wrote:

> . . . the socializing agents and the wider society . . . make competing demands on the Black high school pupil. The competitive school system encourages the adoption of achievement oriented behaviors, of skills and knowledge appropriate to a Western technological society. The wider society, implicitly in segregation and explicitly in the political ideology, insists on the recognition of separateness and inequality . . . The schools can dispense rewards in terms of skills, knowledge, and the qualifications necessary for advance. The society in turn can bar [their] use . . . (p. 126).

There is no need to stress the links between the psychological conflicts inherent in this situation and the explosions of violence which shook Soweto during the 1970s.

Intergroup Conflict and Competition

The research on ethnocentrism took its point of departure in the individuals' group membership. This is also true of research on intergroup conflict based on scarcity of goods or resources for which the groups compete. There exists, however, another basis for competition in which, as Turner (1975) put it, the scarce resources have no value outside of the context of the competition itself. This is the case of groups competing to win a contest, to achieve higher rank, status, or prestige—the case of "social competition," as Turner (1975) named it. The conflict for the "scarce resources" of rank, status, prestige, or winning a contest is "realistic" when it is institutionalized, i.e., when it is explicitly defined as a contest or determined as such by the norms of the social situation. An example of this institutionalization of a conflict about "winning" are the studies by Sherif and his collaborators (see e.g. Sherif 1966); countless other examples are familiar from everyday life. Although the distinction between "objective" conflict and "social competition" contains overlaps and ambiguities (see Tajfel & Turner 1979), its two poles define the range of the "realistic" conflict and competition which concerns us in the present section.

INTERPERSONAL AND INTERGROUP BEHAVIOR A long-standing divergence of approaches to intergroup conflict and competition is perhaps best exemplified in the contrast between the work of Sherif on the one hand and the extrapolations from interindividual competitive games to intergroup conflict represented, among others, by the research of Deutsch (e.g. 1973). Sherif started from the structure of the relations between groups in conflict and treated the behavior of the members of the competing groups as dependent variables of the intergroup situation. His field-experimental methods were used later by Diab (1970), who was able to replicate most of Sherif's results in a Lebanese setting.

The divergence of approaches just mentioned can be subsumed in a distinction between two hypothetical extremes of a continuum of social interaction: the "interpersonal extreme" defined as "interaction between two or more individuals which is very largely determined by their individual characteristics and the nature of the personal relations between them"; and the "intergroup extreme" defined as "interactions which are largely determined by group memberships of the participants and very little—if at all—by their personal relations or individual characteristics" (Tajfel 1979, p. 401). This second "extreme" is a paraphrase of Sherif's (1966) definition of intergroup behavior quoted earlier in this chapter.

This definition leads to empirical questions concerning the special *characteristics* of intergroup behavior and its *antecedents*. Two of these characteristics seem particularly important: the first consists of the uniformities displayed by members of the ingroup in their behavior and attitudes toward an outgroup. This transition toward uniformity mirrors the transition from the interpersonal to the intergroup ends of the continuum as the behavior is increasingly determined by the reciprocal group membership of the constituent individuals. The second major characteristic of intergroup behavior, which also becomes more salient as the "interpersonal" extreme becomes more distant, is another kind of uniformity: the decrease in variability in the characteristics and behavior of the members of the outgroup as they are perceived by members of the ingroup. In this process, members of the outgroup become "undifferentiated items in a unified social category" (Tajfel 1981, p. 243). The phenomena of depersonalization, dehumanization, and social stereotyping which tend to increase in scope as and when intergroup relations deteriorate are no more than special instances of this wider principle of the increased *un*differentiation of the outgroup. Some research relevant to this "undifferentiation" will be discussed later.

The *antecedents* of these two kinds of uniformity seem to fall into four large classes. They are: (*a*) social differentials in status, power, rank, privilege, access to resources, etc., when the group boundaries are firmly drawn and/or perceived as such (see Brewer 1979b) and *when the social organization on which these differentials are based loses its perceived legitimacy and/or stability* (see e.g. Turner & Brown 1978, Commins & Lockwood 1979a, Caddick 1980, Tajfel 1981, Chap. 13); (*b*) intergroup conflict or competition, not necessarily related to previously existing status differences, as was the case in the work of Sherif and many other experimental studies to date; (*c*) movements for change initiated by social groups which, as distinct from case *a* above, are not *always* related to impermeable boundaries between groups (e.g. D. Taylor et al 1973, Mugny & Papastamou 1976–77, 1980, Giles et al 1977, D. Taylor 1980); and (*d*) individually determined patterns of prejudice which have tended for a long time to occupy the center of the stage in much of the traditional research on the subject (see Ehrlich 1973 for a review).

The varieties of the "mix" of interpersonal and intergroup behavior are well exemplified in the recent review by Stephenson (1981) of research on intergroup negotiation and bargaining. Much of this research used to concentrate on the unfolding of interpersonal relations between the negotiators or generalized to intergroup negotiations the findings of the substantive body of work (see Pruitt & Kimmel 1977) on interpersonal gaming research. Although negotiators do enter into personal relations which have their varied effects on the outcomes of the negotiating process, there are, as Stephenson (1981) argued, some very distinctive aspects to intergroup negotiations which can only be neglected at the cost of misinterpreting the nature of the relevant situations (also see Louche 1978). The most important feature of the situation is the fact that the underlying conflict between the groups which the negotiators represent has little to do with the negotiators' interpersonal relations, even if those relations do affect the course of the bargaining. This becomes even clearer when, as in a field study by Stephenson & Brotherton (1975), the number of negotiators on each side is increased. It has also been found that clear intergroup differentiation may actually *strengthen* the interpersonal bonds between the negotiators (Batstone et al 1977) or at least make it easier for them to develop such bonds (Louche 1982). This does not mean that the intergroup conflict can thereby be eliminated or at times even reduced. In many situations, as Louche (1982) put it, "negotiation is not an alternative to intergroup conflict; it is one of the forms in which conflict is expressed."

One of the most striking instances of the effects on interpersonal behavior of the structure of intergroup relations is also one of the earliest. In some of Sherif's studies (Sherif & Sherif 1953, Sherif et al 1961), boys who had become friends before the "official" intergroup competition was started were placed in opposing groups. Their subsequent behavior was affected by the intergroup conflict and not by their previous interpersonal attachments. There is also more recent evidence that the effects of groups membership can overwhelm the unfolding of interpersonal relations, or as Turner (1981) put it "that social groups seem to be more competitive and perceive their interests more competitively than individuals under the same functional conditions" (e.g. Dustin & Davis 1970, Doise & Weinberger 1972–73, Janssens & Nuttin 1976, Lindskold et al 1977, Brown & Deschamps 1980–81). There are also data showing that aggression or retaliation involving groups can be stronger in some conditions than is the case for individuals (e.g. Jaffe & Yinon 1979). But we must still await a great deal of further conceptual clarification and research in order to be able to specify the relative weight of interpersonal and intergroup determinants of social interaction in the enormous variety of situations in which both seem to play a part (see Brown & Turner 1981).

INTERGROUP CONFLICT AND GROUP COHESION This need for further clarification finds an example in what has been traditionally one of the central issues in the study of intergroup conflict. Does conflict promote greater cohesion inside the groups engaged in it? At the limit, can conflict *create* a cohesive group where only a loose structure existed before?

There exists a long tradition of positive answers to these questions. Reflecting the views of his times, Sumner (1906) wrote: "The relationship of comradeship and peace in the we-group and that of hostility and war towards other-groups are correlative to each other. The exigencies of war with outsiders are what makes peace inside" (p. 12). Freud's views, expressed in various periods of his work, were not different. The early frustration-aggression theorists also agreed (e.g. Dollard 1937). The substantial consensus about the existence of this functional relationship does not seem to have weakened. Stein (1976) was able to conclude his recent review of relevant work in a number of social science disciplines by stating that:

> . . . there is a clear convergence in the literature in both the specific studies and in the various disciplines that suggests that external conflict does increase internal cohesion under certain conditions . . . The external conflict needs to invoke some threat, affect the entire group and all its members equally and indiscriminately, and involve a solution . . . The group must be able to deal with the external conflict, and to provide emotional comfort and support to its members (p. 165).

Stein's statement, positive as it is, is also hedged with reservations. What are the "conditions"? What happens if all members of a group are not equally and indiscriminately affected by the conflict? Or if the group is unable to deal with the threat or to provide emotional support? Or when the consensus about threat, when it is dubious, cannot be transformed by the leadership into an "authoritatively enforced cohesion" (Stein 1976, p. 165)?

These are perennial questions and it is not surprising that recent social psychological research continued to find no more than piecemeal answers to them. Some of this research has been concerned with the effects of increased intergroup competition on the positive evaluation of the ingroup or its products (e.g. Doise et al 1972, Kahn & Ryen 1972, Ryen & Kahn 1975, Worchel et al 1975, 1977); with loss of cohesion in cases of group failure (e.g. Diab 1970, Kahn & Ryen 1972, Worchel et al 1975); with subjective enhancement of ingroup qualities deriving from the motivation of individual members (see Hinkle & Schopler 1979 for a review). A good deal of useful data have been collected without achieving what would amount to a major theoretical breakthrough providing a new perspective on the old established functional relationship.

It is therefore interesting to find a dissenting voice. In a series of studies, Rabbie and his colleagues (Rabbie & de Brey 1971, Rabbie & Wilkens 1971, Rabbie & Huygen 1974, Rabbie et al 1974) found that intergroup competition did not create greater ingroup cohesion or affiliation than either simple coaction or cooperation between the groups. Squarely set in the Lewinian tradition (Lewin 1948) of the primary importance in intergroup phenomena of the "interdependence of fate," this work emphasizes the interdependence between the individuals and their groups, and consequently the importance —theoretically prior to intergroup conflict—of such variables as common fate, the anticipation and the nature of the interaction within the ingroup, its perceived boundaries and "entitivity," and the attitudes toward the outgroup based on the perception of the outcomes for the ingroup of the outgroup's actions (see Horwitz & Rabbie 1982).

This work requires further extensions and replications. It is potentially important not because it denies the existence of a relationship between ingroup cohesion and intergroup conflict—which it does not do—but because it considers this relationship as itself being the result of more basic processes. It therefore attempts to specify some conditions in which the relationship does not obtain, these conditions depending upon the relevance of the external conflict to the functioning of these more basic processes.

POWER AND STATUS IN INTERGROUP BEHAVIOR[3] The interpersonal-intergroup distinction is also relevant to issues of status and power.

[3]The writer is keenly aware of the fact that important distinctions need to be made between power, status, rank, prestige, privilege, majority/minority, etc. However, as the editors insisted that the review of the social psychology of intergroup relations should be confined to one chapter only of this year's *Annual Review of Psychology,* a leisurely discussion of finer points of distinction must be avoided.

Apfelbaum (1979) pointedly wondered about *une si longue absence* of power differentials between groups in the study of intergroup behavior. The complaint seems (in part) justified, when one considers the predominantly interpersonal emphasis in, for example, the social psychological chapters of the interdisciplinary compendium on power edited by Tedeschi (1974).

Nevertheless, Apfelbaum's strictures contain an element of exaggeration, as she does not take into account the abundant tradition of research on outgroup favoritism of underprivileged groups summarized earlier in this chapter. It remains true, however, that social differentials have been at the periphery of the interests of social psychologists; but in recent years some promising departures both in theory and research have been made. Four recent trends of research seem to move in this direction. They concern the functioning of minorities, the experimentally induced effects of intergroup power relations, the effects of status on intergroup attitudes, and the role played in intergroup behavior by the perceived illegitimacy and/or instability of social differentials.

A promising start in the research on minorities was stimulated by Moscovici's work (e.g. 1976) on minority influence, which stresses the innovating potentialities of minorities in distinction from the traditional emphasis on a one-way majority influence on minorities. The major determinant of minority influence is, for Moscovici, the unwavering consistency of its viewpoint which confronts the differing views of a majority. This work has now been extended to issues of intergroup relations in studies by Mugny and his collaborators (e.g. Mugny 1975, 1981, Mugny & Papastamou 1976–77, 1980, Papastamou et al 1980). An attempt is made in this research to achieve a synthesis of ideas about innovating minority groups with tendencies sometimes shown by individuals to protect their uniqueness and differentiation (Fromkin 1972, Lemaine 1974, 1975, Lemaine et al 1978, Codol 1975). This is expressed in intergroup behavior through actions aiming to achieve a distinctive group identity associated with positive value connotations (Tajfel 1981, Chap. 12, Turner 1981).

Mugny's work shows that in order to understand the functioning of minorities in intergroup situations, assumptions about a particular "behavioral style" such as consistency must be supplemented by an analysis of the effectiveness of *any* style as it relates to the intergroup situation. This view was confirmed in a recent field study by Di Giacomo (1980) conducted in a Belgian university. An active and consistent minority attempting to gain the adherence of the general student body to a protest movement failed in its endeavors because the wording and contents of its statements led to its definition as an outgroup by the majority of the students.

The recent work of Ng (e.g. 1978, 1980) on the social psychology of power provides an example of another synthesis which seems to be required. In its application to intergroup relations, this research draws on several background conceptions. They include Mulder's theory of "power distance reduction tendencies" (e.g. Mulder et al 1971, 1973a, b) which is concerned with the conditions leading individuals who have little power to attempt an equalization with those who are more powerful; the effects of group membership on competition for power; and the conditions of social exchange (e.g. Thibaut & Kelley 1959) in which "exit" from a relationship (Hirschman 1970) is either more or less likely than attempts to change an existing social situation "from the inside." One of the points of departure in Ng's work is the acknowledgment of the simple fact that, as distinct from many interpersonal situations, real-life "exit" by a group from a multigroup structure is often extremely difficult if not impossible. Thus, in one of his studies Ng (1978) found that the strength of the attempts to change the power structure of a social relationship was *not* affected by a "social categorization that relies only on the social-evaluative force of positive social identity" (Ng 1980, p. 241). This was the case because of the structural constraints of the strongly stratified social setting. In the "no-exit" intergroup situations there is also stronger intergroup discrimination in the case of "property for power" (i.e. property which can be used for increasing the effective exercise of power over another group) than in the case of "property for use" (i.e. property acquired for direct use by its owners).

Status differences are *one* of the reflections of differences in power: differences in power are *one* of the determinants of relative status; and sometimes, when status confers power, these relationships may be reversed. The focus on ethnocentric variables sometimes led to a neglect of the role of the structural constraints of social situations, such as those exemplified in Ng's (1980) work on power. The structural constraints of status are equally important in their psychological effects.

In an extensive field study, van Knippenberg (1978) employed engineering students from two Dutch institutions of higher learning of differing status and prestige. One of the conclusions which emerged clearly from a complex set of results was that the two groups presented what amounted to obverse mirror images in their *evaluations* of four clusters of group characteristics. Among these characteristics, "status" was evaluated more highly by the lower status group. As van Knippenberg (1978) pointed out, a functional view of these differences between the groups needs to be taken. It is in the interest of the higher status group to minimize the importance of consensual status differentials, and it may be in the interest of the lower status group to magnify them. Data on attitudes concerning status-related characteristics obtained from groups in other social settings point in the same direction: university and polytechnic teachers in Britain (Bourhis & Hill 1982); nurses of different grades in a hospital (Skevington 1980); pupils from vocational and grammar schools in Geneva (Doise & Sinclair 1973, in a supplementary analysis of data by van Knippenberg & Wilke 1980); community workers in Italy differing in their professional identifications (Palmonari & Zani 1980).

These studies all point to an implicit conflict between ingroup-favoring tendencies and the acknowledged realities of social differentials in power, status, rank, or privilege. This conflict, in turn, reflects the fact that these differentials are often not accepted as immutable and legitimate. The perceived *il*legitimacy of intergroup differentials leads to a variety of consequences in the reciprocal behavior and attitudes of the groups involved. A classic study in this area is that of Lemaine & Kastersztein (1972). In a field experiment conducted in a holiday camp and resembling in some ways the Sherifian situations, one of the two competing groups of boys was provided, at random but explicitly, with poorer materials for the building of a hut, the excellence of which was to determine the outcome of the competition. The underprivileged group built a hut of indifferent quality but surrounded it with a garden. This act of social creativity, preceded by secret conclaves of the ingroup, was followed by sustained attempts to legitimize the garden as an integral part of the competition in the eyes of the outgroup and the adult judges.

Other studies have shown that experimentally induced illegitimacy of intergroup status differentials increases ingroup-favoring bias. Turner & Brown (1978) found this to be the case for both higher and lower status groups in an experiment in which Arts and Science undergraduates were competing in a task involving "reasoning skill." Induced conditions of higher and lower status between the groups were based on manipulations of legitimacy vs illegitimacy and stability vs instability of status. The findings concerning the effects of instability were less clear-cut than was the case for illegitimacy. Commins & Lockwood (1979b) found that in groups of boys who were equitably or inequitably advantaged or disadvantaged in rewards for the quality of their performance, the inequitably disadvantaged groups showed the most ingroup bias in a subsequent distribution of points worth money between the groups, but the group which had inequitable advantage also showed ingroup bias. Brown & Ross (1982) and Caddick (1980) sharpened the issue by assigning, through their procedures, the responsibility for illegitimate advantage or disadvantage directly to the groups of Ss rather than having it imposed by the experimenters as was the case in the previous studies. In the Brown & Ross study, in conditions of "high threat" caused by the outgroup's defense of illegitimate differentials, both the higher and the lower status groups showed marked outgroup discrimination; the lower status group actually *reversed* the pattern of ingroup derogation which it had shown in the "low threat" condition. Caddick (1980) compared control situations in groups which showed "high" and "low" performance on two tasks, and were rewarded accordingly, with situations in which outgroups were involved in creating an "illegitimate intergroup differentiation." In "illegitimate" conditions both the higher and lower status groups differed significantly from the controls in their distribution of rewards; they maximized differences in favor of the ingroup.

Directly related to these effects of the perceived illegitimacy of social differentials is an important series of studies by I. Katz and his colleagues (e.g. I. Katz et al 1973, I. Katz & Glass 1979) on the "ambivalence-amplification theory of behavior toward the stigmatized." These studies concern the consequences of a conflict experienced in the higher status group—i.e. by members of the white majority. The conflict stems from the discrepancy between accepted values and the treatment of racial minorities. Starting from Myrdal's (1944) ideas about "the American dilemma" and some earlier evidence (e.g. Dienstbier 1970, A. Campbell 1971), I. Katz and his colleagues were able to show that inputs of information about blacks and Chicanos lead to a polarization of reactions toward them by members of the majority. This is so because, according to the authors, the attitudinal ambivalence "potentiates threat to self-esteem in situations of contact" (I. Katz & Glass 1979, p. 57).

Social Categorization and Intergroup Behavior

Our discussion so far of intergroup behavior as a function of group membership revolved around two major themes: the interpersonal-intergroup continuum of social interaction, and the functional characteristics of "realistic" group conflicts (LeVine & D. Campbell 1972). The former of these themes will remain relevant to our present review of research on the effects of social categorization on intergroup behavior. As will be seen, these effects cannot be said to proceed directly from *explicit* conflicts between groups.

SOCIAL CATEGORIZATION: COGNITIONS, VALUES, AND GROUPS In an earlier section of this review, cognitive research was reviewed which stressed the transition "from individual to group impressions" in the formation and functioning of stereotypes. An older tradition of cognitive research on intergroup stereotypes can be traced back at least as far as Allport's (1954) insistence that the "selecting, accentuating and interpreting" of the information obtained from the social environment, which is found in sterotyping, must be understood as a special instance of the functioning of the process of categorization. An early study of D. Campbell (1956) drew attention to the enhancement of similarities within, and differences between, items in an array which could be assigned to the same or to different categories respectively. A transposition to the study of stereotypes of this accentuation of intracategory similarities and intercategory differences (see Tajfel 1981, Chaps. 4, 5, and 6) was based on hypotheses concerning two functions of "social accentuation." The *cognitive* function, resulting in the accentuation of similarities and differences, was the utilization of the category membership of individual items for ordering, systematizing, and simplifying the complex network of social groups confronting individuals in their social environment. The *value* function resulted in a still more emphatic accentuation of these same similarities and differences when they were associated with subjective value differentials applying to social categories. This served to protect, maintain, or enhance the value systems applying to distinctions between social groups. Recent summaries of the earlier research can be found in Eiser & Stroebe 1972, Irle 1975, 1978, Billig 1976, Doise 1978, Stroebe 1980, Wilder 1981.

Recent evidence confirms the accentuation principles. For example, S. Taylor et al (1978), starting from a partial restatement of the earlier hypotheses, found that "as a result of [the] categorization process, within-group differences become minimized and between-group differences become exaggerated" (p. 779). Similar results were obtained by Doise et al (1978), working with Swiss linguistic groups, and Doise & Weinberger (1972–73) with groups of boys and girls. Wilder (1978a) found that members of a group were assumed to hold more similar beliefs than individuals not presented as a group and that the same pattern applied to future behavior as predicted by the subjects. Hensley & Duval (1976) reported an accentuation of assumed similarities to, and differences from, the subjects' own beliefs attributed respectively to members of an ingroup and an outgroup. Similar or related findings were reported in other studies (e.g. Allen & Wilder 1975, 1979, Snyder & Uranowitz 1978, Wilder & Allen 1978).

The social accentuation of intracategory similarities is not, however, a symmetrical phenomenon applying evenly to ingroups and outgroups. One of the principal features, discussed earlier, of intergroup behavior and attitudes was the tendency shown by members of an ingroup to consider members of outgroups in a relatively uniform manner, as "undifferentiated items in a unified social category." The endpoint of this process is the "depersonalization" and "dehumanization" of the outgroup which often occur in conditions of acute intergroup tensions. The incipient forms of this denial of individuality to members of the outgroup have been shown to exist in some recent studies. D. Hamilton & Bishop (1976) reported that in the early stages of an integrated housing project, the white residents knew the names of other white families but referred to black families in terms of their racial category. D. A. Wilder (unpublished manuscript) found that his Ss assumed a greater homogeneity of beliefs and attitudes in the outgroup than in the ingroup about a variety of issues unrelated to the criterion on which was based the ingroup-outgroup division. Concordant findings about the outgroup's greater perceived homogeneity were also reported by Linville & Jones (1980) and Quattrone & Jones (1980).

The value and cognitive functions of social accentuation provide a basis for the understanding of the structure and direction of biases in intergroup attitudes and stereotypes, but they cannot tell us very much about the contents of the groups' reciprocal conceptions. This is why the early descriptive studies of social stereotypes (see Allport 1954) and the purely cognitive studies need to be supplemented by a theory of the *contents of stereotypes,* particularly as we know from historical and anthropological evidence (e.g. Banton 1967, Mason 1970, LeVine & D. Campbell 1972) that the diversity of *patterns* or *types* of intergroup stereotypes is fairly limited. Conceptions of outgroups are generated in their social and historical contexts and then transmitted to individual members of groups and widely shared through a variety of channels of social influence. At least three social functions of these conceptions can be distinguished (Tajfel 1981, Chap. 7): justification of actions planned or committed against outgroups; perception of social causality, especially as it relates to large-scale distressing events (such as inflation, unemployment, a lost war, etc) whose complexity needs to be reduced to simpler proportions; and a positive differentiation of a social group from relevant outgroups. This threefold framework is useful in the integration of some recent research which relates to one or more of these group functions. Thus, Billig (1978) and Guillaumin (1972) presented extensive descriptions, based on data from contents analyses, of the "conspiracy theories" of social causation in which the evil intentions and actions of selected target groups become the assumed "cause" of the ills befalling society at large (see also Cohn 1967, for a parallel historical analysis). Deschamps (1977), Hewstone & Jaspars (1982), and Pettigrew (1979) used a number of relevant experimental studies (e.g. Deaux & Emswiller 1974, Mann & D. Taylor 1974, D. Taylor & Jaggi 1974, Dion & Earn 1975, Duncan 1976, Stephan 1977, Dion et al 1978, V. Hamilton 1978) to extend the interindividual emphasis of attribution theory (e.g. Kelley & Michela 1980) in order to stress the importance of ingroup vs outgroup membership in the kinds of attributions of responsibility that are made for favorable and unfavorable events. This work is also relevant to the group functions of "justification" and "causality" mentioned above. As Hewstone & Jaspars (1982) wrote, "in an intergroup context, attributions are made as a function of the social group membership of both the actor and the observer. Thus, *social categorization* is the key variable." Finally, the group "differentiation" function is directly connected with the work on tendencies to achieve a "positive group distinctiveness" which will be discussed below in the framework of the C.I.C. (social categorization-social identity-social comparison) approach to intergroup behavior.

SOCIAL CATEGORIZATION AND INTERGROUP DISCRIMINATION

Despite the accumulation of commonsense and research evidence that *explicit* intergroup conflicts and competition lead to intergroup discrimination, there have been indications that they are not the *only* necessary conditions. For example, in one of Sherif's studies (Sherif et al 1961) boys came to the holiday camp in two separate groups. As soon as the groups became aware of each other's existence, and *before* the competition between them was institutionalized by the camp authorities, there was some evidence of the development of competitive ingroup-outgroup attitudes. There has also been other evidence (e.g. Ferguson & Kelley 1964, Rabbie & Wilkens 1971) pointing in the same direction, including studies showing that intergroup cooperation does not preclude ingroup bias (see Worchel 1979, Turner 1981 for reviews).

The question therefore arose about the *minimal* conditions that would create intergroup discrimination. In the first experiment in which a "minimal" intergroup categorization was introduced (Rabbie & Horwitz 1969), Ss were divided into two groups on the basis of being labeled "blue" and "green." It was found that discrimination between them only occurred when each of the groups shared some form of a "common fate," while this was not the case in the control condition where the blue-green categorization was the only criterion of intergroup division. These results were questioned later (e.g. Turner 1975, pp. 24–30) on the argument that the methodological criteria for an appropriate intergroup categorization were not met in the study.

Additional criteria were introduced in an experiment by Tajfel et al (1971), in which intergroup categorization was based on over- or underestimation of numbers of dots in clusters and on differing aesthetic preferences. In a subsequent experiment by Billig & Tajfel (1973), division into groups was determined by random tosses of a coin. In these experiments (and others) there was no social interaction either within or between "groups"; no instrumental links between the Ss' responses and their self-interest; the anonymity of group membership was preserved; and there was no previous hostility between the groups. The major dependent variable was the distribution by each S of points worth money between two other anonymous Ss who were either one from the ingroup and one from the outgroup, both from the ingroup, or both from the outgroup. The points were distributed on "matrices" which allowed an assessment of the relative importance of various distribution strategies employed by the Ss. The results showed clear and consistent evidence of bias in favor of the ingroup.

These results gave rise to several methodological controversies (see Billig 1973, Gerard & Hoyt 1974, Branthwaite et al 1979, Aschenbrenner & Schaefer 1980, Brown et al 1980, Turner 1980, Tajfel 1981). The finding that intergroup discrimination can be caused by a "minimal" social categorization retains, however, a considerable robustness. A count made for this review results in a conservative estimate of at least 30 studies which used minimal or near-minimal categorizations with diverse populations of Ss, independent variables and dependent measures, and which all show ingroup-favoring bias (see Brewer 1979b, Brown et al 1980, Turner 1981, for some of the recent reviews).

SOCIAL IDENTITY AND SOCIAL COMPARISON An intriguing aspect of the early data on minimal categorization was the importance of the strategy maximizing the *difference* between the awards made to the ingroup and the outgroup even at the cost of giving thereby less to members of the ingroup. This finding was replicated in a field study (Brown 1978) in which shop stewards representing different trades unions in a large factory filled distribution matrices which specified their preferred structure of comparative wages for members of the unions involved. It was not, however, replicated in another field study in Britain (Bourhis & Hill 1982) in which similar matrices were completed by polytechnic and university teachers.

The data on maximization of differences contributed to the development of the C.I.C. theory. The major assumption is that even when there is no explicit or institutionalized conflict or competition between the groups, there is a tendency toward ingroup-favoring behavior. This is determined by the need to preserve or achieve a "positive group distinctiveness" which in turn serves to protect, enhance, preserve, or achieve a positive social identity for members of the group (Tajfel 1974, 1981, Turner 1975, Tajfel & Turner 1979). "Social identity" is defined as "that *part* of the individuals' self-concept which derives from their knowledge of their membership of a social group (or groups) together with the value and emotional significance of that membership" (Tajfel 1981, p. 255). In conditions in which social interactions are determined to a large extent by the individuals' reciprocal group memberships, positive social identity can be achieved, in a vast majority of cases, only through appropriate inter*group* social comparisons. Thus, the positive or negative conceptions of a social group are seen as being primarily *relational* in nature. In the succinct statement by Commins & Lockwood (1979b): "The social group is seen to function as a provider of positive social identity for its members through comparing itself, and distinguishing itself, from other comparison groups along salient dimensions which have a clear value differential" (pp. 281–82).

A direct inference from these views is that a "minimal" social categorization exerts its discriminatory intergroup effects because it provides a way to enhance "positive ingroup distinctiveness." This is done through the creation of favorable comparisons with the outgroup for which the Ss use the dimensions of comparison which are available to them, as was the case with the distribution matrices in the studies just described. This was the case in a study by Oakes & Turner (1980), who found direct evidence for increased self-esteem being related to the opportunity of engaging in intergroup discrimination.

There also exists a number of recent studies which show in various ways that an increase in the salience of group membership leads, through intergroup comparisons, to more marked ingroup favoritism. These studies used several independent variables, singly or in combination, such as: increasing the salience of an experimentally induced group membership through the mere presence of another group; using in a similar way social situations in which a long-standing "real-life" group membership was made more salient; comparing attitudes and behavior relating to "collections" of individuals showing similarities or differences with an imposition, in the same conditions, of explicit divisions between the individuals in terms of groups (e.g. Boyanowski & Allen 1973, Doise & Sinclair 1973, Hensley & Duval 1976, McKillip et al 1977, White 1977, Worchel et al 1977, Brown & Deschamps 1980–81, Doise et al 1978, McGuire et al 1978, Turner et al 1979).

This work has implications for Rokeach's (1960, 1968) "belief congruence" theory of prejudice which derives from the view that prejudice is based on the assumption of dissimilarity in beliefs between oneself and members of outgroups rather than on socially derived value connotations which are directly associated with intergroup categorizations. The empirical issue can, however, be focused more specifically: if intergroup categorization and interpersonal similarity or attraction are pitted directly against each other, which of the two is more likely to prevail in determining attitudes and behavior? Allen & Wilder (1975) studied directly the interaction between similarity-dissimilarity of beliefs and ingroup-outgroup membership. Using a "minimal categorization" procedure, they found that ingroup favoritism persisted even when there was similarity of beliefs with members of the outgroup and dissimilarity with members of the ingroup. Billig & Tajfel (1973) reported that the presence or absence of a minimal intergroup categorization was a stronger determinant of favoritism shown by the Ss in their distribution of rewards to other people than was interindividual similarity or dissimilarity. In field studies on helping anonymous strangers, Sole et al (1975) discovered a steep increase in the extent of helping when the strangers could be unambiguously categorized by the Ss as members of the "we" group rather than just as being similar in some of their beliefs.

An inference from the C.I.C. theory is that in conditions of salient intergroup categorization, groups will tend to work harder at establishing their distinctiveness from the outgroups which are perceived as similar than from those which are seen as dissimilar. This is in direct contradiction to the "belief congruence" view. There is some support for the C.I.C. prediction from three experimental studies. Turner (1978) found that in competitive situations, groups with similar values displayed more intergroup discrimination than groups with dissimilar values. In a study by Turner et al (1979) Ss were readier to sacrifice self-interest for a strategy maximizing ingroup-favoring differences when they were dealing with outgroups which were more directly comparable with the in-group. In another study (Brown, as reported in Brown & Turner 1981), attitudinal similarity between groups in conditions of intergroup cooperation did induce favorable attitudes toward the outgroup; but this did not apply to Ss who had been previously ascertained as being highly competitive. They were found to like similar groups less than dissimilar ones. In contradiction to all this evidence, D. Taylor & Guimond (1978) reported that in various conditions of increased salience of group membership, belief similarity was more important in determining the Ss' responses than group affiliation.

Thus, the issue still remains unresolved. The direction that needs to be taken by future research was well summarized by D. Taylor & Guimond (1978), who wrote that, as distinct from the procedures of their own study, "it will be important to manipulate important beliefs *shared* by members of a group and require Ss to make judgements about ingroups and outgroups on a collective basis" (p. 24).

An area of work which has proved sensitive to testing the C.I.C. interaction is that of the linguistic aspects of ethnic and national identity. There is a vast amount of evidence from history, anthropology, and political science that various forms of linguistic distinctiveness are perceived as a crucial mainstay in the revival or preservation of a separate ethnic or national identity. This has led in recent years to a considerable amount of research, conducted in many sociocultural contexts, which attempted to integrate sociocultural aspects of language use with the study of psychological intergroup processes. Several discussions and reviews of this work are now available (e.g. Bourhis & Giles 1977, Giles 1979, Husband 1979, Lambert 1980, Giles & Johnson 1981). The achievement by ethnic or national groups of "psycholinguistic distinctiveness" (Giles et al 1977) is equivalent to the "positive group distinctiveness" discussed earlier in relation to the C.I.C. processes. The nature of the existing relations between the groups determines the choice of one or more between a number of possible strategies which are available to an ethnolinguistic minority for coping with its disadvantages. When the boundaries between the groups are not firmly drawn, in the sense that access to the dominant language group does not present too much difficulty, a strategy of individual assimilation is often adopted (see Giles & Johnson 1981). Another individual strategy is that of "illegitimate" assimilation (Breakwell 1979, Tajfel 1981, Chap. 15) which consists of concealing one's background or origin in the use of language as well as through other forms of concealment (e.g. changes of name, the "passing" of light-skinned blacks, etc).

These individual strategies differ sharply from group strategies which are sometimes determined by difficulty of access to the outgroup, sometimes by strong internal pressures for preserving group identity, and very often by a combination of both these conditions. The attempts to achieve positive group distinctiveness are translated here into various forms of linguistic "social creativity," some of which are conceptually similar to the behavior shown by the disadvantaged group in the Lemaine & Kastersztein (1972) study mentioned earlier in this chapter. In some cases there is a positive reevaluation of the group's language or dialect (e.g. Bourhis & Giles 1977). In others, linguistic divergences from the outgroup are accentuated (e.g. Doise et al 1976, Bourhis et al 1979). In still others, this accentuation of divergence takes the form of intense efforts to revive the separate language of the group, as was the case, perhaps most dramatically, with modern Hebrew in Israel and with the corresponding attitudes widely shared in the national group (e.g. Seckbach 1974). Several similar examples from other national and ethnic groups can be found in the review by Giles & Johnson (1981). It has also recently been shown (see Giles & Byrne 1980) that these attempts to achieve or maintain a separate group identity in relation to outgroups can markedly affect the rate of progress and effectiveness of second-language acquisition in immigrant groups.

It would be an oversimplification, however, to exaggerate the ingroup's uniformity of attitudes and behavior in these psycholinguistic expressions of the push toward a distinctive ethnic or national identity. In this and other areas, multiple group membership, differences of individual positions within the group, and the salience of subgroup membership (Zavalloni 1972, 1973, 1975) determine a diversity of patterns. Any conceptual scheme can only account for a limited part of the variance. Its range of validity and the appearance of alternative patterns can be interpreted adequately only when the relevant psychological processes are looked at in conjunction with the study of their socio-cultural contexts.

THE REDUCTION OF INTERGROUP DISCRIMINATION

The term "discrimination" rather than "conflict" is used in the above title because referring to a reduction of intergroup *conflict* would imply adopting a standpoint about the results of the relevant work which appears to prejudge the fundamental issues: can it be said that this research has succeeded in giving us new insights about the reduction of the underlying conflicts between groups, or is it more appropriate to consider it as applying to the reduction, under *some* conditions, of mutual discrimination between *some* members of groups in conflict? For the present there is no evidence that the first of these questions can be answered in the affirmative.

It cannot be said that great strides forward have been accomplished in recent years in our understanding of these issues. This is perhaps due to the fact that we still do not have a general integrating perspective. In a review of the work on the role of intergroup contact in prejudice and ethnic relations, Amir (1976) concluded that "despite a substantial amount of research . . . our theoretical understanding of what contact involves as a potential agent of change and what are the underlying processes is still very limited" (p. 289). This conclusion applies to the area as a whole. Among several strands of recent research which can be identified, three will be discussed here briefly as they represent changes of emphasis from earlier work.

Intergroup Cooperation and Superordinate Goals

Intergroup cooperation leads, as might be expected, to less discrimination than intergroup competition. However, Sherif's (e.g. 1966) early conclusions about the effectiveness of "superordinate goals" shared by the previously competing groups have been found to apply in a more limited way than he had originally envisaged. It has been pointed out (e.g. Tajfel 1981, Chap.14) that in the final stage of Sherif's study, when the two groups of boys worked together for the achievement of a common goal which neither of them could have achieved separately, their competitive conflict was over and there were no other criteria left to perpetuate their division into two groups. In other words, there are no reasons to assume that they have not come to feel as one group and that therefore their full cooperation need not be representative of other situations in which groups retain separate entities despite the occasional situations when they must work together for a common goal.

Experimental research on these issues has now been initiated by Worchel (Worchel et al 1977, 1978), who found that the salience of previously existing group identities strongly affected the conflict-reducing effects of subsequent intergroup cooperation, and that an interaction between these previous identities and the success or failure of the cooperation was also important. A recent review of these and other studies can be found in Worchel (1979).

Intergroup Contact

A large number of studies have also been conducted in recent years on the effects of interpersonal contact on the reduction of intergroup discrimination, particularly in situations of interethnic or interracial tension or conflict (see Amir 1976, Riordin 1978). Comparing recent work with earlier research in the fifties, Amir (1976) drew attention to two general changes of emphasis. The first consists of more attention having been paid recently to the attitudes and behavior of minority group members as compared with the earlier emphasis on the changes of attitudes in the high status majorities. The second major change could be described as a loss of innocence. In the earlier period, many investigators "sought and expected a reduction of prejudice" (Amir 1976, p. 285), and therefore they tended to select social situations in which these results might be expected to occur. There has been in recent years a large increase in research on everyday life situations, as a result of which, to quote Amir again, "a much larger percentage of studies report either no-difference findings, qualified results, or unfavorable changes" (1976, p. 283). This brings us to a conclusion similar to that reached by Diab (1978): whenever the underlying structure of social divisions and power or status differentials is fairly resilient, it is not likely to be substantially affected by piecemeal attempts at reform in selected situations of "contact."

Multigroup Membership and "Individualization" of the Outgroup

There is evidence from anthropological field studies that a certain amount of control of intergroup conflict and hostility has often been achieved in tribal societies through various methods of "crossing" the membership of groups, so that some individuals find themselves belonging to one group on the basis of one set of criteria and to a traditionally hostile group according to other critera (e.g. LeVine & D. Campbell 1972). This "criss-crossing" can be achieved through, for example, various types of exogamous marriages with the result that a structure of social categories may obtain in which individuals who belong to categories A and B are further subdivided into categories AC, AD, BC and BD. Starting from this evidence and predictions which could be drawn from the social accentuation theory described earlier in this chapter, Deschamps & Doise (1978) conducted an experimental study in which "criss-cross" categorizations of the Ss were introduced in terms of two separate and overlapping criteria. They found that as a result there was a decrease in intergroup discrimination as compared with a dichotomous social categorization. Brown & Turner (1979) questioned the interpretation of these results and confirmed their own hypothesis that the reduction in discrimination was due to the cognitive difficulties of the "criss-cross" arrangements experienced by the children who acted as Ss in the previous study. There is, however, some tentative evidence that the "criss-cross" effects may be important. Commins & Lockwood (1978) superimposed an experimentally induced transient categorization upon the important and pervasive Catholic/Protestant division in Northern Ireland and found as a result *some* decrease in the traditionally determined intergroup discrimination; but this did not reach statistical significance. The paradigm may, however, prove important for future research on the reduction of discrimination. As Commins & Lockwood (1978) pointed out, the "real-life" religious categorization in Northern Ireland is much more salient and powerful than the relatively trivial one which was experimentally induced, and stronger results remain possible when two equally powerful social categorizations can be made to overlap and compete.

The "criss-cross" categorizations attempted to break down the perceived homogeneity of the outgroup which, as was seen earlier in this chapter, is an important feature of intergroup behavior. A similar principle was used by Wilder (1978b) in a series of studies on the "reduction of intergroup discrimination through individuation of the outgroup." He found that when Ss who had been initially categorized into groups on "minimal" criteria were later informed that there was dissent within the outgroup about issues which were unrelated to the initial criterion for categorization, intergroup discrimination was less than in the condition in which the outgroup was assumed to be unanimous. As there was no interaction between the groups, nor was there any opportunity for members of the ingroup to form their own opinions about the issues involved, the decrease in discrimination seems a fairly "pure" effect of the decrease in the perceived outgroup homogeneity. The studies by Commins & Lockwood (1978) and by Wilder (1978b) point to the importance for future research of using "natural" situations in which the "criss-cross" and the "individuation" effects are present or can be introduced. If they can be replicated, they could provide a fresh approach to studies on the reduction of intergroup discrimination.

SUMMARY

This has been a selective review of several years of work in an area of research which contains an enormous range and scope of problems and has always defied attempts at neat and tidy integration. I was grateful to the editors of the *Annual Review of Psychology* for their encouragement to present a perspective of newly emerging trends rather than an encyclopedic compilation.

Such an endeavor must, however, result in a reflection of the author's judgments (and biases) as to what is more or less important. The present review was guided by the conviction that intergroup processes present problems which often need their own level of theorizing and research, and that equally often it is not very useful to treat them in terms of extensions from research in which group membership is not a primary independent variable.

The early section of the review concentrated on research which emphasizes cognitive processes as being both necessary and sufficient for the understanding of the formation and functioning of social stereotypes. Important findings and conclusions have emerged from this research, but they are concerned with a fairly narrow range of intergroup situations. These conclusions do not seem able at present to provide generalizations to interactions between groups which are powerfully determined by conflicts and by value-laden social differentiations.

It seemed, therefore, important to stress that the study of intergroup behavior needs to achieve a synthesis of these attentional processes with the socially determined value connotations of divisions between human groups, and with an insight into the conditions in which relations between groups strongly determine the reciprocal behavior of the individuals involved. This is why most of the review was devoted to intergroup behavior seen against the background of *group membership.* Recent research on ethnocentrism, of which some cross-cultural and developmental aspects were summarized, led to the conclusion that this "umbrella concept" must be considered in its connections with the psychological aspects and effects of social stability and social change, and of the *functions* served by group affiliations. These functions were discussed in turn in a perspective stressing the conditions in which the behavior of individuals is closely related to their group membership rather than to their personal relations with other individuals, i.e. the "interpersonal-intergroup continuum." This framework was then used to consider the relations between intergroup conflict and group cohesion and the differentials between social groups in status and power.

There can be no intergroup behavior without categorization into groups, i.e. "social categorization." A section of the review was devoted to processes of intergroup discrimination which in some ways transcend the existence of explicit conflict or competition between groups. These processes seem to depend upon the contribution that group affiliation makes to the self-concept of its individual members, and to their subjective location in the social networks of which they are a part. The study of social identity and social comparison does not *replace* the need for an analysis of explicit conflicts and competition, but complements it. In the final section of the review, devoted to research on the reduction of intergroup discrimination, a very large amount of good research had to be omitted or selectively presented. This was so because we are still badly in need of an integration of this vast area of work. What we have at present is a long list of empirical statements varying considerably in their degree of generality, practical applicability, or theoretical significance.

It seems that the future will have to be much longer than the past in the field of intergroup behavior. The increasing global interdependence since the end of World War II has enormously increased the diversity and complexity of intergroup relations. The psychological study of these problems, which will manage to *combine* some of our traditional preoccupations with an increased sensitivity to the nature of social realities, is one of our most important tasks for the future.

Literature Cited

Aboud, F. E., Taylor, D. M. 1971. Ethnic and role stereotypes: Their relative importance in person perception. *J. Soc. Psychol.* 85:17–27

Aboud, F. E., Taylor, D. M., Doumani, R. G. 1973. The effect of contact on the use of role and ethnic stereotypes in person perception. *J. Soc. Psychol.* 89:309–10

Allen, V. L., Wilder, D. A. 1975. Categorization, belief similarity, and group discrimination. *J. Pers. Soc. Psychol.* 32:971–77

Allen, V. L., Wilder, D. A. 1979. Group categorization and attribution of belief similarity. *Small Group Behav.* 110:73–80

Allport, G. W. 1954. *The Nature of Prejudice.* Cambridge, Mass: Addison-Wesley. 537 pp.

Amir, Y. 1976. The role of intergroup contact in change of prejudice and ethnic relations. See Katz 1976, pp. 245–308

Apfelbaum, E. 1979. Le pouvoir entre les groupes: L'histoire d'une si longue absence. *Rech. Psychol. Soc.* 1:99–121

Aschenbrenner, K. M., Schaefer, R. E. 1980. Minimal intergroup situations: Comments on a mathematical model and on the research paradigm. *Eur. J. Soc. Psychol.* 10:389–98

Austin, W. G., Worchel, S., eds. 1979. *The Social Psychology of Intergroup Relations.* Monterey, Calif: Brooks/Cole. 369 pp.

Banton, M. 1967. *Race Relations.* London: Tavistock. 434 pp.

Barbiero, M. C. 1974. *Noi e Gli Altri: Attegiamenti e Pregiudizi nel Bambino.* Naples: Guida. 107 pp.

Batstone, E., Boraston, I., Frenkel, S. 1977. *Shop Stewards in Action.* Oxford: Blackwell. 316 pp.

Berry, J. W., Kalin, R., Taylor, D. M. 1977. *Multiculturalism and Ethnic Attitudes in Canada.* Ottawa: Min. Supply & Services. 359 pp.

Billig, M. 1973. Normative communication in a minimal intergroup situation. *Eur. J. Soc. Psychol.* 3:339–44

Billig, M. 1976. *Social Psychology and Intergroup Relations.* London: Academic. 428 pp.

Billig, M. 1978. *Fascists: A Social Psychological View of the National Front.* London: Academic. 393 pp.

Billig, M., Tajfel, H. 1973. Social categorization and similarity in intergroup behavior. *Eur. J. Soc. Psychol.* 3:27–52

Bourhis, R. Y., Giles, H. 1977. The language of intergroup distinctiveness. In *Language, Ethnicity, and Intergroup Relations,* ed. H. Giles, pp. 119–35. London: Academic. 370 pp.

Bourhis, R. Y., Giles, H., Leyens, J-P., Tajfel, H. 1979. Psycholinguistic distinctiveness: Language divergence in Belgium. In *Language and Social Psychology,* ed. H. Giles, R. St.Clair, pp. 158–85. Oxford: Blackwell. 261 pp.

Bourhis, R. Y., Giles, H., Tajfel, H. 1973. Language as a determinant of Welsh identity. *Eur. J. Soc. Psychol.* 3:447–60

Bourhis, R. Y., Hill, P. 1982. Intergroup perceptions in British higher education: A field study. In *Social Identity and Intergroup Relations,* ed. H. Tajfel. Cambridge: Cambridge Univ. Press; Paris: Éd. Maison Sci. l'Homme. In press

Boyanowsky, E. O., Allen, V. L. 1973. Ingroup norms and self-identity as determinants of discriminatory behavior. *J. Pers. Soc. Psychol.* 25:408–18

Branthwaite, A., Doyle, S., Lightbown, N. 1979. The balance between fairness and discrimination. *Eur. J. Soc. Psychol.* 9:149–63

Breakwell, G. 1979. Illegitimate membership and intergroup differentiation. *Br. J. Soc. Clin. Psychol.* 18:141–49

Brewer, M. B. 1968. Determinants of social distance among East African tribal groups. *J. Pers. Soc. Psychol.* 10:279–89

Brewer, M. B. 1979a. The role of ethnocentrism in intergroup conflict. See Austin & Worchel 1979, pp. 71–84

Brewer, M. B. 1979b. Ingroup bias in the minimal intergroup situation: A cognitive-motivational analysis. *Psychol. Bull.* 86:307–24

Brewer, M. B. 1981. Ethnocentrism and its role in interpersonal trust. In *Scientific Inquiry and the Social Sciences,* ed. M. B. Brewer, B. E. Collins, pp. 345–60. San Francisco: Jossey-Bass. 502 pp.

Brewer, M. B., Campbell, D. T. 1976. *Ethnocentrism and Intergroup Attitudes: East African Evidence.* New York: Wiley. 218 pp.

Brigham, J. C. 1971. Ethnic stereotypes. *Psychol. Bull.* 86:15–38

Brown, R. J. 1978. Divided we fall: An analysis of relations between sections of a factory workforce. In *Differentiation Between Social Groups: Studies in the Social Psychology of Intergroup Relations,* ed. H. Tajfel, pp. 395–429. London: Academic. 474 pp.

Brown, R. J., Deschamps, J-C. 1980/81. Discrimination entre individus et entre groupes. *Bull. Psychol.* 34:185–95

Brown, R. J., Ross, G. F. 1982. The battle for acceptance: An investigation into the dynamics of intergroup behavior. See Bourhis & Hill 1982. In press

Brown, R. J., Tajfel, H., Turner, J. C. 1980. Minimal group situations and intergroup discrimination: Comments on the paper by Aschenbrenner and Schaefer. *Eur. J. Soc. Psychol.* 10:399–414

Brown, R. J., Turner, J. C. 1979. The crisscross categorization effect in intergroup discrimination. *Br. J. Soc. Clin Psychol.* 18:371–83

Brown, R. J., Turner, J. C. 1981. Interpersonal and intergroup behavior. See Turner & Giles 1981, pp. 33–65

Caddick, B. 1980. Equity theory, social identity, and intergroup relations. *Rev. Pers. Soc. Psychol.* 1:219–45

Campbell, A. 1971. *White Attitudes Toward Black People.* Ann Arbor: Univ. Mich. Inst. Soc. Res. 177 pp.

Campbell, D. T. 1956. Enhancement of contrast as composite habit. *J. Abnorm. Soc. Psychol.* 3:350–55

Cantor, N., Mischel, W. 1979. Prototypes in person perception. *Adv. Exp. Soc. Psychol.* 12:3–52

Capozza, D., Bonaldo, E., Di Maggio, A. 1979. *Problemi di Identità e di Conflitto Sociale: Ricerche Condotte su Gruppi Etnici in Italia.* Padua: Antoniona Spa. 67 pp.

Codol, J-P. 1975. On the so-called "superior conformity of the self" behavior: Twenty experimental investigations. *Eur. J. Soc. Psychol.* 5:457–501

Cohn, N. 1967. *Warrant for Genocide.* New York: Harper. 303 pp.

Commins, B., Lockwood, J. 1978. The effects on intergroup relations of mixing Roman Catholics and Protestants: An experimental investigation. *Eur. J. Soc. Psychol.* 8:383–86

Commins, B., Lockwood, J. 1979a. Social comparison and social inequality: An experimental investigation in intergroup behavior. *Br. J. Soc. Clin. Psychol.* 18:285–90

Commins, B., Lockwood, J. 1979b. The effects of status differences, favored treatment, and equity on intergroup comparisons. *Eur. J. Soc. Psychol.* 9:281–89

Davey, A. G., Mullin, P. N. 1980. Ethnic identification and preference of British primary school children. *J. Child Psychol. Psychiatry* 21:241–51

Davey, A. G., Norburn, M. V. 1980. Ethnic awareness and ethnic differentiation amongst primary school children. *New Community* 8:1–10

Deaux, K., Emswiller, T. 1974. Explanations of successful performance on sex-linked tasks: What is skill for the male is luck for the female. *J. Pers. Soc. Psychol.* 29:80–85

Deschamps, J-C. 1977. *L'Attribution et la Catégorisation Sociale.* Berne: Lang. 186 pp.

Deschamps, J-C., Doise, W. 1978. Crossed category memberships in intergroup relations. See Brown 1978, pp. 141–58

Deutsch, M. 1973. *The Resolution of Conflict: Constructive and Destructive Processes.* New Haven, Conn: Yale Univ. Press. 420 pp.

Diab, L. N. 1970. A study of intragroup and intergroup relations among experimentally produced small groups. *Genet. Psychol. Monogr.* 82:49–82

Diab, L. N. 1978. Achieving intergroup cooperation through conflict-produced superordinate goals. *Psychol. Rep.* 43:735–41

Dienstbier, R. A. 1970. Positive and negative prejudice: Interactions of prejudice with race and social desirability. *J. Pers.* 38:198–215

Di Giacomo, J-P. 1980. Intergroup alliances and rejections within a protest movement (analysis of social representations). *Eur. J. Soc. Psychol.* 10:329–44

Dion, K. L., Earn, B. M. 1975. The phenomenology of being a target of prejudice. *J. Pers. Soc. Psychol.* 32:944–50

Dion, K. L., Earn, B. M., Yee, P. H. N. 1978. The experience of being a victim of prejudice: An experimental approach. *Int. J. Psychol.* 13:197–214

Doise, W. 1978. *Groups and Individuals: Explanations in Social Psychology.* Cambridge: Cambridge Univ. Press. 226 pp.

Doise, W., Csepeli, G., Dann, H-D., Gouge, G. C., Larsen, K., Ostell, A. 1972. An experimental investigation into the formation of intergroup representations. *Eur. J. Soc. Psychol.* 2:202–4

Doise, W., Deschamps, J-C., Meyer, G. 1978. The accentuation of intracategory similarities. See Brown 1978, pp. 159–68

Doise, W., Sinclair, A. 1973. The categorization process in intergroup relations. *Eur. J. Soc. Psychol.* 3:145–57

Doise, W., Sinclair, A., Bourhis, R. Y. 1976. Evaluation of accent convergence and divergence in cooperative and competitive intergroup situations. *Br. J. Soc. Clin. Psychol.* 15:247–52

Doise, W., Weinberger, M. 1972/73. Représentations masculines dans différentes situations de recontres mixtes. *Bull. Psychol.* 26:649–57

Dollard, J. 1937. *Caste and Class in a Southern Town.* Garden City, NY: Doubleday Anchor. 466 pp. 3rd ed. 1957

Duncan, B. L. 1976. Differential social perception and attribution of intergroup violence: Testing the lower limits of stereotyping of Blacks. *J. Pers. Soc. Psychol.* 34:590–98

Dustin, D. S., Davis, H. P. 1970. Evaluative bias in group and individual competition. *J. Soc. Psychol.* 80:103–8

Ehrlich, H. J. 1973. *The Social Psychology of Prejudice: A Systematic Theoretical Review and Propositional Inventory of the American Social Psychological Study of Prejudice.* New York: Wiley. 208 pp.

Eiser, J. R., Stroebe, W. 1972. *Categorization and Social Judgment.* London: Academic. 236 pp.

Ferguson, C. K., Kelley, H. H. 1964. Significant factors in over-evaluation of own group's products. *J. Abnorm. Soc. Psychol.* 69:223–28

Fox, D. J., Jordan, V. B. 1973. Racial preference and identification of black, American Chinese, and white children. *Genet. Psychol. Monogr.* 88:229–86

Fromkin, H. L. 1972. Feelings of interpersonal undistinctiveness: An unpleasant affective state. *J. Exp. Res. Pers.* 6:178–85

Geber, B. A., Newman, S. P. 1980. *Soweto's Children: The Development of Attitudes.* London: Academic. 215 pp.

Gerard, H. B., Hoyt, M. F. 1974. Distinctiveness of social categorization and attitude toward ingroup members. *J. Pers. Soc. Psychol.* 29:836–42

Giles, H. 1979. Ethnicity markers in speech. In *Social Markers in Speech,* ed. K. R. Scherer, H. Giles, pp. 251–89. Cambridge: Cambridge Univ. Press; Paris: Éd. Maison Sci. l'Homme. 395 pp.

Giles, H., Bourhis, R. Y., Taylor, D. M. 1977. Toward a theory of language in ethnic group relations. See Bourhis & Giles 1977, pp. 307–48

Giles, H., Byrne, J. L. 1980. An intergroup approach to second language acquisition. *Rev. Educ.* 265:00–00

Giles, H., Johnson, P. 1981. The role of language in ethnic group relations. See Turner & Giles 1981, pp. 199–243

Giles, H., Powesland, P. F. 1975. *Speech Style and Social Evaluation.* London: Academic. 218 pp.

Greenwald, H. J., Oppenheim, D. B. 1968. Reported magnitude of self-misidentification among Negro children: Artifact? *J. Pers. Soc. Psychol.* 8:49–52

Guillaumin, C. 1972. *L'Idéologie Raciste: Genèse et Langage Actuel.* Paris: Mouton. 247 pp.

Hamilton, D. L. 1976. Cognitive biases in the perception of social groups. In *Cognition and Social Behavior,* ed. J. S. Carroll, J. W. Payne, pp. 81–93. New York: Erlbaum. 290 pp.

Hamilton, D. L. 1979. A cognitive-attributional analysis of stereotyping. *Adv. Exp. Soc. Psychol.* 12:53–83

Hamilton, D. L., Bishop, G. D. 1976. Attitudinal and behavioral effects of initial integration of white suburban neighborhoods. *J. Soc. Issues* 32:47–67

Hamilton, D. L., Gifford, R. K. 1976. Illusory correlation in interpersonal perception: A cognitive basis of stereotypic judgments. *J. Exp. Soc. Psychol.* 12: 392–407

Hamilton, V. L. 1978. Who is responsible? Toward a *social* psychology of responsibility attribution. *Soc. Psychol.* 41: 316–28

Hensley, V., Duval, S. 1976. Some perceptual determinants of perceived similarity, liking, and correctness. *J. Pers. Soc. Psychol.* 34:159–68

Hewstone, M., Jaspars, J. M. F. 1982. Intergroup relations and attribution processes. See Bourhis & Hill 1982. In press

Hinkle, S., Schopler, J. 1979. Ethnocentrism in the evaluation of group products. See Austin & Worchel 1979, pp. 160–73

Hirschman, A. O. 1970. *Exit, Voice, and Loyalty: Responses to Decline in Firms, Organizations, and States.* Cambridge, Mass: Harvard Univ. Press. 162 pp.

Horwitz, M., Rabbie, J. M. 1982. Individuality and membership in the intergroup system. See Bourhis & Hill 1982. In press

Howard, J. W., Rothbart, M. 1980. Social categorization and memory for in-group and out-group behavior. *J. Pers. Soc. Psychol.* 38:301–10

Hraba, J., Grant, G. 1980. Black is beautiful: A reexamination of racial preference and identification. *J. Pers. Soc. Psychol.* 16:398–402

Husband, C. 1979. Social identity and the language of race relations. In *Language and Ethnic Relations,* ed. H. Giles, B. Saint-Jacques, pp. 179–95. Oxford: Pergamon. 251 pp.

Irle, M. 1975. *Lehrbuch der Sozialpsychologie.* Göttingen: Hogrefe. 558 pp.

Irle, M., ed. 1978. *Kursus der Sozialpsychologie.* Darmstadt: Luchterhand. 621 pp.

Jaffe, Y., Yinon, Y. 1979. Retaliatory aggression in individuals and groups. *Eur. J. Soc. Psychol.* 9:177–86

Jahoda, G., Thompson, S. S., Bhatt, S. 1972. Ethnic identity and preferences among Asian immigrant children in Glasgow: A replicated study. *Eur. J. Soc. Psychol.* 2:19–32

Janssens, L., Nuttin, J. R. 1976. Frequency perception of individual and group successes as a function of competition, coaction, and isolation. *J. Pers. Soc. Psychol.* 34:830–36

Jaspars, J. M. F., van de Geer, J. P., Tajfel, H., Johnson, N. B. 1973. On the development of national attitudes. *Eur. J. Soc. Psychol.* 3:347–69

Jaspars, J. M. F., Warnaen, S. 1982. Intergroup relations, ethnic identity, and self-evaluation in Indonesia. See Bourhis & Hill 1982. In press

Kahn, A., Ryen, A. H. 1972. Factors influencing bias toward one's own group. *Int. J. Group Tensions* 2:35–50

Kanter, R. M. 1977. Some effects of proportions on group life: Skewed sex ratios and responses to token women. *Am. J. Sociol.* 82:965–90

Katz, I. 1973. Alternatives to a personality-deficit interpretation of Negro under-achievement. In *Psychology and Race,* ed. P. Watson, pp. 377–91. Harmondsworth: Penguin. 491 pp.

Katz, I., Glass, D. C. 1979. An ambivalence-amplification theory of behavior toward the stigmatized. See Austin & Worchel 1979, pp. 55–70

Katz, I., Glass, D. C., Cohen, S. 1973. Ambivalence, guilt, and the scapegoating of minority group victims. *J. Exp. Soc. Psychol.* 9:423–36

Katz, P. A. 1976. The acquisition of racial attitudes in children. In *Toward the Elimination of Racism,* ed. P. A. Katz, pp. 125–54. New York: Pergamon. 444 pp.

Katz, P. A., Zalk, S. R. 1974. Doll preferences: An index of racial attitudes? *J. Educ. Psychol.* 66:663–68

Kelley, H. H., Michela, J. L. 1980. Attribution theory and research. *Ann. Rev. Psychol.* 31:457–501

Kidder, L. H., Stewart, V. M. 1975. *The Psychology of Intergroup Relations: Conflict and Consciousness.* New York: McGraw-Hill. 128 pp.

Klineberg, O., Zavalloni, M. 1969. *Nationalism and Tribalism Among African Students.* Paris: Mouton. 324 pp.

Lambert, W. E. 1980. The social psychology of language: A perspective for the 1980's. In *Language: Social Psychological Perspectives,* ed. H. Giles, W. P. Robinson, P. M. Smith, pp. 415–24. Oxford: Pergamon. 442 pp.

Lao, R. C. 1970. Internal-external control and competent and innovative behavior among Negro college students. *J. Pers. Soc. Psychol.* 14:263–70

Lemaine, G. 1974. Social differentiation and social originality. *Eur. J. Soc. Psychol.* 4:17–52

Lemaine, G. 1975. Dissimilation and differential assimilation in social influence (situations of "normalization"). *Eur. J. Soc. Psychol.* 5:93–120

Lemaine, G., Kastersztein, J. 1972. Recherches sur l'originalité sociale, la différenciation, et l'incomparabilité. *Bull. Psychol.* 25:673–93

Lemaine, G., Kastersztein, J., Personnaz, B. 1978. Social differentiation. See Brown 1978, pp. 269–300

LeVine, R. A., Campbell, D. T. 1972. *Ethnocentrism: Theories of Conflict, Ethnic Attitudes, and Group Behavior.* New York: Wiley. 310 pp.

Lewin, K. 1948. *Resolving Social Conflicts.* New York: Harper & Row. 230 pp.

Lindskold, S., McElwain, D. C., Wagner, M. 1977. Cooperation and the use of coercion by individuals and groups. *J. Conflict Res.* 21:531–50

Linville, P. A., Jones, E. E. 1980. Polarized appraisals of out-group members. *J. Pers. Soc. Psychol.* 38:689–703

Louche, C. 1978. La négociation comme processus interactif. *Psychol. Fr.* 23:261–68

Louche, C. 1982. Open conflict and the dynamics of intergroup negotiations. See Bourhis & Hill 1982. In press

Louden, D. M. 1978. Self-esteem and locus of

control in minority group adolescents. *Ethn. Racial Stud.* 1:196–217

Mann, J. F., Taylor, D. M. 1974. Attribution of causality: Role of ethnicity and social class. *J. Soc. Psychol.* 94:3–13

Mason, P. 1970. *Patterns of Dominance.* London: Oxford Univ. Press. 377 pp.

McGuire, W. J., McGuire, C. V., Child, P., Fujioka, T. 1978. Salience of ethnicity in the spontaneous self-concept as a function of one's ethnic distinctiveness in the social environment. *J. Pers. Soc. Psychol.* 36:511–20

McKillip, J., Dimiceli, A. J., Luebke, J. 1977. Group salience and stereotyping. *Soc. Behav. Pers.* 5:81–85

Middleton, M., Tajfel, H., Johnson, N. B. 1970. Cognitive and affective aspects of children's national attitudes. *Br. J. Soc. Clin. Psychol.* 9:122–34

Milner, D. 1973. Racial identification and preference in "black" British children. *Eur. J. Soc. Psychol.* 3:281–95

Milner, D. 1975. *Children and Race.* Harmondsworth: Penguin. 281 pp.

Milner, D. 1981. Racial prejudice. See Turner & Giles 1981, pp. 102–43

Moscovici, S. 1976. *Social Influence and Social Change.* London: Academic. 239 pp.

Mugny, G. 1975. Negotiations, image of the other, and the process of minority influence. *Eur. J. Soc. Psychol.* 5:209–28

Mugny, G. 1981. *El Poder de las Minorias.* Barcelona: Rol. 171 pp.

Mugny, G., Papastamou, S. 1976/77. Pour une nouvelle approche de l'influence minoritaire: les déterminants psychosociaux des stratégies d'influence minoritaire. *Bull. Psychol.* 30:573–79

Mugny, G., Papastamou, S. 1980. When rigidity does not fail: Individualization and psychologization as resistances to the diffusion of minority innovations. *Eur. J. Soc. Psychol.* 10:43–61

Mulder, M., Veen, P., Hartsdniker, D., Westerduin, T. 1971. Cognitive processes in power equalization. *Eur. J. Soc. Psychol.* 1:107–30

Mulder, M., Veen, P., Hijzen, T., Jansen, P. 1973a. On power equalization: A behavioral example of power distance reduction. *J. Pers. Soc. Psychol.* 26:151–58

Mulder, M., Veen, P., Rodenburg, C., Frenken, J., Tielens, H. 1973b. The power distance reduction hypothesis on a level of reality. *J. Exp. Soc. Psychol.* 2:87–96

Myrdal, G. 1944. *An American Dilemma: The Negro Problem and Modern Democracy,* Vols. 1,2. New York: Harper. 705 pp., 774 pp.

Ng, S. H. 1978. Minimal social categorization, political categorization, and power change. *Hum. Relat.* 31:765–79

Ng, S. H. 1980. *The Social Psychology of Power.* London: Academic. 280 pp.

Novarra, V. 1980. *Women's Work, Men's Work: The Ambivalence of Equality.* London: Boyars. 160 pp.

Oakes, P., Turner, J. C. 1980. Social categorization and intergroup behavior: Does minimal intergroup discrimination make social identity more positive? *Eur. J. Soc. Psychol.* 10:295–301

Palmonari, A., Zani, B. 1980. *Psicologia Sociale di Communità.* Bologna: Il Mulino. 207 pp.

Papastamou, S., Mugny, G., Kaiser, C. 1980. Echec à l'influence minoritaire: La psychologisation. *Rech. Psychol. Soc.* 2:

Pettigrew, T. F. 1978. Placing Adam's argument in a broader perspective: Comment on the Adam paper. *Soc. Psychol.* 41:58–61

Pettigrew, T. F. 1979. The ultimate attribution error: Extending Allport's cognitive analysis of prejudice. *Pers. Soc. Psychol. Bull.* 5:461–76

Pruitt, D. G., Kimmel, M. J. 1977. Twenty years of experimental gaming: Critique, synthesis, and suggestions for the future. *Ann. Rev. Psychol.* 28:363–92

Pushkin, I., Veness, T. 1973. The development of racial awareness and prejudice in children. See Katz 1973, pp. 23–42

Quattrone, G. A., Jones, E. E. 1980. The perception of variability within in-groups and out-groups: Implications for the law of small numbers. *J. Pers. Soc. Psychol.* 38:141–52

Rabbie, J. M., Benoist, F., Oosterbaan, H., Visser, L. 1974. Differential power and effects of expected competitive and cooperative intergroup interaction on intragroup and outgroup attitudes. *J. Pers. Soc. Psychol.* 30:46–56

Rabbie, J. M., de Brey, J. H. C. 1971. The anticipation of intergroup cooperation and competition under private and public conditions. *Int. J. Group Tensions* 1:230–51

Rabbie, J. M., Horwitz, M. 1969. Arousal of ingroup-outgroup bias by a chance win or loss. *J. Pers. Soc. Psychol.* 13:269–77

Rabbie, J. M., Huygen, K. 1974. Internal disagreements and their effects on attitudes toward in- and outgroups. *Int. J. Group Tensions* 4:222–46

Rabbie, J. M., Wilkens, G. 1971. Intergroup competition and its effect on intragroup and intergroup relations. *Eur. J. Soc. Psychol.* 1:215–34

Rim, Y. 1968. The development of national stereotypes in children. *Megamot* 12:45–50

Riordin, C. 1978. Equal-status interracial contact: A review and revision of the concept. *Int. J. Int. Rel.* 2:161–85

Rokeach, M. 1960. *The Open and Closed Mind.* New York: Basic Books. 447 pp.

Rokeach, M. 1968. *Beliefs, Attitudes, and Values: A Theory of Organization and Change.* San Francisco: Jossey-Bass. 214 pp. 4th ed. 1972

Rosch, E. 1977. Human categorization. In *Studies in Cross-Cultural Psychology,* ed. N. Warren, 1:1–49. London: Academic. 212 pp.

Rosch, E. 1978. Principles of categorization. In *Cognition and Categorization,* ed. E. Rosch, B. Lloyd, pp. 27–48. New York: Wiley. 328 pp.

Rosch, E., Mervis, C., Gray, W., Johnson, D., Boyes-Brae, P. 1976. Basic objects in natural categories. *Cogn. Psychol.* 8:382–439

Rothbart, M., Evans, M., Fulero, S. 1979. Recall for confirming events: Memory processes and the maintenance of social stereotypes. *J. Exp. Soc. Psychol.* 15:343–55

Rothbart, M., Fulero, S., Jensen, C., Howard, J., Birrell, P. 1978. From individual to group impressions: Availability heuristics in stereotype formation. *J. Exp. Soc Psychol.* 14:237–55

Ryen, A. H., Kahn, A. 1975. Effects of intergroup orientation on group attitudes and proxemic behavior. *J. Pers. Soc. Psychol.* 31:302–10

Seckbach, F. 1974. Attitudes and opinions of Israeli teachers and students about aspects of modern Hebrew. *Int. J. Sociol. Lang.* 1:105–24

Sherif, M. 1966. *In Common Predicament: Social Psychology of Intergroup Conflict and Cooperation.* Boston: Houghton Mifflin. 192 pp.

Sherif, M., Harvey, O. J., White, B. J., Hood, W. R., Sherif, C. W. 1961. *Intergroup Conflict and Cooperation: The Robbers' Cave Experiment.* Norman: Univ. Okla. Press. 212 pp.

Sherif, M., Sherif, C. W. 1953. *Groups in Harmony and Tension.* New York: Harper. 316 pp.

Simon, M. D., Tajfel, H., Johnson, N. B. 1967. Wie erkennt man einen Österreicher? *Köln. Z. Soziol. Sozialpsychol.* 19:511–37

Skevington, S. M. 1980. Intergroup relations and social change within a nursing context. *Br. J. Soc. Clin. Psychol.* 19:201–13

Snyder, M., Uranowitz, S. W. 1978. Reconstructing the past: Some cognitive consequences of person perception. *J. Pers. Soc. Psychol.* 36:941–50

Sole, K., Marton, J., Hornstein, H. A. 1975. Opinion similarity and helping: Three field experiments investigating the bases of promotive tension. *J. Exp. Soc. Psychol.* 11:1–13

Stallybrass, O. 1977. Stereotype. In *The Fontana Dictionary of Modern Thought,* ed. A. Bullock, O. Stallybrass, p. 601. London: Fontana/Collins. 684 pp.

Stein, A. A. 1976. Conflict and cohesion: A review of the literature. *J. Conflict Res.* 20:143–72

Stephan, W. 1977. Stereotyping: Role of ingroup-outgroup differences in causal attribution of behavior. *J. Soc. Psychol.* 101:255–66

Stephenson, G. M. 1981. Intergroup bargaining and negotiation. See Turner & Giles 1981, pp. 168–98

Stephenson, G. M., Brotherton, C. J. 1975. Social progression and polarization: A study of discussion and negotiation in groups of mining supervisors. *Br. J. Soc. Clin. Psychol.* 14:241–52

Stillwell, R., Spencer, C. 1973. Children's early preferences for other nations and their subsequent acquisition of knowledge about those nations. *Eur. J. Soc. Psychol.* 3:345–49

Stroebe, W. 1980. *Grundlagen der Sozialpsychologie,* Vol. I. Stuttgart: Klett-Cotta. 406 pp.

Sumner, W. G. 1906. *Folkways.* New York: Ginn. 3rd ed. 1940. 692 pp.

Tajfel, H. 1974. Social identity and intergroup behavior. *Soc. Sci. Inf.* 13:65–93

Tajfel, H. 1979. Human intergroup conflict: Useful and less useful forms of analysis. In *Human Ethology: Claims and Limits of a New Discipline,* ed. M. von Cranach, K. Foppa, W. Lepenies, D. Ploog, pp. 396–422. Cambridge: Cambridge Univ. Press; Paris: Éd. Maison Sci. l'Homme. 764 pp.

Tajfel, H. 1981. *Human Groups and Social Categories: Studies in Social Psychology.* Cambridge: Cambridge Univ. Press. 369 pp.

Tajfel, H., Flament, C., Billig, M., Bundy, R. P. 1971. Social categorization and intergroup behavior. *Eur. J. Soc. Psychol.* 1:149–77

Tajfel, H., Turner, J. C. 1979. An integrative theory of intergroup conflict. See Austin & Worchel 1979, pp. 33–47

Taylor, D. M. 1980. Ethnicity and language: A social psychological perspective. See Lambert 1980, pp. 133–39

Taylor, D. M., Aboud, F. E. 1973. Ethnic stereotypes: Is the concept necessary? *Can. Psychol.* 14:330–38
Taylor, D. M., Bassili, J. N., Aboud, F. E. 1973. Dimensions of ethnic identity in Canada. *J. Soc. Psychol.* 89:185–92
Taylor, D. M., Guimond, S. 1978. The belief theory of prejudice in an intergroup context. *J. Soc. Psychol.* 105:11–25
Taylor, D. M., Jaggi, V. 1974. Ethnocentrism and causal attribution in a South Indian context. *J. Cross-Cult. Psychol.* 5:162–71
Taylor, S. E. 1981. A categorization approach to stereotyping. In *Cognitive Processes in Stereotyping and Intergroup Behavior,* ed. D. L. Hamilton, pp. 83–114. Hillsdale, NJ: Erlbaum, 353 pp.
Taylor, S. E., Crocker, J., Fiske, S. T., Sprinzen, M., Winkler, J. D. 1979. The generalizability of salience effects. *J. Pers. Soc. Psychol.* 37:357–68
Taylor, S. E., Fiske, S. T., Etcoff, N. L., Ruderman, A. J. 1978. Categorical and contextual bases of person memory and stereotyping. *J. Pers. Soc. Psychol.* 36:778–93
Tedeschi, J. T., ed. 1974. *Perspectives on Social Power.* Chicago: Aldine. 427 pp.
Thibaut, J. W., Kelley, H. H. 1959. *The Social Psychology of Groups.* New York: Wiley, 313 pp.
Turner, J. C. 1975. Social comparison and social identity: Some prospects for intergroup behavior. *Eur. J. Soc. Psychol.* 5:5–34
Turner, J. C. 1978. Social comparison, similarity, and ingroup favoritism. See Brown 1978, pp. 235–50
Turner, J. C. 1980. Fairness or discrimination in intergroup behavior? A reply to Branthwaite, Doyle, and Lightbown. *Eur. J. Soc. Psychol.* 10:131–47
Turner, J. C. 1981. The experimental social psychology of intergroup behavior. See Turner & Giles 1981, pp. 66–101
Turner, J. C., Brown, R. J. 1978. Social status, cognitive alternatives, and intergroup relations. See Brown 1978, pp. 201–34
Turner, J. C., Brown, R. J., Tajfel, H. 1979. Social comparison and group interest in ingroup favoritism. *Eur. J. Soc. Psychol.* 9:187–204
Turner, J. C., Giles, H., eds. 1981. *Intergroup Behavior.* Oxford: Blackwell. 288 pp.
Tversky, A., Kahneman, D. 1973. Availability: A heuristic for judging frequency and probability. *Cogn. Psychol.* 5:207–32
Upmeyer, A., Krolage, J., Etzel, G., Lilli, W., Klump, H. 1976. Accentuation of information in real competing groups. *Eur. J. Soc. Psychol.* 6:95–97
Upmeyer, A., Layer, H. 1974. Accentuation and attitude in social judgment. *Eur. J. Soc. Psychol.* 4:469–88
van Knippenberg, A. F. M. 1978. *Perception and Evaluation of Intergroup Differences.* Leiden: Univ. Leiden. 154 pp.
van Knippenberg, A. F. M., Wilke, H. 1980. Perceptions of *collégiens* and *apprentis* re-analyzed. *Eur. J. Soc. Psychol.* 9:427–34
Vaughan, G. M. 1978a. Social categorization and intergroup behavior in children. See Brown 1978, pp. 339–60
Vaughan, G. M. 1978b. Social change and intergroup preferences in New Zealand. *Eur. J. Soc. Psychol.* 8:297–314
Weinreich, P. 1979. Cross-ethnic identification and self-rejection in a black adolescent. In *Race, Education, and Identity,* ed. G. K. Verma, C. Bagley, pp. 157–75. London: Macmillan, 268 pp.
White, M. J. 1977. Counter-normative behavior as influenced by de-individualizing conditions and reference group salience. *J. Soc. Psychol.* 103:75–90
Wilder, D. A. 1978a. Perceiving persons as a group: Effects on attribution of causality and beliefs. *Soc. Psychol.* 1:13–23
Wilder, D. A. 1978b. Reduction of intergroup discrimination through individuation of the outgroup. *J. Pers. Soc. Psychol.* 36:1361–74
Wilder, D. A. 1981. Perceiving persons as a group: Categorization and intergroup relations. See S. E. Taylor 1981, pp. 213–57
Wilder, D. A., Allen, V. L. 1978. Group membership and preference for information about other persons. *Pers. Soc. Psychol. Bull.* 4:106–10
Williams, J., Giles, H. 1978. The changing status of women in society: An intergroup perspective. See Brown 1978, pp. 431–46
Williams, J. E., Morland, J. K. 1976. *Race, Color, and the Young Child.* Chapel Hill: Univ. N. Carolina Press. 360 pp.
Wolman, C., Frank, H. 1975. The solo woman in a professional peer group. *Am. J. Orthopsychiatry* 45:164–71
Worchel, S. 1979. Cooperation and the reduction of intergroup conflict: Some determining factors. See Austin & Worchel 1979, pp. 262–73
Worchel, S., Andreoli, V. A., Folger, R. 1977. Intergroup cooperation and intergroup attraction: The effect of previous interaction and outcome of combined effort. *J. Exp. Soc. Psychol.* 13:131–40

Worchel, S., Axsom, D., Ferris, S., Samaha, C., Schweitzer, S. 1978. Factors determining the effect of intergroup cooperation on intergroup attraction. *J. Conflict Res.* 22:429–39

Worchel, S., Lind, E. A., Kaufman, K. 1975. Evaluations of group products as a function of expectations of group longevity, outcome of competition, and publicity of evaluations. *J. Pers. Soc. Psychol.* 31:1089–97

Zavalloni, M. 1972. Cognitive processes and social identity through focused introspection. *Eur. J. Soc. Psychol.* 2:235–60

Zavalloni, M. 1973. Social identity: Perspectives and prospects. *Soc. Sci. Inf.* 12:65–92

Zavalloni, M. 1975. Social identity and the recoding of reality: Its relevance for cross-cultural psychology. *Int. J. Psychol.* 10:197–217

Ann. Rev. Psychol. 1982. 33:41–85

COLOR VISION

J. D. Mollon

Department of Experimental Psychology, University of Cambridge, Downing Street, Cambridge CB2 3EB, United Kingdom

---

CONTENTS

0066-4308/82/0201-0041$02.00

This review is dedicated to Dr. W. S. Stiles on the occasion of his eightieth birthday. It concentrates on human psychophysics and primate electrophysiology. While remembering those who use chapters in the *Annual Review of Psychology* as bibliographic instruments, I have tried also to write for the student reader who knows something of visual psychology but has not yet been initiated in the delicious mysteries of color. To this end I have corralled most of the general references into the second section and have attempted in the first to introduce the basic concepts needed later. For less compressed introductions, try Cornsweet (1970), Rushton (1972), or Mollon (1979, 1982a). For a *coup d'oeil* of the last 50 years of visual research try Rushton (1977a). The most recent survey of color vision in the *Annual Review of Psychology* was that by Jacobs (1976), which remains a most profitable source.

INTRODUCTION

Trichromacy and the Trichromatic Theory

The most fundamental property of human color vision remains that of trichromacy. Consider a circular matching field subtending two degrees of visual angle and divided into two halves. Suppose that we illuminate the left half of the field with three fixed wavelengths, and the right half with any other wavelength or spectral mixture. The three fixed wavelengths, by an unhappy convention, are called primaries, but the actual wavelengths chosen are arbitrary, provided only that no one of them can be matched by mixing the other two. Now, by adjusting only the intensities of the three primaries, the observer will be able to achieve a color match between the two sides of the field, although sometimes he will have to move one of the primaries to the right-hand side of the field. This is what is meant experimentally by saying that human foveal vision is trichromatic. By systematic experiments of this kind we can derive *color matching functions,* which give the amounts of our three primaries required to match each wavelength in the visible spectrum.

Trichromacy arises because there are just three types of cone photoreceptor in the normal retina, each type containing a different photosensitive pigment (Figure 1). The three pigments are maximally sensitive in different parts of the spectrum, but their sensitivities overlap. Because of this overlap, no one of the primaries in a color-matching experiment will uniquely stimulate a single class of cone, and thus psychophysical color-matching functions cannot tell us directly how the sensitivities of the cones vary with wavelength.

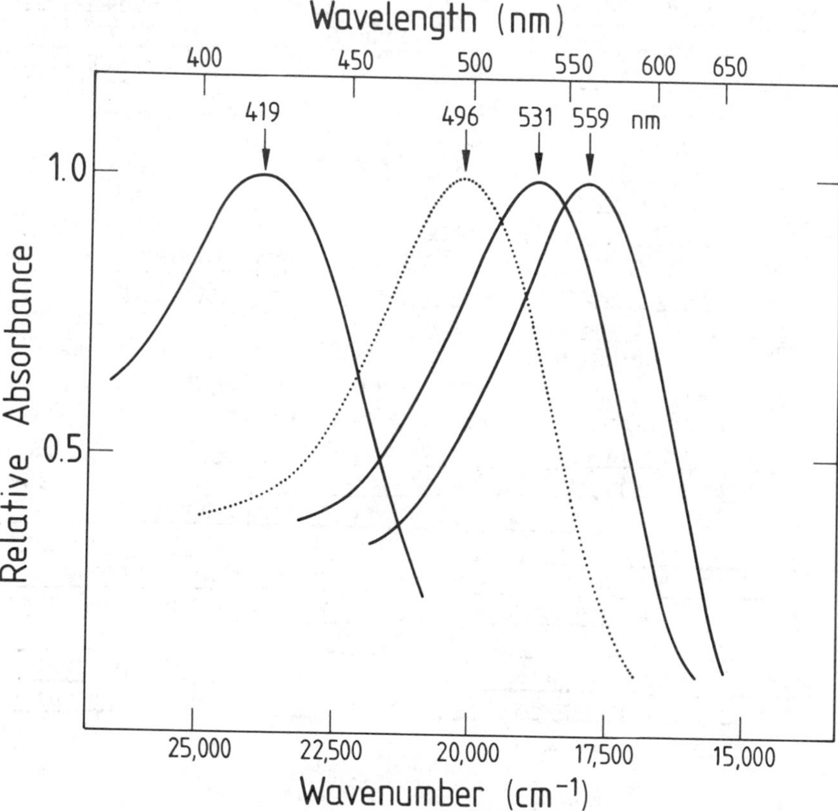

Figure 1 The absorbance spectra of the four photopigments of the normal human retina; the solid curves are for the three kinds of cone, the dotted curve for the rods. The quantity plotted is *absorbance,* i.e. log (intensity of incident light/intensity of transmitted light), expressed as a percentage of its maximum value; when "normalized" in this way, absorbance spectra have the useful property that their shape is independent of the concentration of the pigment (Knowles & Dartnall 1977, Chap. 3). It has become customary to plot absorbance spectra not against wavelength, but against its reciprocal, wavenumber, in part because it was once thought that photopigment spectra were of constant shape on such an abscissa, and in part because frequency (which is directly proportional to wavenumber) is independent of the medium.

These curves are based on microspectrophotometric measurements of 137 receptors from seven human retinae. The data will be published in detail elsewhere, and I am most grateful to Professor H. J. A. Dartnall and Dr. J. Bowmaker for permission to reproduce the absorbance spectra shown here.

The curves plotted in Figure 1 are *absorbance spectra*, which show for a given pigment how the quantity log (incident light/transmitted light) varies with wavelength. Also shown is the absorbance spectrum for the rods, which subserve our colorless vision at low levels of illumination; notice the essential similarity of shape of the four curves. All four photopigments, it is thought, consist of a protein molecule (called the "opsin") to which is bound a derivative of vitamin A_1, 11-*cis*-retinal (called the "chromophoric group"). The same chromophoric group is common to all the pigments but absorbs maximally at different wavelengths according to the protein to which it is bound.

The peak sensitivities of the cones lie in the violet (at a wavelength of approximately 420 nanometers), in the green (ca 530 nm) and in the yellow-green (ca 560 nm). The effect of selective absorption by the lens of the eye is to shift the peak sensitivity of the short-wavelength (violet-sensitive) cones to 440 nm when measurements are made in terms of the radiance incident at the cornea. It is traditional to speak of "blue," "green," and "red" cones, but this practice misleads equally the trusting student and the unguarded expert, and from now on I shall write of short-wavelength (S), middle-wavelength (M), and long-wavelength (L) cones.

In man and primates, any individual cone is thought to obey the *Principle of Univariance:* although the input to the cone can vary in wavelength and in intensity, the cone's electrical polarization increases simply with the rate at which photons are absorbed. All that varies as wavelength varies is the probability that an individual photon will be absorbed (the absorbance spectra of Figure 1 reflect this changing probability). Thus an individual class of cones is as color blind as are the rods. But whereas there is but one class of rod, there are three types of cone; and by comparing the rates of absorption in different classes of cone, the visual system becomes able to discriminate wavelength.

Psychophysical Estimates of the Cone Sensitivities

Reliable physical measurements of human absorbance spectra (Figure 1) have become available only in the last 2 years, and they certainly do not make redundant the many psychophysical estimates of the spectral sensitivities of the cones. For what we ultimately want to explain is seeing, and only psychophysical measurements can assure us that our physical measurements are relevant to color vision.

As we have seen, the overlap of the cone sensitivities means that we cannot discover the properties and spectral sensitivity of a class of cone simply by stimulating the retina with single colored lights. (There are many similar difficulties in other fields of experimental psychology. For example, we cannot study primary memory merely by asking our subject to report back a list of words within a few seconds of presentation; some items may be recovered from primary memory, some from secondary memory.) To "isolate" one class of cone—to cause the subject's response to be determined by only that one class—typical psychophysical strategies have been to select observers who appear to lack either one or two of the three classes, to use temporal or spatial parameters to which some cones are thought to be insensitive, or to use colored adapting fields that selectively depress one or two classes of cone. Often two such devices are combined. I give below an account of one celebrated and easily understood technique, that of W. S. Stiles. There are two reasons for describing this in detail. First, it well illustrates some basic concepts and procedures, which are echoed in later methods. Second, although Stiles's system was set out more than 40 years ago, his work was curiously neglected for many years and has been more frequently cited in the last 6 years than during any previous period; so I shall have to refer to it frequently. In part, Stiles's papers may have gone unread earlier because they were obscurely published; this has been remedied by their recent republication in a single volume (Stiles 1978).

The Two-color Procedure and the π Mechanisms

Stiles typically presented a 200-msec foveal test flash of wavelength λ on a larger adapting field of wavelength μ (Figure 2a). For a given combination of λ and μ, the threshold intensity for detecting the incremental test flash is measured at a number of intensities of the field; this gives a "threshold-vs-intensity" (t.v.i.) curve (see Figure 2b).

To account for how t.v.i. curves change with variations in λ and μ, Stiles postulated that there exist, at a peripheral stage of the visual system, associations of cones (or π mechanisms) that obey two principles: first, the Principle of Univariance, and second, what I shall refer to as the *Principle of Adaptive Independence*. The latter specifies that the sensitivity of each π mechanism depends only on the rate at which photons are absorbed from the adapting field by that mechanism and is independent of the rates of absorption by other π mechanisms. It was from strictly psychophysical observations that Stiles inferred the existence of mechanisms with these two properties; so the π mechanisms are what psychologists call "hypothetical constructs." Since three of them are now known to have spectral sensitivities quite close to those of the cones, their status approaches that of the gene, which existed as a hypothetical construct for 50 years before it could, with qualifications, be identified with a section of a DNA molecule.

In the field sensitivity version of Stiles's method, λ is held constant and is chosen to favor one of the π mechanisms. T.v.i. curves are obtained for different values of μ. Two such curves are shown in Figure 2b. Provided detection remains dependent on a single π mechanism with the properties

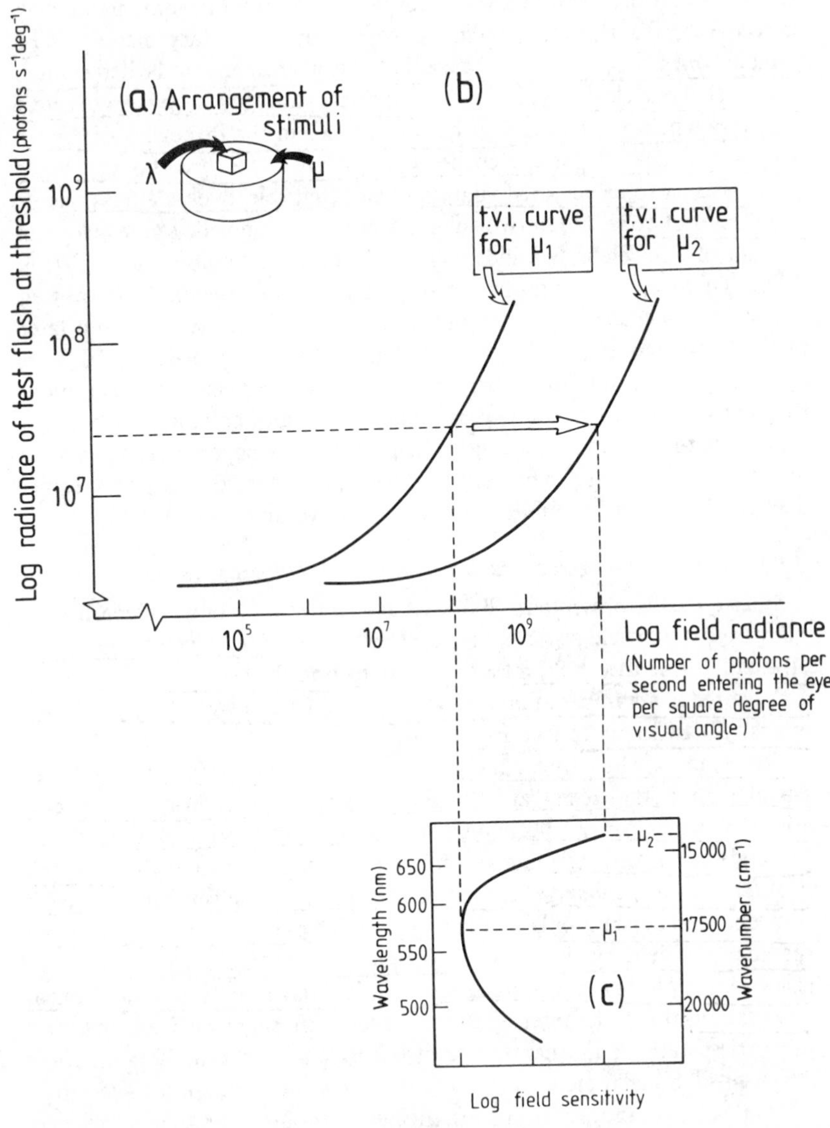

Figure 2 (a) The spatial arrangement of stimuli in Stiles's two-color experiments. (b) t.v.i. curves for two values of the field wavelength (μ_1 and μ_2). The horizontal broken line shows the criterion elevation of threshold (1 log unit) usually used by Stiles for deriving the "field sensitivity" of a π mechanism. (c) Derivation of field sensitivity.

defined above, then all that will happen as μ is varied is that the entire t.v.i. curve will move to and fro along the logarithmic abscissa without any other distortion. Stiles called this a *displacement rule;* in recent literature the same property of the t.v.i. curve is sometimes called *shape invariance.*

The "field sensitivity" of the π mechanism is directly given by the lateral movements of the t.v.i. curve as μ changes. A helpful way to look at it is this. If we could plot on the abscissa and ordinate of Figure 2b the actual rates at which photons are absorbed from the field and from the test flash, then the curve would always be the same (owing to the two defining properties of a π mechanism). But in fact we know only the rate at which photons are delivered to the observer's cornea. What the lateral movements of the curve show us is how the probability of absorption of an individual photon varies as we vary μ. Remember that a constant shift on a logarithmic axis is equivalent to multiplication by a constant factor. Figure 2c shows graphically the derivation of field sensitivity for the long-wave π mechanism. Fields of wavelength μ_2 need to be 100 times ("2 log units") more intense than for μ_1 to raise the threshold by the same criterion amount (Figure 2b); this means that the mechanism is 2 $\log_{10}$ units less sensitive to μ_2 than to μ_1 (Figure 2c). The spectral sensitivity curve derived in Figure 2c is called an action spectrum: it shows the intensity required at different wavelengths to achieve a criterion effect (in this case a rise of 1 $\log_{10}$ unit in the threshold). Its relation to the absorbance spectrum of the L cones will be a matter for discussion later in the review.

By holding μ constant and manipulating λ, Stiles derives a second measure, test sensitivity, from entirely analogous movements of the t.v.i. curve along the ordinate. Sooner or later, however, as λ and μ are varied, shape invariance will fail—the t.v.i. curve may, for example, break up into two branches that move independently. When this happens, Stiles's postulates require him to suppose that a different π mechanism has taken over detection. The three main π mechanisms so derived have peak sensitivities, measured at the cornea, of approximately 440 nm (π_3), 540 nm (π_4), and 570 nm (π_5). However, Stiles found more failures of shape invariance than were compatible with three independent cone systems and was led, for example, to postulate three blue-sensitive mechanisms (π_1, π_2, π_3), which all peak near 440 nm but differ in their sensitivity to longwave fields. Modern opinion attributes these additional failures of shape invariance to limited failures of adaptive independence, and I shall have much to say about this later. For a more detailed introduction to Stiles's method, see Marriott (1976). A brief history of the π mechanisms is given by Stiles (1980).

Postreceptoral Processes

Since individual classes of cone are color blind, there must exist neural machinery to compare the outputs of different classes. The way this comparison is made is thought to be analogous to the way local differences in retinal illumination are detected: some ganglion cells in the primate retina appear to receive excitatory inputs from one or two classes of cone and inhibitory signals from the remaining cones.

In the last two decades it has become very clear that the pattern of activation of the photoreceptor array is examined by a variety of postreceptoral pathways or "channels" that extract different attributes of the stimulus (for a review, see Lennie 1980). These channels, functionally parallel and anatomically intermingled, may correspond to morphologically distinct classes of fibers with perhaps different conduction speeds, different integrative properties, and different central destinations. Only a subset of these channels—the color-opponent channels—are concerned to extract information about wavelength. Accordingly, a dominant objective of color psychophysicists in recent years has been to find ways of isolating particular classes of postreceptoral channel, much as they earlier sought strategies that caused the response to depend on individual classes of cone.

The relative weightings of signals from the three cone types may be different for different postreceptoral channels and thus for different visual functions. If we ask subjects to equate lights of different wavelength for luminosity (e.g. by flicker photometry, in which a comparison light is alternated with a standard and the intensity of the comparison light is adjusted to minimize flicker), then we find that the spectral luminosity function thus obtained behaves as if it is dominated by the response of the L cones; the M cones apparently contribute less and the S cones possibly nothing at all. At any rate, this is the conclusion we must reach if we take modern estimates of the spectral sensitivities of the cones and if we adopt the common (though not entirely satisfactory) hypothesis that the spectral luminosity function represents the linear sum of signals from different classes of cone.

The contributions of the different cones to hue appear to be ordered in the opposite way. The S cones make a very large contribution to hue despite their low absolute sensitivity; and if—as many do—we wanted to suppose that L and M cones are making equal contributions to color-opponent channels when a light appears yellow, we should have to suppose that the M signal has been given a greater weighting before presentation to the opponent channel. However, another conclusion is clear from modern estimates of the cone sensitivities: it is quite impossible to maintain that the ratio of L to M cone signals is the same at the two points in the spectrum that appear neither reddish nor greenish ("unique yellow" and "unique blue" ca 575 and 470 nm respectively). Given this, there is little firm ground for taking the ratio of signals to be unity at either of these wavelengths. To explain the spectral position of unique yellow we probably should look outside the observer: unique yellow is close to the wavelength that produces the same quantum catches in the L and M cones as does the average illumination from our world.

Color Deficiency

About 2% of men and 0.03% of women are dichromats, who require only two variables in a color-matching experiment and who (in this and other ways) behave as if they lack one of the three classes of cones of the normal. The terms protanope, deuteranope, and tritanope are used for observers who behave as if they lacked L, M, or S cones respectively. Protanopia and deuteranopia are inherited as recessive, sex-linked characteristics; inherited tritanopia is rare and is not sex-linked.

Against the idea that deuteranopia represents the simple absence of the M pigment (the "loss" or "reduction" hypothesis), the reader will often find it argued that the spectral luminosity curve of the deuteranope is little changed from that of normals. The curve for the protanope, on the other hand, does show a marked loss at long wavelengths, as would be expected if the L cone were absent. The considerations of the last section show why it is mistaken to advance this argument against the reduction hypothesis for deuteranopia: the spectral luminosity curve of the normal peaks at 555 nm and behaves as if it is dominated by the L cone, which the deuteranope retains.

A second major class of abnormal subjects are the anomalous trichromats, who require three primaries to make all possible color matches but whose matches are different from those of normal observers. All modern evidence is compatible with the hypothesis that the anomalous retina contains three cone photopigments, but at least one of them is abnormal in its spectral position. The term protanomaly is used to indicate the form of anomalous trichromacy in which the L pigment appears to be modified; deuteranomaly and tritanomaly correspond to analogous abnormalities of the M and S cones.

RECENT REVIEWS AND BIBLIOGRAPHIC SOURCES, TESTS, PERSONALIA

Books

A general textbook on color vision by Boynton (1979) is comprehensive and well balanced; with occasional exceptions it represents current orthodoxy. Those who enjoy a mild flirtation with heresy may turn to the text by

Wasserman (1978), which has some good expository passages and some mistaken ones. An authoritative handbook on photopigments has been published by Knowles & Dartnall (1977). Pokorny et al (1979a) have provided a very welcome survey of color deficiency, in which they attend equally to theoretical problems and to the details of clinical testing. A comparative review of vertebrate color vision is to be published by Jacobs (in press). A number of significant papers on color vision appear in a *Festschrift* for Lorrin Riggs (Armington et al 1978), in the proceedings of a conference held in Houston (Cool & Smith 1978), and in the proceedings of the Third AIC Congress (Billmeyer & Wyszecki 1978). The biennial proceedings of the International Research Group for Color Vision Deficiencies (e.g. Verriest 1980, 1982) are of mixed quality but always contain some papers of importance. A short, attractive introduction to colorimetry, *Measuring Colour* by R.R. Blakey (3rd ed., 1980), is available free from Tioxide, 10 Stratton Street, London W1A 4XP, UK. Troubling remarks on surface colors and on transparency will be found in Wittgenstein (1977). The curious, Joycean essay *On Being Blue* by Gass (1976) is a typographically exquisite collectors' item; it is certainly about color and is classified as psychology by the Widener Library.

Journals

A new interdisciplinary journal, *Color Research and Application* (J. Wiley), carries articles on vision as well as on industrial aspects of color. Well worth the $15 subscription is the running bibliography *Daltonia,* circulated by the International Research Group for Color Vision Deficiencies (available from: Dr. G. Verriest, Dienst Oogheelkunde, De Pintelaan 135, B-9000 Gent, Belgium); it concentrates on color deficiency but abstracts many straight papers on color vision. Tachistoscopically frozen glimpses of the latest state of the science will be found in the annual proceedings of the Association for Research in Vision and Ophthalmology, published as a supplement to *Investigative Ophthalmology and Visual Science.*

Reviews and Specialist Bibliographies

Much relevant background material will be found in a distinguished review of visual sensitivity by MacLeod (1978). A recommended review of colorimetry is that by Wyszecki (1978); for a gentle introductory treatment of chromaticity diagrams and color appearance systems try Padgham & Saunders (1975) or Sharpe (in press). Ronchi (1975) provides an annotated bibliography of papers on rods and cones, which is a useful guide to the literature on rod-cone interactions and on the possible role of rods in color vision. Serra (1980) has compiled an annotated bibliography on heterochromatic photometry (the matching of the brightness of lights that differ in color), with special reference to what is nowadays called the minimally distinct border technique, in which the subject adjusts the intensity of a colored field until it forms a minimally distinct border with a juxtaposed reference field of a second color. Reviews by Verriest (1974) and Lyle (1974) are bibliographic sources for information on the many toxins, drugs, and diseases that can impair color vision. Hansen (1979) describes studies in which a perimetric form of the Stiles procedure was used to study cone mechanisms in visual disorders. Walraven (1981) reviews a series of studies on chromatic induction. Turn to Christ (1975) for a bibliography on color coding in visual search and identification tasks; see O'Neem (1981) for discussion of the use of color in street signs.

New Tests and Other Materials

The Okuma charts for detecting color deficiency (Okuma et al 1973) are constructed after the manner of classical pseudoisochromatic plates, such as the Ishihara, but the target is in the form of a Landolt C, a traditional test stimulus for measuring acuity, and thus the same card can be presented repeatedly to the patient in different orientations, if, say, one wishes to examine the effects of visual angle or position in the field. These plates are available from Amoriex Co., Kyodo Bldg., 5 Nihonbashi-Honcho 2 Chome, Chuo-ku, Tokyo, 103 Japan; a rough English translation of the instructions can be obtained from the present writer. The City University booklet test (Keeler Instruments, Windsor, Berks., SL4 4AA, UK) is intended to distinguish different types of deficiency, including the tritan type, which is not detected by most of the traditional booklet tests. A new microprocessor-controlled scorer for the Farnsworth-Munsell 100-hue test (Biophysic Medical S. A., 64 Saint-Jean, 6305 Clermont-Ferrand, France) should allow more use of this classical test when large numbers of subjects are to be screened.

The Optical Society of America has produced its own series of uniform color scales (the OSA UCS system), in which the perceptual separation of the colors is more even than in the Munsell system. These standards are available from OSA, 1816 Jefferson Place, N W, Washington DC 20036, USA.

Necrology

During the period of this review the death has occurred of H. Hartridge (1886–1976) and of his sometime pupil, W. A. H. Rushton (1901–1980). Rushton lived long enough to write two engaging obituaries of his former teacher (Rushton 1977b,c) and to recall that Hartridge, if not a Trinity man, was once a "sound Young-Helmholtz man" before he left Cambridge, entered "the most dangerous domain of color vision, the *appearance* of colors," and yielded to "the special pleading of each lovely color to make it legitimate by granting it a separate parent cone." Apostasy is unforgivable in one who initiated you in the true faith. Many of the problems that exercised Hartridge during the 1940s—prereceptoral filters, chromatic aberration, the antichromatic response, Sloan's notch—are again to the fore, and it is worth returning to his papers. It is a pity that Rushton's bibliography of Hartridge omits his valuable book *Recent Advances in the Physiology of Vision* (1950), which contradicts any idea that Hartridge was preoccupied only with his polychromatic theory.

Rushton has left a brief, characteristically elegant autobiography—and an apology to colleagues for "the ungovernable sharpness of my scientific criticism" (Rushton 1975a). It is astonishing to remember that Rushton entered the field of vision only at the age of 50 and published over 100 papers on the subject before his death. He was especially attracted to color by the elegant manipulations that the trichromatic system allows (see next section), and he in turn has visibly influenced the style of several colleagues and pupils.

THE FUNDAMENTAL SENSITIVITIES

Psychophysical Estimates

There is a sophisticated history to psychophysical derivations of the "fundamentals," the spectral sensitivities of the receptors, and many contemporary discussions are addressed strictly to the cognoscenti. The clearest recent introduction I have come across is that by Sharpe (1980), who is especially concerned with the longwave fundamental. The serious student of this field should not fail to consult the monograph of Estévez (1979) and the recent paper of Wyszecki & Stiles (1980).

DERIVATIONS FROM COLOR-DEFECTIVE OBSERVERS Dichromats offer two classical routes to the fundamentals. Both start from the hypothesis that dichromats retain two of the normal pigments and have simply lost the third.

The first method is to measure directly the spectral luminosity function of a deuteranope or a protanope, eliminating the response of the S cones by using high spatial or temporal frequencies (see below) and thus securing the putative sensitivity of the L cones from the deuteranope and that of the M cones from the protanope (Smith & Pokorny 1975, Tansley & Glushko 1978). An interesting variation of this first method takes advantage of the fact that deuteranopes and protanopes are effectively monochromats in the red-green part of the spectrum: a shortwave "primary" light of fixed intensity and wavelength is mixed with a longwave light of variable wavelength (λ), and for each value of λ the dichromat is asked to adjust the intensity of the longwave component until the mixture matches a fixed white. This

"Maxwell-match" method was used to examine the L cones of deuteranopes by Alpern & Pugh (1977). At wavelengths greater than 530 nm the deuteranope was always able to complete the match with the one adjustment, and Alpern and Pugh infer that the adjustments needed at different values of λ are simply those required to yield a constant quantum catch in the L cones.

A second way of deriving fundamentals from dichromatic matches is to relate the confusions made by each kind of dichromat to the color-matching functions of the normal observer. Insofar as the normal observer can discriminate a set of lights that a certain dichromat confuses, he must be doing so with the single pigment that is lacked by that type of dichromat. Spectral sensitivities derived analytically in this way are called "König fundamentals." Needless to say, several slightly different sets of König fundamentals can be derived by taking different data for the dichromatic and normal color-matching functions. The set of König fundamentals most often adopted by modelers during the period of this review have been those of Smith & Pokorny (1975). The L and M functions of Smith and Pokorny are consistent with their direct measurements of deuteranopic and protanopic luminosities (see above). Two caveats may be helpful to anyone entering this literature. First, there is more than one set of "Smith-Pokorny fundamentals" in circulation: those tabulated by Boynton (1979) are the pure König fundamentals of Smith & Pokorny (1975), whereas those given by Ingling & Tsou (1977) were derived by a hybrid method (Smith et al 1976) in which the shortwave limbs of the L and M König fundamentals were slightly modified to make them more consistent with the absorbance spectrum of a known photopigment, iodopsin. The second caveat is that the formula given by Boynton (1979) for the Smith-Pokorny middlewave function has the wrong sign in front of the $\bar{z}$ term.

Another recent set of König fundamentals are those of Vos (1978), who like Smith and Pokorny, takes his normal color-matching functions from Judd's 1951 modification of the 1931 CIE "standard observer" but adopts different values for dichromatic confusions. Estévez (1979) has argued that König fundamentals are more appropriately derived from the 1955 color-matching functions of Stiles and Burch than from the CIE functions, because only the Stiles and Burch data were obtained directly using radiometrically calibrated primaries.

Some additional evidence for the reduction hypothesis—on which all the above derivations depend—is provided by a reflection densitometric study of 15 deuteranopes by Alpern & Wake (1977), who measured the reflectivity of the fovea at various wavelengths, first in the dark-adapted state and then after partial bleaching with red or green lights that were chosen to bleach approximately half of the L pigment. The measured changes in spectral reflectivity, the difference spectra, were the same (within experimental error) whether red or green bleaching light was used. This result, which elaborates earlier measurements of Rushton, does not rule out the possibility of a small quantity of M pigment in the deuteranope—a quantity unmeasurable by this technique—but it does exclude forms of the classical "fusion" theory of deuteranopia in which it is supposed that L and M pigments are present in almost normal quantities but that pigments or neural signals are mixed to yield centrally a two-variable system. (Such hypotheses were traditionally supported by the deuteranope's luminosity function; see Introduction.) However, Alpern and Wake draw attention to differences in the anomaloscope settings made by different deuteranopes, and this raises a quite separate problem for derivations of the fundamentals from dichromatic data (see below).

SILENT SUBSTITUTION The Principle of Univariance (see Introduction) provides the theoretical basis for some new methods of experimentally isolating an individual class of cone. In these procedures, thresholds are measured not for simple increments, as in Stiles's method, but for a spatial or temporal transition between two lights that have been equated for their effect on one or two of the three classes of cone. If two different wavelengths or spectral mixtures are adjusted in intensity so that they lead to the same rates of quantum catch in, say, the M cones, then a "silent substitution" can be made between the two lights as far as the M cones are concerned. Detection of a transition from one light to the other must then depend on another class of cone—and if, say, measurements are confined to long wavelengths this will be the L cones. One can then use field-sensitivity measurements (see above) to derive the spectral sensitivity of the isolated cones: i.e. one finds for different values of μ the intensity of a background field needed to bring the transition to threshold. At this stage, one must, like Stiles, assume adaptive independence. The method may sound worryingly circular to the reader, for we seem to need to know the spectral sensitivity of at least one class of cone before we can set up the silent substitution in the first place. But in fact it is sufficient that one class of cone should be much more sensitive to the transition than the others; and by an iterative procedure it is possible to improve on an initially rough estimate of the spectral sensitivity of the silenced cones.

Rushton and his collaborators call their version of this technique the "exchange threshold method" (Rushton 1975b), and they obtain field sensitivities at only two field wavelengths (540 and 640 nm). Thereafter, to obtain sensitivities at intermediate wavelengths, they ask their subject to match a given monochromatic light (λ) with a mixture of the green (540 nm) and red (640 nm) lights, and they cunningly arrange that the latter mixture, whatever proportion of red to green the subject requires, always produces the same total effect on the chosen cones. (They can do this because they know the field sensitivities for the red and the green lights and they implicitly assume adaptive independence). Having adjusted the red/green ratio to match the hue of λ, the subject completes his match by adjusting the intensity of λ to equate brightness. And now λ must be producing the same quantum catch in the chosen cones as does the mixture; and a spectral sensitivity can be obtained by repeating this operation for different values of λ. This procedure is complicatedly elegant and is marvelously characteristic of Rushton; I have attempted a less compressed exegesis in Mollon (1979).

Cavonius & Estévez (1975) use a more straightforward version of the silent substitution technique, calling it the "spectral compensation" method. They arrange that the spatiotemporal modulation of a grating should be invisible to two of the three cone types, and they measure field sensitivity throughout the spectrum for the isolated cones. Their three spectral sensitivities thus derived resemble the π_3, π_4, π_5 mechanisms of Stiles, although they find a systematic discrepancy at short wavelengths for the M cones. Piantanida et al (1976) used a similar method to obtain field sensitivities for normals, dichromats, and anomals. Silent-substitution methods are reviewed by Estévez & Spekreijse (in press).

A conceptually related method for securing the fundamentals is that of Williams & MacLeod (1979). Here the principle of silent substitution is used twice over, once in a spatial mode, once in a temporal mode. First, an afterimage is obtained of an intense, bipartite field, half of which is illuminated with green light (538 nm) and half with a longer wavelength, λ (which is different on different occasions). It is well known that afterimages, being perfectly stabilized on the retina, soon disappear if viewed against a homogeneous field but can be revived by a sudden lightening or darkening of the background field. Working in the longwave part of the spectrum, where only two mechanisms are in play, Williams and MacLeod set out to find combinations of (A) the ratio of the green light and λ in the original bleaching light, and (B) the ratio of two background fields, such that the afterimage appears homogeneous and not bipartite, when, after initial fading of the afterimage, a transition is made from one background field to the other. When such a combination is found it is assumed that *(a)* a spatially silent substitution has been achieved for one class of cone during the original bleach, and *(b)* a temporally silent substitution has been achieved for the second class of cone at the moment of transition between the two backgrounds. Only with both types of cone thus silenced does the bipartite division of the afterimage become invisible. By discovering the critical combinations of ratios A and B at different values of λ, Williams and

MacLeod derive spectral sensitivities similar to those obtained by inviting protanopes and deuteranopes to make brightness matches in the same apparatus. Their method depends on, and their results support, the assumption that the losses of sensitivity produced by bleaching are independent for different classes of cone.

COLOR NAMING A very different route to the fundamentals is described by Krauskopf (1978). If very brief (10 msec), very small (1.3') flashes of liminal intensity and constant wavelength (say, 580 nm) are delivered to the central foveola, then from trial to trial their appearance varies strikingly: sometimes the 580-nm flash appears a saturated red, sometimes a saturated green, sometimes desaturated or white, and sometimes it is not seen. Krauskopf supposes that three statistically independent channels are available for detection, that the saturated colors are seen when only one channel is activated, and that desaturated sensations arise when more than one channel is activated. Now, as wavelength is varied, the probabilities of the different types of subjective report also vary. Of course, these probabilities cannot directly give spectral sensitivities for individual channels, since the probability of seeing, say, a saturated red flash at a given intensity and wavelength depends on the sensitivity of the M channel as well as that of the L channel. However, Krauskopf reasons as follows. Allow that the probability of seeing a saturated red flash is identical with the probability (P'_L) of the L channel being activated *in the absence of activation of any other channel.* (He gives evidence for this identity.) Then

$$P'_L = P_L\,(1-P_M)\,(1-P_S) \qquad 1.$$

where P_L, P_M, and P_S are the independent probabilities of detection by L, M, and S channels respectively. The probability of not activating any channel is the probability of not seeing anything at all (P_{ns}) and is given by

$$P_{ns} = (1-P_L)\,(1-P_M)\,(1-P_S) \qquad 2.$$

Dividing Equation 1 by Equation 2 we get

$$P'_L/P_{ns} = P_L/1-P_L \qquad 3.$$

So a constant value for the left-hand term of Equation 3 means a constant rate of activation of the L channel. Since both P'_L and P_{ns} are measured in the experiment, we can obtain an action spectrum for the L channel by finding at different wavelengths the flash intensity needed for a constant value of P'_L/P_{ns}. Krauskopf's general method of identifying sensory detectors is at a special advantage when two sensory channels have closely similar sensitivities—and thus when other methods of isolation fail. In the paper cited, evidence is given that the psychophysically identified channels correspond to single classes of cone, but this is a separate assumption and not intrinsic to the method.

Microspectrophotometry

Ostensibly the most direct technique for discovering the fundamentals is microspectrophotometry, in which a very small beam (typically 2 μm wide) is passed through the outer segment of an individual photoreceptor and absorption is recorded at different wavelengths. In his 1976 review, G. H. Jacobs regretted that little had been done in primate microspectrophotometry since the classical reports of 1964. This has recently been remedied, and it is a happy turn of fate that Dr. Jacobs has become a collaborator in the new work.

Bowmaker et al (1978) published measurements for a large sample of rods and cones from Rhesus monkeys (*Macaca mulatta*); and results have followed for man (Bowmaker & Dartnall 1980), for the cynomolgus monkey *Macaca fascicularis* (Bowmaker et al 1980), and for the New World monkeys *Cebus apella* (Bowmaker & Mollon 1980) and *Saimiri sciureus* (Jacobs et al 1981). The measurements are made with a microspectrophotometer designed by P. Liebman; a description of the instrument is given by Knowles & Dartnall (1977, p. 564 ff.) Whereas the classical microspectrophotometric records were obtained by passing the measuring beam axially along the 30-μm length of the outer segment, in the newer measurements the beam passed transversely through the receptor; it turns out that the absorbance or "optical density" of the pigment is high enough (about 0.015 μm^{-1}) that a satisfactory signal can be obtained from this much shorter path length, and the advantage is that the experimenter, viewing through an infrared converter, can be confident that the beam is passing through only one outer segment.

Listed in Table 1 for the several species are the values of λ_{max} (= wavelength of peak sensitivity) and bandwidth for the different photopigments found. Figure 1 shows mean absorbance spectra for a large sample of cones from seven human eyes. The spectrum for the rods has been added to emphasize that the spectra for all four pigments are of approximately the same form when plotted, as here, against frequency (which is inversely proportional to wavelength). However, it has become very clear during the period of this review that the bandwidths of photopigment absorbance spectra are not constant in frequency units but increase systematically with increasing frequency. This is apparent from the exclusively primate data of Table 1, but a similar relationship has been shown to hold for a variety of

Table 1 Values of λ_{max} and bandwidth for primate photopigments[a]

Species	S cones		Rods		M cones		L cones	
	λ_{max} (nm)	half bandwidth (cm^{-1})	λ_{max} (nm)	half bandwidth (cm^{-1})	λ_{max} (nm)	half bandwidth (cm^{-1})	λ_{max} (nm)	half bandwidth (cm^{-1})
Man	419	2180	496	1770	531	1740	559	1680
Macaca mulatta (Rhesus)			503	1750	535	1720	566	1570
Macaca fascicularis (Cynomolgus)	419	2160	500	1720	535	1600	567	1420
Saimiri sciureus (Squirrel monkey)	429	2180	499	1830	535[b]	1730	552, 568[b]	1530, 1380
Cebus apella (Capuchin)			499	1680	535	1670		

[a] Data are taken from references cited in the text, except in the case of Man, where the values are taken from Figure 1. Absence of values for S cones should not be taken to indicate a tritan species, since these receptors are rare in all samples. The value given for the half-bandwidth is that for the half-bandwidth on the longwave limb (see Bowmaker et al 1980).

[b] The M cones were found only in a behaviorally protan specimen, the L cones in a deutan; the separation of the L cones into two classes is tentative.

nonprimate photopigments (Ebrey & Honig, 1977, Knowles & Dartnall 1977).

The most obvious way in which the new microspectrophotometric results differ from the 1964 data of Brown and Wald and of Marks, Dobelle, and MacNichol is in the value obtained for the λ_{max} of the S cones: as will be seen from Figure 1, these receptors are most sensitive at approximately 420 nm. The earlier reports and the newer ones do agree that the S cones are rare.

Concordance of Estimates of the Human Fundamentals

It is by no means a straightforward matter to compare psychophysical and microspectrophotometric estimates of the cone fundamentals. On the one hand, we have psychophysical action spectra expressed in terms of light incident at the cornea; on the other, we have physical measurements of absorption for a beam passed transversely through an outer segment. To reconstruct one type of sensitivity from the other, one must consider several factors:

(*a*) SELF-SCREENING It is necessary to allow for the fact that in vivo where the light passes axially along the outer segment, the photopigment in the anterior part will significantly screen the photopigment in the posterior part; this "self-screening," which is maximal at the λ_{max} of the pigment, has the effect of broadening the absorbance spectrum (see e.g. Knowles & Dartnall 1977, Chap. 3). Since current thought favors an axial absorbance in the range 0.3–0.5 for primate foveal photoreceptors, self-screening will be significant. Wyszecki & Stiles (1980) compare color matches made at moderate illuminances (ca 10^3 td) with those made at levels that would bleach most of the pigment (ca 10^5); they derive absorbances of 0.44 and 0.38 for the (unbleached) L and M cones respectively.

(*b*) RECEPTORAL OPTICS We must allow for any wavelength-dependent optical funneling that occurs for an axial beam. The magnitude of any such effect is still uncertain, and most recent calculations have ignored it.

(*c*) PRERECEPTORAL ABSORPTION Correction must be made for wavelength-dependent absorption by the media of the eye and the macular pigment. The latter is an inert yellow pigment in the central region of the retina; its peak absorption is at 460 nm, and it is thought to be concentrated in the outer plexiform layer, perhaps in the fibers of Henle (see Snodderly et al 1979). A small new complication is introduced by a distinct photostable violet-absorbing pigment in the inner segments of some primate photoreceptors (Mollon & Bowmaker 1979). This pigment, with peak absorption at 420 nm, could selectively screen individual outer segments. [In its morphological location and absorption spectrum, though not its absolute density, it resembles roughly the pigment of the "ellipsosomes" described in fish outer segments by MacNichol et al (1978).]

If factor *b* is taken to be negligible and if conventional values are assumed for factors *a* and *c*, the corneal sensitivities that are reconstructed from the microspectrophotometric results suggest that the converging psychophysical fundamentals are close to the truth. Equally, however, because of residual uncertainties about factors *a-c* and because the several psychophysical estimates are now very similar, it is unrealistic to try to use the microspectrophotometric measurements to choose among the psychophysical estimates. Thus Bowmaker et al (1978) and Bowmaker & Dartnall (1980), assuming an axial optical density of 0.525 and taking Wyszecki & Stiles's (1967) tabulated values for average prereceptoral absorption, showed that the reconstructed corneal sensitivities were in good first-order agreement with the mechanisms π_3, π_4, and π_5 of Stiles; but using lower values for the optical density and slightly different values for prereceptoral absorption, Estévez (1979) has shown good agreement between the microspectrophotometric spectra and his König fundamentals, and Sharpe (1980) has shown good agreement with the Smith-Pokorny (1975) fundamentals.

I should like to emphasize how similar are the psychophysical estimates now in play. It is remarkable that this agreement has gone almost unheralded, given the wide variety of candidate fundamentals that were available only 20 years ago, and given the badly mistaken sets of fundamentals that are reproduced in textbooks (e.g. Gregory 1977a, Hochberg 1978, Cotman & McGaugh 1980). From a casual reading of the specialist literature one would gain little impression of the convergence that has come about: it is a basic psychological law that small differences are harder to see than large ones, and so it is necessary to shout louder about small differences in order to attract attention to them.

Briefly, the residual differences between psychophysical fundamentals are as follows. In the range 400–500 nm, there is little dispute about the shortwave fundamental, and the discrepancies are no more than could be attributed to experimental error and to the known individual differences in prereceptoral absorption: thus there is reasonable agreement between Stiles's shortwave mechanisms (π_1 or π_3) and (*a*) the photopic sensitivity of rare monochromatic observers who appear to retain only rods and S cones (Alpern 1978, Figure 14) and (*b*) the König S fundamental of Estévez (1979). Stiles's π_4 is extremely similar in bandwidth and spectral position to the König M fundamental of Estévez (1979), but is rather broader than the M fundamental of Smith & Pokorny (1975). When normalized at their peaks the different longwave fundamentals are similar in their longwave limbs, but the shortwave limb of π_5 is shallower than that of König fundamentals or deuteranopic luminosity functions, though the discrepancy is only slight in the case of Estévez's L fundamental. A set of useful plots comparing different estimates of the L fundamental will be found in Sharpe (1980); plots comparing π mechanisms with all three König fundamentals are given by Wyszecki & Stiles (1980). Further discussion of the status of the π mechanisms will be postponed until postreceptoral processes have been dealt with.

Individual Differences

Recent literature provides a further reason why we should not exaggerate the residual differences between psychophysical fundamentals: this is the unwelcome possibility that the absorbance spectra of the photopigments may vary slightly in their spectral positions from one "normal" observer to the next. Bowmaker et al (1975), in a study of frog retinae, reported an 8-nm (275-cm^{-1}) range between animals in the value obtained for the λ_{max} of the rod pigment; the variation appeared both in difference spectra for whole retinae and in mean absorbance spectra obtained microspectrophotometrically from samples of individual outer segments for a given retina.

Alpern & Pugh (1977) have suggested that the L pigment in a group of deuteranopes varied in spectral position over a total range of 7.4 nm (230-cm^{-1}). Their measurements were made psychophysically with the Maxwell-matching technique described above. Against the possibility that the inter-observer differences arose from differences in prereceptoral absorption, Alpern and Pugh offer (*a*) direct physical measurements of the spectral reflectivity of the bleached fovea, and (*b*) measurements of the ratio of two monochromatic primaries needed to match different spectral lights. Against the possibility of systematic differences in the axial density of outer segments they point to the coincidence of the individual action spectra when adjusted horizontally on a wavenumber abscissa. But this latter argument is question-begging, since the spectra have flat, indeterminate peaks, and the technique precludes much reliable measurement of the shortwave limb. If only vertical adjustment is allowed in their Figure 3, the discrepancies can be described as a broadening of the action spectrum and thus possibly attributed to self-screening; it all turns on a very few shortwave points. However, whether or not the differences in action spectra are due to density differences, further convincing evidence that they were real differences is given by Alpern & Moeller (1977), who show that two of the deuteranopes differed consistently on (*a*) Maxwell matches, (*b*) incremental test sensitivities (see Introduction), and (*c*) spectral luminosity functions made by matching lights of different wavelengths to be of the same brightness. For further discussion of Alpern and Pugh's study see Estévez (1979), who suggests that the proposed spectral shifts of the L pigment cannot quantitatively account for the variation in color-matching functions independently found by these authors.

On the basis of color-matching functions for three deuteranomalous trichromats, Alpern & Moeller (1977) suggest that all deuteranomals cannot have the same three pigments. And contrary to what would be the common expectation, they report that a given deuteranope will not accept the color matches of all deuteranomals, while Alpern & Pugh (1977) similarly report that not all deuteranopes will accept the matches of a given normal. Since a trichromatic match requires that absorptions be equated in all three classes of cone, a dichromat ought to accept such matches if he merely lacks one of the normal's three classes of receptor. Alpern and his collaborators are led to suggest that there are not single L and M pigments that characterize normal observers; rather there is a range of possible L pigments and a range of M pigments. They additionally suggest that deuteranomals draw both their longwave pigments from the L range and that protanomals similarly draw two from the M range. Alpern and Moeller indeed found a deuteranomalous observer whose matches were accepted by two deuteranopes who would not accept each other's matches—a result to be expected if the deuteranomal's match is constrained by two L pigments, one common to each of the dichromats.

The microspectrophotometric results of Bowmaker et al (1978, 1980) are consistent with a limited variability of λ_{max} within each class of receptor; the variability is apparent both within and between retinae. In a study of 300 receptors (L and M cones and rods) from 17 Rhesus monkeys, Mollon & Bowmaker (1981) found a statistically significant variation among animals; standard deviations across monkeys for mean estimates of λ_{max} were 3.6 nm (L cones), 2.7 nm (M cones), and 1.7 nm (rods).

A limitation that faces the microspectrophotometric results, and some of the psychophysical ones, is that measurements are not made concurrently on all subjects, and we must rely on stability of experimental conditions. To assess instrumental error, what are clearly needed are independent psychophysical and microspectrophotometric measurements on the same subjects. Experiments of this kind have just begun. The species chosen is the squirrel monkey, *Saimiri sciureus,* for in this species Jacobs has recently found large behavioral differences between individuals in wavelength discrimination, in Rayleigh matches, and in incremental sensitivity at long wavelengths (Jacobs 1977, Jacobs & Blakeslee 1980). If categorized in human terms, some animals behave like mildly deuteranomalous trichromats and enjoy good wavelength discrimination in the red-green range, whereas some animals resemble severely protan observers. This is the first demonstration of major individual differences in the color vision of a nonhuman primate. In a double-blind study, squirrel monkeys from Dr. Jacob's laboratory in Santa Barbara have been flown to London, where microspectrophotometric measurements are made. In a behaviorally protan animal, the cones were microspectrophotometrically found to cluster at 430 nm and 535 nm; in a deuteranomalous animal one shortwave receptor was recorded, no receptors with λ_{max} near 535 nm, and a range of receptors with λ_{max} values in the range 546 to 577 nm, possibly falling into two groups with means 552 and 568 nm (Jacobs et al 1981).

THE ANOMALIES OF THE SHORTWAVE SYSTEM

This is a topic that came to the fore at the beginning of the period of this review, but has moved so rapidly that some phenomena that were initially taken to be singularities of the shortwave system are now seen as general characteristics of color-opponent channels. Nevertheless there remains plenty that is odd about the shortwave mechanism. For the reader's convenience, the principal anomalies are listed summarily below and are arranged into two major subgroups, although the various phenomena are more interconnected than this superficial classification might at first suggest. By "anomalies of the shortwave mechanism" is meant "unusual features of our vision when detection or discrimination depends only on signals originating in the S receptors"; isolation has usually been achieved either by Stiles's method or by some form of silent substitution for L and M cones. For earlier lists and further discussion, see Willmer (1961), Mollon (1977a, 1982b), Gouras & Zrenner (1978), Pugh & Mollon (1979), Polden & Mollon (1980); a bibliography on tritanopia by Barca (1977) is very useful.

Group A: Sensitivity of Short-wavelength System

1. ABSOLUTE SENSITIVITY The quantum efficiency of the shortwave mechanism is much lower than that of the L and M mechanisms (Barlow 1958), although it is now clear that some part of this difference is due to lenticular and macular absorption (see above).

2. INCREMENTAL SENSITIVITY The Weber fraction ($\Delta I/I$) for Stiles's shortwave system is about 4.6 times that for π_4 and π_5. This is the value for Stiles's standard conditions of a 200-msec 1° flash (Stiles 1978) and corresponds, of course, to only one point on a temporal contrast-sensitivity-function (CSF) and one point on a spatial CSF (or more strictly, it represents a single point in a spatiotemporal contrast-sensitivity space). If we make the shortwave target very small or very brief, the Weber fraction and

the absolute threshold of the shortwave mechanism rise much more than those of π_4 and π_5 and we obtain the near-tritan states:

3. SMALL-FIELD TRITANOPIA, 4. TACHISTOSCOPIC TRITANOPIA,

5. SPACE CONSTANTS The reason that the Weber fraction is only 4.6 times poorer for the shortwave system under Stiles's conditions is that greater spatial and temporal integration compensate for the essential insensitivity of the shortwave mechanism. The penalty, of course, is poorer resolution. Thus Cavonius & Estévez (1975), using their silent-substitution technique described above, confirm earlier reports that the spatial CSF for the shortwave system peaks at ~1 cycle.deg^{-1}, has a high-frequency cutoff at ~10 cycles deg^{-1}, and shows a low absolute contrast sensitivity (see also Klingaman & Moskowitz-Cook 1979). A consequence of its spatial CSF is that the shortwave mechanism cannot contribute to the detection of sharp edges. Thus Tansley & Boynton (1978), having adjusted the relative intensity of two juxtaposed, differently colored fields until the boundary was minimally distinct, found that the rated distinctiveness of the residual border between any two colors could be represented by placing all colors on a continuous curved line rather than in the two-dimensional space normally needed to represent differences between equiluminant colors; and when the two colors constituted a tritan pair (i.e. were confusable by a tritan observer and thus probably provided a spatially silent substitution for L and M cones) the border dissolved completely. Similarly, Valberg & Tansley (1977) showed that when monochromatic lights were juxtaposed to a standard white light, the rated distinctiveness of the border, when plotted against the wavelength of the monochromatic light, resembled a tritanope's saturation function; and Boynton et al (1977) found (for some conditions and observers) that introducing a gap between two fields actually improved the chromaticity discrimination of tritan pairs.

6. TIME CONSTANTS Elegantly arranging a temporal silent substitution for L and M cones (by alternating between 439- and 492-nm lights, a tritan pair), Wisowaty & Boynton (1980) measured the temporal CSF for the shortwave mechanism without the use of the longwave field traditionally employed. They confirm earlier suggestions that the peak of the temporal CSF lies at low frequencies, in fact at 2 Hz under the conditions they examined. They also report that the addition of longwave adapting fields attenuate contrast sensitivity in a way that is frequency-selective, being greatest at low and high frequencies. But this latter finding is best taken only in the strictest operational sense: owing to the inverted-U shape of the CSF,

the magnitude of the loss of sensitivity is confounded with depth of modulation, and we do not know whether equal distances on the ordinate correspond to equal attenuations at the site where the longwave signal acts. Mollon & Polden (1976a) describe a subjective illusion resulting from the longer latency of the shortwave system.

7. TRITANOPIA OF THE CENTRAL FOVEOLA Williams et al (1981a) have tackled the vexed question of whether there is a tritanopia of the center of the foveola that is additional to the general insensitivity of the shortwave system to small targets. Measuring increment thresholds for the same wavelength but under conditions that isolate either M or S receptors, they show apparently complete absence of the shortwave mechanism in a central area of 20 min, a result that cannot be attributed to macular pigment, since the M mechanism is not concomitantly affected; and by using successive color matching (to exclude fading of a possible S-receptor signal and to avoid any spatial difficulty in discriminating two parts of a small bipartite field), they show that matches made with the center of the foveola are truly tritanopic. When viewed from a distance, Plate 6 of the City University color-deficiency test (see above) prettily demonstrates the tritanopia of the foveolar center. The common term for the phenomenon is foveal tritanopia, but this is unfortunate, because (contrary to the belief of many psychologists) the anatomical fovea corresponds to a visual angle of ca 5.0° and includes the annular zone of maximal S-receptor sensitivity that lies at an eccentricity of 1°.

8. ACQUIRED TRITANOPIA Although congential tritanopia may not be as rare as once thought (van Heel et al 1980), there is an interesting contrast between the genetic stability of the shortwave system and its disproportionate vulnerability to disease, both specifically ocular diseases such as retinitis pigmentosa (e.g. Wolf et al 1980) and systemic disorders such as diabetes mellitus (e.g. Birch et al 1980). What in older reports are described as "blue-yellow" defects are very likely to be tritanopia. Alpern et al (in press) give a particularly thorough demonstration of acquired unilateral tritanopia in a case of central serous chorio-retinopathy. There are two reports of a high incidence of tritan defects in women taking oral contraceptives (Marré et al 1974, Lagerlöf 1980).

9. NEONATAL TRITANOPIA? Preliminary measurements of increment thresholds on longwave fields suggest that some 2-month-old infants behave as if tritanopic (Pulos et al 1980).

Group B: Adaptational Anomalies

A second group of anomalies concerns the light and dark adaptation of the blue mechanism. It has become somewhat artificial to list these separately, since they are now seen to be interconnected. Moreover, it will be argued below that they represent general properties of opponent-color systems. Four examples are listed here and will be discussed further in later sections.

10. LIMITED CONDITIONING EFFECT Stiles found that the t.v.i. curve for violet flashes on a longwave field shows a plateau at field illuminances of 4–5 log td, before rising again at higher illuminances. He denoted the lower and upper branches of the curve π_1 and π_3 respectively (see Stiles 1978), but his original term for the plateau—the "limited conditioning effect"—now seems more appropriate, for reasons that will emerge below.

11. RESPONSE SATURATION Unlike the other cone mechanisms, but like the rod system, the shortwave system can be saturated by steady adapting fields: when violet targets are presented on violet or blue fields of increasing intensity—in the presence of a fixed longwave "auxiliary" field—the incremental threshold rises more quickly than is predicted by Weber's Law (Mollon & Polden 1977a). There is a further odd aspect to this "saturation": the state of insensitivity to violet increments is reached only after many seconds of adaptation and after the threshold has passed through a much lower value (Mollon & Polden 1978, 1980, Stromeyer et al 1979).

12. TRANSIENT TRITANOPIA If the eye is adapted for some time to light of long wavelength and the adapting field is then turned off, the threshold of the shortwave mechanism does not recover according to the normal dark adaptation curve but actually rises by as much as 2 $\log_{10}$ units; so a stimulus that is readily seen when the field is present becomes quite invisible for several seconds after the field is extinguished. This phenomenon, early described by Stiles, was named transient tritanopia by Mollon & Polden (1975). For detailed experimental results see Augenstein & Pugh (1977), Mollon & Polden (1977b), and Stiles (1977).

13. LIGHT ADAPTATION The adaptation of the shortwave mechanism to longwave fields has been known for some time to be unusually slow (see Augenstein & Pugh 1977), and in fact the time course of adaptation turns out to have a very curious structure to it: for 575-nm fields of intensities greater than $10^{10.8}$ quanta.sec^{-1}.deg^{-2} (which place the observer on the "π_3" plateau), the threshold for violet targets *rises* during the first 10 sec of exposure to the field and only thereafter recovers (unpublished results by Mollon, Polden & Stockman; Mollon 1980a).

Two Explanatory Principles

There is nothing grossly odd about the shape or size of individual S receptors when they are seen in the course of microspectrophotometry, but to explain the anomalies of the psychophysically defined shortwave mechanism we may turn to two hypotheses:

THE SHORT-WAVE CONES ARE RARE Evidence for this hypothesis is provided by microspectrophotometry (see above), by a histochemical staining technique (Marc & Sperling 1977), and by the histological damage produced by intense blue light (Sperling 1980). Although each of these methods may be open to unknown sampling biases, the last two gain credibility from the way in which the numerosity of the putative S cones in primate retinae parallels Brindley's (1954) psychophysical results for the variation of π_1 sensitivity with retinal eccentricity: the frequency of S cones is as low as 2–3% in the very center of the foveola, rises to a peak of approximately 16% in a zone equivalent to an eccentricity of 1°, and then falls to 8–10% in the parafovea. There is also evidence for a regular, widely spaced mosaic of S-receptors. Williams et al (1981b) offer convincing psychophysical evidence that the sensitivity of the shortwave mechanism in the foveola has a punctuate distribution. Electrophysiologically, primate ganglion cells receiving S-receptor input are found relatively rarely (Gouras & Zrenner 1978) and are reported to be most common at eccentricities between 2 and 5° (de Monasterio 1978a).

SIGNALS ORIGINATING IN THE S CONES HAVE ACCESS ONLY TO A CHROMATICALLY OPPONENT SUBSET OF POSTRECEPTORAL CHANNELS Whittle (1973) reported that suprathreshold flashes seen only by π_1 cannot be dichoptically matched in brightness to flashes seen by the longwave mechanisms, although their intensities can be discriminated by differences in phenomenal salience (Whittle 1974). Gouras & Zrenner (1978) state explicitly that S-cone inputs are detectable only in chromatically opponent ganglion cells of the primate retina; de Monasterio (1978a) basically agrees, but allows that a "fraction" of his nonopponent cells "received weak input" from S cones (the example he shows is somewhat ambiguous).

An agreed upon and interesting result is that it is very much more common to record blue ON-center ganglion cells than blue OFF-center units (Malpeli & Schiller 1978, de Monasterio 1978a, Gouras & Zrenner 1978). Also very suggestive is the finding that S-cone signals are virtually absent from fibers projecting to the superior colliculus (de Monasterio 1978a,c); this, rather than a difference between types of geniculo-striate neurons, may account for the very marked slowness of simple reactions to liminal π_1 flashes (Mollon & Krauskopf 1973).

Hypotheses *a* and *b* might both in turn be related to the chromatic aberration of the eye, which ensures that the shortwave component of the retinal image is of little use for spatial discriminations when longer wavelengths are present.

COLOR-OPPONENT CHANNELS

Primate Electrophysiology

The color-opponent cells of the primate visual system differ from nonopponent cells in attributes other than wavelength selectivity; and this, of course, is of interest to psychophysicists seeking to isolate "color-opponent channels." Schiller & Malpeli (1977) confirm earlier reports that color-opponent retinal ganglion cells tend to be more sustained in their responses than do nonopponent cells. de Monasterio (1978a) essentially agrees, but reports that a more reliable distinction can be made on the basis of linearity of spatial summation within the receptive field—the classical basis for distinguishing X and Y cells. In a large sample of Rhesus ganglion cells, X cells had fully opponent responses, in that center and surround signals were drawn from different classes of cone. However, a less complete opponency was also seen in some Y cells: here the opponency arose because one of the types of cone mediating response in one part of the field made no contribution in the other. A second important difference between X and Y types of opponent cell is that the "surround" mechanism of the Y cell has a sensitivity that extends across the receptive field and indeed is maximal in the center, whereas the X cells have an annular input from a true surround (de Monasterio 1978b). Of the heterogeneous class of W cells, some have spatially coextensive, chromatically opponent inputs, and appear to deliver purely chromatic information to the geniculostriate pathway (de Monasterio 1978c). Color-opponent cells project predominantly to the parvocellular layers of the lateral geniculate nucleus and apparently not at all to the superior colliculus, either directly (Schiller & Malpeli 1977, de Monasterio 1978c) or indirectly (Schiller et al 1979).

Psychophysical Techniques for Isolating Color-Opponent Channels

Psychophysicists have recently developed a number of stratagems to try to ensure that detection depends on channels that receive antagonistic inputs from different classes of cone. However, as we leave the receptors and enter the jungle of nerves, we do not have the trusty parang of univariance with which to cut our passage; the techniques of isolation are thereby less secure. Moreover, there are several reasons for caution in identifying the psychophysicist's "opponent channels" with the electrophysiologist's "opponent cells." First, although the psychophysical literature often simplistically contraposes chromatic and achromatic channels, there are many different types of retinal ganglion cell and there are degrees of opponency. Second, the properties revealed psychophysically may be properties that emerge from a *population* of neurons and may not be properties of individual cells. Third, different psychophysical "channels" may correspond to the same class of cell operating in different modes; an example of this possibility comes from Gouras & Zrenner (1979), who show in Rhesus that "red-green" color-opponent ganglion cells are more sensitive to alternation between colored lights ("chromatic flicker") at low temporal frequencies but become more sensitive to achromatic, luminance flicker at high frequencies, the action spectrum shifting from one with two peaks to one resembling $V\lambda$.

Given the present state of knowledge, claims that detection "depends on color-opponent channels" should be taken (here and elsewhere) to mean only that detection depends on the comparison of absorptions in different classes of receptor. Nevertheless, detection by this mode is proving to have a clear signature: test spectral sensitivity shows multiple peaks (particularly characteristic is a depression ca 575 nm and a longwave peak ca 610 nm); and, as we shall see below, pairs of test flashes or pairs of adapting fields are often nonadditive in their effects.

The following techniques of isolation may be usefully listed:

USE OF INCREMENTAL TARGETS OF LOW SPATIAL AND TEMPORAL FREQUENCY Detection by chromatically opponent channels is thought to be favored when a colored, incremental target is large (say, 1°) and of long duration (say, 200 msec), whereas detection is held to be by achromatic channels when the target is small (0.05°) and brief (10 msec) (King-Smith & Carden 1976). Ingling (1978) has cautioned us against relating these suggestions directly to the integrative properties of individual neurons, since the color-opponent, X ganglion cells have *small* receptive fields. Here perhaps is a case where we must consider populations of cells: as one increases the area of a circular colored target, the number of color-opponent cells available for detection should be proportional to πr^2, since any such cell can compare local differences between signals from different types of cone; but the number of nonopponent cells available for detection may increase only as $2\pi r$, since such cells are more sensitive to spatial transients than to homogeneous illumination (cf Dain & King-Smith 1981).

ACHROMATIC ADAPTING FIELD Detection by opponent channels is thought to be favored when the field is neutral and bright (e.g. King-Smith & Carden 1976, King-Smith & Kranda 1981).

SPATIALLY COINCIDENT ADAPTING FIELD If monochromatic test flashes are delivered on a small, congruent "auxiliary" field and if field-sensitivity is measured with a larger, concentric "main" field, then the field sensitivities obtained with long and middlewave targets are not those of π_5 and π_4 but are spectrally narrower and have peaks at approximately 605 and 520 nm (Foster, in press). The effect is absent when the auxiliary field is presented dichoptically and is reduced when the target is small or brief. It appears that the presence of a contour coincident with that of the target masks a spatial transient that would otherwise allow detection by a nonopponent channel. Foster's configuration resembles that of the classical Dittmer-Westheimer effect (see Fry & Bartley 1935), which does occur for relatively large targets (e.g. Crawford 1940), and his results point to the interesting possibility that the Dittmer-Westheimer effect is absent or attenuated when detection depends on chromatic channels. This hypothesis, of course, becomes very plausible if you believe that the Dittmer-Westheimer effect arises because a spatial transient saturates edge-detecting cells that would otherwise respond to the circumference of the test flash.

TEMPORALLY COINCIDENT AUXILIARY FIELD No one seems to have tried systematically superimposing the chromatic target on a temporally coincident pedestal or on a randomly flickering field. These devices, which might eliminate detection by temporal transients, are listed here for completeness.

CONFINEMENT OF INPUT TO S CONES. EQUILUMINOUS TARGETS These last two strategies are discussed above and below respectively.

Chromatically Opponent Processes Manifested in Threshold Measurements.

One of the most remarkable features of the last 6 years has been the evidence for opponent processes that has come from applications of Stiles's two-color technique, which was originally introduced for the analysis of receptoral processes.

INTERACTION OF TEST FLASHES Earlier work on the interaction of test flashes of different wavelengths has been continued by Stromeyer et al (1978a), who show that the detectability of a large, long (1°, 200 msec) red flash on a bright yellow field is reduced if it is accompanied by a similar green flash. Red flashes similarly reduce the detectability of green targets. By now the reader will not be surprised to learn that the cancelative effect disappears if the flashes are very brief or very small.

INTERACTION OF ADAPTING FIELDS: COMBINATIVE EUCHROMATOPSIA If the threshold is found for violet (λ=423 nm) flashes on a steady blue (μ_1=473 nm) field and if enough yellow light is now added to the first field to produce a composite field that is brighter but achromatic, then the threshold actually falls by several tenths of a log unit (Mollon & Polden 1977c, Mollon 1979). The intensity of the yellow field required for maximum facilitation increases with the intensity of the blue field (Polden & Mollon 1980). Sternheim et al (1978) and Stromeyer & Sternheim (1981) have described a very similar phenomenon when detection depends on the L cones: a 633-nm grating of low spatial frequency (1 c.deg^{-1}) was presented on a 615-nm field of $10^{3.7}$td and the detection threshold was found to be reduced when a 565-nm field was added to the first field. The phenomenon was not observed when the grating was presented very briefly or was of higher spatial frequency, nor when detection was mediated by the M cones; but an analogous facilitation was obtained for both red and green targets when the task was to detect a sinusoidally flickering stimulus of low temporal frequency (Sternheim et al 1978). Similarly, Wandell & Pugh (1980b) have found facilitated detection of 200-msec 667-nm test flashes when a 540-nm field is added to a fixed, bright 650-nm field, a facilitation that is absent for 10-msec flashes (Wandell & Pugh 1980a). Particularly dramatic examples of such effects are seen for shortwave targets when flashed yellow fields are used to cancel the response saturation that is produced by flashed violet fields (Stromeyer et al 1978b, 1979).

The available evidence suggests some properties common to these phenomena: the facilitation occurs when the first colored field is of moderate to high intensity, and is absent if the second field is presented dichoptically; most important, it occurs under conditions that favor detection by chromatically opponent processes. Polden & Mollon (1980) propose the term *combinative euchromatopsia* for this facilitation of chromatic discrimination that occurs when certain adapting fields are combined. Combinative euchromatopsia points to a general hypothesis: a color-opponent channel is most sensitive to input perturbations when in the middle of its response range; sensitivity is lost if the channel is polarized, i.e. driven toward one or other extreme of its response range by large differences between the quantum catches of different classes of cone (Pugh & Mollon 1979, Polden & Mollon 1980).

THE DYNAMIC DYSCHROMATOPSIAS Transient tritanopia (see above) proved to have an analog in transient protanopia, a loss in sensitivity to longwave flashes after extinction of a dim cyan or a dim red field (Mollon & Polden 1977b, Reeves 1980); and indeed losses of sensitivity at the onsets and offsets of colored fields may prove to be the rule when detection is mediated by chromatic channels (although, except in the case of the shortwave system, the availability of alternative channels will usually obscure the magnitude of the effects). A generic term is needed for this family of effects and I tentatively suggest that *dynamic dyschromatopsia* would capture their defining properties. It is particularly significant that transient tritanopia does not occur when a blue field is added to the usual yellow field so as to yield a composite field of neutral color (Augenstein & Pugh 1977); that transient tritanopia was not found in one of the rare patients, "blue cone monochromats," who appear to lack L and M cones (Hansen et al 1978); and that transient protanopia is absent when the adapting field is yellow (i.e. neither reddish nor greenish) and when the targets are small or brief (Reeves 1980). Transient tritanopia and transient protanopia are both reduced if the adapting field is flickered (Loomis 1980, Reeves 1980), and transient tritanopia is paradoxically absent if the longwave adapting field is too intense (Mollon & Polden 1976b).

An explanation of transient tritanopia has been proposed by Pugh & Mollon (1979). During initial adaptation to a longwave field, signals from L and M cones are thought to polarize an opponent site through which signals from the S cones must pass, but a restoring force acts to reduce the polarization. The restoring force depends on the input of a leaky integrator with a long time constant, and the input to the integrator is a function of the difference between the signal from the S cones and that from the L and M cones. When the adapting field is suddenly removed, the restoring force continues to act for some seconds and, being now unopposed, polarizes the opponent site and leads to a loss of sensitivity. The loss of sensitivity that accompanies polarization is the same as that postulated above to account for combinative euchromatopsia. Valeton & van Norren (1979) demonstrate transient tritanopia at the level of the b-wave of the local electroretinogram recorded from the fovea of a Rhesus monkey; this suggests that the chromatic interaction occurs at or before the level of the bipolar cells.

Possible Identity of Opponent Mechanisms Revealed by Changes in Sensitivity, by Phenomenological Cancellation, and by Chromaticity Discrimination

Are the opponent channels revealed by recent threshold measurements the same as those (Hurvich 1978) examined in classical studies of phenomenal cancellation? Using slightly different experimental techniques, Polden & Mollon (1980) and Pugh & Larimer (1980) have asked whether longwave lights of the radiance required to cancel the phenomenal blueness of a shortwave light are also lights that produce maximal facilitation under conditions of combinative euchromatopsia; Pugh and Larimer give a positive answer, Polden and Mollon a negative one. Williams et al (1980) have asked whether the "cardinal directions" of color space, as revealed by selective alterations of sensitivity, are the same as those suggested by earlier phenomenological studies. They use a new colorimeter in which lasers provide the three primaries. The crucial idea of their technique is to adapt a putative channel by repeated brief excursions along a particular direction in an equiluminant color space and then to probe sensitivity to liminal excursions in this and other directions. Dynamic adaptation along a red-green axis produces maximal loss of sensitivity to liminal excursions along that axis, whereas thresholds are hardly changed for excursions along a tritan confusion line; conversely, adaptation along a tritan line produces maximum loss on that axis and little on the red-green axis. When adaptation is along other lines, the loss of sensitivity is much less selective; and in particular this is so when the adaptation is along a line connecting phenomenally pure blue and pure yellow, an axis that does not coincide with a tritan confusion line.

The hypothesis suggested by combinative euchromatopsia (see above) has an analog in a quite different literature, that concerned with predicting thresholds for chromaticity discrimination; the idea is explicit, for example, in the 1961 "line-element" of Friele (see Polden & Mollon 1980). Similarly, in reconstructing a tritan wavelength-discrimination function from π_4 and π_5, Cavonius & Estévez (1978) found that thresholds did not depend simply on the rate of change of the ratio of the two sensitivities; it was necessary to assume that the discrimination threshold rose with $r^{1.5}$, where r is the ratio of the adaptation levels of the two cone mechanisms.

DO STILES'S π MECHANISMS CORRESPOND TO CONE FUNDAMENTALS?

Ostensibly it looks as if Stiles settled on spatial and temporal parameters that would invite detection of his target by color-opponent channels. If this is so, then the sensitivity of postreceptoral channels will be varying as μ is varied in field-sensitivity measurements, and thus the measured sensitivity cannot be that of a single class of cone.

Experimental Tests

Recent literature offers several experimental tests of whether the π mechanisms satisfy the properties expected of individual classes of cone.

FIELD DISPLACEMENT RULE Sigel & Pugh (1980) report that "shape invariance" of the t.v.i. curve (see Introduction) does hold for a wide range of values of μ under conditions that isolate the longwave mechanism, π_5. If, however, the t.v.i. curves for λ=667 nm are extended to higher field radiances, a single template will not fit the data for all values of μ (Wandell & Pugh 1980b); it was those discrepancies that led Stiles to postulate his "high-intensity" red-sensitive mechanism, π_5'. Shape invariance does hold for the full range of the t.v.i. curve if 10-msec flashes are used instead of the 200-msec flashes used by Stiles (Wandell & Pugh 1980a).

FIELD ADDITIVITY This test, like the previous one, depends on the Principles of Univariance and Adaptive Independence. It was introduced by de Vries (1949), although his characteristically elliptical account has enjoyed little credit in recent discussions. Suppose we measure t.v.i. curves for two different field wavelengths, μ_1 and μ_2. Knowing thereby, for a given π mechanism, the relative efficiencies of the two wavelengths, we can calculate what should be the effect of a given mixture of μ_1 and μ_2, if indeed the π mechanisms are adaptively independent and if, once absorbed, all photons are equal. The most thorough study of field additivity is that of Pugh (1976) who demonstrated that additivity held for π_1 if both μ_1 and μ_2 were $<$500 nm, but "superadditivity" held for $\mu_1<500$ nm and $\mu_2>550$ nm. Sigel & Pugh (1980) show that additivity holds for π_5 at the low field intensities used in Stiles's measurements.

SILENT SUBSTITUTION Can a transition be made between two fields of different wavelength without disturbing the sensitivity of a π mechanism, as is theoretically possible for a cone? No such case has yet been reported. *Failures* of silent substitution under conditions isolating π_1 and π_5' were found by Mollon & Polden (1975) and Sternheim et al (1977) respectively, but a failure of silent substitution is little argument against the independence of π mechanisms, for Stiles explicitly required that adaptation be at equilibrium.

COINCIDENCE OF TEST AND FIELD SENSITIVITIES If π mechanisms are adaptively independent, the relative spectral sensitivity obtained by manipulating λ (test sensitivity) should coincide with relative field sensitivity, in those parts of the spectrum where both can be measured. This test was central to Stiles's original discussions and he showed, for example, impressive agreement between test and field sensitivities for π_1 and π_3 in the range 400–500 nm (see Stiles 1978, p. 205). Now that we know more about how to reduce contamination by opponent processes, further application of this test to π_4 and π_5 might be valuable.

PREDICTION OF COLOR MATCHING If a subset of the π mechanisms has the sensitivities of cones, it is necessary, though not sufficient, that they should be linear transformations of color-matching functions. With only minor discrepancies this condition has been shown to hold for π_3, π_4, and π_5 by Estévez & Cavonius (1977), who empirically obtained both types of measurement from the same observers, and by Pugh & Sigel (1978), who related Stiles's tabulated π mechanisms to the Stiles and Burch 1955 color-matching functions.

A Theory of π_1 and π_3

To explain the two-branched t.v.i. curve found when violet flashes are presented on longwave fields, Pugh & Mollon (1979) suppose that a signal originating in the S cones must pass through two successive sites, at each of which the signal may be attenuated. The first site probably corresponds to the outer segments of the S cones, and here the attenuation depends only on the rate at which photons are absorbed from the background by the S cones. At the second site, which is chromatically opponent, the attenuation depends on the magnitude of the difference between the signal from S cones and that from the L and M cones. For $\mu > 550$ nm, the lower (π_1) branch of the t.v.i. curve depends only on increasing polarization of the second site, since such fields produce negligible absorptions in the S cones. However, owing to bleaching and perhaps other processes of response compression, the signal from the L and M cones cannot grow indefinitely; hence the "limited conditioning effect" discussed earlier. Eventually, however, as the longwave field is made still more intense, it produces a significant level of direct absorptions in the S cones and then the π_3 branch is obtained. The "superadditivity" found by Pugh (1976) arises because long- and shortwave fields largely act at different sites. The "response saturation" described by Mollon & Polden (1977a) occurs when attenuation is increasing concomitantly at both sites as the intensity of a shortwave field is increased.

Self-Screening

Some part of the difference in shape between König fundamentals and the mechanisms π_4 and π_5 may arise because the former correspond to a 2° foveal field and the latter to a 1° field; the average length of outer segments will be higher for the smaller field and the absorbance spectrum should therefore be broader (see above).

It is interesting that a field sensitivity narrower than that of π_5 has been reported when the subject's task is to detect not a 200-msec flash but the flicker of a 10 Hz longwave target (Ingling & Tsou 1977, Sharpe 1980). To explain this result one might suppose that the use of a relatively high-frequency target reduces the contribution of opponent channels, but here again a change of self-screening may play a part. Baylor et al (1979), recording membrane current from individual toad rods and stimulating restricted parts of the outer segment, found that the time constant of response was much shorter at the vitreal end of the outer segment; if this were so for mammalian cones, narrow field-sensitivity functions might arise because threshold flicker was always detected at the vitreal end of the receptor and the effective absorbance was low. This hypothesis assumes that adaptation is local within the outer segment.

Conclusions

The evidence suggests that π_5 corresponds closely to the L cones. Systematic tests for π_4 are not yet available, but its sensitivity is unlikely to be far from that of the M cones, except in the region of 475 nm, where the ratio of π_4 to π_5 does not well predict the color matches of a tritanope. The failures of adaptive independence seen for π_1 should be set in perspective: they affect only the longwave limb of the field-sensitivity function, and in the region 400–500 nm the (corneal) sensitivity of the S cones is almost certainly given by π_1.

Why did Stiles come so close to the cone fundamentals despite adopting what in retrospect seem to be unsuitable target parameters? One previously unappreciated strength of the two-color method is perhaps the polarization of chromatic channels that is caused by the monochromatic fields; for most values of μ, detection will depend on nonopponent channels that probably vary little in their sensitivity as μ is varied in a field-sensitivity experiment. It also now seems important that Stiles used a relatively low value for his criterion field intensity. The slight flattening of the peak of π_5 in the region of 575 nm may represent local contamination by red-green opponent channels left unpolarized by the yellow field. It might also represent absorption by the α band of oxyhemoglobin at 576 nm.

SILENT SUBSTITUTION FOR POSTRECEPTORAL CHANNELS? THE REIFICATION OF LUMINANCE

Many recent papers have proposed that chromatically opponent channels can be isolated by arranging a silent substitution for the putative nonopponent channel: the observer is required to respond to a temporal or spatial transition between stimuli that are of different wavelength but equal luminance. The technique is venerable: in its temporal form it was used by Piéron (1931), who explicitly postulated independent analysis of hue and brightness; and in its spatial form it was used by Lehmann (1904). In a spatiotemporal version of the method, Nissen & Pokorny (1977) have measured reaction time for stimuli presented in "hue-substitution" mode, and Bowen et al (1977) have similarly measured two-pulse discrimination: a monochromatic light is briefly substituted for the central area of an equiluminant white field, and it is found that latency is longest and two-pulse resolution poorest when the substituted light is yellowish (ca 570 nm), whereas at longer and shorter wavelengths the subject's performance approaches that for luminance increments. A spatial form of the technique, in which a colored bar of variable luminance is set in a fixed white field, has been used to study color vision in infants (Teller et al 1978): in the case of some colored bars there was no luminance at which the bar did not significantly attract the infant's gaze, but for other colors, lying vaguely but not precisely on a tritan axis, such a luminance could be found. Lehmann (1904) found that the *verschobene Schachbrettfigur* of Münsterberg lost its distortion under "isoluminant" conditions whereas the Müller-Lyer illusion survived. Both these results have been rediscovered by Gregory (1977b), using similar apparatus, but one nice contradiction remains for someone to sort out: Lehmann writes "wenn Figur und Grund dieselbe Helligkeit haben, sind die Hauptlinien des Zöller'schen Musters vollständig parallel," whereas Gregory says the distortions of the Zöllner figure were "essentially unchanged."

Hue-substitution techniques, though they may throw up interesting phenomena, do not safely isolate chromatic channels. Suppose that a red field is briefly substituted for a white field of equal luminance. During the substitution an increment is presented to the L receptors and a decrement to the M receptors; transient responses will arise from both classes of receptor. In the spatial case, analogous transients will be present, if only as the result of eye movements. Those who intend to isolate chromatic channels must make the following assumptions: (*a*) the positive and negative transients are symmetrical in magnitude and waveform at the nonopponent site where they cancel; (*b*) the weightings of different cone inputs are identical for all nonopponent cells; and (*c*) linear summation occurs in the nonopponent channel for transient signals from different cones even though many nonopponent neurons (the Y cells) are known not to show linear summation for signals from different local areas. In short, we must reify luminance in the form of a single channel that has the spectral sensitivity of V_λ and obeys the Principle of Univariance. Given the variety of postreceptoral neurons and the biological significance of transients, it seems deeply implausible that assumptions *a*-*c* will always be valid. I am not saying that detection of "isoluminous" targets will invariably depend on nonchromatic channels; if the targets are at threshold and if one uses other devices that we believe favor chromatic channels (if e.g. the liminal target is large and blurred as in the study of duration thresholds by Pokorny et al 1979b), then isolation may be possible; but if the isoluminous target is well above threshold, as in studies cited earlier, then one has no guarantee that chromatic channels are isolated. Bowen et al (1980) cut away their own position by admitting that isolation will fail "at high luminances"; they offer no valid way of knowing when the safety margin has been crossed.

The receptor-transient hypothesis is very difficult to eliminate, because the magnitude of transient responses and the phenomenal saturation of the substituted color both necessarily depend on how far the new quantum catches differ from those produced in the different cones by the white light. However, the properties of the shortwave system (see above) suggest one prediction: if the response depends on nonchromatic channels, its variation with wavelength should resemble the tritanope's saturation function, since only L and M cones will be involved (Mollon 1980b). Now, indeed, the poorest performance does occur when 570-nm light is substituted for white —these lights lie approximately on a tritan confusion line and their interchange should produce minimal transients in L and M cones—but 570-nm light is minimally saturated even for the normal, and more interesting would be a transition from white to the shortwave tritan neutral point, where the substituted light is very saturated. This has not been specifically tested. However, we know from other literature that a spatial tritan transition is extremely difficult to detect (see above); and similarly Boynton & Kaiser (1978) report that a "flickerless exchange" occurs when members of a tritan pair are alternated at low frequency. Is it likely that rapid reactions can be made to such exchanges?

The receptor-transient hypothesis offers an interesting interpretation of the results of Teller and her associates on neonatal tritanopia. Perhaps the infant is not tritanopic but indeed is effectively color blind, as might be expected if its visual behavior depended on the superior colliculus. Spatial transients detected by L and M cones could reach the colliculus and control eye movements.

TO WHAT EXTENT IS COLOR ANALYZED INDEPENDENTLY OF OTHER ATTRIBUTES OF THE RETINAL IMAGE?

There is space here only to indicate some recent papers that might be judged relevant to this celebrated question. For earlier evidence and further discussion, see Mollon (1977b).

Cortical Electrophysiology

Michael (1978a,b,c, 1979) reports a systematic study of the spatial properties of color-opponent cells in the striate cortex of the macaque. Color opponency, though present in only a subset of all cells, was associated with each of the receptive-field types classically distinguished by Hubel and Wiesel: concentric, simple, complex, hypercomplex. The first two types were concentrated in layer IV of the cortex and were almost always monocular, whereas complex and hypercomplex cells were most common in other layers and often could be driven from both eyes. The orientational and directional preferences of a given cell were independent of the wavelength used for stimulation. Conversely, however, Krüger & Gouras (1980) report that the wavelength selectivity of a given cell increases with the length of a stimulating bar.

Bearing on our question in a distinct way is the work of Zeki (1978, 1980), who identifies two adjacent areas in the prestriate cortex of the Rhesus monkey that appear to be specialized for the analysis of color. The first of these ("V4") lies on the anterior bank of the lunate sulcus and the second in the lateral part of the posterior bank of the superior temporal sulcus. At least 56% of all cells in these areas were color opponent. Some color-opponent cells had an orientational preference, but most were not selective for either orientation or direction of motion. Krüger & Gouras (1980) have questioned whether spectral selectivity is in fact more common in V4 than in other areas; this controversy is not yet settled, but it may be significant that Krüger and Gouras confined themselves to foveal projection areas, and it is a pity they did not attempt one of Zeki's most striking comparisons, that between the lateral and medial regions of the posterior bank of the superior temporal sulcus, regions which Zeki reports to be specialized for color and movement respectively.

Color-Contingent Aftereffects

Color aftereffects have been reported that are contingent on the orientation or spatial frequency or direction of movement of a test stimulus. In each case the aftereffect is popularly attributed to the presence in our visual system of neurons specific to more than one stimulus attribute (although in several respects these phenomena resemble Pavlovian conditioning). A recommended review is given by Stromeyer (1978).

Pathology

After central damage, color vision may be lost completely with little or no loss of acuity. A disorder of this kind has been described by Young & Fishman (1980) in a 70-year-old patient who had suffered a cerebral infarct, and by Mollon et al (1980) in a younger man who had suffered a febrile illness, probably herpes encephalitis. By the technique of Stiles, it is possible to discover whether color-blind patients of this kind retain access to signals from more than one class of cone, since we can measure increment thresholds without asking anything about color. The patient of Mollon et al definitely retained both M and L cones but apparently lacked the machinery to compare their signals. In the light of current theories of the shortwave system, it is of special interest to know whether signals from the S cones can control the responses of such patients: increment-threshold measurements suggested that the short-wavelength mechanism was absent in the case of Young and Fishman and present in that of Mollon et al.

The Problem of Perceptual Synthesis

A priori considerations rule out complete independence and complete integration of the analyses of color and form. It would be no good having a system in which there were, say, single units specific to chartreuse-colored Volkswagens moving left at a distance of three meters, since we need to explain how the system recognizes a Volkswagen for what it is independently of its accidental features such as hue. But equally, we cannot postulate complete independence of analysis, since the subject, observing a complex scene, can quickly tell us that the Volkswagen is yellow and the Mini Metro is scarlet. Insofar as the analyses of different attributes are independent, there must be a mechanism for perceptual synthesis, for relating the outcomes of the separate analyses. Treisman & Gelade (1980), reviving a hypothesis of Exner, propose that selective attention provides the necessary mechanism and that indeed we carry out the synthesis for only one part of the field at once. They report that if a subject is required to scan an array for the presence of a single feature (e.g. a color or a form), reaction time varies little with the number of items in the array; but if he must identify a conjunction of features (e.g. pink O in a background of pink Ns and green Os), then reaction time increases with the number of items. The identification of a conjunction of hue and form requires the serial application of focal attention to individual items in our visual field.

ACKNOWLEDGMENTS

I am very grateful to the following friends who have commented on sections of the manuscript: M. Alpern, C. R. Cavonius, L. Fallowfield, M. Hayhoe, J. Krauskopf, D. MacLeod, A. Reeves, L. T. Sharpe, A. Stockman, and P. Whittle.

Literature Cited

Alpern, M. 1978. The eyes and vision. In *Handbook of Optics,* ed. W. G. Discoll, W. Vaughan, Sect. 12, pp. 1–37. New York: McGraw-Hill

Alpern, M., Kitahara, K., Krantz, D. H. 1981. Classical tritanopia. *J. Physiol.* In press

Alpern, M., Moeller, J. 1977. The red and green cone visual pigments of deuteranomalous trichromacy. *J. Physiol.* 266:647–75

Alpern, M., Pugh, E. N. 1977. Variation in the action spectrum of erythrolabe among deuteranopes. *J. Physiol.* 266:613–46

Alpern, M., Wake, T. 1977. Cone pigments in human deutan colour vision defects. *J. Physiol.* 266:595–612

Armington, J. C., Krauskopf, J., Wooten, B. R. 1978. *Visual Psychophysics and Physiology.* New York: Academic. 488 pp.

Augenstein, E. J., Pugh, E. N. 1977. The dynamics of the π_1 colour mechanism: further evidence for two sites of adaptation. *J. Physiol.* 272:247–81

Barca, L. 1977. *Sguardo Bibliografico al Problema della Tritanopia.* Firenze: Fond. 'Giorgio Ronchi' 67 pp. (In Italian).

Barlow, H. B. 1958. Intrinsic noise of cones. In *Visual Problems of Colour,* pp. 615–39. Natl. Phys. Lab. Symp. London: H. M. Stationery Off. 749 pp.

Baylor, D. A., Lamb, T. D., Yau, K.-W. 1979. The membrane current of single rod outer segments. *J. Physiol.* 288:589–611

Billmeyer, F. W., Wyszecki, G. 1978. *Colour 77.* Proc. 3rd Congr. Int. Colour Assoc. Bristol: Hilger

Birch, J., Hamilton, A. M., Gould, E. S. 1980. Colour vision in relation to the clinical features and extent of field loss in diabetic retinopathy. See Verriest 1980, pp. 83–88

Bowen, R. W., Lindsey, D. T., Smith, V. C. 1977. Chromatic two-pulse resolution with and without luminance transients. *J. Opt. Soc. Am.* 67:1501–7

Bowen, R. W., Pokorny, J., Smith, V. C. 1980. Isolating colour vision mechanisms with hue substitution. *Nature* 285:440

Bowmaker, J. K., Dartnall, H. J. A. 1980. Visual pigments of rods and cones in a human retina. *J. Physiol.* 298:501–12

Bowmaker, J. K., Dartnall, H. J. A., Lythgoe, J. N., Mollon, J. D. 1978. The visual pigments of rods and cones in the rhesus monkey, *Macaca mulatta. J. Physiol.* 274:329–48

Bowmaker, J. K., Dartnall, H. J. A., Mollon, J. D. 1980. Microspectrophotometric demonstration of four classes of photoreceptor in an Old World primate, *Macaca fascicularis. J. Physiol.* 298: 131–43

Bowmaker, J. K., Loew, E. R., Liebman, P. A. 1975. Variation in the λ_{max} of rhodopsin from individual frogs. *Vision Res.* 15:997–1003

Bowmaker, J. K., Mollon, J. D. 1980. Primate microspectrophotometry and its implications for colour deficiency. See Verriest 1980, pp. 61–64

Boynton, R. M. 1979. *Human Color Vision.* New York: Holt, Rinehart & Winston, 438 pp.

Boynton, R. M., Hayhoe, M. M., MacLeod, D. I. A. 1977. The gap effect: chromatic and achromatic visual discrimination as affected by field separation. *Opt. Acta* 24:159–77

Boynton, R. M., Kaiser, P. K. 1978. Temporal analog of the minimally distinct border. *Vision Res.* 18:111–13

Brindley, G. S. 1954. The summation areas of human colour-receptive mechanisms at increment threshold. *J. Physiol.* 124: 400–8

Cavonius, C. R., Estévez, O. 1975. Contrast sensitivity of individual colour mechanisms of human vision. *J. Physiol.* 248:649–62

Cavonius, C. R., Estévez, O. 1978. π-mechanisms and cone fundamentals. See Armington et al 1978, pp. 221–31

Christ, R. E. 1975. Review and analysis of color coding research for visual displays. *Hum. Factors* 17:542–70

Cool, S. J., Smith, E. L. 1978. *Frontiers in Visual Science.* New York: Springer. 798 pp.

Cornsweet, T. N. 1970. *Visual Perception.* New York/London: Academic. 475 pp.

Cotman, C. W., McGaugh, J. L. 1980. *Behavioral Neuroscience.* New York: Academic. 838 pp.

Crawford, B. H. 1940. The effect of field size and pattern on the change of visual sensitivity with time. *Proc. R. Soc. London Ser. B* 129:94–106

Dain, S. J., King-Smith, P. E. 1981. Visual thresholds in dichromats and normals; the importance of *post*-receptoral processes. *Vision Res.* 21:573–80

de Monasterio, F. M. 1978a. Properties of concentrically organised X and Y ganglion cells of macaque retina. *J. Neurophysiol.* 41:1394–1417

de Monasterio, F. M. 1978b. Center and surround mechanisms of opponent-color X and Y ganglion cells of retina of macaques. *J. Neurophysiol.* 41:1418–23

de Monasterio, F. M. 1978c. Properties of ganglion cells with atypical receptive field organisation in retina of macaques. *J. Neurophysiol.* 41:1435–49

de Vries, H. 1949. An extension of Helmholtz's theory of colorvision. *Rev. Opt.* 28:91–100

Ebrey, G. T., Honig, B. 1977. New wavelength dependent visual pigment nomograms. *Vision Res.* 17:147–51

Estévez, O. 1979. *On the fundamental database of normal and dichromatic color vision.* PhD Thesis. Amsterdam Univ., The Netherlands. Amsterdam: Krips Repro. 147 pp.

Estévez, O., Cavonius, C. R. 1977. Human color perception and Stiles' π mechanisms. *Vision Res.* 17:417–22

Estévez, O., Spekreijse, H. 1982. The "silent substitution" method in visual research. *Vision Res.* In press

Foster, D. H. 1982. Changes in field spectral sensitivities of red-, green-, and blue-sensitive colour mechanisms obtained on small background fields. *Vision Res.* In press

Fry, G. A., Bartley, S. H. 1935. The effect of one border in the visual field upon the threshold of another. *Am. J. Physiol.* 112:414–21

Gass, W. 1976. *On Being Blue.* Boston: Godine. 91 pp.

Gouras, P., Zrenner, E. 1978. The blue sensitive cone system. In *XXIII Concilium Ophthalmologicum, Kyoto,* ed. K.

Shimizu, pp. 379–84. Amsterdam: Elsevier

Gouras, P., Zrenner, E. 1979. Enhancement of luminance flicker by color-opponent mechanisms. *Science* 205:587–89

Gregory, R. L. 1977a. *Eye and Brain.* London: Weidenfeld & Nicolson. 256 pp. 3rd ed.

Gregory, R. L. 1977b. Vision with isoluminant colour contrast: 1. A projection technique and observations. *Perception* 6:113–19

Hansen, E. 1979. *Selective chromatic adaptation studies with special reference to a method combining Stiles' two-colour threshold technique and static colour perimetry.* Oslo: Dept. Ophthalmol., Rikshospitalet

Hansen, E., Seim, T., Olsen, B. T. 1978. Transient tritanopia experiment in blue cone monochromacy. *Nature* 276: 390–91

Hartridge, H. 1950. *Recent Advances in the Physiology of Vision.* London: Churchill. 401 pp.

Hochberg, J. E. 1978. *Perception.* Englewood Cliffs NJ: Prentice-Hall. 280 pp. 2nd ed.

Hurvich, L. M. 1978. Two decades of opponent processes. See Billmeyer & Wyszecki 1978, pp. 33–61

Ingling, C. R. 1978. Luminance and opponent color contributions to visual detection and to temporal and spatial integration: Comment. *J. Opt. Soc. Am.* 68:1143–46

Ingling, C. R., Tsou, B.H-P. 1977. Orthogonal combination of the three visual channels. *Vision Res.* 17:1075–82

Jacobs, G. H. 1976. Color Vision. *Ann. Rev. Psychol.* 27:63–89

Jacobs, G. H. 1977. Visual sensitivity: significant within-species variations in a nonhuman primate. *Science* 197:499–500

Jacobs, G. H. 1982. *Comparative Color Vision.* New York: Academic. In press

Jacobs, G. H., Blakeslee, B. 1980. Within-species variations in color vision among New World monkeys. *Investig. Ophthalmol. Vis. Sci. Suppl.,* p. 136 (Abstr.)

Jacobs, G. H., Bowmaker, J. K., Mollon, J. D. 1981. Colour vision deficiencies in monkeys: behavioural and microspectrophotometric measurements on the same individuals. *Nature.* 292:541–43

King-Smith, P. E., Carden, D. 1976. Luminance and opponent-color contributions to visual detection and adaptation and to temporal and spatial integration. *J. Opt. Soc. Am.* 66:709–17

King-Smith, P. E., Kranda, K. 1981. Photopic adaptation in the red-green spectral range. *Vision Res.* 21:565–72

Klingaman, R. L., Moskowitz-Cook, A. 1979. Assessment of the visual acuity of human color mechanisms with the visually evoked cortical potential. *Invest. Ophthalmol. Vis. Sci.* 18:1273–77

Knowles, A., Dartnall, H. J. A. 1977. The photobiology of vision. In *The Eye,* ed. H. Davson, Vol. 2B. London/New York: Academic. 689 pp.

Krauskopf, J. 1978. On identifying receptors. See Armington et al 1978, pp. 283–95

Krüger, J., Gouras, P. 1980. Spectral sensitivity of cells and its dependence on slit length in monkey visual cortex. *J. Neurophysiol.* 43:1055–69

Lagerlöf, O. 1980. Drug-induced colour vision deficiencies. See Verriest 1980, pp. 317–19

Lehmann, A. 1904. Die Irradiation als Ursache geometrisch-optischer Täuschungen. *Pflugers Arch.* 103:84–106

Lennie, P. 1980. Parallel visual pathways: a review. *Vision Res.* 20:561–94

Loomis, J. M. 1980. Transient tritanopia: failure of time-intensity reciprocity in adaptation to long-wave light. *Vision Res.* 20:837–46

Lyle, W. M. 1974. Drugs and conditions which may affect color vision. *J. Am. Optom. Assoc.* 45:47–60, 173–82

MacLeod, D. I. A. 1978. Visual sensitivity. *Ann. Rev. Psychol.* 29:613–45

MacNichol, E. F., Kunz, Y. W., Levine, J. S., Harosi, F. I., Collins, B. A. 1978. Ellipsosomes: Organelles containing a cytochrome-like pigment in the retinal cones of certain fishes. *Science* 200:549–52

Malpeli, J. G., Schiller, P. H. 1978. Lack of blue OFF-center cells in the visual system of the monkey. *Brain Res.* 141:385–89.

Marc, R. E., Sperling, H. G. 1977. Chromatic organisation of primate cones. *Science* 196:454–56

Marré, M., Neubauer, O., Nemetz, U. 1974. Colour vision and the 'pill'. *Colour Vision Deficiencies II,* ed. G. Verriest. *Mod. Probl. Ophthalmol:* 13:345–48. Basel: Karger

Marriott, F. H. C. 1976. The two-colour threshold techniques of Stiles. In *The Eye,* ed. H. Davson, 2A:477–588. London: Academic. 616 pp.

Michael, C. R. 1978a. Color vision mechanisms in monkey striate cortex: dual-opponent cells with concentric receptive fields. *J. Neurophysiol.* 41:572–88

Michael, C. R. 1978b. Color vision mechanisms in monkey striate cortex: simple cells with dual opponent-color receptive fields. *J. Neurophysiol.* 41:1233–49

Michael, C. R. 1978c. Color-sensitive complex cells in monkey striate cortex. *J. Neurophysiol.* 41:1250–66

Michael, C. R. 1979. Color-sensitive hypercomplex cells in monkey striate cortex. *J. Neurophysiol.* 42:726–44

Mollon, J. D. 1977a. The oddity of blue. *Nature* 268:587–88

Mollon, J. D. 1977b. *The Perceptual World,* ed. K. von Fieandt, I. Moustgaard, pp. 45–97. London: Academic. 680 pp.

Mollon, J. D. 1979. The theory of colour vision. In *Psychology Survey No. 2,* ed. K. Connolly, pp. 128–50. London/Boston: Allen & Unwin

Mollon, J. D. 1980a. On the light adaptation of the 'blue' mechanism. In *Recent Advances in Vision.* Washington: Opt. Soc. Am. (Abstr.)

Mollon, J. D. 1980b. Isolating colour vision mechanisms with hue substitution: reply to Bowen, Pokorny and Smith. *Nature* 285:440

Mollon, J. D. 1982a. Colour vision and colour blindness. In *The Senses,* ed. H. B. Barlow, J. D. Mollon. Cambridge: Cambridge Univ. Press. In Press

Mollon, J. D. 1982b. A taxonomy of tritanopias. See Verriest 1982

Mollon, J. D., Bowmaker, J. K. 1979. Photostable violet-absorbing structures in primate retinae. *Investig. Ophthalmol. Vis. Sci. Suppl* 18:31 (Abstr.)

Mollon, J. D., Bowmaker, J. K. 1981. Distribution characteristics of a large microspectrophotometric sample of Rhesus photoreceptors. *Investig. Ophthalmol. Vis. Sci. Suppl.* 20:205 (Abstr.)

Mollon, J. D., Krauskopf, J. 1973. Reaction time as a measure of the temporal response properties of individual colour mechanisms. *Vision Res.* 13:27–40

Mollon, J. D., Newcombe, F., Polden, P. G., Ratcliff, G. 1980. On the presence of three cone mechanisms in a case of total achromatopsia. See Verriest 1980, pp. 130–35

Mollon, J. D., Polden, P. G. 1975. Colour illusion and evidence for interaction between colour mechanisms. *Nature* 258:421–22

Mollon, J. D., Polden, P. G. 1976a. Some properties of the blue cone mechanism of the eye. *J. Physiol.* 254:1–2P (Abstr.)

Mollon, J. D., Polden, P. G. 1976b. Absence of transient tritanopia after adaptation to very intense yellow light. *Nature* 259:570–72

Mollon, J. D., Polden, P. G. 1977a. Saturation of a retinal cone mechanism. *Nature* 265:243–46

Mollon, J. D., Polden, P. G. 1977b. An anomaly in the response of the eye to light of short wavelengths. *Philos. Trans. R. Soc. London Ser B* 278:207–40

Mollon, J. D., Polden, P. G. 1977c. Further anomalies of the blue mechanism. *Investig. Ophthalmol. Vis. Sci. Suppl.* 16:140 (Abstr.)

Mollon, J. D., Polden, P. G. 1978. An anomaly of light adaptation. *Investig. Ophthalmol. Visual Sci. Suppl.* 17:177 (Abstr.)

Mollon, J. D., Polden, P. G. 1980. A curiosity of light adaptation. *Nature* 286:59–62

Nissen, M. J., Pokorny, J. 1977. Wavelength effects on simple reaction time. *Percept. Psychophys.* 22:457–62

Okuma, T., Masuda, H., Kawada, C., Shinjo, U. 1973. Ishihara-Okuma's new test-plates for colour defectives. *Acta Soc. Ophthalmol. Jpn.* 77:1359–65

O'Neem, E. P. 1981. Drei Abhandlungen zur Wegweiserfarbentheorie. *Z. Fussgängerforsch* 1:69–173 (In German)

Padgham, C. A., Saunders, J. E. 1975. *The Perception of Light and Colour.* London: Bell. 192 pp.

Piantanida, T. P., Bruch, T. A., Latch, M., Varner, D. 1976. Detection of quantum flux modulation by single photopigments in human observers. *Vision Res.* 16:1029–34

Piéron, H. 1931. La sensation chromatique. *Année Psychol.* 32:1–29 (In French)

Pokorny, J., Bowen, R. W., Lindsey, D. T., Smith, V. C. 1979a. Duration thresholds for chromatic stimuli. *J. Opt. Soc. Am.* 69:103–6

Pokorny, J., Smith, V. C., Verriest, G., Pinckers, A. J. L. G. 1979b. *Congenital and Acquired Color Vision Defects.* New York: Grune & Stratton. 409 pp.

Polden, P. G., Mollon, J. D. 1980. Reversed effect of adapting stimuli on visual sensitivity. *Proc. R. Soc. London Ser. B* 210:235–72

Pugh, E. N. 1976. The nature of the π_1 mechanism of W. S. Stiles. *J. Physiol* 257:713–47

Pugh, E. N., Larimer, J. 1980. Test of the identity of the site of blue/yellow hue cancellation and the site of chromatic antagonism in the π_1 pathway. *Vision Res.* 20:779–88

Pugh, E. N., Mollon, J. D. 1979. A theory of the π_1 and π_3 colour mechanisms of Stiles. *Vision Res.* 19:293–312

Pugh, E. N., Sigel, C. 1978. Evaluation of the candidacy of the π-mechanisms of

Stiles for color-matching fundamentals. *Vision Res.* 18:317–30

Pulos, E., Teller, D. Y., Buck, S. L. 1980. Infant color vision: a search for short-wavelength-sensitive mechanisms by means of chromatic adaptation. *Vision Res.* 20:485–93

Reeves, A. 1980. Transient protanopia results from desensitization of a red-green opponent process. *Invest. Ophthalmol. Vis. Sci. Suppl.* 19:135 (Abstr.)

Ronchi, L. 1975. *150 Years of Rods and Cones. An Annotated Bibliography* Firenze: Fond. 'Giorgio Ronchi'. 88 pp.

Rushton, W. A. H. 1972. Pigments and signals in colour vision. *J. Physiol.* 220:1–31P

Rushton, W. A. H. 1975a. From nerves to eyes. In *The Neurosciences: Paths of Discovery,* pp. 277–92. Cambridge, Mass: MIT Press

Rushton, W. A. H. 1975b. Visual pigments and color blindness. *Sci. Am.* 232 (3): 64–74

Rushton, W. A. H. 1977a. Some memories of visual research in the past 50 years. In *The Pursuit of Nature,* ed. Hodgkin et al, pp. 85–104. Cambridge: Cambridge Univ. Press.

Rushton, W. A. H. 1977b. H. Hartridge. *Vision Res.* 17:507–13

Rushton, W. A. H. 1977c. Hamilton Hartridge (1886–1976). *Biogr. Mem. Fellows R. Soc.* 23:193

Schiller, P. H., Malpeli, J. G. 1977. Properties and tectal projections of monkey retinal ganglion cells. *J. Neurophysiol.* 40:428–45

Schiller, P. H., Malpeli, J. G., Schein, S. J. 1979. Composition of geniculostriate input to superior colliculus of rhesus monkey. *J. Neurophysiol.* 42:1124–33

Serra, A. 1980. An annotated bibliography on MDB technique and related topics. *Atti Fond. Giorgio Ronchi* 35:664–76, 786–827

Sharpe, L. T. 1980. *The effect of test-flash duration upon long-wavelength cone mechanisms field sensitivity.* PhD thesis. Univ. Rochester, New York. 329 pp.

Sharpe, L. T. 1982. Colorimetry. In *Encyclopaedia of Physics in Medicine and Biology,* ed. T. F. McAnish. Oxford: Pergamon. In press

Sigel, C., Pugh, E. N. 1980. Stiles's π_5 color mechanism: tests of field displacement and field additivity properties. *J. Opt. Soc. Am.* 70:71–81

Smith, V. C., Pokorny, J. 1975. Spectral sensitivity of the foveal cone pigments between 400 and 500 nm. *Vision Res.* 15:161–71

Smith, V. C., Pokorny, J., Starr, S. J. 1976. Variability of color mixture data. I. Interobserver variability in the unit coordinates. *Vision Res.* 16:1087–94

Snodderly, D. M., Auran, J., Delori, F. C. 1979. Localization of the macular pigment. *Investig. Opthalmol. Vis. Sci. Suppl.* 18:80 (Abstr.)

Sperling, H. G. 1980. Blue receptor distribution in primates from intense light and histochemic studies. See Verriest 1980, pp. 30–44

Sternheim, C. E., Gorinson, R., Markovitz, N. 1977. Visual sensitivity during successive chromatic contrast: evidence for interactions between photopic mechanisms. *Vision Res.* 17:45–49

Sternheim, C. E., Stromeyer, C. F., Spillmann, L. 1978. Increment thresholds: sensitization produced by hue differences. See Armington et al 1978, pp. 209–20

Stiles, W. S. 1977. Early threshold observations of transient tritanopia. *Philos. Trans. R. Soc. London Ser. B* 278:233–38

Stiles, W. S. 1978. *Mechanisms of Colour Vision* London: Academic. 298 pp.

Stiles, W. S. 1980. The two-colour threshold and π mechanisms: historical note. See Verriest 1980, pp. 111–14

Stromeyer, C. F. 1978. Form-color aftereffects in human vision. In *Handbook of Sensory Physiology,* ed. R. Held, H. Leibowitz, 8:98–142. Berlin: Springer. 993 pp.

Stromeyer, C. F., Khoo, M. C. K., Muggeridge, D., Young, R. A. 1978a. Detection of red and green flashes: evidence for cancellation and facilitation. *Sens. Processes* 2:248–71

Stromeyer, C. F., Kronauer, R. E., Madsen, J. C. 1978b. Apparent saturation of blue-sensitive cones occurs at a color-opponent stage. *Science* 202:217–19

Stromeyer, C. F., Kronauer, R. E., Madsen, J. C. 1979. Response saturation of short-wavelength cone pathways controlled by color-opponent mechanisms. *Vision Res.* 19:1025–40

Stromeyer, C. F., Sternheim, C. E. 1981. Visibility of red and green spatial patterns upon spectrally mixed adapting fields. *Vision Res.* 21:397–407

Tansley, B. W., Boynton, R. M. 1978. Chromatic border perception: the role of red- and green-sensitive cones. *Vision Res.* 18:683–97

Tansley, B. W., Glushko, R. J. 1978. Spectral sensitivity of long-wavelength-sensitive photoreceptors in dichromats determined by elimination of border percepts. *Vision Res.* 18:699–706

Teller, D. Y., Peeples, D. R., Sekel, M. 1978. Discrimination of chromatic from white light by two-month-old human infants. *Vision Res.* 18:41–48

Treisman, A. M., Gelade, G. 1980. A feature-integration theory of attention. *Cognit. Psychol.* 12:97–136

Valberg, A., Tansley, B. W. 1977. Tritanopic purity-difference function to describe the properties of minimally distinct borders. *J. Opt. Soc. Am.* 67:1330–35

Valeton, J. M., van Norren, D. 1979. Retinal site of transient tritanopia. *Nature* 208:488–90

van Heel, L., Went, L. N., van Norren, D. 1980. Frequency of tritan disturbances in a population study. See Verriest 1980, pp. 256–60

Verriest, G. 1974. *Recent Advances in the Study of the Acquired Deficiencies of Colour Vision.* Firenze: Fond. 'G. Ronchi'. 80 pp.

Verriest, G., ed. 1980. *Colour Vision Deficiencies V.* Bristol: Hilger. 410 pp.

Verriest, G., ed. 1982. *Colour Vision Deficiencies VI.* The Hague: Junk. In press

Vos, J. J. 1978. Colorimetric and photometric properties of a 2 deg fundamental observer. *Color Res. Appl.* 3:125–28

Walraven, J. 1981. *Chromatic Induction.* Utrecht: Elinkwijk

Wandell, B. A., Pugh, E. N. 1980a. A field-additive pathway detects brief-duration, long-wavelength incremental flashes. *Vision Res.* 20:613–24

Wandell, B. A., Pugh, E. N. 1980b. Detection of long-duration incremental flashes by a chromatically coded pathway. *Vision Res.* 20:625–35

Wasserman, G. S. 1978. *Color Vision.* New York: Wiley. 224 pp.

Whittle, P. 1973. The brightness of coloured flashes on backgrounds of various colours and luminances. *Vision Res.* 13:621–38

Whittle, P. 1974. Intensity discrimination between flashes which do not differ in brightness. Some new measurements on the "blue" cones. *Vision Res.* 14:599–602

Williams, D. R., Krauskopf, J., Heeley, D. W. 1980. In search of the cardinal directions of color space. *J. Opt. Soc. Am.* 70:1574 (Abstr.)

Williams, D. R., MacLeod, D. I. A. 1979. Interchangeable backgrounds for cone after-images. *Vision Res.* 19:867–77

Williams, D. R., MacLeod, D. I. A., Hayhoe, M. 1981a. Foveal tritanopia. *Vision Res.* 21:1341–56

Williams, D. R. MacLeod, D. I. A., Hayhoe, M. 1981b. Punctate sensitivity of the blue-sensitive mechanism. *Vision Res.* 21:1357–75

Willmer, E. N. 1961. Human colour vision and the perception of blue. *J. Theor. Biol.* 2:141–79

Wisowaty, J. J., Boynton, R. M. 1980. Temporal modulation sensitivity of the blue mechanism: measurements made without chromatic adaptation. *Vision Res.* 20:895–909

Wittgenstein, L. 1977. *Bemerkungen über die Farben.* Oxford: Blackwell. 63 pp. (In German and English)

Wolf, E., Scheibner, H., Pascke, G. 1980. Colour vision in a case of retinopathia pigmentosa. See Verriest 1980, pp. 280–84

Wyszecki, G. W. 1978. Colorimetry. In *Handbook of Optics,* ed. W. G. Driscoll, W. Vaughan, Sect. 9, pp. 1–40. New York: McGraw-Hill

Wyszecki, G. W., Stiles, W. S. 1967. *Color Science.* New York: Wiley. 628 pp.

Wyszecki, G. W., Stiles, W. S. 1980. High-level trichromatic color matching and the pigment-bleaching hypothesis. *Vision Res.* 20:23–27

Young, R. S. L., Fishman, G. A. 1980. Loss of color vision and Stiles' π_1 mechanism in a patient with cerebral infarction. *J. Opt. Soc. Am.* 70:1301–5

Zeki, S. M. 1978. Uniformity and diversity of structure and function in rhesus monkey prestriate visual cortex. *J. Physiol.* 277:273–90

Zeki, S. 1980. The representation of colours in the cerebral cortex. *Nature* 284:412–18

Ann. Rev. Psychol. 1982. 33:87–101

ENDORPHINS AND BEHAVIOR

Robert C. Bolles

Department of Psychology, University of Washington, Seattle, Washington 98195

Michael S. Fanselow

Department of Psychology, Dartmouth College, Hanover, New Hampshire 03755

CONTENTS

INTRODUCTION

> "None of them spoke much . . . A curious, dreamy, irresponsible feeling crept over them. It was as if they had all taken some narcotic drug—the merciful anodyne [analgesic] which Nature uses when a great crisis has fretted the nerves too far . . . A subtle sweetness mingled with the sadness of their fate. They were filled with the serenity of despair."
>
> A. C. Doyle, The tragedy of the Korosko, *The Strand Magazine,* Sept. 1897.

0066-4308/82/0201-0087$02.00

Just a few years ago, Pert & Snyder (1973) reported that certain areas of the brain are peculiarly sensitive to opiates (e.g. morphine) and opiate antagonists (e.g. naloxone). The critical areas were soon implicated in a variety of pain mechanisms (see Liebeskind & Paul 1977), so that part of the puzzle began to go together. But there was a more difficult, and still largely unresolved, question—why? The pharmacological paradigm required that these areas contain opiate receptors. But why should there be opiate receptors anywhere in the brain? If their existence meant that there are opiate-like substances normally occurring in the brain, why were such substances there? What is their function?

The next step was taken by Hughes and his associates (Hughes et al 1975), who isolated and identified the opiate-like substances in brain tissue. There were indeed endogenous morphine-like agents, endorphins, residing there ("endorphin" is a contraction of endogenous and -orphine). The brain's opiates were part of a chain, the details of which had already been worked out. The segments Hughes had identified were positions 61 through 65 on the long polypeptide called β-lipotropin; they are usually designated met-enkephalin and leu-enkephalin. The other parts of β-lipotropin were well known. The first 41 positions of it is ACTH; the part in the middle, occupying positions 42 to 60, is the middle pituitary hormone MSH; the rest of it, 61 to 91 taken together, is designated β-endorphin, which had also been located in the pituitary. Some writers (Jacquet 1978, 1979) have postulated antagonistic and counterbalancing effects of the β-endorphin and the ACTH parts of the whole; but others hold that the two work in concert (Guillemin et al 1977). More recent evidence (see Amir et al 1980) suggests taking a more cautious position. Indeed, we will make no assumptions about any such interaction, nor will we say much more at all about the biochemistry of the endorphins (see Olson et al 1980, Snyder 1977, Terenius 1978).

We will note, however, a curious anomaly that might be called, facetiously, the mind-body problem. On the one hand, the short peptide chains that Hughes located in the brain appear to have relatively little effect when they are injected into the relevant brain sites (Fratta et al 1977, Rossier et al 1977a); they have much more potency on intestinal tissue. On the other hand, the long chain, the large segment 61 to 91, which appears to occur in high concentrations only in certain limited areas of the brain (Rossier et al 1977b), is a very effective analgesic when injected into the brain. But this substance resides in the pituitary and might therefore be expected to have an effect on the digestive system. Perhaps the short pieces Hughes found are only degradation products of functionally more important peptides, or perhaps they are more like neurotransmitters, with a rapid onset and brief duration of action.

In this review we will do three things. First, we will consider analgesia, review some of the behavioral techniques that have been used to assess analgesia, and look at some of the problems that arise in using these techniques. Second, we will discuss the different kinds of stimulation that appear to trigger the endorphins. Third, we will note the variety of effects the endorphins have on behavior, and raise the big question of functional significance, i.e. what purpose do the endorphins serve?

ANALGESIC EFFECTS

The Experimental Paradigm

Morphine, the model opiate, has many effects on the body, but the most remarkable of these is its analgesic (pain-defeating) effect. β-endorphin and the different enkephalins should have similar effects and, most importantly, they should mimic morphine's dramatic analgesic effect. Some of the most compelling experiments were those early studies in which β-endorphin was synthesized and then either injected into the cerebral ventricles (Belluzzi et al 1976, Graf et al 1976), injected into the periaqueductal gray area (Loh et al 1976, Jacquet & Marks 1976), or given systemically (Tseng et al 1976b). In all cases analgesia was found, and it was reversed by naloxone. Another research strategy is to develop tolerance in animals and then show that there is a reduced effect of endorphin treatment (Tseng et al 1976a, Szekely et al 1977).

This early research, which was carried out in several laboratories, provided the essential core of behavioral research on endorphins. It established β-endorphin as the primary analgesic, and it showed that the enkephalins, even though they occur naturally in the brain, produce much smaller and much shorter term analgesic effects. This early research provided a substantial physiological basis for the basic analgesic phenomenon, and it legitimized more behavioristic and biochemically less authoritative research strategies. For example, one research strategy is to produce analgesia by behavioral means (e.g. with a stressor), and show that the analgesia is reversed by naloxone. Some caution is required in interpreting such studies, however, because naloxone may have effects other than antagonizing opiates. There is already evidence that a naloxone effect does not necessarily implicate an opiate type of mechanism (Hayes et al 1977). The basic dependability of this strategy is attested to, however, by the series of early experiments just cited and by the consistency of results it provides.

Testing Analgesia

TAIL FLICK Some of the analgesia tests conventionally used by pharmacologists may not be familiar to psychologists. Perhaps the most common of these is the tail-flick test. A rat is constrained in a tube, its tail is subjected to focused light from a hot light bulb, and the latency of the reflex tail movement is reported. When 100 micrograms of β-endorphin is administered centrally, it produces markedly increased tail-flick latencies.

HOT PLATE The hot-plate technique consists of placing a rat on a hot plate set at some fixed temperature, such as 50°C, and recording the latency of paw licking (usually a short-latency response) or jumping off the plate (usually a slower response). An increase in response latency indicates analgesia. β-endorphin increases the response latency on the hot plate when it is injected either centrally (Loh et al 1976) or peripherally (Tseng et al 1976b).

Naloxone decreases the latency of jumping from the hot plate (Amir & Amit 1978, Grevert & Goldstein 1977). This hyperalgesic effect seems to be reversed by hypophysectomy (Grevert et al 1978). Naloxone's effect on hot-plate-induced paw licking is less clear, since there are both positive reports (Frederickson et al 1977, Leybin et al 1976) and negative reports (Amir & Amit 1978, Grevert et al 1978, Jacob et al 1974). There are three factors that may be responsible for this inconsistency in the data. 1. The temperatures used have varied from 44.5° (Leybin et al) to 80° (Jacob et al). Lower temperatures produce longer latencies, and thus may allow more time to detect naloxone's effect on these short-latency responses. 2. Naloxone's effect on the hot-plate test depends in part on a diurnal rhythm, although this periodicity is more apparent in the jump latency than the paw-lick latency (Frederickson et al 1977). 3. Simply exposing a rat to the hot-plate apparatus may produce fear due to novelty that can result in an endogenous analgesic response (Bardo & Hughes 1979, Sherman 1979). Perhaps naloxone only has a hyperalgesic effect if the situation is fearful (Fanselow, in press).

CHEMICALLY INDUCED PAIN Analgesia can be assessed by injecting a pain-producing substance and then gauging the animal's reaction. For example, acetic acid injected intraperitoneally causes writhing, and β-endorphin suppresses this writhing response (Loh et al 1976) while naloxone increases it (Kokka & Fairhurst 1977).

Bradykinin injected into the common iliac artery causes a flexing of the hind limbs. Some rats show habituation of this flexion response with repeated injections of bradykinin, and naloxone reverses this habituation (Satoh et al 1979). Naloxone does not affect the nonhabituated response, but this absence of effect may reflect a performance ceiling.

Another analgesic-assessment technique is the formalin test (Dubuisson & Dennis 1977). A small amount of formalin is injected into the animal's paw to produce limping and licking of the assaulted paw. Morphine, meperidine, and analgesic brain stimulation all suppress this response but naloxone alone causes no hyperalgesic response (Dennis et al 1980, Dubuisson & Dennis 1977, North 1977).

TRIGGERING THE ENDORPHINS

There is a fascination with stress as a possible trigger of endogenous opiate activity (see Amir et al 1980). Unfortunately, "stress" is a vague term which includes many stimuli ranging from electrical shock (Madden et al 1977) and cold water immersion (Bodnar et al 1978a) to food deprivation (Bodnar et al 1978b). The variety of these different stressors and their different effects force us to look at them individually rather than applying stress as a global explanatory concept. We will consider several kinds of stimulation that appear to induce endorphin-mediated analgesia.

Shock-Induced Analgesia

Madden et al (1977) reported that extremely intense (3.0 ma) and prolonged (30 min) discontinuous shock caused an increase in the level of endogenous opioids, as measured by a radioactive naloxone binding assay, and that it produced analgesia on the tail-flick test. However, this effect dropped out over the course of 13 shock sessions, as if the animals were becoming tolerant to their own endorphins. They also became hyperalgesic.

This is just the kind of thing a clinician might be interested in: long-term behavioral effects and failures to adapt that are derived from chronic stress. It would be easy to conclude that chronic stress disturbs the body's natural biochemical balance to produce a sensitization to pain and an adaptation of the normal pain-inhibiting mechanism. Unfortunately, the peptide assay used by Madden et al does not distinguish different peptides very well, so the endorphin involvement here is largely hypothetical. On the other hand, there is further support for such a position in the reports that chronic pain patients have unusually high circulatory and cerebro-spinal endorphin levels (Terenius & Wahlstrom 1975). The problem here is that it is not clear to what extent chronic pain patients can be characterized as victims of chronic stress, or what these high levels of endorphin have to do with pain sensitivity. But the possibilities are intriguing.

A series of experiments by Lewis and his colleagues (see Lewis et al 1980, in press) suggests that electric foot shock may or may not induce an opiate analgesia, depending on the temporal parameters of the shock. High intensity, discontinuous shock produced an analgesia that was reversed either by hypophysectomy or by injection of dexamethasone or naloxone. This analgesia was reduced by several exposures to shock and was cross-tolerant with morphine. But similarly intense *continuous* shock produced an analgesia with none of these properties. Lewis et al propose that discontinuous shock causes an endorphinergic hypophyseal analgesia, whereas continuous shock causes an analgesia mediated by some other substrate. However, several methodological problems with this work make it impossible to determine if the temporal characteristics of shock are crucial. The discontinuously shocked rats received more total shock than the continuously shocked animals; is it simply that more shock is necessary to trigger the opioids? Also, the discontinuously shocked animals were tested 27 min after shock onset, while the continuously shocked rats were tested 3 min after shock onset. Perhaps continuous shock produces the same opiate analgesia as discontinuous shock, but the analgesia takes more than 3 min to take effect.

It may be noted that the analgesia produced by either continuous or discontinuous shock dissipates in less than 7 min (Lewis et al in press). In this regard, Fanselow (1979) has suggested that shock can trigger an opiate analgesia that has a quite brief duration, perhaps corresponding to the short-term action of met-enkephalin (Dupont et al 1977).

Amir & Amit (1979) maintained rats on a chronic regimen of naltrexone for 3 weeks and then terminated the drug 3 days prior to shock. They found a potentiation of shock-induced analgesia. On the other hand, naltrexone given immediately before a shock session or immediately before an analgesia test can eliminate shock-induced analgesia (Maier et al 1980). The analgesia induced by these severe shock schedules seems to be differentially sensitive to naltrexone as opposed to naloxone (Maier et al 1980). Maier & Jackson (1979) have suggested that the analgesia produced by severe shock schedules is in part dependent upon the shock's uncontrollability. They speculate that this analgesia may account for some of the effects of massive inescapable and uncontrollable shock that have previously been attributed to learned helplessness.

All of the just-cited studies used prolonged, severe shock to produce analgesia. But such brutal treatment is not necessary. Mah et al (1980) found analgesia in mice after a single 6-sec shock. Fanselow (in press) found that naloxone-reversal effects in Pavlovian fear conditioning are most apparent with brief, mild shock (0.5 sec and 0.3 mA). There are other mild-shock effects. Shocks given at the vocalization threshold of mice produce a naloxone-reversible analgesia (Buckett 1979). Naloxone increases the startle response of rats to 0.5 sec, 1–3 mA shock (Bass et al 1978), and naloxone increases the vocalizations of rats and mice to mild to moderate shock (Bass et al 1978, Buckett 1979).

Fear-Induced Analgesia

The fact that Pavlovian conditioned fear stimuli can produce analgesia plays a prominent role in several recent theories of aversive learning and motivation (Bolles & Fanselow 1980, Riley et al 1980, Schull 1979). Chance et al (1978) first reported that exposure to environmental stimuli previously associated with shock could produce analgesia on the tail-flick test. Unfortunately, in this and in Chance's subsequent research, associative controls have not been included, so that the reported effects could be attributed to unconditioned reactions to shock or to sensitization effects rather than to conditioned fear. Further, while Chance and his coworkers have assessed pain reactivity, they have not measured fear. Using conditioning controls and testing animals 24 hr after conditioning to minimize unconditioned responses to shock, Fanselow & Bolles (1979a) demonstrated both conditioned fear (increased freezing) to a tone predicting shock, and a naloxone-reversible conditioning of fear to contextual cues (animals receiving naloxone showed more fear conditioning so, we may assume, shock was more aversive to them). Subsequently, MacLennan et al (1980) used a differential fear-conditioning procedure—equivalent exposure was given in two contexts, but shock was only received in one of them—and found that exposure to the shock-associated apparatus caused analgesia on both the hot-plate and tail-flick tests. A recent study by Fanselow and Baackes (see Fanselow 1981) also included independent assessments of fear and pain-related behavior. Fear was assessed by the occurrence of freezing and pain was assessed by the reaction to formalin injected into a paw. Shock-associated stimuli both increased freezing (indicating fear) and decreased formalin-induced behavior (indicating analgesia). Additionally, Fanselow (1979) reported that naloxone blocks the usual preference rats show for signaled over unsignaled shock. This finding is also consistent with the idea that the fear stimulus preceding a signaled shock causes an endorphin analgesia that reduces the subjective intensity of the shock.

Some writers (Chance et al 1978, Maier et al 1980) have reported that fear-induced analgesia is not reversed with ordinary dosages of naloxone (or naltrexone). But it seems likely (Fanselow in press) that naloxone will reverse analgesia in freely moving rats that are given modest amounts of shock. It appears to be only when prolonged, intense shock is given, and particularly when the animal is restrained, that shock-induced analgesia is not naloxone reversible (see also DeVries et al 1979).

Unsettled Problems

Part of the uncertainty about the endorphinergic basis of some of these analgesic effects may be due to an over-reliance upon naloxone reversibility as a criterion for opiate involvement. Naloxone reversibility is a necessary but not a sufficient condition for opiate mediation (Jacquet 1980, Sawynok et al 1979). Part of the uncertainty reflects the wide variety of stimulation that is called stressful and the perhaps overoptimistic strategy of trying to link them all to some one substrate. Some stressors appear to produce an analgesia that is not naloxone reversible (Hayes et al 1978). However, in some cases of stress-induced analgesis, naloxone may be effective only in doses exceeding those typically used (Maier et al 1980). Caution should be exercised in discounting opiate involvement, since there appear to be opiate systems that are naloxone insensitive (DeVries et al 1979, Terenius 1977). A failure to reverse an effect with naloxone does not necessarily rule out opiate involvement. And a successful reversal of some effect with a small dose of naloxone may not be sufficient to implicate opiates, even though it is strongly suggestive.

When electric shock is used as a stressor, some parameters of shock delivery appear to trigger a naloxone-sensitive opiate analgesia, while other parameters trigger a naloxone-insensitive opiate analgesia. Cold water immersion appears to produce a nonopiate analgesia (Bodnar et al 1978a, Lal et al 1978) that interacts with the endorphin system (Bodnar et al 1980). When so many kinds of stimuli are called stressors, when the test for stress-induced analgesia is usually stressful itself, when there may be several analgesic systems, each of which is differentially sensitive to different stressors, and when these different systems may interact, is it any wonder that there is uncertainty in the literature?

OTHER BEHAVIORAL EFFECTS

Effects on Fear-Motivated Behavior

Young (1980) found that naloxone enhanced, in a dose-dependent manner, the punishing effects of electric shock on a food reinforced operant, but had no effect on the response itself. Soubrie et al (1980) found that doses of naloxone lower than those needed to enhance punishment could reverse the tolerance of punishment caused by diazepam. Seemingly to the contrary, Goldstein et al (1976) had found no effect of naloxone on the shock intensity threshold for a pole-climbing escape task. However, Goldstein et al pretrained their animals to respond to a strong shock, and only those that had a desirable, high level of responding were tested. These animals showed very low thresholds (at or below .125 mA), suggesting that the well-trained escape response was elicited by the sensory qualities of the shock rather than by its painfulness. It has been shown that naloxone does not affect performance of a well-trained avoidance response (Holtzman & Jewett 1973, Izquierdo 1980), so, again, one would not be surprised that Goldstein et al found no effect of naloxone on escape responding. The effect of naloxone on avoidance acquisition is equivocal (Izquierdo 1980, Kostowski & Plaznik 1979), but then so is the effect of shock intensity.

Bolles & Fanselow (1980) have suggested that the major function of the endorphins is to provide for analgesia and the inhibition of pain-motivated behavior at those times when the animal should be defending itself. For example, when wounded by a predator, an animal should display defensive behavior and inhibit recuperative behavior. Fear is therefore seen as the main trigger of the endorphins. Naloxone increases two of the rat's predominant shock-elicited defensive behaviors, freezing (Fanselow & Bolles 1979b) and defensive boxing (Fanselow et al 1980). That these two behaviors have markedly different topographies argues against any account based on nonspecific motor effects. The boundary conditions for these effects are most instructive. In order for naloxone to increase freezing, the rat must be given naloxone before shock, and it must also be shocked more than once. This finding suggests that the first shock of a series triggers an endorphin analgesia which makes later shocks less aversive. Naloxone antagonizes the analgesia to make these shocks more aversive than they would normally be. Since more aversive shock produces more freezing, naloxone increases freezing. In support of the general proposition that fear triggers endorphins is the finding (Fanselow, in press) that naloxone's effect on freezing is also dependent on the presence of stimuli, such as apparatus cues, that have been associated with shock.

Memory Effects

Some researchers have argued for the involvement of endorphins in memory, particularly the memory of aversively motivated instrumental behavior. If β-endorphin is given shortly after passive avoidance training (presumably during the consolidation period), there is a decrement in passive avoidance performance in a later test (Martinez & Rigter 1980). Gallagher & Kapp (1978) found that the opiate agonist levorphenol had a similar effect when administered directly into the amygdala. Morphine (Izquierdo 1979), Leu-enkephalin, and β-endorphin (Izquierdo et al 1980) given following shuttle avoidance training all decrease performance on a subsequent test. On the other hand, naloxone given following avoidance training seems to enhance performance on a subsequent test (Gallagher & Kapp 1978, Izquierdo 1979, Messing et al 1979). These findings have fostered the idea that endorphins may impair memory consolidation. However, one could entertain a more parsimonious account based on a state-dependent generalization decrement. If endorphins are released by shock during avoidance training, then any stimulus consequence of this release should become associated with the avoidance response and be part of the total stimulus context controlling the avoidance response at the time of testing. If opiates released during training persist for some time following the training session, the association between the stimulus aspects of the endogenous opiates and the avoidance response should begin to extinguish. Naloxone, given immediately after training, would eliminate some of the stimulus consequence of the endorphins and curtail this extinction. One would see this as increased responding during the test. However, if opiates are administered after training, there would be greater associative loss due to longer persistence of these stimulus consequences, and this would result in reduced performance during testing.

Hedonic Effects

If the endorphins modulate painful sensations and ameliorate negative affect, perhaps they also play a part in pleasurable sensations and hold the key to the physiological basis of the whole pleasure-pain modality. One can envision several kinds of models. Perhaps the sudden release of endorphins, triggered by delivering some reinforcing stimulus, constitutes reward. Maybe the long-sought secret of pleasure and pain is right before us. Increasing levels of brain endorphin make the connections that are attributed to reinforcement and are detected by the individual as pleasure. Things are never so simple, however. There is only a scrap of evidence for such a model. Rats bar press for self-administration of leu-enkephalin at a slightly higher rate than for saline (Belluzzi & Stein 1977). There are also evidently certain conditions under which naloxone will depress bar pressing for reinforcing electrical brain stimulation (Belluzzi & Stein 1977, van der Kooy et al 1977).

An alternative model, which looks more promising, is that endorphin release has some kind of enabling action on certain kinds of reinforcement. This idea has been developed in some detail by Panksepp et al (1980). Several kinds of evidence support the model's application to social behavior. For example, young puppies give distress vocalizations when isolated, and morphine reduces this crying (Panksepp et al 1978). Naloxone also increases such vocalization in some species (see Panksepp et al 1980). The interpretation given such findings is not just that the opiate state is euphoric, "substituting" for the reward value of returning to the family. Rather, it is that the opiate state mediates how rewarding the social contact will be. For example, young chicks given naloxone hurry to regain social contact, but appear to get little comfort from the contact. Thus, the endorphins are said to have as their primary function making social reinforcement more rewarding.

Metabolic Effects

Stimulation raises the rat's body temperature. Even the minor stress of handling and rectal probing can cause an "emotional hyperthermia," increased plasma endorphin levels, and potentiate morphine's thermic effects (Blasig et al 1978, Stewart & Eikelboom 1981). Naloxone reverses this emotional hyperthermia. The thermal response to stimulation habituates, but it is known that naloxone, in addition, lowers the body temperature of rats that are habituated to the handling procedure (Stewart & Eikelboom 1979). Such findings implicate the endorphins in thermoregulation, particularly in stimulation-induced temperature changes. Hypophysectomy does not block these thermic effects (Eikelboom & Stewart 1981), which suggests that the effect is mediated by some endogenous brain opiate rather than a pituitary endorphin.

There is now a substantial literature showing that naloxone reduces food and water intake (e.g. Rogers et al 1978, Stapleton et al 1979). However, the fact that naloxone will support conditioned taste aversions (see Riley et al 1980, Stolerman et al 1978) suggests a need for caution in interpreting much of the data.

Tossing all caution aside, Margules (1979) has proposed that the primary function of endorphins is metabolic. He suggests that the endorphins serve to conserve body resources and energy. Naloxone, or some related but as yet undiscovered hormone, tips the balance the other way, toward expenditure of body resources and increased energy output. When the balance shifts every day, we have a substrate to control the circadian ingestion and activity cycles. When it shifts seasonally, we have an account of such things as hibernation.

Effects and Functions

It is apparent that the function of the endorphins remains obscure and hence open for speculation. One could believe (as the reviewers do) that analgesia is the primary effect and that the metabolic, hedonic, and other effects are all secondary to it. These other effects can be regarded as accidental by-products of a powerful analgesic mechanism.

But it is still possible to turn it around, making the hedonic effect or the metabolic effect or something else the raison d'être of endorphins and regarding analgesia as the epiphenomenon. There are further possibilities. Mishkin and his associates (see Lewis et al 1981) have reported radioactive binding assays for naloxone that examine both the locus and structure (cytoarchitectonics) of the cortex; the data reveal a clear pattern. Naloxone is most involved in those areas and structures that do the most advanced processing of sensory information. It is concluded that just as the opiates gate pain information at a spinal level, so at the cortical level they gate all sorts of perceptual information. In short, the endorphins are said to mediate attention. Could this be their primary function? Or do the endorphins exist because they restrain male sexual performance (Myers & Baum 1980)? Nobody really knows at this point what their primary function is. We suspect that if the functional question could be answered satisfactorily, much of the literature on the endorphins would make more sense.

On the other hand, interest in these peptides should certainly not be restricted to their primary functional role. If it is true, for example, that naloxone reduces hallucinations in some schizophrenics (Watson et al 1978), that could be important with respect to schizophrenia, and that importance would pertain whatever the primary function of the endorphins might be.

Literature Cited

Amir, S., Amit, Z. 1978. Endogenous opioid ligands may mediate stress-induced changes in the affective properties of pain related behavior in rats. *Life Sci.* 23:1143–52

Amir, S., Amit, Z. 1979. Enhanced analgesic effects of stress following chronic administration of naltrexone in rats. *Eur. J. Pharmacol.* 59:137–40

Amir, S., Brown, Z. W., Amit, Z. 1980. The role of endorphins in stress: Evidence and speculations. *Neurosci. Biobehav. Rev.* 4:77–86

Bardo, M. T., Hughes, R. A. 1979. Exposure to a nonfunctional hot plate as a factor in the assessment of morphine analgesia in rats. *Pharmacol. Biochem. Behav.* 10:481–85

Bass, M. B., Friedman, H. J., Lester, D. 1978. Antagonism of naloxone hyperalgesia by ethanol. *Life Sci.* 22:1939–46

Belluzzi, J. D., Grant, N., Garsky, V., Sarantakis, D., Wise, C. D., Stein, L. 1976. Analgesia induced in vivo by central administration of enkephalin in rats. *Nature* 260:625–26

Belluzzi, J. D., Stein, L. 1977. Enkephalin may mediate euphoria and drive-reduction reward. *Nature* 255:556–58

Blasig, J., Hollt, V., Bauerle, U., Herz, A. 1978. Involvement of endorphins in emotional hyperthermia of rats. *Life Sci.* 23:2525–32

Bodnar, R. J., Kelly, D. D., Spiaggia, A., Ehrenberg, C., Glusman, M. 1978a. Dose-dependent reductions by naloxone of analgesia induced by cold-water stress. *Pharmacol. Biochem. Behav.* 8:667–72

Bodnar, R. J., Kelly, D. D., Spiaggia, A., Glusman M. 1978b. Biphasic alterations of nociceptive thresholds induced by food deprivation. *Physiol. Psychol.* 6:391–95

Bodnar, R. J., Lattner, M., Wallace, M. M. 1980. Antagonism of stress-induced analgesia by D-phenylalanine, an antienkephalinase. *Pharmacol. Biochem. Behav.* 13:829–33

Bolles, R. C., Fanselow, M. S. 1980. A perceptual-defensive-recuperative model of fear and pain. *Behav. Brain Sci.* 3:121–31

Buckett, W. R. 1979. Peripheral stimulation in mice induces short-duration analgesia preventable by naloxone. *J. Pharmacol.* 58:169–78

Chance, W. T., White, A. C., Krynock, G. M., Rosecrans, J. A. 1978. Conditional fear-induced antinociception and decreased binding of (^{3}H) N-Leu-enkephalin to rat brain. *Brain Res.* 141: 371–74

Dennis, S. G., Choiniere, M., Melzack, R. 1980. Stimulation-produced analgesia in rats: Assessment by two pain tests and correlation with self-stimulation. *Exp. Neurol.* 68:295–309

DeVries, G. H., Chance, W. T., Payne, W. R., Rosecrans, J. A. 1979. Effect of autoanalgesia on CNS enkephalin receptors. *Pharmacol. Biochem. Behav.* 11: 741–44

Dubuisson, D., Dennis, S. G. 1977. The formalin test: A quantitative study of the analgesic effects of morphine, meperidine, and brain stem stimulation in rats and cats. *Pain* 4:161–74

Dupont, A., Cusan, L., Garon, M., Alvarado-Urbina, G., Labrie, F. 1977. Extremely rapid degradation of (^{3}H) methionine-enkephalin by various rat tissues *in vivo* and *in vitro*. *Life Sci.* 21:907–14

Eikelboom, R., Stewart, J. 1981. Hypophysectomy increases the sensitivity of rats to naloxone-induced hypothermia. *Life Sci.* 28:1047–52

Fanselow, M. S. 1979. Naloxone attenuates rat's preference for signaled shock. *Physiol. Psychol.* 7:70–74

Fanselow, M. S. 1981. *A role for endogenous opiates in defensive behavior.* Presented at meet. East. Psychol. Assoc. New York

Fanselow, M. S. 1982. Naloxone and Pavlovian fear conditioning. *Learn. Motiv.* In press

Fanselow, M. S., Bolles, R. C. 1979a. Triggering of the endorphin analgesic reaction by a cue previously associated with shock: Reversal by naloxone. *Bull. Psychon. Soc.* 14:88–89

Fanselow, M. S., Bolles, R. C. 1979b. Naloxone and shock-elicited freezing in the rat. *J. Comp. Physiol. Psychol.* 93: 736–44

Fanselow, M. S., Sigmundi, R. A., Bolles, R. C. 1980. Naloxone pretreatment enhances shock-elicited aggression. *Physiol. Psychol.* 8:369–71

Fratta, W., Yang, H. T., Hong, J., Costa, E. 1977. Stability of Met-enkephalin content in brain structures of morphine-dependent or foot shock-stressed rats. *Nature* 268:452–53

Frederickson, R. C. A., Burgis, V., Edwards, J. D. 1977. Hyperalgesia induced by naloxone follows diurnal rhythm in responsivity to painful stimuli. *Science* 198:756–58

Gallagher, M., Kapp, B. S. 1978. Manipulation of opiate activity in the amygdala alters memory processes. *Life Sci.* 23:1973–78

Goldstein, A., Pryor, G. T., Otis, L. S., Larsen, F. 1976. On the role of endogenous opioid peptides: Failure of naloxone to influence shock escape threshold in the rat. *Life Sci.* 18:599–604

Graf, L., Szekely, J. I., Ronai, A. Z., Dunai-Kovacs, Z., Bajusz, S. 1976. A comparative study on analgesic effect of Met^5-enkephalin and related lipotropin fragments. *Nature* 263:240–41

Grevert, P., Baizman, E. R., Goldstein, A. 1978. Naloxone effects on a nociceptive response of hypophysectomized and adrenalectomized mice. *Life Sci.* 23: 723–28

Grevert, P., Goldstein, A. 1977. Some effects of naloxone on behavior in the mouse. *Psychopharmacology* 53:111–13

Guillemin, R., Vargo, T. M., Rossier, J., Minick, S., Ling, N., Rivier, C., Vale, W., Bloom, F. E. 1977. β-endorphin and adrenocortitropin are secreted concomitantly by the pituitary gland. *Science* 197:1367–69

Hayes, R. L., Bennett, G. J., Newlon, P. G., Mayer, D. J. 1978. Behavioral and physiological studies of non-narcotic analgesia in the rat elicited by certain environmental stimuli. *Brain Res.* 155: 69–90

Hayes, R. L., Price, D. D., Dubner, R. 1977. Naloxone antagonism as evidence for narcotic mechanisms. *Science* 196:600

Holtzman, S. G., Jewett, R. E. 1973. Stimulation of behavior in the rat by cyclazocine: Effects on naloxone. *J. Pharmacol. Exp. Ther.* 187:380–90

Hughes, J., Smith, T. W., Kosterlitz, H. W., Fothergill, L. A., Morgan, B. A., Morris, H. R. 1975. Identification of two related pentapeptides from the brain with potent opiate agonist activity. *Nature* 258:577–79

Izquierdo, I. 1979. Effect of naloxone and morphine on various forms of memory in the rat: Possible role of endogenous opiate mechanisms in memory consolidation. *Psychopharmacology* 66:199–203

Izquierdo, I. 1980. Effect of β-endorphin and naloxone on acquisition, memory, and retrieval of shuttle avoidance and habituation learning in rats. *Psychopharmacology* 69:111–15

Izquierdo, I., Paiva, A. C. M., Elisabetsky, E. 1980. Post-training intraperitoneal administration of Leu-enkephalin and β-endorphin causes retrograde amnesia for two different tasks in rats. *Behav. Neural Biol.* 28:246–50

Jacob, J. J., Tremblay, E. C., Colombel, M. C. 1974. Facilitation de reactions nociceptives par la naloxone chez la souris et chez le rat. *Psychopharmacology* 223: 217–23

Jacquet, Y. F. 1978. Opiate effects after adrenocorticotropin or β-endorphin injection in the periaqueductal gray matter of rats. *Science* 201:1032–34

Jacquet, Y. F. 1979. β-endorphin and ACTH: Opiate peptides with coordinate roles in the regulation of behavior? *Trends Neurosci.* 2:140–43

Jacquet, Y. F. 1980. Stereospecific, dose-dependent antagonism by naloxone of non-opiate behavior in mice. *Pharmacol. Biochem. Behav.* 13:585–87

Jacquet, Y. F., Marks, N. 1976. The C-fragment of β-lipotropin: An endogenous neuroleptic or antiphychotogen. *Science* 194:632–35

Kokka, N., Fairhurst, A. S. 1977. Naloxone enhancement of acetic acid-induced writhing in rats. *Life Sci.* 21:975–80

Kostowski, W., Plaznik, A. 1979. Naloxone-induced facilitation of conditioned avoidance behavior in rats. *Pol. J. Pharmacol. Pharm.* 31:293–96

Lal, H., Spaulding, T., Fielding, S. 1978. Swim-stress induced analgesia and lack of its naloxone antagonism. *Commun. Psychopharmacol.* 2:263–66

Lewis, J. W., Cannon, J. T., Liebeskind, J. C. 1980. Opioid and nonopioid mechanisms of stress analgesia. *Science* 208:623–25

Lewis, J. W., Sherman, J. E., Liebeskind, J. C. 1982. Opioid and nonopioid stress analgesia: Assessment of tolerance and cross-tolerance with morphine. *J. Neurosci.* In press

Lewis, W. E., Mishikin, M., Bragin, E., Brown, R. M., Pert, C. B., Pert, A. 1981. Opiate receptor gradients in monkey cerebral cortex: Correspondence with sensory processing hierarchies. *Science* 211:1166–69

Leybin, L., Pinsky, C., LaBella, F. S., Havlicek, V., Rezek, M. 1976. Intraventricular Met-enkephalin causes unexpected lowering of pain threshold and narcotic withdrawal signs in rats. *Nature* 264:458–59

Liebeskind, J., Paul, I. 1977. Psychological and physiological mechanisms of pain. *Ann. Rev. Psychol.* 28:41–60

Loh, H. H., Tseng, L. F., Wei, E., Li, C. H. 1976. β-endorphin is a potent analgesic agent. *Proc. Natl. Acad. Sci. USA* 73: 2895–98

MacLennan, A. J., Jackson, R. L., Maier, S. F. 1980. Conditioned analgesia in the rat. *Bull. Psychon. Soc.* 15:387–90

Madden, J., Akil, H., Patrick, R. L., Barchas, J. D. 1977. Stress-induced parallel changes in central opioid levels and pain responsiveness in the rat. *Nature* 265:358–60

Mah, C., Suissa, A., Anisman, H. 1980. Dissociation of antinociception and escape deficits induced by stress in mice. *J. Comp. Physiol. Psychol.* 94:1160–71

Maier, S. F., Davies, S., Grau, J. W., Jackson, R. L., Morrison, D. H., Moye, T., Madden, J., Barchas, J. D. 1980. Opiate antagonists and the long-term analgesic reaction induced by inescapable shock. *J. Comp. Physiol. Psychol.* 94:1172–83

Maier, S. F., Jackson, R. L. 1979. Learned helplessness: All of us were right (and wrong): Inescapable shock has multiple effects. In *The Psychology of learning and motivation,* ed. G. Bower, 3:155–218. New York:Academic. 426 pp.

Margules, D. L. 1979. Beta-endorphin and endoloxone: Hormones of the autonomic nervous system for the conservation or expenditure of bodily resources and energy in anticipation of famine or fast. *Neurosci. Biobehav. Rev.* 3:155–62

Martinez, J. L., Rigter, H. 1980. Endorphins after acquisition and consolidation of an inhibitory avoidance response in rats. *Neurosci. Lett.* 19:197–201

Messing, R. B., Jensen, R. A., Martinez, J. L., Speihler, V. R., Vasquez, B. J., Soumireu-Mourat, E., Liang, K. L., McGaugh, J. L. 1979. Naloxone enchancement of memory. *Behav. Neural Biol.* 27:266–75

Myers, B. M., Baum, M. J. 1980. Facilitation of copulatory performance in male rats by naloxone: Effects of hypophysectomy, 17 alpha-entradial, and lateinizing hormone releasing hormone. *Pharmacol. Biochem. Behav.* 12:365–70

North, M. A. 1977. Naloxone reversal of morphine analgesia but failure to alter reactivity to pain in the formalin test. *Life Sci.* 22:295–302

Olson, G. A., Olson, R. D., Kastin, J. J., Coy, D. H. 1980. Endogenous opiates: Through 1978. *Neurosci. Biobehav. Rev.* 3:285–99

Panksepp, J., Herman, B., Connor, R., Bishop, P., Scott, J. P. 1978. The biology of social attachments: Opiates alleviate separation distress. *Biol. Psychiatry* 13:607–18

Panksepp, J., Herman, B. H., Vilberg, T., Bishop, P., DeEskinazi, F. G. 1980. Endogenous opioids and social behavior. *Neurosci. Biobehav. Rev.* 4:473–87

Pert, C. B., Snyder, S. H. 1973. Opiate receptor: Demonstration in nervous tissue. *Science* 179:1011–14

Riley, A. L., Zellner, D. A., Duncan, H. J. 1980. The role of endorphins in animal learning and behavior. *Neurosci. Biobehav. Rev.* 4:69–76

Rogers, G. H., Frenck, H., Taylor, A. N., Liebeskind, J. C. 1978. Naloxone suppression of food and water intake in deprived rats. *Proc. West. Pharmacol. Soc.* 21:457–60

Rossier, J., French, E. D., Rivier, C., Ling, N., Guillemin, R., Bloom, F. E. 1977a. Foot shock induced stress increases β-endorphin levels in blood but not brain. *Nature* 270:618–20

Rossier, J., Vargo, T. M., Minick, S., Ling, N., Bloom, F. E., Guillemin, R. 1977b. Regional distribution of β-endorphin and enkephalin content in rat brain and pituitary. *Proc. Natl. Acad. Sci. USA* 74:5162–65

Satoh, M., Kawajiri, S., Yamamoto, M., Makino, H., Takagi, H. 1979. Reversal by naloxone of adaptation of rats to noxious stimuli. *Life Sci.* 24:685–89

Sawynok, J., Pinsky, C., LaBella, F. S. 1979. On the specificity of naloxone as an opiate antagonist. *Life Sci.* 25:1621–32

Schull, J. 1979. A conditioned opponent theory of Pavlovian conditioning and habituation. In *The Psychology of Learning and Motivation,* ed. G. Bower, 3:57–90. New York: Academic. 426 pp.

Sherman, J. E. 1979. The effects of conditioning and novelty on the rat's analgesic and pyretic responses to morphine. *Learn. Motiv.* 10:383–418

Snyder, S. H. 1977. Opiate receptors and internal opiates. *Sci. Am.* 236:44–56

Soubrie, P., Jobert, A., Thiebot, M. H. 1980. Differential effects of naloxone against the diazepam-induced release of behavior in rats in three aversive situations. *Psychopharmacology* 69:101–5

Stapleton, J. M., Lind, M. L., Mirriman, V. J., Bozarth, M. A., Reid, L. D. 1979. Affective consequences and subsequent effects on morphine self-administration of d-ala^2-methionine enkephalin. *Physiol. Psychol.* 7:146–52

Stewart, J., Eikelboom, R. 1979. Stress masks the hypothermic effect of naloxone in rats. *Life Sci.* 25:1165–72

Stewart, J., Eikelboom, R. 1981. Interaction between the effects of stress and morphine on body temperature in rats. *Life Sci.* 28:1041–45

Stolerman, I. P., Pilcher, C. W. T., D'Mello, G. D. 1978. Stereospecific aversive property of narcotic antagonists in morphine-free rats. *Life Sci.* 22:1755–62

Szekely, J. I., Ronai, A. Z., Dunai-Kovacs, Z., Miglecz, E., Bajusz, S., Graf, L. 1977. Cross tolerance between morphine and β-endorphin in vivo. *Life Sci.* 20:1259–64

Terenius, L. 1977. Opioid peptides and opiates differ in receptor selectivity. *Psychoneuroendocrinology* 2:53–58

Terenius, L. 1978. Endogenous peptides and analgesia. *Ann. Rev. Pharmacol. Toxicol.* 18:189–204

Terenius, L., Wahlstrom, A. 1975. Morphine-like ligand for opiate receptors in humans. *Life Sci.* 16:1759–64

Tseng, L. F., Loh, H. H., Li, C. H. 1976a. β-endorphin: Cross tolerance to and cross physical dependence on morphine. *Proc. Natl. Acad. Sci. USA* 73:4187–89

Tseng, L. F., Loh, H. H., Li, C. H. 1976b. β-endorphin as a potent analgesic by intravenous injection. *Nature* 263: 239–40

van der Kooy, D., LePiane, F. G., Phillips, A. G. 1977. Apparent independence of opiate reinforcement and electrical self-stimulation systems in the rat. *Life Sci.* 20:981–86

Watson, S. J., Berger, P. A., Akil, H., Mills, M. J., Barchas, J. D. 1978. Effects of naloxone on schizophrenia: Reduction in hallucinations in a subpopulation of subjects. *Science* 201:73–75

Young, G. A. 1980. Naloxone enhancement of punishment in the rat. *Life Sci.* 26:1787–92

Ann. Rev. Psychol. 1982. 33:103–22

PSYCHOLOGY IN LATIN AMERICA TODAY

Ruben Ardila

National University of Colombia, Bogota, Colombia

CONTENTS

This is the first chapter in the *Annual Review of Psychology* on psychology in Latin America. I will present a comprehensive coverage, including historical factors, social and ideological influences, professional issues, training of psychologists, congresses and publications, scientific research, and perspectives.

I want to make clear from the beginning that there is no such thing as "Latin American psychology" in the same sense that there is no European psychology or Asian psychology. There is psychology *in* Latin America, meaning the investigation and application of psychological principles in a particular context, in this case the Latin American continent.

On the other hand, there is no such a region as "Latin America." There are more than 20 nations in different stages of sociocultural development that speak Spanish, Portuguese, and French, and whose inhabitants belong

0066-4308/82/0201-0103$02.00

to different racial groups—Caucasian, Indian, Negro, Chinese, and others. This heterogeneous group of nations share some traditions and have some common features that facilitate their identification.

Psychology began in Latin America as part of philosophy. Later on it was considered an important complement to medicine and education. The first laboratory of experimental psychology was founded in Argentina in 1898. The earliest training programs were organized in 1946 and 1948. At the present time psychology is a well-developed discipline in the majority of the Latin American countries. The problems of Latin American psychology are developmental problems, both in the scientific and in the professional sense, related to the socioeconomic issues of the region.

This chapter presents a critical discussion of some specific topics that are relevant to contemporary psychology in Latin America: origins and development, professional issues, main areas of research, main areas of application. No encyclopedic coverage is intended, but the review will focus on a few specific topics. Both professional and scientific aspects will be considered.

The major Latin American nations will be considered in this chapter, as well as all the areas of psychology, and all the approaches and "systems," without giving priority to a country, to an approach, or an area. Because a chapter on psychology in Mexico will be published in a future volume of this series, Mexico will not be considered in detail, although it should be studied in the context of Latin America.

Three main cultural influences have shaped Latin American psychology: psychoanalysis, behaviorism, and "French" psychology. In the early stages of development, psychology was taught by medical doctors trained in Freudian psychoanalysis. This tradition still remains, particularly in Argentina. The second influence, behaviorism (particularly Skinner's radical behaviorism), came to Latin America by the middle of the 1960s and the beginning of the 1970s, and continues to be influential in the majority of the nations. "French" psychology, on the other hand, is a mixture of neopsychoanalysis, Marxism, and anthropology that has been taken very seriously in some countries.

The present author has published a number of articles and books in Spanish and English on psychology in Latin America (see for instance Ardila 1968, 1970a, 1973, 1976, 1978, 1980a,b, 1982). Only the most important features of Latin American psychology will be presented here.

At this time Mexico and Brazil are the leading countries, as far as research, training, and professional applications of psychology are concerned. Work is done in the majority of the continent, of course, and Chile, Colombia, Venezuela, Cuba, Panama, Peru, and Argentina have made important contributions that will be reviewed here. Many traditions and many fields will be integrated in order to give a coherent picture of psychology in Latin America today. General trends will be presented, not "national histories" of psychology.

THE CULTURAL TRADITION

Latin America is a large continent with countries in very different stages of development that share common traditions. The name is applied to the whole Western hemisphere with the exception of the United States, Canada, and in some cases to a few of the new Caribbean nations (of Anglo-Saxon origin). As I have indicated previously (Ardila 1982), science is not a cultural value in Latin America. Literature, art, and the humanities are very positively evaluated, and traditional education is very much a part of Latin American culture, but science and technology do not receive much esteem.

Psychology in a broad sense has existed for several centuries. In some of the pre-Columbian cultures much philosophical and psychological thinking went on; the Incas, Aztecs, and Mayas were concerned with man and his place in the world, and some primitive inhabitants of the Americas were relatively advanced in some of these matters.

During the colonial period Spain and Portugal were very influential in the formation of a philosophical tradition, following closely the main ideas cultivated in Europe at that time. In this context, philosophical psychology —the study of the soul and its functions—was one of the main areas of study. Philosophical idealism and the ideas of Aristotle and St. Thomas dominated the philosophical stage in Latin America. Some consequences of this idealism still remain and have hindered the development of science in the most traditional countries of Spanish America.

ORIGINS

From its beginnings in philosophy, medicine, and education, Latin American psychology has evolved into a science and a profession that follows international standards and is contributing to the socioeconomic progress of the region.

The development of Latin American psychology is varied and heterogeneous. In countries with a strong philosophical tradition, like Mexico, Peru, and Argentina, psychology began as part of philosophy taught at the universities of the colonial period following the ideas of Aristotle and St. Thomas. In countries with no philosophical tradition, psychology was at the beginning a discipline that helped medicine and education in the handling of behavioral problems. Philosophy, medicine, and education are the three roots of Latin American psychology. In line with this, the pioneers were philosophers, medical doctors, and educators. The early origins can be traced to the establishment of the first mental hospital in the American continent, the Hospital de San Hipólito in Mexico City in 1566; Bernardino Alvarez was its founder.

From the point of view of experimental psychology it is important to indicate that the earliest experimental psychology laboratory in Latin America was founded by Horacio Piñero (1869–1919) in 1898. The laboratory was founded at the Colegio Nacional de Buenos Aires (Argentina). Wundt had established the first psychological laboratory only 19 years earlier, and Stanley Hall had started the first laboratory on the American continent (at the Johns Hopkins University, in the USA), only 15 years before the Latin American laboratory.

The first laboratory of Mexico was founded by Enrique C. Aragón in 1916. The earliest laboratory in Brazil belongs to the decade of the 1920s (founded by Waclaw Radecki in 1923), and the first laboratories in the other countries are even more recent, in the majority of the cases founded around 1960 to 1965. In some countries there are still no psychological laboratories in a formal sense.

Books were published during the colonial period that were relevant to psychology. Argentina, Mexico, and Brazil were the countries with a more active tradition in the production of books and ideas concerning psychological issues. As we have said, Mexico and Brazil have maintained the leadership of Latin American psychology up to the present time.

Probably the most important psychological book published during the colonial period in Latin America was *Instituciones Psicológicas;* its author was Father Joaquín Millás, who first published it in 1797 in Argentina. The book studied the problems of the relationships between body and mind. Its author insisted that the existence of soul could be proved just by introspection. He utilized the anatomical and physiological knowledge of his time to establish that the soul was located in the body. On the other hand, he studied issues of memory, sensation, and perception, animal and human behavior, and the like.

In Mexico, Fray Bernardino de Sahagún described Aztec beliefs and customs using a methodology similar to the contemporary approach of the social psychologist and cross-cultural researcher. In 1774 an Oratorian priest, Benito Díaz de Gamarra, published a book entitled *Elementa Recentioris Philosophiae,* in which he presented the views of Descartes, Malebranche, Leibniz, Newton, and Gassendi, and his own point of view concerning psychological matters. Díaz de Gamarra studied the mind-body problem, the nature of consciousness, the knowledge of self, etc.

A Mexican professor of medicine, José Ignacio Bartolache, introduced in his country the physiological ideas of Thomas Sydenham and Hermann

Boerhaave, conducted experiments in animals, and made the first study of hysteria in Mexico in 1773 (Robles 1943, Díaz-Guerrero 1976). Besides experiments and dissections of bodies, Bartolache carried out clinical observations and described the neurotic symptoms of functional paralysis, anxiety, fixed ideas, anesthesias, and so forth, a century before Freud. He also said that hysteric symptomatology was more frequent in people from upper and middle classes because of excessive spoiling. Bartolache considered that sex had something to do with hysteria and emphasized its role.

THE PIONEERS

After the independence of the Latin American nations, many changes occurred in education. Science began to be taken into account, especially in countries like Argentina and Mexico, with the arrival of positivism. This new philosophy had to struggle with the idealistic philosophy that was dominant at that time. A few isolated men did very important psychological work at the end of the nineteenth century and the first decades of the twentieth. This could be called the stage of the pioneers.

In the early period of Latin American psychology, one of the most original figures was José Ingenieros (1877–1925). He was a man of many talents: a philosopher, educator, socialist leader, and the author of the earliest system of psychology postulated by a Latin American. In 1910 he presented his "genetic psychology," a new psychological "school" based on the objective approach and evolutionism. For Ingenieros, psychology was a natural science, devoted to the study of psychic functions of the living organisms; it did not concern itself with the soul, and its main method was behavioral observation. Psychological functions adapt the organism to its environment and are elementary processes of all living beings. A maximum of consciousness is obtained through a maximum of experience. Ingenieros' genetic psychology was first presented at the University of Buenos Aires and published in his book *Psicología Genética* (1911), which in later editions was called *Principios de Psicología Biológica,* and finally *Principios de Psicología.*

Another important thinker, also from Argentina, was Enrique Mouchet (1886–1977). He directed the Institute of Psychology of the University of Buenos Aires, founded the first journal of psychology in Latin America, and did important experimental research, especially on perception. Mouchet wanted to convert his institute into the main center for psychological research in the Spanish-speaking world. His journal, *Anales del Instituto de Psicología de la Universidad de Buenos Aires,* published only three volumes. In 1924 Mouchet presented the working plan for his institute; he insisted on the importance of all methods—genetic, experimental, pathological, introspective, psychoanalytic. After doing research in several areas, Mouchet postulated his system in 1941 in his book *Percepción, Instinto y Razón.* The book attempted to present a new point of view in psychology, a new system. Mouchet insisted that the term "psicología vital," the name of his school of psychology, did not have anything to do with vitalism. The center of the system was *cenestesia,* defined as a vital sentiment, a notion of our own personal existence that comes from the biological foundation of consciousness. Mouchet devoted chapters of his book to the study of the vital nature of unity, causality, time, and space. In his study of time he pointed out that vital time is individual time, while rational time is social time. The meaning of duration is discovered by man and reinforced by culture.

For many years Argentina was the country in which most psychological research was carried out (see Papini 1976, 1978, Papini & Mustaca 1979). Brazil and Mexico also had important work in progress which began later than the work done by Argentinians, but it was original and ahead of its time.

Three pioneers of psychology in Mexico in the early twentieth century were Ezequiel A. Chávez (1868–1946), who taught educational and experimental psychology, translated Titchener into Spanish, and had an important role in the development of psychology in Mexico; José Mesa-Gutiérrez, who organized the Manicomio General and wrote several books on medical psychology; and Enrique C. Aragón, founder of a laboratory of experimental psychology, director of the Instituto de Psicología y Psiquiatría of the National University, and author of a number of books on different areas.

In Brazil, Waclaw Radecki (1887–1953) had a decisive influence. He was a Polish psychologist who went to Brazil, did research in experimental psychology, and founded the first psychological laboratory of Brazil (1923). He also worked in Uruguay and Argentina in experimental research, medical psychology, and in the translation of psychology books into Spanish and Portuguese. Radecki was a very active man, deeply involved in the new psychology, who published many books and scientific papers and represented South America at the international congresses of the first decades of the twentieth century.

Emilio Mira y López (1896–1964) belongs to a more recent period. He lived in Spain, Argentina, and Brazil. His main contribution is in the area of psychometrics; he devised important instruments, among them the PMK, a test still used in many countries of the world. He also did administrative work and wrote a large number of books on different psychological topics (see Ardila 1971).

Other pioneers were Walter Blumenfeld (1882–1967), a German psychologist who lived in Peru, and Béla Székely (1892–1955), who was born in Hungary and died in Buenos Aires. Blumenfeld worked in psychometrics and Székely in psychoanalysis.

THE PROFESSIONALIZATION OF PSYCHOLOGY

The pioneers were isolated figures who did much psychological work, wrote scientific books, and in some cases were socially influential. They were not always concerned with psychology as a profession but chiefly with the advancement of their particular line of research. The professionalization of psychology is very recent in Latin America. In some cases it belongs to the decade of the 1960s and 1970s. Today there is professional training of psychologists in almost all Latin American countries, with the exception of the newer nations that are only beginning to organize their educational systems.

TRAINING OF PSYCHOLOGISTS

In Mexico, Chile, Brazil, Argentina, and other countries, Institutes of Psychology were founded in the decade of the 1930s or 1940s approximately. Usually such an institute inherited the instruments and the library of a psychological laboratory, following as a model the laboratory of Wundt in Leipzig. Later on, the Institute gave origin to a Department of Psychology with didactic functions that trained psychologists for the first time in that country. Thus, the pattern was this: first a laboratory based on the Leipzig lab, then an Institute of Psychology, and then a Department of Psychology with training goals.

The first training programs were founded in 1946 and 1948 in Guatemala, Colombia, and Chile. The programs in other countries began later, in 1958 and in the 1960s in the majority of the cases. In Mexico a graduate program began in 1937, but the training programs as such, at the "licenciatura" level (undergraduate or professional), began in 1958 (Díaz-Guerrero 1976). In Argentina the first psychology programs were created also in 1958 at the University of Litoral and the University of Buenos Aires.

A decade and half later, psychology graduate programs were established in many other countries. At the present time there are professional programs in practically all Latin American countries. Graduate programs (at the Master's and/or PhD levels) exist only in a few countries: Mexico, Brazil, Colombia, Venezuela, and few more.

The teaching of psychology in Latin America follows what can be called a "Latin American model." It implies 5 years of professional training after high school graduation. This training is given in all areas of psychology and in related disciplines such as biology, physiology, mathematics, and sociology. The student receives theoretical and practical training, and at the end of the 5-year period he has to write a thesis—usually of an experimental nature—in order to receive his degree. In the majority of cases the degree is "Psychologist," in a few cases it is "Licenciate in Psychology." The title enables him to work in any area of psychology: clinical, industrial, educational, social, experimental, physiological, etc. The training is professionally oriented, is "terminal" (meaning that it does not require graduate training), and emphasizes both scientific and practical aspects. In this last sense the Latin American model could be considered analogous to the Boulder model of United States psychology (see Ardila 1978 for a presentation of the Latin American training model in psychology).

Psychology in Latin America has two main characteristics: 1. it emphasizes practical aspects and applications to the social reality of the country; 2. it is closely related to other disciplines, mainly to education and medicine. The psychologists work in the social area, in the area of education, in the health area, and in others. Even in the national planning programs, psychologists have important roles in some Latin American countries.

Government agencies are the main employers of psychologists in Latin America, and private practice occupies fewer. Although the situation may differ from one country to another, in general terms we could say that Latin American psychologists work in the following settings: government agencies, 24%; industries, 15%; clinics and hospitals, 13%; nonclinical institutions, 11%; universities, 10%; schools, 9%; private practice, 6%; others, 12%.

Many psychologists are interested in working in areas related to the social welfare of the people. Due to the problems of contemporary Latin American society, psychologists are concerned with the applications of psychology that are relevant to the improvement of their fellow human beings. We could say that more psychologists see their profession as a service activity than as a scientific activity. Only a small percent of psychologists are devoted exclusively to research, although the number is increasing.

On the other hand, psychologists realize that the problems of the people arise from political, economical, and social issues that are not in the hands of psychologists. In other words, the shortcomings of Latin America are more political than behavioral and cannot be solved by psychological methods exclusively (see Ardila's *Walden Tres,* 1979).

Information about number of psychologists in Latin America and comparisons with other regions of the world can be found in Rosenzweig (1982).

CONGRESSES, ASSOCIATIONS, AND JOURNALS

There are psychological societies in all the Latin American countries. There are also associations that go beyond the national borders and cover all Latin America, like the Latin American Association for Social Psychology

(ALAPSO), the Latin American Association for the Analysis and Modification of Behavior (ALAMOC), and the Latin American Society for Psychobiology.

From a historical point of view, it is important to indicate that the oldest association of psychologists in Latin America, the Argentine Society of Psychology, was founded in 1908 by José Ingenieros, Horacio Piñero, and other pioneers of psychology in Argentina. It was reorganized in 1930 by Enrique Mouchet, also of Buenos Aires. The large majority of national associations were founded in the decade of the 1960s.

The Interamerican Society of Psychology (SIP) is the most important psychological association of the area. It has among its members psychologists from Latin America, the United States, and Canada. The Interamerican Society of Psychology was founded in 1951 in Mexico City. It organizes the Interamerican Congresses of Psychology, which are very well attended; the Interamerican Congress held in Lima (Peru) in July 1979 had more than 3400 participants. SIP also publishes a journal called *Revista Interamericana de Psicología/ Interamerican Journal of Psychology,* and a newsletter that in the past was called *Bulletin* and now has the name of *The InterAmerican Psychologist.* Recently SIP has founded another journal, *Spanish-Language Psychology,* that contains summaries in English of all the psychological literature originally published in Spanish; the journal is similar to the *German Journal of Psychology* and to *French-Language Psychology.*

There are many journals of psychology currently being published in Latin America. Some appear regularly, some do not. In a previous article, I listed 35 psychological journals (Ardila 1976). Some have ceased publication, and others have been founded since then. Table 1 presents an up-to-date list of 18 psychological journals.

Even this is a tentative list. As the psychological journals that are most regular in their publication and most representative of contemporary Latin American psychology, I would point out the following ones: *Revista Latinoamericana de Psicología* (International, Colombia); *Revista Interamericana de Psicología* (International, USA); *Revista Argentina de Psicología* (Argentina); *Arquivos Brasileiros de Psicologia* (Brazil); *Revista del Hospital Psiquiátrico de la Habana* (Cuba); *Enseñanza e Investigación en Psicología* (México); *Revista de Psicología Clínica* (Perú); *Aprendizaje y Comportamiento* (International, Venezuela); and *Psicología* (Venezuela). Three of these journals are considered "international" because they do not actually belong to a country: *Revista Latinoamericana de Psicología* (published by the Foundation for the Advancement of Psychology), *Revista Interamericana de Psicología* (published by SIP), and *Aprendizaje y Comportamiento* (published by ALAMOC).

Table 1 Main Latin American journals of psychology

Journal	Country	Founded
Aprendizaje y Comportamiento	International	1978
Revista Interamericana de Psicología	International	1967
Revista Latinoamericana de Psicología	International	1969
Acta Psiquiátrica y Psicológica de América Latina	Argentina	1954
Revista de Psicoanálisis	Argentina	1943
Revista Argentina de Psicología	Argentina	1969
Arquivos Brasileiros de Psicologia	Brazil	1949
Boletim de Psicologia (São Paulo)	Brazil	1949
Boletim de Psicologia (Rio de Janeiro)	Brazil	1951
Journal Brasileiro de Psicologia	Brazil	1964
Revista de Psicologia Normal e Patológica	Brazil	1955
Revista del Hospital Psiquiátrico de la Habana	Cuba	1975
Enseñanza e Investigación en Psicología	México	1976
Revista de Psicoanálisis, Psiquiatría y Psicología	México	1965
Revista Mexicana de Análisis de la Conducta	México	1975
Revista Peruana de Análisis de la Conducta	Perú	1979
Revista de Psicología Clínica	Perú	1978
Psicología	Venezuela	1976

These journals, the associations of psychologists, and the congresses that they sponsor, at the national and the international level, are indications of the current state of the discipline (see Ardila 1968, 1970a, 1973; Heineken 1979).

RESEARCH

Science is not a cultural value in Latin America, as we have indicated previously, but in spite of that there are important research centers in Mexico, Brazil, Argentina, Venezuela, Colombia, Cuba, Chile, Puerto Rico, and other countries. They are devoted to many areas of psychology. The most important are social psychology and the experimental analysis of behavior; other areas, for instance, psychometrics, developmental psychology, physiological psychology, industrial and organizational psychology, are also relatively advanced. No encyclopedic coverage of contemporary research will be attempted in this part, and only representative work will be presented, with emphasis on contemporary investigations.

Sensation and Perception

In the development of psychology, perceptual processes have occupied an especially important role. Psychology began as the study of sensation and perception, as has been documented previously. In the particular case of Latin America, this field has been cultivated by groups of investigators in several nations for many decades. Enrique Mouchet was the first important investigator in this area, around 1930.

At the present time the most important South American center for research on sensation and perception is the Laboratory of Sensory Investigations at the University of Buenos Aires, directed by Miguelina Guirao. She is an Argentinian psychologist who studied with S. S. Stevens at Harvard and founded her laboratory in 1967 following the Harvard model. This laboratory has been extremely productive.

As an indication of the investigations of Guirao's laboratory, it is possible to mention her study of sensory receptors and transducers (1971); Guirao & Mattiello (1974) on the scales of color saturation; Mattiello & Guirao (1974) on direct stimulation of lightness of surface colors; Guirao & Valciukas (1975) on perceived vibration and the loudness of low-frequency tones; Guirao & Manrique (1975) on the identification of Spanish vowels.

A few books have been published on perception by Latin American psychologists. The most important one is by Guirao (1980), called *Los Sentidos, Bases de la Percepción.* Also worth mentioning are the books by Oñativia (1963) and Galíndez (1963).

Physiological Psychology

The investigation of the physiological bases of behavior had a distinguished representative in Raúl Hernández-Peón (1924–1968), whose studies on attention are well known. Physiological psychology has been studied in Latin America both by psychologists and by physiologists. There is a Latin American Society of Psychobiology that has its main headquarters in Brazil. There are some journals that publish the outcome of research in the field by Latin American investigators. The most important one is *Acta Physiologica Latino Americana,* published in Buenos Aires in English.

Several groups of physiological psychologists are actively involved in research projects. One of them is associated with the Institute of Brain Investigations, previously directed by Hernández-Peón. This group is working on sleep and dreaming, evoked potentials, attention, intracranial self-stimulation, and similar topics.

Another important group is formed around Juan D. Delius, an Argentinian who works at Ruhr University (Bochum, Federal Republic of Germany). Delius and his collaborators have investigated asymmetry in classical and operant conditioning, vision, audition, orientation in birds, aggression, and other problems in animals. An example of their research is the work by Delius & Habers (1978) on the conceptualization of asymmetry in pigeons.

Alfredo Ardila has worked on the physiological bases of complex processes in Colombia, Venezuela, and Mexico. His research on these problems (A. Ardila 1979) and on sleep and wakefulness (A. Ardila 1976) has important behavioral implications.

A number of Mexican psychologists are actively involved in psychophysiological research. Their work will be reviewed in a future chapter devoted to psychology in Mexico.

Learning

The psychology of learning, including the experimental analysis of behavior associated with the name of B. F. Skinner, is probably the main area of research in Latin American psychology. The experimental analysis of behavior began in Brazil in 1961 through the efforts of Fred S. Keller at the University of São Paulo. It continued in 1967 in Mexico through the work of Sidney Bijou at the Veracruzana University (Jalapa, Mexico).

The experimental analysis of behavior—and in general the psychology of learning—has been very well received by young psychologists who are looking for professional identity. Basic research and its applications to socially relevant problems has expanded very quickly. Behavior therapy and behavior analysis applied to education were the main technological innovations of Latin American psychology in the 1970s. A number of laboratories were created in Mexico, Brazil, Venezuela, Colombia, and Bolivia. A graduate training program in behavior analysis was founded in Mexico at the Veracruzana University, and later at the National University of Mexico-Iztacala campus (see Ribes et al 1980). Several programs began also in Peru, Venezuela, Brazil, and the Dominican Republic. Research and applications had considerable social acceptance at the beginning, although they were later criticized from a political point of view.

As a sample of the research carried out from an operant point of view, we could mention Graeff (1965, 1974) on behavioral pharmacology. He investigated the role of dopamine in the motor excitation induced by brain catecholamine releasers in mice. He also did research in the area of punishment and its tryptaminergic mechanisms (Graeff & Schoenfeld 1970). His investigation on the effects of amphetamine and apomorphine on operant behavior has stimulated further research (De Oliviera & Graeff 1972).

Colotla has done much experimental work on polydipsia (1974) and alcoholism (1976), both in animals and in humans. He investigated schedule-controlled behavior, using several schedules and taking into consideration the duration and the pattern of schedule-induced drinking. In another setting, Colotla et al (1976) studied auto-shaping and self-control in birds. Three experimentally naive food-deprived doves pecked a key when a light was present in the key just before response-independent food presentations; the auto-shaped key-peck response was maintained through 19 sessions; then two of the doves were exposed to two lights, one of which indicated to the subject that it could approach the food magazine and eat freely; the other light (red) indicated to the subject that it could not eat from the food magazine; both birds showed "self-control" behavior, because, with training, they decreased attempts to eat the food available after the red light was presented.

In Brazil Todorov (1971) studied the maintenance of key-pecking responses in pigeons, under concurrently available VI schedules, each one associated with a color, red or green. Pecks at the second key (changeover key) would alternate the colors on the main key. In the first and the second experiments, an electric shock of 50 msec duration followed immediately after changeovers. The proportion of response in the presence of the color associated with the higher frequency of reinforcement per hour was a direct function of shock intensity contingent on changeover. When both schedules provided an equal number of reinforcements per hour, there were no systematic effects of shock intensity on response distribution. In the third experiment, a time-out period was contingent on changeovers, and response distribution was a function of the length of the time out. Todorov has also done research related to Herrnstein's law.

Azcoaga from Argentina has presented a systematic treatment of learning and its physiological bases (see also Ardila 1970b). Research on learning has had a large number of applications, particularly in clinical, educational, and industrial psychology, that have been carried out by Latin American psychologists.

Language and Thinking

Work on cognitive processes and their measurement is in process at the Interdisciplinary Center for Investigations on Mathematical and Experimental Psychology at the University of Buenos Aires. Directed by Horacio Rimoldi, a sophisticated researcher who lived and worked in the United States for more than two decades, the Center is one of the best organized psychological institutions in Latin America. It began its operations in 1972. The Center has carried on research in thinking processes and psychological measurement. As a sample we can refer to Rimoldi (1972, 1974), Rodríguez Feijóo et al (1972), Lopez-Alonso (1979), Rimoldi et al (1979). Computer modeling of thinking processes has been done in Mexico in the last few years, and some work is also in process in Venezuela.

In the area of language, Alcaraz (1980), the physiological psychologist, has done important work. His book discusses the role of speech in human behavior, including signals and symbols, based on Pavlov's investigations. Combinatory behavior in animals is considered as a step in the direction of synthetic behavior in humans. The role of language in discrimination, conservation, memory, and control of nonverbal behavior is also being investigated experimentally. Alcaraz presents his own theory of language and its relevance for the understanding of behavior as a whole.

Developmental Psychology

The most systematic research on child development has been carried out by Díaz-Guerrero and his associates (see Díaz-Guerrero 1965, 1967, 1972, 1973, 1974, 1979; Díaz-Guerrero & Lara-Tapia 1972; Díaz-Guerrero et al 1975; Holtzman et al 1975). The book by Holtzman, Díaz-Guerrero & Swartz (1975), published simultaneously in Spanish and English, contains the results of the 6-year research program on cognitive development in Mexico and the United States. A total of 417 children from Austin, Texas, and 443 children from Mexico City were included in the investigation. They were 6.7, 9.7, and 12.7 years old at the beginning of the study. Holtzman et al used an overlapping longitudinal design of repeated testing that permitted them to cover 12 years of development in 6 calendar years. They studied age-grade, sex, culture, social class, parental attitudes toward child rearing, urban-rural origin and resources for intellectual stimulation.

Díaz-Guerrero's theory of sociocultural premises (the premises that are taken for granted in a certain culture) and his Philosophy of Life Inventory were given great relevance, as well as his concept of active and passive coping. In synthesis, the results of this investigation, considered by many to be the most important research project ever done in Latin America, are as follows:

In Mexico, sex is a strong determinant for the rate of cognitive development in children (except during the period between 3.5 and 5.5; the investigators did not expect this exception to occur). Social class is also a strong determinant for the rate of cognitive development. There is an interaction between sex and social class. Urban 4- and 5-year-olds present a faster rate of cognitive development than rural children. Sociocultural patterning has a stronger effect upon cognitive development in female than in male children in Mexico. The existence in the home of objects that will stimulate the child is a strong determinant of cognitive-intellectual development. Mexicans tend to be more self-modifying (passive) copers with the environment, while Americans tend to be more active copers. Boys are usually more active in their coping style than girls. The lower social class children show more clearly the typical coping style of traditional culture. There are larger differences in coping style between males and females in traditional cultures, and the interaction of sex, social class, and culture explains a large part of the variance found among the groups. This research project has a number of implications for social psychology and for the development of children in Spanish America.

Because of the problems of *malnutrition* in many countries of the area, research has been carried out concerning food deficits in infancy and their effect on psychological development. In Latin America the majority of the population is very young, with an average age of less than 15 years. Also, malnutrition is very widespread. The most important programs that study the relationship between malnutrition and development are in Guatemala, Brazil, and Colombia. McKay et al (1978), in their article published in *Science,* present one of the most advanced reports of the research carried out in Cali, Colombia.

A large number of investigations are concerned with *educational* aspects, school achievement, and similar topics, many of them from a Piagetian point of view. As an example, it is worth mentioning the special issue of the *Revista Latinoamericana de Psicología* devoted to educational psychology, edited by Luis Bravo from Chile (Bravo 1979). Quite a few articles deal with learning disabilities, in many cases from a Piagetian perspective.

In Peru, Bonneveaux (1980) investigated the influence of formal school education, of age, and of socioeconomic level on memory and concept learning. Subjects were 244 children, 5 and 6 years old. Half of the sample came from the low socioeconomic level and the other half from middle class. The memory task and the concept learning tasks were constructed for the present investigation and were complemented by interviews with the mother. Results showed that school attendance was associated with improved performance in both tasks. Age differences were relevant only among children who attended school. Social class differences were found significant for the results in the memory task but not for the concept learning task. The author pointed out the importance of environmental factors and the fact that school attendance and early home stimulation enhance the opportunity to acquire memory and cognitive abilities.

Gerontological psychology is a young area of development psychology in Latin America. Dulcey & Ardila (1976) did one of the first empirical investigations on the attitudes of young and old people toward the elderly. A book was published in Puerto Rico on social and psychological aspects of gerontology (Serra Deliz 1978). Finley & Delgado (1981) have recently presented a review of the area including intelligence, memory, learning, personality, mental health, psychopathology, driving behavior, cross-cultural research, and methodological and interpretative issues; also behavior genetics, nutrition, motivation, attitudes, retirement, stress, and life-span education are considered in the paper. See also Finley (1981) for a review of aging in Latin America, published in English, and addressed to the English-speaking psychological community.

Social Psychology

This last area to be considered is one of the most advanced as far as research is concerned. Social psychology began in Latin America as cross-cultural psychology, but lately it has expanded into different fields and approaches, community psychology being one of the most important ones.

The focus of social psychology in the last few years has been in Venezuela (see, for instance, the book by Salazar et al 1979). There is a Latin American Association for Social Psychology that has been active in the promotion of research and application to relevant problems. In some countries there are associations of social psychologists, some of them politically oriented and others interested in specific topics. A panorama of social psychology in Latin America can be found in the book edited by Marín (1975) and in the bibliography compiled by him (Marín 1978) that is in the *JSAS Catalogue of Selected Documents in Psychology* (American Psychological Association).

Cross-cultural psychology in Latin America has been an active area from the early 1950s up to the present time. Usually an investigation is initiated by a North American or European researcher interested in the comparison of psychological processes across cultures. The goal of testing the "universality" of psychological laws has been one of the inspirations of cross-cultural psychology (see Triandis 1980). In Latin America there are many works done in collaboration with North American psychologists. Angelini (1971) has done important research in Brazil, including achievement motivation (1973) studied from a cross-cultural point of view. Work in progress exists in practically all the Latin American countries with a psychological community relatively developed. As Holtzman (1973) had indicated, even in a bicultural study a great deal of insight can be gained into the role of specified cultural variables if subcultural variations are included which can be matched cross-culturally, if well-trained native examiners are utilized, and if only techniques are used which can be reasonably defended in both cultures.

The main work in cross-cultural psychology in Latin America has been concerned with personality development, moral development, anxiety, perception, social development, Piagetian concepts, educational factors, and others.

Applied social psychology is a different approach to collective phenomena that emphasizes practical aspects. The grave problems of Latin America have made psychologists very sensitive to social issues, including political ones. Applied social psychology is a way of being useful in the tasks of socioeconomic development, using the instruments of psychology in relevant contexts.

Social technology is associated with the name of Jacobo Varela (1971, 1977) from Uruguay. His book (1971), entitled *Psychological Solutions to Social Problems,* presents his system. Varela uses the findings of social psychology, including cognitive dissonance, attitude change, reactancy, rejection latitude, syllogistic equilibrium, and others. The combination of principles and findings produces a social technology analogous to engineering in the physical sciences.

Community social psychology is the fourth approach to social psychology in Latin America. Planning for social change, intervention, and the measurement of results are emphasized. The needs of the community and the active collaboration of the participants are given great importance.

Dialectic materialistic psychology is the fifth approach. Influenced by Soviet psychology, it has been relatively important in some countries in the last few years. The criticisms to traditional approaches in psychology and the importance given to Marxism and to social relevance have been structured in this approach to psychological phenomena.

Social psychology is a growing area in Latin America. The five approaches—cross-cultural research, applied social psychology, social technology, community social psychology, and dialectic psychology—do not represent different stages, but exist simultaneously. A good deal of controversy is the result, which is some cases throws more heat than light on social issues.

PERSPECTIVES

Psychology in Latin America has grown considerably from its modest origins in philosophy, education, and medicine. At the present time there are training programs in the majority of the countries. Research is in progress on topics of scientific relevance such as sensation and perception, physiological psychology, learning, language and thinking, developmental psychology, and social psychology. Some of this work has contributed to psychology in an international perspective. Practical applications are made in clinical, educational, industrial, and social settings.

Many of the problems of contemporary Latin American psychology are developmental problems. This part of the world has been a stage of conflict between ideologies and philosophies that have influenced psychology. Also, the different Latin American countries are in very different levels of development—along divergent lines in some cases—and it is impossible to talk about a unified Latin America. Only general trends have been considered in this chapter.

Psychology in Latin America faces several important problems that have been analyzed in a contemporary perspective in a forthcoming book by Ardila (1982). All of them are developmental problems, both in the sense of psychology as a science and as a profession and in the sense of Latin American culture. Because science is not a cultural value in Latin America, it is difficult to obtain grants for basic research (although the money is available). The scientific status of psychology and its social relevance are discussed over and over again. An investigator does not always find a stimulating environment for his research. Only in the countries with a scientific tradition is the work of investigators not questioned. In the rest of the Latin American countries the social acceptance of basic research is questionable.

Psychology in Latin America today shares many problems with the rest of the Third World. Psychology is a discipline cultivated mainly in the industrialized countries (in the "First World") and not so much in other nations. Contemporary psychology is largely an Anglo-Saxon discipline that shares the values and assumptions of English-speaking countries (see Ardila 1980b), particularly of the United States; some of these values and conceptions seem to be alien to the Latin American way of thinking.

In any case, the scientific principles of psychology are beyond the boundaries of culture and politics. Cultural limitations are being studied and analyzed. What is "universal" and what is "cultural" concerns many investigators today, particularly in the area of cross-cultural psychology. Without doubt, many nations are beginning to make important contributions to the science of psychology. In the case of Latin America, a frame of reference that includes a proper balance of universal and relative factors is much needed.

Literature Cited

Alcaraz, V. M. 1980. *La Función de Síntesis del Lenguaje.* Mexico: Trillas. 542 pp.

Angelini, A. L. 1971. Pesquisa intercultural en psicologia. *Arq. Bras. Psicol.* 23:73–84

Angelini, A. L. 1973. *Motivacao Humana.* Rio de Janeiro: Olympio Editora. 228 pp.

Ardila, A. 1976. *Sueño y Activación.* Bogota: Ciencia Contemporánea. 148 pp.

Ardila, A. 1979. *Psicofisiología de los Procesos Complejos.* Mexico: Trillas. 183 pp.

Ardila, R. 1968. Psychology in Latin America. *Am. Psychol.* 23:567–74

Ardila, R. 1970a. Landmarks in the history of Latin American psychology. *J. Hist. Behav. Sci.* 6:140–46

Ardila, R. 1970b. *Psicología del Aprendizaje.* Mexico: Siglo XXI. 236 pp.

Ardila, R. 1971. *Los Pioneros de la Psicología.* Buenos Aires: Paidos. 239 pp.

Ardila, R. 1973. *La Psicología en Colombia, Desarrollo Histórico.* Mexico: Trillas. 191 pp.

Ardila, R. 1976. Latin America. In *Psychology Around the World,* ed. V. S. Sexton, H. Misiak, pp. 259–79. Monterey, Calif: Brooks/Cole. 470 pp.

Ardila, R. 1978. *La Profesión del Psicólogo.* Mexico: Trillas. 233 pp.

Ardila, R. 1979. *Walden Tres.* Barcelona: CEAC. 184 pp.

Ardila, R. 1980a. Historiography of Latin American psychology. In *Historiography of Modern Psychology,* ed. J. Brozek, L. J. Pongratz, pp. 111–18. Toronto: Hogrefe. 336 pp.

Ardila, R. 1980b. *International psychology: Current trends and perspectives.* Presented at Ann. Conv. Am. Psychol. Assoc., 88th, Montreal

Ardila, R. 1982. *La Psicología en América Latina, Pasado, Presente y Futuro.* Mexico: Trillas

Bonneveaux, B. 1980. Influencia de la escuela, de la edad y del medio socioeconómico sobre el desarrollo del niño peruano. *Rev. Latinoam. Psicol.* 12:313–26

Bravo, L., ed. 1979. Special issue of *Rev. Latinoam. Psicol.* 11:201–309

Colotla, V. A. 1974. Análisis experimental del comportamiento inducido por programas de refuerzo. In *El Análisis Experimental del Comportamiento, la Contribución Latinoamericana,* ed. R. Ardila, pp. 98–120. Mexico: Trillas, 532 pp.

Colotla, V. A. 1976. Modelos experimentales del alcoholismo. *Enseñ. Invest. Psicol.* 2:87–104

Colotla, V. A., McArthur, D., Casanueva, H. 1976. Auto-moldeamiento y "auto-control" en la tórtola y el pichón. *Rev. Latinoam. Psicol.* 8:249–60

Delius, J. D., Habers, G. 1978. Symmetry: Can pigeons conceptualize it? *Behav. Biol.* 22:336–42

De Oliveira, L., Graeff, F. G. 1972. Comparison between the effects of apomorphine and amphetamine on operant behavior. *Eur. J. Pharmacol.* 18:159–65

Díaz-Guerrero, R. 1965. Sociocultural and psychodynamic processes in adolescent transition and mental health. In *Problems of Youth,* ed. M. Sherif, C. Sherif, pp. 129–52. Chicago: Aldine

Díaz-Guerrero, R. 1967. Sociocultural premises, attitudes and cross-cultural research. *Int. J. Psychol.* 2:79–97

Díaz-Guerrero, R. 1972. Una escala factorial de premisas histórico-socioculturales de la familia mexicana. *Rev. Interam. Psicol.* 6:235–44

Díaz-Guerrero, R. 1973. Interpreting coping styles across nations from sex and social class differences. *Int. J. Psychol.* 8:193–203

Díaz-Guerrero, R. 1974. La mujer y las premisas histórico-socioculturales de la familia mexicana. *Rev. Latinoam. Psicol.* 6:7–16

Díaz-Guerrero, R. 1976. Mexico. In *Psychology Around the World,* ed. V. S. Sexton, H. Misiak, pp. 280–92. Monterey, Calif: Brooks/Cole. 470 pp.

Díaz-Guerrero, R. 1979. Socio-cultura, personalidad en acción y la ciencia de la psicología. In *Avances en Psicología Contemporánea,* ed. G. E. Finley, G. Marín, pp. 82–109. México: Trillas. 320 pp.

Díaz-Guerrero, R., Bianchi, R., Ahumada, R. 1975. *Investigación Formativa en Plaza Sésamo.* México: Trillas. 372 pp.

Díaz-Guerrero, R., Lara-Tapia, L. 1972. Diferencias sexuales en el desarrollo de la personalidad del escolar mexicand. *Rev. Latinoam. Psicol.* 4:345–51

Dulcey, E., Ardila, R. 1976. Actitudes hacia los ancianos. *Rev. Latinoam. Psicol.* 8:57–67

Finley, G. E. 1981. Aging in Latin America: A review. *Span. Lang. Psychol.* 1: In press

Finley, G. E., Delgado, M. 1981. La psicología del envejecimiento. *Rev. Latinoam. Psicol.* 13:415–32

Galíndez, J. 1963. *El Papel del Cuerpo en la Percepción.* Tucumán, Argentina: Universidad Nacional de Tucumán. 86 pp.

Graeff, F. G. 1965. The role of dopamine in motor excitation of mice induced by brain catecholamine releasers. *J. Pharm. Pharmacol.* 18:627–28

Graeff, F. G. 1974. El comportamiento operante en psicofarmacología. In *El Análisis Experimental del Comportamiento, la Contribución Latinoamericana,* ed. R. Ardila, pp. 130–61. Mexico: Trillas. 532 pp.

Graeff, F. G., Schoenfeld, R. I. 1970. Tryptaminergic mechanisms in punished and nonpunished behavior. *J. Pharmacol. Exp. Ther.* 173:227–83

Guirao, M. 1971. Receptores sensoriales, transductores de energía y sensación. *Cienc. Invest.* 27(3):67–77

Guirao, M. 1980. *Los Sentidos, Bases de la Percepción.* Madrid: Alhambra. 349 pp.

Guirao, M., Manrique, A. M. B. 1975. Identification of Argentine Spanish vowels. *J. Psycholing. Res.* 4:17–25

Guirao, M., Mattiello, M. L. F. 1974. Saturation scales for surface colors. *Vision Res.* 14:487–93

Guirao, M., Valciukas, J. A. 1975. Perceived vibration and the loudness of low-frequency tones. *Percept. Psychophys.* 17:460–64

Heineken, E. 1979. Zur Lage der Psychologie in Lateinamerika. *Psychol. Rundsch.* 30:257–68

Holtzman, W. H. 1973. *Personality development of children in Mexico and the United States.* Presented at Interam. Congr. Psychol., 14th, Sao Paulo, Brazil

Holtzman, W. H., Díaz-Guerrero, R., Swartz, J. D. 1975. *Personality Develop-*

ment in Two Cultures. Austin: Univ. Texas Press. 427 pp.

Ingenieros, J. 1911. *Psicología Genética.* Buenos Aires

López-Alonso, A. O. 1979. "Scaling" de juicios simples y juicios condicionales. *Pub. Cent. Interdisc. Invest. Psicol. Mat. Exp.* 75

Marín, G., ed. 1975. *La Psicología Social en Latinoamérica.* Mexico: Trillas. 274 pp.

Marín, G. 1978. Social psychology in Latin America: An annoted bibliography for 1976. *JSAS Cat. Sel. Doc. Psychol.* 8 (8)

Mattiello, M. L. F., Guirao, M. 1974. Direct stimulation of lightness of surface colors. *J. Opt. Soc. Am.* 64:206–9

McKay, H., Sinisterra, L., McKay, A., Gómez, H., Lloreda, P. 1978. Improving cognitive ability in chronically deprived children. *Science* 200:270–78

Mouchet, E. 1941. *Percepción, Instinto y Razón.* Buenos Aires: Ed. Joaquín Gil. 240 pp.

Oñativia, O. V. 1963. *Dimensiones de la Percepción.* Tucumán, Argentina: Univ. Nac. Tucumán. 135 pp.

Papini, M. R. 1976. Datos para una historia de la psicología experimental argentina (hasta 1930). *Rev. Latinoam. Psicol.* 8:319–35

Papini, M. R. 1978. La psicología experimental argentina durante el período 1930–1955. *Rev. Latinoam. Psicol.* 10:227–58

Papini, M. R., Mustaca, A. E. 1979. La psicología experimental argentina entre 1956 y 1978. *Rev. Latinoam. Psicol.* 11: 349–61

Ribes, E., Fernández, C., Rueda, M., Talento, M., López, F. 1980. *Enseñanza, Ejercicio e Investigación de la Psicología.* México: Trillas. 324 pp.

Rimoldi, H. J. A. 1972. Aspectos cognoscitivos en la solución de problemas. *Pub. Cent. Interdisc. Invest. Psicol. Mat. Exp.* 10

Rimoldi, H. J. A. 1974. Solución de problemas y procesos cognoscitivos. *Proc. 15th Interam. Congr. Psychol., Bogota,* pp. 4–5

Rimoldi, H. J. A., Minzi, M. C. R., Radovanovic, E. G. 1979. Decisión e información en solución de problemas. *Pub. Cent. Interdisc. Invest. Psicol. Mat. Exp.* 77

Robles, O. 1943. *Historia de la Filosofía en México.* Mexico: Imprenta Univ.

Rodriguez Feijóo, N., Minzi, M. C. R., Stefani, D. 1972. Sobre el supresto de normalidad en la distribución de juicios de preferencias. *Publ. Cent. Interdiscip. Invest. Psicol. Mat. Exp.* 9

Rosenzweig, M. R. 1982. Trends in the development and status of psychology: An international perspective. *Int. J. Psychol.* 17: In press

Salazar, J. M., Montero, M., Muñoz, C., Sánchez, E., Santoro, E., Villegas, J. F. 1979. *Psicología Social.* México: Trillas. 427 pp.

Serra Deliz, W., ed. 1978. *La Problemática de los Envejecientes en Puerto Rico.* Rio Piedras, Puerto Rico: Cent. Invest. Soc. Univ. Puerto Rico. 132 pp.

Todorov, J. C. 1971. Concurrent performances: effect of punishment contingent on the switching response. *J. Exp. Anal. Behav.* 16:51–62

Triandis, H. C., ed. 1980. *Handbook of Cross-Cultural Psychology.* 6 vols. Boston: Allyn & Bacon

Varela, J. 1971. *Psychological Solutions to Social Problems.* New York: Academic. 317 pp.

Varela, J. A. 1977. Social technology. *Am. Psychol.* 32:914–23

Ann. Rev. Psychol. 1982. 33:123–54

SOCIAL MOTIVATION

Janusz Reykowski[1]

Department of Psychology, Polish Academy of Science, 00-063 Warsaw, Poland

---

CONTENTS

INTRODUCTION

The concept "social motivation" has a variety of meanings (Berkowitz 1969, Brody 1980). Some authors describe it as the "social aspect of human motivation" (deCharms & Muir 1978, p. 283). It is a very broad definition. One may argue that human motivation is social by its nature, and therefore the term "social motivation" is redundant. Even so-called biological motives (drives, instincts) do not exist in humans in "pure, natural" form—they are shaped by culture (Leont'ev 1975). This point has been stressed particularly by authors representing Marxist orientation. According to the

[1]This paper was prepared while the author was a visiting professor at the Institute of Child Development, University of Minnesota, Minneapolis, Minnesota.

0066-4308/82/0201-0123$02.00

Marxist view, the biological endowment of humans is only a potential for learning and development. All human qualities are achieved as a result of embedding the individual in a social world. In other words, all human needs, drives, and motives emerge in social interaction and all of them have social aspects.

The concept of "social motivation" can be used, however, in a more specific meaning, which can be defined in the context of a general theory of motivation.

The most advanced formulation of a general theory of motivation has been developed by J. W. Atkinson. He and his numerous collaborators have been elaborating the theory for over three decades. This is a rare example of steady progress in a course of long-lasting, continuous study of the same subject, reaching its present highly sophisticated form (Atkinson & Birch 1978, Atkinson & Raynor 1974; see also deCharms & Muir 1978, Brody 1980). According to Atkinson and his colleagues, motivation is responsible for the instigation of action, consumation in action, and resistance to action (Atkinson & Birch 1978, p. 33). "Action" is regarded as a key concept by many European psychologists, especially in the USSR, where it has been discussed extensively by such authors as Leont'ev[2] (1975), Rubinstein (1973), and in Poland by Tomaszewski (1963).[3] There is also a growing interest in action theory in the Federal Republic of Germany.

One of the critical characteristics of an action is its directivity—action is goal oriented. Goal-oriented behavior is determined primarily by two factors: expectations that a given performance "will lead on to the goal" and incentive value of the goal (Atkinson & Birch 1978, p. 93).[4]

We will not discuss the expectancy issue. It is the subject of cognitive studies concerning the factors that determine estimation of a probability of occurrence of a certain state of affairs. One of the most popular theories in contemporary social psychology—attribution theory—seems to deal with the problem extensively. For the theory of motivation, the main issue appears to be an incentive value of a goal.

In discussing goal, we should keep in mind a difference between goal-state and goal-object; that is, the difference between what is going to be achieved in a given action and what things or places or persons or groups are serving as targets of an action. As long as a target of an action, i.e. a goal object, is a social being, we can talk meaningfully about social motivation.

[2]In some English translations of the Russian term "dejatelnost," the term activity is used.

[3]For the reader's information, in most cases when the author mentioned in the paper works outside of the US, his country of origin will be indicated.

[4]The formulation is based upon a cognitive or expectancy-value approach as developed by E. Tolman, W. Edwards, K. Lewin, and J. B. Rotter (cf Atkinson & Birch 1978).

The term "social being" is a very broad one: it includes persons, social groups, institutions, social organizations, symbolic systems, etc. In this paper we will concentrate upon a specific class of social objects: upon persons. Our consideration of social motivation will be, therefore, limited to the question: what makes one human being become interested and involved in another human? Why should states, conditions, reactions, or attitudes of one human being become a goal of an action by another human being?

Social Motivation and Value Assignment to a Social Object

On the basis of a general theory of motivation, we may assume that the major precondition of a social motivation is value assignment to a social object. The term "value" when applied to objects can evoke some confusion. It is very often used interchangeably with such terms as "valence" or "attraction," i.e. in relation to objects that are instigating approach or avoidance tendencies.

The term "value" is also applied to objects that are treated as things that evoke protective tendencies, that should be preserved or expanded, that deserve maintenance and growth. Frequently, attractive objects are treated as having value, but it is also possible that attraction leads to some consumatory activity which is not associated with any tendency for protection of the object. In our further discussion we will keep in mind this difference between "value" and "valence."

Apparently the social objects (persons) can possess a valence since they are able to satisfy various needs of the individual: they can feed him/her, protect, help, give approval, engage in sexual activity, and so on; they evoke, therefore, preference, attraction, and liking. These kinds of objects are more or less necessary for an individual's personal well-being, and for this reason they are treated as having value. We may say that human beings can possess an *instrumental value* for another human being.

There is reason to believe that a social object can have also an *autonomous value,* i.e. it evokes a tendency for maintenance and development because of its intrinsic properties, without recurrence to the needs of an individual (other than well-being of the object). In subsequent parts of this paper we will deal with the above-described kinds of value assignment processes and their consequences for social motivation.

INSTRUMENTAL VALUE OF A SOCIAL OBJECT

It is an obvious truth that for humans as well as for numerous subhuman species the conspecific object is attractive (e.g. Latane & Steele 1975). Since attractive objects possess an incentive value, we may assume that factors contributing to an object's attractiveness are regulating social motivation.

It is possible to find some evidence that attractiveness of a social object is influenced by biological factors. The obvious case is sex. There are many data indicating that hormonal excretions affect social behavior. In subhuman species the gender-related behavior (such as rough play, mounting) can be influenced by procedures that affect hormonal level. The relationship is not a direct one, however. Castration of rhesus monkeys between the day of birth and 3 months of age did not affect their gender-related behavior, but prenatal injection of androgen (male hormone) did increase the frequency of male type behavior among females (Goy & McEwen 1980, pp. 49–54).

Somewhat similar relationships have been observed among humans. Observations show that congenital or drug-induced abnormality of body sex differentiation, e.g. adrenogenital syndrome (in which there has been some masculinization of reproductive tract and other body characteristics), has an effect upon behavior associated with higher activity level, tomboyishness, and preference for male friends. Children of mothers who received progesteron during pregnancy manifested more feminine type behavior: lower energy level, lesser tomboyishness, preference for feminine clothing (Goy & McEwen 1980).

Further, some authors believe that psychosexual orientation in humans may be related, at least in part, to the sex hormone level during the brain development in prenatal life: they claim that there exists an endocrine profile associated with homosexual behavior (cf Goy & McEwen 1980, pp. 64–70).

The data suggest that attractiveness of certain activities and certain (conspecific) objects is influenced by endocrine factors. The suggestion seems to be controversial for those who believe that learning is a decisive factor in the development of human motivation. But even greater controversy surrounds the issue of allegedly biogenic origin of human aggressivity. The arguments amount to this: is a tendency to attack, to kill, to destroy determined by forces that orginate within the organism?

Motivation to Aggression

It should be noted in the first place that there are good reasons to believe that the attractiveness of a conspecific can be related to the fact that he can serve as a candidate for aggressive encounters—more specifically, as a victim. It has been shown, for example, that an angry animal will cross the grid in the obstruction box in order to get to another animal that is suitable for attack (Lagerspetz 1979). The latency of resumption of a fight is affected by suitability of a victim—the greater the difference in size between aggressor and victim (aggressor being bigger) and the weaker the victim's ability for fighting back, the greater its attractiveness as measured by speed of grid crossing.

Similar phenomena are observed among humans. Bordon & Taylor (1976) found that students showed the highest level of aggression if the chances for retaliation were smallest (i.e. if they could consistently defeat their opponents). In a study made by the Norwegian psychologist Olweus (1978) on bullying among schoolboys in Sweden, it was found that there is a set of characteristics that makes a child become a likely victim of a bully: attractiveness of a child for a bully was related to the fact that he was suitable for aggression.

Attractiveness of a victim may increase if he manifests pain. Sebastian found that angered subjects were not only more punitive than nonangered ones, but they also showed more enjoyment as their victim's pain increased. Higher punitiveness was not a momentary reaction to the angering incident but persisted for some time; it was observed on the next day after the incident occurred, and it was directed not only to the person who was a source of anger but to an innocent victim as well (Sebastian 1980).

In another study made by Berkowitz, Cochran & Embree (1981), it has been found that painful environmental conditions evoke aggressive inclination directed toward doing harm: information about the possibility of hurting the partner served as a goal cue faciliting the overt expression of the inclination.

The data show rather clearly that for an aggressively aroused person a victim is an attractive object that can be sought for. But is the aggressive arousal solely under control of environmental factors? Some authors would argue that endocrine secretion (especially male sex hormones) also play a certain role in those processes. Numerous observations have been made on relationships between testosterone and aggression (Wilson 1975, p. 251). Castration studies seem to indicate that testosterone level has some controlling influence upon aggression since castration typically is associated with decrement of aggressivity while injection of testosterone apparently produces enhancement of aggression, at least with subhuman species.

There are, however, arguments that the relationship is more complex, especially among higher primates. Mendoza et al (1979) have shown that testosterone level was low among dominant and aggressive male squirrel monkeys in well-established groups, but it increased greatly when new groups were formed and still more when females were introduced into the group. In the last two conditions only, their testosterone level was higher than in animals of lower status. Hormonal level prior to group formation was not associated with subsequent dominance status and levels of aggression. The study suggests that testosterone fluctuates according to social circumstances of animal life; it is emitted during conflict situations and in response to the presence of females in breeding season.

In another study by the same authors (Coe et al 1981), there is some evidence that although the endocrine system has an influence upon behavior, behavior influences the endocrine system as well.

Although the data suggest that there is a two-way relationship between hormones and aggressive behavior, there is still some reason to believe that aggressive behavior in animals is partly under the control of endocrine factors. Is it possible that the same is true of humans? In other words, since people do enjoy aggression (sometimes), is it determined by their glands? Some authors would argue that this may be the case since some changes in hormonal status are associated with changes in aggressivity (Hamburg & Van Lawick-Goodall 1978, Money 1974). But what are the possible links between them? Some new light on the issue is provided by studies on the phenomenon called "demand for stimulation."

Demand for Stimulation

The idea that animals and humans are seeking not only a decrement of stimulation (drive reduction) but its increment as well is not new at all. From the early 1950s it became more and more obvious that lack of stimulation can be as aversive as its abundance. It has been proved that people (and animals) are seeking novelty, incongruity, etc (Fowler 1965, Berlyne 1967, Sales 1971).

In the last decade new dimensions have been added to the issue. Strelau and his coworkers from the University of Warsaw have described a relationship between what they call reactivity and demand for stimulation (Strelau 1974, 1980). Strelau (1972) developed a special instrument for measurement of reactivity that is supposed to assess how much stimulus overload a person is able to withstand and enjoy.

In a series of studies (Eliasz 1974) it has been established that people differing with respect to reactivity behave differently in a broad range of situations. Those with high reactivity try to minimize the amount of stimulation and to avoid situations which are "saturated" with stimuli. On the other hand, people with low reactivity are seeking stimulation. For instance, it was found that among professions which carry the largest amount of stimulation (jet pilots, defense attorneys) there was a much greater proportion of people with high demand for stimulation than with low demand. The opposite was true with respect to professions which carry small amounts of stimulation (librarians). The same pattern has been observed when people involved in dangerous sports (mountaineers, parachutists) were compared with those who are not involved in sport activities (Strelau 1980) or when people with a tendency to risky choice in experimental gambling situations were compared with those who avoided risk (Kozlowski 1977).

On the basis of these and other data (see Zuckerman 1979), we can speculate that some people, namely those who have high demand for stimulation, will look for opportunities to increase the amount of available stimuli, choosing situations which are rich in stimulation and activities which have high stimulating properties. There are various possible ways of achieving those results.

High degree of stimulation is produced by extreme situations (high temperature, strong light, noise), by rapid change of stimulation, by new and unexpected events, by danger, risk, etc (Zuckerman 1979). It is also possible to increase the amount of stimulation by activities which can induce a high degree of excitement.

It seems reasonable to assume that when the demand for stimulation is very high people can enjoy rapid movement, sudden change in environment (e.g. destruction of physical objects), strong noise, and strong emotional expression of others (crying, shouting, expression of fear or pain, but also excitation of any kind). One can see that aggressive activity can be a source of a very powerful stimulation; for people who are "stimulation hungry," an aggression can be a "favorite dish."

What are the sources of the demand for stimulation? There are no clear answers to this question, but it is possible to formulate some suggestions. Strelau argues that reactivity is a temperamental characteristic based upon inborn properties of the nervous system. This assumption suggests that there might be some link between hormonal secretion and reactivity. In fact, at least some of the observed differences in so-called gender-related behavior seem to indicate that the typical level of psychological reactivity is sex related. The description of male behavior in animals and humans resembles the description of individuals with elevated demands for stimulation. This would mean that the connection between hormones and aggression is an indirect one. Supposedly, hormonal level influences psychological reactivity and psychological reactivity contributes to the development of aggressivity.[5]

But there are some indications that reactivity level can be modified by environment, especially at an early age. Eliasz (1981), one of Strelau's coworkers, examined children from different neighborhoods (from downtown and residential areas in Warsaw) and observed some systematic differences in reactivity: lower level of reactivity (i.e. higher demand for stimulation) was more frequent in children living in a highly stimulating environment. It suggests that in young people who are exposed to extensive

[5]It should be borne in mind that we are discussing here a special kind of aggressivity: so-called spontaneous aggression performed for an intrinsic satisfaction (joy of aggression) (Reykowski 1979b). The explanation is not applicable to other kinds of aggression [instrumental, emotional, prosocial (Fraczek 1979, 1980)].

stimulation for a period of time, their reactivity level undergoes some adjustment. The phenomenon can be interpreted in the framework of Helson's Level of Adaptation theory (Helson 1966). Eliasz's findings do not rule out that reactivity is controlled by biological factors, primarily by inborn characteristics of the central nervous system. But they point out the possibility that early experience can have its share in shaping those characteristics.

It should be noted that although high demand for stimulation can be to a great extent determined by biological factors (including genetic ones), it does not mean that aggression is "an inborn drive." Demand for stimulation can be gratified in a number of ways. Aggression is only one possible means of such gratification. The demand for stimulation can also be gratified by risky and difficult prosocial action, as the studies on the so-called "angry samaritans" seem to imply (Huston et al 1976). We may argue that low reactivity can facilitate a development of aggressive tendencies if a person has no other opportunity of obtaining stimulation and if motives that could check the aggressive tendencies do not develop (Reykowski 1979b).

In cases of sexual and aggressive motives, a conspecific that possesses certain characteristics can become a goal object, but its attractiveness is a transient one. The consumatory activity diminishes or erases all interest in an object, providing that no other mechanisms are operating. But with higher animals and with humans this is not the typical case. More often than not the interaction between conspecifics leads to a formation of some kind of bonds, and attachment as well as detachment become very important factors of social motivation.

Attachment

An elaborated model of those processes has been proposed by the Swiss psychologist Bischof (1978, 1980). He argues that a basic precondition of attachment is the ability to recognize another animal individually. It requires fairly well-developed cognitive functioning that makes possible some kind of object representation.

Among mammals, the tendency to be attached to conspecifics (need for affiliation) persists life-long. The object of the need changes before or during adolescence. With increased maturity, earlier companions evoke less interest while strangers now induce fascination and a tendency to exploration. The transformation from affiliation with original family members to affiliation with strangers (which eventually leads to formation of a new family) takes different forms among different species. In some cases when transformation of filial bonds does not take place, infantilism and impotence may result.

The basic mechanisms of attachment and detachment are related to two motivational states: security and arousal.[6] Security increases with the proximity of familiar objects, arousal with proximity of strangers. With increasing experience and coping abilities, familiar environment and familiar objects may lose any capability of producing arousal and become boring. At the same time, the level of arousal produced by strangers is not too high because the individual has already learned how to deal with unknown conspecific objects. The attraction to such objects becomes a precondition for formation of new bonds.

The theory tries to explain why family members are attractive in the early stage of life (as "security tokens," as play objects keeping arousal on the comfortable level) and why they later lose their attractiveness while peers and strangers become more attractive. According to Bischof, this developmental dynamic protects against inbreeding and explains the fact that incest avoidance is a rather universal phenomenon not limited to human species.

The Bischof model includes some other phenomena omitted in the above description; nevertheless, its basic assumptions are rather parsimonious. It elucidates the significance for social development of such apparently "neutral" psychological processes as optimal level of stimulation and object representation. It should be added that similar ideas were formulated by other authors, too (see Mason 1971).[7]

On the basis of the above-described data and reasoning, we suggest that some elementary forms of social motivation can be based upon attractiveness of the objects who can regulate the level of arousal: decrease it in some cases, increase it in others. The reaction to such objects depends upon the demand for stimulation. The demand is oscillating; hence the attractiveness of objects based solely on this mechanism is highly unstable. Some consistency in behavior regulated by the demand for stimulation can be attributed to the fact that a relatively stable modal level of the demand can be "set" by temperamental factors. It explains some persisting behavioral patterns —for example, preference for aggressive encounters. The available evidence suggests that hormonal factors seem to contribute to setting the demand. Early experience also has some role.

The impact of hormonal factors upon social behavior is probably not limited to the sphere of demand for stimulation. Something more specific than that is possible, too. We already noted that sensitivity to sex-related characteristics of a social object is associated with the endocrine status of

[6]Human studies demonstrate the importance of attachment for feelings of security. Recent works making differentiations between so-called secure and unsecure attached infants point to numerous consequences of this difference (Sroufe & Waters 1977, Arend, Gove & Stroufe 1979).

[7]Bischof (1975) regards his work as an extension of a theory proposed by Mason.

an individual. We can add that sensitivity to infantile characteristics seems also to be related to sex differences; e.g. according to some authors, females show pupil dilation when shown pictures of a little child (a baby), while males do not (cf Goy & McEwen 1980, p. 61).

It should be noted that the child may play an important role in gratification of attachment need. Female rhesus monkeys isolated from their group showed faster adaptation to captivity (evaluated on the basis of biochemical measures) if they were with their infants than females not having infants (Gonzalez, Gunnar & Levine 1981).

As a consequence of cognitive development, a more or less stable relationship is formed with an attractive object; it acquires value related to its role in the affective functioning of an individual. We can say that such an object possesses an *affective value* for an individual. The affective value of a social object can be associated with its intrinsic qualities as a direct source of gratification: it can serve as a sexual object, as a victim, as a play partner, as "a security token," etc. It can also control sources of important nonsocial gratifications (for example, food). For these reasons, some forms of behavior of a social object seem to acquire secondary reinforcement value. It is claimed that human striving for social approval and a fear of disapproval stem from the very fact that approval/disapproval plays a mediating role in obtaining some very critical gratifications.

Social Approval

A recent attempt to show that social approval is sought for its mediating value (and not as value by itself) has been made by Jellison & Gentry (1978). These authors performed a study showing that undergraduate students are ready to win disapproval if it can give them some material gain. The argument has serious shortcomings. First, the social approval here is regarded as unspecified stimulus, and no consideration is given to the question of from whom and under what conditions it is manifested. There is no doubt that disapproval from an unknown person in an artificial, transient situation has very limited value; it can be much smaller than the material value of a would-be reward. Moreover, the study made by Jellisen and Gentry did not control experimental demand factor, and thus it is quite possible that subjects were ready to sacrifice the approval of a hypothetical boss for whom they allegedly were to work for approval from experimenters.

But the crucial issue that seems to be overlooked entirely is related to the question: why does a material gain possess a value? Is it simply due to the fact that it gives access to a tasty food or sensual pleasures? That might be true in some cases. Everyday life observations, as well as experiments conducted in laboratories and in natural settings (Bandura 1969), indicate that sensitivity to social approval can be contingent upon its capability of mediating some material reinforcements. But real power of the reinforcement system of this kind has been demonstrated primarily in relation to small children or retarded and disturbed people. Properly used, the system may enhance social interaction. It was recently demonstrated by Cone (1978) that formal training, stimulus control, and reward generalization procedures can increase social interaction among profoundly retarded males (12–18 years of age), and the obtained changes were maintained even if continuous reinforcement was markedly reduced.

The procedure gives unequivocal results as long as it is applied to persons who have limited capacity for information processing. But what about people who have achieved the full range of cognitive capabilities? For them, the meaning of the social object plays a much more important role than the specific reward system. For example, in one study concerning children's reaction to the competetive reward system, it was found that an important factor influencing the children's reaction was the relationship with a partner; children interacting with friends behaved differently than when interacting with acquaintances (Newcomb et al 1979).

One Czechoslovak author (Kotaskova 1977) summarized her results thus: "positive and negative reinforcement of the child behavior played a lesser role than previously indicated . . . Parental personalities and attitudes played a greater role in the child's subsequent behavior." Sometime ago a Polish psychologist came to the same conclusion. Mika (1969), who was studying the role of punishment, found that its effectiveness depends not on the punishment itself but on the relationship between the child and punishing agent.

Personal Meaning System

One basic phenomenon of human development is an emergence of the personal meaning system. It develops as the result of the formation of cognitive organizations. In fact, we can use the term "personal meaning system" to describe a specific aspect of human cognitive network. As it is formed, people, things, and events are no longer an array of separated stimuli but are conceived as meaningful. Their meaning comes from the fact that they have their places in the system. It is a precondition of relating to the world in an orderly and stable fashion.

It has been widely recognized that confirmation of beliefs that are an important part of the personal meaning system is a necessary condition for psychological well-being. Serious disconfirmation may result in breakdown of the system. The most important role in the system is played by beliefs (or schemata) concerning one's own self. Information that an individual obtains from his environment has a bearing on beliefs concerning himself: they contribute both to the self description (i.e. are related to the self-identity) and to the evaluation of the self (i.e. they are related to self-esteem).

The major source of information is other people. The essential role in providing such information is played by so-called significant persons. Confirmation of identity comes, in a high degree, from persons with whom the individual remains in a long-term intensive relationship; the confirmatory information is contained in the interaction itself. It means, for example, that to preserve one's own identity as a father, one has to interact with one's children. Confirmation of own self-esteem comes from the people who are the source of approval; it should be stressed that approval is communicated not only by verbal declarations but, more importantly, by attitudes expressing affection, respect, admiration, etc.

Social objects that are the source of confirmatory information for the self possess a value for the individual. The basis of the value is the fact that such objects uphold the personal meaning system, primarily the self system. As a matter of fact, interaction with some of those objects may be essential for existence of the system. As was formulated by Markus: "with the loss of parent, one also loses the concept of oneself as a child and the good feelings associated with it. If a couple becomes separated, they lose or disturb in some ways the concepts of themselves as lovers and partners . . ." (Markus 1980, p. 126). Dependence on confirmatory information concerning self-esteem is described as need for approval.

The need for approval orients people toward activities that can gain acceptance for them. The high level of this "need" probably reflects their uncertainty concerning own value (uncertain self-esteem). This hypothesis is supported by a study which shows that subjects with high need for approval cheated in a task for avoiding disapproval but not for gaining approval (Berger et al 1977). Another study demonstrated that children with high need for approval responded better to the task when they were supposed to achieve a group standard than when they were supposed to compete with others (Coady & Brown 1978). Apparently the main motive here is to avoid being worse than others (and not the desire to be better). In our laboratory we found that the tendency to treat other people as a source of information and evaluation about oneself is higher among the subjects showing uncertainty concerning the self (Czyzewska 1978).

Our analysis suggests that other people can become goal objects as a source of approval and support for beliefs concerning the self. We can say that other people have a *personal value* for an individual in the sense that their presence and their attitudes are indispensable conditions of psychological well-being, and, in fact, for the psychological existence of the self. They perform those functions either as members of a certain category (e.g. audience, neighbors, peers, authority figures) or as specific individuals who have significant positions in the personal meaning system (child, spouse, best friend).

It should be added that people are performing supportive functions for the self not only by their action and attitudes toward the individual but by the very fact of their existence in the individual's awareness. By making self-other comparisons an individual "feeds" himself with information that can either enhance or decrease his self-esteem (Brickman & Bulman 1977). Since self-esteem depends to a high degree on comparisons between self and others, an individual can enhance it by devaluating others symbolically (by derogating, humiliating, ridiculing) or practically, by action that is aimed at worsening other peoples' situations (for more extensive discussion of the phenomenon, see Reykowski 1979b).

We may, however, pose the question: is the value of social objects dependent solely on their role in adaptation for an individual? Is the affective or personal value of others the only reason that they are regarded as deserving protection, care, and growth? We believe that present psychological knowledge does not support such a view. In the next section we will present some arguments for the proposition that social objects can have an autonomous value that cannot be reduced to its function for an individual's well-being.

AUTONOMOUS VALUE OF A SOCIAL OBJECT

The view that people relate to other people primarily or solely on the basis of their usefulness for personal well-being has been challenged by studies concerning intergroup behavior. According to one theory, differential intergroup behavior, i.e. such phenomena as ingroup bias and outgroup discrimination, cannot be explained satisfactorily on the assumption that people try to maximize their individual material or psychological gain. People tend to act on behalf of members of their own group and discriminate against members of the outgroup without any profit in return, and the only condition of this behavior is "social categorization."

The Theory of Social Categorization

In the early 1970s, Tajfel and his associates presented data indicating that differential intergroup behavior can be produced in the absence of the typical conditions that supposedly are responsible for intergroup conflict. They developed the experimental procedure called "minimal group paradigm" which allowed isolation of the phenomenon of "social categorization" from other variables (Tajfel et al 1971). Tajfel (1974) has formulated a theory that not only interprets the data but also gives a very broad view of the nature of human social behavior. His theory won widespread interest among European psychologists and has been developed extensively since that time.

There are four basic assumptions to the theory:

1. People cognitively order their social environment; this ordering consists in classification of other humans into various categories; people possess a network of categories that is socially constructed. Persons (or groups) that we meet or hear or read of are placed in the network. The process has been called *social categorization.*
2. The network defines not only the position of other people but also the position of the individual himself as a member of a given category (or categories). The category membership becomes a basis for self-definition (or self-concept) and a precondition of *social identity.*
3. The positions in the network of categories have evaluative characteristics, that is, depending on category membership, a social object can possess higher or lower values. One's own position in the network becomes, therefore, a basis for self evaluation as well as evaluation of others. People are comparing groups in terms of their value; that is, they make *social comparisons.*
4. Social comparison gives rise to a tendency to protect and enhance positive self-evaluation by preservation of positively valued distinctiveness from other categories. It is a tendency to keep *positive group distinctiveness.*

A person might maintain and expand his/her positive distinctiveness by joining groups that are located higher on any of the evaluative dimensions of social comparison, i.e. he/she can do it by changing category membership. This upright movement accounts for social mobility. If, however, an individual cannot leave his/her present group for external or internal reasons, he may fight for a change of position of his whole group, engaging in an appropriate social action. This accounts for the phenomena of social change. In such cases, when any practical change is improbable or impossible, people tend to reinterpret their situation, transforming symbolically unwelcome features of own category into positive ones (Tajfel 1974).

This theory has generated hypotheses that were tested in laboratories of different (West) European countries. Especially in several recent studies (using a minimal group paradigm), it was demonstrated that subjects who had to allocate reward between ingroup and outgroup members consistently tend to resign from material gain in order to achieve the positive group distinctiveness. Discrimination against the outgroup was more evident with a higher reward (Turner, Brown & Tajfel 1979). There are some empirical arguments that discriminatory responses in minimal group paradigm situations do increase self-esteem (Oakes & Turner 1980) and that the conditions where profit from cooperation is higher, the discriminatory behavior can be weaker but the discriminatory attitudes may still persist (Brewer & Silver 1978).[8]

It should be stressed that favoritism and discrimination were observed even in situations when classification to ingroup and outgroup was based upon trivial characteristics: preference for Klee or Kandinsky paintings, overestimation or underestimation of number of dots in perceptual test (Tajfel 1974), etc.

The social categorization theory is based upon the assumption that the human mind orders phenomena in a set of discrete categories. This assumption, however, can be challenged (Reykowski & Smolenska 1980). It seems to be derived from a traditional view of the characteristics of a cognitive system.

Psychological Space

According to a traditional view of a cognitive system, its basic unit, a concept, can be looked upon as an abstract representation of a class of objects (events, processes) in terms of common properties of members of the class. A concept enables, therefore, a sharp differentiation between objects which belong and those which do not belong to a given class. These so-called logical concepts are the object of study of logic, philosophy (since Aristotle), linguistics, etc. Psychologists of an older school studying concept formation process were operating on the same assumptions. But recent studies on so-called natural concepts, as developed in the framework of research on long-term memory and artificial intelligence, as well as other investigations of a cognitive psychology, brought a substantial modification to this picture. It has been shown that typical natural concepts do not have this all-or-nothing characteristic: category membership is a matter of degree (Mervis & Rosch 1981, Trzebinski 1980). In other studies it has been proved that a given domain of concepts can be represented as multidimensional space, and this is not merely a convenient way of describing available data but has a powerful explanatory value: it could be used for predicting a problem-solving behavior: e.g. solution of analogy (Rumelhart & Abrahamson 1973) or classification problems (Sternberg et al 1978), metaphoric thinking (Sternberg et al 1978), creative thinking (Trzebinski 1981), etc.

It seems plausible to assume that the idea of a cognitive system as semantic space can be extended to include phenomena of greater complexity than lexical symbols. It can serve as an explanatory tool not only for information

[8]For a recent criticism of this theory and discussion, see Branthwaite, Doyle & Lightbown 1979; Turner 1980.

processing but for affective and behavioral phenomena as well. In fact, it seems possible to construct a model of psychological space[9] that can account for social behavior. The model assumes that within the cognitive network there are representations of social objects including the self. Relatively separate cognitive organizations—we will call them "cognitive structures"—develop as a consequence of interaction with the social world and acquisition of experience related to the given object as a separate whole, with relatively stable identity. The self structure is regarded here as one of the cognitive organizations; this way of looking at the self structure seems to achieve widespread support (Epstein 1980, Markus 1977, 1980, Reykowski 1975a, b, Smith 1978).

A model implies that (*a*) objects and events can be located in various distances from the self (or other cognitive structures), and (*b*) the location has an impact upon judgments and affective reactions toward the objects and events. One may expect that: 1. the smaller the psychological distance of an object from the self the greater the tendency to assign to the object descriptive and evaluative characteristics that are being assigned to the self; 2. the smaller psychological distance of an object or event from the self the stronger the reaction toward an event or toward the state of an object (the greater the involvement).

The term "psychological distance" describes the subjective representation of degree of separation of two or more elements in time, in physical space, in social position, and in semantic system.[10] The representation can be assessed by various psychological techniques. As an index of psychological distance, measures of the "degree of similarity" or a degree of covariance have been applied (Reykowski 1980); also, graphic scales, drawing tests (Haase & Markey 1973), Repertory Grid (Slater 1976), and Semantic Differential (Osgood et al 1964) have been used as well. The assessment of subjective representation of social distance was made possible long ago by means of the Bogardus Scale (Prothro & Miles 1953).

The model that we are presenting has implications for a theory of social motivation. Namely, it suggests that value assignment to a social object is a function of its psychological distance from the self; i.e. the closer the given object is located in physical distance, in time, in space, in social position, or in semantic system, the greater the tendency to assign to that object the similar value that is assigned to oneself.

It is possible to present some evidence on behalf of such a hypothesis. Some of the evidence comes from studies on relationships between similarity and liking—we may expect that degree of liking for a given person

[9]Using a term originally introduced by Kurt Lewin (1935).

[10]Note that the term "semantic system" can refer either to a cognitive system of an individual or to symbolic construction as an intersubjective cultural phenomenon.

should be a function of his/her similarity (semantic distance) to the self. This, in fact, has been found in several studies that demonstrated a positive relationship between similarity and interpersonal attraction (Byrne 1971). The relationship is often explained in terms of greater reinforcing value of people whose views support our belief system. This interpretation, however, overlooks the fact that the relationship is not being held in cases of negative self-evaluation: people who ascribe to themselves negative characteristics tend to have a negative evaluation of similar others (Karylowski 1975a,b).

There is also a relationship between similarity and helping: similarity and other forms of psychological proximity increase a tendency to help others and to share with them. Karylowski (1976) and Smolenska of Warsaw (1979) were able to demonstrate that a subject works with greater effort if he/she perceives the previously unknown partner as socially or psychologically similar. It should be stressed that these studies showed that helping does not depend on liking. This contention is supported by findings that outgroup bias is frequently orthogonal to liking (cf Turner et al 1979, pp. 189–90).

Similarity is regarded here as a specific instance of psychological proximity. But other forms of this proximity have the same impact upon helping. J. Piliavin (unpublished manuscript) found that subjective geographical distance (i.e. distance as imagined by subjects) did influence the tendency to help.

Other observations indicate that witnessing someone's pain produces higher emotional arousal if the subject believes that a suffering person is similar to him/her. It also increases a tendency to take more pain for oneself in order to diminish the partner's suffering (Krebs 1975). Psychological similarity increases a tendency for cooperative choice in game situations (Schwanenberg & Huth 1977), and it inhibits aggression (Kosc 1975, Lange & Verhallen 1978; see also Hornstein 1978). All these findings point to the fact that the treatment of a social being depends upon his/her location in the cognitive network of a subject—the closer the given person is located to the self, the stronger the tendency to attribute to him/her the characteristics that are attributed to the self, the stronger the emotional reaction to his/her predicament, the stronger the tendency to make evaluations resembling those attributed to self, and the greater the inclination to take into consideration the person's well-being. In other words, a social object becomes a value to the degree of his/her proximity to the self.

But what about the object who is very remote from the self, who is lacking any resemblance to the self? We believe that this is a situation that gives rise to the phenomenon of dehumanization. Dehumanization leads to numerous consequences. Applications of rules and norms, as well as a tendency to take a perspective of a given person, in a sense of the term as proposed by Feffer (1970), is markedly reduced. It means that the principles of justice, equality, and loyalty have diminishing impact upon behavior. The tendency to take responsibility will also vanish, as well as empathy and sympathy. One illustration of this phenomenon is an observation of an anthropologist, M. Sahlins (Alexander 1975), concerning the decreasing tendency for equal exchange with increasing social distance. In other words, the further away the person is situated in semantic space the weaker the tendency to self-sacrifice the stronger—leading to cheating and exploitation.

Specific consequences of dehumanization may depend upon the region of a cognitive system where the object is situated. The object can be situated in a region having a positive valence where divine beings, heroes, or "beautiful people," are residing too.[11] But an object can also be situated in a region inhabited by lower or dangerous objects such as beasts, insects, and the like. In this case the tendency to avoid or to control or to destroy or exterminate can be aroused. This attitude toward people is all too well known from the recent history of many nations.

Dichotomization or Continuity

The model based upon a concept of psychological (cognitive) space is in many respects the opposite to Social Categorization theory. According to this model, it is not inevitable that the social world is divided into dichotomous, ingroup-outgroup categories. Of course, one should not deny that dichotomous classification is a very pervasive fact of the social interaction of people. But according to our view, dichotomization is a specific instance of organization of psychological space that appears if: (*a*) the representations of social objects are located in remote distances from the self, i.e. if the gradient of involvement is very steep; (*b*) sharp differentiations have been developed that create strong boundaries between cognitive structures.

The shape of a gradient is influenced by situational factors and personal history. It seems possible to provide evidence that stress makes the gradient steeper and dichotomization more probable (Janis 1972). The same can be true of anxiety, as studies on dogmatism seem to indicate (Rokeach 1960).

Since the content and organization of the cognitive system is primarily a product of a culture, it seems quite obvious that the culture will affect the distances between social objects represented in the network. Culture is also responsible for the development of sharp differentiations within a cognitive system. For example, the language that is developed by prison inmates

[11]The statement that dehumanized objects can be located in remote but positively evaluated regions suggests that proximity to the self is not the only source of value ascribed to the object. We will discuss this possibility in the following pages.

serves to make strong boundaries between true "hard-core" criminals and the rest of the world (Kosewski 1973). The differentiations can be produced by situational factors as well. Experimental demonstrations of the phenomenon are well known (Sherif et al 1961, Zimbardo prison experiment 1973, Tajfel & Billig 1974, Deutsch 1981).

At the other side there are operations that can weaken boundaries by extending the psychological perspective. For example, in the theory of a collective developed by Petrovsky from the Soviet Union (1977), it has been stressed that in groups that perceive themselves as embedded in a larger social system and operate upon the principles that are congruent with a larger system, the sharp differentiation "we-they" does not have to develop. While some differentiating processes are occurring—since people discriminate between members and nonmembers of a given collective—at the same time there exists a base for extension of psychological perspective beyond the scope of one's own group. It can be added that Sherif's idea of superordinate goals seems to describe the same process.

The reasoning and data described above suggest that a social object acquires value if it is classified in the same category as the self, or if it is close to the self. Should we come to the conclusion that the self is the only primary source of value? Some authors are assuming that it is so. Rokeach, a long-time student of human values, argues that a main function of the value system is to maintain and enhance societal originating self-conception (Rokeach 1980, p. 296). He is referring to results of many studies that he performed showing that people change their values if it serves their self-maintenance and self-enhancement. We could debate the universality of the statement as well as the methodology of the studies that were supposed to provide the evidence for it. But because of space limitation, we will concentrate only on the theoretical aspects of the issue.

Emerging Values

We will start our discussion here by pointing to the nature of the system that is responsible for the regulation of human behavior. According to our previous argument, the regulation comes about as a consequence of formation of a cognitive system (network) being a product of accumulation and organization of experience and possessing not only reproductive but generative qualities as well. Its elements and its organization are not merely a representation of the outside world; it is a subjective reflection as well as a construction of objective reality.

The cognitive structures function according to the "principle of equilibrium" (in the Piagetian sense of the term, 1967). Maintenance of equilibrium is a necessary condition for proper functioning of the whole system. Equilibrium of the structure is preserved if information concerning the object represented by it match (within certain limits) standards embedded in the structure. The standards represent the normal (and ideal) state of the object, i.e. its normal (or ideal) functioning, physical or psychological well-being, position, etc. Standards can be looked upon as well-established expectations. Deviation from the standards produces a state of tension. For many years now it has been demonstrated that discrepancy from the well-established cognitive expectations produces a state of arousal (Hebb 1949, Festinger 1957, Hunt 1965; see also the review by Zajonc 1968a).

Regulatory potential of a cognitive discrepancy (dissonance) has been questioned—some critics contend that dissonance in belief systems does not affect behavior if beliefs are not related to self-esteem. It should be borne in mind, however, that the typical studies concerning those phenomena deal with rather trivial beliefs. The dissonance or incongruencies that are studied in laboratories are related to surface level of the cognitive system dealing with short-lasting, ad hoc-produced processes. The real meaning of the phenomenon cannot be appreciated as long as we do not take into consideration the "deep structures" and reactions of people to the events that involve the discrepancies with standards representing the most basic "identity standards" of social objects.

This reasoning leads us to the proposition that an object represented on the deep level of the cognitive system possesses a value due to the very fact that it became part of the system and it results in a tendency for protection and enhancement of the well-being of such an object. Such a tendency is manifested in prosocial behavior, i.e. behavior that is aimed at benefit of a social object (Reykowski 1979a). But the statement claiming that there is a "natural" inclination to act on behalf of a social object (providing that it is represented in the subject's cognitive system) seems to be in apparent contradiction with observations of everyday life; they show in a discouraging number of cases that people manifest total indifference to the fate of another social being. To resolve this contradiction we should take into consideration that while at any given moment there are many motivational tendencies aroused, only a few of them—those which have high enough potential—will manifest in a behavior. The others can be suppressed by more powerful ones. Thus, when interests of other people are at stake, providing help to them might result in adverse effects for one's own interests, and that in turn will generate motivation against any action in such a direction (Schwartz 1977). We should not be surprised, therefore, that it is much easier to evoke intensive feelings of compassion and solidarity if there are only remote possibilities that it can imply any serious practical involvement of oneself.

The model implies that motivational effects of arousal produced within the representation of social objects depends upon the importance of this object as related to the importance attributed to oneself, in other words, upon a value of the self and value of others. The implication hardly needs any special evidence. The main point, however, is where the importance comes from. We argue that it emerges as a result of formation of cognitive structures. The degree of importance depends upon the degree of elaboration of the structure.

We believe that the greater a cognitive elaboration, the greater a motivational potential of a given representation. To support the proposition we can refer to several sources. Staub, a long-time student of prosocial behavior and author of the two fundamental volumes on this subject (Staub 1978b, 1979), developed the view that prosocial behavior is a function of the importance of the goal and the activation potential of the environment for that goal. One of the measures of importance of that goal proposed by Staub is a cognitive network associated with the goal. He was able to demonstrate that if such a network is better developed, the subject is more likely to respond positively to another person's needs (Staub 1978a). In our laboratory, Czapinski (1976) found that subjects who worked on behalf of two other persons spent more effort on behalf of a person whose cognitive representation was better integrated with the rest of the cognitive system of a subject. The positive, significant correlation between the degree of integration and the degree of effort remained even when differences in liking were partialed out.

The importance of a social object is not merely a dispositional variable —it can be modified by situational factors. The stimuli that produce an increased concentration upon the social object tend to enhance its regulatory potential, and by the same token, increase a tendency to act on his/her behalf.

This effect was obtained in various psychological laboratories. Jarymowicz in Warsaw (1979) found that subjects who concentrated on social objects by preparing arguments against egocentric views were more sensitive to the needs of other people—their ability to diagnose needs and interests of characters presented on the film increased significantly. It should be borne in mind that the finding cannot be simply explained away by saying that looking for arguments for prosocial behavior reminded the subjects about the social norm or informed them about experimenter expectations; that could be a valid argument if the prosocial behavior were measured. But the greater accuracy of perceptual functioning seems to support the view that some tuning of the representation of social object was achieved.

Observing the harmful acts toward some unrelated people may enhance a tendency to prosocial behavior (Konecni 1972), but the effects tend to disappear if the subject lacks an opportunity to learn about the victim's reaction (cf Rosenhan et al 1981). Apparently feedback from the victim results in increasing concentration upon a social object.

The important fact here, however, is a direction of attention. It may depend on some more or less permanent characteristics of individuals. Staub (1978a) suggests that "prosocial orientation" makes people more sensitive to the information about the fate of others—such people are likely to attend to victim fate. But others can be more attentive to other features of the situation.

It has been shown that people's reaction to the same situation may differ depending upon the focus of their attention. Subjects who were asked to imagine their own reaction to a terminally ill friend were significantly less helpful in a subsequent opportunity of being anonymous altruists than subjects who were asked to imagine the friend's feelings (Thompson et al 1980).

There are also data which show that concentration on the other person is an effective tool of increasing children's prosocial behavior. Kochanska from Warsaw (1980) found that 9-year-old children who had an opportunity to learn that their prosocial acts (drawing pictures for children in an orphanage) contributed to the positive feelings of the recipients showed increased tendency to sharing in the next opportunity for prosocial behavior toward other groups of needy persons.

Nievierovitch from Moscow (1979) has shown that preschool children's motivation for helping other children can be a function of the saliency of an outcome: she increased saliency by introducing more elements to the pictures illustrating the outcome. A somewhat similar finding was obtained by Lewittes & Israel (1978), who report that children 5 years, 8 months old can increase the delay of gratification by taking into account other oriented consequences.

Karylowski (1981), who studied the antecedents of prosocial behavior, found that people who are more likely to take into account other persons' needs and interests were reared by mothers who used significantly more often the procedure called "induction"—the term introduced by Hoffman (1970). According to Hoffman, induction, i.e. using reasoning as disciplinary procedure, especially to make salient for a child the feelings and situation of another person, can facilitate the development of so-called humanistic flexible orientation. The point can be made that the systematic use of procedures concentrating children's attention upon the social objects can have a lasting effect in contributing to the development of their social attitudes.

Similar conclusions can be drawn from an extensive study of results of a special experimental program developed in some elementary schools in Poznan (Poland) by H. Muszynski and associates. In this program (for children from grades 1 to 4) teachers put a special emphasis upon cooperation between pupils, involving all pupils in tasks for a common good or for others. Teachers were encouraged to respect the children's views and treat them as partners of a common task. The evaluation study made after 4 years (with specially devised measurement techniques) showed that children from experimental classes surpassed the children from control classes in a number of indices of prosocial behavior: they understood better other people's needs and expectations, and they were also more tolerant toward differences between people of different nationalities, customs, and religions, and were more helpful (L. Muszynska 1976).

The studies described seem to point to the fact that adults and children, when concentrating on the social object, show an increasing tendency to act on his/her behalf. This concentration can have a transient effect, being a result of saliency of the given social stimulus, but it can also have an enduring effect if used as a socializing procedure. Our analysis suggests the opposite effect can be obtained if concentration upon the self is produced.

The Role of Self-Concentration

The fact that self-concentration may inhibit prosocial behavior is not at all surprising. Sometime ago, Berkowitz (1970) argued that preoccupation with self (self-concern) makes prosocial behavior less probable. Our analysis (Reykowski 1979a) suggests that self-concentration is a heterogeneous phenomenon, that is, it can be produced as a result of two different psychological conditions: self-concentration can appear as a consequence of very high value attached to oneself as compared to value of any other social object (elevated self-esteem), and also it can be a result of tension produced in the self as a consequence of uncertainty concerning one's own value or attributing negative evaluation to oneself[12] (low or unstable self-esteem). In our earlier studies (Szustrowa 1972; cf Reykowski 1981) we found that people with both low and high self-esteem are less likely to behave prosocially. It implies that increment in self-esteem increases prosocial tendencies with people who were originally uncertain about the value of self or had low self-esteem. But the same procedure should be either unsuccessful or even detrimental if applied to people having high self-esteem.

There are facts that corroborate this conjecture. Jarymowicz (1977, 1979), using procedures that were supposed to enhance self-esteem, found that high school students with originally uncertain self-esteem tend to act more prosocially than controls. Groups with high original self-esteem did not show any improvement.

[12]We are accepting an assumption that there is a "natural" tendency to attribute positive value to the self. Whenever a person is prompted to apply negative self-evaluating statements to the self, tension arises. We have no room here to discuss sources of this tendency.

In fact, over the last decade there were a number of studies that showed that positive events such as success and information about one's own competence increase prosocial behaviors (Staub 1978b, Rosenhan et al 1981). The studies were very often interpreted as evidence that positive mood increases a prosocial behavior. This interpretation seems to be inconsistent with data since it is easy to show that a positive mood can facilitate not only prosocial, but in many cases egocentric, behavior as well (Rosenhan et al 1981, Wispe et al 1975).

Such inconsistencies are not unexpected if we take into consideration the model presented above. Positive mood produced by success can have an opposite impact upon people with low and high self-esteem. In fact, we found that if people with high self-esteem receive information that contributes to their positive view about themselves, their readiness to prosocial behavior decreases (Hamer 1978). There are, however, some phenomena that make the picture still more complicated. Complications appear when the role of norms in regulation of social behavior is taken into consideration.

Psychologists, whatever their theoretical orientation, have no doubt that the human value system and evaluation principles are shaped by society, although they differ in their explanations of how this process is effectuated. According to some recent formulations, norms that society imposes upon an individual become associated with one's self-esteem; thus, the realization of such norms (so-called *personal norms*) become a precondition of positive feelings about oneself, while breaking them results in decrement of self-esteem in the form of guilt, shame, remorse, etc (Karylowski 1977, Schwartz 1977). The activation of personal norms requires, according to Schwartz, that some conditions have to be met; two of them are crucial: awareness of consequences of own action for others and assignment of responsibility for the situation to oneself. Research conducted by Schwartz provided evidence concerning the role of those factors.[13]

Since the norms can be associated with the self, the self should play a mediating role in regulating prosocial behavior. It means that self-concentration should facilitate rather than inhibit prosocial behavior. It sometimes happens to be true.

It has been observed that self-concentration produced by guilt increases prosocial behavior (for reviews see Staub 1978b, Rosenhan et al 1981). Obviously, the feelings of guilt indicate that self-esteem is involved. The critical role of self-esteem in guilt-regulated prosocial behavior is well illustrated by a study made by Harris et al (1975), who found that churchgoers

[13]It should be noted that inclusion into a theoretical model of norm activation of two above-mentioned factors provides a theoretical link with two relevant areas of research: role taking and diffusion of responsibility.

are less likely to contribute to charity following confession than prior to it. Similar findings concerning confession were obtained earlier by Carlsmith & Gross (1969). Apparently, as soon as the tension in one's self-esteem is reduced, the readiness for prosocial behavior is reduced as well.

While feelings of guilt facilitate prosocial behavior, other forms of self-concentration such as hearing one's own voice (Gibbons 1978) or looking into the mirror (Rosenhan et al, 1981) usually suppress it. But not in all cases. Karylowski (1979), who made his subjects work for themselves and for an unknown partner for monetary rewards, found that introducing a mirror in the middle of an experiment produces a decrement in the amount of work for a partner, while the amount of work for oneself remains unchanged; but the effect does not appear with subjects who attribute very high values to the norm of helpfulness; to the contrary, they work for a partner more than without the mirror. Apparently in those cases self-concentration resulted in increased saliency of prosocial norms and contributed to the enhancement of prosocial behavior.

Hamer, in her previously quoted study (1978), made one group of subjects believe that they had high potential for prosocial behavior, while the second group believed that they had high potential for coping with life problems. While the second group was *less* helpful than the controls (receiving information not related to self), the first group was *more* helpful than the controls. The findings seem to be consistent with the view that self-perception of helpfulness increases prosocial behavior (see Wegner 1980).[14]

The data described above indicated that if individuals include in their self-concept some norms of prosocial behavior, self-concentration may result in an increased tendency to perform such behavior (concentration upon moral aspects of the self). It should be added that norms that an individual has assimilated can have two different forms: they can have a form of prescriptions concerning the specific type of behavior (e.g. politeness, helpfulness, honesty), or can define the value of the object. In the latter case, an individual learns the rules of value assignment to a social object. Society defines who should be regarded as more important or more valuable and why.

Cognitive or Affective

Internalization of social norms results in assimilation of values that are respected in a society. A substantial part of the values that an individual recognizes as his/her own are imposed by society. But there are also values which emerge as a result of the development of a cognitive system. We are

[14]Other consequences of self-concentration are described by Brody (1980).

suggesting that social objects represented in the system acquire an intrinsic value. The idea that cognitive systems may generate value is implicit in works by Piaget (1965) and Kohlberg (1976). The idea seemed to find substantial support in the discovery made by Zajonc (1968b) of the so-called "mere exposure" effect. For more than a decade, in numerous studies, it has been demonstrated that repeated contact with some objects or events leads to increased liking of those objects or events without any other "reinforcing" experience. One is led to believe that preferences are inherent in the representation of an object. Zajonc himself (1971) indicated the importance of this discovery for the theory of social motivation.

But in his recent paper, Zajonc (1980) makes a strong case for the existence of parallel, separate, partly independent affective systems in the organism. Cognitive and affective systems operate on the basis of two different types of data: Zajonc calls them "discriminanda" (processed by a cognitive system) and "preferenda" (processed by affective system). On the basis of this reasoning, one should expect that a value of a social object is a function of its "incorporation" in the affective system rather than in the cognitive one. But taking into consideration the fact that purely cognitive processes ("cold cognitions") can, under certain conditions, generate affect (in case of incongruency), one may wonder if we should really assume that there exist *two* different systems. Data presented by Zajonc and his reasoning can quite likely be interpreted as indicating that there is basically one system that has two different modes of operation: it operates as an information-processing device and as a source of affective states (and desires). In a given moment, one or the other mode of operation can be predominant. It is possible to describe conditions that can favor the given mode of operation of the system, but the question arises: should we still call it "cognitive"?

CONCLUDING REMARKS

In discussing the origin and the nature of social motivation, some authors claim that humans have the "need to affiliate with other humans" and that need differs from other human instinctual drives like sex (Martimor 1979). Our analysis suggests that what manifests itself as a "tendency toward sociability" is not a homogeneous disposition (or trait, or need, or drive). A human being is attractive to another human being for a variety of reasons. In the first place, he or she is a source of stimuli that bring a strong sensory and functional pleasure; this is a basis for the development of a strong demand for objects who possess such qualities. It can be argued that the difference in sensitivity to such stimuli is affected by some biological factors, especially those which control the demand for stimulation (sensation seeking). Attractiveness of humans can also be related to the fact that some of them (well-known, nurturing persons) can serve as a "device" for controlling stimulation—especially in an unfamiliar and threatening environment.

The other mechanism of social motivation, uniquely human, is related to the fact that human beings play a critical role as a source of support for individual systems of meaning—they provide information necessary for the validation of personal beliefs. Information concerning the self—self-identity and self-esteem—seem to have special importance for an individual. Inflow of information concerning individual beliefs seems to be as important for the existence of a cognitive system as food intake for an organism.

Considering the fact that one human being is an extremely valuable object for another human being, it is hardly suprising that a tendency to associate with people, to care for them (as for anything that has a value for an individual), to exploit them, to take advantage of them, or to abuse them should be (and really is) the most common event of a social life.

But it is not the whole story. The fact is that the value that an individual attaches to human beings can be independent from their relation to his/her personal needs or desires. It can originate from internalized normative systems or it can emerge as a result of the development of cognitive[15] representation of social objects. We have reason to believe that the very fact of ordering social phenomena in a cognitive network leads to the value attribution to objects represented in the network. The process gives rise to a genuine prosocial motivation; that is, a motivation that is not controlled by anticipation of personal gain or avoiding personal loss but by gain or loss as affecting an external social object.

Some people claim that we cannot speak about a genuine prosocial motivation since self-interest is served here as well: individuals acting prosocially are either protecting self-esteem or getting personal satisfaction from another person's gain (well-being). The argument seems to miss a point, however, since it does not take into account where the satisfaction comes from. As long as an individual's satisfaction depends upon another person's benefit, it is qualitatively different from self-interest where the satisfaction comes from personal gain.

The main conclusion of this paper says that the traditional view of social motivation as originating from a number of social needs (or drives, or motives), probably inborn, is much too simplistic. A number of factors have been identified that contribute to the treatment of other humans, at the one side as instruments for need satisfaction or as a prey, while at the other side as an ultimate value justifying complete self-sacrifice. Knowing those fac-

[15]The term "cognitive" is probably not fully adequate. See reservations indicated in preceding section.

tors, we are in a better position to explain under what conditions those or other motivational tendencies will prevail. What is lacking, however, is a theory that could give a proper account of how all those tendencies or motives are organized within the individual, i.e. how they are related to one another. We seem to have a long way to go until such a theory can be developed.

Literature cited

Alexander, R. D. 1975. The search for a general theory of behavior. *Behav. Sci.* 20:77–99

Arend, R., Gove, F. L., Sroufe, A. 1979. Continuity of individual adaptation from infancy to kindergarten: A predictive study of ego-resiliency and curiosity in preschoolers. *Child Dev.* 50:950–59

Atkinson, J. W., Birch, D. 1978. *Introduction to Motivation.* New York: Van Nostrand

Atkinson, J. W., Raynor, J. O., eds. 1974. *Motivation and Achievement.* Washington DC: Winston (Halsted Press/Wiley)

Bandura, A. 1969. *Principles of Behavior Modification.* New York: Holt

Berger, S. E., Levin, R., Jacobson, L. I., Millham, J. 1977. Gain approval or avoid disapproval: Comparison of motive strengths in high need for approval scorers. *J. Pers.* 45:458–68

Berkowitz, L. 1969. Social motivation. In *The Handbook of Social Psychology,* ed. G. Lindzey, E. Aronson, 3:50–135. Reading, Mass: Addison-Wesley

Berkowitz, L. 1970. The self, selfishness and altruism. In *Altruism and Helping Behavior,* ed. J. Macaulay, L. Berkowitz, pp. 143–51. New York: Academic

Berkowitz, L., Cochran, S. T., Embree, M. C. 1981. Physical pain and the goal of aversively stimulated aggression. *J. Pers. Soc. Psychol.* In press

Berlyne, D. E. 1967. Arousal and reinforcement. In *Nebraska Symposium on Motivation,* ed. D. Levine, 1967:1–110. Lincoln: Univ. Nebraska Press

Bishof, N. 1975. A systems approach toward the functional connections of attachment and fear. *Child Dev.* 46:801–17

Bishof, N. 1978. On the phylogeny of human morality. In *Morality as a Biological Phenomenon,* ed. G. S. Stent, pp. 53–74. Berlin: Dahlem Konferenzen

Bishof, N. 1980. *Detachment: The breaking of bonds as a biocultural phenomenon.* Presented at Int. Congr. Psychol., 22nd, Leipzig

Bordon, R. J., Taylor, S. P. 1976. Pennies for pain: A note on instrumental aggression toward a pacifist by vanquished victorious, and evenly-matched opponents. *Victimology* 1:154–57

Branthwaite, A., Doyle, S., Lightbown, N. 1979. The balance between fairness and discrimination. *Eur. J. Soc. Psychol.* 9:149–63

Brewer, M. B., Silver, M. 1978. Ingroup bias as a function of task characteristic. *Eur. J. Soc. Psychol.* 8:393–400

Brickman, P., Bulman, R. J. 1977. Pleasure and pain in social comparison. In *Social Comparison Processes,* ed. J. M. Suls, R. L. Miller, pp. 149–86. Washington DC: Hemisphere

Brody, N. 1980. Social motivation. *Ann. Rev. Psychol.* 31:143–68

Byrne, D. 1971. *The Attraction Paradigm.* New York: Academic

Carlsmith, J. M., Gross, A. E. 1969. Some effects of guilt on compliance. *J. Pers. Soc. Psychol.* 11:232–39

Coady, H., Brown, M. 1978. Need for approval and the effects of nominative and competitive incentives on children's performance. *J. Gen. Psychol.* 132: 291–98

Coe, Ch. L., Mendoza, S. P., Levine, S. 1981. Hormonal correlates of dominance status in the squirrel monkey. *Horm. Behav.* In press

Cone, J. 1978. Developing and maintaining social interaction in profoundly retarded young males. *J. Abnorm. Child Psychol.* 6:351–60

Czapinski, J. 1976. Strukturalne wlasnosci reprezentacji poznawczej obiektow spolecznych a gotowosc do dzialania na rzecz tych obiektow. *Stud. Psychol. Warszawa* 15:83–99

Czyzewska, M. 1978. *Kryteria nadawania wartosci drugiemu czlowiekowi.* Univ. Warsaw. In manuscript

deCharms, R., Muir, M. S. 1978. Motivation: Social approaches. *Ann. Rev. Psychol.* 29:91–113

Deutsch, M. 1981. Interdependence and psychological orientation. In *Living With*

Other People, ed. V. Derlega, J. Grzelak. New York: Academic. In press

Eliasz, A. 1974. Aktywnosc (reaktywna i sprawcza) a wybor sytuacji o roznym stopniu stymulacji. In *Rola cech temperamentalnych w dzialaniu,* ed. J. Strelau, pp. 135–41. Wroclaw, Warszawa: Ossolineum

Eliasz, A. 1981. *Temperament a system regulacji stymulacji.* Warszawa: PWN

Epstein, S. 1980. The self-concept: A review and the proposal of an integrated theory of personality. In *Personality: Basic Aspects and Current Research,* ed. E. Staub, pp. 81–132. Englewood Cliffs, NJ: Prentice-Hall

Feffer, M. 1970. Developmental analysis of interpersonal behavior. *Psychol. Rev.* 77:197–214

Festinger, L. 1957. *A Theory of Cognitive Dissonance.* Stanford: Stanford Univ. Press

Fowler, H. 1965. *Curiosity and Exploratory Behavior.* New York: Macmillan

Fraczek, A. 1979. Functions of emotional and cognitive mechanisms in the regulation of aggressive behavior. In *Aggression and Behavior Change,* ed. S. Feshbach, A. Fraczek, pp. 139–57. New York: Praeger

Fraczek, A. 1980. Aggressive actions—a topic in experimental social psychology studies. *Pol. Psychol. Bull.* 11:99–110

Gibbons, F. X. 1978. *Self-awareness, self-concern and pro-social behavior.* Presented at Am. Psychol. Assoc. Meet., Toronto

Gonzalez, C. A., Gunnar, M. R., Levine, S. 1981. Behavioral and hormonal responses to social disruption and infant stimuli in female rhesus monkeys. *Psychoneuroendocrinology.* In press

Goy, R. W., McEwen, B. S. 1980. *Sexual Differentiation of the Brain. Based on the Work Session of the Neurosciences Research Program.* Cambridge, Mass/ London: MIT Press

Haase, R. F., Markey, M. J. 1973. A methodological note on the study of personal space. *J. Consult. Clin. Psychol.* 40: 122–25

Hamburg, D. A., Van Lawick-Goodall, J. 1978. Factors facilitating development of aggressive behavior in chimpanzees and humans. In *Origin of Aggression,* ed. W. W. Hartup, J. deWit, pp. 57–83. Paris/New York: Mouton

Hamer, H. 1978. Wywolywanie motywacji do dzialan prospolecznych u kobiet aktywnie egocentrycznych. In *Teoria osobowosci a zachowania prospoleczne,* ed. J. Reykowski, pp. 169–85. Warszawa: IFIS PAN Press

Harris, M. B., Benson, S. M., Hall, C. 1975. The effects of confession on altruism. *J. Soc. Psychol.* 96:187–92

Hebb, D. O. 1949. *The Organization of Behavior.* New York: Wiley

Helson, H. 1966. Some problems in motivation from the point of view of the theory of adaptation level. In *Nebraska Symposium on Motivation,* ed. D. Levine, pp. 137–82. Lincoln: Univ. Nebr. Press

Hoffman, M. L. 1970. Moral development. In *Carmichael's Manual of Child Psychology,* ed. P. H. Mussen, 2:261–359. New York: Wiley

Hornstein, H. A. 1978. Promotive tension and prosocial behavior: A Lewinian analysis. In *Altruism, Sympathy, and Helping,* ed. L. Wispe, pp. 177–208. New York: Academic

Hunt, J. McV. 1965. Intrinsic motivation and its role in psychological development. In *Nebraska Symposium on Motivation,* ed. D. Levine, 1965: 189–282. Lincoln: Univ. Nebr. Press

Huston, T. L., Geis, G., Wright, R. 1976. The angry Samaritans. *Psychol. Today* 10(1):61

Janis, I. L. 1972. *Victims of Groupthink.* Boston: Houghton Mifflin

Jarymowicz, M. 1977. Modification of self-worth and increment of prosocial sensitivity. *Pol. Psychol. Bull.* 8:45–55

Jarymowicz, M. 1979. *Modyfikowanie wyobrazen dotyczacych ja dla zwiekszania gotowosci do zachowan prospolecznych.* Wroclaw, Warszawa: Ossolineum

Jellison, J. M., Gentry, K. W. 1978. A self-presentation interpretation of the seeking of social approval. *Pers. Soc. Psychol. Bull.* 4:227–30

Karylowski, J. 1975a. *Z badan nad mechanizmami pozytywnych ustosunkowan interpersonalnych.* Wroclaw, Warszawa: Ossolineum

Karylowski, J. 1975b. Evaluations of others' acts as function of self-other similarity and self-esteem. In *Studies on the Mechanisms of Prosocial Behavior,* ed. J. Reykowski, pp. 25–45. Warsaw: Warsaw Univ. Press

Karylowski, J. 1976. Self-esteem, similarity, liking and helping. *Pers. Soc. Psychol. Bull.* 2:71–74

Karylowski, J. 1977. Explaining prosocial behavior: A review. *Pol. Psychol. Bull.* 8:27–34

Karylowski, J. 1979. Self-focused attention, prosocial norms and prosocial behavior. *Pol. Psychol. Bull.* 10:57–66

Karylowski, J. 1981. On the two types of altruistic behavior: Doing good to feel good versus to make the other feel good. See Deutsch 1981. In press

Kochanska, G. 1980. Experimental formation of cognitive and helping social motivation in children. *Pol. Psychol. Bull.* 11:75–85

Kohlberg, L. 1976. Moral stages and moralization: The cognitive-developmental approach. In *Moral Development and Behavior,* ed. T. Lickona. New York: Holt, Rinehart & Winston

Konecni, V. J. 1972. Some effects of guilt on compliance: A field replication. *J. Pers. Soc. Psychol.* 23:30–32

Kosc, Z. 1975. Podobienstwo agresora do ofiary a natezenie czynnosci agresywnej. In *Z zagadnien psychologii agresji,* ed. A Fraczek, pp. 115–37. Warszawa: PIPS Press

Kosewski, M. 1973. Funkcje agresji w spolecznosci zamknietego zakladu karnego. *Psychol. Wychow* 26:332–43

Kotaskova, J. 1977. Changing influence and importance of some stimuli for the child during socialization. *Psychol. Patopsychol. Dietata* 11:405–17

Kozlowski, C. 1977. Demand for stimulation and probability preferences in gambling decisions. *Pol. Psychol. Bull.* 8:67–73

Krebs, D. L. 1975. Empathy and altruism. *J. Pers. Soc. Psychol.* 32:1134–46

Lagerspetz, K. 1979. Modification of aggressiveness in mice. See Fraczek 1979, pp. 62–82

Lange, A., Verhallen, W. 1978. Similarity of attitudes and instrumentality as determinants of aggression by policemen. *Eur. J. Soc. Psychol.* 8:489–505

Latane, B., Steele, C. 1975. The persistence of social attraction in socially deprived and satiated rats. *Anim. Learn. Behav.* 3:131–34

Leont'ev, A. N. 1975. *Deyatel'nost, Soznaniye, Litschnost.* Moskva: Izd. Politischeskoy Literatury

Lewin, K. 1935. *A Dynamic Theory of Personality.* New York: McGraw Hill

Lewittes, D. J., Israel, A. C. 1978. Maintaining children's ongoing delay of prolification through other-oriented consequences. *Dev. Psychol.* 14:181–82

Markus, H. 1977. Self-schemata and processing information about the self. *J. Pers. Soc. Psychol.* 35:63–78

Markus, H. 1980. The self in thought and memory. In *The Self in Social Psychology,* ed. D. M. Wegner, R. R. Vallacher, pp. 102–31. New York/Oxford: Oxford Univ. Press

Martimor, E. 1979. Sociability: The need for human social interchange. *Ann. Med. Psychol.* 2:807–20

Mason, W. A. 1971. Motivational factors in psychosocial development. In *Nebraska Symposium on Motivation,* ed. W. J. Arnold, M. M. Page, 1970: 35–68. Lincoln: Univ. Nebr. Press

Mendoza, S. P., Coe, Ch. L., Lowe, E. L., Levine, S. 1979. The physiological response to group formation in adult male squirrel monkeys. *Psychoneuroendocrinology* 3:221–29

Mervis, C. B., Rosch, E. 1981. Categorization of natural objects. *Ann. Rev. Psychol.* 32:89–115

Mika, S. 1969. *Skutecznosc kar w wychowaniu.* Warszawa: PWN

Money, J. 1974. Prenatal hormones and postnatal socialization in gender identity differentiation. In *Nebraska Symposium on Motivation,* ed. J. C. Cole, R. Dienstbier, 1973: 221–95. Lincoln: Univ. Nebr. Press

Muszynska, L. 1976. *Altruism i kolektywizm dzieciecy.* Warszawa: WSiP

Newcomb, A. F., Brady, J. F., Hartup, W. W. 1979. Friendship and incentive condition as determinants of children's task-oriented social behavior. *Child Dev.* 50:878–81

Nievierovitch, J. Z. 1979. Motywacja a emocjonalna regulacja zachowan w wieku przedszkolnym. In *Badania nad osobowoscia dzieci i mlodziezy,* I. Obuchowska, Owczynnikowa, J. Reykowski, pp. 20–38. Warszawa: WSiP

Oakes, P. J., Turner, J. C. 1980. Social categorization and intergroup behaviour: Does minimal intergroup discrimination make social identity more positive? *Eur. J. Soc. Psychol.* 10:295–301

Olweus, D. 1978. Personality factors and aggression: With special reference to violence within peer group. See Hamburg & Van Lawick-Goodall, 1978, pp. 274–77

Osgood, Ch. E., Suci, G. J., Tannenbaum, P. H. 1964. *The Measurement of Meaning.* Urbana: Univ. Ill. Press

Petrovsky, A. V. 1977. Psihologitscheskaya teoriya grup i kollektivov na novom etape. *Vopr. Psychol.* 5

Piaget, J. 1965. *The Moral Judgment of the Child.* New York: Free Press

Piaget, J. 1967. *Six Psychological Studies.* New York: Vintage

Prothro, E. T., Miles, O. K. 1953. Social distance in the deep South as measured by a revised Bogardus scale. *J. Soc. Psychol.* 37:171–74

Reykowski, J. 1975a. Position of self-structure in a cognitive system and prosocial orientation. *Dialectics & Humanism* 4:19–30

Reykowski, J. 1975b. Prosocial orientation and self-structure. In *Studies on the Mechanisms of prosocial Behavior,* ed. J. Reykowski, pp. 5–25. Warsaw: Warsaw Univ. Press

Reykowski, J. 1979a. *Motywacja, postawy prospoleczne a osobowosc.* Warszawa: PWN

Reykowski, J. 1979b. Intrinsic motivation and intrinsic inhibition of aggressive behavior. See Fraczek 1979, pp. 158–82

Reykowski, J. 1980. *Cognitive space and regulation of social behavior.* Presented at Int. Congr. Psychol., 22nd, Leipzig

Reykowski, J. 1981. Motivation of prosocial behavior. See Deutsch 1981

Reykowski, J., Smolenska, Z. 1980. *Psychological space and regulation of social behavior.* Presented at Int. Conf. Sociopsychological aspects of cooperative behavior, Bolonia

Rokeach, M. 1960. *The Open and the Closed Mind.* New York: Basic Books

Rokeach, M. 1980. Some unresolved issues in theories of beliefs, attitudes, and values. In *Nebraska Symposium on Motivation,* ed. M. M. Page, 1979: 261–304

Rosenhan, D. L., Salovey, P., Karylowski, J., Hargis, K. 1981. Emotion and altriusm. In *Altruism and Helping Behavior,* ed. J. P. Rushton, R. M. Sorrentino. Hillsdale, NJ: Erlbaum. In press

Rubinstein, S. L. 1973. *Problemy Obstchey Psychologii.* Moskva: Izd. Pedagogika

Rumelhart, D. E., Abrahamson, A. A. 1973. A model for analogical reasoning. *Cogn. Psychol.* 5:1–38

Sales, S. M. 1971. Need for stimulation as a factor in social behavior. *J. Pers. Soc. Psychol.* 19:124–34

Schwanenberg, E., Huth, W. 1977. The hard and the soft in interdependence: Locating game behavior in semantic space. *Percept. Mot. Skills* 45:131–53

Schwartz, S. H. 1977. Normative influence on altruism. *Adv. Exp. Soc. Psychol.* 10: 221–79

Sebastian, R. 1980. Immediate and delayed effects of victim sufferings on the attacker's aggression. *J. Res. Pers.* 12:312–28

Sherif, M., Harvey, O. J., White, B. J., Hood, W. R., Sherif, C. W. 1961. *Intergroup Conflict and Cooperation. Robbers Cave Experiment.* Norman: Univ. Okla. Book Exchange

Slater, P., ed. 1976. *Explorations of Intrapersonal Space.* London: Wiley

Smith, M. B. 1978. Perspectives on selfhood. *Am. Psychol.* 33:1053–63

Smolenska, Z. 1979. *Dystans psychologiczny partnera a dzialanie na jego rzecz.* PhD thesis. Univ. Warsaw, Poland

Sroufe, A., Waters, E. 1977. Attachment as an organizational construct. *Child Dev.* 48:1184–99

Staub, E. 1978a. Predicting prosocial behavior: A model for specifying the nature of personality-situation interaction. In *Perspectives in Interactional Psychology,* ed. L. A. Pervin, M. Lewis, pp. 87–110. New York: Plenum

Staub, E. 1978b. *Positive Social behavior and Morality. Social and Personal Influences,* Vol. 1. New York: Academic

Staub, E. 1979. *Positive Social Behavior and Morality. Socialization and Development,* Vol. 2. New York: Academic

Sternberg, R. J., Tourangeau, R., Nigro, G. 1978. *Metaphor, induction and social policy: The convergence of macroscopic and microscopic views.* Manuscript, Yale Univ.

Strelau, J. 1972. A diagnosis of temperament by nonexperimental techniques. *Pol. Psychol Bull.* 3:97–105

Strelau, J. 1974. Temperament as an expression of energy level and temporal features of behavior. *Pol. Psychol. Bull.* 5:119–27

Strelau, J. 1980. *A regulative theory of temperament.* Manuscript, Univ. Warsaw

Szustrowa, T. 1972. Zdolnosc do dzialania ma rzecz celow pozaosobistych a niektore wlasciwosci rodzinnego treningu wychowawczego. *Zesz. Nauk. Uniw. Warszawskiego,* 1

Tajfel, H. 1974. *Intergroup behaviour, social comparison and social change.* Katz-Newcomb Lectures. Ann Arbor: Univ. Mich. Press

Tajfel, H., Billig, M. C. 1974. Familiarity and categorization in intergroup behaviour. *J. Exp. Soc. Psychol.* 10:159–70

Tajfel, H., Flament, C., Billig, M. C., Bundy, R. 1971. Social categorization and intergroup behaviour. *Eur. J. Soc. Psychol.* 1:149–75

Thompson, W. C., Cowan, C. L., Rosenhan, D. L. 1980. Focus of attention mediates the impact of negative affect on altruism. *J. Pers. Soc. Psychol.* 38:291–300

Tomaszewski, T. 1963. *Wstep do psychologii.* Warszawa: PWN

Trzebinski, J. 1980. Natural concepts and creativity. *Pol. Psychol. Bull.* 11:41–51

Trzebinski, J. 1981. *Tworczosc a struktura pojec.* Warszawa: PWN

Turner, J. C. 1980. Fairness or discrimination in intergroup behaviour? A reply to Branthwaite, Doyle and Lightbown. *Eur. J. Soc. Psychol.* 10:131–47

Turner, J. C., Brown, R. J., Tajfel, H. 1979. Social comparison and group interest in ingroup favouritism. *Eur. J. Soc. Psychol.* 9:187–204

Wegner, D. M. 1980. The self in prosocial action. See Markus 1980, pp. 131–57

Wilson, E. O. 1975. *Sociobiology. The New Synthesis.* Cambridge, Mass./London: Harvard Univ. Press

Wispe, L., Kiecolt, J., Long, E. E. 1975. *Moods and Helping Revisited: Who is Deceiving Whom?* Manuscript, Univ. Okla.

Zajonc, R. B. 1968a. Cognitive theories in social psychology. In *The Handbook of Social Psychology,* ed. G. Lindzey, E. Arnson, pp. 320–411. New York: Addison-Wesley

Zajonc, R. B. 1968b. Attitudinal effects of mere exposure. *J. Pers. Soc. Psychol. Monogr.* 9:1–27

Zajonc, R. B. 1971. Attraction, affiliation and attachment. In *Man and Beast. Comparative Social Behavior,* ed. Eisenberg, Dillon, Ripley, pp. 143–79. Washington DC: Smithson. Inst. Press

Zajonc, R. B. 1980. Feeling and thinking. Preferences need no inferences. *Am. Psychol.* 35:151–75

Zimbardo, P. G. 1973. Social Psychology: Tool for improving the human condition. In *Mental Health Program Reports 6,* ed. J. Segel, M. Reich. Rockville: Natl. Inst. Mental Health

Zuckerman, M. 1979. *Sensation Seeking: Beyond the Optimal Level of Arousal.* Hillsdale, NJ: Erlbaum

Ann. Rev. Psychol. 1982. 33:155–94

TOUCH IN PRIMATES

Ian Darian-Smith

Sensory Processes Laboratory, Department of Physiology, University of Melbourne, Parkville, Victoria 3052, Australia

---

CONTENTS

0066-4308/82/0201-0155$02.00

What is the typical response when one is asked to identify by touch alone an object such as a peach? First, the peach is picked up using the thumb, index, and middle fingers, and held loosely to evaluate its weight and general size and shape. Then it is manipulated so that each part of its surface is successively explored with the pads of the fingers. As a result, a perceptual image of the peach is built up, based on assessment of its shape, including the various irregularities, on the texture and "firmness" of each part of its surface, and on its thermal characteristics. With familiar objects, such as a peach, this tactile identification may last only a few seconds, but with uncommon objects the serial assessment of the different features may take quite a long period of time before a full "image" of the object is established.

The familiar sequence just outlined illustrates some important aspects of the sense of touch. First, the hand in man and in most other primates is the all-important organ of touch. Not only are the finger pads tactually the most sensitive parts of the whole body surface, but also the precise motor control of the hand ensures that these highly sensitive finger pads can be used to explore every detail of the surfaces of an object.

Second, the special domain of the sense of touch is the identification and differentiation of the textured surfaces of objects around us. It is true that the tactile exploration of an object held in the hand also provides information about its shape, but in daily experience form perception usually depends as much, or more, on looking at the object as on touching it. The information about the object derived solely by touching it concerns (*a*) the texture of its surfaces, and (*b*) its thermal features.

A third important aspect of tactile sensibility, illustrated in the tactile exploration of the peach described above, is that the finger pads are moved laterally across any textured surface which is to be identified. Simple contact of the finger pads with the surface certainly will be detected, and coarse spatial patterns may be correctly identified without moving the fingers across the patterned surface (Johnson & Phillips 1981). However, for identifying a finely textured surface, particularly if it is to be differentiated from others, lateral movement of the finger pad relative to the surface is essential. This is equally true in assessing by touch alone the shape of objects.

This translational movement of the fingers relative to surfaces and objects may be either (*a*) entirely directed by the observer ("active" touch), or (*b*) produced by the passage of the stimulating surface or object across the immobilized fingers ("passive" touch). Form perception based on touch alone is virtually impossible unless the observer can actively manipulate and explore with the fingers the object being examined in order to optimize the sensory inflow to the brain. However, at least with simply patterned textured surfaces, the observer's spatial tactile acuity apparently differs little whether "active" or "passive" touch is used, as long as the relative movement between the surface and the finger pad is comparable.

Finally, the evolution of the hand as an organ adapted for manipulating and exploring objects and surfaces within our reach is unique to the primate. Only primates (excluding the primitive tree shrew) can hold an object in one hand and actively explore and identify its form and texture (Bishop 1964). Only the anthropoid primates specifically use their finger pads to do this.

This review focuses on the neural basis of some of the features of touch outlined above. Touch in the primate hand is the theme. Some of the peripheral and central neural mechanisms relevant to the recognition of textured surfaces and to the exploratory manipulation of objects and surfaces are examined. The reader will probably be impressed, as was the reviewer, not only by recent advances made in this field, but also by the limitations in our understanding of some of the more central aspects of tactile sensory processing.

PERIPHERAL NEURAL PROCESSING

During the last decade, substantial progress has been made in our understanding of the coding of sensory information within the nerve fiber populations that innervate the primate hand. These neuron populations are the interface between the external world, the hand, and the central nervous system. They alone signal to the brain *all* the immediate sensory information available to the observer as he explores surfaces and objects with the fingers, and because of this, it is the responses of these fibers that set the upper limit to the tactile sensory performance of the observer. As is apparent from the incomplete sensory deficits resulting from focal lesions within the somatosensory pathways (see later), no neuron populations relaying tactile information in the central nervous system has such a direct relationship with sensory behavior. It is precisely because of this unique direct relationship between neural events and sensory performance that peripheral nerve fiber populations are of special interest in the examination of the neural representation and coding of single- and many-dimensioned stimuli.

There are three successive phases in the functional characterization of the afferent fiber populations innervating a particular tissue or organ (Darian-Smith 1981). The first phase is concerned with the identification of the functionally distinctive fiber populations—their taxonomy. After classifying the functionally different fiber types, the next phase of the analysis is concerned with defining (*a*) what sensory information is signaled to the brain by individual fibers in each of the different fiber populations, and (*b*) how this sensory information is represented in the temporal sequencing of action potentials within the fiber response to each stimulus. The third phase in characterizing these fiber populations is directed to identifying how the central nervous system combines the sensory information it receives from the many individual fibers responding to a common stimulus. This last analysis, yet to be fully achieved for any fiber population, would require two steps. First, the response characteristics of the whole fiber population responding to the stimulus need to be described realistically. It would then be necessary to determine which parameters of the population response are useful to the central nervous system in its assessment of the stimulus. In the following account, investigations relating to each of these three phases in the functional characterization of fiber populations innervating the tissues of the hand, and in particular of the finger pads, are considered.

Several recent technical developments have been of importance in the analysis of peripheral nerve fiber populations. First, the electron microscopy of the various receptor terminals in skin, joints, ligaments, and muscle has brought to focus the common features of the receptors found in each of these tissues; Halata (1975) and Chouchkov (1978) have summarized these findings. Secondly, in 1968 Vallbo and Hagbarth reported the successful recording of single fiber responses in superficial nerves in man, the particular advance being that recording was simply achieved using a microelectrode introduced through the skin. This elegant procedure has proved of great value in the identification of functionally distinctive fiber groups within human somatic nerves (see Kenshalo 1979, Knibestöl 1973, 1975, Johansson 1978, Johansson & Vallbo 1980, Vallbo & Johansson 1978), and also in correlating single fiber responses with the subject's verbal report concerning a particular stimulus (Vallbo & Johansson 1976, Knibestöl & Vallbo 1980, Gybels et al 1979, Johansson et al 1980). A third important contribution has been the development of precisely controlled mechanical and thermal stimulus procedures. Effective stimulus control is essential in any quantitative study of the representation of the different parameters of the stimulus in the responses of single fibers, and of responding populations of these fibers (e.g. LaMotte & Mountcastle 1975).

Taxonomy of Afferent Fibers Innervating the Primate Hand

Classifying the different types of afferent fiber innervating the hand should be based on their essential and primary function, of transmitting information about specific stimulus events in the tissue they innervate to their various terminations within the central nervous system. Ideally, this classification will reflect the following characteristics of each fiber: (*a*) the tissue innervated, (*b*) the structure of the receptor terminal and of the fiber itself, (*c*) the stimulus information that the fiber relays to the central nervous system, and (*d*) the way in which this information is coded in the fiber's responses. In practice, a pragmatic approach must be used to identify individual fibers isolated during an experiment, because all the above information will not be known. Simple, mostly reliable "field" tests have been devised to obtain sufficient information about each fiber to identify it and differentiate it from other fiber groups. It is obvious, however, that this specification of the fiber may provide only limited insight into its normal functional role. Table 1 briefly sets out the afferent fiber types that have been identified in the median and ulnar nerves and their digital branches in man and the monkey: the listed references give a detailed description of the different fiber types. Brief comments on these fiber types follow.

MECHANORECEPTORS Extensive accounts of the mechanoreceptors innervating the skin and underlying tissues have been published recently (Burgess & Perl 1973, Iggo 1974, Darian-Smith 1981, Vallbo et al 1979); Vallbo et al (1979) and Darian-Smith (1981) focused mainly on the innervation of the hand in man and other primates.

In Table 1 the four functionally distinctive mechanoreceptor types innervating ridged digital and palmar skin [quickly or rapidly adapting (QA or RA) fibers, Pacinian afferents, two types of slowly adapting fiber (SAI and SAII)] have been identified with the four structurally specialized receptor endings found in these tissues (Meissner corpuscles, Pacinian corpuscles, Merkel endings, and Ruffini end organs). While probably correct, this identification remains circumstantial. The most compelling correlation is that of the frequency response characteristics of digital "Pacinian" afferents and of Pacinian corpuscles isolated along with their fiber from the cat's mesentary (Sato 1961, Talbot et al 1968). This strongly suggests that those digital mechanoreceptive fibers with an optimal frequency response in the range 200–300 Hz innervate one of the 200–300 Pacinian corpuscles occurring in the primate finger. The remaining correlations are based on extrapolations from studies of cat hairy skin (Iggo & Muir 1969, Chambers et al 1972) and on the frequency of occurrence of the different structural and functional populations innervating the digits and palmar skin.

In two recent studies, one in man (Johansson & Vallbo 1979) and the other in the macaque (Darian-Smith & Kenins 1980), the densities of mechanoreceptor innervation of the finger and palm have been estimated. Although there are substantial sources of error in the methods used, the human and monkey data matched quite well, illustrating the high innervation densities of quickly adapting (QA) and slowly adapting (SA) fibers in the finger pad relative to that of the Pacinian fiber populations (Table 1). With such a disparity, in which the innervation density of Pacinian fibers is 5–7 times less than for QA and SA fibers, the spatial pattern of responses in the Pacinian fiber population is unlikely to provide key information about the fine spatial features of a textured surface being examined with the finger pads. A second finding of these studies was that the mechanoreceptive QA and SA fiber innervation densities fall off rapidly in the proximal part of the finger, and even more in the palmar glabrous skin.

Table 1 Afferent fibers innervating digital and palmar skin of primate

Receptor class	Fiber properties (conduction Vel.) m/s	Site of terminal	Finger pad innervation density[a]	Skin receptive field	Response to indentation	Frequency response Hz	Representation of spatial features of texture
Mechano-receptors							
Meissner	Large myelinated (35–70)	dermis	178 cm^2	small, circumscribed	quickly adapting	20–40	high fidelity
Pacinian	(35–70)	dermis	13 cm^2	large, poorly defined edge	quickly adapting	200–300	poor
Merkel ending	(35–70)	epidermis	134 cm^2	small, circumscribed	slowly adapting	complex; 0–20	high fidelity
Ruffini/Golgi	—	dermis		small, but poorly defined edge			
					Response characteristics		
Thermo-receptors							
"Cold" fibers	Small myelinated (5–30)	dermis	50 cm^2 (monkey palm)	<1 mm in diameter	Respond briskly to cooling pulse with onset transient; "Paradoxical Discharge" at 45°–50°C		
"Warm" fibers	Unmyelinated (0.4–2.5)	dermis	(?) similar to "cold" fibers	<1 mm in diameter	Respond briskly to warming pulse with small onset transient; stops firing at 48°–50°C		
Nociceptors							
Mechanical nociceptor	Small myelinated (10–30) *and* Unmyelinated (0.3–2.0)	dermis	(?)	small <5 mm^2	Respond only to noxious distortion of skin; no thermal response.		
Polymodal nociceptor	(10–30) *and* (0.3–2.0)	dermis	(?)	small <5 mm^2	Responds to noxious distortion of skin, to heating to 46°–50°C and cooling to 0°–10°C		

[a] Darian-Smith & Kenins (1980).

THERMORECEPTORS Knowledge of cutaneous thermoreceptors has expanded considerably in the last decade for two main reasons. First, quantitative studies of the responses of these fibers to controlled rapid changes in skin temperature have become a reality with the development of several good thermal stimulators (Hilder et al 1974, Kenshalo & Bergen 1975). Second, analyses of the fiber populations in cutaneous nerves in the primate begun in the late 1960s immediately revealed that cold fibers, uniquely excited by cooling the skin, suppressed by warming the same skin, and unresponsive to mechanical deformation of the same region, are common in these nerves (Iggo 1969, Hensel & Iggo 1971, Darian-Smith et al 1973, Johnson et al 1973, Dubner et al 1974, 1975, Kenshalo & Duclaux, 1977). In the median nerve at the wrist in the macaque, for example (Darian-Smith et al 1973), cold fibers constitute about one-third of all myelinated fibers with conduction velocities in the range 5–30 m/s (A delta fibers), the mean innervation density of the monkey palm being of the order of 50 cold fibers/cm^2. Later studies showed that warm fibers, uniquely excited by localized warming of the skin, are also common in primate cutaneous nerves (Iggo 1969, Torebjork 1974, Konietzny & Hensel 1977, Darian-Smith et al 1979a,b, Darian-Smith & Johnson 1977, LaMotte & Campbell 1978, Johnson et al 1979, Darian-Smith 1980. Duclaux & Kenshalo 1980), making up a substantial fraction of the total population of unmyelinated fibers in the nerve.

These findings provide the answer to a dilemma confronting previous investigators of the cutaneous fiber populations subserving thermal sensibility. Daily experience and also laboratory measurement indicate that we can detect quite small changes in skin temperature that may occur on touching a warm or cool object with the fingers or forearm (Johnson et al 1973, 1979). Nonetheless, previous investigators over many years failed to identify more than a handful of thermoreceptor fibers in the cutaneous nerves of the hairy skin and footpads of common laboratory animals such as the cat. The reason for this apparent mismatch in sensory behavior and receptor machinery was, of course, due to the fact that thermal sensory performance differs substantially among different mammalian species. Macaques and man are essentially similar in their capacities to identify quite small changes in the temperature of the palmar and digital skin (Kenshalo & Hall 1974, Kenshalo 1976, Molinari et al 1976). Furthermore, to the extent that present studies allow comparison (Konietzny & Hensel 1977), the thermoreceptive fiber populations innervating palmar skin in man and the macaque are also quite similar. The cat on the other hand is quite unresponsive to changes in the temperature of the skin of the limbs and footpad until the skin temperature rises to a noxious level (Kenshalo et al 1967, Kenshalo 1970). The virtual absence of thermoreceptor fibers in limb cutaneous nerves in the cat is therefore no surprise.

NOCICEPTORS The reader is referred to the recent extensive review by Perl (1981) for appraisal of recent investigations in this field.

Representation of "Tactile" Stimuli in the Responses of Digital Nerve Fiber Populations

Having identified the functionally different mechanoreceptive fiber populations innervating the ridged skin of the finger pads, the next step in characterizing the digital nerve fiber population is to assess what features of a particular "tactile" stimulus are represented, first in the response of individual fibers and then in the responses of populations of these fibers. Recent work on the representation within the macaque's digital nerve fiber population of the spatial pattern of a textured surface moving across the finger pad is selected to illustrate such an analysis.

Texture Discrimination

Each of the many textured surfaces that we touch and individually identify has a unique combination of physical properties on which its identity is based. However, specifying those physical features which characterize, for example, a velvet surface, and in turn account for its unique tactile characteristics, is quite difficult. Manufacturing a series of velvets in which one or several of its specifying parameters is systematically altered is even more difficult. The technical problems in constructing suitable graded surfaces have certainly limited investigations of texture discrimination in which the observer's performance was correlated with systematic changes in the spatial characteristics of the surface. Recently experiments of this type have been done using surfaces with simple geometric patterns (Darian-Smith & Oke 1980, Darian-Smith et al 1980, Johnson & Lamb 1981).

SPATIAL GRATINGS A ridged spatial grating with a period of 0.25-1.00 mm, constructed of metal or plastic, is one of the simplest of textured surfaces, its pattern being fully specified in a single dimension by the spatial period and the cycle profile (sinusoidal, square-wave, sawtooth, etc). In differentiating two such surfaces that differ incrementally in their spatial periods, the observer typically rubs the sensing finger to and fro across each surface before making any judgment. For gratings with spatial periods within the range 0.70–1.00 mm, a trained observer will correctly identify with a probability of 0.75 a 3% change in the spatial period. The observer's resolution is only slightly modified by quite large changes in the pattern of movement of the finger over the surfaces, or by changes in contact force between the finger pad and the surface (G. Casper, I. Darian-Smith, and A. W. Goodwin, unpublished data; Morley 1980).

Rather than simply differentiating gratings, the observer may attempt to assess the roughness of the surface and scale surfaces accordingly. With gratings with a ridge to groove ratio of about 1:7, the subjective estimate of the roughness of the surface increases linearly with the spatial period (Morley 1980). With rectangular periodic gratings, in which the widths of the grooves and intervening ridges may be altered independently, Lederman (1974, 1976), Lederman & Taylor (1972), and Taylor and coworkers (1973, 1975) have shown that the subjective estimate of roughness depends on each of these parameters. The apparent roughness of the surface increases with the widening of the grooves in the grating, and decreases, to a lesser degree, with widening of the ridges between the grooves. The pattern of movement of the sensing finger over the surface again had little effect on the subjective roughness, but the latter did increase as the contact force between the finger pad and the surface was increased to the upper limits of normal usage.

As the finger pad moves across the gratings or other textured surface, all low-threshold mechanoreceptors innervating the digital skin contacting the surface will discharge. Since an observer can resolve small changes in the spatial frequency of the surface largely independently of the movement pattern of the finger, this dimension of the surface must be represented within the discharge of the digital nerve in some way which is little influenced by the profile of movement of the sensing finger or by fluctuations in contact force. Darian-Smith & Oke (1980) examined this neural representation in the responding populations of QA, SA, and Pacinian fibers in the digital nerve of the macaque. The grating was mounted on a rotating drum that could be lowered onto and raised from the skin, providing precise control of (*a*) the velocity of the surface moving across the skin, (*b*) the contact force and the duration of contact, and (*c*) the spatial relationship of the surface to the underlying skin at any instant during the period of contact.

Figure 1 illustrates the response of a single QA fiber innervating the macaque's finger pad to three gratings of differing spatial periods (1025, 790, and 550 microns), each moving across the skin with velocities of 22, 66, and 142 mm/s (within the range normally used by the human observer in exploring a surface). With each stimulus combination of spatial period and velocity of movement, the feature represented in the fiber responses was the stimulus temporal frequency, a derivative of these two parameters (temporal frequency = spatial frequency X velocity = velocity/spatial period). For the QA fiber responses in Figure 1, this correspondence with the stimulus temporal frequency was simplest in the range 64–140 Hz (middle and upper right columns). The stimulus temporal frequency was also represented in the fiber response evoked by each of the surfaces moving slowly across the skin (left column), but now instead of a 1:1 correlation, 2–3 impulses occurred during each stimulus cycle. With the finer gratings moving rapidly across the skin (lower right column), the stimulus temporal

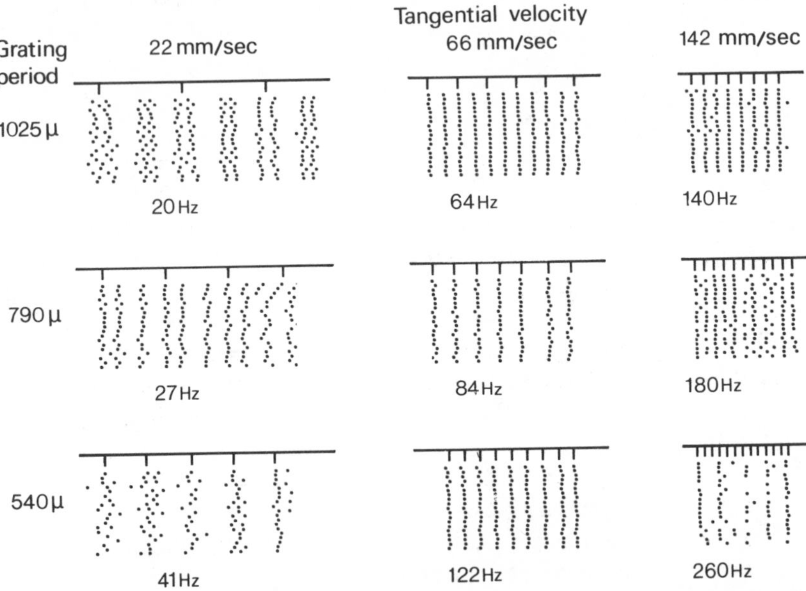

Figure 1. Responses of a Meissner afferent to three different gratings (spatial period of 1025, 790, and 540 microns) moving across the receptive field at three different velocities (22, 66, and 142 mm/sec). The fiber's receptive field was on the fingerpad of the index finger. The radial force was 60 g wt and contact area was approximately 5 X 5 mm. Each response block is a segment of the response beginning approximately 500 msec after the onset of stimulation. The stimulus temporal frequency is indicated by the vertical bars above each response block, and its numerical value is stated below the block. The response frequency accurately reflected the stimulus frequency in the range 64–140 Hz. At frequencies below 64 Hz the stimulus temporal frequency was represented in the modulation of discharge but not in the mean discharge frequency; at stimulus temporal frequencies above 140 Hz, although the response was phase-locked to the stimulus, the fiber did not respond to each successive cycle of the stimulus and hence mean discharge frequency did not equal the stimulus temporal frequency (Darian-Smith & Oke, 1980).

frequency was now no longer well represented in the fiber discharge. A correspondence between the stimulus temporal frequency and the discharge patterns of Pacinian and SA fibers was also observed, the frequency range over which the mean response frequency of the fiber equaled the stimulus temporal frequency being a characteristic of the fiber type. With Pacinian fibers this 1:1 relationship was in the range 140–260 Hz and the SA fibers in the range 20–60 Hz.

These data imply that the spatial frequency of the grating is never unambiguously represented in the responses of single cutaneous mechanoreceptive fibers: information about the spatial features of the surface and the velocity with which it moves across the skin are always confounded. It follows that the observer's resolution of the spatial features of the surface depend on the pattern of discharge in the whole *fiber population* engaged by the moving surface. Darian-Smith & Oke (1980) modeled this representation of the spatial frequency of the moving grating in the responding fiber population. From this synthesis it was apparent that the fidelity of neural representation of the spatial frequency of the grating depends on (*a*) the precision of representation of the stimulus temporal frequency in the responses of individual fibers, (*b*) the uniformity of response among the constituent fibers of the population, (*c*) the innervation density of the skin contacting the surface, and (*d*) the area of contact between the surface and the skin. Because of their low innervation density in the finger pad (Table 1), Pacinian fibers probably contribute little to the peripheral neural representation of the spatial features of gratings. QA and SA fibers, on the other hand, specify the spatial frequency of the grating quite well, and their joint response probably accounts for the resolution of incremental changes in these surfaces.

TWO-DIMENSIONED SPATIAL PATTERNS Most of the textured surfaces that we touch and identify differ from gratings in that they have two independently changing spatial dimensions rather than one. A simply constructed surface with these characteristics is a square or rectangular array of embossed circular dots, as shown in Figure 2. G. Lamb (unpublished data) has shown that incremental changes in the longitudinal or transverse spacing of these dots (relative to the direction of movement of the surface) of the order of 2–3% of the spacing could be correctly identified. As with the differentiation of gratings, this resolution was little influenced by the pattern of movement of the actively exploring finger, or whether the surface was actively explored or rather passed across the immobilized finger pad.

To account for this resolution, both spatial dimensions of the patterned surface must be represented in the responding digital nerve fiber population. Both spatial dimensions do, in fact, systematically modify the responses of single cutaneous mechanoreceptive fibers when the surface traverses the fiber's receptive field. This is shown in Figure 2 for an SA fiber responding to a series of patterned surfaces that moved across the receptive field with a fixed velocity. Using such observations on QA, SA, and Pacinian fibers, Darian-Smith, Davidson & Johnson (1980) attempted to build up a picture of the responses of *populations* of these fibers to "dot" patterns moving across the finger pad. Faithful representation of the two dimensions of the patterned surface, independent of the movement of the surface across the skin, was possible only within a population of fibers whose receptive fields had a specified spatial distribution within the skin of the finger pad in

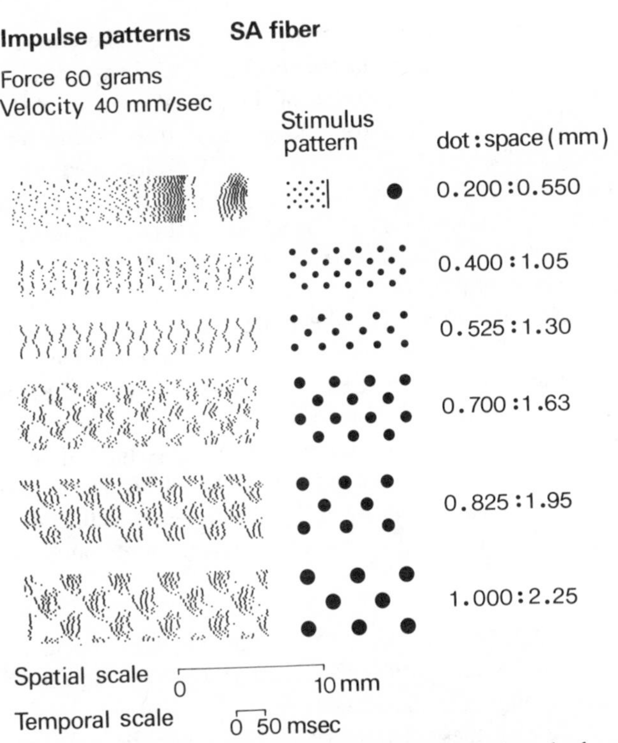

Figure 2. Series of discharge patterns (left-hand column) evoked in a slowly adapting mechanoreceptive fiber that specify its responses to six differently patterned textured surfaces: these surfaces moved across the skin with a velocity of 40 mm/sec and with a contact force of 60 g wt. The fiber's receptive field was on the index finger pad in a macaque. The fiber response to each sweep of the surface across the skin is indicated by a single row of small dots, with each dot representing the occurrence of a single action potential. Each response pattern was generated by the passage of the textured surface 20–40 times across the finger pad. Between successive sweeps the moving surface was displaced 0.25 mm lateral to its direction of movement, so that with 40 sweeps the total lateral shift of the surface was 5.00 mm. With each sweep the instantaneous position of the surface relative to the skin was defined and could be related to each action potential in the fiber discharge. The patterns of the moving nyloprint surfaces are shown in the middle column: the common pattern was a diamond-shaped array of elevated dots whose diameter and separation are indicated in the right-hand column. The surface used in the second row differed from the others in that a transverse ridge and a standard "braille" dot were also presented (data from Darian-Smith et al 1980).

contact with the surface. It was concluded from these studies that most information about the spatial features of the dot pattern is relayed to the central nervous system by SA and QA fiber populations. In their studies of the peripheral neural representation of braille patterns, Johnson & Lamb (1981) argued for an even more restrictive representation, mainly within the responding SA fiber population.

The foregoing account of the representation of the spatial pattern of a textured surface within the different populations of responding digital nerve fibers is qualitative. There are still far too many unknown dimensions of the population response to attempt a quantitative description of the representation of even the simplest textured surface.

If a quantitative synthesis of the peripheral neural representation of a particular stimulus is to have any approximation to the real events in that nerve, at present we must use a simple stimulus with few changing parameters, and furthermore a stimulus which selectively activates a single, functionally homogeneous population of fibers within the whole nerve. Once the total representation within a digital nerve of a stimulus applied to the finger pad can be synthesized with fidelity, a measure of the total information signaled to the central nervous system about each feature of the stimulus can be determined. By comparing the subject's behavioral capacity to assess each stimulus parameter with the information relayed to the brain in the digital nerve discharge about the same parameter, some insight into the central neural processing of sensory information is obtained.

Fortunately, the conditions necessary for reconstructing from single fiber responses a realistic model of the responses of a functionally homogeneous population of sensory nerve fibers are met when a cooling or warming pulse is applied to the digital or palmar skin in the monkey. An account of such an investigation follows.

Sensing Changes in Skin Temperature

The two rather different circumstances in which assessing changes in skin temperature are of importance in our daily lives occur (*a*) when there is cooling or warming of much of the exposed skin resulting from changes in the ambient temperature, and (*b*) when quite rapid steplike shifts in temperature occur in localized regions of skin in contact with an object typically being explored with the fingers. Changes in ambient temperature usually cause a fairly slow drift in the temperature of the exposed skin: an extensive literature covers the behavioral and neurophysiological responses to these changes. However, studies of the subjective discrimination and of thermoreceptor responses to sudden changes in skin temperature, such as occurs when one touches a metal surface at room temperature, were delayed until useful laboratory thermal stimulators were developed (Hilder et al 1974, Kenshalo & Bergen 1975).

A subject trained to identify the more intense of successive pairs of cooling or warming "pulses" applied to the palmar skin resolves minute temperature increments in a wide range of experiments (Johnson et al 1973, 1979, Darian-Smith 1980). In these experiments, intensity discrimination was estimated as that increment in the intensity of the temperature pulse differentiated correctly with a probability of 0.75 (difference limen). With cooling pulses applied to a zone of skin about 1 cm^2 in area, the Weber function relating the discriminated temperature increment (range 0.03°–0.07°C) to the mean amplitude of the stimulus (range 1°–8°C) was linear, and not modified by changes in the baseline temperature of the skin in the range 29°–39°C (in the laboratory environment palmar skin temperature was normally 32°–35°C). With warming pulses discrimination was of the same order, but the Weber function was no longer linear, and discrimination fell off somewhat at the lower baseline skin temperature of 29°C.

Kenshalo & Hall (1974) and Molinari et al (1976) have shown that the rhesus monkey is also sensitive to small changes in the temperature of the skin of the palm and of the thigh. Although direct comparison with human measurements is not possible because of the different procedures used, the data suggest that man and the macaque are quite similar in their thermal sensory capacities.

Compared with the mechanoreceptive fiber populations subserving touch, thermoreceptive fiber populations are simple in their organization and in their relation to the subject's assessment of thermal stimuli. When the palmar or digital skin of the monkey is warmed, a single functionally homogeneous population is excited, and similarly when the skin is cooled, a second quite separate fiber population is excited (Iggo 1969, Hensel & Iggo 1971, Darian-Smith et al 1973, 1977, 1979b,c, Darian-Smith 1980, Kenshalo & Duclaux 1977, Duclaux & Kenshalo 1980). We have then unique "labeled lines," populations of warm and cold fibers respectively, which are the sole relay of all the stimulus information on which the subject's sensory performance is based.

Darian-Smith, Johnson and colleagues (Darian-Smith et al 1973, 1979b,c, Johnson et al 1973, 1979) closely compared the human subject's ability to resolve incremental changes in the amplitude of warming and cooling pulses with the representation of this intensity change in the responses of single warm and cold fibers and populations of these fibers in the monkey. In these comparisons it was assumed that the thermoreceptor fiber populations innervating the digital and palmar skin in man and the monkey are essentially similar. The measure in these experiments of the capacity of single fibers, or populations of fibers, to resolve incremental changes in the intensity of the temperature pulse was the discriminable stimulus increment (DSI) defined as that incremental difference in the intensities of a pair of temperature pulses that can be resolved correctly with a probability of 0.75. The DSI is therefore the precise neural equivalent of the different limen, the measure described above of stimulus resolution achieved by the human subject. In the experiments of Darian-Smith and coworkers, the DSI = 0.67 $\sigma_{\Delta r}/(dr/dI)$, where $\sigma_{\Delta r}$ is the standard deviation of the difference in the responses of the fiber (or population of fibers) to pairs of stimuli, and dr/dI is the fiber's (or population's) sensitivity to incremental stimulus change. The basic assumption in using the DSI as the measure of neural resolution is that the larger of the neural responses generated by each pair of thermal stimuli was that evoked by the more intense stimulus; when this is not so, an incorrect judgment would be made.

A critical problem in any comparison of the behavioral discrimination of stimuli and the neural events evoked by these same stimuli is the identification of the response measure (i.e. the "neural code") actually used by the brain in performing this task. Because of the remarkable regularity of the responses of thermoreceptive fibers to temperature pulses, it was apparent in this investigation that most information about the intensity of the pulse was relayed to the brain by the fiber discharge in terms of a rate measure based on the number of impulses occurring during some specific "integration" interval during the period of stimulation. Even when this response measure was maximal in terms of the amount of stimulus information signaled by each response of the fiber, it was found that single thermoreceptive fibers rarely, if ever, signaled sufficient information to the brain to alone account for the subject's ability to resolve incremental changes in the intensity of the warming pulse. Rather, the brain must use information relayed to it by all of the thermoreceptive fibers engaged by the stimulus to achieve the resolution indicated by the subject's performance.

If now a synthesis of the response of the population of thermoreceptive fibers engaged by each successive temperature pulse is attempted, the next key question is: How does the brain combine the information it receives from each responding fiber? The experiments of Darian-Smith and coworkers showed that simply summing or averaging these different inputs, giving equal weighting to the responses of each fiber, would provide marginally sufficient information about the stimuli to account for the subject's discriminative behavior, provided that (*a*) there is little dependent variability among the responding fibers, and (*b*) the transmission of stimulus information by central pathways to the forebrain, the storage of this information, the decision process, and the motor expression of the resulting judgment are all highly efficient and involve minimal loss of sensory information. If these conditions do not pertain, the central process of combining the inputs of individual thermoreceptive fibers must be selective and more efficient, by giving maximal weighting to those fibers relaying the most sensory information and less weight to the more noisy fibers.

CENTRAL NEURAL PROCESSING

In recent years, some of the most active and productive investigations of the central neural processing of somesthetic information have been directed to the functional organization of the spinal dorsal horn, and to those regions of the primate neocortex concerned with the perception of the object world around us. For studies of transmission in the spinal dorsal horn and its trigeminal analog the reader is referred to the following recent papers on the topics indicated: (*a*) terminations of afferent fibers—Brown et al (1977, 1978), Light & Perl (1979a,b); (*b*) functional organization of neuron populations in spinal dorsal horn—Kerr & Casey (1978), C. LaMotte (1977), C. LaMotte et al (1976), Light et al (1979), Snyder & Childers (1979), Chung et al (1979), Price et al (1978), Willis et al (1974), Applebaum et al (1979), Sessle et al (1981); (*c*) supraspinal modulation of transmission in the dorsal spinal horn—Fields & Basbaum (1978), Haber et al (1980), Rivot et al (1980).

TOUCH AND THE PRIMATE CEREBRAL CORTEX

The role of the neocortex in sensorimotor behavior in man and other primates has continuously attracted investigators since the era of Fritsch and Hitzig, Ferrier and Hughlings-Jackson, but the remarkable coincidence of technical advances during the last decade undoubtedly accounts for the recent resurgence of interest. First, several neuroanatomical techniques have been developed for the more effective tracing of axon connections (see review of Jones & Hartman 1978). Already the application of these methods has greatly expanded our knowledge of the intrinsic and extrinsic structural organization of the neocortex in the monkey. The second major advance was initiated by Evarts' (1966) development of methods for recording from single neurons in the forebrain of the alert monkey, interested in its surroundings and anxious to explore everything within reach. Central neural events are now no longer distorted by the action of general anesthetics. However, the investigator must now appreciate the true complexities of sensing the world around us, that touching and identifying an object or surface typically involves coordination of sensory and motor mechanisms, and that the world we perceive very much depends on what we select to perceive. It follows that the stereotyped neural events evoked by tapping or brushing the finger pads of a deeply anesthetized monkey, with activity limited to Somatosensory Areas I and II, are likely to differ substantially from the activity that actually occurs in the monkey manually exploring and identifying an object or surface. Once more, 40 years after the investigations of Woolsey, Marshall & Bard (1942), the following questions are relevant: (*a*) *which regions* of the primate neocortex contribute to the tactual identification of objects and surfaces? (*b*) *what information* about the object or surface, and the exploratory behavior necessary for their identification, is represented in each of the responding regions of neocortex?

(*c*) *how is this information represented* in the responding neuron populations within each of these cortical regions?

Roland et al (1980a,b) have recently reported an elegant assessment of which cortical regions in man are activated during the performance of certain hand movements with proprioceptive and cutaneous feedback. The clearance of ^{133}Xe from 254 sites in the cerebral hemispheres following intracarotid injection was used to measure changes in blood flow in each of these regions; the regional blood flow was taken as an index of local changes in neuronal activity. With the hand still, and the finger pads passively stimulated by moving a surface or object across them, increased regional blood flow was observed only within the contralateral post- and precentral gyri. If the subject now moved his hand to explore a surface or object placed before him (i.e. located in "extrapersonal space"), blood flow in the posterior parietal cortex increased bilaterally. With stereotyped repetitive movements of the fingers, no additional focal activation of the cortex was observed, but if the finger movements were complex, requiring careful sequencing and positioning of one finger relative to the others (i.e. movement in "intrapersonal" space), then the region of the "supplementary motor cortex" became active bilaterally. This latter observation, and that of the bilateral activation of posterior parietal cortex occurring with movements in "extrapersonal" but not "intrapersonal" space, point to the need for assessing the respective contributions to tactile exploratory behavior, not only of the established somatosensory cortical regions (somatosensory areas I and II), but also the posterior parietal cortex, the precentral "motor" cortex, and the supplementary motor cortex. We need to assess what information is processed within each zone, how this information is represented within the response of the constituent neuron populations, and how different behavioral states, such as the subject's direct attention to the object being examined, influence each neuron population. In the remainder of this chapter, recent developments in our understanding of these six cortical zones are reviewed briefly.

Postcentral Gyrus

The first somatosensory area of the cerebral cortex (SI) of anthropoid primates is differentiable into three cytoarchitectonic subfields, areas 3, 1, and 2 of Brodmann (Brodmann 1905, Powell & Mountcastle 1959a). The view that each structurally distinctive cortical field subserves a specific function was greatly reinforced by the report by Powell & Mountcastle (1959b) of functionally different neuron populations within areas 3, 1, and 2 of the macaque neocortex. Since that report all systematic studies of the functional organization of the postcentral gyrus have taken account of the underlying structural subdivisions. This, in turn, has led to more rigorous analysis of the structural uniqueness of areas 3, 1, and 2, as well as that of the adjacent cortical areas 4 (motor), 6, and the parietal areas 5 and 7.

CONNECTIONS OF POSTCENTRAL GYRUS Two groups (Jones and coworkers 1976, 1977, 1978, 1979a,b, and Kaas and coworkers 1979) have recently sought to define systematically each cortical subfield within the postcentral gyrus in terms of both intrinsic structure and of connectivity. Similar histological methods were used, the anterograde radiographic technique with local injection of tritiated proline or leucine being used to visualize the pattern of termination of fibers, and the retrograde transport of horseradish peroxidase to examine the cells or origin of these fibers. Lin et al (1979) combined their histological studies with detailed microelectrode mapping of the postcentral gyrus.

The cytoarchitectonic fields areas 3a (between precentral motor area 4 and area 3b), 3b, 1, 2, and 5 are not sharply demarcated, the least defined boundaries being between areas 2 and 5 (parietal) and between areas 3a and 3b. Functionally the most important extrinsic connections of the postcentral gyrus are with the dorsal thalamus. There is consensus (Jones and coworkers 1979b, Lin et al 1979) that areas 3b and 1 receive input from thalamic neurons strictly limited to the ventrobasal complex (caudal division of ventroposterolateral nucleus and the ventroposteromedial nucleus; Mountcastle & Henneman 1952). Jones et al (1979b) found area 2 to have a similar input from the ventrobasal complex, but Lin et al (1979) report a thalamic projection from the lateral posterior nucleus in the owl monkey. This apparent disparity probably stems from the uncertainties concerning the boundary between areas 2 and 5, as Jones & Burton (1976) actually define area 2 by its ventrobasal thalamic connections and the adjacent area 5 by its connections with the lateral posterior nucleus. The more caudal part of area 5 differs again in having a thalamic input from the anterior nucleus of the pulvinar. More anteriorly, that part of area 3a adjacent to area 3b also receives input from the ventrobasal complex and is regarded by Jones et al (1979b) as part of area 3b. The rostral part of area 3a, on the other hand, distinguished by the presence of large pyramidal cells, is considered by these investigators to be part of the precentral motor area 4, as it lacks input from the ventrobasal complex, but like area 4, does have input from the oral division of the ventroposterolateral nucleus and the caudal nucleus of the ventrolateral complex. The topographical organization of the ventrobasal complex in terms of thalamocortical connections reported both by Jones et al (1979b) and Lin et al (1979), is quite compatible with the earlier description of Mountcastle & Henneman (1952), of a single representation of the contralateral body surface. The differences in the two recent sets of data are in detail rather than in essentials. Finally, associated with all the thalamocortical projections to the postcentral gyrus described above there was a reciprocal corticothalamic connection (Jones et al 1979b, Lin et al 1979).

The corticospinal projection provides an additional cue to the functional differentiation of areas 4, 3a, 3b, 1, 2, and 5. Earlier studies (Kuypers 1960) demonstrated the separate projection from the postcentral gyrus to the intermediate zone of the contralateral spinal dorsal horn, and the precentral corticomotoneuronal projection to the spinal ventral horn. Coulter & Jones (1977) examined the sites of termination within the monkey spinal cord of corticospinal fibers arising from each cortical subfield. The well-documented projection from the precentral motor area 4 (see Phillips & Porter 1977) terminates in the lateral part of the neck and intermediate zone of the contralateral dorsal horn, and among motoneurons in the more dorsal part of the ventral horn. Corticospinal fibers from areas 3b, 1, and 2 terminate quite differently, mainly in the medial half of the Rexed laminae 4 and 5, but also in laminae 3 and 6. The corticospinal projection from area 5 in the parietal cortex is also mainly to spinal laminae 4 and 5, but to their lateral side. Finally, area 3a has a corticospinal projection overlapping both those of the precentral motor cortex (area 4) and of areas 3b, 1, and 2 (Somatosensory Area I); some fibers in addition terminate more ventrally in the motor nucleus.

The pattern of corticocortical connections (Jones, Coulter & Hendry 1978) of the pre- and postcentral cortical fields further reinforces the conclusions based on their intrinsic structure and their connections with the dorsal thalamus, namely, that areas 3b, 1, and 2 are distinctive, that probably area 3a is not, and that the boundary between areas 2 and 5 is best defined by the cortical terminations of projections from the ventrobasal complex and lateral posterior nucleus of the thalamus. Corticocortical connections between these zones and the precentral areas 4 and 6 are extensive, but surprisingly there are no such connections between areas 3b and 4. The medial part of area 6, identified as the supplementary motor cortex, has quite extensive connections: this zone is reciprocally connected with areas 4 (Jones et al 1978) and 3a and 5, and receives input from areas 1 and 2 also. Finally, areas 3b, 1, and 2 each project to the second somatosensory Area II (SII), a connection considered more fully in a later section.

REPRESENTATION OF BODY SURFACE IN POSTCENTRAL GYRUS

More than 40 years ago, Woolsey, Marshall & Bard (1942) prepared "somatotopic" maps of the postcentral gyrus of the monkey, illustrating the zones of neocortex activated by brief tactile stimulation of the body surface. Important conclusions from these studies were: (*a*) the "tactile" sensory cortex includes Brodmann areas 3, 1, and 2; (*b*) there is sequential representation of the contralateral body surface from toes (or tail) to tongue, which is imperfect and does display some discontinuities in the cervical and limb projections; and (*c*) regions of the body surface with the greatest tactile acuity are maximally represented in the cortical projection to the postcentral gyrus. These conclusions remain valid, but the concept of a single rather than a multiple representation of the body surface within the postcentral cortex has been revised in the light of subsequent physiological studies and of the anatomical studies reviewed earlier. Powell & Mountcastle (1959b) demonstrated a segregation of different mechanoreceptive neuron populations within areas 3, 1, and 2, each of which received input from the same site on the contralateral body surface. This finding certainly did not appear to be compatible with a single "somatotopic" representation of the contralateral body surface. Subsequently, Werner and Whitsel and coworkers (Werner & Whitsel 1968, Whitsel et al 1971, Dreyer et al 1975) and Paul et al (1972) reported replication of the hand within areas 3 and 1 of the postcentral gyrus. A recent intensive study of this representation in new and old world monkeys (Merzenich et al 1978, Kaas et al 1979, Nelson et al 1980), using microelectrode recording in anesthetized animals, has demonstrated one full representation of the contralateral body surface within area 3b and a second in area 1; within each projection neurons responded to tactile cutaneous stimulation. Less convincing evidence was obtained in this study of a third tactile representation in area 2, and possibly a fourth in area 3a. In the last-named projections the input was considered to be mainly from deep somatic tissues, and with area 3a particularly from muscle afferents (cf Phillips et al 1971, Lucier et al 1975).

Figure 3 illustrates part of this somatotopic representation within areas 3b and 1 in the macaque (Nelson et al 1980): the projection is from the contralateral hand. The glabrous and hairy skin of the hand are fully represented in each subfield, the finger pads being rostral in area 3b and caudal in Area 1, so that one projection is the mirror image of the other.

The elegance of the recent studies of somatotopy within the postcentral gyrus must not mask their limitations. Anesthetized monkeys have been used for these studies, and as Iwamura, Tanaka & Hikosaka (1980) emphasize, the anesthetic may well distort the responses of cortical neurons, particularly of cells transmitting complex information. These investigators describe neurons in area 2 in active, alert monkeys that did not respond to simple punctate stimuli, but only to more complex stimulation of the skin or by manipulation of several adjacent joints. Some cells responded to both cutaneous and joint stimulation. Within this population of cells there was no simple somatotopic replication of the peripheral receptor sheet. Indeed, even with populations of cortical neurons in which somatotopic organization is a feature, the precise definition of this organization may provide little insight into the real functions of these populations.

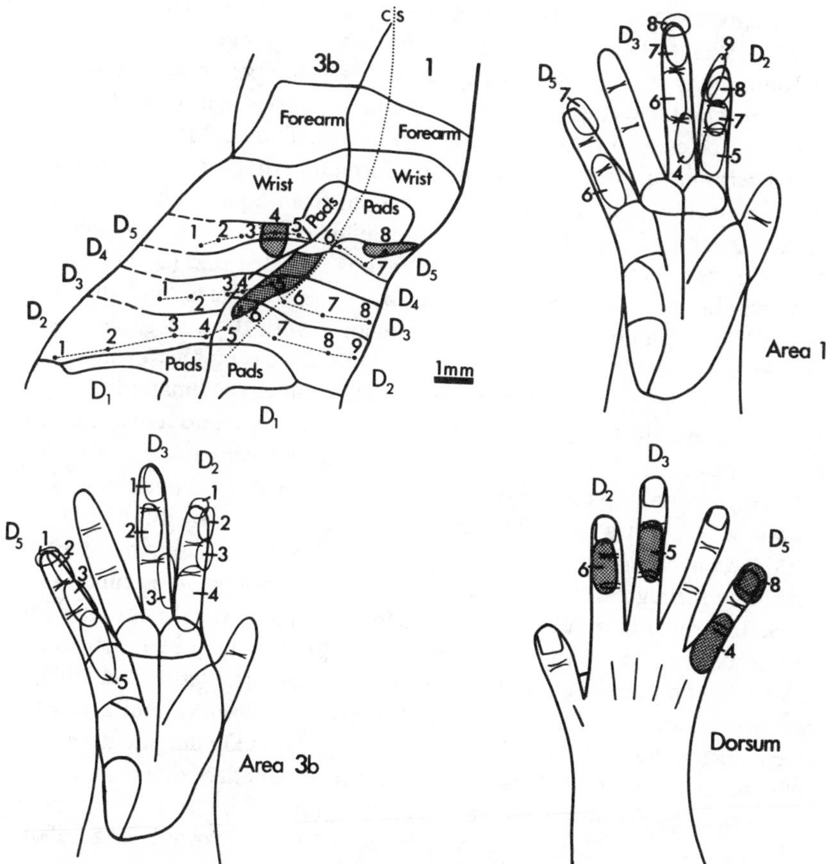

Figure 3. Receptive fields for the representations of the glabrous and hairy surfaces of the hand in Areas 3b and 1 in the macaque. The shaded areas represent the dorsum of the digits. The solid lines in the Area 3b digit representations indicate the maximum depth at which effective recordings were obtained in this experiment. The solid lines to the left indicate the Area 3b-3a border as defined architectonically in this case. Other experiments indicate that the most rostral portion of Area 3b contains the representation of the digit tips and of the nailbeds (Nelson et al 1980).

Finally, what does a multiple somatotopic representation within the post-central gyrus imply? Most investigators interpret such a finding to indicate that the neurons contributing to each representation subserve different functions, that discrete lesions in areas 3b, 1, 2, or 5 might well have different effeets on tactile sensory behavior, and further that the neuron populations within each subfield would have different response characteristics.

REPRESENTATION OF OTHER STIMULUS FEATURES IN POSTCENTRAL GYRUS Demonstrating a replicated representation of the contralateral body surface and underlying tissues in the postcentral gyrus has been important, but the location of a stimulus is but one of its many features that must be coded in the somatosensory cortex. The next step in analysis is to determine the processing of tactile information that occurs within each of the neuron populations that receives input from a particular site, such as the finger pad. In the earlier investigation of Powell & Mountcastle (1959a,b) and Mountcastle et al (1969) it was reported that (*a*) most neurons within area 3b have small cutaneous receptive fields, and that the proportion of the mechanoreceptive population with these receptive fields falls successively in areas 1 and 2; (*b*) complementing this change, an increasing proportion of neurons with input from deep somatic tissues is found in areas 3b, 1, and 2 (and area 5); (*c*) area 3a does not contribute to this rostro-caudal distribution gradient, since a high proportion of its neurons respond only to input from deep tissues [from skeletal muscle, as was shown subsequently by Phillips et al (1971) and Lucier et al (1975)]; (*d*) within each cortical area there are vertically oriented columns of cells extending through all layers of the cortex, which have common functional properties, such as similar receptive fields; and (*e*) cortical neurons with cutaneous input from digital and palmar ridged skin may be functionally subdivided on the basis of input from slowly adapting (Merkel and Ruffini receptor endings), quickly adapting (Meissner corpuscles), and Pacinian mechanoreceptor fiber populations; of these the quickly adapting cortical cells are the commonest. Subsequent studies in anesthetized and alert, active monkeys largely confirmed these observations (Whitsel, Dreyer & Roppolo 1971, Paul et al 1972, Hyvarinen & Poranen 1978a,b, Soso & Fetz 1980).

Although most mechanoreceptive neurons in the postcentral gyrus have the characteristics described above, more complex neurons have been described. Hyvarinen & Poranen (1978a,b) observed a few cells with input from the fingers with both excitatory and inhibitory receptive fields that were discontinuous. Other cells with input from both the skin and deep tissues were reported, but of course for cells innervating the fingers this distinction is difficult to confirm. Several investigators (Hyvarinen & Poranen, 1978a,b, Iwamura & Tanaka 1978, Whitsel, Dreyer & Hollins 1978, Costanzo & Gardner 1980, Gardner & Costanzo 1980) have reported postcentral neurons, especially within areas 1 and 2, which, although relatively insensitive to punctate stimulation of the skin, responded briskly to stimuli moving across the skin. Some neurons responded to the movement of a brush in any direction across the receptive field, but others were selective, discharging vigorously to the movement of the brush in one direction but not to movement in the reverse direction. If the brush moved across the skin at some intermediate angle, the cell response was submaximal and graded according to the angle of the axis of movement. Although peripheral factors that reduce the effectiveness of the mechanical stimulus when it moves in some directions across the skin cannot be entirely discounted, Hyvarinen & Poranen (1978a) and Gardner & Costanzo (1980) favor a central neural mechanism to account for this sensitivity. Barlow & Levick (1965) and others have previously described such mechanisms to account for the direction sensitivity of retinal ganglion cells. They proposed a simple neuronal circuit in which rapidly developing lateral inhibition is generated by the stimulus moving in one direction but not in the reverse.

In a recent study, Hyvarinen, Poranen & Jokinen (1980) have examined the effect of selective attention on the responses of postcentral neurons. A monkey was trained to attend, on cue, to a vibratory stimulus applied to the digital or palmar skin. With more than 80% of neurons responding to the cutaneous stimulus, there was no change in the evoked discharge when the monkey selectively attended to the stimulus or alternatively ignored it. Some augmentation of the response was observed in 16% of the sample when the animal attended to the stimulus, but the functional relevance of this minimal response, and the mediating neural mechanism, are not obvious.

Compared with the substantial transformation observed in the information relayed about the spatial features of visual stimuli by single retinal ganglion cells and by striate neurons, the reported response characteristics of postcentral mechanoreceptive neurons are uninteresting. Intuitively, however, it seems unlikely that the cortical processing of tactile sensory information is as limited as the available studies suggest. A possible reason why so little neural transformation has been observed is that inappropriate cutaneous stimuli have been used. As was considered earlier, we touch surfaces to discern their fine spatial features, to identify their texture, and to achieve this the finger pads must be moved across the surface. Central neural processing in some way extracts information about these spatial features from the total neural representation of the stimulus. The extensive representation of the spatial dimensions of visual stimuli in striate cortex certainly leads one to expect more from the somatosensory cortex than has been reported so far.

SENSORY LOSS FOLLOWING LOCALIZED LESIONS OF THE POSTCENTRAL GYRUS Analysis of the sensory deficit resulting from focal lesions of the neocortex provides, at best, quite indirect information about the functions of the cortex that has been removed (Eidelberg & Stein 1974). Nonetheless, the study of patients and of experimental animals with such lesions has contributed greatly to our present understanding of cortical function. One is reminded of the importance of this approach by the recently published *Selected Papers of Gordon Holmes* (1979). Two recent clinical studies (Corkin, Milner & Rasmussen 1970, Roland 1976) of patients with focal parietal lesions involving the hand area in the postcentral gyrus have demonstrated a permanent tactile deficit in the contralateral hand in which punctate pressure sensitivity, two-point localization, point localization, and position sense in the fingers were impaired. In addition, these patients were unable to assess the size and shape of objects held in the hand. With parietal lesions which spared the hand area of the postcentral gyrus, there was no impairment of tactile sensibility. LaMotte & Mountcastle (1978, 1979) examined the effects of similar lesions of the parietal cortex in the macaque on the animal's capacity to detect vibratory stimuli applied to the ridged skin of the palm and to discriminate changes in amplitude and in frequency of these stimuli. Following the ablation of the postcentral gyrus, the monkey's capacity to detect vibratory stimuli with frequencies of 10, 30, and 200 Hz was temporally impaired only in the contralateral hand, as was the ability to resolve incremental changes in the amplitude of the vibratory stimulus (at frequencies of 30–40 Hz). Frequency discrimination in the range of 30–40 Hz was also impaired following the ablation of SI. If both SI and SII were ablated, frequency discrimination was permanently reduced, but the capacity to detect the occurrence of vibratory stimuli, and changes in their amplitude, did recover considerably in the weeks following the operation. No ipsilateral sensory deficit was observed.

Randolph & Semmes (1974) and Semmes et al (1974) made the next logical step in ablation studies of the postcentral gyrus. They looked for more selective deficits in tactile sensibility in the macaque following removal of the hand area in Brodmann areas 3b, 1, or 2. Microelectrode mapping of the cortex was used to ensure the accurate placing of the lesion. The most severe permanent sensory deficit resulted from a focal lesion in area 3b, when the monkey's ability to both assess "textures" and the size and shape of objects held in the hand were impaired. With a lesion of area 1 the major sensory loss appeared to be the identification and differentiation of textured surfaces, whereas with lesions of area 2 the main sensory loss was reflected in the monkey's inability to differentiate square and diamond shapes. Randolph and Semmes judged this to indicate an inability to assess angle between converging surfaces (a kinesthetic deficit?). This study now needs to be extended to examine the monkey's capacity to detect and differentiate vibratory stimuli, and also to differentiate a variety of textured surfaces.

Somatosensory Area II

The second somatosensory area (SII) was first described in the macaque by Woolsey (1943). Recent anatomical and microelectrode studies have greatly improved our knowledge of the organization of this region of cortex, and ablation studies have at least demonstrated that the integrity of this area of cortex is necessary for normal tactile sensibility. As with SI, however, the neural processing of sensory information within SII is still poorly understood.

CONNECTIONS OF SOMATOSENSORY AREA II (SII) SII is a relatively inaccessible region of cortex in the primate, being located mainly in the parietal operculum overlying the insula (Figure 4). Anatomically SII is differentiated from adjacent cortex by its particular cytoarchitecture, but more specifically by its substantial reciprocal connections with the ventrobasal complex of the thalamus (Jones & Powell 1970, Jones & Burton 1976, Friedman et al 1980). This thalamocortical projection is somatotopically organized.

SII also has well-developed connections with areas 3b, 1, and 2 of the postcentral gyrus. These connections are both reciprocal and bilateral (Jones & Powell 1969a,b, Jones, Coulter & Wise 1979a). Somatotopy is sustained in these corticocortical projections, but there is apparently convergence of input from area 3b, 1, and 2 onto the topographically equivalent area in SII. The transcallosal connections between SI and SII link somatotopically equivalent cortical areas, with the exception that the hand and foot areas lack this connection (Jones & Powell 1969a,b, Jones et al 1979a).

A remaining corticocortical connection of SII is with area 4 which is again reciprocal. Surprisingly, SII apparently has no other direct cortical link.

RESPONSE CHARACTERISTICS OF NEURONS IN SII Single neuron recording in the parietal operculum in the alert macaque (Robinson & Burton 1980a,b,c) immediately demonstrates that many neurons both within SII and in the surrounding cortex respond to gentle mechanical stimulation of the skin, and that they cannot be simply differentiated by their response properties. Robinson and Burton identified and characterized neurons strictly within SII, as defined by its reciprocal connections with the ventrobasal complex of the thalamus. They found that the majority of SII neurons responded to light mechanical stimulation of the skin, that most cells had receptive fields on the contralateral body surface that were comparable in size and sharpness of their boundaries with cells located in areas 3b and 1, and that there was an orderly but complex topographic representation of the contralateral body surface within SII. Neurons with receptive fields on the face or within the mouth were located in the anterior part of SII, and mostly had bilateral symmetrical receptive fields. A small fraction

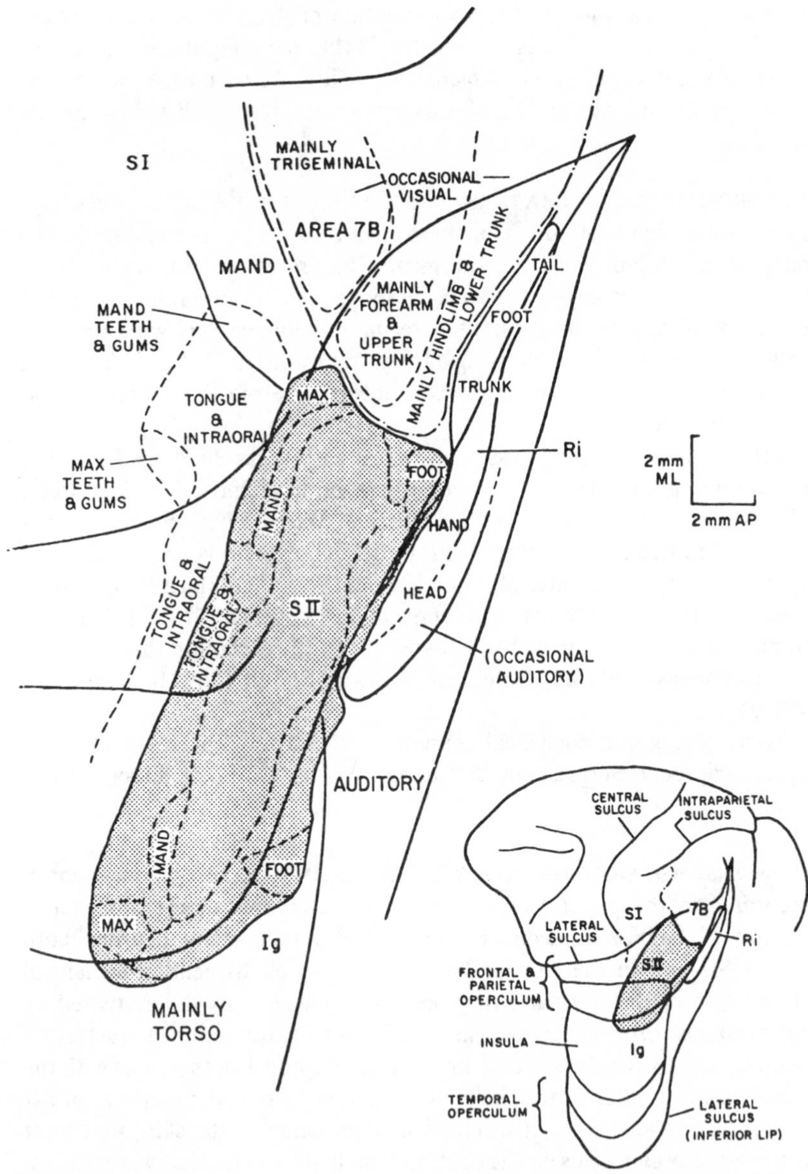

Figure 4. Summary figure of SII and the somatosensory areas surrounding its posterior boundary. Insert figure shows schematically the location of the detailed map on an exposed view of the cortical surface that is normally buried within the lateral sulcus. Scale refers to large figure only (Robinson & Burton 1980a).

of cells with input from the rest of the body surface also had bilateral receptive fields, being least common with input from the hands and feet (cortical zones lacking commissural connections). Figure 5 illustrates the response characteristics of neurons within the hand area of SII in the macaque (Robinson & Burton, 1980a).

As in SI (Mountcastle et al 1969) most cutaneous mechanoreceptive neurons in SII had response characteristics similar to one of the mechanoreceptive fiber types innervating skin. SII neurons with receptive fields on the ridged skin of the fingers or palm, for example, were either slowly adapting or rapidly adapting to sustained indentation of the skin. Although not yet observed in the monkey, Bennett and coworkers (Bennett et al 1980, Ferrington & Rowe 1980) have shown in the cat that the parallel between peripheral mechanoreceptor fiber populations and SII neurons may be extended by examining their responses to cutaneous vibratory stimuli. These investigators observed SII neurons with a frequency response profile matching that of cutaneous Pacinian fibers, with maximal sensitivity in the frequency range 200–300 hz. "Pacinian" SII neurons responded to cutaneous vibratory stimuli in this high frequency range with a periodicity exactly matching the stimulus frequency. Since phase-locking at such high stimulus frequencies is not observed in comparable "Pacinian" neurons in SI (Mountcastle et al 1969), it was proposed that the SII neuron population selectively codes this information.

In addition to the SII neurons described above, Robinson & Burton (1980a) observed cells in two zones adjacent to the hand and digit areas, but still within SII, which were most responsive only when the monkey actively moved the hand across a surface or manipulated a hand-held object. With some of these cells passive mechanical stimulation of the hand elicited no response; the monkey's active involvement was essential. Robinson and Burton also found that many neurons isolated in area 7b, the retroinsular cortex and postauditory cortex, each adjacent to SII, were strikingly similar in their response properties to SII cells. The proportions of the different cell types changed somewhat, with some increase in the representation of deep tissues and of "complex" cells requiring the monkey's active interaction with the stimulus object for their maximal activation. Without response properties that specify them as SII neurons, in experimentally characterizing these cells it becomes important to histologically confirm their location in SII. Probably earlier reports (e.g. Whitsel et al 1969) of more heterogeneous populations of cells in SII resulted from the insufficient anatomical definition of SII at that time.

BEHAVIORAL DEFICITS RESULTING FROM SII LESIONS Ettlinger and coworkers (Ridley & Ettlinger 1978, Garcha & Ettlinger 1978) examined

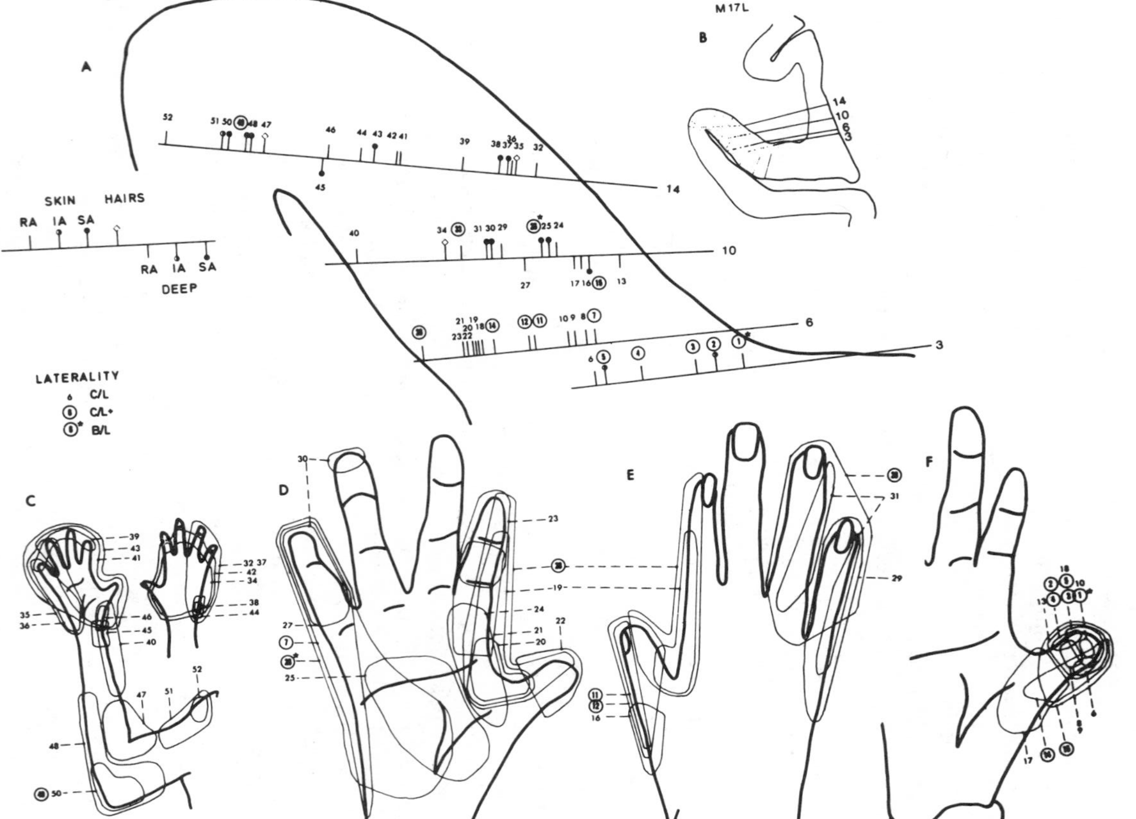

Figure 5. Receptive field and submodality properties of neurons within the "digits," "hand," and "arm" representations within SII of the macaque. A, B: Enlarged portion (A) of coronal section (B) illustrating the locations of 52 cells characterized in four nearly parallel penetrations into the parietal operculum. Neurons indicated by circle and star had symmetrical bilateral receptive field (2 cells); neurons indicated by circle were predominantly contralateral (12 cells); the remaining 38 neurons had strictly contralateral receptive fields. All neurons had cutaneous receptive fields except the 6 cells indicated by a downgoing bar which innervated deep tissues. C-F. Receptive fields of neurons represented in A and B. Most receptive fields were circumscribed (Robinson & Burton 1980a).

the effects of unilateral and bilateral lesions limited to the SII cortex in monkeys, using a complex series of behavioral tests. These monkeys were consistently observed to have difficulty in learning to differentiate by touch variously shaped objects, but there was no impairment in performing tasks that depended on proprioceptive information, such as weight discrimination, or on learning complex motor tasks.

Other Regions of Neocortex Responding to Somatic Stimulation

The remaining areas of neocortex known to be specifically activated during the manipulation and identification by touch of a hand-held object or of a textured surface are Brodmann areas 5 and 7 (posterior parietal cortex), the precentral motor area 4, and area 6, including the supplementary motor cortex. The clinical and experimental evidence that each of these areas is relevant to tactual exploratory behavior has accumulated over many years; however, the observations of Roland et al (1976, 1980a,b), described earlier, on regional cerebral blood flow provides a summary demonstration that this is so. Of these different cortical zones, only areas 5 and 7b (along with the adjacent retroinsular cortex) have been selected for review. Area 5 is immediately posterior to area 2 in SI, and similarly area 7b abuts on SII. Both areas have close structural and functional association with the adjacent primary somatosensory cortex, receiving substantial input from SI and SII respectively. In area 5 about 90% of neurons respond to passive somatic stimulation, most cells responding to movement about joints but a few to mechanical stimulation of other deep tissues and of skin. Neurons in area 7b and the retroinsular cortex also mostly respond to passive somatic stimulation. This response pattern more closely resembles that of neuron populations in SI and SII than of neuron populations in the rest of the posterior parietal cortex, in which most neurons, although responding during manual or visual exploration of the monkey's extrapersonal world, only rarely are responsive to passive mechanical stimulation of somatic tissues.

For the extensive literature on area 7 the reader is referred to the following recent reviews and important papers: Hyvarinen & Poranen (1974), Mountcastle (1975, 1976, 1978), Mountcastle et al (1975, 1980), Motter & Mountcastle (1981), Hyvarinen & Shelepin (1979), Robinson et al (1978), Yin & Mountcastle (1977), Lynch (1980), Lynch et al (1977), Wurtz et al (1980), Rolls et al (1979), Sakata et al (1980), Darian-Smith et al (1979a). Likewise, for the literature relating to sensory input to motor area 4 key references include: Lemon & Porter (1976, 1978), Lemon et al (1976), Brinkman et al (1978), Fromm & Evarts (1978), LaMarre et al (1978), Wong et al (1978), Soso & Fetz (1980), Fetz et al (1980). Finally, recent papers on the functional properties of neurons in the supplementary motor area in the alert responding monkey include: Brinkman & Porter (1978), Tanji et al (1980).

Brodmann Areas 5 and 7b and Retroinsular Cortex

CONNECTIONS If the posterior boundary of area 2 is defined by the caudal limit of the projection from the ventrobasal complex (Jones et al 1979b), then area 5 receives input from projections to two thalamic nuclei, the lateral posterior and the anterior pulvinar nuclei (Burton & Jones 1976). Whether these latter thalamic nuclei have a somatic afferent input is not known. Cortico-cortical connections of area 5 are with areas 2, 3a, 4, and 6, including the supplementary motor cortex (Jones et al 1978). With the exception of area 2, which projects to area 5 but receives no input from it, these connections are reciprocal. An additional cortico-cortical connection for area 5 is with area 7b and the retroinsular cortex (Jones et al 1978). Commissural connections of area 5 are with the contralateral area 5 and also SI. Finally, as mentioned earlier, the macaque area 5 has a corticospinal projection to the lateral part of laminae 4 and 5 in the spinal dorsal horn (Coulter & Jones 1977).

Area 7b, as with area 5, receives thalamic input from both the anterior pulvinar and lateral posterior nuclei, and also from the caudal component of the ventrolateral nuclei (Kasdon & Jacobson 1978, Burton & Jones 1976). Although there is some physiological evidence of somatic input to these thalamic nuclei, the somatic afferent pathways involved are not known. The retroinsular cortex, by contrast, receives thalamic input from the medial component of the posterior nucleus, a region well known to have somatic afferent input (Poggio & Mountcastle 1960, Burton & Jones 1976, Berkley 1980). Cortico-cortical connections of areas 7b and the retroinsular cortex have already been mentioned.

RESPONSE CHARACTERISTICS OF NEURONS IN AREA 5 Neurons in area 5 differ from those in SI in several ways (Mountcastle 1975, 1976): those cells driven by peripheral stimuli are less tightly locked to the stimulus than are SI cells, and their responsiveness may vary greatly with the monkey's behavioral state. About two-thirds of the neurons in area 5 respond to passive movements of one or more joints. Many of these cells resemble SI cells in that they respond to passive movement of a single contralateral joint. Some area 5 neurons, however, respond only if movement at two or more contralateral or ipsilateral joints occurs simultaneously (Mountcastle et al 1975, Sakata 1975, Sakata et al 1973, 1978, 1980). Only a few area 5 neurons have cutaneous input, and these cells typically differ from SI cells in having extensive receptive fields from which they can be best activated when the stimulus moves across the skin; these receptive fields are usually contralateral.

About 10% of the neurons in area 5 are unique in their response patterns (Mountcastle et al 1975). Although these cells are not excited by any form of mechanical stimulation of the hand or limb, some discharge vigorously when the monkey reaches toward an object, such as food, that interests it (projection cells), and other neurons fire only when the object of interest is grasped and manipulated (manipulation cells). Similar movements of the same arm for other purposes did not activate the cell. Mountcastle has also observed neurons in area 5 responding when the animal reached for or manipulated an object of interest, but which also responded to passive stimulation of the limb. Projection neurons and manipulation neurons have not been observed within SI, but are common in area 7a.

RESPONSE CHARACTERISTICS OF NEURONS IN AREA 7B AND IN RETROINSULAR CORTEX In recent investigations specifically directed to neuron populations within area 7b (Leinonen et al 1979, Rolls et al 1979, Robinson & Burton 1980b,c), the cells were found to resemble area 5 cells in some features and to contrast with them in others. Neurons similar to the projection and manipulation cells of area 5 were observed. Cells in areas 5 and 7b were also similar in their response variability and sensitivity to the behavioral state of the animal. A substantial proportion of neurons in both areas 5 and 7b were activated by passive somatic stimulation, but whereas movement of one or several joints was the effective stimulus for most of the area 5 cells, innocuous cutaneous mechanical stimulation, particularly if the stimulus was moving across the skin in a particular direction, was the common effective stimulus for neurons in area 7b. Most of these "tactile" cells had extensive, poorly defined receptive fields that commonly involved both contralateral and ipsilateral parts of the body surface. Robinson & Burton (1980b,c) also found that about 12% of neurons in area 7b were excited only by noxious stimuli.

Neurons in the retroinsular cortex have much in common with SII cells. Virtually all of these cells respond to innocuous, cutaneous stimuli, and most have a circumscribed contralateral receptive field. Robinson & Burton (1980b,c) found a proportion of these cells to be quite sensitive to low-frequency vibratory stimuli. Leinonen (1980) observed a rather different neuron population, responsive mainly to "compression" of the skin, and with receptive fields somewhat larger than those of SII cells.

SOMESTHETIC DEFICITS RESULTING FROM LOCALIZED LESIONS IN POSTERIOR PARIETAL CORTEX Few studies have been done in which the parietal lesion was restricted to area 5 (see Stein 1978), and none with lesions only in area 7b. The behavioral effects of lesions localized to area 5 have yet to be fully documented. Stein examined the effects of reversibly blocking neural processing in area 5 of the macaque by cooling, observing that the immediate effects of such a block were the development of clumsiness in the movements of the contralateral arm and hand and impairment of the tactile exploration and identification of textured surfaces (gratings). Stein argued that these effects resulted from the cooling of area 5 only and did not reflect any impairment of function in the adjacent areas 3, 1 and 2. Similar cooling of the whole of area 7 impaired the monkey's ability to reach for and manipulate objects within the contralateral visual hemifield, but not in tactually guided movements nor in the identification of textures. Impairment of visually guided movements in the contralateral arm and impairment of visually guided movements in the contralateral arm and hand also observed if both areas 5 and 7 were ablated (LaMotte & Acuna 1978; Faugier-Grimaud et al 1978). No ipsilateral deficits were observed in these monkeys.

Recent studies in patients following the ablation of different regions of parietal cortex (Roland 1976, Corkin et al 1970) suggest that whenever a deficit in tactile sensibility was observed in these patients, including the failure to correctly assess the size and shape of a hand-held object, then injury of the hand area of the postcentral gyrus was present. Neither Corkin et al (1970) nor Roland (1976) observed tactile deficits with lesions of the parietal cortex which spared the postcentral gyrus. This finding contrasts with earlier clinical observations and with Stein's observations in the macaque.

COMMENT

The key issue in examining the peripheral and central neural processes of touch is the representation of the features characterizing the tangible world around us. However, as this review has attempted to show, the issue of neural representation is rather more straightforward for investigators of peripheral neural processes than for those examining central processes. For example, in examining stimulus representation in a digital nerve fiber population, one knows that *all* sensory information that the observer obtains about an object by touching it with the finger pad must be represented within the responses of that peripheral fiber population. The investigator has a measurable expression of the sensory information relayed to the brain by the digital nerve in the subject's tactile sensory performance; he seeks in responses of the fiber population a representation of this information. The problem becomes one of identifying which of the (usually) several representations of the stimulus in the responses of the population of fibers is used by the brain.

Analyses of the central neural events of touch start from a much less certain base. Two questions that are usually trivial in the study of peripheral neural processes become important. These are: *Which* populations of central neurons contribute to the tactile identification of a particular surface or object?, and *What* information about the surface or object do these neuron populations process? As this review illustrates, these questions have been a continuing preoccupation in the analysis of the central processes of touch. Even so, most investigations of somatosensory cortex, for example, have been focused on the identification of cortical neuron populations responding to tactile stimulation of the stationary hand. The elegant study of Roland et al (1980a,b) alerts one to the fact that a number of other regions of the cortex are concomitantly active with the primary somatosensory cortex when the observer manipulates and identifies by touch an object or surface held in the hand. Each of these cortical zones poses a question for the investigator concerning its particular role in tactile discriminative behavior.

So far, studies such as those reviewed in this chapter fail to provide us with a coherent model of how each of these populations of cortical neurons relate anatomically and functionally to each other. Recent anatomical studies have certainly greatly expanded our knowledge of their connections, but important information is lacking. One need but consider present knowledge of the total somatic afferent inflow to the neocortex to appreciate this (see Graybiel 1974, Berkley 1980). Not surprisingly, the functional characterization of the various populations of cortical neurons that subserve touch has only just begun. Nonetheless, we do now have powerful tools for examining tactile neural processes in the monkey as he reaches for, manipulates, and identifies the world of objects around him. The next decade should see substantial progress.

Literature Cited

Applebaum, A. E., Leonard, R. B., Kenshalo, D. R., Martin, R. F., Willis, W. D. 1979. Nuclei in which functionally identified spinothalmic tract neurons terminate. *J. Comp. Neurol.* 188: 575–86

Barlow, H. B., Levick, W. R. 1965. The mechanism of directionally selective units in rabbit's retina. *J. Physiol.* 178:477–504

Bennett, R. E., Ferrington, D. G., Rowe, M. 1980. Tactile neuron classes within second somatosensory area (SII) of cat cerebral cortex. *J. Neurophysiol.* 43: 292–309

Berkley, K. J. 1980. Spatial relationships between the terminations of somatic sensory and motor pathways in the rostral brainstem of cats and monkeys. I. Ascending somatic sensory inputs to lateral diencephalon. *J. Comp. Neurol.* 193:283–317

Bishop, A. 1964. Use of the hand in lower primates. In *Evolutionary and Genetic Biology of Primates,* ed. J. Buettner-Janusch, 2:133–225. New York: Academic

Brinkman, J., Bush, B. M., Porter, R. 1978. Deficient influences of peripheral stimuli on precentral neurones in monkeys with dorsal column lesions. *J. Physiol.* 276:27–48

Brinkman, J., Porter, R. 1978. Movement performance and afferent projections to the sensorimotor cortex in monkeys with dorsal column lesions. In *Active Touch: The Mechanism of Recognition of Objects by Manipulation,* ed. G. Gordon, pp. 119–38. Oxford: Pergamon

Brodmann, K. 1905. Beitrage zur histolischen Lokalisation der Grosshirnrinde. IIIte Mitteilung: Die Rindenfelder der neideren Affen. *J. Psychol. Neurol.* 4:177–226

Brown, A. G., Rose, P. K., Snow, P. J. 1977. The morphology of hair follicle afferent fibre collaterals in the spinal cord of the cat. *J. Physiol.* 272:779–97

Brown, A. G., Rose, P. K., Snow, P. J. 1978. Morphology and organization of axon collaterals from afferent fibres of slowly adapting Type I units in cat spinal cord. *J. Physiol.* 277:15–27

Burgess, P. R., Perl, E. R. 1973. Cutaneous mechanoreceptors and nociceptors. In *Handbook of Sensory Physiology, Somatosensory System,* ed. A. Iggo, 2:29–78. Berlin: Springer-Verlag

Burton, H., Jones, E. G. 1976. The posterior thalamic region and its cortical projections in New World and Old World monkeys. *J. Comp. Neurol.* 168:249–302

Chambers, M. R., Andres, K. H., von Duering, M., Iggo, A. 1972. The structure and function of the slowly adapting Type II mechanoreceptor in hairy skin. *J. Exp. Physiol.* 57:417–45

Chouchkov, Ch. 1978. Cutaneous receptors. *Adv. Anat. Embryol. Cell Biol.* 54, Fasc. 5. 62 pp.

Chung, J. M., Kenshalo, D. R., Gerhart, K. D., Willis, W. D. 1979. Excitation of primate spinothalamic neurons by cutaneous C-fiber volleys. *J. Neurophysiol.* 42:1354–69

Corkin, S., Milner, B., Rasmussen, T. 1970. Somatosensory thresholds: contrasting effects of postcentral-gyrus and posterior parietal-lobe exicisions. *Arch. Neurol.* 23:41–58

Costanzo, R. M., Gardner, E. P. 1980. A quantitative analysis of responses of direction-sensitive neurons in somatosensory cortex of awake monkeys. *J. Neurophysiol.* 43:1319–41

Coulter, J. D., Jones, E. G. 1977. Differential distribution of corticospinal projections from individual cytoarchitectonic fields in the monkey. *Brain Res.* 129:335–40

Darian-Smith, I. 1980. Thermoreceptive fibers innervated the palm and fingers: differentiating small changes in skin temperature. *Symp. Thermoreception, 28th Int. Congr. Physiol. Sci., Budapest.* In press

Darian-Smith, I. 1981. The sense of touch: performance and peripheral neural processes. In *Handbook of Physiology,* Sect. 1, Nervous System, ed. V. B. Mountcastle, J. M. Brookhart. Vol. 2, Sensory Processes, ed. I. Darian-Smith. In press

Darian-Smith, I., Davidson, I., Johnson, K. O. 1980. Peripheral neural representation of the two spatial dimensions of a textured surface moving over the monkey's finger pad. *J. Physiol.* 309:135–46

Darian-Smith, I., Johnson, K. O. 1977. Temperature sense in the primate. *Br. Med. Bull.* 33:143–48

Darian-Smith, I., Johnson, K. O., Dykes, R. 1973. 'Cold' fiber population innervating palmar and digital skin of the monkey: responses to cooling pulses. *J. Neurophysiol.* 36:325–46

Darian-Smith, I., Johnson, K. O., Goodwin, A. W. 1979a. Posterior parietal cortex: relations of unit activity to sensorimotor function. *Ann. Rev. Physiol.* 41: 141–57

Darian-Smith, I., Johnson, K. O., LaMotte, C., Kenins, P., Shigenaga, Y., Ming, V. C. 1979b. Coding of incremental changes in skin temperature by single warm fibers in the monkey. *J. Neurophysiol.* 42:1316–31

Darian-Smith, I., Johnson, K. O., LaMotte, C., Shigenaga, Y., Kenins, P., Champness, P. 1979c. Warm fibers innervating palmar and digital skin of the monkey: responses to thermal stimuli. *J. Neurophysiol.* 42:1297–315

Darian-Smith, I., Kenins, P. 1980. Innervation density of mechanoreceptive fibres supplying glabrous skin of the monkey's index finger. *J. Physiol.* 309:147–56

Darian-Smith, I., Oke, L. E. 1980. Peripheral neural representation of the spatial frequency of a grating moving at different velocities across the monkey's finger pad. *J. Physiol.* 309:117–34

Dreyer, D. A., Loe, P. R., Metz, C. B., Whitsel, B. L. 1975. Representation of head and face in postcentral gyrus of the macaque. *J. Neurophysiol.* 38:714–33

Dubner, R., Sumino, R., Starkman, S. 1974. Responses of facial cutaneous thermoreceptive and mechanoreceptive afferent fibers in the monkey to noxious heat stimulation. In *Advances in*

Neurology, ed. J. J. Bonica, pp. 61–71. New York: Raven

Dubner, R., Sumino, R., Wood, W. I. 1975. A peripheral 'cold' fiber population responsive to innocuous and noxious thermal stimuli applied to monkey's face. *J. Neurophysiol.* 38:1373–89

Duclaux, R., Kenshalo, D. R. 1980. Response characteristics of cutaneous warm fibers in the monkey. *J. Neurophysiol.* 43:1–15

Eidelberg, E., Stein, D. G. 1974. Functional recovery after lesions of the nervous system. *Neurosci. Res. Program Bull.* 12: 191–303

Evarts, E. V. 1966. Methods for recording activity in individual neurons in moving animals. In *Methods in Medical Research,* ed. R. F. Rushmer, pp. 241–50. Chicago: Year Book Publ.

Faugier-Grimaud, S., Frenois, C., Stein, D. G. 1978. Effects of posterior parietal lesions on visually guided behavior in monkeys. *Neuropsychologia* 16:151–67

Ferrington, D. G., Rowe, M. 1980. Differential contributions to coding of cutaneous vibratory information by cortical somatosensory Areas I and II. *J. Neurophysiol.* 43:310–31

Fetz, E. E., Finocchio, D. V., Baker, M. A., Soso, M. J. 1980. Sensory and motor responses of precentral cortex cells during comparable passive and active joint movements. *J. Neurophysiol.* 43: 1070–89

Fields, H. L., Basbaum, A. I. 1978. Brainstem control of spinal pain transmission neurons. *Ann. Rev. Physiol.* 40:193–221

Friedman, D. P., Jones, E. G., Burton, H. 1980. Representation pattern in the second somatic sensory area of the monkey cerebral cortex. *J. Comp. Neurol.* 192:21–41

Fromm, C., Evarts, E. 1978. Motor cortex responses to kinesthetic inputs during postural stability, precise fine movement and ballistic movement in the conscious monkey. See Brinkman & Porter 1978, pp. 105–18

Garcha, H. S., Ettlinger, G. 1978. The effects of unilateral or bilateral removals of the second somatosensory cortex (Area SII): a profound tactile disorder in monkeys. *Cortex* 14:319–26

Gardner, E. P., Costanzo, R. M. 1980. Neuronal mechanisms underlying direction sensitivity of somatosensory cortical neurons in awake monkeys. *J. Neurophysiol.* 43:1342–54

Graybiel, A. M. 1974. Studies in the anatomical organization of posterior association cortex. In *The Neurosciences Third Study Program,* ed. F. O. Schmidt, F. G. Worden, pp. 205–14. Cambridge, Mass: MIT Press

Gybels, J., Handwerker, H. O., van Hees, J. 1979. A comparison between the discharges of human nociceptive nerve fibres and the subject's ratings of his sensations. *J. Physiol.* 292:193–206

Haber, L. H., Martin, R. F., Chung, J. M., Willis, W. D. 1980. Inhibition and excitation of primate spinothalamic tract neurons by stimulation in region of nucleus reticularis gigantocellularis. *J. Neurophysiol.* 43:1578–93

Halata, Z. 1975. The mechanoreceptors of mammalian skin; Ultrastructure and morphological classification. *Adv. Anat. Embryol. Cell Biol.* 50, Fasc. 5. 77 pp.

Hensel, H., Iggo, A. 1971. Analysis of cutaneous warm and cold fibers in primates. *Pfluegers Arch.* 329:1–8

Hilder, R. E., Ramey, E., Darian-Smith, I., Johnson, K. O., Dally, L. J. 1974. A contact stimulator for the study of cutaneous thermal sensibility. *J. Appl. Physiol.* 37:252–55

Holmes, G. 1979. *Selected Papers of Gordon Holmes,* ed. C. G. Phillips. Oxford: OUP. 488 pp.

Hyvarinen, J., Poranen, A. 1974. Function of the parietal associative Area 7 as revealed from cellular discharges in alert monkeys. *Brain* 97:673–92

Hyvarinen, J., Poranen, A. 1978a. Movement-sensitive and direction and orientation-selective cutaneous receptive fields in the hand area of the post-central gyrus in monkeys. *J. Physiol.* 283:523–37

Hyvarinen, J., Poranen, A. 1978b. Receptive field integration and submodality convergence in the hand area of the postcentral gyrus of the alert monkey. *J. Physiol.* 283:539–56

Hyvarinen, J., Poranen, A., Jokinen, Y. 1980. Influence of attentive behavior on neuronal responses to vibration in primary somatosensory cortex of the monkey. *J. Neurophysiol.* 43:870–82

Hyvarinen, J., Shelepin, Y. 1979. Distribution of visual and somatic functions in the parietal association area 7 of the monkey. *Brain Res.* 169:561–64

Iggo, A. 1969. Cutaneous thermoreceptors in primates and subprimates. *J. Physiol.* 200:403–30

Iggo, A. 1974. Cutaneous receptors. In *The Peripheral Nervous system,* ed. J. I. Hubbard, pp. 347–404. New York: Plenum

Iggo, A., Muir, A. R. 1969. The structure and function of a slowly adapting touch corpuscle in hairy skin. *J. Physiol.* 200:763–96

Iwamura, Y., Tanaka, M. 1978. Postcentral neurons in hand region of area 2: their possible role in the form discrimination of tactile objects. *Brain Res.* 150: 662–66

Iwamura, Y., Tanaka, M., Hikosaka, O. 1980. Overlapping representation of fingers in the somatosensory cortex (area 2) of the conscious monkey. *Brain Res.* 197:516–20

Johansson, R. S. 1978. Tactile sensibility in the human hand: Receptive field characteristics of mechanoreceptive units in the glabrous skin area. *J. Physiol.* 281:101–23

Johansson, R. S. 1979. Tactile afferent units with small and well demarcated receptive fields in the glabrous skin area of the human hand. In *Sensory Functions of the Skin of Humans,* ed. D. R. Kenshalo, pp. 129–52. New York: Plenum

Johansson, R. S., Vallbo, A. B. 1979. Tactile sensibility in the human hand: Relative and absolute densities of four types of mechanoreceptive units in glabrous skin. *J. Physiol.* 286:283–300

Johansson, R. S., Vallbo, A. B. 1980. Spatial properties of the population of mechanoreceptive units in the glabrous skin of the human hand. *Brain Res.* 184:353–66

Johansson, R. S., Vallbo, A. B., Westling, G. 1980. Thresholds of mechanosensitive afferents in the human hand as measured with von Frey hairs. *Brain Res.* 184:343–51

Johnson, K. O., Darian-Smith, I., LaMotte, C. 1973. Peripheral neural determinants of temperature discrimination in man: A correlative study of responses to cooling skin. *J. Neurophysiol.* 36:347–70

Johnson, K. O., Darian-Smith, I., LaMotte, C., Johnson, B., Oldfield, S. 1979. Coding of incremental changes in skin temperature by a population of warm fibers in the monkey: correlation with intensity discrimination in man. *J. Neurophysiol.* 42:1332–53

Johnson, K. O., Lamb, G. D. 1981. Neural mechanisms of spatial tactile discrimination: Neural patterns evoked by Braille-like dot patterns in the monkey. *J. Physiol.* In press

Johnson, K. O., Phillips, J. R. 1981. Tactile spatial resolution: I. Two-point discrimination, gap detection, grating resolution and letter recognition. *J. Neurophysiol.* Accepted for publication

Jones, E. G., Burton, H. 1976. Areal differences in the laminar distribution of thalamic afferents in cortical fields of the insular, parietal and temporal regions of primates. *J. Comp. Neurol.* 168:197–248

Jones, E. G., Coulter, J. D., Hendry, S. H. C. 1978. Intracortical connectivity of architectonic fields in the somatic sensory, motor and parietal cortex of monkeys. *J. Comp. Neurol.* 181:291–348

Jones, E. G., Coulter, J. D., Wise, S. P. 1979a. Commissural columns in the sensory-motor cortex of monkeys. *J. Comp. Neurol.* 188:113–36

Jones, E. G., Hartman, B. K. 1978. Recent advances in neuroanatomical methodology. *Ann. Rev. Neurosci.* 1:215–96

Jones, E. G., Powell, T. P. S. 1969a. Connexions of the somatic sensory cortex of the rhesus monkey. I. Ipsilateral cortical connexions. *Brain* 92:477–502

Jones, E. G., Powell, T. P. S. 1969b. Connexions of the somatic sensory cortex of the rhesus monkey. II. Contralateral cortical connexions. *Brain* 92:717–30

Jones, E. G., Powell, T. P. S. 1970. Connexions of the somatic sensory cortex of the rhesus monkey. III. Thalamic connexions. *Brain* 93:37–56

Jones, E. G., Wise, S. P., Coulter, J. D. 1979b. Differential thalamic relationships of sensory-motor and parietal cortical fields in monkeys. *J. Comp. Neurol.* 183:833–82

Kaas, J. H., Nelson, R. J., Sur, M., Lin, C-S., Merzenich, M. M. 1979. Multiple representations of the body within the primary somatosensory cortex of primates. *Science* 204:521–23

Kasdon, D. L., Jacobson, S. 1978. The thalamic afferents to the inferior parietal lobule of the rhesus monkey. *J. Comp. Neurol.* 177:685–706

Kenshalo, D. R. 1970. Psychophysical studies of temperature sensitivity. *Contrib. Sens. Physiol.* 74:19–74

Kenshalo, D. R. 1976. Correlations of temperature sensitivity in man and monkey, a first approximation. In *Sensory Functions of the Skin,* ed. Y. Zotterman. Wenner-Gren Symp. Ser. 27:305–30. New York: Pergamon

Kenshalo, D. R. 1979. *Sensory Functions of the Skin of Humans.* New York: Plenum. 439 pp.

Kenshalo, D. R., Bergen, D. C. 1975. A device to measure cutaneous temperature sensitivity in human and subhuman species. *J. Appl. Physiol.* 39:1038–40

Kenshalo, D. R., Duclaux, R. 1977. Response characteristics of cutaneous cold receptors in the monkey. *J. Neurophysiol.* 40:319–32

Kenshalo, D. R., Duncan, D. G., Weymark, C. 1967. Thresholds for thermal stimulation of the inner thigh, footpad and face of cats. *J. Comp. Physiol. Psychol.* 63:133–38

Kenshalo, D. R., Hall, E. C. 1974. Thermal thresholds of the rhesus monkey (*Macaca mulatta*). *J. Comp. Physiol. Psychol.* 81:119–32

Kerr, F. W. L., Casey, K. L. 1978. Pain. *Neurosci. Res. Program Bull.* 16:1

Knibestöl, M. 1973. Stimulus-response functions of rapidly adapting mechanoreceptors in the human glabrous skin area. *J. Physiol.* 232:427–52

Knibestöl, M. 1975. Stimulus-response functions of slowly adapting mechanoreceptors in the human glabrous skin area. *J. Physiol.* 246:63–80

Knibestöl, M., Vallbo, A. B. 1980. Intensity of sensation related to activity of slowly adapting mechanoreceptive units in the human hand. *J. Physiol.* 300:251–67

Konietzny, F., Hensel, H. 1977. Response of rapidly and slowly adapting mechanoreceptors and vibratory sensitivity in human hairy skin. *Pfluegers Arch.* 368:39–44

Kuypers, H. G. J. M. 1960. Central cortical projections to motor and somatosensory cell groups. *Brain* 83:161–84

Lamarre, Y., Bioulac, B., Jacks, B. 1978. Activity of precentral neurones in conscious monkeys: Effects of deafferentiation and cerebellar ablation. *J. Physiol.* 74:253–64

LaMotte, C. 1977. Distribution of the tract of Lissauer and the dorsal root fibers in the primate spinal cord. *J. Comp. Neurol.* 172:529–62

LaMotte, C., Pert, C. B., Snyder, S. H. 1976. Opiate receptor binding in primate spinal cord: Distribution and changes after dorsal root section. *Brain Res.* 112:407–12

LaMotte, R. H., Acuna, C. 1978. Defects in accuracy of reaching after removal of posterior parietal cortex in monkeys. *Brain Res.* 139:309–26

LaMotte, R. H., Campbell, J. N. 1978. Comparison of responses of warm and nociceptive C-fiber afferents in monkey with human judgements of thermal pain. *J. Neurophysiol.* 41:509–28

LaMotte, R. H., Mountcastle, V. B. 1975. Capacities of humans and monkeys to discriminate between vibratory stimuli of different frequency and amplitude: A correlation between neural events and psychophysical measurements. *J. Neurophysiol.* 38:539–59

LaMotte, R. H., Mountcastle, V. B. 1978. Neural processing of temporally-ordered somesthetic input: Remaining capacity in monkeys following lesions of the parietal lobe. See Brinkman & Porter 1978, pp. 73–78

LaMotte, R. H., Mountcastle, V. B. 1979. Disorders in somesthesis following lesions of parietal lobe. *J. Neurophysiol.* 42:400–19

Lederman, S. J. 1974. Tactile roughness of grooved surfaces: The touching process and effects of macro- and microsurface structure. *Percept. Psychophys.* 16: 385–95

Lederman, S. J. 1976. The 'callus-thenics' of touching. *Can. J. Psychol.* 30:82–89

Lederman, S. J., Taylor, M. M. 1972. Fingertip force, surface geometry, and the perception of roughness by active touch. *Percept. Psychophys.* 12:401–8

Leinonen, L. 1980. Functional properties of neurones in the parietal retroinsular cortex in awake monkey. *Acta Physiol. Scand.* 108:381–84

Leinonen, L., Hyvarinen, J., Nyamn, G., Linnankoski, I. 1979. I. Functional properties of neurons in lateral part of associate area 7 in awake monkeys. *Exp. Brain Res.* 34:299–320

Lemon, R. N., Hanby, J. A., Porter, R. 1976. Relationship between the activity of precentral neurones during active and passive movements in conscious monkeys. *Proc. R. Soc. London Ser. B* 194:341–73

Lemon, R. N., Porter, R. 1976. Afferent input to movement-related precentral neurones in conscious monkeys. *Proc. R. Soc. London Ser. B* 194:313–39

Lemon, R. N., Porter, R. 1978. Short-latency peripheral afferent inputs to pyramidal and other neurones in the precentral cortex of conscious monkeys. See Brinkman & Porter 1978, pp. 91–104

Light, A. R., Perl, E. R. 1979a. Spinal termination of functionally identified primary afferent neurons with slowly conducting myelinated fibers. *J. Comp. Neurol.* 186:133–50

Light, A. R., Perl, E. R. 1979b. Reexamination of the dorsal root projection to the spinal dorsal horn including observations on the differential termination of coarse and fine fibers. *J. Comp. Neurol.* 186:117–32

Light, A. R., Trevino, D. L., Perl, E. R. 1979. Morphological features of functionally defined neurons in the marginal zone and substantia gelatinosa of the spinal dorsal horn. *J. Comp. Neurol.* 186: 151–72

Lin, C-S, Merzenich, M. M., Sur, M., Kaas, J. H. 1979. Connections of Areas 3b and 1 of the parietal somatosensory strip with the ventroposterior nucleus in the owl monkey (*Aotus trivirgatus*). *J. Comp. Neurol.* 185:355–72

Lucier, G. E., Ruegg, D. C., Weisendanger, M. 1975. Responses of neurones in motor cortex and in Area 3a to controlled stretches of forelimb muscles in cebus monkeys. *J. Physiol.* 251:833–53

Lynch, J. C. 1980. The functional organization of posterior parietal cortex. *Behav. Brain Sci.* 3:485–98

Lynch, J. C., Mountcastle, V. B., Talbot, W. H., Yin, T. C. T. 1977. Parietal lobe mechanisms for directed visual attention. *J. Neurophysiol.* 40:362–89

Merzenich, M. M., Kaas, J. H., Sur, M., Lin, C-S. 1978. Double representation of the body surface within cytoarchitectonic Areas 3b and 1 in "SI" in the owl monkey (*Aotus trivirgatus*). *J. Comp. Neurol.* 181:41–74

Molinari, H. H., Rozsa, A. J., Kenshalo, D. R. 1976. Rhesus monkey (*Macaca mulatta*) cool sensitivity measured by a signal detection method. *Percept. Psychophys.* 19:246–51

Morley, J. 1980. *A psychophysical study on the tactile perception of textured surfaces.* M.Sc. thesis. Univ. Melbourne, Australia

Motter, B. C., Mountcastle, V. B. 1981. The functional properties of the light sensitive neurons of the posterior parietal cortex studied in waking monkeys: foveal sparing and opponent vector organization. *J. Neurosci.* In press

Mountcastle, V. B. 1975. The world around us: neural command functions for selective attention. *Neurosci. Res. Program Bull.* 14: Suppl. pp. 1–47

Mountcastle, V. B. 1976. The view from within: Pathways to the study of perception. *Johns Hopkins Med. J.* 136:109–31

Mountcastle, V. B. 1978. Brain mechanisms for directed attention. *J. R. Soc. Med.* 71:14–28

Mountcastle, V. B., Henneman, E. 1952. The representation of tactile sensibility in the thalamus of the monkey. *J. Comp. Neurol.* 97:409–40

Mountcastle, V. B., Lynch, J. C., Georgopoulos, A., Sakata, H., Acuna, C. 1975. Posterior parietal association cortex of the monkey: command functions for operations within extrapersonal space. *J. Neurophysiol.* 38:871–908

Mountcastle, V. B., Motter, B. C., Anderson, R. A. 1980. Some observations on the functional properties of neurons in the parietal lobe of the waking monkey. *Behav. Brain Sci.* 3:520–23

Mountcastle, V. B., Talbot, W. H., Sakata, H., Hyvarinen, J. 1969. Cortical neuronal mechanisms in flutter-vibration studied in unanesthetized monkeys. Neuronal periodicity and frequency discrimination. *J. Neurophysiol.* 32:452–84

Nelson, R. J., Sur, M., Felleman, D. J., Kaas, J. H. 1980. Representations of the body surface in postcentral parietal cortex of *Macaca fascicularis. J. Comp. Neurol.* 192:611–43

Paul, R. L., Merzenich, M., Goodman, H. 1972. Representation of slowly and rapidly adapting cutaneous mechanoreceptors of the hand in Brodmann's areas 3 and 1 of *Macaca mulatta. Brain Res.* 36:229–49

Perl, E. R. 1981. Pain and nociception. In *Handbook of Physiology,* Sect. 1, Nervous System, ed. V. B. Mountcastle, J. M. Brookhart. Vol. 2, Sensory Processes, ed. I. Darian-Smith, Chap. 21. In press

Phillips, C. G., Porter, R. 1977. *Corticospinal Neurones: Their Role in Movement.* London: Academic. 450 pp.

Phillips, C. G., Powell, T. P. S., Weisendanger, M. 1971. Projection from low-threshold muscle afferents of the hand and forearm to area 3a of the baboon's cortex. *J. Physiol.* 217:419–46

Poggio, G. F., Mountcastle, V. B. 1960. A study of the functional contributions of the lemniscal and spinothalamic systems to somatic sensibility. *Bull. Johns Hopkins Hosp.* 106:266–316

Powell, T. P. S., Mountcastle, V. B. 1959a. The cytoarchitecture of the postcentral gyrus of the monkey *Macaca mulatta. Bull. Johns. Hopkins Hosp.* 105:108–31

Powell, T. P. S., Mountcastle, V. B. 1959b. Some aspects of the functional organization of the cortex of the postcentral gyrus of the monkey: a correlation of findings obtained in a single unit analysis with cytoarchitecture. *Bull. Johns Hopkins Hosp.* 105:133–62

Price, D. D., Hayes, R. L., Ruda, M., Dubner, R. 1978. Neural representation of cutaneous aftersensations by spinothalamic tract neurons. *Fed. Proc.* 37:2237–39

Randolph, M., Semmes, J. 1974. Behavioral consequences of selective subtotal ablations in the postcentral gyrus of *Macaca mulatta. Brain Res.* 70:55–70

Ridley, R. M., Ettlinger, G. 1978. Further evidence of impaired tactile learning after removals of the second somatic sensory projection cortex (SII) in the monkey. *Exp. Brain Res.* 31:475–88

Rivot, J. P., Chaouch, A., Besson, J. M. 1980. Nucleus raphe magnus modulation of response of rat dorsal horn neurons to unmyelinated fiber inputs: partial involvement of serotonergic pathways. *J. Neurophysiol.* 44:1039–57

Robinson, C. J., Burton, H. 1980a. Somatotopographic organization in the second somatosensory area of *M. fascicularis. J. Comp. Neurol.* 192:43–67

Robinson, C. J., Burton, H. 1980b. Organization of somatosensory receptive fields in cortical areas 7b, retroinsula, postauditory and granular insula of *M. fascicularis. J. Comp. Neurol.* 192:69–92

Robinson, C. J., Burton, H. 1980c. Somatic submodality distribution within the second somatosensory (SII), 7b, retroinsular, postauditory, and granular insular cortical areas of *M. fascicularis, J. Comp. Neurol.* 192:93–108

Robinson, D. L., Goldberg, M. E., Stanton, G. E. 1978. Parietal association cortex in the primate: sensory mechanisms and behavioral modulations. *J. Neurophysiol.* 41:910–32

Roland, E. 1976. Astereognosis: tactile discrimination after localized hemispheric lesions in man. *Arch. Neurol.* 33:543–50

Roland, E., Larsen, B. 1976. Focal increase of cerebral blood flow during stereognostic testing in man. *Arch. Neurol.* 33:551–58

Roland, E., Larsen, B., Lassen, N. A., Skinhoj, E. 1980a. Supplementary motor area and other cortical areas in organization of voluntary movements of man. *J. Neurophysiol.* 43:118–36

Roland, P. R., Skinhoj, E., Lassen, N. A., Larsen, B. 1980b. Different cortical areas in man in organization of voluntary movements in extrapersonal space. *J. Neurophysiol.* 43:137–50

Rolls, E. T., Perrett, D., Thorpe, S. J., Puerto, A., Roper-Hall, A., Maddison, S. 1979. Response of neurons in area 7 of the parietal cortex to objects of different significance. *Brain Res.* 169:194–98

Sakata, H. 1975. Somatic sensory responses of neurons in the parietal association area (area 5) of monkeys. In *The Somatosensory System,* ed. H. H. Kornhuber, pp. 250–61. Stuttgart: Thieme

Sakata, H., Shibutani, H., Kawano, K. 1978. Parietal neurons with dual sensitivity to real and induced movements of visual target. *Neurosci. Lett.* 9:165–69

Sakata, H., Shibutani, H., Kawano, K. 1980. Spatial properties of visual fixation in posterior parietal association cortex of the monkey. *J. Neurophysiol.* 43:1654–72

Sakata, H., Takaoka, Y., Kawarasaki, A., Shibutani, H. 1973. Somatosensory properties of neurons in the superior parietal cortex (area 5) of the rhesus monkey. *Brain Res.* 64:85–102

Sato, M. 1961. Response of Pacinian corpuscle to sinusoidal vibration. *J. Physiol.* 159:391–409

Semmes, J., Porter, L., Randolph, M. C. 1974. Further studies of anterior postcentral lesions in monkeys. *Cortex* 10:55–68

Sessle, B. J., Hu, J. W., Dubner, R., Lucier, G. E. 1981. Functional properties of neurons in cat trigeminal subnucleus caudalis (medullary dorsal horn). II. Modulation of responses to noxious and non-noxious stimuli by periaqueductal gray, nucleus raphe magnus, cerebral cortex, and afferent influences, and effect of naloxone. *J. Neurophysiol.* 45:211–25

Snyder, S. H., Childers, S. R. 1979. Opiate receptors and opioid peptides. *Ann. Rev. Neurosci.* 2:35–64

Soso, M. J., Fetz, E. E. 1980. Responses of identified cells in postcentral cortex of awake monkeys during comparable active and passive joint movements. *J. Neurophysiol.* 43:1090–1110

Stein, J. 1978. Effects of parietal lobe cooling on manipulative behavior in the conscious monkey. See Brinkman & Porter 1978, pp. 79–90

Talbot, W. H., Darian-Smith, I., Kornhuber, H. H., Mountcastle, V. B. 1968. The sense of flutter-vibration: comparison of the human capacity with response patterns of mechanoreceptive afferents from the monkey hand. *J. Neurophysiol.* 31:301–34

Tanji, J., Taniguchi, K., Saga, T. 1980. Supplementary motor area: neuronal response to motor instructions. *J. Neurophysiol.* 43:60–68

Taylor, M. M., Lederman, S. J. 1975. Tactile roughness of grooved surfaces: a model and the effect of friction. *Percept. Psychophys.* 17:23–36

Taylor, M. M., Lederman, S. J., Gibson, R. H. 1973. Tactual perception of texture. In *Handbook of Perception,* Vol. 3, *Biology and Perceptual Systems,* ed. E. C. Carterette, M. P. Friedman, Chap. 12, pp. 251–72. New York: Academic

Torebjork, H. E. 1974. Afferent C units responding to mechanical, thermal and chemical stimuli in human non-glabrous skin. *Acta Physiol. Scand.* 92:374–90

Vallbo, A. B., Hagbarth, K-E. 1968. Activity from skin mechanoreceptors recorded percutaneously in awake human subjects. *Exp. Neurol.* 21:270–89

Vallbo, A. B., Hagbarth, K-E., Torebjork, H. E., Wallin, B. G. 1979. Somatosensory, proprioceptive, and sympathetic activity in human peripheral nerves. *Physiol. Rev.* 59:919–57

Vallbo, A. B., Johansson, R. S. 1976. Skin mechanoreceptors in the human hand: neural and psychophysical thresholds. See Kenshalo 1976, pp. 185–200

Vallbo, A. B., Johansson, R. S. 1978. The tactile sensory innervation of the glabous skin of the human hand. See Brinkman & Porter 1978, pp. 29–54

Werner, G., Whitsel, B. L. 1968. Topology of the body representation in somatosensory area 1 of primates. *J. Neurophysiol.* 31:856–69

Whitsel, B. L., Dreyer, D. A., Hollins, M. 1978. Representation of moving stimuli by somatosensory neurons. *Fed. Proc.* 37:2223–27

Whitsel, B. L., Dreyer, D. A., Roppolo, J. R. 1971. Determinants of body representation in postcentral gyrus of macaques. *J. Neurophysiol.* 34:1018–34

Whitsel, B. L., Petrucelli, L. M., Werner, G. 1969. Symmetry and connectivity in the map of the body surface in somatosensory area II of primates. *J. Neurophysiol.* 32:170–83

Willis, W. D., Trevino, D. L., Coulter, J. D., Maunz, R. 1974. Responses of primate spinothalamic tract neurons to natural stimulation of hindlimb. *J. Neurophysiol.* 37:358–81

Wong, Y. C., Kwan, H. C., MacKay, W. A., Murphy, J. T. 1978. Spatial organization of precentral cortex in awake monkeys. *J. Neurophysiol.* 41:1107–19

Woolsey, C. N. 1943. 'Second' somatic receiving areas in the cerebral cortex of cat, dog and monkey. *Fed. Proc.* 2:55

Woolsey, C. N., Marshall, W. H., Bard, P. 1942. Representation of cutaneous tactile sensibility in the cerebral cortex of the monkey as indicated by evoked potentials. *Bull. Johns Hopkins Hosp.* 70:399–441

Wurtz, R. H., Goldberg, M. E., Robinson, D. L. 1980. Behavioral modulation of visual responses in the monkey: stimulus selection for attention and movement. *Prog. Psychobiol. Physiol. Psychol.* 9:43–83

Yin, T. C. T., Mountcastle, V. B. 1977. Visual input to the visuomotor mechanisms of the monkey's parietal lobe. *Science* 197:1381–83

Ann. Rev. Psychol. 1982. 33:195–230

GROUP RESEARCH

Joseph E. McGrath and David A. Kravitz[1]

Department of Psychology, University of Illinois, Champaign, Illinois 61820–6267

CONTENTS

[1]We are very grateful for the excellent critical reviews and helpful comments that we received on earlier drafts of this chapter from five of our colleagues: Irwin Altman, James H. Davis, J. Richard Hackman, Samuel Komorita, Patrick Laughlin; and for the invaluable editorial and manuscript preparation assistance by Kathleen Karr.

David Kravitz is now at the Department of Psychology, University of Kentucky, Lexington, KY, 40506–0044. Correspondence regarding this chapter should be addressed to: Joseph E. McGrath, 219 Psychology Building, 603 East Daniel Street, Champaign, IL 61820–6267.

0066-4308/82/0201-0195$02.00

INTRODUCTION

In 1961, the treatment of Social Psychology within the *Annual Review of Psychology* was divided, like ancient Gaul, into three parts, each to be treated every third year. One of the parts was Group Research. Since then, there have been six triannual reviews of the group area. (There was one 6-year gap, from 1967 until 1973, the reasons for which we have not been able to discern.) These reviews were by an impressive lineup of scholars, including: Shaw (1961), Steiner (1964), Gerard & Miller (1967), Helmreich, Bakeman & Scherwitz (1973), Davis, Laughlin & Komorita (1976), and Zander (1979). Many of them were themselves major contributors to the development and shaping of the small group research field during those 20 years. Before that, in the first 11 volumes of *Annual Review of Psychology,* chapters were presented on the whole of Social Psychology, including the group area. These chapters had an even more impressive list of authors: Bruner (1950), D. Katz (1951), M. B. Smith (1952), Newcomb (1953), Crutchfield (1954), Festinger (1955), R. L. French (1956), Cartwright (1957), Heyns (1958), Gilchrist (1959), and Riecken (1960). This list, too, contains a number of researchers who have been major forces in shaping the small group field during the past 30 years. Together those 17 treatments of the group research area constitute a formidable historical record of that field's progress, problems, and prospects.

Each of the six reviews of the group area, and before them each of the 11 reviews of social psychology, has explicitly or implicitly offered a "recent past" perspective and has covered a specific period in detail; and most of them have done some prophesying regarding the near future. We can regard them as a time series (with some amount of shingle-like overlap because of preparation time and publication lag), in which the retrospective looks of some reviews are the covered periods of others and the periods of prophesy of still others. Examining those past reviews from such an overlapping period, time-series perspective may be instructive. It may at least give us pause about how well we can project our field into the future. More cogently, it might even make us somewhat skeptical about the extent to which retrospective and future, as well as current, interpretations of the field are a product of the viewers rather than of the field. So we shall devote a few pages of this review to such a backward look, despite the very pressing page limitations under which this review is being prepared.

A Backward Look

Each of the early volumes of *Annual Review of Psychology* had a social psychology chapter with about one-third of it on "groups." Some of the early reviews found the group area to be one of the most rapidly developing parts of the field and a potential focal point for the expanding and fractionated field of social psychology. Several of them decried the lack of theory, in the group area as well as in social psychology as a whole. But one of them (French 1956) did not see this as a fatal flaw; and several others (e.g. Katz 1951, Cartwright 1957) seem to suspect that there might be too much pretense of theoretical rigor, such as the use of hypothetic-deductive formulations, when, in fact, there was little theory from which to deduce those hypotheses. Several saw signs of hope for theoretical advance in the near future.

The early reviewers (e.g. Bruner 1950, Katz 1951, Crutchfield 1954) saw a healthy and proper balance of laboratory, field, and survey methodology. But by the last of that 11-year series (Riecken 1960), there appeared to be a serious imbalance of laboratory over field. That same review also noted the impressive dominance of discipline oriented (i.e. "basic" research) over problem oriented (i.e. "applied" research). Almost all of the reviewers of those first 11 volumes praised the increasing methodological sophistication, referring to advances in design, statistics and measurement. This was the single most consistent positive observation.

In the first of the chapters dealing exclusively with groups, Shaw (1961) saw the area as growing, indeed growing up. It was still disorganized and lacked broad theory, but there were some signs of advance in that regard. He echoed the fundamental optimism of the preceding decade with his final sentence: "The future looks bright!"

Three years later, Steiner (1964) stated that he found no basis to refute Shaw's optimistic epilogue, even though he also found no major conceptual breakthroughs in the intervening years. He did find, along with Shaw, advance in development and use of formal mathematical models. He noted that both research and theory tended to be concerned with small, discrete, and unrelated areas, with little integration. He criticized the continued use of retrospective reports and the continued neglect of process. Steiner felt the prevailing mood was one of peaceful harmony and laissez-faire, but was uncertain whether this was an indication of maturity or apathy. He predicted a better theory-data balance for the future.

Three years further into the '60s, Gerard & Miller (1967) found an overburdening expansion of publications in the area, and found the intervening period one of consolidation, not innovation or advance. They undertook a comprehensive and systematic coverage of the small group literature, with an emphasis on laboratory studies now clearly dominant. They, too, noted a lack of theoretical advance. Although they noted some methodological contributions, they were less enthusiastic in this regard than previous reviewers had been.

There was no groups chapter in the 1970 volume of the *Annual Review of Psychology.* After a 6-year hiatus, Helmreich, Bakeman & Scherwitz

(1973) wrote a review that carried a sharply different tone, and to some extent addressed a different spectrum of topics, than had any previous review. The "spirit" of the preceding 14 reviews could be paraphrased as follows: "The group area is important, perhaps central, to social psychology. Publications in it are expanding very rapidly. While it seems chaotic, needs integration, and lacks theory, it is gaining in methodological rigor and sophistication. While the . . . (period covered by any particular review) was mainly consolidating, good work but not breakthroughs, there is reason to expect great advances soon." The Helmreich et al (1973) review essentially states that the emperor has no clothes! All those laboratory studies, they imply, yielded a pile of data—lacking external validity and applicability—but not a body of knowledge. The attention to methodological rigor had hoist us on the twin petards of practical irrelevance and theoretical barrenness. They suggest a psychological Gresham's Law: bad research drives out good! Yet, in the closing section, even their pessimistic review *predicts* a pattern of breakthrough and advance: increased emphasis on processes; more studies of change over time; more multivariate studies; more emphasis on cognitive variables; more concern with the interaction of individual and situations; and more nonexperimental studies of natural groups over time. Apparently, the emperor's new suit will be ready Tuesday!

Three years later, Davis, Laughlin & Komorita (1976) ignored the previous pessimistic review and offered a more hopeful—though hardly pollyanna—prognosis. They delimited the domain to be treated so as to exclude the large volume of work of the preceding period that essentially dealt with "one-person groups." They also delimited the domain to include only that part of group research that deals with task performance. Work on other problems—group formation and development, participation and communication in groups, interpersonal attraction and interpersonal influence studies that involve multiple persons—was excluded if it was not tied more or less directly to group task performance. At the same time, they extended past coverage in that they gave a full-scale treatment to groups engaged in conflictful or mixed motive tasks. In their review they document some theoretical advances, and they see theoretical models as the route by which we may be rescued from the limitations of both laboratory and field studies. In that same light, they seem to regard basic and applied research as complementary rather than in opposition. And they, too, predict optimistically, including a resurgence of interest in research on groups and a shift toward concerns similar to those of the political economist, with the key problem being the interplay between the goals of the individual and those of the collective.

In the most recent triennial review, Zander (1979) offers a sweeping review of the preceding ones and provides a tally of topic-by-date. That tally shows how treatment of topics has waxed and waned. Zander also points out that new topics grow out of old ones, usually formulated with more precision than the parent. He suggests some reasons why some topics get studied, and he offers a provocative list of unstudied potential topics in the group area. Like many of his predecessors, Zander notes the preponderance of lab experiments and the lack of theory. Like some before him, he notes that few studies are done with a group level unit of study. And he notes the conceptual chaos that comes from the predilection of group researchers to invent new names for old concepts. He did not make predictions.

While each of those earlier reviews had some limitations, each also had some major virtues that commend it to the scholars of this field. It is quite a high ambition to hope that our review will be marked by the best of each of those six treatments of groups: by the inspiring optimism of Shaw; by the prescience and wisdom of Steiner; by the impressive thoroughness of Gerard & Miller; by the openness of Helmreich, Bakeman & Scherwitz to topics along the borders of the field; by the solid, systematic treatment of our colleagues, Davis, Laughlin & Komorita; and by the wide-ranging historical perspective of Zander. It is too much to expect our offering to attain such sixfold success; so we shall be pleased if we can approach, even though not reach, that set of standards.

Content and Organization of the Chapter

While we would prefer to be broadly eclectic in these matters, it is necessary to bound our efforts and our product, for reasons of coherence as well as for space and time constraints. Besides the "standard" social-psychological journals, we made an effort to cover some journals from other areas of psychology, the speech communications field, sociology, education, and administrative sciences. We included the years not covered by the last review as thoroughly as possible, beginning with 1977 and continuing as far toward our manuscript deadline as we could, approximately through 1980.

Ultimately, our criteria for inclusion of an item were: (*a*) that we located it; (*b*) that it had not already been covered in preceding annual reviews of groups; (*c*) that it "fit" our fairly broad working definition of research on groups; and (*d*) that it could help make some useful point in the review.

Our working definition of research on groups requires that two or more people be in dynamic interaction with one another. This implies that the persons are mutually aware of one another and take one another into account, and that the relationship has some temporal (past and/or anticipated future) continuity to it. However, we did not treat the last point too stringently; we included studies in which the temporal continuity of the group was rather fleeting. Furthermore, we viewed groups as "fuzzy sets." Some, but not all, multiperson aggregates are groups; but some of them are "groupier" than others; and all of them are "groupier" at some times than at other times.

We have divided the materials and organized our review into four broad sections. The first section lists some general contributions. The second section deals with *groups as task performance systems.* This includes both cooperative and conflict-inducing tasks and coincides, more or less, with the Davis et al (1976) coverage. The third section deals with *groups as systems for structuring social interaction.* It deals with studies both of group structure and of group interaction process, the latter being an area we are pleased to find undergoing a renaissance. The chapter ends with brief comments on the field.

SOME GENERAL CONTRIBUTIONS

There are a number of books, chapters, and articles that represent a general contribution to group research. For one thing, the "*Advances . . .*" series edited by Berkowitz continued, with some group-relevant contributions in recent volumes (e.g. Leventhal 1976, Berkowitz 1978a). Furthermore, Berkowitz (1978b) produced a volume that reprints a half dozen outstanding group contributions from past volumes of the series, and also offers "updates" by the same authors (Fiedler 1978b, Hackman & Morris 1978, Hoffman 1978, Hollander & Julian 1978, Shaw 1978, Waxler & Mishler 1978). Fishbein (1980) has begun a similar series ("*Progress in . . .*"), and its first volume has several chapters relevant to the group area.

There are several recent volumes from group-relevant conferences (e.g. Brandstätter, Davis & Stocker-Kreichgauer 1981). Hackman (1976) provided an excellent chapter on group effects on individuals. One whole issue of *American Behavioral Scientist,* edited by D. Katz, was devoted to social psychology, with at least two of the articles (McGrath 1978, Newcomb 1978b) pertaining to group research. Davis & Hinsz (1981) provide an overview of current research issues. A second edition of Hare's *Handbook of Small Group Research* (1976) and a third edition of Shaw's comprehensive group dynamics textbook (1981) were published, and a new edition of Hare's collection of group research readings is due soon (Blumberg et al, in press). Zander (1977) provided a readable and interesting treatment of groups in the work context.

Four publishing events during this period deserve special note and offer promise for the short-run future of the field. One is the publication of Kelley & Thibaut's (1978) long awaited companion volume to Thibaut & Kelley's (1959) key monograph on exchange theory. We find it a very powerful formulation. But we suggest that this book, like the earlier one, will take quite a long time before it is fully understood by, absorbed into, and appreciated within the group research field. We suggest that its value will be more appropriately assessed in the next review of this series on group research. Second is the publication of Bales' new formulation on interaction process (Bales & Cohen 1979). Perhaps it will both herald and accelerate a resurgence of effort in that area. The third is the initiation of a "groups" portion of APA's social psychology journal (*Journal of Personality and Social Psychology*) with Ivan Steiner as its first editor. The fourth is the publication (imminent at the time of this writing) of a third edition of the *Handbook of Social Psychology,* with at least one chapter (by Burnstein) pertaining to groups.

GROUPS AS TASK PERFORMANCE SYSTEMS

Historically, one major thrust of group research has been a concern with the task performance effectiveness of groups, as opposed to single individuals, and with effects of a variety of input factors and operating conditions on such task performance. The period covered by this review also was marked by a high proportion of studies (about 40%) focusing on group task performance of some kind of task. Given this high and continuing level of interest, and the importance of task factors in group task performance effectiveness, it is heartening to see a renewal of interest in conceptual and empirical work on task differences and models of group task productivity. Shiflett (1979) has offered an excellent general model of group productivity, building on many earlier models. It defines a matrix (P) of group products that is derived from a matrix (R) of all relevant group resources, by means of a transform matrix (T) that reflects the weighting of members' resources. Hackman & Morris (1978) make at least implicit use of a classification system with three task types and three group product types, drawn from their earlier work, in their excellent treatment of group process and productivity. Davis's work on social decision schemes (e.g. Davis 1980, 1981; see also Laughlin 1980) offers a conceptual schema for relating intellective or problem-solving tasks with decision-making tasks.

Yet even with this recent work, and in spite of the many calls for such efforts in the past, there still is not a comprehensive and generally accepted task taxonomy or task classification schema for group tasks. McGrath (in press) has proposed an eight-category "task circumplex" that may in time provide such an overall comparisons schema (once it has been "polished" by grinding against the critical reviews of colleagues in the field). We will make use of a simplified version of that task circumplex here as a basis for organizing material to be reviewed in this section.

McGrath's Task Circumplex has four quadrants defined in terms of the dominant performance process involved in the group's task, and it divides each quadrant into two task types. Those eight task types, and subtypes within them, reflect a complex ordering relating to the primary performances processes involved, disjunctive and conjunctive relations, and cognitive, affective, and conative emphases. The quadrants, with their types and some subtypes, are:

I. *To Generate* (1. Plans; 2. Creative ideas)
II. *To Choose* (3. Interest tasks; 4. Decision tasks, including juries and choice shift tasks)
III. *To Resolve* (5. Cognitive conflict tasks; 6. Interest conflict tasks, including negotiation and bargaining, dilemmas, and coalition formation and allocation tasks)
IV. *To Execute* (7. Contests, such as competitive sports, wars; 8. Physical tasks)

Research on groups as task performance systems will be reviewed here in terms of these eight task types. We begin, for convenience, with the tasks of quadrant II.

Intellective Tasks

Tasks of the first type are what Laughlin (1980) has called *intellective tasks* (and what others have called problem solving). These are tasks for which there is, or is considered to be, a correct answer. The key work in this area during the period of our review has been done by Laughlin and his colleagues. Laughlin (1978) summarizes his work on the effects of different combinations of members' abilities on group performance. Laughlin & Sweeney (1977) dealt with individual-group transfer in problem solving. Several studies (Laughlin 1980, Laughlin & Adamopolus 1980, 1981) have applied Davis's (1973) social decision scheme theory to problems for which a correct solution—rather than a group preference—is sought. This work is well summarized by Laughlin (1980). One very robust finding from that work is that the "best fit" decision scheme for almost all such problems is: "truth, supported, wins." The exception is for true "eureka" problems, in which not only is there a correct answer, but that answer is easily demonstrable and, once proposed, is intuitively compelling. In such "eureka" problems, a "truth wins" schema best fits results. Many past studies of group problem solving tested groups against a "truth wins" criterion and found groups "less effective" (than their "best" member). This has been taken as a sign of "process losses," an indicator of inefficiency in groups (e.g. Bray, Kerr & Atkin 1978). From the Laughlin work, one can equally well regard this in a different light. The group's unwillingness uncritically to "buy" the noncompelling solution touted by a single member (even when that member has "truth," in the sense that the *experimenter* knows that that particular answer is correct), but to do so when the solution has some support, can be viewed as evidence of the good sense or pragmatic wisdom of groups, rather than of their inefficiency due to process losses.

Another class of problem that partly fits this category is that in which groups are asked to judge some event or condition (almost always in quantitative form), with the experimenter determining the "correct" answer by means of a consensus of experts. Here there is putatively a correct answer, but it may neither be known to nor demonstrable by members of the group. These are often considered accuracy of judgment tasks. Einhorn, Hogarth & Klempner (1977) provide a brief review of research and of previous models in this area. They discuss several models for assessing group "accuracy," provide a method to evaluate them, and apply them to study effects of variables such as group size on group accuracy. Here, groups tend to do "better" than the average individual, but less well than the "best" member.

Decision-Making Tasks

Next we shall consider decision-making tasks, those for which the group is seeking not a correct answer but a preferred one. Work here is mostly on two topics: jury performance and choice shifts. We shall discuss them in turn.

Empirical reviews of the jury research have been provided by Davis, Bray & Holt (1977) and by Gerbasi, Zukerman & Reis (1977). Davis (1980) has provided a thorough theoretical and empirical review of the research done by himself and his colleagues (see also Stasser, Kerr & Davis 1980). Penrod & Hastie (1979) have provided an excellent and broad-based theoretical review (see also Nagel & Neef 1976, Saks 1977, Klevorick & Rothschild 1979).

Jury research consists almost entirely of *mock* jury studies. Attempts to study real juries face formidable legal, logistical, and methodological barriers. J. H. Davis and colleagues, whose work provides a dominant *leit motif* for the area (cf Davis et al 1977, Bray & Noble 1978, Kerr 1978, Bray & Kerr 1979, Nagao & Davis 1980a, Vollrath & Davis 1980, Davis et al 1981), work with the constraint of studying "juries" that are investigator-concocted rather than "naturally occurring" (that is, court-concocted). Any actual case is heard by only one jury and tried by only one judge and one set of attorneys, one time. Results necessarily confound *particulars* of case, jurors, jury, judge, and many aspects of the occasion. It goes without saying that use of mock juries places constraints on interpretation of results in some significant respects (e.g. see Gerbasi, Zuckerman & Reis 1977). But given that limitation, not only does use of mock juries permit experimentally managed jury composition, but it also permits comparison of outcomes for multiple cases tried by the same jury, for multiple juries trying the same case, and even, in principle, for the same jury trying a given case more than once.

Davis's work is also characterized by intensive use of formal models—in this case, what has come to be called Social Decision Scheme (SDS) theory. SDS theory is a mathematical statement of a family of combinatorial models that can be used: (*a*) to induce the "decision rule" that best characterizes the result of a group-decision process, or (*b*) to test whether one or more hypothesized decision rules "fit" such results to some preestablished criterion level (Davis 1973, Schönemann 1979, Kerr, Stasser & Davis 1979).

Results of those and other studies of mock juries suggest strongly that juries operate on a "two-thirds majority" or, in general, a "very strong majority" decision rule, but not on "unanimity," which is the formal legal decision rule for juries. There is some evidence also from postjury interviews that "real" juries also operate on such a "strong majority but not unanimity" rule (see Davis 1980).

The general SDS scheme has been used by Laughlin to explore combinatorial rules for groups doing intellective tasks (discussed earlier). It has also been applied by Davis and colleagues (e.g. Vollrath & Davis 1979, 1980, Nagao & Davis 1980b) as a basis for extrapolating to conditions not yet empirically examined. For example, the SDS model permits one to run out the inevitable consequences of using juries of *any given size* with *any given distribution of predeliberation juror opinions,* assuming only that some one particular decision rule (say, for example, two-thirds majority) will hold for juries of various sizes and composition. While empirical studies of mock juries, and archival data from actual juries, fail to show differences in verdicts due to jury size differences, Davis's SDS model shows that such differences are inevitable, though small and complex. To detect such small and interactive differences by straightforward empirical procedures (e.g. mock jury studies) would require enormous sample sizes, not to mention extreme experimental obtrusiveness. A strong formal model, such as SDS, permits the investigator to identify such differences and state explicitly the conditions and assumptions upon which those "findings" are based.

Penrod & Hastie (1979, 1980) offer a computer simulation model of jury decision making, and have put it to use to test a series of questions about the potential effects of jury size and assigned decision rules. The Penrod and Hastie model, like Davis's SDS, can potentially be used to explore a very large range of research questions at very manageable levels of cost. Such models can be powerful tools in group research in general, as well as in jury research (see also Nagel & Neef 1976, Klevorick & Rothschild 1979). It is the development and use of such formal conceptual models that has been urged for the group research field for several decades (e.g. Steiner 1964, McGrath & Altman 1966, Davis, Laughlin & Komorita 1976). Perhaps the time is at hand when such models, and the cadre of investigators trained to use them and develop others, will become frequent if not standard in group research.

The second problem within the decision task category that received substantial attention during the period of this review is work on choice shifts or, as the phenomenon has come to be called, *polarization*. The key work here has been done by Myers & Lamm (1976, Lamm & Myers 1978, Myers 1978) and by Burnstein and Vinokur (1977, Vinokur & Burnstein 1978a,b). Lamm & Myers (1978) offer an excellent summary of the past history of the risky-shift-choice-shift-polarization phenomenon; and Miller (1978) looked retrospectively at the problem area. Several central notions seem worth stating here. First, the overall thrust of that evidence shows that after group discussion, group members shift toward whichever end of the issue they already favored; and the degree of shift on an item correlates strongly with the degree of prior tendency in that direction characteristic of that item (hence, it is if anything depressed by the operation of regression effects). So the very robust phenomenon of the 1960s is not really a "risky shift" in groups, but rather an accentuation of direction of prior individual views *after exposure to group discussion*. Hence, it is not so much a matter of group task performance, but is largely a matter of group effects on individual members—the topic of a later section of this review where some of the choice shift literature is treated.

Two matters still remain controversial, hence deserving of and receiving research attention (Paicheler 1976, 1977, 1979, Burnstein & Vinokur 1977, Forgas 1977, Jellison & Arkin 1977, Johnson, Stemler & Hunter 1977, Kaplan 1977, Kaplan & Miller 1977, Sanders & Baron 1977, Dickson 1978, Hong 1978, Madsen 1978, Myers 1978, Sanders 1978, Vinokur & Burnstein 1978a,b, Felsenthal 1979, Goethals & Zanna 1979, Greenberg 1979). First is the question of how broadly generalizable the polarization phenomenon is over tasks of different types (e.g. gambling, reward allocation, juries) and over a broader range of issues, including some drawn from current topics (e.g. Paicheler 1976, 1977, 1979). The answer appears to be: very broadly indeed. Second is the question of which of two still plausible theoretical formulations best accounts for polarization—or, more likely, how the two fit together to account jointly for those robust results. One is the theory derived from social comparison theory, favored by Myers & Lamm (1976) among others. The other is a persuasive arguments theory, favored by Burnstein & Vinokur (1977). The evidence seems to show good support for each theory and for the importance of, though not necessarily the necessity for, group discussion. These two theories are similar to the ideas of normative and informational forces in conformity. In some other areas the two seem to be intertwined (e.g. see Hackman 1976). Perhaps here, too, both are a part of the picture. It has been suggested, for example, in several of the sources cited, that social comparisons may be the distal cause and persuasive arguments the proximal cause of the remarkably robust and now more clearly conceptualized polarization effects.

Cognitive Conflict Tasks

Hammond, Brehmer, and colleagues have argued that many group decisions involve cognitive conflict between members (as opposed to motive conflict, which will be the subject of the next part of this section). They have developed a theory, a related set of group treatments, and a set of experimental procedures for creating, studying, and potentially attenuating such cognitive conflicts. They call their approach Social Judgment Theory (Hammond et al 1975), and their work virtually defines that area of study. Brehmer (1976) presents an extremely thorough analysis of that theory and of the large body of experimental work done within its paradigm. He shows that cognitive conflict, and its reduction, is affected by the structure of the task, by the cognitive structures of the parties, and by the consistency with which they use their policies. Rohrbaugh (1979) offers another application of that schema within group research, and Padgett & Wolosin (1980) report a related experiment. It seems likely that such powerful tools—though having important limitations on the range of problems that they can be used to study—will find wider use within the group research field within the coming years.

Mixed-Motive Tasks

Research on mixed-motive groups divides rather naturally into three sets of studies which we will treat seriatum; (*a*) research on bargaining and negotiation; (*b*) research on dilemmas, including the prisoner's dilemma and related two-person games, N-person dilemma games, and social traps; and (*c*) research on coalition formation.

BARGAINING AND NEGOTIATION RESEARCH There are a number of integrative and theoretical contributions in this area. Morley & Stephenson (1977) and Rubin & Brown (1975) have presented useful theoretical perspectives and summarized relevant research. Compilations by Druckman (1977) and Sauermann (1978) contain a number of useful chapters. Roth & Malouf (1979) examined the implications of game-theoretic models for bargaining research. Chertkoff & Esser (1976) and Miller & Crandall (1980) provide reviews of the bargaining literature. We shall use their six-category organization in the following discussion of bargaining research.

The first category is work on individual differences such as gender (Kimmel et al 1980), orientation along a cooperative-competitive dimension

(Lewis & Fry 1977, Schulz & Pruitt 1978), and personality (Hermann & Kogan 1977). The second is research on aspects of the bargaining situation such as payoffs (Schulz & Pruitt 1978, Kimmel et al 1980) and the availability of alternatives (Komorita & Kravitz 1979, Komorita, Lapworth & Tumonis 1981). We found little research dealing with their third category, the effects of social relationships with the opponent (Deutsch & Kotik 1978, Tjosvold 1977). On the other hand, there was a considerable amount of work dealing with significant third parties, including research on the relationship between the negotiator and his or her constituents (Breaugh & Klimoski 1977, Klimoski & Breaugh 1977, Tjosvold 1977, Wall 1978). Rubin (1980) presents a summary of research on third-party intervention, organized around three themes: (*a*) third parties help concession-making without loss of face; (*b*) traditional intervention techniques work under low conflict, but may backfire under high conflict conditions; and (*c*) third-party intervention is often an unwanted intrusion, and the parties will settle to prevent it if they can. There is some research on the fifth category, effects of situational factors (Lewis & Fry 1977, Schulz & Pruitt 1978). Finally, four studies dealt with bargaining strategies and tactics (Hamner & Yukl 1977, Komorita 1977, Wall 1977, Lindskold 1978).

DILEMMAS Two books focusing on matrix games appeared during this period (Rapoport, Guyer & Gordon 1976, Kelley & Thibaut 1978), and Edney (1980) presents a valuable conceptual discussion of the dilemma situation. Pruitt & Kimmel's (1977) review earlier in this series noted the proliferation of studies of two-person, two-choice games, especially the prisoner's dilemma, and criticized the mono-method state of the problem area. The torrent of studies on the prisoner's dilemma game, that threatened to engulf us all, has now abated. There is still some work utilizing the PD, but as was the case with the very early PD work, many current studies use the PD as a vehicle for addressing specific conceptual questions (e.g. Bennett & Carbonari 1976, Chertkoff & Lane 1978, Schlenker & Goldman 1978, Toda et al 1978, Lendenmann & Rapoport 1980).

The problem of choice under social dilemma conditions has received increased attention in models and empirical research on N-person dilemma games (NPD), social traps, and "public goods" approaches (Goehring & Kahan 1976, Komorita 1976, Stern 1976, Alcock & Mansell 1977, Brechner 1977, Dawes, McTavish & Shaklee 1977, Fox & Guyer 1977, Marwell & Ames 1979, Dawes 1980, Fleishman 1980, Komorita, Sweeney & Kravitz 1980, Dawes & Orbell 1981). These paradigms offer promise as bases for exploring choice under dilemma conditions far less restricted than the two person, two-choice paradigms that characterized most of the work in this area during the previous three decades.

COALITION FORMATION Even though the PD torrent has abated, the current flood of coalition research suggests that we cannot yet ignore our flood-control concerns. However, as Davis et al (1976) noted, while the PD area is atheoretical, coalition studies are very much theory-anchored. Miller & Crandall (1980) and Murnighan (1978a) provide useful reviews. Friend, Laing & Morrison (1977) and Komorita (1979) offer new coalition theories, with the former concentrating on process rather than on outcome. Nichols (1977) relates coalition formation to traditional learning research, and Komorita (1978) and Bonacich (1979) both offer indices for use in evaluating the fit of coalition theories. One major body of theory and research in this area is by Komorita and his colleagues (Komorita 1977, 1978, 1979, Komorita & Brinberg 1977, Komorita & Kravitz 1978, 1981, Komorita & Meek 1978, Komorita & Tumonis 1980). This work provides strong experimental comparisons, under a range of conditions, for a set of rival coalition theories (minimum power theory, minimum resources theory, bargaining theory, weighted probability theory, and equal excess theory). Further theory testing work along those lines has been carried out by Chertkoff & Esser (1977), Kahan & Rapoport (1977), Toda & Shinotsuka (1978), and by Murnighan and colleagues (Murnighan, Komorita & Szwajkowski 1977, Murnighan 1978b). The latter have explored factors affecting coalitions in veto games (Murnighan & Roth 1977, 1978, 1980, Murnighan & Szwajkowski 1979). There is also an excellent set of theory comparison studies by Miller (1979a,b, 1980a,b,c).

There is also much other work on coalitions. Some of it involves applications of formal mathematical models and decision theory to the coalition area and further explorations of game properties (Kushner & De Maio 1977, Michener, Yuen & Ginsberg 1977, Roth 1977, Sticha 1977, Michener, Ginsberg & Yuen 1979, Michener, Sakurai, Yuen & Kasen 1979). Some of it involves attempts to broaden the narrow method base of coalition research (Nitz 1976, Cole, Phillips & Hartman 1977, Cole & Barnett 1978, Lawler, Youngs & Lesh 1978, Levinsohn & Rapoport 1978, Miller 1979a). There also appears to be a shift toward multivalued games (in characteristic function form rather than in weighted majority form) and toward studies comparing effects of different sources of power in coalition situations (Komorita & Brinberg 1977, Nydegger & Owen 1977, Rapoport, Kahan & Wallsten 1978, Roth 1979, Funk, Rapoport & Kahan 1980, Kahan & Bonacich 1980, Komorita & Tumonis 1980, Kravitz 1981, Miller 1980a,c).

The upshot of all of this work suggests several things: (*a*) No one of the theories yet formulated is adequate to handle all variations in conditions (number of persons; type, distribution and relevance of resources; characteristic function vs quota games; etc). (*b*) The two that offer most promise for sizable ranges of conditions are equal excess and bargaining theory.

(*c*) Minimum resource and minimum power theories do not work well under most of the conditions studied in experiments, although they may provide very useful guides for research in larger political systems (see Murnighan 1978a). (*d*) The area has been quite narrowly mono-method, and this has had some of the same consequences here as in the PDG area; but there has been marked improvement in this regard to recent work. (*e*) One focal need at this time is not to try to concoct an experimentum crucium in a search for the "one true theory," but rather to try to pin down the range of conditions under which each of the present theories is effective and then to try to induce from that framework the multiple processes that apparently operate in the formation of coalitions and the distribution of payoffs within them. (*f*) There is a need for more research on the processes involved in forming and using coalitions, in order to supplement the strong emphasis on outcomes that has characterized the field to date.

Additional Comments About Group Task Performance

The task circumplex schema that provides the basis for the task classification being used here (McGrath, in press) calls for eight major task types. Thus far we have covered four: intellective tasks, decision tasks, cognitive conflict tasks, and mixed-motive tasks. These are the types most often represented in the group literature. Two of the other four types, competitive physical tasks and noncompetitive physical tasks, have been markedly underrepresented in research on groups, relative to their baserates in "nature"; and such continues to be the case in the materials we located. The other two types are planning tasks and creativity tasks (both "generation" tasks in McGrath's task circumplex). The first, planning tasks, also have been underrepresented in past group research, and continue to be. The latter, creativity tasks, were at one time a favorite task type for group studies during the "brainstorming" craze; but that type, too, is now infrequent in group research.

We found only a few studies that fit any of those latter four types: Rosenbaum et al (1980), Flowers (1977), Goldman, Stockbauer & McAuliffe (1977), and Katz & Tushman (1979). We also found several valuable efforts involving tasks of more than one type (Williams 1977, Kabanoff & O'Brien 1979, Nadler 1979, Murnighan 1981, Rutter & Robinson 1981). Several of those studies are also germane to research on group interaction process, the area to be discussed next.

As an overly simplified summary of the work in this very broad and richly articulated area—group task performance—we want to note that there seems to have been substantial advance in our *knowledge* about task performance of groups, not merely an increment in the volume of research on that topic. Given what has been said about group research in both the recent and the distant past, that statement reflects what we regard as a major advance. Furthermore, we regard even more optimistically the current status of the study of group interaction process—the next major topic to be discussed in this chapter.

GROUPS AS SYSTEMS FOR STRUCTURING SOCIAL INTERACTION

The intense early interest in group interaction process, epitomized by the work with Bales' interaction process analysis (IPA) (e.g. Bales 1950), and the extensive interest in effects of group structure, perhaps epitomized by the extensive work on communication networks (e.g. Leavitt 1951, Shaw 1978), both have been in decline for over a decade. There are several salient reasons for this decline. Among them are the practical difficulties and costs of such studies, the apparent theoretical sterility of many earlier efforts, and the attractiveness of individual-level paradigms for studying related processes. In several earlier reviews of group research in this series (e.g. Helmreich et al 1973, Davis et al 1976) and elsewhere (e.g. Hackman 1976, McGrath 1978) there has been a call for a rekindling of research fervor aimed at developing a better understanding of the interaction processes by which groups act, and by which they have their consequences for tasks, for members, and for the group itself. We have the pleasant duty of reporting that such a resurgence of interest in group interaction has indeed occurred during the period covered by this review, and the even more pleasant duty of reporting that a sizable fraction of that work is interesting, innovative, and of great promise. That resurgence is heralded by Bales' major contribution (Bales & Cohen 1979), and that work may provide the same impetus now that his earlier seminal work (Bales 1950) did three decades ago. The most interesting and exciting part of that work involves studies of the communication process, verbal and nonverbal, and studies of what we will call the morphology of interaction—participation patterns and temporal features of the process. We deal with those areas first before covering the somewhat more traditional work on the acquaintance process and on the influence of group interaction on the individual member.

Patterning of Interaction: The Communication Process

MORPHOLOGY: PATTERNS OF PARTICIPATION AMONG MEMBERS AND OVER TIME Of especially great interest and potential is the blossoming of research on what we have termed the "morphology" of group interaction; that is, studies of the patterning of interaction per se, or, to use a rather awkward phrase, the "structure of interaction process." This has two main parts. One deals with patterns of participation—the who and how much of it. The other part deals with temporal patterns—the when of it. Both are fundamental sets of questions, in our view. Both are sets of questions that were addressed vigorously in an earlier era but have been in eclipse. Both are showing renewed vigor by virtue of the use of more sophisticated methods for recording, processing, and analyzing information. And both are using these methods, and their "morphological" results, to shed new light on a number of substantive questions: patterns of interpersonal trust, cognitive load in interactions, self-monitoring in interactions, patterns of dominance and influence, and the like.

The problem of predicting the distribution of participation among group members has long been with the group research field. Recently both Tsai (1977) and Nowakowska (1978) have tested hierarchical models of participation derived from observations of discussions in natural groups. Koomen & Sagel (1977) offer evidence that participation rates are predictable from the individual participants' prediscussion latencies of verbal response and talkativeness. Conroy & Sundstrom (1977) found territorial dominance of dyadic conversations (i.e. domination by persons in their own territories) for conditions of interpersonal disagreement. Adams (1980), Chell (1979), and Stein & Heller (1979) examined other aspects of participation and dominance in groups.

There also have been some studies of participation at more macro temporal levels. Two studies of college freshmen, using journal-type records, found differences in amount of social interaction over time (two semesters) as a function of gender and of physical attraction (Wheeler & Nezlek 1977, Reis, Nezlek & Wheeler 1980). Lytton, Conway & Sauvé (1977) found less verbal interaction and fewer expressions of affection from mothers to twins vs singleton male children. Baum & Valins (1979) reviewed a range of literature bearing on how design aspects of residential complexes affect level and pattern of social interaction.

Dabbs, Gottman, and their colleagues have made especially valuable contributions regarding temporal patterns of interactions. Gottman has analyzed patterns of dominance in conversations (Gottman et al 1976). He also has developed the use of spectral and cross-spectral analyses for the quantitative study of cyclicality, cross-cyclicality, lead-lag relations, and other temporal aspects of dyadic interaction (Gottman 1979a) and has applied these methods to the study of marital conflict (Gottman 1979b). J. M. Dabbs (draft) has carried out second-by-second analyses of "content free" patterns of speech and gaze during formal and informal conversation, and by use of Fourier analyses has developed means to quantify the "cognitive load" as well as the cyclicality of conversations. He and his colleagues (Dabbs et al 1980) have used such methods to analyze what it is that "self-monitors" monitor during interaction.

McDowall (1978) studied the temporal patterning of body movements among interactors (in one six-person group) and found no evidence for synchrony (simultaneous movements), though he apparently did not explore possible lead-lag patterning. Several other studies examined various temporal aspects of interaction including: speech interruption (Ferguson 1977, Natale, Entin & Jaffe 1979); participation and influence (Carlston 1977, Spitzer & Davis 1978); assertive behavior (Doherty & Ryder 1979); and timing of behavior in conflict situations (Brickman, Becker & Castle 1979). At a more structural level, Skvoretz & Fararo (1980) attempt to build a "grammer of action" from analysis of the logical and linguistic properties of "action strings." Kraemer & Jacklin (1979), Thomas & Malone (1979), and Warner, Kenny & Stoto (1979) all offer models for analysis of dyadic social behavior that permit systematic scrutiny of the effects arising from each of the partners separately as well as conjointly. Freeman (1977) has developed a set of measures of centrality within networks of symmetrical relations. Shaw (1978), in a reprise of the preceding quarter-century of work on communication networks, finds such measures of centrality to be the most important contributions to that problem area.

Work on participation and temporal patterns, especially work such as that by Dabbs and Gottman that uses quite sophisticated tools for collection, processing, and analysis of observations, represents, in our view, an area of key importance for enhancing our understanding of group interaction processes and their effects.

NONVERBAL ASPECTS OF INTERACTION PATTERNING One of the most impressive and welcome changes in research on group interaction is the increased interest in study of nonverbal aspects of interaction in groups. While social psychologists and other social scientists have studied nonverbal communication for some time, much more of the recent work on these questions has been done in a group context than was the case in earlier years.

The largest share of the research is on gaze and eye contact. One set of studies (Rutter et al 1977, Lazzerini, Stephenson & Neave 1978) argues that eye contact—that is, *mutual* gaze by the members of a dyad—can be accounted for as a chance result of independent gaze (Looking) by the two individuals. Most of the rest explore the *functions of looking* within the interpersonal interaction situation. Three main functions of looking have been posited: to express interpersonal attitudes, to collect information about the other, and to regulate-synchronize the dyadic conversation. Although Rutter & Stephenson (1979) assert that most research has been on the expressive function, that is not the case for material found in our search. Rather, there are a number of studies showing the importance of the information collection and the regulatory functions of looking (Allen & Guy 1977, Beattie 1978, 1979, Cary 1978, Ellsworth et al 1978, Kendon 1978, Rutter et al 1978, Rutter & Stephenson 1979). There has been a similar exploration of the information and regulatory functions of some other nonverbal cues in interpersonal interaction: smiles (Brunner 1979, Kraut & Johnston 1979), body posture (Bull & Brown 1977), and other nonverbal strategy signals (Duncan, Brunner & Fiske 1979).

There have been some studies of patterns of "proxemic" variables that seem to be used to regulate interpersonal interaction, with interpersonal distance, axis of body orientation, and visual gaze being the main ingredients of the pattern. Results suggest there may be something like a "set point" or "desired level" for the pattern, which differs for different cultures, for different situations, and perhaps for differences in characteristics of the members of the dyad (LaFrance & Mayo 1976, Campbell & Rushton 1978, Hayduk 1978, Stockdale 1978, Voesjirwan 1978, Worchel & Yohai 1979). In related work, Ickes & Barnes (1977, 1978) examined effects of dyad composition (varied in terms of gender, sex roles, and self-monitoring level) on amount of interaction, initiation latencies, interaction difficulties, and attraction.

Several studies have been concerned with factors affecting accuracy and effectiveness of nonverbal communication (e.g. Rosenthal & DePaulo 1979). Hall (1978) reviewed literature on gender effects in nonverbal decoding accuracy, and conducted an experiment (Hall 1980) showing that nonverbal communication depends heavily on the decoding skills of the receiver. When cues in different modalities are discrepant, decoders are apparently more influenced by visual than by auditory cues (DePaulo et al 1978); and, in general, visual access can help overcome audio difficulties (Krauss et al 1977). Full channel access is vastly superior to a written verbal transcript (Archer & Akert 1977).

PATTERN AND STRATEGIES IN VERBAL COMMUNICATION Stiles has developed a set of categories consisting of eight verbal response modes (e.g. disclosure, question, confirmation) mapped to three interpersonal role dimensions (attentiveness, acquiescence, and presumptuousness). These offer a method for analysis of the content of verbal interaction comparable in scope to, but in certain ways more systematic than, Bales' IPA categories (Stiles 1978, Stiles, Waszak & Barton 1979). Such tools have long been needed. In a similar vein, Albert & Kessler (1978) propose six classes of verbal behavior related to endings of social encounters.

Haas (1979) reviewed past literature on male and female differences in spoken language, concluding that there are some systematic differences: in content (e.g. topics of unstructured discourse), in "interpersonal style" (e.g.

supportive and polite vs directive), and in "linguistic style" (e.g. use of compound forms, tag questions, etc). But Newcombe & Arnkoff (1979) report that "gender" of speech style rather than gender of the speaker influenced ratings of speech. Harrison et al (1978) found certain speech features (e.g. length, hesitation) characteristic of deceptive answers and of reduced believability. Such nonsemantic aspects of speech deserve further study.

There are also several studies of differences in strategies in interperson interaction that are associated with race, gender, sex roles, and status differences (Meeker & Weitzel-O'Neill 1977, Haan 1978, Falbo & Peplau 1980).

Content of Interpersonal Interaction: The Acquaintance Process

STUDIES OF INTERPERSONAL ATTRACTION There were several general offerings on this topic during the period covered. Huston & Levinger (1978) provided an excellent review of research on interpersonal attraction and relationships in Volume 29 of this series. Newcomb (1978a) published a retrospective look at his seminal work on the acquaintance process.

Clore and colleagues (1978) have taken the Byrne-Clore attraction paradigm to a field experimental setting (a biracial summer camp for kids); developed multiple measures of interpersonal attraction, several quite ingenious, and showed substantial convergence among them; and at least partially tested several hypotheses about effect of intergroup (in this case, interracial) contact. This kind of study, with a balance of natural conditions, experimental rigor and theoretical relevance, models some of the classic group studies of the past and stands in pleasant contrast to the plethora of studies of artificial relationships, contrived conditions, and single and reactive measures.

Several studies (e.g. Duck & Craig 1978, McCarthy & Duck 1979) were concerned with tracing the relation between similarity (of personality and attitude measures) and attraction over time. In a similar vein, Teichman (1977) studied shifts in what "resources" are exchanged between friends (in a military unit) as a friendship relationship develops; and Eidelson (1980) found a curvilinear relation between increasing involvement in and satisfaction with friendship relations among college men. Insko & Wilson (1977) studied the effects of social interaction on interpersonal attraction. There also were a few studies of the effects of such "composition" variables as age, gender, and race on relations among school children (Schofield & Sagar 1977) and sibling pairs (Tesser 1980).

There were three studies of romantic attraction. Kendrick & Cialdini (1977) argued for a reinforcement interpretation of love as well as liking.

White (1980) traced the effects of ("objective") physical attraction on courtship progress. Walster, Walster & Traupmann (1978) failed to confirm some predictions from equity theory regarding courtship progress (particularly premarital sexual intimacy) in relationships perceived as equitable or inequitable. Rusbult (1980) tested an investment model of interpersonal attraction. Levinger & colleagues have provided an important theoretical contribution in this area. Huesmann & Levinger (1976) presented a complex, sophisticated computer simulation model (called RELATE) of the development of a dyadic interactional relationship. It draws on incremental exchange theory and uses it to take into account diverse interpersonal phenomena such as altruism, similarity, self-disclosure, and romantic involvement. Recently Levinger (1980) has provided a review and conceptual integration of research on interpersonal acquaintance and has applied the RELATE model in some new forms.

INTIMACY, RECIPROCITY, AND SELF-DISCLOSURE There is now a sizable literature showing that the level of intimacy of self-disclosure in a dyad is an orderly function of characteristics of both the persons and the situation. One central theme of that literature is the idea that there will be an increase in intimacy as the relationship continues over time. This increase can be characterized by the notion of reciprocity. Increases in the amount and intimacy of self-disclosure by A to B will be responded to by increased, and increasingly intimate, self-disclosure by B to A. A number of studies have explored conditions that promote, hinder, or limit such reciprocity of self-disclosure and increasing intimacy: Balswick & Balkwell 1977, Foot, Chapman & Smith 1977, Skotko & Langmeyer 1977, Archer & Berg 1978, J. D. Davis 1977, 1978, Lynn 1978, Morton 1978, Taylor, De Soto & Lieb 1979, Won-Doornink 1979. This work marks some progress in our understanding of the dynamics by which people interact with one another. But this work has limited theoretical underpinnings. We need more theoretically based work on these issues.

PRIVACY AND SOCIAL PENETRATION One of the few major theoretical efforts in the study of interpersonal interaction is the work of Altman and his colleagues. A recent chapter (Altman, Vinsel & Brown 1981) builds on and unites two important previous theoretical efforts: social penetration theory (Altman 1973, Altman & Taylor 1973), which deals with the development of social relations from strangerhood through casual and on to more intimate social bonds, and privacy as boundary regulation process (Altman 1975). Altman et al (1981) have woven these two into a dialectic fabric that features two basic oppositions (openness-closedness, stability-change); that tries to replace the basic concept of homeostasis with concepts of dynamic opposition of forces; and that traces these dynamic oppositions over the "life course" of a developing and/or deteriorating relationship.

Outcomes of Interaction: The Influence Process

ALLOCATION OF REWARDS Equity threatens to become, to present-day group research, what risky shift, altruism, dissonance, conformity, communication nets, and cohesion have been to it in various decades past. Hatfield (formerly E. Walster) and her colleagues have brought equity theory to the relatively understudied area of intimacy and romantic love as well as to other areas (e.g. Berkowitz & Walster 1976). Harris (1976) provided a logical critique of equity models. A number of other researchers have explored a large number of conditions that effect the use of equity vs equality vs other allocation norms in work, family, classroom, and friendship situations. These factors include: friendship (Austin 1980); gender (Kahn, Lamm & Nelson 1977, Carles & Carver 1979, Kahn, Nelson & Gaeddert 1980); status (Parcel & Cook 1977); situational factors such as reward value and retaliatory potential (Greenberg 1978a); and cognitive processes and personality predispositions (Friend, Laing & Morrison 1977, Greenberg 1978b, Moschetti & Kues 1978). Leventhal (1976) provided a careful and comprehensive conceptual treatment of equity, equality, reciprocity, and need as bases for allocation of rewards and resources in groups.

On a related topic, Walker, Thibaut, and their colleagues have studied the relative importance of aspects of procedural justice and distributive justice in the resolution of conflicts and disputes (LaTour et al 1976, Houlden et al 1978, Lind et al 1980). This excellent work ties both to the jury studies and to the coalition studies discussed in an earlier section.

INFLUENCES ON MEMBERS' ATTITUDES AND BEHAVIOR Traditionally, one of the main reasons for interest in research on groups has been the persistent belief that groups are one major source of "environmental forces" that help shape the individuals who are their members. But most current research in areas such as attitude change, attraction, conformity, and social facilitation is done within an individual rather than a group research paradigm.

There is some group research in this area, however. For example, much of the work on polarization, already discussed in the task performance section, deals with effects of group discussion on subsequent individual judgments. There is also some work on influence on jurors (Kaplan 1977, Kerr 1978), gamblers (Sanders 1978), and members of groups engaged in other kinds of tasks (Castore & Murnighan 1978, O'Neill & Levings 1979). Eagly (1978) makes effective use of the distinction between conformity based on group pressures and conformity or persuasion based on other sources in her interesting review of sex differences in influencability. She finds scant evidence for gender differences in nongroup conformity research, but some evidence for such differences in a substantial minority of studies involving group pressures to conform.

There is also some research on effects of group interaction and of such factors as group size, gender composition and number of observers, on self-esteem, interpersonal stress, and perceptions of crowding by individual members (Dabbs 1977, Lundgren 1978, Van Egeren 1979, Diener et al 1980, Schaeffer & Patterson 1980).

There are some studies of somewhat more complex and perhaps more subtle manifestations of interpersonal influence. Snyder and his colleagues continue their thorough exploration of behavioral confirmation phenomena —self-fulfilling prophesies—in a series of experiments dealing with physical attraction, hostility, friendship, and the like (Snyder, Tanke & Berscheid 1977, Snyder & Swann 1978).

Other studies have explored how the effects of cognitive and perceptual factors influence communication effectiveness of laboratory partners (Padgett & Wolosin 1980) and resolution of marital conflicts (Knudson, Sommers & Golding 1980), and how the motivational attributes of husbands influence career levels of wives 14 years later (Winter, Stewart & McClelland 1977).

Still other aspects of influence in groups received attention. Leadership continues to be an important topic in group research, though perhaps not as central as it once was. And Fiedler's contingency theory continues to dominate the area, with Fiedler and his associates developing and extending both the theoretical conceptions and the practical applications, and critics continuing to question both the evidence and its interpretation (Fiedler, Chemers & Mahar 1976, Mitchell, Larson & Green 1977, Vecchio 1977, Fiedler 1978a,b, Schneier 1978). Hollander & Julian (1978) provide a retrospective look at their earlier formulations regarding leader legitimacy. There also were studies of: the emergence of leadership over generations of a group (Insko et al 1980); effects of demographic (e.g. gender), attitudinal, and personality characteristics of the leader on leader and group effectiveness (Green & Mitchell 1979, Lord & Rowzee 1979, Rice, Bender & Vitters 1980); effects of conflict and inequity on the leader's effectiveness (Katz 1977, Lawler & Thompson 1978); and several studies of the relations among power, status, conformity, and interaction (Fleishman & Marwell 1977, Miles 1977, Forgas 1978, Gray & Sullivan 1978, McCall 1979, Ridgeway 1978, Roger & Reid 1978).

EFFECTS OF GROUP INTERACTION ON ATTITUDES TOWARD THE GROUP Brewer's (1979) study provides an excellent review of the rather robust "ingroup bias." She draws three conclusions: (*a*) that a number of factors such as competition, similarity, and status differentials affect ingroup bias indirectly by altering salience of distinctions between ingroup and outgroup: (b) that the degree of ingroup/outgroup differentiation in a particular response dimension depends on the ingroup position on that dimension; and (c) that the enhancement of ingroup bias comes from more positive feelings toward the ingroup, rather than from more negative feelings toward the outgroup. A number of other studies (Segal 1977, Worchel, Andreoli & Folger 1977, Breakwell 1979, Commins & Lockwood 1979, Wilder & Thompson 1980, Worchel & Norvell 1980) document and further explore some of the factors involved in Brewer's three conclusions, including: effects of group size, degree of competition, outcomes of past intergroup contacts, ingroup/outgroup distinctiveness on particular dimensions, legitimacy of membership, perceived effects of environmental conditions, and the like.

LONG-RUN RELATIONS AMONG MEMBERS Several studies have dealt with really long-term interpersonal relations. Kandel (1978) studied similarity in adolescent, same-gender, friendship pairs. Schutte & Light (1978) studied the relative effects of status and proximity on friendship choices in business organizations. Grotevant, Scarr & Weinberg (1977) studied similarity in interest and personality profiles for biological and adoptive parent-child and sibling pairs. Meyer & Pepper (1977) studied the relation between marital adjustment and need similarity and need complementarity. All of these studies suggest a complex relation between acquaintance and both actual and perceived similarity. They also all offer evidence of the hazards involved in trying to untangle a complex causal network when one has only correlational studies of questionnaire responses to do it with.

CONCLUDING COMMENTS

Readers certainly have adduced by now that we view the most recent period as a productive one for group research and see the near future as promising for advances in our knowledge in that area. That optimistic view is based, we believe, on the evidence—much of which we have tried to cite here—of more and better group research during this period than has been the case for several decades. We are especially impressed with the increased sophistication about and interest in formal models—sometimes mathematical models, sometimes computer simulations—in several subareas of the field (some of which we have noted as we covered those topics). We are also impressed with the renewed interest in certain problem areas (verbal and nonverbal communication, interaction patterns, task differences and models of productivity, social dilemmas) and with the abating tide of studies of some other much-studied areas (PDG, risky shift, attraction to hypothetical others, bystander studies, effects of crowding). While there seems to have been some increase in the use of field settings for group research studies, this does not reflect so much an abandonment or rejection of the laboratory —still the most prominent research strategy of the field—but rather an increasing sophistication about methodology in general, and especially about the importance of using multiple approaches in any given problem area.

On the other hand, while the increased use of formal models will certainly tip the field more toward a concern with theoretical matters, the field is still a long way from having a proper balance among theory, method, and data. The dominance of atheoretical (even antitheoretical) viewpoints in the group area, virtually since the days of Lewin, still persists. We hoped to find signs of abatement of such views but did not. We also found far too little diversity in methods choices, although we did find signs that this is changing, as suggested above. But without the guiding hand of theory, it seems likely that the field will continue to move from one fashionable topic to the next, with fashions determined more by availability of paradigms than by conceptual import of the issues.

We noted at the beginning of this chapter that various past reviews of the group area in this series have seen it as the central hope of social psychology, as productive but not yet coherent, as disappointing, as immature, as chaotic, as dynamic, and as meriting various other shades of praise or concern. We have implied that it is undergoing a renaissance. We also cited Shaw's (1961) prediction that "the future looks bright." We see that prophesy as neither fulfilled nor disconfirmed as yet. We see no reason why this—like other behavioral confirmation phenomena—should not become another self-fulfilling prophesy. For the group research field, the future certainly can be bright. But there is no compelling reason why it must!

Literature Cited

Adams, K. A. 1980. Who has the final word? Sex, race, and dominance behavior. *J. Pers. Soc. Psychol.* 38(1):1–8

Albert, S., Kessler, S. 1978. Ending social encounters. *J. Exp. Soc. Psychol.* 14:541–53

Alcock, J. E., Mansell, D. 1977. Predisposition and behavior in a collective dilemma. *J. Conflict Resolut.* 21(3): 443–57

Allen, D. E., Guy, R. F. 1977. Ocular breaks and verbal output. *Sociometry* 40(1): 90–96

Altman, I. 1973. Reciprocity of interpersonal exchange. *J. Ther. Soc. Behav.* 3:249–61

Altman, I. 1975. *The Environment and Social Behavior: Privacy, Personal Space, Territory and Crowding.* Monterey, Calif: Brooks/Cole

Altman, I., Taylor, D. A. 1973. *Social Penetration: The Development of Interpersonal Relationships.* New York: Holt

Altman, I., Vinsel, A., Brown, B. B. 1981. Dialectic conceptions in social psychology: An application to social penetration and privacy regulation. *Adv. Exp. Soc. Psychol.* 14: In press

Archer, D., Akert, R. M. 1977. Words and everything else: Verbal and nonverbal cues in social interpretation. *J. Pers. Soc. Psychol.* 35(6):443–49

Archer, R. L., Berg, J. H. 1978. Disclosure reciprocity and its limits: A reactance analysis. *J. Exp. Soc. Psychol.* 14:527–40

Austin, W. 1980. Friendship and fairness: Effects of type of relationship and task performance on choice of distribution rules. *Pers. Soc. Psychol. Bull.* 6(3): 402–8

Bales, R. F. 1950. *Interaction Process Analysis: A Method for the Study of Small Groups.* Cambridge, Mass: Addison-Wesley

Bales, R. F., Cohen, S. P. 1979. *SYMLOG: A System for the Multiple Level Observation of Groups.* New York: Free Press

Balswick, J. O., Balkwell, J. W. 1977. Self-disclosure to same- and opposite-sex parents: An empirical test of insights from role theory. *Sociometry* 40(3): 282–86

Baum, A., Valins, S. 1979. Architectural mediation of residential density and control: Crowding and the regulation of social contact. *Adv. Exp. Soc. Psychol.* 12:131–75

Beattie, G. W. 1978. Floor apportionment and gaze in conversational dyads. *Br. J. Soc. Clin. Psychol.* 17:7–15

Beattie, G. W. 1979. Contextual constraints on the floor-apportionment function of speaker-gaze in dyadic conversations. *Br. J. Soc. Clin. Psychol.* 18:391–92

Bennett, R. P., Carbonari, J. P. 1976. Personality patterns related to own-, joint-, and relative-gain maximizing behaviors. *J. Pers. Soc. Psychol.* 34(6):1127–34

Berkowitz, L., ed. 1978a. *Advances in Experimental Social Psychology,* Vol. 11. New York: Academic

Berkowitz, L., ed. 1978b. *Group Processes.* New York: Academic

Berkowitz, L., Walster, E., eds. 1976. *Advances in Experimental Social Psychology, Vol. 9. Equity Theory: Toward a General Theory of Social Interaction.* New York: Academic

Blumberg, H. H., Hare, A. P., Kent, V., Davies, M., eds. 1981. *Small Groups.* Chichester, England: Wiley. In press

Bonacich, P. 1979. A single measure for point and interval predictions of coalition theories. *Behav. Sci.* 24:85–93

Brandstätter, H., Davis, J. H., Stocker-Kreichgauer, G., eds. 1981. *Group Decision Making.* London: Academic. In press

Bray, R. M., Kerr, N. L. 1979. Use of the simulation method in the study of jury behavior: Some methodological considerations. *Law Hum. Behav.* 3:107–19

Bray, R. M., Kerr, N. L., Atkin, R. S. 1978. Effects of group size, problem difficulty, and sex on group performance and member reactions. *J. Pers. Soc. Psychol.* 36(11):1224–40

Bray, R. M., Noble, A. M. 1978. Authoritarianism and decisions of mock juries: Evidence of jury bias and group polarization. *J. Pers. Soc. Psychol.* 36(12): 1424–30

Breakwell, G. M. 1979. Illegitimate group membership and inter-group differentiation. *Br. J. Soc. Clin. Psychol.* 18:141–49

Breaugh, J. A., Klimoski, R. J. 1977. The choice of a group spokesman in bargaining: Member or outsider? *Organ. Behav. Hum. Perform.* 19:325–36

Brechner, K. C. 1977. An experimental analysis of social traps. *J. Exp. Soc. Psychol.* 13:552–64

Brehmer, B. 1976. Social judgment theory and the analysis of interpersonal conflict. *Psychol. Bull.* 83:985–1003

Brewer, M. B. 1979. In-group bias in the minimal intergroup situation: A cognitive-motivational analysis. *Psychol. Bull.* 86:307–24

Brickman, P., Becker, L. J., Castle, S. 1979. Making trust easier and harder through two forms of sequential interaction. *J. Pers. Soc. Psychol.* 37(4):515–21

Bruner, J. S. 1950. Social psychology and group processes. *Ann. Rev. Psychol.* 1:119–50

Brunner, L. J. 1979. Smiles can be back channels. *J. Pers. Soc. Psychol.* 37(5):728–34

Bull, P. E., Brown, R. 1977. The role of postural change in dyadic conversations. *Br. J. Soc. Clin. Psychol.* 16:29–33

Burnstein, E., Vinokur, A. 1977. Persuasive argumentation and social comparison as determinants of attitude polarization. *J. Exp. Soc. Psychol.* 13:315–32

Campbell, A., Rushton, J. P. 1978. Bodily communication and personality. *Br. J. Soc. Clin. Psychol.* 17:31–36

Carles, E. M., Carver, C. S. 1979. Effects of person salience versus role salience on reward allocation in a dyad. *J. Pers. Soc. Psychol.* 37(11):2071–80

Carlston, D. E. 1977. Effects of polling order on social influence in decision-making groups. *Sociometry* 40(2):115–23

Cartwright, D. 1957. Social psychology and group processes. *Ann. Rev. Psychol.* 8:211–36

Cary, M. S. 1978. The role of gaze in the initiation of conversation. *Soc. Psychol.* 41(3):269–71

Castore, C. H., Murnighan, J. K. 1978. Determinants of support for group decisions. *Organ. Behav. Hum. Perform.* 22:75–92

Chell, I. 1979. Organizational factors and participation in committees. *Br. J. Soc. Clin. Psychol.* 18:53–57

Chertkoff, J. M., Esser, K. J. 1976. A review of experiments in explicit bargaining. *J. Exp. Soc. Psychol.* 12:464–86

Chertkoff, J. M., Esser, J. K. 1977. A test of three theories of coalition formation when agreements can be short-term or long-term. *J. Pers. Soc. Psychol.* 35(4): 237–49

Chertkoff, J. M., Lane, L. L. 1978. The interactions and perceptions of cooperators and competitors in a prisoner's dilemma game versus an expanded prisoner's dilemma game. See Sauerman 1978a, 7:1–19

Clore, G. L., Bray, R. M., Itkin, S. M., Murphy, P. 1978. Interracial attitudes and behavior at a summer camp. *J. Pers. Soc. Psychol.* 36(2):107–16

Cole, S. G., Barnett, L. W. 1978. The subjective distribution of achieved power and associated coalition formation behavior. See Sauermann 1978b, 8:40–54

Cole, S. G., Phillips, J. L., Hartman, E. A. 1977. Test of a model of decision processes in an intense conflict situation. *Behav. Sci.* 22:186–96

Commins, B., Lockwood, J. 1979. Social comparison and social inequality: An experimental investigation of intergroup behaviour. *Br. J. Soc. Clin. Psychol.* 18:285–89

Conroy, J. III, Sundstrom, E. 1977. Territorial dominance in a dyadic conversation as a function of similarity of opinion. *J. Pers. Soc. Psychol.* 35(8):570–76

Crutchfield, R. S. 1954. Social psychology and group processes. *Ann. Rev. Psychol.* 5:171–202

Dabbs, J. M. Jr. 1977. Does reaction to crowding depend upon sex of subject or sex of subject's partners? *J. Pers. Soc. Psychol.* 35(5):343–44

Dabbs, J. M. Jr., Evans, M. S., Hopper, C. H., Purvis, J. A. 1980. Self-monitors in conversation: What do they monitor? *J. Pers. Soc. Psychol.* 39(2):278–84

Davis, J. D. 1977. Effects of communication about interpersonal process on the evolution of self-disclosure in dyads. *J. Pers. Soc. Psychol.* 35(1):31–37

Davis, J. D. 1978. When boy meets girl: Sex roles and the negotiation of intimacy in an acquaintance exercise. *J. Pers. Soc. Psychol.* 36(7):684–92

Davis, J. H. 1973. Group decision and social interaction: A theory of social decision schemes. *Psychol. Rev.* 80:97–125

Davis, J. H. 1980. Group decision and procedural justice. See Fishbein 1980, 1:157–229

Davis, J. H. 1981. Social interaction as a combinatorial process in group decision. See Brandstätter et al 1981

Davis, J. H., Bray, R. M., Holt, R. W. 1977. The empirical study of decision processes in juries: A critical review. In *Law, Justice, and the Individual in Society: Psychological and Legal Issues,* ed. J. L. Tapp, F. J. Levine, pp. 326–61. New York: Holt

Davis, J. H., Hinsz, V. B. 1981. Current research problems in group performance and group dynamics. See Brandstätter et al 1981

Davis, J. H., Holt, R. W., Spitzer, C. E., Stasser, G. 1981. The effects of consensus requirements and multiple decisions on mock juror verdict preferences. *J. Exp. Soc. Psychol.* 17(1):1–15

Davis, J. H., Kerr, N. L., Stasser, G., Meek, D., Holt, R. 1977. Victim consequences, sentence severity, and decision processes in mock juries. *Organ. Behav. Hum. Perform.* 18:346–65

Davis, J. H., Laughlin, P. R., Komorita, S. S. 1976. The social psychology of small groups: Cooperative and mixed-motive interaction. *Ann. Rev. Psychol.* 27:501–41

Dawes, R. M. 1980. Social dilemmas. *Ann. Rev. Psychol.* 31:169–93

Dawes, R. M., McTavish, J., Shaklee, H. 1977. Behavior, communication, and assumptions about other people's behavior in a commons dilemma situation. *J. Pers. Soc. Psychol.* 35(1):1–11

Dawes, R. M., Orbell, J. 1981. Social dilemmas. See Stephenson & Davis 1981, 1: In press

DePaulo, B. M., Rosenthal, R., Eisenstat, R. A., Rogers, P. L., Finkelstein, S. 1978. Decoding discrepant nonverbal cues. *J. Pers. Soc. Psychol.* 36(3):313–23

Deutsch, M., Kotik, P. 1978. Altruism and bargaining. See Sauermann 1978a, 7:20–40

Dickson, J. W. 1978. The effect of normative models on individual and group choice. *Eur. J. Soc. Psychol.* 8:91–107

Diener, E., Lusk, R., DeFour, D., Flax, R. 1980. Deindividuation: Effects of group size, density, number of observers, and group member similarity on self-consciousness and disinhibited behavior. *J. Pers. Soc. Psychol.* 39(3):449–59

Doherty, W. J., Ryder, R. G. 1979. Locus of control, interpersonal trust, and assertive behavior among newlyweds. *J. Pers. Soc. Psychol.* 37(12):2212–20

Druckman, D., ed. 1977. *Negotiations: Social-Psychological Perspectives.* London: Sage

Duck, S. W., Craig, G. 1978. Personality similarity and the development of friendship: A longitudinal study. *Br. J. Soc. Clin. Psychol.* 17:237–42

Duncan, S. Jr., Brunner, L. J., Fiske, D. W. 1979. Strategy signals in face-to-face interaction. *J. Pers. Soc. Psychol.* 37(2): 301–13

Eagly, A. H. 1978. Sex differences in influenceability. *Psychol. Bull.* 85:86–116

Edney, J. J. 1980. The commons problem: Alternative perspectives. *Am. Psychol.* 35:131–50

Eidelson, R. J. 1980. Interpersonal satisfaction and level of involvement: A curvilinear relationship. *J. Pers. Soc. Psychol.* 39(3):460–70

Einhorn, H. J., Hogarth, R. M., Klempner, E. 1977. Quality of group judgment. *Psychol. Bull.* 84:158–72

Ellsworth, P. C., Friedman, H. S., Perlick, D., Hoyt, M. E. 1978. Some effects of gaze on subjects motivated to seek or to avoid social comparison. *J. Exp. Soc. Psychol.* 14:69–87

Falbo, T., Peplau, L. A. 1980. Power strategies in intimate relationships. *J. Pers. Soc. Psychol.* 38(4):618–28

Felsenthal, D. S. 1979. Group versus individual gambling behavior: Reexamination and limitation. *Behav. Sci.* 24:334–45

Ferguson, N. 1977. Simultaneous speech, interruptions and dominance. *Br. J. Soc. Clin. Psychol.* 16:295–302

Festinger, L. 1955. Social psychology and group processes. *Ann. Rev. Psychol.* 6:187–216

Fiedler, F. E. 1978a. The contingency model and the dynamics of the leadership process. See Berkowitz 1978a, 11:59–112

Fiedler, F. E. 1978b. Recent developments in research on the contingency model. See Berkowitz 1978b, pp. 209–25

Fiedler, F. E., Chemers, M. M., Mahar, L. 1976. *Improving Leadership Effectiveness: The Leader Match Concept.* New York: Wiley

Fishbein, M., ed. 1980. *Progress in Social Psychology,* Vol. 1. Hillsdale, N.J.: Erlbaum

Fleishman, J. A. 1980. Collective action as helping behavior: Effects of responsibility diffusion on contributions to a public good. *J. Pers. Soc. Psychol.* 38(4): 629–37

Fleishman, J. A., Marwell, G. 1977. Status congruence and associativeness: A test of Galtung's theory. *Sociometry* 40(1): 1–11

Flowers, M. L. 1977. A laboratory test of some implications of Janis's groupthink hypothesis. *J. Pers. Soc. Psychol.* 35(12):888–96

Foot, H. C., Chapman, A. J., Smith, J. R. 1977. Friendship and social responsiveness in boys and girls. *J. Pers. Soc. Psychol.* 35(6):401–11

Forgas, J. P. 1977. Polarization and moderation of person perception judgements as a function of group interaction style. *Eur. J. Soc. Psychol.* 7:175–87

Forgas, J. P. 1978. Social episodes and social structure in an academic setting: The social environment of an intact group. *J. Exp. Soc. Psychol.* 14:434–48

Fox, J., Guyer, M. 1977. Group size and others' strategy in an N-person game. *J. Conflict Resolut.* 21(2):323–38

Freeman, L. C. 1977. A set of measures of centrality based on betweeness. *Sociometry* 40(1):35–41

French, R. L. 1956. Social psychology and group processes. *Ann. Rev. Psychol.* 7:63–94

Friend, K. E., Laing, J. D., Morrison, R. J. 1977. Bargaining processes and coalition outcomes: An integration. *J. Conflict Resolut.* 21(2):267–98

Funk, S. G., Rapoport, Am., Kahan, J. P. 1980. Quota vs positional power in four-person apex games. *J. Exp. Soc. Psychol.* 16:77–93

Gerard, H. B., Miller, N. 1967. Group dynamics. *Ann. Rev. Psychol.* 18:287–332

Gerbasi, K. C., Zuckerman, M., Reis, H. T. 1977. Justice needs a new blindfold: A review of mock jury research. *Psychol. Bull.* 84:323–45

Gilchrist, J. C. 1959. Social psychology and group processes. *Ann. Rev. Psychol.* 10:233–64

Goehring, D. J., Kahan, J. P. 1976. The uniform N-person prisoner's dilemma game: Construction and test of an index of cooperation. *J. Conflict Resolut.* 20(1):111–28

Goethals, G. R., Zanna, M. P. 1979. The role of social comparison in choice shifts. *J. Pers. Soc. Psychol.* 37(9):1469–76

Goldman, M., Stockbauer, J. W., McAuliffe, T. G. 1977. Intergroup and intragroup competition and cooperation. *J. Exp. Soc. Psychol.* 13:81–88

Gottman, J. M. 1979a. Detecting cyclicity in social interaction. *Psychol. Bull.* 86:338–48

Gottman, J. M. 1979b. *Marital Interaction: Experimental Investigations.* New York: Academic

Gottman, J. M., Notarius, C., Markman, H., Bank, S., Yoppi, B., Rubin, M. E. 1976.

Behavior exchange theory and marital decision making. *J. Pers. Soc. Psychol.* 34(1):14–23

Gray, L. N., Sullivan, M. J. 1978. Can you create structural differentiation in social power relations in the laboratory. *Soc. Psychol.* 41(4):328–37

Green, S. G., Mitchell, T. R. 1979. Attributional processes of leaders in leader-member interactions. *Organ. Behav. Hum. Perform.* 23:429–58

Greenberg, J. 1978a. Effects of reward value and retaliative power on allocation decisions: Justice, generosity, or greed? *J. Pers. Soc. Psychol.* 36(4):367–79

Greenberg, J. 1978b. Equity, equality, and the protestant ethic: Allocating rewards following fair and unfair competition. *J. Exp. Soc. Psychol.* 14:217–26

Greenberg, J. 1979. Group vs individual equity judgments: Is there a polarization effect? *J. Exp. Soc. Psychol.* 15:504–12

Grotevant, H. D., Scarr, S., Weinberg, R. A. 1977. Patterns of interest similarity in adoptive and biological families. *J. Pers. Soc. Psychol.* 35(9):667–76

Haan, N. 1978. Two moralities in action contexts: Relationships to thought, ego regulation, and development. *J. Pers. Soc. Psychol.* 36(3):286–305

Haas, A. 1979. Male and female spoken language differences: Stereotypes and evidence. *Psychol. Bull.* 86:616–26

Hackman, J. R. 1976. Group influences on individuals. In *Handbook of Industrial and Organizational Psychology,* ed. M. D. Dunnette, 1455–525. Chicago: Rand-McNally

Hackman, J. R., Morris, C. G. 1978. Group process and group effectiveness: A reappraisal. See Berkowitz 1978b, pp. 57–66

Hall, J. A. 1978. Gender effects in decoding nonverbal cues. *Psychol. Bull.* 85:845–57

Hall, J. A. 1980. Voice tone and persuasion. *J. Pers. Soc. Psychol.* 38(6):924–34

Hammond, K. R., Stewart, T. R., Brehmer, B., Steinmann, D. O. 1975. Social judgment theory. In *Human Judgment and Decision Processes,* ed. M. F. Kaplan, S. Schwartz, pp. 271–312. New York: Academic

Hamner, W. C., Yukl, G. A. 1977. The effectiveness of different offer strategies in bargaining. See Druckman 1977, pp. 137–60

Hare, A. P. 1976. *Handbook of Small Group Research.* New York: Free Press. 2nd ed.

Harris, R. J. 1976. Handling negative inputs: On the plausible equity formulae. *J. Exp. Soc. Psychol.* 12:194–209

Harrison, A. A., Hwalek, M., Raney, D. F., Fritz, J. G. 1978. Cues to deception in an interview situation. *Soc. Psychol.* 41(2):156–61

Hayduk, L. A. 1978. Personal space: An evaluative and orienting overview. *Psychol. Bull.* 85(1):117–34

Helmreich, R., Bakeman, R., Scherwitz, L. 1973. The study of small groups. *Ann. Rev. Psychol.* 24:337–54

Hermann, M. G., Kogan, N. 1977. Effects of negotiators' personalities on negotiating behavior. See Druckman 1977, pp. 247–74

Heyns, R. W. 1958. Social psychology and group processes. *Ann. Rev. Psychol.* 9:419–52

Hoffman, L. R. 1978. The group problem-solving process. See Berkowitz 1978b, pp. 101–13.

Hollander, E. P., Julian, J. W. 1978. A further look at leader legitimacy, influence, and innovation. See Berkowitz, 1978b, pp. 153–65

Hong, L. K. 1978. Risky shift and cautious shift: Some direct evidence on the culture-value theory. *Soc. Psychol.* 41(4): 342–46

Houlden, P., LaTour, S., Walker, L., Thibaut, J. 1978. Preference for modes of dispute resolution as a function of process and decision control. *J. Exp. Soc. Psychol.* 14:13–30

Huesmann, L. R., Levinger, G. 1976. Incremental exchange theory: A formal model for progression in dyadic social interaction. See Berkowitz & Walster 1976, 9:191–229

Huston, T. L., Levinger, G. 1978. Interpersonal attraction and relationships. *Ann. Rev. Psychol.* 29:115–56

Ickes, W., Barnes, R. D. 1977. The role of sex and self-monitoring in unstructured dyadic interactions. *J. Pers. Soc. Psychol.* 35(5):315–30

Ickes, W., Barnes, R. D. 1978. Boys and girls together—and alienated: On enacting stereotyped sex roles in mixed-sex dyads. *J. Pers. Soc. Psychol.* 36(7):669–83

Insko, C. A., Thibaut, J. W., Moehle, D., Wilson, M., Diamond, W. D., Gilmore, R., Solomon, M. R., Lipsitz, A. 1980. Social evolution and the emergence of leadership. *J. Pers. Soc. Psychol.* 39(3): 431–48

Insko, C. A., Wilson, M. 1977. Interpersonal attraction as a function of social interaction. *J. Pers. Soc. Psychol.* 35(12): 903–11

Jellison, J., Arkin, R. 1977. Social comparison of abilities: A self-presentation approach to decision making in groups. In

Social Comparison Processes: Theoretical and Empirical Perspectives, ed. J. M. Suls, R. L. Miller, pp. 235–57. New York: Wiley

Johnson, N. R., Stemler, J. G., Hunter, D. 1977. Crowd behavior as "risky shift": A laboratory experiment. *Sociometry* 40(2):183–87

Kabanoff, B., O'Brien, G. E. 1979. The effects of task type and cooperation upon group products and performance. *Organ. Behav. Hum. Perform.* 23:163–81

Kahan, J. P., Bonacich, P. 1980. Palette: A resource-free experimental paradigm for studying coalition formation. *Simulation & Games* 11:259–78

Kahan, J. P., Rapoport, Am. 1977. When you don't need to join: The effects of guaranteed payoffs on bargaining in three-person cooperative games. *Theory Decis.* 8:97–126

Kahn, A., Lamm, H., Nelson, R. E. 1977. Preferences for an equal or equitable allocator. *J. Pers. Soc. Psychol.* 35(11): 837–44

Kahn, A., Nelson, R. E., Gaeddert, W. P. 1980. Sex of subject and sex composition of the group as determinants of reward allocations. *J. Pers. Soc. Psychol.* 38(5):737–50

Kandel, D. B. 1978. Similarity in real-life adolescent friendship pairs. *J. Pers. Soc. Psychol.* 36(3):306–12

Kaplan, M. F. 1977. Discussion polarization effects in a modified jury decision paradigm: Informational influences. *Sociometry* 40(3):262–71

Kaplan, M. F., Miller, C. E. 1977. Judgments and group discussion: Effect of presentation and memory factors on polarization. *Sociometry* 40(4):337–43

Katz, D. 1951. Social psychology and group processes. *Ann. Rev. Psychol.* 2:137–72

Katz, R. 1977. The influence of group conflict on leadership effectiveness. *Organ. Behav. Hum. Perform.* 20:265–86

Katz, R., Tushman, M. 1979. Communication patterns, project performance, and task characteristics: An empirical evaluation and integration in an R&D setting. *Organ. Behav. Hum. Perform.* 23:139–62

Kelley, H. H., Thibaut, J. W. 1978. *Interpersonal Relations: A Theory of Interdependence.* New York: Wiley

Kendon, A. 1978. Looking in conversation and the regulation of turns at talk: A comment on the papers of G. Beattie and D. R. Rutter et al. *Br. J. Soc. Clin. Psychol.* 17:23–24

Kendrick, D. T., Cialdini, R. B. 1977. Romantic attraction: Misattribution versus reinforcement explanations. *J. Pers. Soc. Psychol.* 35(6):381–91

Kerr, N. L. 1978. Severity of prescribed penalty and mock jurors' verdicts. *J. Pers. Soc. Psychol.* 36(12):1431–42

Kerr, N. L., Stasser, G., Davis, J. H. 1979. Model testing, model fitting, and social decision schemes. *Organ, Behav. Hum. Perform.* 23:399–410

Kimmel, M. J., Pruitt, D. G., Magenau, J. M., Konar-Goldband, E., Carnevale, P. J. D. 1980. Effects of trust, aspiration, and gender on negotiation tactics. *J. Pers. Soc. Psychol.* 38(1):9–22

Klevorick, A. K., Rothschild, M. 1979. A model of the jury decision process. *J. Legal Stud.* 8:141–64

Klimoski, R. J., Breaugh, J. A. 1977. When performance doesn't count: A constituency looks at its spokesman. *Organ Behav. Hum. Perform.* 20:301–11

Knudson, R. M., Sommers, A. A., Golding, S. L. 1980. Interpersonal perception and mode of resolution in marital conflict. *J. Pers. Soc. Psychol.* 38(5):751–63

Komorita, S. S. 1976. A model of the N-person dilemma-type game. *J. Exp. Soc. Psychol.* 12:357–73

Komorita, S. S. 1977. Negotiating from strength and the concept of bargaining strength. *J. Ther. Soc. Behav.* 7:65–79

Komorita, S. S. 1978. Evaluating coalition theories: Some indices. *J. Conflict. Resolut.* 22(4):691–706

Komorita, S. S. 1979. An equal excess model of coalition formation. *Behav. Sci.* 24:369–81

Komorita, S. S., Brinberg, D. 1977. The effects of equity norms in coalition formation. *Sociometry* 49(4):351–61

Komorita, S. S., Kravitz, D. A. 1978. Some tests of four descriptive theories of coalition formation. See Sauermann 1978b, 8:207–30

Komorita, S. S., Kravitz, D. A. 1979. The effects of alternatives in bargaining. *J. Exp. Soc. Psychol.* 15:147–57

Komorita, S. S., Kravitz, D. A. 1981. The effects of prior experience on coalition behavior. *J. Pers. Soc. Psychol.* 40(4): 675–86

Komorita, S. S., Lapworth, C. W., Tumonis, T. M. 1981. The effects of certain vs. risky alternatives in bargaining. *J. Exp. Soc. Psychol.* In press

Komorita, S. S., Meek, D. D. 1978. Generality and validity of some theories of coalition formation. *J. Pers. Soc. Psychol.* 36 (4): 392–404

Komorita, S. S., Sweeney, J., Kravitz, D. A. 1980. Cooperative choice in the N-person dilemma situation. *J. Pers. Soc. Psychol.* 38(3):504–16

Komorita, S. S., Tumonis, T. M. 1980. Extensions and tests of some descriptive theories of coalition formation. *J. Pers. Soc. Psychol.* 39(2):256–68

Koomen, W., Sagel, P. K. 1977. The prediction of participation in two-person groups. *Sociometry* 40(4):369–73

Kraemer, H. C., Jacklin, C. N. 1979. Statistical analysis of dyadic social behavior. *Psychol. Bull.* 86(2):217–24

Krauss, R. M., Garlock, C. M., Bricker, P. D., McMahon, L. E. 1977. The role of audible and visible back-channel responses in interpersonal communication. *J. Pers. Soc. Psychol.* 35(7):523–29

Kraut, R. E., Johnston, R. E. 1979. Social and emotional messages of smiling: An ethological approach. *J. Pers. Soc. Psychol.* 37(9):1539–53

Kravitz, D. A. 1981. The effects of resources and alternatives on coalition formation. *J. Pers. Soc. Psychol.* 40(1):87–98

Kushner, H. W., De Maio, G. 1977. Using digraphs to determine the crucial actors in a voting body. *Sociometry* 40(4): 361–69

LaFrance, M., Mayo, C. 1976. Racial differences in gaze behavior during conversations: Two systematic observational studies. *J. Pers. Soc. Psychol.* 33(5): 547–52

Lamm, H., Myers, D. G. 1978. Group-induced polarization of attitudes and behavior. See Berkowitz 1978a, 11:145–95

LaTour, S., Houlden, P., Walker, L., Thibaut, J. 1976. Some determinants of preference for modes of conflict resolution. *J. Conflict Resolut.* 20:319–56

Laughlin, P. R. 1978. Ability and group problem solving. *J. Res. Dev. Educ.* 12(1):114–20

Laughlin, P. R. 1980. Social combination processes of cooperative problem-solving groups on verbal intellective tasks. See Fishbein 1980, 1:127–55

Laughlin, P. R., Adamopoulos, J. 1980. Social combination processes and individual learning for six-person cooperative groups on an intellective task. *J. Pers. Soc. Psychol.* 38(6):941–47

Laughlin, P. R., Adamopoulos, J. 1981. Social decision schemes on intellective tasks. See Brandstätter et al 1981

Laughlin, P. R., Sweeney, J. D. 1977. Individual-to-group and group-to-individual transfer in problem solving. *J. Exp. Psychol.: Hum. Learn. Mem.* 3(2): 246–54

Lawler, E. J., Thompson, M. E. 1978. Impact of leader responsibility for inequity on subordinate revolts. *Soc. Psychol.* 41(3): 265–68

Lawler, E. J., Youngs, G. A. Jr., Lesh, M. D. 1978. Cooptation and coalition mobilization. *J. Appl. Soc. Psychol.* 8:199–214

Lazzerini, A. J., Stephenson, G. M., Neave, H. 1978. Eye-contact in dyads: A test of the independence hypothesis. *Br. J. Soc. Clin. Psychol.* 17:227–29

Leavitt, H. J. 1951. Some effects of certain communication patterns on group performance. *J. Abnorm. Soc. Psychol.* 46:38–50

Lendenmann, K. W., Rapoport, An. 1980. Decision pressures in 2 X 2 games. *Behav. Sci.* 25:107–19

Leventhal, G. S. 1976. The distribution of rewards and resources in groups and organizations. See Berkowitz & Walster 1976, 9:91–131

Levinger, G. 1980. Toward the analysis of close relationships. *J. Exp. Soc. Psychol.* 16:510–44

Levinsohn, J. R., Rapoport, Am. 1978. Coalition formation in multistage three-person cooperative games. See Sauermann 1978b, 8:107–43

Lewis, S. A., Fry, W. R. 1977. Effects of visual access and orientation on the discovery of integrative bargaining alternatives. *Organ. Behav. Hum. Perform.* 20:75–92

Lind, E. A., Kurtz, S., Musante, L., Walker, L., Thibaut, J. W. 1980. Procedure and outcome effects on reactions to adjudicated resolution of conflicts of interest. *J. Pers. Soc. Psychol.* 39(4):643–53

Lindskold, S. 1978. Trust development, the GRIT proposal, and the effects of conciliatory acts on conflict and cooperation. *Psychol. Bull.* 85:772–93

Lord, R. G., Rowzee, M. 1979. Task interdependence, temporal phase, and cognitive heterogeneity as determinants of leadership behavior and behavior-performance relations. *Organ. Behav. Hum. Perform.* 23:182–200

Lundgren, D. C. 1978. Public esteem, self-esteem, and interpersonal stress. *Soc. Psychol.* 4(1):68–73

Lynn, S. J. 1978. Three theories of self-disclosure exchange. *J. Exp. Soc. Psychol.* 14:466–79

Lytton, H., Conway, D., Sauvé, R. 1977. The impact of twinship on parent-child interaction. *J. Pers. Soc. Psychol.* 35(2): 97–107

Madsen, D. B. 1978. Issue importance and group choice shifts: A persuasive arguments approach. *J. Pers. Soc. Psychol.* 36(10):1118–27

Marwell, G., Ames, R. E. 1979. Experiments on the provision of public goods. I. Resources, interest, group size, and the free-rider problem. *Am. J. Sociol.* 84:1335–60

McCall, M. W. Jr. 1979. Power, authority, and influence. In *Organizational Behavior,* ed. S. Kerr, pp. 185–206. Columbus, Ohio: Grid

McCarthy, B., Duck, S. 1979. Studying friendship: Experimental and role-playing techniques in testing hypotheses about acquaintance. *Br. J. Soc. Clin. Psychol.* 18:299–307

McDowall, J. J. 1978. Interactional synchrony: A reappraisal. *J. Pers. Soc. Psychol.* 36(9):963–75

McGrath, J. E. 1978. Small group research. *Am. Behav. Sci.* 21(5):651–74

McGrath, J. E. 1982. *The Study of Groups: Task Performance, Social Interaction and Member Change.* New York: Prentice-Hall. In press

McGrath, J. E., Altman, I. 1966. *Small Group Research.* New York: Holt

Meeker, B. F., Weitzel-O'Neill, P. A. 1977. Sex roles and interpersonal behavior in task-oriented groups. *Am. Sociol. Rev.* 42:91–105

Meyer, J. P., Pepper, S. 1977. Need compatibility and marital adjustment in young couples. *J. Pers. Soc. Psychol.* 35(5): 331–42

Michener, H. A., Ginsberg, I. J., Yuen, K. 1979. Effects of core properties in four-person games with side-payments. *Behav. Sci.* 24(4):263–80

Michener, H. A., Sakurai, M. M., Yuen, K., Kasen, T. J. 1979. A competitive test of the $M_1^{(i)}$ and $M_1^{(im)}$ bargaining sets. *J. Conflict Resolut.* 23:103–19

Michener, H. A., Yuen, K., Ginsberg, I. J. 1977. A competitive test of the $M_1^{(im)}$ bargaining set, kernel, and equal share models. *Behav. Sci.* 22:341–55

Miles, R. H. 1977. Role-set configuration as a predictor of role conflict and ambiguity in complex organizations. *Sociometry* 49(1):21–34

Miller, C. E. 1979a. Coalition formation in triads with single-peaked payoff curves. *Behav. Sci.* 24:75–84

Miller, C. E. 1979b. Probabilistic theories of coalition formation in groups. *Behav. Sci.* 24:359–68

Miller, C. E. 1980a. A test of four theories of coalition formation: Effects of payoffs and resources. *J. Pers. Soc. Psychol.* 38(1): 153–64

Miller, C. E. 1980b. Coalition formation in characteristic function games: Competitive tests of three theories. *J. Exp. Soc. Psychol.* 16:61–76

Miller, C. E. 1980c. Effects of payoffs and resources on coalition formation: A test of three theories. *Soc. Psychol. Q.* 43:154–64

Miller, C. E., Crandall, R. 1980. Experimental research on the social psychology of bargaining and coalition formation. See Paulus 1980, pp. 333–74

Miller, N. 1978. A questionnaire in search of a theory. See Berkowitz 1978b, pp. 301–12

Mitchell, T. R., Larson, J. R. Jr., Green, S. G. 1977. Leader behavior, situational moderators, and group performance: An attributional analysis. *Organ. Behav. Hum. Perform.* 18:254–68

Morley, I., Stephenson, G. 1977. *The social Psychology of Bargaining.* London: Allen & Unwin

Morton, T. L. 1978. Intimacy and reciprocity of exchange: A comparison of spouses and strangers. *J. Pers. Soc. Psychol.* 36(1):72–81

Moschetti, G. J., Kues, J. R. 1978. Transrelational equity comparisons: Extensions to the third partner relationship and a decision-making model. *J. Pers. Soc. Psychol.* 36(10):1107–17

Murnighan, J. K. 1978a. Models of coalition behavior: Game theoretic, social psychological, and political perspectives. *Psychol. Bull.* 85:1130–53

Murnighan, J. K. 1978b. Strength and weakness in four coalition situations. *Behav. Sci.* 23:195–208

Murnighan, J. K. 1981. Game theory and the structure of decision making groups. In *Improving Group Decision Making,* ed. R. Guzzo. New York: Academic. In press

Murnighan, J. K., Komorita, S. S., Szwajkowski, E. 1977. Theories of coalition formation and the effects of reference groups. *J. Exp. Soc. Psychol.* 13:166–81

Murnighan, J. K., Roth, A. E. 1977. The effects of communication and information availability in an experimental study of a three-person game. *Manage. Sci.* 23:1336–48

Murnighan, J. K., Roth, A. E. 1978. Large group bargaining in a characteristic function game. *J. Conflict Resolut.* 22(2):299–317

Murnighan, J. K., Roth, A. E. 1980. Effects of group size and communication availability on coalition bargaining in a veto game. *J. Pers. Soc. Psychol.* 39(1):92–103

Murnighan, J. K., Szwajkowski, E. 1979. Coalition bargaining in four games that include a veto player. *J. Pers. Soc. Psychol.* 37(11):1933–46

Myers, D. G. 1978. Polarizing effects of social comparison. *J. Exp. Soc. Psychol.* 14:554–63

Myers, D. G., Lamm, H. 1976. The group polarization phenomenon. *Psychol. Bull.* 83(4):602–27

Nadler, D. A. 1979. The effects of feedback on task group behavior: A review of the experimental research. *Organ. Behav. Hum. Perform.* 23:309–38

Nagao, D. H., Davis, J. H. 1980a. The effects of prior experience on mock juror case judgments. *Soc. Psychol. Q.* 43:190–99

Nagao, D. H., Davis, J. H. 1980b. Some implications of temporal drift in social parameters. *J. Exp. Soc. Psychol.* 16:479–96

Nagel, S. S., Neef, M. 1976. Deductive modeling to determine an optimum jury size and fraction required to convict. *Wash. Univ. Law Q.* 1975:933–78

Natale, M., Entin, E., Jaffe, J. 1979. Vocal interruptions in dyadic communication as a function of speech and social anxiety. *J. Pers. Soc. Psychol.* 37(6):865–78

Newcomb, T. M. 1953. Social psychology and group processes. *Ann. Rev. Psychol.* 4:183–214

Newcomb, T. M. 1978a. The acquaintance process: Looking mainly backward. *J. Pers. Soc. Psychol.* 36(10):1075–83

Newcomb, T. M. 1978b. Individual and group. *Am. Behav. Sci.* 21(5):631–50

Newcombe, N., Arnkoff, D. B. 1979. Effects of speech style and sex of speaker on person perception. *J. Pers. Soc. Psychol.* 37(8):1293–1303

Nichols, A. L. 1977. Coalitions and learning: Applications to a simple game in the triad. *Behav. Sci.* 22:391–402

Nitz, L. H. 1976. Resource theory and ameliorative strategy in a minimal information political convention game. *Behav. Sci.* 21(3):161–72

Nowakowska, M. 1978. A model of participation in group discussions. *Behav. Sci.* 23:209–12

Nydegger, R. V., Owen, G. 1977. The norm of equity in a three-person majority game. *Behav. Sci.* 22:32–37

O'Neill, P., Levings, D. E. 1979. Inducing biased scanning in a group setting to change attitudes toward bilingualism and capital punishment. *J. Pers. Soc. Psychol.* 37(8):1432–38

Padgett, V. R., Wolosin, R. J. 1980. Cognitive similarity in dyadic communication. *J. Pers. Soc. Psychol.* 39(4):654–59

Paicheler, G. 1976. Norms and attitude change I: Polarization and styles of behaviour. *Eur. J. Soc. Psychol.* 6:405–27

Paicheler, G. 1977. Norms and attitude change II: The phenomenon of bipolarization. *Eur. J. Soc. Psychol.* 7:5–14

Paicheler, G. 1979. Polarization of attitudes in homogeneous and heterogeneous groups. *Eur. J. Soc. Psychol.* 9:85–96

Parcel, T. L., Cook, K. S. 1977. Status characteristics, reward allocation, and equity. *Sociometry* 40(4):311–24

Paulus, P. B., ed. 1980. *Psychology of Group Influence.* Hillsdale, NJ: Erlbaum

Penrod, S., Hastie, R. 1979. Models of jury decision making: A critical review. *Psychol. Bull.* 86:462–92

Penrod, S., Hastie, R. 1980. A computer simulation of jury decision making. *Psychol. Rev.* 87:133–59

Pruitt, D. G., Kimmel, M. J. 1977. Twenty years of experimental gaming: Critique, synthesis, and suggestions for the future. *Ann. Rev. Psychol.* 28:363–92

Rapoport, Am., Kahan, J. P., Wallsten, T. S. 1978. Sources of power in four-person apex games. See Sauermann 1978b, 8:75–106

Rapoport, An., Guyer, M. J., Gordon, D. G. 1976. *The 2 X 2 Game.* Ann Arbor: Univ. Mich. Press

Reis, H. T., Nezlek, J., Wheeler, L. 1980. Physical attractiveness in social interaction. *J. Pers. Soc. Psychol.* 38(4):604–17

Rice, R. W., Bender, L. R., Vitters, A. G. 1980. Leader sex, follower attitudes toward women, and leadership effectiveness: A laboratory experiment. *Organ. Behav. Hum. Perform.* 25:46–78

Ridgeway, C. L. 1978. Conformity, group-oriented motivation, and status attainment in small groups. *Soc. Psychol.* 41(3):175–188

Riecken, H. W. 1960. Social psychology. *Ann. Rev. Psychol.* 11:479–510

Roger, D. B., Reid, R. L. 1978. Small group ecology revisited: Personal space and role differentiation. *Br.J. Soc. Clin. Psychol.* 17:43–46

Rohrbaugh, J. 1979. Improving the quality of group judgment: Social judgment analysis and the Delphi technique. *Organ. Behav. Hum. Perform.* 24:73–92

Rosenbaum, M. E., Moore, D. L., Cotton, J. L., Cook, M. S., Hieser, R. A., Shovar, M. N., Gray, M. J. 1980. Group productivity and process: Pure and mixed reward structures and task interdependence. *J. Pers. Soc. Psychol.* 39(4): 626–42

Rosenthal, R., DePaulo, B. M. 1979. Sex differences in eavesdropping on nonverbal cues. *J. Pers. Soc. Psychol.* 37(2): 273–85

Roth, A. E. 1977. Bargaining ability, the utility of playing a game, and models of coalition formation. *J. Math. Psychol.* 16:153–60

Roth, A. E., Malouf, M. W. K. 1979. Game-theoretic models and the role of information in bargaining. *Psychol. Rev.* 88(6):574–94

Roth, B. M. 1979. Competing norms of distribution in coalition games. *J. Conflict Resolut.* 23(3):513–37

Rubin, J. Z. 1980. Experimental research on third-party intervention in conflict: Toward some generalizations. *Psychol. Bull.* 87:379–91

Rubin, J. Z., Brown, B. R. 1975. *The Social Psychology of Bargaining and Negotiation.* New York: Academic

Rusbult, C. E. 1980. Commitment and satisfaction in romantic associations: A test of the investment model. *J. Exp. Soc. Psychol.* 16:172–86

Rutter, D. R., Robinson, B. 1981. An experimental analysis of teaching by telephone: Theoretical and practical implications for social psychology. See Stephenson & Davis 1981, 1: In press

Rutter, D. R., Stephenson, G. M. 1979. The functions of Looking: Effects of friendship on gaze. *Br. J. Soc. Clin. Psychol.* 18:203–5

Rutter, D. R., Stephenson, G. M., Ayling, K., White, P. A. 1978. The timing of Looks in dyadic conversation. *Br. J. Soc. Clin. Psychol.* 17:17–21

Rutter, D. R., Stephenson, G. M., Lazzerini, A. J., Ayling, K., White, P. A. 1977. Eye-contact: A chance product of individual Looking? *Br. J. Soc. Clin. Psychol.* 16:191–92

Saks, M. J. 1977. *Jury Verdicts: The Role of Group Size and Social Decision Rule.* Lexington, Mass.: Lexington Books

Sanders, G. S. 1978. An integration of shifts toward risk and caution in gambling situations. *J. Exp. Soc. Psychol.* 14:409–16

Sanders, G. S., Baron, R. S. 1977. Is social comparison irrelevant for producing choice shifts? *J. Exp. Soc. Psychol.* 13:303–14

Sauermann, H., ed. 1978a. *Contributions to Experimental Economics: Bargaining Behavior,* Vol. 7. Tubingen, West Germany: Mohr

Sauermann, H., ed. 1978b. *Contributions to Experimental Economics: Coalition Forming Behavior,* Vol. 8. Tubingen, West Germany: Mohr

Schaeffer, G. H., Patterson, M. L. 1980. Intimacy, arousal, and small group crowding. *J. Pers. Soc. Psychol.* 38(2):283–90

Schlenker, B. R., Goldman, H. J. 1978. Cooperators and competitors in conflict: A test of the "triangle model." *J. Conflict Resolut.* 22(3):393–410

Schneier, C. E. 1978. The contingency model of leadership: An extension to emergent leadership and leader's sex. *Organ. Behav. Hum. Perform.* 21:220–39

Schofield, J. W., Sagar, H. A. 1977. Peer interaction patterns in an integrated middle school. *Sociometry* 40(2):130–38

Schönemann, P. H. 1979. Alternative decision schemes for six-person mock juries. *Organ. Behav. Hum. Perform.* 23: 388–98

Schulz, J. W., Pruitt, D. G. 1978. The effects of mutual concern on joint welfare. *J. Exp. Soc. Psychol.* 14:480–92

Schutte, J. G., Light, J. M. 1978. The relative importance of proximity and status for friendship choices in social hierarchies. *Soc. Psychol.* 41(3):260–64

Segal, M. W. 1977. A reconfirmation of the logarithmic effect of group size. *Sociometry* 49(2):187–90

Shaw, M. E. 1961. Group dynamics. *Ann. Rev. Psychol.* 12:129–56

Shaw, M. E. 1978. Communication networks fourteen years later. See Berkowitz 1978b, pp. 351–61

Shaw, M. E. 1981. *Group Dynamics: The Psychology of Small Group Behavior.* New York: McGraw-Hill. 3rd ed.

Shiflett, S. 1979. Toward a general model of small group productivity. *Psychol. Bull.* 86(1):67–79

Skotko, V. P., Langmeyer, D. 1977. The effects of interaction distance and gender on self-disclosure in the dyad. *Sociometry* 40(2):178–82

Skvoretz, J., Fararo, T. J. 1980. Languages and grammars of action and interaction: A contribution to the formal theory of action. *Behav. Sci.* 25:9–22

Smith, M. B. 1952. Social psychology and group processes. *Ann. Rev. Psychol.* 3:175–204

Snyder, M., Swann, W. B. Jr. 1978. Behavioral confirmation in social interaction: From social perception to social reality. *J. Exp. Soc. Psychol.* 14:148–62

Snyder, M., Tanke, E. D., Berscheid, E. 1977. Social perception and interpersonal behavior: On the self-fulfilling nature of social stereotypes. *J. Pers. Soc. Psychol.* 35(9):656–66

Spitzer, C. E., Davis, J. H. 1978. Mutual social influence in dynamic groups. *Soc. Psychol.* 41(1):24–33

Stasser, G., Kerr, N. L., Davis, J. H. 1980. Influence processes in decision making groups: A modeling approach. See Paulus 1980, pp. 431–77

Stein, R. T., Heller, T. 1979. An empirical analysis of the correlations between leadership status and participation rates reported in the literature. *J. Pers. Soc. Psychol.* 37(11):1993–2002

Steiner, I. D. 1964. Group dynamics. *Ann. Rev. Psychol.* 15:421–46

Stephenson, G. M., Davis, J. H., eds. 1981. *Progress in Applied Social Psychology.* New York: Wiley. In press

Stern, P. C. 1976. Effect of incentives and education on resource conservation decisions in a simulated commons dilemma. *J. Pers. Soc. Psychol.* 34(6): 1285–92

Sticha, P. J. 1977. Coalition formation and the distribution of influence in decision making groups. *Mich. Math. Psychol. Program Rep.* MMPP77-1

Stiles, W. B. 1978. Verbal response modes and dimensions of interpersonal roles: A method of discourse analysis. *J. Pers. Soc. Psychol.* 36(7):693–703

Stiles, W. B., Waszak, C. S., Barton, L. R. 1979. Professorial presumptuousness in verbal interactions with university students. *J. Exp. Soc. Psychol.* 15:158–69

Stockdale, J. E. 1978. Crowding: Determinants and effects. See Berkowitz 1978a, 11:197–247

Taylor, R. B., De Soto, C. B., Lieb, R. 1979. Sharing secrets: Disclosure and discretion in dyads and triads. *J. Pers. Soc. Psychol.* 37(7):1196–1203

Teichman, M. 1977. Affiliative behaviours among soldiers during wartime. *Br. J. Soc. Clin. Psychol.* 16:3–7

Tesser, A. 1980. Self-esteem maintenance in family dynamics. *J. Pers. Soc. Psychol.* 39(1):77–91

Thibaut, J. W., Kelley, H. H. 1959. *The Social Psychology of Groups.* New York: Wiley

Thomas, E. A. C., Malone, T. W. 1979. On the dynamics of two-person interactions. *Psychol. Rev.* 86(4):331–60

Tjosvold, D. 1977. The effects of the constituent's affirmation and the opposing negotiator's self-presentation in bargaining between unequal status groups. *Organ. Behav. Hum. Perform.* 18:146–57

Toda, M., Shinotsuka, H. 1978. Three person bargaining for coalition formation. See Sauermann 1978b, 8:144–71

Toda, M., Shinotsuka, H., McClintock, C. G., Stech, F. J. 1978. Development of competitive behavior as a function of culture, age, and social comparison. *J. Pers. Soc. Psychol.* 36(8):825–39

Tsai, Y. 1977. Hierarchical structure of participation in natural groups. *Behav. Sci.* 22:38–40

Van Egeren, L. F. 1979. Cardiovascular changes during social competition in a mixed-motive game. *J. Pers. Soc. Psychol.* 37(6):858–64

Vecchio, R. P. 1977. An empirical examination of the validity of Fiedler's model of leadership effectiveness. *Organ. Behav. Hum. Perform.* 19:180–206

Vinokur, A., Burnstein, E. 1978a. Depolarization of attitudes in groups. *J. Pers. Soc. Psychol.* 36(8):872–85

Vinokur, A., Burnstein, E. 1978b. Novel argumentation and attitude change: The case of polarization following discussion. *Eur. J. Soc. Psychol.* 8:335–48

Voesjirwan, J. 1978. Laboratory study of proxemic patterns of Indonesians and Australians. *Br. J. Soc. Clin. Psychol.* 17:333–34

Vollrath, D. A., Davis, J. H. 1979. Evaluating proposals for social change with minimal data: An example from grand jury reform. *Law Hum. Behav.* 3:121–34

Vollrath, D. A., Davis, J. H. 1980. Jury size and decision rule. In *The Jury: Its Role in American Society,* ed. R. Simon, pp. 73–106. Lexington, Mass: Lexington Books

Wall, J. A. Jr. 1977. Operantly conditioning a negotiator's concession making. *J. Exp. Soc. Psychol.* 13:431–40

Wall, J. A. Jr. 1978. An negotiator's bargaining: The effects of representation and the opponent's sex. See Sauermann 1978a, 7:270–83

Walster, E., Walster, G. W., Traupmann, J. 1978. Equity and premarital sex. *J. Pers. Soc. Psychol.* 36(1):82–92

Warner, R. M., Kenny, D. A., Stoto, M. 1979. A new round robin analysis of variance for social interaction data. *J. Pers. Soc. Psychol.* 37(10):1742–57

Waxler, N. E., Mishler, E. G. 1978. Experimental studies of families. See Berkowitz 1978b, pp. 363–418

Wheeler, L., Nezlek, J. 1977. Sex differences in social participation. *J. Pers. Soc. Psychol.* 35(10):742–54

White, G. L. 1980. Physical attractiveness and courtship progress. *J. Pers. Soc. Psychol.* 39(4):660–68

Wilder, D. A., Thompson, J. E. 1980. Intergroup contact with independent manipulations of in-group and out-group interaction. *J. Pers. Soc. Psychol.* 38(4): 589–603

Williams, E. 1977. Experimental comparisons of face-to-face and mediated communication: A review. *Psychol. Bull.* 84:963–76

Winter, D. G., Stewart, A. J., McClelland, D. C. 1977. Husband's motives and wife's career level. *J. Pers. Soc. Psychol.* 35(3): 159–66

Won-Doornink, M. J. 1979. On getting to know you: The association between the stage of a relationship and reciprocity of self-disclosure. *J. Exp. Soc. Psychol.* 15:229–41

Worchel, S., Andreoli, V. A., Folger, R. 1977. Intergroup cooperation and intergroup attraction: The effect of previous interaction and outcome of combined effort. *J. Exp. Soc. Psychol.* 13:131–40

Worchel, S., Norvell, N. 1980. Effect of perceived environmental conditions during cooperation on intergroup attraction. *J. Pers. Soc. Psychol.* 38(5):764–72

Worchel, S., Yohai, S. M. L. 1979. The role of attribution in the experience of crowding. *J. Exp. Soc. Psychol.* 15:91–104

Zander, A. F. 1977. *Groups at Work.* San Francisco: Jossey-Bass

Zander, A. F. 1979. The psychology of group processes. *Ann. Rev. Psychol.* 30:417–51

Ann. Rev. Psychol. 1982. 33:231–64

ABNORMAL BEHAVIOR: SOCIAL APPROACHES

Leonard D. Eron[1]

Department of Psychology, University of Illinois at Chicago Circle, Chicago, Illinois 60680

Rolf A. Peterson

Department of Psychology, University of Health Sciences, Chicago Medical School, Chicago, Illinois 60064

CONTENTS

[1]Preparation of this review was supported by Grant No. 34410, *Aggression and Psychopathology,* from the *National Institute of Mental Health.*

0066-4308/82/0201-0231$02.00

INTRODUCTION

Previous volumes of the *Annual Review of Psychology* have referred to the body of literature covered by this chapter as *Social and Cultural Influences on Psychopathology.* We have decided to eschew the term psychopathology because it implies an etiological bias—i.e. the assumption that there is an underlying disease process which may or may not be influenced by environmental factors. The use of the term abnormal behavior implies no such necessary process, although it does not deny the existence of one. Our interest here will be in psychologically non-normative behaviors and how they covary with various social and cultural factors. From the nature of the covariation it would be hoped that some statements about cause and effect could be made which would be susceptible to falsification. To date this has not occurred. Although previous reviews have reported numerous studies relating socioeconomic and cultural variables to the incidence and prevalence of abnormal behaviors, symptoms and syndromes, there has not been any clear statement indicating how the sociocultural variables have their effect on the individual. In the most recent review, Strauss (1979) attempted to establish links between sociocultural phenomena and psychopathology in the individual patient. He hypothesized that the important variables were levels of stress to which individuals are exposed and the efficiency of coping skills available to them, each of which varies, presumably, with social factors. However, no evidence was presented to substantiate this particular hypothesis. We would agree that how an individual copes with stress is important to his or her mental health. But coping skills and abnormal behaviors are learned, and it is the learning conditions which are the essential mediating variables between the sociocultural environment and the behavior. The person who is disturbed has not learned appropriate ways to interact with others and to achieve his or her goals without undue interference with and from the environment. The kind of behaviors which the disturbed individual has not learned well would come under the rubric of social skills or social competence. Social competence has been defined as "the ability to produce the desired effects on other people in social situations" (Argyle 1980). It is likely that the learning conditions for developing social skills vary with those environmental conditions which have been consistently related to frequency of abnormal behaviors in past research. It has been estimated that more than one-fourth of all neurotics and most psychotics are severely handicapped by lack of social skills (Argyle 1980). Furthermore, social competence, especially in children, is related to social class position (Herbert 1980), as are the frequency and seriousness of stresses to which an individual is exposed (Cochrane & Sobol 1980).

The literature published on social and cultural influences on abnormal behavior between 1978 and 1980 will be reviewed with an eye to establishing this link. Specifically, we will be looking at social class, race, religion, and culture as social factors affecting abnormal behaviors. Then a particular body of literature dealing with stress and the way individuals learn to cope with it will be examined to determine if differential training and experience in social skills according to various sociocultural categories is a likely contributor to the differential incidence of behavior disorders.

SOCIAL CLASS AND ABNORMAL BEHAVIOR

In the early 1950s three important epidemiological studies were conducted in different localities in North America. Each of the studies demonstrated an inverse relation between social class and the frequency of behavior disorder (Leighton 1959, Redlich et al 1953, Srole et al 1962). It is interesting that in 1980 follow-up studies were reported for all three investigations. Murphy (1980) showed that the modified version of DSM I which was utilized in the Stirling County, Nova Scotia study (Leighton 1959) to classify subjects' mental health status in 1952 was easily assimilable to DSM III 25 years later and that the "use of comparable diagnostic approaches makes it possible to trace continuities between early and recent studies." In the Midtown Manhattan research (Srole et al 1962), conducted in 1954, the investigators did not categorize subjects but rather scored their interviews on a single dimension of severity of symptoms or degree of functional impairment. Both the Stirling County and Midtown Manhattan first-wave samples contained a similar percentage of persons judged to have been suffering from some psychological disorder (20% in Stirling County and 23% in Midtown Manhattan), and this percentage is similar to that found by Weissman et al (1978) in New Haven; Schwab et al (1979) in Alachua County, Florida; Helgason (1978) in Iceland; and Orley & Wing (1979) in two Ugandan villages! Srole & Fischer (1980) report that a reexamination of the same subjects 20 years later revealed a reasonable degree of consistency in judgments of degree of functional impairment. Actually more subjects improved than deteriorated in status. Further, by dividing their subjects into four generational cohorts (the oldest cohort born between 1895 and 1904 and the youngest between 1925 and 1934) and examining ratings applied during the first and second waves of data collection, the authors demonstrated that there is no truth to the widely held assumption of a historical trend toward deteriorating mental health in the general population. As a matter of fact, subjects in the younger cohorts obtained better scores in the first wave than the older cohorts and tended to maintain the advantage.

Unlike the previous investigations, the original New Haven Study (Redlich et al 1953) did not purport to estimate the extent of mental illness or behavior disturbance in the total population, but it did get an almost 100%

count of all persons resident in the New Haven metropolitan area who on December 1, 1950, were in some kind of treatment with a psychiatrist. Thus there were no figures that could be compared to the prevalence estimate of the other two major epidemiological studies of that decade.

Another difference between the New Haven research and the other two investigations is that it is cross-sectional rather than longitudinal. In 1975, the New Haven researchers collected data on all patients in treatment on June 1 of that year and did not, as in the other studies, reexamine the patients originally seen in 1950. In addition to a comparison of patient characteristics at these two different points in time (Redlich & Kellert 1978), there was also a comparison of institutions treating such patients. Additionally, in 1975, data were collected on other mental health professionals as well as psychiatrists (Blum & Redlich 1980). Only data on psychiatrists were collected in 1950 because "in 1950 psychiatrists were virtually the only providers of active treatment" (Mollica & Redlich 1980, p. 1258). However, at both times lower-class patients received treatment judged to be inferior to that received by middle and upper-class patients. In 1950 decisions about type of treatment for lower-class patients related more to their social status than to their symptoms; lower-class patients were less likely to receive psychotherapy and more likely to receive medication than upper-class patients. Mollica & Redlich (1980) suspect that the same inequities exist today since the state hospital is the primary inpatient facility for lower-class patients and the categorical treatment unit is their primary outpatient treatment facility. Categorical units are designed to deal with highly specific patient populations (e.g. schizophrenics, drug addicts, alcoholics). The care provided in these units, according to Mollica & Redlich (1980), is not of as high quality as that provided in more general psychiatric units.

Social Class and Prevalence

According to Redlich & Kellert (1978), the relative proportion of patients in each socioeconomic class remained approximately the same in the later survey year (i.e. 1700 per 100,000 for the lower class (class V) and only 600 per 100,000 for the top three classes). However, there was a marked change in the most prominent diagnostic category of these patients from schizophrenia in 1950 to alcoholism in 1975. It is unclear whether this reflects a change in diagnostic style and acumen and increasing recognition of alcoholism as a mental health problem or an increase in availability of specialized facilities and interested practitioners.

An opposite direction in the relation between socioeconomic status and prevalence of behavior disorder was found in three rural villages in West Bengal, India (Nandi et al 1979). In this study the prevalence of mental illness was determined by direct interview of every person in each family (3718 persons in 609 families). Social class was determined by a scale standardized for use in the rural areas of India. It was found that upper classes had significantly higher rates of mental illness. However, when the sample was broken down into four groups by caste and religion, the socioeconomic differences disappeared. It would appear that the variables of religion and social caste moderate any relation between socioeconomic status and extent of disorder. It is interesting that the only other published study with results showing that persons in the lower social classes had the least risk of developing mental illness (Hagnell 1966) was conducted in two Swedish parishes where, just as in this study, the entire population was interviewed by psychiatrists using newly developed clinical criteria for detecting cases and making a diagnosis.

Social Class and Treatment

The most disturbing aspect of the New Haven studies is the relation the researchers found between social class and type of treatment and care received. This was first noted in 1950. At that time, since only psychiatrists' patients were studied, the investigators could only compare various forms of psychiatric treatment, and it was clear that lower-class patients tended to receive directive/organic therapy while upper-class patients were the presumed beneficiaries of insight oriented psychotherapy. In 1974 when patients of other mental health professionals were studied, the researchers

> found a direct correlation between the status of the mental health professional and the socioeconomic and clinical status of the patient. The 20- to 40-year-old middle- to upper-socioeconomic-class psychoneurotic and schizophrenic patient was most likely to be treated by a psychiatrist or psychologist; the lower-socioeconomic-class alcoholic and aged patient, by the mental health worker and nurse; and the adolescent, moderately disturbed, middle-class patient, by the social worker. The treatment of the alcoholic was particularly illustrative of this relationship. Not one psychiatrist was involved in the therapeutic care of alcoholics in the state hospital, although alcoholics (who were primarily from the lower socioeconomic classes and 30% of whom were non-white) accounted for over 45% of all diagnosed patients. In contrast, psychiatrists in private hospitals were the most frequently cited principal therapists for alcoholics (most of these patients were of high socioeconomic status, and nearly all were white) (Redlich & Kellert 1978, p. 27).

The differences in treatment afforded lower-class and upper-class patients were highlighted in an article by Schubert & Miller (1980), who examined six treatment outcome measures among approximately 7500 patients seen by the Department of Psychiatry in a large Metropolitan general hospital between 1970 and 1974. On all measures Class V patients were significantly different than other patients (including number of visits, degree of improvement, type of treatment, discipline of therapist, and whether or not termination was planned). As in the New Haven studies, these patients received significantly more pharmacotherapy and significantly less psychotherapy. However, unlike findings of that study, psychiatrists were more often assigned to Class V patients and social workers less often (possibly a function of perceived need for medications). Medical students also were assigned significantly more often to Class V patients. There was no differential distribution of psychologists and nurses as assigned therapists. Further, Class IV patients were more similar to Class III than Class V on all measures. The therapist and treatment differences cannot be attributed to disorder differences since in a previous study (Schubert & Miller 1978) the authors had found no social class differences in extent of psychosis, neurosis, or personality disorder, although organic brain syndrome and mental retardation were more frequently diagnosed among lower-class individuals.

Similar differences in delivery of services according to social class of patients were found by Mayfield & Fowler (1977), who compared patients admitted over a one-year period to the psychiatric services of a public (VA) and private hospital both staffed by the same Department of Psychiatry. The authors found that the two hospitals "serve different populations who come to the hospital for different reasons by different referral sources, manifest different behavior, acquire different diagnoses, and receive different treatment over different lengths of time" (p. 322). When social class was controlled, however, the differences in diagnoses, behaviors, and treatment between the two hospitals disappeared except, interestingly enough, the private hospital showed a significantly greater use of somatic therapy and much shorter period of hospitalization. The authors feel this may be due to the pressure to move patients out of the private hospital because of the high cost of care in the private hospital and a complementary inclination in the public hospital for the staff to be more leisurely and lackadaisical. The authors concluded: "in any event, our findings suggest that the financial structure of the two facilities may have more to do with the treatment delivered than do the behavioral, diagnostic, and social class differences in the patient populations they serve" (p. 322).

Since the publication of the three by now classic epidemiological studies of the 1950s, the preponderance of the literature has continued to affirm an inverse relation between prevalence and/or treatment of mental disorder and socioeconomic status (e.g. Carr & Krause 1978, Heller et al 1980, Ilfeld 1978, Schwab et al 1979, Strauss 1978). However, recently there has been a spate of studies disconfirming a relation between social class and diagnosis (e.g. Beitchman et al 1978, Cadoret 1978, Craig & Van Natta 1979, Finlay-Jones & Burvill 1978, Levine & Kozak 1979, Schubert & Miller 1980), as well as between social class and treatment (Day & Reznikoff 1980, Edwards et al 1979, Frank et al 1978, Gomes-Schwartz et al 1978). A thorough search of the literature from 1978 through 1980 would seem to indicate many studies with negative findings. The reason for this change might have to do with increased availability of resources to all segments of the population since the decade of the 1950s (Buck & Hirschman 1980, Mollica & Redlich 1980), albeit as pointed out above, these services have not been of uniform quality.

Social Class and Programs

We have been concerned with the relation between socioeconomic status at the time of admission and extent and type of behavior disorder as well as between socioeconomic status and choice of intervention strategy or treatment. An equally important and interesting problem is the relation of behavior disorder to change in socioeconomic status subsequent to discharge. Tsuang (1980) reported on 500 psychiatric cases and 60 surgical patient controls who were followed up 40 years after discharge from the hospital. Three types of psychiatric diagnosis were included: schizophrenia, depression, and mania. The occupational status of the psychiatric group had declined significantly more than that of the control group, especially in the schizophrenic subsample. However, there was a sizable number of cases in each diagnostic group who sustained or regained their previous status. This was especially true of those who were symptom-free at the time of follow-up.

To summarize recent findings in regard to the relation between social class and abnormal behavior, it is fair to say that the earlier findings of a direct realtion between increased prevalence and decreased social status have been called into question. A number of studies have shown no relation, while still others have shown one in the opposite direction. However, there remains strong evidence for a relation between the type of treatment received and the social class status of the patient.

The solution to the problem of differential access to treatment facilities because of economic conditions has been addressed by Buck & Hirschman (1980). They advocate a consumer-oriented, competitive, market system entailing liberalized licensing programs, greater use of paraprofessionals, removal of restrictions on advertising of services, and national health insurance. By increasing demand for services, these innovations will also increase consumption and supply of services. Further, competition among providers, enhanced by eliminating their subsidization and encouraging advertising, would counteract any price increase resulting from an increase in demand. Buck & Hirshman's suggested approach may increase service availability, but because cost of service is still likely to vary with level of training and type of professional, social class will probably still be associated with type of professional seen for services.

RACE AND ABNORMAL BEHAVIOR

For many years there has been discussion of the conflicting evidence in regard to differential prevalence of abnormal behaviors in black and white portions of the population (Fischer 1969). When differential rates between the races have been noted, the differences have often been ascribed to the use of screening instruments, inappropriately used for one group when they have been normed on another (Gynther 1972); or they have sometimes been explained away by such statements as "what is called sick or deviant behavior for one group may actually be adaptive—or functional—in another" (Fischer 1969). The effect of both of these arguments has often been to overlook serious problems in some patients and make inappropriate dispositions for others (Adebimpe et al 1979). The extent of bias against blacks, whether overt or due to a subtle stereotyping, was dramatically illustrated in two studies published in 1980 (Flaherty & Meagher, Lewis et al). Flaherty & Meagher (1980) examined case records of 101 schizophrenic patients consecutively admitted over 6 months to an all-male unit in a general teaching hospital. There were 66 black and 35 white patients. There were no differences between the two racial groups in global psychopathology, chronicity, age, or employment. However, the blacks had significantly shorter lengths of stay, significantly greater use of medication, seclusion and restraints, and a significantly lower rate of occupational and recreational therapy ordered by the therapist.

Lewis et al (1980) compared psychiatric symptoms, medical histories, and violent behaviors of a total one-year sample of adolescents from the same community who were sent either to a correctional school or to an adolescent psychiatric unit of the only state hospital serving the area. They found the only factor differentiating the incarcerated from the hospitalized group was the presence of significantly more blacks in the incarcerated group. There were an equivalent number of violent crimes among those who were sent to the hospital or the correctional facility, a similar number of behavioral symptoms, and a similar type and frequency of medical problems (except for head injuries of which there were more in the incarcerated group). In a multiple regression the single most powerful predictor differentiating inhabitants of the two facilities was race.

From these two recent studies it would seem that although race may not be related to the etiology of abnormal behaviors, like social class, it is certainly related to type of intervention implemented to deal with these behaviors.

Schwab et al (1979) interviewed a random sample (N = approximately 2000) of all the residents of Alachua County, Florida, with a schedule that included, among other demographic and health items, a comprehensive mental health inventory of 100 items from which was derived a measure of social psychiatric impairment. Blacks, especially females, received the highest scores on this measure. However, when socioeconomic status was controlled, the difference between the races disappeared. This confounding of socioeconomic status and race makes the contribution of either race or socioeconomic status by itself to the impairment score unclear. The pile-up of racial minority group members in the lower socioeconomic levels and the comparative dearth of representatives of those groups in the upper socioeconomic levels does not permit accurate control of race across social class.

Use of Standardized Tests

In addition to questions of difference in prevalence of behavior disorders and access to equivalent treatment between races, there is a related question of the appropriateness of using standardized tests with culturally different groups.

The controversy over the appropriate use of the MMPI for black subjects has continued right up until the time that this review was sent to press (Patterson et al 1981). It was in 1972 that Gynther stated that it was necessary to use separate norms for black subjects. Since that time there have been reports supporting both sides of the argument, usually inconclusive because of various types of confounding such as education, socioeconomic status, reasons for taking the test, and psychiatric status of the subjects. The thrust of the argument has been well put by Penk et al (1978):

> How can a test developed with "contrasted groups" methods using adult, white Minnesotans of the 1930's serve as the standard for interpreting scores of individuals assessed in the 1970's—particularly persons of minority ethnic groups such as Blacks? Should clinicians compare clients of the current generation on a test 'norm-referenced' in 1939 with 724 people waiting while relatives and friends were being seen in the University of Minnesota University Hospital, with 265 high school graduates seeking precollege guidance in the University of Minnesota Testing Bureau, and with 265 skilled workers from Work Projects Administration jobs in Minneapolis (p. 506)?

However, Pritchard & Rosenblatt (1980a,b) in their recent review of the literature concluded there was no evidence to support the notion of differential performance on the MMPI between blacks and whites. In their response to Pritchard and Rosenblatt, Gynther & Green (1980) argued that degrees of ethnic bias in the MMPI vary as a function of the kinds of sample being compared, e.g. drug addicts, psychiatric patients, or normals.

The validity of the MMPI for American Indian subjects has also been questioned recently. Pollack & Shore (1980) found that the MMPI could not discriminate among 142 patients from Pacific Northwest tribes who on the basis of case study and psychiatric examination had been assigned various diagnoses. The profiles of all the patients were similar even though they included diagnosed schizophrenics, depressives, and alcoholics. The similarity of all subgroup profiles demonstrates that results of the MMPI with American Indians are of doubtful validity.

Further research into the appropriate use of standardized tests with minority group members is represented by two recent studies comparing Anglo and Chicano children. One of the studies concerned children who were referred for psychological services and tested with the WISC-R (Reynolds & Gutkin 1980). The other compared Anglo and Chicano children enrolled in a suburban Houston elementary school on the basis of a behavior problem check list filled out by the teacher (Touliatos & Lindholm 1980). Both studies found no difference between the two groups in intelligence and psychopathology. However, the latter sample may not have been representative of Chicano children in general since there is no indication of effect of social class. All children who did not come from intact two-parent families were excluded, and there were only 200 Chicano children as compared to 3000 Anglo children in the study.

Nevertheless, recently reported research does indicate that tests standardized on members of the majority culture may be appropriate for members of some minority groups, but not others.

RELIGION AND ABNORMAL BEHAVIOR

Over the period of this literature search, 1978–1980, there seems to have been much less interest in religious preference or church attendance than in social class membership or racial or ethnic identification as a factor related to psychopathology. Only two articles (Buckalew 1978, Wadsworth & Checketts 1980) and one doctoral dissertation (Berger 1979) were uncovered. All three studies found no relation between religion and extent of abnormal behavior. It is questionable whether Jews should be considered a religious or ethnic group. In any case, a review of studies of psychiatric disorders among Jews in America, conducted over the past 50 years since the great immigration from Eastern Europe, shows rates for Jews to be invariably lower than those for non-Jews (Selavan 1979). As a group, according to this review, Jews appear to display a greater awareness and acceptance of psychological theory and treatment as a way of dealing with emotional problems and therefore utilize to a larger degree than other groups the nonsomatic forms of therapy (e.g. psychotherapy).

Aside from any relation between religious preference or upbringing and frequency of abnormal behavior is a related question of how religion affects the content of abnormal behavior. For example, religious delusions have been most frequently reported in depression and paranoid schizophrenia (Group for the Advancement of Psychiatry 1968), although religious content is also found in obsessive compulsive and phobic disturbances (Mailloux & Ancorra 1960). However, other than for one article published in 1977 (Beit-Hallahami & Argyle), we found no study of this aspect of disordered behavior in our literature search. Hallahami & Argyle pointed out the social environment aspect of religious content in behavior disorders (e.g. religious delusions were found more often among lower and lower middle class patients). Furthermore, there is an inverse relation between the social nature of a religious experience and its psychopathological nature, i.e. the more solitary the religious experience, the more disturbed is the individual.

In summary then the only new evidence for a relation between religion and prevalence of abnormal behavior is one study which shows that Jews have lower rates than the general population but make more use of psychotherapy than the somatherapies.

CULTURE AND ABNORMAL BEHAVIOR

The effect of culture on the prevalence of emotional disorder and abnormal behavior started to come under scientific scrutiny in the early 1930s when Sapir (1932), Benedict (1934), and other cultural anthropologists began to question the universality of Western conceptions of what constitutes normal and abnormal behavior. Soon afterwards, articles by psychiatrists and anthropologists started to appear, maintaining that mental illness was absent in a number of primitive and rural societies. For example, the Okinawans were believed to include no individuals with psychoses and few with psychosomatic illnesses. Schizophrenia was supposedly rare in homogeneous, nonliterate societies which had had little contact with Western civilization, such as the Bantus of the African Congo. This was attributed by Devereaux (1939) to the consistent value structure of these cultures. Kardiner (1939) reported depression and suicide were nonexistent among the Alorese. However interesting these reports, they were at best impressionistic and were not based on a population census in which the entire social system is observed, including healthy as well as sick persons.

Culture and Prevalence

The estimation of the prevalence of mental illness in primitive societies is extremely difficult, and later studies which have met reasonable standards of precision and comprehensiveness did indeed find rates not too different from those encountered in industrialized societies (e.g. Lin 1953, Eaton & Weil 1955). It seems that culture, as represented by different types of societal organization and devlopment, is not related to total amount of behavior disorder but to the ways in which the behavioral aberrations are manifested and in the distribution of specific diagnostic categories. This is strikingly illustrated by the ubiquitous 20–25% figure for prevalence of emotional and/or behavioral disorder found during the last 35 to 40 years in Midtown, Manhattan (Srole et al 1962), Nova Scotia (Leighton 1959), New Haven (Weissman et al 1978), Iceland (Helgason 1978), and two Ugandan villages (Orley & Wing 1979). In fact, Odejide (1979), who reviewed a number of studies with special emphasis on those carried out in his native Nigeria, found data identical to that collected in more industrialized societies, e.g. rate of 0.3% for schizophrenia and similarities in patterns of drug prescription and usage. Similarities in the forms and manifestations of abnormal behavior have been noted in psychiatric disorders of children in Western and Oriental cultures (Singer et al 1978) and between depressed patients in Sweden and England (Montgomery et al 1978).

However, differences have also been noted. Allodi & Dukszta (1978) have described mental health services in China and concluded that psychiatric services there are primarily concerned with psychoses and severe neuroses. Neuroses of moderate severity are viewed as general health problems, and conduct and personality disorders are considered social or community matters. Likewise, different patterns in the diagnosis of schizophrenia and affective disorder have been noted in Britain and America (Gelfand & Kline 1978). It seems that diagnoses of schizophrenia are more common in America and of affective disorder in Britain. In the past this has no doubt been due to the broader definition of schizophrenia in the U.S. However, with the new limiting diagnostic criteria for schizophrenia set forth in D.S.M. III (A.P.A. 1980), as well as the more comprehensive view of affective disorders in that manual, these cross-national diagnostic differences will probably disappear.

Mezzich & Raab (1980) compared the symptoms of depression in Peruvian and US samples of adult diagnosed depressive patients and found that the core depressive symptoms and signs were similar across samples as well as overall level of depressive severity. However, more somatic complaints were seen in the Peruvian group while the US group showed more suicidal signs. Further intercultural differences in the manifestations of depression were pointed out by Marsella (1978), who indicated in his review that depression appears to be less prevalent in smaller non-Western cultures, whether considering treated or nontreated prevalence. There were a few non-Western cultures where the rates were found to be high, but these included highly urbanized populations. Marsella (1979) cites further evidence provided by himself and others to prove that cultures differ in the amount and expression of specific mental disorders. He concludes: "cultures do vary in the manifestation of mental disorders and this finding should not surprise even the most ardent supporters of the universalist position. To deny such a finding would not only be tantamount to rejecting the research which has been conducted, but also to denying that cultural differences exist in behavior" (p. 251). Marsella also speculates on the reason for the variation: "cultural groups which have subjective, as opposed to objective, epistemological orientations toward life will tend to depsychologize experience, and thus not experience the sense of loneliness, isolation, guilt, and detachment associated with depression" (p. 256).

Thus, although the rate of psychotic disorders such as schizophrenia seems to be consistent across cultures, affective disorders which under the new diagnostic system include both psychiatric and neurotic disturbances appear to have differential rates according to the culture, although the evidence is not that clear cut.

Juris Draguns (1980), in a comprehensive synthesis of the literature to date, concludes that the essentials of abnormal behavior can be reduced across cultures to four dimensions. These correspond approximately to affective disorder, schizophrenia, neurosis, and personality disorder. However, within each of these broad categories, there is room for cultural variation. Among Draguns' conclusions is the assertion that there is no disorder which is entirely immune from cultural influence. On the other hand, no known disorder has been shown to be entirely the result of cultural influence. Psychoses are less influenced by culture than nonpsychotic disorders; but of the psychoses, affective disorders seem to show the most influence of cultural factors. Furthermore, variations in the psychotic syndromes are related to economic, social, technological, religious, and other features of the different societies. Those symptoms least influenced by culture are in the areas of cognition, perception, and affect while those most influenced by culture pertain to role and social behavior.

Cross-cultural epidemiological studies have been less than definitive, not only because of logistical problems in carrying them through but because of lack of comparability of diagnostic schemes used in different areas of the world and differential training and experience of observers. In 1966 the International Pilot Study of Schizophrenia (W.H.O. 1973) was begun in nine countries differing widely in sociocultural characteristics in order to devise universally applicable measuring instruments and procedures and then to determine if schizophrenic disorders exist in different parts of the world, and if so how they are differentially manifested and treated. On the basis of standardized assessments and clearly specified criteria, according to Sartorius et al (1978), it was concluded

> that schizophrenic patients with similar characteristics could be identified in all nine of the cultures in which the study took place and that the degree of similarity among them could be specified due to the application of standardized assessment methods ensuring cross-cultural comparability. Furthermore, in all cultures patients diagnosed as suffering from schizophrenia could be distinguished clearly in terms of clinical symptomatology from patients with a diagnosis of affective psychosis or other functional mental disorder (p. 103).

Culture and Prognosis

Two years later approximately 85% of the group of patients in the Sartorius et al research (1978) who had been screened into the study originally were reevaluated to compare course and outcome of disorder across diagnostic groups and countries. It was found that schizophrenic patients in the undeveloped countries (China, Columbia, India, and Nigeria) had, on the average, considerably better course and outcome than schizophrenic patients in the developed countries (Czechoslovakia, Denmark, USSR, UK, and U.S.A.). Associated with prediction of outcome were such variables as social isolation, marital status, educational level, and occupation, indicating again that social factors, while perhaps not as important as previously thought in the etiology of behavior disorders, certainly are of importance in prognosis. Beck (1978) has reviewed the literature on social influences on the prognosis of schizophrenia and has concluded that social events other than the care system are clearly related to outcome, while evidence of the efficiency of various treatments is much less clear. By social events, Beck is referring to such disparate variables as fluctuations in the business cycle, community attitudes, and family overprotection.

Waxler (1979) also maintains that outcome for schizophrenics is better in nonindustrial societies. Results of her 5-year follow-up of 88 patients discharged from a Sri Lanka psychiatric ward were consistent with those of Sartorius et al (1978) for undeveloped societies. She invokes social labeling theory to explain the findings. In peasant societies the expectation is that the patient will get better, so their treatment practices encourage short-term illness and quick return to normality. She interprets the cultural differences in prognosis to be the result of culturally based self-fulfilling prophecies. Since it is believed in Sri Lanka that mental illness results from external causation, either natural or supernatural, the patient's personality or social past is not implicated and the cure is ritualistic and standard for all patients. Thus, within the family and within the treatment network, the Sinhalese patient is more likely to hear messages about quick recovery consistent with Sinhalese cultural beliefs about mental illness.

Culture and Treatment

Socioeconomic factors, as we saw in our discussion of social class and race, are related not only to the etiology and distribution of maladaptive behaviors but also to the type of interventions utilized to change such behaviors or prevent them from occurring in the first place. So too it is with culture as noted by Waxler (1979). Higgenbotham (1979) has discussed the relation between culture and mental health services and has concluded that the kind of services which have been developed by Western agencies are inappropriate for Non-western societies. These societies have neither the trained personnel nor the financial resources to implement such programs, and furthermore the programs themselves have disrupted the integrated elements in the indigenous culture. What is required, according to Higgenbotham, is "a treatment system continuous with cultural beliefs and with existing patterns of helping" (p. 328).

On this continent, cultural factors have been noted in the differential mental hospitalization patterns of Canadians of Dutch, Greek, and Italian ancestry (Murphy 1978), and the ward behavior and att itudes of Anglo and Mexican Americans (Denny 1978). In Asia differences have been noted in the treatment of schizophrenia in India (Dube 1978) and among the aboriginal population in Australia (Burton & Burton 1979).

Culture and Attitudes

It has been pointed out in the recent literature that attitudes toward mental illness vary among cultures and these attitudes are important in determining what is considered mental illness and how it is treated. Such differences were noted between Greek and American samples of professional persons as well as laymen (Koutrelakos & Gedeon 1978); between samples of German and American high school students and mental hospital staff (Townsend 1978); and among various ethnic groups in the US (Jalali, Jalali & Turner 1978, Fandetti & Gelfand 1978).

As mentioned in our discussion of the study by Waxler in Sri Lanka (1979), the belief system in any society is an important determinant of the treatments used to eliminate or ameliorate abnormal behaviors in individuals who are deemed to be disturbed. The variety of culturally specific psychotherapies has been detailed by Prince (1980), who points out that indigenous practitioners often capitalize on the organism's endogenous healing mechanisms which develop spontaneously when the individual is distressed. Prince says, "healers around the world have learned to manipulate and build upon these endogenous mechanisms in a variety of ways to bring about resolution of life's problems and alleviation of suffering" (p. 292). Prince is referring here to altered states of consciousness such as dreams, trance states, dissociations, and mystical experiences of various sorts which are cultivated and elaborated by indigenous healers for therapeutic purposes. In general, Western type practitioners have denigrated these procedures, but recently there has been an increase in interest in them, and efforts have been made to adapt some of their features so they can be integrated with more traditional Western practices.

LABELING VS THE MEDICAL MODEL

The effects of labeling an individual as deviant on the subsequent behaviors of that individual as well as others who interact with him or her have been documented in previous volumes of this series (King 1978, Strauss 1979).

For a number of years this was a popular topic among sociologists who applied labeling theory to an understanding of the causes of crime and delinquency (e.g. Farrington 1977) and behavioral psychologists who invoked the construct to explain the maintenance of certain bizarre behaviors (e.g. Ullman & Krasner 1969). According to the latter authors, once a person is labeled a schizophrenic, we automatically tend to put him in that category in our thinking and expect him to display the behaviors usually ascribed to schizophrenics. Subsequently, we tend to treat him in ways that are deemed to be appropriate for persons with such labels. Further, the label provides the individual with an undesirable social role he or she feels expected to play and indeed does continue to play in order to live up to the stated expectations of others which are implied in the ascribed label. For many behavioral psychologists labeling theory was the rational alternative to an unproven medical model of behavior disorder.

Since 1978, however, other than the broad reference made by Waxler and noted above, there has not been much published research on the topic of labeling. One notable exception has been a book by Sarbin & Mancuso (1980). In this provocative treatise the authors approach schizophrenia through an analysis of metaphoric language, emphasizing the context in which behaviors called schizophrenic by the "experts" evolve. In a brilliant "tour de force" they review all the empirical articles published on the topic of schizophrenia in the *Journal of Abnormal Psychology* over a 20-year span from 1959 through 1978, pointing out flaws in the design, statistical analysis, logic, or interpretation in each, or criticizing the triviality of the behaviors investigated and/or the inappropriateness of their measures. However, the critique is not as devastating as it would appear. The cumulative evidence, both from the series of studies Sarbin and Mancuso criticize as well as those studies appearing in publications other than the *Journal of Abnormal Psychology,* is so great that it is impossible to deny the basic biological, physiological, constitutional, and/or genetic underpinnings to the entity (or construct) called schizophrenia. Certainly these published findings do not tell the whole story, but it would be folly to ignore them in programs of prevention, treatment, or amelioration (Eisenberg 1977). We agree with Draguns (1980) that results of recent studies give comfort neither to the extreme opponents or defendants of the medical model, and that the truth lies somewhere in between the two extremes of medical diagnosis and contextual ascription. Just as in the age-old controversy between nature and nurture as regards intelligence or personality, current knowledge would indicate that abnormal behavior can best be regarded as the result of an interaction between what the individual carries around inside and the specifics of the situation in which the individual is embedded.

SOCIAL CLASS, STRESS, COPING, AND ABNORMALITY

As noted above, although the results are not unequivocally positive, there has been a preponderance of evidence linking social class and abnormal behaviors. The reason for less than universal demonstration of the relation, we believe, is that the essential variable is not social class but a third set of conditions which varies both with abnormal behavior and social class. Thus a positive relation between the latter two is not always obtained. The third set of variables includes the learning environments for acquiring behaviors which permit the individual to cope with stress, i.e. frustrations, attitudes, rewards, and punishments which are administered and endorsed by socializing agents in the individual's milieu.

Stress and Coping

The notion that stress level, the person's experienced level of subjective stress or number of stressful events, is the underlying variable which determines the correlation between social class and abnormal behavior has received much attention and support during the past few years (Wills & Langner 1980). Stress has been related to psychiatric symptomatology (Cochrane & Sobol 1980, Ilfeld 1977, 1979), violence and crime (Schlesinger & Revitch 1980), physical illness and personal problems in adolescence (Gad & Johnson 1980), and psychological impairment (Liem & Liem 1978) and physical illness in general (Minter & Kimball 1980). The literature available to date suggests a causal chain of factors along the following pattern: Low social class is associated with a high frequency of stressful events and the learning of inadequate methods for coping with this stress which may then lead to abnormal behavior (Wills & Langner 1980). This model does not deny the existence of "drift" to the lower class because of abnormal behavior (Harkey, Miles & Rushing 1976) but suggests that class is associated with such factors as stress which also produce high rates of abnormality (Kessler 1979). In order to evaluate this causal model of the social class-abnormal behavior relation, the role of socioeconomic status as related to stress and coping ability will be reviewed.

Dohrenwend's (1973) survey study suggested that low social status, both class (lower class) and sex (female), is associated with greater exposure to stressful life events than higher social status. Further, the data were interpreted as suggesting that stress (life changes) leads to psychiatric symptoms as well as vice versa and that stress is more highly correlated with symptoms among the lower than higher social status groups. Thus, Dohrenwend proposed that the members of the lower class were exposed to more stress and were at the same time more vulnerable to stress. Three recent studies

(Pearlin & Schooler 1978, Kessler 1979, Gad & Johnson 1980) have attempted to examine the relation between social class, stress, and psychological adjustment. Pearlin & Schooler (1978) focused on the relation between coping ability and stress. They defined coping behavior as dealing with problems in ways which eliminate or modify problems, control the meaning of the experience, or control the emotional consequences of the problem. In open-ended interviews, people were asked to describe how they dealt with problems. Factor analysis of these data resulted in six types of marital coping patterns, five types of parental coping patterns for parents with 16- to 21-year-old children, four types of household economic coping patterns, and four occupational coping patterns. In looking at the relation between effectiveness of coping patterns and type of stress, it seems that parental and marital coping methods which involve commitment, belief in ability to solve problems, and direct action are more effective than avoidance or explosive emotional reactions. Additionally, except in the area of occupational stress, the use of multiple coping patterns seems to be more effective than the use of one or two coping methods. Thus, Pearlin & Schooler's results (1978) on coping effectiveness suggest that coping patterns which deal with problems in a direct, calm manner, involve the use of multiple strategies, and are associated with a belief in control provide the best method of reducing or containing stress.

Social Class

These are the basic findings on coping and stress; the critical question here is the association of social class with coping methods. Although the correlations are low, the results are consistent across areas of stress and suggest that low education and income are associated with ineffective coping styles. Additionally, as would be expected, belief in mastery ability and self-esteem are also lower for the subjects of low socioeconomic status. Pearlin & Schooler (1978) view the relation as follows: "The less educated and the poorer are more exposed to hardships and, at the same time, are less likely to have the means to fend off the stresses resulting from the hardships. Not only are life problems distributed unequally among social groups and collectivities, but it is apparent that the ability to deal with the problems is similarly unequal" (p. 17). Consistent with Dohrenwend's finding (1973) that women are exposed to more stress, Pearlin & Schooler found that women more often used less effective or even exacerbating type of coping strategies. They suggest the possibility that stress and coping ability may underlie the relation between sex and abnormal behavior i.e. more frequent disturbance among females. Pearlin & Schooler further suggest that females may be socialized in ways that do not permit them to develop as many effective coping patterns as males.

Kessler (1979) also addresses the question of the relation between social class and stress. Kessler obtained interviews on 720 persons during 1967 and 1969 and gathered information on life events over those 2 years, as well as present financial and physical status and a measure of emotional distress. Again, based on life events and present status, the lower-class subjects were exposed to more stressful experiences than the upper-class subjects. Further comparable stressful events in the two also had more impact on the emotional functioning of the lower class than the upper class. Thus, as demonstrated by Pearlin & Schooler (1978), the lower class appeared to experience more physical stress and were also less able to cope with that stress. When evaluating groups on the basis of psychological (emotional) distress, a slightly different pattern was present. The middle and upper social classes were more likely than the lower class to report extreme distress when exposed to comparable stressors, but because of differential exposure and generally less adequate coping strategies, the lower class, and particularly nonwhites, more often reported extreme distress. Kessler (1979) suggests that the lower-class individual may over time adapt to stress and thus avoid extreme distress in particular instances. This advantage appears of limited value because less access to social support (Liem & Liem 1978) and more exposure to stress still results in more extreme total distress for the lower class and nonwhites than other groups.

Females in the Kessler (1979) study also reported more distress and greater exposure to stress. Kessler attributes the greater extreme stress to differential impact of stress rather than to differential exposure. These results are consistent with the Pearlin & Schooler (1978) finding that females had less effective coping skills than did males. Another vulnerable group consists of separated and divorced persons. They were exposed to more stress and appeared less able to cope with stress and reported more distress and extreme distress than did married, single, or widowed persons.

Liem & Liem (1978), in a review of the literature on the role of economic stress and social support as a factor in the relation between social class and behavior disorder, argue for considering class as a structural system that relates class to an organized environment on several dimensions. They point out the effects of economic factors (Brenner 1973), chronic stress, and other variables which differentially affect the lower class. Liem & Liem (1978) ascribe social class influences to the available social support system. The presence of fewer personal and social supports within the lower class structure is suggested as one reason why lower social class individuals are more vulnerable to psychological disorders. Thus, Liem & Liem (1978) argue for a combined effect of individual differences and class structure rather than emphasizing individual abilities to deal with stress.

In line with this view, Gad & Johnson (1980) also assessed social support as a factor in the relation between stress and socioeconomic level. These authors obtained data from 167 adolescents in the Seattle area. The subjects varied on socioeconomic level and race. Measures of life events, both positive and negative, a number of self-report measure on health and psychological status, and a measure of social support were obtained. The lower-class subjects, both black and white, had experienced more negative life events, e.g. death in family, divorce, and illness in family, than middle and upper-class subjects. Further, number of negative life events was related to a wide array of health, psychological, and self-perception variables, e.g. visit to physician, visit to school counselor, stated personal problems, perceived ability to cope with personal problems, and drug use. The correlations between negative life events and the indicators of stress reactions were not significantly influenced by level of social support. Again, the lower-class subjects were subjected to more stress and in this case the number of stress events (negative life events) was related to reports of increased physical, personal, and self-efficacy problems. The extent of social support was not a significant factor as had been suggested by Liem & Liem's (1978) conceptualization of reduced social support for the lower class. On the other hand, Gad & Johnson (1980) did not deal with psychiatric outcomes and did not look at long-term effects.

Additionally, since number of negative life events is associated with social class, insufficient differences in social support within the lower class population (Liem & Liem 1978) may have prevented adequate evaluation of the role of social support by restricting variability on this factor. The interaction between class membership with class structure, personal abilities, and stress needs additional examination. Social class can affect the ways in which an individual defines need for help. This self definition probably influences the effectiveness of professional health systems. It has been demostrated (Kulka et al 1979) that although willingness to use services is equal among classes, the definition of which personal problems require outside help varies according to class with lower-class individuals more often defining such problems as self-help issues.

In addition to studying the interactions between factors which create increased stress and less efficient coping mechanisms among the lower socioeconomic class, longitudinal studies are needed to determine how stress effects influence long-term adjustment. Also, to understand class effects more fully, it will be necessary to determine the influence of chronic stress, e.g. long-term unemployment, poor housing, dangerous neighborhoods (Humphrey & Kupferer 1977, Wenz 1977), and frequent negative life changes, on psychological functioning and coping strategies. As Pearlin & Schooler's (1978) work on coping styles suggests, when stress is dealt with by withdrawal or aggression, little is solved and stress is exacerbated. If these two general approaches are conceptualized as internal psychological disturbance and acting out (crime), then the cost of high stress and poor coping among the lower class is enormous on both a personal and social level. Although socioeconomic level is being used for classification purposes, it is not necessarily socioeconomic class by itself that causes problems but rather the life events and social structures which tend to result in high stress and poor coping for many people within the lower socioeconomic groups.

Two additional lines of research are also relevant to how or why particular stresses and stress effects occur more often for some groups. The first line of research deals with the personality variables associated with negative reactions to stress. Johnson & Sarason (1978) and Kobasa (1979) both looked at personal control, and belief about control, as moderators of stress effects. In the Johnson & Sarason (1978) study, college students with an external locus of control responded to life stress with depression and anxiety more than students with an internal locus of control. Likewise, Kobasa, using a general style called "Hardiness," which includes locus of control, alienation, and attitudes of vigorousness toward the environment, found that executives who less often responded to stress with illness were more hardy than those who became ill. Thus, the person's view of control appears to be an important moderator of stress; and membership in the lower class tends to produce an external locus of control or lack of personal control over the environment. Wills & Langner (1980) provide an explanation of why the relation between beliefs about control and reactions to stress may appear to be vulnerable to stress. Of course, locus of control is not independent of personal history, and it may be that the same conditions and events which produce stress tend also to produce a sense of lack of control. Kohn (1976) has demonstrated that father's social class is related to the extent to which he values self-direction for his children. The parent's lack of ability, or opportunity, to exert self-direction may be transmitted to the children, and the effects of social class on attitudes of self-direction that the parent holds thus has an effect on present and future generations.

The drift hypothesis has been considered in this regard. One possible reason that lower social class individuals are less able to cope with stress may be that people who lack coping skills drift to a lower class (as compared to their parents) and then both produce more stress for themselves and deal with it less well. The probability that downward drift occurs and is logical appears to have some support (Harkey, Miles & Rushing 1976), but the extent to which lower-class individuals are prevented from moving up the scale or drop even lower because of stress and then develop disordered behaviors is unknown. Even in the Harkey et al (1976) study which looks at physical illness and is interpreted as supporting the drift hypothesis, no data are available showing that it was class that produced the increase in role dysfunction. Longitudinal studies are needed to determine the class outcome for lower-class individuals, the extent of movement, and who drifts down the scale or is prevented from moving up. Since the stress occurs in a variety of reactions, e.g. physical, emotional, and behavioral (Cochrane & Sobol 1980, Pearlin & Schooler 1978, Kessler 1979, Gad & Johnson 1980, Schlesinger & Revitch 1980), and since lower-class individuals are exposed to more stressors (Pearlin & Schooler 1978, Kessler 1979, Gad & Johnson 1980), the presence of conditions which produce drift or prevent upward mobility are present to a greater extent in the lower social class environment. This further raises the issue of what capabilities, social skills, or coping styles are learned in the process of growing up in a lower social class environment and how they are learned. The skills and abilities the individual develops will determine the extent to which upward mobility is possible and the individual's social and psychological functioning are affected. The next section will summarize the findings on social class and development.

SOCIAL CLASS AND CHILD DEVELOPMENT

In the introduction to this review it was suggested that the components of social class which influence development of abnormal behaviors need to be understood in terms of the learning environments which shape cognitive, social, and personality development. In other words, it is not social class in and of itself that causes increased child psychopathology at the lower socioeconomic levels (Wills & Langner 1980) or ineffective coping skills among lower-class adults (Pearlin & Schooler 1978), but rather the combination of deficient biological and environmental learning conditions which tend to be associated with low socioeconomic standing.

A number of articles indicate social class is related, as a marker variable, to delayed development or inferior skill development. Kagan (1977), in a review of his own work on cognitive development, reports that social class is a more powerful variable in determining IQ and reading ability than the infant's attentiveness at 4 and 8 months of age. He found that by 13 months degree of attentiveness was related to social class but was unrelated to earlier attentiveness scores. At age 10, social class was related to IQ and reading scores whereas these scores were not related at all to the quality of infant behavior. These findings with Caucasian children in the Boston area (Kagan 1977, Kagan et al 1978) are similar to the results reported by Neel (1977) on the social and intellectual development of healthy and chronically ill black and white children. Neel states, "Social class exerted a marked effect on intellectual scores, with lower class children consistently and significantly lower, showing more visual-motor pathology, less achievement orientation, less love orientation and less feelings of protection" (p. 1145). Lower-class membership also was associated with more frequent incidence of coming from a broken home and fewer educational and cultural experiences for the children. Further, Neel (1977) reported that lower-class parents felt limited in their ability to give material things or time to their children.

In a study which lacked social class comparisons but attempted to evaluate developmental effects of abuse by matching abused infants with infants involved in an accident (fall or blow) not due to abuse, the effects of lower-class membership seemed to outweigh the specific effect of abuse (Elmer 1978). All the subjects were from the lower two socioeconomic classes. Initially, the abuse group showed delayed cognitive ability compared to the accident group, but one year later both groups displayed delays in mental, motor, and language development. Eight years later the entire subject population showed inferior intellectual abilities, problems with language development, and behavior problems. The apparent adverse impact of lower-class membership lead Elmer (1978) to suggest that infants born to parents of the lower social class are generally stifled in development.

Other skills which have been demonstrated to be influenced by social class are semantic mastery (Kirk et al 1979) and imaginative play (Udwin & Shmukler 1981). Kirk et al concluded that black children in the Head Start program displayed a deficiency in semantic mastery and that in their studies the deficiency appeared due to a lack of knowledge of language rather than differential use of language. Further, Kirk et al (1979) noted that the deficiency is a function of being raised by poor, uneducated parents and is not a function of race. In order to prevent deficiencies and reading problems, which they note are widely observed in uneducated parents of poverty, Kirk et al (1979) suggested educating young parents in how to teach the fundamentals of early language.

Udwin & Shmukler (1981) assessed imaginative play in 60 South African and Israeli preschool children of lower and middle-class socioeconomic status. Again, class was the critical variable:

> The results suggested that socioeconomic status was the overriding variable in determining the observed levels of imaginative play, and the contention was raised that the deficits in imaginative play among lower-class children were created not by the lack of experiences or stimulation per se but rather the failure of the lower-class parents to help their children with the integration of the plethora of stimuli that confront them in the course of everyday life (Udwin & Shmukler 1981, p. 66).

Thus, it may not be the total amount of interaction but the form of the interactions which is most relevant. Kilbride et al (1977) assessed parent-child interactions with 2 week-old healthy Caucasian infants and found that amount of interaction did not vary but the lower social class parents talked to their children less and were less knowledgeable about the abilities and skills of a 2-week-old infant. However, Farran & Haskins (1980), in a study of interactions between mothers and their 3-year-old children from different socioeconomic backgrounds, found that middle income mothers spent twice as much time in mutual play with their children as low income mothers. The quality of the interaction, whether controlling on the part of the mother or mutually interactive, was no different between the two classes. There was just less interaction in the low income group. These differences in early interacting may be an important factor in how social class relates to development. What may be especially important is that the early child-parent interactions may form a pattern which will continue over the years. Bradley & Caldwell (1980) have suggested that delayed cognitive development is due to a continuous long-term result of a less responsive and stimulating environment rather than to early experience per se. Thus, if language and other types of skill stimulation are absent, not just during infancy but characterize later child development as well, the impact on cognitive and social skill development will be markedly negative.

The evidence on the relation among social class variables, mental health, and social skills is less clear than the social class-cognitive development relation. Wills & Langner (1980) suggest a higher rate of abnormality among lower-class children. This hypothesis is based on a review of epidemiological studies. The studies cited by Wills & Langner (1980) as examples of the relation between social class and abnormal behavior are several years old, except for Achenbach (1978). Achenbach obtained data on 300 normal and 300 clinical subjects from 6 to 11 years of age. While age was not related to number of behavior problems, social class was, with upper-class children receiving the lowest scores on the scales and lower-class children the highest. Also, the lower-class subjects received significantly higher scores on the scales labeled Somatic Complaints, Hyperactive, and Aggressive and Delinquent (Achenbach 1978). Additionally, as would be suggested by the above scale differences, the lower-class children received significantly higher scores on Externalization (a total score of the scales suggesting externalization of problems) but not on Internalization. An important innovation introduced by Achenbach (1978) is the use of social competence scales (Social, Activities, and School) as well as symptom ratings. He found that clinical subjects were significantly less competent than normal subjects, and lower-class subjects were generally less competent than upper and middle-class subjects. These results are similar to those of other recent studies by Beitchman et al (1978) and Lindholm et al (1977). No differences in age, sex, or social class on type of diagnosis were found by Beitchman et al (1978) for patients at a clinic in Canada. However, the researchers found that lower-class subjects did exhibit more symptoms of all disorders. Likewise, Lindholm et al (1977), who obtained behavior ratings on 1162 white elementary children, found that lower-class subjects were rated as having more problems than the other socioeconomic classes.

Two general interpretations of the increased abnormality and increased deficits in cognitive growth among the lower class and poor are presented in the literature. Most of the studies have implicitly suggested an environmental-learning interpretation. Stott (1978) reported on two studies and reviewed the literature on the origins of maladjustment. He rejects the notion of genetics as the explanation for greater maladjustment among the lower class but does suggest congenital and prenatal factors are extremely important and account for a large share of the variance. Stott (1978) acknowledges many important environmental variables such as stress and value conflict, but emphasizes the effect of prenatal stress as a cause of a large portion of physical and emotional dysfunction. He suggests that the effect of poverty on maladjustment of the child is mediated by stresses of an interpersonal character on the mother during the prenatal development. Certainly the effects of poverty and lower-class membership do adversely affect the biological competence of lower-class children as a group. Yet the previous studies reviewed suggest environmental factors are extremely important in both an independent and interactive fashion. Vaughn et al (1980) studied the effect of out-of-home care on attachment within an economically disadvantaged population. All of these children might be viewed as "at risk" according to Stott's (1978) interpretation. The children whose mothers worked or attended school during the child's first 12 months displayed more anxious-avoidant attachments (Vaughn et al 1980). This group of mothers also reported more stress which was related to the fact that they had taken up a job or returned to school. By 18 months of age a relation between nonintact familes, also a stressor, and maladaptive attachment was demonstrated. Kellam et al (1977) also identified mother's single status (no second adult in the home) as associated with less adequate social adaptation and psychological well-being of the child. The relation between prenatal stress, which presumably influences biological competence, and such variables as age of child when out-of-home care begins, amount of talking to the child, and a host of other variables has not been determined. Until more data are available, it appears the most valid conclusion is that children from poor and low socioeconomic level families are likely to be at risk for both biological and learning environment inadequacies. What is suggested by the studies reviewed thus far is that the higher levels of stress present among lower-class adults have an impact both on the biological and learning environment of the child.

Another variable which is related to competence and mental health is that of self-esteem or self-concept. Kagan (1977) suggested that children become aware of social values during the early school years and that awareness of membership in the lower class will tend to produce a negative view of self. In contrast to the suggestion that class influences self-concept at an early school age, Rosenberg & Pearlin (1978) found no relation between self-esteem and social class for preadolescents (8–11 year olds), only a modest relation during early adolescence (12–14 year olds) and later adolescence (15 through 12th grade), but a strong relation for adults. Rosenberg & Pearlin (1978) suggest social comparison accounts for the change over age. In other words, until adolescence and particularly adulthood, the low levels of income, education, mobility, etc are not available as a source of comparison to other groups. Prior to adolescence the child's comparison is with his or her own peer group, which results in a normal distribution within group rather than as the low end of the distribution in the larger society. The one limitation of the Rosenberg & Pearlin (1978) report is the absence of the actual items which make up the 6-item Guttman scale for self-esteem. The content of the items may be related to the extent to which social comparison is a component of self-esteem. Barring questions about the scale, Rosenberg & Pearlin (1978) suggest that self-esteem may not be the most appropriate measure for the study of class differences. An alternative, which may not be so influenced by social comparison, is a measure of internal control or control over the environment. This variable may be more closely related to the child's experience and parental values and behavior. Kohn (1976) has argued, and has presented supporting data, that social class is related to the extent to which the adult exercises self-direction in his or her occupational life. Further, the extent of one's self-direction in vocational activities is related to the valuation of self-direction in the person's children. Thus, low social class is associated with a parental value which devalues self-direction. Kohn's (1976) definition of self-direction includes the factors of self-control and responsibility, which are similar to the variables of internal control and self-efficacy. In terms of actual parental behavior, Laosa (1978) found parental teaching style differences were related to educational difference among Chicano families. In this case education was not related to class, but the parents with less education (mean education level for entire sample was approximately 9th grade) used more modeling but less praise and inquiry and more physical control methods. The differences in teaching methods may effect actual skill development as well as beliefs about skills and control.

Kohn (1976) and Laosa (1978) provide the only examples of how social class effects may be mediated by differences in "what is taught" and "how it is taught." The "what" and "how" are important in shaping and developing the skills and personality of the individual.

Social skill plays a major role in abnormality (Argyle 1980, Phillips 1978), and abnormality might be redefined as social skill deficits (Phillips 1978). Further, social skills can be viewed developmentally (Reardon et al 1979), and Van Hasselt et al (1979) concluded that the research literature indicates a relation between the children's social functioning and long-term adjustment. A distinct advantage of evaluating social class differences by studying parental behavior and social skill development across socioeconomic groups is that the skills may be more strongly related to problem behavior and future adjustment than general self-report measures. Just as Rosenberg & Pearlin (1978) report a lack of relation between class and self-concept during preadolescence, Reardon et al (1979) failed to find significant correlations between behavioral ratings and self-report for their 5th grade subjects. However, the measures were related for the 8th grade subjects. Thus, although it was previously suggested that belief about control might better tap child developmental differences than self-concept, the most powerful variable for determining adjustment would appear to be a social skills assessment, especially since it is the observed and reported behavior upon which the judgments of adjustment are primarily based.

Direct assessment of social skills and class has not received much attention. The Achenbach (1978) study, previously reported, included an assessment of social competence and found lower-class children to be less socially competent. However, this result is based on parent ratings only. Working backward, several studies suggest level of social skills and problem-solving skills are related to delinquency (Freedman et al 1978, Ollendick & Hersen 1979), adjustment within the delinquent population (Freedman et al 1978), depression (Phillips 1978, Sanchez & Lewinsohn 1980), and addictions (Van Hasselt et al 1978).

These studies do not evaluate the role of social class or the parent behavior associated with social skill deficits but do suggest that a clearer picture of the relations between social class and child maladjustment (competence) may be obtained by evaluating social skills rather than reports of symptoms and/or global judgments of adjustment.

Defining and evaluating particular skills will also aid in understanding how skill level on varying dimensions may interact with special conflicts faced by the lower-class or nonwhite, middle, and upper-class child. Kohn & Rosman (1974) have demonstrated that the social-emotional status and class status of the kindergarten child are related to second grade school performance. In other words, the social skills one brings to the situation influence success and for the lower class it often results in poor school achievement. Jordon & Tharp (1979) discount the cultural deprivation model as an appropriate model and focus on the "cultural difference model." Based on a review of the literature, their studies, and evaluation of a modified educational program, Jordon & Tharp (1979) suggest underachievement by minority groups is due to an incongruence between the norms, values, behaviors, and assumptions about ability held by the school personnel and the minority student. These differences in assumptions, expectations, and behavior affect all aspects of the child's behavior, e.g. motivation, understanding approval of self, and culture, so as to produce a decline in cognitive and academic skills during the first years of school. Another example of how conflict may exist for the lower-class child is provided by Winetsky (1978). Teachers and parents indicated the expectations they held for 3- and 4-year-old children. The teachers and Anglo middle-class mothers were in general agreement, whereas the expectations of non-Anglo and working class mothers were different from those of the teachers. As indicated by Jordon & Tharp (1979) and Winetsky (1978), whether or not lower-class children arrive at school with fewer appropriate skills, they must deal with more conflict and environmentally produced stress than white middle and upper-class children. Again, we may have a situation such as exists for the lower-class adult, e.g. more stress and less ability to cope with stress, in that the lower-class child may have to deal with more conflict in his interaction with the environment and may be less ready to deal with the conflict.

The ability to cope and the social skills one possesses, as well as the type of prosocial and antisocial behavior exhibited, are assumed by the present authors to be primarily a function of learning. What has been largely ignored by investigators interested in social class is the way in which parental stress, which is related to class, influences parent behavior and child learning. Pearlin & Schooler's (1978) finding that withdrawal and impulsive emotional outburst are ineffective coping behaviors and that these coping behaviors tend to be more frequently used by the lower class, suggests that increased stress, and the resulting stress reactions, may be mediating factors in the development of social and cognitive skills among the lower class. Models of effective parenting (e.g. Baumrind 1978, Goldberg 1977, Nakamura & Finck 1980, Patterson 1980) all require that the parent be able to avoid negative reinforcement of inappropriate behavior and provide consistent positive reinforcement of prosocial behavior. Baumrind's (1978) description of the parents of well-adjusted, successful children suggests a parent who can be responsive to needs, uses positive reinforcement but requires self-controls, and adjusts demands to the developmental level. She says, "By recognizing reciprocity as a pattern of mutually contingent exchange of gratification and as a generalized moral norm, the more effective parents in our studies facilitated the development of mature cognitive and moral judgment and action in the child" (Baumrind 1978, p. 267). Likewise, Nakamura & Finck (1980) describe the parents of their sample of competent children as expressing a full range of positive and negative emotions, understanding and sensitive, engaging in a high rate of intrafamily exchange, and as neither over controlling nor overly permissive. In the above descriptions, as well as other models (e.g. Goldberg 1977, Patterson 1980), the effective parent is attuned to the child and provides appropriate contingent responses to the child's behavior. Further, as Feldman (1980) has pointed out, criminal behavior is more likely among persons who have associated with offenders. Such associations are more frequent as a function of increased and earlier out-of-home interactions among lower-class youths (Ottensmann 1978). Also, criminal behavior as well as other abnormal behaviors are a function of ineffective parental and school training in prosocial behavior (Feldman 1980).

Stress, whether it is environmentally produced, interpersonal, or self-produced, can cause inappropriate behavior, noncontingent responding, and an inability to focus on the needs and behavior of the child. Thus stress, whether it is experienced by a lower, middle or upper-class person, will interact with personality and coping abilities and have a positive, neutral, or negative outcome on the parent's ability to develop and maintain an effective parent-child interaction. The relation between stress, social class, and the child's learning experiences is obviously complex. The process of socialization and development of competence requires further elucidation (Dinges & Duffy 1979). The role of particular stressors, number of stressors, social support systems, coping skills, personality attributes and the child's role in the parent-child interactions all need to be further assessed in order to determine the extent to which stress is a key mediator in the relation between social class and personal adjustment.

CONCLUSION

It has been our thesis throughout this review that, although there may be an association between social factors and the appearance and/or frequency of abnormal behaviors, there is no essential connection between the two; nor is one necessarily caused by the other. In fact, some recent studies have found no relation between extent of abnormal behavior or distribution of diagnostic classes and the social factors we have been considering: social class, race, religion, and culture. Other reports have even provided results in the opposite direction to that established in previous studies. The reason for the inconsistency is that the essential mediating variables in the relation between behavior and the environment, i.e. the learning conditions for appropriate behaviors, are not perfectly correlated with social class, race, religion, or culture. Children in disadvantaged subpopulations classified in this way are often exposed to stressful conditions differing in quality and quantity from that experienced by individuals in more fortunate segments of the population. Furthermore, these children are often socialized by adults, as well as peers, who are also experiencing unusual stress with which they are coping in ineffectual and/or antisocial ways. Thus, through modeling, instigation, and inappropriate reinforcement, the socializing agents are providing deleterious learning environments to young persons growing up in these milieus. As a result, ineffectual, inappropriate, indeed abnormal, ways of behaving are learned. Thus, it is through the learning environments with which they are often but not always associated that social factors are related to abnormal behaviors.

In the previous review on this topic, Strauss (1979) pointed out, with some disappointment, that there was no Broad Street pump in psychiatry which could provide a focus for tracing the epidemiology of mental illness. However, as stated above, maladaptive ways of behaving are learned, and when the learning conditions are completely understood, we will have gone a long way toward isolating the germ or bacillus or virus causing abnormal behavior. This does not mean that sociocultural factors are not important in understanding abnormal behavior, especially its definition, the attitudes which surround it, and the attempts which are made to prevent and treat it.

Literature Cited

Achenbach, T. M. 1978. The child behavior profile. I: Boys age 6–11. *J. Consult. Clin. Psychol.* 46:478–88

Adebimpe, V. R., Gigandet, J., Harris, E. 1979. MMPI diagnosis of black psychiatric patients. *Am. J. Psychiatry* 138: 85–87

Allodi, F., Dukszta, J. 1978. Psychiatric services in China. Or, Mao versus Freud. *Can. Psychiatr. Assoc. J.* 23:361–71

American Psychiatric Association. 1980. *Diagnostic and Statistical Manual.* Washington DC: APA. 3rd ed.

Argyle, M. 1980. Interaction skills and social competence. In *Psychological Problems. The Social Context,* ed. P. Feldman, J. Orford, pp. 123–50. New York: Wiley. 405 pp.

Baumrind, D. 1978. Parental disciplinary patterns and social competence in children. *Youth Soc.* 9:239–76

Beck, J. C. 1978. Social influences on the prognosis of schizophrenia. *Schizophr. Bull.* 4:86–101

Beitchman, J., Bell, K., Simeon, S. 1978. Types of disorders and demographic variables in a Canadian child psychiatry population. *Can. Psychiatric Assoc. J.* 23:91–96

Beit-Hallahami, B., Argyle, M. 1977. Religious ideas and psychiatric disorders. *Int. J. Soc. Psychiatry* 23:26–30

Benedict, R. 1934. Anthropology and the abnormal. *J. Gen. Psychol.* 10:59–80

Berger, M. 1979. The relationship of religious attitudes and values with personality adjustment. *Diss. Abstr. Int.* 39:7232. Ann Arbor, Mich., Univ. Microfilms No. 7910138. 124 pp.

Blum, J. D., Redlich, F. 1980. Mental health practitioners: Old stereotypes and new realities. *Arch. Gen. Psychiatry* 37: 1247–53

Bradley, R. H., Caldwell, B. M. 1980. The relation of home environment, cognitive competence and I.Q. among males and females. *Child Dev.* 51:1140–48

Brenner, M. H. 1973. *Mental Illness and the Economy.* Cambridge, Mass: Harvard Univ. Press

Buck, J. A., Hirschman, R. 1980. Economics and mental health services: Enhancing the power of the consumer. *Am. Psychol.* 35:653–61

Buckalew, L. W. 1978. A descriptive study of denominational concomitants in psychiatric diagnosis. *Soc. Behav. Pers.* 6:239–42

Burton, B., Burton, G. 1979. Arecaidinism: Betal chewing in transcultural perspective. *Can. J. Psychiatry* 24:481–88

Cadoret, R. 1978. Inheritance of alcoholism in adoptees. *Br. J. Psychiatry* 132: 252–58

Carr, L. G., Krause, N. 1978. Social status, psychiatric symptomology and response bias. *J. Health Soc. Behav.* 19:86–91

Cochrane, R., Sobol, M. 1980. Life stresses and psychological consequences. See Argyle 1980, pp. 151–82

Craig, T. J., Van Natta, P. A. 1979. Influence of demographic characteristics on two measures of depressive symptoms. *Arch. Gen. Psychiatry* 36:149–54

Day, L., Reznikoff, N. 1980. Social class, the treatment process and parent's and children's expectations about child psychotherapy. *J. Clin. Child Psychol.* 9: 195–98

Denny, N. 1978. Social environment as a therapeutic agent. *Psychiatr. Ann.* 8: 75–78

Devereaux, G. 1939. A sociological theory of schizophrenia. *Psychoanal. Rev.* 26: 315–42

Dinges, N., Duffy, L. 1979. Culture and competence. In *Perspectives in Cross-Cultural Psychology,* ed. A. J. Marsella, R. G. Tharp, T. J. Ciboronski, pp. 209–32. New York: Academic

Dohrenwend, B. S. 1973. Social status and stressful life events. *J. Pers. Soc. Psychol.* 28:225–35

Draguns, J. G. 1980. Psychological disorders of clinical severity. In *Handbook of Cross-Cultural Psychology,* Vol. 6: *Psychopathology,* ed. H. C. Triandis, J. G. Draguns. Boston: Allyn & Bacon, pp. 1–8

Dube, K. C. 1978. Cultural factors in the treatment of schizophrenia. *Indian J. Psychiatry* 20:132–36

Eaton, J., Weil, R. 1955. *Culture and Mental Disorders.* Glencoe, Ill: Free Press

Edwards, D. W., Greene, L. R., Abramowitz, S. I., Davidson, C. V. 1979. National health insurance, psychotherapy and the poor. *Am. Psychol.* 34:411–19

Eisenberg, L. 1977. Psychiatry and society: A sociobiologic synthesis. *N. Engl. J. Med.* 296:903–10

Elmer, E. 1978. Effects of early neglect and abuse on latency age children. *J. Pediatr. Psychol.* 3:14–19

Fandetti, D. V., Gelfand, E. 1978. Attitudes towards symptoms and services in the ethnic family and neighborhood. *Am. J. Orthopsychiatry* 48:477–86

Farran, D. C., Haskins, R. 1980. Reciprocal influence in the social interactions of mothers and three year old children from different socieoeconomic backgrounds. *Child Dev.* 51:780–91

Farrington, D. P. 1977. The effects of public labelling. *Br. J. Criminol.* 17:112–25

Feldman, P. 1980. The making and control of offenders. See Argyle 1980, pp. 185–218

Finlay-Jones, R. A., Burvill, P. W. 1978. Contrasting demographic patterns of minor psychiatric morbidity in general practice and the community. *Psychol. Med.* 8:455–66

Fischer, J. 1969. Negroes and whites and rates of mental illness: Reconsideration of a myth. *Psychiatry* 32:438–46

Flaherty, J. A., Meagher, R. 1980. Measuring racial bias in inpatient treatment. *Am. J. Psychiatry* 137:679–82

Frank, A., Eisenthal, S., Lazare, A. 1978. Are there social class differences in patients' treatment conceptions? *Arch. Gen. Psychiatry* 35:61–69

Freedman, B. J., Rosenthal, L., Donahoe, E. P. Jr., Schlundt, D. E., McFall, R. M. 1978. A social-behavioral analysis of skill deficits in delinquent and nondelinquent adolescent boys. *J. Consult. Clin. Psychol.* 46:1448–62

Gad, M. T., Johnson, J. H. 1980. Correlates of adolescent life stress as related to race, SES and levels of perceived social support. *J. Clin. Child Psychol.* 9:13–16

Gelfand, R., Kline, F. 1978. Differences in diagnostic patterns in Britain and America. *Compr. Psychiatry* 19:551–55

Goldberg, S. 1977. Social competence in infancy: A model of parent-infant interaction. *Merrill-Palmer Q.* 23:163–77

Gomes-Schwartz, B., Hadley, S. W., Strupp, H. H. 1978. Individual psychotherapy and behavior therapy. *Ann. Rev. Psychol.* 29:435–71

Group for the Advancement of Psychiatry. 1968. The use of religion in mental illness. *G.A.P. Rep.* 6:664–88

Gynther, M. D. 1972. White norms and black MMPI's: A prescription for discrimination. *Psychol. Bull.* 78:386–402

Gynther, M. D., Green, S. B. 1980. Accuracy may make a difference but does a difference make for accuracy? A response to Pritchard & Rosenblatt. *J. Consult. Clin. Psychol.* 48:268–72

Hagnell, O. 1966. *A Prospective Study of the Incidence of Mental Disorder.* Lund, Sweden: Svenska Bokfirlaget Norstedts

Harkey, J., Miles, D. L., Rushing, W. A. 1976. The relation between social class and functional status: A new look at the drift hypothesis. *J. Health Soc. Behav.* 17:194–204

Helgason, T. 1978. Prevalence and incidence of mental disorders estimated by a health questionnaire. *Acta Psychiatr. Scand.* 58:256–66

Heller, P. L., Chalfant, P., Worley, M., Quesada, G. M., Bradfield, C. D. 1980. Socioeconomic class, classification of abnormal behaviors and perceptions of mental health care. *Br. J. Med. Psychol.* 53:343–48

Herbert, M. 1980. Socialization for problem resistance. See Argyle 1980, pp. 39–72

Higginbotham, H. N. 1979. Culture and mental health services. See Dinges & Duffy 1979, pp. 307–32

Humphrey, J. A., Kupferer, H. J. 1977. Packets of violence: An exploration of homicides and suicide. *Dis. Nerv. Syst.* 78:833–37

Ilfeld, F. W. 1977. Current social stressors and symptoms of depression. *Am. J. Psychiatry* 134:161–66

Ilfeld, F. W. 1978. Psychological status of community residents along major demographic dimensions. *Arch. Gen. Psychiatry.* 35:716–24

Ilfeld, F. W. 1979. Persons at risk for anxiety/tension. In *Clinical Anxiety/Tension in Primary Medicine,* ed. B. Brown, pp. 24–38. Amsterdam: Excerpta Medica

Jalali, B., Jalali, M., Turner, F. 1978. Attitudes toward mental illness: Its relation to contact and ethnocultural background. *J. Nerv. Ment. Dis.* 166:692–700

Johnson, J. H., Sarason, I. G. 1978. Life stress, depression and anxiety: Internal-external control as a moderator variable. *Psychosom. Res.* 22:205–8

Jordon, C., Tharp, R. G. 1979. Culture and education. See Dinges & Duffy 1979, pp. 265–86

Kagan, J. 1977. The child in the family. *Daedalus* 106:33–56

Kagan, J., Lapidus, D. R., Moore, M. 1978. Infant antecedents of cognitive functioning: A longitudinal study. *Child Dev.* 49:1005–23

Kardiner, A. 1939. *The Individual and His Society.* New York: Columbia Univ. Press

Kellam, S. G., Ensminger, M. E., Turner, R. J. 1977. Family structure and the mental health of children: Concurrent and longitudinal community-wide studies. *Arch. Gen. Psychiatry* 34:1012–22

Kessler, R. C. 1979. Stress, social status, and psychological distress. *J. Health Soc. Behav.* 20:259–72

Kilbride, H. W., Johnson, D. L., Streissguth, A. P. 1977. Social class, birth order, and newborn experience. *Child Dev.* 88: 1686–88

King, L. M. 1978. Social and cultural influences on psychopathology. *Ann. Rev. Psychol.* 29:405–33

Kirk, G. E., Hunt, J. M., Volkmar, F. 1979. Social class and preschool language skill: VI. Child to child communication and semantic mastery. *Genet. Psychol. Monogr.* 100:111–138

Kobasa, S. C. 1979. Stressful like events, personality, and health: An inquiry into hardiness. *J. Pers. Soc. Psychol.* 37:1–11

Kohn, M. L. 1976. Social class and parental values: Another confirmation of the relationship (Comment on Wright and Wright, ASR June, 1976). *Am. Sociol. Rev.* 41:538–48

Kohn, M., Rosman, B. L. 1974. Social-emotional, cognitive, and demographic determinants of poor school achievement: Implications for a strategy of intervention. *J. Educ. Psychol.* 66:267–76

Koutrelakos, J., Gedeon, S. M. 1978. Opinions about mental illness: A comparison of American and Greek professionals and laymen. *Psychol. Rep.* 43:915–23

Kulka, R. A., Veroff, J., Dorwan, E. J. 1979. Social class and the use of professional help for personal problems, 1957 and 1976. *J. Health Soc. Behav.* 20:2–17

Laosa, L. M. 1978. Maternal teaching strategies in Chicano families of varied educational and socioeconomic level. *Child Dev.* 49:1129–35

Leighton, A. H. 1959. *My Name is Legion: The Stirling County Study of Psychiatric Disorder and Social Environment.* New York: Basic Books

Levine, E. M., Kozak, C. 1979. Drug and alcohol use, delinquency, and vandalism among upper middle class pre- and post-adolescents. *J. Youth Adolescence* 8:91–101

Lewis, D. O., Shanok, S. S., Cohen, R. J., Kligfeld, M., Frisone, G. 1980. Race bias in the diagnosis and disposition of violent adolescents. *Am. J. Psychiatry* 137:1211–16

Liem, R., Liem, J. V. 1978. Social class and mental illness reconsidered: The role of economic stress and social support. *J. Health Soc. Behav.* 19:139–56

Lin, T. 1953. A study of the incidence of mental disorders in Chinese and other cultures. *Psychiatry* 16:313–36

Lindholm, B. W., Touliatos, J., Rich, A. 1977. Influence of family structure and school variables on behavior disorders of children. *Psychol. Sch.* 14:99–104

Mailloux, N., Ancorra, L. 1960. A clinical study of religious attitudes and a new approach to psychopathology. In *Perspectives of Personality Research,* ed. H. P. David, J. C. Berngelmann. London: Int. Union Sci. Psychol.

Marsella, A. J. 1978. Thoughts on cross-cultural studies on the epidemiology of depression. *Cult. Med. Psychiatry* 2: 343–57

Marsella, A. J. 1979. Depressive affect and disorder across cultures. See Draguns 1980, pp. 237–90

Mayfield, D. G., Fowler, D. 1977. Psychiatric hospitalization II. Effect of social class and delivery systems. *Dis. Nerv. Syst.* 38:320–23

Mezzich, J. E., Raab, E. S. 1980. Depressive symptomalogy across the Americas. *Arch. Gen. Psychiatry* 37:818–23

Minter, R. E., Kimball, C. P. 1980. Life events, personality traits and illness. In *Handbook on Stress and Anxiety,* ed. I. L. Kutach, L. B. Schlesinger & Associates, pp. 189–206. San Francisco: Jossey Bass. 580 pp.

Mollica, R. F., Redlich, F. 1980. Equity and changing patient characteristics, 1950 to 1975. *Arch. Gen. Psychiatry* 37: 1257–63

Montgomery, S., Asberg, M., Traskman, L., Montgomery, D. 1978. Cross-cultural studies on the use of CPRS in English and Swedish depressed patients. *Acta Psychiatr. Scand. Suppl.* 271:33–37

Murphy, H. B. M. 1978. European cultural offshoots in the new world: Differences in their mental hospitalization patterns: I. British, French and Italian influences. *Soc. Psychiatry* 13:1–9

Murphy, J. M. 1980. Continuities in community-based psychiatric epidemiology. *Arch. Gen. Psychiatry* 37:1215–23

Nakamura, C. Y., Finck, D. N. 1980. Relative effectiveness of socially oriented and task oriented children and predictability of their behavior. *Monogr. Soc. Res. Child Dev.* 45:1–109

Nandi, D. N., Banerjee, G., Boral, G. C., Ganguli, H., Ajmany, S., Ghosh, A., Sarkar, S. 1979. Socio-economic status and prevalence of mental disorders in certain rural communities in India. *Acta Psychiatr. Scand.* 59:276–93

Neel, A. F. 1977. Social and biological factors in child development. *Psychol. Rep.* 40:1143–46

Odejide, A. O. 1979. Cross-cultural psychiatry: A myth or reality. *Compr. Psychiatry.* 20:103–9

Ollendick, T. H., Hersen, M. 1979. Social skills training for juvenile delinquents. *Behav. Res. Ther.* 17:547–54

Orley, J., Wing, J. K. 1979. Psychiatric disorders in two African villages. *Arch. Gen, Psychiatry* 36:513–20

Ottensmann, J. R. 1978. Social behavior in urban space: A preliminary investigation using ethnographic data. *Urban Life* 7:3–22

Patterson, E. T., Charles, H. C., Woodward, W. A., Roberts, W. R., Penk, W. E. 1981. Differences in measures of personality and family environment among black and white alcoholics. *J. Consult. Clin. Psychol.* 49:1–9

Patterson, G. R. 1980. Mothers: The unacknowledged victims. *Monogr. Soc. Res. Child Dev.* 45:1–64

Pearlin, L. I., Schooler, C. 1978. The structure of coping. *J. Health Soc. Behav.* 19:2–21

Penk, W. E., Woodward, W. A., Robinowitz, R., Hess, J. L. 1978. Differences in MMPI scores of black and white compulsive heroin users. *J. Abnorm. Psychol.* 87:505–13

Phillips, E. L. 1978. *The Social Skills Basis of Psychopathology: Alternatives to Abnormal Psychology and Psychiatry.* New York: Grune & Stratton

Pollack, D., Shore, J. H. 1980. Validity of the MMPI with native Americans. *Am. J. Psychiatry* 137:946–50

Prince, R. 1980. Variations in psychotherapeutic procedures. See Draguns 1980, pp. 291–349

Pritchard, D. A., Rosenblatt, A. 1980a. Racial bias in the MMPI: A methodological review. *J. Consult. Clin. Psychol.* 48:129–42

Pritchard, D. A., Rosenblatt, A. 1980b. A reply to Gynther & Green. *J. Consult. Clin. Psychol.* 48:273–74

Reardon, R. C., Hersen, M., Bellack, A. S., Foley, J. M. 1979. Measuring social skill in grade school boys. *J. Behav. Assess.* 1:87–105

Redlich, F. C., Hollingshead, A. B., Roberts, B. H., Robinson, H. A., Freedman, L. Z., Myers, J. K. 1953. Social structure and psychiatric disorders. *J. Psychiatry* 109:729–34

Redlich, F., Kellert, S. R. 1978. Trends in American mental health. *Am. J. Psychiatry* 135:22–28

Reynolds, C. R., Gutkin, T. B. 1980. A regression analysis of test bias on the WISC-R for Anglos and Chicanos referred for psychological services. *J. Abnorm. Child Psychol.* 8:237–43

Rosenberg, M., Pearlin, L. I. 1978. Social class and self-esteem among children and adults. *Am. J. Sociol.* 84:53–77

Sanchez, V., Lewinsohn, P. M. 1980. Assertive behavior and depression. *J. Consult. Clin. Psychol.* 48:119–20

Sapir, E. 1932. Cultural anthropology and psychiatry. *J. Abnorm. Soc. Psychol.* 27:229–42

Sarbin, T., Mancuso, J. C. 1980. *Schizophrenia: Medical Diagnosis or Moral Verdict?* New York: Pergamon

Sartorius, N., Jablensky, A., Shapiro, R. 1978. Cross-cultural differences in the short-term prognosis of schizophrenic psychoses. *Schizophr. Bull.* 4:102–13

Schlesinger, L. B., Revitch, E. 1980. Stress, violence and crime. See Minter & Kimball 1980, pp. 174–80

Schubert, D. S. P., Miller, S. I. 1978. Social class and psychiatric diagnosis. *Int. J. Soc. Psychiatry* 24:117–24

Schubert, D. S. P., Miller, S. I. 1980. Differences between the lower social classes: some new trends. *Am. J. Orthopsychiatry* 50:712–17

Schwab, J. J., Bell, R. A., Warheit, G. J., Schwab, R. B. 1979. *Social Order and Mental Health: The Florida Health Study.* New York: Brunner/Mazel. 218 pp.

Selavan, I. C. 1979. Behavior disorders of Jews: A review of the literature. *Psychol. Judaism* 4:117–24

Singer, K., Ney, P. G., Lieh, M. F. 1978. A cultural perspective on child psychiatric disorders. *Compr. Psychiatry* 19:533–40

Srole, L., Fischer, A. K. 1980. The Midtown Manhattan longitudinal study vs. the 'mental Paradise Lost' doctrine. *Arch. Gen. Psychiatry* 37:209–21

Srole, L., Langer, T. S., Michael, S. T. 1962. *Mental Health in the Metropolis: The Midtown Manhattan Study.* New York: McGraw Hill

Stott, D. H. 1978. Epidemiological indicators of the origins of behavior disturbance as measured by the Bristol Social Adjustment Guides. *Gen. Psychol. Monogr.* 97:127–59

Strauss, J. S. 1978. Patterns of disorder in first admission psychiatric patients. *J. Nerv. Ment. Dis.* 166:611–23

Strauss, J. S. 1979. Social and cultural influences on psychopathology. *Ann. Rev. Psychol.* 30:397–15

Touliatos, J., Lindholm, B. W. 1980. Psychopathology of Anglo and Chicano children. *Child Psychol.* 9:55–56

Townsend, J. M. 1978. Cultural conceptions and the role of the psychiatrist in Germany and America. *Int. J. Soc. Psychiatry* 24:250–58

Tsuang, M. T. 1980. Social effects of schizophrenia and affective disorders. In *The Social Consequences of Psychiatric Illness,* ed. L. N. Robins, P. J. Clayton, J. K. Wing, pp. 209–15. New York: Brunner/Mazel

Udwin, O., Shmukler, D. 1981. The influence of sociocultural, economic, and home background factors on children's ability to engage in imaginative play. *Dev. Psychol.* 17:66–72

Ullman, L. P., Krasner, L. 1969. *A Psychological Approach to Abnormal Behavior.* New York: Prentice-Hall

Van Hasselt, V. B., Hersen, M., Milliones, J. 1978. Social skills training for alcoholics and drug addicts: A review. *Addict. Behav.* 3:221-33

Van Hasselt, V. B., Hersen, M., Whitehall, M. B., Bellack, A. S. 1979. Social skills assessment and training for children: An evaluative review. *Behav. Res. Ther.* 17:413–37

Vaughn, B. E., Gove, F. L., Egeland, B. 1980. The relationship between out-of-home care and the quality of infant-mother attachment in an economically disadvantaged population. *Child Dev.* 51:1203–14

Wadsworth, R. D., Checketts, K. T. 1980. Influence of religious application on psychodiagnosis. *J. Consult. Clin. Psychol.* 48:234–40

Waxler, N. E. 1979. Is outcome for schizophrenia better in nonindustrial societies? The case of Sri Lanka. *J. Nerv. Ment. Dis.* 167:144–58

Weissman, M. M., Myers, J. K., Harding, P. S. 1978. Psychiatric disorders in a U.S. urban community 1975–1976. *Am. J. Psychiatry* 135:459–62

Wenz, F. V. 1977. Neighborhood type, social disequilibrium, and happiness. *Psychiatr. Q.* 49:187–96

Wills, T. A., Langner, T. S. 1980. Socioeconomic status and stress. See Minter & Kimball 1980, pp. 159–73

Winetsky, C. S. 1978. Comparisons of the expectations of parents and teachers for the behavior of preschool children. *Child Dev.* 49:1146–54

World Health Organization. 1973. *Report of the International Pilot Study of Schizophrenia,* Vol 1. Geneva: WHO

Ann. Rev. Psychol. 1982. 33:265–308

BEHAVIORAL STUDIES OF ASSOCIATIVE LEARNING IN ANIMALS

Robert A. Rescorla

Department of Psychology, University of Pennsylvania, Philadelphia, Pennsylvania 19104

Peter C. Holland

Department of Psychology, University of Pittsburgh, Pittsburgh, Pennsylvania 15260

CONTENTS

0066-4308/82/0201-0265$02.00

This review will discuss associative learning processes as studied behaviorally in animal subjects. It is highly selective in two ways. First, it concentrates on providing a framework within which to view the literature and discusses in detail only a few issues which the authors deem especially important. Second, it excludes nonassociative learning processes. Although the considerable recent activity in the study of such processes can easily be viewed within the framework described below, space limitations make that impossible. The interested reviewer can find recent reviews in Groves & Thompson (1970), Horn & Hinde (1970), Peeke & Hertz (1973), Tighe & Leaton (1976), Spear (1978), and Spear & Miller (in press).

As Rescorla (1980a) has noted, the study of any learning process involves attention to three questions: what are the conditions that produce the learning, what is it that is actually learned, and how is that learning revealed in the performance of the organism? The present review is organized around these questions. It emphasizes approaches to their answer in one of the two principal associative learning paradigms, Pavlovian conditioning; but it also discusses parallel issues in the other popular paradigm, instrumental training. This relative emphasis is in accord with the relative numbers of articles published in the last 10 or so years.

CONDITIONS OF LEARNING

Pavlovian Conditioning

Since long before the advent of serious experimental studies of learning, the notion of contiguity has been dominant in discussions of associations. Whatever their other differences, the British Associationists were unanimous in the thought that two items become associated as a result of their contiguous occurrence. The early dominant investigators of associative learning in the laboratory, Pavlov and Thorndike, concurred in this view, and contiguity has persisted as the central concept in modern theories of learning.

However, the last 15 years have seen successive challenges to the importance of contiguity. Several classes of phenomena have arisen that initially appeared to suggest rejection of contiguity as the primary condition for learning. Yet the ultimate result has instead been refinement in the role accorded to contiguity. These challenges have been of two types: those questioning the necessity of contiguity and those questioning its sufficiency.

Several phenomena have suggested that close temporal contiguity between events is not necessary for the formation of associations. Such results initially emerged slowly as students realized that with certain stimuli, such as tones and shocks, temporal separations of up to several minutes would reduce, but not prevent, the formation of an association (e.g. Kamin 1965).

The pace of discovering troubling findings accelerated with the popularization of the flavor-aversion technique, in which associations form between a flavor and a poison even though they are separated by several hours (e.g. Revusky 1971, Rozin & Kalat 1971). More recently, there have been reports that substantial delays can be introduced between the performance of an instrumental response and the delivery of food reward (e.g. D'Amato, in press, Lett 1975). And there are even reports that a Pavlovian system notorious for its constrained CS-US interval, eyeblink in rabbits, can sustain substantial temporal asynchronies (e.g. Kehoe et al 1979).

The reaction of most students of learning to these challenges to the cherished notion of contiguity has been predictable. Initial expressions of disbelief were followed by attempts to identify artifactual ways in which apparent temporal asynchronies actually involved close temporal pairings of the associated events. For instance, in the flavor-aversion preparation it was suggested that although the experimenter delivered the flavor several hours prior to the poison, perhaps the flavor actually persisted on the tongue much longer, perhaps sufficiently long to still be present at the time of the poison. Alternatively, the delivery of the US might result in the animal actually re-presenting itself with the CS because the internal distress would cause either gaseous or solid return of the stomach's contents to the mouth concurrent with the presence of the US. A variety of experimental procedures, however, have made these peripheral persistances of the CS seem implausible (Revusky & Garcia 1970, Rozin & Kalat 1971). Consequently, a more popular view has been that some memorial representation of the CS either persists through the CS-US interval or is reactivated by the US (Capaldi 1971, Lieberman et al 1979, Revusky 1971, Spear 1978). In this way, the pretheoretical commitment to the notion of contiguity can be preserved by constructing accounts that envision theoretical entities to be contiguous.

At a somewhat more empirical level, examples of learning with substantial asynchronies have been incorporated into existing thinking by noting that they may differ quantitatively, but not qualitatively, from other available data on CS-US intervals in learning. Even in those instances in which long intervals produce learning, shorter intervals typically produce better learning (Revusky 1968). In fact, the normal bitonic function relating conditioning to CS-US interval appears to apply to all of the known instances of conditioning; what differs among those instances is the particular parameter values of the function. This observation, together with others suggesting that these apparently deviant instances actually obey principles like those of other conditioning preparations, has allowed students of learning to keep relatively intact the notion of contiguity as a necessary condition for associative learning (Revusky 1977).

Ironically, there has also emerged a set of data that suggests that modern views of contiguity have underestimated its power. Current notions of contiguity have deviated in two important ways from classical British associationism. First, American discussions have emphasized that a slight temporal asynchrony (of the order of a second) actually produces the best learning; indeed, there has been serious doubt that actual simultaneity in time produces any learning. Second, although British authors included spatial proximity within the notion of contiguity, modern discussions have largely equated contiguity with proximity in time.

But some recent data reaffirm the importance of both simultaneous association and spatial contiguity. For instance, recent studies of associations among relatively neutral stimuli have found substantial learning when those stimuli occur simultaneously (e.g. Fudim 1978, Holman 1980); indeed, with some procedures that mode of presentation appears to produce better learning than does the normally employed asynchronous presentation (e.g. Rescorla 1980b, Rescorla & Cunningham 1978). Moreover, several studies have identified a role for spatial contiguity, apparently independent of that of temporal contiguity, in producing associations (e.g. Marshall et al 1979, Rescorla & Cunningham 1979).

The other major attack on contiguity has questioned its sufficiency for producing associative learning. This attack has had a more profound impact on modern theorizing. Indeed, it could well be claimed that a few instances pointing to the insufficiency of contiguity have completely dominated recent theorizing in Pavlovian conditioning, much of which can be viewed as an attempt to bring those instances back into the fold of contiguity. Two phenomena that question the sufficiency of contiguity are frequently cited. The first is the discovery that arranging close temporal contiguity between a CS and US will fail to produce conditioning if the US is also given frequently in the absence of the CS (e.g. Rescorla 1968; Gamzu & Williams 1971). This observation has been taken to mean that it is not contiguity between events that generates conditioning; rather the CS and US must be correlated such that the CS provides the organism with some unique information about the US. The second phenomenon is that of blocking, first well-studied by Kamin (1968, 1969). Kamin followed a compound stimulus, AX, with shock and then tested for the amount of conditioning to X when it was presented alone. However, some animals had a history of conditioning to A whereas others were spared that history. The finding of interest is that prior conditioning of A apparently blocked conditioning to X that otherwise would have occurred on the reinforced AX trials. Notice that both groups had contiguous presentation of X with the US, yet that contiguity was not sufficient to produce conditioning of X; simply giving prior conditioning of A undermined the impact of the X-US contiguity.

The question of why this CS-US contiguity failed to produce conditioning has fascinated students of Pavlovian conditioning. Two broad solutions have been proposed. Each emphasizes variation in the processing of one of the individual events to be associated, rather than variation in the importance of contiguity itself, as the source of the failure. Perhaps the most obvious, and certainly the older, account has emphasized variations in the processing of the CS. This proposal has taken several forms, but the earliest is well characterized by Sutherland & Mackintosh (1971) in terms of limited attentional capacity. According to this view, multiple CSs must compete for the organism's attention, and any procedure that encourages attention to one CS will necessarily reduce attention to others. Consequently, in the blocking experiment, the previously conditioned stimulus A dominates attention, with the result that there is little processing capacity left for X. Effectively, X is not contiguous with the US because it is not well received by the organism; the failure is not in contiguity of received events but rather in the receipt of the CS.

A second attentional alternative that depends less on the notion of limited processing capacity has been suggested by Mackintosh (1975). According to this view, individual stimuli control amounts of attention that vary with the organism's experience with those stimuli but that are independent of the presence of other stimuli. A stimulus will control large amounts of attention to the degree that it has in the past been a superior predictor of important consequences, such as the US. However, to the degree that other stimuli are better predictors, a given CS will lose attention and therefore be difficult to condition subsequently. Applied to a blocking procedure, X will lose attention in the course of the AX trials because pretraining has made A the better predictor. Consequently, X will develop little conditioning on AX trials, not because it competes with A for attention on any given trial, but rather because it has lost its own attention-grabbing power on preceding trials.

Pearce & Hall (1980) have recently proposed a related account according to which stimuli lose attention (conditionability) when they are not followed by surprising consequences. In a blocking paradigm, X rapidly loses attention because A already predicts the US presented on AX trials. Consequently, X has little chance to become conditioned. Unlike Mackintosh's account, however, it is not the inferiority of X to A as a predictor which matters but the overall predictedness of the US. One result is that Pearce & Hall's theory anticipates both A and X will lose attention.

Another class of approaches to the blocking experiment has instead emphasized variation in the processing of the US as responsible for modulating the effectiveness of a CS-US contiguity. Originally suggested by Kamin (1968) and elaborated by Rescorla & Wagner (1972) and most recently by Wagner (1978), this view says that the effectiveness of a US varies with the degree to which it is well signaled. An expected US is less effective than is a surprising US. Thus A blocks X because the US that is contiguous with X on the AX trials is reduced in effectiveness by being signaled by A.

Much of the empirical battle between these two alternative ways of preserving contiguity has been fought on the ground of the blocking paradigm. We will later review some of these findings. But first it is of interest to ask whether there is any evidence outside of the blocking experiment for the operation of the kinds of processes that these two approaches describe. What independent evidence is there that variation occurs in the processing of either the CS or US under circumstances such as the theories propose?

EVIDENCE FOR VARIATION IN CS PROCESSING Despite its inherent plausibility, there is surprisingly little direct evidence from conditioning paradigms for variation in the processing of CSs as a function of the concurrent presence of other CSs or past experience with that CS. Consider first the natural proposition that the organism has limited attentional capacity which it must distribute among concurrently present CSs.

The principal kind of evidence for this proposition in Pavlovian conditioning comes from the so-called overshadowing experiment (Pavlov 1927). In such an experiment, two groups both receive conditioning of stimulus A, but for one group B is present simultaneously with A. The observation of interest is that subsequent testing of A reveals less conditioning when A and B are presented together, a result frequently interpreted in terms of competition between A and B for processing (and hence conditioning). However, it has long been recognized that if such an experiment is carried out over several trials, it can be conceptualized as a blocking experiment in which A and B both acquire conditioning and hence are capable of blocking further conditioning to each other (Rescorla & Wagner 1972). For that reason, multitrial examples of overshadowing have a ready alternative interpretation in terms of attenuated processing of the US. Hence, the critical overshadowing experiments are those that involve only one conditioning trial. Fortunately, there are now available several well-controlled experiments that demonstrate overshadowing on a single conditioning trial (e.g. James & Wagner 1980, Mackintosh 1971, Mackintosh & Reese 1979, Revusky 1971). Those experiments constitute the best available evidence for limited capacity processing of the CS.

However, enthusiasm for these results must be tempered by both alternative interpretations and contrary data. For instance, less responding to A after conditioning of AB than after conditioning of A may result not from A being less conditioned in the former case but rather from its undergoing greater generalization decrement from conditions of training to those of test. Moreover, there have been several recent reports of the opposite phenomenon, called potentiation (e.g. Durlach & Rescorla 1980, Lett 1980, Rusiniak et al 1979). In some overshadowing-like experiments which use the flavor-aversion paradigm, the addition of B seems to augment rather than depress subsequently observed responding to A. That result has been reported for both multitrial and single-trial procedures. There is some evidence that this potentiation results from the formation of associations between the two stimuli, A and B, rather than from the presence of B augmenting the association between A and the US (Durlach & Rescorla 1980). But whatever its interpretation, the occurrence of potentiation demonstrates that in some circumstances A can be well processed despite the presence of B. Unfortunately, at the present time we have only limited information on the circumstances that produce overshadowing and those that produce potentiation (see Rescorla & Durlach, in press, Palmerino et al 1980), but this question certainly deserves further research.

Another line of evidence for limited CS-processing capacity comes from studies of short-term memory. Several investigators have reported that short-term retention of the elements of a very briefly presented compound stimulus is inferior to that of one of the elements presented separately (e.g. Lamb & Riley 1981, Maki & Leith 1973, Maki et al 1976, Roberts & Grant 1978). However, this limitation on processing comes from situations in which exposure is frequently substantially shorter than that employed in many blocking experiments.

Evidence that stimuli lose attention-grabbing capacity with experience is considerably stronger. The most dramatic demonstration is the phenomenon of latent inhibition, in which repeated exposure to the CS without any consequence has a profound decremental effect on subsequent rate of acquisition when that CS is paired with a US. A natural interpretation is that exposure to the CS retards the development of an association with the US because the organism pays less attention to that CS. The fact that exposure seems to retard any subsequent associative learning, whatever the US or whatever the detailed relation to that US (e.g. Best 1975, Reiss & Wagner 1972, Rescorla 1971b), suggests that the organism has learned no specific association to the preexposed CS but only pays less attention to it. Moreover, this loss in associability occurs even when the CS is not simply presented alone but is presented without any unique consequences in a variety of other contexts. For instance, presenting a stimulus as the redundant X in a blocking experiment appears to lead to reduction in its subsequent associability (Pearce & Hall 1979), as well as to permit habituation of any unconditioned reaction it evokes (Sharp et al 1980). Moreover, arranging for the CS to be uncorrelated with USs has a similar consequence (e.g. Baker & Mackintosh 1979). There have even been some recent reports that the CS loses conditionability when it is followed by a mild US (Hall & Pearce 1979).

What is unclear in these results is whether the loss of associability of CSs follows the rules that have been suggested in order for it to explain blocking. According to the accounts mentioned above, the loss in associability results not simply from the CS being presented but from variations in its predictive relation to the US. But there is little in the available data to force the conclusion that anything beyond the separate presentation of the CS is needed to produce the loss. Perhaps any CS presentation, whatever the consequences, results in loss in associability. The fact that this loss apparently varies as a function of events following the CS may reflect variations in the predictive relation between the CS and its consequent; alternatively, it may reflect variations in the degree to which consequents that vary in surprise value disrupt the normal processing of the CS, whatever its own predictive relation to the consequent.

EVIDENCE FOR VARIATION IN US PROCESSING Substantial evidence that signaled USs are processed differently than are unsignaled ones has accumulated. To account for blocking, it is necessary to assume that a consequence of signaling a US is to make it less reinforcing. But there are apparently other consequences: (*a*) The actual response to the US, the UR, has been found to be attenuated if the US presentation is preceded by a well-conditioned CS (e.g. Kimmel 1966, Wagner, in press). This UR-diminution effect is by no means universal (e.g. Thomas 1972), but it has been observed for a variety of preparations. Wagner (in press) has reported data from a dissertation by Donegan suggesting that the results depend on the intensity of the US. (*b*) Relatedly, the UR is attenuated if the eliciting US is preceded closely by another presentation of the same US (Whitlow 1975). One interpretation is that both signaling CSs and actual USs activate some respresentation of the US which in turn attenulates the impact of immediately subsequent USs, resulting in diminution of the UR (Wagner 1978). (*c*) There is some recent evidence that preceding or following a conditioning trial by a separate occurrence of the US attenuates the associative gain from that conditioning trial (Kremer 1979, Terry 1976). But most relevant here is the further observation that in either case signaling that separate US presentation with a well-conditioned CS reduces its attenuating impact (Kremer 1979, Wagner 1978). (*d*) Recent experiments have used a delayed matching to sample technique (Maki 1979) or a related "preparatory-releaser" procedure (Terry & Wagner 1975) to measure the duration of memory for a presentation of the US. In these experiments the signaling of the US by a well-conditioned CS appears to reduce the duration of that memory (e.g. Terry & Wagner 1975). This attenuation may be taken as evidence that signaling the US reduced its impact (but see Colwill & Dickinson 1980a,b). (*e*) A substantial literature on preference for signaled shock in instrumental performance (e.g. Badia et al 1979, Fanselow 1980, Marlin et al 1979; but see Miller & Balaz, in press) also supports the claim that signaled shocks are less effective than unsignaled shocks. (*f*) Finally, there is a variety of evidence that the occurrence of nonreinforcement is less effective both in establishing conditioned inhibition (Wagner & Rescorla 1972; see below) and in controlling performance in preparatory-releaser discriminations (Terry & Wagner 1975) when that nonreinforcement is expected than when it is not. Thus, there is a variety of evidence outside the blocking paradigm indicating that signaling reinforcements and nonreinforcements modifies their impact.

APPLICATION TO BLOCKING EXPERIMENTS So there is some evidence that the processing of both the CS and the US is modified by past associative experience. It is possible that either of these, as suggested by the various theories, accounts for the failure of conditioning to occur in blocking-like procedures, but it is more likely that both contribute. Several variations on the blocking experiment itself point to the involvement of each of these processes.

Several phenomena provide especially strong evidence that various ways of signaling the US in the course of blocking can dramatically affect the reinforcing power of that US. The first is the phenomenon of "overexpectation" in which prior to reinforcement of an AB compound, each of the elements is separately conditioned by the US. Under these circumstances the US is especially well anticipated; indeed, according to some formal models (Rescorla & Wagner 1972), it is too well expected. Those models predict that the occurrence of a such an "overexpected" reinforcer will decrease rather than increase conditioning of the component stimuli. Moreover, should a neutral stimulus be present when the AB compound is reinforced, it should become inhibitory despite its contiguity with the US. Both of these predictions have received support in conditioned suppression experiments (e.g. Rescorla & Wagner 1972, Kremer 1978, Kamin & Gaioni 1974). Although Mackintosh's (1975) version of a CS-processing theory anticipates loss in the salience of stimuli under these circumstances, it does not expect associative loss. The Pearce & Hall (1980) theory does expect such results but only because their purportedly CS-processing theory actually includes a US-attenuation mechanism when the associative strength of a compound exceeds that appropriate to the reinforcer applied.

The second variation on a blocking procedure, in which a reinforced AB compound contains an inhibitory A, produces the phenomenon of "superconditioning." Under those conditions, the US is especially surprising and should therefore be especially effective in conditioning B. Again there is empirical confirmation for this prediction (Rescorla 1971a, Wagner 1971). Third, the occurrence of blocking on a single compound conditioning trial is entirely consistent with a US-attenuation view of blocking (e.g. Gillan & Domjan 1977, Revusky 1971). That observation is important because it is not consistent with accounts that view the organism as changing its attention to CSs only over the course of repeated compound trials. Finally, the phenomeon of conditioned inhibition itself should be mentioned. The standard conditioned inhibition paradigm which mixes A+ and AB– trials may be viewed as a variation on the blocking design in which nonreinforcement replaces reinforcement on the AB compound trials. Conditioned inhibition is established to B only to the extent that the nonreinforcement is surprising by virtue of conditioning to A. Indeed, one of the major attractions of the class of theories that explains blocking in terms of variations in the effectiveness of the reinforcer is their ability to incorporate conditioned inhibition within the same framework (see Wagner & Rescorla 1972, Konorski 1948, 1967). In contrast, pure CS-processing accounts of blocking have little to say about conditioned inhibition.

But there is also evidence that strongly suggests the involvement of changes in CS-processing in a blocking paradigm. The most powerful comes from "unblocking" experiments in which the blocking of B by A on AB+ trials is disrupted by a change in the reinforcer from the A to the AB trials. Several experiments suggest that if the organism is surprised by the nature of the reinforcer on the AB trials, then less blocking occurs (e.g. Dickinson & Mackintosh 1979, Dickinson et al 1976, Kamin 1968, Kremer 1979, Kremer et al 1980). For instance, if the reinforcer consists of either a single or a double shock after A, then blocking is maximal when AB is also followed by the same shock pattern, but is reduced if the alternative shock pattern is used. Evidence of such unblocking when the number of shocks is increased is compatible with US-processing theories since the effective reinforcer following AB would be greater than that following A; however, reduced blocking when A is followed by a double shock and AB terminates in a single shock is not anticipated by those theories. Yet the latter data are consistent with theories which say that such surprises change the subsequent processing of the CS.

The effect of posttrial surprises is not without alternative interpretation. It is important to note that not all of the responding which one observes to B after its embedding in a blocking paradigm is necessarily attributable to B's association with the US. Posstrial surprises may modulate those other sources of B's responding instead of augmenting its association with the US. As noted above, surprising events following a habituation trial reduce the amount of habituation. It is thus possible that the posttrial surprise following a AB+ trial affects not the conditioning of B but rather its habituation. Since the experiments all come from situations in which a novel B would produce responding like that generated by conditioning, such an alternative cannot be ruled out. Similarly, those surprises might affect the formation of associations between A and B (Cheatle & Rudy 1978, Holland 1980c, Rescorla 1981). Those associations provide an alternative source of responding to B other than that given by its association with the US (Rescorla & Durlach, in press). Finally, one recent experiment suggests that a theoretically related procedure, reducing shock intensity, generates conditioned inhibition (Wagner et al 1980). That outcome is more in accord with US-processing than CS-processing accounts.

It may be noted that one current theory (Wagner, in press) attempts to provide a common framework in which to think about variation in both CS and US processing. By treating the CS as an event which is signaled by the context, that theory allows expected CSs to be less well processed in the same manner that expected USs are less well processed. Supporting this claim are the results of experiments analogous to those described above investigating the processing of USs. For example, the CR to a particular CS is apparently reduced by prior presentation of either the same CS (Pfautz & Wagner 1976) or by another CS that previously served as a signal for the original target CS (Holland & Ross 1981). Furthermore, using either extinction or context change to break the predictive relation between a context and CS substantially attenuates latent inhibition and habituation (Wagner 1978).

This view differs from that of Mackintosh in that CS processing varies according to how well predicted a CS is by another event or a context rather than according to how well it predicts some other event. Surprisingly, currently available data do not allow a clear choice between these alternative ways of looking at changes in stimulus processing during a blocking experiment. But Wagner's theory has the advantage of providing a single framework for a broad range of effects on processing of the CS and US.

It is worth commenting briefly on one situation to which the blocking paradigm has frequently been applied. As noted earlier, Rescorla (1968, 1972) found that the introduction of intertrial USs into a procedure which also pairs CS and US undermines the development of a CR to that CS. Moreover, the quantitative data indicate that the degree of conditioning to the CS is predictable from the difference in likelihood of the US in the CS and in its absence. One way of understanding such data views the CS (X) as presented in a context (A) which is continually present. Then such a procedure is an A/AX paradigm in which both stimuli are reinforced on a partial schedule. Rescorla & Wagner (1972) showed in detail how a US-processing model applied with such identifications accurately describes the gross outcomes of such a situation. Moreover, they noted that such models anticipate that initially X will become conditioned but then (through a process like overexpectation) lose it, a result for which there is some support (Rescorla 1972, Keller, Ayres & Mahoney 1977). Just as in the case of overexpectation, the Mackintosh model provides little insight into such results. The recent Pearce-Hall (1980) model is also inadequate, although for a different reason. According to that model the continuing mixture of reinforcement and nonreinforcement would serve to keep X salient and allow it to become well conditioned.

However, Gibbon & Balsam (1981) and Jenkins et al (1981) have recently suggested that some of this reduced performance to X reflects the impact of the intertrial USs not on conditioning of X but on the exhibition of that conditioning in performance. They argue that performance is exhibited to a CS only to the degree that its likelihood of containing a US exceeds the overall likelihood of the US for the session as a whole. The background and CS do not compete for conditioning; both become conditioned, but their equality makes the CS unable to evoke performance. One testing ground for such alternatives is the impact of signaling the intertrial USs with another CS. US attenuation models expect such signaling to blocking conditioning of the background (A) and hence prevent it from in turn blocking conditioning of the target CS (X); being signaled should make intertrial USs less effective. The Gibbon & Balsam (1981) and Jenkins et al (1981) proposals do not anticipate blocking of this sort with the background and consequently expect no effect of signaling. Evidence on the matter is mixed. Although Jenkins et al (1981) and Jenkins & Shattuck (1980) reported no effect of signaling, Rescorla (1972) and Durlach & Rescorla (1981) found an effect. Consequently, although US-processing models do a superior job to CS-processing models in dealing with these correlational data, there is also the possibility that some of the effects do not involve modification of learning at all but rather reflect modulations in performance.

It is not entirely clear that future research will profitably continue to explore the details of the blocking result itself. That phenomenon had a powerful and salutory effect on theorizing which has led to the identification of important processes that modulate the effect of contiguities. But it may well be best to explore these processes themselves rather than to continue to pick at what may well be a multiply determined and complicated phenomenon. One reason for this suggestion is that in recent years the phenomenon of blocking has so dominated our thinking that theorists have assumed its operation far beyond the bounds for which it is actually demonstrated. There have even been reports of instances in which blocking is either small or absent (e.g. Jenkins et al 1981, LoLordo et al 1975). One begins to fear that additional cases that would be important to our understanding about conditioning could be ignored because the blocking phenomenon, rather than the processes which it suggests, has gained such dominance in our thinking.

OTHER ISSUES Aside from the role that contiguity plays, two other issues of the conditions of learning have gained attention. The first is the possibility that qualitative relations among the events to be associated affect the course and nature of associative learning. This possibility is best exemplified by the so-called cue-to-consequence notion in which certain CSs seem best associated with certain USs, even under circumstances in which potencies of the individual evevets are not at fault. The second issue is the possibility mentioned in the previous section that for learning to occur some post-presentation processing time is required after a CS-US contiguity.

The importance of claiming that qualitative relations between events might influence their association is best understood in terms of an historically dominant pretheoretical assumption that the selection of events and organism is arbitrary. The choice of preparation is typically thought to be a matter of convenience but not something that in any important way influences the conclusions of the experiment. It is of course this assumption of interchangeability of individual events that has made it possible to build up a large body of information about a few situations and still have a certain confidence that the information so gathered is not irrelevant to learning in general. Indeed, one might argue that this is exactly the way in which science must proceed, working with a few model systems; the only question is whether these model systems capture enough of the underlying process to have some generality.

It is against this background that findings of a noninterchangeability of events, such as the cue-to-consequence results originally reported by Garcia & Koelling (1966), had their impact. They seemed to imply that not only are some CSs better signals than others and some USs better reinforcers than others, but also certain combinations of CSs and USs are more readily associable. In its strongest form, the claim was made that certain otherwise demonstrably potent CSs and USs could not become associated when they were contiguous. Although the extreme form of this claim can now be rejected (e.g. Revusky & Parker 1976, Krane & Wagner 1975, Willner 1978), such results suggested a major breakdown in the assumption of interchangeability of events.

Claims of this sort met with two reactions. Some authors were eager to accept them because they implied a biological predisposition of the organism that traditional approaches to the study of learning had neglected. Some saw these results as suggesting both the need for a more ethological approach and the presence of a broader variety of learning processes, each specialized for particular purposes (e.g. Rozin & Kalat 1971). Authors in this category were perhaps too ready to accept the initial results uncritically. Other reviewers were more negative. The study of learning has a strong tradition of parsimony, with a bias against the introduction of complexity unless it is well documented. The original cue-to-consequence results in which flavors are apparently especially associable with toxins whereas lights and tones are especially associable with peripheral pain were indeed impressive; but many authors pointed to inadequacies of design that complicated their interpretation (e.g. Bitterman 1975, Rescorla & Holland 1976, Schwartz 1974). The most constructive consequence of the controversy that has followed is the emergence of a paradigm for demonstrating the impact of qualitative relations, the so-called double dissociation experiment. This paradigm exposes each of two groups to two CSs and two USs. One group receives pairings of the form CS_1—US_1 and CS_2—US_2 whereas the other receives the alternative pairings CS_1—US_2 and CS_2—US_1. Here events that share a subscript are qualitatively related. The observation of interest is more rapid learning by the first group, which has related stimuli paired. Since both groups receive the same individual events and differ only in their contiguity, a wide range of alternative interpretations is ruled out. There are, however, surprisingly few experiments that adequately apply this paradigm. Perhaps the best demonstrations come from experiments showing that similarity of the events to be associated improves the formation of the association (e.g. Rescorla & Furrow 1977). But in any case, the general consensus seems to be that qualtitative relations do influence the formation of associations (e.g. LoLordo 1979).

But the important theoretical question is the manner in which these qualitative relations affect the connection. One possibility is that the nature of the learning is different; the rules of associative learning identified using one set of stimuli might be different from those identified using another set having different qualitative relations. This possibility would have important consequences for the value of previous work with arbitrarily selected stimuli. It would mean that the "laws of learning" have little generality (Seligman 1970). As a result there has been considerable effort directed at evaluating that possibility. The bulk of that effort has selected the flavor-aversion paradigm, which has most frequently been claimed to exemplify the special qualitative relation among stimuli, and investigate its laws, comparing them with the laws that have emerged from other paradigms. The principal conclusion from that work has been that, despite early claims to the contrary, the laws look remarkably similar. The major phenomena that dominate theoretical thinking in Pavlovian conditioning have all been demonstrated with the flavor-aversion preparation (e.g. Revusky 1977). To be sure, that preparation shows different detailed parameter values than do some other Pavlovian preparations, but the variation among those other Pavlovian preparations is also substantial.

But given that the laws of association are unchanged, there remains the further question of the nature of the impact that the choice of CS-US pair has on the association. Implicit in many discussions are two sorts of impact that would have quite different implications for associative processes (LoLordo 1979). One possibility is that the organism comes to the experimental situation with preexisting associations among certain pairs of stimuli. It then is able to learn more rapidly when those stimuli are paired simply because it has a head start on the learning that the experimenter requires. A facilitative impact of this sort would require no revision in theories of conditioning. A second possibility is that the rate of formation of associations is a function of the actual events paired, with some pairs permitting the more rapid development of an association. This possibility would entail an effect of the CS-US pair selected on the actual development of associations. That possibility has not been acknowledged in any theory of conditioning.

As LoLordo (1979) points out, these two alternatives are quite difficult to disentangle experimentally. However, one possibility has been suggested by Rescorla (1980a). He argues that it is instructive to ask whether the learning of both an inhibitory and an excitatory relation is facilitated by the selection of a particular CS-US pair. Presumably a facilitation of performance during the learning of either of these relations could be the product of preexperimental associations. However, if both kinds of learning are facilitated, such an account seems implausible; rather the choice of the CS-US pair would appear to facilitate any learning. In one set of second-order conditioning experiments, Rescorla (1980a) found evidence for facilitation in the learning of such opposite relations. But more data of this sort are clearly needed.

In any case, the finding of an interaction between CS and US that many initially felt to be disastrous for general theories of learning has turned out to be considerably more innocuous. In many cases the effect may not be associative. In those cases where the effect can be identified as associative, it is not clear whether it simply represents preexperimental learning or a change in the course of learning. But in no case do fundamentally different laws of learning seem required.

The second issue is less novel or controversial but may have as important an impact on our thinking about the circumstances that produce learning. This is the possibility alluded to above that after a contiguity the organism requires some posttrial processing time for the association to be formed. Of course, the historically most prominent support for such a possibility comes from experiments in which pharamacological or electrical events with massive effects are applied immediately after a trial. Those procedures have spawned a large literature directed at understanding the nature of the depression in subsequently assessed responding that they produce. But that literature has not succeeded in identifying the mode of action uniquely as disrupting the formation of an association that would otherwise have occurred after the trial. Many investigators (e.g. Lewis 1969, 1976, Miller & Springer 1973, 1974, Spear 1978) have instead concluded that much of the loss in responding observed after such treatments reflects deficits in retrieval. They have noted that reinstitution of the original training context at the time of testing often reveals substantial evidence of learning.

However, some recent experiments have uncovered a more subtle set of procedures that do appear to identify a disruptable posttrial processing of the association. For instance, exposure to another associative learning experience after a CS-US contiguity apparently undermines the formation of the CS-US association (Wagner et al 1973). Moreover, the magnitude of that disruption apparently depends on the amount of new learning that the second experience produces. The same component events in the second experience are more effective in disrupting the association if they themselves produce greater learning. It is not just the occurrence of a posttrial event but rather the occurrence of a posttrial episode that calls for associative learning that is disruptive. Moreover, there is some evidence that the disruption is maximal when the posttrial episode calls for associations involving the same reinforcer as does the learning being disrupted (Dickinson & Mackintosh 1979).

This sort of finding has both empirical and theoretical implications for the study of associative learning. Some authors have argued that one could use these more subtle disruptive procedures to explore the conditions for associative learning in the manner in which many had high hopes for ECS. Perhaps the current flurry of investigations of short-term memory in animals is partly a reflection of this. At a theoretical level such findings have encouraged the importation into theories of animal learning of notions of information processing current in the human memory literature (e.g. Wagner 1978).

Instrumental Learning

The issue of which circumstances produce instrumental learning is tied up with that of which associations are formed. In most instrumental learning experiments the investigator explicitly acknowledges the presence of three events: a response, a reinforcer, and some stimulus in the presence of which the response and reinforcer are arranged to be contiguous. Historical conceptions of instrumental learning emphasized what has been called an S-R approach, which assumed an association between the controlling stimulus and the response. The role of the eventual reinforcer was to select among S-R associations; only those S-R contiguities shortly followed by reinforcers were encoded. More recently, investigators have begun to drift toward thinking of instrumental learning as an association between the response and the reinforcer and have assigned to the stimulus a less explicit role (e.g. Bolles 1972, Mackintosh 1974).

Two points should be made about this shift in orientation. First, it has occurred largely in the absence of clear data demanding the change. To be sure, the traditional S-R approach has seemed inadequate on a number of grounds. But those difficulties are not clearly solved by the alternative response-reinforcer view. Second, there has been only slight attention paid to any alternative view of instrumental learning that involves other than associations among pairs of items. Other than occasional remarks by Skinner (1938) and Jenkins (1977), theoretical structures that involve three rather than two terms have not been developed.

In any case, once one considers the possibility that instrumental learning might be response-reinforcer in nature, it is natural to ask questions that parallel those that have been asked about the stimulus-reinforcer learning of Pavlovian conditioning. For instance, we can ask about the necessity and sufficiency of response-reinforcer contiguity for production of the association. There is substantially less information on such issues, but below we briefly mention some relevant studies.

ROLE OF CONTIGUITY Historically, the necessity of response-reinforcer contiguity has seemed firmly established. Such classic experiments as that of Grice (1942) provided strong evidence that learning with apparent lack of contiguity was actually mediated by a secondary reinforcer being contiguous with the response. However, several recent experiments have suggested that instrumental learning can be produced with substantial delays of reinforcement even in the absence of identifiable secondary reinforcers. For instance, Lett (1975) was able to teach rats a discrimination task despite the fact that several minutes elapsed between the correct response and the food reinforcer. The novel feature of that experiment was the administration of the reward in the start box if the preceding response had been correct. Although such a procedure does not have a natural interpretation in terms of secondary reinforcers, it can be viewed as reactivating a memory of the preceding response, thus making it available for the effect of the reinforcer. Thus one solution offered for cases of learning without response-reinforcer contiguity is similar to that for learning without CS-reinforcer contiguity: the response is viewed as leaving a memory that can either persist in time or be reactivated at the time of reinforcer delivery.

We may also ask whether simple response-reinforcer contiguity, as distinct from some more complicated, informational relation, is sufficient for instrumental learning. Experiments parallel to that of Rescorla (1968), in which contiguities of the response and reinforcer are diluted by the addition of separate reinforcers, have seldom been carried out in the context of acquisition of instrumental behavior. But there is a substantial operant literature concerned with the "matching law." Its relevance in the present context is that the rate of execution of a given instrumental behavior is depressed by the delivery of reinforcers either in a noncontingent fashion or contingent on other behavior.

However, these experiments do not have a unique interpretation in terms of something beyond contiguity affecting learning of a particular behavior. It is difficult to be certain that the extra reinforcers have an adverse effect on the learning of the target response as distinct from having a positive effect on some other response that competes with it. Even if the reinforcers are not explicitly contingent on some other response, they may train behaviors that the experimenter does not observe. In fact, a common way of viewing matching experiments is in terms of various responses having different values (established by their contiguities with the reinforcer). The organism then chooses among those responses according to their values (DeVilliers 1980, Herrnstein 1970, Staddon 1980). Freely delivered reinforcers do not adversely affect the absolute value of the target response, although they may reduce its relative value compared to other responses. That is, noncontiguous reinforcers may affect performance rather than learning. An analogous interpretation has recently been suggested for Pavlovian conditioning experiments (Gibbon & Balsam 1981).

There have also been instrumental learning experiments that are analogous to Pavlovian blocking experiments. Here the question is whether one can arrange a response-reinforcer contiguity that nevertheless produces no learning because the reinforcer is otherwise well predicted. Two types of events have been employed to provide that alternative prediction. Williams (1975) arranged for a response that had previously been contiguous with the reinforcer to intervene between a target response and the reinforcer. Under such circumstances, the target response seems less well learned, suggesting that it was blocked by the pretrained response in the manner that pretrained stimuli block others in Pavlovian conditioning. Unfortunately, the way the animal was induced to execute the response was by illuminating a key with different colors, thus permitting an interpretation entirely in terms of blocking of conditioning to the stimuli rather than blocking of response-reinforcer associations (cf Zanich & Fowler 1978). In a second type of experiment, several investigators have used CSs that signal reinforcers as agents to block response-reinforcer associations. For instance, St. Clair-Smith (1979a) used a shock to punish bar-pressing in rats. For some animals a stimulus that had itself previously been paired with shock intervened between the response and the shock; for others it did not. The finding of interest is that this stimulus seemed to block the learning of the response-shock association as evidenced by less suppression of bar-pressing. Analogous results have been reported for the blocking of response-food associations that might be involved in initial acquisition (Pearce & Hall 1978, St. Clair-Smith 1979b). Mackintosh & Dickinson (1979) have improved on such studies by physically forcing the animal to make the response simultaneously with a CS previously paired with the reinforcer. They found results consistent with a blocking view. Unfortunately, these results permit alternative interpretations. For instance, they may derive from differential Pavlovian conditioning of situational cues which provide motivation for the instrumental performance. More generally, these experiments only really demonstrate that signaled instrumental reinforcers can be less effective in training responses. But they do not uniquely identify interference with response-reinforcer associations as the basis for the effect. However, these data are consistent with both the existence of response-reinforcer associations and the proposition that they follow laws similar to those of stimulus-reinforcer associations.

OTHER ISSUES Aside from the role of contiguity, two other issues have occupied recent attention in the study of instrumental learning. The first is related to the cue-to-consequence issue in Pavlovian conditioning—is the choice of the events to be associated in instrumental learning arbitrary? In the case of instrumental learning, there are three primary events, response, reinforcer, and stimulus; consequently, interest has focused on how the choice of each might interact with that of the other two.

There is some evidence that the choice of the reinforcer interacts with that of the response. Performance in experiments that use a particular reinforcer apparently varies widely according to the choice of the response instrumental to the production of that reinforcer. An early example arose in the avoidance learning literature in which certain responses (e.g. bar pressing) seemed difficult to train whereas others (e.g. locomotion) seemed easy (e.g. Bolles 1970). More recent demonstrations have suggested that golden hamsters show quite different performances when different behaviors are made instrumental to the production of either food or shock (Shettleworth 1975, 1979). One interpretation of such findings is that associative learning proceeds at a different rate depending on the particular combination of response and reinforcer selected. Indeed, the learning may be impossible with certain combinations. However, the available evidence does not permit a choice of this interpretation over one in terms of the response-reinforcer pair affecting performance of the response rather than learning of the association (see section on Learning and Performance).

There is also some evidence that when the choice of the reinforcer is held constant, there is interaction between the choice of the response to be trained and the stimulus in the presence of which that response is to occur. Most of this evidence comes from experiments conducted in Konorski's laboratory and is reviewed in detail by Shettleworth (1979). At the present time those data do not appear substantial enough to warrant any firm conclusion.

Finally, there is evidence that the choice of the reinforcer affects the success with which various stimuli might come to control an instrumental response. The issues raised for this instance are essentially the same as those faced in Pavlovian conditioning, in which interactions in the choice of stimulus and reinforcer are also at issue. LoLordo (1979) has recently reviewed experiments from his and other laboratories. As in the case of Pavlovian conditioning, there appears to be little question that stimuli and reinforcers interact in yielding performance in instrumental learning experiments; moreover, at least a portion of that interaction seems to be associative. But the more subtle question of whether the interaction results from preexperimental associations or from more rapid learning is not settled in the case of instrumental learning (LoLordo 1979).

The issues of interaction among elements have been less thoroughly investigated in instrumental learning. But the initial results suggest that interactions occur. Perhaps with the sophistication gained from parallel experiments in Pavlovian conditioning, rapid further progress can be made.

A second issue that has commanded attention is whether organisms not only learn because of the relations arranged between response and reinforcement but also about those relations. The best researched case of this possibility is the phenomenon of "learned helplessness," in which prior administration of shocks independently of responding appears to retard subsequent escape/avoidance learning (Maier & Seligman 1976). This phenomenon has spawned a large and often acrimonious literature. The initial notion that the organism learns that responses and reinforcers are unrelated has been challenged by alternative theoretical notions in terms of changes in general activity (Anisman et al 1978), development of competing responses (Bracewell & Black 1974), and neurochemical changes (Anisman 1975, Weiss et al 1976). There appears to be emerging a consensus that inescapable shock has multiple effects. It has been documented to reduce general activity, but the question of interest in the present context is whether or not it additionally affects subsequent learning. Some authors have reported learning decrements that do not seem explicable in terms of reduction in activity (Jackson et al 1980) but others have found contrary results using similar procedures (Irwin et al 1980). Maier & Jackson (1979) provide a balanced discussion of the issues; but it remains unclear whether or not the animal can learn the apparently higher-order notion that its behavior is unrelated to reinforcers.

It should be noted that there is a parallel literature in Pavlovian conditioning conducted under the rubric of "learned irrelevance" (e.g. Baker 1976, Mackintosh 1973, Tomie et al 1980). Here the attempt is to demonstrate that exposure to uncorrelated CSs and USs retards subsequent excitatory conditioning of those CSs by the US. This suggestion has been plagued by the alternative possibility that the observed effects are attributable to well-documented effects of separate CS (latent inhibition, e.g. Lubow 1973) and US (US preexposure, e.g. Randich & LoLordo 1979). Moreover, it differs from the learned helplessness notion in suggesting that the decremental effects are specific to a particular CS and US rather than resulting from a depression in the general learning ability of the animal. Although some experimental results are encouraging (Baker & Mackintosh 1979), neither of these features has been demonstrated.

The importance of these experiments lies in the fact that traditional theories of learning have attempted to deal with the learning of relations among events in terms of two associative constructs, excitation and inhibition. They have not admitted that organisms learn other relations, although they have allowed those relations to influence the formation of excitatory and inhibitory connections. Documentation of either learned irrelevance or learned helplessness as representing learning about relations would force theories away from the simple excitatory-inhibitory model that has been so successful.

CONTENTS OF LEARNING

Perhaps the central question with any learning process is its content. When we speak, for instance, of associative learning, what is actually associated with what? In the context of Pavlovian conditioning, the issue is which features of the contiguous events become encoded and associated. In the context of instrumental training, as we have seen, one may first ask which of the three primary events—stimulus, response, and reinforcer—enter into the learning; one may then ask which features of those events are encoded.

A surprisingly limited set of techniques has been devised for addressing these questions experimentally. These may be divided into two classes: those which study what is learned by varying the conditions under which learning takes place, and those which first allow learning to occur and then perform manipulations designed to expose its character. We will emphasize the application of these techniques to the analysis of what is learned in Pavlovian conditioning, since it is there that the broadest range of data is available. Then we will also discuss some parallel experiments in instrumental training.

Pavlovian Conditioning

The first technique for understanding what is learned in Pavlovian conditioning depends heavily on the assumption that contiguity is a primary condition for the production of an association (see above). It is based on the notion that only those aspects of an event which actually occur and are contiguous with another event can become associated with that other event. For instance, the principal alternative possibilities for the encoding of the reinforcing event are in terms of one of two features, its stimulus properties (the US) or its response properties (the UR). The common application of this technique involves arranging conditions such that one of these two aspects of the reinforcer has a better contiguous relationship with the antecedent CS. In its extreme form the application of this technique tries to eliminate one aspect of the reinforcer altogether. If such elimination severely disrupts the course of conditioning, then the inference is drawn that the eliminated aspect must normally participate in the association. This procedure has been applied to both the response and stimulus aspects of the reinforcer.

Two types of response-free reinforcers have been employed. In one type, the experimenter searches for naturally occurring stimuli that have greatly reduced response-evoking properties. The best known case is that of sensory preconditioning, in which two relatively neutral stimuli are paired and then one is made valuable by a conditioning operation (e.g. Brogden 1939). The association between the stimuli is then identified in terms of the value acquired by the other paired stimulus. Although historically there has been serious doubt about the size and reliability of such associations, in recent years the evidence has been quite substantial (e.g. Rescorla 1980b, Rizley & Rescorla 1972). There seems little doubt that associations can be formed between stimuli which evoke minimally distinctive responses. The second case is one in which the investigator reduces the response-evoking power of a US by experimental means. The best known examples use drugs such as curare to attenuate the response. Under those circumstances too, one can demonstrate that learning still occurs (e.g. Solomon & Turner 1962).

The major attempt to generate stimulus-free reinforcers involves direct stimulation of the motor cortex. Although the original experiments with this procedure led to considerable controversy (Loucks 1935), more recent evidence suggests that such direct stimulation can serve as a reinforcer (e.g. Doty & Giurgea 1961). But that evidence also suggests that such stimulation has consequences other than evoking a response which may convert the procedure into an instrumental paradigm in which the animal strives to maintain postural adjustment (Thomas 1971, Wagner et al 1967).

Unfortunately, the experimental designs employed with these techniques are rarely sufficient to determine the magnitude of the disruption produced. One can often eliminate either the response or the stimulus aspect of a reinforcer without preventing Pavlovian conditioning. But it is unclear to what degree that elimination attenuates the formation of the association. In this respect, a related technique used by Rescorla (1980a) may prove more useful. This procedure uses two reinforcers that differ only in the feature of interest (e.g. some stimulus property). One can then ask to what degree conditioning is disrupted by using those reinforcers interchangeably rather than using only one. To the degree that mixing reinforcers differing in only one property affects conditioning, one may infer that that property was learned.

The second technique for understanding what is learned in Pavlovian conditioning has been more widely, and more analytically, used in recent years. The idea of this technique was first suggested by Rozeboom (1958) but has recently been popularized by Rescorla and his colleagues. It is most easily illustrated in second-order conditioning, in which the association of interest is that between two originally neutral stimuli, S2 and S1. In a typical experiment, S1 is first paired with a US and then S2 is paired with S1. The question of interest is which aspects of S1 become associated with S2. The procedure suggested by the present technique is to change the current associative strength of one feature of S1, perhaps by extinction or by pairing it with a new US. Then S2 is tested to see whether this change has consequences for responding to it. If it does, the inference is drawn that part of the response to S2 depends upon an association with the changed feature of S1.

This technique has been applied to various Pavlovian conditioning preparations, with a wide variety of results. In many cases, even the most gross manipulation of all of the features of S1 following second-order conditioning had little impact upon subsequently tested responding to S2 (e.g. Amiro & Bitterman 1980, Cheatle & Rudy 1978, Holland & Rescorla 1975b, Nairne & Rescorla 1981, Rizley & Rescorla 1972). One interpretation of those instances is that the organism has encoded none of the stimulus features of S1 in the association with S2. By inference, the learning is identified as S-R in character. In some second-order conditioning preparations, however, there seems to be considerable encoding of the particular features of S1 (e.g. Leyland 1977, Rashotte et al 1977, Rescorla 1979). In fact, Rescorla (1980a) has used the autoshaping preparation to investigate the rules by which particular sensory aspects of S1 might be selected for association with S2. He has suggested that some of these rules, e.g. similarity between S2 and a feature of S1, might be responsible for the variation observed among conditioning preparations; the organism might be encouraged to learn about the stimulus properties of S1 to the degree that they are similar to S2. Although there is evidence to support such suggestions (Nairne & Rescorla 1981, Rescorla 1980a), much additional work needs to be done defining such selection rules and applying them to different conditioning paradigms.

The application of Rozeboom's logic to first-order conditioning is technically more demanding because it is difficult to change the value of USs after conditioning. In cases attempting change, either by satiation or counterconditioning procedures, varying results have been reported. Some motivational and conditioning changes in the US have produced changes in the response to a CS previously paired with that US (e.g. Holland & Rescorla 1975a, Holland & Straub 1979); those results suggest encoding of the stimulus features of the reinforcer. However, attempts to change other USs, for instance certain drugs (e.g. Riley et al 1976), have found essentially no impact upon responding to the CS. Moreover, Holland & Straub (1979) recently reported that manipulations of the US may affect some responses to the CS but not others, suggesting the possibility that a complex array of associations might be responsible for the total performance during the CS.

Consequently, there is no easy summary for describing which aspects of the reinforcer are encoded in Pavlovian conditioning. What is available, however, are promising techniques for carrying out that analysis. Moreover, those techniques have led to a more sophisticated statement of the original "what is learned" problem. Instead of phrasing the alternatives in terms of stimulus versus response, authors have increasingly come to talk about aspects of the reinforcer being encoded and rules for selection among those aspects.

Instrumental Learning

A basic question of both historical and modern concern has been whether or not the reinforcer is part of the content of the organism's instrumental learning. This question originally arose because of the S-R tradition in which reinforcers played the role of catalysts for the learning of associations between stimuli and responses but were not themselves participants in the learned association. Standing against this Hullian (and even Guthrian) alternative was the notion of Tolman (1932) that the organism learned not just because of the reinforcer but also about the reinforcer. Tolman proposed what any layman would think to be obvious, that the learning underlying goal-directed behavior encoded the goal.

There have been a number of more modern theoretical descendants of the notion that reinforcers enter into instrumental associations. Perhaps the most popular early alternatives were "two-process" theories which gave instrumentally trained animals two associations, one between the controlling stimulus and the instrumental response and another between that stimulus and the reinforcer (Mowrer 1947, Spence 1956). The Pavlovian association encoded knowledge about the reinforcer and was important to the exhibition of instrumental learning; but the instrumental response itself was associated only with the eliciting stimulus and not with the reinforcer. A more radical suggestion is that only this Pavlovian portion of the theory is necessary to explain instrumental performance (e.g. Bindra, 1974, Moore 1973). Many instrumental activities can be characterized as approach responses which may be Pavlovian CRs resulting from the pairing of stimulus with the reinforcer in the absence of any important role of a response-reinforcer contingency. Mackintosh & Dickinson (1979) note that with a little imagination a surprising percentage of instrumental behaviors can be so conceived. When pressed, such an alternative can appeal to stimuli that form part of the feedback from instrumental behaviors themselves. Indeed, several early theories conceived of instrumental learning exactly as the association between feedback from instrumental responses and reinforcers (Miller 1963, Mowrer 1960, Sheffield 1966). From those theories it is a small step to the most popular alternative today, that the animal directly associates its own response with the reinforcer (e.g. Bolles 1972, Mackintosh 1974). It is a tribute to the power of the S-R tradition both that all of these possibilities have been offered as alternatives to it rather than competitors with each other, and that it took so long for psychologists to arrive at the possibility that instrumental learning is R-S in nature. Thinking about instrumental learning has slowly moved from S-R to R-S accounts, passing through several intermediate stages.

As in the case of Pavlovian conditioning, the primary tool for investigating the possibility that the reinforcer is encoded involves postconditioning modifications of the reinforcer. The notion again is that to the degree that the reinforcer is encoded, then modifications of the reinforcer should result in modifications of subsequently tested instrumental behavior.

Early examples of this logic include experiments which change either the goal event (e.g. Crespi 1942) or the value of goal-associated stimuli (e.g. Seward & Levy 1949). In the former studies, animals are first taught an instrumental response with one value of a goal event and then receive additional training with either a more or less valuable goal. Such experiments are of interest in their own right and have received considerable experimental analysis (Mackintosh 1974). However, in the present context their importance is that instrumental performance often shifts rapidly to a level which differs depending upon the reinforcer magnitude used prior to the shift. That can be taken to mean that the organism has encoded the reinforcer features in sufficient detail to respond appropriately when the reinforcer magnitude is changed. One theoretical account, for instance, can be made in terms of two-process theories in which anticipation of a particular reward serves a motivational function in generating instrumental performance (e.g. Spence 1956). But such results by no means force the conclusion that the reinforcer has been encoded (see Mackintosh 1974). Rapid adjustment to a decrease in the value of the reinforcer may reflect a combination of generalization decrement and simple adjustment to the weaker reinforcer. Performance shifts when the reinforcer is improved are typically slower and may largely be due simply to more learning under the stronger reinforcer.

Two classic experiments attempted to change the value of goal-associated stimuli after instrumental learning. Tolman & Gleitman (1949) offered rats a choice between two distinctive goal boxes, both of which had previously contained food but only one of which had subsequently been paired with shock; the rats chose the nonshocked chamber. The apparatus was such that the animal's choice indicated its anticipation that a particular goal chamber would follow a particular choice response. Miller (1935) found a similar result with runway performance. An analogous result has been obtained by simply placing the animal in a previously rewarded goal box with food no longer available. Such exposure produces "latent extinction" as evidenced by more rapid subsequent extinction of an approach response (e.g. Seward & Levy 1949). In this case, however, it is infrequent to report the results of the first extinction test trial, thus leaving open the possibility that prior nonrewarded placement has extinguished some conditioned reinforcing power of the goal box which otherwise would have retarded extinction (but see Gonzalez & Shepp 1965). But taken together, the results of such early experiments indicate that animals can encode stimuli that are intimately associated with instrumental rewards. Unfortunately, they give little information about whether the animal has encoded the reinforcer itself.

One reason that early experiments manipulated the value of goal-related events rather than that of goal events may be the difficulty of changing the value of the reinforcer. However, recently techniques have been developed which make such a change possible. The principal technique makes use of a Pavlovian flavor-aversion procedure in which the instrumental reinforcer is paired with an illness-inducing agent prior to retesting of the instrumental response. The results of applying this procedure have been highly mixed. Some attempts have produced primarily negative results (e.g. Garcia et al 1970, Holman 1975, Morrison & Collyer 1974, Wilson et al 1981). In those experiments, poisoning of the instrumental reinforcer had little effect upon subsequent responding during extinction, although Wilson et al (1981) did find an effect on the conditioned reinforcing power of stimuli preceding that reinforcer. However, Adams & Dickinson (in press) have found some circumstances under which bar-pressing trained with a reinforcer is attenuated when that reinforcer is subsequently poisoned. Moreover, that attenuation was shown to be specific to poisoning of the reinforcer paired with the response. Poisoning another reinforcer also present in the situation had less effect, an outcome that is awkward for two-process accounts of encoding of the reinforcer. Chen & Amsel (1980) have reported that running in a runway can also be depressed when the original reward has been poisoned. Both sets of authors suggest that the conditions of training may affect the sensitivity of an instrumental response to changes in the value of the reinforcer. Although the results are still preliminary, massing of trials and percentage of reinforcement may be contributors. However, it is not clear whether such variables affect the actual encoding of the instrumental reinforcer during learning or our ability to modify its value by conditioning procedures after that learning.

Changes in deprivation state can also be used to change a reinforcer's current value. Krieckhaus & Wolf (1968) found that inducing a salt need in animals that had learned a choice response for salt reward increased their resistance to extinction. A similar procedure has been used in the Pavlovian literature (Fudim 1978). However, even when these effects occur in instrumental performance, they are typically incomplete. Animals will engage in an amazing amount of instrumental activity for a reinforcer that they find highly aversive when it is actually received. And there is a growing literature indicating that essentially complete satiation on the goal object does not prevent enthusiastic instrumental activity aimed at receiving that object (Capaldi & Myers 1978, Morgan 1974, Rescorla 1977). Here, too, such features of training as percentage and size of reward appear to govern the degree to which the instrumental behavior is sensitive to changes in the value of the goal.

This relative insensitivity of the instrumental response to dramatic changes in the value of the goal has several possible interpretations. One suggestion is that the behavior is only partly determined by anticipation of a particular goal object. For instance, Adams & Dickinson (in press) argued that under some training conditions instrumental behavior becomes "automatized" so as to become independent of its goal. Alternatively, Rescorla (1977) has suggested that much of the motivation of instrumental behavior is based on second-order Pavlovian conditioning in which the goal is the US. As noted above, there are many instances in which second-order conditioning is insensitive to changes in the US. Another possibility is that instrumental responding is entirely determined by anticipation of a goal, but our techniques fail to change adequately the value of the goal object. Although most of the studies mentioned above document the impact of these manipulations upon consumption of the goal, that impact is not always complete (e.g. Capaldi & Myers 1978, Chen & Amsel 1980). Nor is it clear that changing the response to the presented goal object changes the value of the organism's representation of that goal. For instance, the animal may encode one aspect of the reinforcer in the instrumental situation (e.g. its texture or drive-reducing qualities) but use another feature of the reinforcer as a signal when it is poisoned (e.g. its taste).

It is striking that although many have adopted some form of an R-S description for instrumental training, nevertheless these data are at best equivocal on the most fundamental prediction of such a model. Attitudes toward alternative models are not always determined by data.

LEARNING AND PERFORMANCE

For the most part, the previous discussion has been silent on the particular response systems used to index learning. This silence reflects the fact that most contemporary learning theories are theories of association rather than of behavior. Most students of learning have been content to assume an isomorphic mapping of associative strength on some selected response measure, ignoring the details of how learned associations are translated into performance (but see Frey & Sears 1978). In this section, we consider how learning generates particular performance patterns.

Determination of Response Form: Pavlovian Conditioning

Although associationistic discussions of Pavlovian conditioning (like ours) have seldom shown concern for the nature of the CR, other orientations have. For instance, another important view of conditioning has its roots in the physiological study of reflexes in the nineteenth century. Within this tradition (e.g. Gormezano & Kehoe 1975), Pavlovian conditioning is seen as the addition of a previously neutral stimulus to an existing reflex system, the transfer of control of the unconditioned response from the US to the CS. This view seemed especially attractive in the context of early conditioning results in which the CR appeared to be a replica or subset of the UR. However, as the range of conditioning preparations has widened and researchers have examined larger samples of behavior using improved measurement techniques, it has become obvious that the CR and UR, although frequently similar, are seldom identical. There are various ways in which the CR and UR diverge.

Often the CR lacks obvious features of the UR; for instance, swallowing and jaw movements are typically not observed in canine salivary conditioning (Sheffield 1965, Zener 1937) although these behaviors form a prominent part of the UR (but see Kierylowicz et al 1968). Sometimes the CR includes behaviors not part of the UR; for instance, substantial motor activity often occurs to CSs paired with food, although activity is not part of the response to food itself (Liddell 1942, Zamble 1968, Zener 1937). More recently, pigeons have been observed to approach and peck visual signals for USs that do not themselves evoke pecking, such as water delivered directly into the mouth (Woodruff & Williams 1976) or heat (Wasserman 1973b, Wasserman et al 1975).

Some CRs even involve behavior changes opposite in direction to those engendered by the US. For instance, although the UR to morphine injection includes hypothermia and analgesia, the CR involves hyperthermia and hyperalgesia (Siegel 1975, 1977, 1978). In fact, the occurrence of such "compensatory" CRs has recently been taken as evidence for a conditioning theory of drug tolerance and addiction (Schull 1979, Siegel 1977, Solomon 1980).

Finally, recent evidence indicates that the form of the CR often depends importantly upon the characteristics of the CS as well as those of the US. In defensive conditioning, for instance, features of the CS such as its modality, duration, or temporal relation to the US have been reported to affect the form of paw flexion in cats (Wickens et al 1969), the form of eyelid closure CRs in rabbits (Smith 1968), the occurrence of fear or leg flexion responses in dogs (Konorski 1967), and freezing or flight in rats (Blanchard & Blanchard 1970, Bolles & Collier 1976). In appetitive conditioning, pigeons show conditioned pecking to localized visual CSs, but not to diffuse visual CSs or to auditory CSs (Rashotte et al 1977, Rescorla 1980a, Wasserman 1973a), even though other measures of conditioning demonstrate substantial learning about those stimuli (Blanchard & Honig 1976, Nairne & Rescorla 1981). The most systematically studied example comes from direct observations of rats' behavior anticipatory to food. The form of those behaviors is a function of CS modality, location, localizability, ease with which the CS can be contacted, and CS-US interval (Boakes et al 1978, Holland 1977, 1980a, Peterson et al 1972).

Such variations in CR form seem incompatible with a reflex transfer principle. In fact, many early investigators (e.g. Tolman 1932, Warner 1932, Zener 1937) cited them as grounds for rejection of such an interpretation of conditioning. These variations also highlight the need for an associative approach to deal with the problem of how performance is generated. Some recent attempts have been made, and the discussion below focuses on two classes of accounts for the origin of CRs. Explanations within the first class assume that the primary mechanism of CR determination remains the transfer of the reflex from the US to the CS; they deal with deviations from identity between CR and UR by allowing other factors to modify the observed CR. Explanations within the second class propose mechanisms other than simple transfer of control of the UR.

SUBSTITUTION-TRANSFER ACCOUNTS Three broad proposals for influences which might conceal the identity of the CR and UR can be distinguished: instrumental reinforcement contigencies, factors affecting processing of the CS, and factors affecting processing of the US.

1. *Instrumental reinforcement* A common account of CR-UR dissimilarity has been to attribute the offending behaviors to instrumental contingencies embedded within the Pavlovian experiment. For instance, motor behaviors often accompanying salivary CRs have been attributed to adventitious reinforcement (Konorski 1967) or to the utility of those behaviors in modifying receipt of the US (Perkins 1968). In some cases this attribution is based more on the assumption that such behaviors could not be conditioned in a Pavlovian fashion than on any experimental evidence. But in other instances, instrumental contingencies have been shown to shape the form of the CR (Prokasy 1965).

Holland (1979) recently examined the contribution of instrumental contingencies to the CS-determination of the CR to signals of food in rats. In that case, manipulations designed to minimize the involvement of instrumental contingencies proved to have little effect on the behavior patterns uniquely evoked by auditory and visual signals of food. For instance, the imposition of an omission contingency in which food was deleted if a particular response occurred in the CS food interval disrupted any adventitious response-food relation but had little effect upon the behavior. Consequently, some instances of variation in form of the CR seem not to be attributable to instrumental contingencies.

2. *Influence of CS processing* One way in which processing of the CS might modify the CR is for the CS to directly affect performance. For instance, if the CS evokes an orienting response, the actually observed CR might result from an interaction between that response and the "true CR" (see Guthrie 1940). This possibility is especially attractive in accounting for CRs which are like the original orienting response to the CS, as in the case of some CRs anticipatory to food in rats (Holland 1977, 1980a).

Relatedly, the occurrence of a CR component might depend upon the presence of particular stimulus "supports" during testing (Tolman 1932). For instance, chewing, swallowing, or pecking might not occur as part of the CR to an auditory signal for food because there is nothing to chew, swallow, or peck when the CR is evoked. In support of this possibility, some experimenters have found such components of the CR when "chewable" CSs have been employed (Boakes et al 1978, Breland & Breland 1966, Peterson et al 1972, Stiers & Silberberg 1974).

One way to assess the possibility that variations in CR form are generated in performance rather than in learning is to provide stimulus supports in testing which were absent in learning. For instance, Holland (1977) examined rats' behavior during an auditory-visual compound stimulus after conditioning one of the elements. If the differential behaviors that these components evoke when conditioned alone are due to different stimulus supports, then responding to the compound should be the same whichever of the components had been conditioned. But responding to the compound proved dependent upon whether the auditory or visual component had been paired with food. Similarly, the addition of a discrete "peckable" keylight during a tone previously paired with food does not convert the response to that tone into pecking in pigeons (Schwartz 1973). At least in some cases then, CS-determination of the CR is not solely a performance effect.

Learned changes in CS processing may also generate CR variation. Several experiments have shown that initially unconditioned orienting responses to a CS can be enhanced by appetitive conditioning (e.g. Holland 1977, 1979, 1980a, Patten & Rudy 1967), perhaps as a result of increasing attention to the stimulus. These learned changes in orienting responses might then interact with a "true" UR-like CR.

3. *US processing* An inherent CR-UR similarity can also be preserved if it is recognized that nominal USs may be processed as multifeatured events, each governing components of the response that can be independently transferred to the CS. For instance, swallowing might not be transferred to a CS signaling food because that component occurs too distant temporally from the CS. In fact, there is evidence suggesting that altering the temporal relation of various UR components to the CS can alter the CR form. Conditioned licking, swallowing, or jaw movement have been observed when the US is delivered directly into the oral cavity rather than into a dish (Kierylowicz et al 1968, Debold et al 1965, Gormezano 1972). Differences might also be anticipated in CR form as a function of variations in the CS-US interval since different US components might occur in optimal temporal relation to the CS. Even extreme cases of CR-UR dissimilarity might occur in this way. For instance, some pharmacological URs appear to be multiphasic (Domjan & Gillan 1977, Domjan et al 1980, Wikler 1973), thus including the changes labeled "compensatory" or "opposite" when they occur as CRs. Solomon & Corbit (1974) have proposed that many USs evoke both a primary and a compensatory or opponent secondary reaction. Either of these might be conditioned to antecedent CSs.

It is less obvious that consideration of US components would account for CS-dependent differences in CR form. At least some CSs evoking very different CRs are apparently associated with the same US features. For instance, Blanchard & Honig (1976) and Holland (1977) noted that pretraining of a CS that evokes one response allows that CS to block conditioning of another CS that evokes quite a different response. These findings suggest that those CSs are associated with similar components of the US.

A similar conclusion can be drawn from the fact that two CSs which evoke different CRs can nevertheless serve equally as reinforcers to condition a common response to a third stimulus (e.g. Holland 1977, 1980b, Rescorla 1980a). For example, tones and lights paired with food in pigeons evoke different responses but both condition pecking when they in turn are signaled by a keylight (Nairne & Rescorla 1981, Rashotte et al 1977).

Overall, sufficient discrepancies remain between the CR and the UR to make a simple reflex transfer account of performance implausible.

NONTRANSFER ACCOUNTS Some investigators have rejected simple reflex transfer as a principal determinant of the CR. Tolman (1932), for instance, assumed that conditioning involves the acquisition of an expectancy not linked to particular behaviors. Behaviors were said to be "appropriate" to the signaling and physical characteristics of the CS and US. Others (e.g. Anokhin 1974) have suggested that organisms evolve CRs of a form that reflects adaptive preparation for the impending US. For instance, CRs that act to maximize the value of the US might be of adaptive value to the species and hence be selected in evolution. Such a CR might be based on a preorganized behavior pattern, but not necessarily that of the UR. Unfortunately, such accounts permit CR-UR dissimilarity but fail to provide an explicit set of rules for predicting the CR form.

Another approach assumes that the CS acquires motivational value as a consequence of its relation to the US. For instance, two-process theories of instrumental learning allow animals to act instrumentally so as to modulate receipt of the CS advantageously (Culler 1938). Similarly, Mowrer (1947) has suggested that animals react to a valued CS in a "consummatory" fashion appropriate to the nature of that event rather than in preparation of an impending US. For instance, rats presented with another rat as a signal for the delivery of food do not bite or chew the signal rat but instead engage in social contact (Timberlake & Grant 1975); rats bury or barricade a prod previously delivering shock rather than freezing in its presence (Pinel et al 1980, Terlecki et al 1979); and chicks peck a key signaling a heat lamp rather than engaging in UR-like behaviors (Wasserman 1973b, but see Hogan 1974). This attention to the acquired value of the CS in influencing CR form might be especially useful in dealing with the frequent observation that animals approach signals positively correlated with food (Hearst 1975) or negatively correlated with shock (LeClerc & Reberg 1980), but withdraw from signals positively correlated with shock (LeClerc & Reberg 1980) or negatively correlated with food (Wasserman et al 1974).

Some researchers have suggested that the CS comes to elicit not a replica of the UR but a more complex set of naturally occurring action patterns appropriate to the US. For instance, stimuli paired with food might release a whole sequentially organized action pattern normally involved in food procuring and consumption, not just those portions of the pattern evoked by the US (Hogan 1974, Woodruff & Williams 1976). Behaviors of dogs conditioned with a food US have been observed to resemble food-procuring activities (begging, hunting, sign-pointing) which occur naturally in those animals (Jenkins et al 1978). Similarly, such normally occurring behaviors as locomotion and contact occur in rats (Hyde & Trapold 1975, Patten & Rudy 1967) and pigeons (Woodruff & Williams 1976) even when care is taken to exclude those behaviors from the UR by direct delivery of the US into the mouth. And burying of a shock prod may reflect previously organized defensive activities (Pinel et al 1980).

These CRs might be said to represent naturally occurring (i.e. unconditioned) responses to the anticipation of the US. The CR form might well differ since integrated acts of consumption and of expectation of the US are often quite different. This "natural signals" notion is satisfying in that it captures some of the spirit of both a reflex-transfer theory (since unconditioned behavior patterns come under the control of arbitrary stimuli) and expectancy theories. But there remains the problem of explaining the origin of such "naturally occurring" responses, which may themselves be conditioned responses. Nor is it clear that this notion by itself could deal with the range of CS-determined CRs. But it clearly deserves further theoretical development.

In summary, a varied range of mechanisms has been proposed to account for the richness of behavior observed as CRs. Surprisingly, however, there have been few empirical attempts to evaluate these accounts. It seems unlikely that any one mechanism determines the nature of conditioned responding in all preparations or even for all components of the CR in a single preparation. But a good deal of empirical work remains to identify and evaluate the various contributors.

IMPLICATIONS OF CR VARIATION FOR MEASURING ASSOCIATIONS

The experimenter must select a behavioral measure of association. Although investigators in the reflex tradition have placed substantial constraints on which responses are acceptable for this purpose, most workers have been quite liberal in letting almost any behavior change count. Moreover, there is little evidence to suggest that responses meeting stringent criteria show qualitatively different phenomena than do more liberal measures. For that reason some authors (e.g. Rescorla & Holland 1976) have advised against adopting such criteria.

But regardless of this decision, the occurrence of variation in CR form may prove troublesome for the assessment of learning. The problem is that apparently quantitative variations in responding as a function of some independent variable may be partially the consequence of variation in response form. For instance, if the CR form varies as a function of the CS-US interval, the assessment of how that variable affects associative strength becomes quite complicated. In the extreme case, a particular manipulation might generate a CR of a form not detected by the experimenter. Perhaps more common, various components of the CR may show quantitatively different CS-US interval functions (see Holland 1980b).

Elsewhere (Rescorla & Holland 1976) we suggested that looking at measures of association other than the response-evoking power of the CS may be helpful in such cases. One can ask about the ability of a CS to serve as a second-order reinforcer or to block conditioning of another stimulus. Such techniques have been used to identify CS-US interval functions independently of differences in response form (Holland 1980b), to compare conditioning of stimuli that evoke different behaviors (Holland 1977), and to detect conditioning to stimuli that may not evoke a measured response (Blanchard & Honig 1976, Holland & Rescorla 1975a, Nairne & Rescorla 1981).

Determination of Response Form: Instrumental Learning

Typically, the form of the instrumentally trained response has been viewed as arbitrarily selected by the experimenter. Indeed, this arbitrary nature of the response has been suggested as a way in which instrumental learning differs from Pavlovian conditioning (e.g. Rescorla & Solomon 1967, Skinner 1938). However, a substantial number of recent investigations show that this selection is not entirely arbitrary. Many cases of "constraints on learning" reflect the extent to which the form of the instrumental response is governed by features of the experimental situation other than the specific response-reinforcer relation it arranged. We indicate here some of those "constraints" on the form of the instrumental response.

One contributor may be the general likelihood of the response because of the presence of appropriate stimulus supports or motivational state. Some responses that are difficult to train instrumentally are more tractable if appropriate supports are provided. For instance, Pearce et al (1978) found scratching to be easier to train in rats if an itch was continuously present because of an abrasive collar. Relatedly, Sevenster (1973) found it difficult to train male sticklebacks to bite a rod for the opportunity to court a female, even though that response was easily trained with the opportunity to fight another male as the reinforcer. But Sevenster noted that the mere placement of a female in the situation inhibited biting.

Similarly, anticipation of a reinforcer on the basis of either response-reinforcer or Pavlovian associations can affect the likelihood of various instrumental responses. For instance, an animal that is fearful in anticipation of shock may become inactive, with quite different consequences for various responses which the experimenter might wish to train instrumentally. Likewise, implicit pairings of a rod with presentation of a female stickleback apprently results in Pavlovian conditioning of courting behaviors directed toward the rod, behaviors which are incompatible with the aggressive biting response being trained. A similar account has been given of the difficulty of training face washing in hamsters with food reward (Anderson & Shettleworth 1977, Shettleworth 1975, 1978). The historically important observations of Breland & Breland (1966) also point to the importance of anticipation of the reinforcer in interfering with the display of experimenter-selected responses. Of course, behaviors engendered in these ways need not interfere with instrumental responding; they can also artificially inflate it. Some authors have even argued that many easily trained instrumental responses are in fact generated primarily by Pavlovian contingencies (e.g. Moore 1973).

The degree to which we observe these nonarbitrary influences depends, of course, on how broadly we define our response class; but they may be there even when not noticed. For instance, when a broad class of behaviors is accepted by the instrumental contingency, subjects may nevertheless emit highly stereotyped behavior. Pigeons that are reinforced for any peck topography exceeding some minimum force tend to limit their pecks to particular forms and durations, depending upon the nature of the reinforcer (Schwartz & Williams 1972, Wolin 1968, but see Ziriax & Silberberg 1978). Similarly, the reinforcement of grooming movements can result in changes in the distribution of those movements or in the display of cursory versions of the movement (e.g. Annable & Wearden 1979, Hogan 1964, Konorski 1967, Shettleworth 1975, Thorndike 1911). Finally, even when the class of reinforced behaviors is broad without limit, as in the case of fixed time or temporal conditioning procedures, species-specific stereotyped response patterns nevertheless may develop (e.g. Anderson & Shettleworth 1977, Staddon & Simmelhag 1971). In this context it is worth noting that how broadly one defines the response class will determine to a large extent the degree to which he runs afoul of "constraints" upon instrumental performance. A broadly defined response class will allow a wider range of responses to meet the same instrumental response requirement regardless of such constraints.

As in Pavlovian conditioning, these influences on the form of the instrumental response seem varied. Shettleworth & Juergensen (1980) have noted that the best predictor of the trainability of various responses is the casual observation as to whether those responses are contained in the behavior sequences which are functional in obtaining the goal object in the wild. This is comparable to Jenkin's suggestion about "natural signals" for the Pavlovian case. In both instances, a set of naturally occurring antecedent behaviors is generated by anticipation of reinforcement. Perhaps the embedded Pavlovian contingencies generate such behaviors in the manner described by Jenkins and then instrumental contingencies work on those generated behaviors. But as in the case of Pavlovian conditioning, there is relatively little experimentation that successfully addresses these possibilities.

CONCLUSIONS

This review has provided a three-issue framework in which to think about infrahuman learning. It has discussed those issues as they arise in the two commonly studied learning paradigms: learning the relations between two events, and learning the relations between the organism's behavior and other events. The best studied of those issues is the circumstances that produce learning. Organisms show considerable sophistication in their representations of events and relations among those events; in some cases we have available detailed theoretical treatments which capture that sophistication. Less well developed is our understanding of the second issue, what is the content of that learning. Although what is learned is a continuing central theme in studies of learning, potentially workable approaches to that question are just now beginning to be explored systematically. In most ways the third issue, how does learning map into performance, is the least well understood. Modern theory development, especially in Pavlovian conditioning, has progressed at a rapid pace precisely because it has postponed the issue of how learning is exhibited in performance. Now that issue must be addressed for both Pavlovian conditioning and instrumental learning.

As important as the particular empirical and theoretical developments are, perhaps more important is the change in tone which has taken place in the study of infrahuman learning. The field has undergone a liberalization partially induced by activities in adjacent fields and reflected in the language in which theories are described. Although the field continues to demand a close tie between theory and data, as well as to emphasize simplicity and parsimony in its theories, modern views of learning see the organism as storing information about its world and deriving its performance from that information. Moreover, the organism is increasingly viewed as storing a wide variety of kinds of information and using a broad range of formats for that storage. Yet the field strives to understand that range in terms of simple associative processes. To a large degree the recent history of the field encourages the continued supposition that a rich representation of the world can be encoded in terms of specifiable elementary associative processes.

Literature Cited

Adams, C., Dickinson, A. 1981. Actions and habits: variations in associative representations during instrumental learning. See Spear & Miller, in press.

Amiro, T. W., Bitterman, M. E. 1980. Second-order appetitive conditioning in goldfish. *J. Exp. Psychol.: Anim. Behav. Proc.* 6:41–48

Anderson, M. C., Shettleworth, S. J. 1977. Behavioral adaptation to fixed-interval and fixed-time food delivery in golden hamsters. *J. Exp. Anal. Behav.* 27: 33–49

Anisman, H. 1975. Time-dependent variations in aversively motivated behaviors: nonassociative effects of cholinergic and catecholaminergic activity. *Psychol. Rev.* 82:359–85

Anisman, H., deCatanzaro, D., Remington, G. 1978. Escape performance following exposure to inescapable shock: deficits in motor response maintenance. *J. Exp. Psychol.: Anim. Behav. Proc.* 4:197–218

Annable, A., Wearden, J. H. 1979. Grooming movements as operants in the rat. *J. Exp. Anal. Behav.* 32:297–304

Anokhin, P. K. 1974. *Biology and Neurophysiology of the Conditioned Reflex and its Role in Adaptive Behavior.* New York: Pergamon. 574 pp.

Badia, P., Harsh, J., Abbott, B. 1979. Choosing between predictable and unpredictable shock conditions: Data and theory. *Psychol. Bull.* 86:1107–31

Baker, A. G. 1976. Learned irrelevance and learned helplessness: rats learn that stimuli, reinforcers, and responses are uncorrelated. *J. Exp. Psychol.: Anim. Behav. Proc.* 2:130–41

Baker, A. G., Mackintosh, N. J. 1979. Preexposure to the CS alone, US alone, or CS and US uncorrelated: latent inhibition, blocking by context, or learned irrelevance? *Learn. Motiv.* 10:278–94

Best, M. R. 1975. Conditioned and latent inhibition in taste-aversion learning: clarifying the role of learned safety. *J. Exp. Psychol.: Anim. Behav. Proc.* 1:97–113

Bindra, D. 1974. A motivational view of learning, performance, and behavior modification. *Psychol. Rev.* 81:199–213

Bitterman, M. E. 1975. The comparative analysis of learning: Are the laws of learning the same in all animals. *Science* 188:699–709

Blanchard, R., Honig, W. K. 1976. Surprise value of food determines its effectiveness as a reinforcer. *J. Exp. Psychol.: Anim. Behav. Proc.* 2:67–74

Blanchard, R. J., Blanchard, D. C. 1970. Dual mechanisms in passive avoidance I. *Psychon. Sci.* 19:1–2

Boakes, R. A., Poli, M., Lockwood, M. J., Goodall, G. 1978. A study of misbehavior: token reinforcement in the rat. *J. Exp. Anal. Behav.* 29:115–34

Bolles, R. C. 1970. Species-specific defense reactions and avoidance learning. *Psychol. Rev.* 77:32–48

Bolles, R. C. 1972. Reinforcement, expectancy, and learning. *Psychol. Rev.* 79:394–409

Bolles, R. C., Collier, A. C. 1976. Effect of predictive cues on freezing in rats. *Anim. Learn. Behav.* 4:6–8

Bracewell, R. J., Black, A. H. 1974. The effects of restraint and noncontingent pre-shock on subsequent escape learning in the rat. *Learn. Motiv.* 5:53–69

Breland, K., Breland, M. 1966. *Animal Behavior.* New York: MacMillan. 210 pp.

Brogden, W. J. 1939. Sensory pre-conditioning. *J. Exp. Psychol.* 25:323–32

Capaldi, E. D., Myers, D. E. 1978. Resistance to satiation of consummatory and instrumental performance. *Learn. Motiv.* 9:179–201

Capaldi, E. D. 1971. Memory and learning: a sequential viewpoint. In *Animal Memory,* ed. W. K. Honig, P. H. R. James, pp. 115–54. New York: Academic. 287 pp.

Cheatle, M. D., Rudy, J. W. 1978. Analysis of second-order odor-aversion conditioning in neonatal rats: implications for Kamin's blocking effect. *J. Exp. Psychol.: Anim. Behav. Proc.* 4:237–49

Chen, J., Amsel, A. 1980. Recall (versus recognition) of taste and immunization against aversive taste anticipations based on illness. *Science* 209:831–33

Colwill, R. M., Dickinson, A. 1980a. Short-term retention of "surprising" events following different training conditions. *Anim. Learn. Behav.* 8:561–66

Colwill, R. M., Dickinson, A. 1980b. Short-term retention of "surprising" events by pigeons. *Q. J. Exp. Psychol.* 32:539–56

Crespi, L. P. 1942. Quantitative variation of incentive and performance in the white rat. *Am. J. Psychol.* 55:467–517

Culler, E. A. 1938. Recent advances in some concepts of conditioning. *Psychol. Rev.* 45:134–53

D'Amato, M. R., Safarjan, W. R., Salmon, D. 1981. Long-delay conditioning and instrumental learning: some new findings. See Spear & Miller, in press

Debold, R. C., Miller, N. E., Jensen, D. O. 1965. Effect of strength of drive determined by a new technique for appetitive conditioning of rats. *J. Comp. Physiol. Psychol.* 59:102–8

DeVilliers, P. A. 1980. Toward a quantitative theory of punishment. *J. Exp. Anal. Behav.* 33:15–25

Dickinson, A., Hall, G., Mackintosh, N. J. 1976. Surprise and the attenuation of blocking. *J. Exp. Psychol.: Anim. Behav. Proc.* 2:313–22

Dickinson, A., Mackintosh, N. J. 1979. Reinforcer specificity in the enhancement of conditioning by post-trial surprise. *J. Exp. Psychol.: Anim. Behav. Proc.* 5:162–77

Domjan, M., Gillan, D. J. 1977. Aftereffects of lithium-conditioned stimuli on consummatory behavior. *J. Exp. Psychol.: Anim. Behav. Proc.* 3:322–34

Domjan, M., Gillan, D. J., Gemberling, G. A. 1980. Aftereffects of lithium-conditioned stimuli on consummatory behavior in the presence or absence of the drug. *J. Exp. Psychol.: Anim. Behav. Proc.* 6:49–64

Doty, R. W., Giurgea, C. 1961. Conditioned reflexes established by coupling electrical excitation of two cortical areas. In *Brain Mechanisms and Learning,* ed. J. F. Delafresnaye, pp. 133–51. Oxford: Blackwell

Durlach, P. J., Rescorla, R. A. 1980. Potentiation rather than overshadowing in flavor-aversion learning: An analysis in terms of within-compound associations. *J. Exp. Psychol.: Anim. Behav. Proc.* 6:175–87

Durlach, P. J., Rescorla, R. A. 1981. *The effect of signaling the US when CS and US are uncorrelated.* Presented at Harvard Symp. Quant. Anal. Behav.

Fanselow, M. S. 1980. Signalled shock-free periods and preference for signaled shock. *J. Exp. Psychol.* 6:65–80

Frey, P. W., Sears, R. J. 1978. Model of conditioning incorporating the Rescorla-Wagner associative axiom, a dynamic attention process, and a catastrophe rule. *Psychol. Rev.* 85:321–40

Fudim, O. K. 1978. Sensory preconditioning of flavors with a formalin-produced sodium need. *J. Exp. Psychol.: Anim. Behav. Proc.* 4:276–85

Gamzu, E., Williams, D. R. 1971. Classical conditioning of a complex skeletal response. *Science* 171:923–25

Garcia, J., Koelling, R. A. 1966. Relation of cue to consequence in avoidance learning. *Psychon. Sci.* 4:123–24

Garcia, J., Kovner, R., Green, K. S. 1970. Cue properties versus palatability of flavors in avoidance learning. *Psychon. Sci.* 20:313–14

Gibbon, J., Balsam, P. 1981. Spreading association in time. In *Autoshaping and Conditioning Theory,* ed. C. M. Locurto, H. S. Terrace, J. Gibbon, pp. 219–53. New York: Academic. 313 pp.

Gillian, D. J., Domjan, M. 1977. Taste-aversion conditioning with expected versus unexpected drug treatment. *J. Exp. Psychol.: Anim. Behav. Proc.* 3:297–309

Gonzalez, R. C., Shepp, B. E. 1965. The effects of end-box placement on subsequent performance in the runway with competing responses controlled. *Am. J. Psychol.* 78:441–47

Gormezano, I. 1972. Investigations of defense and reward conditioning in the rabbit. In *Classical Conditioning II,* ed. A. H. Black, W. F. Prokasy, pp. 151–81. New York: Appleton-Century-Crofts. 497 pp.

Gormezano, I., Kehoe, E. J. 1975. Classical conditioning: Some methodological-conceptual issues. In *Handbook of Learning and Cognitive Processes,* ed. W. K. Estes, 2:143–79. Hillsdale, NJ: Erlbaum. 373 pp.

Grice, G. R. 1942. An experimental study of the gradient of reinforcement in maze learning. *J. Exp. Psychol.* 30:475–89

Groves, P. M., Thompson, R. F. 1970. Habituation: A dual process theory. *Psychol. Rev.* 77:419–50

Guthrie, E. R. 1940. Association and the law of effect. *Psychol. Rev.* 47:127–48

Hall, G., Pearce, J. M. 1979. Latent inhibition of a CS during CS-US pairings. *J. Exp. Psychol.: Anim. Behav. Proc.* 5:31–42

Hearst, E. 1975. Pavlovian conditioning and directed movements. *Psychol. Learn. Motiv.* 9:216–62

Herrnstein, R. J. 1970. On the law of effect. *J. Exp. Anal. Behav.* 13:243–66

Hogan, J. A. 1964. Operant control of preening in pigeons. *J. Exp. Anal. Behav.* 7:351–54

Hogan, J. A. 1974. Conditioned responses in Pavlovian conditioning situations. *Science* 186:156–57

Holland, P. C. 1977. Conditioned stimulus as a determinant of the form of the Pavlovian conditioned response. *J. Exp. Psychol.: Anim. Behav. Proc.* 3:77–104

Holland, P. C. 1979. Differential effects of omission contingencies on various components of Pavlovian appetitive conditioned behavior in rats. *J. Exp. Psychol.: Anim. Behav. Proc.* 5:178–93

Holland, P. C. 1980a. Influence of visual conditioned stimulus characteristics on the form of Pavlovian appetitive conditioned responding in rats. *J. Exp. Psychol.: Anim. Behav. Proc.* 6:81–97

Holland, P. C. 1980b. CS-US interval as a determinant of the form of Pavlovian appetitive conditioned responses. *J. Exp. Psychol.: Anim. Behav. Proc.* 6:155–74

Holland, P. C. 1980c. Second-order conditioning with and without unconditioned stimulus presentation. *J. Exp. Psychol.: Anim. Behav. Proc.* 6:238–50

Holland, P. C., Rescorla, R. A. 1975a. Second-order conditioning with food unconditioned stimulus. *J. Comp. Physiol. Psychol.* 88:459–67

Holland, P. C., Rescorla, R. A. 1975b. The effect of two ways of devaluing the unconditioned stimulus after first- and second-order appetitive conditioning. *J. Exp. Psychol.: Anim. Behav. Proc.* 1:355–63

Holland, P. C., Ross, R. T. 1981. Within-compound associations in serial compound conditioning. *J. Exp. Psychol.: Anim. Behav. Proc.* 7:228–41

Holland, P. C., Straub, J. J. 1979. Differential effects of two ways of devaluing the Unconditioned Stimulus after Pavlovian appetitive conditioning. *J. Exp. Psychol.: Anim. Behav. Proc.* 5:65–78

Holman, E. W. 1975. Some conditions for the dissociation of consummatory and instrumental behavior in rats. *Learn. Motiv.* 6:358–66

Holman, E. W. 1980. Irrelevant-incentive learning with flavors in rats. *J. Exp. Psychol.: Anim. Behav. Proc.* 6:126–36

Horn, G., Hinde, R. A. 1970. *Short-term Changes in Neural Activity and Behavior.* Cambridge: Cambridge Univ. Press. 628 pp.

Hyde, T. S., Trapold, M. A. 1975. Effects of reinforcement-paired stimuli on general activity. *Anim. Learn. Behav.* 4:282–86

Irwin, J., Suissa, A., Anisman, H. 1980. Differential effects of inescapable shock on escape performance and discrimination learning in a water escape task. *J. Exp. Psychol.: Anim. Behav. Proc.* 6:21–40

Jackson, R. L., Alexander, J. H., Maier, S. F. 1980. Learned helplessness, inactivity, and associative deficits: Effects of inescapable shock on response choice escape learning. *J. Exp. Psychol.: Anim. Behav. Proc.* 6:1–20

James, J. H., Wagner, A. R. 1980. One-trial overshadowing: evidence of distributive processing. *J. Exp. Psychol.: Anim. Behav. Proc.* 6:188–205

Jenkins, H. M. 1977. Sensitivity of different response systems to stimulus-reinforcer and response-reinforcer relations. In *Operant-Pavlovian Interactions,* ed. H. Davis, H. M. B. Hurwitz, pp. 47–66. Hillsdale, NJ: Erlbaum. 327 pp.

Jenkins, H. M., Barnes, R. A., Barrera, F. J. 1981. Why autoshaping depends on trial spacing. See Gibbon & Balsam 1981, pp. 254–85

Jenkins, H. M., Barrera, F. J., Ireland, C., Woodside, B. 1978. Signal-centered action patterns of dogs in appetitive classical conditioning. *Learn. Motiv.* 9:272–96

Jenkins, H. M., Shattuck, D. 1980. *Reexamination of contingencies in classical conditioning.* Presented at Psychon. Soc. meet., St. Louis

Kamin, L. J. 1965. Temporal and intensity characteristics of the conditioned stimulus. See Prokasy 1965, pp. 118–47

Kamin, L. J. 1968. Attention-like processes in classical conditioning. *Miami Symp. Predict. Behav.: Aversive Stimul.,* ed. M. R. Jones, pp. 9–32. Coral Gables, Fla: Univ. Miami Press. 145 pp.

Kamin, L. J. 1969. Predictability, surprise, attention, and conditioning. In *Punishment and Aversive Behavior,* ed. B. Campbell, R. Church, pp. 279–98. New York: Appleton-Century-Crofts. 597 pp.

Kamin, L. J. Gaioni, S. J. 1974. Compound conditioned emotional response conditioning with differentially salient elements in rats. *J. Comp. Physiol. Psychol.* 87:591–97

Kehoe, E. J., Gibbs, C. M., Garcia, E., Gormezano, I. 1979. Associative transfer and stimulus selection in classical conditioning of the rabbit's nictitating membrane response to serial compound CSs. *J. Exp. Psychol.: Anim. Behav. Proc.* 5:1–18

Keller, R. J., Ayres, J. J. B., Mahoney, W. J. 1977. Brief versus extended exposure to truly random control procedures. *J. Exp. Psychol.: Anim. Behav. Proc.* 3:53–65

Kierylowicz, H., Soltysik, S., Divac, I. 1968. Conditioned reflexes reinforced by direct and indirect food presentation. *Acta Biol. Exp.* 28:1–10

Kimmel, H. D. 1966. Inhibition of the unconditioned response in classical conditioning. *Psychol. Rev.* 73:232–40

Konorski, J. 1948. *Conditioned Reflexes and Neuron Organization.* Cambridge: Cambridge Univ. Press. 277 pp.

Konorski, J. 1967. *Integrative Activity of the Brain.* Chicago: Univ. Chicago Press. 531 pp.

Krane, R. V., Wagner, A. R. 1975. Taste-aversion learning with a delayed-shock US: Implications for the "Generality of the laws of learning". *J. Comp. Physiol. Psychol.* 88:882–89

Kremer, E. F. 1978. The Rescorla-Wagner model: losses in associative strength in compound conditioned stimuli. *J. Exp. Psychol.: Anim. Behav. Proc.* 4:22–36

Kremer, E. F. 1979. Effect of posttrial episodes on conditioning in compound conditioned stimuli. *J. Exp. Psychol.: Anim. Behav. Proc.* 5:130–41

Kremer, E. F., Specht, T., Allen, R. 1980. Attenuation of blocking with the omission of a delayed US. *Anim. Learn. Behav.* 8:609–16

Krieckhaus, E. E., Wolf, G. 1968. Acquisition of sodium by rats: interaction of innate mechanisms and latent learning. *J. Comp. Physiol. Psychol.* 65:197–201

Lamb, M. R., Riley, D. A. 1981. Effects of element arrangement on the processing of compound stimuli in pigeons (*Columba livia*). *J. Exp. Psychol.: Anim. Behav. Proc.* 7:45–58

LeClerc, R., Reberg, D. 1980. Sign-tracking in aversive conditioning. *Learn. Motiv.* 11:302–17

Lett, B. T. 1975. Long delay learning in the T-maze. *Learn. Motiv.* 6:80–90

Lett, B. T. 1980. Taste potentiates color-sickness associations in pigeons and quail. *Anim. Learn. Behav.* 8:193–98

Lewis, D. J. 1969. Sources of experimental amnesia. *Psychol. Rev.* 76:461–72

Lewis, D. J. 1976. A cognitive approach to experimental amnesia. *Am. J. Psychol.* 89:51–80

Leyland, C. M. 1977. Higher order autoshaping. *Q. J. Exp. Psychol.* 29:607–19

Liddell, H. S. 1942. The conditioned reflex. In *Comparative Psychology,* ed. F. A. Moss, pp. 247–96. New York: Prentice-Hall. 529 pp.

Lieberman, D. A., McIntosh, D. C., Thomas, G. V. 1979. Learning when reward is delayed: A marking hypothesis. *J. Exp. Psychol.: Anim. Behav. Proc.* 5:224–42

LoLordo, V. M. 1979. Selective associations. In *Mechanisms of Learning and Motivation,* ed. A. Dickinson, R. A. Boakes, pp. 367–98. Hillsdale, NJ: Erlbaum. 468 pp.

LoLordo, V. M., Jacobs, W. J., Foree, D. D. 1975. *Failure to block control by a relevant stimulus.* Presented at Ann. Meet. Psychon. Soc., Denver

Loucks, R. B. 1935. The experimental delimitation of neural structures essential for learning: The attempt to condition striped muscle responses to faradization of the signoid gyri. *J. Psychol.* 1:5–44

Lubow, R. E. 1973. Latent inhibition. *Psychol. Bull.* 79:398–407

Mackintosh, N. J. 1971. An analysis of overshadowing and blocking. *Q. J. Exp. Psychol.* 23:118–25

Mackintosh, N. J. 1973. Stimulus selection: learning to ignore stimuli that predict no change in reinforcement. In *Constraints on Learning,* ed. R. A. Hinde, J. Stevenson-Hinde, pp. 75–100. New York: Academic. 488 pp.

Mackintosh, N. J. 1974. *The Psychology of Animal Learning.* New York: Academic. 730 pp.

Mackintosh, N. J. 1975. A theory of attention: variations in the associability of stimuli with reinforcement. *Psychol. Rev.* 82:276–98

Mackintosh, N. J., Dickinson, A. 1979. Instrumental (Type II) conditioning. See LoLordo 1979, pp. 143–69

Mackintosh, N. J., Reese, B. 1979. One-trial overshadowing. *Q. J. Exp. Psychol.* 31:519–26

Maier, S. F., Jackson, R. L. 1979. Learned helplessness: All of us were right (and wrong): Inescapable shock has multiple effects. In *The Psychology of Learning and Motivation,* ed. G. H. Bower, 13:155–218. New York: Academic. 426 pp.

Maier, S. F., Seligman, M. E. P. 1976. Learned helplessness: Theory and evidence. *J. Exp. Psychol.: General* 105:3–46

Maki, W. S. 1979. Pigeons' short-term memories for surprising vs. expected reinforcement and nonreinforcement. *Anim. Learn. Behav.* 7:31–37

Maki, W. S., Leith, C. R. 1973. Shared attention in pigeons. *J. Exp. Anal. Behav.* 19:345–49

Maki, W. S., Riley, D. A., Leith, C. R. 1976. The role of test stimuli in matching to compound samples in pigeons. *Anim. Learn. Behav.* 4:13–21

Marlin, N. A., Sullivan, J. M., Berk, A. M., Miller, R. R. 1979. Preference for information about intensity of signaled tail-shock. *Learn. Motiv.* 10:85–97

Marshall, B. S., Gokey, D. S., Green, P. L., Rashotte, M. E. 1979. Spatial location of first- and second-order visual conditioned stimuli in second-order conditioning of the pigeon's keypeck. *Bull. Psychon. Soc.* 13:133–36

Miller, N. E. 1935. A reply to "sign-gestalt or conditioned reflex?" *Psychol. Rev.* 42:280–92

Miller, N. E. 1963. Some reflections on the law of effect produce a new alternative to drive reduction. *Nebr. Symp. Motiv. 1963,* ed. M. R. Jones, pp. 65–112. Lincoln: Univ. Nebr. Press. 202 pp.

Miller, R. R., Balaz, M. A. 1981. Differences in adaptiveness between classically conditioned responses and instrumentally acquired responses. In *Memory Mechanisms in Animal Behavior,* ed. N. S. Spear, R. Miller. Hillsdale, NJ: Erlbaum. In press

Miller, R. R., Springer, A. D. 1973. Amnesia, consolidation, and retrieval. *Psychol. Rev.* 80:69–79

Miller, R. R., Springer, A. D. 1974. Implications of recovery from experimental amnesia. *Psychol. Rev.* 81:470–73

Moore, B. 1973. The role of directed Pavlovian reactions in simple instrumental learning in the pigeon. See Mackintosh 1973, pp. 159–88

Morgan, M. J. 1974. Resistance to satiation. *Anim. Behav.* 22:449–66

Morrison, G. R., Collyer, R. 1974. Taste-mediated conditioned aversion to an exteroceptive stimulus following LiCl poisoning. *J. Comp. Physiol. Psychol.* 86:51–55

Mowrer, O. H. 1947. On the dual nature of learning. *Harv. Educ. Rev.* 17:102–48

Mowrer, O. H. 1960. *Learning Theory and Behavior.* New York: Wiley. 555 pp.

Nairne, J. S., Rescorla, R. A. 1981. Second-order conditioning with diffuse auditory reinforcers in the pigeon. *Learn. Motiv.* 12:65–91

Palmerino, C. C., Rusiniak, K. W., Garcia, J. 1980. Flavor-illness aversions: the peculiar role of odor and taste in memory for poison. *Science* 208:753–55

Patten, R. L., Rudy, J. W. 1967. Orienting during classical conditioning: acquired versus unconditioned responding. *Psychon. Sci.* 7:27–28

Pavlov, I. P. 1927. *Conditioned Reflexes.* London: Oxford Univ. Press. 430 pp.

Pearce, J. M., Colwill, R. M., Hall, G. 1978. Instrumental conditioning of scratching in the laboratory rat. *Learn. Motiv.* 9:255–71

Pearce, J. M., Hall, G. 1978. Overshadowing the instrumental conditioning of a lever-press response by a more valid predictor of the reinforcer. *J. Exp. Psychol.: Anim. Behav. Proc.* 4:356–67

Pearce, J. M., Hall, G. 1979. Loss of associability by a compound stimulus comprising excitatory and inhibitory elements. *J. Exp. Psychol.: Anim. Behav. Proc.* 5:19–30

Pearce, J. M., Hall, G. 1980. A model for Pavlovian learning: variations in the effectiveness of conditioned but not of unconditioned stimuli. *Psychol. Rev.* 6:532–52

Peeke, H. V. S., Hertz, M. F. 1973. *Habituation,* Vol. 1, *Behavioral Studies.* New York: Academic. 290 pp.

Perkins, C. C. 1968. An analysis of the concept of reinforcement. *Psychol. Rev.* 75:155–72

Peterson, G. B., Ackil, J. E., Frommer, G. P., Hearst, E. S. 1972. Conditioned approach and contact behavior toward signals for food or brain-stimulation reinforcements. *Science* 197:1009–11

Pfautz, P. L., Wagner, A. R. 1976. Transient variations in responding to Pavlovian conditioned stimuli have implications for the mechanism of "priming". *Anim. Learn. Behav.* 4:107–12

Pinel, J. P. J., Treit, D., Wilkie, D. M. 1980. Stimulus control of defensive burying in the rat. *Learn. Motiv.* 11:150–63

Prokasy, W. F. 1965. Classical eyelid conditioning: Experimenter operations, task demands, and response shaping. In *Classical Conditioning,* ed. W. F. Prokasy, pp. 208–25. New York: Appleton-Century-Crofts. 421 pp.

Randich, A., LoLordo, V. M. 1979. Associative and nonassociative theories of the UCS preexposure phenomenon: implications for Pavlovian conditioning. *Psychol. Bull.* 86:523–48

Rashotte, M. E., Griffin, R. W., Sisk, C. L. 1977. Second-order conditioning of the pigeon's key-peck. *Anim. Learn. Behav.* 5:25–38

Reiss, S., Wagner, A. R. 1972. CS habituation produces a "latent inhibition effect" but no active "conditioned inhibition" *Learn. Motiv.* 3:237–45

Rescorla, R. A. 1968. Probability of shock in the presence and absence of CS in fear conditioning. *J. Comp. Physiol. Psychol.* 66:1–5

Rescorla, R. A. 1971a. Variation in the effectiveness of reinforcement and nonreinforcement following prior inhibitory conditioning. *Learn. Motiv.* 2:113–23

Rescorla, R. A. 1971b. Summation and retardation tests of latent inhibition. *J. Comp. Physiol. Psychol.* 75:77–81

Rescorla, R. A. 1972. Informational variables in Pavlovian conditioning. *Psychol. Learn. Motiv.* 6:1–46

Rescorla, R. A. 1977. Pavlovian second-order conditioning: Some implications for instrumental learning. See Jenkins 1977, pp. 133–64

Rescorla, R. A. 1979. Aspects of the reinforcer learned in second-order Pavlovian conditioning. *J. Exp. Psychol.: Anim. Behav. Proc.* 5:79–95

Rescorla, R. A. 1980a. *Second-Order Conditioning.* Hillsdale, NJ: Erlbaum 120 pp.

Rescorla, R. A. 1980b. Simultaneous and successive associations in sensory preconditioning. *J. Exp. Psychol.: Anim. Behav. Proc.* 6:207–16

Rescorla, R. A. 1981. Within-signal learning in autoshaping. *Anim. Learn. Behav.* 9:245–52

Rescorla, R. A. Cunningham, C. L. 1978. Within-compound flavor associations. *J. Exp. Psychol.: Anim. Behav. Proc.* 4:267–75

Rescorla, R. A., Cunningham, C. L. 1979. Spatial contiguity facilitates Pavlovian second-order conditioning. *J. Exp. Psychol.: Anim. Behav. Proc.* 5:152–61

Rescorla, R. A., Durlach, P. J. 1981. Within-event learning in Pavlovian conditioning. See Spear & Miller, in press

Rescorla, R. A., Furrow, D. R. 1977. Stimulus similarity as a determinant of Pavlovian conditioning. *J. Exp. Psychol.: Anim. Behav. Proc.* 3:203–15

Rescorla, R. A., Holland, P. C. 1976. Some behavioral approaches to the study of learning. In *Neural Mechanisms of Learning and Memory,* ed. M. R. Rosenzweig, E. L. Bennett, pp. 165–92. Cambridge, Mass: MIT Press. 637 pp.

Rescorla, R. A., Solomon, R. L. 1967. Two-process learning theory. *Psychol. Rev.* 74:151–82

Rescorla, R. A., Wagner, A. R. 1972. A theory of Pavlovian conditioning: variations in the effectiveness of reinforcement and nonreinforcement. See Gormezano 1972, pp. 64–99

Revusky, S. H. 1968. Aversion to sucrose produced by contingent X-irradiation-temporal and dosage parameters. *J. Comp. Physiol. Psychol.* 65:17–22

Revusky, S. 1971. The role of interference in association over a delay. See Capaldi 1971, pp. 155–213

Revusky, S. H. 1977. Learning as a general process with an emphasis on data from feeding experiments. In *Food Aversion Learning,* ed. N. W. Milgram, L. Krames, T. M. Alloway, pp. 1–72. New York: Plenum. 263 pp.

Revusky, S. H., Garcia, J. 1970. Learned associations over long delays. *Psychol. Learn. Motiv.* 4:1–84

Revusky, S. H., Parker, L. A. 1976. Aversions to unflavored water and cup drinking produced by delayed sickness. *J. Exp. Psychol.: Anim. Behav. Proc.* 2:342–53

Riley, A. L., Jacobs, W., LoLordo, V. M. 1976. Drug exposure and the acquisition and retention of a taste aversion. *J. Comp. Physiol. Psychol.* 90:799–807

Rizley, R., Rescorla, R. A. 1972. Associations in second-order conditioning and sensory preconditioning. *J. Comp. Physiol. Psychol.* 81:1–11

Roberts, W. A., Grant, D. S. 1978. Interaction of sample and comparison stimuli in delayed matching to sample with the pigeon. *J. Exp. Psychol.: Anim. Behav. Proc.* 4:68–82

Rozeboom, W. W. 1958. "What is learned?" —An empirical enigma. *Psychol. Rev.* 65:22–33

Rozin, P., Kalat, J. W. 1971. Specific hungers and poison avoidance as adaptive specializations of learning. *Psychol. Rev.* 78:459–86

Rusiniak, K., Hankins, W., Garcia, J., Brett, L. 1979. Flavor-illness aversions: Potentiation of odor by taste in rats. *Behav. Neurol. Biol.* 25:1–17

Schull, J. 1979. A conditioned opponent theory of Pavlovian conditioning and habituation. *Psychol. Learn. Motiv.* 13:57–90.

Schwartz, B. 1973. Maintenance of key pecking by response-independent food presentation: The role of the modality of the signal for food. *J. Exp. Anal. Behav.* 20:17–23

Schwartz, B. 1974. On going back to nature: A review of Seligman and Hager's *Biological Boundaries of Learning. J. Exp. Anal. Behav.* 21:183–98

Schwartz, B., Williams, D. R. 1972. Two different kinds of key peck in the pigeon: some properties of responses maintained by negative and positive response-reinforcer contingencies. *J. Exp. Anal. Behav.* 18:201–16

Seligman, M. E. P. 1970. On the generality of the laws of learning. *Psychol. Rev.* 77:406–18

Sevenster, P. 1973. Incompatibility of response and reward. See Mackintosh 1973, pp. 265–84

Seward, J. P., Levy, H. 1949. Latent extinction: sign learning as a factor in extinction. *J. Exp. Psychol.* 39:660–68

Sharp, P. E., James, J. H., Wagner, A. R. 1980. Habituation of a "blocked" stimulus during Pavlovian conditioning. *Bull. Psychon. Soc.* 15:139–42

Sheffield, F. D. 1965. Relation between classical conditioning and instrumental learning. See Prokasy 1965, pp. 302–22

Sheffield, F. D. 1966. A drive-induction theory of reinforcement. In *Current Research in Motivation,* ed. R. N. Haber, pp. 98–110. New York: Holt, Rinehart & Winston

Shettleworth, S. J. 1975. Reinforcement and the organization of behavior in golden hamsters: Hunger, environment, and food reinforcement. *J. Exp. Psychol.: Anim. Behav. Proc.* 1:56–87

Shettleworth, S. J. 1978. Reinforcement and the organization of behavior in golden hamsters: Punishment of three action patterns. *Learn. Motiv.* 9:99–123

Shettleworth, S. J. 1979. Constraints on conditioning in the writings of Konorski. See LoLordo 1979, pp. 399–416

Shettleworth, S. J., Juergensen, M. R. 1980. Reinforcement and the organization of behavior in golden hamsters: Brain stimulation reinforcement for seven action patterns. *J. Exp. Psychol.: Anim. Behav. Proc.* 6:352–75

Siegel, S. 1975. Evidence from rats that morphine tolerance is a learned response. *J. Comp. Physiol. Psychol.* 89:498–506

Siegel, S. 1977. Morphine tolerance acquisition is an associative process. *J. Exp. Psychol.: Anim. Behav. Proc.* 3:1–13

Siegel, S. 1978. Tolerance to the hyperthermic effect of morphine in the rat is a learned response. *J. Comp. Physiol. Psychol.* 92:1137–49

Skinner, B. F. 1938. *The Behavior of Organisms.* New York: Appleton-Century. 457 pp.

Smith, M. C. 1968. CS-US interval and US intensity in classical conditioning of the rabbit's nictitating membrane response. *J. Comp. Physiol. Psychol.* 66:679–87

Solomon, R. L. 1980. The opponent-process theory of acquired motivation. *Am. Psychol.* 35:691–712

Solomon, R. L., Corbit, J. D. 1974. An opponent-process theory of motivation. *Psychol. Rev.* 81:119–45

Solomon, R. L., Turner, L. H. 1962. Discriminative classical conditioning in dogs paralyzed by curare can later control discriminative avoidance responses in the normal state. *Psychol. Rev.* 69:202–19

Spear, N. E. 1978. *The Processing of Memories: Forgetting and Retention.* Hillsdale, NJ: Erlbaum. 553 pp.

Spear, N. E., Miller, R., eds. 1981. *Information Processing in Animals: Memory Mechanisms.* Hillsdale, NJ: Erlbaum. In press

Spence, K. W. 1956. *Behavior Theory and Conditioning.* New Haven: Yale Univ. Press. 262 pp.

Staddon, J. E. R., Ed. 1980. *Limits to Action.* New York: Academic. 308 pp.

Staddon, J. E. R., Simmelhag, V. L. 1971. The superstition experiment. *Psychol. Rev.* 78:3–43

St. Claire-Smith, R. 1979a. The overshadowing and blocking of punishment. *Q. J. Exp. Psychol.* 4:51–61

St. Claire-Smith, R. 1979b. The overshadowing of instrumental conditioning by a stimulus that predicts reinforcement better than the response. *Anim. Learn. Behav.* 7:224–28

Stiers, M., Silberberg, A. 1974. Lever-contact responses in rats: automaintenance with and without a negative response-reinforcer dependency. *J. Exp. Anal. Behav.* 22:497–506

Sutherland, N. S., Mackintosh, N. J. 1971. *Mechanisms of Animal Discrimination Learning.* New York: Academic. 539 pp.

Terlecki, L. J., Pinel, J. P. J., Treit, D. 1979. Conditioned and unconditioned defensive burying in the rat. *Learn. Motiv.* 10:337–50

Terry, W. S. 1976. Effects of priming unconditioned stimulus representation in short-term memory on Pavlovian conditioning. *J. Exp. Psychol.: Anim. Behav. Proc.* 2:354–69

Terry, W. S., Wagner, A. R. 1975. Short-term memory for "surprising" vs. "expected" unconditioned stimuli in Pavlovian conditioning. *J. Exp. Psychol.: Anim. Behav. Proc.* 1:122–33

Thomas, E. 1971. The role of postural adjustments in conditioning of dogs with electrical stimulation of the motor cortex as the unconditioned stimulus. *J. Comp. Physiol. Psychol.* 76:187–98

Thomas, E. 1972. Excitatory and inhibitory processes in hypothalamic conditioning. In *Inhibition and Learning,* ed. R. A. Boakes, S. Halliday, pp. 359–80. New York/London: Academic. 568 pp.

Thorndike, E. L. 1911. *Animal Intelligence.* New York: Macmillan. 297 pp.

Tighe, T. J., Leaton, R. N., eds. 1976. *Habituation. Perspectives from Child Development, Animal Behavior, and Neurophysiology.* Hillsdale, NJ: Erlbaum. 356 pp.

Timberlake, W., Grant, D. L. 1975. Autoshaping in rats to the presentation of another rat predicting food. *Science* 190:690–92

Tolman, E. C. 1932. *Purposive Behavior in Animals and Men.* New York: Appleton-Century. 463 pp.

Tolman, E. C., Gleitman, H. 1949. Studies in learning and motivation. I: Equal reinforcements in both end boxes, followed by shock in one end box. *J. Exp. Psychol.* 39:810–29

Tomie, A., Murphy, A. L., Fath, S. 1980. Retardation of autoshaping following pretraining with unpredictable food: effects of changing the context between pretraining and testing. *Learn. Motiv.* 11:117–34

Wagner, A. R. 1971. Elementary associations. In *Essays in Neobehaviorism: A Memorial Volume to Kenneth W. Spence,* ed. H. H. Kendler, J. T. Spence, pp. 187–213. New York: Appleton-Century-Crofts. 345 pp.

Wagner, A. R. 1978. Expectancies and the priming of STM. In *Cognitive Processes in Animal Behavior,* ed. S. H. Hulse, H. Fowler, W. K. Honig, pp. 177–209. Hillsdale, NJ: Erlbaum. 465 pp.

Wagner, A. R. 1981. SOP: A model of automatic memory processing in animal behavior. See Spear & Miller, in press

Wagner, A. R., Mazur, J. E., Donegan, N. H., Pfautz, P. L. 1980. Evaluation of blocking and conditioned inhibition to a CS signaling a decrease in US intensity. *J. Exp. Psychol.: Anim. Behav. Proc.* 6:376–85

Wagner, A. R., Rescorla, R. A. 1972. Inhibition in Pavlovian conditioning: application of a theory. See Thomas 1972, pp. 301–36

Wagner, A. R., Rudy, J. W., Whitlow, J. W. 1973. Rehearsal in animal conditioning. *J. Exp. Psychol.* 97:407–26

Wagner, A. R., Thomas, E., Norton, T. 1967. Conditioning with electrical stimulation of the motor cortex: Evidence of a possible source of motivation. *J. Comp. Physiol. Psychol.* 64:191–99

Warner, L. H. 1932. An experimental search for the "conditioned response." *J. Genet. Psychol.* 41:91–115

Wasserman, E. A. 1973a. The effect of redundant contextual stimuli on autoshaping the pigeon's key peck. *Anim. Learn. Behav.* 1:198–201

Wasserman, E. A. 1973b. Pavlovian conditioning with heat reinforcement produces stimulus-directed pecking in chicks. *Science* 181:875–77

Wasserman, E. A., Franklin, S., Hearst, E. 1974. Pavlovian appetitive contingencies and approach US: withdrawal to conditioned stimuli in pigeons. *J. Comp. Physiol. Psychol.* 87:616–27

Wasserman, E. A., Hunter, N. B., Gutowski, K. A., Bader, S. A. 1975. Autoshaping chicks with heat reinforcement: The role of stimulus-reinforcer and response-reinforcer relations. *J. Exp. Psychol.: Anim. Behav. Proc.* 1:158–69

Weiss, J. M., Glazer, H. I., Pohorecky, L. A. 1976. Coping behavior and neurochemical changes: an alternative explanation for the original "learned helplessness" experiments. In *Animal Models in Human Psychobiology,* ed. G. Serban, A. Kling. New York: Plenum

Whitlow, J. W. 1975. Short-term memory in habituation and dishabituation. *J. Exp. Psychol.: Anim. Behav. Proc.* 1:189–206

Wickens, D. D., Nield, A. F., Tuber, D. S., Wickens, C. D. 1969. Strength, latency, and form of conditioned skeletal and autonomic responses as a function of CS-UCS intervals. *J. Exp. Psychol.* 80:165–70

Wikler, A. 1973. Conditioning of successive adaptive responses to the initial effects of drugs. *Cond. Reflexes* 8:193–210

Williams, B. A. 1975. The blocking of reinforcement control. *J. Exp. Anal. Behav.* 24:215–25

Willner, J. A. 1978. Blocking of a taste aversion by prior pairings of exteroceptive stimuli with illness. *Learn. Motiv.* 9:125–40

Wilson, C. L., Sherman, J. E., Holman, E. W. 1981. Aversion to the reinforcer differentially affects conditioned reinforcement and instrumental responding. *J. Exp. Psychol.: Anim. Behav. Proc.* 7:165–74

Wolin, B. R. 1968. Difference in manner of pecking a key between pigeons reinforced with food and with water. In *Contemporary Research in Operant Behavior,* ed. A. C. Catania, p. 286. Glenview, Ill: Scott, Foresman. 358 pp.

Woodruff, G., Williams, D. R. 1976. The associative relation underlying autoshaping in the pigeon. *J. Exp. Anal. Behav.* 26:1–14

Zamble, E. 1968. Classical conditioning of excitement anticipatory food reward: partial reinforcement. *Psychon. Sci.* 10:115–16

Zanich, M. L., Fowler, H. 1978. Transfer from Pavlovian appetitive to instrumental appetitive conditioning: signaling versus discrepancy interpretations. *J. Exp. Psychol.: Anim. Behav. Proc.* 4:37–49

Zener, K. 1937. The significance of behavior accompanying salivary secretion for theories of the conditioned response. *Am. J. Psychol.* 50:384–403

Ziriax, J. M., Silberberg, A. 1978. Discrimination and emission of different key-peck durations in the pigeon. *J. Exp. Psychol.: Anim. Behav. Proc.* 4:1–21

Ann. Rev. Psychol. 1982. 33:309–42

MENTAL RETARDATION

H. Carl Haywood

Department of Psychology and Human Development, Vanderbilt University, Nashville, Tennessee 37203

C. Edward Meyers

Neuropsychiatric Research Institute, University of California, Los Angeles, California 90024

Harvey N. Switzky

Department of Special Education, Northern Illinois University, DeKalb, Illinois 60115

CONTENTS

0066-4308/82/0201-0309$02.00

Since behavioral research on mental retardation has never before been the subject of a chapter in the *Annual Review of Psychology* we have had the entire history of this field to draw upon, but this fact has also imposed severe constraints on selection of material. Our guiding principles for including areas of study have been a combination of theoretical importance, availability of sufficient empirical research of good scientific quality to warrant at least tentative conclusions, and contemporary social significance of the issues. The broad areas and approaches under which we have organized this summary are, in a general sense: experimental psychology of mental retardation, centered chiefly on learning and cognition, with some special reference to research on severely and profoundly retarded persons; developmental issues, including considerations from the more general development of intelligence, individual differences, personality and motivation; and contemporary social problems, including environmental considerations, assessment, and education. The field has produced exciting advances in the last 20 years, but in many respects it is still in a primitive state. The most obvious conclusion drawn from our review is the pressing need for unifying theory that is specific to retarded mental development.

THEORETICAL APPROACHES TO LEARNING AND COGNITION

Prior to 1960, learning research in mental retardation was either scattered theoretically, essentially atheoretical (focused merely on demonstrating that retarded persons do not learn as efficiently as do nonretarded persons), or conducted under theoretical systems that have limited utility today (see Scott 1978 for a review).

Important theoretical models of learning processes of retarded persons that emerged during the 1960s included the attention theory of Zeaman & House (1963) and the process theories of memory of Ellis (1963, 1970) and Spitz (1963, 1966, 1973). Partly as a result of these developments, the distinction between learning and memory became both less clear and less important. During the last 10 years, empirical research in this field has been concentrated more heavily on memory processes, with memory regarded as the very essence of learning (Atkinson & Shiffrin 1968, Brown 1974, Butterfield et al 1973, Fisher & Zeaman 1973, Kail & Hagan 1977, Zeaman 1973).

The Role of Attention in Discrimination Learning

Zeaman and House and their students (Fisher & Zeaman 1973, House & Zeaman 1958, Zeaman 1973, Zeaman & House 1963, 1967) have contributed the most systematic approach to discrimination learning, motivated by a search for "process parameters" of learning that are sensitive to differences in intelligence. They have used computer simulation creatively, with their "Stat Children" generally behaving according to theoretical formulations and process parameters. They clarified the shapes of individual learning functions of subjects near the criterion of learning by using backward learning curves (Hayes 1953), thereby revealing underlying functions whose slopes did not vary with either intelligence or difficulty level. A family of ogival learning curves remained at chance levels for varying durations of practice and then rose swiftly to criterion, individual subjects being either at chance responding or at criterion. Subjects of lower mental age (MA) or intelligence quotient (IQ) stayed at chance levels longer; however, once learning began, all subjects improved at the same rate. From this information, Zeaman and House developed the hypothesis that attention is the fundamental process that influences the length of the chance responding portion of the ogive. By computer simulation they then determined that variations in the parameter related to the initial probability of attending to the relevant dimension yielded learning functions of Stat Children closely resembling those of human subjects at different levels of intelligence. Since varying learning rate parameters for acquisition and extinction of attentional and instrumental responses had no effect on length of initial chance levels of the ogives, intelligence appeared to be related to attention rather than primarily to learning itself.

The attention theory of Zeaman & House (1963) has recently evolved into an attention-retention theory (Fisher & Zeaman 1973), essentially by conceptual merger with the memory theory of Atkinson & Shiffrin (1968), reflecting the contemporary concern for memorial processes in learning. For additional details see Sperber et al (1973) and Zeaman (1973). A useful change in theory is the distinction between structural features (unmodifiable features of the organism that cannot be changed by training) and control processes (optional strategies related to the control of memorial processes that can be changed by training). Functions of retarded persons that relate to fixed components of intelligence include acquisition and extinction rate parameters (attentional and instrumental responding). Rate of forgetting from the short-term store is regarded as a structural feature, whereas memorial processes related to the rehearsal buffer are control process parameters. The Fisher-Zeaman theory is in part an effort to determine which aspects of learning and memory processes of retarded persons are structural features and which are control processes. Research based on these ideas will lead to new ways to define individual differences in mental retardation.

The Use of Mnemonic Strategies

Cognitive research in the last 15 years has been focused increasingly on the structural features of memory systems (Bransford 1979) and their associated control processes. Mildly and moderately retarded persons are inefficient at spontaneous use of mnemonic strategies; they can be taught to use these strategies when explicitly trained to do so (Paris & Haywood 1973), but unfortunately the effects of training are usually limited to the particular training context (Belmont & Butterfield 1977, Borkowski & Cavanaugh 1979, Brown 1974, 1978, Campione & Brown 1977, Kramer et al 1980, Winschel & Lawrence 1975).

Retarded persons are particularly inefficient at mnemonic strategies that require rehearsal, organization, and elaboration. Competent memorizers are able to evaluate the demands of a task and then to select appropriate strategies for solution. Brown (1974, 1975) has argued that retarded persons do this very poorly if they do it at all. These activities may involve what Flavell & Wellman (1977) have called metamemory, and what Butterfield & Belmont (1977) have called executive control, i.e. those functions whereby individuals select, sequence, evaluate, revise, or change mnemonic strategies.

Retarded persons can be taught to use appropriate mnemonic strategies to improve performance in a variety of areas including: rehearsal (Belmont & Butterfield 1971, Brown et al 1973, Butterfield et al 1973, Turnbull 1974); organization (Ashcraft & Kellas 1974, Bilsky & Evans 1970, Gerjuoy & Spitz 1966, Gerjuoy et al 1969, Luszcz & Bacharach 1975); and elaboration (Ross et al 1973, Turnure & Thurlow 1973, 1975, Wanschura & Borkowski 1974).

Campione & Brown (1977) distinguished between maintenance and generalization of trained strategies. Strategy maintenance refers only to situations in which there is no change in the experimental task used during training. Strategy generalization refers to instances that are designed to evaluate the use of a strategy on a task clearly different from the one used during training. Much of the evidence shows that mnemonic strategies can be maintained for considerable periods from 2 weeks to 1 year (Brown et al 1974, 1979, Kellas et al 1973), but evidence for generalization of such strategies is rare (Belmont et al 1978, Brown et al 1979). Evidence that training specific mnemonic skills is not sufficient for promoting generalization (Brown et al 1977, Burger et al 1980, Campione & Brown 1977) has led investigators to search for more general factors involved in memorial processes, metamemorial factors, and executive control functions.

Retarded persons are typically found to be deficient in a number of metamemorial functions, including evaluating their recall readiness (Brown & Barclay 1976), estimating their memory span (Brown et al 1977), apportioning study time appropriately (Brown & Campione 1977), and judging their feelings of knowing experience (Brown & Lawton 1977). The ability of nonretarded children to perform these metamemorial tasks improves dramatically with age (Cavanaugh & Borkowski 1979, Kreutzer et al 1975), but the much slower improvement with age of retarded children's functions in these areas suggests that there may be structural differences in the growth of metamemorial functions. Further, the evidence generally fails to show clear connections between memory awareness and cognitive processes in retarded persons. Retarded persons do not act as they say they would, suggesting absence of an obvious connection between verbalized knowledge of the memory system and mnemonic behavior in retarded persons (Cavanaugh & Borkowski 1979). The research has been generally discouraging regarding generalization of metamemorial skills (Campione & Brown 1977). While there are still too many holes in the available data to permit even partial understanding of these differences between retarded and nonretarded persons, Campione & Brown (1977) have presented a detailed model to guide future research in which they delineate the process variables that are probably necessary to facilitate generalization.

Research on learning and memory in mildly and moderately retarded persons suggests that their deficits may be due to structural differences and/or to control process variables. Retarded persons are less likely than are nonretarded persons to employ mnemonic strategies spontaneously, but they can be taught to use and maintain mnemonic strategies to increase their performance in learning tasks. Generalization rarely occurs. It remains to be seen whether or not the teaching of metamemorial strategies will lead to effective maintenance and generalization.

BEHAVIORAL RESEARCH ON SEVERELY AND PROFOUNDLY RETARDED PERSONS

The volume of behavioral research on severely and profoundly retarded persons has grown rapidly over the last 10 years (see Berkson & Landesman-Dwyer 1977 and Meyers 1978 for reviews), reflecting rapidly shifting ideas of the abilities and behavioral potential of such persons. Our limited review is focused upon characteristics and individual differences, learning and cognition, and selected behavior management problems (e.g. self-injurious behavior).

Characteristics and Individual Differences

In the absence of clear scientific or clinical information on the defining characteristics of severely and profoundly retarded persons, researchers and practitioners tend to group such persons together as if they were all alike, making replication of studies virtually impossible (Cleland & Rago 1978). Actually, severely and profoundly retarded persons differ from each other in several ways. Profoundly retarded persons (PMRs) have a higher incidence of devastating motoric, sensory, and physical handicaps (Cleland & Clark 1966, O'Connor et al 1970, O'Grady & Talkington 1977, Switzky et al 1979, Tarjan et al 1960). Younger PMRs have a lower incidence of severe behavior problems such as aggressiveness to others, hyperactivity, and self-injurious behavior compared to severely retarded persons (SMRs) and older PMRs (Eyman & Call 1977, Eyman et al 1970). Mortality rates of PMRs are almost 50% higher than those of SMRs, with mortality rates for nonambulant persons significantly higher than for ambulant persons (Balakrishnan & Wolf 1976, Cleland et al 1971, Miller 1975). According to Cleland (1979), PMRs have a higher incidence than do SMRs of: pica, mutism, self-biting, echopraxia, fecal smearing, public masturbation, delayed puberty, left-handedness, lack of self-recognition (Harris 1977), institutionalization, rumination, active seizures, abnormal EEGs, lack of socialization skills, enuresis, encopresis, high pain thresholds, and poor communication skills. There is variability in all these domains, with overlap between profound and severe retardation as well as between severe and moderate retardation (Berkson & Landesman-Dwyer 1977, Cleland et al 1978, Miller 1976). Investigators continue to search for functional subcategories of individual differences and for relationships between such subcategorical differences and differences in learning and performance.

PMRs can be divided functionally into two groups (Miller 1976): (*a*) older, less organically damaged persons who show some degree of ambulation, communication, and self-help skill, referred to as the "relative" profoundly retarded, and (*b*) persons who totally lack all adaptive behavior and exist in a medically fragile state, the "absolute" profoundly retarded. The work of Balthazar & Cleland represents the most sustained efforts to describe individual differences in the relative profoundly retarded group (Balthazar & English 1969; Balthazar & Phillips 1976, also unpublished manuscript; Naor & Balthazar 1975; Phillips & Balthazar 1976; Cleland et al 1978; Rago 1977).

Learning and Cognition

By definition, severely and profoundly retarded persons are extremely inefficient at learning, although it is clear that learning is both possible and actually common in such persons. Both policy makers and scientists need to know what are the limits of learning in SMRs and PMRs, by what processes they learn, and whether development of cognitive processes follows the same patterns and sequences as in nonretarded children.

Both classical and operant conditioning has been demonstrated in severely and profoundly retarded persons, with learning functions of SMRs resembling much more closely those of less retarded and nonretarded persons. Using operant procedures, many skills in the domains of adaptive behavior, simple academics, and vocational skill formation have been developed in the repertoires of SMRs and some PMRs. There is evidence that many severely and profoundly retarded children go through the same stages of cognitive development in the same order as do nonretarded children, differing in rate as well as the ultimate ceiling (Weisz & Zigler 1979), with the possible exception of those who suffer from demonstrable and pronounced brain injury.

CLASSICAL CONDITIONING The experimental literature in classical conditioning (Estes 1970, Ross & Ross 1973) generally fails to support clear relationships between acquisition rate and intelligence in retarded persons, although nonretarded persons show faster rates of extinction than do retarded persons of the same age.

Ross & Ross (1973) have argued that organically damaged retarded persons may perform at levels comparable to nonorganically retarded and nonretarded persons if conditioning parameters are varied, and that the "optimal" conditioning situation may vary with the central nervous system integrity of the subjects. Ross and his colleagues have shown that the classical conditioning of eyelid responses in PMRs does vary with the parameters of the conditioning situation (Guminski & Ross 1976, Ross 1972, Ross & Ross 1973, 1975). When they compared the performance of PMRs in trace and delay classical eyelid conditioning, the PMRs showed good acquisition in the delay conditioning and very poor acquisition in trace conditioning, while nonretarded adults (Ross & Ross 1971) showed equal efficacy of trace and delay conditioning. Ross & Ross (1975) favored an explanation based on the stimulus trace decay hypothesis of Ellis (1963), which assumes that a hypothetical stimulus trace originating with the onset of the conditioned stimulus decays more rapidly in the central nervous system of PMRs than in others.

OPERANT CONDITIONING Operant conditioning has been demonstrated both in absolute PMRs and in relative PMRs, as well as in SMRs. Reviewing operant conditioning in nonambulant PMR children and adolescents, Landesman-Dwyer & Sackett (1978) concluded: (*a*) operant conditioning in this group is not similar to that of nonhandicapped persons except at the most molar level, i.e. the simple fact that acquisition and extinction occur (Fuller 1949, Deiker & Bruno 1976); (*b*) individuals have a very limited response repertoire characterized often by very low rates of responding (2 to 3 per hour), which may require extensive shaping or classical conditioning before operant conditioning may proceed (Rice 1968); (*c*) effects of reinforcing agents are inconsistent (O'Grady 1975), i. e. "spontaneous extinction" may occur, after which attempts at reconditioning are fruitless (Rice & McDaniel 1966); and (*d*) there is great selectivity to reinforcing events, suggesting greater awareness of the environment than was previously believed (Rice et al 1967).

In relative PMRs and in SMRs, operant conditioning methods are highly effective (Berkson & Landesman-Dwyer 1977, Estes 1970, Spradlin & Girardeau 1966). Many studies document how readily the adaptive behavior of these more competent persons can be substantially increased (Berkson & Landesman-Dwyer 1977, Favell et al 1980, Gruber et al 1979, Matson & Earnhart 1981, Porterfield et al 1980, Thompson et al 1979, Tucker & Berry 1980).

COGNITIVE DEVELOPMENT Theorists in mental retardation disagree on whether the sequences of cognitive development described by Piaget are indeed universal. Zigler (1969) has argued that both retarded and nonretarded children go through the same stages in the same sequence, but that retarded children develop more slowly and reach a lower ceiling. It is not clear whether SMRs and PMRs show the same sequence of developmental stages, or whether in these groups prerequisite cognitive structures must be operational before efficient and successful training of skill domains is possible. This controversy has centered around the relationship of the presence and acquisition of stages of the sensorimotor period to language acquisition (Kahn 1975, Mahoney et al 1980, Sailor et al 1973). Rogers (1977) found that the reproducibility and scalability of items in the sensorimotor period in PMRs was predominantly in the order Piaget had suggested for nonhandicapped children. Wohlhueter & Sindberg (1975) found three patterns of sensorimotor development of object constancy in institutionalized PMR children: (*a*) plateau—little change over time in cognitive development; (*b*) variable—frequent upward and downward movement over time; and (*c*) upward—an overall upward trend in cognitive development. The majority of the "variable" group had EEG abnormalities and those in the "plateau" group carried diagnoses that suggested substantial brain injury; mild brain injury or Down's syndrome made up the "upward" group. This work suggests that only in the more competent PMR and SMR groups does the invariance hypothesis hold. These and other studies (Weisz & Zigler 1979) support the notion that retarded and nonretarded children go through similar stages of development, differing in rate and ceiling, with PMRs and SMRs developing most slowly; SMRs would attain the fringes of the preoperational stage, while PMRs would approach the limits of the sensorimotor stage (Inhelder 1968, Woodward 1959).

Two schools of thought have emerged regarding the relationship of acquisition of prerequisite cognitive stages to development of useful expressive language. One of these holds that the development of appropriate cognitive structures must precede learning and that the cognitive structures necessary for the development of useful language are not present until the individual is functioning at stage 6 of the sensorimotor period (Bricker & Bricker 1970, Hollis & Carrier 1975, 1978, Kahn 1975, 1977, Morehead & Morehead 1974, Piaget 1951, 1963, 1964, Reichle & Yoder 1979). The other holds that individuals at any level of cognitive functioning should be considered potential participants through intervention with operant techniques since no systematic evidence exists to support the cognitive prerequisite position (Guess et al 1978b, Mahoney et al 1980). Kahn (1975, 1977) found that only PMRs who were functioning at stage 6 of the sensorimotor period showed useful expressive language. Thus stage 6 functioning is necessary but not sufficient for the acquisition of expressive language. Kahn (1975, 1977), Reichle & Yoder (1979), and Hollis & Carrier (1975, 1978) have argued that operant training techniques do indeed establish the rudiments of a communicative information exchange process, but operant training fails to produce generalized initiated language (Guess 1980, Guess et al 1978b).

A major problem is the failure of communication responses to generalize (Guess et al 1978a, Harris 1975), but if appropriate generalization training is done, especially in social settings, generalization can occur (Guess et al 1978a, Sailor et al 1980, Stokes & Baer 1977). Cognitive prerequisites may be necessary but not sufficient for acquisition, maintenance, and generalization of communication responses. There is also the complex problem of defining exactly at what stage of cognitive functioning a person is functioning, or even whether "object permanence" or "means-end relationships" are more closely related to language acquisition than are some other cognitive indicators.

CONTROL OF SELF-INJURIOUS BEHAVIOR: A SPECIAL CASE Self-injurious behavior is a serious management problem, out of all proportion to its frequency of 3 to 10% of the institutionalized population (Bachman 1972, Corbett 1975, Frankel & Simmons 1976, Schroeder et al 1978). Self-injurious behavior (SIB) is behavior that results in physical damage, including pain, to one's own body (e.g. head banging, face slapping, eye gouging, hand biting), usually of a stereotyped character. Many operant techniques have been employed, with varying success, to decrease the frequency and intensity of SIB (e.g. extinction, time out from positive reinforcement, DRO or differential reinforcement of other or incompatible behavior, over-correction, required relaxation, aversive stimulation). Given that SIB is painful, the major conceptual problem for operant psychology is explaining what maintains it. In spite of a general paucity of theory regarding the development and maintenance of SIB, and the failure to generalize decreases in frequency and intensity brought about by stimulus control, there have been a few suggestions as well as a host of applied attempts to solve the problem. (See Baumeister & Rollings 1976 for a comprehensive review of the SIB literature.)

One ingenious explanation that combines psychological and physiological mechanisms is the "endogenous opiates" notion. The idea is that pain is followed immediately by an increase in the secretion of endorphins, which act much like opiates. If that is true, it might be that people engage in SIB "in order to" obtain "hits" of endogenous opiates. Reasoning that blocking the opiate action of endorphins would effectively put the patients on an extinction schedule, and thus decrease the rate of SIB, Sandman et al (1981) gave naloxone, an endorphin antagonist, to SIB patients and did find a resulting decrease in SIB. This work needs parametric follow-up, but certainly offers a challenging explanation as well as a practical treatment for some patients.

In addition to many methodological problems including poor reliability and short follow-up (Berkson & Landesman-Dwyer 1977, Forehand & Baumeister 1976, Horner & Barton 1980, Johnson & Baumeister 1978, Smolev 1971), there is inadequate understanding of how individual differences variables interact with the topography of the self-injurious responses and the nature of reinforcement mechanisms to determine which of several available operant intervention techniques to use (Frankel & Simmons 1976). Few rigorous behavioral analyses of the critical variables controlling SIB have appeared (Horner & Barton 1980, Johnson & Baumeister 1978), so it is not surprising that our understanding of SIB has been limited.

Extinction procedures involving the withdrawing of the reinforcers that might maintain the SIB have been attempted by Lovaas & Simmons (1969), Jones et al (1974), and Ross et al (1974) with some success. Others have found extinction techniques totally unsuccessful (Butcher & Lovaas 1968, Corte et al 1971, Myers 1975, Watson 1967) because of the large number of self-injurious responses that can occur during an extinction period, the initial increase in rate at the beginning of the extinction period, generally poor effects unless total isolation is possible, and lack of generalization across settings. Horner & Barton (1980) consider extinction procedures useful only in those situations in which the rate of SIB is low and of low magnitude and the social responses of others appear to be maintaining behavior.

"Time out" involves either removing the subject from a reinforcing situation or vice versa, contingent upon the occurrence of the SIB. These techniques have been used by Wolf et al (1964, 1967), Hamilton et al (1967), and White et al (1972), with varying success and with limitations similar to those for simple extinction procedures.

By differential reinforcement of other behavior (DRO) one attempts to reduce SIB by systematically reinforcing behavior other than self-injury. In situations in which it is possible, it has been rather consistently effective (Allen & Harris 1966, Duker 1975, Lane & Domrath 1970, Mithaug & Hanawalt 1977, Peterson & Peterson 1968, Repp et al 1976, Tarpley & Schroeder 1979, Warren & Burns 1970). DRO should be used only if the rate of SIB is moderate or low so that the rate of "other" behavior may be sufficiently high to reinforce consistently.

Overcorrection requires that the individual produce a response that is incompatible with or that corrects the effects of the undesired response (Azrin et al 1973, Foxx & Azrin 1972, 1973). Much confusion surrounds the use of overcorrection and exactly what the topographically incompatible response should be. While often successful (Azrin & Wesolowski 1975, Duker & Seys 1977, Harris & Romanczyk 1976, Kelly & Drabman 1977, Webster & Azrin 1973, Zehr & Therbald 1978), overcorrection procedures are limited by their expensive and time-consuming nature, general lack of transfer beyond the training sessions, and confusion about how to use the procedures, especially with respect to specification of incompatible responses.

A highly effective technique (over the short range) is use of aversive stimulation to punish and control the intensity and rate of SIB (Altman et al 1978, Baumeister & Baumeister 1978, Hall et al 1973, Lovaas & Simmons 1969, Murray et al 1977, Sajwaj et al 1974, Tanner & Zeiler 1975). Contingent on occurrence of SIB, aversive stimuli are presented to the subject (e.g. aromatic ammonia, tabasco sauce, lemon juice, or electric shock, with electric shock being the most potent aversive stimulus). At present such procedures may be the treatment of choice in life-threatening situations (Rechter & Vrablic 1974), but problems include: failure of generalization to settings outside the training situation, maintenance of effects of training, and ethical, philosophical, and sociopolitical concerns of service providers, consumers, and advocates (Rechter & Vrablic 1974).

SIB is a good example of application of learning and behavioral principles to practical problems. Our understanding and control of SIB by operant techniques is just evolving. We are hampered by (*a*) lack of adequate theory concerning the genesis and maintenance of SIB, (*b*) lack of scientifically and methodologically sound studies, including concise definition of the SIB response and good reliability of measurement, (*c*) inadequate research on the parameters controlling generalization, and (*d*) lack of concern about how individual differences variables interact with various topographies of self-injurious responses and how reinforcements in the environment may be used to determine the optimal operant procedure to use to control the rate and intensity of the SIB.

SOME CONTEMPORARY DEVELOPMENTAL PROBLEMS

Whatever it may be that underlies individual differences in the structure of the nervous system and therefore determines the structural limits of intelligence, it is increasingly clear that there is a "reaction range" (Gottesman & Heston 1972). In spite of claims of 75% to 80% "heritability" (Herrnstein 1971, Jensen 1969), there is evidence of a wide range of individual differences in the extent of development of the processes of intelligent behavior (McCall et al 1977, Sameroff & Chandler 1975, Wachs & Mariotto 1978). Contemporary notions of the nature of experiential effects suggest that developmental changes in intelligence are primarily qualitative (see e.g. Guilford 1959, Harwood & Naylor 1971, McCall et al 1972, 1977, Meyers & Dingman 1966, Nesselroade et al 1972). Haywood & Wachs (1981) have suggested that if one has a structurally limited nervous system,

> the establishment of a particular schema may require a far larger investment of experience than would be true in the case of an unimpaired child. Fewer schemas will lead to fewer possibilities of interconnection (Hebb 1949). Discrepancies that are optimal for normally developing children may be too great to bring about assimilation of information in the case of retarded children. Thus, behavioral incapacity that was structurally determined in the beginning may become far more serious than the structural limitations on the nervous system would have required simply because of the cumulative nature of the experiential determinants of cognitive growth (Haywood & Wachs 1981, p. 101).

The Mental Age Deficit

Such a developmental "snowball" suggests part of a possible explanation for a familiar phenomenon in mental retardation known as the "MA deficit." If intelligence were a unidimensional trait determined entirely by genetic endowment and the consequent structure and biochemistry of the nervous system (and if intelligence tests measure that trait with high reliability and validity), then retarded and younger nonretarded persons matched on MA should perform at about the same level, using similar cognitive processes, on a wide variety of tasks that require intelligent behavior. Instead, investigators observe regularly that, on most tasks of learning and "psychological" performance, the retarded members of such matches do less well than do their nonretarded but younger peers (Stevenson & Zigler 1958, Zigler et al 1958). Zigler (1966, 1969, 1973, 1975) has regularly maintained that the differences in performance levels between retarded and nonretarded persons of equivalent MA are explainable on the basis of differences in motivation, and he and his colleagues have found some evidence to support that notion.

Intrinsic Motivation

In a similar series, Haywood and his students and collaborators have identified a broad trait variable, task-intrinsic motivational orientation, that they have shown repeatedly to be associated with marked individual differences in the efficiency of learning and performance. They have defined "intrinsically motivated" persons as those who characteristically seek their principal satisfactions through task achievement, learning, responsibility, creativity, and aesthetic aspects of tasks, while "extrinsically motivated" persons are those who, instead of seeking satisfaction, concentrate on avoiding dissatisfaction through non-task aspects of the environment such as ease, comfort, safety, security, practicality, material gain, and avoidance of effort (Haywood 1971). Relatively intrinsically motivated mildly and moderately retarded children have significantly higher school achievement scores than do extrinsically motivated children of the same age, sex, and IQ (Dobbs 1967, Haywood 1968a,b), learn a visual size-discrimination problem in fewer trials and relearn the problem more efficiently (Haywood & Wachs 1966), persist longer and work more vigorously at a simple motor task for a "task-intrinsic" incentive (merely the opportunity to do more work) (Haywood & Weaver 1967), work harder under self-monitored than under externally imposed reinforcement, and set "leaner" reinforcement schedules for themselves under the self-monitored condition (Switzky & Haywood 1974). These findings provide an example of one relatively enduring trait in the personality/motivational realm that is associated with individual differences in learning and performance within the mental retardation category. Other possibly correlated variables also related to such individual differences include locus of control (Bialer 1970, Cromwell 1963), effectance motivation (Harter 1974, 1975, Harter & Zigler 1974, White 1959), and inner and outer directedness (Zigler 1966). Reviews of related work on relationships between personality/motivational (i.e. individual differences) variables and the efficiency of learning and performance have been presented by Cromwell (1967), Balla & Zigler (1979), and Zigler (1966). The essence of the work in this area is that the performance levels, directions, and persistence of mentally retarded persons may be influenced significantly by factors that we have traditionally considered to be "nonintellective," such as personality/motivational factors.

COGNITIVE PROCESSES While finding reliable relationships between individual differences variables and performance variables is helpful, it leaves unresolved the problem of specifying the processes by which one set of variables affects the other. Some systematic ideas about the nature of those mediating mechanisms have begun to appear in the mental retardation literature. One such notion is that changes in intrinsic motivation first bring about (in the sense of a catalyst) changes in specific cognitive structures; i.e. motivational changes affect the processes of thought, the modes of construction of reality, and the strategies of problem solving (see e.g. Haywood & Burke 1977). It is through the modification of specific cognitive functions that one is able to bring about increases in the levels of learning and performance in mentally retarded persons. In fact, Paris & Haywood (1973) have argued that mental retardation is a learning disorder that is partially remediable through systematic teaching of cognitive processes and strategies. The essence of that argument is that evidence has accumulated that mildly and moderately retarded persons (*a*) do not typically use effective strategies of thought, problem solving, and memory, relying more characteristically on unsystematic methods such as trial and error; (*b*) can employ effective strategies when such strategies are given to them and they are instructed to use them; and (*c*) typically fail to generalize such strategies to new learning and memory situations even when the new situations are similar to the original ones (Paris & Haywood 1973). These arguments have been explored in detail by Belmont & Butterfield (1977), Butterfield & Belmont (1977), and Campione & Brown (1978). The research findings of these investigations are discussed in the section on cognition and learning.

A significant problem, then, is how to get retarded persons to learn and retain generalizable modes of thought, i.e. cognitive processes, that they will then use not only to solve specific problems but even, in the manner of a breeder reactor, to develop their own cognitive strategies and apply them to new situations.

COGNITIVE MODIFIABILITY Feuerstein and his colleagues (Feuerstein 1970, Feuerstein & Rand 1974, Feuerstein et al 1979a, 1980) have developed some elaborate notions along exactly these lines; i.e. how "functionally" retarded children come to have ineffective cognitive processes, how one can modify those cognitive processes, and how the newly acquired more effective processes can be generalized both to other problem-solving situations and to the development of new cognitive strategies and processes. Feuerstein assumes first that effective thought, construction of reality, and problem solving depend upon the acquisition and use of a finite number of cognitive and precognitive processes (e.g. spontaneous comparative behavior, "summative" behavior, systematic search, analytic approach to problems, need for precision and accuracy in data gathering, inhibition of impulsive responding), and second that such processes are ordinarily acquired through a process called "mediated learning" (Feuerstein & Rand 1974) in which parents or other child-rearing agents help children interpret their successive encounters with their environment, induce rules of thought, and apply those rules to newly encountered situations. When for a variety of reasons mediated learning is inadequate (either because of inadequate agents or because of uncommonly great needs/deficiencies in the children), a cumulative interaction is set up between extrinsic motivation and environmental demands for cognitive functions that results in increasing disability and deficiency both in cognitive processes themselves and in performance in tasks, such as learning, that require the application of those processes. Such deficiencies can be catalogued and measured, albeit by clinical methods at present (Feuerstein et al 1979a, Haywood & Arbitman-Smith 1981, Haywood et al 1975). Further, such cognitive deficiencies are remediable through educational methods (called "Instrumental Enrichment") that require the active and deliberate teaching of quite basic processes of thought. These cognitive education procedures are currently being tested in the United States on classes of educable retarded adolescents as well as on other groups of students. One such program, given over a 2-year period to adolescents in special education classes for educable mentally retarded, behavior-disordered, learning-disabled, and "normal" low-functioning students, has yielded increases (over those shown by control students) in cognitive functioning, IQ, some areas of school achievement, reasoning, spatial relations, and in some classes, intrinsic motivation (see e.g. Arbitman-Smith & Haywood 1980, Feuerstein et al 1979b, Haywood & Arbitman-Smith 1981). This systematic set of concepts, and the diagnostic and remedial procedures associated with it, seems to hold significant promise for explaining both the MA deficit and some of the deeper deficits of mentally retarded persons, and perhaps even more important, for providing means by which those performance deficits can be at least partially overcome. Conceptually, the fact that mentally retarded adolescents can be taught to use effective processes of thought and problem solving and even to generate new strategies for attacking previously unknown problems has some important implications for our notions of the extent to which intelligence itself is affected by experiential variables in development, its plasticity, and the nature of mild and moderate mental retardation.

The overriding generalization from work reported in this section on developmental problems is that the performance of retarded persons, especially mildly and moderately retarded persons, is more retarded than would be expected on the basis of structural deficits and mental age. This "MA deficit" appears to be in part a *result* of the developmental experience of being retarded and is reflected in personality and motivational patterns and modes of thought that are not conducive to effective learning and psychological performance. The applied implication of this analysis is that at least that part of the performance deficit of retarded persons that is greater than that of nonretarded MA-matched peers is remediable by attending to dimensions of motivation and basic cognitive processes.

SOCIAL ECOLOGY OF MENTAL RETARDATION

One of the most pressing contemporary social problems in mental retardation is the question of where retarded persons will live, go to school, work, and carry on their daily activities. Psychological research on this set of questions has begun to draw heavily—but perhaps not yet heavily enough (Schoggen 1981)—upon the concepts and methods of ecological psychology (e.g. Barker & Schoggen 1973). The principles that guide these investigations include: (*a*) there is a wide range of individual differences within the group of retarded persons; (*b*) appropriateness of a setting for a person will not remain constant over time and developmental stages; and (*c*) both assets and requirements of persons must interact with both advantages and requirements of settings (Haywood 1981a).

Since the vast majority of mentally retarded persons are mildly or moderately retarded, most live in their own homes. Most of those who live in the homes of their parents or with other relatives, independently, or with foster families are not closely tracked and do not always show up in statistics on mental retardation. The majority of such persons function well, go to school during their school-age years, move fairly freely in their communities, and participate in family life. Many hold jobs. After the school years they are difficult to locate, giving rise to the popular notion that they are retarded in a social sense only because of the personal requirements of the education system—an idea belied by the fact that they turn up with disproportionate frequency on welfare rolls and police blotters (Edgerton 1967, Edgerton & Bercovici 1976).

With estimates of the number of retarded persons in the United States varying from 3,390,000 (1.5% of 226,000,000) to 6,780,000 (3%), depending on the definition of mental retardation (see Grossman 1973, 1981, Haywood 1974), there have never been more than about 200,000 persons in institutions for the mentally retarded, and the population of institutions has been decreasing rapidly in recent years. Scheerenberger (1981) reported a drop in the institutional population from 174,000 in 1972–73 to 139,000 in 1978-79. Reporting one state's complete data, Mayeda & Sutter (1981) suggested that this decline reaches a plateau as failures in extrainstitutional placements equal new placements. It is clear that "easy" extrainstitutional placements run out before one exhausts the institutional population. Tarjan et al (1978) studied the relationship of severity of handicap and chronological age to place of residence, and their data suggest some natural limits as well as a necessary variety of settings to accommodate the needs of retarded persons. Once those who are least handicapped have been placed in extrainstitutional settings, those who remain in institutions are characterized by lower competency, poorer health, greater medical needs, and greater frequency of "problem" behavior than is true of those who live "in the community" (Borthwick et al 1981, Eyman et al 1981, Eyman & Borthwick 1980, Tarjan et al 1978). Failures of community placements occur most frequently because of behavior that is physically dangerous, aggressive, or rebellious, with inappropriate, self-injurious, and hyperactive behavior common (Pagel & Whitling 1978, Scheerenberger 1981). In addition to these characteristics that foster care providers prefer not to accept, providers frequently list the tendency to run away as a characteristic that they reject (Lei et al 1981). These studies suggest that special attention will have to be given to the multifaceted requirements of the severely and profoundly retarded and multiply handicapped residents who remain in institutional settings after the "easy" community placements have been accomplished.

Vivid and helpful descriptions of the processes of establishing and evaluating community placement settings have been provided by O'Connor (1976), Schalock & Harper (1981), Heal et al (1978), Sigelman et al (1980), Bruininks et al (1981), and Flynn & Nitsch (1980). Important dimensions of these processes include preparation of community attitudes, identification and training of care providers, development of community services, matching of clients and care providers, and the sense of crisis in natural parents that often accompanies deinstitutionalizing their child (Meyer 1980, Willer et al 1981). Haywood & Newbrough (1981) have provided a comprehensive review of issues around settings for retarded persons, with Janicki's (1981) chapter on effects of different residential settings being perhaps the best summary to date, while Edgerton's (1975) analysis of conflicting and changing values regarding deinstitutionalization provides unique perspectives. Several chapters in the Bruininks et al (1981) and Haywood & Newbrough (1981) books are addressed specifically to procedural and strategic questions in the study of person-settings interactions. In that context, Stucky & Newbrough (1981) have suggested a mental health perspective, i.e. settings might be evaluated with respect to the individual well-being of the persons who function in them. A few studies of settings have been done using criteria that describe input conditions rather than developmental outcomes, often in terms of certain philosophical "principles" such as "normalization" (e.g. McLain et al 1975, Wolfensberger & Glenn 1975) but these have shed little light on the relative adequacy of person-setting matches. One such instrument, Program Analysis of Service Systems (PASS; Wolfensberger & Glenn 1975), has been used to measure the extent to which service systems follow the "normalization" method. Since the criterion is adherence to a method, it remains to others to relate scores on this settings yardstick to client outcomes. Eyman et al (1979) factor-analyzed the PASS and produced separate dimensional scores roughly reflecting the a priori dimensions of the instrument and found most scores to be related positively, if modestly, to client growth, while one score, extent of advocacy activity of care providers, was correlated negatively with client growth.

Other investigators have used careful observational procedures to study the quality of life and interpersonal relationships of mentally retarded persons across settings, and have shown nonambulatory profoundly retarded persons to have previously unappreciated social responsiveness (Landesman-Dwyer & Sackett 1978, Landesman-Dwyer & Sulzbacher 1981), as well as revealing the importance of such nonobjective variables as friendships, both quality and frequency of social interactions with peers and staff members, and indications of mood (Berkson & Romer 1980, Landesman-Dwyer et al 1979, Romer & Berkson 1980a,b).

ADVANCES IN TERMINOLOGY, CLASSIFICATION, AND MEASUREMENT

Mental retardation is more easily seen than measured. Clinicians, researchers, psychometrists, and educators have worried constantly about who is and who is not mentally retarded, mostly around the "borderline" ranges, which sometimes has led to unnecessary confusion among disciplines. The American Association on Mental Deficiency (AAMD) periodically publishes a *Manual on Terminology and Classification in Mental Retardation* (Grossman 1973, 1977, 1981, Heber 1959, 1961) in which mental retardation is defined and described for purposes mainly of record keeping, research, and communication. The current AAMD definition is "Mental retardation refers to significantly subaverage intellectual functioning existing concurrently with deficits in adaptive behavior and manifested during the developmental period" (Grossman 1977, p. 5).

Recent changes in the AAMD *Manual* suggest that there may be less rigid dependence on IQ than in the past, since the editor of the forthcoming edition (Grossman 1981) will abandon specific IQ values and even standard deviation brackets, indicating that mental retardation is defined in part by an IQ below 70, more or less, and that the diagnosis is the result of a clinical process in which not only IQ but adaptive behavior (see below), social and developmental history, and contemporary functioning in a variety of settings are taken into account.

Adaptive Behavior Scales

The necessity to measure individual differences in "adaptive behavior" has been recognized for a long time, beginning in a formal way with Doll's (1929) introduction of the Vineland Social Maturity Scale. The most widely used contemporary instrument is the AAMD Adaptive Behavior Scale (ABS), with versions standardized both on institutional residents (Nihira et al 1975) and students in regular and special classes (Lambert et al 1975, Nihira et al 1975). Among the 100 or so instruments now being used in various settings for measuring adaptive behavior of retarded persons, prominent ones include: Adaptive Behavior Inventory for Children (ABIC; Mercer & Lewis 1978), Balthazar's Scale of Adaptive Behavior (BSAB; Balthazar 1971, 1973), and Watson's Behavior Modification Technology (Watson 1977). Formal characterization and conceptualization of adaptive behavior management have been presented by Coulter & Morrow (1978) and by Meyers et al (1979), with the latter group having analyzed characteristics of 17 published instruments that reflect most, if not all, of the recommended procedures and qualities of scale development (e.g. item selection, validity and reliability, reference norms). Initially developed to assist in diagnosis, the measurements secured have also assisted in placing clients in levels or categories for statistical reporting and, by use of individual items or subscales, to determine the kind of habilitative program clients will receive. Scale developers and researchers in the area of adaptive behavior measurement have begun to face two persistent problems: (*a*) the traditional scales rely on "third-party" informants to report activities of subjects, and those informants are sometimes unreliable or uninformed; (*b*) many retarded persons have limited language and communication function, so securing valid measures of what they do and do not know, or of their cognitive processes, has been difficult. One group of investigators (Halpern et al 1975, Irvin et al 1977, 1979) has developed the Social and Prevocational Information Battery to assess job training aptitudes of young mildly and moderately retarded persons, using a simple two-choice (Yes-No) format.

Research on the Adaptive Behavior Construct and its Measurement

The ABS has been used successfully as a criterion measure for differential effects of residential placements (Eyman et al 1979). Others (Roszkowski

1980, Spreat 1980) have found the scales' criterion and concurrent validity to be less than perfect but in the useful range. As dependent measures, Arndt (1981) has shown a single maladaptive behavior score to be superior to separate domain or factor scores. Both the ABS (Lambert 1979) and the ABIC (Oakland & Feigenbaum 1980) appear to be essentially without ethnic bias. Oakland (1980) concluded that the ABIC's relationship to school achievement is too low for that instrument to be useful in placing children in different educational programs—not a great surprise, since the scale was constructed deliberately to be unrelated to intelligence. Low relationship to achievement was also found in another state by Kazimour & Reschly (1981), who also found the ABIC forms from California to be of doubtful utility in a neighboring state with similar ethnic composition—a relationship that probably is true of other adaptive behavior scales as well.

Several factor analyses have been performed with the broad-ranged ABS. The most commonly accepted pattern for both regular and school versions consists of three developmentally related factors: Personal Self-Sufficiency (e.g. dressing, eating), Community Self-Sufficiency (e.g. shopping, communicating), and Personal-Social Responsibility (e.g. job performance, initiative, use of leisure time) (Nihira 1976, 1978a,b, Lambert & Nicoll 1976). Meyers et al (1979) have provided a synthesis of all factor determinations.

Dynamic Assessment

An advance in assessment of retarded and low-functioning persons potentially equal in importance to advances in measurement of adaptive behavior has been the development and dissemination of methods of "dynamic" assessment, especially of learning aptitudes (Haywood et al 1975). Dynamic assessment refers to the measurement of learning and cognitive processes rather than measurement merely of the products of past opportunities to learn. The general approach requires a mini-experiment design that includes pretest, active intervention, and posttest, the primary questions being not the traditional, How much does the subject know? but rather, How much, by what processes, and with how much help can the subject learn, given help? In what cognitive or motivational areas is the most help required? To what extent can the subject be taught to generalize processes and strategies? These ideas have been developed and systematized by Feuerstein, who has put together a set of instruments for dynamic assessment of learning potential (Feuerstein et al 1979a; see also reviews by Anastasi 1980, Haywood 1981b, and Switzky 1981). Learning potential assessment, far more than "objective" or normative assessment, requires rather than forbids teaching and actually changing the characteristics that one is measuring (Haywood 1977).

MENTALLY RETARDED STUDENTS IN SCHOOL

With social pressure for deinstitutionalization has come concomitant pressure for "mainstreaming," i.e. the education of retarded and other handicapped children in the same schools and classes in which nonhandicapped children are educated, or at least to provide services in school settings at public expense to all handicapped children. While the social, political, and philosophical issues around these pressures are exceedingly complex, the psychological issues turn on four questions: (*a*) Can retarded children learn enough to justify the same educational arrangements society makes for other children? (*b*) Will the intellectual, personal, and social development of retarded children be enhanced by going to school in "normal" settings? (*c*) What will be the effects on other children of attempts to educate retarded children in "mainstream" settings? (*d*) What circumstances should be constructed to accommodate the wide range of individual differences among retarded children? Available research literature is inadequate to provide definitive answers to any of these questions, but there are, as usual, relevant studies that provide partial answers and directions for further exploration.

The most promising information on the first question, how much retarded children can learn, is reviewed in the section on cognition and learning in this chapter. It is not even a sensible question without specification of the levels of impairment of intellectual functions one proposes to analyze, since mental retardation covers a wide range from profound impairment with a very limited behavioral repertoire to mild retardation in which the impairment appears to be just a slight downward extension from normally developing children (Robinson & Robinson 1976).

With respect to the second question, there are two sets of answers: the "classical" special education literature, and recent studies stimulated by social and political pressures toward mainstreaming. Classical reviews of the efficacy of special classes, mostly for mildly retarded children and adolescents (e.g. Dunn 1968, Goldstein et al 1965, Semmel et al 1979), suggest that there is litle difference in the levels of school achievement between special (segregated) and regular (integrated) classes, but that, in general, children in segregated classes tend to do somewhat better with respect to personal and social variables such as self-concept and attitude toward school. The history of segregated versus integrated education of mildly retarded children has been reviewed by Meyers et al (1980). Zigler & Trickett (1978), writing on outcomes of preschool education, have urged that quality-of-life variables should be considered together with outcome and cost-benefit variables.

Meyers et al (1980) studied the progress of educable mentally retarded (EMR) school children in California who had been "decertified" by court order and returned to regular classes, contrasting them with nondecertified retarded children (remaining in special classes) and with regular class (nonretarded) children. While decertified children did not fail in greater numbers than did those who remained in special classes, they did maintain a school achievement level 4 or more years behind their grade placements. Kaufman et al (1981) have studied "mainstreamed" and segregated EMR children in a statewide comparison. While this massive data set is difficult to interpret in any facile way, it appears that the mainstreamed children might have had higher initial scores on tests of school achievement, but the segregated children showed higher gains over time. Semmel et al (1979) reported that in no studies have the mean reading levels of EMR exceeded a grade level of 4.0.

Studies of the personal-social adjustment of EMR children have centered on social acceptance by peers, with some attention to self-esteem and the effects of labeling. Well-designed studies (i.e. those in which there is some control for the fact that segregated students are rated only by other handicapped children while mainstreamed ones are rated by both handicapped and nonhandicapped children) have shown segregated EMR students to be more accepted than are mainstreamed students—a difference often attributed to segregated EMRs being exposed considerably less to nonhandicapped age-peers than are those in integrated classes (Goodman et al 1972, Gottlieb & Budoff 1973, Gottlieb et al 1974). The segregated students also have more positive self-concepts, whether teacher rated or through self-administered instruments.

The persistent hope that increased interaction of retarded and nonretarded persons will enhance social acceptance continues to be frustrated. Social status, measured by peer ratings, self ratings, sociometric choice techniques, teacher judgments, and occasionally direct observation, appears not to yield to integration, although outcomes depend to some extent on the measures employed (Asher & Taylor 1981, Cavallaro & Porter 1980, MacMillan & Morrison 1980, Morrison 1981). Gottlieb (1975) demonstrated that if negative choices are not provided in a peer nomination procedure, investigators cannot distinguish between actively rejected and simply ignored peers.

Both labels and the characteristics to which the labels refer appear to affect attitudes toward and acceptance of EMR students, although this area of research suffers from severe problems of sampling and design. Positive teacher action (Foley 1979) and positive teacher attribution (Freeman & Algozzine 1980) seem to yield a positive peer attitude toward children labeled as mentally retarded. Siperstein et al (1980) found more positive attitudes when the label was "mentally retarded" than when it was "retard." MacMillan & Morrison (1980) found that both academic competence and misbehavior were the principal correlates of both peer acceptance and peer rejection of EMR students in segregated classes. Cavallaro & Porter (1980) showed in a careful observational study that even mixed normally developing and "at-risk" preschool children exercise some subtlety in interaction preference, depending upon the nature of the interaction, but in many situations there is the familiar pattern of handicapped children choosing nonhandicapped age-peers much more often than the reverse is true.

From a general review of the integrated-segregated education issue for EMR students, we conclude: (*a*) the issue cannot be resolved by random assignment to compared programs, since placements are determined by policy, litigation, or other social forces and are also influenced by parental choice; (*b*) how well one or the other situation works is a function of the criterion measures; (*c*) segregated education appears to yield better scores on measures of self-concept, while integrated programs sometimes yield higher academic achievement—but not always; and (*d*) within-setting variables, such as the entering characteristics of the children, classroom climate, and teacher attitudes, far outweigh administrative arrangements such as number of normally developing peers and degree of restriction in the environment (Meyers et al 1981). Similar limitations apply to the new school programs for more severely impaired children. Decades of literature attest to improvement in adaptation and adjustment associated with educational programs, including those in institutions, even in profoundly retarded and multiply handicapped persons, so the empirical basis for educational utility is not in doubt. (See the section on cognition and learning for recent data.)

SUMMARY OF THE STATE OF RESEARCH IN MENTAL RETARDATION

Our review of the foregoing areas has confirmed our impression that psychological research in mental retardation is firmly established within the context of developmental psychology, and is contributing fundamental knowledge about basic developmental processes in areas such as cognition, learning, social interaction, motive systems, and person-environment interactions. Significant problems include paucity of theory that is specific to retarded intellectual development, some remaining ambiguity regarding the precise diagnosis of mental retardation, and difficulty in evaluating applied programs because of (*a*) varying diagnostic criteria, (*b*) imprecise criterion measures, and (*c*) needs to respond to social and political pressures for change instead of moving in data-induced directions.

Literature Cited

Allen, K. E., Harris, F. R. 1966. Elimination of a child's excessive scratching by training the mother in reinforcement procedures. *Behav. Res. Ther.* 4:79–84

Altman, K., Haavik, S., Cook, J. W. 1978. Punishment of self-injurious behavior in natural settings using contingent aromatic ammonia. *Behav. Res. Ther.* 16:85–96

Anastasi, A. 1980. Review of R. Feuerstein, Y. Rand, M. B. Hoffman, *The Dynamic Assessment of Retarded Performers: The Learning Potential Assessment Device, Theory, Instruments, and Techniques. Rehabil. Lit.* 41(1–2):28–30

Arbitman-Smith, R., Haywood, H. C. 1980. Cognitive education for learning-disabled adolescents. *J. Abnorm. Child Psychol.* 8(1):51–64

Arndt, S. 1981. A general measure of adaptive behavior. *Am. J. Ment. Defic.* 85:554–56

Ashcraft, M. H., Kellas, G. 1974. Organization in normal and retarded children: Temporal aspects of storage and retrieval. *J. Exp. Psychol.* 103:502–8

Asher, S. R., Taylor, A. R. 1981. The social outcomes of mainstreaming: Sociometric assessment and beyond. *Except. Educ. Q.* In press

Atkinson, R. C., Shiffrin, R. M. 1968. Human memory: A proposed system and its control processes. In *The Psychology of Learning and Motivation: Advances in Research and Theory,* ed. K. W. Spence, J. T. Spence, 2:90–195. New York: Academic. 249 pp.

Azrin, N. H., Kaplan, S. J., Foxx, R. M. 1973. Autism reversal: Eliminating stereotypic self-stimulation of retarded individuals. *Am. J. Ment. Defic.* 78: 241–48

Azrin, N. H., Wesolowski, M. D. 1975. Eliminating habitual vomiting in a retarded adult by positive practice and self-correction. *J. Behav. Ther. Exp. Psychiatry* 6:145–48

Bachman, J. A. 1972. Self-injurious behavior: A behavioral analysis. *J. Abnorm. Psychol.* 80:211–24

Balakrishnan, T. R., Wolf, L. C. 1976. Life expectancy of mentally retarded persons in Canadian institutions. *Am. J. Ment. Defic.* 80:650–62

Balla, D., Zigler, E. 1979. Personality development in retarded persons. In *Handbook of Mental Deficiency: Psychological Theory and Research,* ed. N. R. Ellis, pp. 143–68. Hillsdale, NJ: Erlbaum. 785 pp. 2nd ed.

Balthazar, E. E. 1971. *Balthazar Scales of Adaptive Behavior. Section I. The Scales of Functional Independence (BSAB-I).* Palo Alto, Calif: Consult. Psychol. Press (4 parts)

Balthazar, E. E. 1973. *Balthazar Scales of Adaptive Behavior. Section II. The Scales of Social Adaptation (BSAB-II).* Palo Alto, Calif: Consult. Psychol. Press

Balthazar, E. E., English, G. E. 1969. A system for the social classification of the more severely mentally retarded. *Am. J. Ment. Defic.* 74:361–68

Balthazar, E. E., Phillips, J. L. 1976. Social adjustment in more severely retarded institutionalized individuals: The sum of adjusted behavior. *Am. J. Ment. Defic.* 80:454–59

Barker, R. G., Schoggen, P. 1973. *Qualities of Community Life.* San Francisco: Jossey-Bass. 562 pp.

Baumeister, A. A., Baumeister, A. A. 1978. Suppression of repetitive self-injurious behavior by contingent inhalation of aromatic ammonia. *J. Child. Schizophr.* 8:71–77

Baumeister, A. A., Rollings, J. P. 1976. Self-injurious behavior. *Int. Rev. Res. Ment. Retard.* 8:1–34

Belmont, J. M., Butterfield, E. C. 1971. Learning strategies as determinants of memory deficiencies. *Cognit. Psychol.* 2:411–20

Belmont, J. M., Butterfield, E. C. 1977. The instructional approach to developmental cognitive research. See Kail & Hagen 1977, pp. 437–81

Belmont, J. M., Butterfield, E. C., Borkowski, J. G. 1978. Training retarded people to generalize memorization methods across memory tasks. In *Practical Aspects of Memory,* ed. P. E. Gruneberg, R. N. Sykes. London: Academic

Berkson, G., Landesman-Dwyer, S. 1977. Behavioral research in severe and profound mental retardation (1955–1974). *Am. J. Ment. Defic.* 81:428–54

Berkson, G., Romer, D. 1980. Social ecology of supervised communal facilities for mentally disabled adults: I. Introduction. *Am. J. Ment. Defic.* 85:219–28

Bialer, I. 1970. Relationship of mental retardation to emotional disturbance and physical disability. In *Social-Cultural Aspects of Mental Retardation,* ed. H. C. Haywood, pp. 607–60. New York: Appleton-Century-Crofts. 798 pp.

Bilsky, L., Evans, R. A. 1970. Use of associative clustering techniques in the study of reading disability: Effects of list organization. *Am. J. Ment. Defic.* 74:771–76

Borkowski, J. G., Cavanaugh, J. C. 1979. Maintenance and generalization of skills and strategies in the retarded. See Balla & Zigler 1979, pp. 569–612

Borthwick, S., Meyers, C. E., Eyman, R. K. 1981. Comparative adaptive and maladaptive behavior of mentally retarded clients of five residential settings in three western states. See Bruininks et al 1981, pp. 351–59

Bransford, J. D. 1979. *Human Cognition.* Belmont, Calif: Wadsworth. 300 pp.

Bricker, W., Bricker, D. 1970. Development of vocabulary in severely retarded children. *Am. J. Ment. Defic.* 74:599–607

Brown, A. L. 1974. The role of strategic behavior in retardate memory. *Int. Rev. Res. Ment. Retard.* 7:55–104

Brown, A. L. 1975. The development of memory: Knowing, knowing about knowing, and knowing how to know. *Adv. Child Dev. Behav.* 10:103–52

Brown, A. L. 1978. Knowing when, where, and how to remember: A problem of metacognition. In *Advances in Instructional Psychology,* ed. R. Glaser, pp. 77–165. Hillsdale, NJ: Erlbaum. 304 pp.

Brown, A. L., Barclay, C. R. 1976. The effects of training specific mnemonics on the metamnemonic efficiency of retarded children. *Child Dev.* 47:71–80

Brown, A. L., Campione, J. C. 1977. Training strategic study time apportionment in educable retarded children. *Intelligence* 1:94–107

Brown, A. L., Campione, J. C., Barclay, C. R. 1979. Training self-checking routines for estimating test readiness: Generalization from list learning to prose recall. *Child Dev.* 50:501–12

Brown, A. L., Campione, J. C., Bray, N. W., Wilcox, B. L. 1973. Keeping track of changing variables: Effects of rehearsal training and rehearsal prevention in normal and retarded adolescents. *J. Exp. Psychol.* 101:123–31

Brown, A. L., Campione, J. C., Murphy, M. D. 1974. Keeping track of changing variables: Long-term retention of a trained rehearsal strategy by retarded adolescents. *Am. J. Ment. Defic.* 78:446–53

Brown, A. L., Campione, J. C., Murphy, M. D. 1977. Maintenance and generalization of trained metamnemonic awareness by educable retarded children. *J. Exp. Child Psychol.* 24:191–211

Brown, A. L., Lawton, S. C. 1977. The feeling of knowing experience in educable retarded children. *Dev. Psychol.* 13:364–70

Bruininks, R. H., Meyers, C. E., Sigford, B. B., Lakin, K. C. 1981. *Deinstitutionalization and Community Adjustment of Mentally Retarded People.* Washington DC: Am. Assoc. Ment. Defic. Monogr. 4. 412 pp.

Burger, A. L., Blackman, L. S., Tan, N. 1980. Maintenance and generalization of a sorting and retrieval strategy of EMR and nonretarded individuals. *Am. J. Ment. Defic.* 84:373–80

Butcher, B., Lovaas, O. I. 1968. Use of aversive stimulation in behavior modification. *Miami Symp. Predict. Behav.: Aversive Stimulation,* ed. M. R. Jones, pp. 77–145. Coral Gables, Fla: Univ. Miami. 145 pp.

Butterfield, E. C., Belmont, J. M. 1977. Assessing and improving the executive functions of mentally retarded people. In *The Psychology of Mental Retardation: Issues and Approaches,* ed. I. Bialer, M. Sternlicht. New York: Psychol. Dimensions. 670 pp.

Butterfield, E. C., Wambold, C., Belmont, J. M. 1973. On the theory and practice of improving short-term memory. *Am. J. Ment. Defic.* 77:654–69

Campione, J. C., Brown, A. L. 1977. Memory and metamemory development in educable retarded children. See Kail & Hagan 1977, pp. 367–406

Campione, J. C., Brown, A. L. 1978. Toward a theory of intelligence: Contributions from research with retarded children. *Intelligence* 2:279–304

Cavallaro, S. A., Porter, R. H. 1980. Peer preferences of at-risk and normally developing children in a preschool mainstream classroom. *Am. J. Ment. Defic.* 84:357–66

Cavanaugh, J. C., Borkowski, J. G. 1979. The metamemory-memory "connection": Effects of strategy training and maintenance. *J. Gen. Psychol.* 101:161–74

Cleland, C. C. 1979. *The Profoundly Mentally Retarded.* Englewood Cliffs, NJ: Prentice-Hall. 211 pp.

Cleland, C. C., Clark, C. H. 1966. Sensory deprivation and aberrant behavior among idiots. *Am. J. Ment. Defic.* 71:213–25

Cleland, C. C., Powell, H. C., Talkington, L. W. 1971. Death of the profoundly retarded. *Ment. Retard.* 9(5):35

Cleland, C. C., Rago, W. V. Jr., 1978. Replication: A methodological note. *Ment. Retard.* 16(3):273

Cleland, C. C., Rago, W. V. Jr., Mukherjee, A. 1978. Tool use in profoundly retarded humans: A method of subgrouping. *Bull. Psychon. Soc.* 12(1):86–88

Corbett, J. 1975. Aversion for the treatment of self-injurious behavior. *J. Ment. Defic. Res.* 19:79–95

Corte, H. E., Wolf, H. H., Lucke, B. J. 1971. A comparison of procedures for eliminating self-injurious behavior of retarded adolescents. *J. Appl. Behav. Anal.* 4(2):201–13

Coulter, W. A., Morrow, H. W. 1978. *Adaptive Behavior: Concepts and Measurements.* New York: Grune & Stratton. 266 pp.

Cromwell, R. L. 1963. A social learning approach to mental retardation. See Ellis 1963, pp. 41–91

Cromwell, R. L. 1967. Personality evaluation. In *Mental Retardation: Appraisal, Education and Rehabilitation,* ed. A. A. Baumeister, pp. 66–85. Chicago: Aldine. 419 pp.

Deiker, T., Bruno, R. D. 1976. Sensory reinforcement of eyeblink rate in a decorticate human. *Am. J. Ment. Defic.* 80:665–67

Dobbs, V. 1967. *Motivational orientation and programmed instruction achievement gain of educable mentally retarded adolescents.* PhD thesis. George Peabody Coll., Nashville, Tenn. 165 pp.

Doll, E. 1929. Three measurements of adaptation. *Train. Sch. Bull.* 26:17–27

Duker, P. 1975. Intra-subject controlled timeout (social isolation) in the modification of self-injurious behavior. *J. Ment. Defic. Res.* 19:107–12

Duker, P., Seys, D. M. 1977. Elimination of vomiting in a retarded female using restitutional overcorrection. *Behav. Ther.* 8:255–57

Dunn, L. M. 1968. Special education for the mildly retarded: Is much of it justified? *Except. Child.* 35:5–22

Edgerton, R. B. 1967. *The Cloak of Competence: Stigma in the Lives of the Mentally Retarded.* Berkeley: Univ. Calif. Press. 233 pp.

Edgerton, R. B. 1975. Issues relating to the quality of life among mentally retarded persons. In *The Mentally Retarded and Society: A Social Science Perspective,* ed. M. J. Begab, S. A. Richardson, pp. 127–40. Baltimore: Univ. Park. 492 pp.

Edgerton, R. B., Bercovici, S. M. 1976. The cloak of competence: Years later. *Am. J. Ment. Defic.* 80:485–97

Ellis, N. R. 1963. The stimulus trace and behavioral inadequacy. *Handbook of Mental Deficiency: Psychological Theory and Research,* ed. N. R. Ellis, pp. 134–58. New York: McGraw-Hill. 722 pp.

Ellis, N. R. 1970. Memory processes in retardates and normals. *Int. Rev. Res. Ment. Retard.* 6:1–32

Estes, W. K. 1970. *Learning Theory and Mental Development.* New York: Academic. 205 pp.

Eyman, R. K., Borthwick, S. A. 1980. Patterns of care for mentally retarded persons. *Ment. Retard.* 18:63–66

Eyman, R. K., Borthwick, S. A., Miller, C. 1981. Trends in maladaptive behavior of mentally retarded persons placed in community and institutional settings. *Am. J. Ment. Defic.* 85:473–77

Eyman, R. K., Call, T. 1977. Maladaptive behavior and community placement of mentally retarded persons. *Am. J. Ment. Defic.* 82:137–44

Eyman, R. K., Demaine, G. C., Lei, T. 1979. Relationship between community environments and resident changes in adaptive behavior: A path model. *Am. J. Ment. Defic.* 83:330–38

Eyman, R. K., Moore, B. C., Capes, L., Zachofsky, T. 1970. Maladaptive behavior of institutionalized retardates with seizures. *Am. J. Ment. Defic.* 75:651–59

Favell, J. E., McGimsey, J. F., Jones, M. L. 1980. Rapid eating in the retarded. *Behav. Modif.* 4:481–92

Feuerstein, R. 1970. A dynamic approach to the causation, prevention, and alleviation of retarded performance. See Bialer 1970, pp. 341–77

Feuerstein, R., Rand, Y. 1974. Mediated learning experiences: An outline of proximal etiology for differential development of cognitive functions. *Int. Understanding* 9–10:7–37

Feuerstein, R., Rand, Y., Hoffman, M. B. 1979a. *The Dynamic Assessment of Retarded Performers: The Learning Potential Assessment Device, Theory, Instruments, and Techniques.* Baltimore: Univ. Park. 413 pp.

Feuerstein, R., Rand, Y., Hoffman, M. B. 1980. *Instrumental Enrichment: An Intervention Program for Cognitive Modifiability.* Baltimore: Univ. Park. 436 pp.

Feuerstein, R., Rand, Y., Hoffman, M. B., Hoffman, M., Miller, R. 1979b. Cognitive modifiability in retarded adolescents: Effects of instrumental enrichment. *Am. J. Ment. Defic.* 83(6):539–50

Fisher, M. A., Zeaman, D. 1973. An attention-retention theory of retardate discrimination learning. *Int. Rev. Res. Ment. Retard.* 6:171–256

Flavell, J. H., Wellman, H. M. 1977. Metamemory. See Kail & Hagan 1977, pp. 3–33

Flynn, R. J., Nitsch, K. E., eds. 1980. *Normalization, Social Integration, and Community Services.* Baltimore: Univ. Park. 416 pp.

Foley, J. M. 1979. Effect of labeling and teacher behavior on children's attitudes. *Am. J. Ment. Defic.* 83:380–84

Forehand, R., Baumeister, A. A. 1976. Deceleration of aberrant behavior among retarded individuals. In *Progress in Behavior Modification,* ed. M. Hersen, R. M. Eisler, P. M. Mittler, 2:223–78. New York: Academic. 500 pp.

Foxx, R. M., Azrin, N. H. 1972. Restitution: A method for eliminating aggressive-disruptive behavior of retarded and brain-damaged patients. *Behav. Res. Ther.* 10:15–27

Foxx, R. M., Azrin, N. H. 1973. The elimination of autistic self-stimulating behavior by overcorrection. *J. Appl. Behav. Anal.* 6:1–14

Frankel, F., Simmons, J. Q. 1976. Self-injurious behavior in schizophrenic and retarded children. *Am. J. Ment. Defic.* 80:512–22

Freeman, S., Algozzine, B. 1980. Social acceptability as a function of labels and assigned attributes. *Am. J. Ment. Defic.* 84:589–95

Fuller, P. R. 1949. Operant conditioning of a vegetative human organism. *Am. J. Phychol.* 62:487–99

Gerjuoy, I. R., Spitz, H. 1966. Associative clustering in free recall: Intellectual and developmental variables. *Am. J. Ment. Defic.* 70:918–27

Gerjuoy, I. R., Winters, J. J., Pullen, M., Spitz, H. 1969. Subjective organization by retardates and normals during forced recall of visual stimuli. *Am. J. Ment. Defic.* 73:791–97

Goldstein, H., Moss, J. W., Jordan, L. J. 1965. *The efficacy of special class training on the development of mentally retarded children.* US Off. Educ. Coop. Res. Proj. No. 619. Urbana: Univ. Ill.

Goodman, H., Gottlieb, J., Harrison, R. H. 1972. Social acceptance of EMRs integrated into a nongraded elementary school. *Am. J. Ment. Defic.* 76:412–17

Gottesman, I. I., Heston, I. I. 1972. Human behavior adaptations: Speculations on their genesis. In *Genetics, Environment and Behavior: Implications for Educational Policy,* ed. L. Ehrman, G. S. Omenn, E. Caspari, pp. 105–22. New York: Academic. 324 pp.

Gottlieb, J. 1975. Progress rep. to Adv. Comm. BEH-USOE Intramural Res. Program, Proj. PRIME, US Off. Educ.

Gottlieb, J., Budoff, M. 1973. Social acceptability of retarded children in nongraded schools differing in architecture. *Am. J. Ment. Defic.* 78:15–19

Gottlieb, J., Cohen, L., Goldstein, L. 1974. Social contact and personal adjustment as variables relating to attitudes toward EMR children. *Train. Sch. Bull.* 71(1):9–16

Grossman, H. J., ed. 1973. *Manual on Terminology and Classification in Mental Retardation.* Washington DC: Am. Assoc. Ment. Defic. 180 pp. rev. ed.

Grossman, H. J., ed. 1977. *Manual on Terminology and Classification in Mental Retardation.* Washington DC: Am. Assoc. Ment. Defic. 204 pp. rev. ed.

Grossman, H. J., ed. 1981. *Manual on Terminology and Classification in Mental Retardation.* Washington DC: Am. Assoc. Ment. Defic. rev. ed. In press

Gruber, B., Reesen, R., Reid, D. H. 1979. Providing a less restrictive environment for profoundly retarded persons by teaching independent walking skills. *J. Appl. Behav. Anal.* 12:285–97

Guess, D. 1980. Methods in communication instruction for severely handicapped persons. In *Methods of Instruction for Severely Handicapped Students,* ed. W. Sailor, B. Wilcox, L. Brown, pp. 195–226. Baltimore: Brooks. 336 pp.

Guess, D., Keogh, W., Sailor, W. 1978a. Generalization of speech and language behavior: Measurement and teaching tactics. In *Bases of Language Intervention,* ed. R. L. Schiefelbusch, pp. 373–95. Baltimore: Univ. Park. 476 pp.

Guess, D., Sailor, W., Baer, D. 1978b. Children with limited language. In *Language Intervention Strategies,* ed. R. L. Schiefelbusch, pp. 104–43. Baltimore: Univ. Park. 420 pp.

Guilford, J. P. 1959. Three faces of intellect. *Am. Psychol.* 14:469–79

Guminski, M. M., Ross, L. E. 1976. Retardate trace classical conditioning with pure tone and speech sound CSS. *Bull. Psychon. Soc.* 7(2):199–201

Hall, H., Thorne, D. E., Shindeling, M., Sayers, P. S. 1973. Overcoming situation-specific problems associated with typical institutional attempts to suppress self-mutilative behavior. *Train. Sch. Bull.* 70:111–14

Halpern, A., Raffeld, P., Irvin, L. K., Link, R. 1975. *Testbook for the Social and Prevocational Information Battery.* Monterey: CTB/McGraw Hill

Hamilton, J., Stephens, L., Allen, P. 1967. Controlling aggressive and destructive behavior in severely retarded institutionalized residents. *Am. J. Ment. Defic.* 71:852–56

Harris, L. P. 1977. Self-recognition among institutionalized profoundly retarded males: A replication. *Bull. Psychon. Soc.* 9:43–44

Harris, S. L. 1975. Teaching language to nonverbal children—With emphasis on problems of generalization. *Psychol. Bull.* 82(4):565–80

Harris, S. L., Romanczyk, R. G. 1976. Treating self-injurious behavior of a retarded child by overcorrection. *Behav. Ther.* 7:235–39

Harter, S. 1974. Pleasure derived by children from cognitive challenge and mastery. *Child Dev.* 45:661–69

Harter, S. 1975. Developmental differences in the manifestation of mastery motivation on problem-solving tasks. *Child Dev.* 46:370–78

Harter, S., Zigler, E. 1974. The assessment of effectance motivation in normal and retarded children. *Dev. Psychol.* 10:169–80

Harwood, E., Naylor, G. 1971. Changes in the constitution of the WAIS intelligence pattern with advancing age. *Aust. J. Psychol.* 23:297–303

Hayes, K. J. 1953. The backward curve: A method for the study of learning. *Psychol. Rev.* 60:269–75

Haywood, H. C. 1968a. Motivational orientation of overachieving and underachieving elementary school children. *Am. J. Ment. Defic.* 72:662–67

Haywood, H. C. 1968b. Psychometric motivation and the efficiency of learning and performance in the mentally retarded. *Proc. Int. Assoc. Sci. Study Ment. Defic.*, ed. B. W. Richards, pp. 276–83. Reigate, Surrey (England): Jackson, 982 pp.

Haywood, H. C. 1971. Individual differences in motivational orientation: A trait approach. In *Intrinsic Motivation: A New Direction in Education.* ed. H. I. Day, D. E. Berlyne, D. E. Hunt, pp. 113–27. Toronto: Holt, Rinehart & Winston

Haywood, H. C. 1974. Intelligence, distribution of. *Encyclopaedia Britannica* 9: 672–77. 15th ed.

Haywood, H. C. 1977. Alternatives to normative assessment. In *Research to Practice in Mental Retardation: Education and Training,* ed. P. Mittler, 2:11–8. Baltimore: Univ. Park. 432 pp.

Haywood, H. C. 1981a. Preface. See Haywood & Newbrough 1981, pp. xiii–xxi

Haywood, H. C. 1981b. Review of R. Feuerstein, Y. Rand, M. B. Hoffman, *The Dynamic Assessment of Retarded Performers. J. Autism Dev. Disord.* In press

Haywood, H. C., Arbitman-Smith, R. 1981. Modification of cognitive functions in slow-learning adolescents. In *Frontiers of Knowledge in Mental Retardation: Social, Educational, and Behavioral Aspects,* ed. P. Mittler, 1:129–40. Baltimore: Univ. Park. 480 pp.

Haywood, H. C., Burke, W. P. 1977. Development of individual differences in intrinsic motivation. In *The Structuring of Experience,* ed. I. C. Uzgiris, F. Weizman, pp. 235–63. New York: Plenum. 449 pp.

Haywood, H. C., Filler, J. W. Jr., Shifman, M. A., Chatelanat, G. 1975. Behavioral assessment in mental retardation. In *Advances in Psychological Assessment,* ed. P. McReynolds, pp. 99–136. San Francisco: Jossey-Bass. 532 pp.

Haywood, H. C., Newbrough, J. R., eds. 1981. *Living Environments for Developmentally Retarded Persons.* Baltimore: Univ. Park. 335 pp.

Haywood, H. C., Wachs, T. D. 1966. Size-discrimination learning as a function of motivation-hygiene orientation in adolescents. *Educ. Psychol.* 57:279–86

Haywood, H. C., Wachs, T. D. 1981. Intelligence, cognition, and individual differences. In *Psychosocial Influences in Retarded Performance: Issues and Theories in Development,* ed. M. J. Begab, H. C. Haywood, H. Garber, 1:95–126. Baltimore: Univ. Park. 331 pp.

Haywood, H. C., Weaver, S. J. 1967. Differential effects of motivational orientation and incentive conditions on motor performance in institutionalized retardates. *Am. J. Ment. Defic.* 72:459–67

Heal, L. W., Sigelman, C. K., Switzky, H. N. 1978. Research on community residential alternatives for the mentally retarded. *Int. Rev. Res. Ment. Retard.* 9:209–49

Hebb, D. O. 1949. *The Organization of Behavior.* New York: Wiley. 335 pp.

Heber, R. A. 1959. *A Manual on Terminology and Classification in Mental Retardation.* Washington DC: Am. Assoc. Ment. Defic. 1st ed. (Monogr. Suppl.)

Heber, R. A. 1961. *A Manual on Terminology and Classification in Mental Retardation.* Washington DC: Am. Assoc. Ment. Defic. 109 pp. 2nd ed. (Mongr. Suppl.)

Herrnstein, R. J. 1971. IQ. *Atlantic Monthly* 228:42–64

Hollis, J. H., Carrier, J. K. Jr. 1975. Research implications for communication deficiencies. *Except. Child.* 41:405–12

Hollis, J. H., Carrier, J. K. Jr. 1978. Intervention strategies for nonspeech children. In *Language Intervention Strategies,* ed. R. L. Schiefelbusch. Baltimore: Univ. Park. 420 pp.

Horner, R. D., Barton, E. S. 1980. Operant techniques in the analysis and modification of self-injurious behavior: A review. *Behav. Res. Severe Dev. Disabil.* 1:61–91

House, B. J., Zeaman, D. 1958. Visual discrimination in learning in imbeciles. *Am. J. Ment. Defic.* 63:447–52

Inhelder, B. 1968. *The Diagnosis of Reasoning in the Mentally Retarded.* New York: Day. 367 pp.

Irvin, L. K., Halpern, A. S., Reynolds, W. M. 1977. Assessing social and prevocational awareness in mildly and moderately retarded individuals. *Am. J. Ment. Defic.* 82:266–72

Irvin, L. K., Halpern, A. S., Reynolds, W. M. 1979. *Social and Prevocational Information Battery.* Monterey, Calif: CTB/McGraw Hill

Janicki, M. P. 1981. Personal growth and community residence environments: A review. See Haywood & Newbrough 1981, pp. 59–101

Jensen, A. R. 1969. How much can we boost IQ and scholastic achievement? *Harv. Educ. Rev.* 39:1–123

Johnson, W. L., Baumeister, A. A. 1978. Self-injurious behavior: A review and analysis of methodological details of published studies. *Behav. Modif.* 2:465–87

Jones, F. H., Simmons, J. Q., Frankel, F. 1974. Case study: An extinction procedure for eliminating self-destructive behavior in a 9-year-old autistic girl. *J. Austism Child. Schizophr.* 4:241–50

Kahn, J. V. 1975. Relationship of Piaget's sensorimotor period to language acquisition of profoundly retarded children. *Am. J. Ment. Defic.* 79:640–43

Kahn, J. V. 1977. Piaget's theory of cognitive development and its relationship to severely and profoundly retarded children. See Haywood 1977, pp. 77–83

Kail, R. V. Jr., Hagan, J. W. 1977. *Perspectives on the Development of Memory and Cognition.* Hillsdale, NJ: Erlbaum. 498 pp.

Kaufman, J. J., Agard, J. A., Semmel, M. I. 1981. *Mainstreaming: Learners and Their Environments.* Baltimore: Univ. Park. In press

Kazimour, K. K., Reschly, D. J. 1981. Investigation of the norms and concurrent validity for the Adaptive Behavior Inventory for Children (ABIC). *Am. J. Ment. Defic.* 85:512–20

Kellas, G., Ashcraft, M. H., Johnson, N. S. 1973. Rehearsal processes in short-term memory performance in mildly retarded adolescents. *Am. J. Ment. Defic.* 77:670–79

Kelly, J. A., Drabman, R. S. 1977. Overcorrection: An effective procedure that failed. *J. Clin. Psychol.* 6:38–40

Kramer, J. J., Nagle, R. J., Engle, R. W. 1980. Recent advances in mnemonic strategy training with mentally retarded persons: Implications for educational practice. *Am. J. Ment. Defic.* 85:306–14

Kreutzer, M. A., Leonard, C., Flavell, J. H. 1975. An interview study of children's knowledge about memory. *Monogr. Soc. Res. Child Dev.* 40:Ser. 159. 60 pp.

Lambert, N. M. 1979. Contributions of school classification, sex, and ethnic status to adaptive behavior assessment. *J. Sch. Psychol.* 17:3–17

Lambert, N. M., Nicoll, R. 1976. Dimensions of adaptive behavior of retarded and nonretarded public school children. *Am. J. Ment. Defic.* 81:135–46

Lambert, N. M., Windmiller, M., Cole, L., Figueroa, R. 1975. *Adaptive Behavior Scale—Public School Version.* Washington DC: Am. Assoc. Ment. Defic. 53 pp. rev. ed.

Landesman-Dwyer, S., Berkson, G., Romer, D. 1979. Affiliation and friendship of mentally retarded residents in group homes. *Am. J. Ment. Defic.* 83:571–80

Landesman-Dwyer, S., Sackett, G. P. 1978. Behavioral changes in nonambulatory, profoundly mentally retarded individuals. See Meyers 1978, pp. 55–144

Landesman-Dwyer, S., Sulzbacher, F. M. 1981. Residential placement and adaptation of severely and profoundly retarded individuals. See Bruininks et al 1981, pp. 182–94

Lane, R. G., Domrath, R. P. 1970. Behavior therapy: A case history. *Hosp. Community Psychiatry* 21:150–53

Lei, T., Nihira, L., Sheehy, N., Meyers, C. E. 1981. A study of small family care for mentally retarded people. See Bruininks et al 1981, pp. 265–81

Lovaas, O. I., Simmons, J. Q. 1969. Manipulations of self-destruction in three retarded children. *J. Appl. Behav. Anal.* 2:143–257

Luszcz, M. A., Bacharach, V. P. 1975. List organization and rehearsal instructions in recognition memory of retarded adults. *Am. J. Ment Defic.* 80:57–62

MacMillan, D. L., Morrison, G. M. 1980. Correlates of social status among mildly handicapped learners in self-contained special classes. *J. Educ. Psychol.* 72: 437–44

Mahoney, G., Crawley, S., Pullis, M. 1980. Language intervention: Models and issues. In *Advances in Special Education,* ed. B. Keogh, Vol. 2. Greenwich, Conn: Jai

Matson, J. L., Earnhart, T. 1981. Programming treatment effects to the natural environment. *Behav. Modif.* 5:27–37

Mayeda, T., Sutter, P. 1981. Deinstitutionalization: Phase II. See Bruininks et al 1981, pp. 373–81

McCall, R. B., Eichorn, D. H., Hogarty, P. S. 1977. Transition in early mental development. *Monogr. Soc. Res. Child Dev.* 42:Ser. 171. 108 pp.

McCall, R. B., Hogarty, P. S., Hurlburt, N. 1972. Transitions in infant sensorimotor development and the prediction of childhood IQ. *Am. Psychol.* 27:728–48

McLain, R. E., Silverstein, A. B., Hubbell, M., Brownlee, L. 1975. The characterization of residential environments within a hospital for the mentally retarded. *Ment. Retard.* 13:24–27

Mercer, J. R., Lewis, J. F. 1978. *System of Multicultural Pluralistic Assessment.* New York: Psychol. Corp.

Meyer, R. J. 1980. Attitudes of parents of institutionalized mentally retarded individuals toward deinstitutionalization. *Am. J. Ment. Defic.* 85:184–87

Meyers, C. E., ed. 1978. *Quality of Life in Severely and Profoundly Mentally Retarded People: Research Foundations for Improvement.* Washington DC: Am. Assoc. Ment. Defic. Monogr. 3. 384 pp.

Meyers, C. E., Dingman, H. F. 1966. Factor analytic and structure of intellect models in the study of mental retardation. *Am. J. Ment. Defic.* 70(4):7–25 (Monogr. Suppl.)

Meyers, C. E., MacMillan, D. L., Morrison, G. M. 1981. Effects of integrated vs segregated education for the mildly impaired student. In *Effect of Different Settings on the Development of Mentally Retarded Persons,* ed. M. Begab, R. Edgerton, K. Kernan. Baltimore: Univ. Park. In press

Meyers, C. E., MacMillan, D. L., Yoshida, R. K. 1980. Regular class education of EMR students, from efficacy to mainstreaming. In *Perspectives on Handicapping Conditions: Educating Mentally Retarded Persons in the Mainstream,* ed. J. Gottlieb, pp. 176–206. Baltimore: Univ. Park. 280 pp.

Meyers, C. E., Nihira, K., Zetlin, A. 1979. The measurement of adaptive behavior. See Balla & Zigler 1979, 2:431–81

Miller, C. R. 1975. Reinstitutionalization and mortality trends for the profoundly mentally retarded. In *Research with Profoundly Retarded,* ed. C. C. Cleland, L. Talkington, pp. 1–8. Austin, Tex: Western Res. Conf. and Brown Schools

Miller, C. R. 1976. Subtypes of the PMR: Implications for placement and progress. In *The Profoundly Mentally Retarded,* ed. C. C. Cleland, J. D. Swartz, L. W. Talkington, pp. 57–61. Austin, Tex: Western Res. Conf. and Hogg Found.

Mithaug, D. E., Hanawalt, D. 1977. Employing negative reinforcement to establish and transfer control of a severely retarded and aggressive nineteen year old girl. *Am. Assoc. Educ. Severely/ Profoundly Handicap. Rev.* 2:37–49

Morehead, D., Morehead, A. 1974. From signal to sign: Piagetian view of thought and language during the first two years. In *Language Perspectives: Acquisition, Retardation and Intervention,* ed. R. L. Schiefelbusch, L. Lloyd, pp. 153–90. Baltimore: Univ. Park. 670 pp.

Morrison, G. M. 1981. Sociometric measurement: Methodological consideration of its use with mildly learning handicapped and nonhandicapped children. *J. Educ. Psychol.* 73:193–201

Murray, M. E., Keele, D. K., McCarver, J. W. 1977. Treatment of ruminations with behavioral techniques: A case report. *Behav. Ther.* 8:999–1003

Myers, D. R. 1975. Extinction DRO, and response cost procedures for eliminating self-injurious behavior: A case study. *Behav. Res. Ther.* 13:189–91

Naor, E. M., Balthazar, E. E. 1975. Provision of a language index for severely and profoundly retarded individuals. *Am. J. Ment. Defic.* 79:717–25

Nesselroade, J., Schaie, W., Baltes, P. 1972. Ontogenetic and generational components of structural and quantitative change in adult behavior. *J. Gerontol.* 27:222–28

Nihira, K. 1976. Dimensions of adaptive behavior in institutionalized mentally retarded children and adults: Developmental perspective. *Am. J. Ment. Defic.* 81:215–26

Nihira, K. 1978a. Dimensions of maladaptive behavior in institutionalized mentally retarded persons. See Miller 1976, pp. 51–60

Nihira, K. 1978b. Factorial descriptions of the AAMD Adaptive Behavior Scale. See Coulter & Morrow 1978, pp. 45–57

Nihira, K., Foster, R., Shellhaas, M., Leland, H. 1975. *AAMD Adaptive Behavior*

Scale Manual. Washington DC: Am. Assoc. Ment. Defic. 54 pp. rev. ed.

Oakland, T. 1980. An evaluation of the ABIC pluralistic norms, and estimated learning potential. *J. Sch. Psychol.* 18:3–11

Oakland, T., Feigenbaum, D. 1980. Comparisons of the psychometric characteristics of the Adaptive Behavior Inventory for Children for different subgroups of children. *J. Sch. Psychol.* 18:307–16

O'Connor, G. 1976. Home is a Good Place: *A National Perspective of Community Residential Facilities for Developmentally Disabled Persons.* Washington DC: Am. Assoc. Ment. Defic. Monogr. 2. 92 pp.

O'Connor, G., Justice, R. S., Payne, D. 1970. Statistical expectations of physical handicaps in institutionalized retardates. *Am. J. Ment. Defic.* 74:541–47

O'Grady, R. 1975. Sensory reinforcement of social behavior in the profoundly mentally retarded. See Miller 1975

O'Grady, R., Talkington, L. W. 1977. Selected behavioral concomitants of profound retardation. See Miller 1976

Pagel, S. E., Whitling, C. A. 1978. Readmissions to a state hospital for mentally retarded persons: Reasons for community placement failure. *Ment. Retard.* 16:164–66

Paris, S. G., Haywood, H. C. 1973. Mental retardation as a learning disorder. In *The Pediatric Clinics of North America* (Symp. Learn. Disord.), guest ed. H. J. Grossman, 20(3):641–51

Peterson, R. F., Peterson, L. R. 1968. The use of positive reinforcement in the control of self-destructive behavior in a retarded boy. *J. Exp. Child Psychol.* 6:351–60

Phillips, J. L., Balthazar, E. E. 1976. Social compatibility in more severely retarded institutionalized individuals: An index of socially ambivalent behavior. *Ment. Retard.* 14:46–47

Piaget, J. 1951. *Play, Dreams, and Imitation in Childhood.* New York: Norton. 296 pp.

Piaget, J. 1963. *The Origins of Intelligence in Children.* New York: Norton. 419 pp.

Piaget, J. 1964. Developmental learning. *J. Res. Sci. Teach.* 2:176–86

Porterfield, J., Blunden, R., Blewitt, E. 1980. Improving environments for profoundly handicapped adults. *Behav. Modif.* 4:225–41

Rago, W. V. 1977. Identifying profoundly mentally retarded subtypes as a means of institutional grouping. *Am. J. Ment. Defic.* 81:470–73

Rechter, E., Vrablic, M. A. 1974. The right to treatment including aversive stimuli. *Psychiatr. Q.* 48(3):445–49

Reichle, J. E., Yoder, D. E. 1979. Assessment and early stimulation of communication in the severely and profoundly mentally retarded. In *Teaching the Severely Handicapped,* ed. R. L. York, E. Edgar, Vol. 2. Columbus, Ohio: Special Press

Repp, A. C., Deitz, S. M., Deitz, D. E. D. 1976. Reducing inappropriate behaviors in classrooms and in individual sessions through DRO schedules of reinforcement. *Ment. Retard.* 14:11–15

Rice, H. K. 1968. Operant behavior in vegetative patients. III. Methodological considerations. *Psychol. Rec.* 18:297–302

Rice, H. K., McDaniel, M. W. 1966. Operant behavior in vegetative patients. *Psychol. Rec.* 16:279–81

Rice, H. K., McDaniel, M. W., Stallings, V. D., Gotz, M. J. 1967. Operant behavior in vegetative patients, II. *Psychol. Rec.* 17:449–60

Robinson, N. M., Robinson, H. B. 1976. *The Mentally Retarded Child: A Psychological Approach.* New York: McGraw-Hill. 592 pp.

Rogers, S. J. 1977. Characteristics of the cognitive development of profoundly retarded children. *Child Dev.* 48:837–43

Romer, D., Berkson, G. 1980a. Social ecology of supervised communal facilities for mentally disabled adults: II. Predictors of affiliation. *Am. J. Ment. Defic.* 85:229–42

Romer, D., Berkson, G. 1980b. Social ecology of supervised communal facilities for mentally disabled adults: III. Predictors of social choice. *Am. J. Ment. Defic.* 85:243–52

Ross, D. M., Ross, S. A., Downing, M. L. 1973. Intentional training vs. observational learning of mediational strategies in EMR children. *Am. J. Ment. Defic.* 78:292–99

Ross, L. E., Ross, S. M. 1973. Classical conditioning and intellectual deficit. In *The Experimental Psychology of Mental Retardation,* ed. D. K. Routh, pp. 3–77. Chicago: Aldine. 353 pp.

Ross, R. R., Meichenbaum, D. H., Humphrey, C. 1974. Treatment of nocturnal head-banging by behavior modification techniques: A case report. *Behav. Res. Ther.* 9:151–54

Ross, S. M. 1972. Trace and delay classical eyelid conditioning in severely and profoundly retarded subjects as a function of interstimulus interval. *Am. J. Ment. Defic.* 77(1):39–45

Ross, S. M., Ross, L. E. 1971. Comparison of trace and delay classical eyelid conditioning as a function of interstimulus control. *J. Exp. Psychol.* 91:109–13

Ross, S. M., Ross, L. E. 1975. Stimulus input recruitment and stimulus trace decay factors in the trace conditioning deficit of severely retarded young adults. *Am. J. Ment. Defic.* 80:109–11

Roszkowski, M. J. 1980. Concurrent validity of the Adaptive Behavior Scale as assessed by the Vineland Social Maturity Scale. *Am. J. Ment. Defic.* 85:86–89

Sailor, W., Guess, D., Baer, D. M. 1973. Functional language for verbally deficient children. *Ment. Retard.* 11(3): 27–35

Sailor, W., Guess, D., Goetz, L., Schuler, A., Utley, B., Baldwin, M. 1980. Language and severely handicapped persons. In *Methods of Instruction for Severely Handicapped Students,* ed. W. Sailor, B. Wilcox, L. Brown, pp. 71–105. Baltimore: Brookes. 336 pp.

Sajwaj, T., Libet, J., Agras, S. 1974. Lemon-juice therapy: The control of life-threatening rumination in a six-month-old infant. *J. Appl. Behav. Anal.* 7(4):557–63

Sameroff, A. J., Chandler, M. J. 1975. Reproductive risk and the continuum of caretaking causality. In *Review of Child Development Research,* ed. F. D. Horowitz, pp. 187–244. Chicago: Univ. Chicago Press. 654 pp.

Sandman, C. A., Datta, P., Williams, C., Barron-Quinn, J., Hoehler, F., Swanson, J. 1981. *The possible role of β-endorphin in self-injurious behavior.* Presented at 14th Ann. Gatlinburg Conf. Res. MR/DD, Gatlinburg, Tenn.

Schalock, R. L., Harper, R. S. 1981. A systems approach to community living skills training. See Bruininks et al 1981, pp. 316–36

Scheerenberger, R. C. 1981. Deinstitutionalization: Trends and difficulties. See Bruininks et al 1981, pp. 3–13

Schoggen, P. 1981. Foreword. See Haywood & Newbrough 1981, pp. xi–xii

Schroeder, S. R., Schroeder, C. S., Smith, B., Dalldorf, J. 1978. Prevalence of self-injurious behaviors in a large state facility for the retarded: A three year follow-up study. *J. Autism Child. Schizophr.* 8:261–69

Scott, K. G. 1978. Learning theory, intelligence, and mental development. *Am. J. Ment. Defic.* 82:325–36

Semmel, M. I., Gottlieb, J., Robinson, N. M. 1979. Mainstreaming: Perspectives on educating handicapped children in the public school. In *Review of Research in Education,* ed. D. C. Berliner. Am. Educ. Res. Assoc.

Sigelman, C. K., Heal, L. W., Switzky, H. N., Novak, A. R. 1980. Factors that affect the success of community placement. In *Integration of the Developmentally Disabled into the Community,* ed. A. R. Novak, L. W. Heal. Baltimore: Brookes. 256 pp.

Siperstein, G. N., Budoff, M., Bak, J. J. 1980. Effects of the labels "mentally retarded" and "retard" on the social acceptability of mentally retarded children. *Am. J. Ment. Defic.* 84:596–601

Smolev, S. R. 1971. Use of operant techniques for the modification of self-injurious behavior. *Am. J. Ment. Defic.* 76:295–305

Sperber, R. P., Greenfield, D. B., House, B. J. 1973. A nonmonotonic effect of distribution of triads in retardate learning and memory. *J. Exp. Psychol.* 99:188–98

Spitz, H. H. 1963. Field theory in mental deficiency. See Ellis 1963, pp. 11–40

Spitz, H. H. 1966. The role of input organization in the learning and memory of mental retardates. *Int. Rev. Res. Ment. Retard.* 2:29–56

Spitz, H. H. 1973. The channel capacity of educable mental retardates. See Ross, L. E. & Ross, S. M. 1973, pp. 133–56

Spradlin, J. E., Girardeau, F. L. 1966. The behavior of moderately and severely retarded persons. *Int. Rev. Res. Ment. Retard.* 1:257–98

Spreat, S. 1980. The Adaptive Behavior Scale: A study of criterion validity. *Am. J. Ment. Defic.* 85:61–68

Stevenson, H. W., Zigler, E. 1958. Probability learning in children. *J. Exp. Psychol.* 56:185–92

Stokes, T., Baer, D. 1977. An implicit technology of generalization. *J. Appl. Behav. Anal.* 10:349–67

Stucky, P. E., Newbrough, J. R. 1981. Mental health of mentally retarded persons: Social-ecological considerations. See Haywood & Newbrough 1981, pp. 31–56

Switzky, H. N. 1981. Review of R. Feuerstein, Y. Rand, M. B. Hoffman, R. Miller, *Instrumental Enrichment. Am. J. Ment. Defic.* In press

Switzky, H. N., Haywood, H. C. 1974. Motivational orientation and the relative efficacy of self-monitored and externally imposed reinforcement systems in children. *J. Pers. Soc. Psychol.* 30:360–66

Switzky, H. N., Rotatori, A. F., Miller, T., Freagon, S. 1979. The developmental model and its implications for assessment and instruction for the severely/-profoundly handicapped. *Ment. Retard.* 17:167–70

Tanner, B. A., Zeiler, M. 1975. Punishment of self-injurious behavior using aromatic ammonia as the aversive stimulus. *J. Appl. Behav. Anal.* 8:53–77

Tarjan, G., Dingman, H. F., Miller, C. R. 1960. Statistical expectations of selected handicaps in the mentally retarded. *Am. J. Ment. Defic.* 65:335–41

Tarjan, G., Wright, S. W., Eyman, R. K., Keernan, C. V. 1978. Natural history of mental retardation: Some aspects of epidemiology. *Am. J. Ment. Defic.* 77:369–79

Tarpley, H. D., Schroeder, S. R. 1979. Comparison of DRO and DRI on rate of suppression of self-injurious behavior. *Am. J. Ment. Defic.* 84:188–94

Thompson, G. A., Iwata, B. A., Poynter, H. 1979. Operant control of pathological tongue thrust in spastic cerebral palsy. *J. Appl. Behav. Anal.* 12:325–33

Tucker, D. J., Berry, G. W. 1980. Teaching severely multihandicapped students to put on their own hearing aids. *J. Appl. Behav. Anal.* 13:65–75

Turnbull, A. P. 1974. Teaching retarded persons to rehearse through cumulative overt labelling. *Am. J. Ment. Defic.* 79:331–37

Turnure, J. E., Thurlow, M. L. 1973. Verbal elaboration and the promotion of transfer of training in educable mentally retarded children. *J. Exp. Child Psychol.* 15:137–48

Turnure, J. E., Thurlow, M. L. 1975. The effects of structural variations in elaborations on learning by EMR and nonretarded children. *Am. J. Ment. Defic.* 79:632–39

Wachs, T. D., Mariotto, M. J. 1978. Criteria for the assessment of organism-environment correlation in human development studies. *Hum. Dev.* 21:263–88

Wanschura, P. B., Borkowski, J. G. 1974. The development and transfer of mediational strategies by retarded children in paired-associate learning. *Am. J. Ment. Defic.* 78:631–39

Warren, S. A., Burns, N. R. 1970. Crib confinement as a factor in repetitive and stereotyped behavior in retardates. *Ment. Retard.* 8:25–28

Watson, L. S. Jr. 1967. Application of operant conditioning techniques to institutionalized severely and profoundly retarded children. *Ment. Retard. Abstr.* 4:1–18

Watson, L. S. Jr. 1977. *BMT Assessment Instrument: Global Evaluation Scale.* Libertyville, Ill: Behav. Modif. Technol.

Webster, D. R., Azrin, N. H. 1973. Required relaxation: A method of inhibiting agitative-disruptive behavior of retardation. *Behav. Res. Ther.* 11:67–78

Weisz, J. R., Zigler, E. 1979. Cognitive development in retarded and nonretarded persons: Piagetian tests of the similar sequence hypothesis. *Psychol. Bull.* 86:831–51

White, G. D., Nielson, G., Johnson, S. M. 1972. Time-out duration and the suppression of deviant behavior in children. *J. Appl. Behav. Anal.* 5:111–20

White, R. W. 1959. Motivation reconsidered: The concept of competence. *Psychol. Rev.* 66:297–333

Willer, B. S., Intagliata, J. C., Atkinson, A. C. 1981. Deinstitutionalization as a crisis event for families of mentally retarded persons. *Ment. Retard.* 19:28–29

Winschel, J. F., Lawrence, E. A. 1975. Short-term memory: Curricular implications for the mentally retarded. *J. Spec. Educ.* 9:395–408

Wohlhueter, M. J., Sindberg, R. M. 1975. Longitudinal development of object permanence in mentally retarded children: An exploratory study. *Am. J. Ment. Defic.* 79:513–18

Wolf, M. T., Risley, T., Johnson, M., Harris, F., Allen, K. E. 1967. Application of operant conditioning procedures to the behavior problems of an autistic child: A follow-up and extension. *Behav. Res. Ther.* 5:103–11

Wolf, M. T., Risley, T., Mees, H. 1964. Applications of operant condition procedures to the behavior problems of an autistic child. *Behav. Res. Ther.* 1:302–12

Wolfensberger, W., Glenn, L. 1975. *PASS 3 —Program Analysis of Service Systems: A Method for Quantitative Evaluation of Human Services: Field Manual.* Toronto: Natl. Inst. Ment. Retard.

Woodward, M. 1959. The behavior of idiots interpreted by Piaget's theory of sensorimotor development. *Br. J. Educ. Psychol.* 29:60–71

Zeaman, D. 1973. One programmatic approach to retardation. See Ross, L. E. & Ross, S. M. 1973, pp. 78–132

Zeaman, D., House, B. J. 1963. The role of attention in retardate discrimination learning. See Ellis 1963, pp. 159–223

Zeaman, D., House, B. J. 1967. The relation of IQ and learning. In *Learning and Individual Differences,* ed. R. M. Gagne, pp. 192–212. Columbus, Ohio: Merrill. 265 pp.

Zehr, M. D., Therbald, D. E. 1978. Manual guidance used in a punishment procedure: The active ingredient in overcorrection. *J. Ment. Defic. Res.* 22:263–72

Zigler, E. 1966. Research on personality structure in the retardate. *Int. Rev. Res. Ment. Retard.* 1:77–108

Zigler, E. 1969. Developmental versus difference theories of mental retardation. *Am. J. Ment. Defic.* 73:536–56

Zigler, E. 1973. The retarded child as a whole person. See Ross, L. E. & Ross, S. M. 1973, pp. 231–322

Zigler, E. 1975. Cognitive-developmental and personality factors in behavior. In *Mental Retardation: Introduction and Personal Perspective,* ed. J. M. Kaufman, J. S. Payne, pp. 360–87. Columbus, Ohio: Merrill. 427 pp.

Zigler, E., Hodgden, L., Stevenson, H. W. 1958. The effect of support on the performance of normal and feebleminded children. *J. Pers.* 26:106–22

Zigler, E., Trickett, P. K. 1978. IQ, social competence, and evaluation of early childhood intervention programs. *Am. Psychol.* 33:789–98

Ann. Rev. Psychol. 1982. 33:343-70

ORGANIZATIONAL DEVELOPMENT AND CHANGE

Claude Faucheux

Foundation for Business Administration, Delft, The Netherlands

Gilles Amado

Centre d'Enseignement Superieures des Affaires, Jouy en Josas, France

André Laurent

European Institute of Business Administration, Fontainebleau, France

---

CONTENTS

In carrying out our assignment to review Organizational Development (OD) and Change, we have extended the scope and coverage in two important directions over what has been done in the two previous reviews (Friedlander & Brown 1974, Alderfer 1977).

0066-4308/82/0201-0343$02.00

First, the coverage has been extended beyond North American publications. Indeed, it is no longer possible to ignore developments outside the United States and Canada when they influence thinking and research in these two countries. For instance, developments in Northern Europe (Industrial Democracy) and Japan (Quality Circles) cannot be ignored. In addition, the special situation in Latin countries can provide significant insights about the field.

Second, the scope of this review goes beyond OD to include Organizational Change. This is an indication that the OD label may no longer be adequate to describe the various developments that have taken place in the field during the past few years. The impact of the Quality of Working Life (QWL) movement has become critical. Some authors even wonder whether OD is becoming an obsolete label (Jones & Pfeiffer 1977) to be replaced by QWL (Burke 1976).

Part I of this review will discuss and compare OD and QWL. The second part will extend this discussion to the cultural foundations of OD and QWL. The third part will look at a variety of developments specific to the Latin countries. Finally, the concluding section will attempt to broaden the perspective.

ORGANIZATIONAL DEVELOPMENT OR QUALITY OF WORKING LIFE?

Friedlander & Brown (1974) had assimilated the sociotechnical approaches with the "technostructural approaches" which, in their own classification, dealt with structures and technology (in opposition to the "human processual approaches" dealing with processes and peoples). However, this classification is puzzling if we recognize that one of the main characteristics of the sociotechnical approaches is precisely to deal *jointly* with *both* people *and* technology. This is an indication indeed that "sociotechnical approaches" have been somewhat foreign to OD practice though they were nonetheless perceived as working toward similar goals.

Kahn (1974) concluded his often quoted paper by welcoming "the work on job design which approaches organizational structure—the division of labor . . . ; not only will this strengthen the practice of OD, it will also bring the language of OD into the larger realm of organizational theory and research. It is a long awaited convergence." This underlines again the lack of theoretical unification within OD, but it also points in a direction where hopefully such a theoretical base might be found.

Burke (1976), a very perceptive observer of the field, opens his description of the main transitions in OD with the statement that what was known as

OD might come to be called QWI (Quality of Work Intervention) or QWL (Quality of Working Life). He then describes the penultimate transition as one where "the role of the practitioner has changed *from* working almost exclusively with the management, *to* working with both managers and persons at all organizational levels . . . This transition in OD means that practitioners must pay considerably more attention to the whole area of socio-technical systems and to human engineering, job design, and ultimately to the quality of working life."

The following year, Burke (1977) used the previous paper as an introductory chapter to *Current Issues*. However, the opening remark about QWL is omitted and the end of the last sentence quoted above becomes: ". . . practitioners must pay considerably more attention to industrial engineering, job design or redesign and the whole area of socio-technical systems."

In 1978 in the introductory chapter of *The Cutting Edge*, Burke (1978) states "Although OD might have another name in the future, I do not think now it is going to be one of these" (QWI or QWL). He continues, asserting: "Be that as it may, the new kid on the block, at the moment, is QWL: It has replaced job enrichment" and asks "But is QWL the same as OD?" He notes that Walton, though he does not make any comparative statement, defines QWL as broadly, if not more so, than OD; finally, after referring to Nadler's chapter which describes some typical QWL projects, he concludes "QWL will not encompass nor replace OD, but perhaps will be integrated within it as job enrichment has been in many instances. . . . This integration will be all to the good, since OD could be improved with more use of QWL principles and practices, that is OD would no longer be seen solely as a management tool, but would become more of a total organizational process." This leads him to recognize that Kahn's (1974) criticism still holds today: "OD is only a convenient label for a bunch of activities."

Two years later, Burke (1980a) still sees QWL as "OD under a new name" and wonders about "what's an OD consultant to do?" Only three alternatives occur to him: Either fine tune and tinker with the system, or quit the system altogether, or attempt to fundamentally change the system itself. In concluding he recommends: "OD consultants should continue fine-tuning, keeping in mind the risk of furthering the organizational imperative, but they should also attempt to change bureaucracies in some fundamental ways. OD is one way that is still worth pursuing."

In a recent interview, Burke (1980b) does provide some clues to the reasons for such a weak, disillusioned conclusion. Referring to the series of conferences on OD (several of which were chaired by Burke) sponsored by NTL and University Associates, Burke notes that OD researchers and practioners might not be as hung-up about being theory based today as they were in the early seventies (p. 276); but he observes also that concepts coming out of sociotechnical systems approach are beginning to impact the field now and predicts an even stronger influence in the future.

Recent Books in the Field

Some recent authors have titled their publications "Organization Change and Development" (Beer 1980) or "Organization Development and Change," as did Huse as early as 1975, who states in the Preface to his second edition (Huse 1980): "Much that appeared new and innovative in 1975 seemed like history and 'old hat' in 1979 and 1980." Huse is indeed among the few who very early on acknowledged the importance of sociotechnical approaches to work redesign, as did the first reviewers of this subject (Friedlander & Brown 1974).

A rapid glance at some books published in the last 5 years will indicate the transformations in the field. Among handbooks, manuals, or textbooks in 1976, little recognition was as yet given to the emergence of sociotechnical approaches. Some do not even mention it (Dunnette 1976, Bowers 1976). This silence extends even later with Bryant & Niemans (1978), Weick (1979), Golembiewski (1979), even Beer (1980), who nonetheless advocates a system view. Some give a passing recognition like Dubin (1976), Burke (1977), and French et al (1978), who devote a few chapters to sociotechnical systems.

The turning point seems to be the second edition of Katz & Kahn (1978), which provides the most adequate and up-to-date coverage of North European literature with a detailed account of the sociotechnical systems approach. Similarly, the second edition of Huse (1980) and Miles (1980) also give an extensive presentation of this approach. Only a few collected papers are entirely devoted to the sociotechnical approach: Davis & Cherns (1975a,b), Clark (1976), Pasmore & Sherwood (1978), and also the last volume of ICQWL (1979)—a new series published in Holland—and Cooper & Mumford (1979).

Perhaps this significant change in the OD field is best reflected in the new quarterly *Group and Organizational Studies*, which features editorial notes, interviews, book reviews, abstracts from significant papers, articles derived from a wide variety of sources, and reflects a meritorious effort to cover what is going on outside the US. This last feature is particularly welcome at a time when the industrial and economic interdependencies in the world should make us aware of the many different cultural contexts in which social change is taking place and when the influence of Japan and Northern Europe can be felt in the US in the field of organizational change. In order to better understand the nature of these influences it is useful to characterize, even briefly, the different intellectual climates in which organization research has developed.

PLANNED CHANGE IN THE ANGLO-SAXON COUNTRIES

Different US and European Orientations

Some useful considerations concerning the history of OD in the US can be found in French et al (1978) and Tichy (1978). In addition, it is important to note that the rapprochement between the Lewin group and the Tavistock Institute had resulted in little more than the journal *Human Relations* after Lewin's death. Lewin's conceptualization of ecological psychology was an early recognition of the open system nature of persons and groups within the social field. This formulation was attractive to the researchers of the Tavistock Institute who had gone a long way in this direction, whereas this orientation in the US was retained by only a few (Katz & Kahn 1978).

Another dimension of the Tavistock Institute's work further differentiates their approach. Strongly influenced by unorthodox and creative psychoanalysts such as Klein, Fairbairn, Winnicott, and Bion, they developed an approach to groups with a dual focus: they differentiate between the level of the activities carrying out a purpose involving a task in an environment and the level of the activities implying unconscious or unlearned assumptions. Such an orientation led to the recognition of complex systemic interdependencies, whereas the T-group posterity in the US was rather restricted to intragroup and interpersonal phenomena, and only slowly became interested in intergroup aspects. Whereas the task was always central in the Tavistock focus, it was secondary at best for the US.

The Tavistock approach was not only deeper with its psychoanalytic framework, but it was also broader in the sense that they preserved a sociological and anthropological interest which made them sensitive to the cultural contexts in which groups and organizations found themselves. This aspect, which was certainly present with Lewin, is not apparent in OD which tends to be satisfied with the analysis of attitudes.

In the US, an implicit belief in technical determinism might have discouraged any inclination to tinker with the technology of the tasks. On the contrary, with its holistic approach, and its appreciation of cultural realities, the Tavistock Institute could more easily evolve the sociotechnical views according to which there is no such thing as technological determinism, but rather a mutual influence of both technological and social requirements which can lead to a joint optimization of the work systems.

The nature of societal demands was also different. The Tavistock Institute team emerged from the demands of a society confronted with exceptional war problems. The level of intervention was that of the "community" (Bridger 1946, 1978a, Gray 1970). On the other hand, the US demand came primarily from postwar needs of industry to increase productivity in an expanding economy, where the group approach was seen as a convenient road toward the solution of individual problems. The concern with the organization as a whole and the realization that its environment was part of the organization's world emerged comparatively later in the US.

Though the theoretical formulation of sociotechnical systems was born in England, it is in Scandinavia that the Tavistock researchers found a major field for intervention. In the early 1960s in Norway, a joint concern at the national level of both management and unions for the working conditions in industry was at the origin of the "Industrial Democracy" project (Emery & Thorsrud 1976). This movement spread at the end of that decade in Sweden (Herbst 1974, 1976).

Only very few OD researchers in the US during the 60s have intervened at the shop floor level or concerned themselves with structural problems of the organization. The Scandinavian experiments received relatively little attention from the US at the time.

In the US, work design was left almost entirely to specialists who favored an individual job approach to the problem and were not favorable to work participation and collaboration with unions as developed in Scandinavia (Weinberg 1974). Davis, who developed a more wholistic approach to work design, felt much more akin to the Tavistock style than to the views which were dominant in the US at the time. His collaboration with Trist at UCLA in the mid-1960s strengthened the sociotechnical approach from the technological side and resulted in the major theoretical thrust of the QWL movement 10 years later (Davis, 1977a,b, 1978, 1979a,b,c, 1980).

Mills (1975) described very clearly the conditions which led to the emergence of a new concern with human resources, which was to gain such momentum that it would indeed be possible to see it as a genuine social movement. Comparing Europe's industrial democracy project with that of the QWL in the US, Mills (1978) very perceptively stresses the deep differences in style: the European approach being more legalistic, formal, and government induced, whereas the American pragmatism let union-management cooperation develop voluntarily, with a concern for the individual worker involvement in day-to-day decision making.

Nonetheless, it is important to bear in mind that the US government was very influential in the development of a concern for the QWL. For instance, Mills worked with the Price Commission (1971–73) and with the National Commission on Productivity and Work Quality (1973). He then became the first director of the National Quality of Work Center in Washington, later known as the American Center for the Quality of Work Life. In this capacity he has played a very important role in stimulating this development which was not concerned with legislation, though this aspect is not completely absent (Lawler et al 1980, p.91), but rather with the development of institutions where unions, management, and government could collaborate. The support of a private institution like the Ford Foundation was also essential in launching the initial conferences in 1971–1972 (Davis & Cherns 1975a,b) and in funding research programs such as the one in Michigan in 1973 (Seashore 1981).

However, without any real concern among industrialists and unionists, the QWL movement could not have gained such momentum. This social movement is not even in full swing in the US as yet, while on the other hand, the industrial democracy movement in Scandinavia seems to have lost some of its initial thrust of the 60s. Gunzburg & Hammarström (I.C.Q.W.L. 1979) describe how two approaches were tried in Sweden—sociotechnical after the Tavistock Institute and representative systems for joint management-union consultation—and observe that work democracy through changes in work design has been slower to develop than worker representation. The interest in a comparative approach to representative systems and workers' participation has developed only recently (Kühne 1980, Jain 1980, Wilpert et al 1978a,b, Garson 1977, Wall & Lischeron 1977).

Research on OD

An important review of research evidence about OD has been done by Porras in a series of papers. Though the period reviewed ranges from 1959 to mid-1975, no posterior publications seem to invalidate the conclusions. A systematic search yielded 160 evaluation studies of planned organizational change (spread over 36 journals, 22 books, and 8 unpublished manuscripts) out of which only 35 were retained which satisfied the following criteria:

(*a*) *human processual approach* (to the exclusion of sociotechnical, participative, or structural change studies);
(*b*) *real life organizations* (excluding laboratory or simulation studies);
(*c*) collecting and presenting *quantitative data* (excluding case studies);
(*d*) relevant to the *change activity* of the organization (excluding mere participants' evaluation of the intervention);
(*e*) related to changes in human processes (excluding studies with only economic or output measures.

Among many interesting findings let us note the following ones from Porras & Berg (1978a):

1. A significant increase in the use of Survey Feedback and Process consultation and a large decrease in the use of the Managerial Grid approach.
2. An increased use of the more common OD approach, *Laboratory training*, but with a task focus becoming more popular (and a process orientation focus becoming less popular).

From Porras & Berg 1978b:

3. Counter evidence is provided to the widely accepted model that changed process causes changed outcome.
4. Task-oriented variables were among the low changers which questions the effects of OD on task-related behavior in general.
5. Relatively little systematic evidence about the efficacy of OD.
   (*a*)OD does not seem to make people happier and more satisfied.
   (*b*)Group process variables change less than half the time they are measured.
   (*c*)OD does not have an important impact on the overall organizational process (only on individuals).
   (*d*)T-groups, Encounter Groups, and Sensitivity Training Groups resulted in the lowest percentage of reported change.

This systematic survey led to further useful considerations about research methodology, stressing the distinction between implementation research (focusing primarily on finding solutions to a specific organizational problem), evaluation research (focusing primarily on the global outcomes of an intervention), assessment research (designed to discover not only outcomes, but also the processes which generated them), and theory building research (oriented toward discovering fundamental relationships existing in any planned change process) (Porras & Roberts 1980). Some of the reasons why so little assessment research is done were also reviewed, a model of OD assessment proposed with several recommendations for overcoming some of the obstacles to this necessary type of research (Porras & Patterson 1979). Finally, a concrete illustration of these recommendations is provided by an empirical study of OD in a large system (Porras & Wilkins 1980), yielding unexpected findings contradictory to generally accepted OD theory and practice.

The complaints about the paucity of good research and particularly fundamental research are not new, but it is only recently that reasonably good evidence has been provided on the poor efficacy of OD intervention as well as the unsubstantiated character of many OD conceptions (cf also Pate et al 1977). Perhaps the only emerging efficacy seems to be related to the degree to which the OD intervention uses participative methods (Dunn & Swierczek 1977).

Research on QWL

While research on OD appears to be primarily critical, research on QWL projects seems to be gathering momentum (Taylor 1977, 1978). With the support of both the Ford Foundation and the US Department of Commerce, a research program for organizational assessment has developed at the Institute for Social Research, known as the "Michigan Quality of Work Program" (cf Lawler et al 1980, Drexler & Lawler 1977, Seashore et al 1981, Seashore 1981). This effort up to now has been primarily methodological and has resulted in the design of field procedures which could also be useful for the evaluation of organizations and organizational change in different contexts. Eight QWL projects were included in the original plan, some of them having been already reported (Trist et al 1977, Goodman 1979, Nadler 1978a,b, Nadler et al 1980), but most of them are not yet advanced enough for the findings to be published. Such a research effort is unprecedented in scope, magnitude, and sophistication. While awaiting these findings, we have not as yet much research evidence at hand.

Cummings et al (1977), satisfying themselves with some 58 field studies on "work experiments," in spite of a degree of validity which left much to be desired, seemed nonetheless to assess as plausible the overwhelming number of positive results reported and their generalizability. Pasmore & Sherwood (1978, p. 259) selected out of these 58 studies 16 which were more sociotechnical in their approach and describe a typical sociotechnical study as follows:

> it includes male, blue collar, unionized workers who perform industrial tasks. These employees number about 40 and they participate directly in the change program. The experimental changes involve forming an autonomous work group; specific modifications include increases in autonomy, interpersonal/group processes, feedback of results, and task variety, with parallel changes in the technical/physical setting to form whole task groups and in the pay/reward system to reinforce group performance. If the necessary conditions for autonomous group functioning are implemented the likely results are increases in productivity and worker satisfaction (p. 268).

Some case studies: The "National Processing Case" (Drexler & Lawler 1977), Bolivar (Duckles et al 1977), and Tarrytown (Guest 1979) concur in stressing the importance of union-management collaboration and employee participation which require patience in building a favorable climate through appropriate new organizational structures and decision making processes.

Sometimes these new structures are labeled "parallel organizations" (Carlson 1978), "collateral" or "reflective" organizations, even "shadow" structures (Schein & Greiner 1977), "flat, flexible, but formal problem solving and governance organizations that serve to supplement bureaucracy and exist side by side with it, not replace it" as described by Stein & Kanter (1980, p. 371), who see this as a developing trend of the 1980s.

Some sobering observations have been made by Walton (1977) at Topeka, but on the other hand he develops a positive and pragmatic overall view of the work improvements over the last 10 years (Walton 1979).

Cultural Contexts

As we have seen, in order to understand the transformation of the field in the US today, it is necessary to realize that the sociotechnical approach has emerged in an intellectual climate different from that of the US. In a way, it could be compared (mutatis mutandis) to the coming of Kurt Lewin in the 1930s with the only difference that Lewin had not found in the US a trend of research complementary to his own as, for instance, Tavistock researchers found with Davis.

However, it is only in Northern Europe that the Tavistock found an opportunity to develop its approach. Southern Europe provides us with a situation where OD (as it was known in the US or Northern Europe) has never developed to the same extent and a different attitude toward social change, particularly in the organization, has yielded different styles of intervention. The part of Europe which has been visible from the US has mostly been Northern Europe, whereas the comparatively smaller number of publications in English coming from Latin Europe (as well as from Latin America) has not facilitated the awareness of important cultural differences (Faucheux & Rojot 1979).

The fact that different approaches to organizational change seem to have emerged in different cultural contexts should not come as much of a surprise. It is all the more surprising that these strategies for organizational change have been proposed for so long as almost independent from their societal and cultural context (Maurice et al 1980). The very same cultural blindness, ethnocentrism, and claim for universality that has plagued the field of management and organization theory (Hofstede 1980) may have plagued also the field of planned organizational change.

In a recent study comparing managerial ideologies across 10 Western countries, Laurent (1979) has shown, for instance, that the widest gap in management and organizational conceptions could be found between the US and the Latin countries of Europe and that these important national differences were not reduced within large multinational companies. On the basis of his research data, he argues with Inzerilli (1979) that while American managers predominantly hold an "instrumental" view of the organization as a set of tasks to be achieved, French managers favor a "social" view of the organization as a collectivity of people. No wonder then that OD emerged in the US with an instrumental focus on organizational process as tools to be improved, whereas the Latin countries have developed institutional approaches that try to deal with the social intricacies of human collectivities.

Having realized the importance of a proper appreciation of the cultural dimension within social change, we are in a better position to examine why, within the Western world, the technological transfer of OD to Latin countries has been difficult and why alternative approaches to social change have emerged there. Having done this, we will be better equipped to wonder how, outside of the Western world but still within the industrialized nations, the Japanese deal with organizational change, leaving for the main conclusions some considerations about the significance of all this for "developing countries."

ORGANIZATIONAL CHANGE IN LATIN COUNTRIES

When we analyze the theoretical developments as well as present practices in the field of OD and change within Latin countries we find power to be the key factor around which all major research work revolves. That is not to say that power is a neglected dimension elsewhere. In the US (Chesler et al 1979) and even more so in Northern Europe (Mulder 1977, Pettigrew 1979, Borum 1980), power training has been seriously considered as an alternative to OD. Van Dongen (1978) has, however, vigorously criticized this conception which considers power only intraorganizationally without giving proper recognition to the societal context where its real significance originates. According to van Dongen, if we are seeking real organizational change, we should rather attempt *to change the rules of the game* more than anything else.

In addition, the power dimension assumes a further significance in Latin cultures where the influence of Roman Law and the lack of consensual basis strengthen state centralization of authority and power (Faucheux & Rojot 1979, Maurice & Sellier 1979). This central notion, incidentally, renders very problematical any practice of planned change in these countries. The very fundamental assumptions of OD are thus questioned: its cultural origin, its presuppositions about development, organization, adaptation, and change, its epistemological basis consequently, but also its methods and aims. To be sure, OD ideas and practices have been introduced in many Latin countries: in France (Morin 1976), in Italy (Salvemini 1980), and most recently in Brazil (Cavalcanti 1979). However, we must take note that reports on intervention in these countries are scarce and that the most interesting works are precisely those which have attempted to explain the deficiency or the ineffectiveness of those interventions by the cultural specificity of each country.

Latin Bureaucracies

Taking a look at Brazil, whose basic culture is closer to the Latin countries than it is to the Anglo-Saxons, we notice that the first reservations concerning the transfer possibilities of OD had been formulated shortly after its introduction (Da Costa Moura 1978, Carvalho da Cunha 1979, Boetger 1978) and elaborated later by Pinto (1979). For this author, a meaningful cross-cultural application of OD requires at least the rudiments of a comparative theory of a caliber higher than presently available. This is why he attempts to compare the basic OD assumptions as they appear in the current OD literature with their equivalent cultural counterparts drawn from empirical and theoretical writings on comparative administration, development, and politics in Latin America. He goes as far as to suggest the risks of "cultural substitution." Starting from the confrontation of four dimensions (norms and values underlying OD, the individual at work, group processes, organizational climate), he shows how the assumptions of OD are in every respect contradictory to the social reality of Latin America. For instance, "traditional" societies in Latin America stand in opposition to the "modern" Anglo-Saxon societies in their lesser capacity for openness, trust, and rational expression of feelings. Contrary to the contractual basis of North American society, Latin America seems marked by the predominance of deeply rooted tradition, class structure, and government centralization. As Pinto says, Theory Y, suited to the Protestant ethic, does not fit the Catholic work ethic; competence is most often overruled by formal status in Latin America, where, according to this author, tolerance for uncertainty, ambiguity, and undefined structure would be very low. Group cohesion results generally from intergroup rivalry, and conflict resolution follows a win-lose model.

These analyses are striking in their similarity to those developed in Latin Europe. The difficult introduction of Management by Objectives (MBO) in France in the 1970s provides a good illustration. Considered as an additional control procedure by managers who alternate authoritarianism and seduction (Trepo 1973), MBO was integrated mostly in a context where centralization of decision making existed together with bureaucratic protection (Horovitz 1978).

Moreover, the tremendous centralization of business, the marked intervention of the State, ideological splits, the preeminence of the external processes of change (social movements) over internal processes, the importance of law (Sudreau Report and the law on continuous education), the representative structure needed for every change, and the distributive model of power constitute many elements likely to jeopardize what is often called the "truth-love-trust" model of OD. Management's lack of inclination toward OD values and their suspicion of the social sciences, their frequent association with academic elite castes, and the manipulative perspective with which they consider change are not foreign to the disappointment of the most enlightened French practitioners, to their withdrawal from industrial organizations (Rouchy et al 1980), or to their intention of fighting against their present mode of operation (Tichy 1974). These reactions, however, are not merely emotional. They rest upon, or result in, a reflective and theoretical analysis of organizations, development, and change as well as in specific methods of action and intervention.

For instance, Crozier, observing a fear of face-to-face relations within French firms, a certain mythical view of the boss, a tendency to regulate rather than negotiate, has developed a theory of bureaucratic organization (Crozier 1964) which he later put in proper perspective in his analysis of French society as a "stalled" society (Crozier 1973). This analysis of bureaucratic phenomena concurs with that made in Brazil (Daland 1973) and in Italy (Ferraresi 1980). For Crozier, the organization, whether administrative or industrial, is typically a power structure. In fact, it is formed of a combination of more or less *hidden games* (Crozier & Friedberg 1980, Crozier 1964, 1973) which the outside observer as well as the actor cannot easily discern. These games are organized around *uncertainty areas* which individuals would try to control for their own goals. *Information* being the key to power, giving it would necessarily mean losing power. Therefore, any intervention based on a purely voluntary process of information sharing might be a failure. To act upon the "real" organization requires first understanding it by gathering data about the actors' experiences, and then working mainly to *rebuild* their rationale, their strategies (conscious or unconscious) which make their behavior a rational one. The outsider here is more a researcher than a consultant, thus sharing no *relation* with the members of the organization before or after the research. The independence of the researcher and his *distrust in obvious data* seem to be two basic elements of an understanding of organization prior to action.

Crozier and his coworkers have therefore developed a very detailed analysis of power structures and organizational games mostly within public administration, and have contributed to the analysis of cultural processes within firms (Sainsaulieu 1977) as well as within the social castes which compose French society (Thoenig 1973). This theory of organization, called "strategic analysis," consequently views the Human Relations movement as being rather naive and presents some similarity with the systems approach even though it is, no doubt, an original contribution. It is understandable that such a theory does not make much provision for intervention of the OD style even though it is not opposed to it.

Influencing the attitudes of organization members is certainly a necessity if one hopes for a real development of the organization. In France, the uncertainties and tensions which go with a more open style of management are not readily acceptable. However, intervening in organizational games might appear to be wishful thinking or an insuperable task, (Morin, in Levy-Leboyer 1980) in any case inseparable from parallel action at the level of social and organizational structures. Finally, by insisting on the "necessary priority to be given to knowledge," Crozier & Friedberg (1980, pp. 351-55) situate their work prior to the change action.

The Psychosociological Approach

The movement of psychosociological intervention, which has preceded that of strategic analysis and remains parallel to it, is more radical through its clinical orientation. Its initial phase originally corresponds with OD and relies largely on OD principles, as noted by Dubost & Levy (in Mendel & Beillerot 1980). Missions of experts to Bethel in the mid-50s had familiarized the French social psychologists with the Lewinian approach, action-research, and T-groups. Still under the influence of the cohesive climate produced by the postwar period of reconstruction, the French specialists were seduced by the democratic view, Floyd Man's survey feedback, and Rogers' nondirective approach. Breaking away from the traditional role of the expert who holds and distributes knowledge was central then, and social psychological intervention was seen as a way to change authority relationships, decision making, and communication styles. Yet an interest in unconscious and collective emotional phenomena was dawning, thanks to a privileged relationship with the Tavistock Institute of Human Relations in London (Amado & Guittet 1975, Anzieu 1975). The aim was nevertheless (as Dubost noted) a "war of cultures" in the attempt to impose a democratic way of being and acting within organizations.

With the 60s, the analogy drawn with the psychoanalytic and psychotherapeutic model had already pointed to a contradiction between a process of adaptation and a process of elucidation. Two phenomena then accelerated the rupture with the classical OD approach. First was Carl Rogers' visit to France in 1966, an event which triggered great disappointment among most French social psychologists, who were shocked by his naivete, his angelicism, his theoretical weaknesses. Secondly and simultaneously was the impact of the clinical, theoretical, and epistemological work of the French psychoanalyst Jacques Lacan, which led to the *suspension of the desire to cure* the individual or the organization, such a desire implying a normativity incompatible with a real analytical process. A counterpart to this psychoanalytic approach could be found at the sociological level with a largely Marxist view colored with anarcho-syndicalism.

In opposition to American functionalism, to its trust in the self-regulating exchanges of a liberal economy and to its humanistic psychology, the gap had been widening and several basic assumptions of OD were exposed and seriously questioned, if not entirely rejected (Dubost & Levy, in Mendel & Beillerot 1980). For instance:

1. *Knowledge* in the Lewinian approach is considered an unquestionable positive value.
2. Reality is considered reachable (attainable) provided that the various different views are *added* together, referring to a Kantian assumption.
3. *Data collection* is supposed to favor an analytical process, whereas it could be argued that it contributes rather to *repression,* first in transferring into points of view all the splits and contradictions resulting from the intraorganizational divisions (particularly the division of labor), then in letting us believe in the imaginary merging of these divergent representations, reduced to closed statements, disconnected from conduct and strategy (Dubost, ibid).
4. The action research perspective has not led to an epistemological revolution. It is still marked by traditional conceptions of *knowledge and action* considered as *complementary* and not contradictory. It is possible on the contrary to argue that action requires some degree of ignorance or blindness.
5. The importance of the here and now is illusory if one admits that the participants in a process of organizational development or change are *thwarted by their membership in various institutions.* Understanding their discourse implies replacing it in its proper sociological context and interpreting it in relation to these determinisms (which explains the failure of ordinary T groups, especially within the firm).

It is therefore appropriate to consider the organization as being the proper scene for *class struggle* and also as a *construction of the imaginary,* a place where the secret is buried and covered up by rationalizations, in the psychoanalytic sense; historicity is most often put aside, leaving the consultant with a partial and temporal image of organizational processes as underlined by Enriquez (1972a) and Rouchy et al (1980). Furthermore, the role and involvement of the consultant in the social field largely determine the product of his or her work and the knowledge brought into light. The position of the consultant is therefore neither socially nor ideologically (Touraine 1981, Mendel 1974) nor unconsciously neutral (Dubost 1972, Enriquez 1972a,b.).

Finally, even a theoretician sympathetic to managerial concerns, such as Crozier, insists (Crozier & Friedberg 1980) on the inevitability of perverse effects, vicious circles inherent in the organization, rejecting thereby the implicit assumption of smoothly linear development found in OD.

Consequently, we may note the interest of the fundamental questions which are raised and of the theoretical contribution to an analysis of organization attempting to relate psychoanalytic approach and social analysis. However, contributions to intervention methods are more limited, less clear, still in gestation. They resemble the sociology of Elliot Jaques, or rely upon techniques closer to OD (meetings, interviews, confrontations) with a psychoanalytic perspective, or rest upon psychotherapeutic sensitization outside the organization (psychodrama, group analysis, Balint groups). The proponents of this psychosociological orientation—academic researchers, consultants, and psychotherapists—belong for the most part to an association (ARIP) and publish *Connexions,* the only review of this kind exploring organizational and social change from a clinical vantage point.

The Institutional Analysis Approach

The movement showing most originality and theoretico-practical depth is probably *institutional analysis* (Lourau 1970). In opposition with the supposedly normal, rational, or natural order in OD concepts (thus aiming at the defense of a certain social order), institutional analysis, backed by the more recent movement of *sociopsychoanalysis,* gives a real status to disorder. In the end, both refuse the treatment of dysfunctionings in favor of, as Ardoino says (in Mendel & Beillerot 1980), a question on the meaning, the unveiling and the uncovering of that till then was left hidden in the institutional phenomena through interests and the resulting "opacity."

Institutional analysis originated in 1940 from the work of a psychiatrist (Tosquelles 1966) convinced that "it is a question of first taking care of the institution of care" if one wants to have a true psychotherapeutic view, the relationship between institution and psychotherapeutic behavior within the institution being dialectically linked. He debureaucratizes the psychiatric hospital, stimulates the cooperation of the patients, establishes microinstitutions (clubs, etc). We can see some relations here with the first experiments led by the Tavistock Institute in hospitals (Bridger 1946, Gray 1970).

To some extent, the institution is put "in negation" according to the expression of Basaglia (1967), a psychiatrist who has a similar orientation in Italy, who includes in his work the discoveries of antipsychiatry and takes into account Marcuse's theories. The institutional approach then invades the universe of pedagogy and is espoused by psychosociologists critical of the school of Human Relations.

It is indeed in the course of the experience of a training group in the early 1960s that Lapassade (1967) demonstrated that a hidden instituted and authoritarian order (visible through session schedules, fees, etc) was overdetermining this nondirective and quasi self- managed experiment, and unfortunately was not considered a proper object for analysis. On that day, a practice of intervention was born which has gained a particular notoriety among Latin countries and which is characterized by several operations:

1. *The analysis of "demand",* including the official request from the client-staff (in charge of the organization), their hidden implicit demand, and the client-group demand (members of the organization). The intervention bears on this "collective."
2. *The self-management* of the intervention by the client-collective. It is the one who makes the decision about the process of action and the pedagogical and financial contract which binds it to the consultants.
3. The rule of "*say everything*" meant to feed back all the institutional unspoken in the sessions.
4. The clarification of multiple memberships, of positive and negative references to groups, categories, ideologies which deny the common belonging to the organization, and the analysis of the resistances to such an elucidation.
5. The analysis of the *involvement,* of the institutional transference and counter- transference of the consultant in the organizational field studied.
6. The construction or elucidation of "*analyzers.*" These are the elements which can reveal the hidden determinants of a given situation. So a rumor, or an unforeseen incident can be seen as revealing an underlying reality that needs to be further explored as well as important hidden power relations. These are *natural* analyzers which have never before been thought of and whose strength is all the greater as they have appeared in life itself. The *built-up* analyzers, on the contrary, are elaborate situations, carefully designed to provoke disclosures of meanings.

Therefore, we can see that this prospect is inspired both from psychoanalysis (while denouncing the collusion of psychoanalysis with the dominant oppressive power structure) and a radical orientation to unmask the unconscious reality of organization (Lapassade 1972) and allow its members to regain power on their own social life.

If the school of institutional analysis is relatively clear about its methodological approach and its aims, its main problem, however, is one of having only very limited markets for its fieldwork. They very rarely include companies of the private sector, which are not that naive to allow themselves to be caught up in interventions that might disclose the undesirable and shatter their present structure, without clearly offering any real developmental therapeutic process. In most cases those organizations which call in socioanalysts are liberal, marginal-type institutions.

The Sociopsychoanalytic Approach

The goal of *sociopsychoanalysis* is not far from that of institutional analysis but borrows a somewhat different methodology and theory which may explain its greater success. Sociopsychoanalysis was born in the early 1970s in keeping with the antiauthoritarian revolt of May 1968 in France. It begins with the diagnosis that society tends more and more to deprive the citizen of *his social power,* confiscated in favor of a small elite. This confiscation is to be found in schools as well as in hospitals, administrations or enterprises. Here, sophisticated techniques of management such as MBO are attacked as the tools of an *insidious seduction and social control.* That seduction which operates through anesthesia (Loue 1974) rests on unconscious psychic mechanisms that need be disclosed if one wants to help everyone to recover lucidity, power over his own action and, in the end, to enter the permanent democratic conflictual negotiation, the only way of making organizations dynamic.

As an intermediate area of the singular and the collective, the institution-organization is considered as a privileged crossroads of observation and action. Here, the intervention (Mendel 1974) is unfolded at the request of an *"institutional class,"* that is, of a category of actors bound together by common interests within the organization. During a fortnight of sessions, successive consultants—gathered in a sociopsychoanalytic "collective"—try to understand the nature of psychological mechanisms which prevent the actors from reaching the political dimension, a dimension which represents the upper stage of personality development (*the political ego* only develops itself through outranging the "psycho-family" ego) (Mendel 1972). One of the originalities of the method lies in the postulate: that which concerns a group can only be understood by another group (as we are reminded by Mendel in Mendel & Beillerot 1980 and the Desgenettes group in Rouchy et al 1980). The verbal material recorded during the sessions is then decoded within another sociopsychoanalytical group in order that the *counterprojective positions* of the intervention group be analyzed. The consultants are paid only after collective negotiations. Involved in other organizations, they essentially intervene during their *free time,* which confers on the teachings of this action-research a greater truth.

Initiated by Mendel, a psychoanalyst, the sociopsychoanalytic method originated many developments in France, but also since 1977 in Belgium,

Switzerland, Brazil, Spain, Algeria, Israel, Columbia, Italy, even in Canada and the United States. The success of most of those interventions has been recently underlined by Mendel (*Sociopsychanalyse* 1980), even if his evaluation methodology is essentially of a clinical nature.

There is no doubt that these practices are different from those of OD. Their aim is to increase the power of the individual over himself and over society rather than to facilitate the development of the organization conceived as necessarily alienating. In many ways the work of Max Pagès and his coworkers (1979; see Johnstadt 1980) comes close to sociopsychoanalysis. According to these authors, we are at a time when "hypermodern" firms develop tools of a soft violence through sophisticated methods of personnel management. Starting from the study of a multinational company, the authors have attempted to understand the relationships among economic, political, ideological, and psychological variables. Observing that there are correspondencies between social organization and unconscious structures forming a "sociomental" system, they conclude that it is impossible to change the organization unless the nature of unconscious ties, through which the individual is attached to it, is understood as well as the policies which reinforce them.

In this perspective Pagès develops a method of "dialectical analysis" (Rouchy et al 1980) using elements of psychoanalysis and social analysis as well as body expression work, and aims at providing those working within organizations with the means for creating their own area of freedom.

It is important to observe, however, that through their contestation of power and their marginality, the most radical approaches find very few opportunities for intervention among firms, and few such interventions have thus far been reported in detail (Lourau 1974, C.E.R.F.I. 1971, Pagès et al 1979). These specialists are less and less keen to intervene in large firms and prefer intervention sites where real change is more likely to be produced: cooperatives, schools, hospitals, unions, minority groups, couples, and individuals.

Psychoanalysis and Organization

As we can see, psychoanalysis has considerably influenced research about organizations within Latin countries, France and Italy above all. This is a different case from what has happened in the US, where OD rests essentially on psychological and "humanistic" approaches. This does not mean that the OD philosophy has not reached some firms in Latin countries. On the contrary, managers and trainers often collude in diffusing what the academic researchers consider as products of US culture. The fear of manipulation expressed by trade unions is then reinforced by what they consider as a managerial ideology. However, even in the US there exists a psychoanalytic approach to organization which is even taught in some business schools. Actually, this approach remains relatively marginal in view of the quantity of publications on organization that ignore it. However, the work of Zaleznik(1966) on leadership, of Levinson (1970) on stress, of Maccoby (1976) on managers' profiles, of Zaleznik & Kets de Vries (1975) on power have offered a more sophisticated framework of interpretation for organizational realities, establishing thereby the clinical approach to management (Kets de Vries 1980) as a legitimate one. Amado (1980) has nonetheless shown that psychoanalytic research applied to organizations carried implicit assumptions largely determined by the cultural context where they originated. In comparing three countries that have yielded the most original contributions in this field—France, Great Britain, and the US—a number of essential differences must be noted.

In the US, the psychoanalytic approach is predominantly normative. Hartman's egopsychology looks at personality development as a progressive adaptation to an external reality considered as given. Impregnated with the values of liberal economy, organizational psychoanalysts focus mostly on the ways managers exert power and on the potentially dangerous consequences for their careers. In this perspective, they draw upon the contributions of psychiatry and theories of organization.

On the other hand, in England, the influence of psychoanalysts free from psychiatric nosography has helped researchers of the Tavistock Institute to look at the organization differently. Instead of considering it merely as a setting for self-actualization, they deal with it as a defense structure against archaic anxieties. They do stress the importance of task and technology and they pay due attention to administrative structures (such as personel management policies) and to the environmental context of the organization. The emphasis there is put on the client system rather than on the change agent as in the US, explicitly giving an equal weight to the different actors in the organization in a way that is consistent with their own approach to the psychotherapeutic process (Bridger 1977, 1978a,b, 1980).

As we have already seen, the basic assumptions are more explicitly formulated among the Latins and the French in particular who devote to them an attention at least as important as to the practice itself. The influence of more or less radical social philosophies (Marxism, anarchism, self-management) has led researchers to question the use of psychoanalysis which is not woven with concepts taking into account the socioeconomic environment. More or less explicitly, they consider organization as the "bad object," using such Kleinian concepts to give credit to the widely shared notion that organization is an inescapable source of alienation for its members unless they gain awareness of several sets of determinisms. A dialectical approach stands in opposition to the North American positivism and leads the researcher consultant to keep a greater independence concerning the object of study (the organization) which sometimes goes so far as to consider it a construction of fantasy.

Organizational Change, Drop-by-Drop

In Latin cultures, the organization is not the primary place for social change, as it is for instance in the US, and also to some extent in Northern Europe. The polarization which is found not only in the social field but also in the organization may help us to understand why the request for interventions of change agents is rather low. Latin social scientists favor the institutional dimension because it is there that society pervades organizations. Consequently, change is more likely to be looked for at the societal level. For instance, Touraine and his coworkers have developed a *method of sociological intervention* (Touraine 1980, 1981). They attempt to identify among various movements—students, antinuclear, regional, women, union—those which have the potential of becoming the one real social movement likely to produce a real social change. To that extent they are willing to help this social movement develop the analytic reflection needed for social action. This is parallel to the aim of most social scientists who see the main legitimate role of interventions in organizations as helping individuals to mature into responsible citizens. A comparative study between France and Germany (Maurice & Sellier 1979) illustrates this point. They show that the relationship between the worker and the enterprise is a function of the position of the enterprise within society. In Germany, workers do maintain a double allegiance to both enterprise and union. This and the joint management climate drives out of the enterprise the political conflict. Conversely, there is in France a refusal of legitimacy from both sides which demands an exclusive loyalty and makes political conflict pervade the enterprise.

On the other hand, there is a growing market in continuous education for trainers who often collude with management in avoiding the questioning of organizational structures. Training packages using Human Potential Movement techniques are thus more appealing than methodologies trying to integrate the educational process within actual work situations and within firms' structures (Meignant 1972, Meignant in Rouchy et al 1980).

In addition, some economists (Savall 1979), managers, and engineers, helped by social psychologists, have gathered in order to devote themselves to the improvement of working conditions, stimulated by the creation of a government agency (instead of the QWL centers led jointly by management and unions as they exist in North America). The peculiarity of the French approach seems to be the close link maintained at this level between a psychosociological approach and ergonomic studies: the improvement of the quality of working life, taking into consideration not only the actors' discourses but also the systematic studies of various physiological (posture, mental load), psychological, and environmental noxiants. Some sophisticated analytical tools have thus been developed (Guelaud et al 1975) for the study of jobs, tools which gradually allow in-depth actions supported or tolerated by the various actors within the firm. However, there is no research program similar to the Michigan one, monitoring major change experiments. Case studies which have been published until now provide definite results in France (Trepo 1980, European Foundation for the Improvement of Living and Working Conditions 1980), as in Italy (Novara & Ratti 1980, Musatti et al 1980). In spite of an ergonomic singularity, the improvement of working conditions does disturb the tradional power games between known players with codified relationships (Gautrat 1980), to the extent that it requires certain tasks to be managed collectively. Thus, a practice of "drop-by-drop self- management" (Mothé 1980) is beginning to appear and perhaps modify working relations more deeply than had actually been anticipated.

CONCLUSIONS

In contrast with the parsimonious and reluctant change in Latin countries, Japan stands as the non-Western industrialized nation able to compete successfully in the liberal economy game—a Western invention—from completely different cultural premises.

The innovativeness of Japanese organizations has to be understood at least as much in the context of Japanese society as in the context of industrial technology. As an example, recently the high level of quality control in some Japanese industries has put some pressure on Western industries. This has led some American firms to pay more attention to quality control and to the "Quality Circles" (QC) which were responsible in Japan for this performance (Yager 1979). Very rapidly the most progressive industries (very often the same that pioneered QWL projects) were able to follow suit. It is interesting to note then that QC have been presented in the West very often as a reimportation toward the US of "technological transfers" made in the early 1960s from US to Japan. Such an interpretation is puzzling. There is no doubt that American experts have adequately transmitted statistical techniques of quality control to Japan, as well as to many other countries, but of course they cannot be credited with the creative use of those inputs into the design of an innovative work structure more consistent with Japanese culture than with usual Western work organizations. It would also have to be explained why others who had benefited from the same inputs were not able to make a comparable innovation. Nonetheless, what is mostly perceived among Western industries is the technological instrumental aspect, not the social dimension. Actually this short-sightedness of some Western industries trying to imitate the Japanese has led them to the bitter discovery of the hidden part of the cultural icebergs.

The case of QC in Japan, only touched upon here, provides however a particularly useful reminder of the fact that strategies for organizational change cannot be analyzed without proper consideration of their sociocultural and socioeconomic context.

It is therefore essential at this point to recollect that OD has emerged within a booming postwar economy where rapid growth needed to be eased with the development of more participative attitudes among the middle management of organizations. Concerned primarily with process, OD consultants happily left to scientific management specialists all problems of structure and task. This nonbelligerent state of mutual ignorance across mutually agreed upon dividing lines between OD specialists and scientific management could not be maintained very long given the mounting necessity to redesign working conditions in many industries.

The field of planned change, which has been commensurate with OD in the US for nearly 20 years, is now undergoing a very significant transformation. It may not be an exaggeration to see in the sociotechnical system approach a new paradigm, and in QWL a significant social movement.

The crucial paradigmatic change lies in the central importance of the notion of *boundary*. It can be said that OD conceptions are the reflection of a split universe: split between the technical and the human, split between Scientific Management and Human Relations, split between atomistic parts whose organic ties are not seen, split between managers and managed, split between the organizations and their environment.

On the contrary, the gist of the sociotechnical approach is to insist always that both sides of the picture be looked at and dealt with *jointly* if one is to gain mastery of our social reality. It refuses the above schizophrenia and seeks negotiation and trade-offs between conflicting demands. Whenever a piece of reality is singled out, the context from which it is carved is never lost from view.

More research of a new kind (for instance, an action research closer to field experiments) is needed before a more substantial knowledge about social change becomes available. Nonetheless, the collaborative and open nature of these new efforts is crucial in order to face the problems confronting all nations today. Beyond the necessary mastery of organizational life, it is urgent to cope with the *interorganizational domains* (Trist 1979) and with the intercultural dimension of collaboration between nations (Emery & Emery 1976, Trist 1976, 1979). An aggiornamento of development conceptions and models is not only needed for organizations. Economic development, community development, even urban development are also fields questioning now their assumptions of the early 60s.

Social debate about the ways of redesigning our social order, wherever it can take place, is what counts most. It is fortunate that Western countries, in their own ways, have begun to question and reflect upon the tacit assumptions made in the early sixties, during the "first decade of development." For those who might find the conclusions of the present review pessimistic, we advise assessing them in the context of the almost universal admission of failure of the present development strategies. At a time when a collaborative spirit is needed (if impending economic and social disasters are to be minimized) not only at the shop floor, but also internationally, the QWL movement and its underlying philosophy provide some ground for optimism.

The recent realization within the Third World that socioeconomic development has to be self-managed is to be related with the recent interest in self-designing organizations (Hedberg et al 1976, Weick 1977) and self-help groups (Lieberman & Borman 1980). However, it might be important to realize that when structural changes of such magnitude are considered, a critical boundary condition lies in the maturity of the individual actors. Then the approach of Argyris (Argyris & Schon 1978) takes on particular significance because of his focus on increasing the reflective and learning capacities of critical actors. This approach is commensurate with the need to learn about our own culture as a critical path toward learning about and from other cultures (Shah 1978). Both intervention approaches—structural and personal—must be seen as complementary and should operate collaboratively if one is to deal adequately with social change. The crucial importance of individuals and minorities as cultural innovators and sources of change must also be realized (Moscovici 1976).

As the limits to growth have been stressed by many, it is about time that the limits to "first-order," "single-loop" type organizational change and development be more fully recognized as well. In most instances organizational change takes place as a result of changes in the context that organizations create for themselves through their interaction. Planned organizational change can only be a gimmick when it does not fully integrate the contextual dimension that provides life, meaning, and raison d'être to organizations.

In order to take into account the increased internationalization of today's organizational environment, this review has stressed the consideration of the cultural and cross-cultural context of organizational change as a challenge to be met by both theoreticians and practitioners. The field of organizational development needs some significant change. The field of organizational change can only develop if it ventures more into its context.

Literature Cited

Alderfer C. P. 1977. Organization development. *Ann. Rev. Psychol.* 28:197–223

Amado, G. 1980. Psychoanalysis and organization. *Sigmund Freud House Bull.* 4(2):17–20

Amado, G., Guittet, A. 1975. *La dynamique des communications dans les groupes,* ed. A. Colin. Paris: Univ. Press

Anzieu, D. 1975. *Le groupe et l'inconscient.* Paris: Dunod

Argyris, C., Schon, D.A. 1978. *Organizational Learning: A Theory of Action Perspective.* Reading, Mass: Addison-Wesley

Basaglia, F. 1967. *L'instituzione negata.* Milan: Einaudi

Beer, M. 1980. *Organization Change and Development: A System View.* Goodyear

Boetger, R. 1978. Desenvolvimento organizacional : alguns aspectos voltados a realidade brasileira. *Rev. Adm. Publica* 12:75–91. Spec. ed.

Borum, F. 1980. A power-strategy alternative to organizational development. *Organ. Stud.* 1(2):123–46

Bowers, D. G. 1976. *Systems of Organization: Management of the Human Resource.* Ann Arbor: Univ. Mich. Press

Bridger, H. 1946. The Northfield experiment. *Bull. Menninger Clin.* 10

Bridger, H. 1977. *Reducing Occupational Stress,* ed. A. McLean. Conf. Proc. NY Hosp. Cornell Med. Cent.

Bridger, H. 1978a. The relevant training and development of people for organizational development roles in open systems. *Proc. 1st Eur. Forum Organ. Dev., Aachen, Germany*

Bridger, H. 1978b. The increasing relevance of group processes and changing values for understanding and coping with stress at work. In *Stress at Work* ed. C. L. Cooper, R. Payne. New York: Wiley

Bridger, H. 1980. *The implications of ecological change on groups, institutions and communities. Reviewing a therapeutic community experience with open-system thinking.* Presented at Int. Congr. Group Psychother., Copenhagen

Bryant, D. T., Niemans, R. J., eds. 1978. *Manpower Planning and Organization Design.* New York: Plenum

Burke, W. W. 1976. Organization development in transition. *J. Appl. Behav. Sci.* 12(1):22–43

Burke, W. W., ed. 1977. *Current Issues and Strategies in Organization Development.* New York: Human Sciences. 448/pp.

Burke, W. W., ed 1978. *Cutting Edge: Current Theory and Practice in Organization Development.* La Jolla, Calif: Univ. Assoc.

Burke, W. W. 1980a. Organization development and bureaucracy in the 1980's. *J. Appl. Behav. Sci.* 16(3):423–38

Burke, W. W. 1980b. Interview by John Jones. *Group Organ. Stud.* 5(3):272–94

Carlson, H. C. 1978. GM's Quality of Working Life efforts . . . An interview by E. C. Miller. *Personnel* 54(4):11–23

Carvalho da Cunha, E. 1979. Desenvolvimento organizacional no contexto brasileiro. *Rev. Adm. Publica* 13(2): 85–99

Cavalcanti, B. S. 1979. DO : consideraçoes sobre seus objectivos, valores e processos. *Rev. Adm. Publica* 13(2):49–84

C.E.R.F.I. 1971. Analyse institutionnelle à la FNAC. In *Education Permanente,* Vol. 9

Chesler, M. A., Crowfoot, J. E., Bryant, B. I. 1979. Power training: An alternative to conflict management. *Calif. Manage. Rev.* 21(2):84–90

Clark, A. W., ed. 1976. *Experimenting With Organizational Life: The Action Research Approach.* New York: Plenum

Cooper, C., Mumford, E., eds. 1979. *Quality of Working Life in Western and Eastern Europe.* Westport, Conn: Greenwood

Crozier, M. 1964. *The Bureaucratic Phenomenon.* Univ. Chicago Press

Crozier, M. 1973. *The Stalled Society.* New York: Viking

Crozier, M., Friedberg, E. 1980. *Actors and Systems.* Univ. Chicago Press

Cummings, T. G., Molloy, E. S., Glen, R. 1977. A methodological critique of 58 selected work experiments. *Hum. Relat.* 30(8):675–708

Da Costa Moura, P.C. 1978. DO nas organizaç oes brasileiras: aceitaçao real ou ficticia? *Rev. Adm. Publica* 12:9–23. Spec. ed.

Daland, R. 1973. Bureaucracy in Brazil : Attitude of civilian top executives toward change. *Rev. Adm. Publica* 7(4):5–34

Davis, L. E. 1977a. Evolving alternative organization designs: Their socio-technical bases. *Hum. Relat.* 30(3):261–73

Davis, L. E. 1977b. Job design: Overview and future directions. *J. Contemp. Bus.* Spring:85–102

Davis, L. E. 1978. Socio-technical systems: The design of work and quality of working life. See Pasmore & Sherwood 1978, pp. 322–25

Davis, L. E. 1979a. Optimizing organization-plant design: A complementary structure for technical and social systems. *Organ. Dyn.* Autumn:3–15

Davis, L. E. 1979b. *Design of Jobs.* US-Goodyear

Davis, L. E. 1979c. A labor management contract and QWL. *J. Occup. Behav.* 1(1)

Davis, L. E. 1980. Individuals and the organization. *Calif. Manage. Rev.* 22(2): 5–14

Davis, L. E., Cherns, A. B., eds. 1975a. *The Quality of Working Life, I: Problems, Prospects and State of the Art.* New York: Free Press

Davis, L. E., Cherns, A. B., eds. 1975b. *The Quality of Working Life, II: Cases and Commentary.* New York: Free Press-Macmillan

Drexler, J. A., Lawler, E. E. 1977. A union-management cooperative project to improve quality of working life. *J. Appl. Behav. Sci.* 13:373–87

Dubin, R., ed. 1976. *Handbook of Work, Organization and Society.* Chicago: Rand McNally

Dubost, J. 1972. Introduction sur la méthode socioanalytique d'E.Jaques. In *Intervention et changement dans l'entreprise,* ed. E. Jaques, pp. 9–40. Paris: Dunod

Duckles, M. M., Duckles, R., Maccoby, M. 1977. The process of change at Bolivar. *J. Appl. Behav. Sci.* 13:387–99

Dunn, W. N., Swierczek, F. W. 1977. Planned organizational change: Toward grounded theory. *J. Appl. Behav. Sci.* 13(2):135–57

Dunnette, M. D., ed. 1976. *Handbook of Industrial and Organizational Psychology.* Chicago: Rand McNally

Emery, F., Emery, M. 1976. *A Choice of Futures.* Int. Ser. QWL No. 4. Leiden: Nijhoff

Emery, F., Thorsrud, E. 1976. *Democracy at Work.* Int. Ser. QWL No. 2. Leiden: Nijhoff

Enriquez, E. 1972a. Imaginaire social, refoulement et répression dans les organisations. *Connexions* 3:65–93

Enriquez, E. 1972b. Problématique du changement. *Connexions* 4:5–45

European Foundation for the Improvement of Living and Working Conditions. 1980. *The Analysis of Change in Work Organizations.* Dublin

Faucheux, C., Rojot, J. 1979. Social psychology and industrial relations: A cross-cultural perspective. In *Industrial Relations: A Social Psychological Approach.* ed. G. M. Stephenson, C. J. Brotherton. New York: Wiley

Ferraresi, F. 1980. *Burocrazia e politica in Italia.* Bologna: Mulino

French, W. L., et al, eds. 1978. *Organization Development: Theory Practice and Research.* Dallas: Business Publ.

Friedlander, F., Brown, L. D. 1974. Organization Development. *Ann. Rev. Psychol.* 25:313–41

Garson, D. G. 1977. *Worker Self-Management in Industry: West European Experience.* New York: Praeger

Gautrat, J. 1980. *L'effet perturbateur de la participation dans l'amélioration des conditions de travail.* Paris: CNRS

Golembiewski, R. T. 1979. *Approaches to Planned Change.* New York: Dekker

Goodman, P. 1979. *Assessing Organizational Change: The Rushton Quality of Work Experiment.* New York: Wiley

Gray, S. G. 1970. The Tavistock Institute of Human Relations. In *50 Years of Tavistock Clinic,* ed. H. V. Dicks. London: Routledge & Kegan, Paul

Guelaud, F., Beauchesne, M., Gautrat, J., Roustang, G. 1975. *Pour une analyse des conditions de travail ouvrier dans l'entreprise.* Paris: Colin

Guest, R. H. 1979. Quality of Work Life—Learning from Tarrytown. *Harv. Bus. Rev.* July/Aug: 76–87

Hedberg, B., et al. 1976. Camping on seesaws: Prescription for a self-designing organization. *ASQ* 21:41–65

Herbst, P. G. 1974. *Socio-Technical Design.* London: Tavistock

Herbst, P. G. 1976. *Alternatives to Hierarchies.* Int. Ser. QWL, Vol. 1. Leiden: Nejhoff

Hofstede, G. 1980. Motivation, leadership and organization: Do American theories apply abroad? *Organ. Dyn.* Summer:42–63

Hofstede, G., Kassem, S., eds. 1976. *European Contributions to Organizational Theory.* Amsterdam: Van Gorcum

Horovitz, J. H. 1978. Management control in France. *Columbia J. World Bus.* Summer:16–32

Huse, E. 1980. *Organizational Development and Change.* St. Paul: West

International Council for the Quality of Working Life. 1979. *Working on the QWL.* The Hague: Nijhoff

Inzerilli, G., Laurent, A. 1979. *The conception of organizational structure: A comparative view.* Presented at 4th EGOS Colloq., Noordwijk

Jain, H. C. 1980. *Worker Participation: Success and Problems.* New York: Praeger

Johnstadt, T., ed. 1980. *Group Dynamics and Society.* Cambridge, Mass: Oegelschlager

Jones, J. E., Pfeiffer, J. W. 1977. On the obsolescence of the terms Organizational Development. *Group Organ. Stud.* 2(3): 263–64

Kahn, R. L. 1974. Organizational development: Some problems and proposals. *J. Appl. Behav. Sci.* 10(4):485–502

Katz, D., Kahn, R. L. 1978. *The Social Psychology of Organizations.* London: Wiley

Kets de Vries, M. 1980. *Organizational Paradoxes. Clinical Approaches to Management.* London: Tavistock

Kuhne, R. J. 1980. *Co-Determination in Business: Workers Representative in the Board Room.* Holt-Saunders (Praeger)

Lapassade, G. 1967. *Groupes, organisations et institutions.* Paris: Gauthier Villars

Lapassade, G. 1972. L'analyse institutionnelle et l'intervention. *Connexions* 4: 65–106

Laurent, A. 1979. *Cultural dimensions of managerial ideologies: National versus multinational cultures.* Presented at 5th Ann. Meet. Eur. Bus. Assoc., London

Lawler, E. E., Nadler, D. A., Camman, C. 1980. *Organizational Assessment: Perspectives on the Measurement of Organizational Behavior and the Quality of Working Life.* New York: Wiley

Levinson, H. 1970. *Executive Stress.* New York: Harper & Row

Levy-Leboyer, C., ed. 1980. *Le psychologue et l'entreprise.* Paris: Masson

Lieberman, M., Borman, L. D. 1980. *Self Help Groups for Coping with Crisis.* San Francisco: Jossey-Bass

Loue, L. 1974. *L'anesthésie sociale dans l'entreprise.* Paris: Payot

Lourau, R. 1970. *L'analyse institutionnelle.* Ed. de Minuit

Lourau, R. 1974. *L'analyseur Lip.* U.G.E., coll. 10/18

Maccoby, M. 1976. *The Gamesman.* New York: Simon & Schuster

Maurice, M., Sellier, F. 1979. Societal analysis of industrial relations: A comparison between France and West Germany. *Br. J. Ind. Relat.* 17(3):322–36

Maurice, M., Sorge, A., Warner, M. 1980. Societal differences in organizing manufacturing units: A comparison of France, West Germany and Great Britain. *Organ. Stud.* 1(1):59–86

Meignant, A. 1972. *L'intervention sociopédagogique dans les organisations industrielles.* The Hague: Mouton

Mendel, G. 1972. De la régression du politique au psychique. In *Sociopsychanalyse* 1:11–63

Mendel, G. 1974. Qui est l'intervenant? *Sociopsychanalyse* 4:11–66

Mendel, G., Beillerot, J., eds. 1980. *L'Intervention Institutionnelle.* Paris: Payot

Miles, R. H. 1980. *Macro-Organizational Behavior.* Goodyear

Mills, T. 1975. Human resources—Why the new concern? *Harv. Bus. Rev.* Mar/Apr:120–34

Mills, T. 1978. Europe's industrial democracy: An American response. *Harv. Bus. Rev.* Nov/Dec: 143–52

Morin, P. 1976. *Le developpement des organizations.* Paris: Dunod

Moscovici, S. 1976. *Social Influence and Social Change.* London: Academic

Mothé, D. 1980. *L'autogestion goutte à goutte.* Le Centurion

Mulder, M. 1977. *The Daily Power Game.* Int. Ser. QWL No.6. Leiden: Nijhoff

Musatti, C., et al. 1980. *Psicologi in Fabrica.* Turino: Einaudi

Nadler, D. A. 1978a. Consulting with labor and management: Some learnings from the quality of worklife projects. See Burke 1978b, pp. 262–77

Nadler, D. A. 1978b. Hospital, organized labor and quality of work: An intervention case study. *J. Appl. Behav. Sci.* 13(3):366–81

Nadler, D. A., Camman, C., Mirvis, P. M. 1980. Developing a feedback system for work units: A field experiment in structural change. *J. Appl. Behav. Sci.* 16(1): 41–62

Novara, F., Ratti, F. 1980. *L'utile e l'umano: l'industria italiana e la qualita del lavoro.* Rome: Cedis

Pages, M. Bonetti, M., Descendre, D., De Gaulejac, V. 1979. *L'emprise de l'organisation.* Presses Univ. Fr.

Pasmore, W. A., Sherwood, J. J., eds. 1978. *Socio-Technical Systems: A Source Book.* La Jolla: Univ. Assoc. 365 pp.

Pate, L. E., Nielsen, W. R., Bacon, P. C. 1977. Advances in research on organizational development: Toward a beginning: *Group Organ. Stud.* 2(4): 449–60

Pettigrew, A. W. 1979. On studying organizational cultures. *ASQ* 24:571–81.

Pinto, R. F. 1979. Desenvolvimento organizacional intercultural : aplicacao na América Latina. *Rev. Adm. Publica* 13:47–68

Porras, J. I., Berg, P. O. 1978a. Evaluation methodology in organization development: An analysis and critique. *J. Appl. Behav. Sci.* 14(1,2):151–73

Porras, J. I., Berg, P. O. 1978b. The impact of organizational development. *Acad. Manage. Rev.* April:249–66

Porras, J. I., Patterson, K. 1979. Assessing planned change. *Group Organ. Stud.* 4(1):39–58

Porras, J. I., Roberts, N. 1980. Toward a typology of organization development research. *J. Occup. Behav.*

Porras, J. I., Wilkins, A. 1980. Organization development in large systems: An empirical assessment. *J. Appl. Behav. Sci.* 16(4):506–34

Rouchy, J. C., et al. 1980. Psychosociologies. *Connexions,* Vol. 29

Sainsaulieu, R. 1977. *L'identité au travail.* Presses Fond. Nat. Sci. Polit.

Salvemini, S. 1980. *Cambiamento e sviluppo organizzativo.* Suppl. bimest. Sviluppo Organ. No. 58. Milan: E.S.T.E

Savall, H. 1979. *Reconstruire l'entreprise. Une analyse socioeconomique des conditions de travail.* Paris: Dunod

Schein, V. E., Greiner, L. E. 1977. Can organizational development be functioned to bureaucracies? *Organ. Dyn.* Winter:48–61

Seashore, S. E. 1981. The Michigan Quality of Work Program: Issues in measurement, assessment and outcome evaluation. In *Perspectives on Organizational Design and Behavior,* ed. A. van de Ven. New York: Wiley

Seashore, S. E., et al eds. 1981. *Observing and Measuring Organizational Change.* New York: Wiley

Shah, I. 1978. *Learning How to Learn.* London: Octagon

Sociopsychanalyse 1980. *Pratiques d'un pouvoir plus collectif aujourd'hui.* Paris: Payot

Stein, B. A., Kanter, R. M. 1980. Building the parallel organization: Creating mechanisms for permanent quality of working life. *J. Appl. Behav. Sci.* 16(3): 321–88

Taylor, J. C. 1977. Experiments in work system design: Economic and human results. *Personnel Rev.* Part I: 6(3):21–34; Part II: 6(4):21–42

Taylor, J. C. 1978. An empirical examination of the dimensions of QWL. *OMEGA* 6(2):153–60

Thoenig, J. C. 1973. *L'ère des technocrates.* Ed. d'organisation

Tichy, N. M. 1974. An interview with Max Pages. *J. Appl. Behav. Sci.* 10(1):8–26

Tichy, N. M. 1978. Demise, absorption or renewal for the future of organizational development. See Burke 1978, pp. 70–87

Tosquelles, F. 1966. Pédagogie et psychothérapie institutionnelle. In *Rev. Psychothér. Inst.* Spec. issue, Vols. 2–3

Touraine, A. 1980. The voice and the eye: On the relationship between actors and analysts. *Polit. Psychol.* 2(1):3–14

Touraine, A. 1981. *The Voice and the Eye.* Cambridge Univ. Press

Trepo, G. 1973. Management style à la française. *Eur. Bus.* 39:71–79

Trepo, G. 1980. *Conditions de travail et expression du personnel.* Paris: Dalloz

Trist, E. 1976. Toward a post-industrial culture. See Dubin 1976, pp. 1011–34

Trist, E. 1979. *Referent organizations and the development of inter-organizational domains.* Lecture to Acad. Manage. 39th Ann. Conv.

Trist, E., Susman, G. I., Brown, G. R. 1977. An experiment in autonomous working in an American underground coal mine. *Hum. Relat.* 30:201–36

van Dongen, H. J. 1978. *The contributions of organizational development at the level of subsystems in the organization.* Presented at AACHEN

Wall, T. D., Lischeron, J. A. 1977. *Worker Participation: A Critique of the Literature and Some Fresh Evidence.* Berkshire, England: Maidenhead McGraw-Hill, UK

Walton, R. E. 1977. Work innovation at Topeka: After 6 years. *J. Appl. Behav. Sci.* 13(3):422–33

Walton, R. E. 1979. Work innovation in the United States. *Harv. Bus. Rev.* July/Aug:88–98

Weick, K. E. 1977. Organization design: Organizations as self-designing systems. *Organ. Dyn.* 6(2):30–46

Weick, K. E. 1979. *The Social Psychology of Organizing.* Reading, Mass: Addison-Wesley 2nd ed.

Weinberg, A. S. 1974. Work experiments and improving the QWL in the U.S. *Eur. Ind. Relat. Rev.* 10:2–5

Wilpert, B., Kudat, A., Özkan, Y. 1978a. *Workers' Participation in an Internationalized Economy.* Kent State Univ. Press

Wilpert, B., Dachler, H. P. 1978b. Conceptual dimensions and boundaries of participation in organizations: A critical evaluation. *ASQ.* 23(1):1–39

Yager, E. 1979. Examining the quality control circle. *Personnel* Oct:682–84,708

Zaleznik, A. 1966. *Human Dilemmas of Leadership.* New York: Harper & Row

Zaleznik, A., Kets de Vries, M. 1975. *Power and the Corporate Mind.* Boston: Houghton Mifflin

Ann. Rev. Psychol. 1982. 33:371–401

BRAIN FUNCTION, SYNAPSE RENEWAL, AND PLASTICITY

Carl W. Cotman and Manuel Nieto-Sampedro

Department of Psychobiology, University of California, Irvine, California 92717

CONTENTS

I. INTRODUCTION

Behavioral plasticity, the susceptibility of behavior to modification, ensures the adaptibility and survival of all living organisms. Over the past few years many studies have shown that nervous system circuitry is also very plastic. The structural and functional adaptations that contribute to such plasticity are numerous and can be elicited by many different stimuli. Circuitry adaptations range from modifications in existing connections in response to repeated stimuli to the replacement or renewal of synapses induced by surgical or environmental manipulations.

In this review we will examine the class of plasticities which appear to involve synapse renewal. When synapse replacement is induced by partial denervation it is clear that new synapses replace those lost. The issue in

0066-4308/82/0201-0371$02.00

these studies is to determine the factors that initiate this process, those that regulate which inputs grow, and the meaning of these changes from a functional point of view. Long-term changes in brain circuitry can also be induced by more subtle perturbations of the organism or of its environment, some of them identical to the stimuli that cause behavioral plasticity. We will evaluate these changes and show that synaptic growth and remodeling explains, at least in part, many such data. As the review proceeds we will develop the position that reactive synaptic growth and synapse renewal are just an extension of the normal operation and maintainance of brain circuits. We find it appropriate to use the term synapse turnover—that is, the loss and replacement of synapses—to describe synaptic dynamics. We will argue that synapse turnover is an ongoing process which can be readily elicited by certain stimuli to produce morphological and physiological plasticity. We will describe the systems where synapse turnover has been observed, attempt to identify the stimuli that induce this type of plasticity, and evaluate the mechanisms by which it may occur. In this discussion we will look at both the peripheral and central nervous system since many of the trends in brain plasticity are first identified in the peripheral nervous system and because in its own right it plays an important role in behavior.

The idea that synaptic turnover and remodeling goes on continuously and provides an important contribution to neural plasticity is by no means new. Indeed, it was proposed by Cajal, Tello, and others, in the early 1900s. What is interesting is the viability of the idea and the new data which now support it. Although many aspects of synapse renewal continue to be as elusive as ever, the data available show that the various forms of behavioral plasticity have neural counterparts in the ability of the nervous system to modify its circuitry.

II. LESION-INDUCED SYNAPTOGENESIS IN THE ADULT

Direct damage to the nervous system causing partial denervation is the coarser of the stimuli known to induce synapse renewal. Partial denervation of a peripheral or central structure causes intact nerve fibers to sprout new endings and form new synapses that replace those lost as a consequence of the lesion. Such responses can be considered a basic property of ensembles of nerve connections, and the rather voluminous documentation on the phenomenon has been recently reviewed in detail elsewhere (Cotman & Nadler 1978, Cotman et al 1981b). We shall mention only a few examples, the validity of which may be generalized to similar areas of the nervous system.

The innervation of the peroneus tertius muscle of the mouse is shared in variable porportions by spinal roots L5 and L6. Electrical stimulation of either of these evokes 20 to 80% of the total muscle contraction (Brown & Ironton 1978). When one of these roots is sectioned, the remaining root sprouts up to 5 times more new nerve endings that replace those lost. By day 12 postlesion, stimulation of the undamaged spinal roots elicits all the muscle contraction that previous to the operation could only be evoked by stimulation of both roots. Eventually the original fibers regenerate and replace the sprouts. However, the fine details of muscle function, with respect to its behavioral role, are probably never completely restored.

The superior cervical ganglion offers the simplest and best documented example where the recovery of function after partial deafferentiation results from the sprouting of substitute pathways. Ganglion cells receive innervation from spinal segments T1 to T7 and regulate, in turn, several autonomic responses, two of which are pupillary dilation and nictitating membrane contraction. These two responses are normally not elicited by electrical stimulation of preganglionic roots T4 to T7 but appear soon after damage of roots T1 to T3, due to sprouting of the undamaged afferents (Murray & Thompson 1957, Cotman et al 1981b). Similar growth responses occur after partial damage of sensory nerve endings that interrupt the contact of the nerve fibers with the specialized non-neuronal sensory receptors of the periphery, or when the lesion affects neuron-neuron synapses in the central nervous system.

Lesion-induced synaptogenesis has also been identified in the spinal cord following dorsal root section, hemisection of the cord, or chemical lesions by 5,6-dihydroxytryptamine or 6-hydroxydopamine (Cotman et al 1981b); in the olfactory bulb after mechanical or chemical damage to primary olfactory neurons (Graziadei & Monti Graziadei 1978, Harding et al 1978); in the hypothalamus after natural lesions caused by diabetes mellitus, tumors, aging, or following experimental or chemical damage (Billenstein & Leveque 1955, Raisman 1973, Dellmann 1973); in the lateral vestibular nuclei after unilateral labyrinthectomy (Dieringer & Precht 1977, 1979a, 1980); in the motor system (red nucleus) after peripheral nerve injury or cerebellar lesions (Tsukahara 1978a,b); in the cerebellum after removal of climbing fibers (Sotelo et al 1975); in the somatosensory system (somatosensory thalamus) after transection of dorsal root column afferents (Tripp & Wells 1978), interruption of cortical afferents to ventrobasal thalamus (Donoghue & Wells 1977), or following heavy particle irradiation of sensory cortex (Rose et al 1960); in the visual system (lateral geniculate) after cortical deafferentiation (Ralston & Chow 1972, Stenevi et al 1972, Baisden & Shen 1978); and in the limbic system (septum or hippocampus) following lesions of extrinsic or intrinsic pathways (Raisman 1969, Raisman & Field 1973, Cotman & Nadler 1978).

In the CNS, the most extensive studies have been carried out in the hippocampal formation of the rat. Here, all types of lesion evoke synaptic growth provided that a sufficient number of afferents is removed. Lesion-induced synaptogenesis in the hippocampal formation, and particularly in the dentate gyrus, will be described in further detail to point out general rules evolved from this type of study on synapse turnover. A review of the hippocampal circuitry (Cotman & Nadler 1978) is summarized in Figure 1. The entorhinal cortex provides the major extrinsic input to the dentate gyrus of the hippocampal formation. This input, the perforant path, is excitatory and probably uses glutamate as the neurotransmitter. It provides about 85% of the innervation to the outer two-thirds of the dentate gyrus molecular layer and a large proportion of the innervation of stratum lacunosum-moleculare of the hippocampus. The other prominent extrinsic afferent originates in the septum, is cholinergic, and projects to both dentate gyrus molecular layer and hippocampus proper. Minor inputs arrive from locus coeruleus, raphe, hypothalamus, and nucleus reuniens (Cotman & Nadler 1978). The remaining innervation originates in the hippocampal formation itself. The inner one-third of the dentate gyrus molecular layer is innervated by fibers that originate in area CA4 of the ipsilateral (associational fibers) or contralateral (commissural fibers) hippocampus.

Unilateral ablation of the entorhinal cortex causes the loss of about 60% of the total synapses in the dentate molecular layer (Matthews et al 1976a). This lost input is totally replaced (Matthews et al 1976b), beginning 3 days postlesion, by new synapses formed by sprouting fibers originating in the contralateral entorhinal cortex (Steward et al 1974, Zimmer & Hjorth-Simonsen 1975, Steward et al 1976a, Cotman et al 1977), the septum (Lynch et al 1972, Cotman et al 1973, Storm-Mathisen 1974, Steward & Messenheimer 1978) and in area CA4 (commissural/associational system; Zimmer 1973, West et al 1975, Lynch et al 1976, Lee et al 1977). The newly sprouted fibers form electrophysiologically functional synapses (Steward et al 1973,

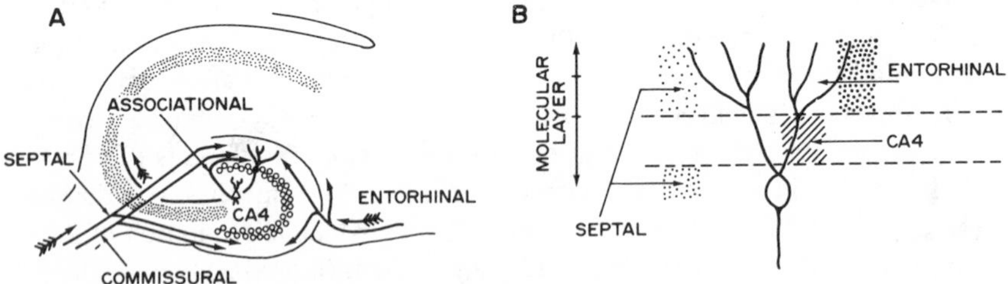

Figure 1 Diagram of the circuitry of the dentate gyrus of the hippocampal formation. (A) The major inputs. The granule cells receive their major input from the ipsilateral entorhinal cortex, associational and commissural CA4 neurons, and the septal area. Some inputs not vital to the concepts elucidated in this review are omitted. (B) Laminar organization of inputs to dentate granule cells.

1974, 1976a,b, West et al 1975, Harris et al 1978, Wilson et al 1979), and in the case of homologous entorhinal fibers, they probably mediate the same function as the entorhinal path that they replace (Goddard et al 1969, Messenheimer et al 1979).

This response exemplifies three general rules. The first rule is that the new synapses completely restore the synaptic input lost following partial denervation (Cotman et al 1981b). The second rule is that an afferent will reinnervate a denervated zone only if its terminal field overlaps that of the damaged afferent. The third general rule is that reactive growth causes only a quantitative increase or rearrangement of previously existing connections. Qualitatively new pathways are not created during lesion-induced synaptogenesis in the adult organism.

Another general rule is illustrated by the response to lesions caused by kainic acid. Intraventricular administration of low doses of this convulsant neurotoxin destroys selectively hippocampal CA3 and CA4 pyramidal cells and, therefore, denervates stratum radiatum and stratum oriens in the hippocampus and the inner third of the dentate gyrus molecular layer. Reinnervation of all denervated structures occurs to a large extent (Cotman 1979, Nadler et al 1980c,d) as in the ablation of the entorhinal cortex. However, the new synapses do not originate from sprouting of entorhinal or septal fibers that constitute the majority near the denervated area. Rather, residual commissural/associational CA4 fibers fill the synapse surface left vacant by denervation. Thus a fourth general rule may be formulated: when a neuron receives more than one type of afferent, there is a definite hierarchy in the relative capacity of the various afferents to grow in response to synapse loss. It seems that "like" afferents, i.e. those from similar cell types, have growth preference. This preference is very definite for systems that project bilaterally such as the CA4 fiber system or the fimbrial input to the lateral septal nucleus. In many cases, however, more than one type of fiber will respond to a lesion, so that the hierarchy is not an absolute preference but rather a weighed apportionment of the available denervated synaptic territory (Cotman & Nadler 1978, Goldberger & Murray 1978, Cotman et al 1981b).

In summary, partial denervation seems to elicit in large-scale plastic capabilities of neurons that are normally either not expressed or perhaps expressed in a more restricted and subtle manner. In the following sections we will show that the latter is probably the case. Our position would imply that the mechanisms and rules that apply to lesion-induced synaptogenesis can be extrapolated to natural occurrences during the life of an animal. This issue is important because to investigate mechanisms at the cellular and biochemical levels we need synchronized ensembles of neurons exhibiting a given phenomenon simultaneously.

III. LESIONS AS TRANSSYNAPTIC STIMULI FOR SYNAPSE RENEWAL

Destruction of nerve endings is definitely a general stimulus for growth of new synaptic connections in the zones directly affected by the lesion, that is, in denervated areas. Taking the analysis one step further, the experiments discussed in this section show that nerve damage may also stimulate synapse turnover in areas located outside the denervated zones.

The first type of experiment involves induction of growth of new peripheral nerve endings in muscle in response to a peripheral lesion in the opposite side of the body. Such an experiment was described by Reichert & Rotshenker (1979) and Rotshenker (1979) in the cutaneous pectoris muscles of the frog. These are two broad flat muscles situated in the frog's chest. Each muscle is supplied by a separate motor nerve whose cell bodies are spinal cord motor neurons located exclusively in the same side as the muscle they innervate (Szekely 1976, Rotshenker 1979). When the muscle in one side of the body was denervated by cutting or crushing its axon afferents, the nerve endings on the muscle of the opposite side sprouted 12 to 30% new synapses. The effect was not mediated by diffusion of factors from the denervated muscle or degenerating nerve fibers (Rotshenker 1979). Rotshenker proposes that the signals for sprouting and new synapse formation may arise in the axotomized motor neurons and are then communicated transneuronally to the intact motorneurones on the opposite side of the spinal cord (Rotshenker 1979).

A similar phenomenon, at least formally, has been observed in the CNS in our laboratory (Hoff et al 1981a). As described in section II, unilateral ablation of the entorhinal cortex deafferents the outer two-thirds of the molecular layer of the hippocampal dentate gyrus. Soon afterwards, intact terminals in the denervated zone and its vicinity sprout new endings that replace those lost as a direct consequence of the lesion. Additionally, the lesion also causes synapse turnover in zones of the hippocampus that are not denervated by the lesion or even directly communicated with the denervated cells. This is the case in the inner one-third of the dentate molecular layer ipsilateral to the lesion. This zone, that receives innervation predominantly from area CA4 of the hippocampus, loses 20% of its synapses within 4 days after the cortical lesion and recovers completely 10 days later. No degenerating terminals are seen at any time, suggesting that remodeling occurs by a mechanism that involves disconnection of terminals rather than degeneration. Small synapses with noncomplex synaptic junctions appear to account for most of the changes. Furthermore, the entorhinal lesion also induces turnover of synapses on the contralateral side of the brain. In this case the time course is slower. Loss of synapses is maximal (about 37%)

after 60 days postlesion and recovery is complete after 180 days. Both the inner and outer zones of the molecular layer are similarly affected. Overall synapse remodeling in the hippocampus is such that the number of synapses at 60 days is approximately the same on both contralateral and operated sides and afterward synapses are replaced symmetrically on both sides. Thus synaptic turnover may represent a homeostatic response to unilateral denervation to facilate the restoration of bilateral function in the dentate gyrus. The asymmetry introduced by the experimental lesion may promote adjustments in the number of synapses at several locations along the circuit as part of the mechanism to restore functional symmetry.

Finally, perturbations of the peripheral nervous system can elicit synapse remodeling in the brain. This was first demonstrated by Tsukahara and coworkers (reviewed in Tsukahara et al 1981), who found that cross-union of peripheral nerve input to flexor and extensor muscles of the same limb caused a redistribution of synapses in the red nucleus. The red nucleus is a small, almost spherical structure, situated in the mesencencephalon at the level of the colliculi. Red nucleus neurons receive two kinds of afferents: one, from the nucleus interpositus of the cerebellum (cerebello-rubral path), contacts red nucleus neurons on their somata; and the other, from the sensorimotor cortex (cortico-rubral path), synapses on the distal part of their dendrites. The efferent axons from the red nucleus project onto spinal motor neurons, forming the rubrospinal tract. The cortico-rubral input can be distinguished from the cerebellar input by its electrophysiological properties: cortical excitatory postsynaptic potentials have a slow-rising time course whereas cerebellar rise time is fast (Tsukahara & Kosaka 1968). Initial studies established that the cortico-rubral path could replace the cerebello-rubral synapses if the latter were removed by a lesion of the nucleus interpositus. Two weeks after destruction of the nucleus interpositus in adult cats the responses in red nucleus cells to cortical stimulation contained a new fast-rising component superimposed on the usual slow-rising cortico-rubral potential (Tsukahara et al 1974, 1975a,b). Extensive electrophysiological and anatomical analysis showed that cortical synapses grew new connections closer to the cell body to replace the lost input from the cerebellum.

Tsukahara et al then proceeded to investigate the possibility that similar effects could be produced by cross-union of the nerve supply to the flexor and extensor muscles in the forepaw of adult cats. Cross-union of nerves is a well-known procedure for testing the recovery and readjustments of muscles. Motor readjustments occur during walking and tactile placing (Tsukahara 1978a, Yumiya et al 1979). Three to 10 months after cross-innervation the cortico-rubral excitatory synaptic potential developed a new fast-rising component in the time-to-peak of excitatory postsynaptic potentials (Tsukahara & Fujito 1976). The new component was confined almost exclusively to neurons which innervate the upper spinal segments related to the forepaw. The change could not be attributed to variations in the cable properties of the dendrites. Furthermore, control self-union surgery had no effect on red nucleus neurons and no degeneration was found in the nucleus interpositus. Therefore, these data provide strong evidence that prolonged changes in the function of a peripheral circuit will elicit synaptic growth in the CNS in the absence of any direct denervation.

Another example of the same phenomenon has been reported recently by Merzenich, Kaas and coworkers (Merzenich et al 1980 and personal communication). They have found that the primate somatosensory cortex is surprisingly plastic to manipulation of the periphery. Amputation of one of the digits or section of the median nerve input to a digit and ligation of the nerve to prevent regeneration results in an enlargement of the surrounding cortical somatopic fields which all but consumes the previous somatotopic representation of the amputated digit. Initially a small rapid expansion occurs which appears related to the unmasking of existing inputs similar to that previously described by Wall and associates in the spinal cord (Merrill & Wall 1978), but the major expansion occurs more slowly and does not appear to be due to the unmasking of inputs already present. It appears likely that fibers surrounding the somatotopic projection area of the affected peripheral nerve expand their terminal fields to occupy zones where they were very sparse under normal circumstances. This hypothesis, although likely, still requires supporting anatomical evidence.

In all these studies, induced synapse growth and/or renewal may be purposeful, that is, may facilitate recovery of a lost function. This is clear in Tsukahara's experiments, where central synaptic changes correlated with the recovery of the cat's ability to adequately control the operated forepaw. Also, it is not very far-fetched to speculate that when a finger is amputated, expansion of the cortical surface devoted to processing sensory input from the remaining digits may help to compensate for the functional loss.

The stimuli that cause this type of synapse turnover are, no doubt, extreme from a physiological point of view. However, they are closer to physiological than direct partial denervation. The experimental paradigms described have the advantage of being reproducible at will and may have considerable bearing on neural correlates of behavioral plasticity. The cat whose forepaw has suffered a cross-union experiment receives a sensory feedback informing him that the pattern of muscle contraction programmed in the past is no longer adequate and must be modified. The adequate signals will reach the neurons of the motor cortex connected to the red nucleus, and these would respond by sprouting new endings and changing their physiological properties.

Presumably, feedback of some type also underlies the nondegenerative turnover in hippocampus after ablation of the entorhinal cortex. It seems that the CNS reacts to the lesion by trying to maintain bilateral symmetry of synapse density.

IV. PLASTICITY AND NATURAL SYNAPSE TURNOVER

We will now examine the notion that synapse loss and replacement is a process that occurs continuously in the mature nervous system in the absence of such drastic stimuli as lesions. It is well known that synapses connect and disconnect in the developing nervous system (Purves & Lichtman 1980), but this is generally thought to cease once the nervous system reaches maturity. The data reviewed here indicate that probably this is not the case. Synapse remodeling observed in the absence of tissue damage will be called "natural" or "spontaneous" to distinguish it from that elicited by lesions. It may be evoked by such natural stimuli as experience, changes in environment, and the normal physiological activity of the organism.

One of the most impressive examples of natural synapse turnover has been described by Townes-Anderson and Raviola in the parasympathetic innervation of the ciliary muscle of adult monkeys. These investigators found that nearly 2% of the axonal profiles observed in the electron microscope were degenerating and a similar number were regenerating (Townes-Anderson & Raviola 1976, 1977, 1978). This is a large portion of the nerve ending population and suggests a relatively rapid turnover. It is possible that this rapid turnover is necessary in this case because of extensive wear and tear associated with eye movements. Earlier, Barker & Ip (1965, 1966) had showed that at the neuromuscular junction of normal adult animals over 20% of the terminal branches of motor nerves bear collateral and terminal sprouts like those seen after partial denervation, suggesting a continuous turnover of the nerve terminals. The number of degenerating endplates in older cats was so large (Tuffery 1971) that if synapse replacement had not occurred, the old animals would have been almost completely denervated (Cotman et al 1981b).

In hibernating animals, seasonal variations occur in the number of neuromuscular junctions, indicating a functional correlate to turnover (Wernig & Stöver 1979). Similarly, the noradrenergic innervation of the guinea pig uterus virtually disappears during advanced pregnancy and recovers slowly to normal after delivery (Owman et al 1975, Sporrong et al 1978, Thorbert et al 1978, Alm et al 1979). It would not be surprising to find the same changes in other animals and women as well. Such variations in innervation illustrate how normal physiological function can be regulated by the disappearance and reappearance of nerve input. Catecholamine fibers are known for their plastic properties in the CNS as well as in the PNS, and it is possible that similar but as yet unidentified variations may occur centrally.

Natural renewal of synapses in the CNS has been identified in several brain areas. In the olfactory system, the bipolar sensory neurons, as well as the synapses that they form in the olfactory bulb, are involved in a continuous cycle of death and replacement every 10–20 days (Tagaki 1971, Graziadei & Monti Graziadei 1978, 1979, Graziadei & Okano 1979, Monti Graziadei & Graziadei 1979). Curiously, though, it has not been possible to distinguish either by ultrastructural or other means the new synapses from those already present. Paramembranous specializations, the so-called postsynaptic densities, are frequently observed unapposed by a presynaptic terminal. These vacant postsynaptic densities may be used in new synapse formation, and therefore are probably a good index of active synapse renewal.

Active nerve ending turnover is also found in neuroendocrine circuits of the central nervous system of normal animals. As far back as 1912, Tello noticed the presence of complex nerve endings in the human neural lobe of the hypophysis which he speculated were indicative of a continuous process of degeneration and regeneration. Subsequent work showed local dilations in axons, called Herring bodies, which are intermediates in a spontaneous degeneration-regeneration cycle (Dellmann & Rodriguez 1970, Baumgarten et al 1972, Dellmann 1973). Ultrastructural analysis revealed three main subclasses of Herring bodies, classified according to the microscopic appearance of their organelles (Dellmann & Rodriguez 1970). Type I bodies, filled with electron-dense neurosecretory granules, degenerate into Type II bodies that are characterized by autophagic vacuoles and other abnormal structures indicative of degeneration. Type III bodies have an appearance similar to regenerating nerve endings, that is, tubular formations, filaments, thin mitochondria, etc (Dellmann & Rodriguez 1970).

It might also seem reasonable to suspect that the vestibular system might possess inherent plastic properties since as the body grows and/or new aspects of balance are acquired, vestibular mechanisms must be reprogrammed. Indeed, it is known that new synaptic growth occurs readily in the vestibular system in response to partial denervation (Precht et al 1966, Dieringer & Precht 1977, 1979a,b, 1980). Moreover, Sotelo & Palay (1971) found in the lateral vestibular nucleus of normal mature rats unusual synaptic profiles in the process of "spontaneous" degeneration and regeneration. Mugnaini et al (1967) had also noted similar structures in their study of the normal ultrastructure of the vestibular system. The ultrastructural peculiarities of the abnormal nerve ending profiles observed here are similar to those described in the hypothalamus (Dellmann & Rodriguez 1970) and the autonomic innervation of ciliary muscle (Townes-Anderson & Raviola 1978), where turnover is well documented. Therefore, the ultrastructural evidence presented by Sotelo & Palay (1971) is strongly suggestive of natural turnover. As Sotelo and Palay discuss, similar degenerating synaptic profiles and growth cones have been noted also in other CNS structures, e.g. cerebellum, nucleus interpositus, cuneate nuclei.

It is now clear that animals placed in various environments can, even as adults, remodel features of their cortex including the number and distribution of synapses. Several reviews have described the effects of environmental changes on various cellular measures in the cortex of mammals (Greenough 1975, Reisen 1975, Rosenzweig & Bennett 1977, 1978), and in adult animals in particular (Uylings et al 1978a,b). The earliest observation of a direct environmental effect on the brain of an adult organism was the report by Bennett et al (1964). These workers found that adult rats (105 days old) placed in an "enriched" environment for 80 days had higher cortical weights, particularly in occipital cortex (+10%), than cage-reared controls of the same age. More elaborate studies have been performed subsequently, where changing environments have been shown to affect dendritic size and/or complexity. Some of the anatomical changes induced appear to involve synapse turnover. In the studies of Uylings et al (1978a,b), 112-day-old rats reared in standard laboratory cages were transferred into an enriched environment and kept there for an additional 30 days. At that time the dendritic branching pattern of these animals was compared to that of animals of the same age maintained in the standard cage condition. As a control for age effects, another group of rats 112 days old, kept in standard cages, was also examined. Microscopic examination showed that the number of terminal segments in layer II and layer III of cortical pyramidal cells increased in number with environmental complexity and age. There was also an increase in the length of terminal branches and first-order intermediate branches of the basal dendrites. Unfortunately, no spine counts were reported, so while it is clear dendrites remodel, the behavior of synapses is less obvious. It is probable that synapses at least turn over with dendritic growth, and it may be that replacing and repositioning synapses is just as purposeful as adding more.

Environmental influences are by no means restricted to cerebral cortex. Mice placed in an environment conducive to a great variety of complex physical activities for 17 days show more spines on cerebellar Purkinje cells (+23%) than mice kept in a cage that allowed only sufficient movement to gain access to food and water (Pysh & Weiss 1979). The dendrites of "active" mice were also about 10% bigger and had larger branches than the "inactive" ones. Similar data were reported by Floeter & Greenough (1979) in the cerebellum of young monkeys reared in a natural environment as compared with controls kept in social isolation with sensory and motor restriction.

Thus there is good, though yet sparse, evidence that synapses in both the peripheral and central nervous system are subject to ongoing turnover in the absence of damage of the tissues and, in some cases, under natural environmental conditions. In the peripheral nervous system the evidence is compelling: at least some neuromuscular junctions are in a state of continuous renewal. In the central nervous system, synaptic "intermediates" in the process of turnover have been identified, though they have not been observed throughout the CNS. Environmental factors can restructure dendrites and add and/or remove synapses. When searching for natural synapse remodeling, some of the difficulties are deciding what to look for, where to look for it, and when to look for it. We have a fairly good idea of what to look for, in terms of microscopic appearance of degenerating endings, vacant postsynaptic densities or growth cones, and synaptic density fluctuations. Where and when to look for these signs of synapse turnover will be discussed in further detail in sections VII and VIII.

V. INFLUENCE OF AGE ON SYNAPTIC STABILITY

Animals exhibit behavioral changes with age, as well as modifications in the rate at which these changes take place, i.e. changes in behavioral plasticity. If synapse remodeling is one of the substrates of behavioral plasticity, then changes in synapse numbers and rate of turnover should be evident as a function of age. The few reports available indicate that this is the case both in animals and man.

First of all, time and with it experience causes an increase in the complexity of nerve circuitry. This has already been commented upon in section IV, when discussing the experiments of Uylings et al (1978a,b) on the effect of environmental modification. One of the controls used by these workers allowed them to assess age effects in the experimental group of rats. They found that aging from 112 days to 142 days caused the dendrites of cortical pyramidal cells of layers II and III to increase the number of terminal segments and their branching complexity (Uylings et al 1978a,b). A similar phenomenon has been described by Buell & Coleman (1979) in humans. The dendrites of the neurons of layer II of the parahippocampal gyrus of normal aged subjects displayed remarkable increases in size and complexity when compared to young adults (Buell & Coleman 1979). The same dendritic arborizations showed clear signs of atrophy in patients suffering from senile dementia (Buell & Coleman 1979). Evidence of continued growth and synapse renewal is not restricted to the brain. The neuromuscular junction of old cats (Tuffery 1971) and rodents (Pestronk et al 1980, G. E. Fagg, S. Scheff, C. W. Cotman 1981) shows evidence of both nerve ending degeneration and replacement as well as enlargement of muscle endplates. Although these reports do not provide firm evidence of synapse remodeling, they establish that, first, the nervous system does not simply deteriorate with age; second, that neuron growth and plasticity continue throughout life and into old age. Other reports, although more indirectly, point to the same conclusion. Thus, in the substantia nigra cell death is common in aged subjects (McGeer et al 1977); the observed increase with age of the ratio of tyrosine hydroxylase activity to cell number suggests that sprouting of remaining neuron terminals compensates at least in part the neuronal loss.

Another example is the abnormal staining pattern reported by Cassell (1981) in the hippocampal formation of a 83-year-old man. As revealed by Timm's stain of autopsy tissue, the dentate gyrus of this individual showed a staining pattern very different from that of subjects in their 40s. A new plexus of mossy fibers was apparent in the supragranular zone, where none are normally found. These fibers most likely arise by sprouting, following the loss of hippocampal hilar cells which is common in many illnesses and in old age. We have described an animal model of this type of lesion, intraventricular injections of small amounts of kainic acid. The loss of hippocampal CA4 cells caused by kainic acid induces granule cells' mossy fibers to sprout and replace the synapses lost in the inner molecular layer of the dentate gyrus (Nadler et al 1980a). It would seem that Cassell has found the same effect in man; if so, it is the first case of sprouting reported in the human CNS.

Thus, experience as brought about by age or age itself is a stimulus for increases in synapse number and probably synapse renewal. The next question is whether and to what extent is the rate of synapse renewal affected by age; that is, how age affects this type of neural plasticity. Again, the data available are scarce and concern the synapse renewal induced by experimental lesions. It appears that in general the rate of lesion-induced sprouting declines with age in both the peripheral and central nervous systems. This is the case for motor neuron axons at the neuromuscular junction after partial section of the sciatic nerve (G. E. Fagg, S. Scheff, C. W. Cotman 1981) or botulinum toxin treatment (Pestronk et al 1980), and in the CNS, for hippocampal CA4 and septal fibers following entorhinal lesions (Scheff et al 1980), or noradrenergic fibers in the septum after transection of the fimbria (Scheff et al 1978a). Turnover stimulated by lesions in nondenervated zones far from the lesion also declines with age (Hoff et al 1981b). It appears as if the threshold for the initiation of growth is raised.

VI. INITIATION OF SYNAPSE RENEWAL AND SUBSEQUENT STEPS

In sections IV and V we have presented evidence that synapse renewal occurs in normal animals in the absence of lesions. If synapse turnover is a natural ongoing process, the stimuli which initiate it should be compatible with this view. That is, the initiating stimuli should arise in the organism itself or from its normal interaction with the environment.

At least one type of stimulus may be involved in the initiation and regulation of local synaptic changes. It appears that changes in circuit activity, i.e. increases or decreases over the most frequent firing pattern will elicit synapse turnover. As in most experimental situations, the stimuli tested, paralysis or artificial electrical stimulation, are rather extreme from the point of view of the normal range of activity in a given nerve circuit. Nonetheless, they demonstrate that synapse turnover can be produced by defined perturbations not involving injury. The effects of changing levels of activity have been tested in different areas of the nervous system.

We will describe first the effect of paralyzing a nerve to induce total inactivity in the circuit concerned. Paralysis can be induced by a variety of neurotoxins that do not cause nerve degeneration. Tetrodotoxin (TTX), for example, is a drug that prevents completely and reversibly the propagation of nerve impulses along the axon. If a cuff impregnated with TTX is applied to a periperal motor nerve, the nerve ceases to conduct impulses and the target muscle becomes inactive as well. If paralysis is maintained for more than 3 days, both blocked and unblocked afferents to the muscle sprout new endings (Brown & Ironton 1977a, Betz et al 1980). A similar effect can be achieved using botulinum toxin, a protein which paralyzes muscle by a totally different mechanism, namely by preventing ACh release. Botulinum toxin, like TTX, causes the growth of terminal sprouts within a few days of its causing muscle paralysis. Sprouting has in this case an important role in functional recovery because toxin binding is irreversible and recovery from botulinum toxin poisoning probably requires the growth of new functional neuromuscular junctions. Blocking of postsynaptic receptors with tubocurarine or α-bungarotoxin also causes terminal sprouting of nerve endings (Wernig & Stöver 1979, Holland & Brown 1980). Terminal sprouting can be prevented by direct electrical stimulation of the paralyzed muscle (Lømo & Slater 1978). These and similar data (Cotman et al 1981b) suggest that target muscle activity controls terminal abundance and that this at least correlates in some way with the number of extrajunctional neurotransmitter receptors. As the number of extrajunctional receptors increases, additional nerve terminals sprout. When this increase is prevented, terminal growth is also suppressed (Berg & Hall 1975, Brown et al 1977, Brown & Ironton

1977b, Lømo & Slater 1978). Perhaps the same mechanism which controls extrajunctional receptors creates diffusible factors which control sprouting.

It should be pointed out that stimuli such as TTX, botulinum toxin, or α-bungarotoxin do not evoke exactly the same growth response as partial denervation does. These toxins induce growth of terminal sprouts only (growth of existing terminals), while partial denervation will also elicit growth of collateral branches in the axons (Figure 2). Apparently collateral growth is less readily initiated and requires as a minimum stimulus the interruption of axonal transport (Aguilar et al 1973, Diamond et al 1976, Cooper et al 1977, Guth et al 1980). Terminal sprouting is particularly suitable for local circuit adjustments and, therefore, is very appropriate to most CNS circuits.

Though in this review we have largely limited the discussion to the mature nervous system, it appears that inactivity can also influence developmental plasticity, at least in the visual and somatosensory systems. Recently Stryker (1981 and personal communication) has shown that treatment with TTX of one eye of kittens from 2 to 6 weeks of age prevents the normal development of occular dominance columns. Segregation of columns fails to occur. Similarily, in the somatosensory system TTX treatment of the trigeminal nerve disrupts the formation of central connections (R. S. Erzurumlu and H. P. Killackey, personal communication). These data suggest that developmental systems may be keyed to functional activity even to a greater degree than mature ones, at least for the duration of the critical period. Aspects of the critical period may be rejuvenated, as suggested by Pettigrew, by local perfusion with norepinephrine (Kasamatsu & Pettigrew 1978, Kasamatsu et al 1978, Pettigrew & Kasamatsu 1978). Perhaps prolonged changes in catecholamine levels may allow subtle remodeling to extend throughout life.

Prolonged artificial stimulation can also elicit new synapse growth. This effect, initially reported by Hoffman (1952) at the neuromuscular junction, has been extended to neuron-neuron synapses of the autononic nervous

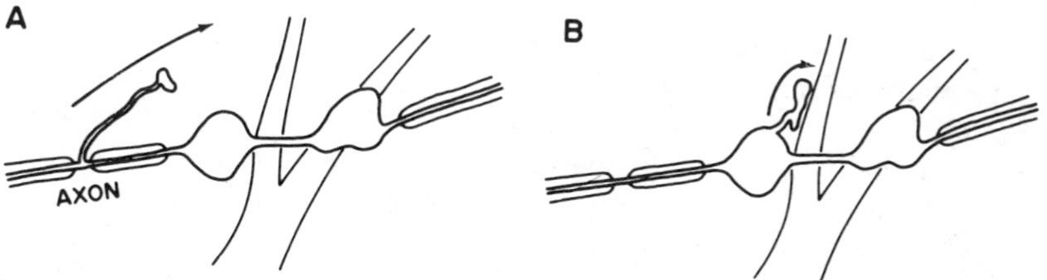

Figure 2 Main types of sprouting. (A) Axon collateral sprouting. This type is readily initiated by partial denervation but not by changes in usage. (B) Terminal sprouting. This type can be initiated by changes in usage as well as by denervation. Thus it is probably most suitable for local interactions and most appropriate for CNS circuitry remodeling.

system by Maehlen & Njå (1979) and to the CNS by Rutledge (Rutledge et al 1974, Rutledge 1978a,b). Rutledge stimulated the callosal fibers of cats by means of electrodes implanted in the suprasylvian gyrus and found that apical dendrites of layers II and III became larger, more complex, and developed more spines (and synapses) than nonstimulated controls (Rutledge et al 1974, Rutledge 1978a,b). These data indicate that unusually high use can also promote synapse growth just as disuse. Both may be mediated by changes in local concentrations of calcium ions, which in turn may activate select proteases which affect directly microtubule or neurofilament stability (Cotman et al 1981b).

In summary, altered levels of usage can produce circuitry adjustments mediated by synaptic growth. In most instances we can only relate a distal disturbance to a type of adjustment at other locations of the circuit. We can expect major advances in detailed mechanisms as additional studies are carried out on polyinnervated systems. Most likely an appropriate metabolic balance between signals for growth and suppression of it is more fundamental than use/disuse analysis. The triggering of terminal and collateral sprouting by interruption of axonal transport by means of colchicine alkaloids points in this direction (Diamond et al 1976, Goldowitz & Cotman 1980). Perhaps nerves carry antigrowth factors, the supply of which when interrupted or reduced allows the other nerves to grow (Diamond et al 1976, Goldowitz & Cotman 1980, Cotman et al 1981b).

Whatever the mechanism of initiation of growth of new nerve endings, a sequence of steps follows, resulting in the formation of a new functional synapse. These steps may include guided axonal growth, recognition of an appropriate target, stabilization of contact with it, and differentiation of synaptic specializations, such as the presynaptic vesicles and postsynaptic densities. These steps have been reviewed in detail elsewhere (Cotman & Banker 1974, Cotman et al 1981b).

VII. HOW FAST IS SYNAPSE TURNOVER?

When a given stimulus evokes a plastic adaptation of brain function, the time course of development of the new response may indicate whether or not synapse turnover is involved. The question from the neurobiological point of view is which of the steps of synapse renewal described in section VI is the slowest, that is, controls the rate of the whole process.

The earliest signs of synaptic growth in response to lesions are observed only after 4–5 days postoperation in the adult CNS (Moore et al 1971, Raisman & Field 1973, Tsukahara et al 1975a, Matthews et al 1976a,b, Cotman et al 1981b), and in the majority of cases 7–9 days are required before any initiation of sprouting is noticed (Cotman et al 1981b). The fastest lesion-induced sprouting of nerve endings occurs in the peripheral nervous system, and even here initiation of growth does not occur before 2 days postlesion (Matthews & Raisman 1972, Brown & Ironton 1978, Grafstein & McQuarrie 1978, Roper & Ko 1978). Accumulation and diffusion of initiation factors probably control the rate initiation of growth, because if a small priming lesion is initially performed, followed by a larger ablation 5–30 days later, then the initiation of sprouting occurs as early as 2 days postoperation (Scheff et al 1977, 1978b). Once initiated, axonal growth proceeds at a rate of 2–5 mm/day (Cotman et al 1981b). In brain, new synapses are formed at short distances from the sprouting nerve endings; hence, the rate of axonal growth is unlikely to be a rate-controlling factor. Finally, given the appropriate nerve endings, synaptic contacts can be formed in less than 24 hours (Rees et al 1976). Therefore, in lesion-induced synapse renewal, the controlling process is the initiation of growth.

Changes in function that develop to their full extent immediately or within a few hours after the lesion are very unlikely to involve new synapse formation. A change in preexisting synapses, brought about by synapse shape modification or metabolic adaptations such as those postulated to explain long-term potentiation, are more likely explanations. On the other hand, functional changes that begin a few days after the operation and continue over weeks or months after a rapid initial phase most likely involve synapse renewal.

Natural synapse turnover or synaptic growth induced by physiological stimuli or environmental changes may obey the same general principles as lesion-induced replacement. However, the regulation of the rate of initiation and overall time-course are probably different. High local concentrations of initiation factors may be achieved in a very short lapse of time compared to that involved in lesion-induced synaptogenesis. Also, neural circuit modifications can take place by repositioning of synapses, without new terminal growth being implicated (Cotman & Nadler 1978). For the time being it is only possible to make rough estimates of the rate of natural synapse renewal in those rare instances where quantitative data are available. In the ciliary muscle of young adult monkeys, about 4% of nerve endings appear to be turning over at any one time, as described earlier. If it is assumed that once initiated a cycle of turnover is completed in 24 hours, then the half-life of this synapse population is 18 days (Cotman et al 1981b). This means that half the total number of synapses is being replaced by new ones every 18 days. Even this conservative assumption indicates that the synapses of the ciliary muscle are renewed many times throughout the life of the animal.

The quantitative data available for the CNS are insufficient to make similar calculations. Terminals degenerating spontaneously are far fewer in the CNS than in the peripheral nervous system. This does not necessarily imply that turnover is slower. It is likely that synapses are eliminated without an intervening stage of degeneration. For example, loss of synapses in the dentate gyrus can take place without showing detectable traces of degenerating terminals (section III). This is probably akin to the synapse elimination mechanisms that operate during development (Purves & Lichtman 1980) or the synapse shedding after axotomy of the recipient neuron (for review see Cotman et al 1981b). There is ample precedent for synapse loss in the absence of degeneration. When the junction breaks, the disconnected nerve endings may either de-differentiate and be reabsorbed, may be reconnected elsewhere, or may be just left unconnected for a considerable time. Examples are known where one or the other of these possibilities occurs (Crepel et al 1976, Sotelo & Triller 1979, Nadler et al 1980c,d, Hoff et al 1981a). Thus synapse turnover is not seriously challenged by the absence of large numbers of degeneration profiles. The real problem is to find alternative means to estimate turnover times.

If one assumes that vacant postsynaptic densities are transient intermediates in synapse turnover with average time of existence of 8 hours (Rees et al 1976, Cotman et al 1981b), the turnover time can be calculated knowing the total number of vacant densities at any time. In the dentate gyrus about 3% of total postsynaptic densities are unoccupied at any time, which gives an estimated synapse half-life of about 1 week. This estimated turnover is probably faster than it actually occurs, but such numerical exercises underscore the remarkable dynamic potential of ensembles of synapses in the nervous system.

VIII. WHERE SHOULD SYNAPSE TURNOVER BE FOUND?

Lesion-induced synapse turnover has a well-established role as a plasticity mechanism in the recovery of the nervous system from injury. It will be found wherever there is injury. Although the molecular mechanisms involved are not known in detail, the practical rules discussed in section II allow us to predict which of several afferents available are most likely to respond to a given lesion.

On the other hand, the observation of synapse growth and replacement in adult animals in the absence of injury (sections III to V) suggests that lesion-induced synapse replacement may be only the massive manifestation of a normal potential of the nervous system. Selective synapse turnover could, in fact, be useful in a number of subtle ways, for example, to repair small damage caused by "wear and tear" of nerve endings, in the adaptation of the brain programs to the current state of the body as reported by peripheral feedback, and perhaps as one of the cellular correlates of learning and experience. The acceptance of these ideas as a working hypothesis helps to organize seemingly unconnected observations and more importantly to predict new situations where natural synapse turnover occurs. We can use to a degree the rules and limitations that apply to lesion-induced phenomenon. We can consider the problem in two parts. The first centers upon the types of perturbations and conditions, other than lesions, that are likely to initiate synapse remodeling; the second centers upon the ways to identify the most reactive neurons.

Regarding initiation of turnover, changes in the pattern of neural activity may be initiating factors (section VI). Changes in environment, variations in the level of muscular activity, or changes in hormonal levels may all translate into changes in the pattern of activity of the relevant neural circuitry. Two conditions, however, can be derived from lesion studies that limit the extent of change which may serve as stimulus for synapse turnover. First, stimuli have to be presented repeatedly and/or during a prolonged period, as indicated by the necessity to maintain nerve paralysis 2–3 days to evoke sprouting (section VII). Second, responses initiated faster than within 2 or 3 days after stimulus presentation are unlikely to involve synapse turnover. The actual physical stimuli could include impulse activity or even drug treatments. For example, prolonged treatments with drugs which compete with neurotransmitters for their receptors cause sprouting in the PNS, and it is possible that they have similar effects on sensitive systems in the CNS. Certainly prolonged drug treatments are known to elicit long-term effects not directly related to the drug's primary action, and perhaps synapse turnover underlies at least some such actions.

The second part of the problem concerns the identification of those locations where natural synapse turnover is most likely to be found. In this respect, the safest approach is to look again to lesion studies. Some brain areas appear inherently more plastic than others. Sensory relay nuclei show little if any potential for sprouting after lesions of major input, e.g. spinal trigeminal nucleus (Kerr 1972, Beckerman & Kerr 1976), lateral cuneate (O'Neal & Westrum 1973), dorsal column nuclei (Rustioni & Molenaar 1975). This is perhaps appropriate in that limited sensory processing should be stable once established during development. In contrast, the hippocampus, cerebral cortex, and to some degree the cerebellum readily show at least some forms of synapse turnover (see below). It is rather risky, however, given the state of the art, to generalize too far between systems because the numbers and types of studies are unequal.

At present synapse turnover is not readily related to parts of circuits implicated in particular behaviors, though it is likely such correlations will be possible in the future as more is understood about CNS circuitry and behavioral plasticity. In our opinion, gross neuronal type (e.g. local circuit vs projection neuron) does not determine synapse turnover potential. Similarly, the type of neurotransmitters used by a neuron does not seem to define its capacity for synapse renewal. For example, locus coeruleus fibers sprout new endings in the septal nucleus after transection of the fimbria, yet they will not do so in the dentate gyrus following an entorhinal lesion. The more critical factor seems to be where the cells reside in a functional system, and this may well define the type of stimulus necessary to produce turnover.

One of the goals of lesion studies has been to identify the plastic afferents and use this information to point to likely spots where synapse dynamics may respond to physiologically relevant stimuli. The work of Tsukahara and coworkers provides at present the most striking illustration of this approach. A lesion was used to demonstrate reactive synaptogenesis in the red nucleus; this was followed by peripheral nerve cross-union, which produced similar though less pronounced changes in the red nucleus as described above (section III). Most recently, Tsukahara et al (1981) have extended their studies on red nucleus plasticity to include studies on classical conditioning. A conditioned stimulus (CS) was applied to the cerebral peduncle of cats which had lesions of corticofugal fibers below the red nucleus 7 days prior to conditioning in order to remove cortical feedback influences. The lesion spared cortico-rubrospinal fibers but eliminated the pyramidal tract, cortico-pontocerebellar, and other descending fibers to the pontine and medullary reticular formation. The unconditioned stimulus (US) applied was an electric shock to the forearm skin causing flexion of the limb. Pairing the CS and US in close temporal association allowed an initially ineffective stimulus to the cerebral peduncle to cause elbow flexion. Extinction was produced by reversing the order of the stimuli or by giving only the CS. The threshold and strength of elbow flexion induced by stimulation of nucleus interpositus was the same as in unconditioned animals. Thus the interposito-rubrospinal system was not the site of the neuronal change. The experimental evidence indicated that the corticorubral synapses undergo a long-term increase in their efficacy. Previously, as discussed above, they had shown that cerebellar lesions or peripheral nerve cross-union caused corticorubral synapses to sprout, and it is entirely possible, as discussed by Tsukahara, that the same mechanism was used during prolonged conditioning. Anatomical studies are needed to confirm this point. Similar studies on other systems would be useful to determine if reactive synaptogenesis elicited by lesions can also be triggered by classical conditioning or other forms of learning.

Sensitive systems may, in fact, show individual variations in their structure which arise because of a difference in their long-term usage patterns.

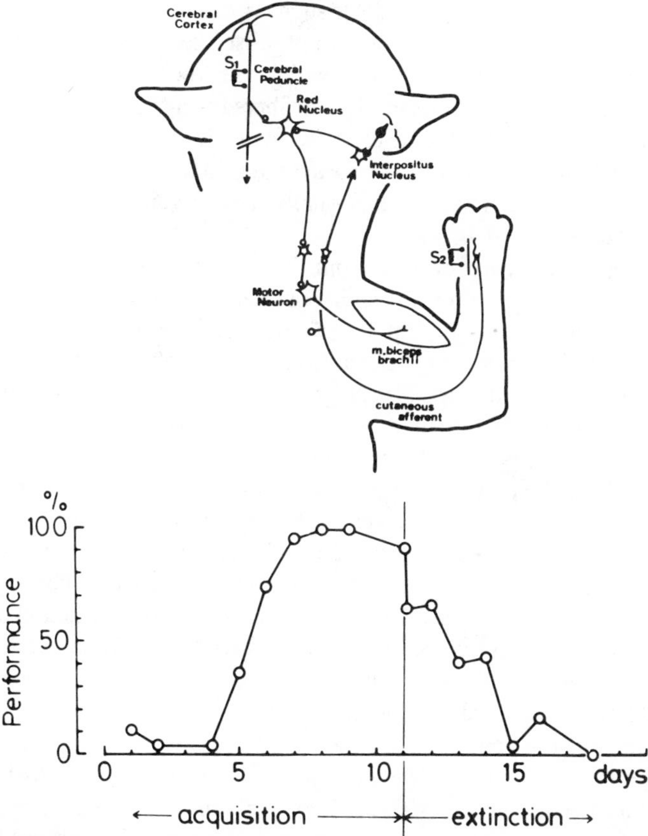

Figure 3 Demonstration of classical conditioning in the red nucleus. (A) Diagram of the principal neuronal circuits involving the red nucleus. S1, conditioned stimulus; S2, unconditioned stimulus. (B) The time course of learning during forward and backward conditioning (Tsukahara et al 1981).

As mentioned previously in section III, the somatosensory cortex shows changes in its somatotopic organization after injury to the nerves of a finger. Recently it has been reported that the detailed somatotopic map in primate cortex shows distinct differences between individuals (Nelson et al 1980). These may represent ongoing turnover or remodeling caused by experience.

Predictions on particularly responsive synapses will come to some degree also from cellular and biochemical levels of analysis. To illustrate the point we will give one example based on our own research in the hippocampal formation. It appears that nerve ending sprouting (or lack thereof) obeys a certain hierarchy (section II) and that this selectivity is due primarily to biochemical properties of the different afferents.

Thus, when a given input is lost, such as the ipsilateral perforant path after entorhinal ablation, the intact input most likely to sprout new endings and replace the lost synapses is that which uses the same neurotransmitter as the lost afferents; in our example, the fibers from the contralateral entorhinal cortex. Stated in general form, we can say that the presynaptic elements which preferentially form new synapses in the course of turnover use the same transmitter (or one functionally indistinguishable) as that of the original axons.

Another principle has evolved from the study of lesion-induced synaptogenesis in the hippocampus which complements and adds precision to neurotransmitter conservation. It appears that in a neuronal population that receives afferents from various sources, one of the afferents, the so-called critical afferent, controls the growth of another (Cotman 1979, Nadler et al 1980a,d, Cotman et al 1981a,b). Thus, in the hippocampus, commisural/associational fibers originating in area CA4 play a pivotal role in establishing the pattern of organization and reorganization of the septal projections to the molecular layer of the dentate gyrus. This is evidenced by the fact that septohippocampal fibers are always sparse in areas rich in commissural/associational fibers. For example, the expansion of the acetylcholinesterase negative zone in the adult, that marks the retraction of septal fibers following an entorhinal lesion, corresponds exactly to the widening of the CA4 fiber plexus. Other fibers are not so affected. Moreover, when CA4 cells are removed, septal fibers fill the zone left vacated by CA4 terminals and the zone sparse in septal fibers fails to form either during development or in adults (Nadler et al 1980b, Cotman et al 1981a). This exclusion of septal fibers by CA4 fibers explains both the development of the observed pattern of septal lamination in the hippocampus and its plasticity properties in the mature brain. This is significant because it shows that the mechanism which explains the development of the system also explains its plasticity in the mature brain.

In summary, while it is clear that much more research is necessary, trends are beginning to develop that provide a theoretical basis for identifying and understanding synapse turnover. Natural turnover is most likely to occur in systems where growth can be induced by lesions and perhaps can be evoked if the stimulus is presented for a prolonged time period.

An understanding of the factors controlling afferent development may help to predict where synapse turnover can occur in the mature nervous system. Growth restraints are imposed in the adult nervous system, and if these are superseded, synapse turnover may result. For example, perhaps it is necessary to release the growth-retarding effect of a critical afferent, as appears to be the case for septohippocampal fibers.

Some hormonally produced changes in behavior might be mediated in part by synapse turnover, particularly when the hormone(s) acts over long periods and produces long lasting changes that continue after the hormone returns to normal levels. We previously noted that the sympathetic innervation of the uterus shows cycles of turnover, and it may be that these peripheral effects have a central counterpart. Some hypothalamic neurons appear capable of natural turnover (see section IV) and these may be sensitive to endocrine influences.

An involvement of synapse turnover in some forms of learning is not a new idea by any means. However, it would seem that only those types of learning which develop over relatively long periods of time and require repeated presentations of the stimulus are likely candidates. Or at least it is in these cases where the extent of the anatomical or electrophysiological effects might be large enough to allow the identification of synaptic changes. Learning of complex motor skills might be one such instance. Such a situation might share common features with Tsukahara's studies on the motor system.

IX. APPROACHES FOR MEASURING NATURAL TURNOVER

At a practical level, how can natural turnover be identified? The problem is that in any given ensemble of synapses only a small proportion of them may be disconnected, being replaced by a similar number of new synaptic contacts. Since microscopically it is impossible to distinguish a new synapse from those that have remained unaltered, the usual methods used to follow synapse growth during development or after lesions are not strictly applicable. The problem is similar to that faced in the study of neuronal birthdays prior to the existence of the labeling technique using radioactive thymidine. The field needs an anatomical technique for establishing "synapse birthday." This has not been achieved, but it is likely that some biochemical markers exist which distinguish old from new synapses. In the absence of such a marker, less direct methods must be used.

Electron microscopy can be used to identify "intermediates" in the sequence of turnover, e.g. degenerating and regenerating terminals. We noted in section IV that "spontaneously" degenerating terminals appear to display grossly altered mitochondria and multilamellated electron dense bodies. Thus the appearance of these structures indicates active turnover. It is not clear, however, that all the synapses which turn over must go through a readily recognized transition state. Synapses which are subject to "wear and tear" appear to degenerate and regenerate, but in the CNS we have observed synapses that are lost without showing degenerating intermediates. Perhaps differentiation is so fast that few such profiles exist at a given time. More likely, however, these synapses do not degenerate, but the nerve endings simply retract and dedifferentiate. At any rate, the important point is that the absence of degeneration may be in fact the more general case.

We suggest that the presence of vacant postsynaptic densities, that is, postsynaptic specializations unapposed by a presynaptic terminal, is another static morphological sign of turnover. These can be found in apparently normal brains, and they are quite abundant during reactive synaptogenesis.

The problem is somewhat simpler if the total number of synapses changes. In these cases quantitative electron microscopy, histochemical methods for specific transmitters, spine number counts, and similar anatomical techniques can be used to indicate turnover. The usual as well as unusual precautions have to be exercised in interpreting results (Cotman et al 1981b). Synapses may redistribute along a dendritic surface, while the total number does not change. In assessing turnover, loss of synapses may be just as important as acquisition.

In the past, changes in levels of neurotransmitter, its receptors, or the enzymes involved in their metabolism have been considered to occur within stable synapse populations. However, in view of the wide ranging existence of synapse renewal in the nervous system, it is plausible that such changes may indicate turnover. We suggest careful reevaluation of old data and evaluation of new data in this perspective.

X. SUMMARY AND CONCLUSION

In this review we have argued that synaptic growth in the mature nervous system of the type elicited by lesions is related to the same phenomenon caused by changes in the environment or other natural stimuli. In order to discuss synapse dynamics we use the term synapse turnover for loss and replacement of synapses either naturally or in response to some stimulus. Lesion-induced synaptogenesis is widespread in the PNS and CNS. It seems that wherever there is nerve injury there is synaptic growth, though it is selective with respect to the afferents that will grow most readily. Synapse turnover is also found distal to lesions as a transsynaptic consequence to denervation or perhaps a homeostatic change in activity patterns of affected circuits. Finally, synapse turnover is in evidence as a natural ongoing process in the PNS and several CNS systems. At least in the red nucleus it is possible that classical conditioning can produce synaptic growth similar to that evoked by lesions. This argues that certain systems reponsive to lesions might be particularly sensitive to other stimuli as well.

Mechanistic studies argue strongly that terminal sprouting can be initiated in the absence of degeneration by changes in the activity patterns of pathways. In this way terminal sprouting appears more readily elicited than collateral sprouting which accompanies partial denervation. The growth of terminal sprouts is particularly suitable for short-range adjustments in the CNS.

In most cases, turnover has been identified by the simultaneous presence of degenerating and regenerating structures. The structures where degeneration per se is in evidence (neuromuscular junction, cutaneous sensory receptors, primary receptors, etc) may be self-repairing from excessive "wear and tear." In other systems it appears that turnover can occur without the presence of identifiable degeneration. Perhaps these synapses simply uncouple and reform elsewhere. Vacant postsynaptic densities may signify turnover in such cases.

In 1941 Carl Caskey Speidel, a well known zoologist, commented during his Harvey Lecture on "Adjustments of Nerve Endings:" "There is little doubt in my mind but that the free nerve endings of the central nervous system may undergo changes during irritation, injury, and recovery much like those of peripherally located endings. The conclusion seems justified that some flexibility in synaptic connections is possible; that certain changes may take place from time to time with the elimination of some old synapses and the establishment of some new ones" (Speidel 1941). Recent research confirms this notion and with time the evidence becomes more and more convincing. Certainly, though, further evidence is necessary to determine how synapse adjustments may be translated to behavioral plasticity.

ACKNOWLEDGMENTS

We are grateful to Susanne Bathgate for assistance in preparation of the manuscript. Our work was supported by grants NIH NSO8957, NIMH MH19691 and NIA AGOO538.

Literature Cited

Aguilar, C. E., Bisby, M. A., Cooper, E., Diamond, J. 1973. Evidence that axoplasmic transport of trophic factors is involved in the regulation of peripheral nerve fields in salamanders. *J. Physiol. London* 234:449–64

Alm, P., Björklund, A., Owman, Ch., Thorbert, G. 1979. Tyrosine hydroxylase and DOPA-decarboxylase activities in the guinea-pig uterus: further evidence for functional adrenergic denervation in association with pregnancy. *Neuroscience* 4:145–54

Baisden, R. H., Shen, C. L. 1978. Sprouting of ipsilateral retinal projections in the optic system of the albino rat. *Exp. Neurol.* 61:549–60

Barker, D., Ip, M. C. 1965. The probable existence of motor end-plate replacement. *J. Physiol. London* 176:11–12P

Barker, D., Ip, M. C. 1966. Sprouting and degeneration of mammalian motor axons in normal and deafferented skeletal muscle. *Proc. R. Soc. London Ser. B* 163:538–56

Baumgarten, H. G., Björklund, A., Holstein, A. F., Nobin, A. 1972. Organization and ultrastructural identification of the catecholamine nerve terminals in the neural lobe and pars intermedia of the rat pituitary. *Z. Zellforsch.* 126:483

Beckerman, S. B., Kerr, F. W. L. 1976. Electrophysiologic evidence that neither sprouting nor neuronal hyperactivity occur following long-term trigeminal or cervical primary deafferentation. *Exp. Neurol.* 50:427–28

Bennett, E. L., Diamond, M. C., Krech, D., Rosenzweig, M. R. 1964. Chemical anatomical plasticity of brain. *Science* 146:610–19

Berg, D. K., Hall, Z. W. 1975. Increased extrajunctional acetylcholine sensitivity produced by chronic postsynaptic neuromuscular blockade. *J. Physiol. London* 244:659–76

Betz, W. J., Caldwell, J. H., Ribchester, R. R. 1980. Sprouting of active nerve terminals in partially inactive muscles of the rat. *J. Physiol.* 303:281–97

Billenstein, D. C., Leveque, T. F. 1955. The reorganization of the neurohypophysial stalk following hypophysectomy in the rat. *Endocrinology* 56:704–17

Brown, M. C., Goodwin, G. M., Ironton, R. 1977. Prevention of motor nerve sprouting in botulinum toxin poisoned mouse soleus muscle by direct stimulation of the muscle. *J. Physiol. London* 267: 42–43P

Brown, M. C., Ironton, R. 1977a. Motor neuron sprouting induced by prolonged tetrodotoxin block of nerve action potentials. *Nature* 265:459–61

Brown, M. C., Ironton, R. 1977b. Suppression of motor nerve terminal sprouting in partially denervated mouse muscles. *J. Physiol. London* 272:70–71P

Brown, M. C., Ironton, R. 1978. Sprouting and regression of neuromuscular synapses in partially denervated mammalian muscles. *J. Physiol. London* 278:325–48

Buell, S. J., Coleman, P. D. 1979. Dendritic growth in the aged human brain and failure of growth in senile dementia. *Science* 206:854–56

Cassell, M. 1981. *The number of cells in the stratum pyramidale of the rat and human hippocampal formation.* PhD thesis. Univ. Bristol, England

Cooper, E., Diamond, J., Turner, C. 1977. The effects of nerve section and of colchicine treatment on the density of mechanosensory nerve endings in salamander skin. *J. Physiol. London* 264:725–49

Cotman, C. W. 1979. Specificity of synaptic growth in brain: Remodeling induced by kainic acid lesion. *Prog. Brain Res.* 51:203–15

Cotman, C. W., Banker, G. 1974. The making of a synapse. In *Reviews of Neuroscience,* ed. S. Ehrenpreis, I. Kopin, 1:1–62. New York: Raven

Cotman, C., Gentry, C., Steward, O. 1977. Synaptic replacement in the dentate gyrus after unilateral entorhinal lesion: electron microscopic analysis of the extent of replacement of synapses by the remaining entorhinal cortex. *J. Neurocytol.* 6:455–64

Cotman, C. W., Lewis, E. R., Hand, D. 1981a. The critical afferent theory: a mechanism to account for septohippocampal development and plasticity. In *Lesion-induced Neuronal Plasticity in Sensorimotor Systems,* ed. H. Flohr, W. Precht, pp. 13–27. Heidelberg: Springer.

Cotman, C. W., Matthews, D. A., Taylor, D., Lynch, G. 1973. Synaptic rearrangement in the dentate gyrus: histochemical evidence of adjustments after lesions in immature and adult rats. *Proc. Natl. Acad. Sci. USA* 70:3473–77

Cotman, C. W., Nadler, J. V. 1978. Reactive synaptogenesis in the hippocampus. In *Neuronal Plasticity,* ed. C. W. Cotman, pp. 227–71. New York: Raven

Cotman, C. W., Nieto-Sampedro, M., Harris, E. W. 1981b. Synapse replacement in the nervous system of adult vertebrates. *Physiol. Rev.* 61:684–784

Crepel, F., Mariani, J., Delhaye-Bouchaud, N. 1976. Evidence for a multiple innervation of Purkinje cells by climbing fibers in the immature rat cerebellum. *J. Neurobiol.* 7:567–78

Dellmann, H.-D. 1973. Degeneration and regeneration of neurosecretory systems. *Int. Rev. Cytol.* 36:215–315

Dellmann, H.-D., Rodriguez, E. M. 1970. Herring bodies: an electron microscopic study of local degeneration and regeneration of neurosecretory axons. *Z. Zellforsch.* 111:293–315

Diamond, J., Cooper, E., Turner, C., MacIntyre, L. 1976. Trophic regulation of nerve sprouting. *Science* 193:371–77

Dieringer, N., Precht, W. 1977. Modification of synaptic input following unilateral labyrinthectomy. *Nature* 269:431–33

Dieringer, N., Precht, W. 1979a. Mechanisms of compensation for vestibular deficits in the frog. I. Modification of the excitatory commissural system. *Exp. Brain Res.* 36:312–18

Dieringer, N., Precht, W. 1979b. Mechanisms of compensation for vestibular deficits in the frog. II. Modification of the inhibitory pathways. *Exp. Brain Res.* 36:329–41

Dieringer, N., Precht, W. 1980. Synaptic mechanisms involved in compensation of vestibular function following hemilabyrinthectomy. *Prog. Brain Res.* 51: 607–15

Donoghue, J. P., Wells, J. 1977. Synaptic rearrangement in the ventrobasal complex of the mouse following partial cortical deafferentation. *Brain Res.* 125:351–55

Fagg, G. E., Scheff, S. W., Cotman, C. W. 1981. Axonal sprouting at the neuromuscular junction of adult and aged rats. *Exp. Neurol.* In press

Floeter, M. K., Greenough, W. T. 1979. Cerebellar plasticity: modification of Purkinje cell structure by differential rearing in monkeys. *Science* 206:227–29

Goddard, G. V., McIntyre, D. C., Leech, C. K. 1969. A permanent change in brain function resulting from daily electrical stimulation. *Exp. Neurol.* 25:295–330

Goldberger, M. E., Murray, M. 1978. Recovery of movement and axonal sprouting may obey some of the same laws. See Cotman & Nadler 1978, pp. 73–96

Goldowitz, D., Cotman, C. W. 1980. Do neurotrophic interactions control synapse formation in the adult rat brain? *Brain Res.* 181:325–44

Grafstein, B., McQuarrie, I. G. 1978. Role of nerve cell body in axonal regeneration. See Cotman & Nadler 1978, pp. 155–95

Graziadei, P. P. C., Monti Graziadei, G. A. 1978. The olfactory system: a model for the study of neurogenesis and axon regeneration in mammals. See Cotman & Nadler 1978, pp. 131–53

Graziadei, P. P. C., Monti Graziadei, G. A. 1979. Neurogenesis and neuron regeneration in the olfactory system of mammals. I. Morphological aspects of differentiation and structural organization of the olfactory sensory neurons. *J. Neurocytol.* 8:1–17

Graziadei, P. P. C., Okano, M. 1979. Neuronal degeneration and regeneration in the olfactory epithelium of pigeon following transection of the first cranial nerve. *Acta Anat.* 104:220–36

Greenough, W. T. 1975. Experimental modification of the developing brain. *Am. Sci.* 63:37–46

Guth, L., Smith, S., Donati, E. J., Albuquerque, E. X. 1980. Induction of intramuscular collateral nerve sprouting by neurally applied colchicine. *Exp. Neurol.* 67:513–25

Harding, J. W., Getchell, T. V., Margolis, F. L. 1978. Denervation of the primary olfactory pathway in mice. V. Long-term effect of intranasal ZnSO irrigation on behavior, biochemistry and morphology. *Brain Res.* 140:271–85

Harris, E. W., Lasher, S. S., Steward, O. 1978. Habituation-like decrements in transmission along the normal and lesion-induced temporodentate pathways in the rat. *Brain Res.* 151:623–31

Hoff, S. F., Scheff, S. W., Kwan, A. Y., Cotman, C. W. 1981a. A new type of lesion-induced synaptogenesis: I. Synaptic turnover in non-denervated zones of the dentate gyrus in young adult rats. *Brain Res.* 222:1–13

Hoff, S. F., Scheff, S. W., Kwan, A. Y., Cotman, C. W. 1981b. A new type of lesion-induced synaptogenesis: II. the effects of aging on synaptic turnover in non-denervated zones. *Brain Res.* 222:15–27

Hoffmann, H. 1952. Acceleration and retardation of the process of axon-sprouting in partially denervated muscles. *Aust. J. Biol. Med. Sci.* 30:541–66

Holland, R. L., Brown, M. C. 1980. Postsynaptic transmission block can cause terminal sprouting of a motor nerve. *Science* 207:649–51

Kasamatsu, T., Pettigrew, J. D. 1978. Preservation of binocularity after monocular deprivation in the striate cortex of kittens treated with 6-hydroxyamine. *J. Comp. Neurol.* 185:139–62

Kasamatsu, T., Pettigrew, J. D., Ary, M. 1978. Restoration of visual cortical plasticity by local microperfusion of norepinephrine. *J. Comp. Neurol.* 185:163–82

Kerr, F. W. L. 1972. The potential of cervical primary afferents to sprout in the spinal nucleus of V. following long term trigeminal denervation. *Brain Res.* 43:547–60

Lee, K. S., Stanford, E. J., Cotman, C. W., Lynch, G. S. 1977. Ultrastructural evidence for bouton sprouting in the adult mammalian brain. *Exp. Brain Res.* 29:475–85

Lømo, T., Slater, C. R. 1978. Control of acetylcholine sensitivity and synapse formation by muscle activity. *J. Physiol. London* 275:391–402

Lynch, G., Gall, C., Rose, G., Cotman, C. 1976. Changes in the distribution of the dentate gyrus associational system following unilateral or bilateral entorhinal lesion in the adult rat. *Brain Res.* 110:57–71

Lynch, G. S., Matthews, D. A., Mosko, S., Parks, T., Cotman, C. W. 1972. Induced acetylcholinesterase-rich layer in rat dentate gyrus following entorhinal lesions. *Brain Res.* 42:311–18

Maehlen, J., Njå, A. 1979. Sprouting after partial denervation in the superior cervical ganglion: effect of perganglionic nerve stimulation. *Acta Physiol. Scand.* 105:18–19A

Matthews, D. A., Cotman, C., Lynch, G. 1976a. An electron microscopic study of lesion-induced synaptogenesis in the dentate gyrus of the adult rat. I. Magnitude and time course of degeneration. *Brain Res.* 115:1–21

Matthews, D. A., Cotman, C., Lynch, G. 1976b. An electron microscopic study of lesion-induced synaptogenesis in the dentate gyrus of the adult rat. II. Reappearance of morphologically normal contacts. *Brain Res.* 115:23–41

Matthews, M. R., Raisman, G. 1972. A light and electron microscopic study of the cellular response to axonal injury in the superior cervical ganglion of the rat. *Proc. R. Soc. London Ser. B* 181:43–79

McGeer, P. L., McGeer, E. G., Suzuki, J. S. 1977. Aging and extrapyramidal function. *Arch. Neurol.* 34:3–35

Merrill, E. G., Wall, P. D. 1978. Plasticity of connections in the adult nervous system. See Cotman & Nadler 1978, pp. 97–111

Merzenich, M. M., Kaas, J. H., Nelson, R. J., Wall, J., Sur, M., Felleman, D. J. 1980. Progressive topographic reorganization of representations of the hand within areas 3b and 1 of monkeys following median nerve section. *Soc. Neurosci. Abstr.* 6:651

Messenheimer, J. A., Harris, E. W., Steward, O. 1979. Sprouting fibers gain access to circuitry transsynaptically altered by kindling. *Exp. Neurol.* 64:469–81

Monti Graziadei, G. A., Graziadei, P. P. C. 1979. Neurogenesis and neuron regeneration in the olfactory system of mammals. II. Degeneration and reconstitution of the olfactory sensory neurons after axotomy. *J. Neurocytol.* 8:197–213

Moore, R. Y., Björklund, A., Stenevi, U. 1971. Plastic changes in the adrenergic innervation of rat septal area in response to denervation. *Brain Res.* 33:13–39

Mugnaini, E., Walberg, F., Hauglie-Hanssen, E. 1967. Observations on the fine structure of the lateral vestibular nucleus (Deiter's nucleus) in the cat. *Exp. Brain Res.* 4:146–86

Murray, J. G., Thompson, J. W. 1957. The occurrence and function of collateral sprouting in the sympathetic nervous system of the cat. *J. Physiol. London* 135:133–62

Nadler, J. V., Perry, B. W., Cotman, C. W. 1980a. Selective reinnervation of hippocampal CA1 and the fascia dentata after destruction of CA3-CA4 afferents with kainic acid. *Brain Res.* 182:1–9

Nadler, J. V., Perry, B. W., Cotman, C. W. 1980b. Interaction with CA4-derived fibers accounts for distribution of septohippocampal fibers in rat fascia dentata after entorhinal lesion. *Exp. Neurol.* 68:185–94

Nadler, J. V., Perry, B. W., Gentry, C., Cotman, C. W. 1980c. Degeneration of hippocampal CA3 pyramidal cells induced by intraventricular kainic acid. *J. Comp. Neurol.* 192:333–59

Nadler, J. V., Perry, B. W., Gentry, C., Cotman, C. W. 1980d. Loss and reacquisition of hippocampal synapses after selective destruction of CA3-CA4 afferents with kainic acid. *Brain Res.* 182:1–9

Nelson, R. J., Merzenich, M. M., Wall, J., Sur, M., Felleman, D. J., Kaas, J. H. 1980. Variability in the proportional representations of the hand in somatosensory cortex of primates. *Soc. Neurosci. Abstr.* 6:651

O'Neal, J. T., Westrum, L. E. 1973. The fine structural synaptic organization of the cat lateral cuneate nucleus. A study of sequential alterations in degeneration. *Brain Res.* 51:97–124

Owman, C., Alm, P., Rosengren, E., Sjöberg, N.-O., Thorbert, G. 1975. Variations in the level of uterine norepinephrine during preganancy in the guinea pig. *Am. J. Obstet. Gynecol.* 122:961–64

Pestronk, A., Drachman, D. B., Griffin, J. W. 1980. Effects of aging on nerve sprouting and regeneration. *Exp. Neurol.* 70:65–82

Pettigrew, J. D., Kasamatsu, T. 1978. Local perfusion of noradrenaline maintains visual cortical plasticity. *Nature* 271: 761–63

Precht, W., Shimazu, H., Markham, C. H. 1966. A mechanism of central compensation of vestibular function following hemilabyrinthectomy. *J. Neurophysicol.* 29:996–1010

Purves, D., Lichtman, J. W. 1980. Elimination of synapses in the developing nervous system. *Science* 210:153–57

Pysh, J. J., Weiss, G. M. 1979. Exercise during development induces an increase in Purkinje cell dendritic tree size. *Science* 206:230–32

Raisman, G. 1969. Neuronal plasticity in the septal nuclei of the adult rat. *Brain Res.* 14:25–48

Raisman, G. 1973. An ultrastructural study of the effects of hypophysectomy on the supraoptic nucleus of the rat. *J. Comp. Neurol.* 147:181–208

Raisman, G., Field, P. M. 1973. A quantitative investigation of the development of collateral reinnervation after partial deafferentation of the septal nuclei. *Brain Res.* 50:241–64

Ralston, H. J. III, Chow, K. L. 1972. Synaptic reorganization in the degenerating lateral geniculate nucleus of the rabbit. *J. Comp. Neurol.* 147:321–50

Rees, R. P., Bunge, M. B., Bunge, R. P. 1976. Morphological changes in the neuritic growth cone and target neuron during synaptic junction development in culture. *J. Cell Biol.* 68:240–63

Reichert, F., Rotshenker, S. 1979. Motor axon terminal sprouting in intact muscles. *Brain Res.* 170:187–89

Riesen, A. H. 1975. *The Developmental Neuropsychology of Sensory Deprivation.* New York: Academic

Roper, S., Ko, C.-P. 1978. Synaptic remodeling in the partially denervated parasympathetic ganglion in the heart of the frog. See Cotman & Nadler 1978, pp. 1–25

Rose, J. E., Malis, L. I., Kruger, L., Baker, C. P. 1960. Effects of heavy, ionizing monoenergic particles on the cerebral cortex. II. Histological appearance of laminar lesions and growth of nerve fibers after laminar destructions. *J. Comp. Neurol.* 115:243–95

Rosenzweig, M. R., Bennett, E. L. 1977. Effects of environmental enrichment or impoverishment on learning and on brain values in rodents. In *Genetics, Environment and Intelligence,* ed. A. Oliveiro, pp. 163–96. Amsterdam: North Holland Biomedical

Rosenzweig, M. R., Bennett, E. L. 1978. Experiential influences on brain anatomy and brain chemistry in rodents. In *Early Influences: Studies on the Development of Behavior and the Nervous System,* ed. G. Gottlieb, 4:289–327. New York: Academic

Rotshenker, S. 1979. Synapse formation in intact innervated cutaneous-pectoris muscles of the frog following denervation of the opposite muscle. *J. Physiol. London* 292:535–47

Rustioni, A., Molenaar, I. 1975. Dorsal column nuclei afferents in the lateral funiculus of the cat: distribution pattern and absence of sprouting after chronic deafferentation. *Exp. Brain Res.* 23: 1–12

Rutledge, L. T. 1978a. Effects of cortical denervation and stimulation on axons, dendrites and synapses. See Cotman & Nadler 1978, pp. 273–89

Rutledge, L. T. 1978b. The effects of denervation and stimulation upon synaptic ultrastructure. *J. Comp. Neurol.* 178: 117–28

Rutledge, L. T., Wright, C., Duncan, J. 1974. Morphological changes in pyramidal cells of mammalian neocortex associated with increased use. *Exp. Neurol.* 44:209–28

Scheff, S., Bernardo, L., Cotman, C. W. 1977. Progressive brain damage accelerates axon sprouting in the adult rat. *Science* 197:795–97

Scheff, S. W., Benardo, L. S., Cotman, C. W. 1978a. Decrease in adrenergic axon sprouting in the senescent rat. *Science* 202:775–78

Scheff, S. W., Benardo, L. S., Cotman, C. W. 1978b. Effect of serial lesion on sprouting in the dentate gyrus: onset and decline of the catalytic effect. *Brain Res.* 150:45–53

Scheff, S. W., Benardo, L. S., Cotman, C. W. 1980. Decline in reactive fiber growth in the dentate gyrus of aged rats compared to young adult rats following entorhinal cortex removal. *Brain Res.* 199:21–38

Sotelo, C., Hillman, D. E., Zamora, A. J., Llinás, R. 1975. Climbing fiber deafferentation: its action on Purkinje cell dendritic spines. *Brain Res.* 98:574–81

Sotelo, C., Palay, S. L. 1971. Altered axons and axon terminal in the lateral vestibular nucleus of the rat. Possible example of axonal remodeling. *Lab. Invest.* 25:653–71

Sotelo, C., Triller, A. 1979. Fate of presynaptic afferents to Purkinje cells in the adult nervous mutant mouse: a model to study presynaptic stabilization. *Brain Res.* 175:11–36

Speidel, C. C. 1941. Adjustments of nerve endings. *Harvey Lect.* 36:126–28

Sporrong, B., Alm, P., Owman, C., Sjöberg, N.-O., Thorbert, G. 1978. Ultrastructural evidence for adrenergic nerve degeneration in the guinea pig uterus during preganancy. *Cell Tissue Res.* 195:189–93

Stenevi, U., Björklund, A., Moore, R. Y. 1972. Growth of intact central adrenergic axons in the denervated lateral geniculate body. *Exp. Neurol.* 35: 290–99

Steward, O., Cotman, C. W., Lynch, G. S. 1973. Re-establishment of electrophysiologically functional entorhinal cortical input to the dentate gyrus deafferented by ipsilateral entorhinal lesions: innervation by the contralateral entorhinal cortex. *Exp. Brain Res.* 18:396–414

Steward, O., Cotman, C. W., Lynch, G. S. 1974. Growth of a new fiber projection in the brain of adult rats: Reinnervation of the dentate gyrus by the contralateral entorhinal cortex following ipsilateral entorhinal lesions. *Exp. Brain Res.* 20:45–66

Steward, O., Cotman, C. W., Lynch, G. S. 1976a. A quantitative autoradiographic and electrophysiological study of the reinnervation of the dentate gyrus by the contralateral entorhinal cortex following ipsilateral entorhinal lesions. *Brain Res.* 114:181–200

Steward, O., Messenheimer, J. A. 1978. Histochemical evidence for a post-lesion reorganization of cholinergic afferents in the hippocampal formation of the mature cat. *J. Comp. Neurol.* 178:697–710

Steward, O., White, W. F., Cotman, C. W., Lynch, G. 1976b. Potentiation of excitatory synaptic transmission in the normal and in the reinnervated dentate gyrus of the rat. *Exp. Brain Res.* 26:423–41

Storm-Mathisen, J. 1974. Choline acetyltransferase and acetylcholinesterase in fascia dentate following lesion of the entorhinal afferents. *Brain Res.* 80:181–97

Stryker, M. P. 1981. Late segregation of geniculate afferents to the cat's visual cortex after recovery from binocular impulse blockade. *Soc. Neurosci. Abstr.* 7:842

Szekely, G. 1976. The morphology of motorneurons and dorsal root fibers in frog's spinal cord. *Brain Res.* 103:275–90

Tagaki, S. F. 1971. Degeneration and regeneration of olfactory epithelium. In *Handbook of Sensory Physiology,* ed. L. M. Beidler, 4:76–94. New York: Springer

Tello, F. 1912. Algunas observaciones sobre la histología de la hipófisis humana. *Trab. Inst. Cajal Invest. Biol.* 10:145–84

Thorbert, G., Alm, P., Owman, C., Sjöberg, N.-O., Sporrong, B. 1978. Regional changes in structural and functional integrity of myometrical adrenergic nerves in pregnant guinea-pig and their relationship to the localization of the conceptus. *Acta Physiol. Scand.* 130: 120–31

Townes-Anderson, E., Raviola, G. 1976. Giant nerve fibers in the ciliary muscle and iris sphincter of *Macaca mulatta. Cell Tissue Res.* 169:33–40

Townes-Anderson, E., Raviola, G. 1977. Degeneration and regeneration of nerve terminals in the ciliary muscle of primates. *Anat. Rec.* 187:732

Townes-Anderson, E., Raviola, G. 1978. Degeneration and regeneration of autonomic nerve endings in the anterior part of rhesus monkey ciliary muscle. *J. Neurocytol.* 7:583–600

Tripp, L. N., Wells, J. 1978. Formation of new synaptic terminals in the somatosensory thalamus of the rat after lesions of the dorsal column nuclei. *Brain Res.* 155:362–67

Tsukahara, N. 1978a. Synaptic plasticity in the red nucleus. See Cotman & Nadler 1978, pp. 113–30

Tsukahara, N. 1978b. Synaptic plasticity in the red nucleus. *J. Physiol. Paris* 74: 339–45

Tsukahara, N. 1981. Synaptic plasticity in the mammalian central nervous sytem. *Ann. Rev. Neurosci.* 4:351–79

Tsukahara, N., Fujito, Y. 1976. Physiological evidence of formation of new synapses from cerebrum in the red nucleus neurons following cross-union of forelimb nerves. *Brain Res.* 106:184–88

Tsukahara, N., Hultborn, H., Murakami, F. 1974. Sprouting of cortico-rubral synapses in red nucleus neurons after destruction of the nucleus interpositus of the cerebellum. *Experientia* 30:57–58

Tsukahara, N., Hultborn, H., Murakami, F., Fujito, Y. 1975a. Physiological evidence of collateral sprouting and formation of new synapses in the red nucleus following partial denervation. In *Golgi Centennial Symposium Proceedings,* ed. M. Santini, pp. 299–303. New York: Raven

Tsukahara, N., Hultborn, H., Murakami, F., Fujito, Y. 1975b. Electrophysiological study of formation of new synapses and collateral sprouting in red nucleus neurons after partial denervation. *J. Neurophysiol.* 38:1359–72

Tsukahara, N., Kosaka, K. 1968. The mode of cerebral excitation of red nucleus neurons. *Exp. Brain Res.* 5:102–17

Tsukahara, N., Oda, Y., Notsu, T. 1981. Classical conditioning mediated by the red nucleus in the cat. *J. Neurosci.* 1:72–79

Tuffery, A. R. 1971. Growth and degeneration of motor end-plates in normal cat hindlimb muscles. *J. Anat.* 110:221–47

Uylings, H. B. M., Kuypers, K., Diamond, M. C., Veltman, W. A. M. 1978a. Effects of differential environments on plasticity of dendrites of cortical pyramidal neurons in adult rats. *Exp. Neurol.* 62:658–77

Uylings, H. B. M., Kuypers, K., Veltman, W. A. M. 1978b. Environmental influences on the neocortex in later life. *Prog. Brain Res.* 48:261–72

Wernig, A., Stöver, H. 1979. Sprouting and repression of the nerve at the frog neuromuscular junction. *Pfluegers Arch.* 379:R38

West, J. R., Deadwyler, S. A., Cotman, C. W., Lynch, G. 1975. Time dependent changes in commissural field potentials in the dentate gyrus following lesions of the entorhinal cortex in adult rats. *Brain Res.* 97:215–33

Wilson, R. C., Levy, W. B., Steward, O. 1979. Functional effects of lesion-induced plasticity: long term potentiation in normal and lesion-induced temporodentate connections. *Brain Res.* 176:65–78

Yumiya, H., Larsen, K. D., Asanuma, H. 1979. Motor readjustment and input-output relationship of motor cortex following cross-connection of forearm muscles in cats. *Brain Res.* 177:566–70

Zimmer, J. 1973. Extended commissural and ipsilateral projections in postnatally deentorhinated hippocampus and fascia dentata demonstrated in rats by silver impregnation. *Brain Res.* 64:293–311

Zimmer, J., Hjorth-Simonsen, A. 1975. Crossed pathways from the entorhinal area to the fascia dentata II. Provacable in rats. *J. Comp. Neurol.* 161:71–102

Ann. Rev. Psychol. 1982. 33:403–40

HUMAN BEHAVIOR GENETICS

Norman D. Henderson[1]

Department of Psychology, Oberlin College, Oberlin, Ohio 44074

CONTENTS

INTRODUCTION

Area of Coverage

Behavior genetics can be divided into three broad areas paralleling (1) general psychology and related social sciences, (2) clinical psychology,

[1]Preparation of this review was supported in part by NSF Grant BNS-78–15366.

0066-4308/82/0201-0403$02.00

psychiatry, and genetic epidemiology, (3) evolutionary biology, psychobiology, and animal behavior. Each area consists of several active subfields, resulting in nearly a dozen research areas that could support a review of the present size. Being able to deal with about one-tenth of the current literature, I have concentrated on the first area because of the number of new large-scale studies reported, the rapid developments in modeling procedures, and the implications of some of this work for the behavioral sciences.

With some reluctance I omit area 3 from this review. Animal research has shown a shift to more ecologically relevant behaviors and reflects some of the rapid progress in psychobiology and neurobiology as well as new genetic methods. Sociobiological theory is also having an impact on research designs and interpretation of results, but this work is still undergoing a "shakedown," and a brief delay in reviewing this aspect of the field is not totally undesirable. An extensive review of material in area 3 can be found in Ehrman & Parsons (1981), the impact of sociobiology in Thiessen (1979), and a warning against uncritical use of adaptationist explanations for behavior in Gould & Lewontin (1979).

Current Trends

Because human behavior genetic studies are perceived to have implications for public policy, results and conclusions tend to be carefully scrutinized and often spiritedly criticized. Once one gets by trivial criticisms and those based on misunderstanding or misrepresentation, attacks on straw morphs and dead horses, unlikely hypothetical situations and other strategies designed to obfuscate the issues, some legitimate criticisms concerning methodology, assumptions, and interpretations of data remain. One consequence of this is that human behavior genetic research has begun to show some changes.

First, there has been an increase in sophistication of designs and increases in sample sizes and in the number of kinship groups studied. In addition to the variables of interest, designs often include well-studied morphological and behavioral benchmarks against which to judge the adequacy of sampling and analytic procedures. Increased attention to sampling procedures and more detailed reporting of sample characteristics typifies many newer studies. Care is being taken to determine the effects of such factors as nonrandom mating, selective placement, and similarity of twin environments. There is also increased use of multivariate extensions of analyses, allowing the genetic and environmental bases of interrelationships between variables to be more thoroughly explored. Unfortunately, the trend toward larger and more complete genetic designs is not universal, especially in the area of psychopathology and in studies involving ethological data. Despite the value of such research, many studies are too small to permit reliable conclusions.

Second, there has been increased caution in the interpretation of the data. The enthusiasm which often accompanies the rapid development in a new field was not escaped by behavior genetics. Inevitably, overstatements were made concerning the role of genes in behavior which were based on data or analyses that subsequently proved to be inadequate for such purposes. This is changing. The word "familial" has replaced the term "heredity" in some studies where between-family environmental influences are confounded with hereditary influences. Investigators reporting large-scale studies have begun to divide their data into subsamples based on age, sex, socioeconomic level, or other factors in order to compare the stability of parameter estimates across such variables. Finally, there is some tendency for newer studies to be moving away from point estimates of genetic and environmental parameters, providing instead ranges based on procedures incorporating different assumptions.

Third, the new analytical models for human kinship data allow the decomposition of genetic and environmental effects into many components. These models often provide more accurate partitioning of environmental variance into common family, maternal, and within-family environmental effects than they do genetic variance into its additive and nonadditive components. Newer models can also incorporate age and sex influences and their interactions with other factors into the analysis. It is thus more accurate to regard much current research as testing general behavioral transmission models (e.g. Thompson 1979), with a greater emphasis on the psychology rather than the genetics of the behaviors studied. The label "behavior genetic" is thus inappropriately restrictive for much recent research. I later suggest that, in the absence of proper "genetic" designs, a great deal of research on cultural and other environmental influences on behavior is doomed to fail in its objectives.

The rapid growth in behavior genetics is reflected in the appearance of revisions of three textbooks in the field. Fuller & Thompson (1978) provided an extensive review of research and methodology in updating their 1960 classic; Plomin et al (1980) provided a sequel to the earlier text of McClearn & DeFries (1973), and Ehrman & Parsons' (1981) revision takes a strong evolutionary point of view with wide coverage of many species. Other books that cover a range of topics in behavior genetics include Oliverio (1977), Morton & Chung (1978), Mielke & Crawford (1980), Osborne et al (1978), Nance (1978), Royce & Mos (1979), Tsuang & Vandermey (1980). The current review covers material that appeared from mid-1977 to mid-1981.

Several terms are abbreviated in the review because of their frequent use. Unspecified genetic and environmental effects are referred to as G and E, respectively. AG refers to additive genetic influences and DG to genetic dominance. CE refers to common environmental influences shared by family members, sometimes called between-family variance or cultural influences which lead to differences between families in the population. SE refers to specific within-family environmental influences such as differential treatment of sibs, birth order, or idiosyncratic effects as well as error variance due to unreliability of measurement. Interactions are referred to in standard ANOVA notation (e.g. G X CE), monozygotic (identical) twins as MZ and dizygotic (fraternal) twins as DZ twins. Correlations reported are intraclass correlations (i.e. proportions of variance) except when noted.

PERCEPTION AND RELATED PROCESSES

Visual Perception

Two reviewers of the literature on spatial visualization ability (McGee 1979, 1982, Boles 1980) concluded that, although variation on spatial test scores appears to be at least moderately heritable, the X-linked recessive gene hypothesis which has served to explain sex differences in spatial abilities is not supported in recent studies. Work appearing since these reviews (Guttman & Shoham 1979, DeFries 1980, Corley et al 1980) is essentially in accord with these conclusions. A recent segregation analysis (Ashton et al 1979) added support to the suggestion that a major gene does influence performance on some, but not all, spatial tests. Rice et al (1981) applied a genetic model that allowed for polygenic and cultural transmission differentially by sex, phenotypic assortative mating, correlated rearing environments, and variable family structure to the data of Bouchard & McGee (1977) and to the data of Loehlin et al (1978). The results did not support an X-linkage interpretation, nor was there evidence of maternal effects for any of the sex-specific cultural mechanisms tested. There was, however, evidence of nontransmissible environmental factors relevant to the development of spatial ability which were different for males and females.

In a study of twins and their offspring, Rose et al (1979b) found substantial genetic influences on perceptual speed but no evidence of X-linkage. The authors suggested that gender differences in perceptual speed ability might reflect polygenic transmission with differing threshholds arising from sex-role training. The similarity of correlations for maternal and paternal half-sibships indicated the absence of maternal influences, and the fact that children resembled their twin uncle or aunt as closely as their own father or mother suggested that there were no major CE influences. It appears that on neither visual spatial abilities, on which males score significantly higher than females, nor on tests of perceptual speed ability, on which females are superior to males, is there much evidence for X-linked inheritance.

Using 203 mother-father-offspring triads and 303 sibling pairs, Coren & Porac (1979) found significant familial correlations for the Müller-Lyer illusion and the underestimation illusion in the Ebbinghaus configuration, but no evidence of familial similarity for the overestimation illusion. These findings provide an interesting parallel to the perceptual theory which suggests that both the Müller-Lyer illusion and underestimation on the Ebbinghaus illusion involve lateral inhibition whereas the overestimation illusion does not.

Reading Disability

Reviews of earlier work on genetic aspects of reading disability can be found in Finucci (1978) and Herschel (1978). Since then reports of the Colorado Family Reading Study have appeared and are summarized in DeFries & Decker (1982). The study, which involved data from 125 reading disabled children, their parents, and siblings, and members of 125 matched control families, is the most extensive study of this type reported. Three ability dimensions were isolated (reading, spatial/reasoning, and symbol processing speed), with probands scoring lower than controls on all three measures. Parent-offspring regressions and sibling correlations demonstrated a significant, though modest, "familiality" for reading.

Although the data suggested a major gene influence, a sex-linked recessive gene model did not adequately account for the different prevalence rates of reading disability between boys and girls. A segregation analysis required rejection of the hypothesis of a simple autosomal dominant or recessive gene influence but provided weak evidence for a single gene recessive inheritance when only the data from families of female probands was included. Both the poor fit for several single gene models and a cross-classification of subtypes of reading disabled siblings and probands suggested that reading disability is a heterogeneous disorder. A similar conclusion comes from a study of 21 families having multiple members with specific dyslexia. Omenn & Weber (1978) found evidence that dyslexic patients could be delineated into subgroups with predominantly visual or predominantly auditory impairment and that, in addition to providing tests of genetic models, family studies can aid in validating taxonomic systems for reading disability.

COGNITION

New Designs, New Data

The family-of-twins design (adult MZ twins, their spouses and offspring) produces correlations for MZ twins, sibs, half-sibs, and parent-offspring; thus consistency of estimates across familial groups can help determine the adequacy of assumptions underlying each of the familial relationships involved. Numerous other comparisons are also possible, making this one of the most powerful new designs available for the study of behavior transmission. Rose et al (1979a) used the design to examine nonverbal intelligence and found estimates of AG based on various genetic relationships were similar, ranging from .40 based on the half-sib correlation to .56 based on the offspring-parent regression. The design also allows a direct test for maternal effects on behavior, since the offspring of pairs of MZ twins are genetic half-sibs but social cousins reared in different households. When maternal effects are present, offspring of female MZ twin pairs will resemble each other more than will the offspring of male MZs. Rose et al (1980a) found this effect with respect to two Wechsler verbal scales, suggesting that at least some of the CE influence on verbal intelligence is due to a maternal effect. Finally, there was no difference in the degree of resemblance between wives of twin brothers and husbands of twin sisters, suggesting that assortative mating was not asymmetric for intelligence.

In a report marking a beginning step in the use of laboratory derived information processing measures in a single cognitive domain, Cole et al (1979) tested 165 families from the Hawaii Family Study on a variety of measures of short-term memory, tests for immediate and delayed-figure memory, and digit span. The complexity of memory was demonstrated by the low correlations between measures and by the low correlation between each measure and general intelligence. All but two measures showed significant though modest offspring-parent regressions, suggesting maximum heritabilities ranging from .2 to .5.

Several reports involving more traditional tests of cognitive ability have appeared from the Hawaii Family Study (DeFries et al 1979, Ashton et al 1979), the Korean Family Study (Park et al 1978), and the Boulder Family Study (Spuhler & Vandenberg 1980). Although familial resemblances in these studies cannot be separated into G and CE effects, the studies do provide upper-bound estimates for genetic parameters, if one is willing to assume that there are no negative correlations between G and CE. All three studies were done by the same group of investigators using largely the same tests, permitting cross-cultural comparisons of familial resemblances and interrelationships between cognitive abilities, as well as segregation analysis of the tests across cultures. Some of this work and results of several new twin and adoption studies will be summarized below.

In the previous *Annual Review of Psychology* chapter on behavioral genetics, DeFries & Plomin (1978) presented in detail the advantages of adoption studies for disentangling G and E influences on behavior. Their timing was appropriate, for the field was on the eve of receiving data from several major adoption studies, with total samples exceeding all previous published research using this methodology. Results of measures of cognitive abilities have now been reported for four adoption projects (Scarr & Weinberg 1976, 1977, 1978, Scarr & Yee 1980, Willerman et al 1977, Willerman 1979, Horn et al 1979, 1981, DeFries et al 1981) and reviews of this work have already begun to appear (Loehlin 1980, Plomin & DeFries 1980, Scarr & Carter-Saltzman 1981). I refer the reader to these reviews and present here only a brief summary of the extensive new data on cognitive abilities.

Table 1 lists pooled correlations from much of the recent research involving familial resemblances in general intelligence. The table is based on a survey by Plomin & DeFries (1980) summarizing results reported between 1976 and 1980, which I have modified and updated as indicated, and on the correlations reported by Ehrlenmeyer-Kimling & Jarvik (1963), also modified as indicated. Although Burt's data are omitted from Table 1 because of their doubtful authenticity (Dorfman 1978, Hearnshaw 1979), they represent such a small fraction of the kinship data on intelligence and are so comparable with the results of other studies (Rowe & Plomin 1978, Rao & Morton 1978, Rice et al 1980), that the correlations shown in Table 1 change very little with or without their inclusion. Because the correlations in Table 1 are based on a heterogenous collection of studies contributing unequally to various kinship catagories, it is not a particularly good starting point for a genetic modeling exercise. Nevertheless, it can be useful for examining some trends in this research.

With respect to the twin data shown in Table 1, there is agreement in MZ and DZ average correlations across older and newer studies, and there was great consistency among the newer studies which have been pooled, despite relatively wide differences in ages of subjects used. Given these average twin correlations, the reader who applies the frequently used $2(r_{MZ}-r_{DZ})$ estimate of heritability is likely to wonder where the earlier figure of 80% came from.

The answer lies partially with the DZ correlations reported in earlier data. The .61 listed in Table 1 is higher than the unweighted median of studies reported by Erlenmeyer-Kimling & Jarvik (1963). As both their summary and the twin survey of Nichols (1978) indicate, the distributions of intraclass correlations of twins are negatively skewed, with some of the smaller studies being such extreme statistical outliers that they raise serious questions about the methodology involved. After dropping studies with less than 25 pairs of each type of twin, the DZ correlation increases from the earlier .53 to the .61 shown. The second part of the answer comes from the spouse correlations shown in Table 1. Earlier reports of the degree of assortative mating for intelligence were much higher than those in more

Table 1 Kinship correlations for general intelligence

Relationship	Rearing	Pre-1963 studies[a] Correlation	Pre-1963 studies[a] N pairs	Post-1975 studies[b] Correlation	Post-1975 studies[b] N pairs
Same individual[c]	—	—	—	.87	456
MZ Twins	Together	.85[d]	2,059	.86[e]	1,417
DZ Twins	Together	.61[d]	1,894	.62[e]	1,329
Siblings	Together	.49	8,288	.41[f]	5,350
Siblings	Apart	.24[g]	203	—	—
Parent, child	Together	.50	371	.35	3,973
Parent, child	Apart	.45	63	.31	345
F. Parent, A. Child	Together	.20	—	.16	1,594
Unrelated children	Together	.23	195	.25	601
Unrelated persons	Apart	-.01	15,096	—	—
Spouses	Together	.44[h]	1,885	.29[i]	5,318
Kinship comparison	AM included[j]	AG[k]	CE[l]	AG[k]	CE[l]
MZ (t)–DZ (t)	No	.49	.36	.48	.38
MZ (t)–DZ (t)	Yes	.75	.10	.58	.28
P, O (t)–P, O (a)	No	.90	.05	.50	.04
P, O (t)–P, O (a)	Yes	.62	.05	.50	.04
Sibs (t)–Sibs (a)	No	.52	.23	.22	.25
Sibs (t)–Sibs (a)[m]	Yes	.43	.23	.25	.25

[a] Based on Ehrlenmeyer-Kimling & Jarvik (1963) except as noted.
[b] Based on Plomin & DeFries (1980) except as noted.
[c] Test-retest reliability.
[d] Weighted average based on Loehlin & Nichols (1976), excluding Burt's data.
[e] Data of Wilson (1978) added.
[f] Based on Paul (1980).
[g] Data of Burt excluded.
[h] Based on Johnson et al (1980) with Halperin rating data excluded.
[i] Based on Johnson et al (1980) excluding spatial ability data and including DeFries et al (1981) adoption data.
[j] Assortative mating included in model.
[k] Estimated proportion of total variance due to additive genetic influences.
[l] Estimated proportion of variance due to common family environment.
[m] See Bouchard & McGue (1981) for a compilation of results of 111 familial studies of intelligence published through 1979.

recent studies. When this is taken into account, estimates of both AG and CE differ considerably between the older and the newer data, as shown in the lower portion of the table.

Older and newer results of adoption and family studies are also difficult to reconcile, with correlations lower in all categories of relatedness in the newer data. More group (as opposed to single family) testing and more frequent use of age-corrected data in newer studies may partly account for these differences. Recent studies also show considerable restriction of range in their samples. In newer adoption data, for example, the variance in IQ scores is less than two-thirds that of the general population. It is difficult to determine whether earlier investigators avoided range restriction by modifying their sampling procedures or whether, because of cultural differences, persons involved with adoption were more representative of the general population than is now the case. In the absence of population equilibrium, resolving the roles of G and E effects can be difficult (Feldman & Cavalli-Sforza 1979). In any case, two major discrepancies exist in the intelligence data summarized in Table 1 when a simple AG + CE model allowing for assortative mating is applied—heritability estimates differ between older and newer studies and heritability estimates based on twin data differ from those based on other kinships.

Analysis of Multiple Kinships

Will the real estimate of heritability of intelligence please stand up? Older twin data, including the smaller studies deleted from the table, largely provided the basis for the often quoted and often challenged 80% figure. Today an estimate of 50% seems more in vogue. The problem with choosing a heritability estimate based on a particular methodology, or even a rough average across several types of kinship data, is that such choices involve assumptions, generally simplifying ones, concerning gene action, E influences, and population characteristics. As can be seen from the lower portion of Table 1, the inclusion of assortative mating improves the agreement between twin and parent-offspring (P,O) studies, since the effect of assortative mating works in opposite directions on these two types of data. One can further reduce the twin vs P,O discrepancy by allowing for genetic dominance, since this would be reflected in the twin data but not P,O data. Dominance does little to resolve the discrepant estimates from the sib vs unrelated-children data, but these discrepancies can be reduced when one allows for other factors to be operating, such as differential family density effects, age difference effects, or assumptions concerning relative magnitudes of CE in twins and sibs.

Table 2 presents a set of general expectations for factors that contribute to intraclass correlations for the relationships listed. The table is based on a number of simplifying assumptions, since it would require several more columns to provide a more comprehensive model of G and E effects. Table 2 is sufficient, however, to allow one to appreciate how various assumptions can lead to quite different interpretations of kinship data. Some examples: 1. By adopting the list of simplifying assumptions shown on the last line below the table, old standby equations can be generated—e.g. the MZ correlation reflects V(AG) + V(CE) and the DZ correlation reflects ½ V(AG) + V(CE), thus twice the difference in these correlations produces an estimate of V(AG), as will doubling the P,O correlation. In the presence of dominance, however, the situation changes since 2(rMZ-rDZ) includes a dominance component whereas the P,O correlation does not. 2. The effect

Table 2 Generalized expectations for variances in kinship correlations

Phenotypic correlation	AG var	DG var	AMG var	CE var	AG × CE var
MZ Twins together	1	1	1	1	1
MZ Twins apart	1	1	1	Q	Q
DZ Twins together	½ (1 + T × AG)	¼	1	S	½ S (1 + T × AG)
DZ Twins apart	½ (1 + T × AG)	¼	1	Q	½ Q (1 + T × AG)
Siblings together	½ (1 + T × AG)	¼	1	U	½ U (1 + T × AG)
Siblings apart	½ (1 + T × AG)	¼	1	Q	½ Q (1 + T × AG)
Parent, child together	½ (1 + T)	0	½ (1 + T)	R	½ R (1 + T)
Parent, child apart	½ (1 + T)	0	½ (1 + T)	0	0
Child, midparent together (regression)	1	0	0	R	R
F. Parent, A. Child together	P	0	0	R	R
Unrelated together	0	0	0	U	U
Unrelated apart	0	0	0	0	0

Assumptions: Polygenic trait, genetic equilibrium, no GE correlation, negligible epistasis, no sex or age differences in mode of transmission, no AG × SE interaction, no DG interactions, equivalent sampling across kinships.
AMG var = Genetic variance due to assortative mating.
P = G correlation between foster parent and child due to selective placement (0 – .3).
Q = Correlation between environments due to selective placement (0 – .3).
R = Correlation between childhood environments of the two generationss (0 – 1.0).
S = Relative similarity of CE of DZ and MZ twins, i.e. DZ/MZ (.6 – 1.2).
T = Spouse correlation (–.1 – .6).
U = Correlation between CE across age within a generation (.7 – 1.0).
Values in parentheses suggest a reasonable range of values for the expectation.
Typical simplifing assumptions: G × E var, DG var, P, Q, R, T = 0; S, U = 1.

of phenotypic assortative mating can be pronounced on DZ twin, sib, and P,O correlations, but not on MZ correlations or on offspring-parent regressions. 3. Adoption studies are often criticized on the grounds that there may have been selective placement of foster children. Yet ignoring selective placement (letting P=0) results in a lower estimate of AG, a point often not appreciated by critics or by individuals comparing the results of adoption studies to twin or family data.

The reader is invited to choose what he or she believes to be reasonable values for the parameters listed in Table 2 and to determine his or her own estimate of the heritability of intelligence based on the data in Table 1. What will quickly become evident is that in many cases simple differences in correlations between pairs of groups will no longer estimate G and E parameters and that the simultaneous analysis of many kinship groups becomes necessary. This is a basic principle behind most current genetic modeling procedures—the more parameters one wishes to estimate, the more nonredundant simultaneous equations one must have. Technically, adding kinship groups can do little to solve the parameter estimation problem, since additional unknowns are introduced with each new group. To solve the underidentification problem, assumptions are usually made concerning the equality of certain parameters, such as CE influences or GE covariance across certain kinships and/or assumptions that some parameters are equal to zero. Although such assumptions are often reasonable and models are usually insensitive to slight variations in some of these fixed parameters, multiple kinship modeling can be vulnerable (and subject to some mischievous manipulation by critics) on this point. The assumptions behind an analysis can sometimes have a major impact on the estimation of parameters (e.g. Loehlin 1978, Goldberger 1978a,b).

Most modeling procedures use some form of maximum likelihood estimation or weighted least squares method to weight information obtained from various kinship groups, a substantial improvement over unweighted group comparisons. The $2(r_{MZ}\text{-}r_{DZ})$ estimate of AG is a case in point. Given equal size samples, MZ correlations contain more accurate information about AG than do DZ correlations since MZ r's are larger and their standard errors smaller than DZs, when AG is present. In the case of intelligence data in Table 1, for example, the MZ correlation contains about five times more information than the DZ correlation yet they are weighted equally in $2(r_{MZ}\text{-}r_{DZ})$.

All things considered, the estimation of parameters through the simultaneous consideration of many kinship groups weighted according to the amount of information each contains is preferable to simpler methods. Modeling is sometimes criticized for making assumptions in order to solve for parameters. Such criticism misses the point that making *any* statements concerning G and E influences based on *any* kinship data involves assumptions. One difference between modeling and simpler approaches is that in modeling the assumptions are usually explicit and testable, whereas many simpler genetic interpretations contain implicit assumptions that are compensated for by invoking a lack of precision in the interpretations themselves.

With regard then to the question of the heritability of intelligence, a tentative answer might be "between .3 and .6, with broad heritability between .4 and .7." Within these ranges a middle value seems no more likely than one of the extremes. Estimates of CE are usually in the .15 to .30 range, with the contributions of G X E interactions and GE correlations usually small. A bit of sophisticated model fitting for the Texas adoption data, for example (Horn et al 1979), produced estimates of AG ranging from .45 to .53 and estimates of CE ranging from .24 to .29 with relatively small G X E effects ranging from .03 to .12. Cattell (1980) applied his multiple abstract variance analysis to data from male twins, brothers, and unrelated boys, estimating a heritability of .60 for fluid and .45 for crystallized intelligence, with a low negative correlation between AG and CE influences. Fulker (1979a), analyzing earlier data, estimated narrow and broad heritabilities of approximately .50 and .69, respectively, with the proportion of CE around .19. In contrast, the application of models with more complete parameterization of cultural transmission factors (Cloninger et al 1979, Rice et al 1980, Cavalli-Sforza & Feldman 1978) produced heritabilities around .30, with cultural influences of approximately the same magnitude.

The heritability of IQ is, however, one of the least interesting questions to be asked about these data. A greater resolution of different forms of genetic variance is of more interest from the standpoint of understanding evolutionary processes (Broadhurst 1979), for example. Knowing the degree of genotypic assortative mating would be valuable from the standpoint of understanding changes in the gene pool, and the degree and possible asymmetry of phenotypic assortation (e.g. Eaves 1979) would provide valuable insights concerning this important social behavior. Similarly, determining the nature of CE influences remains a major issue in psychology, as does the question of why G X E interactions appear so small for cognitive ability. Proponents of a strong "interactionist viewpoint" in the study of cognition often confuse the trivially elementary concept of co-action of G and E to produce the phenotype (e.g. "innate structures interact with environment to determine potential") with the concept of nonadditive G X E effects, which are rarely found to be large for cognitive measures. Finally, the estimation of the magnitude of G and E effects is only a necessary first step in the construction and validation of environmental indices relevant to intelligence (e. g. Rice et al 1980). Not only is such work of interest in psychology, but implications of this work for public policy decisions involving such areas as economic returns of education cannot be underestimated (e.g. Taubman 1978, Behrman et al 1980).

General Intelligence vs Specific Abilities

Because many studies involve a number of specific aptitude measures in addition to measures of global intelligence, many new data are available to address the issue of differential heritability of cognitive abilities. The Hawaii Family Study (DeFries et al 1979) produced consistently higher familial resemblances for a general intelligence factor ("g") than the median resemblances found for the 15 individual tests, across both European ancestry and Japanese ancestry samples. Assortative mating was also higher for "g" than the median of the individual tests. These results were not consistent with those of Park et al (1978), although the latter study may not be directly comparable because of the high degree of assortative mating in Korean populations and differences in the method of test administration used.

The adoption data reported by Scarr & Yee (1980) provided some evidence for the higher heritability of "g", compared to more specific aptitude and achievement measures, and some weak evidence for differential heritabilities among specific abilities. In contrast, there was little evidence to support an aptitude-achievement distinction, with respect to CE influences, in the Texas adoption data (Willerman et al 1977). The extensive survey of twin data reported by Nichols (1978) provides little support for either differential heritability of specific abilities or for higher heritability of "g" than for specific traits. Fulker (1979a), however, argues that much of the earlier data do suggest greater proportion of CE variance for school achievement measures than for general intelligence. Possibly the factorial "purity" (i.e. the absence of "g") of specific tests becomes a factor in conflicting results across studies, and possibly CE is responsible for family differences reported in the Hawaii data.

Three twin studies addressed the issue of differential heritability of cognitive abilities in children, but sample sizes were too small to detect all but major differences across traits. Garfinkle & Vandenberg (1978) were unable to demonstrate significant MZ-DZ differences on a series of tests involving Piagetian mathematical concepts and other measures. Plomin & Vandenberg (1980) analyzed primary mental abilities test data from 80 pairs of young twins, finding significant MZ-DZ differences only for IQ and spatial ability. Foch & Plomin (1980) found only one measure of specific cognitive ability in young twins which showed evidence of significant heritability, with nine tests indicating substantial CE effects. The overall evidence for differential proportions of AG and CE variance in general intelligence, specific abilities, and school achievement is inconsistant at all ages, and when differences are found they tend to be of small magnitude.

The difficulty in distinguishing between different abilities on the basis of G and CE influences may reflect the fact that most abilities are influenced by the same set of genes and largely the same environmental factors. There is strong support for this possibility with respect to scholastic abilities. Page & Jarjoura (1979) reported the results of an analysis of 3427 pairs of twins participating in the ACT assessment program in 1976. English, mathematics, social studies, and natural science scores were analyzed using a same-sex vs opposite-sex multivariate design, partitioning G, CE, and SE components for each variable and for the correlations between them. The genetic component was predominant for each measure with the remaining variance due largely to SE. Phenotypic correlations between measures were due primarily to G, and a factor analysis of the genetic matrix suggested that a single factor accounted for over 80% of the variance.

Highly similar results were obtained by Plomin & DeFries (1979) when they analyzed G and E correlations between the five National Merit Scholarship Qualifying Tests from Loehlin & Nichols's (1976) twin data. Again a single factor emerged from the genetic correlation matrix, accounting for over 70% of the variance. A single factor also emerged from E correlations from the Loehlin & Nichols data, accounting for nearly 70% of the variance. The subtests in these two large (5587 twin pairs) studies probably represent a mix of aptitude and achievement in each of the areas tested, plus a reading comprehension component, yet a single genetic factor was sufficient in both studies to account for most of the variance in the G correlation matrix. A similar situation may exist for E correlations.

Group Differences

Although the arguments continue, empirical data which may help resolve questions concerning the genetic basis of race or ethnic differences has been sparse. Scarr & Carter-Saltzman (1981) presented data which suggest a largely cultural interpretation for black-white differences in cognitive scores, although education and SES had relatively little influence. Fischbein (1980) compared within-pair similarity for MZ and DZ twins from varying social backgrounds in Sweden and found AG effects accounted for a lower proportion of the variance in IQ scores in the low SES group than in the higher SES groups, providing some support for a restriction of range hypothesis for the development of cognitive functioning.

Lynn (1979, 1980) found regional differences in mean IQs in both the British Isles and in France and traced these differences to selected migration patterns within the countries. The arguments that IQ tests are biased in favor of middle-class whites, because they were standardized on this group, is weakened by data showing that Japanese far removed from white Anglo-American culture do consistently better than white populations on the western IQ tests (Lynn 1977). Lower per capita income, calorie consumption, and years of schooling for the Japanese sample compared to North American populations run counter to a simple deprivation explanation for the group differences (Lynn & Dziobon 1980). Hakstian & Vandenberg (1979) found similarity in higher order cognitive structures across four widely differing cross cultural groups. Acculturation opportunities strongly determined cross-cultural differences obtained on the measured variables.

The study of sex-related differences in cognitive functioning, including genetic influences, is extensively reviewed in Wittig & Petersen (1979). A shorter review can be found in Burstein et al (1980), and Wilson & Vandenberg (1978) summarized sex differences in cognition obtained from the Hawaii study.

PERSONALITY AND TEMPERAMENT

Early Behavior Patterns

Using observational methods on a small sample of 2-year-old twins, Lytton et al (1977) found that most of the variance on a number of interactive behaviors with parents could be attributed to between-family differences, but in most cases CE rather than G effects appeared responsible for the differences. Plomin & Rowe (1979), also using 2-year-old twins, found that heredity affected individual differences in social responses to strangers more than to familiar persons. Environmental influences on the development of social behavior were found to be due to SE rather than CE effects. Using 4- to 7-year-old twins and a relatively reliable parental rating instrument for child temperament, Plomin & Rowe (1977) found genetic factors implicated in five of the six traits measured. Seven- to 10-year-old twins were studied by Matheny & Dolan (1980), using maternal ratings tapping six factors of personality and temperament. Five of the six produced correlations significantly higher for MZs than for DZs, and profiles of scores across the six factors were also more concordant for MZs than for DZs, thus both the individual components and the total organization of early personality and temperament dimensions appear genetically influenced.

Family Influences

In their landmark study of nearly 800 pairs of adolescent twins, Loehlin & Nichols (1976) reported two striking findings with respect to personality variables—heritabilities for the wide range of personality traits studied were all approximately equal and, although about half of the total variance on any trait could be attributed to environmental variables, none of this variation could be reliably attributed to CE. The inability to detect family cultural influences on personality has sufficient importance for behavioral theory to warrant further examination.

Table 3 lists heritability estimates based on a simple AG + CE model from several recent large studies of extraversion and neuroticism, along with a summary of some earlier studies compiled by Fulker (1981) and a pooled analysis of data from two additional American studies. The data are based largely on the Eysenck Personality Questionnaire (EPQ) and the California Psychological Inventory (CPI). The sample of twins from the Institute of Psychiatry Twin Register at the University of London is described in Eaves & Eysenck (1977) and in Eaves (1978). The proportions of AG variance from the Scandinavian data has been recalculated using weighted least squares. The results are consistent both across studies and traits—in none of the studies was there evidence for significant CE variance. If SE is adjusted to discount scale unreliability, the proportion of AG variance is quite high—.65 to 1.00 for neuroticism and .75 to 1.00 for extraversion.

Is the absence of any influence other than AG and SE peculiar to twin data? Data on cognitive traits using twins readily demonstrate the presence of CE, but twin designs are not powerful for distinguishing between models specifying only AG and models including nonadditive sources of genetic variation (Martin et al 1978).

Table 3 Heritability estimates of neuroticism and extraversion from twin data

Study	Sample	N pairs	Neuroticism	Extraversion
Earlier data[a]	English, US	336+	.52	.60
Earlier data[b]	US Mixed	345	—	.66
Loehlin & Nichols (1976)	US Adolescents	793	.53	.59
Eaves (1978)	English children	287	.44	.56
Eaves (1978)	English adults	542	.41	.50
Koskenvuo et al (1979)	Finnish women	5,632[c]	.59	.74
Koskenvuo et al (1979)	Finnish women	5,044[c]	.60	.72
Floderus-Myrhed et al (1980)	Swedish men	6,793	.56	.61
Floderus-Myrhed et al (1980)	Swedish men	5,934	.55	.59

[a] Compiled by Fulker (1981). Some studies include other family data. Extraversion based on 407 pairs.
[b] Pooled results from Gottesman (1966) and Horn et al (1976).
[c] Approximate N.

To determine if more complex models better explain the pattern of variation across a wider set of family relationships, Eaves (1978) analyzed the EPQ data from all 2469 adult subjects for whom data were available from the London sample. Maximum-likelihood kinship analyses of extraversion and neuroticism using a variety of models led Eaves to conclude that CE variance could account for no more than 5% of the variance in extraversion scores and 1% in neuroticism and that models totally excluding CE provided an equally good fit to the data. The analysis did suggest that for neuroticism a model which included either nonadditive genetic variance or a Genotype X Age (G X A) interaction across the three-generation age range provided a slightly better fit to the data than a simple AG + SE model. Although the results of the complete kinship analysis confirmed the absence of CE, it also indicated smaller proportions of AG variance influencing the two traits than the twin data alone suggested.

An analysis of a subset of the London data (twins and their parents) by Young et al (1980) further explored the G X A interaction for the neuroticism and extraversion scales. Neuroticism showed high age stability with respect to AG whereas extraversion did not, with a genotypic correlation of only .44 between juvenile and adult measures. The instability of AG for extroversion across age groups, in the absence of a significant G X A interaction, suggests that an interaction or a correlation between G and SE is influencing this trait. Again, CE influences were found to be small and usually nonsignificant.

Does the absence of detectable CE mean that there are no cultural influences on these two personality traits? Possibly not, if one is willing to hypothesize that a negative correlation between G and E serves to differentiate twins as much as to make them similar. The mechanism could work in two ways. First, there could be negative GE covariance between families, with cultural pressures reducing the scores of families with high-scoring phenotypes and increasing families with low-scoring phenotypes, thus reducing overall between-family variation. Cattell labeled this phenomenon the "socio-psychological law of environmental coercion toward the mean" and has provided some, albeit weak, evidence for the phenomenon with respect to both cognitive and personality traits (e.g. Cattell 1980). Alternatively, sibs might be negatively influencing each other's phenotypes, so that a sib possessing alleles exerting an increasing effect on a trait creates an environment for the other sib that tends to reduce the phenotype. Within-pair and total variance would then be greater for DZ than for MZ twins, increasing AG and lowering CE estimates.

There is some evidence in the twin data that such an effect may be working within families for these traits. If a simple AG + SE model is appropriate, MZ correlations should be twice their corresponding DZ correlations. If CE is present, MZ correlations will be less than twice DZ correlations, and if other factors such as a within-pair negative influence is operating, MZ correlations will be more than twice DZ levels. The results on this point are quite consistent for the studies summarized in Table 3. Of the 30 recent large sample MZ-DZ comparisons available, the DZ correlation was less than half that of the corresponding MZ correlation in all cases for extraversion and in 22 cases for neuroticism. Estimates of CE are consistently slightly negative when fitting a simple AG + CE model. Given the large samples involved in each of these comparisons, this is not the situation one would expect. On the other hand, total DZ variance was not always greater than total MZ variance, thus a competition effect is not sufficient to account for all the data. Young et al (1980) tested for a possible competition effect within families for the London sample, using the model developed by Eaves (1976). Although a significant negative sib influence was observed for extraversion, its effect was only pronounced in the juvenile sample.

Among the other factors which could contribute to the pattern of correlations observed, low spouse correlations rule out strong negative assortative mating but genetic dominance is a possibility, although the degree of dominance required to produce such an effect would have to be substantial. The assumption of the twin method, that CE effects are equal across MZ and DZ twins, may be incorrect but one would have to postulate large differences, inconsistent across samples, to explain the data. The interactions and covariation among genetic, age, and environmental factors influencing extraversion and neuroticism may be complex, but the effect of each of these factors is apparently small and unlikely to be masking CE influences to any large degree.

Before concluding that cultural influences are nominal for these and possibly other major personality traits, it is essential to corroborate these results with adoption studies where G and E influences can be clearly separated. In adoption data, the absence of CE influences results in nonsignificant correlations between unrelated children reared in the same families and between adoptive parents and their foster children.

Data from the two Minnesota and the Texas adoption projects are unambiguous on these points. Pairs of unrelated children reared together in the same households show no more resemblance in personality than pairs of children chosen at random. Correlations between unrelated children within adoptive families hovered around zero in all three studies for nearly all of the personality measures studied (Scarr & Weinberg 1976, 1977, Loehlin et al 1981, Scarr et al 1981). Foster-parent, adoptive-offspring correlations were also near zero for nearly all measures. Data from all three adoption projects were thus consistent with an interpretation of no CE effects on many personality traits, including extraversion and neuroticism.

On the other hand, correlations between biological relatives were also low in these studies. Sib correlations averaged about .15 for neuroticism and extraversion, and P,O correlations for these traits averaged less than .1 with young children and less than .2 with adolescents in the adoption projects. These values were representative of most correlations for the personality traits examined in the three adoption studies and are typical of the results from earlier family studies of personality where P,O correlations average about .13 across traits and studies. The situation is comparable to that described for cognitive abilities—estimates of genetic influences differ in twin data and adoption data under the assumptions of a simple AG + E model. In focusing on just the traits of neuroticism and extraversion we have already seen evidence of G X A and G X SE interactions, as well as negative GE covariance and the possibility of genetic dominance. Although small in size, each of these effects can contribute to apparent discrepancies in twin, family, and adoption data. By examining other personality traits, one discovers even more factors which can contribute to these discrepancies.

Loehlin et al (1981) suggested that a G X E interaction involving a genetically based early sensitivity to the effects of home environment may exist. Unwed mothers exhibiting emotional disturbance, as reflected in MMPI scores, tended to have children who appeared more stable than other adopted children reared in the security of foster homes. A direct correspondence between phenotypes need not occur when environmental conditions change greatly. Of some relevance to this point are the data of Torgerson (1977). Adult MZ twins were interviewed about childhood differences between themselves and their twin for a variety of temperament and personality traits. These twin differences were then correlated with differences in 23 traits measured in adulthood. Some childhood differences were not related to differences in adulthood. Others, such as differences in aggression and childhood neurosis, showed corresponding twin differences in adulthood; still other childhood differences, such as those for orderliness and modesty, were correlated with twin pair differences in quite different social and personality traits in adulthood.

It is unfortunate that most of the research in this area has focused on transmission models, limited to kinship similarities on the same trait, rather than more general behavioral influence models which include genetic cross-correlations between traits. It is hardly unreasonable to suspect that a particular personality trait in one individual may influence quite a different trait or ability in a relative. It is also possible that such relationships may be nonlinear, even nonmonotonic, for some measures. Despite the complexity of such analyses, the presence of nonmonotonic relationships and disordinal interactions can often suggest more appropriate higher order constructs for use in interpreting the data (e.g. Henderson 1979).

Complex G X E interactions may, in part, account for low P,O correlations across generations, and the London data suggest that for some personality traits the same genes may not be operative in both adults and juveniles. The presence of Genotype X Sex (G X S) interactions would also lower estimates of G based on sib and P,O data, but not on data from a classical twin design. There is some suggestion in the adoption studies that same-sex correlations are higher than cross-sex correlations, but sampling error is relatively high on these smaller subgroups. A powerful approach to studying G X S interaction involves the use of multivariate extensions of genetic models. Eaves et al (1977b) and Martin et al (1979) carried out an analysis of the covariation of four aspects of impulsiveness in male and female twins in the London sample and found evidence for trait specific G X S interactions. Similarly, Fulker et al (1980) analyzed four sensation-seeking subscales and found that, whereas about 70% of the genetic variance in sensation-seeking was due to a general factor common to both sexes, the remaining 30% involved an interaction with sex of subjects.

Influences on personality traits are undoubtedly more complex than AG + SE models based on twin data suggest. Despite this, simple cultural explanations are consistently called into question by the substantial body of twin, family, and adoption data, all of which fail to demonstrate CE influences.

The Nature of Environmental Influences

The finding of little CE influence on personality traits apparently extends to common fears and phobias. Rose et al (1980b) administered a fear survey to 151 twin pairs and to their parents. Contrary to the data on many personality traits, heritability estimates from twin differences and from mid-twin, mid-parent regressions were quite comparable for most of the specific fears. Interestingly, when analyzed as general factors (fear of organisms, death, and water) offspring-parent regressions produced lower heritabilities than those based on twin resemblances. In all cases there was little evidence of CE effects for these common fears.

The realization that the environmental factors influencing personality and temperament are largely ones that occur within families has led some investigators to begin to examine these influences. Fulker (1981) suggested that these SE influences may simply represent a combination of test unreliability and biologically based individual differences for some personality traits, with no systematic within-family SE influences. Rowe & Plomin (1979) demonstrated that SE effects on behavior are not purely random in nature, since infant MZ twin within-pair differences on a number of measures of social responsiveness were correlated with each other. Both the analysis of covariance structures of the London adult data and Rowe & Plomin's MZ difference procedure with infant data suggest that at least some of the behaviors influenced by SE show consistency across situations.

Rowe & Plomin (1981) have outlined a theoretical framework for understanding sources of E influences on personality and intelligence, including several types of potential SE influences. The area is ripe for further theoretical developments and more sophisticated research to help determine which of a number of heretofore unsuspected environmental factors co-act with genotype to create personality differences.

Differential G and E Influences Across Traits

Despite evidence for some interactions of small magnitude, a simple AG + SE model with no cultural parameters or interactions does reasonably well in accounting for much of the kinship data in the personality-temperament domain. Is this true of all traits in this domain? An affirmative answer would stretch the credulity of all of the behavioral genetic work in personality because the conclusion would be so contradictory to behavioral science lore. Present methods and models would be severely challenged.

With respect to detecting differential proportions of genetic variance in various traits, most studies lack sufficient power to make such discriminations or to dissect different types of genetic influences on behavior. Detecting cultural influences is easier, yet CE effects were rarely found in the work reviewed. There are traits, however, that have been analyzed by the methods discussed and have not shown the G + SE patterns described above.

Results from three studies of conservatism scores were analyzed by Eaves et al (1978) with the consistent finding that a parameter that included CE influence was necessary to explain the data. Cultural transmission of attitudes from parents to offspring and/or peer influences appeared to be an important factor in the transmission of this social attitude. A second example involves the Lie Scale on the EPQ. Young et al (1980) found that a model that included only CE and SE was adequate to explain twin and sib relationships and that the addition of genetic parameters to the model did not improve the fit. A more elaborate model that included covariation between E effects on an individual and effects of the same factors on a co-twin improved the fit still further. Thus, based on sib and twin data analysis, the trait measured by the Lie Scale appeared to be transmitted by purely environmental factors including cultural effects, cooperation effects within twin pairs (honesty of one twin positively influenced the other), and random SE effects. The adoption data of Scarr et al (1981) showed a sib correlation of .18 and an unrelated child-child correlation of .26 for the Lie Scale, also hardly indicative of a genetic influence.

The answer to whether there is differential heritability of noncognitive behavioral traits depends on the breadth the behavioral domain included. Although a large group of personality traits measured on standardized tests may show more or less similar heritabilities and little cultural influence, other traits, particularly involving social attitudes and beliefs apparently show widely varying degrees of G and CE influences.

LONGITUDINAL STUDIES

New Methods of Analysis

Some of the complex issues raised above concerning cognitive abilities and personality traits can be resolved with longitudinal data from sophisticated developmental designs, such as the cohort sequential method extended to include multiple kinships. Statistical methodology for fitting G X E models to longitudinal data is still in early stages of development, although several recent approaches to the problem have been offered.

Fischbein & Nordqvist (1978) concluded that the deviation measure of Cronbach & Gieser may be the most appropriate measure of profile contour similarity in growth curves for analyzing twin data. Eaves et al (1978) extended biometrical genetic procedures to include covariances between occasions of measurement with procedures for testing the adequacy of the model. Wilson (1979) described a formal model for the analysis of longitudinal twin data based on repeated measures ANOVA. Ho et al (1980) demonstrated the application of hierarchical multiple regression procedures to longitudinal twin data. A maximum likelihood, variance components, latent variable methodology applied to a recursive model involving G and E indices and socioeconomic success is described by Behrman et al (1980). The fusion of sophisticated economic models with twin methodology, the concern for both intra- and intergenerational change, and the use of structural equations for parameter estimation make this a particularly interesting contribution. Also promising in this regard are procedures related to structural modeling such as reticular analysis modeling (Horn & McArdle 1980, McArdle 1980) applied to genetic developmental designs.

Current Research Emphasis

The longitudinal method is particularly valuable for demonstrating the dynamic interrelationship among genetic processes, maturation, and environmental influences in mental development. R. S. Wilson (1978) summarized some of the results of an ongoing longitudinal study of twins and siblings for whom measures of mental development were made at frequent intervals between 3 months and 6 years of age. Prior to 18 months of age interclass correlations averaged .69 and .63 for MZs and DZs respectively. Between 18 months and 4 years these correlations averaged .83 and .72 for MZs and DZs and stabilized at .85 and .63 at age 6. These values are nearly identical to correlations found for MZ and DZ adolescents and adults in other studies. DeFries et al (1981) found low but significant resemblances in cognitive abilities between biological, adoptive, and control parents and their one-year-old children, implicating CE influences on early mental development. There was also evidence that the relationship between maternal responsiveness and infant mental development was primarily due to environmental factors. Except for the contingent vocal responses on the part of adoptive mothers, there was little evidence for CE influences on language competence in this group (Hardy-Brown et al 1981), but language competence did correlate significantly with natural mother's IQ.

One focus of recent longitudinal behavioral genetic studies has been on the role of G X E interaction in the development of twins and its effect on the stability of twin differences across age. The most extensive data on young twins has come from the Louisville Twin Project, which has included numerous cognitive, temperament, and sociability-personality measures (R. S. Wilson 1978, 1980, Matheny 1980, Matheny et al 1981). Several factors have been isolated in both the temperament and cognitive domains which show considerable consistency across ages ranging from 3 months to 6 years. These factors generally show greater concordance for MZ pairs than for DZ pairs, with differences becoming more evident with increasing age. The data suggest that developmental processes are initiated and guided to a large degree by gene-action systems despite the influence of maturational and environmental effects. MZ twins parallel each other for spurts and lags in growth, cognitive, and sociability measures to much higher degree than do DZ twins.

Goldsmith & Gottesman (1981) reported an analysis of longitudinal twin data from the Collaborative Perinatal Project on 350 twin pairs who were rated at 8 months, 4 years, and 7 years of age. At all ages certain broadly based temperament factors showed evidence of moderate genetic influences although nonfamilial sources of variation were generally large. Longitudinal results on a smaller sample of Norwegian twins (Torgerson & Kringlen 1978, Torgerson 1981) showed interpair differences between MZ and DZ twins emerging for many measures at 2 months of age; these became increasingly pronounced through age 6. Temperament traits showing little evidence for genetic influences tended to be those identified as risk factors for the development of behavior disorders.

Fischbein (1978, 1979) has reported results of a longitudinal study of 10- to 18-year-old Swedish twins with respect to growth and cognitive measures. She hypothesized that MZ twins as a pair will tend to be affected and react similarly to the same environment, while DZ twins will be affected and react differently on the basis of their nonidentical inheritance. G X E interactions and GE correlations should thus increase DZ within-pair differences with age, particularly for behaviors expected to be differentially influenced by environments. Her results did show an increasing difference in MZ-DZ concordances across ages for a verbal ability factor and less change for inductive reasoning. Unfortunately, in both this and the Norwegian study small sample sizes do not permit conclusions to be regarded as more than tentative.

Results of Behrman et al (1980), based on several thousand adult male twin pairs, suggest that methods of estimating the effects of schooling on socioeconomic success which do not control for background variables and cognitive ability lead to substantial upward biases. Genetic factors accounted for about half of the total family effects on earnings at maturity with no more than 20% of the variance due to inequality of opportunity.

The potential of longitudinal behavioral genetic research is substantial, but the requirements for adequate studies are formidable. The high long-term cost for substantive longitudinal research is amplified in developmental-genetic studies because of the demands for the extremely large samples necessary to compare magnitudes of parameter estimates across traits and across ages. Futhermore, because twin data alone cannot resolve issues concerning genetical influences on behaviors or their time of emergence in development, collection of family data from sibs and parents substantially increases the power of the twin method. Adequate research thus requires a level of support rarely forthcoming, judging from the paucity of data in this area.

In determining whether larger investments in longitudinal behavioral genetic research is cost effective, three points should be considered. First, it is no longer contested that the study of behavioral development must include longitudinal data which can be incorporated into a general developmental model (Baltes et al 1980). Second, an epigenetic or biocultural perspective is receiving considerable primacy in life-span developmental psychology. Third, one must look at the alternative use of resources in developmental psychology. Although there has been some recognition of the contributions of behavioral genetics to child development (Masters 1981), a considerable proportion of current developmental research and theorizing suggests that many investigators are unaware of the substantial body of data concerning the relative magnitudes of CE and SE influences on behavior. One of the most consistent results in these data with respect to cognition, personality, and temperment is that systematic cultural influences usually account for less than one-third and frequently none of the variance in a behavioral phenotype. The a priori assumption that behaviors are due primarily to CE influences can no longer be defended. Research which does not permit the separation of CE and SE influences or research designed only to detect potential CE effects cannot hope to unravel the role of various environmental influences on most behaviors. General transmission designs are often necessary, even for the analysis of behaviors showing little genetic influence. Viewed in this light, longitudinal behavioral genetic designs may represent an excellent investment.

PSYCHOPATHOLOGY

The output of research related to the genetics of psychopathology and related disorders continues to be considerable. Readers are referred to the following reviews of areas not covered in the present chapter: minimal brain dysfunction (Nichols & Chen 1980); psychopharmacogenetics (Omenn 1978, Falek et al 1979); genetic counseling (Crowe 1978, Tsuang 1978); Turner's Syndrome and extra sex chromosomes (Nielsen et al 1977, Nyborg & Nielsen 1981a,b, Garron 1977, Hook, 1979, Rovet & Netley 1981); criminal behavior (Mednick & Christiansen 1977); neurosis, psychopathy, and alcoholism (Zerbin-Rudin 1980b, Carey & Gottesman 1981, Cloninger et al 1979, Schuckit 1980); genetic markers and chromosome banding techniques in psychiatric research (Turner 1979a, Dorus 1980); aging (Ford & Jarvik 1979, Omenn 1981).

Affective Disorders

Research on genetic aspects of affective illness has been the subject of a number of general reviews, including the volume edited by Mendlewicz & Shopsin (1979) and papers by Zerbin-Rudin (1979, 1980a) and Gershon et al (1977). Reviews covering more specific aspects of affective disorders can be found in Kidd & Weissman (1978) on research strategies, Behar & Winokur (1979) on alcoholism and depression, Taylor & Abrams (1980) on the bipolar-unipolar dichotomy, and in Crowe (1981) on genetic models.

The distinction between bipolar (BPD) and unipolar (UPD) disorders has become increasingly blurred, particularly with respect to morbidity risks.

Earlier data suggested that relatives of patients diagnosed as bipolar were a higher morbidity risk than comparable relatives from families of unipolar patients. The risk difference is considerably smaller and even reversed in several recent studies (e.g. Gershon 1977, Smeraldi et al 1977, Cadoret 1978, Scharfetter & Nuesperli 1980, Taylor et al 1980). The majority of lithium studies have also shown similar clinical responsiveness in both diagnostic groups (e.g. Mendels 1976, Donnelly et al 1978).

Winokur's proposal that BPD is transmitted as an X-linked dominant trait (Winokur & Reich 1970) has been controversial since other investigators found instances of father-son transmission. Linkage studies with X chromosome markers based largely on Winokur's data (Mendlewicz & Fleiss 1974) and a pedigree analysis of Winokur's data (Crowe & Smouse 1977) both tended to support the sex-linked dominant hypothesis. Recent pedigree data have not supported a linkage hypothesis (Gershon et al 1979, Leckman et al 1979, Mendlewicz et al 1979), producing results more congruent with family studies which largely suggested polygenic transmission. Leckman & Gershon (1977) applied single-locus and multifactorial models with differential sex threshholds and an X-chromosome dominance model to the data of five earlier studies. Three of the studies were compatible with a sex-threshhold model and one compatible with a sex-linkage model. Finally, Bucher et al (1981) reported that a segregation analysis of three sets of data indicated that neither an X-linked nor an autosomal dominant gene can account for the transmission of BPD.

The considerable heterogeneity of results may in part be due to genetic heterogeneity within both unipolar and bipolar disorders (e.g. Winokur 1979, Angst et al 1980, Andreasen & Winokur 1979). Schlesser et al (1979, 1980) found a distinction between three subtypes of UPD patients in terms of age of onset and serum-cortisol response to dexamethasone suppression, suggesting that UPD may be three or more separate illnesses which differ in clinical course, mode of inheritance, and underlying neurochemistry.

Despite the several categories of affective disorders now in use, genetic heterogeneity within categories continues to pose a serious problem for analysis. Without diagnostically homogeneous subgroups and large samples, genetic modeling is likely to continue to be unproductive. With respect to BPD, Turner & King (1981a) found five pedigrees traced through three generations with no father-son transmission and other evidence suggesting the possibility of X-linked inheritance. This group, however, represented only a fraction of their total BPD population. The major group was apparently affected by a single dominant gene with a locus on the P2 region of chromosome 6 distal to human leukocyte antigen (HLA) locus. Turner & King (1981b) also reported a double BPD pedigree with father-son transmission traced through four and five generations. Linkage analysis enabled placement of this form of BPD distal to HLA on chromosome 6. Although genetic modeling has been unable to distinguish between single locus and polygenic alternatives, Turner's linkage data suggest a single major dominant locus and the possibility of a secondary sex-related factor. If these findings prove reliable, linkage studies of extended pedigrees using a large number of genetic markers may be the most promising research strategy for this area in the near future.

Such studies should also investigate genetic variation in biological characteristics such as monamine metabolites and neurotransmitter receptors, as these may well aid in both genetic understanding of affective disorders and establishing more useful diagnostic criteria. Genetic factors contribute to the variability in the activity of monoamine oxidase (MAO), an enzyme that metabolizes amines in the brain. The studies examining the relationship between platelet MAO activity and psychopathology have mainly shown equivocal results, although low MAO activity appears to be associated with BPD (Leckman et al 1977) and alcoholism (Sullivan et al 1978a,b). Further support for this relationship has come from Pandey et al (1980), who showed that first-degree relatives of BPD patients having both incapacitating manic and depressive states had lower mean MAO activity than relatives of patients with other affective disorders or having no history of affective disorders. Relatives of the patients who had a major affective illness also had a significantly higher ratio of mean red-celled lithium to plasma lithium than did relatives with no major affective illness, suggesting that genetically controlled cell membrane properties may be a factor in vulnerability to BPD (Dorus et al 1979). Both studies lend support to the hypothesis that BPD is heterogeneous genetically and neurochemically. Given the variability of outcomes regarding the relationship between MAO activity and BPD (Gershon et al 1980; Breakefield et al 1980), however, these results await replication.

Schizoaffective Disorders

Schizoaffective disorder (SA) has increasingly been considered a form of affective disorder, in contrast to its traditional classification under schizophrenia (e.g. Pope & Lapinski 1978). The question of whether SA is a special form of schizophrenia or of affective disorders or due to a mixture of genes from both disorders or a completely separate entity with a genetic homotypology has been the subject of several investigations. Tsuang (1979) reported on 35 sib pairs who both were diagnosed as schizophrenic, affective, or SA disorder. Based on the frequency of the six possible types of pairings, he concluded that the data do not support genetic independence of SA disorder, but that the disorder cannot be considered as a simple variant of either affective disorders of schizophrenia. The sample size was quite small for this type of analysis, however.

Angst et al (1979a,b) studied over 1000 first-degree relatives of 150 SA patients, finding increased morbidity risks for both schizophrenia (5.3%) and affective disorder (6.6%) with a high incidence of catatonia and unipolar depression. These results suggest that from a genetic viewpoint SA disorder takes an intermediate position between schizophrenia and affective disorders. An attempt to study the mode of transmission suggested that their sample of probands consisted of four subgroups: cases belonging to the affective disorders, to schizophrenia, to pure SA patients, and a group consisting of a mixture of genetic dispositions. Clinically these four subgroups could not be distinguished from each other. Turner (1979b) has presented evidence for the occurrence of a locus for schizotaxia on the short arm of chromosome 6, whereas no such linkage was found for SA disorders in two generations.

Schizophrenia

A review of genetic research in schizophrenia can be found in a volume by Gottesman & Shields (1982) and a shorter review in Gottesman (1979). McGuffin (1979) has reviewed the evidence associating schizophrenia subtypes with the HLA system. Because of the extensive kinship results available for schizophrenia, attempts to fit transmission models to these data have had a relatively long history (Crowe 1981). In general, both multifactorial and single major locus transmission models have "fit" the data, with the relative degree of fit dependent of specifics of both the model and the breadth of diagnostic categories included in the data analyzed. The models are rather consistent in showing evidence for a large genetic component and evidence for genetic heterogeneity in schizophrenia. Matthysse & Kidd (1976), for example, analyzing data from five studies summarized in Gottesman & Shields (1972), found that neither the multifactorial nor the single major locus model adequately accounted for the data, since the predicted incidence of MZ twin concordance was too low for a SML model and too high for a multifactorial model. Both models predicted genetic heterogeneity among schizophrenics, and the multifactorial model predicted that 9% of the schizophrenic population would be at an extremely high genetic risk.

As Morton et al (1979) point out, finding several alternative models which account for the data poses a problem for genetic counseling. Incorporating thresholds for borderline schizophrenia and schizoid personality into single major locus and multifactorial polygenic models, the authors found that occurrence risk was frequently model dependent, even when the models fit the available data equally well.

Current models generally contain less restrictive assumptions than earlier ones (e.g. Fishman et al 1978, Matthysse et al 1979, Kidd & Gladstien 1980,

Rao et al 1981). The latter authors, for example, applied a path analytic model for attribute data which combined both forms of assortative mating (phenotypic and social homogamy), maternal effects, and intergenerational differences in genetic and cultural effects to the summary of family resemblances compiled by Gottesman & Shields (1981), shown in Table 4. With population lifetime risk taken at .85% the general model fit quite well, although schizophrenic first-degree relatives were slightly underpredicted and second-degree relatives slightly overpredicted, suggesting possible under-ascertainment of more distant relatives. Parameter estimates from the model suggested a genetic component of .71, a cultural effect of .20, and a unique twin component of .09. All three parameters and assortative mating were highly significant. Some caution must be observed in interpreting such results since sampling procedures are not random but are based on families containing an affected proband.

In contrast to the highly significant effect obtained with models analyzing only the prevalence of the disorder in various types of relatives of affected individuals, segregation analysis of family data does not provide such a definitive picture (Elston & Namboodiri 1977, Elston et al 1978). Because segregation analysis deals with nuclear families or large pedigrees rather than pooled data, methods can be considerably more powerful for rejecting specific G or E models than models analyzing pooled family data. A series of such models developed by Elston and colleagues can be applied to disorders of multifactorial etiology with segregation at one or two loci, variable age of onset, and two levels of severity of illness. The application of these models to the schizophrenia data of Kallmann required the rejection of all G and E models tried. It is uncertain whether this rejection was due to the greater power of the method and the fact that transmission of schizophrenia and schizoidia was more complex than any of the models and their assump-

Table 4 Morbidity risk for relatives of schizophrenics[a]

Relationship	N	Percent morbidity	Tetrachoric r	Predicted percent[b]
Spouses	194	2.1	.13	2.4
MZ Twins	261	45.6	.85	45.4
DZ Twins	329	13.7	.53	12.1
Siblings	8,817	8.4	.41	8.3
Children	1,578	11.3	.48	10.1
Half-sibs	499	3.4	.22	3.6
Nieces/nephews	3,966	2.7	.18	3.1
Grandchildren	739	2.8	.19	3.5
First cousins	1,600	1.6	.09	1.7

[a] Based on Gottesman & Shields (1982) and Rao et al (1981).
[b] Based on model of Rao et al with assortative mating, population morbidity rate of .85%, AG = .71, CE = .20, Special Twin E = .09.

tions allowed for (e.g. a substantial proportion of the cases of study have an environmental etiology or that a nonsusceptible genotype is often a heterozygote passing on susceptibility genes), or whether the results simply reflect the peculiarity in the specific data set analyzed. Only further exploration of other segregation analysis models will help resolve discrepancies between these analyses and those pooling family data.

Borderline and nonpsychotic disorders are commonly found in children of schizophrenics. To establish a genetic link with chronic schizophrenia, however, requires a control for illness in spouses of schizophrenics as well as a control group of children to determine the frequency of such disorders in the population. Although data of this type are not yet available, Fowler et al (1977a,b) have examined parental psychiatric illness associated with schizophrenia in the siblings of the schizophrenics and the pattern of psychiatric illness in the offspring of schizophrenics. They found no definitive evidence for a genetic link between alcoholism or borderline psychotic disorders and chronic schizophrenia, although psychiatric illness (most often alcoholism) was frequently found in the spouses of schizophrenics. Antisocial personality in offspring of female schizophrenics was frequently associated with alcoholic fathers.

Summarizing their research on high risk for schizophrenia, Erlenmeyer-Kimling et al (1979) have identified a subgroup of high risk children who show cognitive deficits, early behavioral deviations, some maturational lag, and unusual patterns of auditory evoked potential. Rieder & Nichols (1979) have also found some evidence for neurological soft signs and hyperactivity in male offspring of continuous schizophrenics. Left-handedness also appears to be associated with a mild form of schizophrenia in twins where at least one of the pair was diagnosed as schizophrenic (Boklage 1977, Luchins et al 1980). Structured clinical evaluation of adoptive and biological parents of hospitalized young schizophrenics showed the latter to have considerably more Rorschach pathology (Wender et al 1977).

Erlenmeyer-Kimling et al (1980) found that assembled data from recent studies suggest that the reproductive rate of schizophrenic women is increasing relative to the general population, raising several social policy issues, given the current evidence for genetic factors in schizophrenia.

CONCLUSION

Human behavior genetics appears to be in an interesting transition stage brought about by the rapid development of models in human quantitative genetics. These models set high demands on the quality and type of data collected. For example, although useful for other purposes, neither classical twin studies nor family studies can adequately disentangle various G and E influences in behavioral transmission (although a combination of the two approaches can do so rather well). Similarly, studies with small samples often lack power to reject null hypotheses concerning kinship differences and are of little use for parameter estimation.

In the quest for data to fit models, heterogeneous groups of studies have been pooled where the dependent variable has been more or less similar. Apart from statistical problems with this procedure, it can be used for only a few measures such as general intelligence, a few personality scales, and some well-defined diagnostic categories. It would appear desirable to compromise between generating many diverse small studies with limited kinship groups, where biases, errors, and shortsightedness are randomized across data sets, and supporting a few monolithic studies where they are not. One approach would be to have several cooperative intermediate sized projects gathering similar behavioral data with the same extended kinship design. Variation in G and E parameters estimated in each replicate project would indicate the stability of the estimates.

Whether or not such changes in research strategy occur, two immediate changes would benefit the area greatly: increased use of comparable behavioral data across studies and more complete reporting of data. The first is obvious and the second is overdue. It is inexcusable that such a large proportion of papers continue to be focused on kinship correlational data alone. Although an investigator may not use descriptions of sample characteristics, estimates of assortative mating, first-order statistics, kinship regressions, and between- and within-group variances in his or her particular analysis, this information can be enormously valuable to others.

Recently a distinguished contributor to behavior genetics remarked that the best single move the field could make would be to limit investigators to two publications per year. There are few areas in the behavioral sciences that are more appropriate for monograph reporting than behavior genetics, with its extensive data sets derived from large projects. Judging from their subsequent use in additional analysis and citation, monographs with extended appendices of data have been a more useful publication form than a number of short papers based on a single study where the individual reports together fail to reflect all the data. An interesting question is whether investigators collecting large data sets are obligated to share these widely or whether they are entitled to dole out results indefinitely in small chunks, preprocessed to fit a particular orientation.

The rapid development of human genetic models has not been without problems. Errors, inconsistencies, and unreasonable assumptions have caused serious difficulties. The path analytic, biometrical genetic, and structural equation approaches with many variations in notation and terminology have made it difficult to follow these developments and have masked the fundamental similarities of the methods. Only recently have elementary introductions to the concepts of multiple kinship modeling become widely available (e.g. Cloninger et al 1978, Loehlin 1979, Fulker 1979a,b, 1981, Crowe 1981). More advanced descriptions showing the power and flexibility of these methods can be found in Eaves et al (1977a, 1978), Elston & Rao (1978), Elston (1980), Reich et al (1980), and Behrman et al (1980).

Although current models are robust to some data fluctuations and minor changes in assumptions, there are frequent occasions when very different models can fit empirical data equally well. The extraversion data discussed above provide a case in point. Fitting a simple AG + CE model to these data usually leads to slight negative values for CE variance. For some of these data, two alternative models eliminate this problem and both provide equal inprovements in fit to the data, but one involves AG and a small competition effect within sibs, whereas the other requires genetic variance to be largely nonadditive. It is such major differences in interpretations of similar data that lead to a lack of confidence in modeling outcomes and provide raw material for criticism. An astute armchair critic can easily create situations where small changes in the data and in the model can lead to radically different parameter estimates. Overlooked is the fact that many alternative models may have been clearly rejected by the data, leaving only a few plausible ones. Choosing among the remaining models may have to depend on other genetic or psychological knowledge or further data collection. That one narrows the number of possible explanations for familial resemblances down from a large number to a few rather different explanations should hardly be used as evidence for the weakness of the method. Surely there will be continued development of genetical model fitting and greater use of extended kinship designs by behavior geneticists. It will be interesting to see whether investigators primarly interested in environmental components of behavioral influence become convinced of the value of such research strategies.

Literature Cited

Andreasen, N. C., Winokur, G. 1979. Newer experimental methods for classifying depression. *Arch. Gen. Psychiatry* 36: 447–52

Angst, J., Felder, W., Lohmeyer, B. 1979a. Schizoaffective disorders. *J. Affect. Disord.* 1:139–53

Angst, J., Felder, W., Lohmeyer, B. 1979b. Are schizoaffective psychoses heterogeneous? *J. Affect. Disord.* 1:155–65

Angst, J., Frey, R., Lohmeyer, B., Zerbin-Rudin, E. 1980. Bipolar manic-depressive psychoses: results of a genetic investigation. *Hum. Genet.* 55:237–54

Ashton, G. C., Polovina, J. J., Vandenberg, S. G. 1979. Segregation analysis of family data for 15 tests of cognitive ability. *Behav. Genet.* 9:329–47

Baltes, P. B., Reese, H. W., Lipsitt, L. P. 1980. Life-span developmental psychology. *Ann. Rev. Psychol.* 31:65–110

Behar, D., Winokur, G. 1979. Research in alcoholism and depression: a two-way street under construction. In *Psychiatric Factors in Drug Abuse*, ed. R. W. Pickens, L. L. Heston, pp. 125–52. New York: Grune & Stratton

Behrman, J. R., Hrubec, Z., Taubman, P., Wales, T. J. 1980. *Contributions to Economic Analysis: Socioeconomic Success: A Study of the Effects of Genetic Endowments, Family Environment, and Schooling.* Amsterdam: North Holland

Boklage, C. E. 1977. Schizophrenia, brain asymmetry development, and twinning: cellular relationship with etiological and possible prognostic implications. *Biol. Psychiatry* 12:19–35

Boles, D. B. 1980. X-Linkage of spatial ability: a critical review. *Child Dev.* 51: 625–35

Bouchard, T. J., McGue, M. 1981. Familial studies of intelligence: a review. *Science* 212:1055–59

Bouchard, T. J., McGee, M. G. 1977. Sex differences in human spatial ability: not an X-linked recessive gene effect. *Soc. Biol.* 24:332–35

Breakefield, X. O., Giller, E. L. Jr., Nurnberger, J. I. Jr., Castiglione, C. M., Buchsbaum, M. S., Gershon, E. S. 1980. Monoamine oxidase Type A in fibroblasts from patients with bipolar depressive illness. *Psychiatry Res.* 2: 307–14

Broadhurst, P. L. 1979. The experimental approach to behavioral evolution. See Royce & Mos 1979, pp. 43–95

Bucher, K. D., Elston, R. C., Green, R., Whybrow, P., Helzer, J., Reich, T., Clayton, P., Winokur, G. 1981. The transmission of manic depressive illness II. Segregation analysis of three sets of family data. *J. Psychiatr. Res.* 16:65

Burstein, B., Bank, L., Jarvik, L. F. 1980. Sex differences in cognitive functioning: evidence, determinants, implications. *Hum. Dev.* 23:289–313

Cadoret, R. J. 1978. Evidence for genetic inheritance of primary affective disorders in adoptees. *Am. J. Psychiatry* 135: 463–66

Carey, G., Gottesman, I. I. 1981. Twin and family studies of anxiety, phobic, and obsessive disorders. In *Anxiety: New Research and Changing Concepts,* ed. D. F. Klein, J. Rabkin, pp. 117–36. New York: Raven

Cattell, R. B. 1980. The heritability of fluid, g_f, and crystallized, g_c, intelligence, estimated by a least squares use of the MAVA method. *Br. J. Educ. Psychol.* 50:253–65

Cavalli-Sforza, L. L., Feldman, M. W. 1978. Dynamics and statistics of traits under the influence of cultural transmission. See Morton & Chung 1978, pp. 133–43

Cloninger, C. R., Christiansen, K. O., Reich, T., Gottesman, I. I. 1978. Implications of sex differences in the prevalences of antisocial personality, alcoholism, and criminality for familial transmission. *Arch. Gen. Psychiatry* 35:941–51

Cloninger, C. R., Reich, T., Wetzel, R. 1979. Alcoholism and affective disorders: familial associations and genetic models. In *Alcoholism and Affective Disorders,* ed. D. W. Goodwin, C. K. Erickson, pp. 57–86. New York/London: Spectrum

Cole, R. E., Johnson, R. C., Ahern, F. M., Kuse, A. R., McClearn, G. E., Vandenberg, S. G., Wilson, J. R. 1979. A family study of memory processes and their relations to cognitive test scores. *Intelligence* 3:127–38

Coren, S., Porac, C. 1979. Heritability in visual-geometric illusions: a family study. *Perception* 8:303–9

Corley, R. P., DeFries, J. C., Kuse, A. R., Vandenberg, S. G. 1980. Familial resemblance for the identical blocks test of spatial ability: no evidence for X-linkage. *Behav. Genet.* 10:211–15

Crowe, R. R. 1978. Is genetic counseling appropriate for psychiatric illness? In *Controversy in Psychiatry,* ed. J. P. Brady, H. K. H. Brodie, pp. 763–75. Philadelphia: Saunders

Crowe, R. R. 1981. Genetic models of mental illness. In *American Handbook of Psychiatry,* ed. S. Arieti, H. K. H. Brodie, 7:75–94

Crowe, R. R., Smouse, P. E. 1977. The genetic implications of age-dependent penetrance in manic-depressive illness. *J. Psychiatr. Res.* 13:273–85

DeFries, J. C. 1980. Mental abilities: A family study. See Mielke & Crawford 1980, pp. 397–417

DeFries, J. C., Decker, S. N. 1982. Genetic aspects of reading disability: the Colorado Family Reading Study. In *Reading Disorders, Varieties and Treatments,* ed. P. G. Aaron, H. Halatesha. New York: Academic. In press

DeFries, J. C., Johnson, R. C., Kuse, A. R., McClearn, G. E., Polovina, J., Vandenberg, S. G., Wilson, J. R. 1979. Familial resemblance for specific cognitive abilities. *Behav. Genet.* 9:23–43

DeFries, J. C., Plomin, R. 1978. Behavioral genetics. *Ann. Rev. Psychol.* 29:473–515

DeFries, J. C., Plomin, R., Vandenberg, S. G., Kuse, A. R. 1981. Parent-offspring resemblance for cognitive abilities in the Colorado Adoption Project: biological, adoptive, and control parents and one-year-old children. *Intelligence.* In press

Donnelly, E. F., Goodwin, F., Waldman, I., Murphy, D. 1978. Prediction of antidepressant responses to lithium. *Am. J. Psychiatry* 135:552–56

Dorfman, D. D. 1978. The Cyril Burt question: new findings. *Science* 201:1177–86

Dorus, E. 1980. Applications of chromosome banding techniques in psychiatric research. In *Physico-Chemical Methodologies in Psychiatric Research,* ed. I. Hanin, S. H. Koslow, pp. 179–97. New York: Raven

Dorus, E., Pandey, G. N., Shaughnessy, R., Gaviria, M., Val, E., Ericksen, S., Davis, J. M. 1979. Lithium transport across red cell membrane: a cell membrane abnormality in manic-depressive illness. *Science* 205:932–34

Eaves, L. J. 1976. A model for sibling effects in man. *Heredity* 36:205–14

Eaves, L. J. 1978. Twins as a basis for the causal analysis of human personality. See Nance 1978, pp. 151–74

Eaves, L. J. 1979. The use of twins in the analysis of assortative mating. *Heredity* 43:399–409

Eaves, L. J., Eysenck, H. J. 1977. A genotype-environmental model for psychoticism. *Adv. Behav. Res. Ther.* 1:5–26

Eaves, L. J., Last, K., Martin, N. G., Jinks, J. L. 1977a. A progressive approach to non-additivity and genotype-environmental covariance in the analysis of human differences. *Br. J. Math. Stat. Psychol.* 30:1–42

Eaves, L. J., Last, K. A., Young, P. A., Martin, N. G. 1978. Model-fitting approaches to the analysis of human behavior. *Heredity* 41:249–320

Eaves, L. J., Martin, N. G., Eysenck, S. B. G. 1977b. An application of the analysis of covariance structures to the psychogenetical study of impulsiveness. *Br. J. Math. Stat. Psychol.* 30:185–97

Ehrman, L., Parsons, P. A. 1981. *Behavior Genetics and Evolution.* New York: McGraw-Hill

Elston, R. C. 1980. Segregation analysis. See Mielke & Crawford 1980, pp. 327–54

Elston, R. C., Namboodiri, K. K. 1977. Family studies of schizophrenia. In *Proc. 41st Sess. Int. Stat. Inst.* New Delhi, India

Elston, R. C., Namboodiri, K. K., Spence, M. A., Rainer, J. D. 1978. A genetic study of schizophrenia pedigrees II. One-locus hypotheses. *Neuropsychobiology* 4:193–206

Elston, R. C., Rao, D. C. 1978. Statistical modeling and analysis in human genetics. *Ann. Rev. Biophys. Bioeng.* 7: 253–86

Erlenmeyer-Kimling, L., Cornblatt, B., Fleiss, J. 1979. High-risk research in schizophrenia. *Psychiatr. Ann.* 9: 79–102

Erlenmeyer-Kimling, L., Jarvik, L. F. 1963. Genetics and intelligence: a review. *Science* 142:1477–79

Erlenmeyer-Kimling, L., Wunsch-Hitzig, R. A., Deutsch, S. 1980. Family formation by schizophrenics. In *The Social Consequences of Psychiatric Illness,* ed. L. Robins, P. Clayton, J. Wing, pp. 114–34. New York: Brunner/Mazel

Falek, A., Shafer, D. A., Madden, J. J. 1979. *Genetic effects of substances of abuse in humans.* Presented at Conf. Genetic, Developmental and Perinatal Aspects of Substances of Abuse, Atlanta

Feldman, M. W., Cavalli-Sforza, L. L. 1979. Aspects of variance and covariance analysis with cultural inheritance. *Theor. Popul. Biol.* 15:276–307

Finucci, J. M. 1978. Genetic considerations in dyslexia. In *Progress in Learning Disabilities,* ed. H. R. Myklebust, 4:41–63. New York: Grune & Stratton

Fischbein, S. 1978. Heredity-environment interaction in the development of twins. *Int. J. Behav. Dev.* 1:313–22

Fischbein, S. 1979. Intra-pair similarity in IQ of monozygotic and dizygotic male twins at 12 and 18 years of age. *Ann. Hum. Biol.* 6:495–504

Fischbein, S. 1980. IQ and social class. *Intelligence* 4:51–63

Fischbein, S., Nordqvist, T. 1978. Profile comparisons of physical growth for monozygotic and dizygotic twin pairs. *Ann. Hum. Biol.* 5:321–28

Fishman, P. M., Reich, T., Suarez, B., James, J. W. 1978. A note on the essential parameters of the two-allele autosomal locus model. *Am. J. Hum. Genet.* 30:283–92

Floderus-Myrhed, B., Pedersen, N., Rasmuson, I. 1980. Assessment of heritability for personality, based on a short form of the Eysenck Personality Inventory: A study of 12,898 twin pairs. *Behav. Genet.* 10:153–62

Foch, T. T., Plomin, R. 1980. Specific cognitive abilities in 5- to 12-year-old twins. *Behav. Genet.* 10:507–20

Ford, C. V., Jarvik, L. F. 1979. Genetic aspects of psychopathological disorders in later life. In *Psychopathology of Aging,* ed. O. J. Kaplan, 2:7–13. New York: Academic

Fowler, R. C., Tsuang, M. T., Cadoret, R. J. 1977a. Psychiatric illness in the offspring of schizophrenics. *Compr. Psychiatry* 18:127–34

Fowler, R. C., Tsuang, M. T., Cadoret, R. J. 1977b. Parental psychiatric illness associated with schizophrenia in the siblings of schizophrenics. *Compr. Psychiatry* 18:271–75

Fulker, D. W. 1979a. Nature and nurture: heredity. In *The Structure and Measurement of Intelligence,* ed. H. J. Eysenck, 5:102–32. New York: Springer

Fulker, D. W. 1979b. Some implications of biometrical genetical analysis for psychological research. See Royce & Mos 1979, pp. 337–76

Fulker, D. W. 1981. The genetic and environmental architecture of psychoticism, extraversion and neuroticism. In *A Model for Personality.* ed. H. J. Eysenck 4:88–122. New York: Springer

Fulker, D. W., Eysenck, S. B. G., Zuckerman, M. 1980. A genetic and environmental analysis of sensation seeking. *J. Res. Pers.* 14:261–81

Fuller, J. L., Thompson, W. R. 1978. *Behavior Genetics.* St. Louis: Mosby

Garfinkle, A. S., Vandenberg, S. G. 1978. Development of Piagetian logicomathematical concepts: preliminary results of a twin study. See Nance 1978, pp. 95–100

Garron, D. C. 1977. Intelligence among persons with Turner's Syndrome. *Behav. Genet.* 7:105–27

Gershon, E. S. 1977. Genetic and biologic studies of affective illness. In *The Impact of Biology on Modern Psychiatry,* ed. E. S. Gershon, R. H. Belmaker, S. S. Kety, M. Rosenthal, New York: Plenum

Gershon, E. S., Goldin, L. R., Lake, C. R., Murphy, D. L., Guroff, J. J. 1980. Genetics of plasma dopamine-β-hydroxylase (DBH), erythrocyte catechol-O-methyltransferase (COMT), and platelet monoamine oxidase (MAO) in pedigrees of patients with affective disorders. In *Enzymes and Neurotransmitters in Mental Disease,* ed. E. Usdin, P. Sourkes, M. B. H. Youdin. London: Wiley

Gershon, E. S., Targum, S. D., Kessler, L. R., Mazure, C. M., Bunney, W. E. Jr. 1977. Genetic studies and biologic strategies in the affective disorders. In *Progress in Medical Genetics,* New Ser. 2:104–64. Philadelphia: Saunders

Gershon, E. S., Targum, S. D., Matthysse, S., Bunney, W. E. Jr. 1979. Color blindness not closely linked to bipolar illness—Report of a new pedigree series. *Arch. Gen. Psychiatry* 36:1423–30

Goldberger, A. S. 1978a. Pitfalls in the resolution of IQ inheritance. See Morton & Chung 1978, pp. 195–215

Goldberger, A. S. 1978b. The nonresolution of IQ inheritance by path analysis. *Am. J. Hum. Genet.* 39:442–45

Goldsmith, H. H., Gottesman, I. I. 1981. Origins of variation in behavioral style: a longitudinal study of temperament in young twins. *Child Dev.* 52:91–103

Gottesman, I. I. 1966. Genetic variance in adaptive personality traits. *J. Child Psychol. Psychiatry* 7:199–208

Gottesman, I. I. 1979. Schizophrenia and genetics: toward understanding uncertainty. *Psychiatr. Ann.* 9:54–78

Gottesman, I. I., Shields, J. 1972. *Schizophrenia and Genetics.* New York: Academic

Gottesman, I. I., Shields, J. 1982. *The Schizophrenic Puzzle.* New York: Cambridge Univ. Press

Gould, S. J., Lewontin, R. C. 1979. The spandrels of San Marco and the Panglossian paradigm: a critique of the adaptationist programme. *Proc. R. Soc. London Ser. B.* 205:581–98

Guttman, R., Shoham, I. 1979. Intrafamilial invariance and parent-offspring resemblance in spatial abilities. *Behav. Genet.* 9:367–78

Hakstian, A. R., Vandenberg, S. G. 1979. The cross-cultural generalizability of a higher-order cognitive structure model. *Intelligence* 3:73–103

Hardy-Brown, K., Plomin, R., DeFries, J. C. 1981. Genetic and environmental influences on rate of communicative development in the first year of life. *Dev. Psychol.* In press

Hearnshaw, L. S. 1979. *Cyril Burt, Psychologist.* Ithaca: Cornell Univ.

Henderson, N. D. 1979. Adaptive significance of animal behavior: the role of gene-environment interaction. See Royce & Mos 1979, pp. 243–99

Herschel, M. 1978. Dyslexia revisited: a review. *Hum. Genet.* 40:115–34

Ho, H., Foch, T. T., Plomin, R. 1980. Developmental stability of the relative influence of genes and environment on specific cognitive abilities during childhood. *Dev. Psychol.* 16:340–46

Hook, E. B. 1979. Extra sex chromosomes and human behavior: the nature of the evidence regarding XYY, XXY, XXYY, and XXX genotypes. In *Genetic Mechanisms of Sexual Development,* ed. H. L. Vallet, I. H. Porter. pp. 437–63. New York: Academic

Horn, J. L., McArdle, J. J. 1980. Perspectives on mathematical/statistical model building (MASMOB) in research on aging. In *Aging in the 1980's: Psychological Issues,* ed. L. W. Poon, 37:503–41. Washington DC: Am. Psychol. Assoc.

Horn, J. M., Loehlin, J. C., Willerman, L. 1979. Intellectual resemblance among adoptive and biological relatives: The Texas Adoption Project. *Behav. Genet.* 9:177–207

Horn, J. M., Loehlin, J. C., Willerman, L. 1981. Aspects of the inheritance of intellectual abilities. *Behav. Genet.* In press

Horn, J. M., Plomin, R., Rosenman, R. 1976. Heritability of personality traits in adult male twins. *Behav. Genet.* 6:17–30

Johnson, R. C., Ahern, F. M., Cole, R. E. 1980. Secular change in degree of assortative mating for ability? *Behav. Genet.* 10:1–8

Kidd, K. K., Gladstien, K. L. 1980. Alternative genetic models for the analysis of complex traits. In *Etiology of Cleft Lip and Cleft Palate,* ed. M. Melnick, D. Bixler, E. Shields, pp. 407–35. New York: Liss

Kidd, K. K., Weissman, M. M. 1978. Why we do not yet understand the genetics of affective disorders. In *Depression: Biology, Psychodynamics, and Treatment,* ed. J. O. Cole, A. F. Schatzberg, S. H. Frazier, pp. 107–19. New York: Plenum

Koskenvuo, M., Langinvainia, H., Kaprio, J., Rantasalo, I., Sama, S. 1979. *The Finnish twin registry: baseline characteristics. III. Occupational and psychosocial factors.* Helsinki: Dep. Public Health Sci., Univ. Helsinki, Finland

Leckman, J. F., Gershon, E. S. 1977. Autosomal models of sex effect in bipolar-related major affective illness. *J. Psychiatr. Res.* 13:237–46

Leckman, J. F., Gershon, E. S., McGinniss, M. H., Targum, S. D., Dibble, E. D. 1979. New data do not suggest linkage between the X_g blood group and bipolar illness. *Arch. Gen. Psychiatry* 36: 1435–41

Leckman, J. F., Gershon, E. S., Nichols, A. S., Murphy, D. L. 1977. Reduced MAO activity in first-degree relatives of individuals with bipolar affective disorders. *Arch. Gen. Psychiatry* 34:601

Loehlin, J. C. 1978. Heredity-environment analyses of Jencks's correlations. *Behav. Genet.* 8:415–36

Loehlin, J. C. 1979. Combining data from different groups in human behavior genetics. See Royce & Mos 1979, pp. 303–36

Loehlin, J. C. 1980. Recent adoption studies of IQ. *Hum. Genet.* 16:1–6

Loehlin, J. C., Horn, J. M., Willerman, L. 1981. Personality resemblance in adoptive families. *Behav. Genet.* 11:309–30

Loehlin, J. C., Nichols, R. C. 1976. *Heredity, Environment, and Personality: A Study of 850 Sets of Twins.* Austin, Tex./London: Univ. Texas

Loehlin, J. C., Sharan, S., Jacoby, R. 1978. In pursuit of the "spatial gene": a family study. *Behav. Genet.* 8:27–41

Luchins, D., Pollin, W., Wyatt, R. J. 1980. Laterality in monozygotic schizophrenic twins: an alternative hypothesis. *Biol. Psychiatry* 15:87–93

Lynn, R. 1977. The intelligence of the Japanese. *Bull. Br. Psychol. Soc.* 30:69–72

Lynn, R. 1979. The social ecology of intelligence in the British Isles. *Br. J. Soc. Clin. Psychol.* 18:1–12

Lynn, R. 1980. The social ecology of intelligence in France. *Br. J. Soc. Clin. Psychol.* 19:325–31

Lynn, R., Dziobon, J. 1980. On the intelligence of the Japanese and other Mongoloid peoples. *Pers. Individ. Differ.* 1:95–96

Lytton, H., Martin, N. G., Eaves, L. 1977. Environmental and genetical causes of variation in ethological aspects of behavior in two-year-old boys. *Soc. Biol.* 24:200–11

Martin, N. G., Eaves, L. J., Fulker, D. W. 1979. The genetical relationship of impulsiveness and sensation seeking to Eysenck's personality dimensions. *Acta Genet. Med. Gemellol.* 28:197–210

Martin, N. G., Eaves, L. J., Kearsey, M. J., Davies, P. 1978. The power of the classical twin study. *Heredity* 40:97–116

Masters, J. C. 1981. Developmental psychology. *Ann. Rev. Psychol.* 32:117–51

Matheny, A. P. Jr. 1980. Bayley's infant behavior record: behavioral components and twin analyses. *Child Dev.* 51: 1157–67

Matheny, A. P. Jr., Dolan, A. B. 1980. A twin study of personality and temperament during middle childhood. *J. Res. Pers.* 14:224–34

Matheny, A. P. Jr., Wilson, R. S., Dolan, A. B., Krantz, J. Z. 1981. Behavioral contrasts in twinships: stability and patterns of differences in childhood. *Child Dev.* 52:579–88

Matthysse, S. W., Kidd, K. K. 1976. Estimating the genetic contribution to schizophrenia. *Am. J. Psychiatry* 133:185–91

Matthysse, S. W., Lange, K., Wagener, D. K. 1979. Continuous variation caused by genes with graduated effects. *Proc. Natl. Acad. Sci. USA* 76:2862–65

McArdle, J. J. 1980. Causal modeling applied to psychonomic systems simulation. *Behav. Res. Methods Instrum.* 12:193–209

McClearn, G. E., DeFries, J. C. 1973. *Introduction to Behavioral Genetics.* San Francisco: Freeman

McGee, M. G. 1979. Human spatial abilities: psychometric studies and environmental, genetic, hormonal, and neurological influences. *Psychol. Bull.* 86:889–918

McGee, M. G. 1982. Spatial abilities: the influence of genetic factors. In *Spatial Abilities: Development and Physiological Bases,* ed. M. Potegal. New York: Academic. In press

McGuffin, P. 1979. Schizophrenia an HLC-associated disease? *Psychol. Med.* 9: 721–28

Mednick, S. A., Christiansen, K. O., eds. 1977. *Biosocial Bases of Criminal Behavior.* New York: Gardner

Mendels, J. 1976. Lithium in the treatment of depression. *Am. J. Psychiatry* 133:373–78

Mendlewicz, J., Fleiss, J. L. 1974. Linkage studies with X-chromosome markers in bipolar (manic-depressive) and unipolar (depressive) illnesses. *Biol. Psychiatry* 9:261–94

Mendlewicz, J., Linkowski, P., Guroff, J. J., Van Praag, H. M. 1979. Color blindness linkage to bipolar manic-depressive illness: new evidence. *Arch. Gen. Psychiatry* 36:1442–47

Mendlewicz, J., Shopsin, B., eds. 1979. *Genetic Aspects of Affective Illness.* New York/London: Spectrum

Mielke, J. H., Crawford, M. H., eds. 1980. *Current Developments in Anthropological Genetics.* Vol. 1. New York: Plenum

Morton, L. A., Chung, C. E., eds. 1978. *Genetic Epidemiology.* New York: Academic

Morton, L. A., Kidd, K. K., Matthysse, S. W., Richards, R. L. 1979. Recurrence risks in schizophrenia: are they model dependent? *Behav. Genet.* 9:389–406

Nance, W. E., ed. 1978. *Twin Research Proceedings of the Second International Congress on Twin Studies August 29-September 1, 1977 Washington, D.C., Part A Psychology and Methodology.* New York: Liss

Nichols, P. L., Chen, T. C. 1980. *Minimal Brain Dysfunction: A Prospective Study.* Hillsdale, NJ: Erlbaum

Nichols, R. C. 1978. Twin studies of ability, personality, and interests. *Homo* 29:158–73

Nielsen, J., Nyborg, H., Dahl, G. 1977. Turner's Syndrome: a psychiatric-psychological study of 45 women with Turner's Syndrome. *Acta Jutlandica,* Medicine Ser. 21, 45:3–190

Nyborg, H., Nielsen, J. 1981a. Spatial ability of men with karyotype 47,XXY, 47,XYY, or normal controls. In *Human Behavior and Genetics,* ed. W. Schmidt, J. Nielsen, pp. 85–106 Amsterdam: Elsevier/North Holland Biomed.

Nyborg, H., Nielsen, J. 1981b. Sex hormone treatment and spatial ability in women with Turner's syndrome. See Nyborg & Nielsen 1981a, pp. 167–82

Oliverio, A. 1977. *Genetics Environment and Intelligence.* Amsterdam: Elsevier

Omenn, G. S. 1978. Psychopharmacogenetics: an overview and new approaches. *Hum. Genet. Suppl.* 1:83–90

Omenn, G. S. 1981. Behavior genetics of aging. In *Perspectives in the Psychobiology of Aging,* ed. D. G. Stein. New York: Elsevier. In press

Omenn, G. S., Weber, B. A. 1978. Dyslexia: search for phenotypic and genetic heterogeneity. *Am. J. Med. Genet.* 1:333–42

Osborne, R. T., Noble, C. E., Weyl, N., eds. 1978. *Human Variation: The Biopsychology of Age, Race, and Sex.* New York: Academic

Page, E. B., Jarjoura, D. 1979. Seeking the cause of correlations among mental abilities: large twin analysis in a national testing program. *J. Res. Dev. Educ.* 12:108–17

Pandey, G. N., Dorus, E., Shaughnessy, R., Gaviria, M., Val, E., Davis, J. M. 1980. Reduced platelet MAO activity and vulnerability to psychiatric disorders. *Psychiatry Res.* 2:315–21

Park, J., Johnson, R. C., DeFries, J. C., McClearn, G. E., Mi, M. P., Rashad, M. N., Vandenberg, S. G., Wilson, J. R. 1978. Parent-offspring resemblance for specific cognitive abilities in Korea. *Behav. Genet.* 8:43–52

Paul, S. M. 1980. Sibling resemblance in mental ability: a review. *Behav. Genet.* 10:277–90

Plomin, R., DeFries, J. C. 1979. Multivariate behavioral genetic analysis of twin data on scholastic abilities. *Behav. Genet.* 9:505–17

Plomin, R., DeFries, J. C. 1980. Genetics and intelligence: recent data. *Intelligence* 4:15–24

Plomin, R., DeFries, J. C., McClearn, G. E. 1980. *Behavior Genetics: A Primer.* San Francisco: Freeman

Plomin, R., Rowe, D. C. 1977. A twin study of temperament in young children. *J. Psychol.* 97:107–13

Plomin, R., Rowe, D. C. 1979. Genetic and environmental etiology of social behavior in infancy. *Dev. Psychol.* 15:62–72

Plomin, R., Vandenberg, S. G. 1980. An analysis of Koch's (1966) primary mental abilities test data for 5- to 7-year-old twins, *Behav. Genet.* 10:409–12

Pope, H. G. Jr., Lipinski, J. F. Jr. 1978. Diagnosis in schizophrenia and manic-depressive illness: a reassessment of the specificity of "schizophrenic" symptoms in the light of current research. *Arch. Gen. Psychiatry* 35:811–28

Rao, D. C., Morton, N. E. 1978. IQ as a paradigm in genetic epidemiology. See Morton & Chung 1978, pp. 145–81

Rao, D. C., Morton, N. E., Gottesman, I. I., Lew, R. 1981. Path analysis of qualitative data on pairs of relatives: application to schizophrenia. *Hum. Hered.* In press

Reich, T., Suarez, B., Rice, J., Cloninger, C. R. 1980. Current directions in genetic epidemiology. See Mielke & Crawford 1980, pp. 299–324

Rice, J., Cloninger, C. R., Reich, T. 1980. Analysis of behavioral traits in the presence of cultural transmission and assortative mating: applications to IQ and SES, *Behav. Genet.* 10:73–92

Rice, J., Cloninger, C. R., Reich, T. 1981. General causal models for sex differences in the familial transmission of multifactorial traits: an application to human spatial visualizing ability. *Soc. Biol.* In press

Rieder, R. O., Nichols, P. L. 1979. Offspring of schizophrenics III: hyperactivity and neurological soft signs. *Arch. Gen. Psychiatry* 36:665–74

Rose, R. J., Boughman, J. A., Corey, L. A., Nance, W. E., Christian, J. C., Kang, K. W. 1980a. Data from kinship of monozygotic twins indicate maternal effects on verbal intelligence. *Nature* 283:375–77

Rose, R. J., Harris, E. L., Christian, J. C., Nance, W. E. 1979a. Genetic variance in nonverbal intelligence: data from the kinships of identical twins. *Science* 205:1153–55

Rose, R. J., Miller, J. Z., Dumont-Driscoll, M., Evans, M. M. 1979b. Twin-family studies of perceptual speed ability. *Behav. Genet.* 9:71–86

Rose, R. J., Miller, J. Z., Pogue-Geile, M. F., Cardwell, G. F. 1980b. *Twin-family studies of common fears and phobias.* Presented at 3rd Int. Cong. Twin Studies, Jerusalem

Rovet, J., Netley, C. 1981. Processing deficits in Turner Syndrome. *Dev. Psychol.* In press

Rowe, D. C., Plomin, R. 1978. The Burt controversy: a comparison of Burt's data on IQ with data from other studies. *Behav. Genet.* 8:81–83

Rowe, D. C., Plomin, R. 1979. A multivariate twin analysis of within-family environmental influences in infants' social responsiveness. *Behav. Genet.* 9:519–25

Rowe, D. C., Plomin, R. 1981. The importance of nonshared (E1) environmental influences in behavioral development. *Dev. Psychol.* 17:517–31

Royce, J. R., Mos, L. P., eds. 1979. *Theoretical Advances in Behavior Genetics.* Alphen aan den Rijn, The Netherlands: Sijthoff & Noordhoff

Scarr, S., Carter-Saltzman, L. 1981. Genetics and intelligence. In *Handbook of Intelligence,* ed. R. S. Sternberg. Cambridge: Cambridge Univ. In press

Scarr, S., Webber, P. L., Weinberg, R. A., Wittig, M. A. 1981. Personality resemblance among adolescents and their parents in biologically-related and adoptive families. *J. Pers. Soc. Psychol.* In press

Scarr, S., Weinberg, R. A. 1976. IQ test performance of black children adopted by white families. *Am. Psychol.* 31:726–39

Scarr, S., Weinberg, R. A. 1977. Intellectual similarities within families of both adopted and biological children. *Intelligence* 1:170–91

Scarr, S., Weinberg, R. A. 1978. The influence of "family background" on intellectual attainment. *Am. Sociol. Rev.* 43:674–92

Scarr, S., Yee, D. 1980. Heritability and educational policy: genetic and environmental effects on IQ, aptitude and achievement. *Educ. Psychol.* 15:1–22

Scharfetter, C., Nuesperli, M. 1980. The group of schizophrenias, schizo-affective psychoses and affective disorders. *Schizophr. Bull.* 6:586–91

Schlesser, M. A., Winokur, G., Sherman, B. M. 1979. Genetic subtypes of unipolar primary depressive illness distinguished by hypothalamic-pituitary-adrenal axis activity. *Lancet* 1:739–41

Schlesser, M. A., Winokur, G., Sherman, B. M. 1980. Hypothalamic-pituitary-adrenal axis activity in depressive illness: its relationship to classification *Arch. Gen. Psychiatry* 37:737–43

Schuckit, M. A. 1980. Alcoholism and genetics: possible biological mediators. *Biol. Psychiatry* 15:437–47

Smeraldi, E., Negri, F., Melica, A. M. 1977. A genetic study of affective disorder. *Acta Psychiatr. Scand.* 56:382–98

Spuhler, K. P., Vandenberg, S. G. 1980. Comparison of parent-offspring resemblance for specific cognitive abilities. *Behav. Genet.* 10:413–18

Sullivan, J. L., Stanfield, C. N., Maltbie, A. A., Hammett, E. B., Cavenar, J. O. Jr. 1978a. Stability of low blood platelet monoamine oxidase activity in human alcoholics. *Biol. Psychiatry* 13:391

Sullivan, J. L., Stanfield, C. N., Schanberg, S., Cavenar, J. O. Jr. 1978b. Platelet monoamine oxidase and serum dopamine-β-hydroxylase activity in chronic alcoholics. *Arch. Gen. Psychiatry* 35: 1209

Taubman, P. 1978. Determinants of socioeconomic success: regression and latent variables analysis in samples of twins. See Nance 1978, pp. 175–78

Taylor, M. A., Abrams, R. 1980. Reassessing the bipolar-unipolar dichotomy. *J. Affect. Disord.* 2:195–217

Taylor, M. A., Abrams, R., Hayman, M. A. 1980. The classification of affective disorders—a reassessment of the bipolar-unipolar dichotomy. *J. Affect. Disord.* 2:95–109

Thiessen, D. 1979. Biological trends in behavior genetics. See Royce & Mos 1979, pp. 169–217

Thompson, W. R. 1979. Familial likeness: etiology and function. See Royce & Mos 1979, pp. 221–38

Torgerson, A. M. 1981. Genetic factors in temperamental individuality: a longitudinal study of same-sexed twins from two months to six years. *J. Am. Acad. Child Psychiatry.* In press

Torgerson, A. M., Kringlen, E. 1978. Genetic aspects of temperamental differences in infants: a study of same-sexed twins. *J. Am. Acad. Child Psychiatry* 17:433–41

Torgerson, S. 1977. Intrapair difference in personality traits, and emotional and social adjustment in monozygotic twins. *Acta Genet. Med. Gemellol.* 26:55–61

Tsuang, M. T. 1978. Genetic counseling for psychiatric patients and their families. *Am. J. Psychiatry* 135:1465–75

Tsuang, M. T. 1979. "Schizoaffective disorder": dead or alive? *Arch. Gen. Psychiatry* 36:633–34

Tsuang, M. T., Vandermey, R. 1980. *Genes and the Mind.* Oxford: Oxford Univ. Press

Turner, W. J. 1979a. Toward a molecular biology of the psychoses: searches for genetic markers. *Psychiatr. J. Univ. Ottawa* 4:248–55

Turner, W. J. 1979b. Genetic markers for schizotaxia. *Biol. Psychiatry* 14: 177–206

Turner, W. J., King, S. 1981a. Two genetically distinct forms of bipolar affective disorder? *Biol. Psychiatry.* 16:417–39

Turner, W. J., King, S. 1981b. A double pedigree of bipolar affective disorder segregating with HLA in four and five generations. *Biol. Psychiatry.* In press

Wender, P. H., Rosenthal, D., Rainer, J. D., Greenhill, L., Sarlin, M. B. 1977. Schizophrenics' adopting parents: psychiatric status. *Arch. Gen. Psychiatry* 34:777–84

Willerman, L. 1979. Effects of families on intellectual development. *Am. Psychol.* 34:923–29

Willerman, L., Horn, J. M., Loehlin, J. C. 1977. The aptitude-achievement test distinction: a study of unrelated children reared together. *Behav. Genet.* 7:465–70

Wilson, J. R., Vandenberg, S. G. 1978. Sex differences in cognition: evidence from the Hawaii Family Study. In *Sex and Behavior,* ed. T. E. McGill, D. A. Dewsbury, B. D. Sachs, pp. 317–35. New York/London: Plenum

Wilson, R. S. 1978. Synchronies in mental development: an epigenetic perspective. *Science* 202:939–48

Wilson, R. S. 1979. Analysis of longitudinal twin data: basic model and applications to physical growth measures. *Acta. Genet. Med. Gemellol.* 28:93–105

Wilson, R. S. 1980. *Synchronized developmental pathways for infant twins.* Presented at 3rd Int. Cong. Twin Studies, Jerusalem

Winokur, G. 1979. Unipolar depression: is it divisible into autonomous subtypes? *Arch. Gen. Psychiatry* 36:47–52

Winokur, G., Reich, T. 1970. Two genetic factors in manic-depressive disease. *Compr. Psychiatry* 11:93–99

Wittig, M. A., Petersen, A. C., eds. 1979. *Sex-related Differences in Cognitive Functioning: Developmental Issues.* New York: Academic

Young, P. A., Eaves, L. J., Eysenck, H. J. 1980. Intergenerational stability and change in the causes of variation in personality. *Pers. Individ. Differ.* 1:35–55

Zerbin-Rudin, E. 1979. Genetics of affective psychoses. In *Origin, Prevention and Treatment of Affective Disorders,* ed. M. Schou, E. Stromgren, pp. 185–97, London: Academic

Zerbin-Rudin, E. 1980a. Genetics of affective psychoses. In *Handbook of Biological Psychiatry,* Part III, ed. H. von Praag, M. H. Lader, O. J. Rafaelson, E. J. Sachar. pp. 35–57. New York: Dekker

Zerbin-Rudin, E. 1980b. Genetic factors in neurosis, psychopathy and alcoholism. See Zerbin-Rudin 1980a

Ann. Rev. Psychol. 1982. 33:441–75

THE PSYCHOLOGY OF LAW

John Monahan

School of Law, University of Virginia, Charlottesville, Virginia 22901

Elizabeth F. Loftus

Department of Psychology, University of Washington, Seattle, Washington 98195

CONTENTS

0066-4308/82/0201-0441$02.00

INTRODUCTION

If the first *Annual Review* chapter on psychology and law (Tapp 1976) could dub itself an "overture," this, the second, might be declared a "crescendo." In the past 6 years, the American Psychology-Law Society has burgeoned to record membership levels, an American Board of Forensic Psychology was created to certify expertise in courtroom matters, and, in 1981, the American Psychological Association conferred official legitimacy on the area by forming Psychology and Law as its 41st Division. It is now estimated that fully one-third of all graduate psychology departments in the United States offer courses related to law (Grisso et al in press). Indeed, the turning of psychologists toward law is an international phenomenon. The British Psychological Society created a Division of Criminological and Legal Psychology in 1977, and Beijing University began developing a curriculum in psychology and law in 1980.

The body of published knowledge in the area has expanded apace. In addition to *Law and Human Behavior*, a specialized journal, publications of more general interest, such as the *Journal of Personality and Social Psychology*, have devoted entire issues to legal topics. It is no longer remarkable to find articles relating psychology to the law in such repositories of mainline scholarship as *Psychological Bulletin* and *Psychological Review.*

Paralleling this growth of psychological interest in the law has been the law's steadily developing acceptance of psychology. In the 1978 *Ballew v. Georgia* jury size case, the U.S. Supreme Court cited numerous psychological studies to justify its decision that juries in state criminal cases must contain at least six members. The use of psychological data rather than legal precedent was defended by a plurality of the Court "because they provide the only basis, besides judicial hunch, for a decision about whether smaller and smaller juries will be able to fulfill the purpose and functions of the Sixth Amendment" (p. 4220). In the 1979 decision of *Addington v. Texas,* the same Court stated that cases involving a question of psychological disorder must be decided not so much on the basis of observable facts "but on the *meaning* of the facts which must be interpreted by expert psychiatrists and psychologists" (p. 1811, italics in original).

To make manageable our task of critical and selective review, we consider here only the psychology of law and not the law of psychology, such as the legal regulation of psychological practice (e.g. Bersoff 1980, Schwitzgebel & Schwitzgebel 1980) or research (e.g. Wilson & Donnerstein 1976). Rather than organize our material according to conventionally defined categories of psychology, such as social or clinical, or of law, such as criminal or civil, or of the relationship between the two, such as law as an independent, dependent, or intervening variable for psychological analysis (Feeley 1976,

Friedman & Macaulay 1977), we have chosen a more functional framework. The contributions that psychology is making to understanding and predicting legal phenomena can be said to cluster in three domains (cf Farrington & Hawkins 1979, Grisso et al in press). Psychology is addressing the validity of assumptions underlying substantive law. It is clarifying the nature of the formal legal process by which disputes regarding the application of these substantive laws are resolved. As well, it is mapping the contours of the informal legal system in which a series of decision makers act in furtherance of the substantive law and within the constraints set by the legal process. While the boundaries between these domains are unmarked at places, we have found this taxonomy useful in organizing a vast literature and for sharpening our own understanding of the psychology of law.

SUBSTANTIVE LAW

Law is based upon "an underlying set of assumptions about how people act and how their actions can be controlled" (National Science Board 1969, p. 35). These fundamentally empirical assumptions are of two types. Some are descriptive of human behavior or personality (". . . how people act"), such as the "facts" that normal people intend their actions, but mentally ill people may not, or that children lack the capacity to make informed decisions about their lives. Other assumptions are of a consequential sort (". . . how their actions can be controlled"). Criminal law assumes that if people expect punishment to follow from certain actions, then they will be less likely to do them. Tax law assumes that if people are allowed to deduct mortgage interest payments, then they will be more likely to buy houses.

In the largest sense, all of psychology is relevant to substantive law, since any aspect of human behavior may be the subject of legal regulation. Basic research in psychopathology, child development, and statistics, for example, may have legal ramifications for the insanity defense, child custody, and employment discrimination. We shall concentrate here on forms of psychological research whose relevance to substantive law is more direct. Studies of competence to make decisions will be taken as illustrative of research bearing on descriptive assumptions, and studies of the effects of the criminal sanction will exemplify research relevant to consequential assumptions.

Competence

"Most children," the Supreme Court observed in *Parham v. JR* (1979, p. 2505), "even in adolescence, simply are not able to make sound judgments concerning many decisions . . . Parents can and must make those judgments." Descriptive assumptions like this regarding the "competence" of two groups, children and the psychologically disordered, at various decision-making tasks, such as making a contract, marrying, or serving on a jury, are common in law. The standard against which competence is measured is usually the decision-making ability of "normal" adults. Recent psychological research on the assumption of competence has focused upon decisions regarding medical and psychological treatment and regarding the waiver of legal rights.

TO CONSENT TO TREATMENT Grisso & Vierling (1978) and Melton (1981), in comprehensive reviews of developmental research on decision-making capabilities, conclude that children under the age of 11 do not give adult-like reasons when deciding upon their medical or psychological treatment. At age 15 and above, however, there is no substantial difference between children and adults. Ages 11–14 appear to be a transition period in the development of cognitive and social abilities, and individual differences are pronounced. In the most sophisticated study to date on the competence of children to consent to treatment, Weithorn (1980) compared 9-and 14-year-olds to adults on four legal standards of competency: 1. capacity to express a treatment preference; 2. capacity to reach a "reasonable" decision (regardless of how the decision was reached); 3. capacity to reason logically in reaching a decision; and 4. capacity to understand relevant information regarding treatment alternatives (Roth et al 1977). She found 14-year-olds to be as competent as adults according to these four standards, and 9-year-olds to be less competent than 14-year-olds and adults in terms of logical reasoning and the understanding of information. The 9-year-olds, however, were as likely to express a preference for treatment as were the older subjects, and the direction of the preferences did not differ among the groups.

Research on the competence of psychologically disordered adults to admit themselves voluntarily to mental hospitals has produced similar findings: they make the "right" choice as judged by others (i.e. they seek treatment), but for reasons that are unclear. Appelbaum et al (1981) found that half of those who had voluntarily admitted themselves to a mental hospital denied that they had mental health problems or needed hospitalization. Only 38 percent of these patients were judged to meet minimal clinical criteria of competence (e.g. appreciating the nature of hospital treatment) and only 14 percent met the more stringent legally oriented definition of competence (e.g. awareness of possible adverse effects of hospitalization). The researchers suggest that rather than a competency-based "informed consent" test for hospital admission (which most psychologically disordered persons could not pass), a less rigorous "assent" procedure be imposed, requiring only that the prospective patient "voluntarily" agree to hospitalization, without inquiring into the cognitive processes that mediated the decision.

TO WAIVE RIGHTS In the 1967 *Gault* case, the U.S. Supreme Court stated that judges must take "the greatest care" in evaluating whether a waiver of rights by a child was voluntary "in the sense not only that it was not coerced or suggested, but also that is was not the product of ignorance of rights or of adolescent fantasy, fright, or despair" (p. 55). One of the most comprehensive programs of psychological research on children's competence to waive legal rights has been that of Grisso (1980, 1981). He found that over half of a large sample of incarcerated juveniles aged 11–16 did not comprehend at least one of their *Miranda* rights. The two most common misunderstandings concerned the warning that statements made to the police "can and will be used against you in a court of law" (often understood to mean that disrespect to a police officer would be punished) and the warning of a right to consult an attorney before and during an interrogation (often understood to apply only to future court appearances). Comprehension of rights increased with age through age 13, and began a plateau at age 14, thus paralleling the findings on juvenile competence to consent to treatment. Comprehension correlated strongly with IQ ($r = .47$). Prior experience with the juvenile justice system, however, had no direct effect on comprehension.

Psychological research on competence to consent to treatment and to waive rights is of very recent origin and has yet to capture the attention of the courts. Research on competence can both validate and refine substantive law, and serves as an exemplar of the contribution psychology has to make in analyzing other descriptive assumptions of the law, such as the assumption that mental health professionals can predict violent behavior (Shah 1978, Monahan 1981) or that various groups of people "intend" the consequences of their acts (Keasey & Sales 1977; cf Nisbett & Ross 1980).

The Criminal Sanction

While Gibbs (1975) has identified numerous consequences of the criminal sanction, most accounts focus on three of them. The punishment of a criminal offender may (*a*) *deter* both the offender in question ("special deterrence") and other persons ("general deterrence") from engaging in prohibited behavior in the future; (*b*) *incapacitate* the offender in prison, thus making certain crimes temporarily impossible (or permanently so, in the case of a life or death sentence); or (*c*) *rehabilitate* the offender, so that he or she will not be motivated to commit additional crime. Recent psychological research has focused upon the first and last of these consequences.

It should be noted that there is another assumption underlying the existence of the criminal sanction that is not consequential in nature, but rather reflects explicitly moral considerations. The assumption is that people who commit crime should be punished because they deserve it, regardless of any utilitarian consequences (Vidmar & Miller 1980). Modern retributive theories, such as the currently influential "just deserts" model (von Hirsch & Hanrahan 1979), however, incorporate deterrence as a limiting principle (i.e. punish only because offenders deserve it, but punish no more than necessary to deter others.)

DETERRENCE A major development in the study of deterrence has been the report of the National Academy of Sciences Panel on Research on Deterrent and Incapacitative Effects (Blumstein et al 1978; cf. Ehrlich 1979). The Panel noted four obstacles in interpreting as "deterrence" the frequently found negative correlation between crime rates and the probability of punishment: 1. common third causes (e.g. a changing age distribution in society might influence both crimes and sanctions); 2. error in measuring crimes (many crimes are not reported); 3. the confounding of deterrence and incapacitation (imprisoning offenders can lower the crime rate through incapacitation without any deterrent effect); and 4. simultaneous effects (the crime rate may affect the level of sanction, rather than vice versa, due to an overburdening of police and court resources). While observing that "the evidence certainly favors a position supporting deterrence more than it favors one asserting that deterrence is absent" (p. 7), the Panel concluded that given the above methodological problems, the general question of deterrent effects is still an open one. In particular, the Panel stressed that "the available studies provide no useful evidence on the deterrent effect of capital punishment" (p. 9). Since it is intuitively clear that some criminal sanctions do deter some criminal behavior by some people (as anyone who has ever lightened a foot on a gas pedal after observing a police car in the rear-view mirror can attest), the question for research is best put as what sanctions deter what crimes by what people, under what conditions, and how much.

Carroll (1978a), in one of the few explicitly psychological studies of deterrence, found that both offenders and nonoffenders evaluated the desirability of crime opportunities along simple dimensions, with those dimensions varying greatly across subjects. Both offenders and nonoffenders were generally more responsive to changes in the rewards produced by crime than in the punishments for it if caught. "This suggests that social policies might be directed toward the relative profits of criminal and noncriminal activities as well as toward traditional punitive ends" (p. 1520).

REHABILITATION The National Academy of Sciences followed its Panel on Deterrence with another on Research on Rehabilitative Techniques (Sechrest et al 1979, Martin et al 1981). Rehabilitation was defined as "the result of any planned intervention that reduces an offender's further criminal activity, whether that reduction is mediated by personality, behavior, abilities, attitudes, values, or other factors" (p. 4). The effects of maturation and the effects associated with "fear" were specifically excluded, lest long or cruel sentences be viewed as "rehabilitative" per se (cf Wilson 1980). This group took as its starting point the work of Lipton et al (1975, see also Greenberg 1977), which spawned the now common wisdom that "nothing works" in criminal rehabilitation. While concluding that Lipton et al (1975) were "reasonably accurate and fair in their appraisal of the rehabilitation literature" (p. 5), the Panel noted two qualifications to the "nothing works" interpretation: the interventions studied to date have been insipid and poorly implemented (Quay 1977), and there are "suggestions" among the mass of negative results that some treatments may be effective for some groups of offenders. Specifically, work and financial support programs for certain types of released offenders were targeted as promising approaches. Others (e.g. Ross & Gendreau 1980) read the research more cheerfully.

The rehabilitative consequence of the criminal sanction is a maturing area of research, but psychological analysis of deterrence is in its infancy and of incapacitation is as yet unborn. Given the recognized limitations on the use of aggregate data, and the need for analyses of these topics at the level of the individual (Blumstein et al 1978), psychological approaches to deterrence and incapacitation can be expected to come of age in this decade. As Carroll (1978a, p. 1520) has noted, "the debate between sociologists and economists has now become a forum." In addition to analyzing the effects of the criminal sanction, this forum is addressing many other consequential assumptions of substantive law, such as the effect of school desegregation on student attitudes and achievement (Stephan 1978).

THE LEGAL PROCESS

Research on the legal process considers the more formal aspects of how the law resolves conflicts between individuals (as in contract or tort law) or between an individual and the state (as in criminal or administrative law) in the application of substantive legal principles. Its primary focus, therefore, is on the trial as the ritualized crucible in which conflicts are resolved, rather than on less formal or rule-bound procedures such as police discretion, out-of-court negotiation, or parole (Wrightsman 1978, McGillis 1980, Elwork et al 1981).

While relatively few cases that enter the legal system ever reach the stage of a formal trial—an observation that can be taken either as testimony to the sufficiency of informal mechanisms of resolution (Saks & Hastie 1978) or as an indictment of duplicity in the law (Haney & Lowry 1979)—in absolute terms the numbers are large. An estimated 2 million persons serve as jurors in some 200,000 civil and criminal cases each year (Abraham 1980). The reason that trial processes have so captured the attention of both lay and scholarly audiences, however, has more to do with their symbolic than their numeric importance (Nemeth 1976). Through its ability to establish legal precedent, one trial whose verdict is appealed may have consequences vastly more far reaching than many cases informally disposed (Silberman 1978). As well, the behavior of prosecutors and defense attorneys in plea bargaining and of opposing counsel in private disputes is heavily influenced by expectations of what would happen if negotiation broke down and trial had to be invoked (Heumann 1978).

While some pioneering studies have addressed the role of judges (e.g. Ryan et al 1981) and lawyers (e.g. Partridge & Bermant 1978) at trial, most recent research on the legal process has converged on two role components —jurors and defendants—and three process components—evidence, procedure, and decision rules.

Role Components

JURORS Juror characteristics have been studied both in their own right —with numerous reports that the more similar the juror to the defendant in race, gender, occupation, or attitudes, the more lenient the treatment accorded (Nemeth in press)—and for their relevance to jury selection procedures (Bermant & Shapard 1981). They have studied in the latter context for two seemingly contradictory reasons. On the one hand, surveys and demographic data have been analyzed to demonstrate that the pool from which jurors were selected *was biased* in either its racial (McConahay et al 1977) or attitudinal (Vidmar & Judson 1981) composition. On the other hand, some proponents of "scientific jury selection" have researched the relationship between the characteristics of jurors and the decisions they reach in order *to bias* the jury in favor of a desired decision (see Saks 1976). This second enterprise has generated much empirical debate, with Saks & Hastie (1978, p. 66, cf Hepburn 1980) concluding that the composition of a jury is "a relatively minor determinant" of the verdict reached, especially in comparison with the evidence presented to the jury. It has also engendered ethical concerns (e.g. Herbsleb et al 1979) focusing upon the potential imbalance created when only one side has access to psychological technology.

Jury size is a second topic that has captured much psychological research attention (Davis et al 1977, Suggs 1979) with studies tending to show that the smaller the jury, the less adequate the deliberation and the greater the probability of convicting an innocent person. The use of this research, particularly that of Saks (1977), by the U.S. Supreme Court in the *Ballew v. Georgia* (1978) case has been subjected to a barrage of criticism. The research, for example, showed 12-person juries superior to 6-person juries and not, as the Court claimed, 6-person juries superior to 5-person juries (Lermack 1979, Kaye 1980).

DEFENDANTS A highly popular research topic in the legal process, particularly with social psychologists, has been the effect of defendant characteristics upon juror (sometimes jury) judgments (Izzett & Sales 1981, Greenberg & Ruback in press). Both factors relevant to one's status and history with the law, and factors presumed by the law to be irrelevant have been studied. Among the law-related defendant characteristics that have been found to raise the probability of guilty verdicts by simulated jurors are being in custody, rather than free on bail (Koza & Doob 1975); having evidence of extenuating circumstances offered personally by the defendant rather than by an impartial witness (Frankel & Morris 1976; cf Suggs & Berman 1979); and protesting innocence too severely (Yandell 1979).

Research on extralegal characteristics has not found defendant sex, race, or socioeconomic status consistently to affect simulated juror decisions. The one extralegal variable that has preoccupied simulation researchers has been the defendant's physical or social attractiveness. The modal finding is that attractive defendants receive more lenient treatment than unattractive ones. Exceptions to this tendency are found when the defendant is perceived to have used his or her attractiveness to further criminal aims, as in swindle cases (Sigall & Ostrove 1975) or in cases of physicians using their role to facilitate murder (Bray et al 1978). The few nonsimulation studies investigating attractiveness, however, find that it has little (Kalven & Zeisel 1966) or no effect (Konečni & Ebbesen 1982a) on the treatment of defendants.

Process Components

EVIDENCE Recent research on the evidence introduced at civil and criminal trials and its effect on jury decision making has centered on the mode (e.g. live versus videotaped) by which evidence in general is presented to the jury and the adequacy of evidence produced by eyewitnesses in particular. Other studies have found that jurors do not ignore evidence they have heard that is later ruled inadmissible (Fontes et al 1977, Thompson et al in press), give reduced weight to witnesses who qualify their speech (Erickson et al 1978), and are affected by pretrial publicity (Loftus 1979a).

Changing the mode by which evidence is presented to the jury from "live" participants to videotape would facilitate the testimony of witnesses (e.g. when they are ill) and reduce the probability of a mistrial, since inadmissible evidence would be edited from the tape before it was played to the jury (Jacoubovitch et al 1977). Research generally has been supportive of the use of videotape. It has been found to be more effective than written transcripts in affecting juror judgments (Farmer et al 1977) and as effective as live testimony in keeping the jurors' interest and motivation and in fostering witness credibility (Miller 1976).

With its solid grounding in the fields of perception and memory, research on evidence produced by eyewitnesses to an event is among the most systematic and theoretically developed in the psychology of law (Clifford & Bull 1978, Loftus 1979b, Yarmey 1979, Penrod & Loftus in press, Wells 1980). Among the factors that have been found to affect the reliability of eyewitness identifications are age, with adults being more accurate than children or the elderly (Smith & Winograd 1978), and race, with crossracial identifications being poorer than same-race ones (Goldstein 1979). The manner of questioning by which a recognition is elicited can have a great effect on its reliability (Loftus et al 1978), while training witnesses in recognition techniques does not appear to be effective (Woodhead et al 1979). Despite the fact that jurors give great weight to the "confidence" of an eyewitness in assessing his or her credibility, confidence in recognition has been found unrelated to accuracy of recognition (Deffenbacher 1980).

A substantial discrepancy, therefore, exists between the research literature, which has demonstrated the frequent unreliability of eyewitness identification, and the traditions of the legal process, which highly value such evidence (Wells et al 1979, Hatvany & Strack in press). This discrepancy has led to the increasing use of eyewitness researchers as expert witnesses in trials that revolve around issues of perceptual accuracy (Fishman & Loftus 1978, Woocher 1977, Loftus 1980, Wells et al 1980). The question of "who to believe"—the eyewitness or the eyewitness researcher—is then left for the jury to decide.

PROCEDURE The towering figures in the psychological study of how procedures affect the resolution of legal disputes have been Thibaut & Walker (cf Hayden & Anderson 1979). The early research (Thibaut & Walker 1975) contrasted an "adversary" model, in which the parties to a dispute controlled the procedures for its resolution, to an "inquisitorial" model (common in some European countries), in which procedural discretion rested with a third-party decision maker. Results indicated that people both in the United States and in Europe perceived the adversarial model to be more "fair" than the inquisitorial one (La Tour et al 1976).

More recent studies have distinguished between process control (i.e. control of the presentation of information) and decision control (i.e. control of the ultimate judgment), and between the objective of establishing truth (i.e. a correct view of some set of facts) and that of providing justice (i.e. an equitable distribution of resources or losses). Where the primary disagreement concerns the distribution of resources or losses, as in most legal disputes, justice is the goal and it is best obtained by a procedure that places control of the process in the hands of the disputants and control of the decision in the hands of a third party (e.g. a judge). When the disagreement concerns the nature of facts rather than the distribution of resources or losses, as in many scientific or technological disputes, the goal is truth, and it is best achieved when both process and decision control are in the hands of a third party. Cases in which there is a significant conflict about both facts and the distribution of resources, as in some environmental disputes, may require a two-stage resolution in which truth is first determined and justice then pursued (Thibaut & Walker 1978, Lind et al 1980).

Finally, Walker et al (1979) have investigated the relationship between perceptions of the fairness of a procedure and the perceptions of the fairness of an outcome reached through that procedure. Perceptions of the fairness of a procedure were found to enhance perceptions of the fairness of outcome, but only when subjects actually participated in the decision-making process. The relationship did not obtain for observers nor for persons affected by the decision but not participating in the process of reaching it.

DECISION-RULES Before they retire to deliberate on civil or criminal cases, jurors are presented by the judge with what are in effect decision-rules concerning how the law applies to the factual issues before them (Kerr et al 1976, Kassin & Wrightsman 1979, Penrod & Hastie 1979, 1980, Levine et al 1981). Several studies have found these instructions almost wholly incomprehensible to jurors. Strawn & Buchanan (1976) reported that only half the jurors instructed in the burden of proof in a criminal trial understood that the defendant did not have to prove his or her innocence. Likewise, Charrow & Charrow (1979) found jurors to understand only half of what was explained to them, largely due to the prolix construction of what passes in the law for prose. Multiple negatives, as in "innocent misrecollection is not uncommon," were a frequent obstacle to comprehension. Happily, studies have found that when instructions are rewritten with attention to clarity, comprehension markedly improves (Elwork et al in press).

Comprehension, however, is not the only issue in instructing juries. Borgida (in press; see also Borgida 1979, 1980) found that simulated jurors in a rape case who were explicitly instructed that admission of prior sexual history on the part of the victim did not prove that she consented to the act at issue were *less* likely to convict the defendant than jurors who were not so instructed. He hypothesized that the more explicit the judicial instruction, the stronger the threat to the jury's decision freedom, and thus the development of a reactance response.

THE LEGAL SYSTEM

Studies of the legal process have tended to focus on formal rules, to employ a variety of theoretical frameworks, and to favor simulation methods. In contrast, recent research on the legal system—on the ways in which the law actually disposes of individual cases—has been characterized by an emphasis upon informal discretion, a reliance upon decision making as the analytic framework of choice, and a preference for naturalistic rather than laboratory settings. While many discrete "systems" of law are now receiving research attention (e.g. Arvey 1979 on employment law; Clingempeel & Reppucci in press and Mulvey in press on family law), most recent scholarly activity has been clustered in the criminal justice system, the mental health system, and that hybrid system in which the jurisdictions of criminal law and mental health law overlap.

Criminal Justice System

Surely "criminal justice" has been the mainstay of psychological research on the legal system (Bickman & Rosenbaum 1977, Sales 1977, Toch 1979, Cohn & Udolf 1979), deriving in part from psychologists' long-standing interest in crime and delinquency as forms of abnormal behavior (Feldman 1977, Farrington 1979, Nietzel 1979, Monahan & Splane 1980). While psychologists have been active in studying law enforcement (Bard & Connolly 1978, Novaco 1977, Stotland & Berberich 1979, Mulvey & Reppucci in press) and corrections (Toch 1977, Reppucci & Clingempeel 1978, Brodsky & Fowler 1979, Megargee & Bohn 1979, Bukstel & Kilmann 1980), they have focused in greatest depth upon judicial and quasi-judicial (e.g. Parole Board) decisions regarding whether and for how long an offender should be confined.

The perceived problem that has given rise to much of this research has been that of disparity. Findings that persons convicted of the same offense, with similar criminal histories, receive drastically different sentences (e.g. Diamond & Zeisel 1975) have motivated a search for the sources of this disparity and for methods to reduce it.

Diamond (1981) has characterized sentencing decisions as highly complex. Disparity may occur because judges differ in their overall levels of severity, in how they weight particular aspects of a case, or simply because they are inconsistent in applying their own decision rules. Ebbesen & Konečni (1981), on the other hand, report that judges employ a simple decision strategy in sentencing. They found that the severity of the offense for which an individual was convicted, the extent of the individual's prior record, and whether he or she was released or remained in jail during the period between arrest and conviction largely determined the probation officer's recommended sentence. This, in turn, was generally rubber-stamped by the judge. Such "disparity" as existed was accounted for more by different judges receiving different types of cases than by disagreements among judges on how to decide them.

Despite the growing movement in the United States to substitute sentences of a determinate length, such as 5 years, for sentences of relatively indeterminate duration, such as 1 to 10 years, the precise length of time an offender spends in prison is still usually fixed by an administrative parole board. Here, too, concern with disparity or "unfairness" has been intense (Berman 1977). Carroll, in a systematic series of studies (e.g. 1978b; Carroll & Payne 1977), found that decision making in the context of parole differed from that employed in sentencing in that parole decisions were primarily predictive in nature rather than concerned with punishment for past behavior. Ratings of disciplinary infractions in prison, which could be viewed either as a justification for punishment or as a predictive variable, were strongly related to parole decisions.

Likewise, Gottfredson, Wilkins, and their colleagues (e.g. Gottfredson et al 1978) have studied the decision making processes of the U.S. Board of Parole and concluded that three factors, parole prognosis, institutional behavior, and offense seriousness could account for time served in prison. (That "offense seriousness" was a factor in these studies but not in Carroll's reflects the fact that in the federal system inmates were eligible for parole almost immediately, whereas in Carroll's state system the parole board did not receive cases until inmates had already served a minimum sentence based on the seriousness of their offense.) Gottfredson & Wilkins then fed their information back to the decision makers in the form of a matrix that made explicit the factors and weights that had previously been the implicit bases of their judgments. Decisions made with the use of this informational device were substantially more uniform than those made without it. The "guidelines" approach to structuring discretion has now become a major researched-based approach to parole and sentencing reform.

Mental Health System

Since the late 1960s, 48 states have changed the legal criterion for involuntary mental hospitalization from one emphasizing a professional judgment that a "need for treatment" exists to one focusing upon a prediction that a person found to be mentally ill is "dangerous" to him or herself or to others (Schwitzgebel & Schwitzgebel 1980). As well, courts have promulgated a wide variety of both "positive rights," e.g. the right to treatment, and "negative rights," e.g. the right to refuse certain treatments, for committed persons (Monahan, in press). These wholesale shifts in policy have been the subject of vigorous political and professional debate (Roth 1979, 1980, Wexler 1981) and the object of active research attention.

Nowhere is the "gap problem" approach (Abel 1980) to social science research on law better illustrated than in civil commitment. Without exception, each study lays claim to the discovery of a new discrepancy or "gap" between the legal rhetoric of increased patient autonomy and improved patient care, and the reality encountered by those in contact with the mental health system (Bloom & Asher in press). Attorneys, for example, tend not to act as advocates for patients at commitment hearings, but rather to defer to the decisions of mental health professionals (Stier & Stoebe 1979), which are made on the traditional grounds of a perceived need for treatment (Lipsitt 1980). Training attorneys in techniques for challenging mental health professionals appears not to increase the likelihood that they will do so (Poythress 1978). Judges, in turn, confirm the decisions that mental health professionals have reached, seemingly without regard to whether these decisions comport with statutory requirements (Warren 1977).

If there is one overarching impression to be gleaned from the research of psychologists and others on the mental health system, it is the difficulty of achieving fundamental change through law in a system where decisions —of psychologists and psychiatrists and of judges and attorneys—are so unstructured and inaccessible to direct legal regulation. Saks & Miller (1979, p. 80) are correct when they state that "it is not true that we cannot legislate behavior change; it is only that the legislation must change the conditions that maintain the behavior in question." In the case of initiating civil commitment, however, these conditions appear entrenched. Zwerling et al (1978), in this regard, persuaded the staff at a mental health center to agree to abstain from involuntarily committing anyone for a one week experimental period. Only one exception was allowed: if a prospective patient was believed to be one of the rare cases in clear danger of immediate suicide or other violence, a staff member could ask for approval from his or her superior, and, if they both agreed, commitment would be permitted. Results showed that there were no differences between the number of persons committed during "no commitment week" and the weeks prior and subsequent to it! *Every* prospective patient was found to be the "rare" exception that clearly demanded commitment.

The "guidelines" approach, so successful in structuring decision in the context of sentencing and parole, has yet to be applied to decision making in the mental health system, perhaps due in part to the traditional antipathy of mental health professionals to placing statistical constraints upon clinical judgment (Meehl 1973).

Interactions Between Criminal Justice and Mental Health

Penrose observed in 1939 that rates of imprisonment and rates of mental hospitalization were inversely correlated, with the total volume of institutionalization remaining constant (cf Grabosky 1980). Work on the interaction of the two systems remained dormant for several decades while researchers examined each in isolation. The past several years, however, have seen an awakening of interest in their relationship, first by sociologists (Scull 1977) and now by psychologists as well (Monahan & Steadman in press, 1982). Research has congealed upon how judges decide which individuals should be hospitalized before trial or instead of trial and how juries decide which offenders after trial should be sent to a hospital rather than a prison.

Judges become involved in deciding between mental health and criminal justice processing when confronted with a defendant who alleges or appears to be incompetent to stand trial, or one who may qualify by virtue of the crime charged and the state of mind present during it as a "mentally disordered sex offender." Research on incompetence to stand trial repeatedly has found, as did research on commitment, that judges rubber-stamp the conclusory opinions of psychologists and psychiatrists, whose opinions are strongly affected by a diagnosis of psychosis or a history of mental hospitalization (Roesch & Golding 1980). The question of a defendant's competence to stand trial is often raised as a matter of trial strategy rather than a genuinely perceived issue in its own right. Defense attorneys raise it to assist in plea bargaining or to test the court's receptivity to an insanity plea. Prosecutors raise it to lengthen the period the defendant will be institutionalized, since the examination itself may entail several months of hospitalization. Persons charged with violent felonies are highly overrepresented in findings of incompetence, indicating either that such persons are, in fact, more likely to be incompetent or that incompetency procedures are more likely to be used as legal maneuvers in cases where long sentences are possible (Steadman 1979).

The recent literature on judicial decision making in mentally disordered sex offender cases parallels in several ways that on incompetence to stand trial. Raising the issue of mental disorder at all is often a question of legal strategy; judges tend overwhelmingly to endorse the decisions of the examining mental health professionals, and the decisions of these psychologists and psychiatrists are predictable from knowledge of a few simple variables. To illustrate, Konečni et al (1980) found that the existence of convictions for prior sex offenses almost invariably led to a positive clinical evaluation of mentally disordered sex offender status, with which the judge routinely concurred.

Jury decision-making studies on the relationship between the criminal justice and the mental health systems have focused on the insanity defense. Despite the public impression that the use of the insanity plea is widespread, it is actually raised in only about 1 percent of criminal cases brought to trial, and it is usually unsuccessful in persuading jurors to decide for "acquittal." Those who raise the insanity plea tend to be older, more often white, and more often female than the general population of offenders, but to have relationships with their victims similar to defendants who do not plead insanity, i.e. they are often related or acquaintances (Pasewark & Pasewark in press).

Much of the recent research on decision making in insanity cases has been descriptive in nature. One theoretical notion that has been advanced is that the degree to which decision makers have adopted a general "mental health ideology," rather than any specific legal provisions, accounts for variations in the use and success of the plea (Pasewark & Pasewark in press). Perhaps more intriguing is the hypothesis of Pasewark et al (1979) to explain their finding that mothers who committed infanticide and police officers involved in off-duty killings are overrepresented in insanity acquittals. They suggest that decisions by jurors in these cases represent a collective need to idealize certain archetypal role relationships. In order to preserve the concepts of "mother love" and "police protection," jurors selectively turn their attention from the facts that a child is often the most available victim of a mother's aggression and that providing weapons to a police officer may increase the probability of the weapons being used to resolve an officer's personal conflicts. Instead, people categorize such individuals as "insane" and thereby exclude them from the population of "normal" mothers and police officers who, they may continue reassuringly to believe, behave in the idealized manner.

RECURRING ISSUES

Certain issues arise with regularity in recent studies in the psychology of law, regardless of the specific topic under investigation. We have been able to distill three of them, which we believe are the core concerns with which the field must come to terms in the 1980s. They involve the theoretical integrity, methodological orthodoxy, and policy influence of the psychology of law.

Questions of Theory

The contributions of psychology to the study of law, we have suggested, inhere in its analysis of the law's substantive assumptions, procedural rules, and systemic relationships. But what is the precise nature of these contributions? What, put another way, should psychologists set out to accomplish when they study legal phenomena?

Let us approach this question by considering in some detail two exemplars of sophisticated, meticulous, and programmatic research efforts in the field, the procedural justice studies of Thibaut, Walker, and their colleagues, and the legal decision-making studies of Ebbesen & Konečni. Since much of this research has been discussed earlier, we now consider only their respective approaches to studying problems in the psychology of law.

The research of the Thibaut-Walker group has a clear purpose: testing theory. They begin by extracting and articulating theories of human behavior that are implicit in the law, such as the theory of "adversariness." They then subject deductions from these theories to empirical test (see also Austin 1979).

The research of Konečni & Ebbesen has an equally clear but seemingly very different purpose: predicting behavior. Rather than test (or develop) a theory relevant to law, their goal is "to account for the greatest percent of the variance of the processing of cases through the [legal] system as a whole" (1981, p. 494).

Konečni & Ebbesen criticize theory-testing research such as that of Thibaut and Walker on the grounds that its procedures are chosen "not because they provide externally valid representations of processes in the real-world legal system, but because they may result in internally valid tests of hypotheses," whereas their own strategy emphasizes "the actual operation" of the intact legal system in a manner that can be "invaluable from a predictive point of view" (1981, p. 484). Unlike Thibaut & Walker, who would prefer to account for less of the variance in legal behavior in a theoretically satisfying manner than more of it without recourse to theory, Konečni & Ebbesen seek to maximize predictive efficiency using whatever "concrete and low level" (1979, p. 66) factors best accomplish that task.

The choice of research objectives—testing theory or predicting behavior—is of great importance for the selection of research methods (see below). But it is even more important in its own right, for it determines the criteria against which scholarship is to be evaluated.[1]

While space precludes an extended discussion of issues in the philosophy of science, our own view is that social science, like all science, has dual goals. The goals are prediction and understanding (Brody 1970). Prediction

[1]There may be a third objective of research in the psychology of law as well. "Descriptive" (Friedman & Macaulay 1977) or "exploratory" (Lind & Walker 1979) research that is neither driven by an explicit theory nor concerned with the prediction of specific target behaviors may also be of scientific value, particularly in the early stages of investigation. Such research may identify the parameters of a problem and unearth basic relationships that give rise to later theoretical and predictive studies.

without understanding may lead to effective interventions [as it did in the prevention of cholera (Caplan 1964)]. Understanding without prediction may also be of great scientific value [as it was in Copernican astronomy (Kuhn 1970)]. But ultimately, science must embrace both objectives. Indeed, the two are inextricably linked. Recall Lewin's (1935) dictum that "there is nothing so practical [in predicting behavior] as a good theory." Likewise, unexplained predictions are the principal impetus to theoretical development and ultimately to "paradigm shifts" (Kuhn 1970).

Rather than seeing Thibaut & Walker's emphasis on testing theory and Ebbesen & Konečni's emphasis on predicting behavior as alternative research strategies for the psychology of law, therefore, we would view them as complementary. What the disagreement comes down to is not one of objectives. Thibaut & Walker see their theory-testing research as having implications for predicting behavior. Those implications would come, however, *after* a theory has been developed and shown to be internally valid (Lind & Walker 1979, p. 8). Likewise, Konečni & Ebbesen state that they wish only "to *begin* a research program by doing real-world [i.e. predictive] studies" (1979, p. 65, italics in original). The disagreement is, or should be, one of research strategy. Is it most fruitful to develop a theory first and test the internal validity of the hypotheses deduced from it, and only then to investigate its real-world predictive power, as Thibaut & Walker hold? Or is more to be gained by initially attempting to predict as much externally valid legal behavior as possible before inductively generating and testing a theory that allows for understanding, as Ebbesen & Konečni suggest? On this question psychologists of law with equal commitment to the scientific method will differ.

While each strategy has clear advantages over the other (conceptual elegance in the case of theory testing; practical applicability in the case of behavior predicting), each has its own liabilities. Theory testing may be forced to employ concepts at such high levels of abstraction that their relevance to the legal phenomena of interest becomes strained. Behavior predicting may be left without overarching constructs to explain discrepant findings. If judges in Virginia, for example, are found to take community ties into account in setting bail and judges in California are not (Ebbesen & Konečni 1982), what does one conclude? That there are California judges and there are Virginia judges? Perhaps there are, but without the attempt to develop a theory to help us understand the nature of these differences, the observation itself is unsatisfying. Taking into account these assets and liabilities, it is entirely possible for a psychologist of law to prefer theory testing as the initial strategy of choice for one problem and behavior prediction as the initial strategy of choice for another, depending, perhaps, on the existing state of theory development and the existing state of predictive accuracy.

Questions of Method

There can be little doubt that the bedrock methodological issue confronting the psychology of law in the 1980s is the external validity of laboratory simulations. (Anderson & Hayden 1980, Houlden 1980). The intense questioning of "analog" research in the psychology of law reflects similar concerns regarding its appropriateness in other areas of psychology (Tunnell 1977, Kazdin 1978, Bem & Lord 1979). Since most of the recent contributions to this debate in the psychology of law have focused on the study of jury behavior, we shall take this area as illustrative of the more general issue [cf Ellis (1980) on eyewitness research.]

Simulation is only one of several methods researchers have used to study jury decision making (Baldwin & McConville 1979, in press), but it is far and away the preferred method of psychologists. The reasons for the domination of simulation methods in the psychological studies of juries are not hard to come by. Simulation allows for 1. randomization of experimental variables, thus assuring high internal validity; 2. replication of procedures, again assuring high internal validity; 3. access to a process (i.e. deliberation) that is legally inaccessible in the natural environment; and 4. substantial savings in the time and money necessary to do research.

Bray & Kerr (1979) examined the procedures used in jury simulation studies and concluded that while some of them were "realistic" or face valid representations of actual jury process, most were not. An example of the former would be Zeisel & Diamond's (1978) research in which persons from the jury rolls sat in court and observed an actual and entire trial and then deliberated at length until reaching a verdict. Regarding the latter, "unrealistic" simulations, Konečni & Ebbesen (1981, p. 488) have noted that "finding oneself in a 2X3X4 within-subjects simulated-jury experiment and making the guilty/not guilty decision 24 times in a row within 10 minutes on a 100-mm scale is clearly somewhat different from being in a jury once in a lifetime, watching a 7-day trial, and deliberating for 2 days behind closed doors with 11 complete strangers." The preponderance of these latter studies that lack "verisimilitude" in terms of the structure and functioning of actual juries (Bermant et al 1974) and that fail to use concepts of actual relevance to the law has led Vidmar (1979, p. 96) to state that the entire area of jury simulation research "can be fairly described as marked by (*a*) legal naivete, (*b*) sloppy scholarship, and (*c*) overgeneralization combined with inappropriate value judgments."

Simulation studies tend to be characterized by their authors as having either applied value in predicting actual jury behavior, or theoretical value in testing conceptual frameworks of relevance to psychology or to the law (although even here applied "implications" have flowed freely). In a perceptive review assessing both claims, Weiten & Diamond (1979; cf Vidmar

1979) have noted several major threats to the external validity of simulation research (see also Davis et al 1977, Gerbasi et al 1977). Most simulation studies have employed inadequate sampling in using subjects—undergraduates—who are unrepresentative on numerous dimensions of the population selected for jury duty. They have presented inadequate trial simulations that omit integral elements of an actual trial. In particular, many studies have lacked jury deliberation and therefore are investigations of "juror" rather than "jury" decision making. This is despite the fact that other research has shown deliberation to have a substantial effect upon trial outcome (McGuire & Bermant 1977, Bray & Noble 1978, Kaplan & Schersching 1981). Further, jury simulation studies have used inappropriate dependent measures, such as continuous rather than dichotomous ratings of guilt, and have lacked corroborative field data that would allow an assessment of the success of the simulation in mimicking the real world.

The "most crucial difference" and "the gap most difficult to close" (Weiten & Diamond 1979) between actual and simulated juries, however, is the difference in the perceived consequences of the two decision tasks. In a series of experiments, Wilson & Donnerstein (1977) presented undergraduate subjects with material concerning a fellow student accused of stealing and distributing an examination. Half the subjects were led to believe that their decision would have real consequences for the student in question, and the others were told to act "as if" they were jury members. In two of their three studies, "real" jurors were significantly more likely to convict than those who knew they were in a simulation. A study by Zeisel & Diamond (1978), on the other hand, found simulated juries less likely to convict than actual ones, and Kerr et al (1979) found no effect of perceived real or hypothetical decision consequences. While a main effect of role-playing, if one exists, could be taken into account in interpreting the results of a simulation, the possibility that role-playing interacts with other variables poses more serious difficulty. Wilson & Donnerstein (1977), for example, found that juror role-playing status interacted with defendant characteristics in producing judgments of guilt.

While simulation has borne the brunt of recent methodological criticism in the psychology of law, field methods have not gone unscathed. The principal liability of naturalistic research, of course, is that "nature" is often illegal, unethical, or impossible to control in order to provide the opportunity for internally valid research. But there are other problems as well. Gertz & Talarico (1977), in a study of the reliability of archival data in the criminal justice system, note the frequency of clerical carelessness (e.g. records revealing a defendant to have been convicted before having been arrested) and problems of shifting crime definitions. These problems are compounded when the research assumes not only the reliability but the validity of archival measures as estimates of actual behavior, rather than simply as pieces of information that influence decision makers (Gottfredson & Gottfredson 1980a,b). The manipulation of crime data and other "social indicators" for political purposes is well known. In addition, the pervasiveness of plea bargaining and prosecutorial discretion makes the offense of which a subject is convicted bear only the most metaphoric resemblance to the behavior actually performed.

Our own view of the laboratory-versus-field debate in the psychology of law is that the relative merits of alternative research methods can be evaluated only in the context of the purpose for which the research is undertaken. Where the investigator's primary concern is with the application of research findings to the real-world legal process or system—which is to say, with predicting the behavior of actual legal decision makers—the issue of external validity weighs heavily. Here in vivo naturalistic designs, such as those of Konečni & Ebbesen (1982b) or very close simulations, fulfilling the stipulations set by Weiten & Diamond (1979) and Vidmar (1979), would seem to be the methods of choice. However, where the investigator's primary purpose is to test legal or psychological theory, concern with internal validity looms. "So long as the study meets the specifications of the theory and provides a reasonable test of some logical consequence of the theory, the study is valid. Unless the theory places some explicit restriction on the situations, settings, or subject populations to which it is intended to apply, the study is not properly criticized on these grounds" (Lind & Walker 1979, p. 8). Research of this kind legitimately may employ simulations that lack a high degree of external validity with regard to the intact legal system.

Can "unrealistic" simulations ever provide results that are useful in predicting the behavior of actual legal decision makers? Perhaps. Bem & Lord (1979) have stated that the external or "ecological" validity of simulation research in any area of psychology "requires that the *relationships* between situational variables and the behavior in the [simulated] setting replicate the relationships between situational variables and the behavior outside the laboratory" (p. 841, italics in original). To establish the generalizeability of a simulation, therefore, it is necessary to establish an equivalence between the relationships created in the laboratory and the relationships that exist in the natural environment. Put another way, to use simulation results to predict real-world behavior it is necessary to verify empirically that the decision-rules invoked by the subjects in the simulation correspond to the decision-rules invoked by the makers of actual legal decisions (V. J. Konečni & E. B. Ebbesen, personal communication). This correspondence could be established only by studying real-world as well as simulated settings.

One can in this light view more clearly the frequently given analogy between laboratory research in psychology and in the biological and physical sciences. Bray & Kerr (1979, p. 116), for example, state that "[e]ven if saccharin is not a major cause of human bladder cancer, demonstrating that massive saccharin doses reliably lead to bladder cancer in rats can alert us to possible risks and can guide future research. Demonstrations that artificially powerful treatments reliably affect mock juror/jury judgments can serve similarly valuable functions."

Whether the relationship between saccharin and the rat bladder, however, is equivalent to the relationship between saccharin and the human bladder, no less than whether the relationship between attractiveness and mock jury judgments is equivalent to the relationship between attractiveness and the judgments of actual juries, is an empirical question. In either case, the equivalence may or may not obtain (e.g. saccharin may interact with a substance found in rat bladders, but not in human bladders, in producing cancer). Should this reasoning be accepted, methods to establish the equivalence between simulated and naturalistic relationships in the psychology of law would seem to warrant a high priority on the agenda of those simulation researchers interested in the external validity of their findings.

There is one other purpose of research for which the use of "unrealistic" laboratory simulations may be appropriate. By virtue of its ability to combine variables in novel ways, simulation can allow the "discovery" of relationships that do not exist in the natural environment. Much may be learned, for example, about how to improve the comprehension of jury instructions by actual jurors from studies that present alternative instructions to simulated jurors. Naturalistic research could not address this problem, since the alternative instructions do not exist in the naturally occurring legal environment. "Whenever a potentially beneficial effect is observed in the laboratory, the objective might be *to make the external world match the laboratory, not to make the laboratory match the external world*" (Henshel 1980, p. 475, italics in original). Matching the external world to the laboratory, however, must be done in an experimental manner, to verify that the "potentially beneficial effect" discovered in the laboratory is realized in the field.

What we find to be methodologically problematic are studies that use theory-testing procedures for behavior-predicting purposes. Studies that employ very unrealistic jury simulations to answer very applied questions of jury behavior trade off external validity for little corresponding gain in the internally valid testing of theoretical hypotheses. A distressingly large portion of jury research appears to fall into this category of generating theoretically uninteresting and predictively useless "findings" (Weiten & Diamond 1979, p. 75). Given that a single piece of research may have multiple purposes, we would offer that to the extent the research proffers applied "implications," it legitimately is subject to scrutiny on the grounds of external validity. To the extent the research emphasizes theoretical integrity, it legitimately is subject to scrutiny on the grounds of internal validity. To the extent the research emphasizes neither, its value to psychology or to the law is in doubt.

Questions of Influence

There has been much concern to increase the influence of psychology upon the law. Saks (1980) has distinguished the participation of psychologists in the determination of clinical or "case facts" regarding an individual litigant from his or her role as provider of "social facts" based upon research findings. Clinical psychologists have for some time been actively involved in case evaluations for many legal purposes (Haward 1981). All indications are that the law is now becoming increasingly receptive to psychologists as purveyors of "social facts" to the legislative (Saks 1978), judicial (Tanke & Tanke 1979), and executive (Etzioni 1980) branches of government.

It is less clear that this growing quantity of psychological input is improving the quality of legal decisions. Whether a cited piece of research, for example, helped to shape a judicial decision or was added after the fact to give scientific gloss to a judgment arrived at on other grounds is largely unknowable. This is brought out most clearly in the unanimous U.S. Supreme Court decision in the *Ballew v. Georgia* (1978) jury-size case, in which several justices said they based their opinion on the findings of social psychological research, several other justices said they employed constitutional principles having nothing to do with what they fobbed off as "numerology," and the remaining justices signed the decision without addressing the scientific issue at all (Loftus & Monahan 1980).

There are indeed substantial jurisprudential reasons to suggest caution in relying too heavily upon social science research in deciding cases (Loh 1979, Suggs 1979, Saks & Baron 1980). Thus, the first case in which the U.S. Supreme Court was urged to consider "social facts" concerned the validity of an Oregon statute limiting the number of hours per day women could be made to work in factories and laundries (Muller v. Oregon 1908). Louis Brandeis was supported by contemporary feminists when he represented Oregon in defending the statute. In this original social science "Brandeis brief," however, he cited "scientific" research documenting the "periodical semi-pathological state of health of women" (p. 87), the existence of "general 'female weakness' " (p. 38), and the fact that "the particular construction of the knee and the shallowness of the pelvis, and the delicate nature of the foot" (p. 19) made women less able than men to work long hours. Were Brandeis representing modern day feminists in the fight for equal rights in the workplace, he no doubt would choose different sources of scientific authority. More recently, Kenneth Clark's (1950) study finding that black children from segregated schools chose dolls of a lighter shade than their own skin color was cited in "the most controversial footnote in American constitutional law" (Rosen 1980) in the *Brown v. Board of Education* (1954) school desegregation case. If a replication should now find that black children in predominately black schools chose dolls of the same shade as their own skin, what should the courts do? Call for an end to busing? If not, why was the research cited in the first place?

As long as legal decisions are made in part on the basis of factual assumptions, however, the law has no choice but to be open to any refinement of these assumptions that social science can bring to bear (Schlegel 1979, Davis 1980, Saks & Kidd 1981). It may be, in this regard, that social science research can most influentially be applied to cases of "the middle range" (Kalven 1968), that is, cases in which deeply held values do not predominate and in which the facts are not so generally known as to make research superfluous (Bermant 1975). Also the law may be receptive to social science input when resolutions reached on traditional legal grounds have failed. Ellsworth & Getman (in press) have observed that courts are more willing to consider social science in the criminal law than in other areas such as labor law. This may reflect a general belief that the criminal justice system has failed and that new approaches are needed. There may be less willingness to be "experimental" about labor law because there is a general belief that the current legal approach is adequate. Finally, research that suggests a feasible alternative to an existing policy may rise to influence. Many studies in the psychology of law appear to be unconstructively negative. "People are, it seems, worse than is generally assumed at remembering, recognizing, understanding and processing information according to legal criteria" (Farrington et al 1979, p. xvi). Without suggesting alternatives that take into account these failings, research is unlikely to have "impact."

The first problem that confronts a psychologist of law desirous of having his or her research used by legal decision makers is making them aware of the existence of the research. Tanke & Tanke (1979) have suggested three steps toward this end. Psychologists should (*a*) identify empirical issues in the legal process through legal publications and interest groups; (*b*) consult with lawyers in carrying out research and in criticizing and summarizing the research of others; and (*c*) present their research to the courts by publishing in legal journals, working with parties to appellate cases, filing *amicus curiae* briefs, and participating as expert witnesses at trial. Prescriptions on how clinicians can best inform judges regarding "case facts" at trial are provided by Brodsky (1977) and Poythress (1980).

Assuming they can be made aware of its existence, judges must then be made to comprehend research procedures and findings. One court, when presented with a social science brief, found it to be "an overgrown garden of numbers and charts and jargon like standard deviation of the variable, statistical significance, and Pearson product moment correlations" (*Hobson v. Hansen,* 1971). While one can agree with the U.S. Supreme Court in *Craig v. Boren* (1976) that "it is unrealistic to expect either members of the judiciary or state officials to be well versed in the rigors of experimental or statistical technique," one can also wonder how research findings intelligently can be used by courts or legislatures until the inhabitants of those chambers are educated at least to the nonrigorous level of knowing what "statistical significance" means. Without such education, judges are likely to continue in evaluating either the expert him or herself or the general field of inquiry—with credibility being given to the famous and to all physicists (Saks 1980)—rather than the specific research or clinical methods used to produce the findings offered in evidence.

There are indications that at least some actors in the legal system are beginning to acquire the rudiments of social science methodology. Rossi (1980), for example, noted that before he testified in an Administrative Law Court in a deceptive advertising case against the manufacturer of Anacin, the attorney defending the manufacturer took an advanced course in multivariate analysis, the better to cross-examine him. This attorney also had a battery of statisticians behind him in court passing notes with questions to be asked. Rossi was on the stand for 3 days. As Moynihan (1979, p. 30) has noted, "lawyers with no more than a good undergraduate grounding in social-science methodology could have quite an impact in this area simply by establishing standards of cross-examination which are infrequently attained today. This would be no small thing."

Questions of the influence of the psychology of law cannot fully be answered—indeed, cannot begin to be answered—without attending to questions of the values of the field (Haney 1980). Morse (1978; see also Gass 1979) for example, articulately argues for restricting the participation of clinical psychologists and others in mental health law on the grounds that the issues to be decided are moral rather than empirical in nature, and thus outside the realm of scientific expertise. Bonnie & Slobogin (1980; cf Morse in press), in contrast, argue with equal conviction for improving the quality rather than precluding the admission of clinical testimony. The latter course, they hold, ineluctably would work to the disadvantage of a defendant who has a moral claim to reduced culpability for criminal behavior. In the research area, Saks & Hastie (1978) are disparaged by Luginbuhl & Mullin (1980, p. 153) as "dispassionate observers"—a compliment in other areas of scholarship—because their jury research does not focus upon the "[r]acism, classism, and preformed opinions about defendants [that] plague the courtroom." Likewise, Haney & Lowy (1979, p. 648) castigate Heumann's (1978) study of plea bargaining as legitimating an immoral procedure that serves to "avoid the socioeconomic restructuring required to achieve a meaningful reduction in crime."

Three broad positions on the role of values in the psychology of law can be discerned (cf Friedman & Macaulay 1977). The *instrumental* position (e.g. Stier & Stoebe 1979) holds that the psychologist should assist in the achievement of the values that are espoused by the law. The *natural law* position (e.g. Hickey & Scharf 1980) is to promote values that are perceived by the psychologist as in some sense "natural" or "absolute." The *positivist* position (e.g. Konečni & Ebbesen 1982b) would have the psychologist not attempt to further values of any sort, but rather simply to array the facts as they are found.

Each position has appealing attributes. Instrumentalism has a pragmatic, useful quality to it, with a ring of humble subservience to the legislative and judicial processes. The natural law position affirms the righteousness of the scholar as an independent moral being. Positivism is associated with an image of the objective scientist who lets chips fall where they may. Each also has a darker side. Instrumentalism may inculcate a technocratic and reactive approach to problem solving. Natural law may legitimize the arrogant imposition of personal predilection in the name of principle. Positivism may foster an asceptic aloofness from the human problems with which the law attempts to deal.

While we are unable to recommend for the psychology of law among these three positions—our own work has at different times reflected each of them—we believe that as much attention should be given to "value" as to "influence" issues in graduate education, research, and practice in the field. We take heart in the fact that the literature on this aspect of the psychology of law has burgeoned in the past few years (American Psychological Association 1978, Anderten et al 1980, Monahan 1980).

CONCLUSION

We have structured our synthesis around the question of how psychology can increase our understanding of law. Yet what of the other side? Does the study of law have any contribution to make to our understanding of human behavior more generally, or is it just one more "applied" field of psychological inquiry?

One might say that there are two psychologies of law. The first takes as a priority the study of law as an end in itself, without regard to whether the theories developed or the behaviors predicted have more wide-ranging application. The second studies law primarily to illustrate the operation of general principles of human behavior, and so to assist in the development of those principles. While there is no bright line separating the two psychologies of law, the difference in their emphases is striking, and is reflected both in their research topics and in their research methods.

To which psychology of law does the distribution of recent research most closely correspond? Beyond question, psychologists are using law as grist for the mills of "general" theory. The disjuncture between the legal topics that psychologists study and the topics that have importance to the law itself reflect this. Less than 10 percent of the course offerings at all major law schools concern criminal law, and less than 5 percent of American attorneys handle more than an occasional criminal case (Wice 1978). A substantial majority of research in the psychology of law, however, has dealt with criminal law and most of this was concerned with criminal trials (Loh 1981). While we have acknowledged that trials can have important effects throughout the criminal justice system, the fact is that up to 97 percent of criminal convictions are achieved by means of negotiated guilty pleas, without trial (Miller et al 1978). Yet a bibliography of over 400 articles on plea bargaining (Matheny 1979) lists none published in a psychological journal (cf Gregory et al 1978).

Why such a pronounced skew? Much of the reason may lie in the newness of the field. Many interested researchers may have been reluctant to get "too involved" with an uncharted area lest their careers wind up on the shoals should the tide of scholarly fashion recede. With its growing "mainstream" legitimacy, perhaps the law will now receive their undivided attention. Other factors may be operating as well. Education in law has not been a part of education in psychology. The exposure to law of many psychologists appears restricted to the popular media, which emphasizes criminal cases and jury drama. Perry Mason, along among attorneys, never bargained a plea. Perhaps the dramatic growth of formal educational opportunities in the psychology of law (Fowler & Brodsky 1978, Poythress 1979, Levine et al 1980) will rectify this situation.

A final and more subtle bias may be reflected in the "criminalization" of the psychology of law (Tapp 1980). The virtual nonexistence of psychological research on such topics as contracts, torts, and tax law may be traced at least in some part to the traditional antipathy of "liberal" social scientists to questions that smack of "business" (Moynihan 1979). We believe this bias to be seriously mistaken both for the development of a comprehensive psychology of law and for the furtherance of those very values. A change in tax law—which is to say, in the distribution of resources in society—or in statutes governing corporate liability for harmful decision making (Monahan & Novaco 1980) may have vastly more beneficial or adverse impact on the fabric of society than a change in jury size. In our opinion, the study of "private law" (e.g. contracts, torts) and of noncriminal public law (e.g. administrative law, tax) is among the most pressing research priorities in the field.

Yet we would not make too strongly the point that the psychology of law should be as concerned with law as it is with psychology, for at the most fundamental level the dichotomy between the two fields begins to crumble. Law, as Kelson (1945, p. 1) stated, is "an order of human behavior. An order is a system of rules." The system of rules that people have generated over the centuries to structure their interactions is surely the source of many insights into the nature of human beings in social context. The analysis of "legal reasoning" may well reveal important features of *all* reasoning, and not just things particular to the law (Hamilton 1980). As Scriven (1970, p. 192, italics in original) has noted with regard to the two fields of our concern, "*extremely wide ranging subjects,* concerned with *human behavior,* in which a *systematic rational approach* is employed, aimed in part at yielding *socially useful results,* exhibit a great similarity of method." It is this fundamental similarity in a sea of surface differences that lures together psychology and law.

Acknowledgments

For generously providing us with the benefit of their insight on an earlier version of this work, we thank John Carroll, Ebbe Ebbeson, Phoebe Ellsworth, Jeffrey Fredrick, Edith Green, Vladimir Konečni, Gary Melton, Stephen Morse, N. Dickon Reppucci, David Rosenhan, Bruce Sales, Elizabeth Scott, and Laurens Walker. A grant from the National Science Foundation provided partial support for Elizabeth Loftus during the writing of this chapter.

Literature Cited

Abel, R. L. 1980. Redirecting social studies of law. *Law Soc. Rev.* 14:805–29

Abraham, H. J. 1980. *The Judicial Process.* New York: Oxford

Addington v. Texas, 99 S. Ct. 1804 (1979)

American Psychological Association. 1978. Report of the Task Force on the Role of Psychology in the Criminal Justice System. *Am. Psychol.* 33:1099–1113

Anderson, J. K., Hayden, R. M. 1980. Questions of validity and drawing conclusions from simulation studies in procedural justice: A comment. *Law Soc. Rev.* 15:293–303

Anderten, P., Staulcup, V., Grisso, T. 1980. On being ethical in legal places. *Prof. Psychol.* 11:764–73

Appelbaum, P. S., Mirkin, S. A., Bateman, A. L. 1981. Empirical assessment of competency to consent to psychiatric hospitalization. *Am. J. Psychiatry* 138: 1170–76

Arvey, R. D. 1979. Unfair discrimination in the employment interview: Legal and psychological aspects. *Psychol. Bull.* 86:736–65

Austin, W. 1979. Justice, freedom, and self-interest in intergroup conflict. In *The Social Psychology of Intergroup Relations,* ed. W. Austin, S. Worchel, pp. 121-42. Monterey, Calif: Brooks/Cole

Baldwin, J., McConville, M. 1979. *Jury Trials.* Oxford: Oxford Univ. Press

Baldwin, J., McConville, M. 1981. Criminal juries. In *Crime and Justice: An Annual Review of Research,* ed. N. Morris, M. Tonry, Vol. 2. Chicago: Univ. Chicago Press. In press

Ballew v. Georgia 435 U.S. 223 (1978)

Bard, M., Connolly, H. 1978. The police and family violence: Policy and practice. In *Battered Women: Issues of Public Policy.* Washington DC: US Comm. Civil Rights

Bem, D. J., Lord, C. G. 1979. Template matching: A proposal for probing the ecological validity of experimental settings in social psychology. *J. Pers. Soc. Psychol.* 37:833–46

Berman, J. 1977. Aspects of the parole experience. In *Psychology in the Legal Process,* ed. B. D. Sales, pp. 111–25. New York: Spectrum

Bermant, G. 1975. Data in search of theory in search of policy: Behavioral responses to videotape in the courtroom. *Brigham Young Univ. Law. Rev.* 1975:467–85

Bermant, G., McGuire, M., McKinley, W., Salo, C. 1974. The logic of simulation in jury research. *Crim. Just. Behav.* 1:224–33

Bermant, G., Shapard, J. 1981. The voir dire examination, juror challenges, and adversary advocacy. In *The Trial Process,* ed. B. D. Sales, pp. 69–114. New York: Plenum

Bersoff, D. N. 1980. Regarding psychologists testily: Legal regulation of psychological assessment in the public schools. *Md. Law Rev.* 39:27–120

Bickman, L., Rosenbaum, D. P. 1977. Crime reporting as a function of bystander encouragement, surveillance, and credibility. *J. Pers. Soc. Psychol.* 35:577–86

Bloom, B. L., Asher, S. J. eds. 1981. *Patient Rights and Patient Advocacy: Issues and Evidence.* New York: Hum. Sci. Press. In press

Blumstein, A., Cohen, J., Nagin, D., eds. 1978. *Deterrence and Incapacitation: Estimating the Effects of Criminal Sanctions on Crime Rates.* Washington, DC: Natl. Acad. Sci.

Bonnie, R. J., Slobogin, C. 1980. The role of mental health professionals in the criminal process: The case for informed speculation. *Va. Law Rev.* 66:427–522

Borgida, E. 1979. Character proof and the fireside induction. *Law Hum. Behav.* 3:189–202

Borgida, E. 1980. Evidentiary reform of rape laws: A psychological approach. See Lipsitt 1980, pp. 171–97

Borgida, E. 1981. Legal reform of rape laws: Social psychological and constitutional considerations. In *Applied Social Psychology Annual,* ed. L. Bickman, Vol. 2. Beverly Hills: Sage. In press

Bray, R. M., Kerr, N. L. 1979. Use of the simulation method in the study of jury behavior: Some methodological considerations. *Law Hum. Behav.* 3:107–20

Bray, R. M., Noble, A. M. 1978. Authoritarianism and decisions of mock juries: Evidence of jury bias and group polarization. *J. Pers. Soc. Psychol.* 12:1424–30

Bray, R. M., Struckman-Johnson, C., Osborne, M. D., McFarlane, J. B., Scott, J. 1978. The effects of defendant status on the decisions of student and community juries. *Soc. Psychol.* 41:256–60

Brodsky, S. L. 1977. The mental health professional on the witness stand: A survival guide. See Berman 1977, pp. 269–76

Brodsky, S. L., Fowler, R. D. 1979. Social psychological consequences of confinement. In *Social Psychology and Discretionary Law,* ed. L. E. Abt, I. R. Stuart, pp. 260–69. New York: Van Nostrand Reinhold

Brody, B. A. 1970. *Readings in the Philosophy of Science.* Englewood Cliffs, NJ: Prentice-Hall

Brown v. Board of Education, 347 U.S. 483 (1954)

Bukstel, L. H., Kilmann, P. R. 1980. Psychological effects of imprisonment on confined individuals. *Psychol. Bull.* 88:469–83

Caplan, G. 1964. *Principles of Preventive Psychiatry.* New York: Basic Books

Carroll, J. S. 1978a. A psychological approach to deterrence: The evaluation of crime opportunities. *J. Pers. Soc. Psychol.* 36:1512–20

Carroll, J. S. 1978b. Causal attributions in expert parole decisions. *J. Pers. Soc. Psychol.* 36:1501–11

Carroll, J. S., Payne, J. P. 1977. Crime seriousness, recidivism risk, and causal attributions in judgments of prison term by students and experts. *J. Appl. Psychol.* 62:595–602

Charrow, R. P., Charrow, V. R. 1979. Making legal language understandable: A psycholinguistic study of jury instructions. *Columbia Law Rev.* 79:1306–74

Clark, K. B. 1950. Effect of prejudice and discrimination on personality development. *Midcentury White House Conference on Children and Youth.* Washington DC: GPO

Clifford, B. R., Bull, R. 1978. *The Psychology of Person Identification.* London: Routledge & Kegan Paul

Clingempeel, W. G., Reppucci, N. D. 1981. Joint custody after divorce: Major issues and goals for research. *Psychol. Bull.* In press

Cohn, A., Udolf, R. 1979. *The Criminal Justice System and Its Psychology.* New York: Van Nostrand Reinhold

Craig v. Boren, 429 U.S. 190 (1976)

Davis, J. H., Bray, R. M., Holt, R. W. 1977. The empirical study of decision processes in juries: A critical review. In

Law, Justice and the Individual in Society: Psychological and Legal Issues, ed. J. L. Tapp, F. J. Levine, New York: Holt, Rinehart & Winston
Davis, K. C. 1980. Facts in lawmaking. *Columbia Law Rev.* 80:931–42
Deffenbacher, K. A. 1980. Eyewitness accuracy and confidence: Can we infer anything about their relationship? *Law Hum. Behav.* 4:243–60
Diamond, S. S. 1981. Exploring sources of sentencing disparity. See Bermant & Shapard 1981
Diamond, S. S., Zeisel, H. 1975. Sentencing councils: A study of sentence disparity and its reduction. *Univ. Chicago Law Rev.* 43:109–49
Ebbesen, E. B., Konečni, V. J. 1981. The process of sentencing adult felons: A casual analysis of judicial decisions. See Bermant & Shapard 1981, pp. 413–58
Ebbesen, E. B., Konečni, V. J. 1982. An analysis of the bail system. See Konečni & Ebbesen 1982a, pp. 191–229
Ehrlich, J. 1979. The economic approach to crime: A preliminary assessment. In *Criminology Review Yearbook,* ed. S. L. Messinger, E. Bittner, 1:25–60
Ellis, H. 1980. Psychology and the law. *Science* 208:712–13
Ellsworth, P. C., Getman, J. 1981. Social science in legal decision making. In *Handbook of Law and Social Science,* ed. Soc. Sci. Res. Counc. New York: Sage. In press
Elwork, A., Sales, B. D., Alfini, J. 1981. *Making Jury Instructions Understandable.* Charlottesville, Va: Michie. In press
Elwork, A., Sales, B. D., Suggs, D. 1981. The trial: A research review. See Bermant & Shapard 1981, pp. 1–68
Erickson, B., Lind, E. A., Johnson, B. C., O'Barr, W. M. 1978. Speech style and impression formation in a court setting: the effects of 'powerful' and 'powerless' speech. *J. Exp. Soc. Psychol.* 14:266–79
Etzioni, A. 1980. Mass psychology in the White House. *Transaction* 18:82–85
Farmer, L. C., Williams, G. R., Cundick, B. P., Howell, R. J., Lee, R. E., Rooker, C. K. 1977. The effect of the method of presenting trial testimony on juror decisional processes. See Berman 1977, pp. 59–76
Farrington, D. P. 1979. Longitudinal research on crime and delinquency. In *Crime and Justice: An Annual Review of Research,* ed. N. Morris, M. Tonry, 1:289–348. Chicago: Univ. Chicago Press
Farrington, D. P., Hawkins, K. 1979. Psychological research on behavior in legal contexts. See Farrington et al 1979, pp. 3–34
Farrington, D. P., Hawkins, K., Lloyd-Bostock, S., eds. 1979. Doing psychological research. In *Psychology, Law, and Legal Processes,* ed. D. P. Farrington, K. Hawkins, S. M. Lloyd-Bostock, pp. xiii-xvii. London: Macmillan
Feeley, M. M. 1976. The concept of laws in social science: A critique and notes on an expanded view. *Law Soc. Rev.* 11:497–523
Feldman, M. P. 1977. *Criminal Behavior: A Psychological Analysis.* New York: Wiley
Fishman, D. B., Loftus, E. F. 1978. Expert testimony on eyewitness identification. *Law Psychol. Rev.* 4:87–103
Fontes, N. E., Miller, G. R., Bender, D. C. 1977. Deletion of inadmissible materials from courtroom trials: Merit or myth? *Detroit Coll. Law Rev.* 67–81
Fowler, R. D., Brodsky, S. L. 1978. Development of a correctional-clinical psychology program. *Prof. Psychol.* 9: 440–47
Frankel, A., Morris, W. N. 1976. Testifying in one's own defense: The ingratiator's dilemma. *J. Pers. Soc. Psychol.* 34: 475–80
Friedman, L. M., Macaulay, S. 1977. *Law and the Behavioral Sciences.* Indianapolis: Bobbs–Merrill
Gass, R. M. 1979. The psychologist as expert witness: Science in the courtroom. *Md. Law Rev.* 38:539–621
Gerbasi, K. C., Zuckerman, M., Reis, H. T. 1977. Justice needs a new blindfold: A review of mock jury research. *Psychol. Bull.* 84:323–45
Gertz, M. G., Talarico, S. M. 1977. Problems of reliability and validity in criminal justice research. *J. Crim. Just.* 5:217–24
Gibbs, J. P. 1975. *Crime, Punishment, and Deterrence.* New York: Elsevier
Goldstein, A. G. 1979. Race-related variation of facial features: Anthropometric data. *Bull. Psychon. Soc.* 13:187–90
Gottfredson, D. M., Gottfredson, M. R. 1980a. Data for criminal justice evaluations: Some resources and pitfalls. In *Handbook of Criminal Justice Evaluation,* ed. M. W. Klein, K. S. Teilman, pp. 97–118. Beverly Hills, Calif: Sage
Gottfredson, D. M., Wilkins, L. T., Hoffman, P. B. 1978. *Guidelines for Parole and Sentencing.* Lexington, Mass: Lexington Books
Gottfredson, M. R., Gottfredson, D. M. 1980b. *Decisionmaking in Criminal Justice: Toward the Rational Exercise of Discretion.* Cambridge, Mass: Ballinger

Grabosky, P. N. 1980. Rates of imprisonment and psychiatric hospitalization in the United States. *Soc. Indic. Res.* 7:63–70

Greenberg, D. 1977. The correctional effects of corrections. In *Corrections and Punishment,* ed. D. Greenberg, pp. 111–48. Beverly Hills: Sage

Greenberg, M. Ruback, B. R. 1981. *Social Psychology and Criminal Justice.* Monterey, Calif: Brooks/Cole. In press

Gregory, W. L., Mowen, J. C., Linder, D. E. 1978. Social psychology and plea bargaining: Applications, methodology and theory. *J. Pers. Soc. Psychol.* 36: 1521–30

Grisso, T. 1980. Juveniles' capacity to waive Miranda rights: An empirical analysis. *Calif. Law Rev.* 68:1134–66

Grisso, T. 1981. *Juveniles' Waiver of Rights: Legal and Psychological Competence.* New York: Plenum

Grisso, T., Sales, B. D., Bayless, S. 1981. Law-related courses and programs in graduate psychology departments. *Am. Psychol.* In press

Grisso, T., Vierling, L. 1978. Minors' consent to treatment: A developmental perspective. *Prof. Psychol.* 9:412–27

Hamilton, V. L. 1980. Intuitive psychologist or intuitive lawyer? Alternative models of the attribution process. *J. Pers. Soc. Psychol.* 39:767–72

Haney, C. 1980. Psychology and legal change: On the limits of factual jurisprudence. *Law Hum. Behav.* 4:147–99

Haney, C., Lowy, M. J. 1979. Review of M. Heumann, *Plea Bargaining: The Experiences of Prosecutors, Judges, and Defense Attorneys. Law Soc. Rev.* 13: 633–50

Hatvany, N., Strack, F. 1981. The impact of a discredited key witness. *J. Appl. Soc. Psychol.* In press

Haward, L. R. 1981. *Forsenic Psychology.* London: Batsford

Hayden, R. M., Anderson, J. K. 1979. On the evaluation of procedural systems in laboratory experiments: A critique of Thibaut and Walker. *Law Hum. Behav.* 3:21–38

Henshel, R. L. 1980. The purposes of laboratory experimentation and the virtues of deliberate artificiality. *J. Exp. Soc. Psychol.* 16:466–78

Hepburn, J. R. 1980. The objective reality of evidence and the utility of systematic jury selection. *Law Hum. Behav.* 4:89–101

Herbsleb, J. D., Sales, B. D., Berman, J. J. 1979. When psychologists aid in the voir dire: Legal and ethical considerations. See Brodsky & Fowler 1979, pp. 197–217

Heumann, M. 1978. *Plea Bargaining: The Experiences of Prosecutors, Judges, and Defense Attorneys.* Chicago: Univ. Chicago Press

Hickey, J. E. Scharf, P. L. 1980. *Toward a Just Correctional System.* San Francisco: Jossey-Bass

Hobson v. Hansen, 327 F. Supp. 844 (1971)

Houlden, P. 1980. A philosophy of science perspective on the validity of research conclusions: Response to Anderson and Hayden. *Law Soc. Rev.* 15:305–16

In re Gault, 387 U.S. 1 (1967)

Izzett, R. R., Sales, B. D. 1981. Person perception and jurors' reactions to defendants: An equity theory interpretation. See Bermant & Shapard 1981, pp. 209–33

Jacoubovitch, M. D., Bermant, G., Crockett, G. T., McKinley, W., Sanstad, A. 1977. Juror responses to direct and mediated presentations of expert testimony. *J. Appl. Soc. Psychol.* 7:227–38

Kalven, H. 1968. The quest for the middle range: Empirical inquiry and legal policy. In *Law in a Changing America,* ed. G. Hazard, pp. 56–74. Englewood Cliffs, NJ: Prentice-Hall

Kalven, H., Zeisel, H. 1966. *The American Jury.* Boston: Little, Brown

Kaplan, M. F., Schersching, C. 1981. Juror deliberation: An information integration analysis. See Bermant & Shapard, pp. 235–62

Kassin, S. M., Wrightsman, L. S. 1979. On the requirements of proof: The timing of judicial instruction and mock juror verdicts. *J. Pers. Soc. Psychol.* 37:1877–87

Kaye, D. 1980. And then there were twelve: Statistical reasoning, the Supreme Court, and the size of the jury. *Calif. Law Rev.* 68:1004–43

Kazdin, A. E. 1978. Evaluating the generality of findings in analog therapy research. *J. Consult. Clin. Psychol.* 46: 673–86

Keasey, C. B., Sales, B. D. 1977. An empirical investigation of young children's awareness and usage of intentionality in criminal sanctions. *Law Hum. Behav.* 1:45–62

Kelson, H. 1945. *General Theory of Law and State,* transl. Anders Wedberg. Cambridge, Mass: Harvard Univ. Press

Kerr, N. L., Atkin, R. S., Strasser, G., Meek, D., Holt, R. W., Davis, J. H. 1976. Guilt beyond a reasonable doubt: Effects of concept definition and assigned decision rule on the judgments of mock jurors. *J. Pers. Soc. Psychol.* 34:282–94

Kerr, N. L., Nerenz, D., Herrick, D. 1979. Role playing and the study of jury behavior. *Soc. Methods Res.* 7:337–55

Konečni, V. J., Ebbesen, E. B. 1979. External validity of research in legal psychology. *Law Hum. Behav.* 3:39–70

Konečni, V. J., Ebbesen, E. B. 1981. A critique of theory and method in social-psychological approaches to legal issues. See Bermant & Shapard 1981, pp. 481–98

Konečni, V. J., Ebbesen, E. B. 1982a. An analysis of the sentencing system. In *The Criminal Justice System: A Social-Psychological Analysis,* ed. V. J. Konečni, E. B. Ebbesen, pp. 293–332. San Francisco: Freeman

Konečni, V. J., Ebbesen, E. B., eds. 1982b. See Konečni & Ebbesen 1982a

Konečni, V. J., Mulcahy, E. M., Ebbesen, E. B. 1980. Prison or mental hospital? Factors affecting the processing of persons suspected of being "mentally disordered sex offenders." See Lipsitt 1980, pp. 87–124

Koza, P., Doob, A. N. 1975. Some empirical evidence of judicial interim release proceedings. *Crim. Law. Q.* 17:258–72

Kuhn, T. S. 1970. *The Structure of Scientific Revolutions.* Chicago: Univ. Chicago Press. 2nd ed.

La Tour, S., Houlden, P., Walker, L., Thibaut, J. 1976. Procedure: Transnational perspectives and preferences. *Yale Law J.* 86:258–90

Lermack, P. 1979. No right number? Social science research and the jury-size cases. *NY Univ. Law Rev.* 54:951–76

Levine, D., Wilson, K., Sales, B. D. 1980. An exploratory assessment of APA internships with legal/forensic experiences. *Prof. Psychol.* 11:64–71

Levine, M., Farrell, M. P., Perotta, P. 1981. The impact of rules of jury deliberation on group developmental processes. See Bermant & Shapard 1981, pp. 263–304

Lewin, K. 1935. *A Dynamic Theory of Personality.* New York: McGraw Hill

Lind, E. A., Kurtz, S., Musante, L., Walker, L., Thibaut, J. W. 1980. Procedure and outcome effects on reactions of adjudicated resolution of conflicts of interest. *J. Pers. Soc. Psychol.* 39:643–53

Lind, E. A., Walker, L. 1979. Theory testing, theory development, and laboratory research on legal issues. *Law Hum. Behav.* 3:5–20

Lipsitt, P. D. 1980. Emergency admission of civil involuntary patients to mental hospitals following statutory modification. In *New Directions in Psycholegal Research,* ed. P. D. Lipsitt, B. D. Sales, pp. 247–64. New York: Van Nostrand Reinhold

Lipton, D., Martinson, R., Wilks, J. 1975. *The Effectiveness of Correctional Treatment.* New York: Praeger

Loftus, E. F. 1979a. Insurance advertising and jury awards. *Am. Bar Assoc. J.* 65:68–70

Loftus, E. F. 1979b. *Eyewitness Testimony.* Cambridge, Mass: Harvard Univ. Press

Loftus, E. F. 1980. Impact of expert psychological testimony on the unreliability of eyewitness identification. *J. Appl. Psychol.* 65:9–15

Loftus, E. F., Miller, D. G., Burns, H. J. 1978. Semantic integration of verbal information into a visual memory. *J. Exp. Psychol.: Hum. Learn. Mem.* 4:19–31

Loftus, E. F., Monahan, J. 1980. Trial by data: Psychological research as legal evidence. *Am. Psychol.* 35:270–83

Loh, W. D. 1979. Some uses and limits of statistics and social science in the judicial process. See Brodsky & Fowler 1979, pp. 18–42

Loh, W. D. 1981. Psycholegal research: Past and present. *Mich. Law Rev.* 79: 659–707

Luginbuhl, J., Mullin, C. 1980. Review of M. J. Saks, R. Hastie, *Social Psychology in Court. Contemp. Psychol.* 25:152–53

Martin, S., Sechrest, L., Redner, R. 1981. *New Directions in the Rehabilitation of Criminal Offenders.* Washington, DC: Natl. Acad. Sci.

Matheny, A. R. 1979. A bibliography on plea bargaining. *Law Soc. Rev.* 13:661–87

McConahay, J. B., Mullin, C. J., Frederick, J. 1977. The uses of social science in trials with political and racial overtones: The trial of Joan Little. *Law Contemp. Probl.* 41:205–29

McGillis, D. 1980. Neighborhood justice centers as mechanisms for dispute resolution. See Lipsitt 1980, pp. 198–233

McGuire, M., Bermant, G. 1977. Individual and group decisions in response to a mock trial: A methodological note. *J. Appl. Soc. Psychol.* 7:220–26

Meehl, P. 1973. *Psychodiagnosis: Selected Papers.* Minneapolis: Univ. Minn. Press

Megargee, E. I., Bohn, M. J. 1979. *Classifying Criminal Offenders.* Beverly Hills: Sage

Melton, G. 1981. Children's participation in treatment planning: Psychological and legal issues. *Prof. Psychol.* 12:246–52

Miller, G. R. 1976. The effects of videotaped trial materials on juror response. In *Psychology and the Law: Research Fron-*

tiers, ed. G. Bermant, C. Nemeth, N. Vidmar, pp. 185–208. Lexington, Mass: Lexington Books

Miller, H. S., McDonald, W. F., Cramer, J. A. 1978. *Plea Bargaining in the United States.* Washington DC: GPO

Monahan, J., ed. 1980. *Who is the Client? The Ethics of Psychological Intervention in the Criminal Justice System.* Washington DC: Am. Psychol. Assoc.

Monahan, J. 1981. *The Clinical Prediction of Violent Behavior.* Washington DC: GPO. DHHS Publ. No. ADM 81–921

Monahan, J. 1981. Three lingering issues in patients' rights. In *Patient Rights and Patient Advocacy: Issues and Evidence,* ed. B. L. Bloom, S. J. Asher. New York: Hum. Sci. Press. In press

Monahan, J., Novaco, R. W. 1980. Corporate violence: A psychological analysis. See Lipsitt 1980, pp. 3–25

Monahan, J., Splane, S. 1980. Psychological approaches to criminal behavior. In *Criminology Review Yearbook,* ed. E. Bittner, S. L. Messinger, 2:17–47. Beverly Hills: Sage

Monahan, J., Steadman, H. J. 1981. *Mentally Disordered Offenders: Perspectives from Law and Social Science.* New York: Plenum. In press

Monahan, J., Steadman, H. J. 1982. Crime and mental illness: An epidemiological approach. In *Crime and Justice: An Annual Review of Research Vol. 3,* ed. N. Morris, M. Tonry. Chicago: Univ. Chicago Press. In press

Morse, S. J. 1978. Crazy behavior, morals and science: An analysis of mental health law. *South. Calif. Law Rev.* 51:527–654

Morse, S. J. 1981. Failed explanations, weak science and criminal responsibility. *Va. Law Rev.* In press

Moynihan, D. P. 1979. Social science and the courts. *Public Interest* 54:19–20

Muller v. Oregon, 208 U.S. 412 (1908)

Mulvey, E. P. 1981. Family courts: The issue of reasonable goals. *Law. Hum. Behav.* In press

Mulvey, E. P., Reppucci, N. D. 1981. Police crisis intervention training: An empirical investigation. *Am J. Community Psychol.* In press

National Science Board. 1969. *Knowledge into Action: Improving the Nation's Use of the Social Sciences.* Washington DC: Natl. Sci. Found.

Nemeth, C. 1976. Rules governing jury deliberations: A consideration of recent changes. See G. R. Miller 1976, pp. 169–84

Nemeth, C. 1981. Jury trials: Psychology and law *Adv. Exp. Soc. Psychol.* In press

Nietzel, M. T. 1979. *Crime and its Modification: A Social Learning Perspective.* New York: Pergamon

Nisbett, R., Ross, L. 1980. *Human Inference: Strategies and Shortcomings of Social Judgment.* Englewood Cliffs, NJ: Prentice-Hall

Novaco, R. W. 1977. A stress inoculation approach to anger management in the training of law enforcement officers. *Am J. Community Psychol.* 5:327–46

Parham v. JR, 99 S. Ct. 2493 (1979)

Partridge, A., Bermant, G. 1978. *The Quality of Advocacy in the Federal Courts.* Washington DC: Fed. Judicial Cent.

Pasewark, R. A., Pantle, M. L., Steadman, H. J. 1979. Characteristics and disposition of persons found not guilty by reason of insanity in New York State, 1971–1976. *Am J. Psychiatry* 136:655–60

Pasewark, R. A., Pasewark, M. D. 1981. The insanity plea: Much ado about little. See Bloom & Asher, in press

Penrod, S., Hastie, R. 1979. Models of jury decisionmaking: A critical review. *Psychol. Bull.* 86:462–92

Penrod, S., Hastie, R. 1980. A computer simulation of jury decisionmaking. *Psychol. Rev.* 87:133–59

Penrod, S., Loftus, E. 1981. The reliability of eyewitness testimony: A psychological perspective. In *The Psychology of the Courtroom,* ed. R. Bray, N. Kerr. New York: Academic. In press

Poythress, N. G. 1978. Psychiatric expertise in civil commitment: Training attorneys to cope with expert testimony. *Law Hum. Behav.* 2:1–23

Poythress, N. G. 1979. A proposal for training in forensic psychology. *Am. Psychol.* 34:612–21

Poythress, N. G. 1980. Coping on the witness stand: Learned responses to "learned treatises". *Prof. Psychol.* 11:139–49

Quay, H. 1977. The three faces of evaluation: What can be expected to work. *Crim. Just. Behav.* 4:341–54

Reppucci, N. D., Clingempeel, W. G. 1978. Methodological issues in research with correctional populations. *J. Consult. Clin. Psychol.* 46:727–46

Roesch, R., Golding, S. L. 1980. *Competency to Stand Trial.* Urbana, Ill: Univ. Ill. Press

Rosen, P. L. 1980. History and state of the art of applied social research in the courts. See Saks & Baron 1980, pp. 9–15

Ross, R. R., Gendreau, P. 1980. *Effective Correctional Treatment.* Ontario, Canada: Butterworths.

Rossi, P. 1980. Market research data in deceptive advertising cases. See Saks & Baron 1980 pp. 98–101

Roth, L. H. 1979. A commitment law for patients, doctors, and lawyers. *Am. J. Psychiatry* 136:1121–27

Roth, L. H. 1980. Mental health commitment: The state of the debate, 1980. *Hosp. Community Psychiatry* 31: 385–96

Roth, L. H., Meisel, A., Lidz, C. W. 1977. Test of competency to consent to treatment. *Am. J. Psychiatry* 134:279–84

Ryan, J. P., Ashman, A., Sales, B. D., Shane-DuBow, S. 1981. *American Trial Judges: Organizational Influences on Their Work Styles and Performance.* New York: Free Press

Saks, M. J. 1976. The limits of scientific jury selection: Ethical and empirical. *Jurimetrics J.* 17:3–22

Saks, M. J. 1977. *Jury Verdicts.* Lexington, Mass: Heath

Saks, M. J. 1978. Social psychological contributions to a legislative subcommittee on organ and tissue transplants. *Am. Psychol.* 33:680–90

Saks, M. J. 1980. The utilization of evaluation research in litigation. *New Directions for Program Evaluation.* 5:57–67

Saks, M. J., Baron, C. H., eds. 1980. *The Use/Nonuse/Misuse of Applied Social Research in the Courts.* Cambridge, Mass: Abt Books

Saks, M. J., Hastie, R. 1978. *Social Psychology in Court.* New York: Van Nostrand Reinhold

Saks, M. J., Kidd, R. F. 1981. Human information processing and adjudication: Trial by heuristics. *Law Soc. Rev.* 15:123–60

Saks, M. J., Miller, M. 1979. A systems approach to discretion in the legal process. See Brodsky & Fowler 1979, pp. 71–91

Sales, B. D., ed. 1977. *The Criminal Justice System.* New York: Plenum

Schlegel, J. H. 1979. American legal realism and empirical social science: From the Yale experience. *Buffalo Law Rev.* 28:459–586

Schwitzgebel, R. L., Schwitzgebel, R. K. 1980. *Law and Psychological Practice.* New York: Wiley

Scriven, M. 1970. Methods of reasoning and justification in social science and law. *J. Legal Educ.* 23:189–99

Scull, A. 1977. *Decarceration: Community Treatment and the Deviant—A Radical View.* Englewood Cliffs, NJ: Prentice-Hall

Sechrest, L., White, S., Brown, G. B., eds. 1979. *Rehabilitation of Criminal Offenders: Problems and Prospects.* Washington DC: Natl. Acad. Sci.

Shah, S. A. 1978. Dangerousness: A paradigm for exploring some issues in law and psychology. *Am. Psychol.* 33: 224–38

Sigall, H., Ostrove, N. 1975. Beautiful but dangersous: Effects of offenders attractiveness and nature of the crime on juridic judgment. *J. Pers. Soc. Psychol.* 31:410–14

Silberman, C. E. 1978. *Criminal Violence, Criminal Justice.* New York: Random House

Smith, A. D., Winograd, E. 1978. Adult age differences in remembering faces. *Dev. Psychol.* 14:443–44

Steadman, H. J. 1979. *Beating a Rap? Defendants Found Incompetent to Stand Trial.* Chicago: Univ. Chicago Press

Stephan, W. G. 1978. School desegregation: An evaluation of predictions made in *Brown v. Board of Education. Psychol. Bull.* 85:217–38

Stier, S. D., Stoebe, K. J. 1979. Involuntary hospitalization of the mentally ill in Iowa: The failure of the 1975 legislation. *Iowa Law Rev.* 64:1284–1458

Stotland, E., Berberich, J. 1979. The psychology of the police. See Toch 1979, pp. 24–67

Strawn, D. V., Buchanan, R. W. 1976. Jury confusion: A threat to justice. *Judicature* 59:478–83

Suggs, D. L. 1979. The use of psychological research by the judiciary: Do the courts adequately assess the validity of the research? *Law Hum. Behav.* 3:135–48

Suggs, D., Berman, J. J. 1979. Factors affecting testimony about mitigating circumstances and the fixing of punishment. *Law Hum. Behav.* 3:251–60

Tanke, E. D., Tanke, T. J. 1979. Getting off a slippery slope. *Am. Psychol.* 34: 1130–38

Tapp, J. L. 1976. Psychology and the law: An overture. *Ann. Rev. Psychol.* 27: 359–404

Tapp, J. L. 1980. Psychological and policy perspectives on the law: Reflections on a decade. *J. Soc. Issues* 36:165–92

Thibaut, J., Walker, L. 1975. *Procedural Justice: A Psychological Analysis.* New York: Erlbaum/Wiley

Thibaut, J., Walker, L. 1978. A theory of procedure. *Calif. Law Rev.* 66:541–66

Thompson, W. C., Fong, G. T., Rosenhan, D. L. 1981. Inadmissible evidence and juror verdicts. *J. Pers. Soc. Psychol.* In press

Toch, H. 1977. *Living in Prison: The Ecology*

of Human Survival. New York: Free Press

Toch, H., ed. 1979. *Psychology of Crime and Criminal Justice.* New York: Holt, Rinehart & Winston

Tunnell, G. B. 1977. Three dimensions of naturalness: An expanded definition of field research. *Psychol. Bull.* 84:426–37

Vidmar, N. 1979. The other issues in jury simulation research: A commentary with particular reference to defendant character studies. *Law Hum. Behav.* 3:95–106

Vidmar, N., Judson, J. W. 1981. The use of social science data in a change of venue application: a case study. *Can. Bar Rev.* 59:76–102

Vidmar, N., Miller, D. T. 1980. Social psychological processes underlying attitudes toward legal punishment. *Law Soc. Rev.* 14:565–602

von Hirsch, A., Hanrahan, K. J. 1979. *The Question of Parole: Retention, Reform, or Abolition?* Cambridge, Mass: Ballinger

Walker, L., Lind, E. A., Thibaut, J. 1979. The relationship between procedural and distributive justice. *Va. Law Rev.* 65:1401–20

Warren, C. 1977. Involuntary commitment for mental disorder: The application of California's Lauterman-Petris-Short Act. *Law. Soc. Rev.* 11:629–50

Weiten, W., Diamond, S. S. 1979. A critical review of the jury simulation paradigm: The case of defendant characteristics. *Law Hum. Behav.* 3:71–94

Weithorn, L. A. 1980. *Competence to render informed treatment decisions: A comparison of certain minors and adults.* PhD thesis. Univ. Pittsburgh, Pittsburgh, Pa.

Wells, G. L. 1980. Eyewitness behavior: The Alberta Conference. *Law Hum. Behav.* 4:237–394

Wells, G. L., Lindsay, R. C. L., Ferguson, T. J. 1979. Accuracy, confidence, and juror perceptions in eyewitness identification. *J. Appl. Psychol.* 64:440–48

Wells, G. L., Lindsay, R. C. L., Tousignant, J. P. 1980. Effects of expert psychological advice on human performance in judging the validity of eyewitness testimony. *Law Hum. Behav.* 4:275–85

Wexler, D. B. 1981. *Mental Health Law: Major Issues.* New York: Plenum

Wice, P. B., 1978. *Criminal Lawyers: An Endangered Species.* Beverly Hills: Sage

Wilson, D. W., Donnerstein, E. 1976. Legal and ethical aspects of non-reactive social psychological research: An excursion into the public mind. *Am. Psychol.* 31:765–73

Wilson, D. W., Donnerstein, E. 1977. Guilty or not guilty? A look at the "simulated" jury paradigm. *J. Appl. Soc. Psychol.* 7:175–90

Wilson, J. Q. 1980. "What works?" revisited: New findings on criminal rehabilitation. *Public Interest* 61:3–17

Woocher, F. D. 1977. Did your eyes deceive you? Expert psychological testimony on the unreliability of eyewitness identification. *Stanford Law Rev.* 29:969–1030

Woodhead, M. M., Baddeley, A. D., Simmonds, D. C. 1979. On training people to recognize faces. *Ergonomics* 22: 333–43

Wrightsman, L. S. 1978. The American trial jury on trial: Empirical evidence and procedural modifications. *J. Soc. Issues* 34:137–64

Yandell, B. 1979. Those who protest too much are seen as guilty. *Pers. Soc. Psychol. Bull.* 5:44–47

Yarmey, A. D. 1979. *The Psychology of Witness Testimony.* New York: Free Press

Zeisel, H., Diamond, S. S. 1978. The effect of peremptory challenges on jury and verdict: An experiment in a Federal District Court. *Stanford Law Rev.* 30: 491–530

Zwerling, I., Conte, H., Plutchik, R., Karaser, T. 1978. "No-commitment week": A feasibility study. *Am. J. Psychiatry* 135:1198–1201

Ann. Rev. Psychol. 1982. 33:477–514

INFORMATION PROCESSING MODELS—IN SEARCH OF ELEMENTARY OPERATIONS

Michael I. Posner[1]

Department of Psychology, University of Oregon, Eugene, Oregon 97403

Peter McLeod

Applied Psychology Unit, 15, Chaucer Road, Cambridge, England

---

CONTENTS

[1]Support for this project was provided by the Alfred P. Sloan Foundation and by the National Science Foundation through grant BNS-7923527. The paper was written while the second author was a visiting Fulbright scientist at the University of Oregon.

0066-4308/82/0201-0477$02.00

INTRODUCTION

In a criticism of cognitive psychology, Newell (1973) suggested that there are few common principles emerging from myriads of often dichotomous distinctions. Newell's remedy, and the one that Simon (1979) followed in his *Annual Review* chapter on this topic, is the construction of complex information processing models that might eventually simulate a wide range of human mental activity. The reverse emphasis, and the one explored in this chapter, is that detailed studies of particular task configurations will lead to the identification of fundamental operations that can be used to characterize the human mind. We do not assume that there will be the same set of such operations for all tasks. What are the goals of isolating elementary mental operations? They could give a basis for the analysis of individual differences, for the study of changes over development and learning, and for the division of mental processes into reasonable sets of cognitive systems. In addition, they might provide the links to underlying neural systems. Recently, there has been an increased contact between cognitive psychology and neuropsychology based upon this proposition. Proposals concerning mental operations involved in reading have been a basis for joint work by cognitive and neuropsychologists on acquired dyslexia (Coltheart et al 1980). Similarly, questions of attention and motor control often bring cognitive and neuroscientists together (Scheer 1981, Stelmach & Requin 1980).

History

Whereas Simon (1979) traces the origin of information processing models of cognition to early efforts to produce digital simulations of human intelligence, the experimental study of mental operations has its origin in the subtractive method of Donders (1969) and more recently in the use of information measures to summarize the relationship between uncertainty and reaction time (Hick 1952, Hyman 1953). Failure of such information theory guided research to provide either an absolute capacity of the human mind or an ability to predict performance from stimulus structure alone led to efforts to break apart the human information processing system into components that might perform different mental operations (Neisser 1967).

We take it as fundamental to all information processing models that they incorporate a certain number of elementary mental processes or operations, a concatenation of which can produce complex behavior. At least since the time of John Locke (1924), students of human cognition have wanted to specify a set of elementary operations that could combine to produce the myriad of performances of which the human is capable. Chase (1978) suggests, "It is possible to isolate and measure elementary processes underlying speeded mental tasks." The restriction to speeded mental tasks reflects the importance of careful time-locking between input and response that has been critical to the use of various chronometric measures in psychology (Posner & Rogers 1977). In his discussion of elementary mental processes, Chase identified as possible candidates "finding the next location in memory, comparing two symbols in memory, constructing a negation and so on." Chase recognizes in his chapter that at the moment there is no definition of what constitutes an elementary mental operation.

Taxonomy

We propose a simple taxonomy of mental operations that will aid the reader in following this chapter, but it is by no means universal in the literature. One important distinction between operations relates to the specificity of the functions they perform (Garner 1980, Sanders 1977). Specific computations operate on a narrow range of input to achieve some transformation, while other processes are concerned with very general influences on almost all tasks. Thus, an operation may be performed only upon one kind of input (e.g. light) to achieve one kind of code (e.g. color) or a function like arousal may affect many forms of processing. A second distinction separates relatively enduring components that tend to change slowly, if at all, during a given task (e.g. concepts or semantic knowledge) from more dynamic components that are organized and changed in order to produce a particular performance (e.g. hypotheses).

Dichotomizing these two dimensions (specificity and dynamics) gives the fourfold classification of internal operations shown in Diagram 1. Those operations that perform a specific computation and are enduring we call "structures." If they are assembled for a given task we use the term "strategy." More general influences on performance that vary over time we call "states," while if they are enduring properties we call them "traits."

Most of the literature on information processing has been concerned with structures. The field tends to be divided by the particular computation that is involved in a given task (e.g. reading or problem solving). George Miller (personal communication) has proposed that we consider an analogy between cognitive systems (e.g. language, object recognition, attention, etc) and organ systems like digestion and reproduction. This idea (see Posner, Pea & Volpe 1981) is based on enduring structures that perform particular cognitive functions and have distinct neurological bases.

TAXONOMY OF MENTAL OPERATIONS

Specificity	Dynamics: Enduring	Dynamics: Temporary
Specific	Structure	Strategy
General	Trait	State

One set of structures that has played a very important role, especially in information processing models of language, are those that perform changes of code (Posner 1978). Just as sensory systems transduce one form of energy to another, letter strings are organized into visual codes that represent their orthography (LaBerge & Samuels 1974) and are then transformed into more abstract codes that are common to auditory and visual input (Morton & Patterson 1980, McClelland & Rumelhart 1981).

Dynamic processes that perform specific operations we call "strategies." The idea is that elementary mental operations may be assembled into sequences and combinations that represent the strategy developed for a particular task. It is often difficult to determine whether the elementary mental operations isolated are strategies or whether they are structures. Consider, for example, operations that can perform the same logical computation on a wide range of inputs or outputs such as the "next" operation (Chase 1978). This could increment a position on a verbal list or cause a change of perspective in scanning a visual scene or output the next command in a motor program. Should we look for structures at this level of generality, or should we suppose that such operations are assembled for the task being performed? Probably one should not draw the distinction between structure and strategy too strongly. For just as structures may evolve through learning, so strategies may be relatively enduring, particularly if they represent very high levels of skill. The chess master who has developed a strategy for the analysis of the chessboard over many years of practice may be unable to modify. Thus it becomes more structural in character. Indeed, high levels of skills seem to be characterized by the development of a structural basis for what in most of us is a painfully assembled strategy.

While structure and strategy place emphasis on specific computations, more general influences upon information processing may also be divided into static and dynamic components. These internal characteristics have an influence over a broad range of specific computations. For example, following a warning signal there are changes in the information processing system that affect the efficiency of nearly any task that a subject is asked to perform. This dynamic general affect we call a "state." A change in state following a warning signal has often been called a change in "arousal" or "alertness." Changes in these states may also be induced by other independent variables such as the loss of sleep or presence of stress factors such as vibration and noise, etc. The degree to which these various independent variables influence a common state is still a matter of dispute (Broadbent 1971, Poulton 1979).

Static aspects of information processing affecting a broad range of variables we call "traits." There has been much dispute in personality theory about the existence and enduring quality of such traits (Bem & Allen 1978, Kendrick & Stringfield 1980, Mischel 1973). It can be argued that a given individual is characterized by a cluster of traits that are exhibited in many situations. This view makes the core of traits that characterize a person relatively enduring and thus of particular interest to those who would apply information processing models to the study of personality.

Motivation and emotion have usually been treated as changes in traits or states rather than of strategy and structure. Thus emotions can be seen as changes in state induced by aspects of stimulus situations (Schachter & Singer 1962) or as relatively enduring dispositions or temperaments (Rothbart & Derryberry 1981). There have been some efforts to examine emotional changes as relating to concepts stored in semantic memory and induced by the activation of structures (Bower 1981). Nonetheless, even in these views the effects of the emotion are to vary the quality of perception or memory rather generally.

Chapter Organization

This chapter reviews research conducted mainly since Simon's 1979 presentation by considering it in relation to the question of isolating elementary mental operations. In the second section we discuss methods for isolating mental operations and survey their use in language, analog processes, motor control, and problem solving. This reflects both the likelihood that these topics include a range of cognitive systems and their importance in the contemporary literature. Next we consider research on the coordination of mental operations. The fourth section deals with developmental and individual differences. In the last section we examine proposals for linking mental operations to the study of brain systems.

SOURCES OF ELEMENTARY MENTAL OPERATIONS

Methodology

Many of the ideas for putative mental operations have been intuited by cognitive psychologists from the observation of their own mental processes or from observing the behavior of others. While there is a long tradition (Sackett 1978) of careful coding of behavior in ethology, developmental psychology, and other areas, such systematic coding has been less used in cognitive psychology. Newell & Simon (1972) based much of their work in problem solving on the use of verbal protocols in which subjects speak aloud as they solve problems. Recently, Ericsson & Simon (1980) have presented a justification of the verbal protocol as a basis for understanding human performance in problem solving situations. Could such systematic protocols become the basis for the identification of elementary mental operations? Ericsson and Simon argue that verbal protocols provide a relatively complete record of the information that comes to short-term memory during the solution of problems, and that concurrent verbalization studies provide more accurate information than retrospective analyses of mental operations. The verbal protocol is limited to conscious processes; nonetheless, many important transformations of information certainly can be described by the subject as he solves problems. In addition, eye movement protocols have been used during reading (Just & Carpenter 1980), chess playing (Chase & Simon 1973), and decision making (Russo & Rosen 1975). It seems likely that verbal and eye movement protocols do provide an effective way of gaining a handle on the specific strategies that people use as they perform complex tasks. A comparison of strategies used in many problem-solving tasks has not provided much in the way of common constraints in different task environments. This has led Newell & Simon (1972) to conclude that the human information processing system is rather simple and that only a few basic constraints such as the number of items held in short-term memory and the time to process each chunk are important limits on human information processing. It could be argued that the use of the protocol method itself tends to limit analysis to strategies developed by the subject in the execution of problems and is not a very good way for understanding more structural limits on performance.

More typical of studies of human information processing are efforts to extract elementary mental operations from speeded performance. Such operations are not necessarily conscious. Although the method goes back all the way to Donders' classical subtractive technique, Sternberg's (1969) additive factors methodology has given it greater impetus in recent years. In an excellent review of this literature, Sanders (1980) provides a strong defense of the additive factors method against critics, both of the logic and of the empirical results. He reviews criticisms and conflicts in the literature and attempts to establish the proposition that all current empirical studies using the method can be reconciled through the assumption that choice reaction time tasks consist uniformly of six serial stages. These stages are processing structures that lie behind the myriad of different tasks that subjects perform. In accordance with the additive factors methodology, Sanders associates each stage with an independent variable thought to manipulate its duration. These are shown in Table 1. The first two of these stages are sensory, while the last two are purely motor. The figure clearly illustrates the degree to which the additive factor methods produce a sequencing of relatively abstract structures that may be thought of as general to nearly any task in which subjects respond rapidly to simple input. A subject would probably have great difficulty in identifying any of these as components of his own performance.

A somewhat different conception of the nature of information processing has arisen from those who have not been willing to accept the idea that discrete stages operate in sequence and deliver information to the next stage only after they finish (McClelland 1979, Posner 1978, Taylor 1976, Wickelgren 1976). These views conceptualize the system in terms of hierarchical structures whose activation overlaps in time. This conception is more similar to the parallel channels notion that is now popular in psychophysics (Ball & Sekuler 1980) and sensory physiology.

McClelland (1979) proposes a cascade model in which, for example, a visual word activates light, feature, letter, lexical, decision, and response levels. These levels are very similar to stages obtained from the additive factors analysis, but they overlap in time rather than following one another in discrete fashion. Unfortunately, the less restrictive assumptions in this model also produce a considerable increment in the difficulty of telling if operations are independent. The major technique suggested by McClelland for studying cascading processes is to examine the relative effects of inde-

Table 1 Suggested stages on the basis of typical additive effects[a]

Stage	Typical additive variables
Preprocessing	Signal contrast
Feature extraction	Signal quality
Identification	Signal discriminability, word frequency
Response choice	S-R compatibility
Response programming	Response specificity
Motor adjustment	Instructed muscle tension

[a] From Sanders 1980.

pendent variables upon parameters of a function relating accuracy to time to process input (speed-accuracy tradeoff). Some important studies using the speed-accuracy idea have emerged (Wickelgren 1981), and one recent report seeks to relate the cascade idea to language tasks in some detail (McClelland & Rumelhart 1981), but it is still too early to tell how successful this methodology will be in isolating mental operations.

A somewhat simpler variant of the McClelland proposal is the idea that operations can be isolated if it proves possible to manipulate their time courses independently by changes of plausible variables. Posner (1978) has argued that the physical and name codes of letters and words are represented in separate structures. One can vary time for physical comparisons by manipulating color, for example, without changing the time to derive the names, and can also vary naming times by loading memory with other verbal items without affecting physical match times. Similarly, it has been proposed that letters are encoded by separate local and global operations because the time for detail information can be manipulated independently from the time for information about the overall configuration (Hoffman 1980, Kinchla & Wolf 1979, Navon 1977).

Another method used to isolate internal processes involves examination of the pattern of facilitation and inhibition created by the event (Posner & Snyder 1975, Taylor 1978). According to this view, any stimulus event activates internal codes used to recognize that item. Such pathway activation facilitates the coding of any other item using the same pathway. Automatic activation is distinguished from active attentional processes because only the latter accompany the facilitation with inhibition of items not sharing the same pathway.

These methods should not be seen as either mutually exclusive or exhaustive. It is probably better to view them as a set of tools that can be aids in the decomposition of performance into sets of internal operations. They are often based on different views of the processing system as a whole, but the use of a method such as protocol analysis or additive factors probably does not depend upon the acceptance of the associated viewpoint in its entirety.

Reading and Listening

The study of elementary mental operations has progressed further in the areas of reading and listening than in any other area. Prior to the time under review, very substantial work on the recognition of individual letters and phonemes and of lexical items presented visually and orally had already been accomplished. Much of this work has been summarized in a large number of new textbooks of cognitive psychology that have appeared during the period under review (Anderson 1980, Glass, Holyoke & Santa 1979,

Lachman, Lachman & Butterfield 1979, Wickelgren 1979). It appears that the process of recognizing a visually or orally presented word involves the operation of hierarchically organized structures that process sensory specific (auditory or visual) or more abstract semantic codes.

Within the visual domain, it is often argued that individual letters are analyzed by some form of distinctive feature analysis and that multiple letter strings are organized into units ranging from single letters all the way through whole words or familiar phrases.

There remains a large amount of active research about the specific nature of these internal recognition systems and the methods that might be most appropriate to isolate them. For reading, the most typical methods to explore visual codes have involved masking (Johnston & McClelland 1981), matching of letter strings (Bruder 1978, Carr et al 1979, Henderson 1980), and letter detection (Healy 1976). For speech, much work centers around adaptation techniques in which an input phoneme (e.g. ba) is repeated in order to observe shifts in the boundary between the repeated phoneme and a phoneme differing in a single distinctive feature. At first this method was thought to have a direct effect on the phonetic level, but criticisms of this idea (Diehl 1981, Sawusch & Jusczyk 1981) have dominated the period under review. There is increasing interest in higher levels of pattern recognition in the auditory system (Cole 1980). For this purpose tasks not too different from the visual ones discussed above have been adopted. For example, Foss & Blank (1980) have subjects monitor speech for a particular phoneme. There is also interest in the detection of (Cole & Jakimik 1980) or failure to detect (Marslen-Wilson & Welsh 1978) mispronunciations.

This variety of tasks has also been accompanied by a large variety of dependent variables. Most of these variables would be called chronometric in that they use some aspects of the speeded nature of the task to serve to isolate the level of processing. Most frequently the method used involves direct measures of reaction time, but not infrequently it involves changes in accuracy as the time the subject is given to perform the task is altered, either by use of masking stimulus (Johnston & McClelland 1981) or by forcing the subject to respond quite rapidly, even at the risk of high error rates. Speeded presentation of linguistic information for comprehension or target detection is also widely used (Potter, Kroll & Harris 1980). It seems to us to be an impressive feature of this literature that the general conclusions that one would reach from these tasks do not seem to vary greatly, depending upon the particular type of dependent measure used in the analysis.

The idea that mental operations at different levels of analysis can be isolated by these techniques has become very well represented in the technical literature and in textbooks, but there are those who remain skeptical

(Kolers 1975, Weisburg 1980). Among those who accept such a position, the theoretical questions have begun to focus upon details of the mechanisms working within a structural level (code) of the system. For example, Carr et al (1979) argued that although both orthographic rules and familiarity from past experience operate to improve the recognition of words, within the visual code only rule-based orthography and not prior experience is effective. This rather surprising assertion is based on the failure of familiar, but not orthographically regular, letter strings (e.g. FBI) to exhibit the characteristics of superior performance in visual matching that are shown by orthographically regular strings such as FIB.

This argument has been vigorously disputed (Henderson 1980, Carr et al 1981). Whatever the eventual outcome of the dispute, it represents the kind of discussion that depends upon already having been successful in developing tasks that isolate particular structural codes which operate during word recognition.

One interesting aspect of the use of common methods to develop models of visual and auditory language tasks is the ability to examine the convergence of information upon mechanisms common to the two modalities. Hanson (1981) examined the effect of irrelevant and supposedly unattended auditory and visual information upon tasks performed in the opposite modality. She found influence of unattended visual information on both phoneme monitoring and semantic classification of auditory items, and of unattended auditory information on letter search and semantic classification in the visual modality. It is not clear exactly whether letter detection and phoneme monitoring depend on processes that occur prior to lexical access (Foss & Blank 1980), but if they do, these results suggest that there is convergence of auditory and visual information at the level at which lexical items are recognized and semantic information accumulated (see also Tanenhaus, Flanigan & Seidenberg 1980). Reading and listening represent tasks in which very highly overlearned correspondences exist between stimuli whose sensory processes are quite distinct. The convergence of evidence from visual and auditory language tasks may give us a clue as to how structures that are not sensory-specific interact with sensory-specific information.

A major method for observing the effects of a word on the processing system is to use one word as a priming event for the processing of the second word. This can be accomplished either by having the subject process a word on one trial and follow it with a related word on the next trial (Fischler & Goodman 1978), or by explicitly presenting a prime event which the subject must read before responding to the second word (Neely 1977). Both these methods work very well, and priming is well established for a wide variety of internal codes (Nissen 1979).

It seems clear that there are both automatic and strategic effects involved in priming. Neely attempted to separate the automatic from the attended effects by examining the time course of facilitation and inhibition following the prime. His results favored two separate priming processes—one fast, predominantly facilitory, and automatic, the other slow, predominantly inhibitory, and involving attention. Subsequent work by Antos (1979) showed a fast inhibition effect that might represent an exception to the identification of inhibition with a limited capacity attention system. Another problem with viewing automatic priming as unaffected by task demands is the result of work by Smith (1979). When the task of looking for a target letter was performed on the prime, it did not succeed in facilitating a semantically related word in a subsequent letter detection task.

There are other puzzling differences between tasks that affect the qualitative details of priming. Warren (1974) showed that the associative strength from the prime to the target word affected the degree of priming when the target word is the base for a color-naming task. The stronger the associative strength the more interference the prime word gives with the naming of the color. Warren found that the backward association from target to prime had no influence on the degree of priming as measured by the Stroop interference. On the other hand, in the widely used lexical decision task the amount of priming is relatively independent of the strength of the association between prime and target. It is also true that backward associations from target to prime can influence priming (Koriat 1981).

The most impressive results in favor of an automatic effect of semantic primes are the results reported by Fischler & Goodman (1978) and Marcel (1980). In these experiments there are systematic manipulations of the length of time for which the prime is presented prior to a mask. In its most impressive form a mask follows the prime so quickly that the subject is unable to discriminate between a trial in which a prime precedes the mask and one in which only the masking field is presented. Thus there is no conscious knowledge either of the semantic content of the prime nor even any better than chance knowledge of its presence, and yet a semantic priming effect is found. This evidence is powerful confirmation of the theme that semantic priming can occur automatically even below the threshold of consciousness.

Despite the evidence for automatic priming based on structural codes, the importance of strategies in determining the exact use of the prime shown in the Smith study is reinforced in work by Becker (1980). Becker shows that in different experimental situations it is possible to get a priming effect that is either mainly facilitory or mainly inhibitory. The facilitory pattern occurs when the relationship between prime and target is consistently strong throughout the list. When the materials include a wide range of semantic relationships, interference dominates over facilitation. Becker attributes these two different patterns to different strategies that the subject adopts in the presence of lists of differing type. Whether these strategies in turn relate to attentional or other structural factors in the system is not clear.

Studies of reading and listening up until 1975 mostly involved isolated words or phrases. Recently, however, there has been more concentration on the analysis of sentences or longer passages (Cole 1980, Just & Carpenter 1980, Marslen-Wilson & Welsh 1978, Potter et al 1980).

These experiments are important as tests of whether mental operations extracted from experiments in single tasks provide insight into more complex performance. There has been a general feeling (Neisser 1976) that concentration of chronometric studies on small units of fleeting behavior have not given us the tools for examination of ecologically valid performances such as reading and listening.

Our examination of the literature suggests the contrary. Rayner (1978) showed that the semantic information available within any fixation comes from only a relatively small number of items around the fovea. This finding supports the view that each fixation is roughly a 250-millisecond tachistoscopic glance at a small amount of relevant information. For English readers the semantic influence of the word to the right of fixation primes naming the foveal word in the same way whether the eyes move or not (Rayner, McConkie & Ehrlich 1978, Rayner, Well & Pollatsek 1980).

There is also very clear evidence that the prior context has an important role in creating expectancies that allow integration of information yet to be read. This top-down expectancy is similar to what has been found from the spreading activation studies of single letters and words. Stanovich & West (1979, 1981) and Fischler & Bloom (1979) have attempted to trace the facilitory and inhibitory effects of sentence fragments on lexical decisions for individual words. It appears clear that the sentence context can facilitate lexical decisions to individual items (Kleiman 1980). Moreover, Davidson (1978) in the context of reading stories has shown that lexical decisions to words that fit within the story are facilitated and that this facilitation is not shared by homonyms of those words. His results suggest, as have a number of previous studies of individual words (Kleiman 1975), that lexical access does not require development of the phonological code but rather can come from a direct visual to semantic access. The phonological code appears useful in integrating the story line in memory. In line with this view, reaction time to probes occurring during a reading task are longer when the subjects are trying to integrate information from sentences to follow a narrative than when they read more difficult material that has no narrative or storyline (Britton et al 1979).

Although it seems clear that important new questions of syntax and meaning arise when one examines sentences, paragraphs, and stories rather than letters or words, it appears that some of the structural and strategic components isolated in the study of individual words will provide a theoretical basis for dealing with the more complex levels of information processing of language material.

Analog Processing

There has been much discussion in the current literature (Anderson 1978, Kosslyn 1980, 1981, Pylyshyn 1981) of the distinction between analog and propositional coding. One group of researchers believes that there are fundamental distinctions between cognitive systems used for mental imagery and those for linguistic processing. Others hold that a single propositional code would be appropriate to both types of processing.

One major issue has been the similarity between operations performed upon mental images and those that occur in visual perception. Early work in this area showed that subjects could match, rotate, or scan for the presence of a feature as rapidly and efficiently with an imagined representation as when the stimulus was actually present, provided the amount of material to be represented in the image was within the rather limited capacity for the visual representation of independent items (see Shepard & Podgorny 1978 for a review).

More recent studies have somewhat extended the number of similarities between visual perception and images. For example, Finke (1980) reported that acuity functions for images fall off with distance from the fovea in the same way as is found for sensory stimuli and that visual images can be used to produce adaptation in prism experiments. The methods used require subjective judgments and may be subject to demand characteristics based upon the person's expectation of what data should be found (Pylyshyn 1981).

The ability to study images objectively provides cognitive psychologists with a method of examining perceptual transformations free of sensory input. Most sensory studies have followed the strategy of tracing the input message inward, thus placing most weight upon passive rather than upon active processes. Studies of imagined representations are able to examine some of the rules by which the perceptual system may operate in dealing with objects. For example, Shepard (1981) has compared mental rotations of imagined objects with those found by alternating between two orientations of the same object. In both cases he found linear relationships between the degree of orientation and speed of mental rotation or the quality of apparent motion. Apparent motion is not an option that the subject chooses to experience but is imposed by the stimulus. Yet the effects of angle of orientation are quite similar in apparent motion and in mental rotation of images. This observation also supports the argument that imagery employs some of the same machinery as is involved in perception.

Recently subjects have been asked to image more complex visual displays in an effort to understand how they can scan through such representations. The studies suggest the importance of physical distance in determining the time to move between objects (Kosslyn 1980, Pinker 1980) and the close relations between internal scans and eye movements (Weber & Malmstrom 1979). If it is agreed that the studies of scanning visual images provide information on the nature of central mechanisms that select information in the visual world, it should be possible to study such scanning under simpler conditions. It has been shown that subjects can move attention in accordance with cues in order to enhance detection of increments in luminance (Bashinski & Bachrach 1980, Posner 1980, Remington 1980). These shifts of covert attention can be studied by examining changes in the efficiency of taking in information at different places in visual space with eyes fixed. By the use of probes between fixation and target events it is possible to show that as attention moves from one position in the visual field to another it passes through intermediate positions (Shulman, Remington & McLean 1979). These results suggest the analog nature of shifts of covert attention in the visual field and are similar to the results obtained from scanning imaged scenes. Moreover, in this simple situation it has proved possible to link purely behavioral studies to those studying cognition deficits following brain injury and recording electrical activity from alert animals (Posner 1980).

A major role for covert attention shifts is to direct the eyes to information of interest. It has been known for some time that the visual periphery can detect physical properties of objects such as motion, color, presence or absence, rapid contour change and shape. These factors can serve to control and direct covert orientings and eye movement. Recent studies have shown that comparatively complex cognitive decisions about the nature of objects can be made while they are still in the periphery.

Loftus & Mackworth (1978) studied the control of eye fixation during picture viewing. People studied pictures for 4 sec with instructions to remember them as they would have to recognize them later. In half the pictures an object appeared which would not have been expected given the rest of the picture—an octopus in a farmyard, or a tractor in an underwater scene, for example. (The set was balanced so that in other pictures the objects appeared in their expected surroundings.) Loftus and Mackworth found that after the first fixation an object was fixated sooner if it was out of context than if it were to be expected, given the rest of the picture. The conclusion must be that peripheral visual process can identify enough about an object to decide that it is inappropriate for a given scene. The fact that foveal attention is then drawn to it suggests that some properties of the object which are likely to be of interest are not available to peripheral processing.

Similar conclusions can be drawn from the results of Parker (1978) and Friedman (1979). Parker shows that during a recognition memory test for a picture a change in one of the objects such as the replacement of a boy by a girl would draw a foveal fixation faster than if the object was unchanged from the original. Friedman, who also studied recognition memory for pictures, showed that if the change in the recognition test picture involved replacement of one in-context object by another, the change was less likely to be noticed than if it involved the substitution of an object which was out of context with the rest of the picture. Presumably part of the reason for this is the effect found by Loftus and Mackworth—peripheral processes draw foveal attention less frequently to in-context objects. Thus, changes of in-context items are less likely to be noticed than changes in objects whose presence in the picture is surprising.

The evidence for control of fixation by semantic information from the periphery during reading is rather less clear. As in picture viewing, the physical appearance of words to the right of fixation can be identified. Rayner (Rayner 1978, Rayner, McConkie & Ehrlich 1978) has shown that information about the first and last letters and about the shape of a word to the right of fixation can be picked up. O'Regan (1979, 1980) has demonstrated that the length of the word to the right of the current fixation can be identified because it influences the size of the next saccade. O'Regan (1979) has also provided some evidence that semantic processing of words in peripheral vision can be performed. He compared eye fixations on pairs of sentences such as:

THE OTHER DAY WAS CAUGHT

THE BEAR THAT JOE WAS HUNTING

HAD OFTEN BEEN SEEN

The word after the verb was always three letters long. It was either "the" or a frequently occurring auxiliary (was, had, are) or a less frequently occurring verb (met, ran, ate). He demonstrated that when the eye approached the redundant word "the" there were larger saccades than to other three-letter words. He also showed that saccade length was different for the frequently occurring auxiliary and the less frequently occurring verb. This suggests that the mechanism controlling saccade length does involve lexical access and is not simply a "the" detector.

Motor Control

It has been argued that cognitive life is based upon three forms of internal codes: iconic, symbolic, and enactive (Bruner, Oliver & Greenfield 1966). The last two sections reviewed evidence from imagery (iconic) and language (symbolic) processes, and it is appropriate that we now turn to motor processes. There has been an important resurgence of interest in this area from a variety of viewpoints (Miles & Evarts 1979, Keele, 1981, Stelmach & Requin 1980).

The structural operations in movement control can be studied by examining motor programs. Although the concept of a motor program as a set of instructions which leads to an appropriate action being performed is clear, there is no agreement on what commands a program contains and how it interacts with the feedback produced by a movement.

A strong statement concerning the contents of the motor program is made by the "mass-spring" model. Following the work of Feldman and Bizzi, the model has been developed by Kelso et al (1980). It suggests that the program simply specifies an equilibrium point for muscles to aim at when the limb will again be at rest. Dynamic properties of a movement such as its velocity are determined by setting some aspect of the muscles such as their tension as they move toward their new resting position. For such a model there is no direct role for feedback in the control of movement. Kelso (1977) demonstrated that people wearing wrist cuffs to block proprioceptive feedback and without visual input can still move their fingers accurately to locations they had previously selected despite external disturbance of the movement, as can people with joint capsules removed. Bizzi has demonstrated similar phenomena in deafferented monkeys (Bizzi, Polit & Morasso 1976, Polit & Bizzi 1979). Such findings are naturally interpreted as favoring a mechanism of motor control which seeks endpoints, rather than one which monitors feedback or sends a series of timed instructions to different muscle groups.

An important aspect of the mass-spring model which separates it from other conceptualizations of motor control is that the control program does not contain the time at which successive muscles are activated. The correct order of activation occurs as a natural consequence of the limb system as a whole moving from its initial to its final position. In support of this prediction Newell & Zelaznik (1980) have shown that transfer performance in a task where the subject is trained on one movement and then learns another is not related to the similarity of the pretransfer/posttransfer movement times. Rather, what appears to be learned in the pretransfer phase is some property of the movement which controls its velocity. Schmidt (1980) has also demonstrated that subjects in a movement production task do not appear to learn the duration of the learned movements.

Despite the evidence consistent with the mass-spring model, the undoubted presence of feedback information in the nervous system during normal movement, and the fact that much of it appears to be in a form which *could* be used for movement control (see Miles & Evarts 1979 for a review), makes it hard to believe that the mass-spring model is the whole story. Bizzi (1980) discusses some of the roles for proprioceptive feedback within a mass-spring framework of movement control.

Schmidt (Schmidt et al 1978, 1979) had considerable success with the suggestion that the terminal accuracy of a movement (at least for movements too quick to be under visual control) is determined by the variability in the force which is required to initiate it. The classical Fitts relation that movement time is proportional to the ratio of movement amplitude to target width follows from this when it is coupled with the demonstration that the variability in force is proportional to the magnitude of the force. This theory makes the somewhat counter intuitive prediction (a prediction borne out empirically, Schmidt et al 1979) that the accuracy of a movement will be independent of the mass being moved. The point is that although a large mass requires a larger force to move it, which gives rise to greater movement variability, this variability acts on a larger mass which resists its effects, with the net result on movement accuracy being zero.

Using Schmidt's framework for analysis, Annett et al (1979) have studied the reduced accuracy of aiming movements with the nonpreferred hand. They found it due to a greater variability associated with a given initiating pulse for the nonpreferred hand rather than any intrinsic difference in information processing capacity. A hint that Schmidt's hypothesis holds in continuous skills can be seen in Viviani & Terzuolo's (1980) data on handwriting. They show that while producing letters like "a," the sharper the curve the slower the pen speed. If the writer maintained constant pen velocity, the angular acceleration and hence the force required on the pen would increase with the sharpness of the curve. The only way, according to Schmidt, for the writer to maintain constant accuracy would be to slow down around the curves.

Rosenbaum (1980) has used a cuing technique to study the way that motor programs are assembled. His subjects executed a movement with three dimensions of uncertainty. The movement might be with either hand, either forwards or backwards, and either near or far. He cued the subjects about the value on some dimensions and measured the reaction time when the movement signal resolved the uncertainty on the others. He concluded that arm, direction, and extent information tended to be specified serially, but not in a fixed order, and that it took longest to specify arm, then direction, and that least time was required to specify extent.

Problem Solving

Most of the studies described in this chapter have involved the presentation of a relatively simple stimulus to the subject who identifies it and then selects and executes an appropriate response—a fairly straightforward flow of information from stimulus to response is assumed to underlie the action. In studies of problem solving, in contrast, no simple linear flow is assumed. The subject is presented with information which may require testing and rejecting of potential solutions or storage of partial solutions before a response can be emitted. In general, analyses of problem solving have been more concerned with the strategies involved in controlling the flow of information than in finding out about how the structures used by these strategies work. Studies of problem solving concerned with the "higher" level of control strategy have been reviewed recently by Simon (1979). However, there have been studies in which the object has been to understand the properties of strategies at a microlevel.

Hitch (1978) used mental arithmetic as a vehicle for studying the origin of the loss of information from short-term memory storage. He presented subjects with a series of tasks which typically were to add two 3-digit numbers in her head and then write down the answer. Hitch's conceptualization of the flow of information involved three states: 1. a long-term store which contains a library of strategies such as "compute units first, then tens, then hundreds" and a collection of number facts such as $2 + 5 = 7$; 2. a working store for the temporary registration of information about the particular problem in hand, e.g. "the current stimuli are 345 and 142" and "answer so far is—7"; 3. an executive processor which selects the appropriate facts from long-term storage to transform the current contents of working storage into their required form. Hitch varied the length of time that an item had to be held in working storage and the number of operations between presentation of an item and production of its transformed value by controlling the order in which the calculations were performed (e.g. hundreds first or units first) and the order in which the computed results could be output. He also varied the number of items which had to be held in working storage by allowing different parts of the problem to be written down. Hitch fitted the error data to two models of working storage information loss. One represented the loss of items as due to decay over time; the other attributed forgetting to retrieval difficulty, independent of the length of time an item had spent in store. He demonstrated that the bulk of the error data and the effects of the experimental variables could be represented best by the model which has the decay of items over time as the main source of information loss in working storage.

Chase and his colleagues have demonstrated that the difference between the expert problem solver and the person with more ordinary skills does not lie in any fundamental difference in the elementary operations which they perform while solving problems. For an expert chess player (Chase & Simon 1973) it is the organization of information about chess positions held in long-term memory which separates the master from the amateur. For a mental calculation expert who can square 5-digit numbers in his head (Chase & Ericsson 1980), the difference between him and you or us is a system for storing and retrieving the results of partial calculation en route to the complete solution coupled to an ingenious algorith for reducing the complexity of the calculation. Ericsson, Chase & Fallon (1980) make the same point in a study of a student who, after training an hour a day for 18 months, had increased his memory span for digits from 7 to 79. The authors claim that underlying this phenomenal performance, apparently comparable to that of such famous mnemonists as Luria's patient S or Professor Aitken, there was still a short-term working memory store with a capacity of 4 items which had not been affected by practice. The other 75 items were held in a complex hierarchical mnemonic structure of subunits in long-term memory, each of which held 3 or 4 items. The key unit at the bottom level of the hierarchy was a 4 or 3-digit string usually associated with the time for running an athletic race. (The subject was a keen runner with a large number of categories of times for races from half mile to marathon.) Thus, for example, the string 3492 would be stored as "3 min 49.2 sec—nearly a world record for the mile." This was supplemented by 3 and 4-digit strings corresponding to ages (893-"89.3-a very old man") and dates (1944-"nearly the end of World War II"). The mnemonic system for digits would not generalize to other materials, of course, and his span for consonants remained 6. The study leaves a number of intriguing unanswered questions about the way the mnemonic system works. Why does "nearly the world record" retrieve 3492 rather than 3501?

Summary

We have identified several efforts to provide methods for isolating and studying elementary mental operations. These methods have been applied to four areas of research in which many studies have been conducted within the general information processing framework. Although it is difficult to summarize this work in brief form, it is our general conclusion that in the areas of language, imagery, and motor control, enough has been learned to support the idea that they represent three cognitive systems with probably unique sets of structures, but that the task of isolating such structures can be approached with a common set of tools.

THE COORDINATION OF ELEMENTARY MENTAL OPERATIONS

This is the section which might have contained a summary of exciting advances in our understanding of the control structure which assembles and coordinates elementary operations required for the performance of a task. However, although a number of authors have made general proposals which involve the concept of a control structure or executive which is separate from the operations they control, they have mostly been put forward on theoretical grounds with little direct experimental demonstration of their role (Broadbent 1977, McLeod 1977). Most of the experimental investigation of the coordination of independent elementary mental operations has been involved with two questions, both rather simpler than the nature of the control structure. The first question is what is the form of the performance impairment when elementary operations compete for a common resource, and how does this impairment change with practice? The second is a general question about the architecture of the nervous system—do all tasks compete for a common resource?

Competition for a Common Resource

The origin of interference between simultaneosly presented stimuli has been investigated by Duncan (1980) with the task of perceiving digits from a visual array of letters and digits. He has two findings: 1. the perception of a target (i.e. a digit) is little affected by the number of simultaneously presented nontargets; 2. the perception of one target greatly inhibits the perception of a second. These results complement those of Shiffrin & Schneider (1977), who showed that perception of between one and four target items during visual search for letters was more or less independent of the number items in the target set, provided that during practice the memory and distractor items were kept as mutually exclusive sets. (The development of this effect with practice has also been demonstrated by Rabbitt, Cumming and Vyas 1979.) Similar results were found in an auditory analog of Duncan's task by Ostry, Moray & Marks (1976). In this study, simultaneous pairs of different items were presented to the two ears with either item being a digit or a letter. It was found that the identification of a target (a digit) was unaffected if the item on the other ear was a nontarget but was seriously affected by the simultaneous presentation of another target.

To explain these results Duncan proposed that identification of all items up to the level of meaning proceeds in parallel (because several nontargets can be rejected as easily as one) but that items can only be transferred from this identification stage to a stage when they are available for awareness in a strictly limited fashion (because the perception of one target inhibits the perception of a second). This is a modern version of the theories of late perceptual selection proposed by Deutsch and Deutsch in the 1960s. It is supported (as opposed to early perceptual selection theories in which the meaning of unattended items is not available) by many studies showing that the meaning of the word on the unattended ear in shadowing tasks has some effect on the perception of the attended word. These results have been interpreted as showing that the meaning or semantic class of an unattended word may be available even if the word itself does not reach awareness. The separation of the availability of the meaning of an item and the item itself has been demonstrated in studies of semantic priming which are reported earlier. The idea that identity and category information about letters and digits is extracted simultaneously and independently has been proposed by Taylor (1978). He suggests that subjects can direct their attention to a single category area (e.g. digits), and thus their report of an event in that category will be independent of the number of nontargets. It might also follow from this that identification of how many targets occurred would be much harder than identifying that at least one target had occurred, just as Duncan found.

A different sort of attentional limitation has been suggested by Treisman and her coworkers in a series of experiments on the integration of visual features (Treisman & Gelade 1980). It is generally agreed that the different features which make up the visual world are extracted independently and represented in a series of separate structural "maps" giving the spatial distribution of different features on the retina (see Cowey 1979 for a review of the evidence). Treisman has demonstrated that when a target can be identified on the basis of a single feature (e.g. a green object in a field of brown objects, or a circular object in a field of objects composed of straight line segments), then perception of a target proceeds across the whole visual field simultaneously. However, if a target is only defined by the conjunction of features from separate maps (e.g. a green O in a field of brown Os and green Xs), then an operation which performs the conjunction scans serially through each item in the field looking for a target. Treisman supports the notion that the registration of features is a separate process from their conjunction by demonstrating conditions under which subjects can be persuaded to report false conjunctions of features which were present in the visual array, but not in the same object.

Unfortunately, it seems rather difficult to reconcile these results with those mentioned earlier by Duncan, Shiffrin and Schneider, and Ostry, Moray and Marks. Given the sets which they used (letters and digits), it seems clear that no single feature separates targets and nontargets—only conjunctions of features could be used as the basis of discrimination. And yet they all found evidence for parallel processing of targets and nontargets of the sort Treisman's theory would rule out. Indeed, Duncan performed an experiment explicitly to test Treisman's theory by using targets which were composed of a conjunction of nontarget features (e.g. 5 in a background of E & S). He found no difference from performance when there was no special relationship between target and nontarget features. Treisman has addressed the awkward question of why words on the unattended channel in a shadowing task can influence the interpretation of the attended word. One would assume that words could only be defined as a conjunction of features and therefore, according to Treisman, the system should have difficulty indentifying two words simultaneously. She points to the fact that the hit rate for unattended words is usually low and the false alarm rate for words sounding similar to target words is high. This suggests an incomplete analysis of the unattended word, just as Treisman's theory would predict.

Multiple Sources of Processing Capacity

A number of information processing models have been presented which propose that multiple sources of processing capacity exist to deal with different sorts of tasks. Before outlining these we will describe some recent experiments demonstrating a wide range of conditions under which interference in simultaneous task performance can be switched in and out by experimental manipulation. Demonstrations such as these have suggested that some modification was required to traditional models of information processing involving a single common structure or resource for all tasks.

1. Aldridge (1978) investigated why the retention of verbal material was interfered with by speech tasks but not by nonverbal tasks (such as detection of tones at threshold), even when the nonspeech task appeared to be harder either subjectively or in terms of performance. Having eliminated task difficulty and similarity of material as determinants of interference, he established that the key factor is whether the interfering task required phonetic manipulation. If it does, there will be interference with memorized verbal material; if it doesn't, there is little evidence of such interference. However, two aspects of this study must be borne in mind before acceptance of the idea that interference results only when the tasks involve elements that require the same specialized processor. First, Reitman (1974) has

shown evidence of interference in a similar task even when the interpolated condition involved no phonetic processing. Second, the two tasks are not really fully concurrent since one is studying the presumed rehearsal of one task while the second is being performed. The use of a memory load as one of two dual tasks may be a rather special situation.

2. Moscovitch & Klein (1980) presented subjects with a visual array of three items which might be any combination of words, shapes, and faces. On the basis of previous research, they assumed that the faces and shapes were processed primarily in the right hemisphere, while the words were handled by the left. The major determinant of recognition for a given item was whether the other items in the array were handled by the same hemisphere or the opposite. Perception was worse when both items were handled by the same hemisphere than when items were handled by separate hemispheres.

3. Wickens & Kessel (1980) had four groups of subjects perform the four pairwise combinations of (as primary task) either a tracking task or watching an autopilot control the same task, with (as secondary task) either another tracking task or a running memory task in which a string of digits was occasionally stopped and the subject required to give the last digit but one. The main task for a subject was to identify step changes in the dynamics of the control system used in the primary task. In each case the secondary task only interfered with the conceptually similar primary task. The secondary tracking task interfered with the primary tracking task but not with monitoring the autopilot performing the tracking task, while the running memory task interfered with monitoring for a system change in the primary task, but not with controlling the system.

The common element of these three very different experiments is that a major source of dual task interference was not in any absolute property of either of the tasks but in the demand for specific structures or operations common to both tasks—when the tasks are altered to remove structural overlap much of the interference goes away.

This idea has been formalized in a number of theories of multiple task performance. Kinsbourne & Hicks (1978) have proposed that different cerebral locations are in some neuronal sense linked, with functionally more similar areas being more closely linked than functionally dissimilar. Thus in performance of independent simultaneous tasks, noise cross-talk, and hence performance decrement, is determined by functional separation. Navon & Gopher (1979) have discussed how the existence of multiple resources would affect the interpretation of the Performance Operating Characteristics proposed by Norman & Bobrow (1975). These were originally interpreted with the underlying assumption of a single resource for all tasks.

A link between the approaches to attention discussed in these two sections is provided by Logan (1979). His subjects performed a choice reaction time task varying from 2 to 8 choices combined with a memory load of 8 items. Logan found that after 6 days of practice there was no interaction between the two tasks. Although performance of the choice reaction task was worse when the subject had a memory load, the performance decrement was the same for 2-choice, 4-choice and 8-choice. Using the logic of additive factors methodology, this implies that the two tasks fail to make demands on any common structures. Logan's view, echoing that of Shiffrin and Schneider, is that attention is required to assemble the structures required for the task, but not for their execution. With practice, the assembly demand for the 8-choice task is no greater than that for the 2-choice, hence the lack of interaction between the tasks.

These studies suggest the importance of specialized processors in determining the degree of interference between tasks. In some sense they conflict both with the unified processing ideas that underlie the distinction between automatic and attended processes and the viewpoint that detection is a sufficient basis for producing interference with other events however different they are. It seems that the idea of a single unified attention system receives its best support from experiments in which concurrent tasks are performed where the arrival of stimuli is sudden, discrete, or brief. Evidence for specialized processor is strongest when one of the dual tasks involves a stimulus stream which is more or less continuous [e.g. reading (Hirst et al 1980); typing (Shaffer 1975); piano playing (Allport, Antonis & Reynolds 1972)]. These observations suggest that the system may be seen as a hierarchy of processors that become increasingly abstract. Systems at the top of the hierarchy may perform operations on a broad range of signals and tasks, and once occupied may be refractory to other signals. But signals not selected for this system may still be analysed by other more specialized systems (Broadbent 1977).

INDIVIDUAL AND DEVELOPMENTAL DIFFERENCES IN MENTAL OPERATIONS

While information processing models had their origin in the study of the common performance of normal adult humans, they have by now been applied in many other areas. These applications have the advantages of providing insights into new areas, but can also provide tests of generality of putative elements. We review briefly three areas of particular interest: infancy, individual differences in cognition, and personality traits.

Infancy

During the period under review there have been active efforts to develop analyses of the initial stage of language processing and spatial vision in infancy. Excellent reviews of the field have been published in a special issue of the *Canadian Journal of Psychology* (Muir 1979). Some of the observations make important contact with adult theory and models. For example, Miller & Eimas (1979) review the ability of infants to make complex linguistic discriminations. It appears that at least some of these discriminations do not, as once thought, represent unique aspects of language processing, but reflect more general auditory structures (Trehub 1979). It remains to be learned how these general auditory structures are modified into systems that allow the fluent perception of speech in adults.

Haith (1980) reviews the spatial characteristics of the visual scanning behavior of newborn infants. The first few months bring a rapid shift from control by inborn scan patterns and relatively simple physical characteristics of stimuli to complex information processing. Cohen & Gelber (1975) have shown that up to 4 months infants habituated to a compound pattern show strong habituation of the familiar attributes even when in novel compounds. Cohen argues that by 5 months the compound is treated as a whole. These experiments taken with those cited earlier (Treisman & Gelade 1980) suggest that attributes, not objects, are primary elements both in development and in the sequence of processing stages. Strauss (1979) habituated 10-month-old infants to a set of face stimuli and showed strong transfer to a prototype face that had never been seen before. Bornstein (1981) argues generally for the important role of such prototypes in the control of early visual development.

Much of the work with infants is based upon some version of habituation of looking or listening behavior following repeated trials. Habituation is usually defined as the waning of responsivity to stimuli upon repeated presentation. There has been relatively little attention to what internal mechanisms are being adapted. The adult literature provides abundant evidence that the study of habituation is complex and involves a number of internal mechanisms, each of which may undergo habituation at very different rates and under different input conditions. One effort to apply an information processing analysis to child habituation has been pursued by Kraut (1978). These studies distinguish between a pathway activation effect specific to a given stimulus and a general change of state called alerting that would affect all stimuli. The idea is that repeated presentation of a stimulus habituates its alerting capability, but does not habituate specific internal codes representing the stimulus. Kraut (1978) used 6-year-old children as subjects. He found that familiarization of one of the two stimuli used in the choice reaction time task increased its reaction time. Kraut reasoned that this might be due to habituation of alerting response to the familiarized stimulus. In accord with this notion, he found that when the habituated stimulus was used as a warning signal it produced poor performance on an imperative signal. However, when a nonhabituated warning signal was used, the response to the familiarized or habituated signal was actually superior to that of the nonhabituated signal. These results suggest that the habituation effects are upon a general state of alerting rather than on specific pathways. Some efforts to carry forward the logic of this analysis have been presented in more detail (Posner & Rothbart 1981).

Individual Differences

If the elementary operations used in simple laboratory tasks such as memory search, choice reaction time, or letter matching are also involved in more complex cognitive processes (and if they aren't, much of cognitive psychology based on laboratory experimental paradigms seem rather pointless), then individual differences in the speed and effectiveness of elementary mental operations should be reflected in individual differences in more complex tasks. This assumption underlies an area of research which started with Hunt, Frost & Lunneborg's (1973) demonstration that differences in the time required to make a physical or name match correlated with scores on scholastic aptitude measures of verbal ability. The two main aims of this area of research have been to identify the elementary operations used in complex tasks such as reading or reasoning by correlating individual differences in elementary and complex tasks, and to find information processing concepts which relate to general intelligence. Sufficient progress has been made that some psychometricians, Carroll (1980) and Jensen (1980) for example, see the time approaching when conventional intelligence tests may be largely replaced by the measurement of reaction time in a number of simple laboratory tasks.

The first of these approaches is exemplified by the work of Hunt, Davidson & Lansman (1981). They demonstrated that reaction time on a range of laboratory tasks which required access to semantic or lexical memory via either words or pictures correlated with tests of verbal comprehension skills. The tasks involved deciding whether (*a*) a picture or a word belonged to a given semantic category; (*b*) two words were in the same semantic category; (*c*) two words in different case had the same name. They found that performances on the semantic classification tasks correlated at about –.3 with reading comprehension, although not with vocabulary or reading speed. Hunt et al (1981) concluded, for two reasons, that a single factor—speed of access to long-term memory—was underlying performance in all these tasks and was the basis of the correlation with reading comprehension.

First, performance on the semantic verification task was exactly the same for pictures and for words. Second, a principal components factor analysis of the four tasks (word and picture versions of the semantic classification, semantic verification and word-name matching) provided a single factor accounting for 75% of the common variance. (Subjects also performed a choice reaction task. After removing the partial correlation of the tasks with choice reaction time, the main effects were practically unchanged, indicating that the key single factor determining performance was not speed of reaction.) However, if Hunt et al are correct that the important factor in these tasks is speed of long-term memory access, it is difficult to see why reading speed does not correlate with the tasks.

Clearly, there is more to verbal skill than speed of retrieving information from long-term memory. Hunt et al also included a picture-sentence verification task (e.g. star is above cross: $\overset{+}{*}$)—a task which is presumably less dependent on long-term memory for an understanding of the words, as the total vocabulary used in the experiment was a permutation of possible combinations of six words. They found that this task accounted for variance not accounted for by the semantic task—a multiple correlation of .46 was found between the semantic matching, sentence picture comprehension, and performance on the reading comprehension task.

The second approach is exemplified by Jensen's attempt to relate reaction time to general intelligence (Jensen 1980). Jensen has collected reactions times from groups ranging from bright university students to the severely retarded. He found that for any two groups reliably differing in IQ, the higher IQ group had the faster reaction time. Also, within each group there was a correlation between IQ and RT, although it is usually fairly low, around –.3. With a Hick's Law experiment (i.e. varying the number of choices from 1–8 in a choice reaction experiment) Jensen found that both the slope and the intercept of the function relating reaction time to number of choices correlated with IQ. He also found that the variability of an individual subject's reaction times at a given choice level correlated with IQ. He noted that retardates and normals produced very different distributions of reaction times. The retardate's distribution is much more skewed than the normal, and no reaction times produced by the retarded subjects (IQ typically around 70) are as fast as the fastest reaction times produced by normal subjects. Taking small samples of reaction times (15 trials), he finds that all responses produced by a group with IQ 70 are slower than any responses produced by a group with IQ 120. Jensen believes that the processes involved in simple reaction time experiments are so elementary that the correlation between IQ and reaction time variables indicates that at least part of the difference between the intelligence of individuals is due to simple differences at a neuronal level. He suggests that a small difference in information processing speed, multiplied by years of interaction with learning experiences, could result in substantial differences in acquired knowledge and intellectual skills.

There are many problems in linking relatively small correlations in reaction time to such sweeping abilities as verbal general intelligence. For example, differences in motivation could account for reaction time through changing the relative preference for speed and accuracy. Rabbitt (1981) has demonstrated that following an error in a choice reaction time task, subjects reset their criterion for responding to a more conservative level. The criterion level is then gradually lowered, allowing faster responses, until another error occurs. By this process the subject hunts for an acceptable trade-off between speed and accuracy. Thus, slow responses can be as much the result of an actively conservative strategy or an inappropriately conservative strategy (e.g. large changes in criterion following an error, or slow reduction of criterion following correct responses) as the result of inherently slow processing of information. It is known that older subjects are slow in part because they tend to emphasize accuracy. Thus, it would be wrong to conclude that RT data even in simple tasks necessarily get around the complex differences in the background and assumptions of the subjects which have plagued the interpretation of intelligence tests.

Personality

The study of traits as enduring mental sets fits well with the approach of elementary mental operations (Diagram 1), but there has been difficulty in obtaining adequate stability across tasks. Perhaps this arises in part because of the difficulty of separating more enduring operations (e.g. traits and structures) from changes of strategy and state. Some idea of the complexity of these relationships is apparent in a recent attempt to link theories of personality differences to information processing concepts by Humphreys et al (1980). This started from the observation of an interaction between time of day, the effect of caffeine, and impulsiveness on a test involving sentence completion, analogy formation, and the generation of antonyms (Revelle et al 1980). (Impulsiveness is one of the subscales which make up the personality dimension of introversion/extraversion, the other being sociability). Low impulsives performed worse in the morning after taking caffeine while high impulsives performed better after taking it. In the early evening the position was reversed—caffeine improved the performance of low impulsives while making the performance of high impulsives worse. Revelle et al attempted to explain this interaction by assuming that low and high impulsives reach their peak of arousal at different times of day, and by assuming that the relationship between performance and arousal took the form of an inverted U.

These assumptions came under criticism from Eysenck & Folkard (1980) on a number of grounds, one being that there is no simple relation between performance and arousal. Tasks involving little temporary storage of information and those involving the active use of short-term storage appear to respond in different ways to factors which might be expected to increase arousal. Thus, as body temperature increases during the day (usually taken as an index of arousal), tasks involving immediate processing tend to improve while performance on short-term memory tasks gets worse. In response to this criticism, Humphreys et al proposed a model in which personality traits (anxiety and impulsiveness) interact with situational mediators (time of day and caffeine) to inhibit or excite activational states (arousal and effort), which in turn act either to improve or inhibit the function of information processing constructs such as attention and short-term memory. With such a model they can at least get a qualitative description of the interactions in their own data. Of potential interest is the observation that with such a model the inverted U relation between performance and arousal emerges from a monotonic excitatory effect of arousal on one process which affects performance (attention) coupled to a monotonic inhibitory effect on another process (short-term memory). It seems possible that this approach might build a bridge between information processing theories and personality theories if it is successfully extended to tasks in which the elementary information processing operations are more clearly defined than they were in Revelle et al's study.

NEURAL BASIS OF MENTAL OPERATIONS

During the period under review, links between neuroscience and cognitive psychology have begun to develop. This should not be taken as an indication that cognitive psychology now or ever will be reduced to synaptic interactions or the activity of neural transmitter systems. What is called for is neither reduction of psychological phenomenon to physiological actions nor absorption of physiology into semantic networks, but a constructive interaction between two fields whose major focus is rather different.

Consider the fruitful contact that is taking place in the area of motor control as an example. As was discussed earlier, psychological studies of performance have benefited greatly from contact with ideas arising from the mass-spring model (Bizzi et al 1978). Important tests of this model have been conducted with humans (Kelso 1979), and they have been applied to illuminate complex human performance in tasks like handwriting (Hollerbach 1978, Wing 1978). In turn, ideas about voluntary control and divided attention from cognitive psychology have begun to make their way into the physiological study of reflex behavior (Miles & Evarts 1979). These links are likely to be aided by an important synthesis of this literature (Gallistel 1980).

Models

In the last several years, elementary mental operations in cognitive tasks have been modeled in ways that allow simple neural circuits to perform them (Szengothai & Arbib 1975). The development of these models has been fostered by papers on associative memory systems (Anderson 1977; Anderson et al 1977). In general, the models have employed concepts of lateral inhibition, inhibitory and excitatory contacts between adjacent elements of letters and words, and other ideas that are explicitly based on neuronal properties (McClelland & Rumelhart 1981). Just at the time when elementary mental operations in tasks like reading seem to be coming into contact with simple ideas of interactions among neurons there has been an explosion in the data on the complexity of synaptic connections. For example, Bloom (1978) argues that the locus coeruleus interacts to amplify both excitatory and inhibitory influences on cells to which it connects. It would be a pity if now that the complexity of synaptic interactions is increasing, cognitive psychologists are overconstrained by too simple a model of how neurons might interact.

Methods

Perhaps more relevant for the empirical goal of studying the neural substrate of mental operations are the new techniques that have become available. During the last few years clinical neurology has been greatly aided by the presence of computerized tomography as a method of examination of lesions. (Oldendorf 1978, Osborne 1979). In this technique, X rays are made from a number of different angles and used to reconstruct sectional images by computer. The spatial representation of the cortex thus achieved allows accurate location of lesions (Swets et al 1979).

Radioactive tracer methods of measuring cerebral blood flow or metabolic activity provide more dynamic methods of tracing cerebral activity during sustained cognitive tasks (Lassen, Ingvar & Skinhøj 1978). One method involves the use of a radioactive xenon source, the concentration of which is measured during sustained activity. For example, increased rates of blood flow have been measured during silent reading and other cognitive tasks. The potential of this method for articulating the spatial location of brain areas during cognitive activity is obvious and is already beginning to be exploited (Risberg 1980).

Another approach to the study of brain activity during cognition involves the use of positron emission tomography (Raichle 1979). A glucose molecule is labeled with a radioactive tracer. Distribution of the labeled substance is monitored by annihilation radiation generated when positrons are absorbed. This method can be used to measure blood flow, or with certain limiting assumptions, it also has the potential of examining dynamically the metabolism in different areas of the brain.

While new methods have become available for spatial imaging of the brain, there has also been increased use of electrical recording techniques to study the fine temporal structure of mental activity. For example, developments have taken place in our understanding of the function of the parietal lobe in its relationship to motor control and central attentional mechanisms (Lynch 1980, Mountcastle 1978, Wurtz et al 1980, Posner 1980).

An impressive result is that the time relationships obtained from these physiological studies have converged with cognitive studies. For example, Goldberg & Wurtz (1972) have shown that cells in the superior colliculus whose receptive fields are targets for an eye movement show increased activity about 200 msec prior to the beginning of the eye movement. Posner (1980) reviewed studies showing improvement of target detection in the neighborhood of the target 200 msec prior to moving the eye (Posner 1980, Remington 1980).

Chronometric studies of event-related potentials have also been applied both to the separation of stimulus analysis and response generation (Kutas, McCarthy & Donchin 1977, Ritter et al 1979) and to problems of language (Kutas & Hilyard 1980). These methods have provided converging operations for more standard techniques described previously and also give some idea of the possible localization of the operations. Changes in the cortical evoked potentials induced by an instruction to attend to a simple sensory cue began about 90 msec after input, while semantic target effects occur at 300-400 msec after input. These time values fit with inferences one would make from early and late selection models developed by Broadbent (1971).

It is too early to say how detailed the convergence of these chronometric analyses by cognitive and physiological techniques will be; the results to date only suggest that the two have a roughly similar time scale.

Brain Injury

A combination of spatial and temporal methods should expand our capability of exploring the physical basis of cognition. One of the incentives for so doing is that the confidence of investigators developing information processing models of cognition has been increased by the ability to establish links between independent elements and dissociations produced by brain injury. Although arguing from deficits can certainly be questioned (Wood 1980), there can be no doubt that, for example, the split brain syndrome has increased confidence in the experimental evidence for independence of the structures underlying physical and phonological codes of language stimuli. Similarly, experiments showing that subjects with occipital lesions can orient to stimuli (with their eyes) that they are unable to bring to consciousness (see Weiskrantz 1980) gives concrete evidence of dissociations between covert orienting and detection that is also found by cognitive experiments (Posner 1980). Results in the study of deep dyslexia (Coltheart et al 1980) have shown that patients demonstrate a knowledge of the meaning of a word that they cannot name. This view has helped support the idea of different roots to the meaning of lexical items. One view of deep dyslexia suggest that the patient has available information from semantic memory about a visual word but does not have available the more peripheral visual and phonological codes that would normally be available. What is most striking is how well this fits with the idea of spreading activation within a complex semantic network. The inaccuracy of the semantic memory system in pinpointing a specific item would predict that patients would produce semantic associations rather than the word actually presented, as indeed they do.

The relationship between neurological and cognitive explanations of intelligence has been summarized by Simon (1969, p. 49). "As our knowledge increases, the relations between psysiological and information processing explanations will become just like the relation between quantum mechanical and physiological explanations in biology—they constitute two linked levels of explanation."

CONCLUSIONS

There seem to be two major approaches to the development of information processing models in psychology. They represent the traditional values of synthesis and analysis. The first involves the synthesis of models usually with the aid of computer simulations. The second involves the development of simple experimental model systems of what appear to be elementary mental operations that produce the performance to be described. These two approaches should not be seem as opposed but as complementary. Simon's discussion of the sciences of the artificial has placed cognitive psychology at the boundary between natural and artificial science. It is at once a natural science constrained by the nature of the human brain and its evolutionary process and an artificial science because people are changed through learning. Information processing models look inward to the neurosciences and outward to the complex environments in which humans find themselves. For this reason, it is not an easy field to survey, nor could we have done justice to the many approaches that have applied information processing models to development, personality, social, industrial, organizational, and other areas of psychology. There is no doubt, however, that the efforts remain both exciting and at the core of the psychological enterprise.

Literature Cited

Aldridge, J. W. 1978. Levels of processing in speech perception. *J. Exp. Psychol.: Hum. Percept. Perform.* 4:104–77

Allport, D. A., Antonis, B., Reynolds, P. 1972. On the division of attention: a disproof of the single channel hypothesis. *Q. J. Exp. Psychol.* 24:225–35

Anderson, J. A. 1977. Neural models with cognitive implications. In *Basic Processing in Reading: Perception and Comprehension,* ed. D. LaBerge, S. J. Samuels. Hillsdale, NJ: Erlbaum

Anderson, J. A., Silverstein, J. W., Ritz, S. A., Jones, R. S. 1977. Distinctive features, categorical perception and probability learning: some applications of a neural model. *Psychol. Rev.* 84:413–51

Anderson, J. R. 1978. Arguments concerning representations for mental imagery. *Psychol. Rev.* 85:249–77

Anderson, J. R. 1980. *Cognitive Psychology and its Implications.* San Francisco: Freeman

Annett, J., Annett, M., Hudson, P. T. W., Turner, A. 1979. The control of movement in the preferred and non-preferred hands. *Q. J. Exp. Psychol.* 31:641–52

Antos, S. J. 1979. Processing facilitation in a lexical decision talk. *J. Exp. Psychol.: Hum. Percept. Perform.* 5:527–41

Ball, K., Sekuler, R. 1980. Models of stimulus uncertainty in motion perception. *Psychol. Rev.* 87:535–69

Bashinski, H. S., Bachrach, V. R. 1980. Enhancement of perceptual sensitivity as the result of selectively attending to spatial locations. *Percept. Psychophys.* 28:241–48

Becker, C. A. 1980. Semantic context effects in visual word recognition: an analysis of semantic strategies. *Mem. Cognit.* 6:493–512

Bem, D. J., Allen, A. 1978. On predicting some of the people some of the time: the search for cross-situational consistencies in behavior. *Psychol. Rev.* 85: 485–501

Bizzi, E. 1980. Central and peripheral mechanisms in motor control. See Stelmach & Requin 1980, pp. 131–42

Bizzi, E., Dev, P., Morasso, P., Polit, A. 1978 Effect of load disturbances during centrally initiated movements. *J. Neurophysiol.* 41:542–56

Bizzi, E., Polit, A., Morasso, P. 1976. Mechanisms underlying achievement of final head position. *J. Neurophysiol.* 39: 435–44

Bloom, F. E. 1978. Modern concepts in electrophysiology for psychiatry. In *Biochemistry of Mental Disorders,* ed. E. Usdin, A. Mandell

Bornstein, M. H. 1981. Perceptual organization near the beginning of life. *Minn. Symp. Child Psychol.* 14: In press

Bower, G. H. 1981. Mood and memory. *Am. Psychol.* 36:129–48

Britton, B. K., Holdredge, T. S., Curry, C., Westbrook, R. R. 1979. Use of cognitive capacity in reading: identical texts with different amounts of discourse level meaning. *J. Exp. Psychol.: Hum. Learn. Mem.* 5:262–70

Broadbent, D. E. 1971. *Decision and Stress.* New York: Academic

Broadbent, D. E. 1977. Levels, hierarchies, and the locus of control. *Q. J. Exp. Psychol.* 29:181–201

Bruder, G. A. 1978. Role of visual familiarity in the word superiority effects obtained in the simultaneous matching task. *J. Exp. Psychol.: Hum. Percept. Perform.* 4:88–100

Bruner, J., Oliver, R., Greenfield, P. 1966. *Studies in Growth.* New York: Wiley

Carr, T. H., Pollatsek, A., Posner, M. I. 1981. What does the visual system know about words? *Percept. Psychophys.* 2:183–90

Carr, T. H., Posner, M. I., Pollatsek, A., Snyder, C. R. R. 1979. Orthography and familiarity effects in word processing. *J. Exp. Psychol.: General* 108:389–414

Carroll, J. B. 1980. *Individual difference relations in psychometric and cognitive tasks.* Rep. 163, L. L. Thurstone Psychometric Lab., Univ. North Carolina, Chapel Hill

Chase, W. G. 1978. Elementary information processes. In *Handbook of Learning and Cognitive Processes,* ed. W. K. Estes, 5:19–90. Hillsdale NJ: Erlbaum

Chase, W. G., Ericsson, K. A. 1980. *The squaring algorithm of a mental calculation expert.* Presented at 21st Psychon. Soc. Meet., St. Louis

Chase, W. G., Simon, H. A. 1973. The mind's eye in chess. In *Visual Information Pro-*

cessing. ed. W. Chase, pp. 215–81 New York: Academic

Cohen, L. B., Gelber, E. R. 1975. Infant visual memory. In *Infant Perception from Sensation to Cognition,* ed. L. B. Cohen, P. Salapatek, pp. 347–404. New York: Academic

Cole, R. A., ed. 1980. *Perception and Production of Fluent Speech.* Hillsdale, NJ: Erlbaum

Cole, R. A., Jakimik, J. 1980. A model of speech perception. See Cole 1980, pp. 133–63

Coltheart, M., Patterson, K., Marshall, J. C. 1980. *Deep Dyslexia.* London: Routledge & Kegan Paul

Cowey, A. 1979. Cortical maps and visual perception. The Grindley memorial lecture. *Q. J. Exp. Psychol.* 31:1–31

Davidson, B. J. 1978. *Coding processes during reading.* PhD thesis. Univ. Oregon, Eugene

Diehl, D. L. 1981. Feature detectors for speech. *Psychol. Bull.* 89:1–18

Donders, F. C. 1969. On the speed of mental processes. Trans. in *Acta Psychol.* 30:412–31 (originally published 1868)

Duncan, J. 1980. The locus of interference in the perception of simultaneous stimuli. *Psychol. Rev.* 87:272–300

Ericsson, K. A., Chase, W. G., Fallon, S. 1980. Acquisition of a memory skill. *Science* 208:1181–82

Ericsson, K. A., Simon, H. A. 1980. Verbal reports as data. *Psychol. Rev.* 87:215–52

Eysenck, M. W., Folkard, S. 1980. Personality, time of day, and caffine: Some theoretical and conceptual problems in Reveue et al *J. Exp. Psychol.: General* 109:32–41

Finke, R. A. 1980. Levels of equivalence in imagery and perception. *Psychol. Rev.* 87:113–32

Fischler, I., Bloom, D. A. 1979. Automatic and attentional processes in the effects of sentence contexts on word recognition. *J. Verb. Learn. Verb. Behav.* 18: 1–20

Fischler, I., Goodman, G. O. 1978. Latency of associative activation in memory. *J. Exp. Psychol.: Hum. Percept. Perform.* 4:455–70

Foss, D. J., Blank, M. S. 1980. Identifying speech codes. *Cognit. Psychol.* 12:1–31

Friedman, A. 1979. Framing pictures the role of knowledge in automatized encoding and memory for gist. *J. Exp. Psychol.: General* 108:316–55

Gallistel, C. P. 1980. *The Organization of Action: A New Systhesis.* Hillsdale, NJ: Erlbaum

Garner, W. R. 1980. Functional aspects of information processing. *Attention and Performance,* ed. R. Nickerson, 8:1–26 Hillsdale, NJ: Erlbaum

Glass, A. L., Holyoak, K. J., Santa, J. L. 1979. *Cognition.* Reading, Mass: Addison-Wesley

Goldberg, M. E., Wurtz, R. H. 1972. Activity of superior colliculus in behaving monkeys. II. Effect of attention on neuronal responses. *J. Neurophysiol.* 75:560–74

Grossberg, S. 1980. How does a brain build a cognitive code. *Psychol. Rev.* 87:1–51

Haith, M. 1980. *Rules That Babies Look By.* Hillsdale, N.J: Erlbaum

Hanson, V. L. 1981. Processing of written and spoken words: evidence for common coding. *Mem. Cognit.* 9:93–100

Healy, A. F. 1976. Detection errors in the word the: evidence for reading units larger than letters. *J. Exp. Psychol.: Hum. Percept. Psychophys.* 2:235–42

Henderson, L. 1980. Is there a lexicality component in the word superiority effect? *Percept. Psychophys.* 28:179–84

Hick, W. E. 1952. On the rate of gain of information. *Q. J. Exp. Psychol.* 4: 11–26

Hintzman, D. L. 1981. Orientation in cognitive maps. *Cognit. Psychol.* 13:149–206

Hirst, W., Spelke, E., Reaves, C., Caharack, G., Neisser, U. 1980 Dividing attention without alternation or automaticity. *J. Exp. Psychol.: General* 109:98–117

Hitch, G. J. 1978. The role of short term working memory in mental arithmetic. *Cognit. Psychol.* 10:302–23

Hoffman, J. E. 1980. Interaction between global and local levels of a form. *J. Exp. Psychol.: Hum. Percept. Perform.* 6: 222–34

Hollerbach, J. M. 1978. *A study of human motor control through analysis and synthesis of handwriting.* PhD thesis. Mass. Inst. Technol., Cambridge, Mass.

Humphreys, M. S., Revelle, W., Simon, L., Gilliland, K. 1980. Individual differences in diurnal rhythms and multiple activation states: A reply to M. W. Eysenck and S. Folkard. *J. Exp. Psychol.: General* 109:42–48

Hunt, E. B., Davidson, J., Lansman, M. 1981. Individual differences in long-term memory access. *Mem. Cognit.* In press

Hunt, E. B., Frost, N., Lunneborg, C. 1973. Individual differences in cognition: A new approach to intelligence. In *The Psychology of Learning and Motivation: Advances in Research and Theory,* ed. A. Bower, Vol. 7. New York: Academic

Hyman, R. 1953. Stimulus information as a determinant of reaction time. *J. Exp. Psychol.* 45:188–96

Jensen, A. R. 1980. Chronometric analysis of intelligence. *J. Soc. Biol. Struct.* 3: 103–22

Johnston, J. C., McClelland, J. L 1981. Experimental tests of a hierarchical model of word recognition. *J. Verb. Learn. Verbal Behav.* In press

Just, M. A., Carpenter, P. A. 1980. A theory of reading: from eye fixations to comprehension. *Psychol. Rev.* 87:329–54

Keele, S. 1981. Behavioral analysis of movement. In *Handbook of Physiology: Motor Control.* In press

Kelso, J. A. S. 1977. Motor control mechanisms underlying human movement reproduction. *J. Exp. Psychol.: Hum. Percept. Perform.* 3:529–43

Kelso, J. A. S. 1979. Motor control mechanisms underlying human movement reproduction. *J. Exp. Psych.: Hum. Percept. Perform.* 5:229–38

Kelso, J. A. S., Holt, K., Kugler, P., Turvey, M. 1980. On the concept of coordinative structures as dissipative structures. 2. Empirical lines of convergence. See Stelmach & Requin 1980, pp. 49–80

Kenrick, D. T., Stringfield, D. O. 1980. Personality traits and the eye of the beholder. *Psychol. Rev.* 87:88–104

Kinchla, R. A., Wolf, J. M. 1979. The order of visual processing "top-down", bottom up or middle out. *Percept. Psychophys.* 25:225–31

Kinsbourne, M., Hicks, R. E. 1978. Functional cerebral space: a model for overflow, transfer and interference effects in human performance. *Attention and Performance,* ed. J. Requin, 8:345–62. New York: Academic

Kleiman, G. M. 1975. Speech recoding during reading. *J. Verb. Learn. Verb. Behav.* 14:323–39

Kleiman, G. M. 1980. Sentence frame contexts and lexical decision: sentence-acceptability and word relatedness effects. *Mem. Cognit.* 8:336–44

Kolers, P. A., 1975. Specificity of operations in sentence recognition. *Cognit. Psychol.* 7:289–306

Koriat, A. 1981. Semantic facilitation in lexical decision as a function of prime-target association. *Mem. Cognit.* In press

Kosslyn, S. M. 1980. *Image and Mind.* Cambridge, Mass: Harvard Univ. Press

Kosslyn, S. M. 1981. The medium and the message in mental imagery: a theory. *Psychol. Rev.* 88:46–66

Kraut, A. G. 1978. Effects of familiarization on alertness and encoding in children. *Dev. Psychol.* 12:491–96

Kutas, M., Hillyard, S. 1980. Reading senseless sentences: brain potential and semantic incongruity. *Science* 207:203–5

Kutas, M., McCarthy, G., Donchin, E. 1977. Augmenting mental chronometry: The P300 as a measure of stimulus evaluation time. *Science* 197:792–95

LaBerge, D., Samuels J. 1974. Toward a theory of automatic information processing in reading. *Cognit. Psychol.* 6: 293–323

Lachman, R., Lachman, J. L., Butterfield, E. C. 1979. *Psychology and Information Processing.* Hillsdale, NJ: Erlbaum

Lassen, N. A., Ingvar, D. H., Skinhøj, E. 1978. Brain function and blood flow. *Sci. Am.* 238:62–71

Lea, G. 1975. Chronometric analysis of the method of loci. *J. Exp. Psychol.: Hum. Percept. Perform.* 2:95–104

Locke, J. 1924. *An Essay Concerning Human Understanding,* ed. Pringle-Patterson. Oxford:Clarendon

Loftus, G. R., Mackworth, N. H. 1978. Cognitive determinants of fixation location during picture viewing. *J. Exp. Psychol.: Hum. Percept. Perform.* 4:565–72

Logan, G. D. 1979. On the use of a concurrent memory load to measure attention and automaticity. *J. Exp. Psychol.: Hum. Percept. Perform.* 5:189–207

Lynch, J. C. 1980. The functional organization of the posterior parietal cortex. *Behav. Brain Sci.* 3:485–34

Marcel, A. 1980. Conscious and preconscious recognition of polysemous words: locating selective effects of prior verbal context. *Attention and Performance,* ed. J. Requin, 8:435–58. Hillsdale, NJ: Erlbaum

Marslen-Wilson, W. D., Welsh, A. 1978. Processing interaction and lexical access during word recognition in continuous speech. *Cognit. Psychol.* 10:29–63

McClelland, J. L. 1979. On the time relations of mental processes: an examination of systems of processes in cascade. *Psychol. Rev.* 86:287–330

McClelland, J. L., Rumelhart, D. E. 1981. An interactive model of the effect of context in perception, part I. *Psychol. Rev* 88:375–407

McLeod, P. D. 1977. A dual task response modality effect: support for multiprocessor models of attention. *Q. J. Exp. Psychol.* 29:651–67

Miles, F. A., Evarts, E. V. 1979. Concepts of motor organization. *Ann. Rev. Psychol.* 30:327–62

Miller, J. L., Eimas, P. D. 1979. Organization in infant speech perception. *Can. J. Psychol.* 33:353–67
Mischel, W. 1973. Toward a cognitive social learning reconceptualization of personality. *Psychol. Rev.* 80:252–83
Morton, J., Patterson, K. 1980. A new attempt at an interpretation, or an attempt at a new interpretation. See Coltheart et al 1980
Moscovitch, M., Klein, D. 1980. Material-specific perceptual interference for visual words and faces; implications for models of capacity limitation, attention and laterality. *J. Exp. Psychol.: Hum. Percept. Perform.* 6:590–664
Mountcastle, V. B. 1978. Brain mechanisms for directed attention. *J. R. Soc. Med.* 71:14–28
Muir, W. 1979. Infant development. *Can. J. Psychol.* 33:211–412
Navon, D. 1977. Forest before trees: The precedence of global features in visual perception. *Cognit. Psychol.* 9:353–83
Navon, D., Gopher, D. 1979. On the economy of the human processing system. *Psychol. Rev.* 86:214–56
Neely, J. H. 1977. Semantic priming and retrieval from lexical memory: roles of inhibitionless spreading activation and limited capacity attention. *J. Exp. Psychol.: General* 106:226–54
Neisser, U. 1967. *Cognitive Psychology.* New York: Appleton-Century-Crofts
Neisser, U. 1976. *Cognition and Reality.* San Francisco: Freeman
Newell, A. 1973. You can't play 20 questions with nature and win. In *Visual Information Processing,* ed. W. G. Chase. New York: Academic
Newell, A., Simon, H. A. 1972. *Human Problem Solving.* Englewood Cliffs, NJ: Prentice-Hall
Newell, K. M., Zelaznik, H. N. 1980. Is time a parameter of the motor program? Presented at 21st Meet. Psychon. Soc., St. Louis
Nissen, M. J. 1979. Interactions among levels of processing. *Mem. Cognit.* 7:124–32
Norman, D. A., Bobrow, D. G. 1975. On data-limited and resource-limited processes. *Cognit. Psychol.* 7:44–64
Oldendorf, W. H. 1978. The quest for an image of the brain. *Neurology* 28:511–33
O'Regan, K. 1979. Saccade size control in reading: evidence for the linguistic control hypothesis. *Percept. Psychophys.* 25:501–9
O'Regan, K. 1980. The control of saccade size and fixation during reading: The limits of linguistic control. *Percept. Psychophys.* 28:112–17
Osborn, A. G. 1979. Computed tomography in neurological diagnosis. *Ann. Rev. Med.* 30:189–98
Ostry, D., Moray, N., Marks, G. 1976. Attention, practice and semantic targets. *J. Exp. Psychol.: Hum. Percept. Perform.* 2:326–36
Parker, R. E. 1978. Picture processing during recognition. *J. Exp. Psychol.: Hum. Percept. Perform.* 4:284–93
Pinker, S. 1980. Mental imagery and the third dimension. *J. Exp. Psychol.: General* 109:354–71
Polit, A., Bizzi, E. 1979. Characteristics of motor programs underlying arm movements in monkeys. *J. Neurophysiol.* 42:183–94
Posner, M. I. 1978. *Chronometric Explorations of Mind.* Hillsdale, NJ: Erlbaum
Posner, M. I. 1980. Orienting of attention. *Q. J. Exp. Psychol.* 32:3–25
Posner, M. I., Pea, R., Volpe, B. 1981. Cognitive neuroscience: developments toward a science of synthesis. In *Perspectives on Mental Representation,* ed. J. Mehler, E. Walker, M. Garrett. Hillsdale, NJ: Erlbaum
Posner, M. I., Rogers, M. G. K. 1977. Chronometric analysis of abstraction and recognition. In *Handbook of Learning and Cognitive Processes,* ed. W. K. Estes, 5:143–88. Hillsdale NJ: Erlbaum
Posner, M. I., Snyder, C. R. R. 1975. Attention and cognitive control. In *Information Processing and Cognition: The Loyola Symposium,* ed. R. Solso. Hillsdale, NJ: Erlbaum
Posner, M. I., Rothbart, M. K. 1981. The development of attentional mechanisms. *Nebr. Symp. Motiv.: Cognit. Processes,* ed. H. E. Howe, J. H. Flowers. Lincoln: Nebr. Univ. Press
Potter, M. C., Kroll, J. F., Harris, C. 1980. Comprehension and memory in rapid sequential reading. *Attention and Performance,* ed. R. S. Nickerson, 8:395–418. Hillsdale, NJ: Erlbaum
Poulton, E. C. 1979. Composite model for human performance in continuous noise. *Psychol. Rev.* 86(4):361–75
Pylyshyn, Z. W. 1981. The imagery debate: analogue media versus tacit knowledge. *Psychol. Rev.* 88:16–45
Rabbitt, P. M. A. 1981. *Attention and Performance,* ed. A. Baddeley, J. Long, Vol. 9
Rabbitt, P. M. A., Cumming, G., Vyas, S. 1979. Improvement, learning and retention of skills at visual search. *Q. J. Exp. Psychol.* 31:441–59
Raichle, M. E. 1979. Quantitative in vivo au-

toradiography with positron emission tomography. *Brain Res. Rev.* 1:47–68

Rayner, K. 1978. Foveal and papafoveal cues in reading. *Attention and Performance,* ed. J. Requin, 7:149–62. Hillsdale, NJ: Erlbaum

Rayner, K., McConkie, G. W., Ehrlich, S. 1978. Eye movements and integrating information across fixations. *J. Exp. Psychol.: Hum. Percept. Perform.* 4: 529–44

Rayner, K., Well, A. D., Pollatsek, A. 1980. Asymmetry of the effective visual field in reading. *Percept. Psychophys.* 27: 537–44

Reitman, J. S. 1974. Without surreptitious rehearsal, information in short-term memory decays. *J. Verb. Learn. Verb. Behav.* 13:365–77

Remington, R. W. 1980. Attention and saccadic eye movements. *J. Exp. Psychol.: Hum. Percept. Perform.* 6:726–44

Revelle, R., Humphreys, M. S., Simon, L., Gilliland, K. 1980. The interactive effects of personality, time of day, and caffeine: a test of the arousal model. *J. Exp. Psychol.: General* 109:1–31

Risberg, J. 1980. Regional blood flow measurements by 133 Xe inhalations: methodology and application in neuropsychology and psychiatry. *Brain Lang.* 9:9–37

Ritter, W., Simson, R., Vaughan, H. G., Friedman, D. 1979. A brain event related to making of a sensory discrimination. *Science* 203:1358–61

Rosenbaum, D. 1980. Human movement initiation: Specification of arm, direction and extent. *J. Exp. Psychol.: General* 109:444–76

Rothbart, M. K., Derryberry, D. 1981. Theoretical issues in temperament. In *Developmental Disabilities,* ed. M. Lewis, L. Taft, New York: SP Med. Books

Rumelhart, D. E., McClelland, J. L. 1980. *An interactive-activation model of the effect of context in perception, part II.* Presented at Cent. Hum. Inform. Process., La Jolla, Calif.

Russo, J., Rosen, L. 1975. An eye fixation analysis of multialternative choice. *Mem. Cognit.* 3:267–76

Sackett, G. P. 1978. *Observing Behavior.* Baltimore: Univ. Park Press

Sanders, A. F. 1977. Structural and functional aspects of the reaction process. *Attention and Performance,* ed. S. Dornic, 6:1–25. Hillsdale, NJ: Erlbaum

Sanders, A. F. 1980. State analyses of reaction processes. See Stelmach & Requin 1980, pp. 331–54

Sawusch, J. R., Juszyck, P. 1981. Adaptation and contrast in the perception of voicing. *J. Exp. Psychol.: Hum. Percept. Perform.* 7:408–21

Schachter, S., Singer, J. 1962. Cognitive, social and physiological determinents of the emotional state. *Psychol. Rev.* 69: 379–99

Scheer, D., ed. 1981. *Attention: Theory Brain Functions and Clinical Applications.* Hillsdale, NJ: Erlbaum. In press

Schmidt, R. 1980. On the theoretical status of time in motor program representations. See Stelmach & Requin 1980, pp. 145–66

Schmidt, R., Zelaznik, H., Frank, J. 1978. Sources of inaccuracy in rapid movement. In *Information Processing in Motor Control and Learning,* ed. G. Stelmach. New York: Academic

Schmidt, R., Zelaznik, H., Hawkins, B., Frank, J., Quinn, J. 1979. Motor output variability: a theory for the accuracy of rapid motor acts. *Psychol. Rev.* 86: 415–49

Shaffer, L. H. 1975. Multiple attention in continuous verbal tasks. In *Attention and Performance,* ed. P. Rabbitt, S. Dornic, 5:157–67. New York: Academic

Shepard, R. N. 1981. Psychophysical complementarity. In *Perceptual Organization,* ed. J. Kubovy, J. Pomerantz. Hillsdale, NJ: Erlbaum

Shepard, R. N., Podgorny, P. 1978. Cognitive processes that resemble perceptual processes. See Chase 1978, 5:189–238

Shiffrin, R. M., Schneider, W. 1977. Controlled and automatic human information processing: II, Perceptual learning, automatic attending, and a general theory. *Psychol. Rev.* 84:127–90

Shulman, G. L., Remington, R. W., McLean, J. 1979. Moving attention through visual space. *J. Exp. Psychol.: Hum. Percept. Perform.* 5:522–26

Simon, H. A. 1969. *The Science of the Artificial.* Cambridge, Mass: MIT Press

Simon, H. A. 1979. Information processing models of cognition. *Ann. Rev. Psychol.* 30:363–96

Smith, M. C. 1979. Contextual facilitation in a letter search task depends on how the prime is processed. *J. Exp. Psychol.: Hum. Percept. Perform.* 5:239–48

Stanovich, K. E., West, R. F. 1979. Mechanisms of sentence context effects in reading: automatic activation and conscious attention. *Mem. Cognit.* 7:77–85

Stanovich, K. E., West, R. F. 1981. The effect of sentence context on ongoing word recognition tests of a two process theory. *J. Exp. Psychol.: Human Percept. Perform.*

Stelmach, E., Requin, J., eds. 1980. *Tutorials in Motor Behavior.* Amsterdam: North Holland

Sternberg, S. 1969. The discovery of processing stages: Extensions of Doners method. *Acta Psychol.* 30:276–315

Stevens, A., Coupe, P. 1978. Distortion in judged spatial relations. *Cognit. Psychol.* 10:422–37

Strauss, M. S. 1979. Abstraction of prototypical information by adults and 10 month old infants. *J. Exp. Psychol.: Hum. Percept. Perform.* 6:618–32

Swets, J. A., Pickett, R. M., Whitehead, S. F., Getty, D. J., Schnur, J. A., Swets, J. B., Freeman, B. A. 1979. Assessment of diagnostic technologies. *Science* 205: 753–59

Szengothai, J., Arbib, M. A. 1975. *Conceptual Models of Neural Organization.* Cambridge, Mass: MIT Press

Tanenhaus, M. K., Flanigan, H. P., Seidenberg, M. S. 1980. Orthographic and phonological activation in auditory and visual word recognition. *Mem. Cognit.* 6:513–20

Taylor, D. A. 1976. Stage analysis of reaction time. *Psychol. Bull.* 83:161–91

Taylor, D. A. 1977. Time course of context effects. *J. Exp. Psychol.: General* 106: 404–26

Taylor, D. A. 1978. Identification and categorization of letters and digits. *J. Exp. Psychol.: Hum. Percept. Perform.* 4: 423–39

Trehub, S. E. 1979. Reflections on the development of speech perception. *Can. J. Psychol.* 33:368–81

Treisman, A. M., Gelade, G. 1980. A feature integration theory of attention. *Cognit. Psychol.* 12:97–136

Viviani, P., Terzuolo, C. 1980. Space-time invariance in learned motor skills. See Stelmach & Requin, pp. 525–36

Warren, R. E. 1974. Association, directionality and semantic encoding. *J. Exp. Psychol.* 102:151–58

Weber, R. J., Malmstrom, F. V. 1979. Measuring the size of mental images. *J. Exp. Psychol.: Hum. Percept. Perform.* 5: 1–12

Weisburg, R. W. 1980. *Memory Thought and Behavior.* New York: Oxford Univ. Press

Weiskrantz, L. 1980. Varieties of residual experience. *Q. J. Exp. Psychol.* 32:365–86

Wickelgren, W. A. 1976. Network strength theory of storage and retrieval dynamics. *Psychol. Rev.* 83:466–78

Wickelgren, W. A. 1979. *Cognitive Psychology.* Englewood Cliffs, NJ: Prentice-Hall

Wickelgren, W. A. 1981. Human learning and memory. *Ann. Rev. Psychol.* 32: 21–52

Wickens, C. D., Kessel, C. 1980. Processing resources demands of failure detection in dynamic systems. *J. Exp. Psychol.: Hum. Percept. Perform.* 6:564–77

Wing, A. M. 1978. Response timing in handwriting. In *Information Processing in Motor Control and Learning,* ed. G. E. Stelmach, pp. 153–72 New York: Academic

Wood, C. C. 1980. Interpretation of real and simulated lesion experiments. *Psychol. Rev.* 87:474–76

Wurtz, R. H., Goldberg, M. E., Robinson, D. L. 1980. Behavioral modulation of visual responses in the monkey: stimulus selection for attention and movement. *Prog. Psychobiol. Physiol. Psychol.* 9: 43–83

Ann. Rev. Psychol. 1982. 33:515-39

LARGE GROUP AWARENESS TRAINING

Peter Finkelstein, Brant Wenegrat, and Irvin Yalom

Department of Psychiatry, Stanford University Medical Center, Stanford, California 94305

CONTENTS

INTRODUCTION

In the past decade, hundreds of thousands of people have participated in intensive large group awareness trainings. "Lifespring," "Actualizations," and "est" (Erhard Seminars Training) are the best known of these enterprises. Although these groups have aroused popular interest, enjoyed wide media coverage, and stimulated much curiosity and private speculation within the psychotherapeutic professions, they have been given little serious attention by the professional literature. In this article we review the extant literature on these awareness trainings, discuss similarities between these trainings and psychotherapy, and suggest directions for further inquiry.

0066-4308/82/0201-0515$02.00

The large group awareness movement has not arisen denovo but represents a new development in the Human Potential Movement which began in the United States in the 1950s. Although this movement has been partially characterized by its unstructured, "soft" approach to human problems, it is possible nonetheless to trace its evolution and describe its conceptual sources.

Influenced by the work of Rogers, Maslow, and May, the Human Potential Movement sought to provide alternatives to orthodox psychoanalysis at one extreme and behaviorist psychology at the other, and for this reason, was often called the "third force" in American psychology. According to Maslow, the cure for neurosis was self-actualization, or growth towards one's full potential, and the diverse components of the Human Potential Movement were united by this shared vision. Practitioners used methods as disparate as gestalt, encounter, and yoga to accomplish their therapeutic goals, and a deeply eclectic bent has characterized the entire movement. Drawing from sources in sensitivity training, Eastern Philosophy, and European Existentialism, the Human Potential Movement organized itself around the search for less intellectualized and less verbal growth experiences. A new emphasis on the individual's relation to his/her body became expressed in body therapy and drew upon the work of Reich, Lowen, Feldenkrais, and others (Sayre 1977). Spiritual dimensions of the individual were emphasized as well, and popularizers of Eastern Philosophy, such as Allen Watts, were incorporated into the movement as resident philosophers. By the 1960s the runaway scientific technocracy and the breakdown of intimacy-sponsoring social institutions resulted in widespread anomie. Large numbers of individuals turned toward the Human Potential Movement for a sense of purpose and community.

For these reasons the Human Potential Movement has always been loosely tied to a critique of modern society. Life in an achievement oriented, competitive society, based on materialistic values and shot through with inequity, was seen as inimical to full human development. Not surprisingly, a strain of political activism has often accompanied the growth activities, and workers in this tradition have been reluctant to return "adjusted" people to function in a society whose commitment to human values is so capricious.

Enhanced communication and intensified experience became the Human Potential Movement's mid-range goals, and these were embodied first in sensitivity groups and later in encounter groups: honesty and expanded consciousness were meant to free the person for further growth and creativity. Encounter groups flourished during the late sixties and early seventies, sometimes aided by professional support, sometimes surviving despite professional opposition. Groups were led by clergy, business people, lay people, and psychotherapists, and existed outside the domains of academic psychology or psychiatry. Their measure of performance was consumer satisfaction and formal research was seldom pursued, perhaps owing to the basic incompatibility of world views: measurement, categorization, and quantification all ran contrary to the encounter group ethos.

The last decade has seen the waning of the encounter group and, perhaps in its place, the growth and expansion of large group awareness trainings. As this chapter goes to press, nearly 450,000 people have participated in these trainings, and there is evidence to suggest that this pace is accelerating. A recent est publication claimed that one in 900 Americans had been through their training (est 1980). Children, prisoners, air force and police personnel alike have been trained with the specific approval of government institutions.

Despite these compelling facts, social scientists have virtually ignored this phenomenon. Little research has been reported and much of it is of poor quality. The reasons for this scarcity of research include the following: 1. These trainings are an amalgam of elements as diverse as education, spiritual enlightenment, and psychotherapy, and therefore fall outside the boundaries of academic disciplines which would normally perform this research (Bartley 1978). 2. Large group awareness trainings rest upon vitalistic or antipositivistic assumptions: a central place is accorded to subjective experience and objective research is not highly valued. 3. Social scientists have seemed disinclined to acknowledge these groups, perhaps out of discomfort with appearing to endorse the commercial, nonprofessional use of potentially powerful tools for personal growth. 4. Finally, the organizations themselves have little motive for research since they use an economic rather than a scientific yardstick. Unfortunately, these formidable obstacles to research have discouraged social scientific investigation of Large Group Awareness Trainings. In spite of these obstacles, the study of such trainings may yield important data for the psychotherapeutic disciplines. Because of the sheer numbers involved, many therapists will treat clients who have been through the trainings or who will engage in them while in therapy; because such trainings often evoke powerful emotions, it is advisable that therapists be knowledgeable about the nature of the training. Furthermore, if these group trainings are indeed successful, their study might suggest useful techniques or even the reconsideration of aspects of personality theory (e.g. stability of defensive structure). Finally, this movement would appear to indicate that there are large numbers of people whose needs are being met neither by society nor by the professional psychotherapy disciplines.

Given the paucity of research, is there a literature which might serve as a springboard for a more serious exploration? Because est is the only commercial large group training which has been studied in the professional literature, we shall, of necessity, focus this review upon the est training. This focus does not mean that est and other large group trainings are viewed as identical, but rather that these issues warrant consideration through whatever literature is available.

We begin by reviewing demographic data about est and follow this with a description of est training itself. We then review outcome studies and conclude with discussions of three paradigms for viewing the similarities between est and psychotherapy.

DEMOGRAPHIC DATA ON EST

As of December 1980, over 250,000 persons had completed est training. An est organization survey of 5800 graduates (est 1980), to which there were 2200 responses, established the following demographic characteristics: the average age of est graduates, of whom 54% are females, is 36 years. Thirty-six percent of graduates are married, 28% have never married and live alone, and 24% are divorced, separated, or widowed. The average graduate has 3½ years of college education. Thirty percent of graduates earn over $35,000 annually, and 94% are Caucasian. As of July 1976, 2700 children between 6 and 12 years of age had completed est training (Babbie & Stone 1977).

A DESCRIPTION OF EST TRAINING

The following is a description of the standard adult est training, based on three sources endorsed in some way by the founder of est, Werner Erhard (Erhard & Gioscia 1978, Rhinehart 1976, Bry 1976).

The trainee's first contact with the est organization comes with his attendance at a guest seminar. As many as several hundred prospective trainees are addressed by volunteer est graduates, who give personal testimonials and summarize the purpose of est training ["...to transform your ability to experience living so that the situations you have been trying to change or have been putting up with clear up just in the process of life itself" (Bry 1976, p. 35)]. The format of est training is briefly described, and a structured exercise, usually a brief guided imagery experience, is conducted to adumbrate the training itself. Called "processes" in est terminology, structured exercises of several different kinds play an important role in conjunction with more didactic material in est training. Finally, prospective trainees are urged to reserve space in upcoming training seminars by making a deposit. The full cost of the seminars, $350 in 1981, is paid before the seminars actually begin.

Those who sign up for the weekend seminars are urged to attend a three-hour "pretraining" session Monday evening before their first training weekend. There the ground rules of est training are read: trainees agree to forego alcohol, marijuana, and other nonprescription drugs for the period of training; to bring no timepiece into the training room; to use the bathroom, eat, and smoke only during breaks set aside for that purpose; to stay seated and silent unless called upon by the trainer; to wear name tags; to not sit in proximity to any familiar person.

The first training session begins at 8:30 A.M. on the Saturday following the pretraining. Two hundred and fifty trainees are given large name plates bearing their first name and take their seats facing a dais, which is empty except for blackboards, stools, and lectern. The session begins with a rereading of the ground rules by an assistant trainer, who stresses the voluntary nature of these agreements. After the assistant trainer leaves the dais, the trainer enters the room and takes his place.

No account of est training could be complete without a description of the trainer's extraordinary demeanor. Neatly dressed and clean shaven, the est trainer is distinguished from his assistants only by an air of absolute authority. He betrays no affect, even when he excoriates the trainees. During the course of the training, he will repeatedly refer to them as "assholes," and he will devalue their accomplishments with the repeated assertion that their lives "do not work." He maintains complete control of the floor; trainees, who may only address the trainer, must raise their hands to stand and speak. Once recognized, they are expected to remain standing until their interaction with the trainer is terminated by his saying "thank you." The audience then applauds and the trainee resumes his or her seat. The trainer meets anger and criticism with studied indifference, reminding the trainees that they have chosen to be there and implying that their feelings are irrelevant in any event, since if they merely stay in the room for the duration of the training, they will "get it." At other times he tells trainees they will get nothing from the training, or that they should last it out and "take what you get."

During the first training day, which will last—with only one meal break and two or three shorter toilet breaks—until the early hours of Sunday morning, several themes are emphasized: choice, agreements, beliefs, and resistance to experience. Trainees are repeatedly reminded, for example, that they have chosen to take est training. When trainees attribute their decision, as they inevitably will, to recommendations, testimonials, or personal pressures to which they have been exposed, they are told that it is ultimately they who have chosen to heed the advice, believe the testimony, or yield to the pressure which they would prefer to see as the determinant of their decision. Because they have freely chosen to seek est training, it follows that the trainees should feel bound by the agreements they have made as part of that training. Yet the trainer predicts they will violate those agreements, and he asserts that, in fact, the trainees are incapable of abiding by any agreements they make, a major reason their lives and the world as a whole "don't work." The trainees are told that they fail to truly experience events because of their beliefs, to which they cling obstinately and which are the enemies of direct experience. The trainer argues that belief systems, understanding, and reasonableness isolate the trainees from the direct experience of reality which alone could make their lives work. Trainees are told that fully experienced—in contrast to intellectually comprehended—pain, fear, depression, or anger will evaporate. Understanding is said to be the "booby prize" for those with troubled feelings.

Two or three "processes," usually relaxation and guided imagery exercises, are conducted during the first day. Later, trainees are encouraged to share their experience of these structured exercises with the group as a whole.

Much of the second day, which begins early Sunday morning, is taken up by individuals describing those persistent problems which are to be the object of the "Truth Process" later in the day. During the "Truth Process" the trainees lie supine on the floor, which has been cleared for that purpose. With eyes closed, they meditate on the individual problem which they have defined as the object of the exercise. At the trainer's command, the trainees imagine a situation in which that problem has occurred and systematically explore the detailed bodily sensations and images associated with the problem itself. As the trainer orders the trainees to examine images from the past and from childhood, powerful affects are released. The room is soon filled with the sound of sobbing, retching, and uncontrolled laughter, punctuated by the exclamations of those remonstrating with figures from their past or the quieter voices of those imagining earnest conversations. Later in the training, trainees are given the opportunity to share their experience of this highly charged exercise, and many will report that their persistent problem, fully experienced for the first time, appears to them in a new light or has disappeared.

Later in the second day, during the so-called "Danger Process," trainees come to the dais in groups of 25 and stand facing the audience. The trainer exhorts those on the dais to "be" themselves, and reprimands those who appear to be posturing or falsely smiling, or who fail to make eye contact with the seated trainees. It is not uncommon, apparently, for trainees to faint or cry when called to the dais in this fashion, and some later recount that they found the experience liberated them from social anxieties.

The trainees recess late Sunday night, only to reconvene for a 3-hour midtraining seminar the following Wednesday evening. At that time trainees report on their experiences since the weekend, often to tell of dramatic improvements in behavior and self-perception and occasionally to complain of deterioration in their mood.

The third training day begins early Saturday morning following the midtraining seminar. After the trainer has demonstrated that few of the trainees have, since the previous weekend, lived up to their agreements concerning abstinence, the themes of reality and responsibility are introduced. In lectures and dialogues lasting nearly half the day, the trainer argues that trainees' belief in the reality of the material, consensual world causes them to depreciate as unreal the world of subjective experience. Yet, he argues, subjective experience, the reality of which does not rest on consensual agreement but on the individual's act of witness, is the most real thing known to the trainees. If, as the trainer argues, the subjective world of the individual is the real world in which he lives, then each trainee is the "source" of his or her subjective experiences and must assume absolute responsibility for the experience of everything that occurs in his or her world. Although the trainees may not have caused their misfortunes in a consensual sense, they remain totally responsible for their experience of them, and therefore for the realities in which they live.

Closely following this epistemologic discussion are processes, or exercises, which subtly reinforce the trainer's argument. In one exercise, for instance, trainees are asked to stand before other trainees and act out roles they would normally consider socially inappropriate, illustrating for them that their embarrassment results from their own construction of the experience rather than from an external source.

The fourth day begins Sunday morning with reports on experiences during the processes of the previous evening. These are followed by a presentation entitled "The Anatomy of the Mind." During this presentation the trainer asserts that the human mind is composed of multisensory records of successive moments in the individual's life. These records are of two kinds, the first containing the imprint of experiences involving a threat to survival and the second containing the imprint of experiences not deemed threatening to survival. Experiences judged threatening to survival include those in which pain, unconsciousness, or threat to survival actually occurred, those in which an affectively powerful loss was sustained, and those reflexly associated by the mind with experiences in which threat or loss occurred.

Because of the ubiquity of associative connections between experiences, the mind illogically categorizes essentially all experiences into the threatening category, although the occasions on which pain, unconsciousness, physical danger, or affective loss are actually sustained by an individual are usually few. Unfortunately, because the individual comes to equate the correctness of his mental records and beliefs with the survival of his being, he comes to place a higher value on being justified than on being correct, and is thus rarely willing to rectify the illogical categorizations of the machinelike processes of the mind. Thus, enlightenment consists in recognition that one is a machine, and that the emotional upsets of day-to-day life result from machinelike, illogical associative processes which link present experiences to past threats or losses. That one is a mechanical, illogical, "feeding-tube" is all there is to "get" from est, although the trainees were that all along and so literally got "nothing" from the training, as they were promised.

This discourse, coming after the previous training, awaited with high expectations, dramatically executed, and lasting 6 hours, appears to create in many of the trainees a euphoric sense of well-being and community. Therefore, when the trainer, who by now has adopted a less serious, even jocular manner, requests those who have "gotten it" to stand, a large proportion of the trainees rise to their feet, laughing and smiling. They are joined moments later by those who got it but don't like it, by those who got it but already had it, by those who got it but found it depressing or confusing, and eventually by those who got the nothing which was all there was to get anyway, according to the trainer.

The remainder of the fourth day is spent reviewing the positions presented on earlier days; the chimerical nature of beliefs, the necessity of fully experiencing problems, the higher reality of subjective life, and each individual's responsibility as the source of his or her constructed world are reexamined and applied to a wide range of interpersonal issues, using the new context provided by the just completed "Anatomy of the Mind." This extended dialogue, with exercises, culminates in an early morning graduation ceremony. The trainees, joined at that time by a hundred or so est graduates, observe the trainer formally acknowledge the end of training by stepping from the dais, in this way explicitly becoming just another among the assembled graduates.

Following an evening post-training seminar, the contact of graduates with the est organization is highly variable. Many graduates pursue no further est activities or training. Others, however, attend a variety of postgraduate seminars and special events of which they are notified by newsletter, and some choose to assume a proselytizing role among their friends and relations. Another means by which the graduate can maintain contact with est is through volunteer work. Both in training sessions and for organizational purposes the est enterprise is heavily dependent on volunteer labor. Volunteers are expected to be punctilious and businesslike, but they nonetheless have the opportunity, by virtue of their volunteer work, to develop social contacts with other est graduates and feel part of a larger community of like-minded persons. Volunteer work may be a major component of the est experience for many graduates.

OUTCOME OF EST TRAINING

We will summarize 12 studies of the outcome of est training, considering them under three headings: 1. testimony of est graduates, 2. psychological change in est graduates, and 3. psychiatric casualties among est trainees.

Testimony of est Graduates

Ornstein et al (1975) mailed a 680-item questionnaire, intended to elicit information on mental and physical well-being, to 1895 est graduates randomly selected from the 12,000 persons who had completed training at the time the study was initiated. This survey, commissioned by the est Foundation and never published in a professional journal, is described with little methodologic detail in est Foundation literature. Twelve hundred and four (64%) of the 1895 graduates responded, comprising 10% of all those who had taken est training at the time the study was initiated.

Details of the measuring instrument and of data analysis are not offered in the brief report available to these authors. Most respondents reported positive changes since est training with regard to a wide variety of variables, including perceived physical health, drug use, alcohol consumption, cigarette and marijuana smoking, work satisfaction, and meaningfulness of life. A spectrum of psychophysiologic complaints, including headaches, insomnia, allergies, dysmennorhea, gastrointestinal disorders, memory problems, and sexual difficulties, were also reported improved, as were colds, sore throats, and acne. Follow-up, both by telephone (54 subjects) and with a shorter questionnaire (153 subjects), of those who failed to respond initially showed the same broad pattern of perceived improvement as did the major questionnaire, suggesting that self-selection of respondents was not wholly responsible for the survey results.

Babbie & Stone (1977) performed a secondary examination of the Ornstein data. They report that when asked to rate the effect of their training on a seven-point scale, ranging from "very unfavorable" to "very favorable," over half of the responding graduates gave a "7" ("very favorable") rating to est. Another 37% of respondents rated the effect of their training as "5" or "6," indicating less intense but still favorable impressions. Only 6 percent rated the effect of their training unfavorably.

As part of another unpublished survey for which few methodologic details are available, Hamsher (est 1977) sent evaluation questionnaires to 725 est graduates who were also mental health professionals. Of the 242 respondents, 50% were psychiatrists or psychologists and 27% were social workers. The reported responses to est training were as favorable from these professionals as from Ornstein's sample. Using a 7-point scale ranging from "very negative" to "very positive," over 90% of respondents reported some degree of positive impact of est training on their personal lives.

The largest survey study of graduate satisfaction with est training was recently performed by the est organization itself (est 1980). Of 185,000 questionnaires sent to subscribers to *The Graduate Review,* an est newsletter, over 20,000 were returned, for a response rate of 11%. When asked to rank order the five most important of nine listed activities, the average respondent rated est training more useful to the quality of his or her life than education, job, recreation, art, religion, or government. Only family and personal relationships were deemed more useful by the average respondent. Nearly 30% of respondents, however, considered est training more useful even than family or personal relationships. Thus, among both lay persons and mental health professionals who have paid for est training, there exist many highly satisfied customers. Absence of attention to and reporting of methodologic detail makes it impossible to gauge the real extent of this satisfaction or to estimate the true numbers of those potentially unhappy with their est experience. When account is made of self-selection, the level of satisfaction with est training may compare favorably with that found in studies of encounter groups (Lieberman et al 1973) but may not be substantially higher. Absence of appropriate control groups, moreover, makes it impossible to know whether self-perceived results stem from specific attributes of est training or from nonspecific activity. For instance, self reported personal changes suggesting enhanced mental health, decreased defensiveness, and decreased dogmatism have been shown to follow even from recreational weekends occupied by volleyball, charades, and ballroom dancing when those activities remove individuals from their ordinary milieu and are associated with positive expectancies (McCardel & Murray 1974).

Psychological Change in est Graduates

The relationship between testimony and other evidence of personal change is seldom straightforward. Therefore, we must ask: do psychological and other test instruments confirm the positive testimonials provided by many est graduates? Behaviordyne, a private psychological testing service, carried out a study which attempted to shed some light on this question (Tondow et al 1973). Like the Ornstein and Hamsher surveys, the Behaviordyne study was never published and few of its methodologic details are available. Subjects were administered the California Psychological Inventory (CPI) prior to participation in est training, immediately after completion of training, and three months following training. The 480 CPI items were scored on 141 (sic) scales and comparisons were made for each sex between pre-training and post-training scale scores, using the *students t test* to determine significance of differences of means. Two hundred and twenty-seven subjects were administered the pretraining CPI, but only 144 of these were willing to take the post-training test, and only 93 were willing to participate in the three month follow-up. An age, sex, and socioeconomically matched control group of 200 subjects was administered the CPI at similar intervals to the experimental group, but did not receive est training. Twenty-six scale changes, significant at the 5% level, were found between pretraining and post-training CPIs for male subjects; 76 changes were found for female subjects. Scale changes for male subjects were consistent with improved self-image, reduced anxiety, dependency and guilt, and a diminished tendency toward psychophysiological reactions. Scale changes for female subjects were consistent with those for males, but additionally revealed increased ambition and self-demand. No significant scale changes were found for the control group (sic). Unfortunately, the high attrition of subjects between pre and post-training tests, the use of inappropriate statistical methods with a low significance level for the number of tests performed, and the failure to control for response sets severely limit the inferences that may be drawn from this study.

A much better study was performed by Weiss (1977), who predicted discrete personality changes as the result of est training and employed pre- and post-training measuring instruments specifically suited to detect those changes. Seventy-seven subjects undergoing est training were compared to a waiting list control group of 18 subjects, using analysis of covariance to determine significance levels. Weiss predicted that as the result of est training, experimental subjects would develop increased self-concept congruence, cognitive orientation, independence, and energy level. Subjective distress was expected to diminish. Scores on the *Self Concept Incongruence Scale* showed a highly significant decrease in incongruence for female est graduates, while male graduates showed a nonsignificant trend in the same direction. Also as predicted, scores on the *Mooney Problem Check List,* using a variety of scales, showed statistically significant changes in experimental subjects consistent with predicted changes in cognitive orientation and independence, but compared to controls, est graduates showed no increase in energy or activity level. An "infrequency" scale on the *Personality Research Form,* used to measure pseudo-random, careless, or confused responding, revealed significant differences between experimental and control subjects on post-training tests consistent with a more careful attitude on the part of est graduates. Weiss suggests that est graduates may be more responsible in their test-taking behavior as the result of est's emphasis on "keeping agreements." Unfortunately, although methodologically more sophisticated than the Behaviordyne study, Weiss's study of est graduates still suffers from a major flaw: like the Behaviordyne study, it lacks a truly adequate control group exposed to an intense, focused experience capable of creating powerful response sets. With psychological test data as with testimonial data, the very intensity of the est experience requires scrupulous attention to adequacy of control groups if specific conclusions about est training per se are to be drawn.

Hosford et al (1980) performed a prospective study of est training in a federal prison. Two hundred and sixty-three inmates who volunteered for est training were randomly assigned to each cell of a Solomon Four-Group Design. Thus, half of the volunteers received est training and half received only the promise of future est training; somewhat over half of each group were pre and post-tested and the others received only post-tests. Dependent measures fell into three categories: 1. Psychological Measuring Instruments included the MMPI, the Self-Evaluation Questionnaire, and a Semantic Differential measurement. The Self-Evaluation Questionnaire, is a forced choice self-report instrument designed to measure state and trait anxiety. The Semantic Differential measurement required subjects to judge 12 separate personal concepts (e.g. "Myself as I want to be") in terms of each of nine polar adjectives (e.g. "valuable-worthless"), thus assigning the concepts to "positions" in a nine-dimensional adjectival space. 2. Physiological measurements, obtained during 10-minute periods of relaxation in a standardized setting, included hand temperature, basal skin resistance, galvanic skin resistance, and respiratory rate, all sensitive measures of current anxiety level. 3. Behavioral measurements, averaged over three-month periods, included the number of inmate-initated sick calls, self-reported drug usage, custody levels, merit awards, furloughs, rule infractions and grievances, and supervisors' ratings of work adjustment, among others.

Although no significant differences were found between est completers and controls on pretest psychological measurements, multivariate statistical analyses revealed a number of significant differences following est training. Inmates completing est training, for instance, showed pre-to post-training MMPI scale changes significantly greater than those occurring in pre- and post-tested control subjects. These included lower Hysteria and Schizophrenia scores and increased scores on scales of Ego Strength and Social Status. Comparison of post-test MMPI's alone revealed that inmates completing est training were significantly more healthy than controls on scales of Psychasthenia, Conscious Anxiety, Ego Strength, Caudality, and Dependency. Semantic Differential measurements following training showed that est completers reported greater congruence between ideal and perceived self, greater self-satisfaction, greater satisfaction with physical health and prison life, and greater self-confidence. Post-training Self-Evaluation Questionnaires likewise revealed that est completers reported significantly less trait and state anxiety than control subjects.

Thus, Hosford et al's psychological test measurements alone lead to conclusions similar to those of Weiss's study: est graduates, compared to control groups awaiting est training, manifest psychological test changes suggesting improved mental health. As with Weiss's results, however, the changes occurring among inmates completing est may result from response sets for which no adequate control group, exposed to an active but non-specific treatment, is provided. In this regard, Hosford's physiological and behavioral outcome measurements are of particular interest. Failure to find est-related physiological and behavioral changes would suggest that response sets may be wholly responsible for positive psychological test findings, emphasizing once more the importance of adequate control groups. In fact, Hosford found no significant differences between est-completers and volunteer controls on any physiological or behavioral measure. Hosford, commenting on the discrepancy between psychological test results and other outcome measures, noted that test results are a "form of self report" affected by "response sets and the predispositions of individuals to maintain cognitive consonance" (Hosford et al 1980, p. 101). Once again, the issue of a truly adequate control group proves critical in evaluating est training as a specific intervention.

The only study of est training which included a more adequate, active, control group was carried out by Hoepfner (1975) using juvenile subjects. Second and third-grade classes in the Castro Valley, California, public school system received either their usual instruction, an "enriched" instructional program stressing independence and interpersonal skills, or the enriched program combined with est training. The enriched program, in effect, served as an active control for est training. One-way analysis of variance was used to determine statistical significance of group differences at six-month follow-up. No significant differences were found between control, enriched, or est-trained classes on the *Interperson Perception Test,* which was employed as a measure of "social intelligence." *The California Test of Personality: Section 2C, Primary,* administered as a measure of interpersonal skills, likewise showed no significant difference between est-trained students and control students, although students in the "enriched" class did show significant improvement on this test. A test of "decision making ability" also showed no significant differences between est-trained students and controls. On three measures, however, est-trained students performed significantly better than students from control or enriched classes: teacher ratings on a five-item measure of independent learning skills, on a scale of interpersonal skills, and on a scale of learning motivation all significantly favored est-trained students over both control and enriched classes. Unfortunately, lack of available methodologic detail renders the interpretation of Hoepfner's positive findings problematic. It is particularly striking that est-trained students were superior only on teacher rating scales and were not significantly improved on more objective tests. On one such objective measure, that of interpersonal skills, est-trained students were actually inferior to their enriched controls. If the few teachers involved with est-trained students were influenced by their knowledge of their students' experiences or had directly been exposed to est, their resulting bias may have affected their ratings in the absence of any real change in student behavior. No information on teacher bias is offered, however, in Hoepfner's description.

Psychiatric Casualties Among est Trainees

If no proof of benefit can be offered, is there any evidence that est causes harm? Glass, Kirsch & Parris (1977) and Kirsch & Glass (1977) described seven patients presenting psychiatric disturbances following closely upon est training. Five of these patients were diagnosed as schizophrenic, three with paranoid symptomatology, one was manic-depressive, and one was thought to have a depressive neurosis. Only one patient, a 30-year-old male with delusions, had a previous history of psychiatric disorder, but psychosocial stresses, some of which had actually motivated these patients to seek est training, may have played etiologic roles in particular cases. In all but one case, symptoms developed no later than one week following training, and in four cases, before the training was completed. Over a follow-up period of from several months to 3 years, six of seven patients were considered to suffer marked psychological impairment. Because mood swings, grandiose delusions, and delusional identification with Werner Erhart were prominent among the symptoms that brought these patients to psychiatric attention, Kirsch & Glass (1977) postulate that the est trainer's authoritarian, confronting manner might cause those overinclined to identify with the aggressor to suffer psychiatric harm from est training.

As intriguing as their cases are, both from an epidemiologic and psychodynamic viewpoint, great caution must be exercised in drawing conclusions from the material presented by these authors. Although they were associated with a major psychiatric treatment center in San Francisco, the very nidus of est activity, they describe only seven patients whose acute decompensations could plausibly be attributed to est training. This paucity of case material suggests that few of those experiencing est training actually do suffer severe psychiatric sequelae, and that however it may have contributed to the form taken by symptoms in these seven cases, over-reliance on defensive identification with the aggressor is not in itself sufficient to place the est trainee at risk.

Babbie & Stone (1977), on the basis of data gathered by Ornstein, Swencionis, Deikman & Morris, estimate the rate of self-reported "nervous breakdown" following est training to be either 0.6 or 0.8 percent, depending on whether those trainees with similar previous problems are excluded or not. The comparable rates of self-reported psychiatric hospitalizations following est training are estimated to be 0.08 and 0.2 percent. According to Babbie and Stone, most of those who suffer psychiatric sequelae to their est training nonetheless believe themselves to have ultimately benefited.

If pathologic defenses increase the likelihood of harm from est training, then psychiatric patients attending est should be especially at risk. Simon (1978) however, reported on 49 of his psychiatric outpatients whom he referred to est training in the course of individual dynamically oriented psychotherapy and found no cases in which a patient was permanently harmed as the result of est training. In fact, he considered 30 of his less disturbed patients to be clinically improved by est. Whether these patients would have benefited from est training outside the context of psychotherapy is, of course, only conjectural. Although 25 of the patients were judged to have moderate or severe psychopathology, only one patient, a previously hospitalized manic-depressive male with traumatic brain damage who was poorly compensated before taking est, had transient psychotic symptoms after est training. Simon saw another 18 patients sometime after they had graduated from est, and reports that four patients had suffered transient severe depression or psychosis after training, but all four had returned promptly to their pre-est level of functioning. Simon concluded that although the most severely disturbed patients are least likely to benefit from est training, they stand little risk of permanent harm from it either.

In a similar study, Simon reports little effect of est training on chronic alcoholics undergoing group psychotherapy (1977).

The Hamsher (est 1977) survey, described above, lends credence to Simon's conclusions. Of the 242 est graduates who were mental health professionals contacted by Hamsher, the majority felt that mildly neurotic, severely neurotic, character disordered, and addiction-prone patients benefit from est training, but relatively few recommend est for the compensated psychotic. These 242 professionals had treated 1739 other graduates and reported that over 90% had benefited from est training. Less than 4% of these graduates were thought to be harmed by est training. Of 163 patients with psychiatric hospitalizations prior to training, 152 were considered to be improved. None were considered worse. Thirteen patients, six of whom had histories of prior hospitalization, required psychiatric impatient treatment shortly after est training, but at least nine of these, after hospitalization, were thought to be improved as the result of est.

Because, as we have noted, the professionals responding to the Hamsher survey are a highly self-selected group with very positive regard for the role est training has played in their own lives, the patient observations they report are likely to be severely flawed by observer bias. Therefore, the characterization of patient benefit which emerges from the Hamsher survey must be viewed with extreme skepticism. Nor does the very low incidence of reported harm, even for the psychiatrically ill, deserve our credulity. Nonethless, from the simple assumption that at least objective events were reported in an unbiased fashion by Hamsher's respondents, the same broad conclusion emerges as from Simon's data: est training is not so noxious as to pose a threat to the health of every compromised patient, nor are those who do suffer adverse reactions to training doomed to permanent disability. It is of interest, however, that the majority of Hamsher's respondents nevertheless hesitated to recommend est training to compensated psychotics. Whether these patients are seen as particularly vulnerable to transient ill effects, or whether they are seen as less likely to benefit, as Simon argues, is not clear from the Hamsher data.

In summary, although three surveys of est graduates establish that many graduates are highly satisfied with the perceived results of their training, methodologic flaws make it impossible to judge the true proportion of satisfied est "consumers" or the frequency with which graduates are dissatisfied with their expenditure. Studies of psychological change after est training are likewise severely methodologically flawed, so that no conclusions can be drawn about the value of the training per se. The objective outcome measurements of the Hoepfner study comprise the best approximation to a controlled investigation and show no effect of est training on juvenile subjects. The literature on casualties and psychiatric patients in est is largely anecdotal and impressionistic. There is no proof that est causes psychiatric disorders, nor that it compromises the long-term mental health of those already ill. The occurrence of some transient decompensations following est training, however, suggests that caution is required in the participation of those with borderline or psychotic traits.

The first investigators of any new psychotherapeutic process are, not surprisingly, those who are also its advocates. Their research typically shows highly positive results, which are gradually qualified by later, more unbiased research. Eventually either the new procedure is shown to be useless or a residue of genuine benefit emerges, usually far more limited and specific than one would have expected from earlier research. Although some investigators have sought genuine objectivity and others seem inimical to est, much of the research we have summarized seems to be of the early, advocacy type. Only from the next generation of studies will the true measure of est training emerge.

EST AS PSYCHOTHERAPY

Many observers of est training have commented on the extent to which it employs techniques and principals of accepted psychotherapeutic value, to which its putative benefits may be attributed. In this section we will discuss the overlap of est training with psychotherapy. Topics covered include behavioral, group therapeutic, and existential paradigms embedded in the standard training.

est as Behavior Therapy

Baer & Stolz (1978) analyze est training from a behavioral point of view. Essentially, they argue that the trainer's instructional control, or his power to punish and reward trainees, is established early on as the result of his extraordinary behavior. The trainer, for instance, refers to the trainees as "assholes." Social or professional roles which ordinarily confer prestige on the trainees are derided as "acts," and spontaneous assertions of personal status are ridiculed. Trainees' belief systems are scorned, as are attempts to escape the trainer's control by withdrawal. An individual standing to leave the training room will be called to account by the trainer, who will emphasize his inability to abide by agreements. The trainees, meanwhile, experience very real physical discomfort from which only the trainer can release them. Nor can the trainee establish contingent countercontrol over the trainer. The most virulent criticisms are met by an apparently unconcerned response, the most impassioned arguments by ridicule. The trainer makes it clear that he has gotten what he came for—the trainees' money—and that he is totally impervious to trainees' objections.

But while the trainer punishes self-assertion, he also rewards undefended self-disclosure. According to Baer and Stolz, the trainer employs his power to prolong or terminate interactions with individual trainees to shape the verbal behavior of trainees in the direction of increased self-revelation, self-exploration, and vulnerability. Until the trainee has moved in the direction desired, the trainer will withhold the words "thank you" or "I got it" by which he signals the trainee to resume his seat. The applause following these words then serves as a powerful social reinforcement for whatever behavior the trainer has chosen to reward. Baer and Stolz argue, in fact, that a major function of the est trainer's contingent control is to shape self-exploratory behaviors by trainees. Eventually, as trainees begin to model self-exploration for each other, a process of intense personal exploration becomes self-sustaining, according to Baer and Stolz.

What part do the structured exercises, which Baer and Stolz call "experience algorithms," play in est training? These authors argue that some of the exercises confront the trainee with memories, thoughts, and feelings that the trainee would otherwise avoid, and thus can be likened to the flooding techniques of behavior therapists. It is, however, that these exercises serve to reveal the trainee's behavioral contingencies that makes them particularly valuable, according to Baer and Stolz. Thus the exercises are seen as opportunities for the trainee to become aware of those contingencies which determine his or her day-to-day affective responses and behavior. Since these may be derived from childhood experience, false self-impressions, and misapprehensions of the interpersonal world, the trainee may then choose to alter his or her behavior in light of more realistic adult expectations.

It is not clear what part the est curriculum, the body of ideas imparted by the trainer, actually plays in the self-exploratory and self-monitoring activities described by Baer and Stolz, except that it may serve to reduce cognitive dissonance by providing an ideology consistent with these efforts.

In their emphasis on self-examination and monitoring, Baer and Stolz overlook entirely other potentially important behavioral aspects of the est training. If the exercises, for instance, can be likened to flooding techniques, what can be said about the training as a whole? The socially anxious trainee, looking for approval and validation from others rather than from himself, comes face to face in the training with a punitive, authoritarian, invulnerable trainer who ridicules, abuses, and shouts at him in front of 250 people, demolishing his feeble counterattacks and reducing him to a state of apparent foolishness. Yet he survives! In fact, the trainer repeatedly reminds the trainee that he constitutes his own world, is the agent of his own distress, and cannot be touched by others unless he decides to be touched. Thus, even while stripping the trainee of his usual defenses, the trainer provides a new cognitive framework which explains to the trainee how he has come unscathed through a public humiliation ordinarily perceived as devastating. Certainly all this amounts to a potent flooding technique, directed not, however, at arcane and private fantasies, but at very public fears of authority and humiliation. Not only the interaction of trainer and trainee, but the emphasis on self-revelation itself, and many of the processes (e.g. the "Danger Process"), can be conceptualized as flooding techniques directed at the desensitization of profound social anxieties.

Although incompletely elaborated, the behavioral approach taken by Baer and Stolz provides a valuable introduction to the study of est training and other large group experiences from a learning theory viewpoint. Identification of that which is learned in large group trainings, and of the means by which it is reinforced, is essential in understanding both effect and outcome associated with these experiences.

est as Group Psychotherapy

Several factors which have previously been related to positive outcome of group psychotherapy (Yalom 1975) are evident in est training: catharsis, identification, universality, instillation of hope, and transference insight.

Catharsis has been central to psychodynamic therapy since Freud and Breuer's *Studies in Hysteria* (1895), but its place among factors responsible for psychological change has been the subject of controversy. Est participants often report powerful cathartic experiences, particularly during the "Truth Process" on the second day of training (Bry 1976, Emery 1973). If the est experience is truly helpful, it may be that affective expression is an important component.

Various studies have attempted to evaluate the role of catharsis in psychotherapy. Several studies (Berzon et al 1963, Lieberman et al 1973) indicate that affective discharge in the absence of other therapeutic factors does not correlate well with positive change, but there is evidence that therapeutic measures which *do* elicit strong affect, *in the presence of* other therapeutic factors, may be important to positive outcome. In one study of 20 successful group therapy patients (Yalom 1975), all but two were able to recall at least one critical incident during their therapy, and nine patients recalled two such incidents. These events were heavily laden with affect and were vividly recalled by those queried. The evidence, therefore, indicates that affect arousal is important in the right therapeutic context, but must be accompanied by, and integrated with, other therapeutic factors.

As discussed above, the est experience encourages affectively charged self-revelation, and trainees are asked to understand their inappropriate responses, to learn from one another, and to integrate their emotionally charged experiences with didactic material offered in the training. It remains uncertain how essential the cathartic component of large group training is, or how well it is supported and integrated with aspects of training design, but short-term, intensive, cathartic experiences appear to be an integral part of the program.

Universality refers to the reassuring recognition that we are rather more like other people than we had thought, that "we are all in the same boat." The conviction that one is different and uniquely unworthy may be central to neurotic discontent. Although the process of transforming these feelings is difficult and intricate, learning that others suffer similarly is apparently helpful (Yalom 1975). Est trainees talk about their problems and fears to a large group of others in a setting which discourages inattention and in which the sense of togetherness is considerable. It would seem then that a sense of brotherhood and shared humanity is vital to this experience and is perhaps augmented by the very size of the group.

The *Instillation of Hope,* also known to be present in successful therapy, is partly dependent upon positive expectational set, which is created in est by attractive marketing and an energetic pretraining pitch. Hope is also augmented by exposure to successful graduates and by the repeated reassurance that trainees have nothing to do but remain in the training room in order to benefit.

Identification refers to learning which occurs as the result of modeling behavior upon others. Glass and associates (1977) and Kirsch & Glass (1977), in reports of est casualties (described above), suggest that "identification with the aggressor" is a central dynamic in all est outcomes. They argue that est trainees exposed to a regimen of deprivation and an attacking charismatic leader attempt to master the situation by unconsciously identifying with, or merging with, the trainer. According to these authors, individual outcome may be determined by the nature of previous relationships with "threatening, ambivalently held" persons; trainees who had previously been traumatized in the course of such relationships might do less well than those who had positive relationships with similar figures.

The claim that an "overdetermined and pathological reliance on" identification with the aggressor is "central to the production of psychiatric casualties" may, however, be erroneous. Patients experiencing psychotic decompensations typically manifest boundary confusion with dominant persons in the environment; to argue that this identification has etiological significance may mistake symptoms for cause. In addition, the focus upon identification with the aggressor stresses the aggressive and threatening aspects of the training experience, perhaps at the expense of other more positive facets of the training.

The psychoanalytic literature has criticized est for ignoring *transference* insight (C. H. Miller 1977), but in its reminders that we behave as "uncorrected cybernetic machinery," est emphasizes the presence of distortions whose roots are in the past (Bartley 1978). Such distortions are essentially equivalent to "parataxic" or transference distortions. Est training makes use of *awareness* of transference phenomena, but in contrast to psychodynamic group therapy, it leaves the *working through* of transference issues for the trainee to resolve alone (J. Miller 1977).

est as Existential Psychotherapy

The standard est training promises to transform the capacity to experience life so that one is more satisfied with life as it is (Sayre 1977). As such it promises a personal upheaval in consciousness which is meant to alter the very way in which the environment is known (epistemology) and being is experienced (ontology) (Lande 1976). Est purports to be a philosophical training (Bartley 1978) and, for this reason, we will consider it within the paradigm provided by existential psychotherapy.

In contrast to psychoanalytic emphasis upon historically determined personality, existential psychotherapy seeks to understand human problems in terms of the inevitable confrontation with existence's "ultimate concerns" (Yalom 1980). Among these ultimate concerns are isolation, meaninglessness, responsibility, and death. Concepts such as the "self" or "responsibility," largely absent from psychological writing, appear in existential psychotherapy and provide a paradigm by which to view est's mechanism of action.

Est training aims to lead trainees to an appreciation of their deep or *core self,* often referred to in est writings as "The Self." This "Self" is depicted as the source of all true identity and is contrasted to our more ordinary consciousness, the "Mind State." The disparity between Mind State and Self is underscored repeatedly in both didactic and experiential portions of the training; only after one has fully grasped the ubiquity of the Mind State can one go beyond to the Self (Bartley 1978, Erhard & Gioscia 1977).

Est asserts that the individual who operates in the Mind State behaves as "uncorrected cybernetic machinery." The purpose of this "machinery" is to protect the individual from possible harm, real or imagined, and to assure the survival of beliefs and ideas held important to the individual. The machine-like quality of Mind derives from its reflexly inclusive associative function. All experience even remotely connected to that which had been traumatic is associatively linked with that traumatic experience. The Mind State narrowly and unimaginatively constitutes reality in an effort to avoid further trauma (Bartley 1978). It values effectance and domination at the expense of aliveness, and the sum of these defensive activities resembles our concept of personality.

The aim of est training is apparently to rekindle aliveness by "besieging" the Mind and laying bare its presuppositions. This attempt to examine the presuppositions which underlie ordinary consciousness has rich historical antecedants. Husserl, founder of Phenomenology, referred to ordinary consciousness as "The Natural Attitude," and devoted much of his writing to the effort of making the presuppositions supporting this consciousness more explicit (Gurwitsch 1966). His motto, "To the things themselves," calls for the direct examination of experience, in place of a conceptually mediated examination, framed by our presuppositions (Heuscher 1978). Toward this goal of exposing the Mind State presuppositions, trainees share their experiences, listen to lecture and discussion, and participate in the guided imagery of the structured exercises. All this is meant to help trainees recognize the difference between "coming from the Mind State" and "coming from the Self." In the Mind State one is protected but deadened; in the state governed by Self one is spontaneous, alive, and creative (Emery 1973). These contrasting states are similar to Heidegger's two modes of existence, *Forgetfulness of Being* and *Mindfulness of Being.* In the first of these modes one lives a "fallen" existence, caught up in a concern for *the way* things are. In the second mode one lives authentically, appreciates fully *that* things are; one is awakened to life (Heidegger 1962).

Est also reminds trainees that they live in a world characterized by scientific abstraction; they "understand" life but distrust subjective experience. The presentation "Anatomy of Experience" emphasizes that "understanding is the booby prize," that "understanding" is far removed from authentic experiences of living. The greater the adherence to the conceptual world the more one loses sight of responsibility for construing the world in a limiting way. Although we may be vaguely dissatisfied by what Rank called our "partializations" of reality (Becker 1973), we have become blind to the gross reduction of experience wrought by Mind.

Identifications are prominent among the beliefs which serve to limit experience, and for this reason one of the goals of est training is "disidentification," which spurs awareness of the extent to which we base our identities on specific social roles and identifications (Bartley 1978). We identify ourselves as psychologists, mothers, wage-earners, or tennis players, but beyond such identifications is a Self unbound by such role descriptions; disidentification is designed to regain for the individual a sense of Self buried under partial identifications and their accompanying behavioral prescriptions (Assagioli 1965). Not only is the unmediated experience of Self (in phenomenological terms the "Transcendental Ego") intrinsically pleasurable, but awareness of its constituting function is essential for the assumption of true *responsibility,* to which we now turn.

"*Responsibility*" or "uncontested authorship" (Sartre 1956) refers to the individual's awareness of authoring and reauthoring personal reality. Responsibility as "existence unveiled," as "getting it," is emphasized in virtually all est literature. Est testimonials about responsibility are numerous, and describe dramatic changes in assumption of responsibility. Bry, for example, writes: "est goes far beyond providing people with ways to deal with their personal problems. Its most far-reaching effect will undoubtedly come from the issue of responsibility, specifically the notions of self-responsibility and of being at the cause of our lives" (Bry 1976, p. 219).

While noting the emphasis on responsibility in est training, Yalom (1980) questions the consistency of this orientation. Calling attention to the hierarchical structures and sometimes submissive behavior of volunteers, he argues that internal inconsistencies may belie a paradoxical attitude. At a superficial level est encourages responsibility but at a deeper level est structures may actually oppose personal choice and reveal a longing for external constraints which runs counter to the authentic assumption of responsibility. Smith, in a similar vein, suggests that the est notion of responsibility is inconsistent or even paternalistic, and this view is echoed in other reports as well (Smith 1975, Rosen 1975, Fenwick 1976).

Although awareness of the personal constitution of reality is no doubt essential in gaining personal freedom, true responsibility for constitution of the world may be more elusive than est and other awareness trainings suggest. The existentialist notion of a constitution of reality shares a large overlapping realm with the notion of defense (Fingarette 1963). Our partializations of reality, much as our character structure, may be significantly defensive (Becker 1973). If this is so, how quickly and under what circumstances can significant changes occur? The suggestion of est enthusiasts is that the reconstruction of consciousness may be facilitated in a short period of time and remain stable thereafter. Depth psychotherapists maintain that real and enduring freedom from personal defensiveness requires lengthy working through—a more arduous process than est can offer during a brief, albeit intensive, training. The est program is far shorter than other analogous enlightenment programs (e.g. Buddhist meditation, psychoanalysis). Do students traveling a 60-hour path to enlightenment truly arrive at the same destination as those traveling more slowly? Psychotherapists and spiritual masters frequently share an assumption about the optimum velocity for individual transformation: too slow a pace and change grinds to a halt, momentum is lost; too fast a change and new defenses are unwittingly brought into play, obstructing the process toward integration.

A long tradition of existential and Eastern philosophy has assumed that superior realms of consciousness may be attained on the far side of our natural attitude. Though trainings such as est attempt to package philosophic knowledge in a manner accessible to nonspecialists, they may err in overlooking cultural and ethical contexts. As Cox (1977) has pointed out, Western psychology's infatuation with radical critiques of consciousness, be they Eastern or existential, must be carefully scrutinized. Just as meditation is offered to the busy professional in order that she or he may work longer hours but feel more refreshed, enlightenment itself may be used as a "high state" which supplies "energy" for further colonial behavior on the part of the personality. As this is done, perhaps for the good of some technical end, the fully radical nature of the alternative view is obscured, perhaps even subsumed into the reigning psychology. Herein lies one of the hazards of a brief training program made up of an amalgam of diverse and borrowed techniques and teachings; it becomes difficult to assess how well the deeper wisdom which had spawned the technique survives in the training recipe. Are we truly reaching for enlightenment, or are we merely "turning the awakening force of great ideas into fuel for the engines of egoism?" (Needleman 1965).

SUMMARY

Nearly 450,000 persons in this country have undergone one of the several available commercial large group awareness trainings. The most popular of these trainings, and the only one which has commanded attention in the professional psychological and psychiatric literature, is est (Erhard Seminars Training). That literature resembles the early literature on encounter groups and other vehicles of the human potential movement; it consists of only a few objective outcome studies which exist side-by-side with highly positive testimonials and anecdotal reports of psychological harm. Reports of testimonials have been compiled by est advocates and suffer from inadequate methodology. More objective and rigorous research reports fail to demonstrate that the positive testimony and evidence of psychological change among est graduates result from specific attributes of est training. Instead, nonspecific effects of expectancy and response sets may account for positive outcomes. Reports of psychological harm as the result of est training remain anecdotal, but borderline or psychotic patients would be well advised not to participate. We have described est training in terms of behavioral, group, and existential therapeutic paradigms in order to elucidate its possible psychotherapeutic content.

Literature Cited

Assagioli, R. 1965. *Psychosynthesis* pp. 116–25. New York: Penguin. 323 pp.

Babbie, E., Stone, D. 1977. An evaluation of the est experience by a national sample of graduates. *Biosci. Commun.* 3: 123–40

Baer, D. M., Stolz, S. B. 1978. A description of the Erhard Seminars Training (est) in the terms of behavioral analysis. *Behaviorism* 6:45–70

Bartley, W. 1978. *Werner Erhard.* New York: Potter. 279 pp.

Becker, E. 1973. *The Denial of Death,* pp. 159–207. New York: Free press. 315 pp.

Berzon, B., Pious, C., Parson, R. 1963. The therapeutic event in group psychotherapy: A study of subjective reports by group members. *J. Individ. Psychol.* 19:204–12

Bry, A. 1976. *est: 60 Hours That Transform Your Life.* New York: Avon. 233 pp.

Cox, H. 1977. *Turning East: The Promise and Peril of the New Orientalism,* p. 75, cited in J. Welwood 1979, *The Meeting of the Ways,* p. 181. New York: Schocken. 240 pp.

Emery J. E. 1973. A physician's view of the est training. *Bull. San Francisco Med. Soc.*

Erhard, W., Gioscia, V. 1977. The est standard training. *Biosci. Commun.* 3: 104–22

Erhard, W., Gioscia, V. 1978. est: communication in a context of compassion. *Curr. Psychiatr. Ther.* 18:117–25

est. 1977. *Herb Hamsher Study of est Mental Health Professionals.* est Found., San Francisco

est. 1980. The dialogue continues. *The Graduate Review,* pp. 3–11

Fenwick, S. 1976. *Getting IT: The Psychology of est.* Philadelphia/New York: Lippincott. 191 pp.

Fingarette, H. 1963. Mystic selflessness. *The Self in Transformation,* pp. 294–338. New York: Harper & Row. 362 pp.

Glass, L. L., Kirsch, M. A., Parris, F. N. 1977. Psychiatric disturbances associated with Erhard Seminars Training: I. A report of cases. *Am. J. Psychiatry* 134:245–47

Gurwitsch, A. 1966. The phenomenological and the psychological approach to consciousness. In *Essays in Phenomenology,* ed. M. Natanson, pp. 40–57. The Hague: Nijhoff. 240 pp.

Heidegger, M. 1962. *Being and Time,* pp. 210–24. New York: Harper & Row. 589 pp.

Heuscher, J. 1978. Contributions of phenomenology to psychotherapeutic theory and practice. *Am. J. Psychoanal.* 38: 67–86

Hoepfner, R. 1975. *Castro Valley Unified School District Title III: Parents as Partners Summative Evaluation Report.* Castro Valley Unified Sch. Dist., Castro Valley, Calif.

Hosford, R. E., Moss, C. S., Cavior, H., Kerish, B. 1980. *Research on Erhard Seminar Training in a Correctional Institution.* Fed. Correct. Inst., Lompoc, Calif.

Kirsch, M. A., Glass, L. L. 1977. Psychiatric disturbances associated with Erhard Seminars Training: II. Additional cases and theoretical considerations. *Am. J. Psychiatry* 134:1254–58

Lande, N. 1976. est. *Mindstyles/Lifestyles,* pp. 135–46. Los Angeles: Price/Stein/Sloan. 495 pp.

Lieberman, M. A., Yalom, I. D., Miles, M. B. 1973. *Encounter Groups: First Facts.* New York: Basic Books. 495 pp.

McCardel, J., Murray, E. J. 1974. Nonspecific factors in weekend encounter groups. *J. Consult. Clin. Psychol.* 42: 337–45

Miller, C. H. 1977. Human potential movement: Implications for psychoanalysis. *Am. J. Psychoanal.* 37:99–109

Miller, J. 1977. Discussion of "The Human Potential Movement: Implications for Psychoanalysis." *Am. J. Psychoanal.* 37:111–14

Needleman, J. 1965. *A Sense of the Cosmos: The Encounter of Modern Science and Ancient Truth,* p. 92. New York: Dutton. 178 pp.

Ornstein, R., Swencionis, C., Deikman, A., Morris, R. 1975. *A Self Report Survey: Preliminary Study of Participants in Erhard Seminars Training.* est Found., San Francisco

Rhinehart, L. 1976. *The Book of est.* New York: Holt, Rinehard & Winston. 271 pp.

Rosen, R. D. 1975. est. *Psychobabble,* pp. 64–83. New York: Avon. 250 pp.

Sartre, J. P. 1956. *Being and Nothingness,* p. 633, Transl. Hazel Barnes. New York: Philosophical Library. 811 pp.

Sayre, J. 1977. Radical therapeutic techniques. *Curr. Psychiatric Ther.* 17: 103–13

Simon, J. 1977. An evaluation of est as an adjunct to group psychotherapy in the treatment of severe alcoholism. *Biosci. Commun.* 3:141–48

Simon, J. 1978. Observations on 67 patients who took Erhard Seminars Training. *Am. J. Psychiatry* 135:686–91

Smith, A. 1975. *Powers of Mind,* pp. 267–83. New York: Ballentine. 419 pp.

Tondow, M., Teague, R., Finney, J., LeMaistre, G. 1973. *Abstract of the Behaviordyne Report on Psychological Changes Measured After Taking the Erhard Seminars Training.* Palo Alto, Calif: Behaviordyne

Weiss, J. A. 1977. *Reported Changes in Personality, Self Concept, and Personal Problems Following Erhard Seminars Training.* PhD thesis. Calif. Sch. Prof. Psychol., San Diego 206 pp.

Yalom, I. D. 1975. *The Theory and Practice of Group Psychotherapy,* pp. 3–104. New York: Basic Books. 529 pp. 2nd ed.

Yalom, I. D. 1980. *Existential Psychotherapy.* New York: Basic Books. 524 pp.

Ann. Rev. Psychol. 1982. 33:541–79

ORGANIZATIONAL BEHAVIOR[1]

L. L. Cummings

Kellogg Graduate School of Management, Northwestern University, Evanston, Illinois 60201

CONTENTS

[1]Reproduction in whole or in part is permitted for any purpose of the United States Government. This report was sponsored in part by the Organizational Effectiveness Research Program, Office of Naval Research (Code 452), under Contract No. N00014-79-C-0750, NR 170-892 with Dr. L. L. Cummings and R. B. Dunham, University of Wisconsin-Madison as Co-Principal Investigators.

0066-4308/82/0201-0541$02.00

INTRODUCTION

The first review of organizational behavior to appear in the *Annual Review of Psychology* was prepared by T. R. Mitchell (1979) and appeared in Volume 30. Reflecting upon that review, one is reminded of Smith's Principles of Bureaucratic Tinkertoys:

1. Never use one word when a dozen will suffice.
2. If it can be understood, it's not finished yet.
3. Never do anything for the first time.

Mitchell violated all three principles in that his review:

1. Used dozens of words, but efficiently and very meaningfully.
2. Was understood and, at least in 1979, was finished.
3. Was the first time.

The scope of this second review of organizational behavior can be better appreciated within the context of the coverage offered by Mitchell. Basically, he covered four topics and drew six conclusions about the field as follows:

A. Personality and individual differences.
B. Job attitudes (satisfaction, commitment, involvement, attributions).
C. Motivation (expectancy, goal setting, equity, operant conditioning, plus new directions).
D. Leadership (contingency model, path goal, new measures, theories, and paradigms).
E. Conclusions:
   1. advances in theory—particularly contingency analyses;
   2. advances in methodology—particularly in field and quasi-experimental designs, increasing use of path analysis and cross-lagged correlations, also increased use of simulations;
   3. problems remain—low quality of theory available in most areas of organizational behavior;
   4. construct validity not well established for many of the field's constructs;
   5. need greater competitive testing and integration across theories;

6. need greater attention to issues of values and ethics of doing and applying organizational behavior research.

This review focuses on topics not redundant with the above. In this review, the literature from 1977 through the first quarter of 1981, inclusively, is covered. The topics selected for review are: new overviews and integrations of the field; task design; feedback; organizational structure, technology, and control; new conceptualizations and emerging topical trends. Conclusions are drawn concerning both theoretical and research needs.

These topics were chosen to reflect both current and controversial issues upon which substantial scholarship has been conducted recently. In each area reviewed, there are partially conflicting frameworks driving current research. In addition, this review explicitly attempts to bring the macro or organizational side of organizational behavior into focus and analysis. The three topics selected which reflect this posture (organizational structure, technology, and control) are each viewed from the perspective of internal organizational characteristics. That is, each will be treated as a determinant of individual behavior within organizations. The environmental and other contextual determinants of each will be treated only lightly.

This review attempts to be projective and prescriptive, in addition to descriptive, of the work covered. New conceptualizations, emerging trends, and conclusions about likely developments within organizational behavior are given weight.

OVERVIEWS

Several attempts at either integration or review of theory and controversies have appeared during the time frame covered here. Miner (1980) has described what he considers to be the major theories of organizational behavior (expectancy, goal setting, several theories of leadership, behavior modification, etc). He has also provided very valuable evaluations of each of the theories and extends his analysis to include suggestions for future developments of theory and research in the areas selected. On the macro side of organizational behavior, Nystrom & Starbuck (1981) have edited an important two-volume collection of essays focusing on organizational design. The coverage is much broader than the usual interpretation of design, however. Most of the standard topics of macro organizational behavior are included. Beyond those, the volumes offer innovative coverage on organizational growth, regulation, control, and politics. These two volumes represent a major addition to the literature of organizational behavior and represent an invitation to scholars in the field to both integrate and extend their paradigms and topical coverages.

Controversy and extensions beyond the traditional topics of organizational behavior are the focus of a book edited by Karmel (1980) and a new series of analytical essays and critical reviews introduced by Staw (1979) and now edited by Cummings and Staw (1980, 1981). The Karmel collection pits two well-known scholars, representing differing perspectives, on a topic against one another in a debate format. The theme centers on the points of theoretical and methodological controversy that currently impact each of the four topics debated. The Staw and Cummings edited series of annual essays attempts to provide a forum for the initial and conceptual contributions which establish new agendas for untracking organizational behavior from some rather unfruitful, or at least stale, directions and topics. As has been noted by Cummings (1981a), these essays are articulating the uncertain and shifting nature of both the substantive content and methodological foundations of organizational behavior as it has developed over the past 20 years. The field seems ripe for new perspectives, new theory, and the accommodation of a much wider variety of methods, research designs, and analytical postures. In some sense reflecting this need and opportunity, two new journals have commenced publication in 1980. The *Journal of Occupational Behavior,* edited by Cary L. Cooper and James C. Taylor, seems to have focused to date on issues of power distribution and the quality of working life. *Organization Studies,* edited by David Hickson, is broader in scope and focuses upon multidisciplinary studies of organizations, the organizing process, and the relations among organizations in society. Both new journals reflect a distinctively international flavor.

TASK DESIGN

This section of the review focuses upon the literature of task design. The review is organized into three subsections, each focusing upon a different theme. In general, the subsections flow from a description of current knowledge on task design through an assessment of the present state of that knowledge and methodology to a discussion of the determinants of task characteristics.

Theoretical Frameworks and Current Findings

Over the last 6 years there have been several major attempts to integrate and theoretically expand the task design literature. As Roberts & Glick (1981) have noted, most of the work during this period has focused on one particular model of task design: namely, the job characteristics model originally developed by Hackman and his associates (Hackman & Oldham 1980). Each of these major reviews emphasizes a slightly different theme and takes a slightly different focus on the task design literature. As noted, the Roberts & Glick (1981) review is an extremely critical assessment of the theoretical formulation and testing of the job characteristics model. A broader and earlier review of the job design literature was presented by Pierce & Dunham (1976). In that review they pointed to several significant issues which were unexplored at that time and which will be noted and reviewed in a later subsection of this review. More recently, Wall, Clegg & Jackson (1978) also have provided an evaluation of the job characteristics model. While their evaluation is less critical and less comprehensive than that of Roberts & Glick (1981), it is also suggestive of the need for expanded theoretical frameworks and improved methodology in the study of the effects of task design.

Although it is true that much of the task design literature of the 1970s was based on the job characteristics model, three significant alternative theoretical frameworks have been presented (Schwab & Cummings 1976, Steers & Mowday 1977, Umstot, Mitchell & Bell 1978). Each of these three models presents alternatives to the job characteristics model. The Schwab & Cummings framework derives from expectancy theory, the Steers & Mowday formulation encompasses a number of motivational frameworks in analyzing the properties of tasks, and the Umstot et al perspective integrates job enrichment and goal setting in formulating an approach to task design. There have been two comprehensive attempts at testing and expanding the job characteristics model beyond the work of Hackman and his associates. Evans, Kiggundo & House (1979) as well as Arnold & House (1980) have provided comprehensive extensions of the job characteristics model of motivation. In particular, they have gone beyond the assumption of the four intervening psychological states which are posited in the job characteristics model. They also have utilized a framework much closer to expectancy theory with some incorporation of goal-setting concepts in these extensions and tests. Finally, Clegg (1979) has provided a searching analysis of the process of job redesign as it typically has been embedded in the above models. His opinion represents an extreme position in that he argues that most of these approaches are, in fact, largely theoretically vacuous.

As noted above, the Roberts & Glick (1981) review has provided a comprehensive analysis of the results generated through the job characteristics model. There are, however, a number of other studies which have examined the attitudinal and motivational effects of various forms of task expansion. Illustrations of these effects are those provided by Champoux (1978) in one of the few field experiments in the job design area. He basically replicated the findings of Hackman, Pearce & Wolfe (1978) in which positive job satisfaction and motivational results were found in a naturally occurring field experiment. These types of findings have been replicated in numerous other studies which have been published in the last 2 years (Katerberg, Hom & Hulin 1979, Orpen 1979, Taylor 1981, Bhagat & Chassie 1980). Two additional studies serve to illustrate the increasing breadth of dependent variables that have been related to task designs. Brousseau (1978) has found that two personality characteristics (i.e. active orientation and freedom from depression) are impacted by job designs. In general, the more enriched the job, the more active and the less depressed individuals appear to be. Weed & Mitchell (1980) have found that the degree of task structure has a major role on uncertainty perceptions experienced by individuals. Their findings are suggestive of the possibility of an optimum degree of task structure in relation to perceptions of ambiguity and uncertainty in employee roles. This possibility of a curvilinear relationship between degree of task structure and various employee responses has largely been ignored in the empirical literature.

Task Design in Relation to Other Variables

Task design has been examined jointly with a large number of other characteristics at both the individual and organizational levels. Much of this research has examined the moderating influence of various individual differences on task design effects. It is now generally clear that few systematic individual difference moderators have been found (White 1978a,b, O'Connor, Rudolf & Peters 1980). An array of individual differences has been examined. Most have tapped motivational and personality characteristics. Examples of studies in this genre are Stone, Mowday & Porter (1977), Stone et al (1979) Steers & Spencer (1977), Sims & Szilagyi (1976), Robey & Baker (1978), Ganster (1980), Mowday, Stone & Porter (1979), Kidron (1977), Kim (1980), Friend & Burns (1977), Abdel-Halim (1979), and Morris & Snyder (1979). In most of these studies, the moderating effects of individual differences were not significant. Where they were, the individual characteristics typically moderated the relationship between task design and satisfaction. Few effects are reported as moderating a task design-performance relation. This may well be partially due to the demonstrated reciprocal relation between perceived job characteristics and job satisfaction (James & Jones 1980). In general, then, enriched jobs seem to exert positive affective and behavior effects regardless of an incumbent's desire for higher order need satisfaction, need for achievement, need for autonomy, etc.

On the other hand, job tenure (Katz 1978a,b), ability (Dunham 1977b, Schuler 1977a), age (Gould 1979), and desire for a stimulating job (Cherrington & England 1980) have been found to positively moderate job design effects. Given these kinds of inconsistencies in the significance of individual differences as moderators, the work of Terborg (1977) on an underlying model of individual differences is welcome. Much of the individual differences-task design interaction research has not been guided by such a theoretical model.

Situational moderators of task design effects have been studied less frequently but the results are more encouraging. Significant results have been reported by Dunham (1977a) for organizational function, by Karasek (1979) for decision latitude, by Rakestraw & Weiss (1981) for social and peer influences, by Griffin (1979) for leader behavior, by Hall et al (1978) for departmental structure, by Rousseau (1977, 1978b) for departmental structure and technology, by Schuler (1977b) for technology and organizational structure, by Scott & Erskine (1980) for compensation, by Umstot, Bell & Mitchell (1976) for task goals, by Armenakis et al (1977) for environmental variables, and, finally, by Champoux (1980) for off-the-job variables. Three theoretical statements have been offered in an attempt to integrate some of these situational and contextual variables known to influence the effects produced by variations on job design (Carnall 1977, Oldham & Hackman 1980, Slocum & Sims 1980). Following upon Porter, Lawler & Hackman's (1975) formulation of a congruence model of job design, two studies have attempted to test the congruence hypothesis (Pierce, Dunham & Blackburn 1979, Champoux 1981). Both found partial support for the predictive validity of a model fitting personal, task design, and organizational design characteristics; i.e. congruence predicted employee responses somewhat better than the main effects of any single factor. Pierce (1979) also has found that the effects of work unit structure on employee responses appear to operate through task design. This finding has been generally replicated by Oldham & Hackman (1981). To some degree, then, findings may be due to a convergence of the measures of the constructs involved (Pierce & Dunham 1978).

Task characteristics also have been positioned as moderators of the effects of other independent variables. A wide range of such main effects have been found to be moderated by task characteristics, including aptitude test scores (Forbes & Barrett 1978, Schmidt, Hunter & Pearlman 1981), feedback provided by others on the job (Kim & Schuler 1979), leader behavior (Johns 1978, Griffin 1979), role overload and ambiguity (Abdel-Halim 1978), and job performance in relation to job satisfaction (Ivancevich 1978, 1979).

This embeddedness of task design and other determinants of individual responses complicates both the predictions which can be made concerning the viability of task redesign as a strategy for organizational change (Hackman 1978) and the techniques for achieving such redesigns even where feasible (Hackman & Lee 1979).

Determinants of Task Perceptions

Because of the frequent discovery of a low correlation between so-called objective task characteristics and perceptions of these characteristics (Roberts & Glick 1981), a number of recent studies have begun to analyze the determinants of task perceptions. Several findings suggest that the following influence an employee's perceptions of task characteristics, frequently in interaction with the objective characteristics of the task: *Social cues* (White & Mitchell 1979, Weiss & Nowicki 1981, Weiss & Shaw 1979, Salancik & Pfeffer 1977, 1978, Oldham & Miller 1979, O'Reilly & Caldwell 1979); *personality characteristics* (O'Reilly 1977, O'Reilly, Parlett & Bloom 1980, Schmitt et al 1978, Stone 1979). Walsh, Taber & Beehr (1980) have developed a model of the interactive effects of organizational setting and informational cues as determinants of perceived job characteristics.

FEEDBACK

The study of feedback within organizations has been active during the period of this review. Developments have occurred on several fronts, and this section will be organized to reflect these.

Concepts, Definitions, and Processes

The major work of the last decade on conceptual developments and feedback processes is the article by Ilgen, Fisher & Taylor (1979). They provide a thorough review of the literature through 1977 and integrate this literature into a model of the intraindividual processes through which feedback is hypothesized to influence individual responses. This piece provides a fruitful base for the expansion of the empirical literature on both the effects produced by feedback and the processes involved. The second major intraindividual model presented focuses on the self-monitoring processes of individuals (Snyder 1979). The research on the antecedents, moderators, and consequences of self-monitoring behavior yields several useful predictions awaiting testing within the context of organizational behavior. Self-monitoring can be expected to influence rates of task learning, the relative importance of objective versus perceived task characteristics as determinants of employee reactions, and the rapidity and ease of socialization experiences as individuals cross organizational boundaries.

Building on the earlier work of Greller & Herold (1975), Herold & Greller (1977) and Greller (1980) have offered a typology of definitions of feedback and sources of feedback from within a person's environment. They have moved beyond merely conceptual definitions and have offered empirical evidence of the dimensionality of both constructs. Their work awaits replication across samples and contexts before we can be reasonably certain of the generality of the dimensionality uncovered.

Two broader conceptualizations of the role of feedback in system change have been offered, one at the individual level and the other at the societal level. Bandura (1977) has incorporated a feedback and self-monitoring process in his behavioral model of individual change. The provision of positive feedback to change targets and its interpretation are central to a sense of personal efficacy. This sense, in turn, provides the personal stability necessary for environmental exploration and information seeking in an uncertain context. Bogart (1980) has offered a three-dimensional conceptualization of information exchange. Feedback, feedforward, and feedwithin are offered as alternative, yet simultaneously occurring informational exchanges in effective systems. While Bogart's contribution is most easily understood at the macro-systems level, the three dimensions of information exchange are applicable to understanding individual behavior. His descriptions are similar to recent conceptualizations within interactional psychology pertaining to situation-situation, situation-person, and person-person interactions.

Two recent papers have interpreted the effects of performance feedback through attribution processes (Ilgen & Knowlton 1980, Ilgen, Mitchell & Fredrickson 1981). Utilizing the basic attributional model, this work has examined the effects of feedback on the attributions made by superiors, given poor performance by subordinates. These effects are strongly influenced by the locus of attribution. The responses of the superior to this feedback are a joint function of the locus of the attribution and a number of environmental and historical cues unique to the superior-subordinate dyad. This research clearly demonstrates the complexity involved in attempting to predict the effects of feedback. Not only must one examine the form and content of the feedback per se, but attention must also be given to the attributional tendencies of the superior *and* the subordinate as well as situational and personal characteristics present in the interaction. There is every reason to suspect that such complex interactions of feedback and other processes operate in nonperformance contexts as well.

Interaction and Joint Effects

Feedback's effects on individual responses have been investigated in combination with a number of other independent variables. This section will review these interaction and joint effects.

One study (Komaki, Waddell & Pearce 1977) reported main effects for both feedback and participation in decision making, as well as interaction effects exhibiting greater response to feedback, given participation. The dependent variables of concern were a number of performance indexes within the context of small business operations.

Pritchard, Montagno & Moore (1978) reported a significant interaction effect between job design (i.e. enrichment) and feedback. Adelman (1981) has found that several properties of experimental tasks influence the effects of feedback on learning of probabilistic tasks. Two studies have reported both main effects and interaction effects (with monetary savings) of feedback in the reduction of electricity consumption (Seligman & Darley 1977, Winett et al 1978). Both studies were conducted using behavioral modification principles. Likewise, both were done in the context of real-world problems, utilizing actual consumers of residential electricity, and thus enhancing the external validity of the demonstrated effects.

Several investigations have reported evidence relating feedback and goal setting as independent variables. Erez (1977) reported evidence interpreted as indicating that feedback is a necessary condition for goal setting to have a positive performance effect. This finding has met with mixed replications. A number of studies have found that the presentation of either feedback or goal setting, given the other, enhances behavioral responses. Strang, Lawrence & Fowler (1978) have demonstrated this on arithmetic problems in a laboratory setting; Becker (1978) has done likewise in a study of residential energy consumption; Dossett, Latham & Mitchell (1979) have reported generally similar results in a more complex experiment involving two types of goals (assigned versus participatively set), feedback, and individual differences; and Nemeroff & Cosentino (1979) have reported the improvement of the skill levels of performance appraisers utilizing feedback and goal setting.

Two highly relevant reviews have appeared recently. One clearly demonstrates the ubiquitous nature of the positive effects of goal setting on performance, with and without feedback (Locke et al 1981). The other compares the relative performance effects of four independent variables typically utilized as performance improvement tools (Locke et al 1980). Compensation and goals were consistently found to be more effective than participation (which can be viewed as enhancing feedback to the performer) and job enrichment.

Three well-designed studies have examined the moderating effects of individual self-esteem on responses to feedback. Taylor & Slania (1981) reported that self-esteem moderates what has been referred to as the psychological success cycle. Individuals possessing high self-esteem set higher goals, perform at a higher level, and experience more positive affect when performing well than do low self-esteem individuals. In essence, high self-esteem individuals seem to gain the benefits of a self-reinforcing cycle of goals-performance-success-satisfaction-goals. Low self-esteem seems to reduce the chances of occurrence of such a cycle. Weiss (1977, 1978) has found that persons possessing high self-esteem seek less information and social modeling from others prior to making decisions and forming judgments. Individuals low in self-esteem seem to be more dependent upon social and environmental cues in forming judgments and making decisions. They, in turn, also seem to respond more quickly and fully to feedback from their environment.

Other Feedback Effects

A number of single studies have been aimed at answering questions focused on the effects of specific forms and contexts of feedback. Pritchard & Montagno (1978) have compared the effects of specific versus general and absolute versus comparative feedback on both performance and satisfaction. Specific, comparative feedback seems to produce the greatest information and contribute most to response effects. Fisher (1979) has confirmed that superiors tend to distort information when sending negative feedback to low performing subordinates. They also show greater reluctance to provide negative feedback as evidenced by increased latency relative to that found when providing positive feedback. Conlon (1980) has found that the longevity of a planned change in behavior is a function of the form and amount of feedback provided to individuals concerning the personal and organizational outcomes associated with such change.

Hanser & Muchinsky (1978) have provided a theoretical model of the nature of work which emphasizes the informational nature of work and its typical contexts for the individual. Work and its achievement provide a number of important feedback cues to individuals concerning their self-images, social standing, and anticipated organizational rewards.

The effects of feedback on groups have been carefully reviewed by Nadler (1979). One important, subsequent study has found that group members form impressions of their group's processes based primarily on feedback cues about the group's performance. These performance cues weighed more heavily in group members' perceptions of process than did either the actual nature of the processes themselves or the degree of familiarity among group members (Binning & Lord 1980).

STRUCTURE, TECHNOLOGY, AND CONTROL

This section reviews the material on three of the more macro variables of organizational behavior. Here we examine the recent literature linking behavior and attitudinal reactions within organizations to organizational structure or design, technology, and formal control systems. Along with leader behavior, reviewed by Mitchell (1979), and task design, these represent the major sources of environmental structure impinging upon an organizational participant. The three general questions addressed in this review regarding these sources of structure are: how is the conceptualizing of these constructs changing, what effects do these sources have on participant responses, and what accounts for systematic variations in structure?

Organizational Structure

In this subsection of the paper we will review the literature on several issues relating to the impact of organizational design. The first issue, in many ways the most central, centers upon the dimensionality of organizational structure and associated concerns with the measurement of structure. There have been major theoretical, and the beginnings of empirical, work on the question of the dimensionality of organizational structure. Ranson, Hinings & Greenwood (1980) have provided a major theoretical piece in which they argue that the *structuring* of organizations is a more important and relevant dependent variable than the more static and mechanistic concept of the *structure* of organizations. Their work has provided a very meaningful input into the recent empirical investigation completed by Blackburn & Cummings (1982). Blackburn & Cummings have found that the empirically derivable dimensions of structure, when utilizing participants' perceptions of structure, overlap little with the dimensions derived from traditional bureaucratic theory. The Blackburn & Cummings methodology centers on a social definitionist orientation toward the generation of knowledge with the minimum imposition of dimensionality from the researcher's theoretical or measurement bias. Meyer & Rowan (1977) have gone even further in a theoretical contribution arguing that the real institutional or formal structure concept in the organizational literature is basically a myth and an organizational ceremony. That is, the actual structuring of participants' responses is provided by the consistent myths and stories that are generated and transmitted in organizations over time. The tangible, physical, or formal structure is mostly a manifestation and articulation of these myths and stories. The realities of structure exist more in the myths and ceremonies than they do in the formal organizational designs.

A related body of literature appeared in the late 1970s focusing upon the actual assessment of given dimensions of structure. Dewar, Whetten & Boje (1980) provided the most thorough empirical study to date assessing the Aiken & Hage scales of centralization, formalization, and task routineness. In general, their assessment of the reliability and validity of these scales indicated that the scales were highly variant in their degree of reliability and validity and raised serious questions about the use of the scales in the assessment of organizational structure. Even more fundamentally, both Ford (1979) and Sathe (1978) have examined the usefulness and psychometric properties of the two major types of measures of organizational design which have impacted the literature. They compared measures of structure based upon questionnaire responses with those based upon institutional records or the counts of institutional demographics. While Sathe (1978) was highly critical of the questionnaire measures relative to institutional measures, Ford's data positions the two measures of structure as much more equivalent and as not necessarily indicating contrary structures in the same organization. An even more far-reaching implicit criticism of the traditional measures of organization structure has been provided by Moch (1980). He argues that the real structure of organizations is to be found in the networks of integrated relationships among employees within an organization. He argues further that most assessments of organizational design have not tapped this systematic integration of employee networks and have, therefore, missed one of the major sources of environmental structuring from the employees' point of view.

The relationship between organizational size and structure and their combined effects on a number of employee responses continued in the late 1970s as an active research area. Kimberly (1976) reviewed the evidence concerning organizational size in relation to structure. In general, his review indicated that while size does exhibit some systematic relationships to organizational design, it is not to be considered as the primary determinant of variations in design, and that size has been overemphasized as a covariant of organizational design in much of the theoretical literature as of that date. An important question in the assessment of size has to do with the relative validity and relationship among several measures of organizational size. Agarwal (1979) reported very low correlations among a number of different measures of size of an organization. His work is important because it points to the tenuous generalizability of studies of the effects of organizational size which are based on different indicators of size. Dewar & Hage (1978) have provided the richest theoretical statement to date relating organizational size, technology, complexity, and other indicators of structural differentiation. Their work is of major scope in that it positions size, technology, and the scope or breadth of an organization's tasks as major factors influencing the design of an organization. The work on the empirical relationship between size and structure has continued to date as reflected in the research of Glisson & Martin (1980) as well as Dewar & Simet (1981). The former have reported one of the few studies of the productivity and efficiency in human service organizations as a function of organizational size. Their work clearly shows that size is positively related to organizational efficiency in the public sector. Dewar & Simet (1981) on the other hand, argue that it is necessary to look at level-specific predictions; that is, predictions contingent upon the hierarchical level of an organization when examining the effects of organizational size and other characteristics on span of control within that organization. In other words, Dewar & Simet indicate that generalizations about the effects of size on organizational structure through span of control are at least partially a function of the hierarchical level within the organization which one is addressing.

THE EFFECTS OF STRUCTURE The effects of organizational structure on human responses have been reviewed three times within recent years. James & Jones (1976) carefully reviewed the literature on the dimensionality of structure as well as the theoretical literature relating structure to employee attitudes and behaviors. More recently, Berger & Cummings (1979) reviewed the empirical literature on the relationship between organizational structure and employee attitudes and behavior. Both of these reviews were highly critical of the existing theoretical and empirical literature on the grounds of theoretical ambiguity, poor psychometric properties of measuring instruments, and inappropriate research designs and analytical procedures, given the complexity of the structure-employee responses relationship. More recently, Dalton et al (1980) have reviewed the empirical literature relating organizational structure and indicators of employee performance. Once again, their review is critical and suggests similar problems to those noted by James & Jones (1976) and Berger & Cummings (1979).

Work does continue relating organizational design to a number of dependent variables. Most of this work is still subject to the same criticisms that the above reviews have noted. Several empirical pieces have, however, attempted to deal with one or more of these problems and are noteworthy in that regard. The following studies are representative of this progress and have related structure to a more innovative and changing set of dependent variables. Dependent variables that have been examined with these improving studies are:

1. The personal characteristics of administrators (Pfeffer & Salancik 1977).
2. The communication networks and systems within an organization (Bacharach & Aiken 1977).
3. The leadership style and participation behaviors of leaders (Jago & Vroom 1977).
4. A number of job attitudes and climate perceptions, including job satisfaction and work motivation (Adams, Laker & Hulin 1977).
5. The compensation associated with different hierarchical positions (Mahoney 1979).
6. The role conflict and ambiguity of different occupational groups (Morris, Steers & Koch 1979).
7. The amount of perceived environmental uncertainty by persons in boundary-spanning roles (Leifer & Huber 1977).

8. The perceptions of conflict and satisfaction by employees (Dewar & Werbel 1979).
9. Employee attitudinal and behavioral reactions to open-plan office physical arrangements (Oldham & Brass 1979).

STRUCTURE AT MULTIPLE LEVELS Some of the most sophisticated recent theoretical work has focused on the issue of the degree to which congruence or fit among measures of structure at the level of the task, the work unit, and the overall organization predict performance and other employee responses. There have been two major attempts to empirically address this issue. The first was reported by Schuler (1977b) and found that congruence between task structure, organization structure, and measures of technology reduced role conflict and ambiguity of participants in the organization. As the lack of fit between these three dimensions increased, employee expressions of conflict and role ambiguity increased accordingly. More recently, Pierce, Dunham & Blackburn (1979) have, in general, supported a congruence model incorporating measures of a systems structure, job design, and individuals' growth need strengths. Their work is very suggestive of continued research on the employee response effects produced by congruent sources of structuring in the work environment.

There also have been a number of theoretical works calling for and examining the need for a multiple-level assessment of structure. Most significant in this regard have been the works by Ouchi & Jaeger (1978) arguing for the simultaneous study of organizational structure and control systems as congruent and mutually interdependent constructs. Aldrich & Herker (1977) have also argued for the utility of examining subunit structures in relationship to their particular environments. Their argument is essentially that studies of overall organizational design do not capture the complexity needed to understand the relationship between differentiated subunits and the environments within which those subunits interact. It is clear that Aldrich & Herker (1977) are implying that a full understanding of the effects of organizational structure is dependent upon the simultaneous examination of multilevels of structure that exist within any one organization. Pitts (1980) has taken this argument even further and has contended that the appropriate strategy for theorizing about organizational structure is to examine structural differentiation across organizations within a contingency framework where the primary contingencies are environmental uncertainty and the nature of market structures within which the organization is operating. A very similar theme was espoused by Miles et al (1978) in arguing that the appropriate understanding of organizational structure can only be realized when structure is examined in relationship to organizational goals and strategy on the one hand and organizational processes utilized to implement that strategy on the other. Clearly, this position takes the congruency and contingency notions out to the level of organizational-environmental strategic relationships. Finally, there have been two persuasive arguments made that the distinction between micro and macro indices of organizational structure is at best artificial and perhaps, at worst, inappropriate. These arguments have been made by Nightingale & Toulouse (1977) and Mealiea & Lee (1979). Both papers argue for a multilevel congruence model of organizational structure and explicitly argue for downplaying the traditional differentiation between micro or task structure and more macro or overall organizational design.

DETERMINANTS OF ORGANIZATION STRUCTURE One major review of the literature on the correlates and determinants of organizational structure appeared in 1977 (Ford & Slocum 1977). They offered a careful review of the literature and a theoretical integration of the relationship among organizational size, technology, and environment as impacting the structure of organizations. There have been a number of attempts since 1977 to examine particular correlates of organization structure. The issue continues to be actively explored, and a number of characteristics at various levels of analysis are being examined as covariates of structure. Representative of this work are studies by Katz & Tushman (1979), Daft & Bradshaw (1980), and Beyer & Trice (1979). These studies share the common characteristic of looking at the task characteristics of an organization and the size of an organization as determinants of structure. This intersection between task characteristics and size as covariates of structure continues to appear to be a worthwhile avenue of pursuit. At a different level of analysis, Allen (1979) has examined the characteristics of top managers as determinants of organizational design. In particular Allen (1979) positioned the usual contextual determinants of structure against these top management characteristics and found that these managerial characteristics were a more important source of structural variation than the contextual variables. Characteristics examined by Allen included top management's personal goals, desires, and beliefs concerning organizational function and individual careers.

A number of scholars have continued to examine characteristics of the environment external to the organization as determinants of organizational design. Representative work in this regard is that of Tung (1979), Bourgeois, McAllister & Mitchell (1978), Daft & Macintosh (1981), Tushman (1979), and Fennell (1980). In each of these cases the researcher has examined some characteristic of an organization's environment (e.g. environmental turbulence, complexity, or the clustering of organizations in the environment) in relationship to the organization structure. In general, the hypothesis that environmental change, turbulence, and complexity cause increases in organizational differentiation and integration mechanisms has been supported by this broad stream of work. While these studies have not been systematically related to one another and, generally, have not been cumulative, the totality of the evidence across researchers, types of organizations, and methods does lend credence to the generalizability of the basic nature of the findings.

Finally, there have been two recent examinations of the role of culture as a determinant of organizational structure. Maurice, Sorge & Warner (1980) found major differences in the organizing and manufacturing units across France, West Germany, and Great Britain. They interpret these data as indications of cultural or societal differences impacting organizational design. In a major theoretical piece, Child (1981) has argued that culture, contingency (that is, environmental and technological determinants), and economic system (capitalism versus socialism) each impact the organizational designs that one should expect to find across national cultures. Child's paper is a major attempt to disentangle the relative effects of the sources of cross-national variation in organizational design. The theoretical richness of the paper should lead to its utilization as a guide for cross-national research on organizational structure.

Organizational Control

The area of the control of and predictability of participant responses in organizations has been undergoing a rather major change in recent years. This is reflected in several major theoretical pieces that posit a much broader conceptualization of organizational control and control mechanisms within organizations. For example, Ouchi (1979) has described a series of control mechanisms that are used in organizations wherein the central issue is the equitable distribution of rewards among members of the organization. The primary concern in developing such control systems is to provide mechanisms for solving evaluation and control issues such that the consequences of applying these mechanisms achieve perceptions of equity among participants. Ouchi goes on to elaborate on the consequences of different organizational control strategies for organizational structure and design. Ouchi (1977, 1980, 1981) has developed this theme in two primary ways. He has described a total management system that is based upon this notion of control when coupled with concepts of trust and organizational loyalty. He elaborates this theme in the form of describing a Theory Z organization which attempts to capture the best of both the Japanese and American models of organizational control and coordination. Ouchi also has developed a trichotomy of control mechanisms, only one of which centers on the traditional bureaucratic form of organizational coordination. The other two mechanisms of coordination and control among organizational participants center on market or competitive mechanisms on the one hand and social or clan-like mechanisms on the other.

Two recent contributions have focused on the concept of control defined as the control over contingencies or over dependencies. Both Pfeffer & Salancik (1978) and Hambrick (1981) have described the development of organizational processes and structure as largely a function of dependencies of the organization upon external forces and the implications of such dependencies for internal organizational power distributions, hierarchies, and control mechanisms. These approaches to the conceptualization of organizational control are rich with implications for the linking of processes across organizational units and between organizations and the environments with which they interact.

Two rather novel approaches to internal control of participants' behavior have been developed recently. Weiss (1977) has conceptualized internal control as primarily a combination of socialization and behavior modeling processes. He has studied this in the context of the similarities of behaviors within subordinate and superior pairs. He has found that one characteristic of the subordinate (i.e. self esteem) tends to moderate the relationship between these perceived similarities and a number of behavioral outcomes. Cherns (1980) has recently argued that a processes approach to intervention in organization development has not been effective in increasing participant organizational control. He advocates a more structural orientation toward increasing organizational control with organizational design and technological interventions as the primary change strategies to implement such.

Finally, two broadly based and very encompassing reviews of the psychological control literature as it pertains to organizational behavior have appeared recently. Dachler & Wilpert (1978) have interpreted the broad literature on participation as essentially a control mechanism. Their work is important because it provides a multidisciplinary examination of both the conceptual dimensions of participation and the boundaries of participation as a control vehicle. Kerr & Slocum (1981) have recently reviewed a number of mechanisms that organizations utilize to increase the control and predictability of individual variations in employee responses. Their contribution is important primarily because it points to the wide range of typical independent variables in organizational behavior that can be interpreted as organizational control devices.

The Technology of Organizations

Organizational technology has been examined as a causal or independent variable in relationship to a number of dependent variables. Beginning at the individual level of analysis, Rousseau (1978b) has found several measures of technology to be good predictors of variations in employee attitudes. Sutton & Rousseau (1979) expanded this framework and examined technology in relationship to organization structure and interorganizational relationships as determinants of individual responses. Again, within this comparison, technology appears to be an important correlate of a number of behavioral and attitudinal responses. Rousseau (1979) has placed these and other findings within the context of a theoretical interpretation. She calls for an expanded conceptual examination of technology to include not only closed systems approaches, as is typical, but also the implications of open systems logic for the assessment of technology.

Two studies have examined organizational structure as a function of technology. Comstock & Scott (1977) have found that the key issue in predicting structure from technological variation is one of compatible levels of analyses. They found that technology at the organization-wide level predicts macro or global organization structure. On the other hand, the technology of subunits within complex organizations predicts the design of those subunits. Over all, Comstock & Scott (1977) report that technology is a more significant predictor of organizational structure than is organizational size. Reimann (1980) has also examined the relationship between technology and organizational structure at two levels of analysis. He found that system technology predicts system design characteristics while the technology of the work flows within an organization predicts subunit design. These two studies combined clearly indicate that in the prediction of organizational structural variations it is important to focus on the technological characteristics at a similar level of analysis.

Two studies have also examined technology as a predictor of job characteristics. Billings, Klimoski & Preaugh (1977) have conducted one of the few time series studies examining the impact of a change in technology on job characteristics. Their general finding is that changes in technology over time have an effect on the structure of work, on the social structure among workers, and on the job satisfaction of workers. Dowell & Wexley (1978) also have examined the effects of technology on jobs. In this study, the jobs in focus were those of supervisors, and Dowell & Wexley (1978) report few technological effects. The structure of leaders' jobs was found to be stable across different technologies as well as across different organizational functions.

Finally, in one of the more interesting studies examining technology and independent variables, Vardi & Hammer (1977) found that the rates and directions of personnel mobility within organizations is a function of the technology within which these personnel work. In general, more loosely defined technologies generate higher rates of personnel mobility than do more tightly defined and rigid technologies as typically found in large-scale manufacturing organizations.

CONCEPTUAL AND METHODOLOGICAL ADVANCES

This section will focus on several conceptual or theoretical and methodological advances that have influenced the contents and methods of research *across* several areas within organizational behavior. In each case, the nature of the contributions will be discussed first, followed by illustrations of their utilization.

New Theory and Basic Methodology

Several authors have contributed by offering either new theoretical frameworks or emphasizing the necessity for attention to fundamental issues of research method and design. In 1978 Staw & Oldham (1978) called for a major reconsideration of the dependent variables typically examined in organizational behavior. A few theoretical works have responded indirectly to this call. Leading the theoretical contributions is a major, new theory of behavior in organizations by Naylor, Pritchard & Ilgen (1980). I have reviewed this book elsewhere and will not repeat the details of that evaluation here (Cummings 1981b). The book represents a thorough articulation of a cognitive theory of choice and behavior with illustrations of usefulness being offered in the analysis of organizational roles, motivation, leader behavior, and our old friend "organizational climate." A leading theoretical treatise on the macro side is Hage's (1980) analysis of the form (structure), processes, and transformation of organizations per se. His emphasis on the development and testing of formal hypotheses and interrelated sets of propostions is a welcome addition to the macro organizational behavior literature. Bandura (1977) has developed the concept of personal efficacy and argued forcefully for its application to several areas of traditional interest in organizational behavior with particular focus being given to strategies for changing behavior within organizational contexts.

Several others have called for more rigorous processes of theorizing, with particular focus on the development of middle-range theories, taxonomies, and construct validation attempts (Pinder & Moore 1979, 1980, Schwab 1980). These calls have been coupled with one major attempt at specifying the conditions and issues constraining the development of an interdisciplinary science of behavior in organizations. Particular concern has been given to methods and designs for conducting research across levels of analysis and aggregation and on dynamic phenomena (Roberts, Hulin & Rousseau 1978). Hunter & Gerbling (in press) have provided a major explication of the conditions necessary for modeling such dynamic phenomena and the analytical paradigms for adequate testing of such. Of course, there are those who would argue that the emphasis upon more carefully and highly constructured methods and models for assessing dynamic phenomena is essentially misplaced (Susman & Evered 1978). Their position is that the adequate study of change in variables in real settings involves "action" research. This, in turn, calls for less positivistic research strategies. Developments along these lines are receiving increasing attention within the discipline and are being utilized by established scholars to study both traditional and newer substantive content areas within organizational behavior (Van Maanen 1979). One of the most promising of these combines the writing of organizational biographies and historical analysis of archival data, as nicely illustrated in the work of Kimberly (1979).

Beyond established theory and method, several authors are calling for major paradigm shifts for the 1980s in the study of organizational behavior (Benson 1977, Brown 1978, Pondy & Mitroff 1979, Morgan 1980) and of organizations per se (Hannan & Freeman 1977). It remains unclear whether these calls will be heeded and reflected in systematic and programmatic research.

Cognitive Processes and Symbolism

One very clear development of the late 1970s has been the emergence of several streams of research heavily influenced by the cognitive reformulation of both established substantive topical areas and the formulation of new areas utilizing developments in cognitive psychology. These developments have added new zest and intellectual excitement to several areas. The most important is the use of attributional processes to study leadership effects (Mitchell, Green & Wood 1981, Mitchell, Larson & Green 1977, Mitchell & Wood 1980, Green & Mitchell 1979) and to study situations in terms of the attributions made by observers regarding the importance of leadership (Staw & Ross 1980). While it is obvious that attribution is a well-established construct in social psychology and personality theory, its status as a facilitating theoretical framework within organizational behavior seems to be at its peak presently (Kelley & Michela 1980).

A second, equally fruitful recent development has been the utilization of information processing theory and research to enlighten several phenomena of traditional interest in organizational behavior. Representative interpretations are those of organizational design (Tushman & Nadler 1978), organizational entry (Louis 1980), organizational climate (James et al 1979), leadership (Weiss 1978), motivation (Zedeck 1977), organizational strategy (Tussle & Gerwin 1980), task design and job attitudes (Salancik & Pfeffer 1978, Shaw 1980), stress (Sarason & Sarason 1979), performance appraisal (Feldman 1981), and organizational design and communication (March & Feldman 1981). In most of these utilizations, individual cognitive processing has been positioned as a major intervening variable between contextual or environmental cues and either individual or organizational responses. This work on cognitive processing of stimuli comes as close as organizational behavior has come to date in understanding the processes which underlie so many of the functional relationships central to the discipline. As will be emphasized in the concluding section of this review, this contribution bids well for further incorporation of cognitive constructs within organizational behavior.

Attitudes as schema for interpreting events in organizational life and as a basis for the construction of personal and shared causal maps has also been emphasized recently in both theory (Calder & Schurr 1981) and research (Bougon, Weick & Binkhorst 1977). One of the most creative applications of the treatment of individual cognitive complexity as an attitudinal or dispositional construct has been Suedfeld & Rank's (1976) analysis of the success and survival of revolutionary leaders utilizing historical, archival data.

One important development in the study of decision making which reflects this cognitive orientation has been the emergence of problem finding, problem defining, and problem formulation (as distinct from problem solving) as researchable processes. Cognitive processes have been found to significantly impact both the predecisional phases of decision making (Payne, Braunstein & Carroll 1978) and the conscious recognition and subsequent articulation of problems and decision opportunities (Alexander 1979, Lyles & Mitroff 1980). In addition, Stabell (1978) has reported data linking the problem formulation stage of decision making with later phases (e.g. alternative generation and the assessment of consequences) through cognitive processes.

The role of symbols as objects of inquiry and of symbolism as an organizational and managerial process has recently emerged to guide several theoretical statements. We can expect to see the generation of empirical research in the 1980s utilizing this approach to understanding organizational behavior. Reflective of current theorizing are the interpretations of managerial actions as mostly symbolic or representational (Pfeffer 1981), the analysis of organizations per se as language systems as opposed to logical arrangements of structural components (Daft & Wiginton 1979), and the symbolic reinterpretation of many macro organizational phenomena (Dandridge, Mitroff & Joyce 1980). While the descriptions of organizational and managerial symbols as representing hierarchy and power differentiation have been commonplace in organizational behavior, the systematic study of the processes of symbol creation and transmission have not. Furthermore, we can look forward to increased research on the functions served and consequences produced by the management of symbols within organizations.

EMERGING TRENDS

Four areas of substantive research and theory have emerged or reemerged in the late 1970s which are likely to continue to accelerate as foci of scholarship. Present work in each will be described briefly, and an attempt will be made to project the general nature of emerging work. The four areas are: organizational effectiveness, individual stress within organizations, the relation of work and nonwork experiences and their contributions to the quality of an individual's life, and finally, the study of time as an important main and moderating effect in understanding behavior in organizations.

Organizational Effectiveness

Of course, concerns about and the general study of organizational effectiveness are not new. Economics, general management theory, and operations research, among others, have attempted to model and prescribe organizational effectiveness for several decades. What is new and rapidly emerging is the descriptive empirical study and behavioral theorizing about the dimensions and determinants of organizational effectiveness.

Effectiveness can be and has been conceptualized at many levels of analysis and aggregation. While the emphasis here is upon organizational behavior perspectives on effectiveness, it should be noted that this focus is not exclusively on the effectiveness of individuals within organizations. Rather, this individual perspective is complemented by models of organizational effectiveness that assume the group, the between-group unit, and the organization per se are the most appropriate units of analysis.

One current theme in this literature is an argumentation concerning the viability of organizational effectiveness as a construct susceptible to scientific analysis (Pennings & Goodman 1977). Some would argue that the overall construct is too global, too multidimensional, and too ideological to be subject to scientific inquiry without substantial additional construct validation and domain clarification. Of course, others disagree and have offered reviews and integrations of present definitional controversies as well as suggestions for needed research (Steers 1977).

Several authors have reviewed and critiqued the quality of work to date on organizational effectiveness (Steers 1977, Scott 1977). In general, these critiques point to the need for a closer connection between theory, operational definitions, and research methods as well as the need for longitudinal designs examining the determinants of effectiveness across organizations and organizational families or clusters. At the most fundamental level, one is struck by the diversity and even incompatibility of perspectives taken toward understanding the effectiveness of organizations (Goodman & Pennings 1977, Cunningham 1977).

Attempts to tackle these problems and to position organizational effectiveness as a researchable topic are being made. Most impressive in this regard is the work of Cameron (1978, 1981). He has empirically examined the dimensionality of effectiveness of universities and colleges and has both built and tested theory concerning the determinants of effectiveness within this domain. Others have begun to point to the importance of organizational effectiveness as a scientific concept in advancing our understanding of corporate strategy (Kirchhoff 1977). Schneider and his colleagues (1980) have reported the results of an empirical assessment of organizational effectiveness through the combined perceptions of the employees and customers of banking organizations. Their definitions and operationalizations represent a major contribution to the assessment of organizational effectiveness through the individual level of analysis. Their treatment of issues of aggregation and the careful use of perceptual measures of effectiveness are a significant advancement. Molnar & Rogers (1976) have empirically examined and contrasted two of the dominant theoretical positions defining organizational effectiveness, i.e. the goal and system resource models. These, then, represent the major attempts to move beyond definitional arguments and pessimistic predictions about the usefulness of the concept. Two clear statements of possible research agendas for continued work have been offered by Cameron (1980) and Connolly, Conlon & Deutsch (1980). The common themes of these more optimistic positions center on the need for systems and contingency conceptualizations of effectiveness, longitudinal designs, and multidisciplinary perspectives.

Stress in Organizations

The work on stress is abundant; yet fully developed models of organizational contributors to stress are only beginning to guide research. Two major theoretical statements in this regard have recently appeared (Ivancevich & Matteson 1980, Brief, Schuler & Van Sell 1981). Both combine organizational determinants (e.g. role overload, conflict, and ambiguity) with individual behaviors and personalities in building predictive models of the occurrence of stress. In addition, both attempt to come to grips with the difficult definitional issues necessary for distinguishing among the constructs frequently used in discussions of stress (e.g. stressors, stress, outcomes of stress, and moderators of such outcomes).

Several research programs have produced many bivariate, correlational findings relating organizational and personal characteristics to perceptions of stress and behavioral coping strategies used in managing stress. The resulting studies have been reviewed and critiqued by Beehr & Newman (1978) and Newman & Beehr (1979). The most comprehensive and theoretically linked review of the current literature has been provided by Cohen

(1980). He reviews the results of research on several stressors across both behavioral and social outcomes. While Cohen's review is not restricted to examining the effects of stress within the organizational context, his theoretical interpretations of the consistent findings in other contexts are central to our future work on stress in organizations.

Two attempts have been made to broaden the organizational domain of stress effects even further. Spector (1978) has creatively interpreted several of the stress studies as indexes of frustration caused by organizational constraints and procedures. He has provided a model within which he interprets and critiques that literature as a special case of the individual frustration-aggression hypothesis. His model is particularly suggestive of work that is needed on industrial sabotage and general employee alienation within the work setting. Jamal & Mitchell (1980) reviewed the literature on work- and nonwork-related factors contributing to mental health, concluding that variables in the work context generally contribute more to positive mental health than nonwork contextual factors. Many of these work-related variables are conceptually similar to the most frequently cited stressors. Clearly, the findings of Jamal & Mitchell (1980) challenge the generally accepted notion of work as a contributor to psychological stress. It is highly likely that the continuing research on stress will find that the relation of work-related variables and stress is curvilinear and strongly contingent upon an individual's nonwork environment.

Work and Nonwork Satisfactions

The questions of the degree of independence of work and nonwork satisfactions and the contributions of each to life satisfactions are emerging as an active research interest. A recent thorough review of the literature to date is highly likely to focus the attention of organizational behavior scholars in the 1980s (Kabanoff 1980). This review contrasts compensation, generalization, and segmentation models of the relation between work and nonwork experiences and offers suggestions for research methods and theoretical frameworks needed to disentangle the relative effects of factors in each domain. Near, Rice & Hunt (1980) have offered a more narrowly focused review examining the relation between the social systems of the nonwork and work environment. They conclude that the social systems of the two domains are much more closely linked and interdependent than is normally thought. Friendship roles, status and privilege systems, and general behavioral styles are frequently found to be generalizable across the work/nonwork boundary.

Several recent studies have focused specifically on the relation of work (or jobs) satisfaction to nonwork (or leisure) satisfaction. Orpen (1978) reported evidence that satisfaction with factors at work impacted satisfaction with factors in the nonwork environment more than the reverse direction of causality. Orpen's study is one of the few allowing any conclusions concerning the directionality of causation between work and nonwork satisfactions.

Three studies have related work and leisure satisfaction to either one another and/or to a more global concept of life satisfaction (or quality of life). Near, Rice & Hunt (1978) examined the work and nonwork correlates of both general life satisfaction and job satisfaction. They report little overlap between life and job satisfaction and little overlap among their respective correlates. They offer the richest conceptual model available to date hypothesizing the composition of life satisfactions to be threefold, i.e. satisfaction with home, satisfaction with job, and physical health. In turn, each of the three dimensions is hypothesized to be related to second-order variables within each of the three domains. London, Crandall & Seals (1977) have reported that both job satisfaction and satisfaction with other dimensions of life contribute to individuals' perceptions of the quality of their lives. However, significant differences were found between so-called advantaged and disadvantaged groups of respondents. Disadvantaged persons report work satisfaction to be less important in their assessments of life's quality. Contrary to the Near et al (1978) findings, Schmitt & Mellon (1980) have reported that life satisfaction contributes more to job satisfaction and the reverse. Clearly, such contradictory findings call for much richer theory and more complex contingency frameworks. Suggestive of the complexity involved, at least at the individual level of analysis, is the work of Dubin & Champoux (1977). They report data showing that job satisfaction can be clearly predicted from clusters of an individual's central life interests. In particular, the degree of centrality of work within an individual's overall interest profile is significantly correlated with the degree and focus of satisfactions derived from the work context. Persons for whom work is not a central life interest exhibit much less predictability in the satisfactions derivable from their jobs.

Time

Time has been neglected as a major theoretical construct, particularly as a casual variable, in organizational behavior. Several recent works suggest that this neglect is disappearing. Albert's (1977) reformulation of social comparison theory into a model of temporal comparisons, while focused on social psychological and personality issues, is rich with hypotheses testable within the context of organizational behavior. In particular, his work represents a promising avenue for reformulation of equity and relative deprivation as partially temporal phenomena and as within individual comparisons.

Both Pfeffer & Lawler (1980) and Alderfer & Guzzo (1979) have explicitly included the passage of time as an important variable in explaining individual commitment to organizations and the shifts in the relative importance of individual desires throughout the life cycle. At the organizational level of analysis, Miller & Friesen (1980) have presented and creatively tested, with archival data, a model of several patterns of organizational transitions. Their model incorporates assumptions about the continuous (versus discrete) nature of time, about the time lags for organizational disruptions and creations to occur, and about the time periods needed for organizational transitions to stabilize.

Katz (1978b) examined the empirical effects of an individual's time in a job and in an organization on the relation between the characteristics of an individual's job and the satisfaction associated with the job. The relative importance of various job characteristics in contributing to job satisfaction varied systematically with both time durations. Clearly, this work possesses significant implications for sampling and implementation in job design/redesign research and application. Katz (1980) has also elaborated upon the centrality of time in understanding both the nature or meaning of work to individuals and reactions to work. This theoretical statement on time and work provides an important base for future research on the role of time in organizational behavior.

CONCLUSION

Looking across the topics reviewed, seven needs seem to emerge as likely candidates for attention in the 1980s in organizational behavior. They capture both methodological and paradigmatic concerns within the discipline. These needs and likely trends have been elaborated elsewhere (Cummings 1981a) and will be highlighted here as derivative from the literature reviewed.

Improved Construct Validity

Probably the most important advancement likely in the 1980s will be the improved construct validity of many of the measures that we use within our field. Just a few examples will suffice to indicate that trends in this direction are beginning to appear. First, as noted earlier, the construct of task design has received considerable emphasis in the latter half of the 1970s. Much of this emphasis has been upon clarification of the relationships among constructs such as perceived characteristics, objective characteristics, personal needs, and work unit structure. I would argue that this development has been essentially an exploration of construct validity as it applies to one of the central concepts in our discipline.

A second area of great importance within organizational behavior focuses upon organizational structure and design. As we all know, the study, and more particularly the results produced by the study, of organization structure has been a major disappointment for many of us working within organizational behavior. I would argue that one of the central reasons for this disappointment has been inadequate attention devoted to questions of construct validity in the study of organizational structure. Several authors have recently noted this problem and have suggested that it may be reasonable to be optimistic about movement toward more construct-valid assessments of organizational characteristics.

More Careful Selection and Measurement of Dependent Variables

I expect that we will see in the decade of the 1980s less attention given to several of the common or standard dependent variables upon which much of organizational behavior has focused its attention. For example, studies predicting dependent variables such as absenteeism, turnover, and attitudes on simple jobs will decrease in frequency.

A different set of dependent variables appears to be emerging as central to the research programs of several active scholars in organizational behavior. Examples are the focus upon the consequences to individuals and organizations of alternative task designs; the determinants of the perceptions of jobs as assessed through the incumbents of those jobs; the study of the perceptions of organizational structure and design processes as a conceptually distinct variable from the physical design or the objective design of that structure; the study of the determinants of feedback seeking, as well as the study of stress and time as central causal variables in explaining behavior in organizations.

The focus upon these slightly changing dependent variables will remain one of increased validity and reliability of measuring instruments and a more careful and rigorous use of theoretical paradigms to study these variables. It may well be that the paradigms used in such studies will draw increasingly from established fields within psychology but outside of the usual boundaries of organizational behavior. Particularly likely candidates in this regard are theoretical frameworks from the fields of personality and social psychology. Organizational behavior has from its beginnings benefited from the creative use of concepts from these disciplines. The time is ripe for a new infusion of constructs and theory into organizational behavior. Clearly the process has begun with the utilization of attributional frameworks, cognitive psychology, and interactionalist perspectives.

Longitudinal and Experimental Research Designs

A third area that will surely see increasing emphasis and utilization during the 1980s will be the careful use of longitudinal and experimental research designs as applied to areas where such designs have been lacking in the past. There is clearly a continuing interest in establishing the cause-and-effect relations that exist among variables and within networks of variables within our discipline. Of course, this concern with establishing causal relationships has been a continuing concern in our field for many years. The use of research designs that have some chance of eliminating causal hypotheses will be applied to an increasing number of established research areas within organizational behavior. Each of the areas reviewed here are candidates for such improvement. It is likely that by the mid-1980s being longitudinal will no longer possess the distinctiveness as it does presently. Being either experimental or longitudinal will be much more typical of the research of the 1980s. The next hope is for increasing proportions of research in organizational behavior to derive from and contribute to theory.

Appropriate Use of Multivariate Statistical Analyses

Paralleling the continued emphasis and the increased application of longitudinal and experimental research design will be the increased and more appropriate use of multivariate statistical analyses.

The 1980s will emphasize such a trend because of two underlying currents that were beginning to appear in the late 1970s. First, behavioral scientists are beginning to realize that real organizations are not static phenomena. That is, organizations develop and change over time and they exert their impacts upon the dependent variables that we have studied as a system of components. The field is beginning to realize the need to recognize such realities in the analyses of our data. This realization rapidly forces us to multivariate analyses both with regard to the independent and dependent variables included within our studies. This accounts for the increasing use that we have seen, and that I suspect will continue, of techniques such as MANOVA and the associated issues of the appropriate second-stage analyses given significant effects found through the application of MANOVA. Second, the realization that organizations impact dependent variables through systems of components brings us to the bruising reality of the multicollinearity among many of our cherished independent variables. It is apparent that much of our knowledge in organizational behavior in the 1980s will be dependent upon our ability to disentangle the effects of a number of jointly impacting independent variables that operate as a system. In this review we have noted the beginnings of this trend in the present scholarship on task design, feedback, and organizational structure.

Organizational Behaviors as Social Constructions of Reality

Several scholars are arguing that the only way to understand organizations and their effects is to study them as social constructions as opposed to objective realities. The position defines organizations as essentially phenomenological in essence. They exist only in the patterning and clustering of participants' perceptions.

Thus, to understand the effects that organizations exert upon individuals, one must shift the typical paradigm in organizational analysis to a focus upon the detailed, fine-grained analysis of these perceptions.

This orientation toward organizations as social realities can be expected to exert its impact in several areas of study in the 1980s. The most likely examples are the continued use of attribution models to study phenomena of leadership, performance appraisal, and job and organizational design. The emphasis upon the social construction and social transmission of the definition of realities in organizations gives added emphasis to information-processing and decision-making models as they apply to most phenomena that organizational psychologists are likely to study. We have already seen the beginnings of that trend in the literature on task design, organizational design, and control systems.

The Symbolic Nature of Management as a Process

We are also likely to witness an increased emphasis on the essentially symbolic nature of management as a process. This theme brings forth the importance of myths and stories in the management of organizations. In particular, the emphasis is likely to be on the importance of these phenomena in the creation and perpetuation of control systems within organizations.

Organizational behavior is very likely in the 1980s to study increasingly the processes of how these stories are collected and how the myths are created and transmitted from one generation of organizational participants to the next.

We will see increasing focus by organizational researchers on the role that these myths, stories, and histories of organizations play in the socialization of new members entering organizations and on the decision-making processes that characterize the strategic levels within organizations.

Processes Linking Levels of Analysis

Organizational behavior will be advanced by focusing on processes that operate across levels of analysis that have been traditional within our field. For example, increasing emphasis is likely to be given to the context of individual behavior within organizations. As a second example, we can expect to see more intersection of the frameworks traditionally used in organizational sociology and the perspective of organizational psychology in studying the impact of environments upon organization. There has been work completed in the late 1970s suggesting that it is important to examine the processes that link levels of analysis. Certainly, topics in organizational behavior such as employee socialization, decision making, the behavioral modeling of leadership processes, and the transmission of values and decision premises across levels within organizations all call for understanding the processes that link individual and social system levels of analysis. Today, only a few areas within the discipline have benefited from this focus. The study of processes across levels of analysis will encourage, if not force, the incorporation of established theoretical frameworks into organizational behavior, e.g. interaction theory, sociotechnical systems theory, and radical theories of organizational design. The emphasis on processes may even provide the stimulation for the development of original theories within organizational behavior itself.

Literature Cited

Abdel-Halim, A. A. 1978. Employee affective responses to organizational stress: Moderating effects of job characteristics. *Pers. Psychol.* 31:561–79

Abdel-Halim, A. A. 1979. Individual and interpersonal moderators of employee reactions to job characteristics: A reexamination. *Pers. Psychol.* 32:121–37

Adams, E. F., Laker, D. R., Hulin, C. L. 1977. An investigation of the influence of job level and functional specialty on job attitudes and perceptions. *J. Appl. Psychol.* 62:335–43

Adelman, L. 1981. The influence of formal, substantive and contextual task properties on the relative effectiveness of different forms of feedback in multiple-cue probability learning tasks. *Organ. Behav. Hum. Perform.* 27:423–42

Agarwal, N. C. 1979. On the interchangeability of size measures. *Acad. Manage. J.* 22:404–9

Albert, S. 1977. Temporal comparison theory. *Psychol. Rev.* 84:485–503

Alderfer, C. P., Guzzo, R. A. 1979. Life experiences and adults' enduring strength of desires in organizations. *Adm. Sci. Q.* 24:347–61

Aldrich, H., Herker, D. 1977. Boundary spanning roles and organization structure. *Acad. Manage. Rev.* 2:217–30

Alexander, E. R. 1979. The design of alternatives in organizational contexts: A pilot study. *Adm. Sci. Q.* 24:382–404

Allen, S. A. 1979. Understanding reorganizations of divisionalized companies. *Acad. Manage. J.* 22:641–71

Armenakis, A. A., Feild, H. S. Jr., Holley, W. H. Jr., Bedeian, A. G., Ledbetter, B. Jr. 1977. Human resource considerations in textile work redesign. *Hum. Relat.* 30:1147–56

Arnold, H. J., House, R. J. 1980. Methodological and substantive extensions of the job characteristics model of motivation. *Organ. Behav. Hum. Perform.* 25: 161–83

Bacharach, S. B., Aiken, M. 1977. Communication in administrative bureaucracies. *Acad. Manage. J.* 20:365–77

Bandura, A. 1977. Self-efficacy: Toward a unifying theory of behavioral change. *Psychol. Rev.* 84:191–215

Becker, L. J. 1978. Joint effect of feedback and goal setting on performance: A field study of residential energy conservation. *J. Appl. Psychol.* 63:428–33

Beehr, T. A., Newman, J. E. 1978. Job stress, employee health, and organizational effectiveness: A facet analysis, model, and literature review. *Pers. Psychol.* 31:665–700

Benson, J. K. 1977. Organizations: A dialectical view. *Adm. Sci. Q.* 22:1–21

Berger, C. J., Cummings, L. L. 1979. Organizational structure, attitudes and behavior. See Staw 1979, 1:169–208

Beyer, J. M., Trice, H. M. 1979. A reexamination of the relations between size and various components of organizational complexity. *Adm. Sci. Q.* 24:48–64

Bhagat, R. S., Chassie, M. B. 1980. Effects of changes in job characteristics on some theory-specific attitudinal outcomes: Results from a naturally occurring quasi-experiment. *Hum. Relat.* 33: 297–313

Billings, R. S., Klimoski, R. J., Preaugh, J. A. 1977. The impact of a change in technology on job characteristics: A quasi-experiment. *Adm. Sci. Q.* 22:318–39

Binning, J. F., Lord, R. G. 1980. Boundary conditions for performance cue effects on group process ratings: Familiarity versus types of feedback. *Organ. Behav. Hum. Perform.* 26:115–30

Blackburn, R. S., Cummings, L. L. 1982. Cognitions of work unit structure. *Acad. Manage. J.* In press

Bogart, D. H. 1980. Feedback, feedforward, and feedwithin: Strategic information in systems. *Behav. Sci.* 25:237–49

Bougon, M., Weick, K., Binkhorst, D. 1977. Cognition in organizations: An analysis of the Utrecht Jazz Orchestra. *Adm. Sci. Q.* 22:606–39

Bourgeois, L. J. III, McAllister, D. W., Mitchell, T. R. 1978. The effects of different organizational environments upon decisions about organizational structure. *Acad. Manage. J.* 21:508–14

Brief, A. P., Schuler, R. S., Van Sell, M. 1981. *Managing Job Stress.* Boston: Little Brown

Brousseau, K. R. 1978. Personality and job experience. *Organ. Behav. Hum. Perform.* 22:235–52

Brown, R. H. 1978. Bureaucracy as proxis: Toward a political phenomenology of formal organizations. *Adm. Sci. Q.* 23:365–82

Calder, B. J., Schurr, P. H. 1981. Attitudinal processes in organizations. See Cummings & Staw 1981, 3:283–302

Cameron, K. S. 1978. Assessing organizational effectiveness in institutions of higher education. *Adm. Sci. Q.* 23: 604–32

Cameron, K. S. 1980. Critical questions in assessing organizational effectiveness. *Organ. Dyn.* Autumn:66–80

Cameron, K. S. 1981. Domains of organizational effectiveness in colleges and universities. *Acad. Manage. J.* 24:25–47

Carnall, C. A. 1977. Contingency theory and job design. In *Organizational Choice and Constraint: Approaches to the Sociology of Enterprise Behavior,* ed. M. Warner. Hants, England: Saxon House

Champoux, J. E. 1978. A serendipitous field experiment in job design. *J. Vocat. Behav.* 12:364–70

Champoux, J. E. 1980. The world of nonwork: Some implications for job redesign efforts. *Pers. Psychol.* 33:61–75

Champoux, J. E. 1981. The moderating effect of work context satisfactions on the curvilinear relationship between job scope and affective responses. *Hum. Relat.* In press

Cherns, A. 1980. Structure and process: The succession of interventionist goals. *J. Occup. Behav.* 1:69–81

Cherrington, D. J., England, J. L. 1980. The desire for nonenriched jobs as a moderator of the enrichment-satisfaction relationship. *Organ. Behav. Hum. Perform.* 25:139–59

Child, J. 1981. Culture, contingency and capitalism in the cross-national study of organizations. See Cummings & Staw 1981, 3:303–56

Clegg, C. W. 1979. The process of job redesign: Signposts from a theoretical orphanage? *Hum. Relat.* 32:999–1022

Cohen, S. 1980. Aftereffects of stress on human performance and social behavior: A review of research and theory. *Psychol. Bull.* 88:82–108

Comstock, D. E., Scott, W. R. 1977. Technology and the structure of subunits: Distinguishing individual and work-group effects. *Adm. Sci. Q.* 22:177–202

Conlon, E. J. 1980. Feedback about personal and organizational outcomes and its effects on persistence of planned behavioral changes. *Acad. Manage. J.* 23: 267–86

Connolly, T., Conlon, E. J., Deutsch, S. J. 1980. Organizational effectiveness: A multiple-constituency approach. *Acad. Manage. Rev.* 5:211–18

Cummings, L. L. 1981a. Organizational behavior in the 1980s. *Decis. Sci.* 12: 365–77

Cummings, L. L. 1981b. Beyond VIE and information processing? A review of J. C. Naylor, R. D. Pritchard, and D. R. Ilgen, *A Theory of Behavior in Organizations. Contemp. Psychol.* In press.

Cummings, L. L., Staw, B. M. 1981. *Research in Organizational Behavior,* Vol. 3. Greenwich, Conn: JAI Press. 356 pp.

Cunningham, J. B. 1977. Approaches to the evaluation of organizational effectiveness. *Acad. Manage. Rev.* 2:463–74

Dachler, H. P., Wilpert, B. 1978. Conceptual dimensions and boundaries of participation in organizations: A critical evaluation. *Adm. Sci. Q.* 23:1–39

Daft, R. L., Bradshaw, P. J. 1980. The process of horizontal differentiation: Two models. *Adm. Sci. Q.* 25:441–50

Daft, R. L., Macintosh, N. B. 1981. A tentative exploration into the amount and equivocality of information processing in organizational work units. *Adm. Sci. Q.* 26:207–24

Daft, R. L., Wiginton, J. C. 1979. Language and organization. *Acad. Manage. Rev.* 4:179–92

Dalton, D. R., Todor, W. D., Spendolini, M. J., Fielding, G. J., Porter, L. W. 1980. Organizations, structure and performance: A critical review. *Acad. Manage. Rev.* 5:49–64

Dandridge, T. C., Mitroff, I., Joyce, W. F. 1980. Organizational symbolism: A topic to expand organizational analysis. *Acad. Manage. Rev.* 5:77–82

Dewar, R., Hage, J. 1978. Size, technology, complexity and structural differentiation: Toward a theoretical synthesis. *Adm. Sci. Q.* 23:111–36

Dewar, R. D., Simet, D. P. 1981. A level specific prediction of spans of control examining the effects of size, technology and specialization. *Acad. Manage. J.* 24:5–24

Dewar, R., Werbel, J. 1979. Universalistic and contingency predictions of employee satisfaction and conflict. *Adm. Sci. Q.* 24:426–48

Dewar, R. D., Whetten, D. A., Boje, D. 1980. An examination of the reliability and validity of the Aiken and Hage scales of centralization, formalization and task routineness. *Adm. Sci. Q.* 25:120–28

Dossett, D. L., Latham, G. P., Mitchell, T. R. 1979. Effects of assigned versus participatively set goals, knowledge of results, and individual differences on employee behavior when goal difficulty is held constant. *J. Appl. Psychol.* 64:291–98

Dowell, B. E., Wexley, K. N. 1978. Development of a work behavior taxonomy for first-line supervisors. *J. Appl. Psychol.* 63:563–72

Dubin, R., Champoux, J. E. 1977. Central life interests and job satisfaction. *Organ. Behav. Hum. Perform.* 18:366–77

Dunham, R. B. 1977a. Reactions to job characteristics: Moderating effects of the organization. *Acad. Manage. J.* 20:42–65

Dunham, R. B. 1977b. Relationships of perceived job design characteristics to job ability requirements and job value. *J. Appl. Psychol.* 62:760–63

Erez, M. 1977. Feedback: A necessary condition for the goal setting-performance relationship. *J. Appl. Psychol.* 62:624–27

Evans, M. G., Kiggundu, M. N., House, R. J. 1979. A partial test and extension of the job characteristics model of motivation. *Organ. Behav. Hum. Perform.* 24:354–81

Feldman, J. M. 1981. Beyond attribution theory: Cognitive processes in performance appraisal. *J. Appl. Psychol.* 66:127–48

Fennell, M. L. 1980. The effects of environmental characteristics on the structure of hospital clusters. *Adm. Sci. Q.* 25:485–510

Fisher, C. D. 1979. Transmission of positive and negative feedback to subordinates: A laboratory investigation. *J. Appl. Psychol.* 64:533–40

Forbes, J. B., Barrett, G. V. 1978. Individual abilities and task demands in relation to performance and satisfaction on two repetitive monitoring tasks. *J. Appl. Psychol.* 63:188–96

Ford, J. D. 1979. Institutional versus questionnaire measures of organizational structure: A reexamination. *Acad. Manage. J.* 22:601–610

Ford, J. D., Slocum, J. W. 1977. Size, technology, environment and the structure of organizations. *Acad. Manage. Rev.* 2:561–75

Friend, K. E., Burns, L. R. 1977. Sources of variation in job satisfaction: Job size effects in a sample of the U.S. labor force. *Pers. Psychol.* 30:589–605

Ganster, D. C. 1980. Individual differences and task design: A laboratory experiment. *Organ. Behav. Hum. Perform.* 26:131–48

Glisson, C. A., Martin, P. Y. 1980. Productivity and efficiency in human service organizations as related to structure, size, and age. *Acad. Manage. J.* 23:21–37

Goodman, P. S., Pennings, J. M., eds. 1977. *New Perspectives on Organizational Effectiveness.* San Francisco: Jossey-Bass. 275 pp.

Gould, S. 1979. Age, job complexity, satisfaction, and performance. *J. Vocat. Behav.* 14:209–23

Green, S. G., Mitchell, T. R. 1979. Attributional processes of leaders in leader-member interactions. *Organ. Behav. Hum. Perform.* 23:429–58

Greller, M. M., Herold, D. 1975. Sources of feedback: A preliminary investigation. *Organ. Behav. Hum. Perform.* 13:244–56

Greller, M. M. 1980. Evaluation of feedback sources as a function of role and organizational level. *J. Appl. Psychol.* 65:24–27

Griffin, R. W. 1979. Task design determinants of effective leader behavior. *Acad. Manage. Rev.* 4:215–24

Hackman, J. R. 1978. The design of work in the 1980s. *Organ. Dyn.* 7:3–17

Hackman, J. R., Lee, M. D. 1979. *Redesigning Work: A Strategy for Change.* Scarsdale, NY: Work in America Inst.

Hackman, J. R., Oldham, G. R. 1980. *Work Redesign.* Reading, Mass: Addison-Wesley

Hackman, J. R., Pearce, J. L., Wolfe, J. C. 1978. Effect of changes in job characteristics on work attitudes and behaviors: A naturally occurring quasi-experiment. *Organ. Behav. Hum. Perform.* 21: 289–304

Hage, J. 1980. *Theories of Organizations: Form, Processes and Transformation.* New York: Wiley

Hall, D. T., Goodale, J. G., Rabinowitz, S., Morgan, M. A. 1978. Effects of top-down departmental and job change upon perceived employee behavior and attitudes: A natural field experiment. *J. Appl. Psychol.* 63:62–72

Hambrick, D. C. 1981. Environment, strategy and power within top management teams. *Adm. Sci. Q.* 26:253–71

Hannan, M. T., Freeman, J. 1977. The population ecology of organizations. *Am. J. Sociol.* 82:929–64

Hanser, L. M., Muchinsky, P. M. 1978. Work as an information environment. *Organ. Behav. Hum. Perform.* 21:47–60

Herold, D. M., Greller, M. M. 1977. Feedback: The definition of a construct. *Acad. Manage. J.* 20:142–47

Hunter, J., Gerbling, D. 1982. Unidimensional measurement, second order factor analysis and causal models. In *Research in Organizational Behavior,* Vol. 4. ed. B. M. Staw, L. L. Cummings. Greenwich, Conn: JAI Press. In press

Ilgen, D. R., Fisher, C. D., Taylor, M. S. 1979. Consequences of individual feedback on behavior in organizations. *J. Appl. Psychol.* 64:359–71

Ilgen, D. R., Knowlton, W. A. Jr. 1980. Performance attributional effects on feedback from superiors. *Organ. Behav. Hum. Perform.* 25:441–56

Ilgen, D. R., Mitchell, T. R., Fredrickson, J. W. 1981. Poor performers: Supervisors' and subordinates' responses. *Organ. Behav. Hum. Perform.* 27:386–410

Ivancevich, J. M. 1978. The performance to satisfaction relationship: A causal analysis of stimulating and nonstimulating jobs. *Organ. Behav. Hum. Perform.* 22: 350–65

Ivancevich, J. M. 1979. High and low task stimulation jobs. A causal analysis of performance-satisfaction relationships. *Acad. Manage. J.* 22:206–22

Ivancevich, J. M., Matteson, M. T. 1980. *Stress and Work.* Glenview, Ill: Scott, Foresman. 244 pp.

Jago, A. G., Vroom, V. H. 1977. Hierarchical level and leadership style. *Organ. Behav. Hum. Perform.* 18:131–45

Jamal, M., Mitchell, V. F. 1980. Work, nonwork and mental health: A model and a test. *Ind. Relat.* 19:88–93

James, L. R., Gent, M. J., Hater, J. J., Coray, K. E. 1979. Correlates of psychological influence: An illustration of the psychological climate approach to work environment perception. *Pers. Psychol.* 32: 563–88

James, L. R., Jones, A. P. 1976. Organizational structure: A review of structural dimensions and their conceptual relationships with individual attitudes and behavior. *Organ. Behav. Hum. Perform.* 16:74–113

James, L. R., Jones, A. P. 1980. Perceived job characteristics and job satisfaction: An examination of reciprocal causation. *Pers. Psychol.* 33:97–135

Johns, G. 1978. Task moderators of the relationship between leadership style and subordinate responses. *Acad. Manage. J.* 21:319–25

Kabanoff, B. 1980. Work and nonwork: A review of models, methods and findings. *Psychol. Bull.* 88:60–77

Karasek, R. A. Jr. 1979. Job demands, job decision latitude, and mental strain: Implications for job redesign. *Adm. Sci. Q.* 24:285–308

Karmel, B., ed. 1980. *Point & Counterpoint in Organizational Behavior.* Hinsdale, Ill: Dryden. 154 pp.

Katerberg, R., Hom, P. W., Hulin, C. L. 1979. Effects of job complexity on the reactions of part-time employees. *Organ. Behav. Hum. Perform.* 24:317–32

Katz, R. 1978a. The influence of job longevity on employee reactions to task characteristics. *Hum. Relat.* 8:703–26

Katz, R. 1978b. Job longevity as a situational factor in job satisfaction. *Adm. Sci. Q.* 23:204–23

Katz, R. 1980. Time and work: Toward an integrative perspective. See Staw & Cummings 1980, 2:81–127

Katz, R., Tushman, M. 1979. Communication patterns, project performance, and task characteristics: An empirical evaluation and integration in an R&D setting. *Organ. Behav. Hum. Perform.* 23: 139–62

Kelley, H. H., Michela, J. L. 1980. Attribution theory and research *Ann. Rev. Psychol.* 31:457–502
Kerr, S., Slocum, J. W. Jr. 1981. Controlling the performances of people in organizations. In *Handbook of Organizational design,* ed. P. C. Nystrom, W. H. Starbuck, 2:116–34. New York: Oxford Univ. Press
Kidron, A. G. 1977. Individual characteristics as moderators of the job characteristic-satisfaction relationship. *Proc. Acad. Manage.* 37:21–75
Kim, J. S. 1980. Relationships of personality to perceptual and behavior responses in stimulating and nonstimulating tasks. *Acad. Manage. J.* 23:307–19
Kim, J. S., Schuler, R. S. 1979. The nature of the task as a moderator of the relationship between extrinsic feedback and employee responses. *Acad. Manage. J.* 22:157–62
Kimberly, J. R. 1976. Organizational size and the structuralist perspective: A review, critique and proposal. *Adm. Sci. Q.* 21:571–97
Kimberly, J. R. 1979. Issues in the creation of organizations: Initiation, innovation, and institutionalization. *Acad. Manage. J.* 22:437–57
Kirchhoff, B. A. 1977. Organization effectiveness measurement and policy research. *Acad. Manage. Rev.* 2:347–55
Komaki, J., Waddell, W. M., Pearce, M. G. 1977. The applied behavior analysis approach and individual employees: Improving performance in two small businesses. *Organ. Behav. Hum. Perform.* 19:337–52
Leifer, R., Huber, G. P. 1977. Relations among perceived environmental uncertainty, organization structure, and boundary-spanning behavior. *Adm. Sci. Q.* 22:235–47
Locke, E. A., Feren, D. B., McCaleb, V. M., Shaw, K. N., Denny, A. T. 1980. The relative effectiveness of four methods of motivating employee performance. In *Changes in Working Life,* ed. K. D. Duncan, M. M. Gruneberg, D. Wallis, pp 363–88. New York: Wiley
Locke, E. A., Shaw, K. N., Saari, L. M., Latham, G. 1981. Goal setting and task performance: 1969–1980. *Psychol. Bull.* 90:125–52
London, M., Crandall, R., Seals, G. W. 1977. The contribution of job and leisure satisfaction to quality of life. *J. Appl. Psychol.* 62:328–34
Louis, M. R. 1980. Surprise and sense making: What newcomers experience in entering unfamiliar organizational settings. *Adm. Sci. Q.* 25:226–51
Lyles, M. A., Mitroff, I. I. 1980. Organizational problem formulation: An empirical study. *Adm. Sci. Q.* 25:102–19
Mahoney, T. A. 1979. Organizational hierarchy and position worth. *Acad. Manage. J.* 22:726–37
March, J. G., Feldman, M. S. 1981. Information in organizations as signal and symbol. *Adm. Sci. Q.* 26:171–86
Maurice, M., Sorge, A., Warner, M. 1980. Societal differences in organizing manufacturing units: A comparison of France, West Germany, and Great Britain. *Organ. Stud.* 1:59–86
Mealiea, L. W., Lee, D. 1979. An alternative to macro-micro contingency theories: An integrative model. *Acad. Manage. Rev.* 4:333–45
Meyer, J. W., Rowan, B. 1977. Institutional organization: Formal structure as myth and ceremony. *Am. J. Sociol.* 83:340–63
Miles, R. E., Snow, C. C., Meyer, A. D., Coleman, H. J. Jr. 1978. Organizational strategy, structure and process. *Acad. Manage. Rev.* 3:546–62
Miller, D., Friesen, P. 1980. Archetypes of organizational transition. *Adm. Sci. Q.* 25:268–99
Miner, J. B. 1980. *Theories of Organizational Behavior.* Hinsdale, Ill: Dryden
Mitchell, T. R. 1979. Organizational behavior. *Ann. Rev. Psychol.* 30:243–82
Mitchell, T. R., Green, S. G., Wood, R. 1981. An attributional model of leadership and the poor performing subordinate. See Cummings & Staw 1981, 3:197–234
Mitchell, T. R., Larson, J. R. Jr., Green, S. G. 1977. Leader behavior, situational moderators, and group performance: An attributional analysis. *Organ. Behav. Hum. Perform.* 18:254–68
Mitchell, T. R., Wood, R. E. 1980. Supervisor's responses to subordinate poor performance: A test of an attributional model. *Organ. Behav. Hum. Perform.* 25:123–38
Moch, M. K. 1980. Job involvement, internal motivation, and employees integration into networks of work relationships. *Organ. Behav. Hum. Perform.* 25:15–31
Molnar, J. J., Rogers, D. C. 1976. Organizational effectiveness: An empirical comparison of the goal and system resource approaches. *Sociol. Q.* 17:401–13
Morgan, G. 1980. Paradigms, metaphors, and puzzle solving in organization theory. *Adm. Sci. Q.* 25:605–22
Morris, J. H., Snyder, R. A. 1979. A second look at need for achievement and need for autonomy as moderators of role per-

ception-outcome relationships. *J. Appl. Psychol.* 64:173–78

Morris, J. H., Steers, R. M., Koch, J. L. 1979. Influence of organization structure on role conflict and ambiguity for three occupational groupings. *Acad. Manage. J.* 22:58–71

Mowday, R. T., Stone, E. F., Porter, L. W. 1979. The interaction of personality and job scope in predicting turnover. *J. Vocat. Behav.* 15:78–89

Nadler, D. A. 1979. The effects of feedback on task group behavior: A review of the experimental research. *Organ. Behav. Hum. Perform.* 23:309–38

Naylor, J. C., Pritchard, R. D., Ilgen, D. R. 1980. *A Theory of Behavior in Organizations.* New York: Academic

Near, J. P., Rice, R. W., Hunt, R. G. 1978. Work and extra-work correlates on life and job satisfaction. *Acad. Manage. J.* 21:248–64

Near, J. P., Rice, R. W., Hunt, R. G. 1980. The relationships between work and nonwork domains: A review of empirical research. *Acad. Manage. Rev.* 5: 415–29

Nemeroff, W. F., Cosentino, J. 1979. Utilizing feedback and goal setting to increase performance appraisal interviewer skills of managers. *Acad. Manage. J.* 22: 566–76

Newman, J. E., Beehr, T. A. 1979. Personal and organizational strategies for handling job stress: A review of research and opinion. *Pers. Psychol.* 32:1–44

Nightingale, D. V., Toulouse, J. M. 1977. Toward a multilevel congruence theory of organization. *Adm. Sci. Q.* 22:264–80

Nystrom, P. C., Starbuck, W. H. 1981. *Handbook of Organizational Design,* Vols. 1, 2. New York: Oxford Univ. Press. 560, 552 pp.

O'Connor, E. J., Rudolf, C. J., Peters, L. H. 1980. Individual differences and job design reconsidered: Where do we go from here. *Acad. Manage. Rev.* 5:249–54

Oldham, G. R., Brass, D. J. 1979. Employee reactions to an open-office plan: A naturally occurring quasi-experiment. *Adm. Sci. Q.* 24:267–84

Oldham, G. R., Hackman, J. R. 1980. Work design in the organizational context. See Staw & Cummings 1980, 2:247–78

Oldham, G. R., Hackman, J. R. 1981. Relationships between organizational structure and employee reactions: Comparing alternative frameworks. *Adm. Sci. Q.* 26:66–83

Oldham, G. R., Miller, H. E. 1979. The effect of significant other's job complexity on employee reactions to work. *Hum. Relat.* 32:247–60

O'Reilly, C. 1977. Personality-job fit: Implications for individual attitudes and performance. *Organ. Behav. Hum. Perform.* 18:36–46

O'Reilly C., Caldwell, D. F. 1979. Informational influence as a determinant of perceived task characteristics and job satisfaction. *J. Appl. Psychol.* 64:157–65

O'Reilly, C., Parlett, C., Bloom, J. 1980. Perceptual measures of task characteristics: The biasing effects of differing frames of reference and job attitudes. *Acad. Manage. J.* 23:118–31

Orpen, C. 1978. Work and nonwork satisfaction: A causal-correlational analysis. *J. Appl. Psychol.* 63:530–32

Orpen, C. 1979. The effects of job enrichment on employee satisfaction, motivation, involvement, and performance: A field experiment. *Hum. Relat.* 32:189–217

Ouchi, W. G. 1977. The relationship between organizational structure and organizational control. *Adm. Sci. Q.* 22:94–113

Ouchi, W. G. 1979. A conceptual framework for the design of organizational control mechanisms. *Manage. Sci.* 25:833–48

Ouchi, W. G. 1980. Markets, bureaucracies and clans. *Adm. Sci. Q.* 25:129–41

Ouchi, W. G. 1981. *Theory Z: How American Business Can Meet the Japanese Challenge.* Reading, Mass: Addison-Wesley

Ouchi, W. G., Jaeger, A. M. 1978. Type Z organization: Stability in the midst of mobility. *Acad. Manage. Rev.* 3:305–14

Payne, J. W., Braunstein, M. L., Carroll, J. S. 1978. Exploring predecisional behavior: An alternative approach to decision research. *Organ. Behav. Hum. Perform.* 22:17–44

Pennings, J. M., Goodman, P. S. 1977. Toward a workable framework. See Goodman & Pennings 1977, pp. 146–84

Pfeffer, J. 1981. Management as symbolic action: The creation and maintenance of organizational paradigms. See Cummings & Staw 1981, 3:1–52

Pfeffer, J., Lawler, J. 1980. Effects of job alternatives, extrinsic rewards, and behavioral commitment on attitude toward the organization: A field test of the insufficient justification paradigm. *Adm. Sci. Q.* 25:38–56

Pfeffer, J., Salancik, G. R. 1977. Organizational context and the characteristics and tenure of hospital administrators. *Acad. Manage. J.* 20:74–88

Pfeffer, J., Salancik, G. R. 1978. *The External Control of Organizations.* New York: Harper & Row. 300 pp.

Pierce, J. L. 1979. Employee affective responses to work unit structure and job design: A test of an intervening variable. *J. Manage.* 5:193–211

Pierce, J. L., Dunham, R. B. 1976. Task design: A literature review. *Acad. Manage. Rev.* 1:83–97

Pierce, J. L., Dunham, R. B. 1978. An empirical demonstration of the convergence of common macro- and micro-organization measures. *Acad. Manage. J.* 21:410–18

Pierce, J. L., Dunham, R. B., Blackburn, R. S. 1979. Social systems structure, job design, and growth need strength: A test of a congruency model. *Acad. Manage. J.* 22:223–40

Pinder, C. C., Moore, L. F. 1979. The resurrection of taxonomy to aid the development of middle-range theories of organizational behavior. *Adm. Sci. Q.* 24:99–118

Pinder, C. C., Moore, L. F., eds. 1980. *Middle-range Theory and the Study of Organizations.* Boston: Nijhoff. 413 pp.

Pitts, R. A. 1980. Toward a contingency theory of multibusiness organization design. *Acad. Manage. Rev.* 5:203–10

Pondy, L., Mitroff, I. 1979. Beyond open systems models of organizations. See Staw 1979. 1:1–36

Porter, L. W., Lawler, E. E. III, Hackman, J. R. 1975. *Behavior in Organizations.* New York: McGraw-Hill. 561 pp.

Pritchard, R. D., Montagno, R. V. 1978. *Effects of specific versus nonspecific and absolute versus comparative feedback on performance and satisfaction.* Tech. Rep. # AFHRL-TR-78-12, Brooks AFB, Texas

Pritchard, R. D., Montagno, R. V., Moore, J. R. 1978. Enhancing productivity through feedback and job design. Tech. Rep. # AFHRL-TR-78-44, Brooks AFB, Texas

Rakestraw, T. L. Jr., Weiss, H. M. 1981. The interaction of social influence and task experience on goals, performance, and performance satisfaction. *Organ. Behav. Hum. Perform.* 27:326–44

Ranson, S., Hinings, B., Greenwood, R. 1980. The structuring of organizational structures. *Adm. Sci. Q.* 25:1–17

Reimann, B. C. 1980. Organization structure and technology in manufacturing: System versus work flow level perspectives. *Acad. Manage. J.* 23:61–77

Roberts, K. H., Glick, W. 1981. The job characteristics approach to task design: A critical review. *J. Appl. Psychol.* 67:193–217

Roberts, K. H., Hulin, C. L., Rousseau, D. M. 1978. *Developing an Interdisciplinary Science of Organizations.* San Francisco: Jossey-Bass

Robey, D., Baker, M. M. 1978. Task redesign: Individual moderating and novelty effects. *Hum. Relat.* 31:689–701

Rousseau, D. M. 1977. Technological differences in job characteristics, employee satisfaction, and motivation: A synthesis of job design research and sociotechnical systems theory. *Organ. Behav. Hum. Perform.* 19:18–42

Rousseau, D. M. 1978a. Characteristics of departments, positions, and individuals: Contexts for attitudes and behavior. *Adm. Sci. Q.* 23:521–40

Rousseau, D. M. 1978b. Measures of technology as predictors of employee attitudes. *J. Appl. Psychol.* 63:213–18

Rousseau, D. M. 1979. Assessment of technology in organizations: Closed versus open systems approaches. *Acad. Manage. Rev.* 4:531–42

Salancik, G. R., Pfeffer, J. 1977. An examination of need satisfaction models of job attitudes. *Adm. Sci. Q.* 22:427–56

Salancik, G. R., Pfeffer, J. 1978. A social information processing approach to job attitudes and task design. *Adm. Sci. Q.* 23:224–53

Sarason, I. G., Sarason, B. R. 1979. The importance of cognition and moderator variables in stress. In *Personality at the Cross-roads: Current Issues in Interactional Psychology,* ed. D. Magnusson, N. S. Endler. Hillsdale, NJ: Erlbaum

Sathe, V. 1978. Institutional versus questionnaire measures of organizational structure. *Acad. Manage. J.* 21:227–38

Schmidt, F. L., Hunter, J. E., Pearlman, K. 1981. Task differences as moderators of aptitude test validity in selection: A red herring. *J. Appl. Psychol.* 66:166–85

Schmitt, N., Coyle, B. W., White, J. K., Rauschenberger, J. 1978. Background, needs, job perceptions and job satisfaction: A causal model. *Pers. Psychol.* 31:889–901

Schmitt, N., Mellon, P. M. 1980. Life and job satisfaction: Is the job central? *J. Vocat. Behav.* 16:51–88

Schneider, B., Parkington, J. J., Buxton, V. M. 1980. Employee and customer perceptions of service in banks. *Adm. Sci. Q.* 25:252–67

Schuler, R. S. 1977a. The effects of role perceptions on employee satisfaction and performance moderated by employee ability. *Organ. Behav. Hum. Perform.* 18:98–107

Schuler, R. S. 1977b. Role conflict and ambiguity as a function of the task-structure-technology interaction. *Organ. Behav. Hum. Perform.* 20:66–74

Schwab, D. P. 1980. Construct validity in organizational behavior. See Staw & Cummings 1980. 2:3–43

Schwab, D. P., Cummings, L. L. 1976. A theoretical analysis of the impact of task scope on employee performance. *Acad. Manage. Rev.* 1:23–35

Scott, W. E. Jr., Erskine, J. A. 1980. The effects of variations in task design and monetary reinforcers on task behavior. *Organ. Behav. Hum. Perform.* 25: 311–35

Scott, W. R. 1977. Effectiveness of organizational effectiveness studies. See Goodman & Pennings 1977, pp. 63–95

Seligman, C., Darley, J. M. 1977. Feedback as a means of decreasing residential energy consumption. *J. Appl. Psychol.* 62:363–68

Shaw, J. B. 1980. An information-processing approach to the study of job design. *Acad. Manage. Rev.* 5:41–48

Sims, H. P., Szilagyi, A. D. 1976. Job characteristic relationships: Individual and structural moderators. *Organ. Behav. Hum. Perform.* 17:211–30

Slocum, J. W. Jr., Sims, H. P. 1980. A typology for integrating technology, organization, and job design. *Hum. Relat.* 33:193–212

Snyder, M. 1979. Self-monitoring processes. *Adv. Exp. Soc. Psychol.* 12:85–128

Spector, P. E. 1978. Organizational frustration: A model and review of the literature. *Pers. Psychol.* 31:815–30

Stabell, C. B. 1978. Integrative complexity of information environment perception and information use: An empirical investigation. *Organ. Behav. Hum. Perform.* 22:116–42

Staw, B. M., ed. 1979. *Research in Organizational Behavior,* Vol. 1. Greenwich, Conn: JAI Press. 478 pp.

Staw, B. M., Cummings, L. L., eds. 1980. *Research in Organizational Behavior,* Vol. 2. Greenwich, Conn: JAI Press. 355 pp.

Staw, B. M., Oldham, G. R. 1978. Reconsidering our dependent variables: A critique and empirical study. *Acad. Manage. J.* 21:539–59

Staw, B. M., Ross, J. 1980. Commitment in an experimenting society: A study of the attribution of leadership from administrative scenarios. *J. Appl. Psychol.* 65:249–60

Steers, R. M. 1977. *Organizational Effectiveness: A Behavioral View.* Santa Monica, Calif: Goodyear

Steers, R. M., Mowday, R. T. 1977. The motivational properties of tasks. *Acad. Manage. Rev.* 2:645–58

Steers, R. M., Spencer, D. G. 1977. The role of achievement motivation in job design. *J. Appl. Psychol.* 62:472–79

Stone, E. F. 1979. Field independence and perceptions of task characteristics: A laboratory investigation. *J. Appl. Psychol.* 64:305–10

Stone, E. F., Ganster, D. C., Woodman, R. W., Fusilier, M. R. 1979. Relationships between growth need strength and selected individual differences measures employed in job design research. *J. Vocat. Behav.* 14:329–40

Stone, E. F., Mowday, R. T., Porter, L. W. 1977. Higher order need strengths as moderators of the job scope-job satisfaction relationship. *J. Appl. Psychol.* 62: 466–71

Strang, H. R., Lawrence, E. C., Fowler, P. C. 1978. Effects of assigned goal level and knowledge of results on arithmetic computation: A laboratory study. *J. Appl. Psychol.* 63:446–50

Suedfeld, P., Rank, A. D. 1976. Revolutionary leaders: Long-term success as a function of changes in conceptual complexity. *J. Pers. Soc. Psychol.* 34:109–78

Susman, G. I., Evered, R. D. 1978. An assessment of the scientific merits of action research. *Adm. Sci. Q.* 23:582–603

Sutton, R. I., Rousseau, D. M. 1979. Structure, technology and dependence on a parent organization: Organizational and environnmental correlates of individual respones. *J. Appl. Psychol.* 64: 675–87

Taylor, M. S. 1981. The motivational effects of task challenge: A laboratory investigation. *Organ. Behav. Hum. Perform.* 27:255–78

Taylor, M. S., Slania, M. A. 1981. *The moderating effects of chronic self-esteem upon the psychological success cycle.* Presented at Ann. Meet. Midwest. Psychol. Assoc., Detroit

Terborg, J. R. 1977. Validation and extension of an individual differences model of work performance. *Organ. Behav. Hum. Perform.* 18:188–216

Tung, R. L. 1979. Dimensions of organizational environments: An exploratory study of their impact on organization structure. *Acad. Manage. J.* 22:672–93

Tushman, M. L. 1979. Work characteristics and subunit communication structure: A contingency analysis. *Adm. Sci. Q.* 24:82–98

Tushman, M. L., Nadler, D. A. 1978. Information processing as an integrating concept in organizational design. *Acad. Manage. Rev.* 3:613–24

Tussle, F. D., Gerwin, D. 1980. An information processing model of organizational perception, strategy, and choice. *Manage. Sci.* 26:575–92

Umstot, D. D., Bell, C. H., Mitchell, T. R. 1976. Effects of job enrichment and task goals on satisfaction and productivity: Implications of job design. *J. Appl. Psychol.* 61:379–94

Umstot, D., Mitchell, T. R., Bell, C. H. Jr. 1978. Goal setting and job enrichment: An integrated approach to job design. *Acad. Manage. Rev.* 3:867–79

Van Maanen, J., ed. 1979. Qualitative methodology. *Adm. Sci. Q.* Spec. Issue, 24:519–671

Vardi, Y., Hammer, T. H. 1977. Intraorganizational mobility and career perceptions among rank and file employees in different technologies. *Acad. Manage. J.* 20:622–34

Wall, T. D., Clegg, C. W., Jackson, P. R. 1978. An evaluation of the job characteristics model. *J. Occup. Psychol.* 51:183–96

Walsh, J. T., Taber, T. D., Beehr, T. A. 1980. An integrated model of perceived job characteristics. *Organ. Behav. Hum. Perform.* 25:252–67

Weed, S. E., Mitchell, T. R., 1980. The role of environmental and behavioral uncertainty as a mediator of situation-performance relationships. *Acad. Manage. J.* 23:38–60

Weiss, H. M. 1977. Subordinate imitation of supervisor behavior: The role of modeling in organizational socialization. *Organ. Behav. Hum. Perform.* 19:89–105

Weiss, H. M. 1978. Social learning of work values in organizations. *J. Appl. Psychol.* 63:711–18

Weiss, H. M., Nowicki, C. E. 1981. Social influences on task satisfaction: Model competence and observer field dependence. *Organ. Behav. Hum. Perform.* 27:345–66

Weiss, H. M., Shaw, J. B. 1979. Social influences on judgments about tasks. *Organ. Behav. Hum. Perform.* 24:126–40

White, J. K. 1978a. Generalizability of individual difference moderators of the participation in decision making-employee response relationship. *Acad. Manage. J.* 21:36–43

White, J. K. 1978b. Individual differences in the job quality-worker response relationship: Review, integration and comments. *Acad. Manage. Rev.* 3:267–80

White, S. E., Mitchell, T. R. 1979. Job enrichment versus social cues: A comparison and competitive test. *J. Appl. Psychol.* 64:1–9

Winett, R. A., Kagel, J. H., Battalio, R. C., Winkler, R. C. 1978. Effects of monetary rebates, feedback, and information on residential electricity consumption. *J. Appl. Psychol.* 63:73–80

Zedeck, S. 1977. An information processing model and approach to the study of motivation. *Organ. Behav. Hum. Perform.* 18:47–77

Ann. Rev. Psychol. 1982. 33:581-618

PERSONNEL SELECTION AND CLASSIFICATION

Mary L. Tenopyr

American Telephone and Telegraph Company, Morristown, New Jersey 07960

Paul D. Oeltjen

Bell Canada, Montreal H3C 3G4, Quebec, Canada

CONTENTS

0066-4308/82/0201-0581$02.00

INTRODUCTION

In the last decade, the field of personnel selection and classification has seen profound change. Traditional concepts in the area have undergone searching reevaluation, the relatively unstudied concepts in the field have been developed, often amid serious debate and controversy, and the quality of research and development work in the field has increased. It is gratifying to note the quality of work in the field and the theoretically high level of the matters which are of controversy.

As the nature of concerns in personnel selection has been upgraded, it has also been broadened. Thus, it becomes difficult for reviewers of literature in the field to delineate that which is the proper subject matter of personnel psychology and that which is more properly assigned to other disciplines. Space limitations prohibit this review from covering in depth the many topics of relevance to personnel selection and classification; consequently, the review will be primarily confined to the core subject matter of the discipline, and under this restriction not even all relevant articles could be included. Space limitations also preclude coverage of much of the vast literature which is outside the refereed journals in psychology. Thus, this review contains little coverage of the journals whose audience is mainly personnel administrators, the many relevant dissertations, and the numerous unpublished papers and reports in the field. The large number of books published during the last 4 years also cannot be covered. Some of the books, however, which should elicit a high degree of interest are those by Cascio (1978), Landy & Trumbo (1980), McCormick & Ilgen (1980), and Bass & Barrett (1981). References dated before January 1978 have been included only where they are needed to develop a topic, and these references should be considered as examples, as no attempt has been made to cover the complete history of any subject.

JOB ANALYSIS

General Issues

A comprehensive overview of job analysis methods was long overdue. It is now available in a book by McCormick (1979). There also appears to be an increase in research on job analysis. The most widely available information about jobs in the United States is contained in the *Dictionary of Occupational Titles* (DOT) (U.S. Department of Labor 1977) of which a new edition was published recently. Unfortunately, its availability is not matched by the availability of research results with data on the reliability and validity of information contained therein. An Occupational Analysis Inventory (OAI) which is applicable to the entire occupational spectrum has been developed by Cunningham and associates. Job clusters identified on the basis of analyzing OAI data were found compatible with the grouping of jobs in the DOT (Pass & Cunningham 1978). It is hoped that a future edition of the DOT will make use of research results obtained by Cunningham and associates and include information of OAI-based work dimensions for each job. The job clustering approach by Cunningham and associates has one advantage over most other applications of job clustering; namely, it starts with a meaningful and well-defined universe of jobs to be clustered. Where this has not been done it is always possible that the results of the job clustering were biased by the selection of jobs to be clustered.

A widely used job analysis methodology is the task inventory approach associated with the CODAP (Comprehensive Occupational Data Analysis Programs) computer software package. This system, originally developed in the U.S. Air Force, has recently found widespread use among public service sector organizations (Gambardella & Alvord 1980). The approach recommended by the Center for Vocational Education of the Ohio State University (Ammerman 1977) for identifying the performance content for job training is based upon this methodology.

To identify performance dimensions, researchers have performed factor analyses or cluster analyses of task inventories (Dowell & Wexley 1978, Kesselman & Lopez 1979, Trattner 1979). The number and type of dimensions identified in these analyses is partially a function of the differential specificity of task statements; a duty will more likely appear as a separate dimension if the analyst has broken it down and has written several task statements representing it; a duty is less likely to appear as a performance dimension if only one statement has been written for it (or none at all). Thus there is a need for a method of generating task statements which describe the job completely, are neither too general nor too specific, and are replicable by different job analysts working independently. An attempt to develop such a method has been made by R. M. McIntyre and associates (unpublished manuscript, 1980). Another approach to solve the problem of replicability may be the use of the Position Analysis Questionnaire or PAQ (see McCormick 1979), which has been used to determine the number of different performance appraisal forms required in the U.S. Coast Guard (Cornelius et al 1979b).

A direct approach to the identification of job requirements is to ask subject matter experts (SMEs) which knowledge, skills, or abilities (KSAs) are required for successful job performance. SMEs are asked to develop descriptions of job-relevant KSAs, but often they must identify abstract constructs without having a full understanding of the meaning of these constructs. This may explain why the job element method, which is the most common job analysis approach among personnel specialists in the public service, is perceived as more difficult to use than task analysis, PAQ, or critical incidents (Levine et al 1980). A preferred alternative would be to present SMEs with a standard comprehensive list of KSAs and to ask them to rate their job relevance, since it allows for the incorporation of well-established constructs based upon previous research on individual differences.

A standard list for rating ability requirements has been applied by Lopez & Kesselman (1980). A further improvement would be to obtain ratings of ability requirements separately for different task dimensions. This approach was used by Cornelius & Lyness (1980). Since an experimental evaluation of different job analysis methods is practically very difficult, Levine and associates (1981) surveyed experienced job analysts and obtained ratings on seven major methods of job analysis.

The most common sources of job analysis information are job incumbents, supervisors, and job analysts. Smith & Hakel (1979) averaged responses to the PAQ for each of several groups of job informants and obtained high convergent validities. Unfortunately, discriminant validity was not reported. Taylor (1978) and Taylor & Colbert (1978) found only moderate interrater agreements among individual respondents. Considering the moderately low interrater agreement on the PAQ, there appears to be a need to increase the standardization of PAQ scales, possibly by developing anchors for the scales. In the meantime, PAQ ratings should be obtained from several job analysts and then averaged. Within a group of job incumbents one might expect different job analysis results contingent upon the performance level of the incumbent. However, Wexley & Silverman (1978) found no differences in the relative time spent in various work activities between effective and ineffective managers.

Cluster analysis and factor analysis are the most commonly used techniques for grouping jobs (Dowell & Wexley 1978, Taylor 1978, Taylor & Colbert 1978, Youngman et al 1978, Brush & Owens 1979, Cornelius et al 1979a,b, Krzystofiak et al 1979). Cornelius and associates (1979a) found that seven clusters of foremen positions clustered differently, depending on whether or not the input to the cluster analysis was responses to an ability requirement inventory, the PAQ, or a task inventory. When reviewing the literature on cluster analysis of jobs, Pearlman (1980) also concluded that different grouping strategies are likely to produce different groupings of jobs. It might be added that the selection of jobs to be clustered is also very important, since the result of any data reduction technique will be dependent upon the types of jobs which were entered into the analysis. Since cluster analysis only provides information on relative similarities, some researchers have suggested evaluating job similarities by means of a multivariate analysis of variance (Lissitz et al 1979). For the purpose of validity generalization Pearlman (1980) suggested that the way to avoid the problem of selecting a job analysis and grouping stategy is to classify jobs rationally and use as a criterion of job differences the empirical validity distribution. It can be concluded that there is no consensus on the proper methods for assessing job similarities and for grouping jobs.

Realistic Job Previews

One purpose of job analysis which has received little or no attention by job analysts is the development of realistic job previews (RJP), as described by Wanous (1980). R. R. Reilly et al (unpublished manuscript, 1980) recommended that RJP development should be similar to the development of a content-oriented test. An example for a systematically developed job preview can be found in Reilly et al (1979a). Latham et al (1979) suggest the use of behavioral observation scales developed via the critical incident technique to show applicants what will be expected of them in the job. The inclusion of evaluative information in RJPs requires additional dependent variables or even additional orientations in job analysis. An example of a new variable can be found in Ash et al (1979), who developed a position analysis checklist on which incumbents had to indicate the most and least liked aspects of the job. An example for an additional orientation in job analysis is the assessment of perceived job characteristics by Taber et al (1978).

Wanous (1980) presented arguments why RJPs should lead to increased job satisfaction and have a variety of other beneficial effects. However, the only effect of RJPs for which there is empirical evidence is a very small effect on turnover which can only be detected in studies with large sample sizes. This was the finding by R. R. Reilly et al (1981) after a review of 11 studies examining the effectiveness of RJPs. Based upon their review, it can be concluded that it would be unrealistic to expect too much from RJPs. Their primary objective should be to take much of the discussion of job content out of the employment interview, which is not the best place to inform applicants about the job anyway, since interviewers often are not a credible source of job information (Fisher et al 1979).

JOB EVALUATION

Most job evaluation systems involve setting the pay for jobs on the basis of skill, effort, and responsibility (Belcher 1974). Relative to skill, there are four basic questions (*a*) What skills are required? (*b*) How much of these skills is required? (*c*) Is more of skill A required in job 1 than there is of skill B in job 2? (*d*) Are skill A and skill B of equal worth to the organization? The relationship between the job evaluation process and the subject matter of personnel selection psychology is readily apparent. Skill requirements in terms of type may be elicited by traditional job analysis methodology or in some cases by test validation. The use of the latter involves some problems, as the range of talent on pertinent skills may be severely restricted for those already in the job or even among those applying for a given job. The question of how much skill is required is analogous to the question of where to set the critical score after a test validation study. This is usually not determined by refined psychometrics, but often rests heavily upon the interpretation of psychometric data. Questions *c* and *d* are at present unanswerable in terms which invoke any scientific rigor. Question *d* involves so many value judgments that it probably can have no completely satisfactory answer.

Nevertheless, personnel psychology is beginning to make more inputs into the job evaluation process. For example, in several studies PAQ predictions of salary were related to actual salaries. Taylor (1978) and Taylor & Colbert (1978) observed high correlations between pay and PAQ dimensions for a heterogeneous group of jobs; Smith & Hakel (1979) found moderate correlations for a more homogeneous group of jobs. A good overview and analysis of the PAQ and other job evaluation methods can be found in Treiman (1979) and in Schwab (1980). While selection research can contribute to the improved evaluation of skill requirements, human performance research on perceived effort and difficulty can make some contribution to the valid assessment of the compensable factor of effort (Hogan et al 1980, Herbert 1978, Brumback 1978).

PERFORMANCE MEASUREMENT

Supervisory Assessment

Supervisory ratings of performance continue to be the most common criterion against which tests are evaluated, and the literature on rating methods and rating effectiveness is extensive. One book (Latham & Wexley 1981) and one technical report (De Vries et al 1980) review much of the literature from a practical perspective of appraising performance with the goal of developing employees or making administrative personnel decisions. Three major reviews with a more theoretical orientation have appeared in the period covered by this review (De Cotiis & Petit 1978, Kane & Lawler 1979, Landy & Farr 1980). All reviewers agree in their conclusion that there has been too much emphasis on rating formats and not enough on the rating context.

Performance appraisal scales have been constructed on the basis of various job analysis methods, such as the critical incident technique (Latham et al 1979, Dickinson & Zellinger 1980, Ivancevich 1980, Shapira & Shirom 1980), task inventories (e.g. Dowell & Wexley 1978, Trattner 1979), or the PAQ (Colbert & Taylor 1978, Cornelius et al 1979b). Reviewers of research on behaviorally anchored rating scales (Atkin & Conlon 1978, Jacobs et al 1980) concluded that their expected superiority over other methods has not been demonstrated. Bernardin & Smith (1981) rose to the defense of behaviorally anchored rating scales and pointed out that most researchers have not used the original Smith & Kendall (1963) procedure properly. De Cotiis (1978) and Latham & Wexley (1981) suggest that the development of behaviorally oriented rating scales should include the collection of a wide range of behavioral statements, and the selection of items for inclusion in the final scale should be on the basis of some form of item analysis or factor analysis.

Two other formats which also failed to show any clear superiority were the forced choice scale (King et al 1980) and the mixed standard scale (Saal 1979, Dickinson & Zellinger 1980, Bernardin et al 1980). No studies were found which evaluated the unique features of the mixed standard scale, which permits the identification of ambiguous dimensions and illogical raters. A completely new format for behavioral rating scales has been proposed by Kane & Lawler (1979). The objective of their behavioral discrimination scales is to assess not only typical or average performance, but also the distribution of performance over an appraisal period. Behavioral rating scales are theoretically not appropriate for jobs where goals can be accomplished through a variety of different behaviors (Keeley 1978, Kane & Lawler 1979). What is required in these cases are result- or outcome-oriented rating scales. Surprisingly little research has been done on result-oriented performance appraisal, and studies comparing behavior versus task-oriented (result-oriented) appraisal have not been found.

Progress has been made in the assessment of the psychometric quality of rating data. Saal et al (1980) recommended an analysis of variance approach to the definition of rater bias. Methods for assessing interrater agreement and consistency have been reviewed by Shrout & Fleiss (1979) and by Fleiss and associates (1979). One way to improve the quality of ratings is to average the ratings of several judges. Libby & Blashfield (1978) found a pooling of ratings by three judges to be optimal.

Peer Assessment and Self-Assessment

There are occasions when peers have more opportunities to observe performance than superiors. But based upon the review by Kane & Lawler (1978) it can be concluded that peer assessments are not an appropriate criterion for selection research. One exception to this general recommendation is performance appraisal by panels of peers, in particular for appraising scientific performance. Kissler & Nebeker (1979) found highly structured peer ratings to be more reliable and valid (using a scientific productivity criterion) than supervisory ratings.

For situations where supervisor or peer ratings are not available, or are deficient, several researchers have suggested the consideration of self-ratings. Davey (1980) found some evidence for convergent and discriminant validity for self-ratings and test scores of verbal and quantitative skills. Holzbach (1978), Thornton (1980), and Meyer (1980) have observed that compared to supervisory ratings, self-appraisals tend to be more lenient. The other potential problem with self-appraisal forms is that they are fakable, as was shown by South (1980). Perhaps a proper use of self-appraisal is as a self-selection instrument, as suggested by Downs and associates (1978), who observed a relationship between objective trainability test scores and the probability of accepting a job offer. Thus, work sample tests might serve a realistic job preview function and discourage non-qualified applicants long before any predictive validity data are available.

Rater Training

In efforts to improve the quality of ratings, training programs for raters of performance have been developed and evaluated. Spool (1978) reviewed research on rater training and concluded that training has some effect on reducing rating errors and increasing interrater reliability. This conclusion is supported by findings by Pursell et al (1980), who were able to train supervisors to exhibit less restriction of range in their ratings. A diminishing effect of rater training over time or a lack of transfer to an administrative context was observed by Bernardin (1978), Ivancevich (1979), and Warmke & Billings (1979). Ivancevich suggested a need for refresher training to maintain a positive effect of rater training.

Ultimately, personnel researchers are interested in increasing rating accuracy which is more difficult to define operationally than rating errors. Bernardin & Pence (1980) and Borman (1979) defined accuracy as agreement with another group of raters. Thornton & Zorich (1980) developed an objective criterion to assess accuracy of observation and found that accuracy can be enhanced by instructions to record specific behaviors and by training to avoid observation errors. What is required for practical applications in organizations is an observer training program supplemented by a program to motivate raters to observe performance more frequently and more systematically. A similar position is presented by Bernardin (1979).

One variable affecting supervisory ratings which has received little attention from rating training program developers is motivational rating bias. Knowlton & Mitchell (1980) observed more extreme (positive or negative) performance evaluations if identical levels of performance were attributed to effort rather than to ability. This finding is naturally of great concern to selection researchers, since it might affect the correlations between tests of ability and performance criteria.

Objective Performance Measurement

Only a few studies have examined performance criteria which do not involve ratings. In an enlightening investigation, Cascio & Valenzi (1978) compared objective counts of positive and negative police officer performance incidents. They found that the objective criteria suffered from low variance and low reliability. Only a small relationship with BARS ratings was observed. Rothe (1978) reported moderate reliabilities of weekly productivity data; thus reasonably high reliabilities could be obtained by summing the data over several weeks. This is the approach recommended by Gustafson (1977) and Gael (1978), who have developed a "Job Performance Evaluation" system which is based on obtaining sufficiently large samples of work products for each individual and determining a significance level of the difference between the individual performance distribution and a normative distribution. Because of the weakness of supervisory ratings and the difficulties of obtaining objective productivity data, several researchers have developed work samples for use as criteria (e.g. Trattner 1979).

Turnover and absenteeism do not seem to be common criteria predicted by selection procedures. An explanation for this can be inferred from the reviews by Muchinsky & Tuttle (1979) and by Mobley and associates (1979). Muchinsky and Tuttle concluded that tests are poor predictors of turnover, whereas biodata have been established as a good predictor of turnover in several studies. In the turnover model by Mobley and associates, individual difference variables which can be assessed during the selection process assume only a minor and indirect role.

A similar situation exists with regard to attendance as a criterion. Steers & Rhodes (1978) reviewed the literature on employee attendance and proposed a model which does not include variables which could be assessed at the selection stage.

VALIDITY CONCEPTS

It appears that few subjects in personnel selection and classification have been the subject of so much recent controversy as the basic concept of validity. There has been discussion of all three of the traditional aspects of validity; criterion-related, content, and construct. Some controversy relates to all three strategies and to the basic nature of validity itself.

Unity of Validity

The provision for dividing validity, like Gaul, into three parts was first evident in the American Psychological Association's first pronouncement which recommended standards for psychological tests (American Psychological Association 1954) and has been carried forth in numerous publications. It has become apparent from the outcries of many persons in the field that compartmentalized thinking about validity has been carried to an extreme. Messick (1975, 1980), Guion (1977, 1978, 1980), Tenopyr (1977), Dunnette & Borman (1979), and Cronbach (1980a,b) have all been saying that rigid division of validity into criterion-related, content, and construct is wrong. *The Principles for the Validation and Use of Personnel Selection Procedures* (*Principles*) (American Psychological Association, Division of Industrial and Organizational Psychology 1980) speak of strategies of validation, not "types."

Guion (1980) defined validity as "the degree to which the result of the measurement (the numbers) satisfactorily represents the various magnitudes of the intended attribute." In a sense then all validity is essentially construct validity, and the various strategies by which one assesses goodness of measurement of the attribute in question appear to be inextricably intertwined. It is difficult to conceive of a measurement situation which would not involve all three aspects of validity.

Criterion-Related Strategies

The Principles for the Validation and Use of Personnel Selection Procedures (American Psychological Association, Division of Industrial and Organizational Psychology 1980) (*Principles*) treat criterion-related strategies in a somewhat different manner than they were in the earlier version of that publication. For example, concurrent validation strategies with appropriate controls are given more acceptability. Barrett and associates (1981) also have argued strongly for such an upgrading of the status of concurrent designs. The *Principles* also differ from their predecessor in lending more status to corrections for restriction in range of measurement and allowing for more generalization of results of criterion-related research.

Content-Oriented Strategies

Content-oriented strategies have received considerable attention during the last 4 years as a result of extensive equal employment litigation often involving civil service jurisdictions (Perticone & Wiesen 1979). The legal problems are exacerbated by professional differences in the conceptualization of content-oriented strategies and by the lack of agreement on the exact procedures to follow in developing a measuring instrument by content-oriented procedures. On the conceptual side, the *Principles* present, in a general manner, the essence of the basis of content strategies. A new section discusses the psychometric considerations associated with the development of content-based instruments for selection purposes. Moving from a content sample to a measuring procedure raises not only psychometric questions but also questions about which aspect of validity, content or construct, is appropriate for interpreting scores (Guion 1978). Strict interpreters of government advisories (Barrett 1980) also raise questions about the roles of content and construct strategies. The basic question appears to involve determining the conditions when content-oriented test construction is enough to justify a selection procedure. Until conceptual issues relative to content-oriented strategies are resolved, the test developer is urged to proceed with caution in employing these strategies.

Relative to procedural mechanics in content-oriented instrument development, there does not seem to be a professional consensus. It appears that there should be some unified effort to conduct the research and development necessary for prescribing appropriate mechanics in this area.

Construct-Oriented Strategies

The difficulties in applying construct strategies in personnel selection are clearly depicted in the proceedings of a 1979 colloquim on the subject (Educational Testing Service 1980). The academician's tendency is to work at the process level, whereas practitioners speak in terms of relatively broad traits. Dunnette (1980) noted the diversity of strategies discussed by the various contributers and correctly welcomed them as crucial for advancing science. However, it appears that the wide difference between the concerns of the psychometricians and those of the practitioners needs some resolution. In view of the immediate pressures on the practitioners, they cannot wait until promising but molecular theories like Sternberg's e.g. (1979) become developed so that they can be a basis for operational employee selection. Guttman's (1955) facet theory which is being applied in selection research (Ridgway 1980) and achievement test construction (Berk 1978), however, may deserve more exploration as an immediate means for ensuring construct-relevance of selection tests in some instances. A discussion of the method may be found in Shye (1978).

Those who espouse factor analytic techniques as a basis for establishing construct-based support for selection should welcome the Ekstrom et al (1979) monograph which contains a thorough review of the literature on factor analytic literature relative to cognitive abilities, a designation of established factors, and a description of marker tests for these factors. The review by Jackson & Paunonen (1980) should be of interest to those attempting to base selection on personality constructs, as should be the taxonomic efforts of Wiggins (1979).

There is likely to be a conceptual framework within which the dilemma posed by the separation of the theoretical and practical can be resolved. Lerner (1977) emphasized that traditional concepts of construct validation represented ideals and could not be imposed as legal standards. Cronbach (1980a, p. 44), speaking of the Cronbach & Meehl (1955) formulation of construct validity, has said:

> Our original presentation made construct validity more esoteric than it really is. Construct validation is nothing more than argument that combines data and accepted beliefs to bridge over uncertainties and reach persuasive prediction. . . . The reason construct validation is thought to be rare is that psychologists have associated the term with an ideal of elegance and certainty that is not likely to be attained and that is not necessary.

Guion (1980) expresses essentially the same view. The *Principles* reflect the same point. There is obviously a middle ground between the made-up-on-the-spot construct and the construct supported by a complex nomological network. With the concepts regarding validity justification in place, it appears necessary now, as it is with content validity, to attempt to reach a consensus on the mechanics of establishing construct support for selection.

GROUP DIFFERENCE ISSUES

Guidelines

The effect of the equal opportunity employment movement on the field of personnel selection was accentuated by the publication in August 1978 of the Uniform Guidelines on Employee Selection Procedures (UGL) (Equal Employment Opportunity Commission et al 1978). Two sets of questions and answers on the guidelines were subsequently published (Equal Employment Opportunity Commission et al 1979, 1980).

The new UGL are highly specific in their content relative to legal, technical, and documentation issues. They are also somewhat at odds with the *Principles.* Major differences are delineated as follows:

Principles	*UGL*
1. Emphasize strategies of validation	Divide validity into three parts
2. Express no preference for strategies	Express a preference for criterion-related validity
3. Do not require search for alternatives to valid selection procedures	Require search for alternatives
4. Do not require fairness studies	Require fairness studies
5. Allow for validity generalization	Make little provision for validity generalization
6. Are flexible in content-oriented test development; recognize that all tests are abstractions	Practically insist on point-to-point correspondence to the job when content procedures are used
7. Do not require special qualifications for ranking on any test	Require justification for ranking on content-developed test

Thus, it appears that serious controversy between professional standards and guidelines and misunderstandings about what is required in a validation effort will be possible in legal proceedings.

Alternatives

The emphasis in the UGL on alternatives is for the purpose of reducing group differences on selection procedures. There are two possible sources of alternatives to a valid selection test: (*a*) other tests or (*b*) other types of selection procedure. Relative to reducing black-white differences in test performance, it has often been suggested that reducing the verbal content of tests would also reduce black-white mean differences. There are obvious sampling problems in obtaining appropriate estimates of population parameters for various ethnic groups; however, the considerable research was summarized by Loehlin et al (1975, p. 194) as follows: "Only in black-white comparisons on the Wechsler scales is there a substantial number of studies using the same instruments, and here, although there is some variation in the findings, there appears to be a tendency for black subjects to score relatively better on the verbal scales than on the nonverbal scales." Furthermore, there is nothing in recent studies of race differences which would support the notion that changing types of test would benefit blacks (Hennessy & Merrifield 1978, Backman et al 1979, Wing 1980).

Sex differences in spatial tests and certain mathematical reasoning tests have been well documented (Backman 1972, Maccoby & Jacklin 1974, McGee 1979, Jensen 1980). Thus, it appears that women are at a disadvantage competing for jobs demanding mathematical and spatial abilities. Changing tests would be useful only if appropriate tests measuring different constructs were equally valid for selection for the given jobs.

Relative to the possibility of using nontest classes of alternatives, R. R. Reilly and G. Chao (unpublished manuscript, 1979) conducted an extensive review of nine classes of alternatives. Results indicated that only biodata and peer evaluations were supported as having validities substantially equal to those for standardized tests. The available studies of fairness offered no clear indication that any of the alternatives have validity equal to that of conventional tests and less adverse impact. The authors further concluded that unless criterion means are equal, a predictor cannot meet both the conditions of fairness and no adverse impact, and that when criterion means differ, the most valid alternative will have the lesser adverse impact. Kesselman & Lopez (1979) found a job knowledge test to be valid and fair, whereas a commercial aptitude test in the same situation produced adverse impact and was not found valid. Importantly, G. H. Ironson and R. M. Guion (unpublished manuscript, 1981), commenting on Schmidt and associates' (1977) conclusion that work sample tests are likely to have less adverse effect than paper-and-pencil trade tests, warned against conclusions in this area when measurement methodology and underlying ability being measured may be confused. They also reached the conclusion that the more valid the test is, the less the adverse impact will be.

Selection Fairness Models

Selection fairness models are often called "test bias" models, e.g. Flaugher (1978). The former term is adopted here, because fairness is not a property of the test but a function of how the test is used. There has been little development of such models since Dunnette & Borman (1979) reviewed the many models which had been proposed in the late 1960s and the 1970s. Schwartz (1978) has developed a probabilistic procedure with the goal of evaluating the interactive effects of adverse impact, job relatedness, and criterion differences. Bartlett and associates (1978) suggested alternate computational procedures for studying group differences in regression systems. Moebus (1978) related various selection fairness models and developed procedures he suggested ensure fairness.

The fact that there has been little new development of fairness models suggests that there has been at least some implicit acceptance of utility formulations to define and apply equity in the given personnel selection situation (Gross & Su 1975, Cronbach 1976, Novick & Petersen 1976, Petersen & Novick 1976, Darlington 1976, Novick & Ellis 1977). Thus it appears fairness in selection is being recognized as involving policy issues as well as psychometric issues.

Apparently the only new model on the horizon is that of L. J. Cronbach and G. W. Schaeffer (unpublished manuscript, 1980). They have developed methodology for "equal marginal risk" hiring which involves estimating the expected criterion score of each applicant by means of the regression equation specific to the applicant's demographic group. All applicants are ordered together in terms of these estimates and the best *N* hired. They have considered between-groups and within-groups utilities separately. Cronbach and associates (1980) have also developed a mathematical structure for analyzing fairness and have shown that, in a representative case, substantial changes in the rate of minority hiring have only small effects on the quality of the workforce.

The various developments in the area of selection models, no matter how mathematically elegant and logically consistent, unfortunately, will probably have little impact on the way employees are selected in the real world. In the first place, the data upon which to base the use of many of the models are often just not available. For example, few employers have large enough *N*s available to make reliable estimates of population parameters required to apply the models. For example, as Trattner & O'Leary (1980) have indicated, sample sizes required for appropriate power in testing for differential validity are large. Also there are problems in making estimates of some of the basic data required by some models. For example, success ratio, selection ratio, and adverse impact are all probably random variables, not constants. Secondly, employers, always in public view, must be able to explain selection procedures in such a way as to be understood by applicants, employees, unions, and shareowners. Procedures such as use of different tests or standards for different groups just cannot be expected to be explained to everyone's satisfaction.

Differential Prediction

DIFFERENTIAL VALIDITY Whether differential validity of ability tests for blacks and whites is a viable phenomenon has had a long history of debate, as reported by Dunnette & Borman (1979). This controversy has continued into the period covered by this review (see Hunter & Schmidt 1978, Boehm 1978, Bobko & Bartlett 1978, Katzell & Dyer 1978). The definitional and methodological questions involved in the various reviews on the subject have been many. For example, Schmitt et al (1978) reported that corrections for restriction in range had no effect on group validities.

In an invited paper which was to be the *Journal of Applied Psychology's* final published word in a series of articles, Linn (1978) reached the following conclusions: (*a*) Single-group validity cannot exist, and it is inappropriate to conclude that a test is more valid for one group than another because the coefficient of correlation is significant for one group and not significant for the other. (*b*) If equal validity is defined as one population coefficient of correlation precisely equaling one for another population, obviously differential validity does not exist; the evidence is, however, very strong that the magnitude of the difference for blacks and whites is very small.

Perhaps Hunter and associates (1979) have had the last word. They concluded on the basis of a large-scale analysis that true differential validity does not exist. Schmidt et al (1980b) also concluded that for employment tests differential validity for Hispanic Americans and the majority group occur no more often than would be expected on the basis of chance plus the operation of various statistical artifacts.

The status of differential validity relative to the sexes is less clear. In reviews of the literature, Schmitt and associates (Schmitt et al 1978, Mellon et al 1980) found female validities slightly but significantly higher than male validities for predicting academic criteria. Jensen (1980, p. 629), however, has pointed out that males and females are not evenly distributed through the various curricula in universities and that unless male and female validities can be compared for persons taking the same courses, such comparisons are meaningless. Schmitt et al found only two studies with both male and female validities in employment settings, so conclusions regarding employment criteria were difficult to reach. A recent review of various studies conducted in one organization (D. L. Zink and M. L. Tenopyr, unpublished manuscript 1981) indicated little evidence of differential validity for the sexes when physical and cognitive abilities and a variety of criteria were involved. Linn's (1978) conclusion that differential validity may well be considered a *pseudoproblem* bears echoing. Not only is there good reason to believe that validity differences for race and ethnic groups are near zero, but also there is apparently no rational scientific hypothesis which would support a contention that differences should be otherwise. Also, in the case of possible sex differences in validity, no one to date has brought forth a reasonable hypothesis as to why there should be such differences.

DIFFERENTIAL REGRESSION SYSTEMS The unfortunate exaggerated attention to the differential validity issue has detracted from study and discussion of a far more important issue relative to selection fairness, that of group differences in regression systems (Schmidt et al 1973, Bobko &

Bartlett 1978, Linn 1978.) Selection is not necessarily unfair for a group with lower validity. At a minimum, comparisons of standard errors of estimate, slopes, and intercepts for different groups are necessary to determine fairness. Ruch (1972) and R. L. Linn (unpublished manuscript, 1981) have found that unfairness for races is uncommon and that when there is unfairness the result obtained most often in the comparison of prediction systems for blacks and whites is that the system for the majority group slightly overpredicts for the minority group. Schmidt and associates (1980b), in reviewing fairness literature for Hispanic Americans, found differences in slopes and intercepts for Hispanics and the majority group to be in the chance range. No appreciable sex differences in regression systems were found in the studies reviewed by Zink & Tenopyr (unpublished manuscript), as cited above. Webster et al (1978) concluded that separate regression equations were not needed for hospital personnel of different sexes. Methodology for comparing regression systems has been discussed by Hollingsworth (1980); Sorbom (1978) and Rogosa (1980) have proposed new procedures.

Should ensuing research reveal any marked tendencies toward differences in prediction systems for different groups, it would be wise to generate testable hypotheses relating to reasons for such differences. The quest for differential validity when there was no rational reason to assume any differences should not be repeated in the investigation of prediction systems.

Simulated Employment Evaluation Studies

At least 16 studies to determine the effects of race and sex on employment decisions have been published in the last 3 years. Space does not permit their evaluation here. In addition, there have been two evaluative reviews relative to group differences in the subjective aspects of employment decision making (Arvey 1979, Nieva & Gutek 1980). The majority of the studies have involved "paper people" and students acting as personnel directors or supervisors who evaluate persons whose credentials are identical but whose sex or race is different.

A fairly consistent finding is that females receive lower evaluations than males. However, there are many variables which appear to affect the incidence and degree of different evaluations of the sexes. Among these are marital status, educational background, predominant sex of potential subordinates, personal attractiveness, type of job (managerial or nonmanagerial, sex-congruent or not), strength of organization's affirmative action policy, authoritarianism of the interviewer, sex composition of the applicant pool, and sex of evaluator.

Findings of overt racial discrimination do not appear to be as prevalent as those of sex discrimination in the studies reviewed; however, this too is dependent upon many factors, including size of company, degree of race-congruence of job, and race of evaluator.

In view of the current national interest in the aging and the handicapped, it is surprising that there is so little research on employment of these persons. The small amount of simulated applicant research done in these areas offers few bases for generalizations.

There are some problems with this general line of research, such as transparency of purpose, as Gorman and associates (1978) and Newman and Krzystofiak (1979) have indicated. Perhaps the greatest value of this type of research is not in the area of determining aspects of possible discrimination, but in generating the greatly needed further hypotheses about the subjective aspects of personnel decision-making processes. Such hypotheses bear testing with other types of experimental techniques.

METHODOLOGICAL CONSIDERATIONS

Validity Generalization

The view that validity study results should not be generalized was challenged in 1977 by Schmidt and Hunter. They developed a validity generalization model which permits estimates of the percentage of observed variation in validities which is due to "statistical artifacts" (sampling error, variation in restriction of range, and differences in test and criterion reliabilities), the size of true validities, and confidence intervals. While the equations associated with the model have changed somewhat since 1977, and alternative equations have been proposed by Callender & Osburn (1980), the conclusions from applying the model have not been affected by the use of different equations. The model has been applied to clerical, supervisory, and programming jobs with consistent results. Most of the between-study variance of validity coefficients was found to be artifactual and due primarily to differences in sample size (Schmidt et al 1979b 1980a, Pearlman et al 1980).

The validity generalization approach by Schmidt and colleagues seems to imply the acceptance of the null hypothesis of no differences in validity coefficients between jobs and the rejection of the alternative hypothesis of situational specificity. However, validity generalization and situational specificity are not mutually exclusive hypotheses. While there is sufficient reason to conclude that validities generalize across a variety of jobs, there is insufficient evidence to reject the possibility of situational effects on the size of the validity coefficients.

An accepted theory of situational effects would make it possible to combine studies in order to obtain sufficient statistical power for testing the effect (Rosenthal 1979). The need for a theory or taxonomy of situations or dimensions of environments has been recognized by Roberts and associates (1978), Schneider (1978), Terborg and associates (1980), and Peters & O'Connor (1980). Peters and associates (1980) identified eight situational variables and demonstrated their effect on performance. The theory by Peters and associates draws attention to ceiling effects in the criterion. Results obtained in laboratory studies of task difficulties are compatible with the Peters theory (Forbes & Barrett 1978, Fleishman 1978). Since the naturally occurring variance in situational effects is probably too small to be of practical significance, researchers should attempt to create them through experimentation or organizational intervention.

In conclusion, while the results of validity generalization studies are of great importance for practitioners, this should not lead researchers to ignore situational variables and moderators. A coexistence of validity generalization and situational specificity is possible. If situational variables are assessed with an instrument like the PAQ, a job component approach to validity generalization might be considered, as was demonstrated by McCormick et al (1979).

A matter which specifically should be a subject for future study is the effect of criteria upon validity generalization results. It appears that criteria such as supervisory ratings, which are subject to a large general factor, may lead to extensive generalizability, whereas those criteria which are more focused upon specific aspects of job behaviors and results may be associated with more situational specificity of validity.

Estimation

"Shrinkage" formulas have been of considerable concern. Cattin (1980b) and Huberty & Mourad (1980) explained the distinction between estimating population multiple correlation coefficients for the prediction model or for the correlation model. Estimates for the prediction model were evaluated in Monte Carlo simulation tests by Rozeboom (1978), Cattin (1980b), and Huberty & Mourad (1980). The recommended equations have been presented by Cattin (1980a,b). Estimates for the correlation model were similarly examined in simulation studies (Claudy 1978, Carter 1979, Cattin 1980b, Huberty & Mourad 1980). These estimation equations apply only in the case of ordinary least squares regression. When predictors have been selected from a larger group of predictors by using a stepwise regression procedure, not only will shrinkage be larger than expected based upon the number of selected predictors, but also traditional formulas may not indicate an appropriate significance level for the multiple coefficient of correlation (Wilkinson 1979). Until appropriate procedures have been established for estimating population correlation coefficients for situations where different weights than the ordinary least squares weights for the complete set of predictors have been used, it is recommended that cross-validation be done (Dorans & Drasgow 1980, Cattin 1980b).

The most common method of cross-validation is to split a single sample (Murphy 1979) in order to get an indication to what extent the results can be generalized and applied to other samples. The problem with single sample cross-validation is that whatever factors cause the sample to be unique and not generalizable impinge upon both parts of the sample. In order to get more meaningful information out of cross-validation, researchers should split their samples systematically. An applicant sample, for example, might be split on the basis of date of application. In this way, cross-validation becomes more like replication.

To reduce problems of shrinkage, methods of robust estimation have been proposed. These have been reviewed by Darlington (1978), Wainer (1978), and Winer (1978). Of all the different alternatives for robust regression, reduced rank regression appears least controversial, can be done by using standard computer programs, and is particularly appropriate for selection research. It is ideally suited for predictive validation strategies where there is a large number of applicants for whom predictor scores are available, but relatively fewer cases with both predictor and criterion scores. The recommended procedure is to do a principal components analysis using all predictor data, to calculate factor scores by using an incomplete unit-weighting method recommended by Morris (1979), and to regress these new predictors against the criterion. The major advantage of this procedure is that it uses all available data and is quite robust. This robustness is partially due to an increase in predictor reliability and a reduction in the number of predictors. It even permits the use of shrinkage formulas (Cattin 1980b). If several criteria are available, predictor-criterion relationships may be explored by analysis techniques recommended by Skinner (1978).

Weighting Predictors

Dawes (1979) argued strongly in favor of using equal weights when linearly combining variables for the purpose of making decisions. Remus (1980) cautioned against using Dawes's recommendations in applied situations and presented examples of predictions in selection situations where a unit rule is inferior to an optimal regression rule (Remus & Jenicke 1978, Remus 1980). Rozeboom (1979) presented mathematical formulas and Bentler & Woodward (1979) a statistical rationale which provide little justification to favor equal weights in applied prediction. Laughlin (1978, 1979) also cautioned against the indiscriminate use of equal weights, based upon results of a simulation study. As an alternative, he described a Bayesian approach to the estimation of regression weights. A Bayesian approach involving the use of prior beliefs has also been suggested by Remus (1980) and Pruzek

& Frederick (1978). Cattin (1978) outlined a procedure which would allow personnel researchers to decide between equal weights and regression weights.

In summary, selection researchers can choose between several well-documented methods for weighting predictors: ordinary least squares regression weights, unit or directional weights on raw scores or on standard scores, weights on principal components, and Bayesian weights (see Darlington 1978, Wainer 1978). The latter two alternatives should seriously be considered by selection researchers.

Power and Related Issues

Another advantage of the method for combining predictors prior to regression analysis, discussed earlier, is that the statistical power of detecting true validities is increased (Cascio et al 1978, 1980). If the researcher is only able to obtain criterion data for a subsample of all applicants who were hired, then power can be increased by obtaining criterion data for extreme groups (Osburn & Greener 1978, Abrahams & Alf 1978).

Issues associated with correcting for restriction of range have been the subject of several papers (Sands et al 1978, Greener & Osburn 1979, Bobko & Rieck 1980, Boone & Lewis 1980). Brown (1979), Roe (1979), and Schultz (1980) observed that in practice the degree of restriction of range is less severe than what would be expected on the basis of the selection ratio. Thus, it is important to calculate the variance of predictor scores for all applicants as well as for those who were selected, and not to make inferences on the basis of selection ratios.

Little research has been directed at problems associated with cutting scores. One exception is an investigation by Campion & Pursell (1980), who determined selection ratio, adverse impact, validity coefficient, and expected job performance as a function of different cut-offs. They pointed out that the final decision is judgmental and trade-offs have to be made between, for example, adverse impact and validity. Melamed & Oeltjen (1980) proposed a model which would replace fixed cut-offs by probabilities of being recommended for hiring conditional upon predictor scores.

Tailored Testing

Computerized tailored (or adaptive) testing is a process in which examinees interact with a computer to answer a series of items, each prompted by the correctness or incorrectness of answer to previous items. After each item is answered, the computer estimates the examinee's ability. Based upon this estimate, the computer selects the next item. As the series of items progresses, the estimate of ability becomes increasingly precise. Because each series of items or test is tailored to the individual examinee, significantly fewer items (and consequently less testing time) are required relative to conventional paper-and-pencil tests. Information on the state of the art may be found in Urry (1977), Hambleton et al (1978), McBride (1979), and Weiss & Davison (1981). An extensive coverage of the models, theory, and algorithms may be found in Urry & Dorans (1981).

Tailored testing is probably of most interest to large employers. Should various test disclosure bills become law for employers or should breaches of test security be a problem, tailored testing could be worth the investment, because each examinee essentially takes a different test.

HUMAN RESOURCE PLANNING

Human resource planning is an emerging field, a discipline coming into its own. In 1978, the Human Resource Planning Society began publishing its own journal, *Human Resource Planning.* Despite increasing development and definition of the field, it is apparent (Kahalas et al 1980) that approaches and orientations vary widely among organizations. It is apparent that the equal employment opportunity movement with its attendant government regulation has given impetus to planning activities, particularly with respect to the labor market analysis aspects of planning. The affirmative action aspects of human resource planning have been reviewed by Dunnette & Borman (1979) and covered in numerous articles in *Human Resources Planning.*

In reviewing the literature on personnel planning, it is dismaying to note how little input into the field is from the traditional areas of industrial and organizational psychology. Milkovich & Mahoney (1978) reviewed the literature on structured task lists as a basis for task and job taxonomies which in turn can be input to many human resource planning activities. Dunnette and associates (1979) gave a complete discussion of the development of such taxonomies. Psychologists can do more than provide languages; possible inputs to planning can come from a variety of activities. For example, Ritchie & Beardsley (1978) have shown how psychological and market research techniques can be used to determine labor pool interest in particular kinds of work. Also, the advent of automation and the possibility of sophisticated human resource information systems (e.g. Walker 1980) provide the vehicles by which psychological information can be incorporated into the total human resources system. Importantly, a well-developed human resources planning system can provide inputs of value to the particular work of the personnel psychologist. It is hoped that in future years a synergistic relationship between the two can be formed.

SELECTION AND CLASSIFICATION RESULTS

General Issues

Possibly one of the most interesting characteristics about the period of this review is the lack of published validation studies. V. R. Boehm (unpublished manuscript, 1981) reports a significant decrease in published validation studies in the major journals over the past 20 years. Mitchell et al (1980) report that, as compared to the number of vocational tests mentioned in the *Eighth Mental Measurements Yearbook* (Buros 1978), there has been a 10% decrease in new submissions of such tests.

One can only speculate as to reasons for the decline in published validation studies, but the possibility that the use of formal selection procedures is declining is dismaying in view of the problematic national decline in productivity and the likely contribution of industrial and organizational psychology in solving the problem (Thayer 1980, Tenopyr 1981). There are many problems in providing the needed emphasis on psychology's role in productivity improvement. The definitional issue is probably the most important. R. J. Bullock (unpublished manuscript, 1980) has reviewed productivity measurement methods and concluded that such techniques should be objective and that organizational theory must be incorporated in such a way that it provides construct support for such measurements. Schmidt and associates (1979a) have shown that even in the absence of objective productivity measurement, substantial productivity gains through the use of testing can be demonstrated. The study of productivity relative to personnel selection should undoubtedly receive much more emphasis in the literature than it already has.

Interviewing

It appears that the vast majority of recent research on the interview has been concerned with what happens in the interview, not what should happen. There is apparently only one recent true validation study on the interview (Latham et al 1980) and that, because of its small sample size, needs replication.

Prominent among recent studies of the interview decision-making process were those of nonverbal behaviors. Tessler & Sushelsky (1978) found that degree of eye contact and social status interacted in their relationship to interviewer's perceptions. Sterrett (1978) found no main effects relating to intensity of body language, but did find interactions between nonverbal behaviors and sex of interviewer relative to ratings on various characteristics. McGovern & Tinsley (1978) found that a high degree of interviewee nonverbal behavior was associated with high interviewer ratings. Forbes &

Jackson (1980) also found some nonverbal behaviors related to interviewer decisions. Hollandsworth et al (1979) indicated that appropriateness of content, fluency of speech, and composure were more important than nonverbal behavior in apparent influence on interview outcome. A number of other studies have involved other aspects of the interview situation.

All of these studies and those concerned mainly with discrimination of various sorts related to the subjective aspects of the employment process have added valuable information to the repertoire of knowledge about the many variables affecting decision making in the interview. If such research continues, it appears that in a few years there will be an almost interminable list of variables which affect decision making in the interview. Such research should undoubtedly be continued, but it appears to be about time to catalog the various variables in relation to their comparative strengths, as Hollandsworth and associates (1979) have started to do, and concentrate attention upon developing a theory of decision making in the interview.

The need for a conceptual approach to provide not only greater interview validity but also understanding of the relationships involved has been expressed by Guion (1976) and Dunnette & Borman (1979). An example of such an approach is in the promising work of Jackson and associates (Jackson et al 1980, Rothstein & Jackson 1980). Another development of note is the judgment model presented by Naylor and associates (1980). The views of Ross (1977) relative to attribution theory may also be a basis for understanding interview dynamics and improving the validity of the interview. The research reported by Pitz (1980) offers the possibility of courses of action which may improve interviewers' judgments. Another theoretical development which merits strong consideration in relation to interviewing is that of Einhorn & Hogarth (1978), who have developed a model for learning to make judgments and maintaining confidence in one's own judgment.

Experience and Education

Probably education and experience are considered in almost all personnel selection decisions made; however, there is a conspicuous lack of recent research relative to them. Caplan & Schmidt (1977) reviewed the literature and found little evidence of validity for education and experience ratings. Johnson et al (1980) generated data which suggested different methods of evaluating training and experience yield different validities. O'Leary (1980), after a review of the literature, concluded that there is a slight positive relationship between grade point average and occupational success. Kaufman (1978) found that apparently some modes of continuing education are more effective than others in improving performance and that level of technology of the job and reward climate may moderate validity of continuing education.

Relative to the probationary period as a selection device, Cormier (1980) found no evidence regarding either its validity or adverse impact on various groups.

Noncognitive Predictors

PERSONALITY AND INTEREST INVENTORIES Despite the fact that personality and interest inventories continue to be used for selection of executives (Wysocki 1981) and groups such as police officers (Parisher et al 1979), there is surprisingly little new information on their usefulness. All in all, inventories have appeared, as in the past, to afford at the best modest levels of prediction of organizational criteria. Perhaps developments like those of Borman et al (1980) in providing construct support for selection may help provide a brighter future for inventories in selection.

BIODATA Biodata continue their relatively successful history as a predictor of job behavior. Life Insurance Marketing and Research Association (1978) clearly documented the relationship of the Aptitude Index Battery to profits. Brown (1978) showed that the validity of this technique has held up well over a number of years. Erwin (1981) reported useful multi-industry validation results relative to management success. Both of these major efforts, significantly, reported no practical discrimination of their instruments against major groups. With large item pools and thousands of subjects, it appears possible to select items in such a way that validity and fairness can both be ensured.

In a series of U. S. Navy studies, Booth et al (1978), Hoiberg & Pugh (1978), and Sands (1978) reported that biodata, at times combined with other variables, could be useful for selecting personnel for a variety of occupations. Continuing Owens' (1968, Owens & Schoenfeldt 1979) pioneering work in the use of subgroups determined on the basis of biographical data, Brush & Owens (1979) evaluated Schoenfeldt's (1974) assessment-classification model and found it useful for a variety of organizational purposes. Matteson (1978) found results suggestive of the usefulness of homogeneous keys in scoring biodata. Brown (1979) found that validity of biodata may be distorted by persons with different score reports getting differential treatment on the job.

Cognitive Predictors

MINIATURE TRAINING Miniature training or trainability testing appears to be emerging as a valuable selection device. New studies by Reilly

& Manese (1979), MacLane (1980), and Robertson & Mindel (1980) indicate successful applications of the technique. The literature relating to the general success of this approach and various issues relative to its development and use has been reviewed by Siegel (1978), Robertson & Downs (1979), and Harris-Thomas (1980).

CONTENT-ORIENTED TESTS Well-developed content-oriented tests are being used for a number of purposes; examples are licensing (Eignor & Seneca 1979), criterion development (Distefano et al 1980), selection (Cascio & Phillips 1979), pretraining diagnosis (Panell & Laabs 1979), and U. S. Army proficiency assessment (Maier & Hirshfeld 1979). Although space does not permit extended discussion of the many content-oriented development procedures recently formulated for special purposes, a conclusion which may be drawn is that much of the work being done in this area is of fairly high quality.

Assessment Centers

The assessment center approach to selection has gained much popularity in the last few years. Dunnette & Borman (1979) reported the variety of uses to which assessment center methodology was being put; this variety is rapidly increasing, particularly in the public sector. Fitzgerald (1980), in surveying large public jurisdictions, found that 44% were using assessment centers in selecting persons for widely divergent departments such as fire, police, streets, and sanitation. The federal government too is a heavy user of assessment centers. Examples of work in this area are reported by Neidig & Martin (1979) and Hall (1980). There is also some research on assessment in the armed services (Dyer & Hilligoss 1980). The assessment center movement has reached a point at which a journal devoted to articles on the technique, *Journal of Assessment Center Technology,* emerged in 1978. The increasing popularity of the method has brought notes of caution from some (Howard 1974, Ross 1979, Cohen 1980).

There is a particular definitional problem with assessment centers. Those who have prepared standards for the technology (Task Force on Assessment Center Standards 1979) have been specific in the requirements for centers. However, the rubric of "assessment center" is apparently being applied to any set of selection procedures which includes some sort of simulation; consequently it is difficult to generalize about methods which are called assessment centers. Those in operation today may involve a variety of techniques and an assortment of different constructs. The matter of validity generalization should be of concern; certainly the validity of the assessment approach should be established by some means whenever a widely divergent use is proposed. Even in use for management selection, despite the generally positive results (Bray et al 1974, Moses & Byham 1977) there should be some checks to determine the extent of validity generalization to the particular situation.

Because of the voluminous literature on assessment and ready access of bibliographies (Earles & Winn 1977, *Journal of Assessment Center Technology* 1980) only a few further research issues will be discussed here. There have been a number of studies involving internal analyses of typical assessment processes.

Klimoski & Strickland's (1977) observation that the overall assessment rating may be a device which essentially reflects the methods by which people normally advance in the given organization has received further attention. The same authors (R. J. Klimoski and W. J. Strickland, unpublished manuscript 1981) found overall assessment ratings to be valid for predicting advancement, but, interestingly and perhaps surprisingly, found little relationship between them and rated performance; they showed that other measures could well serve as alternate predictors. Similarly, Hinrichs (1978), in confirming the long-term validity of assessments for predicting advancement criteria, also found an alternate measure to be essentially an equivalent predictor. Obviously assessment centers, because of their acceptability to management, and because of other features, can further organizational purposes not readily served by other types of predictors. However, it appears that other methods might well be explored with the goal of at least complementing the assessment center.

Physical and Perceptual Tests

The new trend toward the movement of people of small stature into physically demanding jobs has brought with it a new emphasis on individual differences in variables which may be considered more physical than psychological in nature or a combination of both. The lines between occupational medicine, kinesiology, engineering psychology, and personnel psychology have become increasingly blurred. Both the quality and the quantity of the research in this area is widely divergent. Certainly the many physical variables medical practitioners are currently using in selecting employees need the support of validation. It is apparent that some physical variables can provide valid measures relative to job performance criteria e.g. (Reilly et al 1979b, Grossman & Whitehurst 1979); however, much remains to be done in assembling a knowledge base from the varied sources of information in different disciplines and settling on an appropriate set of methodologies for validation of physical and psychophysical variables. Fleishman's (1979) work may assist in providing one of the necessary frameworks for further developments in this field.

Deception-Detection Devices

Polygraphs and other devices designed with the intent of determining dishonesty are being widely used in U.S. corporations (Belt & Holden 1978). Considerable controversy surrounds their use. The following selected conclusions included in a review by Sackett & Decker (1979) bear echoing: (*a*) Polygraph accuracy data gathered in the criminal investigation context cannot be generalized to employment settings. (*b*) In employment, probable low base rate of deception coupled with the use of multiple judgments about many aspects of employability may result in considerable error, especially that of an innocent person being judged guilty. (*c*) Voice analysis instruments cannot detect deception at a greater than chance level. (*d*) Paper-and-pencil detection instruments, while showing some evidence of validity, are in further need of research.

The technical questions relating to the detection of deception interact with the ethical and moral questions concerning the use of such devices as polygraphs for employment purposes. The decision on whether to use such instruments in employment settings should be carefully made with the moral consequences weighed against the possible economic benefits, such as theft prevention.

Organizational Variables

Obviously, the area of personnel selection and classification cannot be divorced from organizational variables. Mitchell (1979) provides a review of organizational behavior and covers the role of personality and individual differences in organizational research. In this era of social change, it appears that the relationship between individual difference and organizational research and theory must change (Tenopyr 1981). As the measurement of individual differences in applied settings becomes more difficult because of legal constraints, it appears that organizational manipulations must share more of the burden in increasing productivity. It is hoped that researchers and theorists in both areas will join in work on the new problems, so that solutions which will be responsive to both social and organizational needs can be achieved.

SUMMARY

Possibly the most important general developments during the period of this review have been the changes in conceptualization of validity. It appears that there is a merging of the theoretical and the applied, especially where construct validity is concerned. It also seems that future professional requirements for validation will have a firm basis in research, be generally agreed upon, and be on the whole less complicated. It is important that the requirement for differential validation studies for the races no longer appears appropriate and that situational specificity of validity has been called into question. It is hoped that the research on job analysis and performance measurement will converge similarly, so that there are agreed-upon principles for development in these areas.

The research on the subjective aspects of employment decision making is even in more need of unification. The large number of unreplicated studies in this area offer little in the way of guidance for a researcher attempting to develop a valid selection system.

There is an uncomfortable lack of published validation research, not only for subjective methods, but also for the more objective selection techniques. It appears necessary to remove any barriers to the dissemination of such information and allow more results of practical studies to be incorporated into the body of scientific knowledge.

Finally, it appears that the boundaries of that which has been called personnel selection are rapidly expanding and becoming less definite. As the core subject matter of personnel psychology is expanding to include that traditionally thought of as belonging in other disciplines, so other areas such as human resource planning are incorporating more of the knowledge which was once exclusively the province of the personnel psychologist. It is hoped that this trend will continue in a managed, orderly manner, so that personnel psychology will have an expanded role both in personnel systems and in science.

Literature Cited

Abrahams, N. M., Alf, E. F. 1978. Relative costs and statistical power in the extreme group approach. *Psychometrika* 43:11–17

American Psychological Association 1954. *Technical Recommendations for Psychological Tests and Diagnostic Techniques,* pp. 13–14. Washington DC: Am. Psychol. Assoc.

American Psychological Association, Division of Industrial-Organizational Psychology. 1980. *Principles for the Validation and Use of Personnel Selection Procedures.* Berkeley, Calif: Div. Ind. Organ. Psychol. 28 pp. 2nd ed.

Ammerman, H. L. 1977. *Performance Content for Job Training. Vol. 2: Stating the Tasks of the Job.* Res. Dev. Ser. 122, Columbus, Ohio: Cent. Vocat. Educ. 69 pp.

Arvey, R. D. 1979. Unfair discrimination in the employment interview: Legal and psychological aspects. *Psychol. Bull.* 86:736–65

Ash, R. A., Levine, E. L., Edgell, S. L. 1979. Exploratory study of a matching approach to personnel selection: The impact of ethnicity. *J. Appl. Psychol.* 64:35–41

Atkin, R. S., Conlon, E. J. 1978. Behaviorally anchored rating scales: Some theoretical issues. *Acad. Manage. Rev.* 3:119–28

Backman, M. E. 1972. Patterns of mental abilities: Ethnic, socioeconomic, and sex differences. *Am. Educ. Res. J.* 9:1–12

Backman, M. E., Lynch, J. J., Loe Ding, D. J. 1979. Sex and ethnic differences in vocational aptitude patterns. *Meas. Eval. Guid.* 12:35–43

Barrett, G. V., Phillips, J. S., Alexander, R. A. 1981. Concurrent and predictive validity designs. *J. Appl. Psychol.* 66:1–6

Barrett, R. S. 1980. Is the test content valid: Or, does it really measure a construct? *Employee Relat. Law J.* 6:459–75

Bartlett, C. J., Bobko, P., Mosier, S. B., Hannan, R. 1978. Testing for fairness with a moderated multiple regression strategy: An alternative to differential analysis. *Personnel Psychol.* 31:233–41

Bass, B. M., Barrett, G. V. 1981. *People, Work, and Organizations.* Boston, Mass: Allyn & Bacon. 673 pp. 2nd ed.

Belcher, D. W. 1974. *Compensation Administration.* Englewood-Cliffs, NJ: Prentice Hall. 606 pp.

Belt, J. A., Holden, P. B. 1978. Polygraph usage among major U.S. corporations. *Personnel J.* 57:80–86

Bentler, P. M., Woodward, J. A. 1979. *Regression on Linear Composites: Statistical Theory and Applications.* Multivar. Behav. Res. Monogr. No. 79–1. 58 pp.

Berk, R. A. 1978. The application of structural facet theory to achievement test construction. *Educ. Res. Q.* 3:62–71

Bernardin, H. J. 1978. Effects of rater training on leniency and halo errors in student ratings of instructors. *J. Appl. Psychol.* 63:301–8

Bernardin, H. J. 1979. Rater training: A critique and reconceptualization. *Proc. Acad. Manage.* 39:216–20

Bernardin, H. J., Carlyle, J., Elliot, L. 1980. A critical assessment of mixed standard rating scales. *Proc. Acad. Manage.* 40:308–12

Bernardin, H. J., Pence, E. C. 1980. Effects of rater training: Creating new response sets and decreasing accuracy. *J. Appl. Psychol.* 65:60–66

Bernardin, H. J., Smith, P. C. 1981. A clarification of some issues regarding the development and use of behaviorally anchored rating scales. *J. Appl. Psychol.* 66: In press

Bobko, P. Bartlett, C. J. 1978. Subgroup validities: Differential definitions and differential prediction. *J. Appl. Psychol.* 63:12–14

Bobko, P., Rieck, A. 1980. Large sample estimators for standard errors of functions of correlation coefficients. *Appl. Psychol. Meas.* 4:385–98

Boehm, V. R. 1978. Populations, preselection, and practicalities: A reply to Hunter and Schmidt. *J. Appl. Psychol.* 63:15–18

Boone, J. O., Lewis, M. A. 1980. Demonstration of possible effects of recruitment and selection procedures on correcting the validity coefficient for restriction in range. *Psychol. Rep.* 46:927–30

Booth, R. E., Mcnally, M. S., Berry, N. H. 1978. Predicting performance effectiveness in paramedical occupations. *Personnel Psychol.* 31:581-93

Borman, W. C. 1979. Format and training effects on rating accuracy and rater errors. *J. Appl. Psychol.* 64:410–21

Borman, W. C., Rosse, R. L., Abrahams, N. M. 1980. An empirical construct validity approach to studying predictor-job performance links. *J. Appl. Psychol.* 65:662–71

Bray, D. W., Campbell, R. J., Grant, D. L. 1974. *Formative Years in Business: A Long-term Study of Managerial Lives.* New York: Wiley. 236 pp.

Brown, S. H. 1978. Long-term validity of a personal history item scoring procedure. *J. Appl. Psychol.* 63:673–76

Brown, S. H. 1979. Validity distortions associated with a test in use. *J. Appl. Psychol.* 64:460–62

Brumback, G. B. 1978. *Circumstances and conditions as factors in work difficulty.* Presented at Ann. Meet. Am. Psychol. Assoc., 86th, Toronto

Brush, D. H., Owens, W. A. 1979. Implementation and evaluation of an assessment classification model for manpower utilization. *Personnel Psychol.* 32:369–83

Buros, O. K., ed. 1978. *Eighth Mental Measurements Yearbook.* Highland Park, NJ: Gryphon. 2182 pp.

Callender, J. C., Osburn, H. G. 1980. Development and test of a new model for validity generalization. *J. Appl. Psychol.* 65:543–58

Campion, M. A., Pursell, E. D. 1980. *Adverse impact, validity, expected job performance, and the determination of cut scores.* Presented at Ann. Meet. Am. Psychol. Assoc., 88th, Montreal

Caplan, J. R., Schmidt, F. L. 1977. *The validity of education and experience ratings.* Presented at Ann. Meet. Int. Personnel Manage. Assoc. Assess. Counc., Kansas City

Carter, D. S. 1979. Comparison of different shrinkage formulas in estimating population multiple correlation coefficients. *Educ. Psychol. Meas.* 39:261–66

Cascio, W. F. 1978. *Applied Psychology in Personnel Management.* Reston, Va: Reston. 434 pp.

Cascio, W. F., Phillips, N. F. 1979. Performance testing: A rose among thorns. *Personnel Psychol.* 32:751–66

Cascio, W. F., Valenzi, E. R. 1978. Relations among criteria of police performance. *J. Appl. Psychol.* 63:22–28

Cascio, W. F., Valenzi, E. R., Silbey, V. 1978. Validation and statistical power: Implications for applied research. *J. Appl. Psychol.* 63:589–95

Cascio, W. F., Valenzi, E. R., Silbey, V. 1980. More on validation and statistical power. *J. Appl. Psychol.* 65:135–38

Cattin, P. 1978. A predictive-validity-based procedure for choosing between regression and equal weights. *Organ. Behav. Hum. Perform.* 22:93–102

Cattin, P. 1980a. Note on the estimation of the squared cross-validated multiple correlation of a regression model. *Psychol. Bull.* 87:63–65

Cattin, P. 1980b. Estimation of the predictive power of a regression model. *J. Appl. Psychol.* 65:407–14

Claudy, J. G. 1978. Multiple regression and validity estimation in one sample. *Appl. Psychol. Meas.* 2:595–607

Cohen, S. L. 1980. Pre-packaged vs. tailor-made: The assessment center debate. *Personnel J.* 59:989–91

Colbert, G. A., Taylor, L. R. 1978. Empirically derived job families as a foundation for the study of validity generalization. Study III. Generalization of selection test validity. *Personnel Psychol.* 31:355-64

Cormier, S. M. 1980. *The Probationary Period: Its Use in Selection and Performance Evaluation.* Personnel Res. Dev. Cent. Rep. PRR-80-5, Washington DC: Off. Personnel Manage.

Cornelius, E. T. III, Carron, T. J., Collins, M. A. 1979a. Job analysis models and job classification. *Personnel Psychol.* 32:693–708

Cornelius, E. T. III, Hakel, M. D., Sackett, P. R. 1979b. A methodological approach to job classification for performance appraisal purposes. *Personnel Psychol.* 32:283–97

Cornelius, E. T. III, Lyness, K. S. 1980. A comparison of holistic and decomposed judgment strategies in job analyses by job incumbents. *J. Appl. Psychol.* 65:155–63

Cronbach, L. J. 1976. Equity in selection—where psychometrics and political philosophy meet. *J. Educ. Meas.* 13:31–42

Cronbach, L. J. 1980a. Selection theory for a political world. *Public Personnel Manage.* 9:37–50

Cronbach, L. J. 1980b. Validity on parole: How can we go straight? *New Dir. Test. Meas.* 5:99–108

Cronbach, L. J., Meehl, P. E. 1955. Construct validity in psychological tests. *Psychol. Bull.* 52:281–302

Cronbach, L. J., Yalow, E., Schaeffer, G. W. 1980. Mathematical structure for analyzing fairness in selection. *Personnel Psychol.* 33:693–704

Darlington, R. B. 1976. Defense of "rational" personnel selection and two new methods. *J. Educ. Meas.* 13:43–52

Darlington, R. B. 1978. Reduced-variance regression. *Psychol. Bull.* 85:1238–55

Davey, B. 1980. *The use of candidate self-ratings as validation criteria.* Presented at Ann. Meet. Int. Personnel Manage. Assoc. Assess. Counc., Boston

Dawes, R. M. 1979. The robust beauty of improper linear models in decision making. *Am. Psychol.* 34:571–82

DeCotiis, T. A. 1978. A critique and suggested revision of behaviorally anchored rating scales developmental procedures. *Educ. Psychol. Meas.* 38: 681–90

DeCotiis, T., Petit, A. 1978. The performance appraisal process: A model and some testable propositions. *Acad. Manage. Rev.* 3:635–46

DeVries, D. L., Morrison, A. M., Shullman, S. L., Gerlach, M. L. 1980. *Performance Appraisal on the Line.* Tech. Rep. 16. Greensboro, NC: Cent. Creat. Leadership. 165 pp.

Dickinson, T. L., Zellinger, P. M. 1980. A comparison of the behaviorally anchored rating and mixed standard scale formats. *J. Appl. Psychol.* 65:147–54

Distefano, N. K. Jr., Pryer, M. W., Craig, S. H. 1980. Job-relatedness of post-training job knowledge criterion used to assess validity and test fairness. *Personnel Psychol.* 33:785–93

Dorans, N. J., Drasgow, F. 1980. A note on cross-validating prediction equations. *J. Appl. Psychol.* 65:728–30

Dowell, B. E., Wexley, K. N. 1978. Development of a work behavior taxonomy for first-line supervisors. *J. Appl. Psychol.* 63:563–72

Downs, S., Farr, R. M., Colbeck, L. 1978. Self-appraisal: A convergence of selection and guidance. *J. Occup. Psychol.* 51:271–78

Dunnette, M. D. 1980. Summary and integration. See Educ. Test. Serv. 1980, pp. 139–42. Princeton, NJ: Educ. Test. Serv.

Dunnette, M. D., Borman, W. C. 1979. Personnel selection and classification. *Ann. Rev. Psychol.* 30:477–525

Dunnette, M. D., Hough, L. M., Rosse, R. L. 1979. Task and job taxonomies as a basis for identifying labor supply sources and evaluating employment qualifications. *Hum. Resour. Plann.* 2:37–54

Dyer, F. N., Hilligoss, R. E. 1980. *Using an Assessment Center to Predict Field Performance of Army Officers and NCO's.* JSAS Cat. Select. Doc. Psychol. 10:Ms. 2163

Earles, I. A., Winn, W. R. 1977. *Assessment Centers: Annotated Bibliography.* JSAS Cat. Select. Doc. Psychol. 7:Ms. 1610

Educational Testing Service, ed. 1980. *Construct Validity in Psychological Measurement.* Princeton, NJ: Educ. Test. Serv. 143 pp.

Eignor, D. R., Seneca, L. 1979. *Insurance License Qualification Examinations.* Princeton, NJ: Educ. Test. Serv. 58 pp.

Einhorn, H. J., Hogarth, R. M. 1978. Confidence in judgment: Persistence of the illusion of validity. *Psychol. Rev.* 85:395–416

Ekstrom, R. B., French, J. W., Harman, H. H. 1979. *Cognitive Factors: Their Identification and Replication.* Multivar. Behav. Res. Monogr. No. 79–2. 84 pp.

Equal Employment Opportunity Commission, Department of Labor, Department of Justice. 1978. Adoption by four agencies of uniform guidelines on employee selection procedures. *Fed. Regist.* 43:38290–39315

Equal Employment Opportunity Commission, Office of Personnel Management, Department of Justice, Department of Labor. 1979. Adoption of questions and answers to clarify and promote a common interpretation of the uniform guidelines on employee selection procedures. *Fed. Regist.* 44:11996–12009

Equal Employment Opportunity Commission, Office of Personnel Management, Department of Justice, Department of the Treasury, Department of Labor. 1980. Adoption of additional questions and answers to clarify and provide a common interpretation of the uniform guidelines on employee selection procedures. *Fed. Regist.* 45:29530–31

Erwin, F. E. 1981. *Management Digest: The Supervisory Profile Record.* Washington DC: Richardson, Bellows & Henry

Fisher, C. D., Ilgen, D. R., Hoyer, W. D. 1979. Source credibility, information favorability, and job offer acceptance. *Acad. Manage. J.* 22:94–103

Fitzgerald, L. F. 1980. *The Incidence and Utilization of Assessment Centers in State and Local Governments.* Washington DC: Int. Personnel Manage. Assoc.

Flaugher, R. L. 1978. The many definitions of test bias. *Am. Psychol.* 33:671–79

Fleishman, E. A. 1978. Relating individual differences to the dimensions of human tasks. *Ergonomics* 21:1007–19

Fleishman, E. A. 1979. Evaluating physical abilities required by jobs. *Personnel Adm.* 24:82–92

Fleiss, J. L., Nee, J. C. M., Landis, J. R. 1979. Large sample variance of kappa in the case of different sets of raters. *Psychol. Bull.* 86:974-77

Forbes, J. B., Barrett, G. V. 1978. Individual abilities and task demands in relation to performance and satisfaction on two repetitive monitoring tasks. *J. Appl. Psychol.* 63:188–96

Forbes, R. J., Jackson, P. R. 1980. Non-verbal behavior and the outcome of selection interviews. *J. Occup. Psychol.* 53: 65–72

Gael, S. 1978. *Improving Output Through Job Performance Evaluation.* JSAS Cat. Select. Doc. Psychol. 8:Ms. 1742

Gambardella, J. J. N., Alvord, W. G. 1980. *TI-CODAP: A Computerized Method of Job Analysis for Personnel Management.* JSAS Cat. Select. Doc. Psychol. 10:Ms. 2118

Gorman, C. D., Glover, W. H., Doherty, M. E. 1978. Can we learn anything about interviewing real people from "interviews" of paper people? Two studies of the external validity of a paradigm. *Organ. Behav. Hum. Perform.* 22:165–92

Greener, J. M., Osburn, H. G. 1979. An empirical study of the accuracy of corrections for restriction in range due to explicit selection. *Appl. Psychol. Meas.* 3:31–41

Gross, A. L., Su, W. 1975. Defining a "fair" or "unbiased" selection model: A question of utilities. *J. Appl. Psychol.* 60:345–51

Grossman, J. D., Whitehurst, H. O. 1979. The relative effects of multiple factors on target acquisition. *Hum. Factors* 21:423–32

Guion, R. M. 1976. Recruiting selection and job placement. *Handbook of Industrial and Organizational Psychology,* ed. M. D. Dunnette, pp. 777–828. Chicago: Rand McNally, 1740 pp.

Guion, R. M. 1977. Content validity, the source of my discontent. *Appl. Psychol. Meas.* 1:1–10

Guion, R. M. 1978. Content validity in moderation. *Personnel Psychol.* 31:205–14

Guion, R. M. 1980. On trinitarian doctrines of validity. *Prof. Psychol.* 11:385–98

Gustafson, H. W. 1977. Job performance evaluation as a tool to evaluate training. *Improv. Hum. Perform. Q. 5:133–52*

Guttman, L. 1955. An outline of some new

methodology for social research. *Public Opin. Q.* 18:395–404

Hall, H. I. 1980. Analysis of an executive level assessment center: A comparison of assessment center ratings to supervisor ratings and biodata. *J. Assess. Cent. Technol.* 3:15–30

Hambleton, R. K., Swainathan, H., Cook, L. L., Eignor, D. R., Gifford, J. A. 1978. Developments in latent trait theory: Models, technical issues, and applications. *Rev. Educ. Res.* 48:467–510

Harris-Thomas, P. 1980. *Trainability Testing: The Miniature Training and Evaluation Approach to Testing.* Personnel Res. Dev. Cent. Rep. PRR-80–9. Washington DC: Off. Personnel Manage. 18 pp.

Hennessy, J. J., Merrifield, P. R. 1978. Ethnicity and sex distinctions in patterns of aptitude factor scores in a sample of urban high school seniors. *Am. Educ. Res. J.* 15:385–89

Herbert, A. 1978. Perceived causes of difficulty in work situations. *Ergonomics* 21:539–49

Hinrichs, J. R. 1978. An eight-year follow-up of a management assessment center. *J. Appl. Psychol.* 63:596–601

Hogan, J. C., Ogden, G. D., Gebhardt, D. L., Fleishman, E. A. 1980. Reliability and validity of methods for evaluating perceived physical effort. *J. Appl. Psychol.* 65:672–79

Hoiberg, A., Pugh, W. M. 1978. Predicting navy effectiveness: Expectations, motivation, personality, aptitude and background variables. *Personnel Psychol.* 31:841–52

Hollandsworth, J. G. Jr., Kazelskis, R., Stevens, J., Dressel, M. E. 1979. Relative contributions of verbal, articulative, and nonverbal communication to employment decisions in the job interview setting. *Personnel Psychol.* 32:359–67

Hollingsworth, H. H. 1980. An analytical investigation of the effects of heterogeneous regression slopes in analysis of covariance. *Educ. Psychol. Meas.* 40:611–18

Holzbach, R. L. 1978. Rater bias in performance ratings: Superior, self-, and peer ratings. *J. Appl. Psychol.* 63:579–88

Howard, A. 1974. An assessment of assessment centers. *Acad. Manage. J.* 17:115–34

Huberty, C. J., Mourad, S. A. 1980. Estimation in multiple correlation/prediction. *Educ. Psychol. Meas.* 40:101–12

Hunter, J. E., Schmidt, F. L. 1978. Differential and single-group validity of employment tests by race: A critical analysis of three recent studies. *J. Appl. Psychol.* 63:1–11

Hunter, J. E., Schmidt, F. L., Hunter, R. 1979. Differential validity of employment tests by race: A comprehensive review and analysis. *Psychol. Bull.* 86:721–35

Ivancevich, J. M. 1979. Longitudinal study of the effects of rater training on psychometric error in ratings. *J. Appl. Psychol.* 64:502–8

Ivancevich, J. M. 1980. A longitudinal study of behavioral expectation scales: Attitudes and performance. *J. Appl. Psychol.* 65:139–46

Jackson, D. N., Paunonen, S. V. 1980. Personality structure and assessment. *Ann. Rev. Psychol.* 31:503–51

Jackson, D. N., Peacock, A. C., Smith, J. P. 1980. Impressions of personality in the employment interview. *J. Pers. Soc. Psychol.* 39:294–307

Jacobs, R., Kafry, D., Zedeck, S. 1980. Expectations of behaviorally anchored rating scales. *Personnel Psychol.* 33: 595–640

Jensen, A. R. 1980. *Bias in Mental Testing.* New York: Free Press. 786 pp.

Johnson, C. A., Tokunaga, H. T., Hiller, J. 1980. *Validation of a job analysis questionnaire through intensive observation.* Presented at Ann. Meet. Mil. Test. Assoc., 22nd, Toronto

Journal of Assessment Center Technology. 1980. Bibliography of assessment center articles. *J. Assess. Cent. Technol.* 3:Suppl. 1

Kahalas, H., Pazer, H. L., Hoagland, J. S., Levitt, A. 1980. Human resource planning activities in U.S. firms. *Hum. Resour. Plann.* 3:53–66

Kane, J. S., Lawler, E. E. III. 1978. Methods of peer assessment. *Psychol. Bull.* 85: 555–86

Kane, J. S., Lawler, E. E. III. 1979. Performance appraisal effectiveness: Its assessment and determinants. Greenwich, Conn: Jai. 478 pp. In *Research in Organizational Behavior,* ed. B. M. Staw, 1:425–78

Katzell, R. A., Dyer, F. J. 1978. On differential validity and bias. *J. Appl. Psychol.* 63:19–21

Kaufman, H. G. 1978. Continuing education and job performance: A longitudinal study. *J. Appl. Psychol.* 63:248–51

Keeley, M. 1978. A contingency framework for performance evaluation. *Acad. Manage. Rev.* 3:428–38

Kesselman, G. A., Lopez, F. E. 1979. The impact of job analysis on employment test validation for minority and nonminority accounting personnel. *Personnel Psychol.* 32:91–108

King, L. M., Hunter, J. E., Schmidt, F. L. 1980. Halo in a multidimensional forced-choice performance evaluation scale. *J. Appl. Psychol.* 65:507–16

Kissler, G. D., Nebeker, D. M. 1979. Peer and supervisory ratings of research scientists. *Proc. Acad. Manage.* 39:392–96

Klimoski, R. J., Strickland, W. J. 1977. Assessment centers—valid or merely prescient. *Personnel Psychol.* 30:353–56

Knowlton, W. A. Jr., Mitchell, T. R. 1980. Effects of causal attributions on a supervisor's evaluation of subordinate performance. *J. Appl. Psychol.* 65:459–66

Krzystofiak, F., Newman, J. M., Anderson, G. 1979. A quantified approach to measurement of job content: Procedures and payoffs. *Personnel Psychol.* 32: 341–57

Landy, F. J., Farr, J. L. 1980. Performance rating. *Psychol. Bull.* 87:72–107

Landy, F. J., Trumbo, D. A. 1980. *A Psychology of Work Behavior.* Homewood, Ill: Dorsey. 626 pp. 2nd ed.

Latham, G. P., Fay, C. H., Saari, L. M. 1979. The development of behavioral observation scales for appraising the performance of foremen. *Personnel Psychol.* 32:299–311

Latham, G. P., Saari, L. M., Pursell, E. D., Campion, M. A. 1980. The situational interview. *J. Appl. Psychol.* 65:422–27

Latham, G. P., Wexley, K. N. 1981. *Increasing Productivity Through Performance Appraisal.* Reading, Mass: Addison-Wesley. 273 pp.

Laughlin, J. E. 1978. Comment on "estimating coefficients in linear models: It don't make no nevermind". *Psychol. Bull.* 85:247–53

Laughlin, J. E. 1979. A Bayesian alternative to least squares and equal weighting coefficients in regression. *Psychometrika* 44:271–88

Lerner, B. 1977. Washington V. Davis: Quantity, quality, and equality in employment testing. *The Supreme Court Review,* ed. P. Kurland, pp. 263–316. Chicago: Univ. Chicago Press. 343 pp.

Levine, E. L., Ash, R. A., Bennett, N. 1980. Exploratory comparative study of four job analysis methods. *J. Appl. Psychol.* 65:524–35

Levine, E. L., Ash, R. A., Hall, H. L., Sistrunk, F. 1981. *Evaluation of Seven Job Analysis Methods By Experienced Job Analysts.* Tampa, Fla: Cent. Eval. Res., Univ. S. Fla. 60 pp.

Libby, R., Blashfield, R. K. 1978. Performance of a composite as a function of the number of judges. *Organ. Behav. Hum. Perform.* 21:121–29

Life Insurance Marketing and Research Association. 1978. *Profits and the AIB in United States Ordinary Companies.* Hartford, Conn: Life Insurance Market. Res. Assoc. Res. Rep. No. 1978–6

Linn, R. L. 1978. Single-group validity, differential validity, and differential prediction. *J. Appl. Psychol.* 63:507–12

Lissitz, R. W., Mendoza, J. L., Huberty, C. J., Markos, H. V. 1979. Some further ideas on a methodology for determining job similarities/differences. *Personnel Psychol.* 32:517–28

Loehlin, J. C., Lindzey, G., Spuhler, J. N. 1975. *Race Differences in Intelligence.* San Francisco: Freeman. 380 pp.

Lopez, F. E., Kesselman, G. A. 1980. *An empirical test of a trait-oriented job analysis technique.* Presented at Ann. Meet. Am. Psychol. Assoc., 88th, Montreal

Maccoby, E. E., Jacklin, C. N. 1974. *The Psychology of Sex Differences.* Stanford, Calif: Stanford Univ. Press. 634 pp.

MacLane, C. N. 1980. *A miniature training and evaluation approach to entry-level selection.* Presented at Ann. Meet. Int. Personnel Manage. Assoc. Assess. Counc., 4th, Boston

Maier, M. H., Hirshfeld, S. F. 1979. *Criterion-referenced Job Proficiency Testing: A Large Scale Application* JSAS Cat. Select. Doc. Psychol. 9:Ms. 1892

Matteson, M. T. 1978. An alternative approach to using biographical data for predicting job success. *J. Occup. Psychol.* 51:155–62

McBride, J. R. 1979. *Adaptive Mental Testing: The State of the Art.* Tech. Rep. TR-423. Alexandria, Va: Army Res. Inst. Behav. Soc. Sci. 47 pp.

McCormick, E. J. 1979. *Job Analysis: Methods and Applications.* New York: Amacom. 371 pp.

McCormick, E. J., Denisi, A. S., Shaw, J. B. 1979. Use of the position analysis questionnaire for establishing the job component validity of tests. *J. Appl. Psychol.* 64:51–56

McCormick, E. J., Ilgen, D. 1980. *Industrial Psychology.* Englewood Cliffs, NJ: Prentice-Hall. 464 pp. 7th ed.

McGee, M. G. 1979. Human spatial abilities: Psychometric studies and environmental, genetic, hormonal and neurological influences. *Psychol. Bull.* 86:889–918

McGovern, T. V., Tinsley, H. E. 1978. Interviewer evaluations of interviewee nonverbal behavior. *J. Vocat. Behav.* 13:163–71

Melamed, L., Oeltjen, P. D. 1980. *Probabilistic selection: A model for continuous validation.* Presented at Ann. Meet. Int. Personnel Manage. Assoc. Assess. Counc., 4th, Boston

Mellon, P. M., Schmitt, N., Bylenga, C. 1980. Differential predictability of females and males. *Sex Roles* 6:173–77

Messick, S. A. 1975. Meaning and values in measurement and evaluation. *Am. Psychol.* 30:955–66

Messick, S. A. 1980. Test validity and the ethics of assessment. *Am. Psychol.* 35:1012–27

Meyer, H. H. 1980. Self-appraisal of job performance. *Personnel Psychol.* 33: 291–95

Milkovich, G. T., Mahoney, T. A. 1978. Human resource planning models: A perspective. *Hum. Resour. Plann.* 1:19–30

Mitchell, J. V., Reynolds, C. R., Elliott, S. N. 1980. Test news from the Buros Institute. *Meas. News* 23:6–16

Mitchell, T. R. 1979. Organizational behavior. *Ann. Rev. Psychol.* 30:243–81

Mobley, W. H., Griffeth, R. W., Hand, H. H., Meglino, B. M. 1979. Review and conceptual analysis of the employee turnover process. *Psychol. Bull.* 86:493–522

Moebus, C. 1978. Zur Fairness psychologischer Intelligenztests: Ein unloesbares Trilemma zwischen den Zielen von Gruppen, Individuen und Institutionen (Fairness of psychological ability tests: An unsolvable trilemma between the aims of groups, individuals and institutions?). *Diagnostica* 24:191–234

Morris, J. D. 1979. A comparison of regression prediction accuracy on several types of factor scores. *Am. Educ. Res. J.* 16:17–24

Moses, J. L., Byham, W. C., eds. 1977. *Applying The Assessment Center Method.* New York: Pergamon. 310 pp.

Muchinsky, P. M., Tuttle, M. L. 1979. Employee turnover: An empirical and methodological assessment. *J. Vocat. Behav.* 14:43–77

Murphy, K. R. 1979. *Fooling yourself with cross-validation: Single-sample designs.* Presented at Ann. Meet. Am. Psychol. Assoc., 87th, New York

Naylor, J. C., Pritchard, R. D., Ilgen, D. R. 1980. *A Theory of Behavior in Organizations.* New York: Academic. 299 pp.

Neidig, R. D., Martin, J. C. 1979. *The FBI's Management Aptitude Program Assessment Center. Res. Rep. No. 2: An Analysis of Assessor's Ratings.* Personnel Res. Dev. Cent. Rep. TM-79-2. Washington DC: Off. Personnel Manage.

Newman, J., Krzystofiak, F. 1979. Self-reports versus unobtrusive measures: Balancing method variance and ethical concerns in employment discrimination research. *J. Appl. Psychol.* 64:82–85

Nieva, V. F., Gutek, B. A. 1980. Sex effects on evaluation. *Acad. Manage. Rev.* 5:267–76

Novick, M. R., Ellis, D. D. 1977. Equal opportunity in education and employment. *Am. Psychol.* 32:306–20

Novick, M. R., Petersen, N. S. 1976. Towards equalizing educational and employment opportunity. *J. Educ. Meas.* 13:77–88

O'Leary, B. S. 1980. *College Grade Point Average as an Indicator of Occupational Success: An Update.* Personnel Res. Dev. Cent. Rep. PRR-80-23. Washington DC: Off. Personnel Manage. 27 pp.

Osburn, H. G., Greener, J. M. 1978. Optimal sampling strategies for validation studies. *J. Appl. Psychol.* 63:602–8

Owens, W. A. 1968. Toward one discipline of scientific psychology. *Am Psychol.* 23:782–85

Owens, W. A., Schoenfeldt, L. F. 1979. Toward a classification of persons. *J. Appl. Psychol. Monogr.* 64:569–607

Panell, R. C., Laabs, G. V. 1979. Construction of a criterion-referenced, diagnostic test for an individualized instruction program. *J. Appl. Psychol.* 64:255–61

Parisher, D., Rios, B., Reilly, R. R. 1979. Psychologists and psychological services in urban police departments: A national survey. *Prof. Psychol.* 10:6–7

Pass, J. J., Cunningham, J. W. 1978. *Occupational Clusters Based on Systematically Derived Work Dimensions: Final Report.* JSAS cat. Select. Doc. Psychol 8: Ms. 1661

Pearlman, K. 1980. Job families: A review and discussion of their implications for personnel selection. *Psychol. Bull.* 87:1–28

Pearlman, K., Schmidt, F. L., Hunter, J. E. 1980. Validity generalization results for tests used to predict job proficiency and training success in clerical occupations. *J. Appl. Psychol.* 65:373–406

Perticone, J., Wiesen, J. P. 1979. *Content Validity Studies in the Courts.* Test Dev. Validation Unit Publ. 11357–28–125–5–79–C.P. Boston: Commonwealth of Mass. Div. Personnel Admin.

Peters, L. H., O'Connor, E. J. 1980. Situational constraints and work outcomes: The influences of a frequently overlooked construct. *Acad. Manage. Rev.* 5:391–97

Peters, L. H., O'Connor, E. J., Rudolf, C. J. 1980. The behavioral and affective consequences of performance-relevant situational variables. *Organ. Behav. Hum. Perform.* 25:79–96

Petersen, N. S., Novick, M. R. 1976. An evaluation of some models for culture-fair selection. *J. Educ. Meas.* 13:3–29

Pitz, G. F. 1980. Sensitivity of direct and derived judgments to probabilistic information. *J. Appl. Psychol.* 65:164–71

Pruzek, R. M., Frederick, B. C. 1978. Weighting predictors in linear models: Alternatives to least squares and limitations of equal weights. *Psychol. Bull.* 85:254–66

Pursell, E. D., Dossett, D. L., Latham, G. P. 1980. Obtaining valid predictors by minimizing rating errors in the criterion. *Personnel Psychol.* 33:91–96

Reilly, R. R., Blood, M. P., Brown, B. M., Maletesta, C. A. 1981. The effects of realistic previews: A study and discussion of the literature. *Personnel Psychol.* 34: In press

Reilly, R. R., Manese, W. R. 1979. The validation of a minicourse for telephone company switching technicians. *Personnel Psychol.* 32:83–90

Reilly, R. R., Tenopyr, M. L., Sperling, S. M. 1979a. Effects of job previews on job acceptance and survival of telephone operator candidates. *J. Appl. Psychol.* 64:218–20

Reilly, R. R., Zedeck, S., Tenopyr, M. L. 1979b. Validity and fairness of physical ability tests for predicting performance in craft jobs. *J. Appl. Psychol.* 64: 262–74

Remus, W. E. 1980. Measures of fit for unit rules. *Am. Psychol.* 35:678–80

Remus, W. E., Jenicke, L. O. 1978. Unit and random linear models in decision making. *Multivar. Behav. Res.* 13:215–21

Ridgway, J. 1980. Construct validity through facet analysis: Scheduling tests do not necessarily measure scheduling ability. *J. Occup. Psychol.* 53:253–63

Ritchie, R. J., Beardsley, V. D. 1978. A market research approach to determining local labor market availability for nonmanagement jobs. *Personnel Psychol.* 31:449–59

Roberts, K. H., Hulin, C. L., Rousseau, D. M. 1978. *Developing an Interdisciplinary Science of Organizations.* Chap. 5: Staffing and Maintaining Organizations, pp. 110–35. San Francisco: Jossey-Bass. 171 pp.

Robertson, I., Downs, S. 1979. Learning and the prediction of performance: Development of trainability testing in the United Kingdom. *J. Appl. Psychol.* 64:42–50

Robertson, I. T., Mindel, R. M. A study of trainability testing. *J. Occup. Psychol.* 53:131–38

Roe, R. A. 1979. The correction for restriction of range and the difference between intended and actual selection. *Educ. Psychol. Meas.* 39:551–59

Rogosa, D. 1980. Comparing nonparallel regression lines. *Psychol. Bull.* 88:307–21

Rosenthal, R. 1979. The "file drawer problem" and tolerance for null results. *Psychol. Bull.* 86:638–41

Ross, J. D. 1979. A current review of public sector assessment centers: Cause for concern. *Public Personnel Manage.* 8:41–46

Ross, L. 1977. The intuitive psychologist and his shortcomings: Distortions in the attribution process. *Adv. Exp. Soc. Psychol.* 10:173–220

Rothe, H. F. 1978. Output rates among industrial employees. *J. Appl. Psychol.* 63:40–46

Rothstein, M., Jackson, D. N. 1980. Decision making in the employment interview: An experimental approach. *J. Appl. Psychol.* 65:271–83

Rozeboom, W. W. 1978. Estimation of cross-validated multiple correlation: A clarification. *Psychol. Bull.* 85:1348–51

Rozeboom, W. W. 1979. Sensitivity of a linear composite of predictor items to differential item weighting. *Psychometrika* 44:289–96

Ruch, W. W. 1972. *A re-analysis of published differential validity studies.* Presented at Ann. Meet. Am. Psychol. Assoc., 80th, Honolulu

Saal, F. E. 1979. Mixed standard rating scale: A consistent system for numerically coding inconsistent response combinations. *J. Appl. Psychol.* 64:422–28

Saal, F. E., Downey, R. G., Lahey, M. A. 1980. Rating the ratings: Assessing the psychometric quality of rating data. *Psychol. Bull.* 88:413–28

Sackett, P. R., Decker, P. J. 1979. Detection of deception in the employment context: A review and critical analysis. *Personnel Psychol.* 32:487–506

Sands, W. A. 1978. Enlisted personnel selection for the U.S. navy. *Personnel Psychol.* 31:63–70

Sands, W. A., Alf, E. F. Jr., Abrahams, N. M. 1978. Correction of validity coefficients for direct restriction in range occasioned by univariate selection. *J. Appl. Psychol.* 63:747–50

Schmidt, F. L., Berner, J. G., Hunter, J. E. 1973. Racial differences in validity of employment tests: Reality or illusion? *J. Appl. Psychol.* 58:5–9

Schmidt, F. L., Gast-Rosenberg, I., Hunter, J. E. 1980a. Validity generalization results for computer programmers. *J. Appl. Psychol.* 65:643–61

Schmidt, F. L., Greenthal, A. L., Hunter, J. E., Berner, J. G., Seaton, F. W. 1977. Job sample vs. paper-and-pencil trade and technical tests: Adverse impact and employee attitudes. *Personnel Psychol.* 30:187–97

Schmidt, F. L., Hunter, J. E. 1977. Development of a general solution to the problem of validity generalization. *J. Appl. Psychol.* 62:529–40

Schmidt, F. L., Hunter, J. E., McKenzie, R. C., Muldrow, T. W. 1979a. Impact of valid selection procedures on work-force productivity. *J. Appl. Psychol.* 64:609–26

Schmidt, F. L., Hunter, J. E., Pearlman, K., Shane, G. S. 1979b. Further tests of the Schmidt-Hunter Bayesian validity generalization procedure. *Personnel Psychol.* 32:257–81

Schmidt, F. L., Pearlman, K., Hunter, J. E. 1980b. The validity and fairness of employment and educational tests for Hispanic Americans: A review and analysis. *Personnel Psychol.* 33:705–24

Schmitt, N., Coyle, B. W., Mellon, P. M. 1978. Subgroup differences in predictor and criterion variances and differential validity. *J. Appl. Psychol.* 63:667–72

Schneider, B. 1978. Person-situation selection: A review of some ability-situation interaction research. *Personnel Psychol.* 31:281–97

Schoenfeldt, L. F. 1974. Utilization of manpower: Development and evaluation of an assessment classification model for matching individuals with jobs. *J. Appl. Psychol.* 59:583–95

Schultz, C. B. 1980. *Three methods for assessing cost effectiveness.* Presented at Ann. Meet. Int. Personnel Manage. Assoc. Assess. Counc., 4th, Boston

Schwab, D. P. 1980. Job evaluation and pay setting: Concepts and practices. In *Comparable Worth: Issues and Alternatives.* ed. E. R. Livernash, pp. 49–77. Washington DC: Equal Employ. Advis. Counc. 260 pp.

Schwartz, D. L. 1978. A probabilistic approach to adverse effect, job relatedness and criterion differences. *Public Personnel Manage.* 7:368–77

Shapira, Z., Shirom, A. 1980. New issues in the use of behaviorally anchored rating scales: Level of analysis, the effects of incident frequency, and external validation. *J. Appl. Psychol.* 65:517–23

Shrout, P. E., Fleiss, J. L. 1979. Intraclass correlations: Uses in assessing rater reliability. *Psychol. Bull.* 86:420–28

Shye, S., ed. 1978. *Theory Construction and Data Analysis in the Behavioral Sciences.* San Francisco: Jossey-Bass. 426 pp.

Siegel, A. I. 1978. Miniature job training and evaluation as a selection/classification device. *Hum. Factors* 20:189–200

Skinner, H. A. 1978. The art of exploring predictor-criterion relationships. *Psychol. Bull.* 85:327–37

Smith, J. E., Hakel, M. D. 1979. Convergence among data sources, response bias, and reliability and validity of a structured job analysis questionnaire. *Personal Psychol.* 32:677–92

Smith, P. C., Kendall, L. M. 1963. Retranslation of expectations: An approach to the construction of unambiguous anchors for rating scales. *J. Appl. Psychol.* 47: 149–55

Sorbom, D. 1978. An alternative to the methodology for analysis of covariance. *Psychometrika* 43:381–96

South, J. C. 1980. Fakability and the Engineer Performance Description Form. *Personnel Psychol.* 33:371–76

Spool, M. D. 1978. Training programs for observers of behavior: A review. *Personnel Psychol.* 31:853–88

Steers, R. M., Rhodes, S. R. 1978. Major influences on employee attendance: A process model. *J. Appl. Psychol.* 63: 391–407

Sternberg, R. J. 1979. The nature of mental abilities. *Am. Psychol.* 34:214–30

Sterrett, J. H. 1978. The job interview: Body language and perceptions of potential effectiveness. *J. Appl. Psychol.* 63: 388–90

Taber, T. D., Beehr, T. A., Walsh, J. T. 1978. The relationship between objective and perceived job characteristics. *Proc. Acad. Manage.* 38:89–93

Task Force on Assessment Center Standards. 1979. Standards and ethical considerations for assessment center operations. *J. Assess. Cent. Technol.* 2:19–23

Taylor, L. R. 1978. Empirically derived job families as a foundation for the study of validity generalization. Study I. The construction of job families based on the component and overall dimensions of the PAQ. *Personnel Psychol.* 31:325–40

Taylor, L. R., Colbert, G. A. 1978. Empirically derived job families as a foundation for the study of validity generalization. Study II. The construction of job families based on company-specific PAQ job dimensions. *Personnel Psychol.* 31:341–53

Tenopyr, M. L. 1977. Content-construct confusion. *Personnel Psychol.* 30:47–54

Tenopyr, M. L. 1981. Trifling he stands. *Personnel Psychol.* 34:1–17

Terborg, J. R., Richardson, P., Pritchard, R. D. 1980. Person-situation effects in the prediction of performance: an investigation of ability, self-esteem, and reward contingencies. *J. Appl. Psychol.* 65: 574–83

Tessler, R., Sushelsky, L. 1978. Effects of eye contact and social status on the perception of a job applicant in an employment interviewing situation. *J. Vocat. Behav.* 13:338–47

Thayer, P. W. 1980. Personnel challenges in the eighties. *Public Personnel Manage.* 9:327–35

Thornton, G. C. III. 1980. Psychometric properties of self-appraisals of job performance. *Personnel Psychol.* 33: 263–71

Thornton, G. C. III., Zorich, S. 1980. Training to improve observer accuracy. *J. Appl. Psychol.* 65:351–54

Trattner, M. H. 1979. Task analysis in the design of three concurrent validity studies of the professional and administrative career examination. *Personnel Psychol.* 32:109–19

Trattner, M. H., O'Leary, B. S. 1980. Sample sizes for specified statistical power in testing for differential validity. *J. Appl. Psychol.* 65:127–34

Treiman, D. J. 1979. *Job Evaluation: An Analytic Review.* Washington DC: Nat. Acad. Sci. 170 pp.

US Department of Labor. 1977. *Dictionary of Occupational Titles.* Washington DC: US GPO 1371 pp. 4th ed.

Urry, V. W. 1977. Tailored testing: Successful application of latent trait theory. *J. Educ. Meas.* 14:181–96

Urry, V. W., Dorans, N. J. 1981. *Tailored Testing: Its Theory and Practice. Part I. The Basic Model, The Normal Ogive Submodel, and The Tailoring Algorithms.* San Diego: Navy Personnel Res. Dev. Cent. In press

Wainer, H. 1978. On the sensitivity of regression and regressors. *Psychol. Bull.* 85:267–73

Walker, P. J. 1980. Arriving soon: The paperless personnel office. *Personnel J.* 59:559–62

Wanous, J. P. 1980. *Organizational Entry: Recruitment, Selection, and Socialization of Newcomers.* Reading, Mass: Addison-Wesley. 240 pp.

Warmke, D. L., Billings, R. S. 1979. Comparison of training methods for improving the psychometric quality of experimental and administrative performance ratings. *J. Appl. Psychol.* 64:124–31

Webster, E. G., Booth, R. E., Alf, E. F. 1978. A sex comparison of factors related to success in normal hospital corps school. *Personnel Psychol.* 31:95–106

Weiss, D. J., Davison, N. L. 1981. Test theory and methods *Ann. Rev. Psychol.* 32:629–58

Wexley, K. N., Silverman, S. B. 1978. An examination of differences between managerial effectiveness and response patterns on a structured job analysis questionnaire. *J. Appl. Psychol.* 63: 646–49

Wiggins, J. S. 1979. A psychological taxonomy of trait-descriptive terms: The interpersonal domain. *J. Pers. Soc. Psychol.* 37:395–412

Wilkinson, L. 1979. Tests of significance in stepwise regression. *Psychol. Bull.* 86: 168–74

Winer, B. J. 1978. Statistics and data analysis: Trading bias for reduced mean squared error. *Ann. Rev. Psychol.* 29: 647–81

Wing, H. 1980. Profiles of cognitive ability of different racial/ethnic and sex groups on a multiple abilities test battery. *J. Appl. Psychol.* 65:289–98

Wysocki, B. 1981. More companies try to spot leaders early, guide them to the top. *Wall Street J.* Feb. 25

Youngman, M. B., Oxtoby, R., Monk, J. D., Heywood, J. 1978. *Analysing Jobs.* West Mead, England: Gower Press, Teakfield. 157 pp.

Ann. Rev. Psychol. 1982. 33:619–49

CONSUMER PSYCHOLOGY

Harold H. Kassarjian

Graduate School of Management, University of California, Los Angeles, California 90024

CONTENTS

INTRODUCTION

Although its roots can be traced back to the great philosophers and psychological laboratories in Europe, consumer psychology as typically recognized today is a much more recent phenomenon. A child of the *Zeitgeist* that

0066-4308/82/0201-0619$02.00

could only emerge in a civilization of abundance, one in which man is freed from survival pressures, the field is about two decades old . . . maybe three. In fact, the terms consumer psychology and consumer behavior had not been in use very long before the first appearance of the topic in the *Annual Review of Psychology* (Twedt 1965). Three years later the second *Annual Review* chapter appeared (Perloff 1968) and the field had truly emerged. Consumer behavior was then being taught in several dozen schools. Myers and Reynolds had published their paperback text (1967) and the first true textbook was about to appear (Engel et al 1968). By the time Jacoby had completed the third review (1976), four texts, several books of readings, and several comprehensive theories of consumer behavior had been published. By then consumer psychology was to be found not only in occasional issues of tangential marketing or psychological journals, but the new *Journal of Consumer Research* had been launched with APA participation and the Association for Consumer Research had emerged as an important medium of dissemination.

Now in early 1981 more than a dozen additional texts are available with several more to appear within the year. Another dozen reading books and case books as well as collections of original papers are available. It is estimated that as many as 150,000 students per year take a course in consumer behavior, and it is no longer possible to estimate accurately the number of papers published that can be considered relevant to the field. Unfortunately, this work is not well known in psychology. Hence the guiding aim of this review is not to present great insights to a few specialists in this field or to provide a rigorous evaluation of selected studies, but rather the aim is to sketch a broad panorama of the field, concentrating on some peak trends and developments. However, some heavily researched areas such as cognitive processing are underemphasized since other reviews are available and widely known. The reviewed literature primarily encompasses the years 1975–1980 and generally ignores the relevant literature in sister disciplines such as social and mathematical psychology, marketing, and experimental psychology. And other topics have been intentionally ignored —those that are part of consumer behavior but not really within the subset of consumer psychology—pricing, brand and store loyalty, and market segmentation. Others were arbitrarily discarded, such as buyer-seller interaction, roles of blacks and women in the media, and methodological approaches such as psychometrics, conjoint analysis, and data collection techniques.

Finally, many relevant and interesting topics have been ignored because of space limitations and the fact that not all that much research has yet been carried out—topics such as humor in advertising, variety seeking, the consumption of esthetics, and dozens more. Whenever possible the interested reader is referred for greater detail to other reviews or papers that cite the literature.

For the purpose of this review, consumer psychology has been divided into three major segments. The first of these is the molecular level of analysis—the physiological approach. Because it offers seemingly simple measures of behavioral antecedents, or perhaps because of an intrinsic fascination with the human nervous system, studies on physiological responses have been carried out in consumer behavior since its inception. These studies have ranged from sensory reactions such as touch (Dawson & Bettinger 1977) to the nervous system and EEG measures of brain wave activity.

The second segment, that with the greatest ferment and fervor, has emerged out of the cognitive revolution in social psychology that replaced behaviorism in the 1960s (McGuire 1977). These studies have examined numerous middle range theories and approaches such as attitudes, attribution, and the presently flourishing state of information processing.

The third division covers the more molar or macro aspects of behavior involving interpersonal influence and the impact of society on the consumer. This work ranges from the influence of family members to the impact of the mass media. Also included in the molar approach is the omnipresent topic of economic psychology, never fully accepted and integrated into the main stream of either consumer psychology or economics and never fully ignored. This review takes each of these segments in turn.

THE PHYSIOLOGICAL APPROACH TO CONSUMER BEHAVIOR

Unfortunately, psychobiology is one of the least well understood areas in consumer psychology and has also been the most oversold and misused. The quality of research has ranged from voice-pitch analysis to the highly sophisticated studies on eye movement and brain lateralization research. The earliest attempts concerned measurement of the electrical properties of the skin, respiration rate, and other reactions of the autonomic nervous system (ANS). Researchers were seeking a measure of valence such as the preference or dislike of an advertisement or package design. As should have been predicted, in time these techniques were deemed unreliable and became rather unpopular. For although in extreme examples, such as advertisements displaying nudity where the tools were able to measure the magnitude of the emotional response with some degree of reliability, the proponents were seeking a measure of direction and persuasiveness.

Arousal and Activation

The more recent and considerably more sophisticated studies of the last few years have tended to focus on arousal and activation. Activation is provoked by stimulating a subcortical unit, the reticular activation system (RAS) in the brain stem, which figuratively "alerts" other functional areas of the brain to take a "stand-by" position (ANS activity). Simultaneously, cerebral areas are aroused involving information processing, perception, thought, and memory (Kroeber-Riel 1979).

The concept of the RAS and its concomitant, the orienting reflex, was first introduced to consumer psychology by Greeno (1970) and Hansen (1972) in his classic monograph. Hansen hypothesized that there is an optimal level (or better yet, range) of arousal in consumer choice behavior, and much of his later theorizing and empirical work is based on this structure. Today much of this work is emerging from the University of Saarland laboratory under Kroeber-Riel (1979, 1980; Ryan 1980).

The belief is that cognitive and psychological processes originate from physiological ones and that there are biological limits on the person's deliberate and conscious control of his behavior. Further, verbal methods of measuring arousal or even cognitive activity such as information processing are either not sensitive enough or involve a needless detour (the measurement of the perception of responses in the nervous system) when the response itself can be measured directly. Often the subject being interviewed simply will not or cannot verbalize his responses. The Kroeber-Riel group, as well as Russo (1978), Bettman (1979), and others have well documented the noncorrespondence between verbal measures and physiological measures such as eye movement.

Eye Movement

Relating eye movement and fixation to psychophysical arousal, Witt (1977) showed that the more intense (erotic) the stimulus the greater the frequency of eye fixations. Further, the more frequently a person fixes his eyes upon a stimulus (advertisement) the better it will be recalled (Barg 1977, Berhard 1978) and the more effective the ad will be (Barton 1980); that is, the higher the activation level the greater the recall. Moreover, Kroeber-Riel would claim that an increase in the consumer's level of activation will increase the processing of information. However, the Kroeber-Riel group does not necessarily deny the optimum level of arousal hypothesized by Hansen. Kroeber-Riel himself points to the work of Peterson & Kerin (1977), indicating that advertisements with extreme nudity were perceived as less appealing and less reputable than less arousing advertisements.

Measurement of eye movement ranges from very simple experimenter observation through one-way mirrors (Smead et al 1980) and video recordings of the eyes for later analysis (van Raaij 1977a,b) to computer controlled systems involving eye position sensors and complex software (Russo 1978). Basically this stream of research records eye movements while subjects are presented with a stimulus (e.g. advertisements, information on brands or products, etc). By analyzing the pattern of fixations the choice strategies are hypothesized. They are typically "validated" against verbal protocols in which the subject "thinks out loud" as he makes his decisions. Compared to other methods of collecting information processing data such as information display boards, Russo feels that eye fixation has the advantages of detailed data and high validity with equipment costs its major drawback. In this Kroeber-Riel and Russo are in agreement; however, Kroeber-Riel would go one step further and claim that physiological measures are always superior since they are a more direct measure of activity than any method dependent upon verbal or motor response.

Some Recent Failures

The measurement of pupil dilation was a natural successor to the earlier ill-fated GSR research in advertising. First introduced in the 1960s (Hess & Polt 1960), commercial researchers reverted back to earlier logic with claims that pupils dilate in response to pleasant stimuli and contract with viewing unpleasant stimuli. Once again, subsequent studies clearly indicated no relationship between pupil dilation and direction of affect (Rice 1974), but by the 1970s proponents were still espousing the use of "pupilometrics" to measure emotional valance (for recent reviews see Arch 1979, Watson & Gatchel 1979).

Nevertheless, pupil dilation does seem to be related to the orienting reflex (Goldwater 1972) as one might expect, while Kahneman & Beatty (1966) related pupil dilation with learning and memory. The more demanding the task the greater the diameter and the greater information stored in memory. But in advertising, perhaps because of oversell, the topic died a timely death by the late 1970s.

The most recent incursion of Madison Avenue oversell into psychobiology is the voice-pitch analyzer, another black box that promises much. Perhaps most familiar to readers of advertisements in Airline magazines, this electronic wonder is sold as a valid lie detector for use in personal interviews, telephone conversations, and television broadcasts. Introduced to the research community by Brickman (1976, 1980), the claim is that the instrument viably predicts commercial success of products and advertisements by measuring tremors in the voices of subjects previewing films. The level of physiological and psychological sophistication of the research is quite naive and its future seems dim.

Brain Hemisphere Lateralization

A very recent trend in consumer behavior involves the differential activities of the right and left brain hemispheres. Several papers have appeared buttressing the dozens of studies in psychology and physiology. The basic research on brain lateralization has involved studies of individuals with brain damage, patients emerging from electoconvulsive therapy, and by controlled stimulation transmitted to the brain of normal individuals (Hansen 1981). These data indicate that among normal subjects (including most but not all left-handed persons) the left hemisphere is primarily responsible for traditional cognitive activities relying upon verbal information, symbolic representations, sequential analysis, and the ability to report consciously. The right brain, without the individual being able to report verbally about it, is more concerned with pictorial, geometric, timeless, and other nonverbal information (Hansen & Lundsgaard 1981). The left brain is causal, logical, and argumentative in contrast with the right brain processes which are more diffuse, spatial, intuitive, and musical. In creativity and problem solving, the left hemisphere prefers the use of language and analysis whereas the right prefers the use of visualization and imagery (McCallum & Glynn 1979). Normally both hemispheres are active together, interacting through the connecting corpus callosum, but according to Lundsgaard (1978), some people tend to be left-brain dominated and others are right-brain dominated. The extent of lateral domination depends partly on inherited factors and partly on the kind of stimulation and training received during childhood.

Up to this point much of the research has involved use of an electroencephalograph (EEG) requiring delicate and expensive equipment, highly skilled technicians, precise placement of electrodes, and a special laboratory environment. Further, since hemisphere differences involve interpretations of the patterns of alpha and beta waves, seemingly no aspect of the procedure using EEG is simple or amenable to large-scale studies.

Use of the EEG in consumer research can be traced back to an article by Krugman describing an incident in which brain wave activity generated by a secretary was recorded while she was browsing through a magazine and while being shown three TV commercials (Weinstein 1980). Krugman (1979) claimed that since reading and speaking are left-brain functions and image perception a right-brain function, print media are left-brain oriented while TV is right-brain oriented. Further, tieing this work into high and low involvement in consumer decision making, Krugman hypothesized that high involvement is left-brain activity and low involvement is right-brain.

Only if sufficient psychic energy or involvement is generated will television advertising invoke the left brain and the ability to verbalize the perception or impact of the stimulus. Without such involvement mere holistic exposure rather than information processing will lead to a decision and with it the inability to verbalize the decision process or even recall the activity.

The validity of these hypotheses have been examined in several studies. For example, Weinstein et al (1980) wired 30 right-handed women for measurement of beta waves. Print ads and TV commercials were presented in a natural context. Results indicated that every magazine ad produced more brain wave activity (in both right and left hemispheres) than did any of the TV commercials. Secondly, relative to television, magazine ads generated more left-brain activity than right-brain. And finally, advertising which generates more total brain-wave activity produced more recall, in part. Magazine ads failed to produce higher levels of recall despite the fact that they produced higher levels of beta activity and generated more left-brain activity. (However, for negative results by the same authors see Appel et al 1979.)

LATERAL EYE MOVEMENT Other physiological measures have been used in brain activity; for example, conjugate lateral eye movement. Although there is disagreement, at least some studies seem to indicate that direction of eye movement implies which cerebral hemisphere is engaged most actively or is dominant (Kling 1979, Richardson 1977). A "left-looker" (right hemisphere dominant) should handle information differently from a "right-looker" (left dominance). For example, Kling presented subjects with proverbs that they were to interpret in their own words while the experimenter was watching eye movement during the thought process. Although the paper is rather confusing, the theoretically expected results seemed to have emerged with left-dominated individuals having greater access to their decision rules than their counterparts. These papers, however, are not just the results of a few more studies, but rather indicate one more attempt at finding a measure of hemisphere dominance.

A PAPER-AND-PENCIL TEST If some people are in fact right-brain and others left-brain dominated, the potential of the concept in consumer behavior is great, moderating many of the present-day findings. The problem is one of measuring hemisphere domination, if indeed it exists, among normal subjects. At present Hansen, Lundsgaard, and their associates in Denmark are in the midst of developing a short paper-and-pencil instrument to measure lateral domination. Using sophisitcated tests such as tachistoscopic stimulation and dichotic listening (tasks in which the right and left ear are simultaneously presented with different pairs of nonsense syllables) and more typical psychological tests (Goldstein-Sheerer cube test, copy recall, etc) validity and reliability measures are under way. If development of the scales is successful, and preliminary data seem to suggest it may be (Hansen & Lundgaard 1981), this would be a major contribution accelerating research in this area and allowing for reasonable sized samples without the difficulties of instrumentation.

In summary, physiological activity continues to attract interest among consumer psychologists, and it appears as if the laboratory offers significant long-run potential for better understanding of human behavior within or without the marketplace.

THE COGNITIVE CONSUMER

Once weaned from mechanistic views of man and the psychoanalytic view of motivation research, the cognitive revolution was under way. From its early beginnings in studying selective perception and applying cognitive dissonance to automobile purchases, to the complexity of memory factors in information processing, research poured forth: perceived risk, cognitive mapping, decision rules, halo effects, etc. This review, however, can concentrate on only a few selected topics, those that have generated the greatest recent interest.

Attitudes

No topic in psychology has captured a greater interest among consumer researchers than the field of attitude formation and attitude change. The interest evolved out of the work of social psychologists of the post World War II era and later out of the functional theory of Katz (for a recent resurgence of this view see Lutz 1978, Locander & Spivey 1978), and eventually turned to the expectency-value theories of Rosenberg and Fishbein. Rosenberg's view is that a person's attitude toward an object is related to beliefs about the potential of that object for the attaining or blocking of valued states. The more the object leads to attainment of a valued state the more positive the attitude and vice versa. Fishbein claims that an attitude toward an object is the belief (subjective likelihood) that the object possesses some attribute times the evaluation of that attribute, summed over all salient attributes. Thus affect is seen as the multiplicative summation of salient beliefs about an object weighted by the value of those beliefs. Although the two models appear to be quite similar, causing considerable confusion at first among consumer researchers, the Fishbein multiattribute attitude model and later his extended model were to be most influential throughout the 1970s. The number of papers exploded from about 40 studies in 1973 to literally hundreds by 1980 (for review see Lutz & Bettman 1977). These studies explored not only the relationship of attitudes to consumer variables but turned to the use of multiattribute models for their diagnostic capabilities and their ability to suggest appropriate attitude change strategies (Lutz 1975).

And just as rapidly as it emerged, interest began to decline by the late 1970s. The original formulation may have been a bit too simple and the attitude-behavior relationship was not that clear. Thus both Fishbein and consumer researchers shifted their interest to Fishbein's extended attitude-behavior model. The basic proposition underlying the extended model is that if one wishes to predict a specific behavior (e.g. purchase of a particular brand during some specified time period), then one must measure the person's attitude toward performing that behavior, not just the general attitude toward the object at which the behavior is directed (Lutz 1981). The best predictor of behavior is the actor's intention to perform the behavior. The intention is based on the person's attitude toward the behavior and the *subjective norm* regarding the behavior—the extent to which the person feels that significant others think that the behavior should be performed. The subjective norm is intended to measure social influence on a person's behavior in recognition of the fact that there are some situations where the behavior is under *normative* and not attitudinal control of the individual along with varying levels of motivation to comply (Ajzen & Fishbein 1977, Fishbein & Ajzen 1975). The model basically represents an attempt to combine cognitive influences with interpersonal and group influences. Attitudes are good predictors only when the attitudinal and behavioral measures show a high degree of correspondence on action, target, context, and time dimensions (Ajzen & Fishbein 1981).

The model has been generally successful in accounting for such things as family planning, alcohol use, reenlistment in the National Guard, and voting on a nuclear power plant proposal (Cialdini et al 1981), as well as formulating strategies designed to increase the number of loan applications at a credit union (Ryan & Bonfield 1980). However, in consumer psychology the extended model has not generated as much research as the earlier formulation (for a sampling see Bearden & Woodside 1977, Lutz 1977, Ryan & Bonfield 1980). For one thing, the Fishbein model was designed to predict widely varying behaviors. Hence, it has not been specifically tailored for purchasing situations and its unique features (e.g. affordability, availability). The model may be too general for consumer purchasing applications (Warshaw 1980). Further in the studies that do exist, predictions have not been very successful (Ryan & Bonfield 1975), undoubtedly dampening some enthusiasm. Miniard & Cohen (1979) point out other difficulties such as multicolinearity and problems of attitudinal contamination in the subjective norm and motivation to comply components of the model.

Sheth (1974b) has presented an alternative model constructed specifically for a product purchase context, but it too has difficulties and has generated very little research. Very recently, Warshaw (1980) has reconceptualized the Fishbein extended model incorporating behavioral intentions, norms, and product-specific variables such as brand availability. The author claims low multicollinearity among predictor variables, high predictive ability, and reasonable stability across test products. Meanwhile Fishbein and his co-workers are still developing their theory and the pace of publications is again accelerating. It is certainly too early to predict either its success or its demise.

Cognitive Response

One of the most important related trends in consumer psychology today is the research being carried out in cognitive response. Introduced into the consumer literature almost a decade ago (Wright 1973), the concept was at first slow in emerging and is now rapidly accelerating. The basic tenet of this approach is that cognitive responses or thoughts are evoked by persuasive communications and these are crucial mediators of attitude change (Petty 1977). The approach postulates that when messages are perceived, the individual may attempt to relate the new information to his existing repertoire of cognitions. These self-generated cognitions may be in agreement with the proposals of the source—a support argument in which the message is supported by already entrenched beliefs and values. Hence attitude change in the advocate direction should be facilitated. Or the cognitive response can be in disagreement with the intent of the communicator. A counterargument is activated when incoming information is compared to the existing belief system and a discrepancy is noted countering the message received. An alternate type of resistive response focuses on the source of the information in a derogatory manner. To the extent that counterargument or source derogation exists, an attitude change should be inhibited. Or as Petty points out, it is even possible that the subject's own cognitions are so much more persuasive than the arguments of the source that attitude change in the direction opposite to that advocated may result.

The studies conducted to date seem to be rather impressive; cognitive arguments do act as mediators between the stimulus and attitude change and are related to a wide range of cognitive variables including beliefs, attitudes, and purchase intentions. Even in messages that are not overly persuasive, the cognitive response process seems to be in operation and consumers may counterargue or support-argue with message content that does not directly attack established beliefs. It may even operate in cases of low involvement, unimportant products—a class where few earlier theories and studies seem generalizable (Olson et al 1978).

The cognitive response methodology seems to have widespread appeal. For example, Wilson & Muderrisoglu (1980) measured the number of arguments generated to test the effectiveness of comparative and noncomparative advertising. Comparative ads (those making specific comparisons with competing brands) were found to produce significantly more counterarguments, source derogations, and negative ad-related statements than did noncomparative ads. The authors conclude that comparative advertising is probably less effective than noncomparative advertising, supporting other research results on that topic.

The impact of source credibility on cognitive response has been addressed by Sternthal et al (1978); Tybout et al (1978) have developed a model bringing in self-perception theory; Wright & Rip (1980) related the concept to decision strategies, Lammers & Becker (1980) to distraction, and Calder (1978) brought in LTM and STM aspects of information processing. Finally, Lutz & Swasy (1977) have developed a model relating cognitive response to cognitive structures and Fishbein's attitude model attempting to capture the power of both approaches—the free response format of cognitive response with the more precise measurement procedures of attitude measurement. Some empirical support for this integration can be seen in the Olson et al (1978) paper previously discussed.

In summary, cognitive response will have considerable potential in consumer psychology for the coming few years, for it not only begs for integration with other favored theories but has the added appeal of being obviously and directly relevant to behavior in the marketplace. The substantive findings have been thoroughly reviewed in the recent literature (Petty et al 1980, Cialdini et al 1981) and need not be belabored here. In particular, Wright (1980) has presented a detailed framework and an exemplary review with the conclusion that thought verbalizations have often been consistent with information processing theories on the effects of stimulus variations and that these processes mediate message or treatment effects on attitudes, intentions, or preferences. All indications are that research on attitudes, persuasion, information processing, and several other areas are converging on cognitive response—where arguments come from, and how and under what conditions they are triggered.

Information Processing

Except for attitude models, information processing has led to more research in consumer psychology than any other topic. Its ascent has been meteoric in recent years, and without question it is now enjoying a peak in popularity. Independently introduced into the consumer behavior literature by Haines

(1969, Alexis et al 1968), and by Bettman (1970), both were heavily influenced by the massive contributions of Newell, Shaw & Simon's earlier work on human problem solving.

At first information processing was described simply as the manipulation of informational inputs to achieve a decision. However, memory factors were soon introduced and the approach became more dynamic. According to this view incoming data or stimuli enter the short-term memory store (STM) where they are encoded into memonics, images, and associations, and with some processing effort such as rehearsal, transferred into long-term memory (LTM). LTM can consist of price and quality information, advertising, earlier learning, and experiences with products or choice strategies. When a decision is called for, incoming data from the receptors entering STM trigger the retrieval of traces of earlier cognitive acts. These traces interact with the new cues, are weighted in some manner, and a new decision signals an action response.

The central focus of the information processing perspective is on viewing consumers as cognitively active problems solvers and understanding the strategies and plans used in decision making, typically product purchases and choice between brands (Mitchell 1978). Relying heavily on cognitive psychology, the research has revolved around information search, information acquisition, encoding, storage, retrieval, integration, and the processes used in the choice of heuristics, the rule of thumb a consumer might use.

For example, information acquisition has been studied by several dozen researchers using a variety of methods: verbal protocols, eye movement recordings, response time, and the highly used information display boards in which subjects are presented with a matrix of information involving brand names and data on various attributes (Lehmann & Moore 1980). These methods are thoroughly reviewed by Bettman (1977) and Russo (1978) and will not be repeated here. The encoding process is discussed by Olson (1980), integration by Cohen et al (1980), choice heuristics by Bettman & Park (1980), etc. The greatest recent ferment is in the examining of memory factors (Johnson & Russo 1978, Bettman 1979) and how consumer's knowledge effects information processing. This literature is so voluminous that any attempt to overview the field would simply be inadequate in the space allocated. The interested reader is advised to turn to one of several massive reviews of this research. For example, the field has been thoroughly reviewed and integrated in Bettman's splendid monograph (1979) on consumer choice. Posner covers information processing models in another chapter in this *Annual Review* volume. Also see McGuire (1977) and Hughes & Ray (1974). The implications of this stream of research extend well beyond the academic laboratory.

IS MORE INFORMATION BETTER? It has long been assumed both by public policy makers and consumer researchers that the consumer has a basic "right to know," a right to be informed of product performance, characteristics, and ingredients. In the realm of consumer products, the greatest source of information is that of advertising. But generally advertisers have been prone to provide precious little product information outside of promising an alluring smile or the prevention of "ring around the collar." The belief of advertisers has been that consumers are not interested nor can they handle large amounts of relevant information, and that the proper strategy is to position a product on some unique selling proposition such as brighter teeth, flavor, or price. Consumerists, on the other hand, seem to be demanding more and more information be made available in the equally adamant belief that more is necessarily better: miles per gallon cars, energy use on appliances, nutritional information on labels and ads, etc. (An excellent analysis of these and related issues can be found in Federal Trade Commission, 1979).

The classic papers on this issue by Jacoby et al (1974a,b; see also Jacoby, Hoyer & Sheluga 1981) have been some of the most discussed and criticized studies in the field. The authors had claimed that although consumers do feel more satisfied and less confused, increasing information tends to produce dysfunctional consequences in terms of the consumer's ability to select that brand which is best for him—an information overload leading to a poorer choice.

Rejoinders were immediately published (Russo 1974, Wilkie 1974a, among others) arguing that unless data is presented in a proper format, it will not be informative or useful, and criticizing the conceptualization and the experimental design. Reanalysis of the data indicated increased accuracy (rather than poorer choice) as attribute information increased when brands were held constant. Hence in a similar study, Scammon (1977) varied the amount of information and the mode of presentation, holding the number of brands constant. Using TV ads for two brands of peanut butter, she presented various levels of nutritional information in either raw "% of RDA" numbers or evaluative adjectives—excellent, fair, etc.

The major conclusion drawn from this study was that subjects were able to recall objective product information presented to them, and further, they appeared to comprehend the overall nutritional message contained in the commercials. The results were more pronounced for respondents exposed to adjectives than those exposed to percentage information and occurred even though the information presented to them was discrepent with their expectations. Scammon feels consumers could handle far more information if presented in an understandable and manageable manner.

The critical issue is whether or not it is possible to extend the ability of consumers to process more information without the negative consequences of "overload." For example, Bettman (1975) concludes that product comparisons by brands are psychologically taxing and inefficient. Processing all brands one attribute at a time reduces this load as alternatives may be dropped if important differences are not perceived. Seeing data for each brand in isolation means that context must be created from memory rather than being readily available (e.g. Bettman & Jacoby 1976, Bettman & Kakkar 1977, Bettman & Zins 1979, Russo 1977). The obvious conclusion is that information overload need not necessarily be a serious problem if communicators are interested in providing information.

CONSUMER USE OF INFORMATION With proper presentation and repetition the evidence is clear that consumers are capable of assimilating massive quantities of data regarding products and services. The question then arises of whether or not consumers use and comprehend the information available to them. Scammon (1977) indicated that consumers are able to comprehend nutritional information, but it did not effect their brand preference or "intentions to buy." Jacoby et al (1977) summarized several studies carried out at Purdue and concluded that consumers consistently say they want and are willing to pay for nutritional information but do not acquire, comprehend, or use such information when making a purchase decision.

Similar results were found earlier with other information programs such as age dating, truth in lending, and unit pricing. In the beginning the information was simply not extensively used, but over time at least some classes of consumers began to make use of the information in their purchase decisions (for a review see Day 1976). Clearly it takes time, some effort on the part of the communicator, and sufficient repetition to have such information assimilated into the memory system and decision process. And once again context, situation, and socioeconomic status play an important role in just how much information the consumer is able and willing to process (Capon & Burke 1980).

Attribution Theory

First introduced into the consumer literature by Settle et al (1971), the roots of attribution theory go back to Bem, Kelley, Heider, and ultimately to the Gestalt psychologists and Kurt Lewin, the birthplace of so much of consumer psychology today. In a classic experiment conducted in the 1940s, Heider presented subjects with a film of moving geometric figures such as squares, circles, and triangles. These figures were interpreted as *chasing* and *interacting* with each other, actions of beings. Heider proposed that individuals seem to operate as "naive psychologists," perceiving actions and events by reverting to causality.

In time, research on causal attribution has taken one of three interrelated streams (Mizerski et al 1979): person perception (interpersonal relations), self-perception (inferring causes for one's own action), and object perception (assumptions about things in the external world). However, the work in consumer behavior has been related primarily to the latter two approaches.

OBJECT PERCEPTION This work is based on Kelley's (1967) covariance model and the ever popular analysis of variance experimental framework in social psychology. The assessment of causality or attribution depends on several criteria: distinctiveness (effect occurs only when "cause" is present), consistency over time (reliability), consistency over modality, and consensus.

The influence of consensus, for example, has been studied on evaluations of the taste of coffee with the conclusion that people use the evaluation of others as a basis for inferring that the product is indeed a better product (Burnkrant & Cousineau 1975). Earlier Settle & Golden (1974) had studied the covariance principle. Their results indicated that the believability of some product claims and the credibility of the source (advertising) may be increased by disclaiming superiority on some product features, the importance of the covariance of claims. However, Hansen & Scott (1976) have challanged both the interpretations of covariance theory and the interpretation of the data in an insightful rejoinder (see also rebuttal, Golden 1977, and extensions related to advertising: Smith & Hunt 1978, Sparkman & Locander 1980).

Perusal of the field indicates that in some cases the theory was misapplied; in others, data indicated that the attribution process was a bit more complicated than first assumed (Calder & Burnkrant 1977); and in still others, advances have been made in applying attribution theory to consumer activities. For example, attribution theory seems to help account for product dissatisfaction among buyers. Using Weiner's internal-external locus of control framework, consumer complaint behavior and postpurchase satisfaction as well as the placing of responsibility have been examined by Krishnan & Valle (1979), Valle & Koeske (1977), and Richens (1980), among many others.

SELF-PERCEPTION In a very similar vein, self-perception theory provides a framework for analyzing how beliefs are derived from experience: "... individuals come to know their own attitudes, emotions, and other internal states partially by inferring them from observations of their own behavior and/or the situation in which the behavior occurs (Bem as cited in Scott 1981). Or as Scott has pointed out, "I must like this comedian because I am always laughing at him," the core of self-perception theory.

In perceiving the causes of past behavior, the presence or absence of plausible factors external to the individual that could have produced the action is critical. When plausible external causes for the behavior (a sale with impressive discounts from list price or payment to do something) are present, the individual attributes his behavior to these factors and discounts the causal role of internal motivations (Scott 1981). This is the discounting principle of Kelley that has been heavily studied in consumer research. Thus the behavior is not perceived as being indicative of the person's own dispositions (I don't really like this dress—I only bought it because it was on sale"). In contrast, when no plausible external causes are present, the behavior is attributed to the person's own motivations and subsequent behavior consistent with these beliefs should result (Scott 1981). Various studies involving participation in a survey (Reingen & Kernan 1977, 1979), brand switching (Dodson et al 1978), and completion of a mail questionnaire (Hansen & Robinson 1980) suggest that behavior may result in favorable attitudes (and repeat purchase) if internal attributions are made and less favorable attitudes (discounting) if the attributions are external.

Using the so-called "foot-in-the-door" technique, one of the first studies in consumer psychology on self-perception was presented by Scott (1976) and Sternthal et al (1976). The premise is that consumers induced into making a small purchase (e.g. at a trial price or trial size) will more likely make larger purchases (I bought it, therefore I must like it). In Scott's study, subjects were contacted by telephone and offered a two-week trial subscription to a local newspaper—some at no charge, others at half-price, still others at regular price. Self-perception theory would predict that the full price group would be most likely to resubscribe at regular prices and the free trial the least likely. The results indicated that only the half-price group generated significantly more subscriptions than a control group, whereas the free trial group generated the fewest follow-up sales. Scott concluded that self-perception theory was only partially confirmed and that some incentive is necessary in a commercial setting to promote interest. The small incentive was enough to produce compliance but not enough to result in discounting of internal motivations (I paid for it, ergo I must like it, even if I did pay less).

The process by which these behaviors occur and situational cues are interpreted has been studied by Scott & Yalch (1978), Reingen & Kernan (1979), Reingen (1979), Scott & Tybout (1979), etc. On overview, the evidence now seems to indicate that consumer experience and feedback mechanisms are neither as simple nor as automatic as early interpretations of attribution theory might indicate. Like so much else in consumer psychology, attribution theory does explain some portion of the variance of the behavior of individuals in the marketplace, but by itself it is simply not sufficient (for reviews see Scott 1978, 1981, and Mizerski et al 1979).

The Counter-Revolution

Very recently there has been a reaction to the overdependence on cognitive psychology from several directions. The first emerges from the fact that consumer researchers generally have been heavily influenced by the computer revolution and its concomitant flow charts, arrows, boxes and feedback loops. Once a mental process is modeled, the model often tends to take on an entelechial character. A flow-chart model, say, stimulus to encoding to STM to LTM to retrieval, may soon be accepted as gospel and research designs created on that assumption. Although such models have a respected tradition behind them and perhaps can be heuristically quite useful in stimulating research, as has often been the case in scientific inquiry, they can trap empiricism within narrow confines (Chestnut & Jacoby 1977).

On a more general level, a second difficulty is the assumption of an involved information-extracting individual seeking the correct decision on brand or product. Of course, in many cases and under many conditions the consumer does behave as a thinking, information processing consumer. But under other conditions, particularily in low-involvement products, he or she simply could care less. Olshavsky & Granbois (1979), in fact, present evidence that a substantial portion of purchases does not involve decision making at all, even on the first purchase. This distinction has not yet been incorporated into the research stream on cognitive processing (for an attempt see Gardner et al 1978).

The concept of low involvement affects many of the views of the cognitive consumer. For example, the assumption that attitudes precede action implies a classical high involvement hierarchy. Ray (1974) and his coworkers suggest that under low commitment conditions the hierarchy of effects is not awareness-attitude-adoption, but rather awareness and minimal comprehension occur first, followed by trial and attitude formation or change in that order. Cognitive processing of information, if it occurs at all in the usual manner, does not necessarily precede a trial adoption or decision. Further, numerous other concepts involving product selection, brand loyalty, advertising, and even the selection of political candidates (Robertson 1976, Rothschild 1978) are areas where the concept of the uninvolved, plodding, muddling consumer challenges our cherished views.

Finally, a third challenge to the cognitive consumer has come from the work of physiological researchers and the reemergence of interest in learning theory and behavior modification (Markin & Nayarana 1976, Nord & Peters 1980) as well as the work on the effects of repetition in advertising. The latter view is that advertising effectiveness is directly related to advertising repetition, and although cognitive factors may or may not be denied, they are essentially ignored (Sawyer & Ward 1979, Zielski & Henry 1980; for review see Sawyer 1977; for a theoretical treatment see Otteson 1980 and Bass 1974).

A SOCIAL PERSPECTIVE

The application of concepts and theories from a social perspective has not been as prolific as from the cognitive perspective. Numerous papers do exist, however, on such topics as reference groups, social influence and power, social class, and the ever popular innovation and diffusion; and a few have taken a true sociological perspective (Nicosia & Mayer 1976, Zaltman & Wallendorf 1979). In this review two of the areas that have been on the frontier of consumer psychology within the past decade will be touched upon: family decision making and consumer socialization.

Family Decision Making

As Robertson & Zielinski (1981) suggest, it is becoming increasingly clear that the appropriate unit of analysis for much of consumer behavior should be the family and not the individual. However, little of the research on family consumption behavior has explored how families make decisions or the process of family decision making, but has rather emphasized influence, marital roles, and to what extent husband and wives agree in perceptions of their own and each other's role in the process. The early study by Davis (1970) focused on the selection of automobiles and furniture, and that has been more or less replicated a number of times (e.g. Woodside & Motes 1979). Others have studied home buying (e.g. Munsinger et al 1975), financial planning (Ferber & Lee 1974), and vacations (Filiatrault & Ritchie 1980). Davis & Rigaux (1974) have an excellent study on Belgian families, and others have considered methodological issues and moderator variables (Sheth 1974a, Burns & Granbois 1977). An excellent review has been done by Davis (1976) and more recently by Jenkins (1980). The results of these studies indicate that household goods and nondurables are generally wife-dominant in the husband-wife influence process while husbands are more dominant in the durable expensive products. The husband dominates in deciding when and where to buy an automobile while the wife dominates in choice of color and model. The "larger" decisions seem to be in the husband's domain, such as the decision concerning price range in the buying of a home, while the wife is more involved in specifics such as floor plan and other house features, the style, fabric, and color of furniture, or brands of household goods to purchase. Further, there seem to be differences between husband and wives on perceptions of who has greater influence. That is, reports from wives and husband differ on the degree of influence and domination each sees in the other.

Joint decision making is more common among middle-class families than among the upper class or the poor; working wives have more influence than nonworking wives; and finally, there appears to be considerably more joint decision making early in married life, but roles are increasingly more differentiated as the family grows older (Kassarjian & Robertson 1981). The findings are not always obvious, however. For example, one might assume that family planning programs and the use of birth control devices fall more heavily on women than men since most modern devices involve the woman and they are believed to be more receptive to birth control practices for obvious reasons. Yet several studies reported by Davis (1976) indicate that husbands play an important and perhaps the major role in the family contraceptive adoption process. In one study the decision to use an IUD was made by the wife alone in only 7 percent of the cases, and husbands were reported to make the final decision in 44% of the families. Other studies support this finding in both developed and nondeveloped countries, with husbands having considerable influence in contraceptive use.

This stream of research is still in a very early stage, and much of it tends to be descriptive: who does what and who decides which. Although that may be very important and interesting, the potential of the field is just beginning to be tapped, for here is a natural field condition in which group decisions are constantly being made and adjusted. Theories such as role bargaining, negotiation, exchange, and the interaction process have yet to be studied. Once one turns from individual decision making to group decision making, much of the prevailing knowledge in consumer psychology simply may not apply. Further, as Robertson and Zielinski point out, when research has been conducted on the "family," with few exceptions, it has in reality included only husband-wife decision making and for the most part examined the role of children, not as members of the family team, but rather focused on the requesting/yielding and "gatekeeper" processes initiated for child-relevant products. Children may have an important influence on the selection of a car, vacation, or home, not to mention brands of cereal or the dinner menu.

Children and Consumer Socialization

The socialization of children as consumers, on the other hand, has generated considerable ferment in the field (for reviews see Adler et al 1980, Ward 1981). Until recently, consumer socialization did not seem particularily relevant either to consumer researchers or to child psychologists. After all, socialization is a product of intrapersonal development and interpersonal communication with family, peers, and teachers. In reality, purposive training in consumer skills occurs infrequently (Ward & Wackman 1973). However, modern technology, particularily television, has exposed the child to an additional important source of norms, values, and behavior other than those reflected in the family or peer group (Myers 1978). Hence the question arises: what is the influence of television and particularily television advertising aimed at children?

The impetus for this work did not just happen to emerge but rather was stimulated by actions of regulatory bodies such as the FCC and FTC. Prodded by an activist group convinced of the evils of television advertising (Action for Children's Television), the FTC focused hearings on potentially deceptive and unfair practices such as offer of premiums, disclaimers, and separation of commercials from program content. Industry representatives, on the other hand, defended such practices with the claim that parents and peers mollify such promotions and that parents have a mediating influence. For example, Banks claimed (FTC statement quoted in Robertson 1979) that the exchange between parent and child (conflict, denial, etc.) may possibly facilitate "the child's ability to cope with realities of independent living."

According to Roberts & Bachen (1981), the FTC decision to consider in their hearings whether young children even understand the nature of commercials and the degree to which any lack of understanding might render all commercials unfair or misleading to children gave the research a more theoretical tone, if only because it addressed the question in terms of various developmental models of cognition, information processing, and social behavior.

Clearly the most influential developmental model has been the cognitive approach of Jean Piaget, and hence age-related differences in children's reactions to television advertising have had an important impetus (Ward et al 1978). Evidence from correlational studies indicate that younger children pay more attention to advertising, are less able to discriminate between programs and commercials, exhibit less understanding of advertising's persuasive intent, believe advertising is more truthful, and recall less of the commercial content than their older counterparts (Roedder 1981).

Turning to the influence of premium offers, an early study by Shimp et al (1976) suggests that the liking of a premium does not necessarily assure that children will also like or desire the product containing the premium. However, a recent study (Miller & Busch 1979) indicated that premium commercials showed a clear superiority over host-selling and announcer commercials as measured by the percentage of children who selected the advertised product. And an even more recent study (Heslop & Ryans 1980) supported the earlier contentions that premium offers are relatively unimportant. These and several other studies carried out with varying methodologies tend to indicate that the influence of premiums in choosing products is simply not clear and probably not very important.

The influence of advertising on product choice, however, is not debatable. The Miller and Busch study indicated that TV commercials exert considerable influence on children's favorable affective and cognitive reactions toward products, supporting Goldberg & Gorn's (1974) finding. Girls manifested more favorable attitudes than boys, but there were no sex differences in product selection. No differences were found between black and white children. Still other studies support Gorn & Goldberg's (1980) contention that even a single exposure is enough to produce positive effects for advertised products.

Perhaps of greater concern should be the potential of unintended effects of advertising on childhood socialization affecting norms, goals, and parent-child relations. For example, one of the more vocal issues of Action for Children's Television is that advertising is a major cause of parent-child conflict and ensuing guilt. Goldberg & Gorn's (1978) work suggests that exposure to toy commercials influenced preschool children to make more "materialistic" than "social" choices, preferring to spend more time with the advertised toys as opposed to playing with their peers. Further, parent-child conflict does develop as a function of TV advertising, but there is little evidence that exposure will generate more negative feelings toward a parent who refuses a request.

An additional unintended but serious potential of television advertising is best expressed by Johnson (as quoted in Myers 1978). The child is taught ". . . that troubles are dissolved by the 'fast, fast, fast relief' that comes from pills (vitamins, headache pills, sleeping pills, stomach pills, tranquilizers, pep pills, or 'the pill') and not from dedication, training, or discipline. . . ." A major research project has addressed this issue (Robertson et al 1979), with the conclusion that there was no evidence of a link between medicine advertising and a child's use of proprietary drugs, but the long-run effects are simply not known.

Finally, the issue of parental mediation was studied by Rossiter & Robertson (1979), who asked to what extent children derive their views of over-the-counter drugs from parental conceptions? Parents apparently have a negligible influence on their children's emerging attitudes and behavioral dispositions toward nonprescription drugs. The authors concluded that children make their own judgments about the efficacy and appropriateness of OTC drug remedies for colds, coughs, headaches, and stomachaches with limited influence from instructional or role model mediation from parents.

On the other hand, Popper (1979) found that television advertising to children does not appear to lead inexorably to purchase, but rather mothers mediate the request. A review of other evidence can be found in Robertson (1979). The conclusion seems to be that the issue is far from resolved and that neither the consumer protection people nor the advertising industry can support their contentions and emotionally held beliefs with any degree of scientific rigor.

Social Issues and Public Policy

Not only with regard to the impact of advertising on children, but in general, consumer researchers have shown a high level of interest in public policy and societal issues, particularily as it relates to advertising. For example, numerous studies have supported the FTC contention that carry-over effects of advertising are not trivial, and one way to counter deception is by requiring corrective advertising designed to undo some of the attitudes, beliefs, and attributes created by errant ads (Mazis & Adkinson 1976, Dyer & Kuehl 1978, Armstrong et al 1979, Mizerski et al 1980, Semenik 1980, etc). However, the research on counteradvertising (Hunt 1974) is relatively sparse. The major evidence involves the anticigarette smoking ads of a few years ago. Aggregrate data indicate domestic per capita sales of cigarettes dropped each year that countercommercials were run and rose when their use was effectively eliminated. Individual data reinforced this shift; a major increase in the percent of former smokers (from 16% to 24%) occurred during the broadcasts. And even larger changes were seen in intentions to discontinue smoking and negative attitudes toward smoking (Wilkie 1974b).

Comparative advertising (an explicit comparison with competing brands) has been encouraged by the FTC as a tool of more informed choice and interadvertising policing of deception. This concept has led to several studies but interestingly few have referred back to research on one-sided vs two-sided communications. Most of the present studies seem to indicate that a comparative ad is not particularly superior to a single brand ad in attitude measures (e.g. Golden 1976, Goodwin & Etgar 1980), although there is some indication that recall measures improved in a comparative format (Jain & Hackleman 1978, Prasad 1976). Unfortunately, there seems to be no indication that comparative advertising has led to more substantiated claims by advertisers or information that can lead to a more informed public.

Numerous other papers on societal issues exist: product safety, labeling, energy conservation, and consumer satisfaction-dissatisfaction (e.g. Day & Landon 1977), further supporting the significance of the interrelationship between the consumer and the social environment. Although governmental activity is bound to be lessened in the coming years, research in this area has yet to reach its peak.

ECONOMIC PSYCHOLOGY

Few areas in consumer psychology can claim the persistence and longevity of economic psychology. Originally the field developed in reaction to traditional economics. For example, if one considers the relationship between inflation and consumer spending, the prevailing belief in economics is: when rational people expect prices to go up (inflation) they will save less and spend more to stock up or hoard at the prevailing lower price.

The decades of research by Katona and his colleagues (e.g. 1951, 1975) indicate this may not necessarily be so: many people under conditions of inflation are pessimistic, feel that as prices increase they will have to spend more on necessities, and therefore would have smaller resources at their disposal for the purchase of nonessential goods and services. Therefore, inflation makes for the postponement of discretionary expenditures and reduces rather than increases the quantity of goods demanded. At the same time, price increases create uncertainty which lead people to feel a great need for savings and reserve funds. Hence, Katona claims the rate of savings is expected to increase in inflationary periods [however, there are great differences between the attitudes of Americans and Western Europeans, and by 1979 the pattern in the US had changed (Katona & Curtin 1980)]. These psychologists have long claimed that consumer sentiment (optimism, confidence) has served to predict the turning points in economic trends.

However, economic psychology was not destined to enjoy rapid expansion. The emerging new breed of consumer researchers tended to be far more interested in social psychological issues than the molar aspects of human behavior in the economic environment. This area of inquiry would have slowly withered were it not for Europe, where interest in economic psychology was rapidly accelerating.

Under the philosophical tutorage of Pierre-Louis Reynaud (1974) at Strassbourg, Wärneryd in Stockholm, and van Veldhoven in The Netherlands, laboratories emerged in Austria, Germany, France, and several other countries. The only group housed within psychology and producing psychologists trained in economics is at Tilborg University in The Netherlands.

A sample of this work can perhaps be seen in Wärneryd's research relating taxation, economic behavior, and motives to work (1980). The data indicate that blue collar workers are more willing to work if taxes on extra work are lowered than are professionals who are much higher paid and pay relatively higher taxes. On the other hand, there is much more planning of expenditures so as to avoid taxes (e.g. buying heavily mortgaged homes, investing in pensions) among professionals than industrial workers. Further, both groups of subjects underestimate actual marginal income tax rates with industrial workers underestimating the marginal tax far more than professionals.

In a similar study, van Veldhoven (1980) found that professionals are more internal oriented (Rotter Locus of Control) than blue collar workers and that psychological variables play an important part in the attitudes and behavior toward taxation schemes. Interestingly, personality measures when applied to taxation accounted for more of the variance than typically found in studies relating personality to brand choice and consumer purchases. It could well be that attitudes toward taxation are far more important and involve basic values and personality structures at a more significant level than say the purchase of canned peaches or brands of socks. The future for research in economic psychology is bright, at least in Europe.

CONCLUSION

Although the term "interdisciplinary" has often been applied to the field of consumer behavior, it is in fact not always interdisciplinary, and perhaps a better term would be "fragmented." The typical pattern of activity has been to modify a middle range theory or concept and apply it to behavior in the marketplace. And in the near future this trend should continue for there are yet many significant topics that have not been sufficiently explored.

For example, the exceptional importance of *situational factors* (Belk 1975, Miller & Ginter 1979, Wright & Weitz 1977) has yet to be fully examined. There is little question that the same individual in differing situations is likely to behave differently with respect to the same product or brand or decision (Kakkar & Lutz 1981). This variable impacts much of the rest of consumer behavior.

Of all topics, one would think that *motivation* would have been thoroughly explored by this time, and yet it has not been studied much in recent years. Now the trend seems to be turning back to basic motivational aspects and concerns about motivation theory (e.g. Bettman 1979, Fishbein & Ajzen 1975). It simply could be ignored no longer.

Continuing, "One of the curious anomolies in the field of consumer research has been the lack of attention devoted to *cultural values.* This is particularily paradoxical considering that most serious students of human behavior have argued for centuries that values play an important role in personal, social and cultural activity" (Clawson & Vinson 1978). A few studies do exist (e.g. Vinson et al 1977, Henry 1976, Munson & McIntyre 1978, Del Signore & Kassarjian 1981), and there is simply no question that the study of values is a fruitful endeavor if one is interested in studying the molar and social patterns of behavior of the consumer rather than the micro-oriented cognitive relationship that have been so heavily studied in the past.

Still another, although perhaps odorous, area would be to study not what the consumer claims to consume but rather what he or she discards—a content analysis of garbage, for garbage cans contain a wealth of information. The idea is not new, hinted at some years ago by Jacoby (1976). The first garbology project was started by anthropologist William Rathje at the University of Arizona, and findings have not always been obvious (e.g. Rathje & Harrison 1978). For example, garbologists have indicated that as the price of meat increases, use of meat substitutes increase (egg shells, chicken bones, milk cartons). However, the amount of meat waste also increases: apparently people tend to buy cheaper and undesirable meats, and more bones, fat, waste, and half-eaten kidneys appear in the garbage can.

Integration

Numerous other middle range concepts could be mentioned and without doubt will appear before the next review; however, the major need of the area now is not one more topic to apply to the consumer. Although the trend has been away from creating comprehensive theories of behavior, what is desperately needed at this point is integration of the various topics in the field. For example, it seems obvious that cognitive processing, physiological arousal, left brain activity and high levels of involvement are somehow interrelated. Low commitment behavior does not necessarily need a new set of theories but does somehow involve right brain activity, situational influences, learning, and perhaps behavior modification. In some manner the fragmented nature of the work needs to be tied together, and individual researchers need to be alert to the implications of their work to researchers in other areas. It is quite clear that research on eye movement emanating from information processing is directly relevant to the psychobiological work of the Kroeber-Riel laboratory. And although the field simply does not need another flow chart, perhaps one should reiterate once again Lewin's dictum that there is nothing so practical as a good theory.

On a more positive note, consumer behavior as it is seems to quickly assimilate new ideas and with welcoming arms seems to embrace researchers both from rigid and traditional areas and those wanting to study off-beat topics such as willingness to donate human body parts (Pessemier et al 1977), gift-giving (Belk 1979), and garbology. In the sphere of human behavior little can be found that in some way cannot be considered somehow relevant to consumer psychology. To the academic researcher, to the regulator, and to the practitioner, it indeed offers an exciting future.

Literature Cited

Adler, R. P., Ward, S., Lesser, G. S., Meringoff, L. K., Robertson, T. S., Rossiter, J. R. 1980. *The Effect of Television Advertising on Children: Review and Recommendations.* Lexington, Mass: Lexington Books. 361 pp.

Ajzen, I., Fishbein, M. 1977. Attitude-behavior relations: a theoretical analysis and review of empirical research. *Psychol. Bull.* 84:888–918

Ajzen, I., Fishbein, M. 1981. *Understanding Attitudes and Predicting Social Behavior.* Englewood Cliffs: Prentice Hall. 278 pp.

Alexis, M., Haines, G. H. Jr., Simon, L. 1968. Consumer information processing: the case of women's clothing. *Proc. Am. Market Assoc. Educ. Conf.* 197–205

Appel, V., Weinstein, S., Weinstein, C. 1979. Brain activity and recall of TV advertising. *J. Advert. Res.* 19:7–15

Arch, D. C. !979. Pupil dilation measures in consumer research: applications and limitations. *Adv. Consum. Res.* 6: 166–68

Armstrong, G. M., Gurol, M. N., Russ, F. A. 1979. Detecting and correcting deceptive advertising. *J. Consum. Res.* 6:237–46

Barg, C. D. 1977. *Measurement and effects of psychological activation through advertising.* PhD thesis. Univ. Saarland, Saarbrücken, West Germany. Cited in Krober-Riel 1979

Barton, B. 1980. *Eye movements and advertising effectiveness.* Presented at Ann. Colloq. Eur. Econ. Psychol., 5th, Leuven, Belgium

Bass, F. M. 1974. The theory of stochastic preference and brand switching. *J. Market. Res.* 11:1–20

Bearden, W. O., Woodside, A. G. 1977. Testing variations of Fishbein's behavioral intention model within a consumer behavior context. *J. Appl. Psychol.* 62: 352–57

Belk, R. W. 1975. Situational variables and consumer behavior. *J. Consum. Res.* 2:157–64

Belk, R. W. 1979. Gift-giving behavior. *Res. Market.* 2:95–126

Berhard, U. 1978. *Exposure to advertising: Eye movement and memory.* PhD thesis. Univ. Saarland, Saarbrücken, West Germany. Cited in Kroeber-Riel 1979

Bettman, J. R. 1970. Information processing models of consumer behavior. *J. Market. Res.* 7:370–76

Bettman, J. R. 1975. Issues in designing consumer information environments. *J. Consum. Res.* 2:169–77

Bettman, J. R. 1977. Data collection and analysis approaches for studying consumer information processing. *Adv. Consum. Res.* 4:342–48

Bettman, J. R. 1979. *An Information Processing Theory of Consumer Choice.* Reading, Mass: Addison-Wesley. 402 pp.

Bettman, J. R., Jacoby, J. 1976. Patterns of processing in consumer information acquisition. *Adv. Consum. Res.* 3:315–20

Bettman, J. R., Kakkar, P. 1977. Effects of information presentation format on consumer information acquisition strategies. *J. Consum. Res.* 3:233–40

Bettman, J. R., Park, C. W. 1980. Effects of prior knowledge and experience and phase of the choice process on consumer decision processes: a protocol analysis. *J. Consum. Res.* 7:234–48

Bettman, J. R., Zins, M. A. 1979. Information format and choice task effects in decision making. *J. Consum. Res.* 6:141–53

Brickman, G. A. 1976. Voice analysis. *J. Advert. Res.* 16(Jun):43–48

Brickman, G. A. 1980. Uses of voice-pitch analysis. *J. Advert. Res.* 20(Apr):69–73

Burnkrant, R. E., Cousineau, A. 1975. Information and normative social influence in buyer behavior. *J. Consum. Res.* 2:206–15

Burns, A. C., Granbois, D. H. 1977. Factors moderating the resolution of preference conflict in family automobile purchasing. *J. Market. Res.* 14:77–86

Calder, B. J. 1978. Cognitive response, imagery, and scripts: what is the cognitive basis of attitude. *Adv. Consum. Res.* 5:630–34

Calder, B. J., Burnkrant, R. E. 1977. Interpersonal influence on consumer behavior: an attribution theory approach. *J. Consum. Res.* 4:29–38

Capon, N., Burke, M. 1980. Individual, product class, and task-related factors in consumer information processing. *J. Consum. Res.* 7:314–26

Chestnut, R. W., Jacoby, J. 1977. Consumer information processing: emerging theory and findings. In *Consumer and Industrial Buying Behavior,* ed. A. G. Woodside, J. N. Sheth, P. D. Bennett, pp. 119–33. New York: Evsevier North Holland. 523 pp.

Cialdini, R. B., Petty, R. E., Cacioppo, J. T. 1981. Attitude and attitude change. *Ann. Rev. Psychol.* 32:348–404

Clawson, C. J., Vinson, D. E. 1978. Human values: a historical and interdisciplinary analysis. *Adv. Consum. Res.* 5:396–402

Cohen, J. B., Miniard, P. W., Dickson, P. R. 1980. Information integration: an information processing perspective. *Adv. Consum. Res.* 7:161–70

Davis, H. L. 1970. Dimensions of marital roles in consumer decision making. *J. Market. Res.* 7:168–77

Davis, H. L. 1976. Decision making within the household. *J. Consum. Res.* 2: 241–60

Davis, H. L., Rigaux, B. P. 1974. Perception of marital roles in decision processes. *J. Consum. Res.* 1:51–62

Dawson, L. E. Jr., Bettinger, C. O. III. 1977. On the relationship of consumer behavior and the sense of touch. *Proc. Am. Market. Assoc. Educ. Conf.,* pp. 27–30

Day, G. S. 1976. Assessing the effects of information disclosure requirements. *J. Market.* 40(Apr):42–52

Day, R. L., Landon E. L. Jr. 1977. Toward a theory of consumer complaining behavior. See Chestnut & Jacoby 1977, pp. 425–37

Del Signore, J., Kassarjian, H. H. 1981. The relationship between opinions, social values and behavior during the 1979 gasoline crisis: an exploratory attempt. *Proc. Am. Market. Assoc. Educ. Conf.,* pp. 295–98

Dodson, J. A., Tybout, A. M., Sternthal, B. 1978. Impact of deals and deal retraction on brand switching. *J. Market. Res.* 15:72–81

Dyer, R. F., Kuehl, P. G. 1978. A longitudinal study of corrective advertising. *J. Market. Res.* 15:39–48

Engel, J. F., Kollat, D. T., Blackwell, R. D. 1968. *Consumer Behavior.* New York: Holt, Rinehart & Winston. 652 pp. 1st ed.

Federal Trade Commission Staff. 1979. *Consumer Information Remedies.* Washington DC: GPO 352 pp.

Ferber, R., Lee, L. C. 1974. Husband-wife influence in family purchasing behavior. *J. Consum. Res.* 1:43–50

Filiatrault, P., Ritchie, J. R. B. 1980. Joint purchasing decisions: a comparison of influence structure in family and couple decision-making units. *J. Consum. Res.* 7:131–40

Fishbein, M., Ajzen, I. 1975. *Belief, Attitude, Intention, and Behavior: An introduction to Theory and Research.* Reading, Mass: Addison-Wesley. 578 pp.

Gardner, M. P., Mitchell, A. A., Russo, J. E. 1978. Cronometric analysis: an introduction and an application to low involvement perception of advertisements. *Adv. Consum. Res.* 5:581–89

Goldberg, M. E., Gorn, G. J. 1974. Children's reactions to television advertising: an experimental approach. *J. Consum. Res.* 1:69–75

Goldberg, M. E., Gorn, G. J. 1978. Some unintended consequences of TV advertising to children. *J. Consum. Res.* 5:22–29

Golden, L. L. 1976. Consumer reactions to comparative advertising. *Adv. Consum. Res.* 63–67

Golden, L. L. 1977. Attribution theory implications for advertisement claim credibility. *J. Market. Res.* 14:115–17

Goldwater, B. C. 1972. Psychological significance of pupilary movements. *Psychol. Bull.* 77:340–55

Goodwin, S., Etgar, M. 1980. An experimental investigation of comparative advertising: impact of message appeal, information load and utility of product class. *J. Market. Res.* 17: 187–202

Gorn, G. J., Goldberg, M. E. 1980. Children's response to repetitive television commercials. *J. Consum. Res.* 6:421–24

Greeno, D. W. 1970. *Psychophysiological measures: an analysis of the orienting reflex.* Presented at Ann. Meet. Assoc. Consum. Res., 1st, Amherst

Haines, G. H. Jr. 1969. *Consumer Behavior: Learning Models of Purchasing.* New York: Free Press. 216 pp.

Hansen, F. 1972. *Consumer Choice Behavior: A Cognitive Theory.* New York: Free Press. 548 pp.

Hansen, F. 1981. Hemispherical lateralization: a review and a discussion of its implications for consumer behavior research. *J. Consum. Res.* 8:23–36

Hansen, F., Lundsgaard, N. E. 1981. Developing an instrument to identify individual differences in the processing of pictorial and other non-verbal information. *Adv. Consum. Res.* 8:367–73

Hansen, R. A., Robinson, L. M. 1980. Testing the effectiveness of alternative foot-in-the-door manipulations. *J. Market. Res.* 17:359–64

Hansen, R. A., Scott, C. A. 1976. Comments on "attribution theory and advertiser credibility." *J. Market. Res.* 13:193–97

Henry, W. A. 1976. Cultural values do correlate with consumer behavior. *J. Market. Res.* 13:121–27

Heslop, L. A., Ryans, A. B. 1980. A second look at children and the advertising of premiums. *J. Consum. Res.* 6:414-20

Hess, E. H., Polt, J. M. 1960. Pupil size as related to interest value of visual stimuli. *Science* 132:349–50

Hughes, G. D., Ray, M. L. 1974. *Buyer/Consumer Information Processing.* Chapel

Hill: Univ. North Carolina Press. 425 pp.

Hunt, H. K. 1974. Measuring the impact and effectiveness of counter messages. In *Advertising and the Public Interest.* ed. S. F. Divita, pp. 203–14. Chicago: Am. Market. Assoc. 264 pp.

Jacoby, J. 1976. Consumer psychology: an octennium. *Ann. Rev. Psychol.* 27: 331–58

Jacoby, J., Chestnut, R. W., Silberman, W. 1977. Consumer use and comprehension of nutrition information. *J. Consum. Res.* 4:119–28

Jacoby, J., Hoyer, W. D., Sheluga, D. A. 1981. Viewer miscomprehension of televised communication: A brief report on findings. *Adv. Consum. Res.* 8:410–15

Jacoby, J., Speller, D. E., Berning, C. A. K. 1974a. Brand choice behavior as a function of information load: replication and extension. *J. Consum. Res.* 1:33–42

Jacoby, J., Speller, D. E., Kohn, C. A. 1974b. Brand choice behavior as a function of information load. *J. Market. Res.* 11:63–69

Jain, S. C., Hackleman, E. C. 1978. How effective is comparison advertising for stimulating brand recall. *J. Advert.* 7(Spr.):20–25

Jenkins, R. L. 1980. Contributions of theory to the study of family decision-making. *Adv. Consum. Res.* 7:207–11

Johnson, E. J., Russo, J. E. 1978. The organization of product information in memory identified by recall times. *Adv. Consum. Res.* 5:79–86

Kahneman, D., Beatty, J. 1966. Pupil diameter and load on memory. *Science* 154:1583–85

Kakkar, P., Lutz, R. J. 1981. Situational influence on consumer behavior: a review. See Kassarjian & Robertson 1981, pp. 204–15

Kassarjian, H. H., Robertson, T. S. 1981. *Perspectives in Consumer Behavior.* Glenview, Ill: Scott-Foresman. 538 pp. 3rd ed.

Katona, G. 1951. *Psychological Analysis of Economic Behavior.* New York: McGraw-Hill. 347 pp.

Katona, G. 1975. *Psychological Economics.* Amsterdam: Elsevier. 438 pp.

Katona, G., Curtin, R. T. 1980. Problem-oriented rather than discipline-oriented research. *Adv. Consum. Res.* 7:44–48

Kelley, H. H. 1967. Attribution theory in social psychology. In *Nebraska Symposium of Motivation,* ed. D. Levine, pp. 192–240. Lincoln: Univ. Nebr. Press. 335 pp.

Kling, N. D. 1979. *Hemispheric asymmetries, relative cerebral hemispheric dominance and information usage.* Presented at Atlantic Sch. Bus. Conf., Halifax

Krishnan, S., Valle, V. A. 1979. Dissatisfaction attributions and consumer complaint behavior. *Adv. Consum. Res.* 6:445–49

Kroeber-Riel, W. 1979. Activation research: psychobiological approaches in consumer research. *J. Consum. Res.* 5:240–50

Kroeber-Riel, W. 1980. *Konsumentenverhalten.* München: Vahlen. 679 pp. 2nd ed.

Krugman, H. E. 1979. Low involvement theory in the light of new brain research. In *Attitude Research Plays for High Stakes,* ed. J. C. Maloney, B. Silverman, pp. 16–36. Chicago: *Am. Market. Assoc.* 279 pp.

Lammers, H. B., Becker, L. A. 1980. Distraction: effects on the perceived extremity of a communication and on cognitive responses. *Pers. Soc. Psychol. Bull.* 6:261–66

Lehmann, D. R., Moore, W. L. 1980. Validity of information display boards: an assessment using longitudinal data. *J. Market. Res.* 17:450–59

Locander, W. B., Spivey, W. A. 1978. A functional approach to attitude measurement. *J. Market. Res.* 15:576–87

Lundsgaard, N. E. 1978. *Psykologiske funktioners asymmetriske repraesentation i den menneskelige hjerne.* PhD thesis. Copenhagen Univ., Denmark. Cited in Hansen 1981

Lutz, R. J. 1975. Changing brand attitudes through modification of cognitive structure. *J. Consum. Res.* 1:49–59

Lutz, R. J. 1977. An experimental investigation of causal relations among cognitions affect, and behavioral intention. *J. Consum. Res.* 3:197–208

Lutz, R. J. 1978. A functional approach to consumer attitude research. *Adv. Consum. Res.* 5:360–69

Lutz, R. J. 1981. The role of attitude theory in marketing. See Kassarjian & Robertson 1981, pp. 233–50

Lutz, R. J., Bettman, J. R. 1977. Multiattribute models in marketing: a bicentennial review. See Chestnut & Jacoby 1977, pp. 137–49

Lutz, R. J., Swasy, J. L. 1977. Integrating cognitive structure and cognitive response approaches to monitoring communications effects. *Adv. Consum. Res.* 4:363–71

Markin, R. J., Narayana, C. L. 1976. Behavior control: are consumers beyond freedom and dignity. *Adv. Consum. Res.* 3:222–28

Mazis, M. B., Adkinson, J. E. 1976. An experimental evaluation of a proposed corrective advertising remedy. *J. Market. Res.* 13:178–83

McCallum, A. S., Glynn, S. A. 1979. Hemispheric specialization and creative behavior. *J. Creat. Behav.* 13:263–73

McGuire, W. J. 1977. Psychological factors influencing consumer choice. In *Selected Aspects of Consumer Behavior,* ed. R. Ferber, pp. 11–31. Washington DC: GPO 543 pp.

Miller, J. H. Jr., Busch, P. 1979. Host selling vs. premium TV commercials: an experimental evaluation of their influence on children. *J. Market. Res.* 16:323–32

Miller, K. E., Ginter, J. L. 1979. An investigation of situational variation in brand choice behavior and attitude. *J. Market. Res.* 16:111–23

Miniard, P. W., Cohen, J. B. 1979. Isolating attitudinal and normative influences in behavioral intentions models. *J. Market. Res.* 16:102–4

Mitchell, A. A. 1978. An information processing view of consumer behavior. *Proc. Am. Market. Assoc. Educ. Conf.,* pp. 188–97

Mizerski, R. W., Allison, N. K., Calvert, S. C. 1980. A controlled field study of corrective advertising using multiple exposures and a commercial medium. *J. Market. Res.* 17:341–48

Mizerski, R. W., Golden, L. L., Kernan, J. B. 1979. The attribution process in consumer decision making. *J. Consum. Res.* 6:123–40

Munsinger, G. M., Weber, J. E., Hansen, R. W. 1975. Joint home purchasing decisions by husbands and wives. *J. Consum. Res.* 1:60–66

Munson, J. M., McIntyre, S. H. 1978. Personal values: a cross cultural assessment of self values and values attributed to a distant cultural sterotype. *Adv. Consum. Res.* 5:160–66

Myers, J. G. 1978. Advertising and socialization. *Res. Market.* 1:169–99

Myers, J. H., Reynolds, W. H. 1967. *Consumer Behavior and Marketing Management.* New York: Houghton Mifflin. 336 pp.

Nicosia, F. M., Mayer, R. N. 1976. Toward a sociology of consumption. *J. Consum. Res.* 3:65–75

Nord, W. R., Peters, J. P. 1980. A behavior modification perspective on marketing. *J. Market.* 44(Spr.):36–47

Olshavsky, R. W., Granbois, D. H. 1979. Consumer decision making—fact or fiction? *J. Consum. Res.* 6:93–100

Olson, J. C. 1980. Encoding processes: level of processing and existing knowledge structures. *Adv. Consum. Res.* 7:154–60

Olson, J. C., Toy, D. R., Dover, P. A. 1978. Mediating effects of cognitive responses to advertising on cognitive structure. *Adv. Consum. Res.* 5:72–78

Otteson, O. 1980. *Views of man and research into the primary and secondary effects of advertising.* Copenhagen: Handelshojskölen. 58 pp.

Perloff, R. 1968. Consumer analysis. *Ann. Rev. Psychol.* 19:437–66

Pessemier, E. A., Bemmoar, A. C., Hanssens, D. M. 1977. Willingness to supply human body parts: Some empirical results. *J. Consum. Res.* 4:131–40

Peterson, R. A., Kerin, R. A. 1977. The female role in advertisements: some experimental evidence. *J. Market.* 41(Oct):59–63

Petty, R. E. 1977. The importance of cognitive responses in persuasion. *Adv. Consum. Res.* 4:357–62

Petty, R., Ostrom, T., Brock, T., eds. 1980. *Cognitive Responses in Persuasion.* Hillsdale, NJ: Erlbaum. 512 pp.

Popper, E. T. 1979. Mothers mediation of children's purchase requests. *Proc. Am. Market. Assoc. Educ. Conf.,* pp. 645–48

Prasad, V. K. 1976. Communications-effectiveness of comparative advertising: a laboratory analysis. *J. Market. Res.* 13:128–37

Rathje, W. L., Harrison, G. C. 1978. Monitoring trends in food utilization: application of an archaeological method. *Proc. Fed. Am. Soc. Exp. Biol.* 37:49–54

Ray, M. L. 1974. Consumer initial processing: definitions, issues and applications. See Hughes & Ray 1974, pp. 145–56

Reingen, P. H. 1979. Inducing compliance with a request: the list technique. *Adv. Consum. Res.* 6:45–49

Reingen, P. H., Kernan, J. B. 1977. Compliance with an interview request: a foot-in-the-door, self-perception interpretation. *J. Market. Res.* 14:365–69

Reingen, P. H., Kernan, J. B. 1979. More evidence on interpersonal yielding. *J. Market. Res.* 16:588–93

Reynaud, P. L. 1974. *Precis de Psychologic Economique.* Paris: Presses Univ. France. 128 pp.

Rice, B. 1974. Rattlesnakes, french fries, and pupillometric oversell. *Psychol. Today.* 7(Feb):55–59

Richardson, A. 1977. Verbalizer-visualizer: a

cognitive style dimension. *J. Ment. Imagery* 1:109–26

Richens, M. L. 1980. Product dissatisfaction: causal attribution structure and strategy. In *Proc. Am. Market Assoc. Educ. Conf.* pp. 105–8

Roberts, D. F., Bachen, C. M. 1981. Mass communication effects. *Ann Rev. Psychol.* 32:307–56

Robertson, T. S. 1976. Low commitment consumer behavior. *J Advert. Res.* 16(Apr):19–24

Robertson, T. S. 1979. Parental mediation of television advertising effects. *J. Commun.* 29:12–25

Robertson, T. S., Rossiter, J. R., Gleason, T. C. 1979. Children's receptivity to proprietary medicine advertising. *J. Consum. Res.* 6:247–55

Robertson, T. S., Zielinski, J. 1981. "New" sociological perspectives for consumer behavior research. Submitted for publication

Roedder, D. L. 1981. *Age difference in children's information processing.* Paper 101, Cent. Market. Stud., UCLA. 35 pp.

Rossiter, J. R., Robertson, T. S. 1979. Children's independence from parental mediation in learning about OTC drugs. *Proc. Am. Market. Assoc. Educ. Conf.* pp. 653–57

Rothschild, M. L. 1978. Political advertising: a neglected policy issue in marketing. *J. Market. Res.* 15:58–71

Russo, J. E. 1974. More information is better: a reevaluation of Jacoby, Speller & Kohn. *J. Consum. Res.* 1:68–72

Russo, J. E. 1977. The value of unit price information. *J. Market. Res.* 14: 193–201

Russo, J. E. 1978. Eye fixation can save the world: a critical evaluation and a comparison between eye fixation and other information processing methodologies. *Adv. Consum. Res.* 5:561–70

Ryan, M. J. 1980. Psychobiology and consumer research: a problem of construct validity. *J. Consum. Res.* 7:92–96

Ryan, M. J., Bonfield, E. H. 1975. The Fishbein extended model and consumer behavior. *J. Consum. Res.* 2:118–36

Ryan, M. J., Bonfield, E. H. 1980. Fishbein's intentions model: a test of external and pragmatic validity. *J. Market.* 44(Spr.)82–95

Sawyer, A. G. 1977. Repetition and affect: recent empirical and theoretical developments. See Chestnut & Jacoby 1977, pp. 229–42

Sawyer, A. G., Ward, S. 1979. Carry-over effects in advertising communication. *Res. Market.* 2:259–314

Scammon, D. L. 1977. "Information load" and consumers. *J. Consum. Res.* 4:148–55

Scott, C. A. 1976. The effects of trial and incentives on repeat purchase behavior. *J. Market. Res.* 13:263–69

Scott, C. A. 1978. Self-perception processes in consumer behavior: interpreting one's own experiences. *Adv. Consum. Res.* 5:714–20

Scott, C. A. 1981. Forming beliefs from experience: evidence from self perception theory. See Kassarjian & Robertson 1981, pp. 296–305

Scott, C. A., Tybout, A. M. 1979. Extending the self-perception explanation: the effect of cue salience on behavior. *Adv. Consum. Res.* 6:50–54

Scott, C. A., Yalch, R. F. 1978. A test of the self-perception explanation of the effects of rewards on intrinsic interest. *J. Exp. Soc. Psychol.* 14:180–92

Semenik, R. J. 1980. Corrective advertising: an experimental evaluation of alternative television messages. *J. Advert.* 9:21–30

Settle, R. B., Faricy, J. H., Warren, G. T. 1971. Consumer information processing: attributing effects to causes. *Proc. Assoc. Consum. Res.* pp. 278–88

Settle, R. B., Golden, L. L. 1974. Attribution theory and advertiser credibility. *J. Market. Res.* 11:181–85

Sheth, J. N. 1974a. A theory of family buying decisions. In *Models of Buyer Behavior,* ed. J. N. Sheth, pp. 17–33. New York: Harper & Row. 441 pp.

Sheth, J. N. 1974b. A field study of attitude structure and the attitude-behavior relationship. See Sheth 1974a, pp. 242–68

Shimp, T. A., Dyer, R. F., Divita, S. F. 1976. An experimental test of the harmful effects of premium-oriented commercials on children. *J. Consum. Res.* 3:1–11

Smead, R. J., Wilcox, J. B., Wilkes, R. E. 1980. An illustration and evaluation of a joint process tracing methodology: eye movement and protocols. *Adv. Consum. Res.* 7:507–12

Smith, R. E., Hunt, S. D. 1978. Attributional processes and effects in promotional situations. *J. Consum. Res.* 5:149–58

Sparkman, R. H. Jr., Locander, W. B. 1980. Attribution theory and advertising effectiveness. *J. Consum. Res.* 7:219–24

Sternthal, B., Dholakia, R., Leavitt, C. 1978. The persuasive effect of source credibility: tests of cognitive response. *J. Consum. Res.* 4:252–60

Sternthal, B., Scott, C. A., Dholakia, R. R. 1976. Self-perception as a means of personal influence: the foot-in-the-door technique. *Adv. Consum. Res.* 3:387–93

Twedt, D. W. 1965. Consumer psychology. *Ann. Rev. Psychol.* 16:265–94

Tybout, A. M., Sternthal, B., Calder, B. J. 1978. A two stage theory of information processing in persuasion: an integrative view of cognitive response and self-perception theory. *Adv. Consum. Res.* 5:721–23

Valle, V., Koeske, R. 1977. Elderly consumer problems: actions, sources of information, and attribution of blame. *Proc. Div 23 Am. Psychol. Assoc.* pp. 7–8

van Raaij, W. F. 1977a. *Consumer choice behavior: An information processing approach.* PhD thesis. Katholicke Hogeschool, Tilburg Univ., Tilburg, Netherlands

van Raaij, W. F. 1977b. Consumer information processing for different information structures and formats. *Adv. Consum. Res.* 4:176–84

van Veldhoven, G. M. 1980. *Psychological aspects of taxation.* Presented at Ann. Colloq. Eur. Econ. Psychol., 5th, Leuven, Belgium

Vinson, D. E., Munson, J. M., Nakanishi, M. 1977. An investigation of the Rokeach value survey for consumer research applications. *Adv. Consum. Res.* 4:247–52

Ward, S. 1981. Consumer socialization. See Kassarjian & Robertson 1981, pp. 380–96

Ward, S., Wackman, D. 1973. *Effects of Television Advertising on Consumer Socializations.* Cambridge, Mass: Market. Sci. Inst.

Ward, S., Wackman, D., Wartella, E. 1978. *How Children Learn to Buy: The Development of Consumer Information Processing Skills.* Beverly Hills: Sage. 271 pp.

Wärneryd, K. E. 1980. *Taxes and economic behavior.* Presented at Ann. Colloq. Eur. Econ. Psychol., 5th, Leuven, Belgium

Warshaw, P. R. 1980. A new model for predicting behavioral intentions: an alternative to Fishbein. *J. Market. Res.* 17:153–72

Watson, P. J., Gatchel, R. J. 1979. Autonomic measures of advertising. *J. Advert. Res.* 19(June):15–26

Weinstein, S. 1980. Brain wave analysis in attitude research: past, present and future. In *Attitude Research Enters the 80's.*, ed. R. W. Olshavsky, pp. 41–47. Chicago: Am. Market. Assoc. 196 pp.

Weinstein, S., Appel, V., Weinstein, C. 1980. Brain activity responses to magazine and television advertising. *J. Advert. Res.* 20(June):57–63

Wilkie, W. L. 1974a. Analysis of effects of information load. *J. Market. Res.* 11:462–66

Wilkie, W. L. 1974b. Research on counter and corrective advertising. See Hunt 1974, pp. 189–214

Wilson, R. D., Muderrisoglu, A. 1980. An analysis of cognitive responses to comparative advertising. *Adv. Consum. Res.* 7:566–71

Witt, D. 1977. *Emotional advertising: the relationship between eye-movement patterns and memory—empirical study with the eye-movement monitor.* PhD thesis. Univ. Saarland, Saarbrücken, West Germany. Cited in Kroeber-Riel 1979

Woodside, A. G., Motes, W. H. 1979. Husband and wife perceptions of marital roles in consumer decision processes for six products. *Proc. Am. Market Assoc. Educ. Conf.* pp. 214–19

Wright, P. L. 1973. The cognitive processes mediating acceptance of advertising. *J. Market. Res.* 10:53–62

Wright, P. L. 1980. Message-evoked thoughts: persuasion research using thought verbalizations. *J. Consum. Res.* 7:151–75

Wright, P. L., Rip, P. D. 1980. Product class advertising effects on first-time buyers' decision strategies. *J. Consum. Res.* 7:176–88

Wright, P. L., Weitz, B. 1977. Time horizon effects on product evaluation strategies. *J. Market. Res.* 14:429–43

Zaltman, G., Wallendorf, M. 1979. *Consumer Behavior: Basic Findings and Management Implications.* New York: Wiley. 567 pp.

Zielski, H. A., Henry, W. A. 1980. Remembering and forgetting television ads. *J. Advert. Res.* 20(Apr):7–13

Ann. Rev. Psychol. 1982. 33:651-88

ENVIRONMENTAL PSYCHOLOGY

James A. Russell and Lawrence M. Ward

Department of Psychology, University of British Columbia, Vancouver, British Columbia, Canada V6T 1W5

CONTENTS

0066-4308/82/0201-0651$02.00

INTRODUCTION

Environmental psychology is that branch of psychology concerned with providing a systematic account of the relationship between person and environment. Of course, an interest in the environment is not new to psychologists and certainly not unique to environmental psychologists. Nor is there some subset of psychological processes unique to environmental psychology as there is, for example, in perception, cognition, or psychophysiology. More like developmental psychology, environmental psychology provides instead a unique perspective on all psychological processes.

Craik (1970) described the perspective taken by environmental psychology as providing a study of "the physical setting of molar behavior" (p. 15). He was extending the boundaries of psychology beyond the study of an immediate response to an immediate stimulus to include a study of behavior as organized over a larger span of time and in relation to the large-scale environment. From this more molar perspective, Palys & Little (1980) introduced the important notion of personal projects, behavioral episodes that organize many behavioral components into a meaningful sequence. Personal projects, in turn, depend on the opportunities afforded by the environment in which one lives. A molar perspective on the organization of behavior thus fosters an understanding of behavior at a subjectively meaningful level—the level at which people plan their day, go to work, and return home—a level of both practical and theoretical importance.

Consider, for example, the important theoretical issue of whether behavior is caused by the situation in which it occurs. As people move from one place to another, their behavior changes accordingly. Behaviors that occur in one place would be out of place elsewhere. This place-specificity of behavior is the fundamental fact of environmental psychology. It is a fact pointed to by psychologists from William James to Roger Barker and Walter Mischel as having important implications for our understanding of the causes of behavior. But this fact requires an explanation rather than provides one, and its implications depend on the perspective from which it is viewed.

Figure 1 illustrates a familiar way of thinking about the relationship between behavior and the environment. Person P is in some environment E and produces some behavior B. The assumption is that $B = f(P,E)$. From

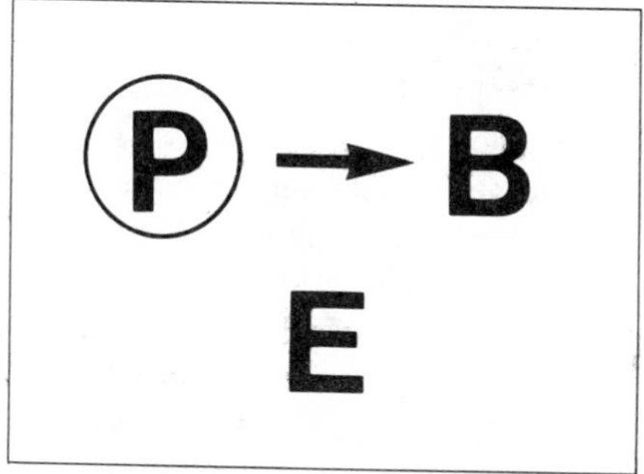

Figure 1 Person P emits behavior B while in environment E.

this perspective, the environment appears to exert a powerful and direct causal influence upon behavior.

Figure 2 illustrates another way of thinking about the place-specificity of behavior. The environment is represented as two places embedded within a third, and two steps have been inserted before we reach the scene depicted in Figure 1. In the first step, person P devises a plan to do something. In the second step, P travels somewhere else, since doing something often requires going somewhere: Shopping and gardening typically require a shop and a garden. In the third step, P arrives at his or her destination and carries out the plan.

Figure 2 contains Figure 1 and thus provides the kind of broader or more molar perspective that we are speaking of. From this perspective, we see

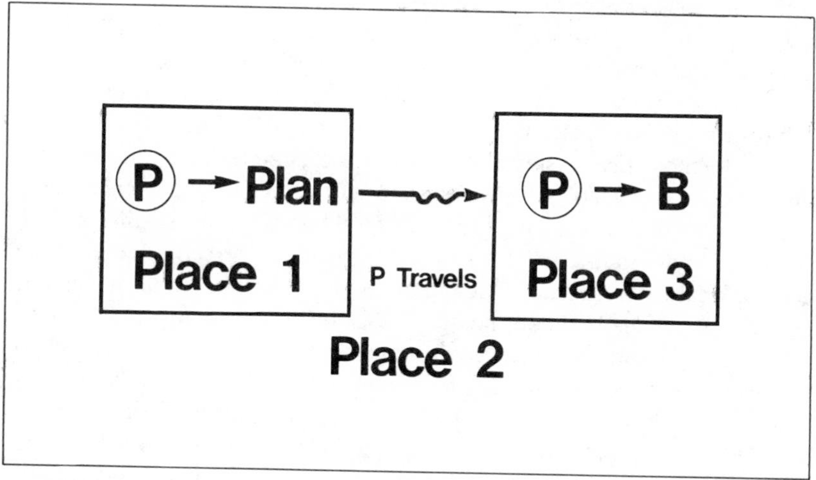

Figure 2 Person P concocts a plan, travels to a place, and carries out the plan through behavior B.

environment exerts a direct causal influence upon behavior. People rarely just find themselves somewhere and then begin behaving accordingly. More often, they go there in order to behave that way. A restaurant does not cause eating; it is a place where you go to eat. Suppose that you did just happen to find yourself in a restaurant. Most likely you'd leave, although, of course, you could change your plans. You might decide to stay and have a meal —provided you were hungry, liked the type of food served, had enough money, etc. We can also see that different persons will arrive at the same place with a similar plan in mind and will then behave similarly. It will then appear as if the place has elicited or caused their behavior, even though we know that the high correlation of place and behavior does not imply that one caused the other.

Figure 2 is undoubtedly an oversimplified and idealized picture, and later we shall have to deal with various complexities. We do not mean to imply, for example, that all psychological processes can be neatly divided into three sequential steps. People sometimes act first and think later, they sometimes plan while they travel, etc. But Figure 2 does highlight certain theoretical that the place-specificity of behavior does not necessarily imply that the issues, in addition to that of causality, that are of current concern to environmental psychologists (e.g. Rapoport 1977, Wapner 1980, Stokols 1981) and that are not as explicit in Figure 1. In Figure 2, people are more cognitively active and goal-oriented. People must often devise plans on the basis not of their current environment but of their image of other places, an image based on information previously obtained from primary or often secondary sources. They typically arrive at a place with considerable information about that place and with some plan in mind about what to do there.

Figure 2 emphasizes the dimension of time as well as space. We know, for example, that a pleasant or unpleasant experience in one place affects behavior in the next place visited (Sherrod et al 1977). The environment is seen to be more than a single stimulus; it is a complex of immediate and distant places, psychologically arranged into a hierarchy such that each place is part of a larger place and can be subdivided into smaller places. (*Place* will refer in this article to a psychological or "perceived" unit of the geographical environment.) One hierarchy, for example, would be nation, region, town, neighborhood, home, dining room, and each person's place at the dining room table. The environment is more than an antecedent to behavior; it affords opportunities for future action. More generally, various relationships may exist between person and environment, and the type of relationship may vary with the level in the hierarchy being studied. The relationship between a person and the room he or she is in probably cannot be described in the same terms as the relationship between a person and the community he or she lives in.

Figure 2 is also an attempt to outline the conceptual boundaries that guided our review of the literature. Its three steps will serve as a convenient organizing framework for that review: 1. Planning and the image, 2. Travel, and 3. Behavior-in-place. We must first mention three qualifications, however. First, boundaries around disciplines are inevitably fuzzy. Figure 2 might better be thought of as portraying a central focus of environmental psychology than as drawing an outline of its boundaries. Second, we review topics here in a highly selective and evaluative manner, ignoring or slighting much good work along the way. Third, not everyone would agree with our view of environmental psychology. To include what all environmental psychologists do, we would have to review a much broader set of problems. Whereas we have emphasized its basic and theoretical side, some would see environmental psychology as principally an applied discipline. Whereas we have emphasized a molar level of analysis, some would see the field as the study of single attributes of physical environments (such as noise, chemical pollution, or color). Whereas we have emphasized environmental psychology as a branch of and a perspective on psychology, some would see the field as an interdisciplinary study of environment and behavior.

STEP 1: PLANNING AND THE IMAGE

Kenneth Boulding's 1956 book, *The Image,* presented the simple thesis that human activity is predicated on an image of, rather than on the objective reality of, the external world. The image referred to a person's known or believed universe, the person's mental encyclopedia. Although this thesis was not new, Boulding's treatment inspired much subsequent theoretical work in environmental psychology. Downs and Stea entitled their 1973 landmark book in environmental psychology *Image and Environment,* explicitly drawing on Boulding's concept. Downs and Stea focused on that part of the image called a *cognitive map,* an internal representation of the spatial organization of the external world. Boulding's concept of the image also inspired a quite different conceptualization in psychology: Miller, Galanter & Pribram's (1960) influential idea of a *plan.* Behavior, they argued, was organized in time by means of a hierarchically arranged set of plans. The image, it would seem, plays a central role in what we would define as the central concern of environmental psychology: organization of behavior in space and time.

This section deals with planning and with the internally stored information on which it relies, the entries for places in the mental encyclopedia. We shall thus consider those psychological processes that *can* occur in the absence of the external environment. Of course, planning and thinking must take place somewhere and can occur in the place being thought about. I can plan my shopping routine while in the grocery store, but I could plan the routine before going there. How much I can plan before arriving depends on how much knowledge I have before going there.

Place Knowledge

People have of necessity acquired extensive and multifaceted knowledge of the environment in which they live. Downs & Stea (1977) distinguish two broad classes of such knowledge: locational (where something is) and nonlocational (what it is). We shall postpone discussion of locational knowledge (the mental atlas) until the section on travel and shall consider here only nonlocational knowledge (the mental encyclopedia).

ENVIRONMENTAL MEANING A major research effort has been the search for the fundamental dimensions along which people conceptualize places, or, put another way, for the fundamental dimensions of the meaning of places. Part of environmental meaning is symbolic—places can stand for an idea (Tuan 1978b, Moore 1979b). This is perhaps most easily seen from a cross-cultural perspective when places take on religious significance. For example, the Navaho attribute religious significance to the location and orientation of a house. Study of this belief system allowed architects to design a Navaho house that preserved traditional values while providing modern conveniences (Snyder et al 1976). Saegert & Winkel (1981) argued that for many women, the home symbolizes self, family, and social relationships; for many men, it symbolizes ownership and childhood memories.

Another approach to environmental meaning has been to examine environmental descriptors found in natural languages. Most such studies have found that environmental meaning is a complex mix of affective and denotative meaning. Russell, Ward & Pratt (1981, Russell & Pratt 1980) attempted to isolate and describe the structure of affective meaning. More denotative aspects of meaning have been explored through factor analytic studies of everyday language traits of places (Horayangkura 1978) and multidimensional scaling studies of the judged similarities (Oostendorp & Berlyne 1978, Ward 1977) or preferences (S. Kaplan 1979) among places. These and earlier studies yielded diverse results that were unique to each study. Ward & Russell (1981b) applied a variety of these scaling techniques to the same set of places and offered an explanation for the diverse results. Each study had sought a set of underlying, uniquely interpretable, *orthogonal* dimensions, but, in fact, environmental attributes are highly interrelated. Multivariate techniques thus yield a structure with only a few orthogonal dimensions but with many different, equally compelling interpretations. Moreover, the relationships among attributes are of such different sorts—causal, definitional, and empirical—that their representation through dimensional models would only serve to confuse matters more. (See Craik 1981, Daniel & Ittelson 1981, and Russell & Ward 1981, for controversy surrounding this interpretation and for possible future directions.) Canter (1981) was also critical of the factor analytic representations of environmental meaning and offered facet theory as an alternative.

GENERAL PLACE CATEGORIES General place categories such as *city, town, office,* and *restaurant* probably have an internal structure (Mervis & Rosch 1981). Central to each category is a prototypical example. Other instances then resemble the prototype to varying degrees. Thus, there would not be rigid boundaries separating, say, cities from towns, offices from nonoffices. Rather, specific places are more or less city-like. Perhaps New York is prototypical, but many cities are less so. Place categories could also be organized in hierarchies. At the lowest level of the hierarchy are specific places; at the highest level are the most general categories (Tversky 1981a). Actually there are at least two distinct senses of place hierarchy: (*a*) geographical inclusion, as when Paris is part of France, and (*b*) categorical inclusion, as when Paris is an instance of a city.

BEHAVIOR PATTERNS Part of the meaning of any place is the standing pattern of behavior that occurs there. The meaning of "home" would include the kinds of things you do there. In fact, activities that occur in a particular place are more likely to be remembered than its architectural features (Moore 1979b); and choice among cities as a place to live in is largely determined by activities that occur there: jobs and entertainment as well as types of persons who live there (Brown et al 1977). Ecological psychologists (Barker et al 1978, Wicker 1979) define a special unit, the *behavior setting,* that is the combination of a specific place, a specific time, and a standing pattern of behavior. Canter & Tagg (1980) provided a geometric representation of the rooms of a house and the activities carried out there: a two-dimensional space contained an inner circle of rooms and an outer circle of activities, with the two circles aligned so that eating was near the kitchen, sleeping near the bedroom, etc. Names of many places are related to the action that occurs there: you shop in shops, launder in laundries, and dine in dining rooms. Cultures differ in the kinds of activities that occur in certain kinds of places. Hence, environmental meaning will be culture-specific. The social interaction that occurs inside the home in much of North America may occur on stoops in the West End of Boston or in the streets in Israeli cities (Rapoport 1980).

A more complex representation of activities is achieved through the concept of a *script* (Schank & Abelson 1977). A script is typically a sequence of actions and actors. Thus, the mental category for restaurant would refer you to the restaurant script, which would specify the roles (customer, maitre d', waiter, wine steward) and each actor's actions. Alternatively, we might not store whole scripts, but might generate plausible scenarios when required. Kahneman & Tversky (1981) provide evidence that we do so (the simulation heuristic) in various judgment situations.

Planning and the Use of Place Knowledge

How does a person choose where to be? Why, in spite of government warnings, did many people refuse to evacuate the area around Mt. St. Helens volcano before its eruption (Saarinen 1980)? Part of the reason that people occupy hazardous areas is that in weighing the benefits and risks, they underestimate the likelihood of a hazardous event (even in the face of good physical evidence) and of being personally affected by it (Burton et al 1978). Thus, "rational" models in which all options are objectively considered and by which "place utility" is maximized have given way to ideas such as Simon's concept of "satisficing," which is selecting the first option encountered that meets a set of criteria (Kaplan & Kaplan 1978).

Traveling to and participating in a place is but one type of plan regarding a place. People also plan to build, develop, or, more generally, alter places. Planning thus ranges from planting a vegetable garden to designing an urban renewal project. Whether formal or informal, planning is presumably organized hierarchically and based on the person's image of the environment (Pocock & Hudson 1978), but little is actually known about the process. Rapoport (1979) has begun to analyze folk design, and Zeisel (1981) describes the design process of professionals. Environmental psychologists would benefit greatly from the sophisticated work being done on decision and choice (Einhorn & Hogarth 1981), while decision theorists might find environmental decision problems a challenging arena for testing the applicability of their theories.

Development

Surprisingly little is known about the development of children's knowledge of the physical environment. Although children are limited in cognitive skills, place knowledge is likely to be extensive: children as young as 5 years appear to employ a system of environmental meaning as complex as that employed by adults (Ward & Porter 1980). Tuan (1978a) contrasts our Tom Sawyer and Huck Finn myths with the reality of children's relationship to nature. Children take a functional view of nature (mountains are for climbing), and children reared in more natural surroundings are often no more creative in play nor more empathic toward plants and animals. Indeed, they are often quite cruel.

Hart (1979) carried out an informal but fascinating observational study of children from kindergarten to sixth grade. Hart described their favorite places, secret places, treasured short cuts, and special scary but alluring places. Much of the children's knowledge stemmed from unaided exploration. Parents restrict the range of childrens' explorations, but loosen restrictions as the children grow older, more quickly for boys than girls. Sex differences in restrictions may account for later sex differences in spatial abilities (Saegert & Hart 1978), although of course, in setting restrictions, parents may be influenced by the demonstrated spatial abilities of their children.

STEP 2: TRAVEL

Let us now assume that our person P has a plan to go somewhere. Getting there involves the simultaneous use of the plan, of current input from actual environmental conditions while traveling, and of stored and organized knowledge of the geography—a mental atlas. Most research has been aimed at the last item, although some more recent research has been aimed at the process of travel, particularly at keeping track of one's own position within the environment. We know of no research on how these three elements are integrated. Another set of questions, which we will not consider at all, concerns the emotional, behavioral, and health consequences of travel conditions (Stokols & Novaco 1980).

The Mental Atlas

O'KEEFE AND NADEL'S THEORY The major recent event in the study of spatial knowledge was the publication of O'Keefe & Nadel's (1978) book *The Hippocampus as a Cognitive Map.* O'Keefe and Nadel place current issues concerning the mental representation of space within an historical and philosophical context. One continuing issue of great philosophical complexity concerns which aspects of space are attributes of the physical universe and which are constructs of the mind. Another is the question of whether space is mentally represented as absolute or relative. Absolute space is a framework within which objects are located. Relative space is a set of relationships among objects. When an object moves in relative space, the space is changed. Not so in absolute space, which exists independently of any object.

Psychologists have made various distinctions similar to the one between relative and absolute space: response learning vs place learning, egocentric space vs fixed frame of reference, route knowledge vs cognitive map, process knowledge vs state knowledge, nondimensional vs dimensional forms of space, and taxon systems vs locale system. In the first item of each pair, the mental atlas is thought of as something like a cookbook, a list of places with instructions on how to get there; in the second item, as something more like a map on which various places may be located. Psychologists such as Hull argued that we need only assume relative space (response learning) to account for wayfinding and other spatial behaviors, but Tolman sought to demonstrate that we must assume absolute space (place learning or a cognitive map). Menzel (1978) reports recent data on chimpanzee spatial learning that favor Tolman's side in this controversy. (The term *cognitive map* has been used to refer to, among other things, a hand-drawn map, a person's entire mental atlas whatever its form, and a person's mental representation of space as absolute space. Here we shall restrict the term to the last meaning.)

Along with most writers today (Downs & Stea 1977), O'Keefe and Nadel argue that we use both absolute and relative representations of space and that wayfinding, sketching maps, estimating distances, and other spatially relevant behaviors can result from either. It is therefore difficult to attribute a specific behavior or judgment to one form or the other, but O'Keefe and Nadel have sought to sharpen the distinction as much as possible. They view the mental representation of absolute space as a product of a *locale system,* which, they argue, is located mainly in the hippocampus. Relative space is a product of *taxon systems,* which are located in other parts of the brain. Construction of the taxon systems is motivated by specific rewards and punishments. Each route learned has a specific goal or end-point. Because a route depends on each element being correctly linked to the next, its use is easily disrupted. Taxon learning is incremental and use of taxon information is relatively rigid, but rapid. In contrast, construction of the locale system is motivated by curiosity. It has no one goal or end-point. Because it does not depend on any one object or place, its use is not easily disrupted. Once the overall map is established, places are added in an all-or-none fashion, and its use is extremely flexible, but slow.

We can do little more than mention the controversy over O'Keefe & Nadel's (1978) hypothesis that the hippocampus is the neural locus of the locale system. They report evidence of hippocampal neurons that respond only when an animal is in a particular place and others that respond only when an object normally present in a particular place is absent. Based largely on the form of amnesia in humans with left hippocampal lesions, they speculate that the left hippocampal hemisphere may have formed the substrate for the spatial nature of semantic deep structures. Controversy over their theorizing is presented in a series of articles published in *Behavioral and Brain Sciences* (1979, Vol. 2) and *Physiological Psychology* (1980, Vol. 8).

ELEMENTS AND USE Kevin Lynch (1960) hypothesized five elements of the mental atlas: paths, nodes (path intersections), landmarks, districts, and boundaries. This typology has received empirical support (Magana 1978).

As cognitive reference points, landmarks play an important role in both the taxon and locale systems. They serve as stimuli in a route (turn right at the statue of Kevin Lynch), provide anchor points around which a cognitive map can be constructed, help in accurately locating nearby places, and are involved in distance and direction judgments (Holyoak & Mah 1980, Sadalla et al 1980, Yamamoto et al 1980).

Estimates of distances between places are frequently inaccurate and generally inconsistent with Euclidean geometry. For example, category judgments of distance often are not in even the same rank order as magnitude estimates of the same distances; pairwise comparisons of distances between places can be intransitive ($a > b$, $b > c$, but $c > a$); and distance estimates may depend on the order of presentation ($ab \neq ba$) (Cadwallader 1979, Holyoak & Mah 1980, Sadalla et al 1980). Multidimensional scaling of estimated distances also suggests that a non-Euclidean metric may represent the data better than a Euclidean metric (Richardson 1979). There is considerable controversy concerning exactly how these distortions and non-Euclidean properties arise and how to study them (Golledge 1978). Distances may be inaccurately perceived in the first place. Distances may be distorted in memory. Perhaps something other than distance is stored in memory accurately, and distortions arise when judgments about distance are called for. Or perhaps method artifacts account for non-Euclidean results; Rieser, Lockman & Pick (1980) found that if specifically instructed to estimate the Euclidean distance (distance as the crow flies) between places, people can do so. If instructed to estimate functional distance (distance to actually travel) between places, they can also do that. When not specifically instructed, people tend to give a compromise between functional and Euclidean distance. These results also suggest that simple instructions may provide a means of separating taxon and locale systems.

Spatial relationships are sometimes assumed to be stored in memory as visual images, an assumption in which the metaphor of the cognitive map may be being taken too literally. Still, there is some support for such an assumption. When they are sketching maps, subjects report visual images. And when they are estimating distances, their response latency is proportional to distance in remembered environments (Baum & Jonides 1979) just as it is in visual images (Kosslyn et al 1978). Rather than visual images, spatial relationships might be mentally coded as propositions. Propositions (x is two blocks from y) are obvious candidates for the taxon systems, but could serve the locale system as well. However, it may be impossible to empirically distinguish propositional storage from image-like storage since propositions might be used to generate an image (Anderson 1978).

There is also evidence of the psychological reality of the hierarchy of places. Judgments of spatial relationships between two places are affected by the relationship between the superordinate categories for the places. You may be surprised to learn that San Diego, California, is *east* of Reno, Nevada. Subjects tend to believe the opposite (Stevens & Coupe 1978), presumably because California is remembered as west of Nevada. Reaction time to verify statements about spatial relationships also depends on whether the places involved are within the same or different superordinate places (Wilton 1979, Maki 1981).

Other spatial distortions are more easily interpreted as produced by encoding or decoding processes than by the way in which information is stored in memory. Tversky (1981a,b) hypothesized that heuristics are used to process spatial information. (A heuristic is a judgment that is relatively easy to make and that provides an approximate solution to a more difficult problem.) In the *alignment* heuristic, spatial relationships among places are approximated by a straight line. In the *rotation* heuristic, straight lines are assimilated to either the north-south or the east-west directions. For example, you may be surprised to learn that New York City is on the same longitude as many points on the *west* coast of South America. Presumably, we are surprised because we assimilate the central axis of North and South America to a straight line and assimilate that straight line to be a north-south longitude.

There may be other heuristics in operation as well. People tend to assimilate turns to 90° angles and to equate distances along a route that fall between turns (Byrne 1979). People thus estimate distance they have traveled by the number of turns (Sadalla & Magel 1980). They also use number of nodes along the route (Sadalla & Staplin 1980b) or, more generally, the amount of information they remember about the route (Sadalla & Staplin 1980a). In judging compass directions, people are quicker at 0°, 90°, 180°, and 270° than at other angles (Loftus 1978). When applying verbal labels, left-right (or east-west) judgments are more difficult than above-below (north-south) judgments in terms of both speed and accuracy, and from both perception and memory (Maki et al 1977). This effect disappears when directional labels do not have to be used (Loftus 1978, Maki et al 1979). Adults' problems using left and right labels are reminiscent of children's problems learning them. The reason may be ecological, since for many things the left half is similar or symmetrical to the right half, but top and bottom and front and back are rarely similar.

Learning New Places

Upon encountering a new environment, a person generally first learns specific routes (i.e. relative space of the taxon system) and only later constructs a cognitive map (i.e. absolute space of the locale system) (Evans 1980). Newcomers to Paris and newcomers to a college campus both appeared to learn major landmarks quite early on, but to add paths and nodes more slowly to their hand-drawn maps (Evans et al 1981). Their early maps demonstrated knowledge of only ordinal distances, and later maps of interval distances. This may indicate the development of an absolute space, although reasonably accurate interval distances could be achieved simply by a more elaborate path system such that each place is "fixed" by more and more connections. Still, whether a person uses the taxon or locale system or both, or whether paths, districts, or landmarks are learned first, may depend largely on the environment (Heft 1979b): some environments lend themselves much more to one way of thinking than the other.

Garling, Book & Lindberg (1979) described how adding tasks or subtracting various types of information impair learning of spatial relationships. Learning can be improved by providing names for places (Pezdek & Evans 1979), by providing multiple rather than single perspectives on a place (Evans & Pezdek 1980), and through strategies that emphasize particular ways of encoding spatial information, evaluating progress, and then focusing attention on unlearned information (Thorndyke & Stasz 1980). On the other hand, whether environmental scenes are seen in a sequential or merely random order (provided of course that the scenes depict overlapping areas) has little effect on formation of a reasonable cognitive map of an environment (Allen et al 1978). The ability to learn from a map seems to depend on good visual memory and is affected surprising little by experience with maps. (Thorndyke & Stasz 1980). Those with a self-reported "good sense of direction" are better than those without it at pointing in the direction of unseen places, thus suggesting individual differences in the use of the locale system (Kozlowski & Bryant 1977).

Development

From a developmental perspective, O'Keefe & Nadel's (1978) locale system is but one stage (and not necessarily the final one) in a developmental sequence. The dominant theoretical position on the topic derives from Piaget's theory that such knowledge progresses through qualitatively different stages. Much research (Hazen et al 1978, Evans 1980) supports some such developmental sequence as the following: (*a*) an egocentric stage, in which all spatial knowledge is in reference to self, (*b*) an allocentric stage, in which a relative space is constructed independent of self, and (*c*) a geocentric stage, in which an absolute space is constructed independent of self and of specific objects.

Evidence inconsistent with this general framework has also accumulated, however (Spencer & Darvizeh 1981). Many of these conflicting findings are clarified by theorizing that there is developmental progress in the use of each type of spatial element (self, landmark, route, frame of reference) as well as a developmental sequence from the use of one type to another. Thus there are naive and sophisticated ways to use any reference point (Pick & Lockman 1981, Pick & Rieser 1981, Siegel et al 1978, Sonnenfeld 1979). An immature way to use a landmark would be to rely on one external object to locate another. A mature way would be to use a relative space consisting of a number of interrelated landmarks. Similarly, there are immature ways to use the self as a spatial reference point (hence the egocentric errors observed by Piaget). But updating one's own position as one moves through space is a mature use of self as a reference point.

Consistent with this view, very young children can avoid egocentric errors under proper circumstances. Before 16 months of age children usually respond egocentrically. When trained to expect an event to occur on their left, they will still look to their left even after they've been turned around 180°. After 16 months, children can rely on external cues, and after being turned 180° will look to their right for the event (Acredolo 1978). At 9 months, children can use an external cue if it is a bold visual pattern (Bremner 1978) or if tested at home (Acredolo 1979). Even at 6 months, a child can employ an external landmark if it is made extremely salient and can use gravity as a cue to spatial position (Rieser 1979). In short, there is evidence of very young children using primitive forms of external frames of reference long before they've overcome all egocentric errors. For example, at 7 years, most children still make egocentric errors when asked to point to a picture of what a scene looks like from someone else's perspective. If, however, the children are asked to indicate the relative positions of objects in the scene one at a time, the number of egocentric errors declines (Huttenlocher & Presson 1979). Providing the children with a small-scale model of the scene practically eliminates their egocentric errors (Presson 1980). Egocentric errors also increase when children are asked to answer quickly, suggesting that they must learn to inhibit the egocentric response so that appropriate cognitive processes can occur (Lasky et al 1980).

STEP 3: BEHAVIOR-IN-PLACE

There has been a prolonged debate between those environmental psychologists taking a cognitive approach and those emphasizing the study of the objective physical environment. Up to now we have taken the cognitive approach, but each approach clearly has its focus of convenience. Step 3 brings us back to Figure 1, in which reality replaces expectations and the actual setting guides behavior. Recall Mark Twain's river pilots who had well-developed plans, skills, and knowledge. Nevertheless, when traveling treacherous waters, their behavior had to be finely tuned to where a sand bar was rather than where they remembered it to be. In this section, we consider first the perception and cognition of the current environment and then the direct effects of such environmental variables as noise, level of stimulation, and amount of crowding.

Place Perception

To complete the journey, our person P must recognize when he or she has arrived at the destination. Rapoport (1977) has outlined at least some of the issues that a study of place recognition and perception must consider. People arrive with a set of expectations, but must verify them, update information about the place, and detect and analyze any unusual aspects of the place. (Dangerous events might call for a complete revision of plans; so might unusually good opportunities.) People must decide whether the place will, in fact, support their current plans, and if so, must add details to the plans and begin carrying them out.

EMPIRICAL RESULTS People's perceptions of their current surroundings depend upon the plans with which they arrived. Wofsey, Rierdan & Wapner (1979) showed that people psychologically distance themselves from an environment they plan to leave. Leff & Gordon (1980) described 35 environmental cognitive sets that can be taught and that influence how a place is perceived, how much it is enjoyed, and how creatively it is responded to. An environmental cognitive set is a plan to notice certain attributes of a place rather than others or to process environmental information in a certain way. Other evidence suggests that cognitive set influences not the attributes people perceive in an environment, but only the relative weight they give the attributes in making global judgments (Ward & Russell 1981a).

Perceived spaciousness can be understood through the concept of the isovist (Benedikt & Burnham 1980), which is the set of light rays or straight lines connecting a person's eye to all opaque surfaces in the environment. Properties of the isovist, such as area and circumference of its horizontal plane, can be measured and varied experimentally. Evidence so far indicates that spaciousness is directly related to area of the horizontal plane, but inversely related to circumference. Aspects of perceived complexity, beauty, and privacy might be understood through the concept of isovist field, which is the sequence of isovists generated when an observer moves through the environment (Benedikt 1979).

FURTHER QUESTIONS The boundaries around places are more perceived than real (Ittelson 1978). Walls and fences and, less obviously, changes in color and texture are some environmental cues to boundaries. Are perceived boundaries influenced by activity patterns? (and vice versa?)

Do we have biases regarding the shapes of boundaries—a tendency to use straight lines, circles, or ellipses as in personal space boundaries? Information on such questions is unavailable. This is unfortunate in light of Newman's (1972) argument that a boundary is one of the things that can influence a sense of ownership over a place, what one does there, the way one deals with strangers who enter, and ultimately the likelihood of crime being committed there.

People often have the sense that they've returned to the "same" place, despite changes in various details. This would suggest "place constancies." The mechanism that accounts for such recognition is unknown, however. Must a person do considerable cognitive work, identifying various attributes and relationships among them to compare with remembered attributes? Or is there an automatic feature matching procedure similar to that hypothesized in the recognition of simple stimuli? Is recognition based on global attributes or more local details? Perhaps a place is defined as a large collection of features, no one of which is sufficient to define the place. Location in space may be a necessary feature, but it is not sufficient, as illustrated by Saarinen's (1980) report of the aftermath of the May 1980 eruption of Mt. St. Helens volcano. Residents returning to the devastated countryside failed to recognize familiar places.

Regarding the hierarchy of places, at what level do we perceive ourselves to be? We are probably influenced by walls and other features that influence boundaries, properties of the isovist, and features that promote place constancies. Speed of movement would be another influence, since when moving quickly we can only focus on more distant features (Rapoport 1977) and might be more likely to perceive ourselves in more superordinate places. Perhaps most important would be the plan we are currently executing. Walking in a hallway chatting, I'm in the hallway. Walking down the same hallway to leave, I'm in the building. Walking in the hallway planning my day, I'm at the university.

THEORETICAL ISSUES Ittelson (1978) pointed out that environments provide information to all the senses, provide peripheral as well as focal information, and provide much more information than can be processed. Environments are typically experienced over a long period of time while the person is moving about, are experienced in large part in terms of their social and symbolic meaning, and are nonetheless experienced as a whole rather than as a succession of parts. These properties of environments provide a profound challenge to the study of place perception, since places are so unlike objects, the traditional focus in perceptual research.

Gibson (1979, Warren 1978) offered an ecological theory of place perception. He argued that our perceptual systems register directly the important information that is contained in the ever-changing array of light, sound, etc that is the environment. His ecological approach thus suggests the study of the distribution and abundance of such information, not as it is perceived but as it exists in the ecology. His approach also emphasizes the usefulness of perception. The environment provides opportunities for action, and the perceptual system has evolved to perceive directly such opportunities.

Gibson's approach contrasts with the current emphasis on cognitive construction of perceptions from sensory information, which provides only probabilistic clues to reality (S. Kaplan 1978). Both types of theories may be valuable (Baron 1980). Gibson's theory might describe the immediate perception of quickly changing environments, while constructivist theories might better describe more reflective judgments of more static environments. Similarly, Gibson's theory may tell us more about perception of natural environments, which are similar to those we evolved in, while constructivist theory may tell us more about perception of the built environment.

Place Interpretation

Research on the psychological interpretation of places has already been reviewed in connection with knowledge of places. Yet it may be worthwhile to mention how little is known about the process of interpretation. What has been studied is the behavioral effect of interpretation. Upon entering a professor's office, for example, students not only evaluate the setting but anticipate different sorts of interaction, depending on furniture arrangement, plants, and tidiness (Campbell 1979). Stokols (1981) argued that the meaning of actual places will vary in clarity, with obvious behavioral consequences.

Even less is known about how prior expectations and current information are integrated. Subjects' expectations or prior information about some aspect of the situation have also been manipulated more directly (Langer & Saegert 1977, Greenberg & Baum 1979). The importance of expectations is underscored by Klein & Harris's (1979) finding that task performance decrements could be attributed to the violation of expectations rather than to the particular environmental manipulation. In most studies, levels of the environmental variable are confounded with the expectedness of each level. Subjects are unlikely to expect an experimental laboratory to be crowded, for example, and it is therefore unclear in most studies whether any observed effects are due to the crowding or to the violation of subjects' expectations. Violation of an expectation could also serve as a clue to the experimental hypothesis, a clue not available to the control group.

Affective response to a place is usually thought to follow its categorization. Kaplan & Kaplan (1978) argue for an evolutionary link of positive affect with such naturally beneficial elements as water and vegetation. Zajonc (1980), however, believes that affective response may precede categorization.

Physical Stimulation

Places can be ordered on a continuum called, among other things, information load. At one end would be no stimulation. At the other end, high load places are filled with intense, complex, novel, ever-changing, unpredictable, and uncontrollable stimulation of all sorts. Most people, it is thought, prefer something in the middle range, generating the notions of underload and overload.

LITTLE STIMULATION The closest we get to the low end of the load continuum is probably in a sensory deprivation chamber. In his thorough review of this area, Suedfeld (1980) remarks that "In the public mind, and even in the minds of many behavioral scientists and clinicians, the term 'sensory deprivation' evokes images of bizarre effects, psychological disturbance, a Svengali-like power over the subject, and torture" (p. ix). Suedfeld argues that this image is profoundly mistaken. When experimental artifacts such as panic buttons and liability-release forms are eliminated, there is no evidence that ill effects result from prolonged periods in which stimulation is reduced as much as possible. Although some subjects find the experience unpleasant, others find it quite pleasant and some volunteer for more. On the practical side, the bad press given restricted stimulation has allowed us to overlook its ability to facilitate creativity and its potential as an adjunct therapeutic tool. On the theoretical side, Suedfeld's argument calls on environmental psychologists to re-think their views of the "under"-load end of the continuum.

MUCH STIMULATION Several not altogether distinct hypotheses predict effects of copious stimulation, regardless of sensory modality: cognitive overload, attention, stress, and arousal. Cognitive overload is the central idea in environmental psychology's most elegant conceptualization, Milgram's (1970) analysis of the psychology of the city. Briefly, Milgram's idea is that the urban dweller, faced with an environment of excessive stimulation, uses various cognitive and behavioral mechanisms to filter out some. In this way, Milgram accounts for such urban phenomena as the unresponsive bystander and the norm of privacy. Milgram's analysis continues to generate both support (e.g. Boles & Hayward 1978) and debate. Proshansky (1978) argued that Milgram overlooked the pleasant and exciting opportunities of cities. Holohan (1977) distinguished an urban setting from a high-load setting and found no effects of urban per se but only of the amount of load in the specific setting. In a similar vein, House & Wolf (1978) found that urban and rural residents differ not in their attitudes regarding helping but in their actual behavior. Moreover, urbanites' unwillingness to help strangers is not so much related to population size, density, or heterogeneity (i.e. indexes of overload) as it is to crime rate in their city.

ATTENTION Cohen (1978) theorized that the effects of increased stimulation are mediated by attention. Cohen adapted the notion of attention as mental effort. Humans have limited attentional capacity, so that when incoming information exceeds capacity, effort must be devoted only to information that on preliminary analysis appears to warrant it. The occurrence or the anticipation of intense, unpredictable, uncontrollable, or important events requires more monitoring of (attention to) environmental inputs, thereby using up attentional capacity. Capacity declines with use and can be restored only with rest. Thus, background noise, high ambient temperature, excessive closeness to other persons, or any environmental stimulus uses up attentional capacity (Bell 1978), thereby diminishing attention available for either the task at hand or for other aspects of the environment such as more subtle social cues.

STRESS AND STRESSORS Stress (a response) and stressor (the stimulus) are the concepts most commonly employed in psychological studies of physical stimulation. In the prototypical case, stress is prolonged physiological, emotional, behavioral, cognitive—in short, organismic—mobilization during a prolonged emergency. But in less extreme cases, the meaning of "stress" is far from clear. As the concept is used today, stress is a hypothetical mediator in a family of conceptualizations (Stokols 1979). The medical branch of the family is concerned with stressors such as toxins or injury and with responses that are mainly physiological. The psychological branch is concerned with events that are stressors because of their meaning (events from challenges to threats) and with responses that involve emotional, cognitive, and behavioral components. The sociological branch is concerned with social stressors and with societal responses. Members of the stress family also range from rather detailed models (e.g. Stokols 1979) to simple hypotheses of the heat-produces-physiological-arousal variety. Altogether, it is difficult to say what response would not fall within someone's use of the term "stress" and what environmental attribute would not fall within someone's use of the term "stressor."

ATMOSPHERIC CONDITIONS Everyone may talk about the weather (see Campbell & Beets' 1977 annotated bibliography), but Bell (1981) says that we can no longer talk in simple terms. Because of various adaptive mechanisms and complex changes over time, no one mediator can explain the psychological effects of even one variable, heat. The effect of heat on task performance involves at least three separate mediators: body temperature, arousal, and attention. The effect of heat on social behavior can mainly be accounted for by changes in affect: unpleasant temperatures decrease attraction toward and willingness to help strangers and increase willingness to harm them. Presumably affect also accounts for Cunningham's (1979) finding that when temperatures are moderate, the more sunshine, the more generous people are. Similarly, Carlsmith & Anderson (1979) found that civil riots are more likely when temperatures are unpleasantly high, with no evidence of a previously reported curvilinear trend such that extremely high temperatures discourage riots. Still, affect is probably not the only mediator of heat effects (Schneider et al 1980, Bell 1981). For example, aggression occurs more indiscriminately in a hot room than in a cold room (Calvert-Boyanowsky et al 1976).

According to Evans & Jacobs' (1981) review, most research on air pollution concerns knowledge, beliefs, attitudes, and actions about air pollution rather than its direct psychological effects. Nevertheless, enough is known on the latter topic to warrant further and systematic investigation. And the sooner the better. Psychological effects can be demonstrated even when the pollution is nonperceptible and at concentrations below those known to impair physical health. Even ionization of the air may alter task performance and mood (Charry 1976, Hawkins & Barker 1978). Air pollution correlates with the number of emergency visits at a psychiatric hospital (Strahilevitz et al 1979). There is other evidence of effects on perception, attention, motor coordination, and memory. Effects on more molar behaviors can so far be accounted for by changes in affect. Thus, unpleasant but harmless odors reduce tolerance for frustration, although the effect is lessened when a person has a greater sense of control over the odor (Jones & Bogat 1978, Rotton et al 1979). Unpleasant odors also produce greater aggression, a more unpleasant mood, decreased liking for an unknown other, less time spent in the setting, lower evaluation of the setting, but increased liking for someone who shares the unpleasant experience (Rotton et al 1978).

In a review of an extensive literature, Campbell & Beets (1978) found no support for the belief that phases of the moon are associated with human behavior—a conclusion consistent with recent empirical evidence (Frey et al 1979, Sharfman 1980). The popularity of lunar research makes a sad contrast with the dearth of information on a more vital topic. Barnes (1978) observed a close temporal correlation between decline in high school students' SAT (Scholastic Aptitude Test) scores and atmospheric radiation levels (produced by nuclear weapons tests) the time of their conception and birth, raising the possibility of widespread genetic damage from radiation. Sternglass & Bell (1979) confirmed the temporal correlation and found an equally striking geographical correlation based on closeness to test sites, wind patterns, and measurements of ground level radiation.

NOISE Urban society is permeated with unpredictable and uncontrollable noise (unwanted sound). Even wilderness is being invaded by snarling snowmobiles and coughing, sputtering trail bikes. As of 1970, noise did not appear to be much of a psychological problem (Kryter 1970). Subsequent research has changed this conclusion. Noise decreases helping behavior (Page 1977), interferes with interpersonal and social discrimination judgments (Siegel & Steele 1980), and decreases attentiveness to social cues (Cohen & Lezak 1977). Children from noisy homes suffer attentional deficits, although with time they do adapt to some extent (Heft 1979a). Children in noisier schools have higher blood pressure, lower tolerance for frustration, and poorer performance on reading-related cognitive tasks (Cohen et al 1980, 1981). The effect of noise on task performance was the subject of a controversy between Poulton (1977) and Broadbent (1978). Poulton proposed that many of the deleterious effects of continuous noise on performance could be accounted for simply by one mechanism: masking of helpful auditory processes such as inner speech (short-term memory rehearsal) or of subtle, auditory, task cues overlooked by the experimenter. The implication of sloppy experimentation resulted in a series of rejoinders and retorts. In the latest round Poulton (1979) posited four mechanisms—masking, distraction, arousal, and positive and negative transfer from noise to quiet—to explain all known effects.

COMMENT Few continue to believe that the effects of all the various physical parameters on all the various possible psychological responses can be reasonably dealt with through an S-R approach. The resulting list of relationships would simply be too long. Recourse has thus been to models involving mediating variables such as perceived control, stress, affect, and cognitive overload. Stokols (1979) pinpoints one major problem in these models: almost without exception, environmental variables are considered one at a time. How stressful, controllable, attention-eliciting, etc is the entire setting? How do various stimulus parameters combine or interact in determining the level of the psychological mediator? Stokols (1979) lays the groundwork for a conceptual analysis of this problem that, moreover, takes into account a person's prior plans and goals.

A second major problem concerns the various mediating processes themselves. Sometimes they are thought of as conflicting hypotheses, sometimes as different words for the same thing. For example, the terms stress and overload are often used interchangeably. And for the type of stimulation employed in a typical study, the amount of stimulation is probably correlated with its unpleasantness. If amount of stimulation and unpleasantness were not confounded, however, unpleasant, neutral, and pleasant stimulation might produce different effects. Russell & Mehrabian (1978) argued that tolerance for stimulation is greater when that stimulation (or the person's mood more generally) is pleasant. Further understanding of the psychological influence of the physical environment awaits a theory specifying the relationships among mediating mechanisms.

Proxemics

Worry over the ever-increasing human population on what now seems a small planet triggered an avalanche of research on issues such as crowding, density, personal space, privacy, and territoriality. The study of these issues is now called proxemics, a field concerned with individuals and groups utilizing space and thus facing the problem of space as a limited resource and structuring their activities accordingly (Baldassare 1978).

CROWDING An initial terminological fog in proxemics is slowly lifting. A distinction between *density* and *crowding* is now generally accepted. *Density* refers to an objective assessment of number of persons and amount of space. *Crowding* refers to a psychological response to a place, such as the feeling that it is crowded. Even so, *crowding* is used in two senses. For some theorists, *crowding* is a scientific construct, the meaning of which is created by the theorist. For example, Stokols (1978) defines crowding as a motivational state involving the need for more space. For other theorists, *crowding* is an everyday word, the meaning of which must be discovered empirically. Both approaches are of course legitimate, but sometimes not properly distinguished, as when the everyday word *crowding* is used as a measure of the scientific construct. The everyday use of the word *crowding* has been studied extensively and shown to vary with not only number of persons and amount of space, but with such things as the type of place, the expected number of persons there (Schmidt & Keating 1979), and the availability of alternative explanations for felt discomfort (Worchel & Yohai 1979). The study of everyday environmental concepts (and there is no reason to focus exclusively on *crowding*) will undoubtedly soon be enriched by taking into account what we now know of the nature of concepts in general (Mervis & Rosch 1981).

Density is the number of persons in a place divided by the amount of space available. With hindsight, we can see that density is a poor psychological concept. Two persons in 2 square meters receives the same density score as 20 persons in 20 square meters. Because density is a single number, numerator is confounded with denominator. Lack of space and number of persons are treated as if interchangeable, which makes no psychological sense. Consequently, two types of density had to be distinguished: social density, which is really just number of persons (with space and all other variables held constant) and spatial density, which is really just amount of space (with number of persons and all other variables held constant). Most studies vary either amount of space or number of persons, but there are two reasons to include both in future research. First, either variable alone is confounded with space per person, and second, the commonsense notion of crowding is probably best captured by an interaction: too many persons in too little space.

SPATIAL DENSITY Everybody assumed that lack of space would be harmful. When in 1975 Freedman announced that he could find no evidence that this was so, there was a collective gasp, similar to the one that must have occurred when a child pointed out that the emperor had no clothes. (Freedman used the term *crowding* but carefully defined it as amount of space.) A reappraisal of the animal literature yielded a similar conclusion (Freedman 1979), and today Freedman's position is widely accepted. The question has become: "When does [spatial] density matter?" (Cohen & Sherrod 1978).

If space is thought of as a resource (Stokols 1978), then lack of space or poor arrangement of space might matter when the person's plans require space (Baum & Valins 1979, Saegert 1980). Even when a person is alone, spatial restriction can be unpleasant (Smith & Lawrence 1978). Such an effect is termed behavior constraint or interference, although it is important to distinguish intentional from unintentional interference. In different types of places lack of space will present different types of problems (Karlin et al 1978). Ten persons living in a home with 500 square feet of floor space are absurdly cramped; ten persons traveling on a train with 500 square feet of floor space may be lonely. Lack of space among family members in their private environments is probably a much more serious problem than among strangers in public places (Stokols 1978). Loo (1980) emphasized that lack of space is more a problem for more vulnerable groups, those who lack other resources with which to compensate: the poor (McCarthy & Saegert 1978), the very young (Evans 1978, Saegert 1980), the very old, and the institutionalized such as patients or prisoners (Cox et al 1979).

Three hypotheses predict general effects of lack of space. (*a*) arousal hypothesis: lack of space increases arousal (Evans 1978); (*b*) density-intensity hypothesis: lack of space intensifies whatever social response would otherwise occur (Freedman 1975); (*c*) perceived control hypothesis: lack of space decreases the perceived controllability of a situation (Baron & Rodin 1978, Cohen & Sherrod 1978). Evidence that clearly differentiates these three hypotheses is lacking, perhaps because they are conceptually overlapping. An uncontrollable situation might also be an unpleasant one, in which case the density-intensity hypothesis would also predict negative effects. The arousal hypothesis is also conceptually quite close to the density-intensity hypothesis if we assume (*a*) that arousal intensifies relevent behavioral responses and (*b*) that arousal is not per se unpleasant. Freedman & Perlick (1979) cleverly pitted the density-intensity hypothesis against the arousal hypothesis. According to Freedman, limited space intensifies only social behaviors, whereas by the arousal hypothesis, it should intensify all behaviors. Subjects in a smaller room laughed more than those in a larger room, but only when a confederate laughed first. Spatial restriction thus intensified social contagion rather than laughter.

SOCIAL DENSITY When the number of persons in a given place is varied, the study is termed one of "social density" by environmental psychologists and "group size" by social psychologists. Initial research on social density focused primarily on the question of whether it was harmful, although this question is unanswerable, as is perhaps made clearer by rephrasing it: Is it harmful to have other people around? Subsequent hypotheses regarding spatial density were formulated to apply equally well to social density, although it would be surprising if that strategy worked since a person and an area of space are such different things. Indeed, the psychological effects of increasing numbers of persons within a place were empirically found to be more powerful than those due to lack of space (Loo & Kennelly 1979).

For example, Sadalla (1978) reviewed the evidence on crowding in cities. He concluded that number of persons, rather than density or amount of space, is the important variable. As number increases, social differentiation occurs in both positive (specialists with exotic skills) and negative directions (criminal networks). An urbanite is more likely to encounter strangers, to remain anonymous, and to experience deindividuation, which is a state of lowered social influence, lowered inhibitions, and lack of caring about the evaluations of others. As a consequence, the urbanite will be less conformist, more expressive of opinions, and more innovative and unconventional.

Other people can interfere with our plans, of course, but they can facilitate plans as well. Ecological psychologists have shown that there is an optimal number of persons in a situation, depending on the number of tasks to be performed (Srivastava 1979, Wicker 1979). Morasch, Groner & Keating (1979) interviewed people at a fair. Those wanting to buy goods were unhappy about the crowd, but those wanting to affiliate were happy about it. When asked to name the least enjoyable aspect of the fair, one subject replied, "the crowd." When asked to name the most enjoyable aspect, the same subject replied, "the crowd."

Increased number of persons within one's living quarters is a quite serious matter. For children, effects include emotional and behavioral disturbances in school and lower reading vocabulary and comprehension (Saegert 1980). For college students, effects include social avoidance, giving up sooner on intellectual tasks, behaviors indicative of learned helplessness, a feeling of loss of control, and lowered scholastic performance (Glassman et al 1978, Baum & Valins 1979, Baum & Davis 1980). Among prisoners, effects include problems of physical and mental health (Paulus et al 1978).

The effects of an increasing number of persons are probably mediated by social variables (Baum et al 1979). Effects vary with sex roles (Patterson et al 1979), perceived similarity among the persons (Rohe 1978), their group structure (McCallum et al 1979), their degree of trust (Saegert 1980), and their social relationships (Epstein 1980). Thus some of the problems of large numbers in an apartment house disappear when next-door neighbors are friends (Saegert 1980). It is unfortunate then that a distinction fundamental to sociology, the distinction between aggregates and groups, has been overlooked in this literature. Baron & Mandel (1978) point out that groups (which have common goals and means of social influence) will respond quite differently to almost any situation than will a mere aggregate of unfamiliar individuals.

TERRITORY Territoriality is difficult to define in a way that makes associated theories falsifiable. Nonetheless, it does invite us to notice that places are perceived as belonging to specific individuals or groups. A place belonging to a primary group (an individual, family, or small face-to-face group) is called *primary territory.* A place belonging to a secondary group (club, work team) is called *secondary territory.* A place open to all is called *public.* Rather than three types, however, we might better think of a continuum since borderline cases abound. Better yet, we might better think of each place as having, as part of its perceived meaning, a definition of whom it belongs to, who belongs there, and who does not. There is another important consideration as well: Who belongs where changes with time. Some territories are claimed permanently (Marshland for the Marshlanders), some are held for generations (estates), years (houses), months (trailer home sites), days (hotel rooms), or an hour (a table in a restaurant). The extreme end of this continuum is personal space, the small area around the body that people lay claim to wherever they are.

Upon entering a place, people must notice the territorial claims of others (McAndrew et al 1978) and establish some claim themselves. That claim could vary from homesteading to picking a table at a restaurant. Violations of prior claims are noticed and responded to (Haber 1980). In their own territory, individuals are less aroused (Edney & Uhlig 1977) and, although evidence is lacking, should feel more in control. Thus the literature on the psychological effects of perceived control should be a rich source of hypotheses on the effects of being in one's own territory. In a double-occupancy room in a home for the elderly, an improvement in self-esteem and sense of adequacy was achieved by visible markers that divided the room into two separate primary spaces (Nelson & Paluck 1980). Behaviors inside vs outside one's own territory also differ in subtle and complex ways. For instance, in a conversation with another of *dissimilar views,* the owner of the place tends to control social interaction by initiating topics and speaking more (a dominance effect). In a conversation with another of *similar* views, however, the owner tends to speak and control the converstaion less than the guest (the hospitality effect) (Conroy & Sundstrom 1977).

Ownership is actually but one of various roles and norms that are closely tied to specific places. One person rarely has absolute power over any piece of land. In short, territory is part of a system of socially defined rights and obligations (Godelier 1979). Behaviors associated with territory are equally complex. Van den Berghe (1977) described a summer fishing club that is divided into private lots. Club members defend the club as a whole, allowing access to certain types of strangers but not to others. Territorial defense is graded such that behaviors and barriers are mounted to protect certain core areas the most, the immediately surrounding area next, and peripheral areas least. Club members use each others' private lots, but only when the owner is absent and even then the core area is avoided. When the owner is present, there is a ritual for an intruder, who must seek out an *adult* of the owner's family. The differing roles of family members in such situations point out how oversimplified it is to speak only of behavior inside and outside one's own territory.

PERSONAL SPACE The term *personal space* is applied to several quite different sorts of things. One meaning is the amount of space between two persons that a culture defines as appropriate. It was once thought that personal space in a culture was indicative of whether the culture was a "contact" or "noncontact" one. In fact, personal space in a culture is not indicative of typical eye contact or angle of orientation and its meaning varies from culture to culture (Noesjirwan 1978). Another meaning of *personal space* is the particular distance that a person chooses to keep from another at a particular time. So defined, personal space is a dependent variable and cannot be discussed here except to say that chosen distance appears to be a subtle part of the complex communication between two persons through which their relationship is negotiated (Firestone 1977, Patterson 1978, Sundstrom & Sundstrom 1977).

Chosen distance is thus particularly situation-specific, but one determinant is the person's characteristically preferred interpersonal distance, which is another meaning of *personal space.* It is unclear why this trait is more interesting than characteristic body lean, level of eye contact, amount of touching, or any other individual difference in communication style. Still, personal space has received enormous attention (Hayduk 1978). There appear to be serious measurement problems in the self-report personal space measures (Aiello & Thompson 1980), although they do predict behaviors in children (Gifford & Price 1979) and may be a clue to the motivations of certain criminals with a violent history (Curran et al 1978).

The environmental psychologist is most directly interested in a person's response to the distance from another (i.e. distance as an independent variable). Initial reports of "invasions of personal space" suggested that the "invadee" felt uncomfortable and would flee. But clearly a distinction must be made between voluntary invasion by a stranger, which is a highly unusual and meaningful act, and a situation (such as an elevator) where there is no choice (Murphy-Berman & Berman 1978). When the invader chooses the distance, its effects will be negligible over a reasonable range if circumstances are appropriate (Tesch 1979). Skolnick, Frasier & Hadar (1977) describe one place, a beach in Los Angeles, where invasions were even welcomed.

When the invader does not choose the distance, it is probably ignored (Nerenz et al 1979). This would happen when, for instance, the size of a room, furniture arrangement, and other environmental features force people together. Even touching and bodily contact are ignored in situations, such as crowded subways, where there is no choice (Maines 1977). Worchel & Teddlee (1976) pointed out that most studies of spatial density confound room size with distance between persons. They separated the two variables by varying room size and the distance between chairs independently. The major behavior differences they observed were due to distance between chairs rather than room size, suggesting that the few effects attributable to spatial density may actually be due to distance. Indeed, consistent with current theories of spatial density, interpersonal closeness was shown to be neither positive nor negative per se but to intensify both prosocial and antisocial behaviors already present (Storms & Thomas 1977, Baron 1978).

PRIVACY Privacy is a central concept in a theory that continues to play a heuristic and organizing role in the field of proxemics, Altman's (1977, 1979, Altman & Chemers 1980) theory of interpersonal boundary regulation. By *privacy,* Altman means a condition of control over interpersonal exchanges. This definition is far from the everyday meaning of the term, but Altman is using the word as a scientific concept, and as such it means whatever he wants it to mean. According to Altman, such control serves a universal human function. Humans use environmental features as a means of achieving such control, but availability and effectiveness of any feature will vary with culture.

The meaning of the everyday term *privacy* is quite complex. Various types of privacy (solitude, anonymity, intimacy, secrecy, reserve) have been identified and inventories developed to assess individual differences in the need for, value of, or expectancy of achieving, each type (e.g. Smith & Swanson 1979). Shumaker (1980) took an alternative theoretical tack by arguing that different goals require different amounts of privacy, that different places provide different amounts of privacy, and that discomfort results when there is a disparity between these two. Still, we may not be able to treat privacy in this way. A person's goals sometimes include being alone, being away from specific others, hiding certain behaviors, hiding information, being free from distraction, being nameless, etc. Places differ in their ability to serve each of these separate goals, a particularly important consideration in homes and especially in institutions. For example, in one hospital, children were observed to feign emotional outbursts in order to be sent to a seclusion room. Although designed as a punishment, this room provided their only opportunity to be alone (Laufer & Wolfe 1977). Places thus cannot usefully be classified as offering or not offering privacy. Places simply differ in numerous ways that facilitate or hinder attainment of various specific goals. Variables already considered (primary/secondary/public space, amount of space, etc) are clearly part of the story. Archea (1977) argued that we must also consider many more specific design features. For example, environmental features can obstruct, hide, or reveal information. The amount of visual access could have numerous effects on behavior but in general would be proportional to normative pressure.

ENVIRONMENTAL PROBLEMS

In their introduction to the inaugural issue of the new *Journal of Environmental Psychology,* Canter & Craik (1981) described the mutual benefit of basic and applied environmental psychology. A large literature is accummulating on topics such as environmental attitudes and ecologically relevant behaviors such as littering and energy use. (See Wohlwill & Weisman 1981 for an annotated bibliography of applied research.) Two topics seem to have made particular progress.

DESIGN OF PLACES Designers have always believed that the design of a building influences its users. The main support for their belief was a statement of Winston Churchill's: First we shape our buildings and then they shape us. Almost any change in the environment, whether founding a city or putting up a shed, could be designed in more than one way. Research on the psychological implications of design alternatives has now accumulated overwhelming evidence that design can influence the users, in some cases quite strongly. Knowledge of such effects then cannot help but be useful to the designer (Moore 1979a).

Still, there is an inevitable "applicability gap" between the designer and the researcher. The first to bridge this gap was the researcher-as-consultant, but enthusiasm for this solution appears to be waning. Zeisel (1981) shows how the gap can be bridged from the designer's side by thinking of design as research. For the most part, however, the applicability gap is slowly but surely being bridged by those who study the design alternatives for specific types of places for particular groups. An excellent example here is Weinstein's (1979) discussion of the design of classrooms, in which design options are carefully evaluated in light of empirical evidence. Another is Lawton's (1980) illustration of how research can effectively be brought to bear on the design of accommodations for an especially vulnerable population, the elderly.

ASSESSMENT OF PLACES In environmental assessment, group consensus is used to provide formal measurement of psychological properties of places. These are properties such as value, beauty, social climate, user satisfaction, and preferability, which often have strong evaluative as well as descriptive aspects. The full assessment paradigm involves developing a multidimensional taxonomic model with predictor variables, criterion variables (the psychological properties of places), and various tactics for gauging the reliability, validity, and usefulness of assessments (Craik 1979). Craik & Appleyard (1980) conceptualize the assessment procedure in terms of Brunswick's lens model. The rater serves as a lens through which varied environmental information, often gathered over a long period of time, is filtered and used to predict the criterion. The model emphasizes the questions of ecological and functional validity: Does the association between a piece of environmental information and the criterion actually hold in the ecology? Does the rater's assessment of the criterion generalize to the population of users of the environment rated?

Patterns and outcomes of social processes associated with a place have been termed "social climate." Moos (1979) describes a Work Environment Scale and a Family Environment Scale, with the latter able to diagnose pathogenic families (e.g. those with drug abusers) and to predict therapeutic prognosis. [But see Richards' (1978) critique of social climate scales.]

Simulations of places provide flexibility and economy in the development of assessment instruments and help in forecasting responses to places before they are built. Encouraging evidence of the validity of simulations has been provided by a large-scale investigation of various presentation media: similar descriptions and evaluations of places resulted from an auto tour of a community in California, from a color film of of the auto tour, and from a color film of a simulated auto tour of a detailed model of the same community (Craik et al 1980).

CONCLUDING COMMENTS

Many of the articles we read for this review ended with the obligatory call for more research on the same topic. Reading the written product of this fetish for more data leads us to express a minority opinion. When a few problems are explored intensively, most problems remain unexplored. When many studies are carried out on the same topic in a short span of time, they are likely to suffer from similar methodological errors and conceptual problems. For example, in the last few years there appeared numerous "ecological-correlational" studies on crowding in which the unit of analysis was a region, a census tract, a city block, or some other aggregate of individuals. At the same time the fatal methodological flaws of these tremendously expensive studies were being pointed out (e.g. Kirmeyer 1978). To avoid this inefficiency, we need fewer studies spread more evenly across a broader range of topics. And one thing a review of the literature in environmental psychology indicates is that time spent thinking rather than data-gathering would not be wasted.

We also encountered the idea that such a young field must settle for data less than rigorously gathered. Again, we disagree. In a young field such a strategy can produce data that are little more than a Rorschach card onto which we project our preconceptions. Our call for rigorous methods is not to say that environmental psychology is the study of the college sophomore in a laboratory. The laboratory experiment in which subjects agree to set aside their own plans for an hour and do whatever is asked of them is clearly not suited to the study of many issues in environmental psychology. Indeed, one of the most exciting aspects of the way in which environmental psychologists think about and study human beings derives from their interaction with nonlaboratory disciplines. We simply call for patience: wait for really telling data.

In this review we chose to restrict environmental psychology to a branch of psychology. Many environmental psychologists would rather view it as part of a larger, interdisciplinary study of all relationships between human beings (defined at any level, individual, group, cultural, societal) and their surrounding environment (also defined at any level). This larger field of "environment and behavior" would thus include urban sociology, human ecology, and ecological anthropology. It is particularly unfortunate that we could not review work in four fields that are especially closely related:

ecological psychology (Wicker 1979), eco-cultural psychology (Berry 1980), behavioral geography (Golledge 1978, Tuan 1978b), and cross-cultural psychology (Rapoport 1979, Altman & Chemers 1980). Nevertheless, we would stop short of equating environmental psychology with any or all of these other fields. Environmental psychology is better thought of, and this was the theme of our article, as a coherent discipline unto itself, the area of overlap between the two larger disciplines, psychology and environment-and-behavior. The environmental psychologist thus draws on and contributes to both of these larger disciplines.

The value of this approach is perhaps best seen by examining the change in our own image of the human beings we study. The subjects who volunteered in the environmental psychology laboratory 10 years ago were fragile creatures, each enclosed in a personal space bubble, protected by invisible walls, and driven by a territorial instinct to defend the seat we provided. They carefully monitored their arousal level, information level, and stimulation level, lest they become overloaded and antisocial or worse still, underloaded and crazy. They didn't really produce their own behavior. They drifted aimlessly about until they encountered a behavior setting. Suddenly they sprang to life, behaving according to the setting's program until, duties completed, the setting ended. Then they fell lifeless again until their next behavior setting. The thought even occurred that we should forget about such puppets and study the behavior setting directly. The creatures were the medium for the behavior setting's message.

In the last few years, the personal space bubble burst and what sallied forth were clever creatures who even enjoy themselves occasionally. Without noticeable harm, they tolerate a broad range of stimulation from relaxation and even sleep to some pretty exciting stuff. They can plan their own behavior and then go to the best place to carry it off. They should prove to be most interesting subjects for future study.

Acknowledgments

We thank, first of all, Nancy Gunn for her painstaking bibliographic work. We also thank Raymond Corteen, Kenneth Craik, Jerry Wiggins, and Peter Suedfeld for their thoughtful comments on an earlier version of this chapter, and the many colleagues who sent us their current work and ideas on the field. Their letters demonstrated the vitality and the diversity of viewpoints characteristic of this field. We regret we did not have space to cite more of this work, and we would like to acknowledge its influence on the ideas we summarize here. Grants from the Social Science and Humanities Research Council of Canada to J. A. Russell and from the Natural Sciences and Engineering Research Council of Canada to L. M. Ward supported the writing of this chapter.

Literature Cited

Acredolo, L. P. 1978. Development of spatial orientation in infancy. *Dev. Psychol.* 14: 224–34

Acredolo, L. P. 1979. Laboratory versus home: The effect of environment on the 9-month-old infant's choice of spatial reference system. *Dev. Psychol.* 15: 666–67

Aiello, J. R., Thompson, D. E. 1980. Personal space, crowding, and spatial behavior in a cultural context. In *Human Behavior and Environment,* ed. I. Altman, A. Rapoport, J. F. Wohlwill, 4:107–78. New York: Plenum. 351 pp.

Allen, G., Siegel, A., Rosinski, R. 1978. The role of perceptual context in structuring spatial knowledge. *J. Exp. Psychol.: Hum. Learn. Mem.* 4:617–30

Altman, I. 1977. Privacy regulation: Culturally universal or culturally specific? *J. Soc. Issues* 33: 66–84

Altman, I. 1979. Privacy as an interpersonal boundary process. In *Human Ethology: Claims and Limits of a New Discipline,* ed. M. von Cranach, K. Foppa, W. Lepenies, D. Ploog, pp. 45–132. Cambridge: Cambridge Univ. Press. 764 pp.

Altman, I., Chemers, M. 1980. *Culture and Environment.* Monterey, Calif: Brooks/Cole. 337 pp.

Anderson, J. R. 1978. Arguments concerning representations for mental imagery. *Psychol. Rev.* 85: 249–77

Archea, J. 1977. The place of architectural factors in behavioral theories of privacy. *J. Soc. Issues* 33: 116–37

Baldassare, M. 1978. Human spatial behavior. *Ann. Rev. Sociol.* 4: 29–56

Barker, R. G. and Associates. 1978. *Habitats, Environments and Human Behavior.* San Francisco: Jossey-Bass

Barnes, T. R. 1978. Dumber by the dozen or by the decade? *Psychol. Rep.* 42:970

Baron, R. A. 1978. Invasions of personal space and helping: Mediating effects of invader's apparent need. *J. Exp. Soc. Psychol.* 14:304–12

Baron, R. M. 1980. *The role of the physical environment in three models of environment perception and behavior.* Presented at Ann. Meet. Am. Psychol. Assoc., Montreal

Baron, R. M., Mandel, D. R. 1978. Toward an ecological model of density effects in dormitory settings. In *Human Response to Crowding,* ed. A. Baum, Y. M. Epstein, pp. 304–26. Hillsdale: Erlbaum. 416 pp.

Baron, R. M., Rodin, J. 1978. Perceived control and crowding stress. In *Advances in Environmental Psychology,* ed. A. Baum, J. Singer, S. Valins, 1:145–90. Hillsdale: Erlbaum. 204 pp.

Baum, A., Davis, G. E. 1980. Reducing the stress of high-density living: An architectural intervention. *J. Pers. Soc. Psychol.* 38:471–81

Baum, A., Shapiro, A., Murray, D., Wideman, M. V. 1979. Interpersonal mediation of perceived crowding and control in residential dyads and triads. *J. Appl. Soc. Psychol.* 9:491–507

Baum, A., Valins, S. 1979. Architectural mediation of residential density and control: Crowding and the regulation of social contact. *Adv. Exp. Soc. Psychol.* 12:131–75

Baum, A. R., Jonides, J. 1979. Cognitive maps: Analysis of comparative judgments of distance. *Mem. Cognit.* 7:462–68

Bell, P. A. 1978. Effects of noise and heat stress on primary and subsidiary task performance. *Hum. Factors* 20:749–52

Bell, P. A. 1981. Physiological, comfort, performance, and social effects of heat stress. *J. Soc. Issues* 37:71–94

Benedikt, M. L. 1979. To take hold of space: Isovists and isovist fields. *Environ. Plan B* 6:47–65

Benedikt, M., Burnham, C. 1980. *Describing and perceiving the physical world: Research with isovists.* Presented at Ann. Meet. Am. Psychol. Assoc., Montreal

Berry, J. W. 1980. Cultural ecology and individual behavior. In *Human Behavior and Environment,* ed. I. Altman, A. Rapoport, J. F. Wohlwill, 4:83–106. New York: Plenum. 351 pp.

Boles, W. E., Hayward, S. C. 1978. Effects of urban noise and sidewalk density upon pedestrian cooperation and tempo. *J. Soc. Psychol.* 104:29–35

Bremner, J. G. 1978. Spatial errors made by infants: Inadequate spatial cues or evidence of egocentrism? *Br. J. Psychol.* 69:77–84

Broadbent, D. E. 1978. The current state of noise research: Reply to Poulton. *Psychol. Bull.* 85:1052–67

Brown, L. A., Malecki, E. J., Philliber, S. G. 1977. Awareness space characteristics in a migration context. *Environ. Behav.* 9:335–48

Burton, I., Kates, R. W., White, G. R. 1978. *The Environment as Hazard.* New York: Oxford Univ. Press

Byrne, R. 1979. Memory for urban geography. *Q. J. Exp. Psychol.* 31:147–54

Cadwallader, M. 1979. Problems in cognitive

distance: Implications for cognitive mapping. *Environ. Behav.* 11:559–76

Calvert-Boyanowsky, J., Boyanowsky, E. O., Atkinson, M., Gaduto, D., Reeves, J. 1976. Patterns of passion: Temperature and human emotion. In *Readings in Social Psychology: Contemporary Perspectives,* ed. D. Krebs, pp. 96–99. New York: Harper & Row. 343 pp.

Campbell, D. E. 1979. Interior office design and visitor response. *J. Appl. Psychol.* 64:648–53

Campbell, D. E., Beets, J. L. 1977. Meteorological variables and behavior: An annotated bibliography. *JSAS Cat. Sel. Doc. Psychol.* 7(1):I. MS 1403

Campbell, D. E., Beets, J. L. 1978. Lunacy and the full moon. *Psychol. Bull.* 85:1123–29

Canter, D. 1981. The potential of facet theory for applied social psychology. *Appl. Soc. Psychol. Ann.* 2:In press

Canter, D., Craik, K. H. 1981. Environmental psychology. *J. Environ. Psychol.* 1:1–11

Canter, D., Tagg, S. 1980. The empirical classification of building aspects and their attributes. In *Meaning and Behavior in the Built Environment,* ed. G. Broadbent, R. Bunt, T. L. Lorens, pp. 1–19. London: Wiley. 372 pp.

Carlsmith, J. M., Anderson, C. A. 1979. Ambient temperature and the occurrence of collective violence: A new analysis. *J. Pers. Soc. Psychol.* 37:337–44

Charry, J. M. 1976. *Meteorology and behavior: The effects of positive air ions on human performance, physiology, and mood.* PhD thesis. New York Univ., New York. *Diss. Abstr. Int.,* Vol. 37. Univ. Microfilms No. 77-5290

Cohen, S. 1978. Environmental load and the allocation of attention. See Baron & Rodin 1978, pp. 1–29

Cohen, S., Evans, G. W., Krantz, D. S., Stokols, D. 1980. Physiological, motivational, and cognitive effects of aircraft noise on children. *Am. Psychol.* 35: 231–43

Cohen, S., Evans, G. W., Krantz, D. S., Stokols, D., Kelly, S. 1981. Aircraft noise and children: Longitudinal and cross-sectional evidence on adaptation to noise and the effectiveness of noise abatement. *J. Pers. Soc. Psychol.* 40:331–45

Cohen, S., Lezak, A. 1977. Noise and inattentiveness to social cues. *Environ. Behav.* 9:559–72

Cohen, S., Sherrod, D. R. 1978. When density matters: Environmental control as a determinant of crowding effects in laboratory and residential settings. *J. Popul.* 1:189–202

Conroy, J.III, Sundstrom, E. 1977. Territorial dominance in a dyadic conversation as a function of similarity of opinion. *J. Pers. Soc. Psychol.* 35:570–76

Cox, V. C., Paulus, P. B., McCain, G., Schkade, J. K. 1979. Field research on the effects of crowding in prisons and on offshore drilling platforms. In *Residential Crowding and Design,* ed. J. R. Aiello, A. Baum, pp. 95–106. New York: Plenum. 250 pp.

Craik, K. H. 1970. Environmental psychology. In *New Directions in Psychology* ed. K. H. Craik, B. Kleinmuntz, R. L. Rosnow, R. Rosenthal, J. R. Cheyne, R. H. Walters, 4:1–121. New York: Holt, Rinehart & Winston. 382 pp.

Craik, K. H. 1979. *Environmental assessment and situational analysis.* Presented at int. symp. on "The Situation in Psychological Theory and Research," Stockholm, Sweden

Craik, K. H. 1981. Comments on "The psychological representation of molar physical environments," by Ward & Russell. *J. Exp. Psychol.: General* 110:158–62

Craik, K. H., Appleyard, D. 1980. Streets of San Francisco: Brunswick's lens model applied to urban inference and assessment. *J. Soc. Issues* 36:72–85

Craik, K. H., Appleyard, D., McKechnie, G. E. 1980. Impressions of a place: Effects of media and familiarity among environmental professionals. Inst. Pers. Assess. Res. Tech. Rep. Berkeley: Univ. Calif.

Cunningham, M. R. 1979. Weather, mood, and helping behavior. *J. Pers. Soc. Psychol.* 37:1947–56

Curran, S. F., Blatchley, R. J., Hanlon, T. E. 1978. The relationship between body buffer zone and violence as assessed by subjective and objective techniques. *Crim. Justice Behav.* 5:53–61

Daniel, T. C., Ittelson, W. H. 1981. Conditions for environmental perception research: Reactions to Ward and Russell. *J. Exp. Psychol.: General* 110:153–57

Downs, R. M., Stea, D. 1977. *Maps in Minds: Reflections on Cognitive Mapping.* New York: Harper & Row. 284 pp.

Edney, J. J., Uhlig, S. R. 1977. Individual and small group territories. *Small Group Behav.* 8:457–68

Einhorn, H. J., Hogarth, R. M. 1981. Behavioral decision theory: Processes of judgment and choice. *Ann. Rev. Psychol.* 32:53–88

Epstein, Y. M. 1980. Physiological effects of crowding on humans. In *Biosocial Mechanisms of Population Regulation,* ed. M. N. Cohen, R. S. Malpass, H. G. Klein, pp. 209–24. New Haven: Yale Univ. Press. 406 pp.

Evans, G. W. 1978. Crowding and the developmental process. See Baron & Mandel 1978, pp. 117–40

Evans, G. W. 1980. Environmental cognition. *Psychol. Bull.* 88:250–81

Evans, G. W., Jacobs, S. V. 1981. Air pollution and human behavior. *J. Soc. Issues* 37:95–125

Evans, G. W., Marrero, D. G., Butler, P. A. 1981. Environmental learning and cognitive mapping. *Environ. Behav.* 13:83–104

Evans, G. W., Pezdek, K. 1980. Cognitive mapping: Knowledge of real world distance and location information. *J. Exp. Psychol.: Hum. Learn. Mem.* 6:13–24

Firestone, I. J. 1977. Reconciling verbal and nonverbal models of dyadic communication. *Environ. Psychol. Nonverb. Behav.* 2:30–44

Freedman, J. L. 1975. *Crowding and Behavior.* San Francisco: Freeman. 177 pp.

Freedman, J. L. 1979. Reconciling apparent differences between the responses of humans and other animals to crowding. *Psychol. Rev.* 86:80–85

Freedman, J. L., Perlick, D. 1979. Crowding, contagion, and laughter. *J. Exp. Soc. Psychol.* 15:295–303

Frey, J., Rotton, J., Barry, T. 1979. The effects of the full moon on human behavior: Yet another failure to replicate. *J. Psychol.* 103:159–62

Garling, T., Book, A., Lindberg, E. 1979. The acquisition and use of an internal representation of the spatial layout of the environment during locomotion. *Man-Environ. Syst.* 9:200–8

Gibson, J. J. 1979. *An Ecological Approach to Visual Perception.* Boston: Houghton-Mifflin. 332 pp.

Gifford, R., Price, J. 1979. Personal space in nursery school children. *Can. J. Behav. Sci.* 11:318–26

Glassman, J. B., Burkhart, B. R., Grant, R. D., Vallery, G. G. 1978. Density, expectation, and extended task performance. *Environ. Behav.* 10:299–316

Godelier, M. 1979. Territory and property in primitive society. See Altman 1979, pp. 133–55

Golledge, R. G. 1978. Representing, interpreting, and using cognized environments. *Pap. Reg. Sci. Assoc.* 41:169–204

Greenberg, C. I., Baum, A. 1979. Compensatory responses to anticipated densities. *J. Appl. Soc. Psychol.* 9:1–12

Haber, G. M. 1980. Territorial invasion in the classroom. *Environ. Behav.* 12: 17–32

Hart, R. 1979. *Children's Experience of Place.* New York: Irvington. 518 pp.

Hawkins, L. H., Barker, T. 1978. Air ions and human performance. *Ergonomics* 21:273–78

Hayduk, L. A. 1978. Personal space: An evaluative and orienting overview. *Psychol. Bull.* 85:117–34

Hazen, N. L., Lockman, J. J., Pick, H. L. Jr. 1978. The development of children's representations of large-scale environments. *Child Dev.* 49:623–36

Heft, H. 1979a. Background and focal environmental conditions of the home and attention in young children. *J. Appl. Soc. Psychol.* 9:47–69

Heft, H. 1979b. The role of environmental features in route-learning: Two exploratory studies of way finding. *Environ. Psychol. Nonverb. Behav.* 3:172–85

Holohan, C. J. 1977. Effects of urban size and heterogeneity on judged appropriateness of altruistic responses: Situational vs. subject variables. *Sociometry* 40: 378–82

Holyoak, K. J., Mah, W. A. 1980. *Cognitive reference points in judgments of symbolic magnitude.* Presented at Meet. Psychon. Soc., St. Louis, Mo.

Horayangkura, V. 1978. Semantic dimensional structures. *Environ. Behav.* 10:555–84

House, J. S., Wolf, S. 1978. Effects of urban residence on interpersonal trust and helping behavior. *J. Pers. Soc. Psychol.* 36:1029–43

Huttenlocker, J., Presson, C. C. 1979. The coding and transformation of spatial information. *Cognit. Psychol.* 11:357–94

Ittelson, W. H. 1978. Environmental perception and urban experience. *Environ. Behav.* 10:193–213

Jones, J. W., Bogat, G. A. 1978. Air pollution and human aggression. *Psychol. Rep.* 43:721–22

Kahneman, D., Tversky, A. 1981. Availability and the simulation heuristic. In *Judgment Under Uncertainty: Heuristics and Biases,* ed. D. Kahneman, P. Slovic, A. Tversky. New York: Cambridge Univ. Press. In press

Kaplan, S. 1978. Perception of an uncertain environment. See Kaplan & Kaplan, 1978, pp. 30–35

Kaplan, S. 1979. Concerning the power of content identifying methodologies. In *Assessing Amenity Resource Values,* ed.

T. C. Daniel, E. H. Zube, pp. 4–13. USDA Forest Serv., Gen. Tech. Rep. RM-68

Kaplan, S., Kaplan, R. 1978. *Humanscape: Environments for People.* North Scituate, Mass: Duxbury. 480 pp.

Karlin, R. A., Epstein, Y. M., Aiello, J. R. 1978. A setting-specific analysis of crowding. See Baron & Mandel 1978, pp. 166–82

Kirmeyer, S. 1978. Urban density and pathology: A review of research. *Environ. Behav.* 10:247–70

Klein, K., Harris, B. 1979. Disruptive effects of disconfirmed expectancies about crowding. *J. Pers. Soc. Psychol.* 37: 769–77

Kosslyn, S. M., Ball, T. M., Reiser, B. J. 1978. Visual images preserve metric spatial information: Evidence from studies of image scanning. *J. Exp. Psychol.: Hum. Percept. Perform.* 4:47–60

Kozlowski, L. T., Bryant, K. J. 1977. Sense of direction, spatial orientation, and cognitive maps. *J. Exp. Psychol.: Hum. Percept. Perform.* 3:590–98

Kryter, K. D. 1970. *The Effects of Noise on Man.* New York: Academic. 633 pp.

Langer, E. J., Saegert, S. 1977. Crowding and cognitive control. *J. Pers. Soc. Psychol.* 35:175–82

Lasky, R. E., Romano, N., Wenters, J. 1980. Spatial localization in children after changes in position. *J. Exp. Child Psychol.* 29:225–48

Laufer, R. S., Wolfe, M. 1977. Privacy as a concept and a social issue: A multidimensional developmental theory. *J. Soc. Issues* 33:22–42

Lawton, M. P. 1980. *Environment and Aging.* Monterey: Brooks/Cole

Leff, H. L., Gordon, L. R. 1980. Environmental cognitive sets: A longitudinal study. *Environ. Behav.* 12:291–328

Loftus, G. R. 1978. Comprehending compass direction. *Mem. Cognit.* 6:416–22

Loo, C. 1980. *Chinatown: Crowding and mental health.* Presented at Ann. Meet. Am. Psychol. Assoc., Montreal

Loo, C., Kennelly, D. 1979. Social density: Its effects on behaviors and perceptions of preschoolers. *Environ. Psychol. Nonverb. Behav.* 3:131–46

Lynch, K. 1960. *The Image of the City.* Cambridge, Mass: MIT Press. 194 pp.

Magana, J. R. 1978. *An empirical and interdisciplinary test of a theory of urban perception.* PhD thesis. Univ. Calif. Irvine. *Diss. Abstr. Int.* 39:1460 B

Maines, D. R. 1977. Tactile relationships in the subway as affected by racial, sexual, and crowded seating situations. *Environ. Psychol. Nonverb. Behav.* 2:100–8

Maki, R. H. 1981. Categorization and distance effects with spatial linear orders. *J. Exp. Psychol.: Hum. Percept. Perform.* 7:15–32

Maki, R. H., Grandy, C. A., Hauge, G. 1979. Why is telling right from left more difficult than telling above from below? *J. Exp. Psychol.: Hum. Percept. Perform.* 5:52–67

Maki, R. H., Maki, W. S. Jr., Marsh, L. G. 1977. Processing locational and orientational information. *Mem. Cognit.* 5:602–12

McAndrew, F. T., Ryckman, R. M., Horr, W., Solomon, R. 1978. The effects of invader placement of spatial markers on territorial behavior in a college population. *J. Soc. Psychol.* 104:149–50

McCallum, R., Rusbult, C. E., Hong, G. K., Walden, T. A., Schopler, J. 1979. Effects of resource availability and importance of behavior on the experience of crowding. *J. Pers. Soc. Psychol.* 37:1304–13

McCarthy, D., Saegert, S. 1978. Residential density, social overload, and social withdrawal. *Hum. Ecol.* 6:253–72

Menzel, E. W. 1978. Cognitive mapping in chimpanzees. In *Cognitive Processes in Animal Behavior,* ed. S. H. Hulse, H. Fowler, W. K. Honig, pp. 375–422. Hillsdale, NJ: Erlbaum 465 pp.

Mervis, C. B., Rosch, E. 1981. Categorization of natural objects. *Ann. Rev. Psychol.* 32:89–115

Milgram, S. 1970. The experience of living in cities. *Science* 167:1461–68

Miller, G. A., Galanter, E., Pribram, K. H. 1960. *Plans and the Structure of Behavior.* New York: Holt, Rinehart & Winston. 226 pp.

Moore, G. T. 1979a. Architecture and human behavior: The place of environment-behavior studies in architecture. *Wis. Archit.* Sept.: 18–21

Moore, G. T. 1979b. Knowing about environmental knowing: The current state of theory and research on environmental cognition. *Environ. Behav.* 11:33–70

Moos, R. H. 1979. Evaluating family and work settings. In *Toward a New Definition of Health,* ed. P. I. Ahmed, G. V. Coelho, pp. 337–60. New York: Plenum. 470 pp.

Morasch, B., Groner, N., Keating, J. P. 1979. Type of activity and failure as mediators of perceived crowding. *Pers. Soc. Psychol. Bull.* 5:223–26

Murphy-Berman, V., Berman, J. 1978. The importance of choice and sex in invasions of interpersonal space. *Pers. Soc. Psychol. Bull.* 4:424–28

Nelson, M. N., Paluck, R. J. 1980. Territorial markings, self-concept, and mental status of the institutionalized elderly. *Gerontologist* 20:96–98

Nerenz, D., Ickes, W., Kerr, L., Oliver, D. 1979. Reactions to personal space invasion: Experimental tests of an attributional analysis. In *Human Consequences of Crowding,* ed. M. R. Gurkaynak, W. A. LeCompte, pp. 125–38. New York: Plenum. 331 pp.

Newman, O. 1972. *Defensible Space.* New York: MacMillan. 264 pp.

Noesjirwan, J. 1978. A laboratory study of proxemic patterns of Indonesians and Australians. *Br. J. Soc. Clin. Psychol.* 17: 333–34

O'Keefe, J., Nadel, L. 1978. *The Hippocampus as a Cognitive Map.* Oxford: Clarendon. 570 pp.

Oostendorp, A., Berlyne, D. E. 1978. Dimensions in the perception of architecture: I. Identification and interpretation of dimensions of similarity. *Scand. J. Psychol.* 19:73–82

Page, R. A. 1977. Noise and helping behavior. *Environ. Behav.* 9:559–72

Palys, T. S., Little, B. R. 1980. *A project-based analysis of community dynamics and satisfactions.* Presented at EDRA 11: Ann. Meet. Environ. Design Res. Assoc., Charleston, S. C.

Patterson, M. L. 1978. The role of space in social interaction. In *Nonverbal Behavior and Communication,* ed. A. Siegman, S. Feldstein, pp. 265–90. Hillsdale, NJ: Erlbaum. 400 pp.

Patterson, M. L., Roth, C. P., Schenk, C. 1979. Seating arrangement, activity, and sex differences in small group crowding. *Pers. Soc. Psychol. Bull.* 5:100–3

Paulus, P. B., McCain, G., Cox, V. C. 1978. Death rates, psychiatric commitments, blood pressure, and perceived crowding as a function of institutional crowding. *Environ. Psychol. Nonverb. Behav.* 3:107–16

Pezdek, K., Evans, G. W. 1979. Visual and verbal memory for objects and their spatial locations. *J. Exp. Psychol.: Hum. Learn. Mem.* 5:360–73

Pick, H. L. Jr., Lockman, J. J. 1981. From frames of reference to spatial representations. In *Spatial Representation and Behavior Across the Lifespan: Theory and Applications,* ed. L. S. Liben, A. H. Patterson, N. Newcombe. New York: Academic. In press

Pick, H. L. Jr., Rieser, J. J. 1981. Children's cognitive mapping. In *The Neural and Developmental Bases of Spatial Orientation,* ed. M. Potega, New York: Academic. In press

Pocock, D., Hudson, R. 1978. *Images of the Urban Environment.* London: MacMillan. 181 pp.

Poulton, E. C. 1977. Continuous intense noise masks auditory feedback and inner speech. *Psychol. Bull.* 84:977–1001

Poulton, E. C. 1979. Composite model for human performance in continuous noise. *Psychol. Rev.* 86:361–75

Presson, C. C. 1980. Spatial egocentrism and the effect of an alternate frame of reference. *J. Exp. Child Psychol.* 29:391–402

Proshansky, H. M. 1978. The city and self-identity. *Environ. Behav.* 10:147–69

Rapoport, A. 1977. *Human Aspects of Urban Form.* Oxford: Pergamon. 438 pp.

Rapoport, A. 1979. Cultural origins of architecture. In *Introduction to Architecture,* ed. J. C. Snyder, A. J. Latanese, pp. 2–20. New York: McGraw Hill. 450 pp.

Rapoport, A. 1980. Environmental preference, habitat selection and urban housing. *J. Soc. Issues* 36:118–34

Richards, J. M. Jr. 1978. Review of the Social Climate Scales. In *Eighth Mental Measurements Yearbook,* ed. O. K. Buros, pp. 1085–87. Highland Park, NJ: Gryphon. 2182 pp.

Richardson, G. D. 1979. *The appropriateness of using various Minkowskian metrics for representing cognitive maps produced by non-metric multidimensional scaling.* MA thesis. Univ. Calif., Santa Barbara

Rieser, J. J. 1979. Reference systems and the spatial orientation of six month old infants. *Child Dev.* 50:1078–87

Rieser, J. J., Lockman, J. J., Pick, H. L. Jr. 1980. The role of visual experience in knowledge of spatial layout. *Percept. Psychophys.* 28:185–90

Rohe, W. M. 1978. *The response to density in residential settings: The mediating effects of social and personal variables.* Presented at Ann. Meet. Am. Psychol. Assoc., 86th, Toronto, Canada

Rotton, J., Barry, T., Frey, J., Soler, E. 1978. Air pollution and interpersonal attraction. *J. Appl. Soc. Psychol.* 8:57–71

Rotton, J., Frey, J., Barry, T., Mulligan, M., Fitzpatrick, M. 1979. The air pollution experience and physical aggression. *J. Appl. Soc. Psychol.* 9:397–412

Russell, J. A., Mehrabian, A. 1978. Environmental, task, and temperamental effects on work performance. *Humanitas* 14:75–95

Russell, J. A., Pratt, G. 1980. A description of the affective quality attributed to environments. *J. Pers. Soc. Psychol.* 38:311–22

Russell, J. A., Ward, L. M. 1981. On the psychological reality of environmental meaning: Reply to Daniel and Ittelson. *J. Exp. Psychol:. General* 110:163–68

Russell, J. A., Ward, L. M., Pratt, G. 1981. The affective quality attributed to environments: A factor-analytic study. *Environ. Behav.* 13:259–88

Saarinen, T. F. 1980. Reconnaisance trip to Mt. St. Helens, May 18–21, 1980. *The Bridge (Natl. Acad. Eng.)* 10:19–22

Sadalla, E. K. 1978. Population size, structural differentiation and human behavior. *Environ. Behav.* 10:271–92

Sadalla, E. K., Burroughs, W. J., Staplin, L. 1980. Reference points in spatial cognition. *J. Exp. Psychol.: Hum. Learn. Mem.* 6:516–28

Sadalla, E. K., Magel, S. G. 1980. The perception of traversed distance. *Environ. Behav.* 12:65–79

Sadalla, E. K., Staplin, L. J. 1980a. An information storage model for distance cognition. *Environ. Behav.* 12:183–93

Sadalla, E. K., Staplin, L. J. 1980b. The perception of traversed distance: Intersections. *Environ. Behav.* 12:167–82

Saegert, S. 1979. A systematic approach to high density settings: Psychological, social and physical environmental factors. See Nerenz et al 1979, pp. 67–82

Saegert, S. 1980. Crowding and cognitive limits. In *Cognition, Social Behavior and the Environment,* ed. J. Harvey. Hillsdale, NJ: Erlbaum

Saegert, S., Hart, R. 1978. The development of environmental competence in girls and boys. In *Play: Anthropological Perspectives,* ed. M. Salter, pp. 157–76. Cornwall, NJ: Leisure Press. 262 pp.

Saegert, S., Winkel, G. 1981. The home: A critical problem for changing sex roles. In *New Environments for Women,* ed. G. Wekerle, R. Peterson, D. Morley. Boulder, Colo: Westview

Schank, R. C., Abelson, R. 1977. *Scripts, Plans, Goals, and Understanding.* Hillsdale, NJ: Erlbaum. 248 pp.

Schmidt, D. E., Keating, J. P. 1979. Human crowding and personal control: An integration of the research. *Psychol. Bull.* 86:680–700

Schneider, F. W., Lesko, W. R., Garrett, W. A. 1980. Helping behavior in hot, comfortable, and cold temperatures. *Environ. Behav.* 12:231–40

Sharfman, M. 1980. Drug overdose and the full moon. *Percept. Mot. Skills* 50: 124–26

Sherrod, D. R., Armstrong, D., Hewitt, J., Madonia, B., Speno, S., Teruya, D. 1977. Environmental attention, affect, and altruism. *J. Appl. Soc. Psychol.* 7:359–71

Shumaker, S. A. 1980. *Adjusting the physical environment to the discomforts of inadequate privacy.* Presented at Ann. Meet. Am. Psychol. Assoc., Montreal

Siegel, A. W., Kirasic, K. C., Kail, R. V. 1978. Stalking the elusive cognitive map: The development of children's representations of geographic space. In *Human Behavior and Environment,* ed. I. Altman, J. F. Wohlwill, 3:223–58. New York: Plenum. 300 pp.

Siegel, J. M., Steele, C. M. 1980. Environmental distraction and interpersonal judgments. *Br. J. Soc. Clin. Psychol.* 19:23–32

Skolnick, P., Frasier, L., Hadar, I. 1977. Do you speak to strangers? A study of invasions of personal space. *Eur. J. Soc. Psychol.* 7:375–81

Smith, D. E., Swanson, R. M. 1979. Privacy and corrections: A social learning approach. *Crim. Justice Behav.* 6:339–57

Smith, F. J., Lawrence, J. E. S. 1978. Alone and crowded: The effects of spatial restriction on measures of affect and simulation response. *Pers. Soc. Psychol. Bull.* 4:139–42

Snyder, P. Z., Stea, D., Sadalla, E. K. 1976. Socio-cultural modifications and user needs in Navajo housing. *J. Archit. Res.* 5:4–9

Sonnenfeld, J. 1979. *Egocentricity and geographic orientation.* Presented at Meet. Assoc. Am. Geogr., Philadelphia

Spencer, C., Darvizeh, Z. 1981. The case for developing a cognitive psychology that does not underestimate the abilities of young children. *J. Environ. Psychol.* 1:21–31

Srivastava, R. K. 1979. Crowding: an ecological approach. See Nerenz et al 1980, pp. 45–55

Sternglass, E. J., Bell, S. 1979. *Fallout and the decline of scholastic aptitude scores.* Presented at Ann. Meet. Am. Psychol. Assoc., New York

Stevens, A., Coupe, P. 1978. Distortions in judged spatial relations. *Cognit. Psychol.* 10:422–37

Stokols, D. 1978. In defense of the crowding construct. See Baron & Rodin 1978, pp. 111–30

Stokols, D. 1979. A congruence analysis of human stress. In *Stress and Anxiety,* ed. I. G. Sarason, C. D. Speilberger, pp.

27–53. Washington DC: Hemisphere. 386 pp.

Stokols, D. 1981. Group x place transactions: Some neglected issues in psychological research on settings. In *Toward a Psychology of situations: An Interactional Perspective,* ed. D. Magnusson, pp. 393–415. New York: Plenum

Stokols, D., Novaco, R. W. 1980. Transportation and well-being: An ecological perspective. In *Human Behavior and Environment,* ed. I. Altman, J. Wohlwill, P. Everett, Vol 5. New York: Plenum

Storms, M. D., Thomas, G. C. 1977. Reactions to physical closeness. *J. Pers. Soc. Psychol.* 35:412–18

Strahilevitz, M., Strahilevitz, A., Miller, J. E. 1979. Air pollutants and the admission rate of psychiatric patients. *Am. J. Psychiatry* 136:205–7

Suedfeld, P. 1980. *Restricted Environmental Stimulation.* New York: Wiley. 513 pp.

Sundstrom, E., Sundstrom, M. G. 1977. Personal space invasions: What happens when the invader asks permission? *Environ. Psychol. Nonverb. Behav.* 2:76–82

Tesch, F. E. 1979. Interpersonal proximity and impression formation: A partial examination of Hall's proxemic model. *J. Soc. Psychol.* 107:43–55

Thorndyke, P., Stasz, C. 1980. Individual differences in procedures for knowledge acquisition from maps. *Cognit. Psychol.* 12:137–75

Tuan, Yi-Fu. 1978a. Children and the natural environment. In *Human Behavior and Environment,* ed. I. Altman, J. F. Wohlwill, 3:5–32. New York: Plenum. 300 pp.

Tuan, Yi-Fu. 1978b. Sign and metaphor. *Ann. Assoc. Am. Geogr.* 68:363–72

Tversky, A. 1981a. Picture memory. In *Learning by Eye,* ed. R. Wu, S. Chipman. In press

Tversky, A. 1981b. Distortions in memory for maps, environments, and forms. *Cognit. Psychol.* 13:407–33

Van den Berghe, P. L. 1977. Territorial behavior in a natural human group. *Soc. Sci. Inform.* 16:419–30

Wapner, S. 1980. *Transactions of person-in-environments: Some critical transitions.* Hartford, Conn: East. Psychol. Assoc. Presidential Address

Ward, L. M. 1977. Multidimensional scaling of the molar physical environment. *Multivar. Behav. Res.* 12:23–42

Ward, L. M., Porter, C. A. 1980. Age-group differences in cognition of the molar physical environment: A multidimensional scaling approach. *Can. J. Behav. Sci.* 12:329–46

Ward, L. M., Russell, J. A. 1981a. Cognitive set and the perception of place. *Environ. Behav.* 13:610–32

Ward, L. M., Russell, J. A. 1981b. The psychological representation of molar physical environments. *J. Exp. Psychol.: General* 110:121–52

Warren, R. 1978. The ecological nature of perceptual systems. In *Handbook of Perception, Vol. X Perceptual Ecology,* ed. E. C. Carterette, M. P. Friedman, pp. 3–18. New York: Academic. 434 pp.

Weinstein, C. S. 1979. The physical environment of the school: A review of the research. *Rev. Educ. Res.* 49:577–610

Wicker, A. W. 1979. *An Introduction to Ecological Psychology.* Monterey, Calif: Brooks/Cole. 228 pp.

Wilton, R. 1979. Knowledge of spatial relations: The specification of the information used in making inferences. *Q. J. Exp. Psychol.* 31:133–46

Wofsey, E., Rierdan, J., Wapner, S. 1979. Planning to move: Effects on representing the currently inhabited environment. *Environ. Behav.* 11:3–32

Wohlwill, J. F., Weisman, G. D. 1981. *The Physical Environment and Behavior: An Annotated Bibliography and Guide to the Literature.* New York: Plenum. In press

Worchel, S., Teddlee, C. 1976. The experience of crowding: A two-factor theory. *J. Pers. Soc. Psychol.* 34:30–40

Worchel, S., Yohai, S. M. L. 1979. The role of attribution in the experience of crowding. *J. Exp. Soc. Psychol.* 15: 91–104

Yamamoto, T., Wapner, S., Stevens, D. A. 1980. Exploration and learning of topographical relationships by the rat. *Bull. Psychon. Soc.* 15:99–102

Zajonc, R. B. 1980. Feeling and thinking: Preferences need no inferences. *Am. Psychol.* 35:151–75

Zeisel, J. 1981. *Inquiry by Design: Tools for Environment-Behavior Research.* Monterey: Brooks/Cole. 250 pp.

CHAPTERS PLANNED FOR THE NEXT
ANNUAL REVIEW OF PSYCHOLOGY

Volume 34 (1983)

Prefatory Chapter, *Neal E. Miller*

Brain Functions, *Aryeh Routtenberg*

Electrophysiology and Behavior, *Steven A. Hillyard*

Auditory Psychophysics, *Dennis McFadden and Fred Wightman*

Perception, *Paul A. Kolers*

Developmental Psycholinguistics, *Eve Clark*

Animal Cognition, *David Premack and Guy Woodruff*

Neurophysiology of Learning and Memory, *James L. McGaugh*

Comparative Psychology, Ethology, and Animal Behavior, *Charles T. Snowdon*

Social and Personality Development, *Ross D. Parke*

Child Development Periods: Adolescence, *John P. Hill*

Gerontology, *James E. Birren and Walter Cunningham*

Personality, *Jane Loevinger*

Personality Structure and Assessment, *Leonard G. Rorer*

Psychopathology: Biological Approaches, *Monte S. Buchsbaum and Richard Haier*

Diagnosis and Clinical Assessment, *H. J. Eysenck and James Wakefield*

Social Cognition and Perception, *Reid Hastie*

Psychology and Culture, *Richard W. Brislin*

Instructional Psychology, *Robert M. Gagné and Walter Dick*

Experimental Design and Data Analysis, *Bert F. Green*

Evaluation Research, *Paul Wortman*

AUTHOR INDEX

(Names appearing in capital letters indicate authors of chapters in this volume.)

D

M

N

O

P

S

SUBJECT INDEX

B

C

M

Q

R

CUMULATIVE INDEXES

CONTRIBUTING AUTHORS, VOLUMES 29–33

CHAPTER TITLES, VOLUMES 29–33